Sociology

An Introduction

Edition
6

Richard J. Gelles

University of Pennsylvania

Ann Levine

McGraw-Hill
College

Boston   Burr Ridge, IL   Dubuque, IA   Madison, WI   New York   San Francisco   St. Louis
Bangkok   Bogotá   Caracas   Lisbon   London   Madrid
Mexico City   Milan   New Delhi   Seoul   Singapore   Sydney   Taipei   Toronto

McGraw-Hill College

A Division of The **McGraw·Hill** *Companies*

SOCIOLOGY: AN INTRODUCTION

This book is printed on acid-free paper.

7 8 9 0 VNH/VNH 9 3 2

ISBN 0-07-024767-6

Editorial director: *Phillip A. Butcher*
Senior sponsoring editor: *Sally Constable*
Developmental editor: *Elaine Silverstein*
Marketing manager: *Leslie Kraham*
Senior project manager: *Beth Cigler*
Senior production supervisor: *Madelyn S. Underwood*
Designer: *Jennifer McQueen Hollingsworth*
Senior photo research coordinator: *Keri Johnson*
Cover image: *David Hockney,* Nichols Canyon, *1980 (detail), Acrylic on Canvas,* © *David Hockney*
Photo research: *Barbara Salz*
Supplement coordinator: *Marc Mattson*
Compositor: *Shepherd, Inc.*
Typeface: *10.5/12 Berkeley Book*
Printer: *Von Hoffmann Press, Inc.*

Library of Congress Cataloging-in-Publication Data

Gelles, Richard J.
    Sociology : an introduction / Richard J. Gelles, Ann Levine. —
  6th ed.
      p. cm.
    Includes bibliographical references (p.   ) and indexes.
    ISBN 0-07-024767-6 (alk. paper)
    1. Sociology. I. Levine, Ann. I. Title.
HM51.G36 1999
301—dc21   98-8254

http://www.mhhe.com/gelles

Preface

Students come to their first course in sociology with a natural curiosity about the social world. In responding to that curiosity, the authors of an introductory sociology textbook have two basic responsibilities. The first is to introduce students to the sociological perspective: to theoretical orientations, to the use of the scientific method in studying human behavior, and to the concepts that guide the thinking and research of sociologists. The second is to describe what sociologists have learned about how the social world is put together and why people behave as they do.

Some texts emphasize the first responsibility on the grounds that students must master theoretical constructs, technical vocabulary, and methodology before they can begin to understand social behavior. We agree that learning the basics is important. But we believe that a true understanding of the discipline of sociology comes from the active effort to understand society and how it got to be the way it is. Hence our emphasis is on how sociology answers real world questions about both public issues and private troubles.

In this edition, as in previous ones, our primary goal is to show how social structures affect people; how the society in which one lives, the position one occupies in that society, and the roles one plays influence individual experience and social behavior. Sociology shows that many of the things we take for granted, such as the differences between the sexes, are in large part social creations. Sociology also shows how apparently irrational behavior—such as the bombing of the federal building in Oklahoma City, the 1992 riot in Los Angeles, and the Heaven's Gate group suicide—is comprehensible, given a certain set of social circumstances.

A number of basic Sociology texts have been published in recent years. Most are shorter, simpler spin-offs of longer, higher-level texts. Ours is one of the only books that was specifically designed for shorter courses (17 versus 22 or more chapters)

and is packaged as a lower-priced paperback. Not a condensation of a "big book," our book does not short-change students on sociology. Limiting the number of chapters has enabled us to provide the in-depth analysis of sociological theories, concepts, and research of longer books. At the same time, our use of clearly written concrete examples makes this book accessible to students at all levels.

The Sixth Edition

This edition has been revised in a number of ways.

Global Perspective

Looking at social issues and social processes in other societies helps us to see our own society more clearly. Furthermore, events and trends within our society are shaped increasingly by global forces, which may be beyond our control but not beyond sociological understanding. The United States is inextricably linked to the global community—economically, politically, culturally, and even morally. Finally, many of today's students have roots in different countries and cultures.

The global coverage in this edition includes the following:

- Each chapter has *A Global View* box, which looks at the social pattern under discussion in another culture(s).
- Key chapters include new sections that compare our institutions with those in other societies. For example, Chapter 9: "Racial and Ethnic Stratification" begins with the conflicts in the former Yugoslavia and introduces patterns of intergroup relations by looking at different societies (rather than focusing exclusively on the United States). Chapter 13: "Religion" has a new comparative section on major world religions. Given the role religion plays in national and global politics today, understanding different belief systems is critical.

Chapter 14: "Politics" compares democracy in the United States with the parliamentary and social democracies of Europe, as well as comparing democracy with contemporary monarchies, dictatorships, and totalitarian political systems.

- For continuity and depth we return to the same societies in different chapters and contexts, especially Japan, China, and postcommunist Russia. For example, Chapter 4: "Socialization through the Life Course" begins with a comparative study of preschool in Japan, China, and the United States. Chapter 12: "Education" compares education in Japan, China, western Europe, and the United States.

- We have added a new map program. Some of the maps are designed primarily for identification, so that students do not wonder "where in the world" is, say, Papua New Guinea? Others reinforce sociological points, such as Figure 3-2, which illustrates global migration patterns, and Map 9-4, which compares pre- and postcolonial maps of Africa.

Many chapters include discussions, figures, and tables that show where the United States stands in relation to other countries—for example, in degrees of economic inequality (Chapter 8), student achievement test scores (Chapter 12), participation in organized religion (Chapter 13), and even vacation time (Chapter 15). Throughout this edition, we point out the differences between the United States and western European democracies, which we too often assume are like the United States in everything but language and cuisine.

The Mass Media

One of the prime forces in globalization has been the mass media. Most of what we know about the world we learn from television, books (rising book sales have defied predictions that reading would become passé), and increasingly the Internet. In recognition of this fact, we place major emphasis on the media.

- To introduce the sociological perspective, Chapter 1 of this edition opens with different approaches to explaining poverty. We begin with journalist Leon Dash's Pulitzer Prize–winning biography of Rosa Lee, whose life exemplified common ideas about the urban poor (and the "welfare queen"). Next we compare Dash's account of Rosa Lee's story to the sociological explanation of poverty in William J. Wilson's latest book, *When Work Disappears*. Finally, we point out that Wilson was one of President Bill Clinton's chief advisers on urban poverty and social policy during the intense debate on welfare reform. Our discussion of Émile Durkheim's classic study of suicide includes a box on the role the media play in copycat suicides (updated with grunge rock star Kurt Cobain). The last section of the chapter analyzes the news from a sociological perspective, including a dynamic graphic on the "web" of connections among giant media corporations.

- We follow through on this opening with a series of boxes entitled *Sociology and the Media* in which we analyze media coverage of a topic, identify the hidden assumptions in media reporting, and/or consider the impact of the media on people's attitudes and behavior. For example, "Prime-Time Families" (Chapter 11) compares and contrasts three generations of TV sitcoms. This popular feature from previous editions is designed to encourage students to become more intelligent consumers of media information.

Gender

In the belief that women's activities are not a subplot to the "serious," male-dominated history of society, we have expanded our coverage of gender.

- Chapter 10: "Gender Stratification" analyzes female inequality in the workplace and the family and describes the origins and current status of the women's movement. We have updated our coverage of sexual harassment (looking, in particular, at the military) and have added a new section on sexual orientation. The basic message of this chapter is that the revolution in gender roles is at best incomplete.

- Unlike other texts, we do not limit coverage of gender issues to a single chapter or to a section on feminist sociology, as if this were a stepsister to "real" sociology. Rather, women and so-called women's issues appear in every chapter. For example, in Chapter 1: "The Sociological Perspective" we use the "discovery" of wife abuse to illustrate the role sociologists play in calling hidden problems to public attention. In Chapter 4: "Socialization through the Life Course" we look not only at gender socialization in infancy and childhood but also at stages of an adult woman's life. In this edition students will "meet" poor, homeless women and famous, wealthy women (Oprah Winfrey); powerful women heads of state and powerless victims of dowry violence and female genital mutilation; women in their roles as athletes, soldiers, clergy, and corporate executives; as well as wives and mothers.

- This book is not "for women only." Also unlike other texts, in our chapter on gender we describe the hazards of the traditional male role and how social definitions of masculinity are changing, including an in-depth look at Promise Keepers.

We would also note that the number of women taking courses in sociology has increased over the last decade to about half the students studying sociology—a trend that we believe reflects the fact that women see understanding society not as something best left to men but as *their* business.

Aging

The graying of the U.S. population is a major social structural change that affects everyone: children who compete with their grandparents for their parents' time, workers who pay Social Security taxes, baby-boomers who wonder whether the country will support them as they age, and the elderly themselves. Never before have so many people lived to such an old age or enjoyed good health and leisure time in their 60s, 70s, and 80s. Rather than setting aside a special chapter on senior citizens, we have woven aging into the text, beginning with changing age structure (Chapter 1) and continuing with resocialization in late adulthood and changing attitudes toward dying (Chapter 4), age stratification (Chapter 5), generational differences in economic prospects (Chapter 9), and a global analysis of age structure (Chapter 16).

Update

Some students (and even some instructors) may find this difficult to believe, but when we wrote the first edition of this text (published in 1980) the civil rights movement was a living memory, the women's movement was just gathering steam, the cold war between the United States and the Soviet Union divided most of the world into two camps, and all-male universities such as Princeton and women's colleges such as Vassar were just beginning to admit students of the opposite sex. Fax machines, post-its, and compact discs (CDs) had not been invented yet; neither had the concepts of sexual harassment and date rape. The Internet was known only to scientists at major universities. Much has changed.

Just as the world has changed over the six editions of this book, so has sociology changed. In each edition, we have updated not only social facts (patterns and trends) but also sociological thinking. For example, in the past the study of social stratification usually focused on the United States; today explanations of inequality in our society requires sociologists to look at global forces. What we wrote even in the last edition does not cover changes that have occurred in the past three years. Nevertheless, knowing what happened three, thirty, or three hundred years ago is essential to understanding the present. In updating this book we have not thrown out the past. Many chapters include the historical background necessary to make sense of current events through a sociological lens. In Chapter 7: "Deviance and Social Control," for example, we open with the "beer crisis" among the Pilgrims who settled in Plymouth, and we then use changes in attitudes toward and patterns of drinking in the United States (including drinking on college campuses today) to introduce the social definition of deviance.

Writing a sixth edition not only requires authors to update material but also provides them the luxury of refining it. In this edition, we decided to focus on the subjects long considered the most difficult for introductory students: social structure, politics, and economics.

Social Structure All sociology textbooks include a chapter on social structure. As all sociologists know, this is one of the field's major contributions to understanding human societies and human behavior. Most texts introduce the basic concepts (social institutions, statuses and roles) and then quickly move on to the more entertaining subject of social interaction. While social interaction is an important part of social structure, this emphasis deprives students of the opportunity to see what sociology really is: the study of social structures and how they affect human social behavior. Typically, groups and formal organizations are covered in a separate chapter.

Our new Chapter 5: "Social Structure" looks at the basic elements of social structure (including formal organizations), the structure of societies (including social institutions and social stratification), and relations among societies (including evolutionary trends and the world system). Thus it is a "macrosocial" chapter, but not an abstract or "dry" one. To bring social structure alive for readers, we open the chapter with discussion of the new

Women's National Basketball Association (the WNBA) and use the rules of the game (here, changing rules for women's basketball) to illustrate the impact of social structure on individual behavior. Later in the chapter we trace basketball's evolution from a minor diversion to a multimillion-dollar enterprise to illustrate the development of formal organization. To introduce social stratification, we look at age stratification, which is as universal and as taken-for-granted as gender stratification. Most people think of aging as a natural biological process, ignoring the impact of social definitions on the experience of growing older. A new discussion of roles as resources looks at Hollywood. We believe these familiar, thought-provoking examples make social structure as interesting and accessible as the most popular topics in sociology, such as deviance.

Our new Chapter 6: "Social Interaction and Social Groups" looks at social structure from the micro-perspective. We begin with apparently insignificant behavior: how husbands monopolize the TV remote control. Then we show how mundane behavior reflects and perpetuates deeper levels of social structure—in this case, the "war of the sexes." The first half of this chapter analyzes everyday interaction, which leads naturally to the topic of social groups. We have expanded our coverage of groups with examples of different leadership styles (the IBM versus Apple models) and new material on behavior in groups (using the Challenger disaster and decision making in juries as primary examples).

Chapter 14: "Politics" has undergone a major revision. First, we open with a vignette about campaign financing during the 1996 presidential election, which is an issue that has moved from the sidelines of American politics to center stage and has virtually overshadowed the election itself. We follow through on this approach in our section on politics in the United States today. Second, we look at politics not just as a matter of power but also as a social institution. We trace the development of specialized political institutions in the first section and compare political systems around the globe in the last section.

Chapter 15: "The Economy and Work" has been moved to the unit on social institutions. Our main goal in revising this chapter is to show the relationship between changes in the economy and changes in work and the workforce. The introduction looks at downsizing in white-collar as well as blue-collar

jobs in the United States, which is a theme picked up later in the chapter, when we discuss cutbacks in Japan and other countries and the recent economic crisis in the Pacific Rim.

Features

As in the previous editions, each chapter in the book begins with a list of key questions, which correspond to the major sections in the chapter. The chapter summary then reviews how the concepts, theories, and data introduced in the chapter answer these key questions.

We have kept the format (but revised the content) of three sets of boxes: *A Global View, Sociology and the Media,* and *Close Up.* These boxes are in-depth discussions of topics and/or research of particular interest, from "The Ethics of Social Research" and Zimbardo's classic study "Are We Prisoners of Society?" to "A Cultural History of Jeans."

Key terms are printed in **boldface** type in the text, listed at the end of each chapter, and defined in a Glossary at the end of the book.

New Features

Our new *map program* is designed to help readers who have not studied geography since second grade (perhaps the majority of American students) to call attention to global issues, and to stimulate interest in other regions, countries, and cultures.

Each chapter now includes a list of *Recommended Readings,* our choice of some of the best sociological work on subjects in the chapter, including both classic and contemporary titles.

In the last five years, lists of web sites have become a routine feature of sociology texts. We have taken this one step further in our *Sociology on the Web* feature in each chapter by providing readers with Internet exercises that contain suggested topics and questions students can investigate on the Internet, as well as sites to help them get started.

Supplements for the Student

Study Guide

Each student will receive along with the text a copy of the free Study Guide prepared by Kenrick Thompson of Northern Michigan University. Each chapter begins with a list of basic questions the student should be able to answer and a list of concepts the student should be able to understand after reading the corresponding chapter in the text. Each chapter includes a chapter review, concept review, matching terms, 20 to 30 review questions with brief explanations of the correct answers, and true/false questions that challenge the student to distinguish between popular myths and social fact.

Web Site

Students are invited to visit the book's web site at http://www.mhhe.com/gelles. The site includes a variety of activities and resources, including online study guide material, chapter quizzes/practice tests, crossword puzzles, web destination links, and updates to material in the text.

WebQuester (Dushkin/McGraw-Hill)

WebQuester is a series of guided web site explorations and online exercises that walk your students through carefully selected sites covering key topics in sociology. For additional information contact your sales representative or visit the Dushkin site at http://www.mhhe.com/webquester.

McGraw-Hill Learning Architecture

Connecting students and instructors in an integrated environment, this web-based product provides course administration, collaborative learning, content management and customization, as well as interactive quizzing at the click of your computer's mouse.

Duskin/McGraw-Hill

Any of these Dushkin publications can be packaged with this text at a discount: Annual Editions, Taking Sides, Sources, Global Studies. For more information please visit the web site at http://www.dushkin.com.

Supplements for the Instructor

The **Instructor's Manual** provides chapter overviews summarizing key principles and research findings, a list of teaching objectives, two or more mini-lectures, research projects to promote student learning through "hands-on" experience, essay questions, and a classroom exercise that can usually be conducted during one class period. The manual was prepared by a team directed by John Maiolo at East Carolina University.

The **Test Bank and Computerized Test Bank** contains approximately 60 multiple-choice questions per chapter, with answers keyed to the relevant pages in the text and the type of question (applied or factual). The Test Bank was prepared by Kenrick Thompson, who also wrote the Study Guide.

PowerPoint slides, available as electronic presentation slides in Windows 3.1, include four-color figures, tables, and maps to use for classroom presentation.

The **McGraw-Hill Video Library** offers adopters a variety of videos, suitable for classroom use in conjunction with the topics in Sociology.

The **Gelles/Levine Web Site,** http://www.mhhe.com/gelles, contains a variety of resources and activities, including many quizzes for students. For instructors, the authors have a feature called Seventh Edition Now! which updates material and examples in the book as new research is made available. This way, you can automatically update your lectures and give your students the latest material on a topic or issue.

Developed through a joint partnership between McGraw-Hill and WBT System, based on WBT's highly successful TopClass product, the **McGraw-Hill Learning Architecture** enables professors to provide content, give online tests, administer the course, encourage collaborative learning, and customize course content.

Please contact your local McGraw-Hill representative for details concerning policies, prices, and availability, as some restrictions may apply.

Acknowledgments and Thanks

We are very grateful to the following reviewers for their insightful comments:

Kay Coder, Richland College
Susan Cunningham, Holy Cross College
Greg Elliott, Brown University
Robert R. Faulkner, University of Massachusetts, Amherst
Jesse Garcia, Morton College
Frank Glamser, University of Southern Mississippi

David N. Johnson, South Suburban College

Ramon S. Guerra, University of Texas, Pan American

Karen Main, Arapahoe Community College

Ron Matson, Wichita State University

Charles L. Mulford, Iowa State University

Charles A. Pressler, Purdue University North Central

Javier Treviño, Wheaton College

David Wachtel, Lexington Community College

We thank Phil Butcher for his commitment to this edition and for moving our book from the netherworld of black-and-white to a large full-color format with an updated design. We especially thank Sally Constable, our sponsoring editor, for her enthusiastic support, unflappable determination to get this edition out on schedule, first-hand insights into what instructors want and need, and "can-do" approach. Sally listened to the authors' problems, asked what we needed, and in the blink of an eye, provided critical resources. In this time of publisher downsizing and editorial staff cutbacks, thank goodness for Amy Smetzley, editorial coordinator extraordinaire. Amy handles the most troublesome or trivial questions—quickly, professionally, and cheerfully.

All textbooks are team efforts. Rita Noonan, University of Iowa, provided the outlines and research for Chapters 16 and 17. Writer Leslie Carr came in midstream, handling a number of revisions with professional aplomb. We thank developmental editor Elaine Silverstein, especially for writing the Internet exercises, and her then 10-year-old son Mickey Thaler, who guided her through cyberspace; project manager Beth Cigler; designer Jennifer Hollingsworth; and the incomparable photo editor Barbara Salz. Steven Grice provided research assistance.

About the Authors

Richard J. Gelles holds the Joanne and Raymond Welsh Chair of Child Welfare and Family Violence in the School of Social Work at the University of Pennsylvania.

His book, *The Violent Home,* was the first systematic empirical investigation of family violence and continues to be highly influential. He is the author or coauthor of 21 books and more than 100 articles and chapters on family violence. His latest books are *The Book of David: How Preserving Families Can Cost Children's Lives* (Basic Books, 1996) and *Intimate Violence in Families, Third Edition* (Sage Publications, 1997). Gelles was a member of the National Academy of Science's panel on Assessing Family Violence Interventions. He is also the Vice President for Publications for the National Council on Family Relations.

Gelles received his A.B. degree from Bates College (1968), an M.A. in Sociology from the University of Rochester (1971), and a Ph.D. in Sociology at the University of New Hampshire (1973). He edited the journal *Teaching Sociology* from 1973 to 1981 and received the American Sociological Association Section on Undergraduate Education Outstanding Contributions to Teaching Award in 1979. Gelles has presented innumerable lectures to policy-making groups and media groups, including *The Today Show, CBS Morning News, Good Morning America, The Oprah Winfrey Show, Dateline,* and *All Things Considered.* In 1984 *Esquire* named him as one of the men and women who are "changing America."

Presently, Gelles lives in Philadelphia with his wife Judy, a photographer. His son Jason graduated from Harvard University in 1996 and works in Los Angeles. His son David is a senior at Tufts University.

Ann Levine is a writer and editor who received her B.A. with Highest Honors in English from New York University in 1966. Before her freelance career, she was an editor in the Journals Department of Rockefeller University and in the College Department of Prentice Hall. Levine has been the principal writer on a number of college textbooks in sociology, psychology, and anthropology. She coauthored *Social Problems,* with Michael Bassis and Richard Gelles, and *Understanding Development,* with Sandra Scarr and Richard Weinberg. The second edition of *You and Your Adolescent: A Parent's Guide for Ages 10 to 20,* by Laurence Steinberg and Levine, was published in 1997. Levine worked with Biruté Galdikas on *Reflections of Eden: My Years with the Orangutans of Borneo* (1994), the subject of an upcoming ABC/Hallmark Productions TV movie. She is currently working with Earl Johnson on a report of his study of fathers of children on welfare (MDRC Russells, 1998).

Levine lives in New York City with her husband, two dogs, and a cat. As a member of the Orangutan Foundation International, she has made several trips to Borneo and learned much from the *Ibu* Professor and from Siswi, Princess, Kusasi, and other orangutans. She also works with Mighty Mutt, a group that rescues stray dogs and cats from the streets of Brooklyn.

Contents in Brief

xiii

Contents

❶ Introducing Sociology

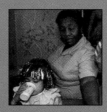

2 Dynamics of Social Behavior

3 **Social Inequality**

Chapter Nine
Racial and Ethnic Stratification   312

4 Social Institutions

5 The Changing Shape of Society

List of Boxes

Close Up

Sociology and the Media

A Global View

Sociology on the Web

List of Maps

Sociology

An Introduction

Part

Introducing Sociology

1

We begin this book by inviting you to look at the world around you through the eyes of a sociologist. The sociological perspective is unique both because of the kinds of knowledge sociologists seek (described in Chapter 1) and because of the ways they go about acquiring that knowledge (the subject of Chapter 2).

Chapter 1 compares the images of social reality that we get from media news and our own commonsense understanding of events with the insights you will gain through sociology. Emile Durkheim's classic study of suicide illustrates what is unique about the sociological perspective.

The mass media often report what sociologists or other scientists have learned about family violence, for example, but rarely tell you how they arrived at these conclusions. Chapter 2 goes "behind the scenes" to show how sociologists approach a subject, how they go about establishing the facts of a situation, and how theory and research work together.

Chapter

One

The Sociological Perspective

Rosa Lee Cunningham described herself as a "survivor." Her story, as told to Washington Post *reporter Leon Dash (1996), is a sometimes chilling, sometimes heartbreaking account of three generations of poverty, teenage pregnancy, drugs, and crime in urban America.*

Rosa Lee's parents were among the many African American sharecroppers who migrated from the deep south to Washington, D.C., during the Depression of the 1930s. An illiterate farmer, her father worked for low wages in construction, gradually succumbing to alcoholism. Her mother supported the family by working as a maid. Their run-down wooden row house had no indoor plumbing. Rosa Lee remembered her mother as stingy and harsh, never missing an opportunity to "smack me upside the head." As the oldest daughter among eleven children, Rosa Lee was responsible for cleaning the house, doing the laundry, and dressing and feeding younger siblings; she often missed school. Her mother did not believe education was important for a black woman; what counted were hard work and clean living.

Rosa Lee had other ideas. She began stealing change from her classmates' desks and soon graduated to emptying pockets in the church cloakroom, rifling through the unguarded pocketbooks of customers on her news-

paper route, and shoplifting clothes. At age 13 Rosa Lee became pregnant and dropped out of school, having never learned to read. She had her second child at age 15, and at age 16 married the father of her third child; the marriage lasted only four months. Rosa Lee moved back into her mother's house with her children and resumed her career of petty theft. Bullied by her mother and overwhelmed by her children, she considered her periodic arrests and jail terms as "vacations."

Ultimately Rosa Lee had eight children with six different men, none of whom stayed around. She supported her family herself, supplementing welfare checks by working as a waitress in nightclubs, selling drugs, shoplifting, and engaging in prostitution. "[O]ur survival was no problem," said one of her grown sons, admiringly. "My mother knows how to survive. She got nine lives. She never abandoned us!" (p. 140).

When Dash met Rosa Lee, she was 52 years old and serving a seven-month term in the D.C. jail for selling drugs—to feed three of her grandchildren, she explained. Since the birth of her first child she had moved eighteen times, twice into a homeless shelter; been convicted twelve times on theft or drug charges, and spent a total of five years in jail; and been a heavy drug user for more than twelve years.

Five of Rosa Lee's eight children seemed to be following in her footsteps. Ranging in age from 28 to 38, they had never held regular jobs, were addicted to drugs, and bounced from friends' apartments to jail, to the street, to Rosa Lee's. With some pride, Rosa Lee told Dash that she never turned her adult children away, even though they often stole money and even food from her to buy drugs and depended on her to pay their drug debts (which "Mama Rose" did by selling drugs herself). She admitted to Dash that she introduced her daughter Patty to prostitution at age 11, but insisted that she never forced her. Patty confirmed this, saying she wanted to help her mother. Getting high and hustling together, mother and daughter felt "like sisters." Both were HIV-positive.

A similar future beckoned the next generation. Rosa Lee matter-of-factly described to Dash how she had taught her 9-year-old grandson to shoplift a jacket he wanted. Another time, she had her 5-year-old granddaughter ferry heroin through the street drug market, so that if Rosa Lee were busted, the police "wouldn't find nothing." Only two of her children, Alvin and Eric, never used drugs, never got arrested, escaped poverty and the ghetto, and lead stable, working- and middle-class lives today. (Her eighth child, a mother of three, was recovering from crack addiction and asked Dash not to include her in his story.)

When Dash approached Rosa Lee about writing her story, she was eager to cooperate. "Maybe I can help somebody not follow in my footsteps if they read my story," she told him (p. 10). After his eight-part series in the Washington Post won a Pulitzer Prize, Rosa Lee became something of a celebrity, speaking to parishioners at local churches and to groups of drug treatment officials and physicians. At the age of 59—two days after the grandson she taught to shoplift was killed in a drug shoot-out, and with her daughter Patty and Patty's son Junior in jail on murder charges—Rosa Lee died of AIDS-related pneumonia.

Dash contrasts Rosa Lee's story to his own. Also African American, he was raised in Harlem and the Bronx. His father, a postal clerk, and his mother, a registered nurse, believed strongly in the importance of education. When Rosa Lee was struggling to feed and clothe her eight children, Dash was attending a private high school in Manhattan. When she was serving her first prison term for theft, he was earning a bachelor's degree at Howard University. When she was selling heroin on the streets of northwest Washington, he was writing about the devastating effects of heroin traffic on those same streets for the Washington Post. Over coffee one morning, Dash told Rosa Lee that his father had become a supervisor in the U.S. Postal Service and his mother, an official at the New York City Department of Health. Rosa Lee didn't believe him. "You mean to tell me they had black people doing that in them days? . . . Mr. Dash, you're lying!" (p. 252).

Dash's portrait of Rosa Lee is sympathetic. He suggests that given her parents' rural background and her own isolation in a Washington ghetto, Rosa Lee was neither aware of nor prepared for the opportunities that became available to African Americans in the 1950s and 1960s. The product of a segregated school system that didn't care whether black children learned to read or write, she was not qualified for most entry-level jobs. She had as little contact with middle-class blacks as she had with whites. The ghetto was all she knew, and she earned money the only ways she knew how. Dash implies that he was "lucky."

If Dash's story is the American dream (overcoming poverty and racial prejudice through education and hard work), Rosa Lee's story is the American nightmare (a way of life based on welfare, crime, and drugs).

Key Questions

1. What does sociology add to common explanations of issues such as poverty?
2. What is sociology?
3. What are the practical uses of sociology? How can it help you understand your own life? the changing world in which you live?
4. How do sociological insights differ from commonsense explanations of social behavior?
5. How did Emile Durkheim use the sociological perspective to add to our understanding of suicide?
6. How does the picture of the world presented by the news media differ from the perspective gained by studying sociology?

Explaining Poverty

As a journalist, Dash's goal was to *describe* one poor woman and her family, not to *explain* urban poverty.

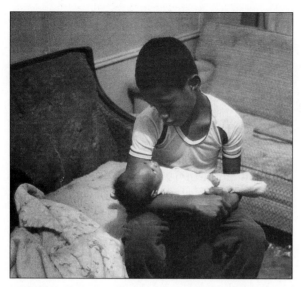

A sociologist sees an issue like poverty as less a matter of individual choices and characteristics than of social and economic circumstances that shape people's lives. In this society, African American mothers and their children are disproportionately poor.

Rosa Lee's story leaves many questions unanswered. Why are people poor? Why does poverty persist in the United States, even during periods of general prosperity? Why is poverty so extreme in minority, inner-city neighborhoods? Why is it that some people are able to work their way out of poverty while others cannot? Equally important, what can be done to reduce or eliminate poverty?

Public Opinion

When pollsters ask why people are poor, Americans tend to give conflicting answers (Yankelovich, 1997). On the one hand, we recognize unequal opportunity and the fact that some children get a better start in life than others do: their parents have the resources to provide them with a stable home, regular meals, more than enough clothes, good medical care, and such "extras" as trips to museums and summer camp; they attend good schools, and their teachers and parents expect them to do well; they very likely go to college; and so they are prepared to succeed in today's economy. The Rosa Lees of this world have no such advantages.

On the other hand, Americans tend to hold individuals responsible for their own economic circum-

stances. We like to think that through education and hard work anyone can get ahead. People who fail have only themselves to blame. Thus poverty is seen as a personal defeat—as a reflection of individual character flaws. In public opinion polls, the most commonly chosen explanation of poverty is "lack of effort," followed by "lack of thrift" and "moral weakness" (Yankelovich, 1997). To be sure, Rosa Lee grew up in extreme poverty. But nobody forced her to have eight children, to become a prostitute, or to use drugs. Besides, eight of her brothers and sisters escaped poverty to become self-supporting, law-abiding, responsible adults, as did two of her own children. If they could make something of themselves, why couldn't she?

Polls show that, in the abstract, Americans are sympathetic toward the poor. A substantial majority of Americans think the government should do more for the poor, especially poor children (Bobo and Smith, 1994). When asked about specific programs, however, people are less generous. In the 1980s and 1990s, public opinion turned sharply against welfare, the main federal program to assist the poor.[1] Originally designed to help poor mothers whose husbands had died or left them to provide for their children, welfare (the argument went) had become an incentive for young women to drop out of school, give birth out of wedlock, and become dependent on government aid and for fathers to desert their families. Associated with fraud and abuse, welfare was seen as one of the causes of inner-city poverty (Wilson, 1996). Americans do not believe that anyone should get something for nothing. Retirees earned their Social Security benefits and the elderly deserve Medicare (programs that also benefit their middle-aged children, who might otherwise be responsible for them). But why should the poor receive benefits for not working, not getting married, and generally not "getting their act together"? Why should the country support a program that undermines the work ethic and family values while promoting irresponsibility and lifelong dependency, generation after generation?

---

[1] "Welfare" refers to the federal program Aid to Families with Dependent Children (AFDC). Under new legislation passed in 1996, AFDC has been phased out and replaced with Temporary Aid to Needy Families (TANF), which sets time limits on cash benefits (among other changes).

Good or bad luck, personal shortcomings and bad choices, may explain why one person is poor. But looking at individuals does not explain the phenomenon of poverty itself. This is where sociology comes in.

Sociological Perspective

In his classic book *Invitation to Sociology* (1963), Peter Berger characterized sociology as a fascination with the familiar. At times, sociologists explore worlds that were previously unknown to them—such as inner-city ghettos, religious cults, or the private, behind-the-scenes world of surgeons, military leaders, or rock bands. But just as often they investigate realms of behavior that are familiar to them and to most people in their society, through either direct experience or news reports. What is unique is that the sociological perspective "makes us see in a new light the very world in which we have lived all our lives" (1963, p. 21). Sociologists attempt to approach the world we take for granted as if it were new, unexplored territory and to look beyond the official motives and explanations that people give for their beliefs and behavior. They examine *social forces*—the variable patterns of individual and collective action and changing attitudes and assumptions that shape our social climate. Like the weather, social forces are omnipresent, permeating everything we do. Without much thought, we look out the window or tune in the weather forecast before deciding what to wear in the morning. In much the same way we routinely test the social atmosphere by following the news, reading magazines and watching television, and talking with family and friends before making decisions—ranging from such mundane considerations as what outfit is appropriate (and stylish) to serious commitments such as what career to pursue or whether to get married. For the most part, we do so unconsciously. As with the weather, only when something unexpected disrupts our routines do we pay close attention. In contrast, sociologists use the scientific method to track social forces, during ordinary as well as extraordinary times. They seek to describe and explain the current social climate, as well as to make predictions about the future. But they cannot control social forces or be certain what tomorrow may bring, any more than meteorologists can control or predict the weather with absolute certainty.

To identify social forces, sociologists look at *trends,* such as changing rates of poverty and the ages, races, and social positions of people who are poor, live in single-parent families, depend on welfare, use drugs, and contract HIV. Looking at overall patterns reveals the limitations of popular individualistic explanations.

Consider the poverty rate, or the percentage of the population who are poor in a given year. The poverty rate in the United States peaked in 1959, hit a low point in 1979, peaked again in 1983, dropped somewhat, and then began climbing again. Individual motivation and effort cannot explain this pattern. Rather, one must look at such patterns as changes in the global economy; what kinds of jobs are available and where; how many men and women, high school or college graduates, are competing for those jobs; and the impact of government tax rates, subsidies, regulations, and social programs on the economy.

The poverty rate also varies from one state to another. In 1995, for example, the poverty rate was 23.5 percent in Mississippi but only 5.3 percent in New Hampshire; 25.3 percent in New Mexico versus 9.6 percent in Nebraska; and 19.9 percent in North Carolina compared with 12.6 percent in South Carolina (Statistical Abstract, 1996). Neither luck nor individual effort explains these variations; one must look at the local economies and populations for answers.

What age group in our society has the highest rate of poverty? Some readers may guess the elderly; others may suspect it is young adults in their twenties, who have yet to establish a foothold in the workplace. In fact, the poverty rate in our country is highest for children 4 years old and younger, second-highest for children 5 to 9 years old, and third-highest for those who are 10 to 14 years old. No one would argue that children are poor because they are "lazy" and that they therefore do not deserve food, clothing, health care, and decent housing.

For many Americans, the word "poverty" conjures up an image of unmarried, unemployed, inner-city minority, "welfare moms." The sociological perspective shows that this image is distorted. The majority of poor Americans (about 70 percent) are white people, not African Americans. Some of America's poor *are* unwed mothers and their children who live in urban ghettos, but many more are single-parent and two-parent families living in sub-

The majority of poor Americans are white, but poor whites are less likely to live in segregated inner-city neighborhoods than are poor African Americans.

urbs, small towns, and rural areas, plus people with long histories of steady employment who recently lost their jobs or suffered a family crisis such as divorce or death. Others have full-time, year-round jobs but do not earn enough to keep themselves and their families out of poverty. A little more than one-third of poor Americans apply for public assistance. Roughly 12 million Americans received Aid to Families with Dependent Children (AFDC) in 1996, the year before this program was canceled (Johnson, 1997). Of these, two out of three were children; nine in ten of the adults were women; and about 40 percent were white and 40 percent, black. This means that the majority of poor Americans and welfare recipients were white, Latino, or "other"; but the rate of poverty for African Americans (29.3 percent) was higher than that for the population as a whole (13.2 percent). Contrary to stereotypes, most AFDC recipients did not become dependent on welfare (Wilson, 1996). Half left welfare within a year, and three-quarters within two years.

To explain social patterns, sociologists draw on the concepts of social structure and culture (among others). Sociologist William J. Wilson (1996), who has studied inner-city poverty for more than two decades, holds that nature of today's urban poverty—"poor, segregated neighborhoods in which a substantial majority of individual adults are unemployed or have dropped out of the labor force altogether" (p. 19)—is a recent social development.

Wilson's explanation of urban poverty begins with *social structure:* the social positions, networks of relationships, and institutions (the economy, politics, family, education, and religion) that hold a society together and shape people's opportunities and experiences. Structural changes in the *economy*— the kinds of jobs available, the distribution of jobs, educational requirements for work, new technologies—have left many inner-city residents stranded. The entry-level factory and government jobs that enabled earlier generations of African Americans to work their way out of poverty have largely disappeared. The inner-city poor do not have the advanced education required for new professional, technical, and managerial jobs in the information sector. Competition for low-wage, often part-time or temporary jobs in the service sector (mail-room clerk, messenger, janitor, hospital orderly) is intense.

Another structural factor is *race,* which, in our society, influences social position and relationships. Poor African Americans are more likely to live in segregated neighborhoods, with high concentrations of joblessness, than are poor whites, who are more widely dispersed. Residential segregation affects not only the homes in which people live but also the kinds of public schools their children attend, the people they know, and their job information networks. On Chicago's South Side, for example, two out of three adults are unemployed, and half have not completed high school. Two-thirds of households are headed by single mothers, six in ten of whom are on welfare. Young males, especially, have a better chance of landing in jail than of landing a job (Wacquant, 1989, 1994). Poverty is more likely to become entrenched under these conditions.

A third structural factor is *work* (Wilson, 1996). Work is more than just a way to make a living and support one's family; it also provides a framework for daily life. Regular employment determines where a person will be during certain hours of the day. This in turn sets a pattern for other activities. Parents get up at 6 or 7 A.M., drop off their children at day care or school, go to work, pick their children up at 5 or 6, make dinner, do household chores and watch TV, and go to bed around 11 or 12 P.M. every day of the week. Weekends are reserved for family outings, shopping, visiting, and more chores. When people are unemployed or irregularly employed, these routines fall apart. Family life becomes more chaotic, and planning ahead is more difficult. When most adults in a community lack regular employment, social organization unravels. Wilson holds that joblessness (not just poverty) is the root cause of many problems in the ghetto.

A complete explanation of urban poverty must also take culture into account. **Culture** consists of the values, attitudes, habits, and behavioral styles people learn from the community to which they belong (Wilson, 1996, p. xiv). Culture is a set of collective ideas about why things are as they are, what people with different social characteristics are like, and how they will act in different situations, as well as how they *should* act. Racial attitudes, acquired as part of culture, contribute to inner-city poverty. Employers tend to be suspicious of African American, inner-city males, who in turn are suspicious of employers. To the degree that different groups in a society are isolated from one another, not only their experiences but also their world views and behavioral styles vary. Inner-city youth learn ways of walking and speaking that may help them survive in the ghetto but hurt them in a job interview. Cultural interpretations—for example, is someone who is looking you directly in the eyes issuing a challenge or showing friendliness and honesty?—may be subtle but powerful. Differences in style and mutual misunderstanding help explain why young African American men are less likely to be hired and more likely to be fired or to quit than are young white men with similar educations and work experience. Wilson's research shows that the inner-city poor support such mainstream values as hard work, initiative, and honesty but live in circumstances where these values are difficult to apply.

Culture and social structure are not separate and independent; they influence one another. In areas with high concentrations of joblessness, adults cannot expect to be steadily employed; as a result, "hustling"—doing whatever is necessary, legal or illegal, to survive and make ends meet—becomes an accepted alternative. When young men are in short supply, because of imprisonment or violent death, young women cannot expect to get married or stay married. When 40 to 50 percent of eligible young men in a community are unemployed, marriage becomes less attractive to both sexes. And so bearing children out of wedlock becomes an accepted alternative. Such "ghetto-related" outlooks and behavior patterns are in large part adaptations to circumstances.

C. Wright Mills (1959) coined the term **sociological imagination** to describe the ability to see the connection between private troubles (such as Rosa Lee's) and social problems (such as urban poverty). To answer the question "Why are people poor?" you have to look beyond individual motivation to the society and times in which people live and to the social forces that shape their lives. When you do this, you are exercising sociological imagination.

The main goal of this book is to show how sociological imagination sheds light on virtually every aspect of our personal lives and the world in which we live—from the most mundane patterns of everyday life to the most troubling events and controversial issues facing the world today. Each chapter of the book is organized around a series of key questions.

What Is Sociology?

Sociology is the systematic study of the groups and societies in which people live, how social structures and cultures are created and maintained or changed, and how they affect our behavior. Whether driving through a ghetto, walking across a college campus, or contemplating a story in the news, sociologists ask: "What are people doing with each other here? What are their relationships to each other? How are these relationships organized in institutions? What are the collective ideas that move [people] and institutions?" (Berger, 1963, p. 20).

Sociology begins with the observation that humans are intensely social creatures. Virtually everything we do—from making love to making war or making a profit—we do with others. We are constantly building and rebuilding groups—from families and lunchroom cliques to multinational corporations and international alliances. We also group people in our minds; that is, we sort them into social categories according to their age, sex, race, occupation, income, and other characteristics. Our private hopes and fears, our experiences and opportunities, our identities and behavior all reflect these social arrangements.

We are who we are in part because of the society into which we were born and because of our particular place in society. Your daily life, your friends, and your future would be very different if you were a homeless street person or a member of the Kennedy clan, a shepherd in Nepal or a factory worker in Beijing, a priest in the ancient Mayan empire of Central America or a serf in medieval Europe. You are who you are in part because you are a college student in contemporary America.

The structure of society both creates and limits opportunities. Consider the age structure of the U.S. population (Treas, 1995). At the turn of the last century, the United States was a "young society": only one in twenty-five Americans was 65 or older. But as shown in Figure 1-1, the proportion of young people in the United States is declining while the proportion of older people is growing. There are two main reasons for the "graying of America." The first is that, on average, Americans live longer today than they did 100 years ago. Thanks to improved sanitation, nutrition, and medical care, life expectancy for white males has increased from forty-seven years in 1900 to seventy-two today, and for white females, from forty-nine years to almost eighty. The second reason is the baby boom that took place in the United States in the prosperous 1950s and 1960s. Members of this generation, numbering about 80 million (one-third of the entire U.S. population), are entering their fifties. In the next 15 to 60 years, baby boomers will reach retirement age. By the year 2030, about one in five Americans will be 65 or older. One consequence will be enormous pressure on the Social Security

system. Social Security is not a pension plan, from which retirees withdraw money they deposited when they were working; rather, benefits for retirees are financed mainly by payroll taxes on current workers and employers. When Social Security was enacted into law in 1935, there were more than thirty workers for every retiree; estimates are that in 2030, there will be only two or three workers for every retiree. To meet its obligations, the government will have to dramatically increase payroll taxes, cut benefits to retired workers, or fund Social Security by other means.

The main lesson, and message, of sociology is that *the structure of society affects people's attitudes and behavior,* often in ways they don't consciously perceive.

Sociology is part of the family of social sciences that includes psychology, anthropology, economics, political science, and parts of history. All social sciences are concerned with human behavior. Although they share the same basic subject matter, each social science focuses on a different aspect of behavior. Psychologists are most interested in the internal sources of behavior; sociologists, in the external sources of behavior. Psychologists study the workings of the nervous system and the effects of neurotransmitters, hormones, or stress on individuals. Sociologists study the workings of society and the effects that social class, gender roles, age, new technologies, changing attitudes toward religion, or political revolutions have on people. Psychologists focus on personality—on the behavior and attitudes that are characteristic of a person regardless of the situation. Sociologists focus on roles—on the behavior and attitudes that are characteristic of people in a given social position or situation regardless of their individual personalities.

Social psychology, which bridges the two fields, studies the impact of groups on individual behavior and of individuals on group behavior. Sociologists study not only group dynamics but also large-scale, or "formal," organizations, in which particular individuals have relatively little influence. Anthropology shares sociology's interest in the impact of social structure and culture on behavior; but anthropologists usually study nonwestern societies, preliterate societies, local communities, or small groups. Sociologists, too, study communities and small groups, but they also examine modern industrial societies and large-scale organizations.

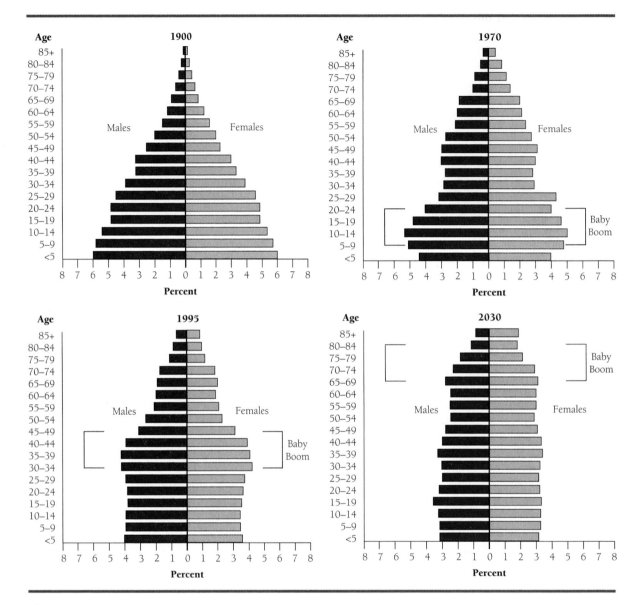

Figure 1-1   *The Changing Age Structure of the U.S. Population*

At the beginning of the 20th century, the age structure of the United States resembled a pyramid, with a small number of elderly people at the top of a much larger base of children and working-age adults. In the 21st century, the age structure will resemble a column, with almost equal proportions of children, working-age adults, and older people.

Source: J. Treas, "Older Americans in the 1990s and Beyond," *Population Bulletin* 50, 1995, fig. 1, pp. 4–5.

Economists and political scientists single out particular kinds of social activity; sociologists look at the nature of social action itself and at the manner in which different kinds of activities fit together to create the larger pattern of society.

Sociologists are primarily interested in areas where social structure and culture intersect. One of

these is social institutions. **Social institutions** are established patterns of action and thought that organize important social activities—the family, education, religion, the political and economic systems. These institutions provide ready-made answers to the recurring problems of life: how to make community decisions (the political system), how to produce and distribute goods and services (the economic system), how to arrange households and provide child care (the family), and so on. Although there are both individual and group variations on these patterns in every society, and although social institutions may change over time, they nevertheless provide a basic framework for social life. (See Chapter 5.)

Perhaps the most unique feature of sociology is its focus on institutionalized inequality, or social stratification. *Social stratification* refers to the division of society into different layers (or strata) whose occupants have unequal access to social opportunities and rewards, unequal power and influence, and unequal life chances. Stratification may be based on social class, racial and ethnic identity, gender, or age. There is nothing "natural" about these divisions: they vary from society to society and change over time. In western societies today, we see childhood as a time of playing and learning. In other societies, however, children are expected to work as soon as they are physically able to do so; education beyond elementary school is a privilege enjoyed only by the wealthy (and in some cases, only by boys). In our own society at the turn of the last century, children were a significant part of the workforce and helped drive the Industrial Revolution. Not until the 1930s was child labor outlawed. For most of U.S. history, white males enjoyed rights and privileges that were denied to African Americans, Native Americans, and women; these and other groups are still struggling for full equality. Sociologists study the social construction and social consequences of stratification. (See Part 3: Chapters 8, 9, and 10.)

The Challenge of Sociology

Sociology began to develop as a science at the end of the nineteenth century, a time of revolutionary outbreaks and social upheaval. Industrialization was changing the shape of society and the nature of social life. Farmers were leaving small, stable communities where their families had lived for generations and where everyone knew everyone else. They were seeking better-paying factory jobs and moving into tenements in big cities. The populations—and problems—of the cities were multiplying. Urban squalor and riots gave rise to an elitist image of "the dangerous classes" (Chevalier, 1981). More organized protests over both political and economic grievances threatened existing property and power arrangements. New nation-states, new governments, and new social classes were being born. Religion was losing some of its moral authority. Moreover, the pace of social change was accelerating. Children could no longer assume that their lives would resemble those of their parents in all but the details.

In many nonwestern nations, children perform arduous tasks for minimal wages, like these young workers in a carpet factory in Egypt. Similar conditions prevailed in New York garment factories during the nineteenth century.

Sociology grew out of the effort to understand the Industrial Revolution and the rise of modern nation-states, as well as revolutions against particular political regimes (Nisbet, 1967; Evans, Reuschemeyer, and Skocpol, 1985). From the beginning, then, the promise of sociology has been to illuminate immediate public concerns as well as to advance social science in general.

Conditions today, at the beginning of the twenty-first century, are not unlike those of the late nineteenth century. New technologies, cultural transformations, and political upheavals are changing the world we took for granted. The most immediate task for sociology is to provide a framework for understanding rapid social change, both in public affairs and in our private lives.

General Enlightenment

One function of sociology is to make us aware of the different ways in which social arrangements shape our lives—that is, to provide a comparative context within which we can assess conditions in our society today and our own personal experiences.

Sociology has direct and indirect effects on public understanding. Every year more than a million undergraduates take courses in sociology. Social policy makers hire sociologists as consultants and use sociological findings to shape public policy regarding such issues as crime, delinquency, welfare reform, teenage pregnancy, and family violence. Almost every day the news media consult sociological experts, report sociological findings, or use sociological techniques. The modern public opinion poll, which has become a fixture of public life, was developed by sociologists. Numerous sociological concepts—social role, class conflict, white-collar crime, the self-fulfilling prophecy, white flight—have made their way into the public vocabulary. For example, when we talk about the teacher's role in the classroom or ask what role a corporation should play in cleaning up toxic waste, we are using a sociological concept (see Chapter 5). This concept allows us to go beyond the teacher's duties and the corporation's legal liabilities to consider social relationships and responsibilities. We use the term "white-collar crime" (coined by sociologist Edwin Sutherland) to distinguish between crimes that are committed by seemingly respectable people in positions of power and authority (fraud, tax evasion, embezzlement, and the like) and common crimes (burglary, auto theft, drug dealing) that are committed primarily by members of lower classes (see Chapter 7).

Questioning Public Assumptions

A second function of sociology is to examine the often unspoken and unconscious assumptions underlying popular opinion. Sociologists not only challenge popular beliefs and attempt to set the record straight, separating fact from fiction; they also investigate the social origins of these beliefs. This accounts for what Peter Berger called the "debunking motif" in sociology (1963, p. 38)—the habit (grounded in theory and research) of exposing the social fictions behind "what everybody knows" and demonstrating that things are not always what they seem.

For example, consider the problem of missing children. When individual cases appear in the media, the public seems ready to assume the worst: the child has been kidnapped by a child molester, an estranged spouse seeking revenge, a pornography ring, or even a satanic cult (Best, 1990). Such was the case when a sobbing woman named Susan Smith told police that a black man wielding a gun had stopped her on a lonely country road, ordered her out of her car, and driven off with her two sons, ages 3 years and 14 months, strapped in their car seats in the back (Adler et al., 1994). The media quickly picked up her story, broadcasting a description of the car and a police sketch of the kidnapper. She and her ex-husband appeared on national television, pleading for the return of their children. During the news conference, the tearful mother described how her oldest son had hugged her and said "I love you" the day of the carjacking. Hundreds of townspeople responded by searching the local woods for a maroon Mazda, while others held prayer vigils and hung yellow ribbons.

Just hours after the press conference, Smith confessed that there hadn't been any kidnapper. Distressed by a broken romance, she had buckled her children into her car and driven around for several hours. Then she parked on the shore of a lake, got out of the car, and apparently watched as the car rolled down a gravel ramp into the water and her two children drowned. Though the police and some reporters were suspicious from the beginning, the public had willingly accepted Smith's story of abduction, in part because it was easier to accept than the horror of a mother murdering her own children.

Even in the absence of actual cases, rumors about child abduction and victimization—what sociologist Joel Best (1990) calls "urban legends"—continue to circulate. Details vary, but the basic plot is the same. An anonymous little girl, age 3 or 4, is left unattended for a few moments in a shopping mall. When the parent turns around, she is gone. In some versions she is never seen again. In others, she is found with her hair cut and clothes changed, disguised as a boy, so that her kidnappers can make their escape. Urban legends are reinforced by exaggerated claims about the extent of the problem. Congressional committees have heard "expert" testimony that between 25,000 and 50,000 children are kidnapped by strangers each year. Adding runaways and children abducted by a noncustodial parent, some have claimed that 1.8 million children in the United States are missing.

In reality, child kidnapping is quite rare. The FBI estimates that, nationwide, about fifty children are abducted by strangers, and an average of four to fifteen are murdered by their kidnappers, in a given year (Best, 1990, p. 55). Statistics cannot ease the terrible pain and suffering of the families of these children, but reinforcing urban legends with dubious numbers will not help, either. To the contrary, creating public panic—regarding child kidnapping, satanic cults, or sexual abuse in day care centers (to name a few recent scares)—does more harm than good. False alarms divert attention and resources from more widespread problems, such as the much greater numbers of children who are neglected, mistreated, molested, and murdered in their homes by their biological, step-, or foster parents (Gelles, 1996).

One of the sociologist's jobs is to speak out when he or she believes the public is misinformed about a social problem. Another job is to identify problems that the public has not recognized, locate the source of those problems, and assess their scope.

Identifying Social Problems

Another goal of sociology is calling attention to social problems that may be hidden, ignored, or misunderstood. How widespread is family violence?

Twenty or twenty-five years ago most Americans—social scientists as well as the public at large—thought physical injury of one family member by another was exceedingly rare. Yet newspapers often carried stories of children who had been battered by their parents and of wives, by their husbands. Were the media exploiting a minor problem for its sensationalism? When sociologists Murray Straus, Richard Gelles, and Suzanne Steinmetz looked for scientific studies, they found very little. The entire literature on domestic violence could be read in a single sitting. Yet they were convinced that something was out there. The 1960s was a violent decade, with the war in Vietnam; mass demonstrations that sometimes turned ugly; the assassinations of John F. Kennedy, Robert Kennedy, and Martin Luther King, Jr.; bloody race riots; and rising crime rates. The sociologists suspected that public violence was rooted in private brutality; people learn to use violence, they reasoned, by experiencing it in the home (Gelles and Straus, 1988, p. 11).

In 1976, Straus, Gelles, and Steinmetz conducted the first national survey of violence in the family (described in Chapter 2). This survey found that slapping, punching, and more serious assaults among family members were far more common—and more accepted—than anyone had suspected. In analyzing the results of this survey, the sociologists emphasized that neither psychological case studies nor individual deviance could explain these patterns; social factors had to be taken into account.

Around the same time, British sociologists Rebecca and Russell Dobash (1979) looked at wife abuse, and violence against women in general, from a feminist perspective. Rather than investigating the character disorders of men who battered their wives, or the social characteristics (such as age, race, or income) of such men, they focused on the patriarchal organization of society that allowed and even required men to control women—financially, psychologically, and physically. Their broader perspective identified the economic constraints that tied women to abusive men and the cultural "blind spot" that viewed subordination of women as natural. This, in turn, paved the way for the identification of other problems, such as date rape and sexual harassment. Until recently, a woman who went to a man's apartment or dorm room was assumed to want sex; bawdy jokes and unwanted come-ons in the workplace were viewed as one of the "prices"

Solving the problems in the inner cities would include, among other things, closing the educational gap between the cities and the surrounding suburbs. The prison-like atmosphere of this inner-city school and campus-like environment of the wealthy suburban school symbolize different attitudes toward and expectations for their students' future prospects.

women who entered the workforce had to pay. No longer.

Sociologists took the lead in documenting the prevalence—and acceptance—of both domestic violence and violence toward women in other settings, transforming public perception of intimate violence from a hidden, private trouble to a social problem.

On issues ranging from wife abuse to white-collar crime (which costs the public far more than common crime; see Chapter 7) and institutionalized racism (accepted practices that perpetuate segregation and inequality; see Chapter 9), sociologists have functioned as professional "whistle-blowers," calling the public's attention to social problems.

Designing Solutions

Correcting social perceptions (debunking) and identifying social problems (whistle-blowing) are only a part of what sociologists do. They also are frequently asked to design and evaluate programs that address social problems. They may be asked to give expert testimony in court or before legislatures, to act as consultants to government agencies or private organizations, to advise the President, or to design and test a program at the local level.

William J. Wilson, for example, has been one of President Bill Clinton's chief advisers on urban

poverty and welfare reform. During the 1994 presidential campaign Clinton often called Wilson for advice, solicited memorandums, met with him, and recommended Wilson's book *The Truly Disadvantaged* (1987) to nearly everyone (Remick, 1996, p. 96). In a more recent book, *When Work Disappears* (1996), Wilson held that any attempt to solve the problems of inner cities must take into account developments in the global economy. To maintain a leading position in the global economy, he argued, the United States must strengthen the ties between education, employment, and family supports and between cities and suburbs. Drawing on social policies in the other major industrial democracies of Europe and Japan, Wilson made five recommendations:

1. *National education standards.* To graduate from high school, students would have to pass demanding exams that demonstrate they are prepared to work in skilled jobs, seek additional technical training, or go to college. National standards would increase the value of a high school diploma and provide a means for local and state governments and for parents to evaluate different schools.

2. *Linking schools to employers.* In Germany and Japan, businesses and schools form partnerships and work together to develop up-to-date, job-oriented programs. Businesses have a vested interest in "their" school and students, and students who do well are virtually guaranteed a job with good wages,

benefits, and career potential in "their" company. Thus education and employment are better-integrated, making the transition from student to worker smoother.

3. *Family support.* For educational reform to be meaningful, families will need support—not just poor and single-parent families but also better-off families in which both parents work. The United States is the only industrial democracy that does not have paid parental leave; child support subsidies; free, national preschool programs; and universal child health insurance.

4. *Programs to integrate cities and surrounding suburbs.* European cities have not deteriorated the way American cities have—in part because the national government subsidizes major cities, in part because of cheap, efficient public transportation systems. Only in the United States are cities and surrounding areas politically and financially separate. City-suburb partnerships would help slow the deterioration of cities; close the economic, educational, and cultural gap between city and suburbs; and give urban workers access to suburban jobs and require suburban residents to pay some of the cost of the city services they use.

5. *Genuine workfare.* Wilson agreed with most Americans that welfare should not be a way of life but a program of temporary support, to protect children from their parents' bad luck or bad choices. However, he argues that if the government places time limits on cash assistance (as the 1996 legislation does), it must also provide jobs for people who have not found work in the private sector when they reach the limit. He calls for a public employment program, similar to the Works Progress Administration (WPA) initiated by Franklin D. Roosevelt at the height of the Great Depression. The new WPA would focus on repairing the nation's aging infrastructure—such public facilities and services as highways and bridges, water and power lines, schools and post offices. Thus it would not compete with or take jobs away from private enterprise and would contribute to overall economic growth.

Wilson recognized that his proposals ran counter to current political thinking, which emphasizes personal responsibility, not inequities in society as a whole, and people helping themselves, not social programs designed to alleviate social problems. His aim is "to galvanize and rally concerned Americans," who believe, as he does, that unless we address the mounting problems in the nation's inner cities, our society as a whole will suffer. Like Wil-

son, sociologists are free to make policy recommendations, based on their research, that may not be popular or politically correct. Although they do not have the power to implement social programs, sociologists can influence policy makers and public opinion.

Sociological Imagination

As a final challenge, sociology seeks to help individuals better understand their own experiences, problems, and prospects. In everyday conversation, people tend to differentiate between private troubles and public issues. We assume that private troubles reflect the character of the individual and his or her direct experiences and personal relationships. The problem and the solution are in the individual's hands. In contrast, public issues transcend personal experience, and so they may seem more vague and abstract. Public values are threatened, although there may be some debate about what those values really are and why they are in danger. We tend to see private troubles and public issues as separate and distinct, but in fact they are intertwined. "Neither the life of the individual nor the history of a society can be understood without understanding both," wrote Mills (1959, p. 3).

For example, homelessness is a personal tragedy. Each homeless person has a story explaining why he or she lives on the streets. Often these stories involve family problems, mental illness, and alcoholism. But homelessness is also a social problem. It results from social causes, such as cutbacks in funds for low-income housing, the closing of hospitals for the mentally ill, rising divorce rates, and low levels of assistance for people who are chronically unemployed; it affects large numbers of people; and it cannot be solved by acts of individual charity alone.

Similarly, every act of domestic violence is a personal tragedy. Each family has its own story to tell. But domestic violence is also a social problem. It is rooted in poverty, social and gender inequality, unemployment, and other external sources of family stress; in sexist attitudes and a culture that has long accepted male privilege and domination of women; and in cultural approval of the use of violence. Further, it affects millions of Americans, and it cannot be solved merely by providing shelter for battered women and children or counseling for violent families.

The circumstances of individual lives are heavily influenced by social forces. Homelessness is the result of changes in the economy, deinstitutionalization of the mentally ill, and urban gentrification, which reduced the stock of low-cost housing, among other factors.

Sociological imagination helps us see that personal failings and personal failures are often the result of social forces, forces that are beyond the control of any individual and can be explained only in terms of social patterns, not in terms of individual psychology. Thus, homelessness is all but inevitable in a society that attempts to "sweep poverty under the rug," for example, by tearing down old housing projects and gentrifying run-down urban neighborhoods. Family violence is all but inevitable in a society that glorifies violence in the mass media, approves the use of physical force as a child-rearing technique, and expects men to be heads of their households, in charge and in control, even though few jobs offer men (or women) a "family wage."

Sociological imagination is not limited to society's downtrodden; it applies equally to people in comfortable circumstances. What we make of the opportunities available to us is a matter of personal talent, effort, and initiative. But as individuals, we do not control the kind of education we receive, the jobs that are available at a given time, the cost of housing and raising a family, or the information to

which we have access. To pick an obvious example, people who started smoking in the 1930s, 1940s, or even 1950s did not know that cigarettes were a serious hazard to their health and highly addictive. Their decision was largely a matter of style (and for women, a statement of rebellious liberation). Today, we know better. In many cases, children, who learn about the dangers of smoking in school, badger their parents into quitting. Moreover, armed with the knowledge that second-hand smoke is almost as dangerous as smoking itself, the public has won the right to smoke-free environments—in offices, restaurants, airplanes, and other public places—through collective action. Adult smoking rates are tapering off, not because individuals have become smarter but because the social climate has changed.

Another example is retirement. Many Americans now in their seventies are beneficiaries of federal mortgage programs that enabled them to buy their own homes at a relatively low cost (and later, if they chose, sell those homes for a substantial profit), as well as legislation that tied Social Security benefits to the cost of living. Even if they were not hugely successful financially and did not plan for their retirement, most of today's retirees are comfortable if not affluent. When members of the baby boom generation began to buy homes, prices soared—if only because their generation is so large. If they are counting on their homes as a "nest egg" for retirement, they will probably find that their investment does not pay off as much as it did for their parents—because baby boomers paid more up front and the generation behind them (and thus the housing market) is smaller. Some have already been pushed into early retirement because of corporate downsizing. In coming decades, Social Security and Medicare may be cut back. Thus, through no fault of their own, twenty-first-century retirees may face reduced financial circumstances and a lower quality of life. Or today's middle-aged Americans may unite, through such organizations as the American Association of Retired Persons (AARP), and use their numbers to demand a secure future, reshaping politics in terms of age.

Many single Americans in their early twenties want and expect to have families. If they are like most young people, they also expect to have two-earner families. But our society and culture have not "caught up" with new families. Steady jobs require full-time commitment; day care is a patchwork of public and private arrangements; and the birth of a child tends to bring out gender-typed roles in the most egalitarian marriages. We have not developed strong cultural guidelines for how new parents should cope with their changing relationship, much less how they should juggle work and parenthood. Although, statistically, two-earner families are the norm, new parents have to find their own way through a maze of traditional cultural expectations and current social realities.

Sociological imagination cannot promise to help people solve personal problems. But it can help us put new information to use, anticipate and plan for social change, and see our personal troubles and frustrations in perspective. For example, the idea that children need a full-time mother, who always knows what is best and has no responsibilities beyond baking cookies, was a product of the prosperity of the United States in the 1950s and 1960s and the huge exodus to suburbs. In most societies and times, women have played essential roles in providing for their families, and children have grown up with multiple adults who cared for a number of children while they worked. Working mothers are not violating a "rule of nature," which holds that infants and young children need full-time mothers; they are struggling to adapt to social change.

To better explain the value and distinctiveness of sociological imagination, we look at two familiar sources of information about the world in which we live: common sense and the news media.

Sociology and Common Sense

You may have heard the charge that "sociology is just common sense" (see Pease, 1981). In the words of one newspaper columnist, "A major characteristic of sociology as a discipline is its remorseless pursuit of proof of what everyone knew all along" (Kempton, 1963, p. 112). It is true that sociologists are interested in topics that concern the average person, and on occasion sociological findings and common sense coincide. For example, the commonsense saying "The rich get richer and the poor get poorer" is a concise summary of sociological research on the impact of social class on the individual's life chances (discussed in Chapter 8). The folk expression "Too many cooks spoil the broth" was

confirmed by Irving Janis's research on "groupthink" (summarized in Chapter 6).

Often, however, sociology challenges popular wisdom. For example, common sense suggests that riots and revolutions occur when people have suffered a prolonged period of poverty and oppression. The more oppressed people are, the more likely they are to take up arms. Right? Wrong. In fact, sociological research shows that riots and revolutions are most likely to occur when living conditions have begun to improve (see Chapter 17). Common sense holds that crime has reached epidemic proportions in the United States and that streets, especially in urban areas, are unsafe. In fact, crime rates have fallen in recent years. Even juvenile crime rates, which rose in the early 1990s, began dropping in the late 1990s (see Chapter 7).

Although sociology, like common sense, sometimes deals with the obvious and mundane, sociology puts the obvious to the test. This is the critical difference between sociology and common sense. The best way to illustrate this difference is to take a fresh look at common sense. How do we arrive at our commonsense perceptions of the world? How accurate are those perceptions?

Seeing and Believing: Which Comes First?

Common sense holds that "seeing is believing." The evidence of our senses is the bottom line: what we see with our own eyes must be true. Yet sociologists have found that the reverse is also true: what we believe often determines what we see. Our perceptions are filtered through the lens of our previous experiences, attitudes, and beliefs.

The human mind is not a videotape machine; even the simplest kinds of perception involve selective interpretation. For example, when a car appears on the horizon, your eyes send an image of a miniature automobile to your brain, an image that grows larger as the car approaches. What you perceive, however, is a normal-size car, because you know that cars do not expand and contract. If the car is yours and you know it's blue, you will perceive it as blue whether it's in bright sunlight, in dark shadow, or under a yellow streetlight.

In much the same way, we adjust our social perceptions to fit what we know—or think we know. A famous riddle illustrates this: A man and his son are in an auto accident. The father is killed; the boy is rushed to the hospital for emergency surgery. The surgeon comes into the operating room, looks at the boy, and exclaims, "I can't operate. That's my son." Who is the surgeon? Many people are stumped by this riddle because they expect a doctor (especially a surgeon) to be a man. The surgeon, of course, is the boy's mother.

Our perceptions of the social world are determined in large part by our position in that world. If you asked the judge, the prosecutor and defense attorney, the accused, the jurors, and the victim's mother to describe a criminal trial, you would get quite different explanations of what was happening and why. Likewise, if you asked a husband, his wife, and their teenage son to describe their home life (who makes decisions, who does what around the house, and the like), you might not know they were describing the same family. How we perceive the world around us depends on where we stand.

The Social Definition of Reality

Much of what we know, we know through others. The values, attitudes, and judgments of the people around us have more impact on what we "see" than most of us realize. Even teenagers have much more in common with their parents than many of them would like to admit (Offer et al., 1988). However much they quarrel about clothes and chores, family members generally share the same world view. Thus a teenager may dress "grunge," whereas her parents wear expensively tailored suits to the office and classic sportswear on the weekends. Although each generation exhibits different tastes, both reveal a similar concern with the impression they make on others (see F. Davis, 1992).

A classic experiment by Solomon Asch (1952) offers dramatic evidence of the impact of the group on the individual. Asch asked student volunteers to participate in a test of perception. When a new volunteer arrived, six or seven other students were waiting. The students were assigned seats, and the experiment began. Asch explained that he would show them pairs of cards (see Figure 1-2). One card had a single line that was, say, 6 inches long; the other had three comparison lines that were, say, 4, 6, and 7 inches long. The students' task was to pick the comparison line that matched the standard.

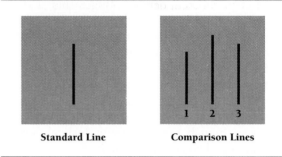

Standard Line   **Comparison Lines**

Figure 1-2   *Cards Used in Asch's Experiment*

Subjects for Asch's experiment were assigned seats in a room with students posing as volunteers. When asked to choose which of the comparison lines matched the standard line, the students, following previous instructions, gave wrong answers, making the real subject a minority of one. The chances were less than one in three that the subject would trust his or her own judgment when faced with unanimous disagreement.

Source: S. E. Asch, *Social Psychology.* Englewood Cliffs, NJ: Prentice-Hall, 1952.

Given the clear differences between the lines, the experiment seemed ridiculously simple. But Asch arranged a twist. The volunteer, always seated near the end of the row, was the only real subject. All the other students were in on the experiment. Asch had instructed these insiders, or "confederates," to give the right answer on the first two trials but then to give the same, obviously wrong answer on subsequent trials. Thus the volunteer was put in the position of being a minority of one and had to choose between the evidence of his or her senses and the opinion of the majority.

Asch found that the chances were less than one in three that subjects would stick to their guns in the face of unanimous disagreement. Most subjects went along with the group on at least some trials. Even those who remained staunchly independent were visibly uncomfortable. Some interrupted the proceedings to ask if they had understood the instructions. Others squinted, shifted in their seats, or got up to inspect the cards. In the debriefing session after the experiment, nearly all the subjects said that they had experienced extreme self-doubt. Some had begun to wonder if there was something wrong with their vision or even if they were "going mad." Only a few suspected a trick; most concluded that something was wrong with them.

Asch's experiment demonstrated how heavily our ideas of reality rely on the assumption that they are shared by others. When everyone else disagreed, the independent subjects began to doubt what they had seen with their own eyes. If other people can have this much impact on a simple visual test, think how group pressure affects our perceptions of human behavior, which is so much more complex and ambiguous.

Common sense itself is a product of social influences. The way we perceive our world has been shaped by our experiences in a particular social niche. Sociology invites you to step out of that niche and to see in a new light what you have taken for granted.

Suicide in Sociological Perspective

In July 1993, Vincent Foster, legal adviser and personal friend of President and Mrs. Clinton, left his office early, drove to a park in northern Virginia, took off his jacket and neatly folded it on a bench, put a gun in his mouth, and shot himself to death. Why did he do it? A number of theories were put forth on talk shows and in other forums. According to one, Foster had thrived in the small-town atmosphere of Little Rock, Arkansas, but was not prepared for the pressures, fast pace, and public scrutiny of Washington, D.C. In another, Foster felt responsible for the Whitewater scandal involving the Clintons and chose death as the only honorable way out. Foster's family revealed that they believed he had been suffering from depression and convinced him to call his family physician in Arkansas, who prescribed antidepressive medication, but the prescription arrived too late. There were also rumors (never substantiated) that Foster actually had been murdered because he "knew too much." We'll never know the full answer, for the obvious reason that people who commit suicide can't tell us why they did it.

When someone we know, or know of, takes his or her own life, we feel a need to perform a "psychological autopsy." Suicide threatens those left behind. As novelist Joyce Carol Oates wrote, "The suicide does not play the game, does not observe the rules. . . . He leaves the party too soon, and leaves the other guests painfully uncomfortable" (in Gelman, 1994, p. 46). To reassure ourselves that life is meaningful, we search for clues in the suicide victim's life that might explain his or her decision to die, for a "diagnosis" that distinguishes the suicide from us. Often we look to psychology for an answer, on the assumption that anyone who kills himself or herself must be emotionally disturbed.

Psychologists have various theories and opinions on the causes of suicide. People who are clinically depressed (that is, not just sad but psychologically incapacitated) seem to be at much higher risk of suicide than others. Moreover, there is considerable evidence that clinical depression is linked to changes in brain chemistry, which may be hereditary and which can be treated with medication. But no one knows whether depression causes or is caused by neurochemical imbalances; why some people whose family history includes depression develop such problems while others do not; and what causes some, but not all, people suffering from depression to commit suicide. Attempts to create a psychological profile of people "destined" to take their own lives have not been successful.

Sociologists look at suicide from a different angle. They do not deny that every suicide has a unique story and leaves a personal mystery in its wake. Nor do they dispute the relationship between depression and suicide. Rather, sociologists maintain that explanations of suicide that focus on individual cases do not tell the full story. Just as Rosa Lee's story does not explain urban poverty, neither does Vincent Foster's story explain the occurrence of suicide.

Commonsense interpretations of suicide usually rely on **idiographic explanations** (from the Greek *idio-,* which means "personal" or "distinctive," as in the word "idiosyncrasy"). Using the idiographic approach, one analyzes the many special circumstances that differentiate a particular person or a specific event from other similar ones. The result is an individualized explanation of a single case.

In everyday life, we use idiographic explanations all the time. When a couple divorce, we look for an explanation in their private lives: he wanted children, she wanted a career; their backgrounds were too different; he had a drinking problem; she was insanely jealous; and so on. When a young child is doing poorly in school, parents usually agree to a battery of tests to determine if the child has a learning disability,

Many people would explain the Persian Gulf war, Iraq's ongoing "war" with UN arms inspectors, and deteriorating living conditions in Iraq on that country's president for life, Saddam Hussein. Sociologists look for more complete answers.

a physical handicap (such as undetected deafness), or psychological problems. Likewise, in analyzing current events we lean to idiographic explanations. Many people blame the Persian Gulf war on one man, Iraq's President Saddam Hussein, whose actions and speeches—including his refusal to allow UN inspectors to visit suspected munitions plants in 1997 and 1998—seem irrational to most westerners. We may believe that Timothy McVeigh, perhaps working with one or more accomplices, was responsible for the 1995 bombing of the federal building in Oklahoma City. Some people think that the thirty-nine members of a cult called Heaven's Gate who committed mass suicide in 1997 had been brainwashed and were under the spell of their charismatic, probably delusional leader, Marshall Herff Applewhite. These explanations are not necessarily incorrect, but sociologists consider them incomplete.

Applied to suicide, an idiographic account might explain why one individual took his or her own life. But suicide is not an isolated event. Each year more than 32,000 Americans kill themselves. (These are merely the known suicides; because some suicides may be recorded as "accidents," the actual number is probably higher.) Suicide is the ninth leading cause of death in the United States

today (surpassing homicide), with an average of eighty-three suicides a day, or one every seventeen minutes (*Statistical Abstract, 1996*). In addition, each year between 250,000 and 600,000 people attempt to kill themselves but fail; an estimated 5 million living Americans have attempted suicide at least once (McIntosh, 1991).

Suicides are not distributed randomly in the population but reveal a number of patterns (see Figure 1-3). For example, white men are 4 times more likely than white women to commit suicide; black men are almost 6 times more likely to take their own lives than are black women. Moreover, suicide rates within segments of the population change over time. From 1933 (the height of the Great Depression) to 1980, the suicide rate for Americans age 65 or older declined steadily. In the 1980s, however, this trend reversed, and suicides in that age group began to climb. Today the suicide rate is 16.6 per 100,000 for Americans age 65 to 69, 21.6 for 75- to 79-year-olds, and 24.6 for 80- to 84-year-olds—almost twice the national rate of 12.1 (U.S. Department of Health and Human Services, 1996b). Although lower than the national average, the suicide rate for teenagers and young adults has tripled in the last four decades. Today suicide is the third leading cause of death among adolescents, after accidents and homicide (*Statistical Abstract, 1996*). Most people who commit suicide, teenagers and older people alike, use guns. More than 60 percent of suicides involve a firearm, compared with 14.5 percent that involve hanging or strangulation, and 7.5 percent that involve gas poisoning.

Striking differences in suicide rates also appear among societies. The United States has almost twice the rate of suicides per year as the United Kingdom, despite cultural similarities, and France has almost three times the rate of its neighbor, Italy (see Figure 1-4). Troubling as an individual suicide is, then, variations within the overall suicide rate are even more puzzling. Why are the British relatively immune to the psychological and situational pressures that we associate with suicide? Why is the suicide rate among the elderly rising? Focusing on individual cases is of little use here. To explain these patterns, we need to know not what makes each suicide unique but what qualities all suicides, or all kinds of suicide, tend to have in common. (See *A Global View:* Suicide Rates in China.)

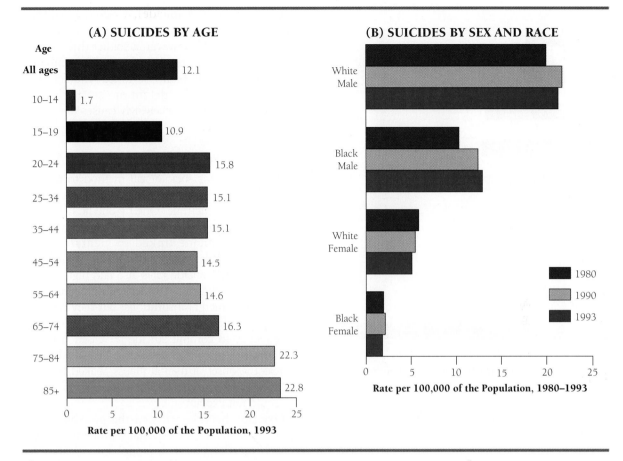

Figure 1-3   *Suicides by Age, Sex, and Race*

Suicides are not distributed randomly in the population. Rates vary, for example, by age, sex, and race.

Source: U.S. Bureau of the Census. *Statistical Abstract of the United States, 1996.* Washington, DC: GPO, table 140, p. 102.

Nomothetic explanations can tell us. They isolate the relatively few factors associated with all or most suicides in order to help us understand the underlying trends and patterns (Babbie, 1995). The result is a general explanation of a class of actions or events—what we might call a law. (The word "nomothetic" comes from the Greek *nomo-,* which means "law.") Research in the physical sciences is based on the nomothetic approach. For example, when medical researchers conduct an experiment with a group of rats, they are not interested solely in the specific rats they are handling. Rather, they want to learn how all rats, and ultimately all mammals (especially humans), respond to a change in diet, a new drug, or some other treatment. Like physical scientists, social scientists look beyond individual circumstances for general explanations of

social phenomena, such as divorce, school achievement, terrorism, or war. They do not generalize from an individual case but examine many cases to discover any underlying pattern. Equally important, they look at the social context in which the cases occurred.

French sociologist Emile Durkheim conducted a classic study of suicide (1897) that illustrates this sociological perspective. Durkheim wanted to distinguish sociology from the psychology of individuals. For this reason he concentrated on explaining variations in suicide *rates* among different social groups during the same time period and variations in the same group at different time periods. Individualistic psychological analysis could not explain these variations. Challenging conventional wisdom ("the debunking motif"), Durkheim argued that

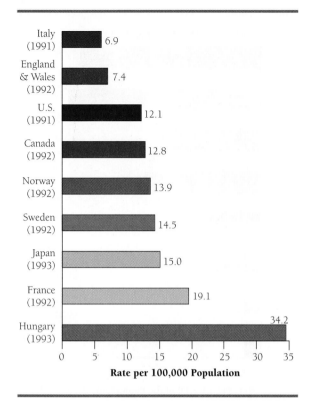

Figure 1-4   *Suicide Rates for Selected Countries*

Suicide rates differ sharply across societies: The United States has almost twice the rate of suicides per year as Great Britain; France has almost 3 times as many as Italy. To explain these patterns, we need to know not what makes each suicide unique, but what suicides have in common.

Source: U.S. Bureau of the Census. *Statistical Abstract of the United States, 1996.* Washington, DC: GPO, table 1328, p. 832.

suicide is as much a social phenomenon as a personal tragedy. He chose the topic of suicide in part because reasonably accurate public records on causes of death had been kept for many years.

Durkheim's Sociological Analysis

Durkheim began by defining suicide. This is a crucial first step, because sociologists need to know which phenomena fit their definition in order to be sure they are examining all the relevant evidence. Gray areas have to be ruled out. For example, soldiers risk their lives when they go into battle;

should this be considered suicide? Durkheim thought not: although accepting a risk, soldiers are not trying to die. If, however, a soldier throws himself on a live hand grenade to save his comrades, knowing he will probably be killed, the action is suicide. In Durkheim's definition, suicide occurs whenever an individual *knowingly* causes the end of his or her own life.

Speculation versus Fact

Durkheim used his sociological method to test the many alternative explanations of suicide that were being debated at the time. One by one he held leading theories up to the data on suicide to see whether they fit. Was suicide linked to mental illness? Durkheim saw little evidence that it was. While some groups with high suicide rates also had high rates of insanity, others did not. Women outnumbered men five to four in mental institutions, but they committed only a small percentage of all suicides. Moreover, the tendency to commit suicide increased with age (in the time period Durkheim was studying), whereas the onset of mental illness peaked between ages 30 and 45. Durkheim concluded that mental illness could not explain suicide.[2]

Next Durkheim considered the possibility that certain nationalities are especially prone to suicide. Is there something about a group's biological or genetic makeup that predisposes its members to suicide? The facts indicated that there is not. Variations within ethnic groups were as great as those between ethnic groups.

Then Durkheim looked at the physical environment, or what he called "cosmic factors"—climate, weather, and so on. Was there any truth, for example, to the belief that the long nights and short days of Sweden's long winters made Swedes gloomy and suicidal? Again, Durkheim found the answer was no. The majority of suicides in virtually all countries, including Sweden, took place in the daylight during the summer months—June, July, and August (though, of course, there were exceptions). (See Figure 1-5.)

---

[2]Likewise today, women are twice as likely as men to be diagnosed as suffering from clinical depression (McGrath et al., 1990) but far less likely to commit suicide. Moreover, suicide rates have increased most rapidly among youth age 15 to 24, who are the least likely age group to suffer from depression (O'Carroll, Rosenberg, and Mercy, 1991).

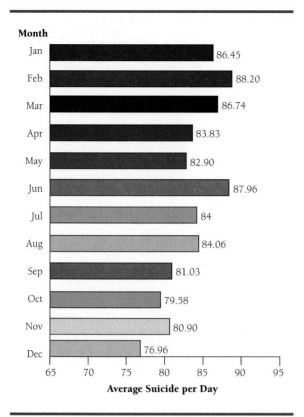

Month

Month	Average Suicide per Day
Jan	86.45
Feb	88.20
Mar	86.74
Apr	83.83
May	82.90
Jun	87.96
Jul	84
Aug	84.06
Sep	81.03
Oct	79.58
Nov	80.90
Dec	76.96

Average Suicide per Day

Figure 1-5   *Holiday Blues?*

Many people believe that the suicide rate goes up around holidays, when family celebrations and holiday cheer make people who are isolated or depressed feel even more estranged. In fact the suicide rate in the United States is lowest in December and highest in the spring and summer.

Source: National Center for Health Statistics. *Vital Statistics of the United States, 1992 Vol II, Mortality, Part A.* Washington, DC: Public Health Service, 1996.

Durkheim had ruled out psychological, biological, and environmental factors as explanations of suicide. What else remained?

For Durkheim, the answer was obvious. Clearly the suicide rate varied from group to group. Thus there must be something about the *groups themselves* that encouraged or discouraged suicide. Analyzing the social life of groups with high and low suicide rates, Durkheim concluded that there are four main types of suicide, which he labeled *egoistic, altruistic, anomic,* and *fatalistic*—each linked to a distinct set of social circumstances. Durkheim's realization that there are four distinct types of suicide, each with its

own causal pattern, not one overall cause, was the key to explaining variations in suicide rates.

Egoistic Suicide

Durkheim found that the suicide rate in Protestant nations was 3 times as high as the rate in Catholic nations. Why? Durkheim reasoned as follows: In nineteenth-century Europe, the Catholic Church regulated every aspect of life, from birth to death. The rules were clear. A sin was a sin; there were no gray, ambiguous areas, although there were ways to obtain forgiveness for one's sins. These beliefs and practices linked devout Catholics to a community that shared their views. As long as they followed the teachings of their church, they had a spiritual home. The expression "Mother Church" captures the sense of belonging thus created.

In contrast, Protestants were encouraged to question authority (within certain limits), to interpret the Bible for themselves, and to relate to God directly, one to one. What constituted a sin for Protestants was debatable (though neither religion sanctioned suicide). There were few absolute rules. The Protestant community did not have the bond with individual members that the Catholic community had. In large part, individuals were on their own.

Durkheim argued that "excessive individualism," or egoism, raises the suicide rate. When people do not feel attached to a group or community that commands their loyalty and participation, they find it easier to opt out, once and for all, via suicide—thus the term *egoistic suicide.* For example, the suicide rate for foreign students, who are far from family and old friends, is higher than that for American students. Note that in this context, "egoistic" does not mean selfish but rather alone and adrift.

Egoism explains why the suicide rate is higher for single people than it is for married people, especially couples with families. Indeed, the more children a couple have, and the more social attachments they have, the less likely they are to kill themselves. Egoism also solves the puzzle of why suicide rates go *down* in times of war. War unites people against a common enemy, creating a heightened sense of togetherness and solidarity.

Altruistic Suicide

After identifying egoism as a catalyst for suicide, Durkheim ran into a seeming contradiction. The

Suicide Rates in China

Until recently, the People's Republic of China, the former Soviet Union, and other totalitarian Communist countries did not release data on suicide and other deviant social behavior. Officially, the social problems that plagued capitalist nations did not exist in a people's republic, and scholars were discouraged from studying them. As China seeks entry into the global economy, however, the government has become more tolerant of sociological research. For the first time, data on suicide based on systematic, scientific sampling are available.

Comparing suicide patterns in China's capital, Beijing, during 1992 and 1993 to patterns in western societies, Jie Zhang (1996) found more differences than similarities.* First, suicide rates in Beijing are comparatively low: 5.1 and 4.6 per 100,000 population in 1992

and 1993, compared with 12.3 in the United States. On a list of suicide rates for sixty-two countries (Diekstra, 1990), Hungary ranked first, with a rate of 45.3 per 100,000, and Egypt ranked last, with a rate of 0.1. China would be ranked forty-fourth on this list, while the United States ranked twenty-fourth.

> **Comparing suicide patterns in China to patterns in western societies, Zhang found more differences than similarities.**

Second, studies of western societies, from Durkheim's day to the present, have always found that suicide rates are significantly higher for men than for women. In China this pattern is reversed: 55.4 percent of successful suicides were committed

by women and 46.6 percent by men. By comparison, females account for only 21.8 percent of suicides in the United States and 21.8 percent in Europe.

Third, the alleged reasons for committing suicide and the methods employed by Chinese are unusual. Officially, the most frequent cause of suicide in China is "mental illness." However, like the Communist regime in the former Soviet Union, the Chinese government often treats political dissidents as emotionally disturbed and confines them to mental hospitals. Suicides committed for "other [unspecified] reasons" may also include political dissidents. Putting these two categories together, perhaps 42 percent of suicides in Beijing were the result of persecution, or fatalistic suicides in Durkheim's terms. This is speculation, of course, but suicide rates have risen in China during periods of

*Zhang used data from Beijing for his study because he concluded that they were the most reliable statistics available at the time and reflected overall patterns in China.

loyalty among soldiers, particularly career soldiers, is legendary. The army (the group) is their whole life. Yet the suicide rate for soldiers was higher than that for civilians. Similarly, Japanese families are large and tightly knit, yet the suicide rate in Japan was higher than in many societies that were less family-oriented. How could this be?

Durkheim reasoned that just as excessive individualism raises the suicide rate, so, too, does excessive attachment to a community. When the group becomes more important than life itself, the individual is willing to sacrifice himself or herself to its needs. Under these circumstances, killing one-

self, according to Durkheim, is **altruistic suicide;** it is an act of self-sacrifice for the welfare of others. For example, traditionally, Eskimos who got too old to hunt or travel went off to die alone, so as not to become a burden to their bands. Traditionally, Japanese soldiers and (less frequently) civilians committed hara kiri (suicide by disembowelment) to punish themselves for violating custom or law and to save their families and regiments from shame.

Mass suicides—from the "Jonestown massacre" of 1979, in which more than 900 members of the People's Temple drank cups of Kool-Aid laced with political turbulence, such as the Cultural Revolution of the 1960s. Fatalistic suicides are the least common type in western societies. The second most frequent cause of suicide in Beijing is family disputes, disappointment in love, and marital infidelity (25 percent of the total), which again are relatively rare in the west. The most common method of committing suicide in the United States is shooting oneself; in China, where guns are banned, the most common method is "light poisoning," such as an overdose of sleeping pills. The Beijing records also include a number of culturally unique methods, hardly ever seen in the west, including self-strangulation, drowning in a well or vat of water, self-immolation, and bashing the head against something hard. Cutting one's throat or belly (not the wrists)

are also more common in China. Only the fact that Chinese suicide rates are higher in warm weather corresponds to the pattern in the west (see Figure 1-5).

Zhang suggests that the very different patterns of suicide in China reflect China's history and culture. Western cultures often idealize self-sacrifice, whether for love or for one's country. In Chinese culture, the main reason for suicide is thought to be shame for having done something wrong. Suicide victims are not seen as tragic heroes or heroines. The relatively low suicide rate may also reflect the fact that China is still largely a preindustrial country with a high degree of social integration and strong family and community ties. As a rule, suicide rates are lower in preindustrial than in industrial countries, where egoism and anomie are more common.

The reversal of gender patterns in China might reflect the greater availability of firearms in the west: in general, men contemplating suicide are more likely to use guns and women more likely to take pills. But Zhang thinks other social forces are at work. Despite government attempts to minimize gender differences, China remains a patriarchal society. Women may work alongside men in factories and fields, but in their homes and family lives women are still subservient to men. In this family-oriented society, women are the first to be blamed for family problems, likely blame themselves, and may go to extremes out of shame.

As China modernizes, will suicide rates begin to resemble those in the west, especially in major cities?

cyanide, to the 39 members of the Heaven's Gate cult who consumed lethal levels of phenobarbital and vodka—generally qualify as altruistic suicide. This does not mean such acts are kind and generous; to the contrary, from the point of view of the families left behind they are often cruel and selfish. Nevertheless, these people sacrificed their lives for what they saw as the good of the group.

Anomic Suicide

One puzzle remained. Durkheim found that suicide rates climbed in times of economic crisis. This was hardly a surprise. But suicide rates also increased

during economic booms. How could this be? Durkheim argued that any major disruption of a people's way of life, for better or worse, is stressful. In a stable society people know more or less what they can expect in life and adjust their aspirations accordingly. However, when the economy opens up, those limits disappear. Traditional guidelines for behavior and shared standards of good and bad no longer apply. The line between success and failure blurs. What once seemed impossible now seems probable. Hopes soar, and people may become angry or lose hope when their unrealistic expectations are not fulfilled. Durkheim called this breakdown of the

Dr. Jack Kevorkian, shown here with two women whom he later helped to take their own lives, has led a campaign to legalize physician-assisted suicide by chronically or terminally-ill individuals who choose to stop living. In Durkheim's terms, their suicides might be altruistic (if they want to relieve their families of the emotional and financial burden of caring for them) as well as fatalistic.

collective order **anomie** (from the Greek word for "lawlessness"). Although it may lead vulnerable individuals to commit suicide, anomie is a social (not a personal) phenomenon. People depend on social guidelines to order their lives. When rules for behavior are weak, ill-defined, or conflicting, one consequence may be **anomic suicide.**

The rising suicide rate for black males, for example, may reflect the social disorganization and lawlessness in today's inner-city ghettos. Celebrity suicides, such as that of rock star Kurt Cobain (see *Sociology and the Media:* Copycat Suicides, p. 32), suggest another source of anomie. Handed sudden fortune and fame, stars have the money to do almost anything they want and the leeway to behave in ways that would not be tolerated in others. But stardom has costs as well as benefits, and being free from ordinary social guidelines may lead to anomie.

Fatalistic Suicide

Fatalistic suicides occur when people believe that there is nothing they can do to alter their life conditions. They may actually be imprisoned or confined to a mental institution, or they may feel trapped by a totalitarian political regime or by a medical system that keeps them alive but cannot cure their ailment and does not ease their physical or psychological pain. "Physician-assisted suicide"—suicide committed with the help of a physician, by someone who is terminally ill, in chronic pain, or so incapacitated that the person feels life is not longer

worth living—might be classified as fatalistic. Or if the person wants to save his or her family the emotional and financial costs of a prolonged illness, the suicide might be seen as altruistic.

Conclusions

Durkheim demonstrated that even as private an act as suicide is shaped by social forces. The four types of suicide he identified are actually variations on a single theme: the relative strength of the social order and the relationship of individuals to the group. Egoistic suicides reflect the fact that people have become detached from society. Altruistic suicides occur when people value the group above their own lives. Anomic suicides take place when the social order has broken down and people no longer know what to expect. Fatalistic suicides occur when people feel they have lost control and have no other way out.

Looking beyond suicide, Durkheim argued that trying to explain society in terms of the personal characteristics and activities of individual members is as absurd as trying to explain the human body by describing individual cells. Like the human body, a society is more than the sum of its individual parts. One has to look at the whole and at how its different parts (the family, codes of honor, economic conditions, and so on) are interrelated. The concept of independent social forces may seem abstract, but the example of suicide shows that they have a powerful impact on private thoughts and individual behavior.

The existence of social forces is, in Durkheim's words, a "social fact"—that is, one can measure social behavior, compare rates across cultures and over time, and analyze these data scientifically.

Contemporary sociologists continue to study social influences on suicide (Breault, 1986; Bearman, 1991; Phillips and Carstensen, 1986, 1988; Stack, 1987b; Trovato and Vos, 1992). In particular, sociologists have spoken out about the dangers of treating suicide solely as a mental health problem. In focusing on depression as the key risk factor in suicide, we tend to ignore the many other risk factors that are consistently linked to suicide, such as the availability of firearms, a recent move, loss of a parent, family disruption, acquaintance with a suicide victim, alcohol and drug use, and social isolation. "If suicide prevention efforts focus solely on mental illness and ignore the . . . other factors that contribute to suicide, many lives will be lost that could otherwise have been saved" (O'Carroll, Rosenberg, and Mercy, 1991, p. 192).

Sociology and TV News

Much of what we know (or think we know) about the world beyond our personal experience comes to us through the mass media—daily newspapers, weekly news magazines, radio news stations and talk shows, the ever-expanding Internet, and television. Of these, television is by far the most influential. On any give weeknight, 38 to 40 million Americans watch a network newscast, and millions more watch the local news (Postman and Powers, 1992). The average American child spends more time watching television than attending school (Bagdikian, 1997). Worldwide, the television audience numbers in the tens of millions. Television offers early-morning and late-night news; news bulletins and specials; news magazine shows; shows featuring news reenactments and inviting viewer participation; countless talk shows; and, of course, twenty-four-hour news networks, especially the Cable News Network (CNN). Because of its enormous power to shape world views, we will focus on TV news in this discussion. But analysis of other news media would reveal similar patterns.

What image of the world does the TV news present? How does this picture differ from the sociological perspective?

News Bite by Bite

On television, news items are presented one by one, with little effort to place them in social or historical context. This is largely due to pressures of time and space. Because scheduling allows at most a minute or two for each item, only the highlights of an event—its most dramatic elements—can be presented. Indeed, the average length of a TV news story has been declining.

Gradual, cumulative change and complex events involving many people and places are underreported on television. It is extremely difficult to portray something like the growing acceptance of single parenthood or the decline of political parties in a two-minute TV news slot. Strictly speaking, these are not events. They did not happen today or yesterday or last month. A presidential decision or a fire in a social club makes a "better" story because it is relatively easy to put into focus. Footage of the President signing a bill or the charred wreckage of the club makes a strong visual statement.

From television we learn the "who, what, where, and when." But what about the "why"? What do the stories mean? The evening news often seems like a play with many characters and scenes, but no plot:

> To make sense of [the news]—which is a very complicated thing—one must learn how to connect the events reported, how to understand them by relating them to more general conceptions of the societies of which they are tokens, and the trends of which they are part. (Mills, 1959)

TV news is designed primarily to show or tell the public what is happening—to describe events, not to explain them. Coverage often is superficial and leaves many questions unanswered. Even when experts, including sociologists, are brought in to interpret events, time usually is limited, so they are forced to give short, simple, quotable answers. In TV lingo, the news is presented "bite by bite."

While sociologists also collect data and report what they find, their ultimate goal is to explain trends and events. They do this not by offering opinions but by testing, revising, and retesting theories of social behavior.

News as the Dramatic Picture

Television is a visual medium, one that plays on the commonsense notion that "seeing is believing." In

The videotape of Rodney King being beaten by Los Angeles police officers was a graphic image that people around the world saw as undeniable proof of police brutality—yet the jury in the officers' criminal trial determined otherwise.

our daily lives, most of us are confined to a small circle of people, places, and experiences; the media make us part of a "global village" (in Marshall McLuhan's famous phrase) and enable us to participate, vicariously, in world events. If an event is not covered in the news media, in terms of public consciousness, it didn't happen. While the news media may not tell us what to think, they have a powerful influence on what we think *about* (Parenti, 1993). The news media set the agenda. In choosing which stories to cover, what angle to take, what images to use, and how extensively to cover them, the news media promote a particular version of reality.

What we see on the home screen often seems more real to us than our own everyday experience. (See *Sociology and the Media:* Copycat Suicides.) Indeed, the videotape of black motorist Rodney King being beaten by white policemen—a tape that was broadcast repeatedly on news shows—made history. The announcement that a predominantly white jury found those policemen innocent touched off one of the worst riots in recent history. Having seen the beating with "their own eyes" on television, many people (not only the rioters) were outraged. Similarly, the image of O. J. Simpson trying to squeeze his hand into a black glove the prosecution claimed he had been wearing when he allegedly murdered his ex-wife and her friend is engraved in many viewers' minds.

Television tends to prove the old saying, "A picture is worth a thousand words." Coverage of an isolated incident or unusual circumstance may become a universal reality for TV viewers (Lake, 1989). Americans who have seen televised images of Burundian refugee camps in Zaire may believe that most of the population of Africa is homeless, hungry, and engaged in civil war. Those who saw TV footage of the fighting between primarily Christian Serbs and primarily Muslim Bosnians, in what used to be Yugoslavia, may believe that eastern Europeans are religious fanatics. Who can forget the image of a lone Chinese citizen blocking a line of army tanks moving toward the students demonstrating for democracy in Tiananmen Square? The single image, chosen for emotional impact, becomes confused with the whole.

Events that receive extensive coverage on TV news have more impact than those that cannot be pictured. Almost every American was aware of O. J. Simpson's criminal trial, which was broadcast live, day in and day out, for months. Many fewer understood or followed the civil trial, from which TV cameras were banned. The Whitewater scandal—allegations that President and Mrs. Clinton were involved in a series of illegal loans and real estate deals while he was governor of Arkansas—was in the newspapers for more than a year. But because financial dealings are difficult to tie to a visual image or to explain in a minute or two, these allegations apparently had little impact on the 1996 presidential election.

Where TV news seeks to dramatize through visual imagery, sociology attempts to explain. Why are famines and civil strife so common in central Africa? (See Chapter 16.) Why is ethnic conflict fomenting civil wars around the globe? (See Chapter 9.) How much does white-collar crime, compared with common crime, cost the country? (See Chapter 7.)

News as the Unique Personality

What famous and important people do and say makes news. Well-known public figures dominate TV news. These "knowns" include entertainers, sports stars, elected officials, presidential candidates, and, of course, the President, who alone accounts for about 20 percent of all domestic news coverage (Gans, 1979). In 1997, the allegation that President Clinton had had an intimate relationship with a young White House intern remained in the headlines for weeks, longer than any previous single news story except the bombing of the federal building in Oklahoma City. Almost half of the sources cited on the news are associated with the government (Berkowitz, 1987). "Unknowns" seldom make the news unless they commit a serious crime or are part of a group of people who do something unusual, like going on strike or dying in a plane crash.

Television is particularly well suited to dramatic portrayal of individuals. This focus on individuals also implies a particular—and questionable—theory of history. It suggests that historical events and social movements are the single-handed work of great men and (less often) great women. According to the "great man theory of history," World War II was started by one disturbed individual, Adolf Hitler; the civil rights movement in the United States can be credited to the personal charisma of Martin Luther King, Jr.; and the problems with Iraq, before and after the war in the Persian Gulf, were caused by Saddam Hussein. By implication, history would have taken different paths if these individuals had not been born.

Likewise, the media (and common sense) tend to attribute personal triumphs, such as winning a sports scholarship or the Nobel Prize for a scientific breakthrough, and personal tragedies, such as suffering through a divorce or contracting AIDS, to the particular talents or weaknesses of individuals.

Sociologists do not deny that individuals may be exceptionally good or evil, brilliant or stupid, caring or careless (of themselves and others). But sociologists also see the social forces that act on indi-

News magazines and newspapers—many of which now print color pictures—as well as TV news dramatize events through use of visual images, especially of public figures. During the media frenzy that followed allegations that President Clinton had had an intimate relationship with a young White House intern, this photograph appeared countless times, overshadowing reporting on affairs of state.

viduals and affect their behavior. These social forces exist independently of individual actors. From the sociological perspective, another person in the same social position, under the same social circumstances, would probably act in a similar fashion. Thus the political figures who dominate the news may, indeed, influence the times in which they live. Sociologists consider it equally possible that these individuals owe their power and influence, at least in part, to social circumstances. They are as much the creatures as the creators of their times.

From the sociological perspective, the cumulative effect of the decisions that ordinary people make in their everyday lives may do more to alter the course of history than any particular event or single individual. An increase in birthrates, the spread of a new technology, and the rise or decline of religious observances act as social forces. It is impossible to pinpoint the dates on which these social forces took shape or to assign responsibility for their creation to particular individuals. You can't photograph social forces for a TV spot. Nevertheless, they sweep through our lives, shaping and reshaping our social landscape.

SOCIOLOGY & THE MEDIA

Copycat Suicides

One of the most common complaints against the mass media concerns violence, and there have been thousands of studies of the effects of TV violence on behavior (Berkowitz, 1993). But studies of the impact of media coverage of suicides have been relatively rare. Sociologist David Phillips broke that trend. Phillips collected data, beginning with the appearance of a suicide story in the mass media, on the amount of coverage the suicide received (front- or inside-page coverage in newspapers, one or more reports on the TV news) and the increase in the suicide rates in the month following the story (Phillips, 1974; Phillips and Cartensen, 1986, 1988). He found an average increase of fifty-eight suicides in the week following a suicide story. The more coverage the suicide received, the greater the increase. Further study has shown that suicides by famous people are more likely to lead to copycat suicides than those committed by noncelebrities (Stack, 1987a).

Phillips and his colleagues found that teenagers are more prone to copycat suicides than are people of other ages (Phillips and Cartensen, 1986, 1988). Whereas the suicide rate for young adults age 20 to 29 rose less than 7 percent after a suicide story appeared in the media, that for teenagers rose 22 percent. Only among adolescents does the power of media suggestion seem to override the effects of sex and race. The tragedy is that these youthful, imitative suicides might be prevented.

Phillips suggests that the impact of suicide stories is in part the result of the way they are reported (Phillips and Cartensen, 1988). He describes suicide stories as "natural advertisements," which inadvertently follow the rules for good commercials. Sales of a product are most likely to increase if the ads (1) appear in prominent places, (2) appear more than once, (3) show attractive people who

> **Media coverage of celebrity suicide stories may function either as "natural advertisements" for suicide or as "inoculations" against copycat suicides.**

appeal to consumers, (4) do not mention negative consequences (such as added calories and slowed reaction times when you drink beer), and (5) do not show alternatives (Big Macs in a Burger King ad, or vice versa).

Likewise, teen suicide rates are most likely to increase if the media coverage (1) appears on the front page of newspapers or as the lead story in newscasts, (2) repeats the story on more than one day, (3) centers on the suicide of a celebrity or a teenager with whom other teenagers can identify, (4) neglects to mention the physical pain and disfigurement of suicide, and (5) does not present alternative ways of coping with unhappiness and stress (counseling, self-help groups, hotlines). The media do not intend to "sell" suicides, of course, but they do want to sell themselves. The natural advertisement of suicide is thus an unintended consequence of the competition among publishers to sell newspapers and among TV stations to improve ratings.

When 27-year-old Kurt Cobain, leader of the band Nirvana, killed himself in 1994, he joined the choir of brilliant but troubled "rock angels" who have taken their own lives, either deliberately or through accidental overdoses of drugs and alcohol—Elvis Presley, Jim Morrison, Jimi Hendrix, and Janis Joplin. Cobain's band had rebelled against the slick, MTV-driven rock establishment. With their stringy hair and torn clothes, heavy-metal sound, and lyrics of disillusionment and despair, they appealed to young people who were tired of such prepackaged icons as Madonna and Michael Jackson (Gelman, 1994; Giles, 1994). Nirvana's third album, *Nevermind,* propelled Cobain into the fame and fortune he disdained. This poet of alienation had convinced thousands of his generation that they were not alone.

Two days after Cobain's body was discovered, the city of Seat-

The greatest increase in suicides ever reported in the United States occurred in August 1962, following the intensive media coverage of actress Marilyn Monroe's alleged overdose of sleeping pills. In contrast, media coverage of rock star Kurt Cobain emphasized the selfish, wasteful, painful aspects of suicide and also publicized where to go for help. This media coverage may have prevented copycat suicides among Cobain's fans.

tle and several local radio stations organized a candlelight vigil at a downtown park that drew some 7,000 fans. The sponsors of this event and public health officials were justifiably concerned that Cobain's death might spark an epidemic of copycat suicides, especially in his hometown. In fact, there were fewer suicides in the seven weeks following Cobain's death than during the same period a year earlier, and only one that appeared linked to Cobain. Analysis suggests that one reason was that "much was done right by the media" (Jobes et al., 1996, p. 263).

First, the media made a concerted effort to distinguish between Cobain, the artist, and Cobain, the depressed drug user who had an ugly history of self-destructive behavior and a troubled marriage to singer Courtney Love and who had repeatedly refused treatment. Second, the media did not glamorize Cobain's suicide (whereas they had romanticized the image of Marilyn Monroe, lonely and misunderstood, drifting into a painless, sleepy death from drug overdose). To the contrary, reporters emphasized that Cobain was so disfigured that the coroner needed to check his dental records to make a positive identification. The candlelight vigil featured an angry, grief-stricken taped message from Courtney Love, who cursed her husband for his selfishness, the pain he caused her and their infant daughter, and the waste of his talent. Finally, broadcasters used every opportunity to advertise the telephone number of the Seattle Crisis Clinic, which was inundated with calls. The general message was clear: great artist; great music; stupid act, don't do it; here's where to get help.

Cobain himself did not benefit from increased awareness of suicides about to happen. But his unheroic death increased public awareness about the true victims of suicide (the survivors), crisis services, and available treatments and help.

The Bad-News Bias

As defined by TV broadcasts, "news" is the exceptional, the dramatically different, the unique, the frightening. Television thrives in hard news—stories about natural disasters, crimes and accidents, and unscheduled events. Reporting tends to focus on "action, people doing something, preferably involving disagreement, conflict or adventure" (Gans, 1970, p. 32). A civil war gets more media attention than an election; a violent election receives more coverage than a peaceful one; and so on. The TV news tends to overemphasize bad news. As one TV producer said, "All journalists assume that the Boy Scouts and the churches are operating normally; our job is to cover what goes awry" (quoted in Gans, 1970, p. 10; see also Gitlin, 1986).

TV journalists do not deliberately distort current events. But they tend to concentrate on dramatic events that make "good stories." As a result, the

This image of the body of an American soldier being dragged through the streets of Mogadishu in 1993 became a rallying cry for those who opposed the U.S. mission to Somalia.

overall impression of the world that we get from television can be misleading. Airplane crashes, terrorist bombings, and hostage situations attract extensive coverage. What we don't see is that even in a troubled region such as the Middle East, most people go to work in the morning, come home to dinner with their families, and visit their relatives on the weekends. Studies show that heavy TV viewers are more likely than light viewers to see their communities, and the world, as dangerous (Postman and Powers, 1992).

Whereas the TV news plays on our emotions, sociology encourages us to look more objectively at a wider range of facts. What we find is that things aren't nearly as bad as the news often suggests. For example, New York City, the city everyone loves to hate, is not such a dangerous place to live; the great majority of New Yorkers have never been mugged or otherwise attacked. Indeed, New York ranks nineteenth in the nation in rates of violent crime. (See Table 1-1.)

Sociologists are as interested in crime as the average person, but they look beyond individual cases for explanations. It is important to understand the cause of one homicide; but over and above that, sociologists want to know why there are 25,000

Table 1-1   *Violent Crime Rate by City, 1994*

City	Total Violent Crime Rate per 100,000
Newark, NJ	3,841
St. Louis, MO	3,750
Atlanta, GA	3,571
Tampa, FL	3,482
Miami, FL	3,413
Baltimore, MD	2,834
Detroit, MI	2,687
Washington, DC	2,662
Baton Rouge, LA	2,449
Birmingham, AL	2,445
Kansas City, MO	2,435
St. Petersburg, FL	2,254
Buffalo, NY	2,124
Los Angeles, CA	2,059
Boston, MA	1,915
Minneapolis, MN	1,907
Portland, OR	1,902
Jersey City, NJ	1,865
New York, NY	1,861

Source: U.S. Bureau of the Census, *Statistical Abstract of the United States, 1996.* Washington DC: GPO, table 313, p. 203.

homicides in the United States each year, why the homicide rate may be rising or falling, who the offenders are, who the victims are, what the circumstances are surrounding the killings, and what the most common relationships are between the victim and the offender.

The TV news claims to tell us what is happening in our world. But on any given day, there may be thirty or forty civil wars, as many riots, a dozen natural disasters, scores of elections, plus hundreds upon hundreds of other potentially newsworthy events. The news media are necessarily selective. As big businesses themselves, the news media tend to support the status quo. One way they do this is by making you feel lucky to be you, given the misfortunes other people are suffering—hence the "bad-news bias" (see Liska and Baccaglini, 1990). Sociology helps explain what is selected as news, how it is packaged, and why.

News as Big Business

To understand what issues and events are reported as news and how they are covered, one must understand the social structure of news organizations themselves. In the early days of television, news programs were seen almost as a public service, supplementing more commercial entertainment and sports programs. Today, however, TV news is big business. Indeed, public communications is fast becoming one of the largest and most powerful industries in the United States—and the world.

Like breakfast cereal, news comes to us in many different packages with an assortment of colorful labels. In fact, our sources of information are limited. Ownership of the communications media is highly concentrated. Twenty-five years ago, newspapers, magazines, radio, television, books, and movies were still separate industries, each dominated by one or a few large companies (Bagdikian, 1997). Since then, the number of controlling firms in all these media has shrunk—from fifty corporations in 1984 to twenty-three in 1990 to between six and ten in 1996. At the same time, the boundaries between different media have largely disappeared. Today's major media companies have holdings in virtually every form of communication and entertainment (from theme parks and video games to newscasts and telephone companies), and they control everything from the content to delivery to consumers.

The Disney empire, for example, has interests in the America Online computer network, Buena Vista home video, Hyperion and Chilton book publishers, four movie and TV production studios, four magazine publishing groups, three record companies, eleven newspapers, and several cable networks (including part ownership of A&E, Lifetime, and ESPN). When Disney bought ABC, it acquired the largest radio network in the United States as well as ABC Network News, whose programs include *Prime Time Live, Good Morning America, 20/20,* and *World News Tonight with Peter Jennings.* General Electric owns the NBC News Network; CBS is owned by Westinghouse; Time Warner, publisher of *Time* magazine, owns Turner Broadcasting (which owns CNN) and runs its own cable company. These huge conglomerates usually are able to buy out or shut out independent producers. In some cases they compete directly with one another, but in many cases they engage in joint ventures (Figure 1-6).

A measure of the power of these media giants was the passage of the Telecommunications Act of 1996, which, for the first time, allowed a single company to own more than one radio station, or both TV stations and cable systems, in the same market and permitted telephone companies to enter the fields of television, radio, and cable. Supporters of the act held that it would promote variety and competition. In most cases, however, the opposite has happened (Bagdikian, 1997). In the United States, of the 1,500 newspapers, 99 percent are the only daily in their cities; all but a handful of the almost 12,000 cable systems are monopolies in their area; and the more than 11,000 commercial radio stations adopt similar formats (all talk, all news, a particular style of music). Instead of competing with one another, these media often collaborate. For example, Disney and News Corporation compete in Europe and North America, but are 50/50 partners in ESPN Star Sports, broadcast in Asia; the News Corporation and Sony are partners in a new satellite venture in Japan; and Europe's third-largest media corporation has a long-term distribution arrangement with Disney. As a result of centralization, network news tends to be homogenized, with overlapping coverage of the same events, told from similar political themes. The only genuine alternatives are public TV channels and radio stations, which must compete for foundation funds and audience contributions.

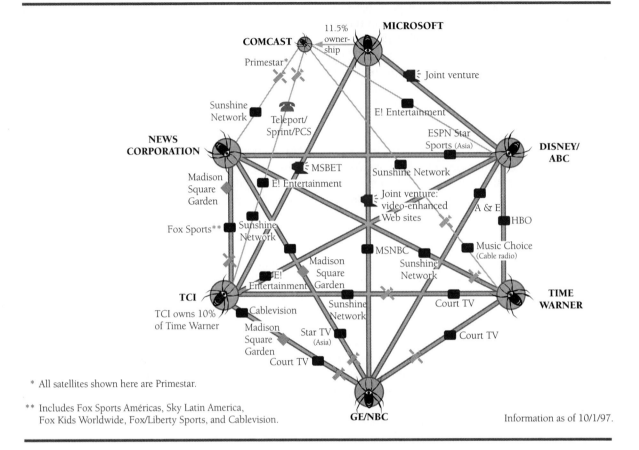

Figure 1-6   *Major Media Conglomerates*

Not only do a small number of giant media conglomerates dominate mass communication, but these companies also collaborate on joint projects, resulting in a complex web of connections that reduces competition and contributes to the homogenization of news and entertainment.

Source: Adapted from K. Auletta, "The Next Corporate Order: American Keiretsu," *The New Yorker,* Fall 1997.

The media are commercial enterprises. (Even public broadcasting must support itself.) Hence the news is a commodity—a product or package—designed to attract an audience for advertisers. Unlike the movies, which require that the audience purchase tickets (albeit for a limited number of films distributed by major media corporations), most television is free to viewers. The networks make money by selling time to advertisers. In some cases, an advertiser exercises direct pressure by refusing to sponsor a program that runs counter to its interest (and by convincing other potential sponsors to do the same). More often, the pressure is indirect: advertisers sponsor news programs that are usually friendly to corporate America and its government supporters. When critical exposés do surface, they are often revealed by low-budget, obscure, offbeat stations and publications, which reach only small audiences. Furthermore, the lines between news, entertainment, and advertising are becoming blurred.

Now and then, a well-known journalist resigns as a protest against corporate attempts to control his or her editorial freedom. But this is the exception. Typically, broadcasters exercise what media analyst Michael Parenti (1993) calls "self-censorship." There are no actual censors checking the news and blacking out criticism of those in power. Rather, the U.S. news media censor themselves. The heads of network news divisions (who set policy), the editors (who make decisions about what stories to cover and which reporters to assign), and the reporters themselves learn to "play by the rules." They may cover a protest demonstration, for example, but underestimate the number of demonstrators or focus on dissenters who appear to be members of an extreme fringe. Reporters exercise autonomy, but mostly within limits acceptable to those who pay their salaries (ultimately the advertisers), who control their careers (media executives), and who can provide or withhold essential information (government officials).

Concentration of ownership has occurred in all media, not just television. Against predictions, radio is making a comeback, led by conservative Rush Limbaugh's call-in show and his estimated 19 million listeners (Bagdikian, 1997). One reason is that the Fairness Doctrine, which required broadcasters to give equal time to opposing views and to allow public figures who were attacked on air to respond, was suspended in 1987. The Fairness Doctrine was based on the concept that the airwaves belonged to the public at large and that broadcasters therefore had a civic duty to be evenhanded; the doctrine was repealed on the grounds that government regulations were limiting freedom of speech. Conservatives were the first to take advantage of this new freedom and still dominate radio talk shows. The book-publishing industry is another example of concentrated ownership. More Americans are buying books than ever before. As a nation, we spend more on books than on any other medium. Yet half of all popular or "trade" books are published by just three companies (Random House, Advance/Newhouse, and the German-owned company, Bertelsmann which purchased Random House in 1998) and one-third are purchased at two chain stores, Borders/Walden and Barnes & Noble. Even the Internet, hailed as the ultimate medium for free and open communication, is not immune to the issue of concentration. Microsoft, which produced almost 80 percent of the computer software now in American homes, is fighting to control the format (if not the content) of the Internet, by requiring computer manufacturers who use its popular windows system to use the Microsoft browser as well. In short, we have access to more sources of information than ever before, but that information is produced by a smaller collection of interconnected corporations.

We are not suggesting that all media, or all news, is biased and misleading or that sociology and the media are "opponents." As readers will note, we frequently use statistics, tables, and illustrations from the news media in this text. The news media are designed for rapid delivery; thus sociological findings and insights may be reported through the media more quickly than they are published in professional journals and books. Likewise, the news media may employ sociologists to conduct polls or may solicit sociologists' insights on an issue or event. But even though the news media and sociology may overlap, there are two main differences between them. First, in collecting and reporting findings, sociologists follow accepted scientific rules of evidence (described in Chapter 2). Second, in deciding what to investigate and how to conduct their investigations, sociologists are guided by established theoretical perspectives (also introduced in Chapter 2). While TV stations and newspapers must concern themselves with what is current and disturbing, as well as which stories and what approach will boost ratings or sell papers, sociologists concern themselves with which questions are important, what research can reveal, and how they can advance our understanding of human social behavior.

In a series of boxed inserts entitled *Sociology and the Media* we illustrate how sociology can fill in the blanks in the news, identify the assumptions underlying the news, and illuminate the impact of the news on people's attitudes and behavior—and how it can help readers be active interpreters of the news, not just passive spectators. In addition, each chapter ends with a section, *Doing Sociology on the Web,* which provides guidelines and web sites which allow you to use the Internet to find more information on topics in that chapter of the text and to compare different sites and evaluate the information you find with a critical, sociological eye. We also invite students to visit the McGraw Sociology web site at http://www.mhhe.com/socscience/sociology/.

SOCIOLOGY ON THE WEB

Sociology and Common Sense

Crime is one of the most serious problems in American societies, right? Violent crime is a threat to every citizen, a pervasive evil that is becoming increasingly prevalent. At least, that's what you're likely to think after watching the local TV news in almost any part of the United States.

Here's a simple exercise that will allow you to get some idea of whether this commonsense idea is true. First, monitor the local news programs in your community for a week. Estimate what percentage of the stories reported on concern violent crimes. (You might want to work with a small group of students, each one monitoring one TV station.) At the end of the week, jot down your answers to the following questions, based on TV coverage and your commonsense ideas: Is violent crime a serious threat to ordinary people? Is crime on the rise? Who is most likely to be the victim of a crime? Who is most likely to be the perpetrator?

Next, test the accuracy of your opinions by using the Internet to look up national and local crime statistics. Determine whether crime rates are going up or down, and what parts of the country are most affected. Here are some sites at which to begin your web search:

http://www.icpsr.umich.edu/NACJD
The National Archive of Criminal Justice Data at the University of Michigan contains data and analy-

sis from many studies and polls about crime and victims. The archive also includes links to many other sites. For instance, under the heading "Official Statistics," you will find a study of homicides in Chicago from 1965 to 1995, done under the auspices of the state of Illinois.

http://www.ojp.usdoj.gov/bjs/
The web site of the U.S. Department of Justice, Bureau of Justice Statistics, contains summary findings about criminal justice, crime statistics, and characteristics of criminals and victims.

http://www.fbi/gov/
http://www.lib.virginia.edu/socsci/crime
The first web site listed here, that of the FBI, allows you to access the federal government's Uniform Crime Reports. These are broken down by county, thus enabling you to compare crime statistics across locations and through time. The second site, maintained by the University of Virginia, also allows you to access the Uniform Crime Reports, in addition to providing much information about sociological research on crime.

Summary

1. **What does sociology add to common explanations of issues such as poverty?**
    Common explanations of poverty focus on individual behavior. Sociologists look at *social forces*—at trends and patterns, *social structure,* and *culture*—to illuminate the connection between personal troubles and social problems.

2. **What is sociology?** *Sociology* is the scientific study of the groups and societies we build and how these alliances affect our behavior. It is part of the family of social sciences, which

    includes psychology, anthropology, economics, and political science. The main goal of sociology is to show how the society in which people live and how the positions they occupy in that society, at a particular period in history, influence individuals' attitudes, beliefs, and behavior. To this end, sociologists focus on *social institutions* and *social stratification.*

3. **What are the practical uses of sociology? How can it help you understand your own life? the changing world in which you live?**

Sociology contributes to an understanding of today's complex world by offering fresh ideas (including new concepts, new research, and new perspectives); challenging popular perceptions (especially about what other people are thinking and doing); identifying social problems (such as violence against women); and designing solutions to persistent problems (such as urban poverty). It takes *sociological imagination* to identify the connection between private troubles and public issues and to put personal problems into perspective.

4. **How do sociological insights differ from commonsense explanations of social behavior?** On occasion, sociology is accused of being "nothing more than common sense." In some cases sociology does, indeed, confirm common sense. But often it does not. Furthermore, sociological analysis reveals the flaws in our commonsense views of the world. Our perceptions are often distorted by our previous experiences, attitudes, values, and beliefs, and our images of reality are strongly influenced by the people around us. Common sense is itself a social phenomenon.

5. **How did Emile Durkheim use the sociological perspective to add to our**

understanding of suicide? Durkheim's classic study of suicide shows how sociologists think and how they work. Rejecting *idiographic explanations* (based on individual cases), Durkheim sought to explain the patterns underlying many cases (*nomothetic explanations*). His analysis of the data identified the social facts that explained variations in suicide rates. Suicides can be classified as *egoistic, altruistic, anomic,* or *fatalistic,* depending on the nature and strength of the individual's involvement in society.

6. **How does the picture of the world presented by the news media differ from the perspective gained by studying sociology?** Much of our information about the world comes from the mass media. TV newscasts tell us the "who, what, where, and when" of an event, but rarely the "why." Sociologists seek to understand the underlying social reality: to make connections, to clarify the similarities between apparently dissimilar and isolated events, to go behind events to identify *social forces,* and to put facts into perspective. Analyzing the social structure of the media is part of this process.

Key Terms

altruistic suicide   26
anomic suicide   28
anomie   28
culture   10
egoistic suicide   25

fatalistic suicide   28
idiographic explanation   21
nomothetic explanation   23
social forces   8
social institution   12

social stratification   13
social structure   9
sociological imagination   10
sociology   10

Recommended Readings

Berger, Peter. (1963). *Invitation to Sociology: A Humanistic Perspective.* New York: Anchor Books.

Dash, Leon. (1996). *Rosa Lee: A Mother and Her Family in Urban America.* New York: Basic Books.

Durkheim, Emile. (1897/1966). *Suicide.* New York: Free Press.

Mills, C. Wright. (1959). *The Sociological Imagination.* New York: Oxford University Press.

Parenti, Michael. (1993). *Inventing Reality: The Politics of News Media,* 2d ed. New York: St. Martins.

Wilson, William J. (1996). *When Work Disappears: The World of the New Urban Poor.* New York: Knopf.

Chapter

TWO

Science and Theory in Sociology

Look through a newspaper or magazine on any given day and the chances are you will find at least one story that reports sociological findings.

YOUNG BEYOND THEIR YEARS

Something happened on the way to the 21st century: American youth, in a sharp reversal of historical trends, are taking longer to grow up. As the 20th century winds down, more young Americans are enrolled in college, but fewer are graduating—and they are taking longer to get their degrees. They are taking longer to establish careers, too, and longer yet to marry. . . . Experts on the family say they've never seen anything like it. "Young people are growing up with much less commitment of any kind," says Rutgers University sociologist David Popenoe. . . . "Never before has it been so hard to leave the period of youth." (*Newsweek* Special Issue, Winter/Spring 1990, p. 54)

IN DEATH, A LINK TO BIRTHDAYS

When gravely ill and approaching their birthday, men tend to give up the ghost whereas women hang on, celebrate the birthday and die the following week, a study has found. . . . [The study] is the first to show sex differences in so-called anniversary effects. . . . "We do not know why these differences exist," said

Dr. David P. Phillips, a sociologist at the University of California in San Diego, who conducted the study. . . . [He theorized that] men may die before birthdays since it is a time of taking stock, with less successful men deciding against another year. Women may be more connected to family and [therefore] rally. (*The New York Times,* Sept. 27, 1992, p. E2)

NEVER TOO YOUNG TO BE PERFECT

Child beauty pageants appear to be another example of an America wanting to have it both ways: a paean to the beautiful innocence that childhood should be, but dolled up with the aura of adulthood. . . .

"The commodification of bodies is big business because society reinforces stereotypes of beauty to keep women in their place," said Shalene Hesse-Biber, associate professor of sociology at Boston University. . . .

Anthony Graziano, professor of sociology and co-director of the Center for Children and Youth, at the State University of New York at Buffalo, said: "We want to be good parents and are quick to criticize those we see as not being good parents. But then something creeps into this. It is, at its most

2

Sociologists study the causes and effects of changing family structure—including a new form, blended families—in a variety of ways.

extreme, a sense that we own these children. They are objects to mold and do with as we like." (*The New York Times*, Jan. 12, 1997, p. E4)

THE FACE OF THE FUTURE

The continuing erosion of the family is another sign of trouble. Although the U.S. divorce rate appears to have leveled off since 1980, it is still very high: nearly half of all American children will experience the breakup of their parents' marriage before the age of 18. Single parenting, almost always by the mother, is on the rise: . . .about a third of all American children now live in single-parent homes. Kids in single-parent households are twice as likely to drop out of school or get pregnant during their teenage years, and the risk is just as high for kids of "blended families" that result from remarriage after divorce. And because two-wage-earner households are now the national norm, intact families are under enormous stress as well. . . . "We say it's up to parents to raise their children well, but we know they don't have the time

or the resources to do it," says Frank Furstenberg of the University of Pennsylvania. "There's a lot of blank time in these kids' lives. We have to be concerned about what children are going to look like as a result of family life in the 21st century." (*Newsweek*, Jan. 27, 1997, p. 60)

How do sociologists determine how many young people are delaying graduation, careers, and marriage? How do they discover a link between deaths and birthdays? explain the phenomenon of child beauty pageants in a society that worries that its children grow up too fast? study the impact of changing family structure on the twenty-first century? News reports often tell you what sociologists have found and what they think. But with rare exceptions, they do not tell you how sociologists arrived at those conclusions.

This chapter goes behind the scenes to show sociologists at work in their role as scientists. The goals of any science are to establish the facts of a situation and to explain why these fact are as they are. Facts are established through research; they are explained through scientific theory. Research and theory are intertwined.

Key Questions

1. What is the science of sociology?
2. How do sociologists conduct research?
3. What role does theory play in science?
4. How do sociologists explain society?
5. How do sociologists explain everyday behavior?
6. How do theory and research influence one another?

Sociology as Science

Sociology is grounded in the scientific method. This is what distinguishes sociologists from journalists, philosophers, gossips, people who debate issues through chat rooms on the Internet, and others who seek to understand the human condition. People have been expressing their opinions on the whys and wherefores of human behavior since the beginning of time. The debate over the differences between men and women, for example, goes back thousands of years. Writing in the fourth century B.C., Plato held that "the gifts of nature are alike diffused in both [sexes]; all the pursuits of men are the pursuits of women"—but then he added that "in all of them a woman is inferior to a man" (quoted in Tavris and Wade, 1984, p. 13). Today this debate is likely to focus on specific issues. Your friend may argue that women have equal opportunity in the workplace: they can enter virtually every field and profession and advance as far as their talents and efforts permit. You may respond that men close ranks and create a "glass ceiling" to prevent women from getting to the top in their organizations or professions. Why, for example, are there so few female company presidents? so few female surgeons? If you and your friends stick to your opinions, the argument may go on all night.

The science of sociology moves such issues as gender inequality out of the muddy waters of speculation onto the more solid ground of objective inquiry. **Science** is a set of agreed-upon procedures for establishing and explaining facts. Sociology shares five key features with other sciences.

First, sociology is an *empirical* discipline that relies on evidence gathered through systematic observation and experimentation. Sociologists work with information that can be verified through independent observation. Insofar as possible, they refuse to take anything for granted or to accept anything on faith. They demand proof. Hunches and speculation do have a function in sociology, as in other sciences: they suggest new directions for research. But all conclusions must be put to the empirical test before they are accepted.

Second, sociology is concerned with *minimizing error and bias*. Sociologists use a variety of techniques (such as the control group and the random assignment, described later in this chapter) to guard against seeing only what they want or expect to see. In addition, the reports of scientific research always include a measure of the trustworthiness of the results (such as the margin of error that is reported with the results of a public opinion poll).

Third, sociology is a *public* venture. Sociologists make their methods as well as their results available so that others can evaluate their conclusions and test them independently. Looking at the same data, other sociologists might draw different conclusions. Or they might decide to undertake a study of their own, to verify the results. Open discussion and examination of research gives sociology a self-correcting mechanism. Conclusions are never taken

as final and absolute but are always open to question, testing, and revision.

Fourth, sociology is concerned with *generalizations*. When sociologists interview members of a family, they are interested not just in learning about those particular individuals but in testing general propositions about all families. When they study social behavior during a hurricane or a flood, they hope to learn something about social responses to all natural disasters. Thus scientists study particular cases in order to arrive at generalizations (Berger, 1963).

Finally, sociology seeks to relate facts to one another and to underlying principles in order to produce *theory*. Sociologists pursue not only descriptions but also explanations. They want to know the *causes* of social facts, the *function* of social institutions, or the *meaning* of social actions. Theory helps sociologists predict, understand, and explain events.

Are the social sciences "true" sciences, like biology or physics? Certainly, sociology has not produced anything comparable to the laws of motion in physics or the technology that sent people to the moon. But the subject of sociological investigation—human behavior—presents obstacles that are different from those encountered in the natural sciences. (See *Close Up:* The Ethics of Social Research.) Unlike molecules or mollusks, the subjects of sociological inquiry are active, conscious participants in the action or event being studied, with goals and understandings of their own (Giddens, 1985a). They may deliberately mislead the researcher because they want to make an impression, to appear to be "politically correct," or simply to stay out of trouble. Their views and behavior may be changed by the process or results of research.

Despite obstacles, the scientific study of groups and societies has produced a large body of concrete, and often unexpected, findings. In their efforts to collect facts, minimize error, and systematically test theories through research, sociologists employ the logic and methods used by all scientists.

The Research Procedure

The phrase "scientific research" can be intimidating. It conjures up pictures of men and women in white coats performing mysterious operations with test tubes or feeding data into computers. In fact the

The Ethics of Social Research

Some scientists study chemicals, cell cultures, or distant stars. Sociologists (and other social scientists) study human behavior. This fact creates a number of special ethical considerations—and an equal number of ethical dilemmas.

Sociologists' primary responsibility is to their human subjects. The first rule in conducting research on humans is to avoid causing subjects extreme or lasting physical pain, psychological distress, or humiliation. But in sociological research "harm" may be difficult to measure. On occasion social scientists have asked subjects to violate social rules and perhaps their own consciences. In one experiment, for example, subjects were instructed to administer what they thought were painful electric shocks to another person (Milgram, 1963). In fact the "shocks" were faked and the "victims" were acting, but the subjects did not know this. The experiment was designed to test whether people would obey orders, even if they thought those orders were wrong. (Surprisingly, most did obey.) But did the results justify the potential psychological distress of subjects who believed they had caused a stranger great pain?

The second rule of research on humans is to obtain informed consent. In medical research, the scientist must make sure that subjects understand the potential risks, that they voluntarily agree to participate, and that they know they are free to withdraw at any time for any reason. In social research, however, deception may be critical

> **Sociologists' primary responsibility is to their human subjects.**

to the success of the study. One researcher (A. J. Reiss, 1971) wanted to investigate charges of police brutality. If he had revealed the purpose of his study to police officers, they probably would have gone out of their way to prove that police always treat civilians with respect and consideration. Instead, he told them he was interested in the way civilians treat the police, implying that he was "on their side." The researcher did witness police assaults on civilians. But did the results justify the deception?

The third rule in research on humans is to respect individual privacy. People have a right to determine for themselves when, how, and what kind of information about their private lives becomes public. But if sociologists studied only public behavior, their image of social life would be superficial. The problem is where to draw the line. One researcher was interested in men who engage in furtive, impersonal homosexual acts in public rest rooms, which the men called "tea-rooms" (Humphreys, 1970). He gained their confidence by volunteering to act as a lookout. On the sly he jotted down the men's license plate numbers and obtained their names and addresses from the motor vehicles department. Almost a year later he interviewed a number of these men in their homes, without letting them know why they had been included in his survey. If he had revealed the purpose of his study, the chances are that most would have refused to answer

---

basic, step-by-step procedure that all scientists follow is not at all mysterious (Table 2-1):

1. *Selecting a topic:* The initial idea for a study may come from an article in a professional journal, a classroom discussion, a historic event, or a personal experience that excites a researcher's curiosity.

Sociologists are most likely to pursue a topic if it is the subject of public concern and controversy or if it has some bearing on a theoretical issue that interests them.

2. *Reviewing the literature:* The second step takes the researcher to the library or, nowadays, onto the Internet. How much is known about the subject?

questions. This researcher took elaborate precautions to conceal the men's identities while he was analyzing his data and in his publications. But, again, did the results of the study justify the invasion of privacy?

The American Sociological Association's code of ethics requires that researchers maintain confidentiality "even when the information enjoys no legal protection or privilege and legal force is applied." In keeping with this code, James Richard (Rik) Scarce, a graduate student in sociology at Washington State University, refused to testify before a grand jury investigating a group of animal liberation activists who had been accused of breaking into university laboratories (*The Chronicle of Higher Education*, May 26, 1993, p. A10). The author of a book on "eco-warriors," Scarce had interviewed numerous environmental activists as part of his research. He maintained that testifying at the trial not only would break his vow of confidentiality to his subjects but also would damage the ability of other social scientists to conduct

research that requires anonymity. Scarce served 159 days in jail before he was released when a judge ruled that further incarceration was not likely to cause him to testify. Some colleagues see Scarce as an authentic American hero, but others disagree on the grounds that sociologists are not above the law. The law protects the confidentiality of communications with one's spouse, physician, lawyer, and minister, priest, or rabbi. No other professionals, including journalists, enjoy this protection. If a sociologist receives confidential information about a planned act of terrorism, should he or she refuse to reveal this information, even under court order? Did Scarce's research justify the potential cover-up of a crime?

Sociologists also have responsibilities toward the discipline and their colleagues. Science is a collaborative enterprise. It depends on the sharing of accurate information. If researchers falsify data, they not only mislead their colleagues but, also undermine public trust in the scientific community. (In-

vasions of privacy and acts of deception may also undermine public trust.)

Finally, sociologists have responsibilities toward the public. Sociology can have direct impact on people's lives. Sociologists are sometimes called upon to design and evaluate social programs. Officials draw on sociological theories and research in formulating public policy. Bits and pieces of research are frequently used—and misused—as ammunition in political battles. While sociologists cannot control the uses to which their research is put, they do have an ethical responsibility to inform the public when statements or data are taken out of context or when tentative findings are misrepresented as fact.

The overarching rule in scientific research is that the potential benefits must outweigh the risks. Universities have independent institutional review boards to assess this question and approve (or reject) research involving human subjects.

How have other investigators explained what they have found? What questions haven't they answered? What questions haven't they asked?

3. *Formulating the problem:* Next the researcher translates hunches and findings that emerge from his or her review of the literature into a question or questions that are suitable for research. For example, rates of

unemployment are exceptionally high in inner-city ghettos. One possible explanation is that ghetto residents do not have the educational credentials necessary for employment in today's job market; another possible explanation is that employers discriminate against African Americans. A review of the data shows that Latinos have about the same levels

Unlike meteorologists, physicists, or chemists, sociologists study human beings who are active, conscious participants in the events being studied.

Table 2-1   *Basic Research Procedure*

1. Selecting a topic
2. Reviewing the literature
3. Formulating the problem (translating theories or hunches into hypotheses)
4. Creating a research design (choosing a research method, sampling procedure, and measurements)
5. Collecting data
6. Interpreting and analyzing data (uncovering and explaining patterns in the data; confirming, rejecting, or modifying hypotheses)
7. Publishing findings (making methods and results available to others)
8. Replicating the research (another researcher repeating the study, perhaps with modifications)

Source: Adapted from Carlo Lastrucci, *The Scientific Approach.* Cambridge, MA: Schenkman, 1967, p. 55. Reprinted by permission of Schenkman Books, Inc.

of education as blacks and are also subject to discrimination—yet Latinos have significantly lower rates of unemployment. This puzzle became the basis for William J. Wilson's ongoing program of research into the effects of class and race on ghetto poor (discussed in detail in Chapter 8).

Next the researcher formulates **hypotheses**— testable statements about the nature of a phenomenon, distribution of behavior, or cause and effect. For example, a researcher might hypothesize that during presidential elections, televised debates play a critical role in helping undecided voters decide how to cast their ballot. In this hypothesis, televised debates are the **independent variable,** the factor that is considered a potential cause; the viewer's decision to vote for one or another candidate is the **dependent variable,** the phenomenon that is treated as an effect or result. A **variable** is any phenomenon in which researchers can observe differences across cases or change over time. For example, people with high incomes might favor one candidate, whereas people with low incomes might prefer another; the proportion of undecided voters may be large at the beginning of the campaign but small near the end. The researcher may find a positive relationship between variables: a majority of undecided voters become committed voters after a debate. If this is the case, the hypothesis is supported. If the researcher finds no relationship, or an insignificant one (most undecided voters are no more committed after debates than they were before), the hypothesis is disproved.

4. *Creating a research design:* The fourth step is deciding what methods to use to collect data. Later in this section we describe the five main research methods sociologists use most often: the survey, the field study, the experiment, the cross-cultural study, and the historical study. Each method has strengths and weaknesses. In some cases the nature of the research topic may force a choice. For example, a survey is the most likely choice when a researcher wants to determine how widespread a behavior pattern is. This is why polls are used so often to measure political opinion. But the choice of methods is only part of the research design. The sociologist must also deal with the problems of sampling and measurement.

In most research, as we have noted, sociologists are not interested in individual cases. They seek information that applies to a large population (all working-class families, all college students, all Chinese Americans). It is seldom possible to study all members of the target population, however; sociologists can study only a **sample,** or portion of that number. How can they ensure that the people they study are typical? One technique is **representative sampling,** in which each member of the population being studied has an equal chance of being selected. If the sample is large enough, this procedure will ensure that all major social groups will be represented. If the sample is small, researchers "oversample" from some social groups and then use statistical weighting procedures to adjust for this. The larger the sample, the smaller the margin of error.

A second issue is measurement. Suppose the researchers are studying child abuse. If they ask parents, "Have you ever abused your child?" they will get a low rate of (honest) positive responses; few people want to admit to socially unacceptable behavior. A better approach would be to present parents with a list of disciplinary techniques, some of which could injure a child, that does not label these actions "abuse" (see Table 2-2).

A number of practical considerations also enter into the research design. A sociologist may not be able to obtain funds for a national survey; police or hospital officials may not be willing to allow a researcher to examine their files; subjects may move and be unavailable for crucial follow-up interviews.

5. *Collecting data:* Step five is putting the research plan into action by sending out questionnaires or knocking on doors, becoming an observer in our own or another culture, gathering historical documents, or conducting an experiment (as we will describe in detail below).

6. *Interpreting and analyzing the data:* Facts do not fall neatly into place, no matter how carefully they are collected. More often than not, data collection produces unexpected or ambiguous findings. Classifying bits and pieces of information so that patterns become visible, and then interpreting these patterns, is one of the most demanding steps in research. The hypothesis may be confirmed, rejected, or left undecided.

The process of interpreting data often requires that sociologists draw on works of sociological theory that both summarize existing knowledge and provide guidelines for collecting and explaining new data. (See the discussion of theory later in this chapter.)

7. *Publishing findings:* Once the information has been interpreted, the researcher makes it available by presenting it in a paper at a professional meeting and/or publishing it in a journal article or a book. Sociologists publish their methods as well as their results so that others can evaluate their conclusions independently by replicating the research. As a rule, the researchers point out any problems they encountered in the course of their study, discuss the limitations of their findings (how widely they can be applied to other people and situations), and suggest questions for future research. Publication does not necessarily complete the research process.

Table 2-2   *Family Violence Against Children*

Percent of Children Whose Parent(s):	1975	1985	1988	1989	1990	1991	1992	1993	1994	1995	1996	1997
Insulted or swore at them	37%	42%	55%	51%	40%	44%	45%	44%	45%	40%	35%	42%
Spanked or hit them	58	56	63	61	51	52	53	52	49	47	42	46
Hit or tried to hit them with an object	13	8	x	x	x	8	10	10	9	10	7	7
Kicked, bit, or punched them	3	3	x	x	x	3	4	2	2	3	1	2

x=Question not asked.

1975: First National Family Violence Survey, Murray A. Straus and Richard J. Gelles, principal investigators; data based on interviews with 1,146 intact families (2 caretakers in the home). 1985: Second National Family Violence Survey, Gelles and Straus; data based on interviews with 3,232 caretakers (including single parents). 1988–1997: National Committee to Prevent Child Abuse annual poll; number of families interviewed in 1988, 490; 1989, 513; 1990, 459; 1991, 480; 1992, 445; 1993, 468; 1994, 474; 1995, 470; 1996, 445; 1997, 470.

8. *Replicating the research:* Other researchers may repeat the study, both to check the results and to determine whether they can be applied to a larger population, or generalized. **Replication**—repeating a study with another group of subjects at another place and time, perhaps with modifications in the methods—is an essential safeguard against error. Other researchers might or might not obtain the same results, as we will see when we discuss a field experiment below.

Doing Sociological Research

The basic steps in scientific research are clear and straightforward. In actual practice, however, the process is not quite so neat. Some steps may be accomplished in a matter of hours; others may drag on for months. A sociologist may make a number of false starts that lead to dead ends or may have a sudden flash of insight. Scientific research is a creative process that requires imagination, a tolerance for hard and often tedious work, skill in organizing resources and winning cooperation, and occasionally luck. Now we look behind the scenes, to show sociologists at work.

Each of the five studies analyzed below addresses the issue of family violence. But each deals with a different aspect of this problem, and each uses a different research design.

Family violence was not considered to be an extensive or serious social problem until sociologists began to study it in the 1970s. Even in the 1990s, however, allegations of family violence were not taken seriously. The murder of Nicole Brown Simpson helped to raise public consciousness. Despite her repeated calls to 911 begging for protection, her husband O.J. Simpson was not arrested, charged, or tried for assaulting his wife.

A Survey: Two National Family Violence Surveys

The Problem

In the 1960s, family violence was not considered a serious problem (as noted in Chapter 1). When sociologists Murray Straus, Richard Gelles, and Suzanne Steinmetz became curious about this topic and discussed the issue with friends and colleagues, however, they were met with skepticism. Family violence is a blind alley, they were told. Besides, how could they study private behavior, especially behavior that reflected badly on the participants? Although aware that this line of research might lead nowhere, the three sociologists nevertheless decided to try.

Methods

Straus, Gelles, and Steinmetz chose the **survey** approach: the use of standardized questionnaires or interviews, or both, to gather data on large populations. They began in the early 1970s with an exploratory study of the hundreds of students enrolled in introductory sociology classes at the University of New Hampshire. Rather than ask students directly whether they had been abused by their parents or had seen their parents abusing each other, they devised the Conflict Tactics Scale (see Figure 2-1). Students were asked to fill out a questionnaire about how their family resolved conflicts. They were given a choice of three basic approaches: rational discussion, verbal or nonverbal expressions of anger and hostility, or the use of physical force or violence. The scale was designed to measure how often and under what circumstances these different strategies were employed.

A major concern is whether the procedures the researchers are using are *valid*. That is, do they measure what the researchers want to measure, and are the results truthful and accurate? For example, students may not know about violent interactions between their parents. To assess the validity of students' responses, the questionnaire was also sent to their parents. A student's and his or her parents' answers were nearly always consistent, indicating the Conflict Tactics Scale was a valid means of measuring family violence. Even so, the researchers assumed that there would be some underreporting and that their estimates would be conservative. People do not "tell all" in social surveys on sensitive topics.

Sample question: No matter how well a couple gets along, there are times when they disagree, get annoyed with the other person, or just have spats or fights because they're in a bad mood or tired or for some other reason. They also use many different ways of trying to settle their differences. I'm going to read some things that you and your partner might do when you have an argument. I would like you to tell me how many times *(read each item)* in the past 12 months you *(read list)*.

Q.35
Respondent

	Once	Twice	3–5 times	6–10 times	11–20 times	More than 20 times	*(Do not read)* Don't know	*(Do not read)* Never
a. Discussed an issue calmly	___–1	___–2	___–3	___–4	___–5	___–6	___–8	___–0
b. Got information to back up your/his/her side of things	___–1	___–2	___–3	___–4	___–5	___–6	___–8	___–0
c. Brought in or tried to bring in someone to help settle things	___–1	___–2	___–3	___–4	___–5	___–6	___–8	___–0
d. Insulted or swore at him/her/you	___–1	___–2	___–3	___–4	___–5	___–6	___–8	___–0
e. Sulked or refused to talk about an issue	___–1	___–2	___–3	___–4	___–5	___–6	___–8	___–0
f. Stomped out of the room or house or yard	___–1	___–2	___–3	___–4	___–5	___–6	___–8	___–0
g. Cried	___–1	___–2	___–3	___–4	___–5	___–6	___–8	___–0
h. Did or said something to spite him/her/you	___–1	___–2	___–3	___–4	___–5	___–6	___–8	___–0
i. *Threatened* to hit him/her or throw something at him/her/you	___–1	___–2	___–3	___–4	___–5	___–6	___–8	___–0
j. Threw or smashed or hit or kicked something	___–1	___–2	___–3	___–4	___–5	___–6	___–8	___–0
k. Threw something at him/her/you	___–1	___–2	___–3	___–4	___–5	___–6	___–8	___–0
l. Pushed, grabbed, or shoved him/her/you	___–1	___–2	___–3	___–4	___–5	___–6	___–8	___–0
m. Slapped him/her	___–1	___–2	___–3	___–4	___–5	___–6	___–8	___–0
n. Kicked, bit, or hit him/her/you with a fist	___–1	___–2	___–3	___–4	___–5	___–6	___–8	___–0
o. Hit or tried to hit him/her/you with something	___–1	___–2	___–3	___–4	___–5	___–6	___–8	___–0
p. Beat him/her/you up	___–1	___–2	___–3	___–4	___–5	___–6	___–8	___–0
q. Choked him/her/you	___–1	___–2	___–3	___–4	___–5	___–6	___–8	___–0
r. *Threatened* him/her/you with a knife or gun	___–1	___–2	___–3	___–4	___–5	___–6	___–8	___–0
s. Used a knife or fired a gun	___–1	___–2	___–3	___–4	___–5	___–6	___–8	___–0

Figure 2-1   *Conflict Tactics Scale*

Straus, Gelles, and Steinmetz devised the Conflict Tactics Scale, a questionnaire for students about how their families deal with conflicts.

Source: R. J. Gelles and M. A. Straus, *Intimate Violence.* New York: Simon and Schuster, 1988, p. 227.

Of course, college students are a captive audience, unlikely to refuse a professor's request to participate in a study. Would the general public be willing to talk about this taboo subject? To find out, Gelles obtained the cooperation of a southern New Hampshire police department, which gave him the names and addresses of families listed for domestic disturbance or assault calls. Neighbors were selected for comparison. Armed with clipboards and tape recorders, Gelles and his assistants began ringing doorbells in the early morning, hoping to find the wife or husband at home alone. The interviewers were nearly always admitted; the interview, designed to take one hour, often continued for three or four as respondents recalled additional incidents, often in graphic detail. Far from being unwilling to talk, some seemed almost unable to stop.

The results of these pilot studies were "sadly surprising" (Gelles and Straus, 1988, p. 208). One in six college students reported that they had witnessed their parents engaging in violence at least once during the preceding year. Half of the students sampled had been hit, and 8 percent reported being injured by a parent during the last year they lived at home, when they were 17 or 18 years old. Half of the families from the police list reported one or more instances of abuse. So did one-third of the neighbors, who had been interviewed because they were thought to be nonviolent! Clearly media reports were only the tip of the iceberg; a broader study was called for.

In 1976, Straus, Gelles, and Steinmetz launched their most ambitious project, the First National Family Violence Survey. To be eligible, respondents had to be currently married or living with a person of the opposite sex. The researchers interviewed a nationally representative sample of 2,146 individual family members face to face, again using the Conflict Tactics Scale.

Then, in 1985, Straus and Gelles conducted the Second National Survey, interviewing 6,002 individuals by telephone. This time, single parents (whether never married, separated, or divorced) were included.

Results

The results of the First National Survey indicated that domestic violence was far more widespread than anyone had imagined, even the researchers:

Drive down any street in America. More than one household in six has been the scene of a spouse striking his or her partner last year. Three American households in five (which have children living at home) have reverberated with the sounds of parents hitting their children. Where there is more than one child in the home, three in five are the scenes of violence between siblings. Over all, every other house in America is the scene of family violence at least once a year. (Straus, Gelles, and Steinmetz, 1980)

Violence, it seemed, was as much a part of family life as love. Americans were at greater risk of assault, physical injury, and even murder in their own homes, at the hands of other family members, than anywhere else. Although shocking at first, other research supported these findings.

When Gelles and Straus conducted their Second National Survey in 1985, the results were equally surprising—but for different reasons (Gelles and Straus, 1987, 1988; Straus and Gelles, 1986). They found that rates of domestic violence were still unacceptably high but that child abuse had *declined* by 47 percent (from 36 to 19 acts of severe violence per 1,000 children) and wife beating, by 21 percent (from 38 to 30 acts of severe violence per 1,000 wives). A number of child advocates and others who work with families were skeptical: "Gelles Study Strikes Discordant Note," proclaimed a headline in *Child Protection Report* (Nov. 22, 1985, p. 3).

What accounted for the difference between the results of the two surveys? One possibility was that the second survey used somewhat different methods, in particular, half-hour phone interviews rather than hour-long face-to-face interviews. But most studies show that respondents are more likely to report taboo behavior over the phone than in person. The responses "never" and "don't know" were not listed but had to be volunteered in the second survey, which again should have produced higher, rather than lower, rates of reported violence.

A second possibility was that people were less willing to report the use of physical force within the family at the later date. In the 1980s, slapping a spouse or smacking a child had become less "socially acceptable."

A third possibility was that changes in the social climate had produced real changes in behavior. Public awareness of domestic violence had increased dramatically. The proportion of the public who considered child abuse a serious problem spiraled from 10 percent in the early 1970s to 90 percent in the 1980s. Whereas wife beating used to be considered a family matter, the International Association of Chiefs of Police now recommended that all assaults be treated equally, regardless of where they took place (at home or in public) and regardless of whether the parties were related. All fifty states now require that social workers, physicians, teachers, and others who work with children report suspected incidents of child abuse or neglect. Families had also changed. Americans were marrying later, having fewer children, and apparently having fewer unplanned children—all of which may reduce family stress. The economy was better in 1985 than in 1975, again reducing pressures on families. Moreover, the number of hotlines and shelters for victims of family violence had grown, as had treatment programs for abusers.

The researchers supported the third view—that the decline in reported family violence reflected real changes in behavior—adding that even if the changes were limited to attitudes, that alone was a step in the right direction. More recent surveys (Gelles, 1997) found that while minor assaults by husbands against wives had increased somewhat, severe assaults and homicides had continued to decline (see Figure 2-2). Despite the growing "parents' rights" movement, which holds that the government has no right to tell parents how to discipline their children, parents' self-reports of spanking their children also declined, from 64 percent in 1988 to 47 percent in 1995.

Strengths and Weaknesses of Surveys

The chief advantage of surveys lies in numbers. With a comparatively small investment of time, a researcher can ask thousands of people hundreds of questions. The impersonality of an anonymous mail survey or phone interview may encourage people to give information about sensitive topics that they might not disclose to someone face to face. Finally, the questions (and in some cases the responses) in surveys are usually standardized. Everyone is asked the same questions, and on some surveys the same choice of responses is given (for example, "always, often, sometimes, or never"). As a result, findings can easily be quantified, or translated into numbers. Gelles and Straus could say precisely that the rate of child abuse had dropped from 36 to 19 children per 1,000, for example. Such numbers permit rapid

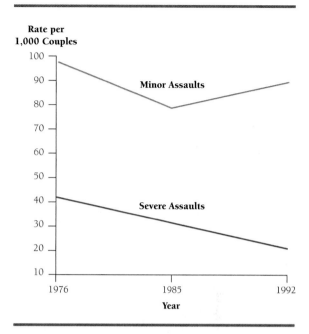

Figure 2-2   *Changing Rates of Husband-to-Wife Violence*

Sources: M. A. Straus and R. J. Gelles, "Societal Change and Family Violence from 1975 to 1985 as Revealed by Two National Surveys," *Journal of Marriage and the Family* 48, 1986, pp. 465–479; M. A. Straus and G. Kaufman Kantor, "Change in Spouse Assault Rates from 1975 to 1992: A Comparison of Three National Surveys in the United States," paper presented at the 13th World Congress of Sociology, Bielefeld, Germany, 1994.

and easy comparisons between groups and quick assessments of change over time, as in the example described here.

Standardization is also the chief weakness of surveys. Surveys often seem to reduce attitudes, beliefs, and experiences to the lowest common denominator. Because the questions have to be simple, the results may seem superficial. The researcher cannot be sure people are taking a survey seriously and answering truthfully. Moreover, survey responses are greatly influenced by the phrasing of questions and even by the order in which they are asked (Schumann and Presser, 1981). The answers do not reveal very much about the social context—the "feel"—of the situation being studied. Researchers can easily overestimate how complete a picture they get from survey data or treat responses as "hard facts" rather than as indicators. But surveys are only an indirect measure of behavior: the researcher learns what people *say* they did or might do under certain circumstances, not what they *actually* do (Babbie, 1995).

A Field Study: Disciplining Children in Public Places

The Problem

The National Family Violence Surveys found that all forms of domestic violence, from wife beating to physical punishment of children, are more common in poor and working-class families than in middle- and upper-class families. Is this in fact the case? Or are wealthier, better-educated respondents simply better at detecting the researchers' motives and giving the "socially correct" responses in a survey?

Sociologist Bruce Brown (1979) was curious about social class differences in the way parents dis-

Are working-class parents more likely than middle-class parents to use coercive methods of disciplining children? A sociological field study explored this question.

cipline children. A number of studies had suggested that working-class parents were primarily interested in teaching their children obedience to parental authority and often used force to obtain compliance, whereas middle-class parents were primarily interested in teaching their children self-control and used reasoning and guilt to control misbehavior (Kohn, 1959; Steinmetz, 1974). But these studies were based on interviews, surveys, and direct observation—methods that are open to distortion because subjects seek to present themselves in a favorable light. In their daily interaction with their children, are working-class parents as authoritarian, and middle-class parents as reasonable, as they claim? To explore this question, Brown (1979) conducted a field study.

Methods

A ***field study*** takes the form of direct, systematic observation of social behavior in its natural setting. In most cases the researchers introduce themselves to their subjects and spend many hours either observing behavior from the sidelines or participating in social activities and conducting in-depth interviews with their subjects. These techniques are called ***participant observation.***

Bruce Brown's field study was somewhat different. To learn how parents actually behave, he wanted to be as unobtrusive as possible. Brown felt that to "infiltrate" people's homes under false pretenses—for example, by claiming to be visiting socially or to be studying some other topic—would be unethical. To avoid this problem, Brown studied parent-child interaction in a public place, the shopping mall. He chose this setting because shopping often is an intergenerational activity, in which parents and children participate together.

Brown conducted weekly one-and-a-half-hour observation sessions for a nine-week period in 1976 and a seven-week period in 1978. Subjects were identified as working class or middle class on the basis of their appearance and clothing. [Although not thoroughly scientific, there is some empirical evidence that most people can accurately identify a stranger's social class from his or her clothing (Sisson, 1970).] Parents' attempts to discipline children were classified as restrictive (hitting, forcing, yelling, commanding) or autonomy-granting (reasoning, requesting, bribing). In all, he observed 116 middle-class and 129 working-class parent-child interactions.

Findings

Brown found that working-class parents were slightly more likely than middle-class parents to use restrictive disciplinary techniques, but the difference was not statistically significant (81 versus 72 percent of cases, respectively). He suggests that the reason for heavy reliance on coercion is that parents see behavior in public as an "emergency situation." Parents of both social classes accept the view that their children's behavior is a reflection on themselves. If they were good parents, their children would be well-behaved (considerate, courteous, obedient). To avoid public embarrassment, parents use the quickest and most effective means of control, namely, restriction. The observation that parents seem embarrassed when their children misbehave, and often look around to see if others have noticed the misbehavior before acting, suggests that—in public at least—parents are more interested in the reactions of onlookers than in their children's development.

Brown's definition of "restrictive discipline" included both nonphysical (yelling, commanding) and physical coercion (hitting). He did not expect to see serious injury or child abuse in a shopping mall. But his findings have implications for family violence. As long as parents see their children's behavior as a reflection of their own competence, rather than as an expression of the child's own temperament and level of development, they are likely to resort to force as a means of controlling their children's behavior in public, and force can easily escalate into violence in private.

The Strengths and Weaknesses of Field Studies

The field study is particularly well suited for making observations, discovering regularities, and generating new ideas. It is a technique that allows a researcher to get close to subjects and observe subtleties in attitude and behavior that might not be discoverable otherwise. A mailed questionnaire, for example, cannot detect a subject's embarrassment or stress. The field study is the only way to study people in their natural settings; and it may be the best way to collect data on social interaction (like courtroom or schoolroom behavior) and unpredictable events (like political demonstrations).

But there are drawbacks as well. First, the researcher can observe only a small sample of behavior, which may not be typical. Brown notes, for example, that yelling and hitting are more noticeable than requesting or reasoning, and so restrictive discipline may be overestimated in his study. Second, findings tend to depend more on the observer's intuitions and therefore to be more subjective than other methods. In retrospect, Brown wishes that after the incidents he recorded, he or another researcher had interviewed subjects to obtain specific information about their socioeconomic background. Third, it is difficult to generalize from or to replicate a field study. Brown's study tells us how parents react to their children's misbehavior in a public place, for example, but not how they react in private. Fourth, if the researchers make their presence known (which Brown avoided doing), their very presence may alter the behavior. And if they are participant observers, who join the activities they study, there is always a danger that they may become overinvolved with the subjects and lose their impartiality. Finally, Brown's conclusions about why parents behaved as they did are largely intuitions; to identify cause and effect, researchers need tighter control of the variables they want to study.

An Experiment: The Minneapolis Police Experiment

The Problem

What can be done to reduce family violence and to protect victims from future injury? Traditionally the police were reluctant to make arrests in cases of domestic violence, especially wife beating. There were a number of reasons for this "hands-off" attitude; in particular, police tended to see family fights as a private matter, and wives were often reluctant to press charges against their husbands. Unless the wife insisted or the husband threatened an officer, police usually separated the spouses and tried to calm them down but did nothing more.

In the mid-1970s, as concern about family violence grew, two main theories emerged about how the problem should be handled. On the one hand, a number of psychologists called for mediation, or counseling the spouses on nonviolent ways of

Sociologists designed a field experiment to assess whether different types of police intervention could reduce wife abuse.

resolving their differences. Their goal was not to punish the abuser but rather to strengthen the family. They held that arresting the abusive husband would only increase tensions in the family and perhaps incite revenge, making the problem worse. On the other hand, feminist groups called for arrests on the grounds that violence against a woman in the home was no different from violence against a stranger in a public place and, therefore, that wife beating was a criminal act. In several class-action suits, battered women sued police and courts for failing to prosecute their husbands or partners. They argued that by not acting, the criminal justice system in effect was giving men permission to abuse their wives.

Does arrest act as a deterrent to wife abuse? To answer this question, sociologists Lawrence Sherman and Richard Berk designed a field experiment.

Methods

An **experiment** is a systematic, controlled examination of cause and effect. The researcher manipulates some aspect of a situation and observes the effects on the subjects' behavior. In most cases experiments are conducted in a laboratory or another controlled environment to eliminate outside influences. The experimenter designs and directs the action. For obvious reasons, Sherman and Berk could not instigate woman battering in a laboratory. Instead, they adapted the experimental method for a study of actual cases of domestic violence in Minneapolis.

The study began with a three-day planning session between the researchers and about thirty police officers who agreed to participate. This group decided to limit the study to cases of "moderate," or misdemeanor, violence (not involving severe or life-threatening injuries, and therefore not in the felony category) and to exclude cases where the victim demanded an arrest or where a police officer was threatened. The officers were instructed to follow one of three procedures selected by the researchers: arrest, advise (sometimes including informal mediation), or separation (requiring the offender to leave the house for at least eight hours). The effect of these different procedures was measured, first, by examining records to learn whether police received additional complaints of violence from the same household and, second, by conducting follow-up interviews with the victims every two weeks for six months. In all, the study covered a sixteen-and-a-half-month period.

Before considering the results of this experiment, let's go over the design. The purpose of an experiment is to test cause-and-effect relationships. To use a medical example, suppose researchers were interested in the effectiveness of a certain flu shot on elderly people. They might inoculate some volunteers with the vaccine and some with a simple sugar solution. This treatment, which the experimenters control or manipulate, is the *independent variable*. Which of the subjects get the flu and which do not is the *dependent variable*. Presumably, this outcome depends on whether or not the subjects got the flu shot. In the Minneapolis experiment, police intervention (arrest, mediation, or separation) was the independent variable. The husband's later behavior (violent or nonviolent) was the dependent variable. Presumably, this outcome depended (at least in part) on how the police handled the situation.

Researchers cannot assume that they have accurately identified cause and effect. They must control for other, intervening variables. Thus in the medical experiment, the researchers compare the impact of the flu vaccine with that of the sugar solution. In the Minneapolis experiment, the researchers compared the impact of arrest with the impact of advice or separation of the spouses, without arrest.

Comparisons help experimenters reduce the possibility that other factors, which are not part of their experimental design, will influence the results. For example, the fact that the police arrived on the scene and a private altercation became a public one might affect the man's future behavior. Two experimental techniques help reduce "contaminating" factors. First, a true experiment involves at least two groups of subjects. One is the **experimental group**—the one exposed to the experimental treatment (in the Minneapolis experiment, arrest). The second group is the **control group**—the one that is exposed to all the experimental conditions except the experimental treatment (a visit by police that ended with advice or separation, but not arrest). Having two or more groups to compare makes it possible to assess whether differences arise from the experimental treatment or from other, perhaps unknown, factors.

Including an experimental and a control group is necessary to hold other factors constant, but it is not sufficient. Some bias could slip into the assignment of subjects to different groups. For example, men with prior arrest records might be assigned to the experimental group, and men with no known history of crime or violence might be assigned to the control groups. In order to eliminate this possibility, experimenters make a **random assignment** of people to the different groups. In the Minneapolis Police Experiment, report forms were color-coded for arrest, advice, or separation; randomly sorted; and bound in numbered pads. When sent to investigate domestic violence, the participating officers followed whichever procedure—arrest, advice, or separation—was indicated on the top form on their pad. In this way the researchers hoped to eliminate police discretion as a factor that might influence both the procedure and the outcome. The basic idea behind random assignment is that the experimental group, which is chosen blindly from the same population of potential subjects as the control group (alleged wife beaters), would behave in the same way as the control group *if not for the experimental treatment* (arrest).

Findings

Sherman and Berk (1984) found small but significant differences between the experimental and control groups. After six months, 10 percent of the spouses who had been arrested had been reported again for domestic violence, compared with 16 percent of those assigned to advice or mediation and 22 percent of those who were merely separated. The researchers concluded that "the arrest intervention certainly did not make things worse and may well have made things better" (1984, p. 269).

In a preliminary report released to the press, Sherman and Berk advised, with appropriate qualifications, "Arresting most suspects of domestic assault *may* reduce the likelihood of the suspect repeating that violence" (*The New York Times,* Apr. 5, 1983, p. C4, emphasis added). The same article quoted criminologist James Q. Wilson as cautioning that "one experiment doesn't settle anything. We'll have to do this many times and reanalyze the data." Nevertheless, ten days later New York City's police commissioner issued new rules based on Sherman and Berk's findings. Other police commissioners were quick to follow. That September, the Attorney General's Task Force on Family Violence (1984) quoted the Sherman and Berk study extensively and strongly recommended that family violence be treated with criminal sanctions. A study by the Crime Control Institute found a fourfold increase between 1984 and 1986 in police department recommendations of arrest for family violence (Sherman and Cohn, 1989).

Wilson's caution turned out to be prophetic. To date, replications of the Minneapolis Police Experiment have failed to support the general hypothesis that arrest deters violent husbands (see Table 2-3). Similar studies in Omaha, Charlotte, and Milwaukee found no evidence that arrests reduce recidivism; to the contrary, they found that arrest may *increase* the chances of a wife's being abused

Table 2-3   *Summary of Results of Six Arrest Experiments for Repeat Violence against the Same Victim*

Finding	Minneapolis	Omaha	Charlotte	Milwaukee	Colorado Springs	Miami
Six-month deterrence, official measures	Yes	No	No	No	No	1 of 2
Six-month deterrence, victim interviews	Yes	Border	No	No	Yes	Yes
Six- to twelve-month escalation, official measures	No	Yes	Yes	Yes	No	No
Six- to twelve-month escalation, victim interviews	*	No	No	No	No	No
Thirty- to sixty-day deterrence, official measures (any or same victim)	Yes	No	Border	Yes	No	1 of 2
Thirty- to sixty-day deterrence, victim interviews	Yes	Border	No	Yes	*	Yes
Escalation effect for unemployed	*	Yes	*	Yes	Yes	*
Deterrence for employed	*	Yes	*	Yes	Yes	*

*Relationship not reported.

Source: L. W. Sherman, J. D. Schmidt, and D. P. Rogan, *Policing Domestic Violence: Experiments and Dilemmas.* New York: Free Press, 1992, p. 129.

again (Dunford, Huizinga, and Elliott, 1990; Hirschell, Hutchison, and Dean, 1992; Sherman et al., 1992). However, replications in Colorado Springs and Miami found that both short- and long-term arrest did deter violence over the next six months, with no escalation of violence, according to victims' reports (Berk et al., 1992; Pate and Hamilton, 1992).

What explains these apparently contradictory findings? Closer analysis of the data on five cities seemed to support the idea of "conditional deterrence": arrest did act as a deterrent with men who were employed, but it had the opposite effect with men who were unemployed. Sherman and his colleagues (Sherman et al., 1992) suggest that the impact of arrest depends on the offender's "stake in conformity" (Toby, 1957). The more ties a man has to the community (through work, family, and so on), the greater the shame and humiliation associated with arrest. But a man who is unemployed, unmarried, and otherwise uninvested in the community has little to lose and may seek revenge. (See the discussion of control theory in Chapter 7.)

In summary, these studies have found that arrest works better in some cases of family violence than in others. But the evidence is not overwhelming in either direction. More research is needed to help police accurately identify "good" and "bad" risks on the scene and handle cases appropriately. But until we have firm data, until we know what type of intervention is most effective, Berk holds that arrest is the best option (R. A. Berk, 1993).

The Strengths and Weaknesses of Experiments

The chief advantage of experiments is control. Because the researchers can hold constant other possible influences, it is easier to isolate cause and effect and to rule out intervening factors in experiments than it is in other types of research. Relatively simple techniques (control groups and random assignment) can be used to guard against researcher bias. Experiments usually are easy to replicate, because procedures are worked out in advance.

On the negative side, most social experiments are conducted in laboratories (often with college students as subjects), which can introduce an element of artificiality into the situation. The subjects are bound to feel a little self-conscious. They may

 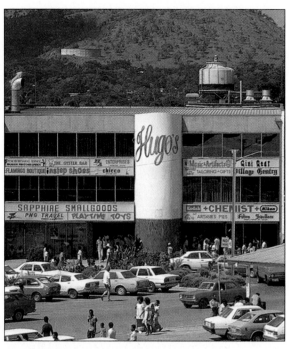

In a cross-cultural study based in Papua New Guinea, Rebecca Morley tested the prevailing view that domestic violence is less common in traditional village societies, where husbands and wives have almost no privacy, than in urban settings, where neighbors are unrelated, or in western societies, where couples are isolated and norms prevent outsiders from intervening in family affairs. Contrary to expectations, she found that wife beating was more frequent in villages than in the capital city Port Moresby, and was twice as common there as in the United States, the United Kingdom, and Australia.

try to second-guess the experimenter. Sherman and Beck avoided artificiality by conducting a field experiment. But what they gained from this realism they may have lost in control. As they themselves have suggested (R. A. Berk, Smyth, and Sherman, 1988), the sample size and the number of police officers who participated regularly were small; officers could undermine the random-assignment procedure by "forgetting" their experimental report sheets or by labeling an assault a felony and therefore not suitable for the experiment; the regular follow-up calls to victims may have introduced a "surveillance effect," preventing repeat violence at least while the study lasted; and many victims could not be reached for follow-up interviews. Each replication of the original experiment has introduced slight variations in an effort to correct these problems.

Experiments are most useful for studying limited, clearly defined questions. They are especially helpful in studies of how individuals or small groups react to a specific situation, such as arrest.

A Cross-Cultural Study: Wife Abuse and Modernization in Papua New Guinea

A **cross-cultural study** is a comparative study of beliefs, customs, and/or behavior among two or more groups of people with different languages and ways of life. The ultimate goal of cross-cultural studies is to learn which patterns of human social life are cultural universals—common to all or most people regardless of where and how they live; which elements of social life are culturally variable; and why. In some cases, cross-cultural studies take the form of an **ethnography,** an extended participant-observer field study, during which the researcher tries to see the world through the eyes of the people he or she is studying and attempts to describe their culture from the inside. The researcher may live in a village or neighborhood of the culture he or she is studying or may spend days, weeks, or months visiting and socializing with local people. In other cases, the researcher examines the results of official records, surveys, or other studies of different cultures.

Papua New Guinea is primarily a Melanesian country composed of more than 700 different linguistic and cultural groups, many of which pursue traditional lifestyles in remote, isolated areas and maintain few contacts with outsiders. (See Map 2-1.) Once a colony of Australia, Papua New Guinea became an independent nation in 1975. Like most developing countries, its economy is primarily agricultural; only 10 percent of the population holds formal jobs, primarily in urban areas. Although virtually all groups in Papua New Guinea have been influenced by modernization and westernization to some degree, traditions remain strong in many rural villages.

British sociologist Rebecca Morley (1994) was interested in the relationship between wife beating and modernization. On the basis of existing evidence, a number of social scientists (for example, Gelles and Cornell, 1983; Levinson, 1989) had postulated that domestic violence was more common in advanced, industrialized nations than in traditional, rural societies, the reason being that in modern societies the nuclear family is isolated from larger networks of kin and subject to numerous sources of conflict and stress. By extension, rapid modernization undermines traditional social values and restraints, causing an increase in family violence and other social problems. An invitation to participate in a national survey conducted by the Law Reform Commission of Papua New Guinea enabled Morley to test these hypotheses through a cross-cultural study.

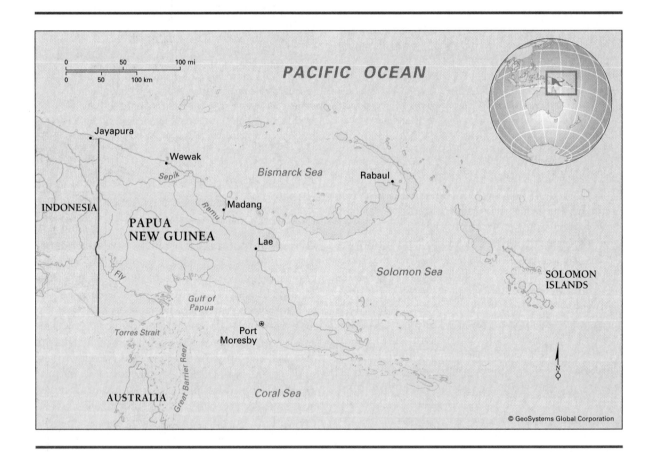

Map 2-1   *Papua New Guinea*

The nation of Papua New Guinea consists of the eastern half of the island of New Guinea. The western half, called Irian Jaya and formerly part of the Dutch East Indies, became a province of Indonesia following a controversial plebiscite (or vote for self-government) in 1969.

The Problem

So far we have been looking at violence in the United States. Is domestic violence a worldwide phenomenon? Is it more common in modern, industrialized nations or in traditional, developing countries?

Methods

The Papua New Guinea domestic violence study was unusual in that Morley and her colleagues used the survey method instead of participant observation for cross-cultural purposes.

Data were collected by students at the University of Papua New Guinea in Port Moresby. Nineteen of the students went to different rural villages and spent a month each administering standardized questionnaires and talking with villagers, much as an ethnographer would. Nearly 1,500 men and women were contacted in these settings. Other groups of students interviewed low-income workers at a variety of companies in Port Moresby and wives in several low-income housing projects, for a total of more than 660 respondents. (A planned study of the "urban elite" was abandoned because few high-level civil servants returned the questionnaires that were mailed to them.) All those surveyed were asked "Have you ever hit your wife?" (for husbands) or "Has your husband ever hit you?" (for wives), plus a number of questions designed to assess attitudes and ways of handling marital problems and marital violence.

For purposes of the study, the impact of modernization was measured by comparing the answers of rural (traditional) and urban (modern) respondents. Urban rates of domestic violence were used for comparisons of Papua New Guinea with other, more developed industrial nations.

Findings

Contrary to what she expected (and to what other research has suggested), Morley found that rates of wife beating in urban Papua New Guinea are twice as high as in industrialized nations (Australia, the United Kingdom, and the United States). Clearly, wife abuse is not a western phenomenon; nor is it tied to the level of modernization. Two-thirds of the rural respondents in the Papua New Guinea survey said they had been victims of abuse, compared with half of the urban respondents. But the gap between the city and the village may not be as wide as these answers indicated. Two-thirds of urban respondents said that their neighbors beat their wives, and those urbanites who did admit to violence beat their wives more often than did rural villagers.

Even so, the survey found that attitudes were changing (see Table 2-4). Urban men as well as women were far less likely than their rural counterparts to say that wife bashing is justified. Why, then, do levels of marital violence remain high? Morley suggests two overlapping reasons. Traditional restraints on wife beating (such as the presence of kin who can intervene and prevent verbal hostilities from escalating into physical violence) have eroded. At the same time, the pressures on couples have grown. In particular, urban women have not only more freedom and autonomy but greater expectations of equality and companionship in their marriages, and this may produce new insecurities in men, who fear that their traditional right to control and dominate their wives is being threatened.

Is wife beating universal? Does it have the same meaning in diverse cultures? Analyzing the reasons men and women give for beatings, Morley concludes they are much the same in rural Papua New Guinea, in Sydney, Australia, and in London, England: "What unites them is the wife's, sometimes defiant, failure to do her husband's bidding and/or her questioning of his actions or authority, and the husband's attempt to beat her into submission" (Morley, 1994, p. 46). If measured in terms of the proportion of people who say wife beating is sometimes necessary and justified, it is more acceptable in traditional societies; but if measured in terms of the reluctance of outsiders to intervene, wife beating is just as acceptable in technologically advanced western societies (Counts, 1990; L. Smith, 1989).

Table 2-4   *Is It Acceptable for a Husband to Hit His Wife?*

Survey	Percent Responding Yes	
	Men	Women
Rural	66	57
Urban	47	25

Source: Rebecca Morley, "Wife Beating and Modernization: The Case of Papua New Guinea." *Journal of Comparative Family Studies*, 1994, table 4, p. 36.

Moreover, in urban New Guinea, as in Australia and Great Britain, both husband and wife often cite alcohol as the excuse for domestic violence. Morley concludes that "both urban and traditional Papua New Guinea would seem to have much in common with other societies in the 'developing' and 'industrialized world' " (1994, p. 47).

The Strengths and Weaknesses of Cross-Cultural Studies

The main advantage of cross-cultural studies is that they enable researchers to identify *cultural universals:* values, norms, beliefs, or practices that are found in all cultures. Thus, Morley found that male dominance is not a peculiar characteristic of "primitive" or industrial societies, European or South Pacific cultures, but that it is found at all levels of technological development and in virtually every culture. Furthermore, gender inequality played a key role in wife abuse in the societies she studied, a finding that is consistent with research in many other societies. Of course, the fact that wife abuse appears to be culturally universal does not mean that it is common behavior: the majority of men do not beat their wives, in any society. It also does not mean that wife beating is "normal" behavior but, rather, means that the problem is widespread.

Cross-cultural research may also help reduce both *ethnocentrism,* the belief that one's own culture is superior to that of other people (see Chapter 3), and reverse ethnocentrism, the view that one's own society is worse than other societies. Many people see the United States as an extremely violent society and assume that wife battery is more common here than in other societies. Morley's research showed that violence toward wives is a serious problem in many—if not most—societies, though it is not always taken seriously as a form of criminal violence.

A major problem in cross-cultural research is definitions. One cannot assume that the same behavior means the same thing to people of other cultures (Counts, 1990). Researchers studying child abuse, for example, find that what people consider abusive behavior or maltreatment varies widely among cultures. Americans think it is normal for infants to sleep alone in a darkened room, and for toddlers to cry themselves to sleep, because it trains them to be independent. In most traditional societies people would consider these practices cruel.

Women carry their babies close to their bodies, in a sling or backpack, at all times, and small children sleep with or within reach of their mothers.

Gaining access to another culture and winning people's trust is a demanding, time-consuming process. To discover how people of another culture see the world, the researcher must learn their language (first choice) or employ translators or key informants (second choice). Either way, it is difficult to translate terms and concepts from the language of the investigator to the language of the people being studied—and back again, for publication. Often there is no exact equivalent for a word or phrase in the other language.

Finally, there is always a risk that the researchers will take an ethnocentric view of the society they are studying, judging other people's ideas and customs in light of their own beliefs and values. Culture is not a set of clothes we can change at will but an integral part of our being: it works its way into our very bones. We take many elements of our culture for granted, as "only natural." (See Chapter 3.) Researchers are not immune to cultural indoctrination. Bias may slip into the questions field researchers ask, the topics they elect to study, and the way they describe their findings. Researchers may be disgusted or enchanted by what they see; they may scorn or idealize the culture they study. Either way, the picture of that society will be distorted.

A Historical Study: The Roots of Violence Against Wives

The Problem

The evidence that domestic violence is widespread continues to mount. Still we believe that the family *ought* to be a "haven in a heartless world" (Lasch, 1977), an island of harmony, bliss, and security. We tend to be nostalgic about the family and to assume that families were happier in the past than they are today. Is that, in fact, the case? To answer this question, sociologists R. Emerson Dobash and Russell Dobash (1979) looked back through history.

Methods

A **historical study** is a review of sources from earlier times that seeks to determine when and why cultural attitudes and social behavior developed and how they have changed over time.

Sociologists use both primary and secondary sources when conducting a historical study. This nineteenth-century woodcut and advertisement from the late 1940s shed light on contemporary attitudes toward wife beating.

Echoing C. Wright Mills (1959; see Chapter 1 of this book), Dobash and Dobash hold, "It is not possible to understand wife beating today without understanding its past and the part the past plays in contemporary beliefs and behaviors" (1979, p. 32). They began their research by examining the work of other scholars who had studied women through history. These *secondary sources,* usually available in university libraries or historical archives, are critical in helping sociologists study a broad topic like attitudes toward, and treatment of, wives over a long period of time. They provide the sociologist not only with important data but also with frames of reference. What information have other scholars discovered? How have they interpreted these data? On what points do they agree and disagree?

Historical sociologists also examine *primary sources*—writings, documents, and records created directly by the people whom they are studying, during the period they are studying. Often primary sources are not published in current books or journals but must be culled from museums, historical archives, government recording offices, and the like.

Findings

Dobash and Dobash conclude that violence against wives is an extension of *patriarchy:* ancient customs and laws designed to give men domination and control over women. The term "patriarch" comes from the Latin for "ruling father." Among the early Romans, the patriarch had absolute authority over everyone and everything in his household. He had the legal right to decide whether a newborn child would be allowed to live or would be put out to die, whom his children would marry, whether they would be sold into bondage, and how they should be punished for wrongdoing. A wife had no more rights than a child or a slave; she was her husband's property. Going to public games without her husband's permission, appearing in public without a veil, or drinking from the family wine cellar were offenses punishable by beating or divorce. Actual or suspected sexual infidelity was punishable by death, without benefit of trial. Wives whose husbands were unfaithful or drunken had no such recourse; indeed, leaving their husbands for any of these reasons was prohibited by law.

Training for patriarchy began at birth. Boys were given three names, one each for the individual, family, and clan; girls usually were given only two names, for the family and clan. For all but practical purposes (such as childbirth), girls did not exist as individuals.

Women's position in early Christian society, according to Dobash and Dobash's research, was only marginally better. The Bible was interpreted as teaching that woman was created from Adam's rib, as an afterthought, to serve man's needs; that she was weak by nature and easily lured into temptation; and that as punishment for Eve's transgression, she must live a life of subjugation. In medieval and Renaissance Europe, a wife's relationship to her husband was considered that of servant to master. Enforcing obedience was a male prerogative, though there were limits on the degree of violence a man could use against his wife.

Not until the late nineteenth century, in the United States and Great Britain, were laws passed banning the use of "excessive" physical force against wives. Even then a woman had no legal rights of her own, independent of her father and later her husband. She could not sign contracts, make decisions regarding her children's education or religion, or vote. Confined to the home, denied positions in the courts or the church (except as nuns, who were considered to be "brides of Christ"), shut out from the wage economy under industrialization (unless she was poor), her identity and sphere of influence resided almost exclusively in the family.

Although much has changed, old patriarchal attitudes linger. For example, family (or last) names pass down the male line. A girl is given her father's family name at birth and often takes her husband's family name at marriage. Current debates about "family values" often focus on the problems that arise when the (male) head of family is absent. The controversy over sexual harassment evokes old images of Eve the temptress. And the statistics on violence against women suggest that many men still feel force is justified when their authority in the home is challenged (even if they must get drunk as an excuse to exercise these supposed male rights).

The Strengths and Weaknesses of Historical Studies

The advantages of historical studies are similar to those of cross-cultural studies. Both seek to put our own society into perspective. Whereas cross-cultural researchers look for cultural universals or variations, historical researchers look for continuity or change over time.

Historical studies permit sociologists to study phenomena that develop over long periods of time, such as the creation of modern family forms, industrialization, or the spread of democracy. They also enable sociologists to investigate rare and/or unpredictable phenomena, which are difficult or impossible to study via surveys, experiments, or participant observation. Revolutions are an example. To be in the right place at the right time, a researcher might have to wait decades.

Equally important, historical studies prevent sociologists from making faulty generalizations. Immigration to the United States has been going on for centuries and has involved a wide variety of groups under a wide range of circumstances (see Chapter 9). A study of one immigrant group at one particular time might yield conclusions that apply only to that group in those circumstances. A study of birthrates in contemporary Europe and contemporary Latin America might conclude that people from these different cultures have different ideas about ideal family size. If one looks at changes in birthrates over the last two centuries, however, a different picture emerges (see Chapter 16).

Like the other methods described, historical studies also have drawbacks. Cross-cultural researchers gather data firsthand; should new questions arise, they can adjust their methods as needed. Historical sociologists have to depend on data gathered at another time, usually for another purpose. The data they need may or may not be available (because they were never collected or were later lost or destroyed). Moreover, it is difficult to check on the accuracy of data collected by people who are no longer alive. (What methods did they use? Was there any reason for them to falsify information?)

For these reasons, historical studies may not be as precise as surveys or experiments, or as rich in detail and emotion as field studies. But they are uniquely suited to addressing some of the most interesting sociological questions.

Other Research Techniques

Following are some commonly used variations on the three basic research strategies we have described:

1. *In-depth interviews:* The questions are open-ended, allowing the people being interviewed to add whatever they want to their answers and the interviewer to follow up on the issues they raise.
2. *Content analysis:* Researchers study written texts, transcripts of conversations, and even TV shows and commercials. The aim of this type of research is to discover the patterns in both that which is being communicated and the method of communication. (See *A Global View:* Dowry Violence, A Content Analysis.)
3. *Simulation:* Sociologists design a formal model of a social process in order to study the impact of possible variations. For example, a social interaction might be conceived as a "game," and a computer used to identify all the possible "moves" or strategies a "player" could employ. Simulation is useful in charting possibilities and examining rational choices and strategies, not for discovering what actual people do.

Ultimately, complete exploration of an area of social life depends on a combination of techniques. Different methods enable sociologists to see the same phenomenon from various angles. The subtle insights of field studies, the abundant data of surveys, the control of experiments, and the depth of cross-cultural and historical studies are all valuable (see Table 2-5 on page 66).

This section has focused on research techniques, setting theory aside. This is something practicing sociologists never do. Without theory, research is like a car without a driver.

The Role of Theory

The aim of all sciences is to explain facts—to answer questions, solve problems, and test hypotheses (tentative explanations) about the world. Collecting data through research is only part of the scientific enterprise. If sociologists and other scientists were concerned only with recording data, this textbook would be an expanded version of an almanac—a collection of undigested facts and figures. Suppose, for example, that a team of researchers conducted a study of the number of muggers who are left-handed or the percentage of redheads who vote Democratic. Their facts might be accurate, but what would they have learned about the social world? Nothing. Facts do not speak for themselves; they must be fit into a meaningful framework. Thus, theory and research are interdependent (see Figure 2-3 on page 67).

A ***theory*** is a summary of existing knowledge that provides guidelines for conducting research and interpreting new information. Theories highlight which elements of a phenomenon such as family violence are relevant and important to study. They also help researchers determine what the data they have collected mean and what they should make of conflicting or ambiguous findings.

The Elements of Theory

Theories are composed of three basic elements: assumptions, concepts, and propositions.

Theoretical assumptions are untested notions about the nature of human behavior or social systems. An example is the belief that human beings are rational creatures whose actions reflect conscious calculations of the relative costs and benefits of behaving one way instead of another (an assumption of social exchange theory, discussed in greater detail in Chapter 6). Assumptions are the foundation of theory, the underlying structure on which other elements of theory build.

Sociological concepts are general notions that apply to a number of individual cases. They are abstract ideas that identify similarities among otherwise diverse social phenomena. One example is *social class.* People do not belong to a social class the way they belong to a country club. But belonging to a country club is one of many indicators of social class, along with income, occupation, education, address, lifestyle, and tastes. The concept of social class summarizes these diverse but interrelated attributes. Another example of a concept is *intelligence,* which today is often quantified in an IQ score. People do not have an IQ in the sense that they have arms and legs. Rather, individuals

A GLOBAL VIEW

Dowry Violence: A Content Analysis

Dowries—marriage payments made to the groom's family by the wife's family—are illegal and publicly condemned in India. Yet it is no secret that the payment of dowries is socially and culturally approved. Marriages are still arranged in India; sometimes the couple do not meet until after their future has been decided. In educated, urban, upper-class families the prospective bride and groom usually are involved in the decision, though the family may exercise "veto" power. The larger a woman's dowry, the greater her attractiveness to future in-laws. The rationale for dowries is that because a woman does not contribute to her husband's family's income, they should be compensated for providing for her.

The dowry is not a one-time payment, but open-ended. Typically, the bride moves into the home of her husband's extended family. At each of a series of culturally required visits, festivals, and ceremonies related to marriage and childbirth, the wife's family is expected to present additional gifts to the groom and members of his family. Many young men and their kin see escalating dowry demands as a legitimate way of acquiring luxury goods, paying off family debts, and climbing the social ladder. Aware that the wife's treatment in her new household is linked to these gifts, her family may try

to comply. If they do not or cannot, the wife may be abused verbally, beaten, tortured, disfigured, confined without food, threatened with desertion—or in some cases murdered or driven to suicide.

In the last fifteen years, dowry-related violence has begun to attract media attention, in large part because of the growing women's movement in India. Reliable data on the extent of dowry violence and the characteristics of victims and their tormentors are difficult to obtain. If dowry violence is reported, the husband and his

"[My husband] told me he would be happy if I die."

family risk being imprisoned, while the wife's family suffers shame. To overcome this difficulty, B. Devi Prasad (1994) used the research technique called *content analysis*. Over a period of six years he collected and analyzed dowry-related stories in three English-language and six regional-language newspapers.

In all, Prasad collected 125 dowry-related stories, including reports of 41 homicides and 40 suicides. Since most incidents are not reported, this is likely a small sample, but nevertheless it provided useful data. The majority of victims of dowry-

related violence were young, recently married housewives who had little education and were totally dependent on their husbands and the husband's relatives. One-quarter were either pregnant or mothers of young children. This echoes the pattern in other societies, where young, recently married, low-status, unemployed homemakers and mothers of small children are most likely to be abused by their husbands.

In other respects, the Indian pattern was culturally unique. In most cases, the husband was cited for abuse. But in contrast to the case in western societies, the husband often was actively assisted by his mother, his brothers, and less often his sisters. A majority of the victims lived (and died) in large, joint households. In the United States and Europe, domestic violence is associated with the isolation of couples and their children, and it is usually kept secret. In India, family members not only know about the pattern of abuse but also apparently approve. A majority of the husbands were employed, middle-income (and sometimes upper-income) men. In contrast to the pattern in other societies, only a few were unskilled and unemployed. The most common means of death (whether murder or suicide) was pouring kerosene over the woman and setting her on fire.

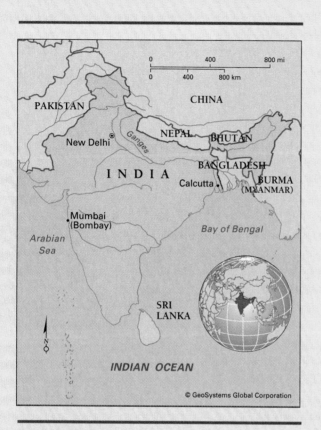

Map 2-2   *India*

if I die" (p. 80). Continuing psychological and physical abuse constitutes a slow, indirect form of murder, especially in a society where being a wife and mother are the only accepted roles open to all but the most highly educated women. Whether suicide or actual (but disguised) murder, dowry death can be profitable. With one wife out of the way, a man is free to seek a new, dowry-bearing wife.

Of the 114 cases for which information was available, police knew of the complaint but made no arrest in 51 percent of the cases; the accused was arrested in 31 percent of the cases, but in only 15 percent of the cases was the accused convicted and sent to prison. To combat dowry violence, Prasad recommends developing community support services; starting self-help groups to act as surrogate families for women separated from their actual families; issuing "peace bonds" to first-time offenders (given that neither family is likely to bring charges); passing a gender-neutral inheritance law that gives women equal rights to their parents' property; and limiting dowries to income-generating assets given and held in the wife's name, so that women are no longer dependent on their husbands' families.

Traditional Indian women spend much of their time in the kitchen, and most households use kerosene as cooking fuel. Thus kerosene is readily available; moreover, death by fire is easy to disguise as an accident or suicide.

Prasad found as many stories about dowry-related suicide as he did about murder, which suggests that isolation from their own family and relatives, combined with psychological and physical abuse, leads to low self-esteem and feelings of helplessness. One victim wrote in her diary, "I have started hating myself. I feel I should die. . . . [H]e is critical of my every act. . . .I want to run away . . .but where should I go?" (p. 80). Another wrote to her sister, "It is immaterial whether I live or die. . . . He [her husband] told me that he would be happy

Table 2-5   *The Strengths and Weaknesses of Different Research Methods*

Research Method	Advantages	Disadvantages
Field Study: Direct observation of social behavior in its natural setting.	*Depth:* A researcher can investigate the social meanings people attach to behavior and events. *Flexibility:* A researcher can change directions if new questions arise.	*Subjectivity:* Findings depend on the researcher's insight and judgments and may reflect personal prejudices. *Limited application:* Findings may apply only to the group studied; generalization is risky. *The observer effect:* The presence of an observer may alter the way people behave.
Survey: A study that uses standardized questionnaires or interviews to collect data on a comparatively large population.	*Economy:* A researcher can collect data on a large population in a relatively short time. *Comparisons:* Because findings can be quantified, a researcher can make precise comparisons of different groups and precise measurements of changes over time.	*Oversimplification:* Standardized questions may obscure subtle differences. *Reliance on self-reports:* Surveys measure what people say they do, not what they actually do. Respondents may give "socially correct" but inaccurate answers.
Experiment: A systematic, controlled examination of cause and effect.	*Control:* A researcher can isolate variables by using control and experimental groups. *Replication:* Other researchers can readily repeat the experiment to verify results.	*Limited scope:* A researcher can manipulate only a small number of variables. *Artificiality:* The situations a researcher creates in a laboratory may not reflect the "real world" outside.
Cross-cultural study: A comparative study of beliefs, customs, and behavior among two or more groups of people with different languages and ways of life.	*Perspective:* A researcher can examine the impact of social structures on human behaviors across societies and cultures. *Breadth:* Researchers can generalize findings beyond a single society.	*Access:* Access to data is time-consuming and difficult, in large part because of language barriers. *Bias:* The risk exists that the researcher will interpret the results from the point of view of his or her own cultural beliefs and values.
Historical study: Use of sources from an earlier time or from an extended time span.	*Breadth:* A researcher can study large-scale social processes and changes in the social context. *Specificity:* A researcher can study rare or especially interesting cases and can avoid faulty generalizations.	*Dependence on existing data:* A researcher cannot create new data but can only uncover and adapt old material. *Selectivity:* Partly because data are limited, often a researcher cannot test propositions or explore behavioral detail as much as with other methods.

demonstrate different levels of problem-solving abilities on a variety of tasks. The concept of intelligence provides a category in which to collect all this information. Concepts are the basic building blocks of theory. Equally important, they can be converted into measurable variables for research (via socioeconomic indicators or IQ tests, for example).

Scientific propositions are statements about the nature of a concept or about the relationship between two or more concepts—for example: "Arrest and punishment deter crime," or "Families are in trouble in the United States today." Propositions are the scaffold or connecting framework that holds other elements of theory together.

Levels of Theory

There are also three different levels of theory. The first is not a complete theory but a *hypothesis*, which

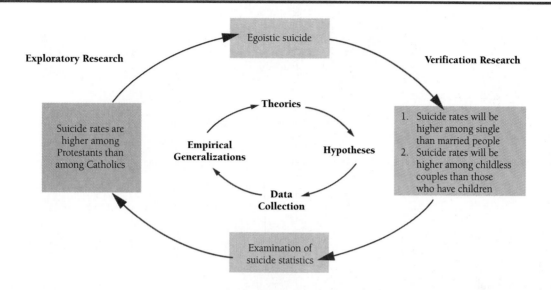

Figure 2-3   *The Research Cycle (Example: Durkheim's Study of Suicide)*

A researcher starts with a hypothesis, a tentative explanation of a given phenomenon. Then data are collected and examined and empirical generalizations emerge. From these generalizations theories, formal statements that summarize and synthesize existing knowledge, may be formed. Further research is then conducted to verify theories, which in turn leads to new hypotheses, and so on.

Sources: Adapted from Walter L. Wallace, *Sociological Theory: An Introduction.* Chicago: Aldine, 1969, p. ix; and from Ann Greer and Scott Greer, *Understanding Sociology.* Dubuque, IA: William C. Brown, 1974, p. 15. Reprinted with permission.

is a limited, testable proposition. Examples of hypotheses are: "The more education a person obtains, the higher-prestige job he or she will be able to obtain," and "Women earn less than men in similar occupations with similar job responsibilities." These are concrete statements about relationships between variables that can be tested empirically.

The second level is what sociologist Robert Merton (1965) called *theories of the middle range.* These theories apply to an array of topics, not just one subject. But they are modest theories, limited in scope and generality and close to the empirical data. They are relatively easy to test and, if necessary, to revise. An example is Merton's theory of relative deprivation (1968), which concerns the way in which individuals judge their own circumstances. According to Merton's theory, how deprived people feel depends not on the objective conditions in which they find themselves but on the condition of the people with whom they compare themselves. This theory can apply to corporations (secretaries compare their salaries with those

of other secretaries, not with their supervisor's), college life (in an honors program at an Ivy League school, a B student may feel like a failure), and countless other social situations. You will encounter this and other middle-range theories throughout this book.

On a higher level still are *theoretical orientations*—broad, general theories that attempt to explain all (or at least the most important) aspects of social life. Theoretical orientations provide sociologists with a vision of society, and with a common vocabulary, approach, and understanding of research topics. They suggest which topics are important and how to approach them. As a rule, middle-range theories draw on one or the other of these broad perspectives.

The founders of sociology put forth two main theoretical orientations: the *functionalist* and *conflict* perspectives, and for almost a century the great majority of sociologists identified with one of these two schools of thought. The early functional and conflict theorists generally focused on large-scale

According to Merton's theory of relative deprivation, if these Amazonian tribespeople compare their living conditions to those of other Amazonian tribes, they are likely to be content. However, if they compare their lifestyle to that in Rio de Janeiro, they are likely to feel deprived.

social phenomena (such as the rise of capitalism or the role of religion in society). In the early twentieth century, American sociologists became interested in small-scale patterns of everyday social behavior. The result was a third theoretical orientation, *symbolic interactionism*. All remain important voices in sociology today. They are summarized in Table 2-6 and described in detail in the sections that follow.

Explaining Society

The founders of sociology were concerned with the question "What holds society together?" What binds individuals and groups with different backgrounds and different goals and interests into the collective enterprise we call society? Functionalism and conflict theory attempt to answer this question, although in different ways.

The Functionalist Perspective

The primary assumption underlying the **functionalist perspective** is that society is a stable, well integrated, self-regulating *system* that endures because it serves people's basic needs. The functionalist orientation took shape in the nineteenth century, in the writings of French sociologists Auguste Comte (1798–1857) and Emile Durkheim (1858–1917) and British sociologist Herbert Spencer (1820–1903). Its leading contemporary advocates have been American sociologists Talcott Parsons (1951) and Robert Merton (1968) and, more recently, Jeffrey Alexander (1988).

Spencer drew an analogy between societies and living organisms. An organism is made up of many specialized parts (the brain, the heart, the lungs, and so on). Each part has a particular *function,* which contributes to maintaining the whole. These parts are *interdependent:* each needs the others. For the organism to survive, the parts must work in harmony with one another.

Table 2-6   *Major Theoretical Orientations*

Functionalism	Conflict Theory	Symbolic Interactionism
Basic Assumptions		
Societies are integrated systems, composed of specialized, interdependent parts.	Societies are competitive arenas where different groups vie for control of scarce resources (wealth, power, and prestige).	The structure of society is determined through social interaction.
Social life depends on consensus and cooperation. Conflict is usually destructive.	Social life inevitably generates divided interests, opposing goals, and conflict. Conflict may be beneficial.	Social life depends on how actors interpret their roles and what audiences they play to.
Sudden change tends to disrupt social life, setting things off balance.	Change is inevitable, even desirable.	Change occurs when actors improvise on the basic script.
The sociologist's job is to explain the different parts of society in terms of their consequences and to show how they are interrelated.	The sociologist's job is to identify competing interests and show how those in power maintain their position.	The sociologist's job is to observe and record the social drama in detail.
Key Questions		
What function does a social pattern perform for the social system, and how is it related to other parts of the system? (What are the consequences of that social pattern?)	Who has the power to create existing social arrangements, and who benefits from them?	What are the unspoken understandings? How do actors interpret their different roles in the social drama?
Major Weaknesses		
Failure to deal adequately with power and social change.	Inability to explain social harmony and cohesion.	Failure to link data on face-to-face interaction to larger social events.

So it is with societies. Key propositions in the functionalist perspective may be summed up as follows: Each society is composed of many specialized structures called *social institutions* (the family, religion, politics, the education system, and so on). Each of these institutions has a function that contributes to maintaining the whole. (The family, for example, bears and raises children.) These social structures are interdependent. (The economy depends on the education system to provide future workers with skills; the education system depends on the economy for funds.) For a society to survive, its interdependent parts must function in harmony. Functionalists hold that survival depends on cooperation and that cooperation depends on consensus (agreement) on basic values and rules for behavior. Under normal conditions the various parts of society work together toward shared goals, producing order, stability, and equilibrium. Viewed from this perspective, conflict is a symptom of "disease" in the social organism.

Modern functionalists stress the delicate balance among different social structures. Because these structures are interdependent, change in one area of

social life inevitably causes adjustments in other areas. For example, changes in the economy (such as a rise in unemployment) bring about changes in the family. Likewise, changes in the family (an increase in divorce and in the number of single parents) bring about changes in the economy. According to this perspective, sudden and rapid change can throw the entire system—the whole society—off balance.

From the functionalist perspective, the following are basic questions for sociological research: "What functions do different parts of the system serve?" (What do they contribute to the whole?) "How are the parts connected to one another?" Functionalists answer these questions by examining the *consequences* of behavior patterns and social arrangements, rather than focusing on people's intentions and motives. Merton (1968) pointed out the important distinction between **manifest functions**—those that are intended and recognized—and **latent functions**—those that are unintended and often unrecognized. For example, the manifest function of education is to provide youngsters with information, skills, and values. The latent functions of

Functionalists hold that cooperation, the basis of survival, depends on agreement on basic rules and values. How does the Japanese custom of bowing express cooperation and harmony?

education include keeping young people out of an overcrowded job market, providing a "baby-sitter" for working parents, and perpetuating class differences by sorting students into academic and vocational tracks according to their perceived potential. The manifest function of our interstate highway system is to provide a convenient mode of transportation. Latent functions include increasing the market for automobiles and gasoline and promoting the growth of suburbs. (See Boudon, 1982.)

Merton also distinguished between behavior patterns that are *functional*—that contribute to the stability or survival of a social system—and those that are *dysfunctional*—that tend to undermine a social system. Patterns that are functional at one time may become dysfunctional at another time. Thus, a transportation system based on private cars was functional when gasoline was cheap and plentiful but became dysfunctional when gasoline was less plentiful and more expensive and began to be recognized as a source of environmental pollution.

Some key concepts for functionalists, which you will encounter frequently in this text, are *systems, function, interdependence,* and *equilibrium* (or balance). New ideas in their day, these concepts have become part of every sociologist's working vocabulary.

The functionalist perspective dominated sociology in the 1950s and 1960s. Functionalist analysis is particularly useful in mapping the connections between various elements of a social system—for example, America's access to oil, its technology, its highway program, and its "love affair" with cars. But functionalists tend to neglect or downplay the role that power plays in creating and maintaining social arrangements—a central concern of the conflict perspective.

The Conflict Perspective

The main assumption underlying the **conflict perspective** is that society is a collection of *competing* interest groups, each with its own goals and agendas. Conflict theorists argue that what holds a society together is not consensus but *constraint.* Clearly some groups benefit more from existing social arrangements than others do. For example, in preindustrial Europe, the aristocracy controlled the most important resource: land. As a result, the aristocrats were in a position to exploit the landless lower classes. In today's "information society," knowledge and expertise are becoming the most important resources (Bell, 1979). As a result, the educated classes often are able to exercise power over groups with less schooling. Whereas functionalists view social arrangements in terms of their functions in society as a whole, conflict sociologists ask, "Functional *for whom?* Who benefits from a given social arrangement? How is the dominant group able to maintain its position?"

Conflict theory is rooted in the writings of Karl Marx (1818–1883). In formulating propositions, Marx stressed the importance of economic resources in social *conflict.* He was concerned not so much

Conflict theories emphasize the struggle between various segments of a society. They point out that the inequities of capitalism, in which owners invariably exploit the working class, are the reason these boys spent their days in a coal mine instead of in school in the early twentieth-century United States.

with wealth that was used to purchase material goods as with wealth that was invested in the *means of production* (for example, raw materials, factories, machines, and other things used to create more wealth). Marx saw a fundamental division in capitalist societies between those who owned the capital (the means of production) and those who did not and were therefore forced to work for wages under conditions set by the capitalists. In his view, capitalist societies fostered economic expansion and growth, but not so that all members of society would benefit. Rather, this arrangement increased the profits and capital of the dominant class. Economic dominance was reflected in religious beliefs, educational policies, and even family life. Workers were exploited, not just as individuals but as a class. Mass exploitation laid the foundation for collective or class struggle against the capitalists. Sooner or later, Marx believed, the majority of workers would overthrow the minority of owners and bosses—either peacefully or through violent revolution.

Although Marxism is still influential, conflict theory has undergone considerable revision. Early in the twentieth century, German sociologists Georg Simmel (1858–1918) and Max Weber (1864–1920) broadened conflict theory by adding *power* and

privilege to the list of scarce resources that provoke competition and conflict among groups in a society. They also stressed the difficulty of organizing large masses of people. The potential for revolution might exist in all capitalist societies, but the practicalities of class action were another story.

Weber thought that Marx overestimated the degree to which material factors (the means of production) determine ideas and beliefs in a society. Weber argued that a purely "objective," materialist account of social life was incomplete.

Contemporary sociologists have revised conflict theory in other ways. Lewis Coser (1967) brought elements of functionalism to conflict theory. Coser holds that one of the functions of conflict between groups is to reinforce solidarity *within* groups. When a nation goes to war, for example, citizens unite against a common enemy and conflicts within the nation are forgotten. Coser also suggests that in modern societies multiple conflicts (between various racial and ethnic groups, males and females, old and young, etc.) crisscross one another, preventing the division of society into hostile camps. Other conflict theorists (for example, I. Wallerstein, 1980) have applied Marx's model of class struggle to the *world system*, focusing on economic relations among nations, rather than on class relations within nations. In this view, technologically advanced nations (chiefly the United States, Europe, and Japan) are seen as an international ruling class, and the developing countries (mainly former colonies in the southern hemisphere) as a pool of exploited laborers.

Some key concepts for conflict sociologists are *power, privilege, prestige, conflict,* and *competition.*

The conflict perspective moved to the foreground of sociology in the 1960s and 1970s, a period when many institutions were being examined critically. It offered a more dynamic view of society, which fit the changing times. But in focusing narrowly on the sources of tension in society, conflict theorists tend to overlook the sources of harmony and consensus.

Today the majority of sociologists recognize a middle ground. Conflict sociologists acknowledge the possibility of collaboration in meeting basic needs, even between groups whose interests clash. Functional sociologists acknowledge that existing social institutions may benefit some groups at the expense of others and that conflict is inevitable and may lead to positive social change. The distinction between these two schools today is largely a matter of emphasis. Functionalists focus on the forces that knit society together, while conflict sociologists focus on the forces that threaten to pull society apart.

Explaining Everyday Social Behavior

The functionalist and conflict perspectives look at the structure of society as a whole and at the role of broad social forces in maintaining stability or provoking change. But all sociologists recognize that societies are composed of individual actors. To understand society, one must also understand how these social actors make decisions, organize their lives, and influence and are influenced by one another. This is the goal of the third classic theoretical perspective in sociology, symbolic interactionism.

Symbolic Interactionism

The symbolic interactionist perspective was developed by American sociologists George Herbert Mead (1863–1931) and Charles Horton Cooley (1864–1924) in the early twentieth century and was elaborated upon in more recent years by Herbert Blumer (1939, 1969), Erving Goffman (1959, 1967), Howard Becker (1963, 1984), and others (see Fine, 1993, for a review). Sociologists in this school are less concerned with large-scale social phenomena than with everyday behavior and interpersonal relationships, which they regard as the basic building blocks of social life.

Symbolic interactionism begins with the assumption that much human behavior is determined not by the objective facts of a situation but by the *meanings* people ascribe to a situation. W. I. Thomas made this point in his often-quoted remark, "If men define situations as real, they are real in their consequences" (Thomas and Thomas, 1928, p. 572). In other words, our subjective interpretations of the world in large part determine how we behave. What we call "reality" is in fact a social construct (Blumer, 1969); that is, we agree collectively to pay attention to certain phenomena and label them "real," while treating other phenomena as irrelevant. For example, in the United States we view people of European, African, and Asian ancestry as belonging to three distinct races. We may believe that all people are equal, regardless of race, but nevertheless assume they have certain innate differences. For example, we tend to think that African Americans have "natural" athletic ability and that Asian Americans excel at math and science. In reality, each of these racial groups includes wide variation in height and coordination, intelligence and perseverance. Only a handful of African Americans are sports superstars, and a minority of Asian Americans are math geniuses. The differences *within* these racial categories outweigh the differences *between* races. But because we *believe* people can be classified as Caucasian, African, or Asian and because we believe that real differences between these categories exist, these perceived differences are real in their consequences (see Chapter 9).

Symbolic interactionism rests on a number of interlocking propositions. In order to engage in any sort of joint action, humans must have some means of communicating with one another. We do so by means of *symbols*—not only words and phrases but also gestures and actions that have acquired social meaning. And we learn what behavior and events mean through *interaction* with other people, which requires fitting our actions and interpretations to

Symbolic interactionists hold that people manipulate the presentation of their selves by means of symbols, such as clothing, gestures, and posture.

those of other people. Even our identity or sense of *self* is based in large part on the reflection of ourselves that we see in other people's eyes—a "looking-glass self," in Charles Horton Cooley's phrase (see Chapter 4). The self is never fixed or stable; it is subject to continual redefinition and revision as the result of social interaction.

Some symbolic interactionists drew an analogy between social life and the theater, in what is called the *dramaturgical approach* (Sennett, 1978, 1980). Just as each actor on a stage has a role to play in the drama, so each member of society has a part to play in relation to other members (husband or wife, student or teacher, and so on). Just as players on a stage follow a script, so actors in society follow rules for acceptable behavior. There is room for improvisation in any role, however. The actor's interpretation depends in part on the script, and in part on what he or she brings to the role, what other actors do with their roles, and how the audience— whether real or imagined—reacts (J. H. Turner, 1978). But if actors depart too far from widely accepted role definitions, they are likely to be labeled "deviant." In society, as on a stage, each person plays many roles over the course of a lifetime.

Another branch of symbolic interactionism, *ethnomethodology*, focuses not on the roles people consciously play but on the routine, mundane behavior that people take for granted. Ethnomethodologists

propose that the "glue" that holds society together and makes human social life possible consists of widely accepted but subconscious rules people notice only when they are violated. Consider, for example, habitual greetings: "Hi, how are ya?" "Fine, an' you?" Everyone knows that these greetings are ritualistic: neither party wants a detailed description of the other's health or financial condition. But failure to extend or respond to such a greeting is considered extremely rude—a signal that something has gone wrong in the relationship. Ethnomethodologists hold that conformity to expectations about greetings and other habitual behavior establishes the basic trust that is necessary for all social interaction (Garfinkel, 1967).

Another area of much interest to symbolic interactionists is *sociolinguistics:* the study of how social factors influence speech patterns. Sociolinguists propose that people use speech (and nonverbal cues) not only to communicate information but also to locate the self in relation to others. For example, men maintain a dominant position in relation to women by speaking clearly and directly, and by making assertions and demands with little hesitation; women unconsciously tend to go along with this by speaking more tentatively and indirectly and by soliciting agreement (Lakoff, 1990). Sociolinguists also study how people use distinctive ways of speaking to establish and maintain their cultural identity. Ebonics (from the words "ebony" and "phonic," what used to be called "black English"), which developed in urban ghettos and was popularized by rap artists, is an example. Other symbolic interactionists are interested in unconscious knowledge, in the skills we use without thinking about what we are doing and would have difficulty explaining. For example, basketball superstar Michael Jordan knows how to make a perfect reverse dunk shot but probably cannot explain exactly how he does it. So it is with many everyday social skills.

One new area of interest is *social coordination theory:* the effort to establish general principles to explain how social actors coordinate their activities, whether those actors are individuals, groups, communities, organizations, or even nations. According to this view, the same basic principles apply at all levels (Couch, 1992). A second area of new interest is the *sociology of emotions:* the study of how emotions relate to social life. In this view, emotions are learned through social interaction, are controllable, and are guided by "feeling rules." Consciously or unconsciously, people may use emotions to manage the impressions they make on others. Conversely, the emotions people express, and perhaps even what they feel, depend on the social roles they are playing and the shared definition of a situation. (See Hochschild, 1983; Gubrium, 1992.) A third new direction is *social constructionism:* how and why social groups construct and defend boundaries between what is seen as normal and what is considered deviant, and how these boundaries change over time. (See the discussion of labeling theory in Chapter 7.)

Key concepts for symbolic interactionists include *meanings, symbols, interaction, self,* and *role.* Although they have many different areas of interest, symbolic interactionists share a common focus. For these sociologists there are specific basic questions: "How do people interpret their social scripts?" "How do they arrive at shared understandings and unconscious knowledge?" "How does everyday interaction support or modify social definitions of reality?" "What principles, feelings, and rules govern all social action, on whatever scale?"

For many years, symbolic interactionism was considered a "stepchild" of sociology, not a serious or important approach. However, many ideas from this school found their way into mainstream sociology, and symbolic interactionism itself has become

broader in scope and more varied in methodology (Fine, 1993). The strength of symbolic interactionism is that it zooms in on the everyday conventions we take for granted, revealing the structure underlying routine, personal actions and beliefs. But symbolic interactionism cannot explain major social events, such as revolutions, or sweeping social change, such as the changing structure of families.

The Interplay of Theory and Research

In everyday conversation people often use the word "theory" to refer to abstract but impractical notions. We say, "That plan sounds good in theory, but it won't work in practice." Scientific theories are firmly grounded in research. One could not exist without the other: theory guides research, and research informs theory. Before embarking on a study, researchers develop hypotheses based on existing assumptions and propositions; the data they collect may or may not prove their hypotheses correct.

The studies we analyzed in this chapter illustrate how theory and research work hand in hand. In the Minneapolis Police Experiment, for example, Sherman and Berk set out to test the hypothesis that arrest acts as a deterrent to future domestic violence. This hypothesis rests on the middle-range theory of social exchange. According to this theory, people weigh the costs and benefits of their behavior before acting. Arrest should deter or control family violence by making it more costly to the abuser. When other studies produced conflicting data, Sherman and Berk had to refine this explanation in terms of the middle-range theory known as "social control." According to this view, social connections act as a control on behavior. The more social attachments people have, the more committed they are, the more involved they are, the less likely they are to engage in deviant behavior. The reason, quite simply, is that they have too much to lose if they get caught. This explains the higher rates of recidivism among unemployed wife beaters.

In her cross-cultural study, Morley set out to test the hypothesis that modernization increases family violence. The idea that social change, in general, and modernization, in particular, are disruptive is grounded in the functionalist orientation. Functional-

SOCIOLOGY ON THE WEB

Exploring Theory and Theorists

You can find a great deal of fascinating information about sociological theorists and their work on the web. Following is a brief list of sites to start you on your search. Find other sites by using the links you will find at these sites and doing your own searches; much of the fun of exploring this or any other topic on the Internet is not knowing what you will find in the next site you reach.

**http://www.stg.brown.edu/projects/hypertext/
landow/victorian/religion/**
At this site you will find background information on the life and work of Auguste Comte. The material on Comte is part of a page on Victorian religious thought, with many interesting entries; the page, in turn, is part of a larger site on Victorian culture and thought.

http://www.marx/org/
The home page for information about Karl Marx and Friedrich Engels. Information about the life and work of these two thinkers, photos that document their lives, and texts of most of their major works are available for downloading.

**http://paradigm.soci.brocku.ca/
~lward/default.html**
At this page maintained by the Mead project at Brock University (Ontario), you will find a great deal of information about George Herbert Mead: a bibliography of his work (with many texts available for download), commentaries, a glossary, and links to supplementary sites.

**http://www.runet.edu/~lridener/DSS/
DEADSOC.HTML**
The Dead Sociologists Home Page is a fun and informative site with many, many links to other material about sociological theory and research. This is a good place to begin a search of the web for information on theory or theorists.

http://weber.u.washington.edu/~hbecker/
Here's the web site of a live sociologist. Howard Becker, a symbolic interactionist, maintains this site, which provides a complete bibliography of his work, with many articles available for downloading, plus news and commentary about his personal life.

ists hold that rapid social change causes stress in the family and other institutions. In this study, the hypothesis was disproved. Modernization and urbanization appeared to reduce spouse abuse to some extent.

Gelles and Straus's research on family violence was designed to measure the extent of family violence (the first survey) and then to investigate whether rates of family violence had changed. The theoretical models they used to explain these patterns derived from social exchange and social control theory. They looked at whether increased privacy, inequality, and legitimization of violence were linked to higher rates of family violence (see Chapter 11). They found that individuals who approved of family violence, who were socially isolated, and who controlled family decision making had the highest rates of family violence.

These examples highlight an important point: Science is a collective and cumulative enterprise. In history books we may read about individual geniuses like Sir Isaac Newton, Charles Darwin, or Karl Marx. But no scientist or theoretician works in isolation. All build on the work of those who preceded them. As Newton acknowledged, "If I have seen farther, it is because I stand on the shoulders of giants." (See Merton, 1965.)

Summary

1. **What is the science of sociology?** Like other *sciences,* sociology is a public enterprise that uses agreed-upon procedures for minimizing errors and bias to establish empirical generalizations. All sociologists follow certain basic procedures in their research. Generating *hypotheses,* identifying *variables,* and selecting *a sample* to study (ideally a *representative sample*) are essential. Which particular method they employ depends on their interest and resources.

2. **How do sociologists conduct research?** Sociologists employ five basic methods or strategies to collect data; each of these methods has its strengths and weaknesses.

   Surveys enable researchers to gather data on a large population and to quantify results for comparative purposes. But surveys measure only what people say they do and think, and so the results may be superficial.

   The *field study* (or *participant observation*) allows a researcher to study behavior in its natural setting and to observe subtleties in attitudes and behavior. But only a small number of people can be studied by this method, and the researcher's presence may affect what subjects say and do.

   Experiments are most useful in studying limited, clearly defined questions. They enable a researcher to isolate *independent* and *dependent variables.* To control for outside influences, the researcher compares the attitudes and/or behavior of *control* and *experimental groups,* which are created through *random assignment.*

   Cross-cultural studies are comparisons of beliefs, customs, and/or behaviors of two or more groups of people with different languages and ways of life. Some take the form of an extended field study, or *ethnography,* while others rely on secondary sources. Cross-cultural research helps social scientists distinguish between *cultural universals* and culturally variable patterns, but there are problems with cultural bias and translation.

   Historical studies permit researchers to study rare, unpredictable, and long-term social phenomena and to answer questions that depend on a particular social context. But collecting essential, accurate data may be difficult.

3. **What role does theory play in science?** *Theories* provide guidelines for research and aid in the interpretation of data. They are composed of three main elements: *theoretical assumptions, sociological concepts,* and *scientific propositions.* Theories range from relatively limited *hypotheses,* to more inclusive *theories of the middle range,* to broad, comprehensive *theoretical orientations.* Sociology has produced three main theoretical orientations: functionalism, conflict theory, and symbolic interactionism.

4. **How do sociologists explain society?** The functionalist and conflict perspectives attempt to explain large-scale, long-term social phenomena, though in different ways. *Functionalists* view society as a cohesive system composed of interrelated parts. They seek to explain the various parts of a social system in terms of the consequences or functions, to distinguish between *manifest* and *latent* functions, and to show how different parts are related to one another. Functionalists emphasize the need for social equilibrium and for consensus among members of a society. The main weakness of functionalism is its tendency to downplay the importance of power and social change.

   For *conflict theorists,* society is a collection of competing interest groups. Constraint, not consensus, holds society together. These theorists seek to understand who benefits from existing social arrangements and how they maintain their position of power. They see conflict and change as inevitable (and often desirable) elements of social life. The main weakness of conflict theory is its failure to explain social cohesion.

5. **How do sociologists explain everyday behavior?** *Symbolic interactionists* focus on the patterns of everyday life, on the process of social interaction, and on the way social actors' definition of a situation shapes their behavior.

Symbolic interactionists are interested in the social construction of meaning and in the conscious and unconscious rules that enable coordination and cooperation.

6. **How do theory and research influence one another?** The relationship between theory and research is a dynamic one: theories stimulate research, and research leads to new or amended theories. A collective undertaking, science promotes the continuous revision and rethinking of previous findings.

Key Terms

conflict perspective 70	historical study 60	science 43
control group 55	hypotheses 46	scientific proposition 66
cross-cultural study 57	independent variable 46	sociological concept 63
cultural universal 60	latent function 69	survey 48
dependent variable 46	manifest function 69	symbolic interactionism 72
ethnography 57	participant observation 52	theoretical assumption 63
experiment 54	random assignment 55	theoretical orientation 67
experimental group 55	replication 48	theory 63
field study 52	representative sampling 47	theory of the middle range 67
functionalist perspective 68	sample 47	variable 46

Recommended Readings

Babbie, Earl. (1995). *The Practice of Social Research,* 7th ed. Belmont, CA: Wadsworth.

Coser, Lewis. (1977). *Masters of Sociological Thought,* 2d ed. New York: Harcourt Brace Jovanovich.

Gelles, Richard J., & Straus, Murray A. (1988). *Intimate Violence.* New York: Simon and Schuster.

Hoover, Kenneth, & Donovan, Todd. (1995). *The Elements of Social Scientific Thinking,* 6th ed. New York: St. Martin's.

Kohn, Melvin L. (1989). *Cross-National Research in Sociology.* Newbury Park, CA: Sage Publications.

Miller, Delbert C. (1991). *Handbook of Research Design and Social Measurement,* 5th ed. Newbury Park, CA: Sage Publications.

Reinharz, Shulamit. (1992). *Feminist Methods in Social Research.* New York: Oxford University Press.

Sherman, Lawrence W. (1992). *Policing Domestic Violence: Experiments and Dilemmas.* New York: Free Press.

Part

Dynamics of Social Behavior

2

This part of the book focuses on the interplay between social action and social structure.

Chapter 3 analyzes the established patterns of thinking and behaving that distinguish one people from another, and it shows how individuals are both the creators and creations of their culture.

Chapter 4 traces socialization—the process of social interaction that shapes identity and behavior—from birth through death.

Chapter 5 uses the game of basketball to illustrate the impact of social structure on behavior, then examines the basic elements of social structure, the structure of societies, the evolution of societies, and the current world system from the macro perspective.

Chapter 6 looks at everyday social interaction, networks, and behavior in small groups from the micro perspective.

Chapter 7 looks at the causes and consequences of deviance (behavior that violates social expectations and generates disapproval) and identifies different types of social control, with special emphasis on crime and the justice system.

Chapter

Three

Culture

"I felt just like I fell in from the sky," says Jonathan Lee, a Vietnamese refugee, describing his arrival in New York City. "On the street people rushed by me like they were running from a fire. The tall building of my caseworker had all these guards with uniforms outside, and the doors were closed. In my country you don't dare open closed doors" (Sontag, 1992, p. 36). An ethnic Cambodian, Mr. Lee fled Communist South Vietnam in 1982, traveling by train, bus, and foot to Thailand, where he spent a year in refugee camps before being admitted to the United States as a political refugee.

Ten years after fleeing his homeland, Mr. Lee was working as a refugee counselor, advising recent immigrants from such far-flung places as South Korea, Ethiopia, El Salvador, and the Republic of Georgia in the former Soviet Union. Some of his clients have no family or friends in the United States; most speak little or no English; and almost all are suffering, as he did, from cultural shock. Mr. Lee initiates his clients into American customs and lifestyles. He teaches them how to ride the subway, how to dial 911 in emergencies, and, in some cases, how to flush a toilet. He advises them to put their money in banks, to be wary of strangers, and to look people in the eye during a conversation, something that would be considered extremely rude in many other cultures.

Mr. Lee and his clients were part of the largest wave of immigration to the United States since the turn of the century (see Figure 3-1). Between 1985 and 1994, the United States admitted nearly 9 million immigrants, bringing the number of foreign-born people legally living in the United States to 20 million (Statistical Abstract, 1996). Always a nation of immigrants, the United States is becoming even more multicultural.

Current immigrants differ from former generations in several ways. In the past, a system of national quotas ensured that the great majority of immigrants were Europeans whose cultural heritage was similar to that of native-born Americans. The 1965 Immigration Act, which abolished quotas for particular nationalities, changed this. Under the act, preference was granted to close relatives of U.S. citizens, people with skills in "essential occupations," and political refugees who had "a well-founded fear of persecution" in their home countries. The majority of today's immigrants are from Latin America, Asia, and the Caribbean, adding to this country's cultural diversity.

In the past, a majority of immigrants were unskilled or low-skilled workers with little

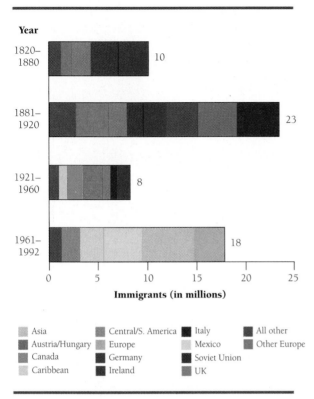

Figure 3-1   *Regions and Countries of Origin for U.S. Immigrants, 1820–1992*

In the first half of this century, most immigrants to the United States were European or Mexican. The 1965 Immigration Act opened the door to immigrants from new places.

Source: P. Martin and E. Midgley, "Immigration to the United States: Journey to an Uncertain Destination," *Population Bulletin* 49, 1994, fig. 7, p. 25.

education. A substantial proportion of today's immigrants are highly educated professionals. The average immigrant today has as much education as the average native-born American (give or take a year). Overall, 25 percent are professional or technical workers (doctors, engineers, and the like), compared with 15 percent of native-born Americans. This is in part the result of the 1990 Immigration Act, which gives priority to "employment-preference workers" and their families. (One latent consequence of the essential-occupation requirement in the U.S. immigration law is a "brain drain" on Third World countries, which are losing some of their brightest and most highly skilled citizens. The law wasn't intentionally written to rob these countries

of skilled workers, but given the attraction of higher wages in the United States, it has this effect.) Other new immigrants were business owners, landowners, or managers in their native countries but lost their positions during political upheavals and hope to start over in the United States.

Finally, a larger proportion of today's newcomers are illegal immigrants. A 1986 immigration act attempted to limit "back-door" immigration by, on the one hand, imposing penalties on U.S. employers who knowingly hired illegal aliens and, on the other, granting amnesty (legal immigrant status) to nearly 3 million illegal immigrants who had established roots in this country. Even so, an estimated 1.5 to 2.5 million illegal aliens still live here, and that number increases by about 300,000 a year (Martin and Midgley, 1994). Most of these people are from developing countries (especially Mexico and other Latin American nations), where conditions are deteriorating due to rapid population growth, economic stagnation, and, in some cases, political instability.

Transplantation from one culture to another is a fact of modern life. Migration, permanent or temporary, is a worldwide phenomenon (Figure 3-2). In the early 1990s, an estimated 100 million people resided outside their homelands; about half were living and working in the industrialized nations of western Europe, North America, and, to a lesser extent, Asia (Martin and Midgley, 1994). Most of the world's major cities house large numbers of people whose cultural roots lie elsewhere—people whose language, customs, family life, cooking, and ways of dealing with the joys, sorrows, and everyday necessities of life are quite different from those of their neighbors.

Migration is not the only source of contact between cultures. The United States exports culture—in the form of television programs, movies, music, and consumer goods—to countries all over the world. Coca-Cola has plants in the People's Republic of China; the Disney Company opened a theme park just outside Paris; Baywatch is the most popular TV show in the world; and CNN news is available just about everywhere. The United States also imports culture—in forms ranging from French cheese and British comedy to Japanese cars and computer chips and Latin and Caribbean rhythms. U.S. cable channels offer soap operas from Brazil and Japan and soccer games from around the world; automated teller machines in New York City give customers a choice of five languages (English, Spanish, Chinese, Japanese, and Russian); almost every shopping mall and

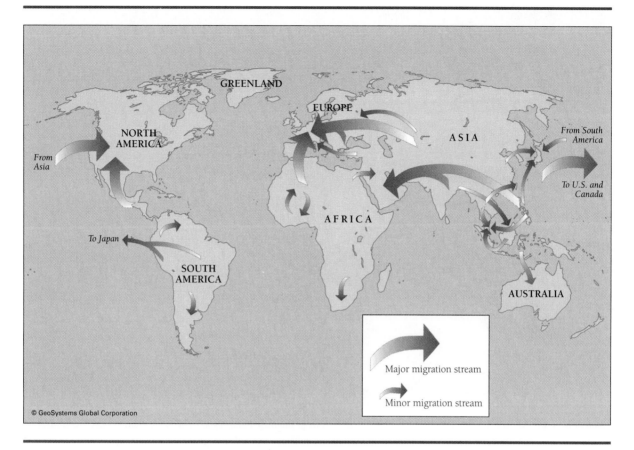

© GeoSystems Global Corporation

Figure 3-2   *Major World Migration Patterns in the Early 1990s*

In the late twentieth century, migration became a global phenomenon.

Source: Population Bulletin 51 (1), April 1996.

rest stop on interstate highways has a taco stand. In-creasingly, globalization is replacing Americanization or westernization—that is, tastes and trends, which may have originated in western countries but now are pro-duced in other countries, are global blends (Crossette, 1997a). In Phnom Penh, the capital of Cambodia, chil-dren crowd into roadside stalls to play video games pro-duced in Japan. Express boats on the rivers of Borneo show films produced in Hong Kong that make Hollywood violence seem mild. Middle-class parents in Bangkok worry about the impact on children of Indian popular films that degrade women and glamorize gangsters. Karaoke—an audio-visual system invented in Japan that provides MTV-like accompaniment and lyrics for amateur performers—is displacing traditional forms of entertainment throughout Southeast Asia and becoming popular in the west as well.

Likewise, business today is multinational. Most large corporations in the United States have offices and factories in other countries, and major European and Asian corpo-rations have headquarters in the United States. Business-people "commute" from New York, Los Angeles, Paris, and London to Athens, Buenos Aires, Madrid, Singapore, and Hong Kong, by plane or e-mail. Joint ventures, involving international partners, are increasingly common.

With all these forms of cross-cultural pollination, the need to understand our own culture and other cultures has never been greater.

Key Questions

1. *Why is culture so important to human beings?*
2. *What elements do all or most cultures share?*
3. *How do people view the differences among cultures?*

Contact between cultures results from cultural export as well as from migration and travel. The United States exports cultural artifacts, such as consumer goods and entertainment products, throughout the world.

4. *How do people improvise within their own culture?*
5. *How do social scientists explain cultural variations?*
6. *What are the sources and consequences of cultural change?*

Culture: An Overview

Culture has been defined as a "design for living" (Kluckhohn, 1949) and as the "shared understandings that people use to coordinate their activities" (Becker, 1986). Members of a society must share certain basic ideas about how the world works, what is important in life, how technology is to be used, and what their artifacts and their actions *mean.* Whereas "social structure" refers to the practical/instrumental aspects of social relations, "culture" refers to the "symbolic/expressive aspects of social relations" (Wuthnow, 1987, p. 4).

All creatures have designs for living—courtship rituals, patterns for rearing offspring, strategies for acquiring food and water and for establishing territories, and so on. What is special about culture is that it is a design for living that is acquired through learning. Few other animals are quite so helpless at birth as the human infant. No other animal can learn, or *needs* to learn, as much. Within a few hours of birth, a horse is capable of running and kicking in self-defense; this behavior is governed by *instincts,* or genetically programmed behavior patterns. A colt or filly doesn't need to be taught to run with the herd. In contrast, human infants are born with only a few simple reflexes. We need to be taught what is dangerous and how to respond to danger, among countless other lessons. A few tragic cases have been discovered of children who were given physical care but left in isolation. Because these children had been deprived of human interaction and learning experiences, their behavior was barely human. They communicated in grunts, made no effort to control their bodily functions, and seemed indifferent to other human beings. With only their biological resources to draw upon, they did not become complete persons. Simply put, humans must *learn* to be human. Human development depends on **socialization**—the ongoing process of interaction through which we acquire a personal identity and social skills. (See Chapter 4.)

The content of socialization varies from one society to another. Through socialization, we acquire the culture of the society in which we are raised; we learn its particular design for living. No other animal is as flexible as humans. Every species of bird has its own, distinctive songs. A baby bird may need to hear its species' songs to perform them, but no amount of exposure can make a crow sing like a nightingale or vice versa (though a few species, like mockingbirds, are natural mimics). Humans do not inherit a predisposition for speaking English rather than Chinese, much less for thinking that pork is unclean or for believing that germs rather than angry ancestors cause sickness and death. What kind of people we become is strongly influenced by **enculturation**—immersion in a culture to the point where that particular design for living seems "only natural."

The genetic predispositions that make a colt run or a bird warble are inherited. The human *ability* to acquire culture is also inherited. But culture itself is passed from one generation to the next through socialization—through children's stories and games, poems, religious rituals, jokes, and other learning activities. Often we are not aware of how much of our behavior is learned. The human sex drive is a good illustration of this. Americans tend to assume that sexual behavior is biologically determined. Many of us believe that the sex drive is a powerful force (as urgent as hunger and thirst), that sex plays a central role in every adult's life, and that everyone has a natural heterosexual destiny (Goode, 1978). In reality, the "sex drive," as we call it, is highly variable across cultures (Ford and Beach, 1951).

Anthropologist Karl Heider (1976) studied a society in which people simply are not very interested in sex. Like many other groups that do not have modern birth control devices, the Dani of New Guinea practice a postpartum taboo on sexual relations (that is, intercourse is forbidden for a certain

period after the birth of a child). In most societies in which it occurs, this taboo lasts about two years. In Dani society it lasts four to six years. Heider found no evidence that the Dani compensate for the suspension of conjugal relations by engaging in extramarital affairs, homosexual relations, or masturbation. Neither do they show signs of stress or unhappiness. Questions about this area of their lives puzzle them. Long periods of celibacy seem normal and natural to the Dani. In contrast, the Aranda of Australia consider it normal to make love, sleep, then make love again, three to five times a night, every night (Hyde, 1979). Sexual techniques, standards of physical attractiveness, attitudes toward masturbation and homosexual relations, and the roles men and women play in sexual relations also vary among societies. The Thonga of Africa find kissing disgusting; the Siriono of South America find grooming (removing ticks and thorns from a lover's body and lice from the hair) a "turn-on." In the Trobriand Islands of the South Pacific, men complain of being "gang-raped" by women (Malinowski, 1929). Cross-cultural variations in sexual behavior illustrate both the flexibility of human behavior and the power of enculturation.

The Elements of Culture

Anthropologists generally have emphasized the differences among groups of people who speak distinct languages and pursue diverse ways of life. But it is important not to overlook the similarities, what Donald Brown (1991) calls "human universals."[1] All human beings live in social groups, though the size and nature of those groups is extremely variable. All societies organize families (minimally a mother and her children) and recognize kinship. Who is considered "family," the strength and duration of family bonds, and the importance of the family group to other aspects of life are variable. But families are universal. Paul Ekman and his associates (1969, 1986) found that the facial expression of certain basic emotions is universal: an urban westerner and a member of a New Guinea tribe can each recognize what the other is feeling from

---

[1]The related term "cultural universals" is generally used to refer to specific values and beliefs that are found in all or most cultures, such as the prohibition of incest and cannibalism.

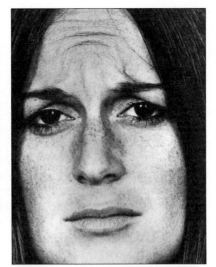

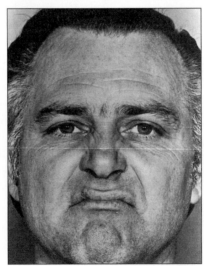

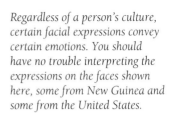

Regardless of a person's culture, certain facial expressions convey certain emotions. You should have no trouble interpreting the expressions on the faces shown here, some from New Guinea and some from the United States.

photographs. People in all cultures make music and dance. Ninety-five percent of known cultures have kept domesticated dogs.

The origin of human universals is the subject of much debate. They may arise from the nature of the human animal (our evolutionary past), the structure of the human brain (our biology), a common culture from which all current and past cultures are descended (our history and prehistory), or all three. What patterns of thought and activity belong on a list of human universals is also controversial. But nearly all social scientists agree that all cultures consist of six main elements:

1. Beliefs (shared explanations of experience)
2. Values (criteria of moral judgment)
3. Norms and sanctions (specific guidelines for behavior)
4. Symbols (representations of beliefs and values)
5. Language (a system of symbolic communication)
6. Technology

To introduce these cultural basics, in the following pages we compare the American and Vietnamese "designs for living." (See Map 3-1.)

Beliefs

Beliefs are shared ideas about how the world operates. They may be summaries and interpretations of the past, explanations of the present, or predictions for the future. They may be based on common sense, folk wisdom, religion, or science, or on some combination of these. Some beliefs apply to intangible things (for example, whether the human spirit lives on after death). All cultures distinguish between ideas for which people have reasonable proof (for example, that smoking increases the risk of cancer) and ideas that have not been, or cannot be, tested (for example, that there is intelligent life on other planets). Where and how people draw the line varies, however.

Because beliefs shape both personal and social experience, basic differences in beliefs account for some of the problems Vietnamese immigrants have had in American society. One example is beliefs concerning the nature of time. People in western cultures believe that time is irreversible. We think of time as a straight line. At 12:01 A.M. every January 1 we add another year to the calendar, with much fanfare and hoopla. By the mid-1990s, we had begun planning for the new millennium. Traditionally, the

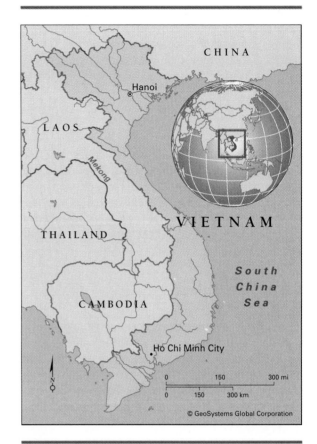

Map 3-1   *Vietnam*

Vietnamese reckon time in sixty-year cycles: every sixty years the cycle starts over with the year with which it began. Such a conception of time suggests that current events are not unique, that things come around again and again. The American belief that time is linear creates the sense that "time is ticking away"; the Vietnamese belief that time is cyclical fosters an entirely different state of mind.

Beliefs apply not only to concepts like time but also to more mundane aspects of the material world. Some years back, residents of San Francisco were outraged to learn that rural immigrants from Laos and Cambodia had been stalking stray dogs in Golden Gate Park to eat for their dinners. San Franciscans could not understand how the newcomers could hunt and eat dogs; the Indochinese could not understand why San Franciscans did not—a classic case of the same animal having different cultural meanings. Even within our own culture we can see great variation in how people think about the same resource (Czikszentmihalyi and Rochberg-Halton, 1982). Some people see dogs as working animals, acquired to protect their warehouse or livestock; others treat their dogs as special friends or even as substitute children.

Values

Whereas beliefs describe what is, values describe what ought to be. **Values** are broad, abstract, shared standards of what is right, desirable, and worthy of respect. Although values are widely shared, they are seldom adhered to at all times by every member of a culture. Rather, values set the general tone for cultural and social life.

Vietnamese Values

The center of Vietnamese life is the family, which traditionally includes three and often four generations living under the same roof. Vietnamese families are also large: many refugees grew up with eight or ten siblings and two or three times as many cousins. *Family loyalty* is at the heart of the Vietnamese system of values. Children are raised to honor and obey their parents even after they are grown and have children of their own; "success" is defined in terms of contributing to family harmony and well-being, not individual achievement. The family's interests come before private needs or ambitions. As one refugee explained,

> To Vietnamese culture, family is everything. . . . We solve problems because [the] family institution is a bank. If I need money—and my brother and my two sisters are working—I tell them I need money to buy a house. I need priority in this case. They say okay, and they give money to me. After only two years, I bought a house. . . . Now I help them. They live with me and have no rent. . . .
>
> The family is a hospital. If mom is sick, I, my children, and my brother and sisters care for her. We don't need a nurse. She stays home, so we don't need to send her to nursing home. (Gold, 1993, p. 304)

In the United States as in their homeland, extended Vietnamese American families function as a unit, not a collection of individuals. They frequently pool labor, capital, and know-how to run restaurants, grocery and dry-goods stores, and other small businesses. Making a profit is not the only or even the main reason for launching these ventures; rather,

These Vietnamese immigrants have brought to their new home in the United States their intense family loyalty—a strongly held cultural value.

the goal is to provide employment for, and maintain social contact with, family members.

Being split up during or after immigration has been a major problem for Vietnamese families. Whether they fled on short notice with the American troops in 1975 or escaped later, often on small, overcrowded boats across open seas, few families remained intact. Vietnamese who left parents, grandparents, brothers, sisters, or cousins behind were as emotionally torn as Americans would be if circumstances forced them to abandon their children. Keeping what remained of their families together after they arrived was another hurdle. U.S. apartments and houses simply aren't designed for families with fifteen or twenty members. Overcrowding caused problems with neighbors, who resented the extra traffic and noise, as well as within families, who were accustomed to more space.

The Vietnamese consider *adaptability* a supreme virtue. Individuals who adjust their principles to the circumstances and who are quick to compromise are admired. People who "stick to their guns" are not. For the Vietnamese, no position is irreversible. In the turbulent years leading up to the war in Vietnam, the last emperor, Bao Dai, first backed the French, then shifted to the Japanese, turned to the Communist Viet Minh, switched to the Americans, and then returned to the French—all in the space of two years! Needless to say, this flexibility was highly frustrating to western political leaders. To the Vietnamese, the emperor's behavior made perfect sense. They have a saying: "The supple bending reed survives storms which break the strong but unyielding oak."

This flexibility has played an important role in helping Vietnamese adapt to life in the United States. To feel more at home, as well as to get started economically, refugees re-created large families by including as family members more distant relatives and unrelated people they had met in refugee camps in Southeast Asia or resettlement programs in the United States and providing them with work and accommodations. In Vietnam, men are the unquestioned heads of their households, though women handle domestic finances. In the United States, refugees have stretched the female role of *Noi Tuong* or "domestic manager" to cover times when the wife is working and the husband is unemployed, without unduly damaging his authority or self-esteem.

The Vietnamese also place a high value on *propriety*. The ability to maintain an even temper and to be polite, no matter what the circumstances, is highly prized. Raising one's voice for any reason at all is considered vulgar. Open displays of affection are an insult to the loved one as well as to anyone who might see them. Extensive use of hand gestures in talking, and poking and touching in jest—both common among Americans—are rude to the Vietnamese, a sign of lack of control over one's body. Some Americans who work with Vietnamese and other Asian refugees consider their traditional reserve "unhealthy." From our cultural perspective, they are "slaves to etiquette."

Tradition, harmony, and respect for elders and ancestors also rank among the most important Vietnamese values.

American Values

American ideas about what is desirable and good are based on western European values that were transplanted to the great open spaces of North America, modified by the presence of seemingly unlimited resources and opportunities, and touched by the pioneer's love of adventure. The set of values that resulted is distinctively American.

Individualism is a dominant theme in American culture. One of our goals in socialization is to raise children who are independent and self-sufficient. We maintain ties with relatives, but "live our own lives." In most societies, elderly parents live with their grown children; in our society, most older people say they prefer to remain independent. We spend a great deal of time and effort on self-improvement, through exercise or adult education or psychotherapy. We are judged—and we judge others—on the basis of individual effort and personal achievement.

Americans admire people who stick to their *principles*. We tend to be highly moralistic and react badly when a public official (or a parent or friend) does not exhibit the ideal behavior we expect. Our judgments have an either/or quality: we tend to classify people and actions as either good or bad, either successes or failures, either practical or impractical. This kind of thinking leads us to take absolute positions. If we accept one principle, we must reject its opposite; the idea that some action may be both good and bad makes Americans uncomfortable. This high-minded adherence to principle exists in uneasy alliance with the value of pragmatism (doing whatever is most practical to accomplish a goal).

Americans tend to be *activists*. When something seems wrong (in our government, in our school, in our family), we assume that if we try hard enough, we'll be able to identify the problem and solve it. This faith in action reflects over 300 years of expansion across first geographic, then technological, frontiers. To Americans, obstacles exist to be overcome. Other peoples are more inclined to accept their fate, to let things happen. Americans say, "It's better to do something than nothing." Our activism and pragmatism lead us to place a high value on assertiveness.

These are only a few of the major values that shape our culture. Americans also believe in human rights, equality, freedom, and patriotism. We value rationality and the scientific approach.

Norms and Sanctions

Whereas values are abstract ideals, **norms** are rules about what people should or should not do, say, or think in a given situation. (For example, patriotism is a value; showing respect for the flag is a norm.) Norms are shared ideas about how people *should* behave. They provide guidelines for virtually every activity: when and where to give birth and how to handle death, making love and making war, what to eat and what to wear, when and where to make a joke. Actual behavior can and does stray from the norms. People don't always do what they're supposed to do. Moreover, individuals or groups may have differing or even conflicting standards. For example, some groups in American society view a citizen's right to bear arms as sacred; others believe private ownership of guns contributes to the high level of violence in our society and represents a threat to everyone.

Some norms are sacred, and violations of them are almost unthinkable. Such norms are called **mores** (pronounced *more-ays)*. Our cultural prohibitions on cannibalism and on an adult's having sex with a child are examples. Other norms, called **folkways,** are not sacred but are so ingrained that people conform to them automatically, out of habit. Examples are saying "Hello?" when answering the telephone and eating sweets at the end of a meal

rather than at the beginning. A norm written into a formal code by officials of the state is a **law.**

Norms vary widely from culture to culture. For example, traditionally Vietnamese parents make all major life decisions for their children, including what job or career they should train for and whom they should marry. It is a parent's job to tell children what to do and how to do it, and a child's job is to obey without question. Thus one Vietnamese father described proudly how he planned and orchestrated every step in his son's education, from his first year in an American high school through his graduation in chemistry from Berkeley (Gold, 1993). American norms, in contrast, emphasize individual choice. "Good parents" do not force children to participate in activities they don't enjoy or tell them what to wear or whom to befriend but, rather, guide them toward making good decisions for themselves. Once a child graduates from high school, a parent's role is to advise, not to direct; as teenagers become young adults, start careers, and launch families, a parent's role is cut back to advising only when asked. In terms of our norms, Vietnamese parents are dictatorial; in terms of Vietnamese norms, American parents are irresponsible to the point of neglect.

Not only do norms vary from culture to culture, but different norms apply to different categories of people within the same culture. In all societies men and women, children and adults, and friends and strangers are expected to behave differently. For example, in our society young children are expected to play and go to school, not work for wages. In ballroom dancing (the tango or the waltz), the man is supposed to lead and the woman to follow. In public places, friends converse as if they were alone, though they whisper if the subject is an intimate one; a stranger who offers his opinion on what you said to your friend about your mother would be considered rude, if not crazy. Moreover, different norms apply in different situations and settings. At parties, strangers are welcome to introduce themselves and join in conversations. Adults are expected to exercise modesty in public but can wear almost nothing on the beach and can disrobe and shower next to total strangers (of the same sex) at a gym or health club. Finally, norms change. Twenty years ago men were allowed to "flirt" with women they met in the workplace; today unwanted sexual advances are considered sexual harassment.

Before the AIDS epidemic, people did not mention condoms in polite conversation, and they were kept behind the counter and out of sight in pharmacies. Today condoms often are available in college dormitories and in bars; they are prominently displayed in drugstores and purchased by women as well as men. On TV programs directed at teenagers and in sex education classes, teachers and peer counselors use bananas to demonstrate how to use condoms. Changes in norms may be either gradual and unintended or the result of active, organized campaigns.

By themselves, norms are only guidelines; sanctions are what provide norms with muscle. *Sanctions* are the socially imposed rewards and punishments by which people are encouraged to conform to norms. Sanctions may be formal or informal.

Formal sanctions are official, public rewards and punishments, such as a passing or failing grade in school, a medal of honor or a dishonorable discharge from the military, or a promotion or dismissal at work. In modern societies, we rely a good deal on formal sanctions, especially through the criminal justice system. People accused of violating the law appear before a judge, who decides whether the charge is warranted and whether the accused should be jailed pending trial and determines the amount of bail (if any). Every citizen has a right to a trial by jury. In practice, most criminal cases are settled informally through plea bargaining (see Chapter 7), but the threat of imprisonment, fines, or other formal penalties provides the incentive to negotiate.

In traditional Eskimo societies a person accused of violating norms confesses to a shaman (a person who mediates between the material and spiritual worlds) while the whole village gathers around, chanting to cleanse the person's soul. Like a courtroom trial, this ceremony involves formal sanctions.

Informal sanctions are unofficial, sometimes subtle or even unconscious checks on everyday behavior. An encouraging or contemptuous look, an approving or embarrassed smile, a shoulder to cry on or "the cold shoulder," a pat on the back or a slap in the face, people laughing with you or laughing at you, and the possibility of praise or the threat of gossip are enough to keep most people in line.

In most cases, violating a norm isn't a crime, but people still feel better when they "do the right thing." You ask yourself: "Should I ask my boss for the day off or lie by calling in sick?" "Would it be wrong for me to go out with my friend's 'ex'?" "Should I give some change to the homeless-looking man on the corner?" In making such decisions, you recall past sanctions—times when your behavior met with reward or punishment—and you act accordingly, if only to avoid embarrassment.

Norms and sanctions establish the boundaries of acceptable social behavior. The fact that most members of a culture share the same ideas about what is appropriate, normal, or polite helps make social behavior and social interaction predictable. In most situations, we know what to expect. This predictability is an essential element of social structure (see Chapter 5).

Symbols

A *symbol* is an image, object, or sound that can express or evoke meaning—a crucifix or a statue of Buddha, a teddy bear, a national anthem. Many symbols are physical objects that have acquired cultural meaning and are used for ceremonial purposes. A flag, although nothing more than a piece of colored cloth, is treated with solemn ritual and inspires feelings of pride and patriotism, solidarity or hatred because of the meaning people associate with it. Some symbols, like the flag or the cross, are condensed representations of cultural beliefs, values, and norms and carry many meanings. Others, like a red hexagonal sign, have a narrower, more specific meaning: Stop!

Symbols may also be ordinary, useful items that have acquired special meaning. Certain cars denote wealth; others may express youth, daring, power, or involvement in a lifestyle (a jeep or dune buggy) for their owners. In other cultures, a cow or a pig of a particular color can evoke similar feelings. In these cases, cultural and personal meanings intertwine. Depending on cultural evaluations and personal experiences, people can develop deep and powerful attachments to ordinary objects (a grandmother's sewing thimble, a baseball cap that recalls summer camp and youth) (Czikszentmihalyi and Rochberg-Halton, 1982).

The same object, even when used for the same purpose, may mean quite different things in

Symbols are often ordinary objects that have acquired special meaning. In the United States, certain cars, such as sport utility vehicles, denote upper-middle-class status.

different cultures. For example, both Americans and Vietnamese bury their dead in coffins, and both may spend a great deal of money on coffins. But traditionally, those Vietnamese who can afford to do so purchase a coffin long before an elderly person dies and they put it on display—much to that person's delight. The Vietnamese honor their departed relatives on "death days" (the day a relative died)—in much the same way Americans celebrate birthdays—by inviting the family, preparing an elaborate meal, decorating the house, lighting candles (or incense), and drinking toasts to the deceased person (Lack, 1978).

Language

Language is a shared set of spoken (and often written) symbols and rules for combining those symbols in meaningful ways. Language has been called "the storehouse of culture" (Harroff, 1962). It is the primary means of capturing, communicating, discussing, and changing shared understandings and passing them along to new generations (and new citizens). We use language not only when we are with other people but also when we are alone. Much of what we call "thinking" is actually a conversation with ourselves.

Anyone who has tried to function in a foreign country with only a pocket dictionary knows that languages vary in complex, and sometimes subtle, ways. Knowing the Italian translation for the appropriate English words does not necessarily enable you to get your laundry done in Rome; you have to know Italian grammar and pronunciation in order to make yourself understood. Every language has words and phrases for which there are no exact equivalents in other languages. Moreover, each language has its own set of sounds, which may be difficult for adults to learn. A number of African languages employ clicking sounds that English speakers find almost impossible to produce; Asian languages include tonal variations that English speakers find difficult to *hear,* much less pronounce.

Learning a new language can force you to think in unaccustomed ways. For example, English speakers use the pronoun "you" when addressing another person—any other person. Many European languages, however, have two forms of address, one formal and one familiar. The French use the formal *vous* to indicate respect, deference, and social distance; the familiar *tu* indicates equality or intimacy. The Vietnamese have a complex system of address that indicates degrees of respect based on age, position, education, and other factors. Any elderly man is politely addressed as *anh* (which translates literally as "elder brother"). A young man is politely addressed as *bae* ("father's older brother"). But a young man who does not, in the speaker's view, deserve respect is called *chu* ("father's younger brother"). Given the Vietnamese concern with politeness, deliberately using the wrong term is a clear insult. Thus the French and especially the

Vietnamese systems of pronouns make distinctions that cannot be made in the same way in English.

These nontranslatable differences among languages raise an interesting question. Are linguistic differences a reflection of different ways of looking at the world, or do linguistic differences *create* different perceptions? Are we to some extent prisoners of our own language? Two anthropologists, Edward Sapir (1921) and Benjamin Lee Whorf (1940), have argued that we are. According to the **Sapir-Whorf hypothesis,** language causes people to pay attention to certain things but ignore others. For example, English speakers have a single word for white flakes that fall from the sky: "snow." Eskimos have more than twenty words that enable them to describe subtle variations in the snow's texture, weight, and other qualities but no single word to cover all these variations. Sapir and Whorf argue that language forces reality into different molds. Hence "our view of reality is an abridged version of the world that has been edited by our language" (Plog and Bates, 1980, p. 210). People who speak different languages do not merely occupy the same world with different labels but to some extent actually perceive different worlds and live in different realities. According to this view, Eskimos see things in a winter landscape that non-Eskimos cannot perceive, and the Vietnamese experience social relationships in a way Americans do not—because of the differences in the languages.

In an empirical test of the Sapir-Whorf hypothesis, John A. Lucy (1992) compared Maya speakers from southern Mexico with English speakers from the United States. Linguistic analysis showed that English speakers almost always identify a noun as singular or plural ("book" or "books"). Maya speakers often ignore number by using so-called mass nouns (such as "cattle" or "the news" in English). The Mayan language has more terms for the materials out of which objects are made (wood, metal), whereas English has more terms for shape (round, flat). When Lucy compared the performance of subjects from the two groups on a variety of cognitive tests, he found that English speakers more often recalled number and classified objects by shape, whereas Maya speakers rarely mentioned number and grouped objects made from similar substances.

This concrete experiment supports the Sapir-Whorf hypothesis, at least on a small scale. But how much linguistic variations contribute to different world views is debatable. Lucy suggests that certain modes of thought (science, philosophy) may be more language-dependent than others and that certain uses of language (poetry, the printed word) may have more impact on thought than others.

In general, the evidence supports a weak version of the Sapir-Whorf hypothesis. Certainly, language calls attention to particular features of the physical and social landscape by labeling these features. It affects what we notice and how we understand what we observe. But language does not dictate what we see and think in a rigid way. It is only one element of culture.

Technology

Technology is a body of practical knowledge and equipment for enhancing the effectiveness of human labor and altering the environment for human use. Many of the Vietnamese who came to the United States in the late 1970s were from rural, peasant communities. They had worked their fields with wooden plows and water buffalo, as had their grandparents and their grandparents' grandparents. Few had had electricity or plumbing in their homes. For these refugees, coming to the United States was a little like visiting Disneyland. Our technology seemed fabulous and unreal. Even our farms and fishing fleets were mechanized. The variety of goods for sale in American stores, the fact that nearly all our goods were machine-made, and their sheer abundance were astonishing. Technology creates a particular physical, social, and psychological environment.

Many Americans feel just as disoriented in the world of computers, especially that vague territory called the Internet or "cyberspace." The Internet began to take shape in the 1960s (Cairncross, 1997). At the time, the only computers were large, expensive, scarce mainframes. The Defense Department commissioned a small company in Massachusetts to devise a way of connecting computers across the country to enhance their power. The first network, linking four universities, was switched on at UCLA in 1969. Networks began to multiply, but well into the 1980s the main users were large research universities. Several innovations were required to transform the Internet from an academic billboard, accessible only to computer scientists, to a popular playground, accessible to anyone. First was the creation of affordable personal computers (PCs), first mass-marketed in the late 1980s. Second was the creation of the World Wide Web, which added multimedia (color, pictures, sound, and animation) to the data and text, making the Internet more inviting. Third was hypertext, a tool for cross-referencing and links; and fourth, browsers, which made all these other tools easy to use. As recently as 1990, only academics regularly used the Internet. By 1997, an estimated 71 million people, more than half of them in the United States, were logging on (see Figure 3-3). Today, the most frequent use of the Internet is sending and receiving e-mail, followed by doing research. But radio programmers, TV producers, and long-distance telephone services are beginning to use and expand the Internet.

The impact of the Internet remains to be seen. One might predict that distance, location, and time will become increasingly irrelevant (Cairncross, 1997). Rapid, relatively inexpensive electronic communication makes it possible for employers and employees to locate anywhere on earth; to work at any hour and receive instant feedback; and to market goods, services, and skills and spread ideas globally. The separation of home and office and the 9-to-5 routines, ushered in by the Industrial Revolution, might fade. Although computers are expensive ($1,000 plus), the Internet itself is public property and use of the Internet is almost free.[2] The result is a new window of opportunity for private entrepreneurs, who can go into business with a relatively small investment (no stores, salespeople, or costly ads); but an opportunity for dominance has also arisen. Microsoft, the company that was founded by Bill Gates and that introduced the user-friendly Windows format for PCs, is now fighting charges of monopoly in U.S. courts for requiring PC manufacturers to install Microsoft's Internet browser as a condition for installing Windows. Because the United States pioneered the Internet, there is a possibility that English will become the language of global communication and subtly impose Anglo-Saxon values on other cultures. But the Internet also provides the means for ethnic groups who are geographically dispersed to maintain their heritage and for other subcultures (from fans of Sherlock Holmes, to animal rights activists, to the modern militias, described below) to flourish.

This comparison of American, Vietnamese, and other cultures suggests why it can be difficult to adapt to a new culture. Often full integration of immigrants into the new culture does not take place until the second or third generation—if the immigrants want to become assimilated and if members

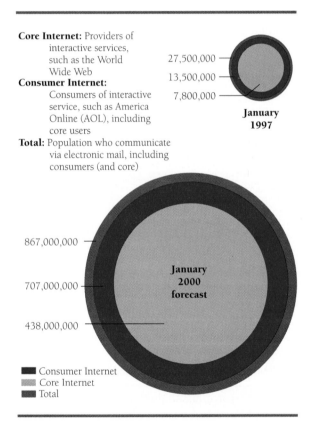

Figure 3-3 *The Growth of the Internet*

The Internet is growing exponentially and is on its way to becoming one of the major communication media around the world.

Source: Adapted from Matrix Information and Delivery Services, Austin Texas (www.mids.org), and F. Cairncross, *The Death of Distance: How the Communications Revolution Will Change Our Lives.* Boston: Harvard University Press, 1997, fig. 4-1, p. 88.

---

[2]This varies, however. In parts of the United States and some other countries, local calls are "free" in the sense that they are included in the basic service charge for a telephone line. Faced with competition, America Online instituted a flat fee, which other computer service providers copied. Access to the Internet is more expensive in other places.

of the host culture choose to accept them. But even then, people may retain certain habits of the mind and heart, souvenirs, and symbolic ties to their "old country." Likewise, adapting to the "new world" created through the Internet can be difficult, especially for adults who grew up before computers were invented, even before television, when the primary media of communication were radio, newspapers, handwritten letters, and face-to-face conversation. Like second- and third-generation immigrants, children seem much more at home with computers and find their way around the web as easily and naturally as their parents and grandparents roamed the neighborhood.

Ethnocentrism and Cultural Relativism

Anthropologists use the term *culture shock* to describe the feelings of disorientation and stress that people experience when they enter an unfamiliar cultural setting. Culture shock often occurs when we visit a foreign land, even one whose culture is similar to our own (as when an American visits Great Britain). Typical "symptoms" of culture shock include feelings of incompetence; fear of being contaminated (for example, by the water), cheated, or laughed at; and loneliness. Suddenly, familiar behavioral cues are taken away and replaced by new patterns that at first make little sense. Ordinary, everyday life becomes unpredictable. Thus culture shock is a form of anomie (see Chapter 1).

For example, older members of the Ndau tribe of Mozambique talk wistfully about "the ceremony." In the old days, the elders say, when droughts came, the tribal chief would go to the cemetery and ask the ancestors for rain. "Before he could come home, it would rain. And after three days he would have to go back to the cemetery and ask it to stop" (*Baltimore Sun*, Oct. 11, 1992, p. K8). Likewise, when someone was sick or injured, the tribal shaman would perform a curing ceremony. But the government of Mozambique has banned such rituals as superstitious and replaced hereditary tribal leaders with appointed officials, most of whom are young and know little about the old traditions. The Ndau elders see the civil wars and droughts that plague

their country as punishment for neglecting their ancestors. Cut off from their cultural roots, from the beliefs and rituals that once gave their lives order and meaning, they feel helpless.

Culture shock occurs because of enculturation: We learn our own cultural patterns so early in life, and so thoroughly, that they become second nature. We consider our distinctive way of thinking and behaving as simple "common sense." We conform out of habit, without stopping to consider alternatives. We don't realize how dependent we are on shared understandings about what is appropriate. Confronted with other ways of doing things, we are sometimes merely amused but sometimes annoyed, repulsed, or shocked.

The problems of functioning in a new culture are compounded by ethnocentrism. *Ethnocentrism* is the tendency to evaluate other cultures in terms of one's own and to conclude that the other cultures are inferior.

Ethnocentrism is widespread. A number of different cultural groups, such as the Caribs, Kiowas, Lapps, and Tunguses, call themselves by names that mean "people," implying that all nonmembers are less than human. Traditionally, the Jews divided all humankind into themselves ("the chosen people") and gentiles; the Greeks called all non-Greeks "barbarians." When Europeans first arrived in Greenland, the native Inuits there assumed that they had come to learn good manners and virtue, which the Inuit believed the Europeans sorely lacked (Sumner, 1906/1959). The European view was somewhat different.

Ethnocentrism is based on cultural misunderstandings. Taken out of context, any custom can seem ridiculous. Consider the Nacirema, a people whose culture is still poorly understood:

> The fundamental belief underlying [the Naciremas'] whole system appears to be that the human body is ugly and that its natural tendency is to debility and disease. Incarcerated in such a body, man's only hope is to avert these characteristics through the use of the powerful influences of ritual and ceremony. Every household has one or more shrines devoted to this purpose. . . .
>
> The focal point of the shrine is a box or chest which is built into the wall. In this chest are kept many charms and magical potions without which no native believes he could live. These preparations are secured from a variety of specialized practitioners.

Ethnocentrism probably causes you to find the woman on the left more attractive than the woman on the right. A person from Yunnan, China, might disagree.

The most powerful of these are the medicine men, whose assistance must be rewarded with substantial gifts. . . .

Beneath the charm-box is a small font. Each day every member of the family, in succession, enters the shrine room, bows his head before the charm-box, mingles different sorts of holy water in the font, and proceeds with a brief rite. . . . It was reported to me that the ritual consists of inserting a small bundle of hog hairs into the mouth, along with certain magical powders, and then moving the bundle in a highly formalized series of gestures. (Miner, 1956, pp. 503–504)

Try spelling "Nacirema" backward, and then see whether you can identify the ritual being described.

Taken out of context, this familiar activity seems as bizarre as the custom of filing or knocking out front teeth for beauty (a custom in some Pacific groups); calling on the ancestors to bring rain and the spirits to cure sickness (the Ndau ceremonies mentioned

above); a taboo against eating meat (a Hindu custom), pork (an Islamic and Jewish custom), or ants and slugs (a "Nacirema" custom); chest-pounding duels (a ritual practiced by the Yanomami of the Amazon rain forest); or body-pounding duels (a "Nacirema" ritual called "football").

Each of these practices or beliefs is part of a larger cultural whole that gives it meaning. We cannot begin to understand, much less judge, items of culture apart from this cultural whole. **Cultural relativism** is the view that a culture must be understood in terms of its own meanings, attitudes, and values. (It is the opposite of ethnocentrism.) Cultural relativism derives in part from the functionalist perspective, which holds that all elements of a culture are interwoven and therefore should not be judged out of context. Understanding a custom does not necessarily mean one should accept or endorse it. Most readers of this book would condemn clitoridectomy, for example. But if one wants to convince people to abandon this ritual, one must first understand what it means to them. (See *Sociology and the Media:* Female Genital Mutilation: Rites versus Rights.)

Cultural Inconsistencies and Diversities

Cultures vary widely in their degree of **cultural integration**—in the extent to which different parts of a culture fit well together and support one another (see Giddens, 1985a). In small, homogeneous societies that have few contacts with outsiders, cultural integration may be near-perfect. The different elements of culture are synchronized; for many purposes, people act and think as one. In some traditional societies, there is no word for "religion" because what we would call religious rituals are woven into the fabric of everyday life. In complex, modern societies like our own, this is rarely the case. Social and technological change may occur too rapidly for norms to keep pace. Outdated norms may remain on the law books and in the language as figures of speech long after they've lost their usefulness. For example, in New York City an old law dating back to Prohibition makes it illegal to call a bar a "saloon." When cited for violation, one restaurant skirted this law (and had to make only a minor adjustment to its neon sign) by renaming itself "O'Neal's Baloon [sic]."

In complex, modern societies people live in different habitats (from urban high rise to rural farm), work at different occupations, enjoy different standards of living, follow different educational paths, and so experience different versions of their culture. Internal inconsistencies and diversities are most visible in such societies. Immigrant groups may keep up the traditions and language they brought from the old country, setting themselves apart. Other groups within a culture may rebel against prevailing standards and create their own. But conflicting views of proper behavior exist in all societies, creating enough ambiguity to allow for the introduction and acceptance of change.

The Ideal and the Real in Culture

There generally is a difference between what people say they think and do and what they actually believe and practice. **Ideal culture** consists of norms and values to which people openly and formally adhere. **Real culture** consists of norms and values that people may not openly or formally admit to but practice nonetheless. For example, Americans believe in being charitable. Everyone wants to help the homeless—unless this means building a shelter on their block; in that case a NIMBY (not-in-my-backyard) reaction is common. American culture idealizes lifelong monogamy. In their marriage ceremonies, most couples vow to stay together "til death do them part." In reality, more than half of first marriages end in divorce, and most Americans feel that if a marriage turns bitter, a man and woman have a right to separate.

The interplay between ideal culture and real culture can result in obvious contradictions. For example, Americans place a high value on health and spend billions every year on hospital care, doctors' bills, and medications. Yet we spend almost as much on things we know to be injurious to our health—cigarettes, alcohol, and junk food. We say, "Honesty is the best policy," but we also say, "Business is business." Americans stand ready to fight "to keep the world safe for democracy," yet only about half of eligible voters in this country turn out for an election. (In 1996, 49 percent of the voting-age population cast ballots in the presidential election, down from 52 percent in 1992.) The list of contradictions within American culture could run on for pages.

Laws that regulate campaign fundraising activities leave politicians room in which to maneuver. As a result, there is also room for doubt and questioning. Here, the Senate Governmental Affairs Committee investigates possible campaign-finance violations during the 1996 presidential campaign.

SOCIOLOGY & THE MEDIA

Female Genital Mutilation: Rites versus Rights

The case of a 19-year-old West African, Fauziya Kasinga, brought a widespread but largely unknown custom to public attention in the United States, sparking public outrage. Ms. Kasinga had fled her home in Togo because her family and the man to whom she had been promised insisted she undergo genital mutilation before she wed. Entering the United States under a false passport, she was held in detention for two years before the U.S. Board of Immigration Appeals, under considerable public pressure, granted her asylum on the grounds that she had "a well founded fear of persecution" in her homeland. How widespread is this practice? What are the consequences for girls and women who undergo such operations? What is the cultural meaning of genital mutilation? What can be done to reduce or eliminate this practice? The media called attention to the problem by focusing on a single case; to answer these questions, however, we turn to sociological research.

The practice of female genital mutilation (FGM), sometimes called "female circumcision," is most common in Africa and the Arab peninsula but also occurs among a few groups in Asia and among Arab and African immigrants in Europe, North America, and Australia (Chalkley, 1997). Worldwide, an estimated 100 million women have undergone such operations, and 2 mil-

Fauziya Kasinga, of Togo, shown here at the Board of Immigration Appeals in Falls Church, Virginia, fled her native land to avoid genital mutilation and sought political asylum in the United States.

> **I am happy. I am a big girl now. Just like my friends.**
> —Hudan, 6-year-old Somalian girl, after undergoing infibulation*

lion girls are operated on each year. In some countries (Eritrea, Mali, and Northern Sudan), FGM is almost universal: 90 to 95 percent of women have experienced clitoridectomies or infibulation. In other countries (Côte d'Ivoire, the Central African Republic, and Tanzania), the practice is limited to certain cultural groups. As many as 150,000 girls now residing in the United States either have undergone FGM or will do so.

Typically FGM is performed by a midwife using a razor or sharp piece of glass, without anesthesia or antiseptics, before a girl enters puberty (between ages 4 and 10). The procedure is so painful that it takes three or four women (sisters, aunts, neighbors) to hold the girl down, while others sing and shout to drown out her screams. The mildest form of FGM, *clitoridectomy,* entails removing part or all of the clitoris. *Excision* involves total removal of the clitoris as well as part or all of the labia minora. In the most severe form, *infibulation,* all of the external genitals are cut away and the vagina is stitched together or closed with thorns, leaving a pencil-size hole for urination and menstruation. The girl's legs are bound together for several weeks until the "wound" heals.

*Los Angeles Times, July 14, 1996, p. A-1.

Women who have undergone infibulation must be "cut open" to have sexual intercourse or give birth; many are re-infibulated after each birth.

The health consequences of FGM last beyond pain, shock, and hemorrhaging, which may cause death, at the time of the operation. Infections from unsterile instruments and "healing" creams can lead to long-term pelvic infections, chronic pain, difficulty urinating or controlling urination; miscarriage, prolonged and obstructed labor, stillborn or brain-damaged infants, or, in other cases, sterility.

To westerners, female genital mutilation is a cruel, barbaric, dangerous practice, a major public health problem, and a human rights issue—the ultimate form of female oppression. Where practiced, however, the strongest supporters of FGM are often women themselves, who believe FGM is necessary to reduce a girl's sexual appetite (and preserve virginity until marriage) and to achieve "full femininity." Moreover, it is women who perform the operation and perpetuate the custom in a female rite from which men are excluded. A survey conducted in Egypt in 1995 found that 97 percent of ever-married women had undergone FGM (Chalkley, 1997). A majority of the women surveyed (82 percent) said the practice should continue, because husbands prefer wives who have been circumcised and because it satisfies Muslim religious traditions. Most believed FGM made a woman more beautiful. Only a small proportion were aware of negative consequences, such as reduced sexual satisfaction (29 percent), the risk of death (24 percent), and a greater risk of problems during childbirth (5 percent). In Somalia, women say that FGM is required for marriage and honor. Daughters who have undergone infibulation have better prospects for marriage than do those who have "merely" submitted to clitoridectomy, while young women who have undergone neither are shunned. To call someone "a son of an uncircumcised mother" is considered the ultimate insult (Davies, 1996).

Another explanation, sometimes overlooked, is simply, "This is our custom, part of our traditions, something we've always done." The result is what sociologist Gerry Mackie calls "belief traps": beliefs that are not revised because the cost of testing them is too high (1996, p. 1009). Allowing one's daughter to forgo FGM may be condemning her to a life of social ostracism. "We can't win," said one father. "If we circumcise our daughters, there is pain. If we don't circumcise our daughters, there is different pain. The community will not accept us" (Davies, 1996). A survey of Somali university students found that a majority of men and women believe FGM should be abolished, but almost the same proportions planned to maintain the tradition with their own daughters. Simply put, no one wants to go first.

Prompted by African and Arab women's groups who broke the long-standing taboo on even talking about this subject, international groups such as UNICEF, the UN Population Fund, and the World Health Organization have condemned FGM as a human rights violation. At least two dozen countries, including nineteen in Africa, have enacted laws or issued official statements against FGM. In 1996, the Egyptian Health Ministry issued a ban on genital surgery. After a campaign by Islamic conservatives, the ban was overturned by an Egyptian court in June 1997. Then, in December 1997, Egypt's supreme court overturned that ruling, restoring the ban on FGM and a three-year prison sentence for violations. In its decision, the court noted that nothing in the Koran authorizes this practice (Crossette, 1997a). A new U.S. law requires that federal officials inform immigrants from the countries where this custom is widespread that FGM is a crime in this country and that they face up to five years in prison for performing such procedures or arranging them for their daughters. But criminal sanctions are unlikely to change strongly held

continued

Female Genital Mutilation: Rites versus Rights *(concluded)*

religious or cultural beliefs. Much as laws banning abortion forced American women to undergo risky, illegal procedures to end a pregnancy, so laws banning FGM may force the practice underground.

What can be done? The most successful campaigns preserve the social and ritual aspects of FGM. In the Meru district of Kenya, for example, local women's groups organize mother-daughter training programs in which participants learn about reproductive health and ways to resist FGM. At the end of this program, they hold a communitywide celebration of the girls' coming of age (Chalkley, 1997). Mackie cites China's success in eliminating—in a single generation—the equally cruel practice of binding women's feet. Education (informing adults and children of the harm caused by binding and the benefits of natural feet) and outside pressure (China did not want to be seen as backward) were important. But Mackie holds that the key was the creation of "pledge associations": groups of parents who pledged not to allow their daughters to be mutilated *or* to allow their sons to marry women who had been mutilated. Pledge associations lowered the risk of breaking with tradition while increasing the benefits: no one had to go first.

On the one hand, opposing norms and values create conflicts. In living up to one norm, a person may automatically violate another. Suppose that after she and her boyfriend break up, a woman in her early thirties discovers that she is pregnant. She does not think abortion is necessarily wrong but, rather, considers it a "last resort" when the mother or parents cannot provide for a child. She has a steady income, a flexible job, and a large supportive family and thinks she could be a good single parent. She knows her boyfriend would support whatever decision she makes regarding abortion but would want to get married if she decides to have their baby. Our norms hold that children need and deserve two parents. For her to have the baby without marrying the father would be "selfish." But contemporary norms also hold that forced or "shotgun" marriages probably aren't good for anyone. Attitudes toward abortion are in a state of flux, but some people would hold that the best solution in this situation would be having an abortion. What should she do?

On the other hand, the existence of contradictory standards leaves individuals considerable room in which to maneuver. Our norms hold traditional marriage as ideal, but many people today see nothing wrong with an unmarried couple living together—unless they have children, either together or from prior marriages. (In Scandinavian and some European countries, unmarried parenthood is more widely accepted; see Chapter 11.) When people within a culture break a rule, they tend to do so in much the same way. For example, hardly anyone drives at precisely the legal speed. If the legal limit is 55 miles per hour, most of us drive at 60 or 65, not 40 or 80. Most Americans wouldn't consider stealing from a department store, but they think nothing of occasionally taking supplies home from work, padding their expense accounts a little, or cheating just a little on income taxes. Many politicians would never consider taking a bribe but see nothing wrong with giving a job to campaign workers or accepting a campaign contribution from a lobbyist (see Chapter 14). Indeed, people who do not bend the norms (that is, people who do not conform to real culture) are often thought peculiar, or even antisocial.

Thus real culture may be said to consist of patterned evasions of the ideal culture. This does not mean that ideal culture does not have an impact; it does. The immigrants who are attempting to adapt to life in the United States must learn both official standards for proper behavior and unofficial but accepted strategies for bending the rules.

Subcultures and Countercultures

Neither real culture nor ideal culture is equally shared and accepted by all groups in a society. Together, the real and the ideal cultures form the common denominator; but there are many variations, particularly in large and complex societies. These cultural variations within the larger culture are known as subcultures. A **subculture** is a set of understandings, behaviors, practical and symbolic objects, and vocabulary that distinguish a particular group from other members of their society. For a subculture to exist, individuals must identify with the group (although they may have other social identifications as well) and must interact and share information with others who identify with the group, both directly and indirectly (Fine, 1987).

Although ethnicity is the most obvious source of subcultures, they may also be based on religion, occupation (medical interns and jazz musicians have their own subcultural worlds), lifestyle (ski or beach "bums"), sexual orientation (the gay subculture), or age. People who enjoy horse racing do not constitute a subculture; people who devote their lives to breeding and training race horses and who associate almost exclusively with other people who do the same might qualify. The key is whether they see themselves, and are seen by others, as "different."

In some instances, subcultures do not merely differ from the mainstream but actively oppose the values and practices of the larger society. Such a group is called a **counterculture,** meaning "against the culture." The militia movement that came to public attention after the bombing of the federal building in Oklahoma City is an example. No one

knows how many people are active members of militias (paramilitary groups, or "posses" as some call themselves) or how many passively support them; how well organized and coordinated such groups may be; or how many who support the militia's goals also support terrorist tactics. In 1997, Klanwatch, a branch of the Southern Poverty Law Center, estimated that there were 380 armed antigovernment groups operating in 50 states, about 100 of which had white supremacist and anti-Semitic ties (Kifner and Thomas, 1998). But there is reason to believe militias represent a counterculture—people whose values, attitudes, and activities cause them to identify with one another and feel a symbolic sense of community.

The militia movement has roots in the "survivalists" of the early 1960s (Zellner, 1995). Convinced that nuclear war was imminent, survivalists held that families must move to isolated, rural areas and prepare to provide everything for themselves, live without modern technology, and defend themselves against both communist invaders and hordes of urbanites who would be forced to flee cities in the event of a nuclear attack. In the wake of the Vietnam war, many came to believe that the enemy was not "out there" but right here, in the form of the federal government. The government, they believed, sent American boys to fight and die in a foreign jungle but "tied their hands behind their backs," as President Reagan often said. One way to avenge defeat by guerrillas abroad is to become

This Dublin, Ireland, street gang displays all the attributes of a subculture—unique understandings, unique material culture, symbols, and behaviors.

guerrillas at home (Wills, 1995). By the 1990s, the term "survival" had come to stand for self-defense against a broad spectrum of issues linked to government control. The militia movement has attracted white supremacists, religious fundamentalists, opponents of gun control and abortion, and others. What unites them is their fear of government oppression.

The main theme of the militia movement is that the federal government has become the enemy of freedom, not its protector. Today's militants see the IRS, government regulatory agencies, and federal law enforcement agencies (especially the FBI, and the Bureau of Alcohol, Tobacco and Firearms) as agents of a police state that uses Social Security numbers, tax forms, the census, and even birth, death, and marriage certificates to "spy" on citizens. Some militia groups attribute this state of affairs to infiltration of U.S. government by ZOG, the Zionist (Jewish) Occupation Government; others, to a takeover by the United Nations or the New World Order; still others, to Satan; and some, simply to government corruption. In their view, the American government isn't "American" anymore, in the sense of government by the people.

A second theme is family autonomy. Militants hold that a man has a God-given right to be head of his household and to rear his children as he sees fit, according to his religious principles. Many of today's militants believe that public schools are "brainwashing" children with a secular world view (by denying the importance of prayer), with anti-American propaganda (by advocating multiculturalism), and with critical thinking—including sex education and instruction on children's rights (which subvert parental authority). In particular, they view laws against child abuse—and, by extension, corporal punishment—as invasions of family privacy.

A third theme is the right to bear arms. Militants hold that citizens have not just a right but a duty to fight tyranny, whether in the form of dictatorship or big government bureaucracy. Gun control is the "last straw," one that would strip citizens of the right to self-defense.

Two incidents galvanized the militia counterculture: the shoot-outs at Ruby Ridge, Idaho, and Waco, Texas. At Ruby Ridge, a man protecting his own family on his own property, and at Waco, the group calling themselves Branch Davidians, defending their religious beliefs, in both cases with constitutionally protected firearms, were assaulted (and some members killed) by federal agents. Both places have become almost sacred, pilgrimage sites.

The bombing of the federal building in Oklahoma City (on the second anniversary of the death by fire of Branch Davidians in Waco, Texas; see Chapter 17) took the country by surprise. No one suspected that terrorism threatened the "heartland" of America or that the terrorists might be Americans, not foreigners (as in the bombing of the World Trade Center in New York City).

From a functionalist perspective, subcultures and even countercultures play an important role in society (see Weinstein, 1991). The "symbolic rebel" ensures that dominant cultural values and symbols are not mistaken for the way things must be. In challenging mainstream culture, subcultures force members of a society to reexamine and perhaps reaffirm, or revise, their views. Opposition to big government and government intrusion—the general feeling that government has overstepped its boundaries—is widespread. Liberals have protested FBI plots against citizens like Martin Luther King, CIA experiments with LSD on unsuspecting citizens, and the shooting of student protestors against the war in Vietnam at Kent State University by National Guardsmen. Ronald Reagan won votes for himself and other conservative Republican candidates in large part by asserting that government itself is the problem and that we must get the federal government "off our backs." Whatever their political leanings, many Americans saw the confrontation in Waco, and the deaths of federal agents as well as Branch Davidians, as a tragic mistake. The militia movement has taken this position to a logical (though violent) extreme.

Although "different" from the main culture, no subculture is wholly independent of it. A subculture's relationship to the main culture may be rejecting, defensive, or ambivalent, but the connection remains. Armed opposition to government is part of our culture, beginning with the American Revolution. As the militia movement demonstrates, subcultures are variations on the main theme.

Explaining Culture

Sociological interest in culture has waxed and waned. The founders of sociology considered understanding of culture critical to understanding of society, and they devoted considerable attention to beliefs and rituals (Durkheim), norms and values (Weber), and ideology (Marx). But with some notable exceptions (Talcott Parsons and Robert Bellah, for example), succeeding generations of sociologists tended to leave the study of culture to anthropologists. In recent years, however, this has changed; attempts to explain both the role culture plays in society and the relationship between individuals and culture have moved to the forefront of sociology (Alexander, 1988; Calhoun, 1994).

Functionalist Views

Functionalists view culture as part of an integrated whole, as an essential piece of the machinery that keeps society running. Talcott Parsons (1951), for example, saw culture as providing the link between the goals and needs of individuals and the requirements of society. Jeffrey Alexander (1988) and other contemporary sociologists emphasize the role of cultural symbols and rituals in maintaining social solidarity.

The functional approach to culture has a long history in sociology. Emile Durkheim is best remembered for his analysis of the impact of social forces over human behavior (see Chapter 1). Toward the end of his life, however, Durkheim became interested in the question of how external social forces become internalized, in how social forces get *inside* people and motivate them.

To answer this question, Durkheim (1912/ 1947) turned to the study of religion. All cultures, he found, distinguish between the sacred (that which is holy and must be treated with reverence) and the profane (ordinary, everyday things that can be treated casually). He concluded that religious symbols function as personifications of the unseen social forces that shape our lives and that religious rituals are an attempt to control or at least appease these forces. Thus religious beliefs satisfy the universal human need to find order and meaning in life, to believe that some higher being is in control of the things we cannot control. Equally important, religious rituals reaffirm and enhance commitment to the group. They play a key role in maintaining social continuity, on the one hand, and in legitimizing social change, on the other. (For more on Durkheim's views of religion, see Chapter 13.)

A primary aim of functionalists has been to explain how cultural events and practices that seem senseless or bizarre in fact perform important social functions. Kai Erikson's analysis (1966) of the witch hunts that swept the Puritan communities of New England in the seventeenth century is a classic example. Erikson argued that the public labeling and excommunication of deviants (in this case, the burning or hanging of witches) functions to maintain cultural boundaries. Every cultural group draws a set of "symbolic parentheses" around the range of possible human activities. Behavior that falls within these parentheses is acceptable; behavior outside these markers is not. The group's symbolic parentheses are its cultural boundaries. Like war or natural disasters, crime and punishment unite people through common feelings of anger and indignation, reminding them of their collective interests and the shared values that make them a special people. The Salem witch hunts occurred during a period when Puritan communities were beginning to break apart and cultural boundaries had to be reestablished.

One group of contemporary functionalist sociologists and anthropologists—called *cultural ecologists*—focuses on the role of the environment in shaping cultures. From this perspective, cultural traits are best seen as adaptations to the physical environment and can be understood only in the environmental context—the ecological system—in which a people live.

Marvin Harris's explanation (1975) of the sacred cow in India is a classic example of the cultural ecology approach. The population of India is chronically malnourished. Against this backdrop of starvation, the Hindu prohibition against slaughtering cattle or eating their meat seems irrational. But Harris showed that live cattle play a vital role in the Indian ecosystem. Cows and oxen provide India with a low-cost substitute for tractors. Their dung is used for both fertilizer and fuel. (Harris estimated that the 350 million tons of dung used in kitchen stoves is the equivalent of 27 million tons of kerosene or 35 million tons of coal.) Cattle do not compete with humans for food in India as they do in the United States, where they are fed grain; they scavenge. Thus the fertilizer and fuel they provide is free. Moreover, they are able to survive long periods of drought with little food and water. For Indians to kill off their cattle during a famine would be a little like unemployed Americans selling the cars they need to get to work. Doing so might provide immediate cash but in the long run would deprive them of their means of making a living. In India, "cow love" makes good ecological sense.

Conflict Theories

Unlike functionalists, who emphasize the role of culture in promoting social solidarity and adaptation to the environment, conflict theorists emphasize the role of culture in the struggle for power and privilege. According to this view, the dominant culture in a society usually benefits some groups at the expense of others. For example, computer technology has become one of the most important elements of culture in the United States and, indeed, the world. Computers have become increasingly important in education and business, as well as entertainment and personal communications. In the job market, computer literacy is not just an asset but a requirement for all but low-level jobs. The cost of computers themselves, as well as training, sets limits on who owns computers, knows how to use them, and so has access to the "information highway." Low-income families cannot afford to buy their children home computers, and schools in low-income neighborhoods cannot afford the most up-to-date hardware or the salaries of additional teachers who specialize in computer training. The "computerization" of culture enhances the power of those already in power.

Whether looking at new technology or old traditions, conflict sociologists study how cultural patterns reinforce or change the balance of power. Sally Moore studied witchcraft among the Chagga of Tanzania from a conflict perspective (Moore and Meyeroff, 1975). Moore found that allegations of witchcraft in Chagga communities were not random. In most cases, such accusations were made by the wives of the oldest or youngest brothers in a family against the wives of middle brothers. These accusations were likely to stick. The reason, Moore thinks, is that farmland is scarce. Wives take advantage of the fact that middle brothers have the least power in Chagga families; they make accusations that will force these brothers to leave home for jobs in urban areas, ensuring adequate land for those remaining behind. Thus accusations of witchcraft benefit some at the expense of others, reinforcing social inequality.

Pierre Bourdieu (1984) has explored the ways in which groups in western societies use cultural products to maintain social class distinctions. Bourdieu traces the emergence of abstract painting to the efforts of social elites to set themselves "above" people of lower social status. Abstract art is an acquired taste. The subject and emotional content of representational art—landscapes, still lifes, portraits, and the like—is apparent to anyone, but one must learn to interpret what an abstract painter is portraying. (Indeed, one must learn whether or not it is "art.") Elites cultivate this special knowledge; by and large, the working and lower classes do not. Likewise, members of the elite tend to prefer furniture that appeals more to the intellect than to the body: straight-backed, elaborately carved antique couches, modern chairs that don't look like chairs, country pine that shows its age. Only someone who "knows" furniture (and furniture prices) can appreciate such pieces. Members of the working class are more likely to choose furniture for comfort, utility,

Does this room belong to a member of the elite or a member of the working class?

and familiarity: recliners, easy-to-clean linoleum kitchen floors, cheerful curtains and cute pictures, and knickknacks. In this way social elites strive to maintain their social distance from lower classes. These principles apply not only to art and antiques but also to fashion and style. (See *Close Up:* A Cultural History of Jeans.)

Following Weber, some conflict theorists see cultural patterns as a major source of political and economic change (for example, Eisenstadt, 1978). Religious fundamentalism—comprising movements that oppose secularization and modernization and seek to restore traditional beliefs and practices—has become a powerful political force in many countries. Conflict theorists see fundamentalist movements as rebellions against modernization, which not only threaten traditional patterns of social life but also create a new, westernized, capitalistic elite. In Iran and Afghanistan, Muslim fundamentalists overthrew secular regimes and now control their countries' governments. In Algeria, tens of thousands have died in a civil war between the secular army and Muslim traditionalists. Although a minority, Orthodox Jews in Israel have become increasingly powerful in the government and society as a whole. In the United States, a conservative movement, emphasizing such traditional cultural values as family togetherness, self-sufficiency, and parental authority, led to the Republican victory in the 1994 congressional elections and to a balanced-budget amendment, the repeal of welfare, and other changes in policy and programs.

Following Marx, other conflict theorists see culture as a reflection of the interests of the ruling class. Without necessarily planning or intending to do so, this elite creates cultural patterns that rationalize its power to exploit the masses. The result is what Marxists call "false consciousness." Cultural patterns may lead peasants or workers to accept a social system that works to their disadvantage because they are preoccupied with religion and the afterlife (in feudal societies) or with consumer goods and short-term gains in pay (in industrial societies).

The Individual and Culture

Where does the individual fit in the cultural framework? Are we prisoners of our culture, blindly endorsing the values and following the rules that have been handed down to us? Or are we the producers of our culture, selectively adopting some aspects of our cultural inheritance and rejecting or amending others?

Most sociologists would agree that the answer is both: "Culture shapes us and we shape culture" (Bourdieu, 1989). On the one hand, culture can be seen as the background against which the social drama is played. From this perspective, culture consists of a body of inherited assumptions and expectations that guide social interaction. The goal of sociological studies is to make these implicit assumptions explicit, to uncover the cultural blueprint for social action.

On the other hand, culture can be seen not as background but as a product of social behavior. Culture does not exist "out there" but is created, maintained, and revised through social interaction. From this perspective, the goal of sociology is to investigate the production of culture by social actors, to analyze cultural products (works of art, books, rituals, speech, ideologies, and the like), and to explain these phenomena.

The Production of Culture

Sociologists who study the production of culture begin with the observation that the "elements of culture do not spring forth full blown, but are made somewhere by somebody" (Peterson, 1979, p. 152). Some individual or group declared the cow sacred, and contemporary social actors make it their business to teach and enforce this belief in India today. Certain painters experimented with abstract art, and specific critics and collectors helped turn their work into status symbols; modern art galleries and magazines carry on this process. Traditions do not endure on their own; they must be re-created in each generation (Shills, 1981).

In this view, culture can be seen "as a 'tool-kit' of symbols, stories, rituals, and world-views, which people may use in varying configurations to solve different problems" (Swidler, 1986, p. 273). Sociologists who emphasize the production of culture study the impact of technology, social structure, and economics on the music, art, and science that are produced in a society. They investigate such things as the social mechanisms for judging originality (from Academy Awards to Nobel Prizes); the role of "cultural gatekeepers" (people who decide which cultural products will reach the public—

A Cultural History of Jeans

In his book *Fashion, Culture, and Identity* (1992), sociologist Fred Davis traces the changing cultural symbolism of blue jeans. Jeans were invented in the mid-nineteenth century by a Bavarian Jewish peddler named Morris Levi Strauss, who had settled in San Francisco. The trousers were made from a sturdy indigo-blue cotton said to have originated in Nîmes, France (the English word "denim" comes

> **The transformation of a sturdy, utilitarian garment into fashion**

from the French *de*—"of" or "from"— *Nîmes*) and resembled pants worn by Italian sailors from Genoa whom the French called *genes* (hence the English "jeans").

For nearly half a century jeans were worn almost exclusively by men who worked out-

The symbolism of jeans has shifted over the years, from down-to-earth work clothes for miners and other laborers to fashion statements.

museum directors, music company executives, church councils, book and magazine editors, movie censors, and the like); the contexts in which cultural products are used (whether music is played in a barroom or a symphony hall, whether religion is preached in a cathedral or a TV studio); and the effects of consumers on the production process (see Griswold, 1987; Peterson, 1979).

Sociologists from this school are not interested in individual producers of culture per se. They are not looking for the person who invented the expression "Have a nice day," the fax machine, or cubist painting. Rather, they are interested in the social condi-

tions, contexts, and interactions that promote cultural continuity or change. Howard Becker makes this important point in his book *Art Worlds* (1984). We tend to think of art history in terms of individual geniuses (da Vinci, Rembrandt, Renoir, Picasso) who saw beyond existing artistic forms and created new ones. But as Becker emphasizes, the individual painter is only one member of a production crew, albeit the starring member. Whether a "genius" or not, a painter depends on the people who manufacture canvas and brushes; the people who operate galleries and museums; the people who collect art and attend showings; and other artists, past and doors (miners, laborers, farmers, and, of course, cowhands). The transformation of a sturdy, utilitarian garment into fashion began in the late 1930s and 1940s when jeans were adopted by painters and other artists in the southwest, then by motorcycle gangs or "bikers" in the 1950s, and finally by New Left activists and hippies in the 1960s. In different ways, each of these groups opposed conservative, respectable middle-class standards, symbolized by the businessman's gray flannel suit and the neat hats and white gloves at women's luncheons. Jeans made a strong antiestablishment statement. Besides, they were cheap, baggy, and comfortable—at least at first.

By the late 1960s jeans had crossed occupational, class, gender, age, and cultural lines to achieve worldwide popularity. Jeans manufacturers certainly played a role in convincing consumers that jeans were for everyone. But jeans also called up visual images of rural democracy, the common man, and, especially for Europeans, the American west. No sooner had jeans achieved widespread acclaim than they began to change. Old, faded, fringed, and tattered jeans sent a message of "conspicuous poverty" (spending more to look poor). Skintight jeans and ultrashort cutoffs for women turned a unisex garment into an erotic one. The Levi Strauss, Lee, or Wrangler label on the back hip pocket was joined by designer labels such as Calvin Klein and Ralph Lauren. Indeed, in the late 1980s Karl Lagerfeld designed "dressed-up denims" for Chanel, including a classic suit ($960), a bustier ($360), and a hat ($400). In terms of their symbolism as well as their design and price, jeans had come full circle, from the world of hard work to the world of postindustrial leisure and affluence.

In the 1990s, super-baggy jeans, bought several sizes too large and worn low on the hips, became the "in" style among would-be hip-hop teenagers. The Calvin Klein company adopted this style for a series of ads (partly to sell underwear). How long this trend will last is impossible to say. As Davis's history makes clear, cultural symbols are constantly evolving. The "message" of blue jeans has shifted over the years, from down-to-earth work clothes for miners and other laborers to fashion statements for cultural icons like Kate Moss.

present, whose paintings provide the context for understanding his or her work. The production of culture is always a collective, social process, not the work of single individuals.

Medical research provides another example. Who decides which conditions or diseases are worthy of research and on what grounds? There is strong evidence that research on AIDS was delayed in the United States because the disease appeared first among homosexuals and then among intravenous drug users—two "outcast" groups in our society (Shilts, 1987). Only when AIDS was seen as a threat to heterosexuals and non-drug-users did the health community mobilize. Meanwhile, as many as a million Americans were infected with HIV, the virus that causes AIDS.

An enduring problem for cultural sociologists is to strike a balance between showing how cultural patterns are socially constructed (for example, by the music and publishing industries or the agencies that fund medical research) and recognizing the irreplaceable function of individual creativity and personal taste (Wolff, 1983). Language illustrates both the dilemma and the solution. No one would argue that one individual or group of individuals got up one morning and decided to create language. But we do use language creatively, every time we speak. The language we speak does not determine what we think, but it does make it easier to conceive and express certain ideas and difficult to imagine and articulate others (the Sapir-Whorf hypothesis, discussed earlier). So it is with other elements of culture, such as beliefs, values, and even technology. We inherit beliefs but test them against our own experiences and other people's beliefs. In trying to understand our own lives, we unconsciously fit people and events into a narrative form that conforms to stories in our culture's "library" (G. S. Howard, 1991). Like ancient Greek tragedies, today's tabloids tell stories of how the rich and powerful fall from grace. When the federal building in Oklahoma City was bombed, many people assumed it was the work of foreign terrorists because this fit a familiar scenario. Just when pundits predicted that reading would soon disappear, replaced by television, a number of booksellers opened "superstores" that combine elements of singles bars and libraries and became as popular on rainy weekends as shopping malls.

The Internet is the newest, fastest-growing, and potentially most powerful medium for the production and transmission of culture. What role does the Internet play today in shaping beliefs, attitudes, and tastes? How much will the Internet change the way we gather information, interact with other people, and maintain or modify culture? We do not know, but its impact is already being felt. When TWA Flight 800 crashed into the Atlantic Ocean, killing all the passengers and crew members, "news" that the plane had been shot down by a Navy missile appeared on the Internet and spread rapidly, bypassing traditional news communication pathways. The traditional news media found themselves responding to what many people already "knew," or thought they knew. The growth of the militia movement is due in part to use of the Internet and e-mail. In the past, organizations have played a central role in transforming social discontent into social movements (see Chapter 17)—organizing networks and rallies, providing supporters with information, and the like. Creating "home pages" on the web is relatively easy and inexpensive, and anyone who is interested—or simply browsing—can log on and leave her or his e-mail address for future communications. Much as megastores replaced local bookshops, Amazon.com,

which sells books via the Internet (using such techniques as reader reviews, author interviews, sample chapters, and personal recommendations based on a profile users fill out), may be undercutting the megastores. For the first five editions of this book, we relied on research available from the library; for this edition, at least 40 percent of the source material and statistics came from the Internet.

Will the power of cultural gatekeepers decline as the number of home pages multiplies? Or will Internet service providers [such as America Online, Compuserve, MSN (Microsoft Network), and Prodigy], Internet browsers (such as Netscape and Microsoft Explorer), and search engines (such as Yahoo!, Lycos, InfoSeek, and AltaVista)—all of which format and preselect Internet links—become the most important gatekeepers? Will our culture become more fragmented as Internet users choose for themselves what they want to know and who they consider reliable sources? Or will cultures around the globe become more homogenized or more Americanized—as French President Chirac suggested, will they become "an Anglo-Saxon network" (in Cairncross, 1997, p. 95)? The answers lie in the future, but a future that is approaching faster, thanks largely to the Internet.

Cultural Change

No culture is static. Each individual, and each generation, makes adjustments in the overall design for living as their personalities and the times dictate. Sometimes the adjustments are major, and many ties with the past are broken. The next generation inherits not simply a new edition of culture but a revised version.

The Sources of Change

There are three main sources of large-scale cultural change. The first is an alteration of the *natural environment*. (As we have seen, this source of change is emphasized by cultural ecologists.) A change in the climate; a shortage of wheat, gasoline, or some other resource; a sudden rise or fall in population—all force people to adapt. They cannot go on living exactly as they did in the past.

The second source of cultural change is contact with groups whose norms, values, and technology are different. *Cultural contact* may be friendly or hostile; voluntary or involuntary; or mutual (trade relations or a student exchange program) or one-sided (an invasion by military forces or technical advisers who impose their way of doing things). In some cases, such as the Republic of China (discussed below), change may be imposed by the government or another group within a society.

The third source of cultural change is discovery and invention. *Discovery* is the uncovering of new knowledge about, or new uses for, something that already exists [such as penicillin (extracted from mold), solar power, or the militia movement]. *Invention* is a recombination of existing knowledge and materials to create something new (such as the steam engine, the fax machine, birth control patches, public opinion polls, rap music, post modernism). Any one of these sources can spark major change in a group's overall design for living.

Cultural change often occurs in fits and starts. There is often a **cultural lag,** or delay, between a change in technology (material culture) and changes in beliefs and values (nonmaterial culture) (Ogburn, 1922). Rapid changes in reproductive technology provide a current example, one that continues to raise moral and ethical issues. In the not-so-distant past, there was only one way to make a baby: a couple had sexual intercourse and about nine months later the mother gave birth to a new human being. Then, in 1978, British physicians announced the birth of the first so-called test-tube

baby, conceived through *in vitro fertilization.*[3] Since then medical breakthroughs have enabled tens of thousands of couples who were infertile or carried a genetic disease, and many older women, to have healthy babies. But the new reproductive technology has raised a multitude of as yet unanswered ethical questions (Robertson, 1994).

Traditionally, parenthood has been defined in terms of biological relatedness (or adoption). With the new technology, a child may have five "parents": the woman who donated an egg, the man who donated sperm, another woman who carried the embryo to term, and the couple who want a baby. Who are the child's "real" parents? If a couple who conceived a child through artificial insemination divorce, what rights does the husband have regarding the child? What if a surrogate mother decides she wants to keep the baby she carried or the couple who arranged for the pregnancy decide they don't want the baby? In vitro fertilization procedures often result in several viable embryos, some of which may be frozen for future use. Do those embryos have a right to be born? If the couple dies, who owns the embryos?

Ultrasound, amniocentesis, and related procedures allow physicians to detect physical abnormalities and

---

[3]Removing eggs from the mother's ovaries, fertilizing them with the father's sperm in a petri dish, and implanting one or more embryos in the mother's womb.

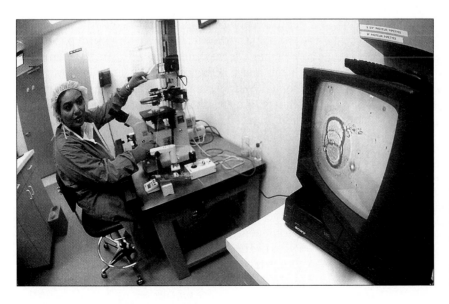

There is currently a cultural lag between the capabilities of reproductive technology and changes in beliefs and values. Therefore, there is controversy over the use of some available technologies, especially cloning.

genetic disorders, as well as the sex of the fetus, long before birth. As a result, what was once left to fate or to God is now a matter of choice. Many people might agree that it is cruel to give birth to a baby known to have Tay-Sachs disease, a hereditary disorder that inevitably causes early, painful death. But what about a child who will be physically disabled or mentally retarded? A girl when the parents wanted a boy? Since China instituted its "one-child policy," sex ratios at birth are skewed, with baby boys way outnumbering baby girls. Presumably, many female fetuses have been aborted. Using prenatal testing to choose a son over a daughter is illegal in China, but apparently it is widespread. (See Chapter 10.)

Through genetic engineering it will soon be possible to alter chromosomes, removing "defective" genes or replacing "missing" genes that cause disorders such as cystic fibrosis and muscular dystrophy. Gene therapy might eliminate diseases that, at present, are incurable. However, the same techniques might be used to produce "designer babies" whose appearance, temperament, and other traits are preselected by the parents, much as people choose options on a new car. One can imagine a "genetic caste system" composed of groups of people who were "designed" to be political leaders, scientists, artists, superstar athletes, office or factory workers, and servants or slaves. Indeed, the fact that genetic engineering undoubtedly will be costly will give the wealthy and powerful more "options" regarding their children than will be available to people with fewer resources.

The announcement in 1996 that a sheep had been cloned greatly complicated the picture. Dolly, as the lamb was named, is a genetic replica of her mother, in effect her mother's identical twin, born without a father. It is only a matter of time before scientists will be able to clone human beings. What will this mean? Consider several scenarios (Kluger, 1997):

> Parents learn that their 6-year-old daughter is suffering from leukemia. The only way to save her is a bone marrow transplant, but they must find a compatible donor. An identical twin would be ideal, but the girl is an only child. The solution? A clone. Instead of losing their one daughter, the parents would raise "two of her."

> A Nobel laureate in physics is terminally ill; when he dies, the world will lose a genius. Through reproductive chance, an equally brilliant scientist might appear someday, but the timing is unpredictable. His clone, and his clone's clone, might continue his research well into the future.

> A dictator who has ruled his country for decades is in his eighties and realizes that his days are numbered. He has seen other countries fall apart when a powerful, popular leader is followed by a weaker leader. A clone will ensure that his leadership will continue after he dies.

Cloning will not produce an identical human being: because we cannot duplicate human experience and socialization, we cannot duplicate a person (see Chapter 4). But the possibilities are tempting—and troubling.

For better or worse, scientists are on the verge of being able to apply the principles of industrial design—quality control, predictability—to human beings. Rapid technological or environmental change leave cultural assumptions and guidelines out on a limb. For example, cloning adds a new dimension to the concept of "immortality" that may undermine religious concepts and the idea that exceptional people (artists, political leaders, even saints) live on through their creations and deeds.

Adjustment to Change

People do not automatically accept new cultural elements introduced by foreigners or new cultural products developed by members of their own society. Acceptance depends on whether the innovation is similar to existing customs and practices, whether the new item is useful in their environment, and whether it fits their ideas of how things should be done. It also depends on attitudes toward change in general (based on previous experiences) and on whether the item is seen as potentially beneficial or harmful.

When changes are dramatic, adjustment can be extremely difficult. Thus contact with technologically advanced societies has in some cases had a devastating effect on small, preliterate societies. Cargo cults are the classic example. When Europeans penetrated remote regions of Melanesia and New Guinea in the nineteenth and early twentieth centuries, tribal people were fascinated by western technology—radios, guns, watches, canned food. Equally fascinating was the fact that Europeans were never observed making these things themselves (as tribespeople crafted their own material goods); the goods arrived on ships and planes, as if by magic. The tribes concluded that Europeans must have superior magic. In place after place, prophets linked visions of European wealth to local myths. They predicted that their ancestors would soon return on ships and planes loaded with a cargo of money and goods, causing the Europeans to flee. Whole villages went to work clearing airstrips, stringing vines on poles to resemble radio transmitters, and imitating Europeans in other ways in order to capture their magic. The routines of everyday life were abandoned. Because the fields were neglected, when the cargo failed to appear, many people went hungry (Worsley, 1968).

Cargo cults may be an extreme example. But it should not come as a surprise that sudden, dramatic cultural change produces dislocation. Culture does not just provide guidelines for action; it provides people with their basic definition of reality and with a sense of meaning and purpose. When continuity with the past is broken, the future is no longer perceived as predictable. Even when change

is peaceful and welcome, adjusting to a new design for living is difficult.

The Case of China

The recent history of the People's Republic of China provides vivid illustrations of planned cultural change enforced by the state and unplanned cultural change in response to cultural contact. (See Map 3-2.)

The death of Mao Zedong in 1976 was a turning point for China. Before 1976, visitors to China sometimes felt as if they were stepping into a black-and-white photograph (Schell, 1989). Everyone dressed in the same quilted "Mao jacket," baggy trousers, white shirt, and canvas shoes. Everyone read the same government-approved publications and watched the same government-sponsored television. Even flowers were banned, as self-indulgent.

This cultural uniformity was the product of the Communist Revolution of 1949. The new leaders set out to reorganize Chinese society, from top (the government) to bottom (the family). China's ancient civilization was attacked as a feudal society that had exploited the masses for thousands of years. Religious shrines, outdoor markets, traditional teahouses, and

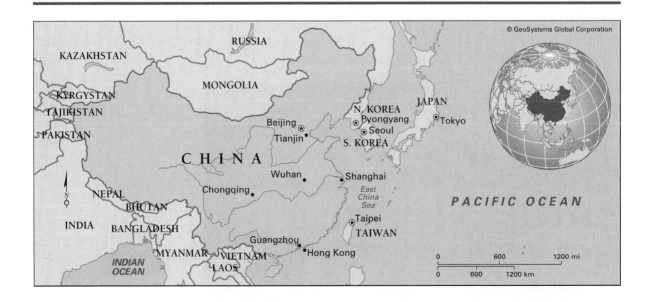

Map 3-2 *China*

other remnants of the old order were systematically destroyed. At the same time, westerners were denounced as "capitalists" and "imperialists"; western customs and tastes were portrayed as the ultimate decadence; and the doors to China were shut tight. Every aspect of Chinese life was measured against the sayings of Chairman Mao, which were summarized in the famous "little red book."

This assault on China's past, foreign influences, and individual expression reached a peak during the Cultural Revolution (1966–1976). With Mao's blessing, millions of scientists, artists, and other alleged "counterrevolutionaries" were stripped of their jobs, publicly humiliated, and sent to jail or banished to the countryside. Many were said to have "disappeared."

Partly in response to the excesses of the Cultural Revolution, and partly to overcome economic stagnation, the leaders who came to power after Mao's death instituted a program of reform. Some private enterprise was permitted, economic planning was decentralized, and controls on art and literature were eased. In 1978, Chairman Deng Xiaoping declared "modernization" a national priority, the beginning of a "second revolution." This meant allowing foreign investors and tourists into China and permitting Chinese students and officials to visit the west. Over the next several years, Mao's picture and sayings quietly disappeared, and party leaders began to talk about how much China could learn from the west.

The first westerners to visit China during this period found themselves the objects of intense curiosity. Having never seen a European before, many Chinese wondered if these large, pale, beak-nosed, round-eyed strangers were really human. But as more and more Chinese observed westerners, in person or on imported TV programs, attitudes changed rapidly in the direction of acceptance. By the mid-1980s, many Chinese had bought the entire western package, "from discos to democracy" (Schell, 1989, p. 73). Translated works by Jefferson, Freud, and other previously forbidden western thinkers appeared regularly in bookstalls; abstract art began to replace "social realism"; the fashionless Chinese now sported designer jeans, turtlenecks, bright ski parkas, and jogging shoes; female "bodybuilders" in scanty bikinis adorned the covers of magazines; college students rode ten-speed bicycles and listened to rock music on portable cassette players; and disco dancing was replacing earnest discussions of the pronouncements of Chairman Mao on courtship. Falling in love (an idea spurned both by traditional Chinese culture, which held that marriages should be arranged by families, and by revolutionary ideology, which emphasized states' needs over individual desires) became an accepted reason for marriage.

This flood of changes reached a peak in the spring of 1989, when thousands of students occupied Beijing's huge Tiananmen Square. The world watched on live television as nearly a quarter-

China in the 1990s is a unique combination of a one-party totalitarian state and a rapidly growing free-market economy. Quality of life has improved rapidly for millions of Chinese people.

million protestors took to the streets, calling for democracy. Then, on the night of June 3, government troops moved in and "cleared" the square. Thousands of students were killed, and thousands more arrested. For a time, censorship was reinstated and university students and their supporters were required to undergo military training and to work as laborers in the countryside. Even handholding was banned at Beijing University. This political crackdown did not stop economic growth, however.

A new picture of China began emerging in the 1990s (Kristof, 1993). China is no longer a "Communist country" in any ideological sense but, rather, a distinctive combination of a one-party, totalitarian state and a growing free-market economy. The Communist party is as brutally repressive as ever. Political dissidents are routinely jailed, beaten, tortured, sent to insane asylums, and confined with criminals who have infectious diseases, such as tuberculosis, until they become infected themselves. Yet the same party that torments its people has engineered one of the most remarkable increases in standard of living in history. Since the "second revolution" in 1978, China's gross domestic product (GDP) has almost tripled. The World Bank (1992) estimates that the number of Chinese living in absolute poverty (without adequate food, clothing, and shelter) dropped from 270 million in 1980 (the size of the entire U.S. population) to 98 million in 1990. (See Figure 3-4.) By almost any measure of the quality of life, China has performed better than India, the second most populous country in the world and a democracy. The once ultra-left People's Republic now boasts a thriving stock market, satellite television, private colleges, Avon ladies, radio talk shows, soap operas, theme parks, frozen food (chiefly dumplings), and an estimated 4 to 5 million "millionaires" (calculated in Chinese currency, about the equivalent of US $175,000).

To many Asians, however, there is no contradiction between political repression and economic freedom. Asian cultures have always emphasized social order and the collective good over individual rights. The Chinese have a saying: *Yi fang, jui luan,* which means "Loss of control leads to chaos." In the quest for national prosperity and strength, Chairman Deng feared chaos and conflict above all else. Having lived through wars, famines, and political upheavals himself (though a longtime colleague of Mao, he had been one of the victims of the Cultural Revolution), he saw disorder as China's worst enemy, a threat not just to the party, but also to China's hopes for modernization. During the student uprising, Deng warned other leaders that if they did not crush the democracy movement, China would become a "dish of loose sand."

With the death of Deng Xiaoping in 1997, China's future is uncertain (Kristof, 1997). The history of China is one of "dynastic cycles": the first emperor, a strong-willed general or peasant leader who seizes power and institutes far-reaching reform, is followed by progressively weaker leaders; increasing government corruption and incompetence undermine the dynasty's "mandate of heaven," its moral authority and popular support; and a new leader emerges to found a new dynasty. In many ways, the Chinese Revolution ushered in a Communist dynasty. If Mao Zedong was the first Communist emperor, Deng Xiaoping may have been the last and the Communist dynasty may have run its course. None of China's current leaders has the quasi-imperial authority Deng exercised for eighteen years. Official corruption is rampant; the army operates beyond civilian control; rapid development has caused severe environmental damage; displaced peasants are flocking to cities; and the gap between prosperous coastal cities and the vast interior, the rich and the poor, is widening. Rapid economic growth combined with sudden exposure to the outside world has fostered a new, competitive individualism that runs counter to both traditional and communist values, creating a cultural vacuum.

What form will the next "dynasty" take? One possibility is that China will follow the path of the former Soviet Union and break apart. But economic growth and new prosperity make this seem unlikely. Another possibility is that rising income and education levels and the emergence of a new middle class will lead—gradually or suddenly, with the appearance of a new "emperor"—toward greater political freedom and tolerance, and even democracy. Yet the threat of a reactionary military coup cannot be discounted. One certainty is that the future of the largest nation on earth, like its past, will be distinctively Chinese.

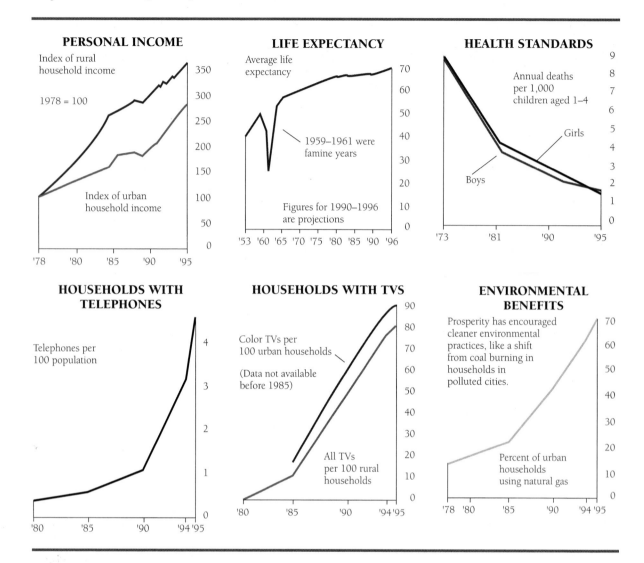

PERSONAL INCOME

Index of rural
household income

1978 = 100

Index of urban
household income

350
300
250
200
150
100
50
0

'78   '80   '85   '90   '95

LIFE EXPECTANCY

Average life
expectancy

1959–1961 were
famine years

Figures for 1990–1996
are projections

70
60
50
40
30
20
10
0

'53 '60 '65 '70 '75 '80 '85 '90 '96

HEALTH STANDARDS

Annual deaths
per 1,000
children aged 1–4

Girls

Boys

9
8
7
6
5
4
3
2
1
0

'73   '81   '90   '95

**HOUSEHOLDS WITH
TELEPHONES**

Telephones per
100 population

4

3

2

1

0

'80   '85   '90   '94 '95

HOUSEHOLDS WITH TVS

Color TVs per
100 urban households

(Data not available
before 1985)

All TVs
per 100 rural
households

90
80
70
60
50
40
30
20
10
0

'80   '85   '90   '94 '95

**ENVIRONMENTAL
BENEFITS**

Prosperity has encouraged
cleaner environmental
practices, like a shift
from coal burning in
households in
polluted cities.

Percent of urban
households
using natural gas

70
60
50
40
30
20
10
0

'78 '80   '85   '90   '94 '95

Figure 3-4   *The Rising Standard of Living in China*

A combination of tight political control and limited economic freedom has led to significant improvements in the standard of living for most Chinese.

Source: The New York Times, Feb. 23, 1997, p. E-5.

SOCIOLOGY ON THE WEB

Exploring Culture

The web is a great place to obtain basic information about other cultures. You can learn about history, architecture, and politics; read people's life histories; hear music; view artwork; even find recipes. Here are a few sites that provide fascinating information about Vietnam and Vietnamese Americans, plus one site that will allow you to begin to explore Latin American cultures:

http://www-personal.umich.edu/~hpp/hispol.html
This site, titled Vietnam Culture and Community, provides links to sites about history, politics, and the Vietnamese American community. You can also search for the home pages of Vietnamese American college students.

http://www.viettouch.com/
Included at this site are pages about Vietnamese art, architecture, history, literature, and music, among

other topics. Click on "History" to view a beautiful timeline that details the history and culture of Vietnam.

http://www.vietgate.net/
This omnibus site contains links to 90,000 other web pages about Vietname and Vietnamese Americans. Find travel information, links to Vietnamese-run businesses in the United States, and much general information about the community.

http://lanic.utexas.edu/
This is a good place to begin a search for information about Latin American culture. Click on the name of any Latin American country, and find wide-ranging lists of linked sites: academic research, cultural resources, maps, charts, economic data, government links, publications. Links are also cross-indexed by topic, such as gender studies.

Summary

1. **Why is culture so important to human beings?** Because humans adapt to their environments primarily through learning, culture is vital to our species. Our survival, our very humanity, depends on it. A people's *culture* is their entire design for living, transmitted from generation to generation through learning.

2. **What elements do all or most cultures share?** All cultures have certain universal features, but the details of these features may vary widely. The basic elements of culture are *beliefs* (shared ideas about how the world operates), *values* (shared standards), *norms* (rules for behavior), *technology* (knowledge and techniques for creating material objects), *symbols* (which express or evoke cultural meanings), and *language* (shared symbols and rules for combining them in meaningful ways). Language shapes the way we perceive the

world, as well as the way we communicate our perceptions (the *Sapir-Whorf hypothesis*).

3. **How do people view the differences among cultures?** A person who enters an unfamiliar cultural setting often experiences *culture shock*. One reason for the difficulty people have in adjusting to other cultures is *ethnocentrism*, the widespread belief that one's own culture is vastly superior to all others. The opposite of ethnocentrism is *cultural relativism*.

4. **How do people improvise within their own cultures?** Since the integration of the varied and complex elements of culture is never perfect, there is always a "gray area" between a people's *ideal culture* and their *real culture*. Real culture consists of patterned evasions of the ideal culture's norms, evasions that are accepted by most members of society. A *subculture* is a

set of understandings and behaviors that distinguishes members of a regional, an occupational, an ethnic, or some other group from other members of society.

5. **How do social scientists explain cultural variations?** Functionalists see culture as maintaining the social system and meeting basic human needs. Cultural ecologists hold that the physical environment has a decisive, even determining, impact on beliefs and practices. Conflict theorists may view culture as serving the needs of the elite or as a basis for revolutionary change. Most contemporary sociologists agree that we are the producers as well as the products of our culture.

6. **What are the sources and consequences of cultural change?** No culture is static. Major shifts in cultural patterns may be caused by changes in the natural environment, contact with other cultures, or discovery and invention. A *cultural lag* may result when adjustment to change is difficult. The case of China shows the interaction of planned cultural change and unplanned social forces.

Key Terms

beliefs 87	folkways 90	real culture 97
counterculture 101	formal sanctions 91	sanctions 91
cultural integration 97	ideal culture 97	Sapir-Whorf hypothesis 93
cultural lag 109	informal sanctions 91	socialization 85
cultural relativism 96	language 92	subculture 101
culture 84	law 90	symbol 91
culture shock 95	mores 90	technology 93
enculturation 85	norms 90	values 88
ethnocentrism 95		

Recommended Readings

Bellah, R. N., Madsen, T., Sullivan, W. M., & Swidler, A. (1985). *Habits of the Heart: Individualism and Commitment in American Life.* New York: Harper & Row.

Bourdieu, P. (1991). *Language and Symbolic Power.* Cambridge, MA: Harvard University Press.

Brown, D. (1991). *Human Universals.* New York: McGraw-Hill.

Harris, M. (1975). *Cows, Pigs, Wars and Witches: The Riddles of Culture.* New York: Random House.

Hoeg, P. (1993). *Smilla's Sense of Snow.* Tiina Nunnally, trans. New York: Delta. (A cross-cultural mystery/thriller, based in part on the Sapir-Whorf hypothesis.)

Hunter, James Davison. (1991). *Culture Wars: The Struggle to Define America.* New York: Basic Books.

Kluckhorn, C. (1949). *The Mirror of Man.* New York: McGraw-Hill.

Lucy, J. (1992). *Grammatical Categories and Cognitive Processes.* New York: Cambridge University Press.

Tannen, D. (1990). *You Just Don't Understand Me: Women and Men in Conversation.* New York: Morrow.

Wuthnow, R. (1987). *Meanings and Moral Order: Explorations in Cultural Analysis.* Berkeley, CA: University of California Press.

Chapter

Four

Socialization through the Life Course

A quiet revolution in child rearing is spreading around the globe. Throughout history, small children have been raised in their homes by their parents and relatives. In recent years, however, an ever-increasing number of small children around the world are enrolled in preschools. About 85 percent of 4-year-olds in Tokyo, 80 percent in Beijing, and 65 percent in New York attend day care centers, nursery schools, or group care homes.

Preschools serve not only children and their parents but also the larger society of which they are a part. Though they are in part baby-sitting services, they are also responsible for molding children's behavior into patterns their culture approves. A comparison of three preschools—one in Japan, one in China, and one in the United States—illustrates how cultural values and beliefs translate into quite different approaches to child rearing. Joseph Tobin and his colleagues (Tobin, Wu, and Davidson, 1989) filmed "daily routines and little dramas" at the three schools. Then they asked preschool administrators, teachers, and parents to comment on the videotapes of their own school and the other two. A summary of the approaches and comments follows.

Komatsudani: *A Japanese Preschool*

At a Japanese preschool, a recent university graduate, Fukui-sensei, is the teacher for a class of twenty-eight 4-year-olds. She has planned two main activities for the day: a number and coloring workbook exercise for the morning, and for the afternoon, construction of an inflatable origami ball, with ample time for free play in between. Fukui-sensei leads the children through the planned activities step-by-step. As the children work, they chatter, joke, move about, and roughhouse. The teacher remains calm and patient, rarely intervening. She seems to ignore one particularly troublesome boy, Hiroki, who performs a loud song and dance routine during the workbook session and pummels his male classmates during playtime. When a girl reports that Hiroki deliberately stomped on another boy's hand, Fukui-sensei whispers into the girl's ear and sends her back outside. A while later, the teacher walks to the door and finds Hiroki wrestling another boy to the floor. "Are you still fighting?" she asks in a neutral tone.

4

Japanese culture is group-oriented. The Japanese generally avoid singling out individuals for praise or for blame. They believe that children learn self-control and social skills best through experience. Fighting and mischief are normal at this age; only by hitting and being hit, misbehaving and experiencing peer rejection, do children learn to work out problems among themselves and get along with the group. A preschool teacher's job is to "let children be children." Japanese educators and parents thought Fukui-sensei handled Hiroki correctly; to restrict or discipline him would only injure his pride and provoke more misbehavior.

Chinese parents and teachers thought the Japanese preschool was chaotic. Said one preschool principal, "Children fighting and running wild in a classroom are not a group—they are a mob. In an atmosphere of bullying and chaos they cannot learn social responsibility and the self-control necessary for being a member of the group" (p. 106). American parents and teachers agreed. In their view, children—especially difficult children like Hiroki—need individual attention; how can one teacher meet the individual needs of twenty-eight small children?

Dong-feng (*East Wind*): A Chinese Preschool

At a Chinese preschool, two teachers and an assistant are in charge of a class of twenty-six children. The day begins with twenty minutes of calisthenics, songs, and dancing. After this, the children take their seats at neat rows of tables and benches. Each child is given a box of blocks with "blueprints" for the child to copy. The children work in silence, while the teachers walk up and down the aisles, correcting their work. At 10 A.M. the whole class files to the bathroom and back. An arithmetic lesson is next. Then a hot lunch is delivered from a central kitchen. The children are admonished to eat correctly, not talk, and not waste food. After lunch and a long nap, the teachers lead the children in reciting a patriotic story in unison and then take them to the courtyard for organized relay races and supervised play. After washing up, they assemble at tables for dinner.

The only incident of misbehavior occurs before the school day began. When Amei, a 4-year-old girl, arrives, she clings to her father's hand, refusing to let go. He talks to her quietly and then hands her over to one of the teachers. The teacher helps her out of her coat and gives her a steamed breakfast bun. When the

teacher's back is turned, however, Amei leaps down and runs after her father, intercepting him in the courtyard. Father and daughter talk earnestly for several minutes and then return to the classroom. Before he leaves again, she pulls his face to her level and whispers, "Don't forget to come and pick me up Wednesday . . ." (p. 73). Amei is one of about seventy boarding or "whole care" students at Dong-feng who go home only on Wednesday nights and weekends.

A central concept in Chinese child rearing is guan, *which, translated literally, means "to govern." But* guan *also means to care for and to love. Thus not supervising a child and not instructing him or her in proper behavior is a sign of lack of affection. Teachers believe they must establish order and control, schedule activities so that children do not have opportunities to misbehave, and constantly monitor and correct behavior. They see their primary goal as producing good citizens. One official explained, "Parents are concerned for their children, but they are not the only ones. Children do not belong to their parents alone" (p. 104). Chinese educators and parents are concerned about the "4-2-1 syndrome": under China's policy of one child per family, four grandparents and two parents may lavish attention on a single child, who may become a household tyrant or a helpless dependent as a result. Having asked parents to sacrifice for the good of the country by having only one child, the government owes parents the very best in child support.*

Japanese and Americans who saw the film of Dong-feng were appalled by the degree of regimentation in this Chinese preschool. One Japanese educator lamented the apparent lack of spontaneity. "The feeling of the school is so cold, so joyless. The children are expected to be so, well, unchildlike. All that emphasis on sitting straight, on being perfectly quiet, on standing in straight lines" (p. 92). Japanese viewers also felt there were too few group activities at the school. "Everyone doing the same thing at the same time isn't the same as real group life, is it?" (p. 39). Americans criticized the suppression of individuality. "What gets me," said one preschool teacher, "is the way the Chinese children are made to . . . follow directions like workers on an assembly line, which negates the whole point of block play" (p. 92). Off the record, Chinese preschool teachers said they were much stricter when they had visitors—an attempt to impress outsiders that, ironically, had the opposite effect.

Japanese and American parents also thought 4-year-olds were far too young to be sleeping away from home.

Many Japanese and Americans are appalled at the degree of regimentation in a Chinese preschool (left). Likewise, many Japanese and Chinese are appalled at American methods of disciplining children (right).

Chinese parents were surprised that neither Japan nor the United States offers overnight "whole care." What if parents' schedules do not mesh with day care or preschool hours? if parents are too rushed to provide nutritious meals?

St. Timothy's: An American Preschool

At an American preschool, two teachers, Cheryl and Linda, are in charge of a class of eighteen 4-year-olds. The classroom is organized into various "learning stations" with materials for painting, blocks, make-believe, and other activities. Each child decides what he or she wants to do, and the children switch activities whenever they like. The two teachers keep busy putting fresh paper on easels, helping children in and out of dress-up clothes, reading stories, and arbitrating disputes. When a fight breaks out among three boys who are playing with blocks, Cheryl intervenes immediately. She asks each child what happened, talks about why it's better to express anger with words than with fists, and then suggests a compromise. At cleanup time, Cheryl spots a pile of abandoned Legos. "Who was playing with these Legos and didn't put them away?" she asks, looking at a boy playing in a corner. "Kerry, was it you? No? You didn't play with these Legos? I think you did. Please come here and put them away." Kerry shakes his head and looks down, avoiding eye contact. Cheryl tries again. "You have nothing to say to me? Then you can sit over there on the time-out chair and think about it until you are

ready to clean up" (pp. 132–133). A minute or two later Kerry gets up and puts the Legos away. At lunchtime, Cheryl sits next to Kerry, her arm around his shoulder. The afternoon is less structured than the morning, with supervised free play indoors and outdoors.

Above all, American parents want their children to become independent individuals. They give St. Timothy's high marks, praising the variety of learning materials, opportunities for individual creativity, and freedom of choice. Parents also praise Cheryl and Linda for giving children individual attention and paying attention to special needs. In their view, St. Timothy's has achieved the right "balance between freedom and order, free play and structured activities, indulgence and discipline" (p. 142).

Chinese educators and parents were impressed with the amount of space, colorful decorations, and variety of play materials and activities at the American school. However, they criticized St. Timothy's for having too few rules and treating discipline as a matter of negotiation between teachers and children. In contrast, Japanese educators and parents faulted the American school for an overabundance of materials. In their view, too many props interfere with make-believe. "Don't teachers in America believe children have imaginations?" one Kyoto teacher asked. They also felt American teachers were intrusive—both in offering too much help with tasks and in intervening too *quickly and too often in children's disputes. Both Chinese and Japanese viewers thought singling Kerry out for misbehavior and the public shame of the "time-out chair" was cruel.*

Clearly, preschools reflect the cultures of which they are a part. But Tobin and his collaborators see a common thread. Parents and educators in all three societies are attempting to deal with sweeping change in family structure and work patterns. In the past, children shared their parents with two, three, or more siblings; they got to know many adults, whether relatives who lived in their household or neighbors who knew and watched over all the children nearby; and they spent much of their time outdoors, playing by themselves in mixed-age groups. But as family size has shrunk and tight-knit communities have been replaced by neighborhoods composed mostly of strangers, children's worlds have become smaller. Preschools can be seen as an attempt to compensate for social change by providing a "substitute" extended family and neighborhood. Children enter preschool belonging to their parents and, through social interaction with teachers and peers, "leave with more diffuse, more complex ties to a world still centered on, but now much larger than, their families" (p. 205).

This study of preschools illuminates one phase in the lifelong process of socialization. **Socialization** *is education in the broadest sense: it is the process whereby one acquires a sense of personal identity and learns what people in the surrounding culture believe and how they expect one to behave (Musgrave, 1988). Through socialization, a helpless infant is gradually transformed into a more or less knowledgeable, more or less cooperative member of society. Through socialization, individuals not only learn the values, norms, and skills of their culture but also acquire a sense of who they are and where they belong. Socialization involves both explicit instruction and unconscious modeling; it influences both personality development and social behavior. Although the foundations of identity are laid and basic social skills are acquired in early childhood, socialization continues throughout life. Each of us plays a number of social roles in life; some role changes are related to age (a child becomes a teenager, a teenager becomes a young adult), while others are the result of choice (getting married and becoming a parent, switching careers, moving from New Delhi to New York). Socialization is an ongoing, lifelong process.*

Key Questions

1. *Why is socialization so important?*
2. *How does socialization occur?*
3. *Who is responsible for socialization?*
4. *How does socialization change over the life cycle?*

The Nature of Human Behavior

Clearly, all human beings are alike in some ways but different in others. Explaining the similarities and differences among human beings is a major goal of social science. Whereas psychologists focus on individual differences, sociologists are more interested in the origins of group differences. Why do people reared in different cultures, or members of different social classes, or men and women behave and think differently?

Nature and Nurture

The debate over human nature has occupied scientists for more than a century. On one side of the debate are those who have argued that individual and social behavior is the product of heredity, or "nature." According to this view, the kind of person we become is genetically preordained, and the human social drama follows a predetermined genetic script. On the other side are those who have argued that individual and social behavior is the product of experience and learning, or "nurture." According to this view, who we become depends on the environment and the way we are raised, and social scripts are largely of our own making. Underlying this debate is the more general question: "How important is socialization?"

The publication of Charles Darwin's *On the Origin of Species* in 1859 pushed the nature viewpoint into the forefront of nineteenth-century thinking. Darwin shook the theological pedestal that held human beings above the animal kingdom (though below the angels). Human beings, he argued, are the product of the same natural processes that produced snails and finches, mice and elephants, and, our nearest relatives in the animal kingdom, the great apes. We are what we are because of evolution, not divine creation.

How does evolution occur? Genetic mutations (mistakes or accidents in genetic copying) produce variations in every generation of living organisms. In most cases, these changes are either insignificant or harmful. In some cases, however, a mutation gives an individual an advantage over others of its kind. The individual is better adapted to its environment and therefore survives longer and produces more offspring. Those offspring may inherit the trait, and hence the advantage. Over time, the adaptive trait spreads, producing changes in the species or even leading to a new species. Thus evolution is the result of natural selection—nature acting on genetic diversity, selecting the most adaptive traits.

Biological Determinism

Some nineteenth-century thinkers expanded on Darwin's theory of evolution, applying the same reasoning to cross-cultural differences and social inequalities. Social Darwinists, as they were called, argued that the dominant position Europeans occupied in the world at that time was the result of natural selection: the Asian, African, and other peoples they ruled were in an earlier stage of evolution and therefore biologically inferior. The fact that within European societies some people were rich and prosperous while others were poor and hungry illustrated "the survival of the fittest."

Other social scientists of this period focused on behavior. If human beings are members of the animal kingdom, then human behavior, like other animals' behavior, must be governed by biological drives and instincts. Warfare and violence were attributed to the "aggressive instinct"; mass behavior to the "herding instinct"; an interest in homemaking to the "nesting instinct"; love of one's infant to the "maternal instinct"; and so on. The notion of "born criminals" was also popular: phrenologists claimed that they could tell whether an individual had criminal tendencies by measuring his or her skull.

The cornerstone of the nature viewpoint was the idea that most individual and social behavior is genetically predetermined. Socialization is little more than "icing on the cake." By implication, attempts to rehabilitate individuals or to reform society are largely futile.

Environmental Determinism

Early in the twentieth century the pendulum swung the other way, and the nurture viewpoint moved to the forefront. Inspired by Russian physiologist Ivan Pavlov, and led by American psychologists John B. Watson and B. F. Skinner, increasing numbers of social scientists came to believe that almost all human behavior is the product of learning. In his famous experiments with dogs, Pavlov demonstrated that even salivation, which appeared to be an automatic reflex, could be shaped by learning. (Pavlov's dogs learned to salivate at the sound of a metronome, which they associated with the delivery of food.) Expanding on this model, Skinner showed that pigeons could be taught to play Ping-Pong, and rats taught to run complex mazes, through a process of conditioning. Simply put, animals repeat behavior that produces rewards (such as food pellets) and cease behavior that induces punishments (such as electric shocks).

Behaviorists, as these psychologists called themselves, argued that human behavior is equally malleable, or plastic. The infant is a *tabula rasa* (Latin for "blank slate") on which experience may write virtually anything. What people become is dictated by events in their environment; heredity, they claimed, is unimportant. The classic statement of this position comes from Watson (1924):

> Give me a dozen healthy infants, well-formed, and my own specified world to bring them up in, and I'll guarantee to take any one at random and train him to become any type of specialist I might select—doctor, lawyer, artist, merchant-chief and, yes, even beggar man, and thief, regardless of his talents, penchants, tendencies, abilities, vocations, and race.

For behaviorists, socialization was all powerful.

Contemporary Views

Most social scientists today reject both genetic determinism (the nature view of the Social Darwinists) and environmental determinism (the nurture view of behaviorists), though in some areas debate continues. (See *Close Up:* Homosexuality: Born or Bred?) Developmental psychologists and others who study individual differences have begun to understand how genes and environments *interact*— that is, how genetic and environmental variables influence each other. Because of his or her unique

C L O S E   U P

Homosexuality: Born or Bred?

Is homosexuality inborn, the result of genetic and physiological differences over which the individual has no control? Or is homosexuality learned, the result of family dynamics or other environmental influences? These questions are not simply matters of scientific inquiry and theoretical debate; they carry social consequences. A recent study of middle-class attitudes, based on in-depth interviews of 200 suburbanites, found that on most issues—mothers working, racial integration, religious choice, and multiculturalism—subjects endorsed the principle, "Thou shalt not judge" (Wolfe, 1998). There was only one exception to this live-and-let-live attitude: four times as many of these suburbanites condemned, rather than accepted, homosexuality. The middle-class Americans most hostile to homosexuality believed sexual preference was a conscious choice, a lifestyle; those most tolerant believed ho-

mosexuality was an inborn trait or "part of their nature."

Several recent studies have suggested that sexual orientation is grounded in biology. In August 1991, Simon LeVay, a neuroscientist at the Salk Institute in La Jolla, California, announced his finding that an area of the brain that controls sexual activity was more than twice as large in heterosexual than in ho-

> **It's a mistake to think that we will be able to modify or change homosexuality.**
> —Sociologist Evelyn Hooker

mosexual men. Homosexual himself, LeVay had been a bookish boy who despised rough sports, adored his mother, and hated his father—almost a textbook illustration of the Freudian view of the psychodynamic origins of homosexuality in the family. Yet

LeVay had long believed that Freud had gotten things backward: hostile fathers didn't make sons gay; fathers became hostile because their sons were born "sissies." When LeVay read that UCLA scientists had discovered differences in male and female hypothalamuses, he decided to compare homosexuals' and heterosexuals' brains. His examination of forty-one cadavers convinced him that sexual orientation was inborn. But others were not persuaded. The discovery of brain differences does not prove cause and effect, for experience affects the development and structure of the brain.

Just months after LeVay's announcement, psychologists Michael Bailey and Richard Pillard (1991) published the results of a study of twins. Comparisons of identical twins (who have the same genes and share the same prenatal environment), of fraternal twins (who are no

Sources: *Newsweek*, Feb. 24, 1992, pp. 46–53; Alan Wolfe, *One Nation, After All: How the Middle Class Really Think About God, Country, and Family.* New York: 1998.

genetic characteristics, each child elicits special responses from the environment. An easy baby may evoke warm, playful parenting, for example, whereas a whiny, difficult baby may evoke harsh treatment or even neglect, with many variations between these extremes. Thus children reared in the same family grow up in different social worlds. As a result of these unique, individual environments, some genetic predispositions will be expressed fully and others will be masked or repressed—hence the almost infinite variety among human beings.

Sociologists focus on the broader picture of human development and emphasize group differences rather than individual differences. The sociological perspective acknowledges that biology sets the stage for human development. Genes give us the capacity to walk, talk, and use our hands and our brains in distinctively human ways. They establish a timetable for development. Thus all normal babies begin to walk at about the same age. All normal children progress from cooing and babbling to one-word exclamations, two-word "telegrams," and more alike genetically than siblings but share the same prenatal environment), and of adoptive siblings (who are genetically unrelated) are a classic source of data on the relative influences of genes and environment. Bailey and Pillard found that if one identical twin was homosexual, the odds were high that the other was homosexual, too. Of the identical twins they studied, 56 percent were both gay, compared with 22 percent of the fraternal twins and only 11 percent of adoptive brothers. What about the identical twins who had different sexual orientations? Bailey and Pillard had evaluated their subjects with the Kinsey scale, which rates people along a 7-point continuum from exclusive heterosexuality at one extreme, through various degrees of bisexuality, to exclusive homosexuality at the other extreme. These twins were at opposite ends of the spectrum, a finding that seems to defy both genetic and environmental arguments.

A third source of evidence for the biological view of homosexuality comes from cross-cultural research. Frederick Whitman, who has studied homosexuality in the United States, Central America, and the Philippines, finds that the rate of homosexuality and homosexual behavior is much the same in these diverse cultures. Yet different cultures vary dramatically in their attitudes toward homosexuals and homosexuality. Says Whitman, "That suggests something biological going on" (p. 52).

What is one to make of these diverse findings? In the 1950s, well before the gay and lesbian rights movement gained public attention, sociologist Evelyn Hooker conducted a classic study that showed that it was impossible to distinguish between heterosexuals and homosexuals on a battery of psychological tests. This study played a key role in the American Psychological Association's decision to remove homosexuality from its list of emotional disorders, in 1973. This decision, in turn, contributed to the growing view that homosexuality is a lifestyle, not an illness or perversion. "Why do we want to know the cause?" asks Hooker, now 84. "It's a mistake to think that we will be able to modify or change homosexuality. . . . If we understand its nature and accept it as a given, then we come much closer to the kinds of attitudes which will make it possible for homosexuals to lead a decent life in society" (*Newsweek*, Feb. 24, 1992, p. 53). In other words, in looking for the cause of homosexuality, we indirectly endorse the view that homosexuality is deviant. Hooker asks us to be both more realistic and more tolerant.

compound sentences with grammatical qualifications, questions, and jokes in roughly the same order. Most humans mature sexually between ages 12 and 18. The basic outline is genetically given.

But the details of development are supplied by socialization. What language children learn and how well they speak it, for example, depend on the culture in which they are reared and on the influence of people around them. How they feel about the bodily changes of puberty and how they express their sexuality also reflect their culture and personal history. Moreover, without opportunities to interact with other people, they will not develop the capacity to speak or to love at all. Socialization is the key that unlocks children's potential—as members of the human species and as unique individuals.

The Impact of Socialization

The main sources of evidence for the impact of socialization are case studies of children kept in

For years, the main debate in the study of socialization has been whether children's temperament (as exemplified in this tantrum) is the product of nature or nurture. The contemporary view focuses on how these two variables interact.

isolation, research on cross-cultural variations in behavior, and recent advances in neurobiology.

Isolated Children

History provides numerous tales of abandoned children who apparently were adopted and raised by animals. When captured, these "feral" children usually resist attempts to civilize them, suggesting that what we call "human nature" depends on a normal, human upbringing. But this conclusion is speculative, for in most cases the children never learned to talk, and so we do not know their full story. But more recent cases of socially isolated children provide strong evidence of the necessity for socialization.

When discovered by authorities in 1938, 6-year-old Anna seemed barely human. An illegitimate and unwanted child, Anna had been confined to a dark-

ened bedroom since birth, a guilty secret. Fed just enough milk to keep her alive, deprived of human contact and stimulation, her development was severely stunted. She did not respond to sound or light, never cried or laughed, and could not walk, talk, or even chew, but lay immobile on her hospital bed, staring into space. Placed in a foster home, Anna began to respond to people, to walk, feed herself, and attempt to speak. She did not recover from early neglect, however, and died before her eleventh birthday. Isabelle, another child found in similar circumstances, fared better. With loving care she caught up with other children her age, entered a regular high school, made friends, and eventually married and raised a family (K. Davis, 1947, 1948).

When "Genie" limped into a Los Angeles county welfare office with her battered mother in the fall of 1970, the welfare worker who interviewed them estimated that Genie was 6 or 7 years old and suspected that she was autistic. In fact, though only 59 pounds, Genie was a teenager. Like Anna confined to an empty room, Genie suffered further abuse. Her father insisted that she be strapped into an infant's potty chair or enclosed in a straight-jacket-like sleeping bag, day after day, year after year. If she attempted to attract attention by making noise, her father beat her with a wooden bat. Somehow she survived this silent, solitary, and abusive childhood. Finally, when Genie was 13½, her mother summoned the courage to escape with her daughter. (Genie's father committed suicide shortly afterward.)

Psychologists and medical practitioners who worked with Genie often described her as "ghostlike" (Rymer, 1993). She treated people as if they were objects, inspecting them with her eyes and hands but not responding to social overtures. With care and attention, Genie began to recover in some ways but not others. She became attached to her caregivers, but sometimes latched onto complete strangers as well. She began to talk, but her grammar never progressed beyond the level of a 2-year-old. She had particular difficulty with pronouns, as if she didn't understand the boundaries between self and others. ("Mommy loves Genie," she would say, pointing to herself in the third person.) She learned to bathe and dress herself but continued to have toilet problems. Alternately clinging and withdrawn, prone to tantrums and infantile bodily regressions, Genie spent time in several foster homes but finally was sent to a home for the mentally re-

"Genie," the young girl raised in almost total isolation until she was 13 years old. Her lack of socialization deprived her of many basic human qualities.

tarded, where she remains today (Curtiss, 1977; Ruch and Shurley, 1985; Rymer, 1993).

Case studies of isolated children illustrate that the most basic human characteristics depend on socialization. The ability to talk develops spontaneously according to nature's plan, but using that ability, actually learning to speak, requires social interaction. Likewise the ability to walk depends on opportunities to move about, crawl, and toddle—with an adult helping hand. Studies of children who have been raised in large, impersonal orphanages where human contact and physical stimulation are minimal confirm this view (Spitz, 1945; Rutter, 1974). Although physically healthy, these babies are much slower to develop than babies raised in a home. They do not walk, talk, or begin to play with other children "on schedule." They are unlikely to achieve their full potential as individual human beings (Rutter, 1988; Provence, 1989).

Cross-Cultural Variations

A second line of evidence for the impact of socialization on human behavior comes from cross-cultural studies. Anthropologist Margaret Mead's *Sex and Temperament in Three Primitive Societies* (1935) is a classic in this field. Are women, "by nature," nurturant? Are men, "by nature," aggressive? Mead set out to test the belief that men and women are emotionally and psychologically different by visiting three tribes in New Guinea. At the time, these peoples had little contact with neighboring tribes, much less with westerners.

In the first tribe she studied, the Arapesh, Mead found that the males were as mild-mannered and nurturant as the females. Little boys treated the infant girls they hoped to marry like dolls, dressing them in bead and feather jewelry. Men couldn't stand to hear a baby cry. Members of both sexes behaved in ways that we would call "feminine."

In the second tribe she studied, the Mundugumor, this pattern was reversed. The women were as hot-tempered, combative, and uncaring as the men. A woman who tried to rescue an infant who had been abandoned or abused was subjected to intense ridicule. In different ways, then, neither the Arapesh nor the Mundugumor recognized differences in temperament or personality between the sexes.

The Tchambuli, the third tribe Mead visited, did make a distinction, but their gender stereotypes were the opposite of ours. The plainspoken, practical Tchambuli women took care of business matters while the men primped and gossiped in their clubhouses. No self-respecting Tchambuli woman pined for love, but the men and boys were in constant romantic turmoil. Mead was a pioneer in anthropological fieldwork; the scientific accuracy of her conclusions has been questioned by more recent researchers (e.g., D. Freeman, 1983). But the anthropological literature provides abundant examples of human plasticity.

Cross-cultural variations in differences between the sexes, in sexual behavior (discussed in Chapter 3), and in many other areas show that human behavior is in large part learned behavior. Specific behavioral patterns are not the only cultural variable; the sense of self—the way people define themselves in relation to others and to nature—also varies cross-culturally (Hsu, 1985). Western cultures, for example, treat each person as a unique, independent individual. In many other cultures, however, the individual exists only as a member of a family group, often extending back through generations of ancestors. (Thus even though their traditions are changing, both Japanese and Chinese preschools put more emphasis on the group and less on the individual than do American preschools.)

Socialization and Brain Development

Some of the strongest evidence for the impact of socialization comes from neurobiology. Recent advances in research technology have enabled scientists to study the development of the brain in some detail (Greenspan, 1997). At birth, a baby's brain contains some 100 billion neurons—about the number of stars in the Milky Way. The basic circuits for seeing, hearing, speaking, muscle coordination, and so on, are in place, but the connections are loose and the newborn's senses are dim. From the moment of birth, experience washes through the brain in waves, carving the mental channels that will enable the baby to see his father's face, recognize his mother's voice, burble, babble, and eventually speak. During the first years of life, neurons branch out, establishing trillions of connections that will change the structure of the baby's brain, influencing everything from temperament to coordination.

Experience is the key. Sensory experience triggers electrical charges, which strengthen connections between neurons; connections, or synapses, in turn form circuits that grow stronger with every repeated experience. Laboratory studies show that rats raised in cages strewn with toys have about 25 percent more synapses per neuron than do rats raised in sterile, empty cages with little stimulation; their behavior is also more complex. Studies of brain waves in human children reveal similar effects. Babies whose mothers and fathers use "parentese" (an animated, high-pitched, sing-song style) learn to connect words with objects earlier than do babies whose parents are more laid-back. Babies whose mothers suffer from depression, and are disengaged or irritable and impatient with their infant, show markedly reduced neural activity in the left frontal lobe, the area of the brain associated with joy and exuberance. The more severely depressed the mother is and the longer her depression lasts, the more likely the child is to have abnormally low levels of brain activity at age 3 (Dawson and Levy, 1989). Babies who are physically abused in infancy develop brains finely attuned to danger. At the slightest threat, their pulse races, their stress hormones surge, and their brains become superactive. Among other implications, these studies suggest that preschools can play a vital role in child development in a world of smaller families where parents, for whatever reason, do not have much time to play with their young children.

Around age 10, this explosive growth of nerve connections stops; indeed, circuits that have not been used atrophy, refining the structure of the brain in terms of previous experience. By the end of adolescence, around age 18, the brain is less flexible but more powerful. With unused connections "weeded out," talents and tendencies that experience has reinforced have space to flower. Hence it is more difficult—though not impossible—for adults to learn certain things (such as a foreign language or computer skills) and perhaps to change their basic cultural and emotional orientations.

In short, heredity sets the stage for human development, but socialization writes the script. Socialization strongly influences what kind of individuals we become, how we feel about such things as being males or females, and, indeed, whether we become human at all.

The Process of Socialization

How is the helpless, dependent human infant transformed into a mature social actor? How does socialization work its magic? The eminent Viennese psychoanalyst Sigmund Freud (1856–1939) viewed socialization as a confrontation between the child and society. American sociologists Charles Horton Cooley (1864–1929) and George Herbert Mead (1863–1931) viewed socialization more as a collaborative effort between the child and society. The following sections compare and contrast these views.

Psychosexual Development: Freud

Sigmund Freud's primary concern was *personality*: an individual's characteristic patterns of behavior and thought (see his *Collected Works*: Freud, 1964). He believed that much of human behavior is guided by unconscious motives—by impulses, passions, and fears of which we are not consciously aware. Further, he believed that childhood experiences, buried in the unconscious, shape adult personality.

Freud pictured socialization as a constant struggle—a battle—between the child, who is driven by powerful, inborn sexual and aggressive urges, and the parents, who seek to impose on the child their standards for proper behavior. Put another way, he saw socialization as a confrontation between biology (represented by the infant's "animal urges") and society (represented by the parents' efforts to "civilize" the child).

According to Freud, infants are sensual, pleasure-seeking beings, intent on gratification. As they mature, the focus of their sexual interest and their psychological orientation toward the world change. Freud believed that there are five stages of psychosexual development. In the *oral stage* (the first year of life), infants focus on taking or incorporating the outside world into themselves. They derive special pleasure from nursing and sucking and will put virtually anything into their mouths. In the *anal stage* (the second year), their attention shifts to maintaining the unity of the body and its parts. Now they find pleasure in releasing or retaining their bowel movements. In the *phallic stage* (age 3 to 6), children seek to demonstrate their power over the external world, their ability to make things happen. They discover their genitals and become aware of the differences between the sexes. In this stage "oedipal conflicts"[1] occur: the child's desire to possess the parent of the opposite sex creates intense rivalry with the parent of the same sex, in the child's mind, if not in reality. At age 6 or 7, children enter the *latency stage.* Sexual urges are dormant, and the child's interest shifts to developing skills for mastering the environment. In the *genital stage,* which begins in adolescence, desires reemerge and the young person begins to seek mutually gratifying sexual relationships and mature love.

At each stage, the child's wishes are thwarted to a greater or lesser degree. Weaning, toilet training, and sexual norms inevitably cause frustration. The child's psychological development depends on how he or she resolves conflicts between powerful, internal urges and equally powerful external demands and controls. The psychological mechanisms children develop for resolving these developmental conflicts become more or less permanent parts of their personalities.

Freud envisioned personality as having three interrelated parts: the id, the ego, and the superego. The **id** is the reservoir of innate, primitive, asocial, sexual, and aggressive urges with which a child is born. The id operates on the pleasure principle, seeking immediate gratification. The **superego** is the internal representation of society's norms and values, especially as taught by the child's parents. (It is roughly equivalent to what we call the "conscience.") The superego operates largely on guilt. Freud believed that children internalize their parents' attitudes, almost literally. Throughout life, individuals "hear" their parents' voices in their minds, telling them the right thing to do and the dire consequences that will befall them if they go wrong. The superego is a demanding, inflexible, punitive "parent." The **ego,** the rational part of the personality that deals with the outside world, channels impulses from the id into socially acceptable activities, and protects the individual from impossible demands by the superego.

In short, Freud viewed socialization as a power struggle. Conflict is inevitable, not only between parent and child and between individual and society but also within the individual, among the id, the superego, and the ego. Biological drives and social demands are forever at war.

The Emergence of Self: Cooley and Mead

Charles Horton Cooley and George Herbert Mead were primarily concerned with the emergence of *self*—of the individual's sense of identity or "who I am." In their views, social interaction is the driving force, and biology takes a back seat.

In his influential *Human Nature and the Social Order* (1902), Cooley argued that the self is defined and developed through social interaction. Our image of ourselves is largely a reflection of how other people react to us—in Cooley's phrase, a **looking-glass self.** (The image is from Shakespeare: "Each to a looking glass/Reflects the other that doth

---

[1] The term "oedipal conflict" is drawn from an ancient Greek myth in which King Oedipus unknowingly kills his father and marries his mother.

pass.") This looking-glass self consists of three parts: how we imagine others see us; how we imagine they judge what they see; and how we feel about those reactions, or what Cooley called "self-feeling" (1902, p. 184). It is by observing our reflection that we come to think of ourselves as attractive or unattractive, smart or slow, considerate or selfish.

Cooley stressed the importance of language in the emergence of self. It is largely through language that children come to think of themselves as separate and unique, as one of the objects in their social world. (Children often speak of themselves in the third person—"Sally is good"—before they use the first-person pronoun: "I am good.") Cooley held that **primary groups** such as the family, which are characterized by "intimate face-to-face associations" and "mutual identification," have the most impact on our sense of self, for the opinions of these people matter most to us. But he did not believe that the self is established, once and for all, in childhood. We continue to check our image, to try out new images, and to revise our feelings about ourselves throughout life. For example, a high school student whose classmates see him as a "brain" but do not place much value on intelligence and scholarship may well wish he were someone else. In college and the working world, however, his self-feelings may change.

In *Mind, Self, and Society* (1934) George Herbert Mead elaborated on Cooley's ideas, suggesting how and when the self takes shape. Mead saw the self as the product of **symbolic interaction**—of the symbolic communications contained in a smile or a frown, in a hug or a slap, and, especially, in language. He believed that the emergence of self begins in the preverbal stage of development and accelerates as children learn to talk.

Observing children's behavior, Mead identified two stages in the emergence of self: the play stage and the game stage. The emphasis in Mead's scenario is on the development of social cooperation. In the early part of the **play stage,** children play at being different people—Mommy, Daddy, the mail carrier, Superwoman, and so on. They imitate their models' speech and activities, delivering imaginary letters, sweeping imaginary floors, and so on. Adults may call this make-believe, but to children it is serious business. By pretending to be other people, children acquire vicarious experience of differ-

ent perspectives. In the later part of the play stage, they actually begin to act out relationships. Thus, one minute the child plays himself hitting his baby brother, and the next minute he plays his mother scolding him for hitting the baby. What the child is doing is *taking the role of the other*—that is, putting himself in the other person's shoes. In the process, children learn to see themselves through other people's eyes. By the age of 7 or 8 they are able to take the role of the other in their imaginations, without acting out the parts. They can see themselves as objects, as well as subjects, and can think about themselves. Only when they can realize that other people have different needs and purposes, likes and dislikes, do they begin to acquire a sense of themselves as distinct people. Most of their experience in this play stage is with specific others (their own mother, the children in their school class).

In the **game stage,** children do not just play *at* roles but actually participate in reciprocal relationships with others. Mead used a baseball game to illustrate the difference: To play baseball, a child must be able to see the game not only from her own perspective as the pitcher but also from the other players' points of view. She has to anticipate what the batter, infielders, and outfielders will do and what they expect from her. The child must also understand the rules of the game. The baseball game is more than a metaphor, for children spend much of their playtime in organized games and, largely through these games, come to see themselves as part of an organized structure that has established roles and is governed by general rules. Children's awareness of these external structures gives structure to their internal lives. Mead believed that children internalize this knowledge in the form of a **generalized other,** an image of the structure and norms and values of society as a whole. As an integral part of the self, the generalized other guides behavior in socially acceptable directions.

Although Mead believed that the self is the product of social interaction, he did not see the individual as a social robot, mindlessly following society's rules. Mead distinguished between **the "me,"** the socialized self that is composed of internalized norms and values and is ever mindful of its social reflection, and **the "I,"** the impulsive, creative, egocentric self. A child's response to criticism illustrates the interplay between the "I" and the "me" (Hewitt, 1976). A mother who is angry at her son's miscon-

During the game stage of social development, children come to see themselves not only from their own perspective but also from the other players' point of view.

duct tells him to go to his room and stay there until dinner. The boy starts to protest but then checks himself and does as he is told. We can imagine his reasoning: "She will only be angrier with me if I object." The spontaneous, willful "I" wants to protest, but the "me" is concerned about his reflection in his mother's eyes and complies. The socialized "me" does not always win out, however. Mead attributed both deviance (or antisocial behavior) and creativity to the unsocialized "I."

Mead's theory may seem to overlap with Freud's. The "I" seems to resemble the id; the "me" resembles the ego and superego. There are important differences, however. Whereas Freud saw the id and the superego as opponents locked in a never-ending battle, Mead saw the "I" and the "me" as collaborators. For Freud, civilization (and socialization) inevitably produces discontent. For Mead, the relationship between the individual and society is one of cooperation, not conflict. The function of socialization is not to beat down powerful antisocial impulses but to give direction to behavior that would otherwise be lacking in significance. Whereas Freud saw personality as more or less fixed in early childhood, Cooley and Mead saw the self as continually changing in response to changing social circumstances.

In short, the sociological perspective challenges the idea that socialization is a passive process whereby children adapt to and internalize adult standards. Rather, it is a community activity, whereby children—with adults and peers— negotiate, share, and help create culture (Corsaro and Elder, 1990).

Agents of Socialization

An ***agent of socialization*** is an individual, group, or organization that influences a person's behavior and sense of self, whether by rewarding and punishing behavior, by providing instruction in social rules and social roles, or simply by serving as a model. The family is the primary agent of socialization in early childhood, and it remains a central influence for years thereafter. But as children grow older, the list of agents expands to include baby-sitters, teachers, peers (others their own age), and, not least, the characters they "meet" through television and books. The number and importance of nonfamily social relationships increase in later childhood and adolescence. The looking-glass self includes a range of ***significant others***—people whose evaluations an individual holds in high esteem.

People an individual knows directly and personally are not the only agents of socialization. Sociologists use the term ***reference group*** to describe a group or social category that individuals use as a guide in developing their values, attitudes, behavior, and self-image (Hyman, 1942; Merton, 1968). Reference groups serve both a normative and a comparative function. Individuals look to these groups for guidance when they are unsure of what to think or do (the normative function). People also look to reference groups in evaluating their own and other people's performances (the comparative function). To a large extent, a person's self-image depends on how he or she measures up to the reference groups' standards. Positive reference groups are those to which a person would like to belong in the future. A student who hopes to attend graduate school may see his professors and teaching assistants as a positive reference group and try to understand and imitate their values, attitudes, and behavior. Internships expose undergraduates both to role models and to the "culture" of the field in which they may choose to work. Negative reference groups are those a person rejects and does not want to join in the future. An aspiring medieval scholar might see certain cliques at her school, who seem interested only in sports or future salaries, as examples of the kind of people she does *not* want to become. Her self-image will depend in part on how well she succeeds in differentiating herself from them (Lindesmith, Strauss, and Denzin, 1975).

The most powerful agents of socialization are the family, peers, school, and the mass media.

The Family

In the 1940s, 1950s, and 1960s, the immediate family exercised a near monopoly on early childhood socialization in the United States, at least in white middle-class families. Small children spent virtually all their time with their mothers and siblings. This contrasts with traditional societies (including preindustrial America), in which grandparents, aunts, uncles, and cousins were also an integral part of the household. In many ethnic groups large households continued to be the norm.

For different reasons, the children of the 1980s and 1990s are once again dependent not so much on the immediate family but on other relatives and/or on day care providers and preschool teachers (as described at the beginning of this chapter). With more and more mothers working, 60 percent of children under age 6 spend most of their time with someone other than a parent (Figure 4-1). Moreover the size, composition, and socioeconomic circumstances of a child's family may change, as parents divorce and remarry. Many children are members of more than one family before they reach maturity. This is not to say that parents' influence on childhood socialization is fading, however. In-

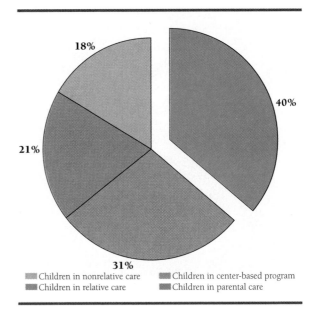

deed, there is some evidence that working mothers and divorced fathers spend more exclusive time with their children than other parents do. (This is discussed further in Chapter 11.)

Figure 4-1   *Child Care Arrangements for Children under 6 Years Old, 1995*

The United States is the only advanced, industrial nation that does not have a national child care program. With more and more mothers working, who is minding the children?

Chart does not add to 100% because some children participate in more than one type of non-parental care arrangement.

Source: U.S. National Center for Education Statistics, *Statistics in Brief,* October 1995 (NCES 95–824).

Styles of Parenting

Diana Baumrind's ongoing studies (1967, 1980, 1989) of socialization have identified three distinct styles of parenting and their effects on children. *Authoritarian* parents see obedience as a prime virtue. They expect children to do as they are told, without discussion. If a child asks why, a parent will often answer "Because I said so." Parents' desires and needs come first in their households. *Permissive* parents, in contrast, see free self-expression as a virtue. They tend to avoid confrontations and discipline and make few demands for responsibility and order. The child's wishes and desires come first in their homes. *Authoritative* parents fall between these two extremes. They expect the child to comply with household rules but encourage the child to express his or her opinions. They do not shy away from discipline but use punishment only when reason fails. In these homes, parents and children both have rights as well as responsibilities.

Baumrind has found that the children of authoritative parents tend to be independent, friendly, and cooperative. Interestingly, children of both authoritarian and permissive parents tend to be dependent and clinging with adults and selfish and uncooperative in groups of other children. Children of authoritarian parents have too little freedom, while children of permissive parents have too much. As a result, neither learns the consequences of inappropriate behavior. Baumrind does not speculate on why some parents are authoritarian whereas others are permissive or authoritative. Melvin Kohn's studies (1963, 1974) of class differences in socialization provide a sociological clue.

Kohn compared working- and middle-class parents, first in the United States only, then in Poland and Japan as well (Kohn et al., 1986, 1990). He found that working-class parents tend to be "traditional." They want their children to be neat and clean, obedient and respectful. Middle-class parents tend to be "developmental." They want their children to be communicative, eager to learn, ready to share and cooperate, and "happy." Working-class parents focus on conformity to external standards. Middle-class parents focus on the child's internal dynamics. They value self-control. The question is why these differences exist. Kohn suggests that the way parents socialize their children reflects their own experiences, specifically, their experiences at work. Middle-class occupations require an ability to manage interpersonal relationships and to exercise self-direction. Getting ahead is largely a matter of individual effort. Working-class occupations require an ability to manipulate things. Blue-collar workers are subject to both standardization and supervision. Opportunities to exercise self-direction and initiative are limited, and keeping a job usually means submitting to both company and authorities.

Thus in both classes, parents socialize their children for the world that they themselves know. The kinds of reading material in a home, the TV shows parents watch, their topics and style of conversation, family activities, and general expectations for a child contribute to these class differences. How children are reared at home, in turn, may affect the way children act and are treated in school (as we will discuss in Chapter 12). By emphasizing different values and encouraging different kinds of behavior, parents unintentionally re-create the social class differences in the next generation.

Other researchers have linked parenting styles to family structure. Single mothers are more likely than two natural parents to be permissive and to grant autonomy too early, if only because they are overloaded (Dornbusch and Gray, 1988). Compared with two natural parents, stepparents tend to be more permissive or more authoritarian (Crosbie-Burnett et al., 1988). Given the lack of clear norms for stepparents, they may be either heavy-handed (authoritarian) or avoid confrontations (permissive), especially with older children and adolescents. But on the whole, social class differences tend to override these other factors.

Peers

Children's relations with their peers highlight the creative and communal aspects of socialization. William Corsaro and others hold that children create their own, private peer culture, which incorporates elements of adult culture but has special rituals, routines, values, and concerns of its own (Corsaro and Elder, 1990; Fine, 1987). In this view, childhood is not merely a period of apprenticeship for adult roles but a time when children collectively build their own world of meanings.

Three of the main themes of children's peer culture are (1) sharing and social participation (few children are loners by choice); (2) dealing with the fears, confusions, and conflicts of their lives (for example, by inventing and conquering "monsters"); and (3) resisting adult rules and authority. Children attempt to gain control over their own lives and autonomy from adults almost from the beginning. Children as young as 14 months laugh at their own, their siblings', or their parents' playful misdeeds and forbidden acts (Dunn, 1988). Agents of peer socialization are, first, older siblings and, later, playmates and friends.

Children of all ages are intrigued by other children. An infant is fascinated by the sight of a smaller baby and will watch children her own age with rapt attention. At age 2, toddlers play together with the same toy. By age 3 or 4, children form small play groups around joint activities and often signal the importance of shared activities by declaring "We're friends, right?" (Corsaro, 1981). For preschool and elementary school children, simply doing things together is cause for joy. Whereas friendships among elementary school children tend to focus on shared activities, friendships among adolescent girls, in particular, center more on shared secrets.

Children's relationships with other children differ in important ways from their interactions with adults (Berndt and Ladd, 1989; Hartup, 1989). Peer relationships are egalitarian. They are not governed by differences in status or by dependency. A child is not expected to obey another child, as she obeys an adult. And she doesn't need other children the way she needs her parents. As a result, there is a good deal more give-and-take, and trial and error, in peer interaction. Parents may teach a child that it is wrong to take something that belongs to someone else; they have the power and authority to enforce that rule. With peers, a child can test the limits of the rule and discover the social consequences of taking a toy from another youngster or being robbed herself. A father may teach his son that he should defend himself by fighting, but he cannot actually show the boy what may happen in a fight.

Much of children's play (alone and together) may be described as ***anticipatory socialization:*** learning about and practicing a new role before one is actually in a position to play the role. Children play at being mommies and daddies, cops and robbers, movie stars and sports heroes. As George Herbert Mead observed, through such play, youngsters learn to take the role of the other. (Adults also engage in anticipatory socialization, for example, when they contemplate becoming a parent, changing jobs, marrying for a second time, or retiring.)

The importance of peers as agents of socialization increases in adolescence. What teachers and parents think may not matter half as much to an adolescent as what his or her friends think. Popularity in high school becomes tangible affirmation of self-worth. A lot depends on whom the adolescent chooses as a reference group. There is no one, single peer culture among adolescents; rather, there are many cultures, supporting a wide range of different values and behavior (Brown, 1990). Like adults, adolescents usually choose friends who are similar to themselves in social class, in race and ethnicity, and in values and aspirations for the future (Savin-Williams and Berndt, 1990). Some adolescents identify with honor students ("brains"), some want to be associated with athletes ("jocks"), and still others hang out with delinquents ("crews" or "gangstas"). A few may be unwillingly categorized as losers or "Herbs." How individual adolescents evaluate themselves depends in part on whether they are accepted by a specific group, not

There are many different peer cultures for adolescents. Like adults, adolescents usually choose friends who resemble them in social class, values, and aspirations.

by the school as a whole. But interactions with peers outside an adolescent's circle of close friends—friends of friends, acquaintances, strangers, and even enemies—also serve as a looking glass, providing the youth with a variety of evaluations and a sense of the broader world (Giordano, 1995).

School

From first grade through high school, most young Americans spend a legal minimum of 180 days a year in school. Getting ready in the morning, traveling to and from school, attending classes, participating in extracurricular activities, and doing homework consume almost the entire day. As the importance of schooling has increased over the last hundred years, its role as an agent of socialization has expanded.

Much of the school curriculum is specifically designed to socialize—to turn individual children into active members of society who are committed to its culture. For generations of children, classes in civics have been classes in being a good American. But socialization occurs in many other ways as well. Textbooks may include thinly disguised messages on appropriate male and female behavior (though efforts have been made in recent years to minimize this stereotyping). Schools have taken over instruction in areas once dealt with in the family, such as sex education (including information about sex abuse and AIDS prevention) and advice on careers. Participating in student government, working on the school newspaper, and similar activities provide the anticipatory socialization for a variety of adult occupations.

Schools bear major responsibility for preparing young people for the world of work. By placing some students in general programs and others in college preparatory classes, schools open or close the doors to many occupations. Conflict sociologists stress the unfairness of this sorting process, which not only assigns people different educational and occupational opportunities but also makes the perpetuation of socioeconomic inequality appear legitimate and fair (Bowles and Gintis, 1976). In contrast, functionalists see it as a benign, necessary method of fitting individuals into appropriate social niches. (See Chapter 12.)

On a subtler level, school is the young person's introduction to large, impersonal organizations. At home, young people, ideally, are valued for who they are (my son, my sister), not on the basis of how well they perform. Rules are adjusted to individual needs. Relations between parent and child, brother and sister are many-layered—personal, emotional, social, practical. In school, by contrast, young people are rated according to how well they perform on papers and tests and how they behave. For the most part, the same rules apply to everyone. Relations between student and teacher are more instrumental than emotional. (Each has a job to do: the teacher to teach, the student to learn.) Punctuality and other rules of behavior are taught partly in preparation for the demands of work (Violas, 1978). Thus the experience of attending school is, in itself, a form of socialization.

Growing Up with Television

In the more than fifty years since its invention, television has skyrocketed in popularity (see Table 4-1). And the United States is the largest consumer of TV programs in the world (Huesmann, 1985). Virtually every American child grows up with television (Andreasen, 1990; Huston, Watkins, and Kunkel, 1989). In addition to receiving regular channels, 62 percent of U.S. households subscribe to cable services and 79 percent have VCRs

Table 4-1 *Households with Television, 1946–1994*

Year	Households with Sets (thousands)	Percent of Households with Sets
1946	8	.02
1950	3,875	9.0
1960	45,750	87.1
1970	58,500	95.3
1980	76,300	97.9
1985	84,900	98.1
1990	92,042	98.0
1994	94,000	98.3

Note: Data for years 1946 to 1950 are from Sterling and Haight (1978, p. 372). Data for subsequent years through 1988 are from Television Bureau for Advertising (1988, p.3). Data for 1990 are estimates from the *Nielsen Station Index* (1989). Data for 1994 are from *Statistical Abstract* 1996, Table 876, p. 561.

Source: Adapted from M. S. Andreasen, "Evolution in the Family's Use of Television: Normative Data from Industry and Academe," in J. Bryant (ed.), *Television and the American Family.* Hillsdale, NJ: Erlbaum, 1990, table 1.3, p.22.

Table 4-2   *Time Spent Viewing Television per Household Daily*

Year	Average Time per Day
1950	4 hr. 35 min.
1960	5 hr. 6 min.
1970	5 hr. 56 min.
1980	6 hr. 36 min.
1985–1986	7 hr. 10 min.
1987–1988	6 hr. 55 min.
1995–1996	7 hr. 17 min.

Note: A. C. Nielsen Co., annual averages for 1950 through 1981. Data for 1985–1986 through 1987–1988 from *Nielsen Report on Televison, 1989* (1989, p. 6). Data for 1995–1996 from Nielsen Media Research.

Source: Adapted from M. S. Andreasen, "Evolution in the Family's Use of Television: Normative Data from Industry and Academe," in J. Bryant (ed.), *Television and the American Family.* Hillsdale, NJ: Erlbaum, 1990, table 1.5, p. 24.

The more children watch violent TV programs, the more they learn scripts for violent behavior and fantasize about violence.

(*Statistical Abstract, 1996*). In the average American household the television is turned on for almost seven hours a day (see Table 4-2). Young children often spend two to three hours a day watching television (the equivalent of 100 to 125 school days a year). Most American children—and parents—cannot imagine life without it.

Children make up a special audience for television. When adults watch television, they presumably evaluate what they see against what they already know about how the world works and about how people behave (or should behave) toward one another. But children lack this accumulated background knowledge. As a result, they may misunderstand what is being presented, assume that everything they see on television is "true" or "real," and fail to take into account both the means and the motives for producing a TV show. Adults distinguish between news and entertainment and between entertainment and advertising. In other words, they edit what they see—both with their minds and with their remote controls or "zappers." Children may not.

The impact of TV violence on children is of special concern. The typical prime-time show on U.S. television consists of brief, fast-paced action sequences with a high rate of physical violence, plus frequent commercial interruptions (Cole, 1997). Young people are exposed to violence not only in movies and sitcoms but also in the increasingly popular "shockumentaries," which feature reality-based footage of violence (whether by humans or animals), and in the sports and news programs their parents and older siblings watch. Even cartoons designed for children feature a significant amount of make-believe carnage. In an ongoing study of child-rearing practices and childhood aggression begun in 1960, the researchers tested and interviewed parents and children of the entire third-grade population of a semirural county in New York State (Huesmann, 1985). Among other questions, the researchers asked parents how often their children watched TV and what their favorite shows were. They also asked the children questions designed to elicit whether they identified with TV characters and whether they perceived TV violence as realistic. And they asked both teachers and children to rate students on measures of aggression. They found that the more aggressive children were in school, the higher level of violence in the TV shows they watched at home. So began one of the longest-running studies of the impact of media violence on real-life behavior. (For the cross-cultural phase of this research, see *A Global View:* Violence and Television: A Public Health Problem?)

Ten years later, when the subjects had graduated from high school, about 500 were reinterviewed; again in 1981 the researchers obtained data on 400 of the original subjects, now age 30, and 80 of their children. The researchers found strong correlations between early exposure to TV violence and adult aggression, especially for males. Thirty-year-olds who watched a lot of violent TV at age 8 had more arrests for drunk driving and violent crime, were more abusive to their spouses, and had more aggressive children than did other subjects. The correlation was confined to childhood: there was no relationship between watching violent TV at age 19 or age 30 and adult aggression. Of course, correlation doesn't prove cause and effect; perhaps more

aggressive children are drawn to violent TV, or some other factor intervenes. But the correlation is strong enough to suggest that TV has a strong impact, perhaps accounting for 10 percent of aggressive behavior (*Newsletter,* p. 7).

The researchers hypothesized that the relationship between media violence and aggression is circular. Children who watch many violent scenes on television learn scripts for aggressive behavior and fantasize about these scenes, especially if the violent character is rewarded for such behavior. They later recall these models when faced with a social problem and respond aggressively. This aggressive behavior makes a child unpopular with peers; it also interferes with academic achievement. As a result, the child receives few rewards in the schoolroom or the playground and escapes by watching more television and identifying with heroic characters, many

A classic series of studies found that heavy TV viewing in the preschool years is associated with aggressive behavior. The researchers concluded that TV provides a model for solving problems through physical force.

Violence and Television: A Public Health Problem?

Is the connection between TV violence and aggressive behavior peculiarly American? Is there something about American culture that makes children more vulnerable and violence more enticing? Or is the same effect found in other cultures?

TV violence is as harmful to children as drinking and smoking.

To answer these questions, L. Raul Huesmann and Leonard Eron are conducting similar studies in six countries (Australia, Finland, Israel, the Netherlands, Poland, and the United States). So far, children have been interviewed and tested three times at one-year intervals. In all six countries at least some aspect of the child's

Map 4-1   *Israel*

Sources: "Television Violence and Kids: A Public Health Problem?" *Profiles: IRTS Newsletter* 18 (1), February 1994, pp. 5–7; L. R. Huesmann, *Children and the Media: First International Conference*, 1985, pp. 103–128.

viewing habits was correlated with aggression. The effects were strongest in Finland, Poland, and the United States. But the most interesting results came from Israel (see Map 4-1).

Half the children in the Israeli sample lived on kibbutzim and half in cities. *Kibbutzim* are rural settlements where the entire community assumes collective responsibility for rearing children. The TV programs and other films small children are permitted to watch are selected by others, not the child; older children and adolescents nearly always watch shows with a group of peers, not alone. The researchers found virtually no correlation between exposure to television and aggression in kibbutz children but a high correlation for urban children who were less closely supervised. This suggests that the communal nature of the kibbutz, with its emphasis on prosocial values, neutralizes the effects of TV violence.

Huesmann and Eron conclude that TV shows for children—not for adults—should be regulated, for several reasons. First, TV influences attitudes and behavior; if it didn't, why would companies spend so much on TV advertisements? Second, young children (age 3 to 12) appear to be most vulnerable to TV violence. No one claims that TV "makes" children aggressive, but evidence of the impact on young children is substantial. Parental supervision might be the best way to monitor what children watch, but given the growing numbers of single-parent families and families in which both parents work, this has become increasingly difficult. Third, the most harmful shows are not necessarily the bloodiest but are those in which the aggressor is rewarded for violence and in which aggression is portrayed as justified. Huesmann and Eron argue that we need to look at TV violence as a public health problem, not an issue of freedom of speech. In their view, consuming large amounts of TV violence is as harmful to children as drinking and smoking. We do not allow children to buy liquor or cigarettes; why should we provide them with unlimited amounts of free violence?

of whom are violent. Thus watching violence on television becomes a vicious circle.

In a classic series of studies, social psychologists Jerome and Dorothy Singer (1984, 1986) followed children from age 4 to age 9. In general, they found that heavy TV viewing, beginning in the preschool years, is significantly associated with aggressive behavior, restlessness, and belief in a "mean and scary world" in elementary school. Heavy TV viewers are more likely to initiate or respond to threats with aggression than are other children. They have difficulty sitting still for any length of time, which can interfere with their performance in school. And they tend to believe that the world is a dangerous place, with little justice or fairness. These effects are most pronounced when the family treats television as a major source of entertainment and parents do not supervise the amount or content of the shows children watch. Children whose mothers watch a good deal of television themselves show poorer comprehension of plots, greater confusion of fantasy and reality, and lower levels of general information than do children whose television viewing is limited and supervised (Singer and Singer, 1986).

The Singers concluded that television affects children's beliefs and behavior in two ways. First, television provides numerous models of resolving conflicts through physical force; even "good guys" have to fight for their rights. Second, television preempts time that children might otherwise spend in imaginative, make-believe play. The more children learn to exercise their imaginations, the better able they are to entertain themselves, cope with fears and frustrations, and develop a sense of mastery over their environment. Children who spend their free time watching television miss such important experiences.

Of course, not all TV shows have a negative impact on children. In one study the Singers divided preschoolers into three groups who watched two weeks of either *Mr. Rogers' Neighborhood, Sesame Street,* or nature programs. The children were observed at play both before and after the viewing period, by researchers who did not know to which group different children had been assigned. They found that children who watched *Mr. Rogers' Neighborhood*—a carefully paced program that encourages "pretending" and clearly separates fantasy from reality—seemed happier, less aggressive, more curious, and more imaginative after the viewing pe-

riod. Clearly, well-designed children's programs can have beneficial effects, at least temporarily reducing aggression (Singer and Singer, 1986, p. 113).

A second area of concern is gender stereotyping in the mass media. Nancy Signorielli (1989) analyzed prime-time TV shows over a period of 15 years. She found that men outnumber women three to one on prime-time television. The women on situation comedies tend to be young and attractive. They are less likely than men to work outside the home, and if they do, they usually work in low-status occupations (such as waitress or secretary). The men tend to be older, wealthier, more powerful, and successfully combining work and family. Television heroes tend to be men of action: cops, doctors, reporters, and cowboys; heroines tend to be concerned with romance and with pleasing their family or their boss. In TV ads women are sometimes shown in work roles and men in family roles, but 90 percent of the time the narrator—the voice of authority—is male (Bretl and Cantor, 1988). More recent studies show that this pattern of gender stereotyping hasn't changed very much. Every year several new shows present women (and less often men) in nontraditional roles, but prime-time working women tend to be more concerned with interpersonal relations (helping, caring, peacemaking), and less involved in decision making, leadership, and political action, than are their male colleagues (Vandenberg and Streckfuss, 1992). Not surprisingly, children who watch a lot of prime-time TV are more likely to describe men and women in gender-stereotyped terms, and to be gender-stereotyped themselves, than are children who rarely watch TV or watch mostly educational TV (Signorielli and Lears, 1992).

Still another concern is sexually explicit material. Adolescents with VCRs report watching more R-rated shows than do other young people (Huston et al., 1992); such shows are also available (at a cost) on cable channels. How does network TV deal with sexual matters? A study of the daytime soap opera *All My Children* (Larson, 1991) revealed mixed messages. Over the course of a year, there was less promiscuity and illicit sex than the "soaps'" bad reputation would suggest. Sexual intercourse was relatively rare and almost always involved married or committed couples; even "intimate kissing" was mostly limited to appropriate partners. But the use of physical coercion (grabbing, pushing, constraining) and scenes where women first resisted but then gave in, suggesting that "no" really meant "yes," were surprisingly common.

Prime-time network TV is designed to appeal to the broadest possible audience. Often this means showing people what they want to see and reinforcing what they already believe. On the positive side, analysis of plots indicates that the great majority of shows teach such widely held values as "Good wins out over evil," "Hard work pays off," and "Honesty is the best policy." TV movies, if not sitcoms, frequently depict heroism and self-sacrifice in the face of such social problems as racism, physical disabilities, and domestic violence. On the negative side, prime-time television often presents a stereotyped version of the social world, in which being male, young, good-looking, and white wins approval, and being female, old, disabled, dark-skinned, or "foreign" invites disapproval and ridicule.

Socialization and the Life Cycle

All societies divide the life course into stages. Stages of the life cycle are institutionalized in formal rules defining the ages at which people are allowed (or required) to participate in different social institutions and to engage in different social relationships. In our society we are required to attend school but not allowed to get married or to work (without a permit) until age 16. We are not entitled to Medicare until age 65, and we used to be forced to retire at age 70.

The institutionalized life cycle, as written into law and supported by culture, creates opportunities for, and limitations on, individual action. Individuals do not always abide by this schedule, but we still use age to organize and evaluate our own lives (Buchmann, 1989; Neugarten and Neugarten, 1987). We keep our eye on the social clock and constantly ask ourselves, "How am I doing for my age?" In explaining our lives, to ourselves and others, we cite the timing of major events ("I married early" or "I graduated late"). Age also shapes the way we relate to other people. We expect a child, a young adult, and an elderly person to behave differently, and we behave differently toward them.

Erik Erikson, a student of Freud's who immigrated to the United States, was one of the first so-

cial theorists to examine the changes people undergo as they move from childhood and adolescence into young adulthood, middle age, and old age. Erikson (1963) divided the life cycle into eight stages—the "eight stages of man" (see Figure 4-2). Erikson believed that each stage is characterized by a central problem or crisis in which the needs and abilities of the individual are pitted against the needs and demands of society. How the individual resolves the conflict in one stage determines how well equipped he or she is to deal with the problem in the next.

Childhood

Erikson divided childhood into four stages—infancy, early childhood, play age, and school age—each with its central problem. For the first year of life, infants are totally dependent on adult caretakers (usually their parents). If they receive adequate and consistent care, they develop a sense of *basic trust*. If not, they are likely to experience lasting mistrust and anxiety.

In the second year of life, children begin "to stand on their own two feet"—quite literally. They are eager to explore but have no sense of the possible dangers of, say, a staircase. Toddlers whose parents guide them gently through this period develop a sense of *autonomy*. Those whose parents exercise too much—or too little—control experience shame and doubt.

Once they have gained control of their bodies, children want to do things on their own. Acts of pure defiance are typical during the "terrible twos." If parents and other agents of socialization understand their wish to be independent, children develop a sense of *initiative*. If parents and others treat them as a constant nuisance, ridiculing their efforts, children are likely to experience guilt.

At about age 6, children enter school full-time. In school, youngsters gain recognition by mastering skills. If their efforts at mastery are encouraged and applauded, they develop a sense of *industry*; if not, they may develop feelings of inferiority.

Erikson's aim was to describe the socialization of "everychild." Yet every child is not exposed to the same influences and pressures. How parents go about raising their children depends on their economic position, religious beliefs, education, racial and ethnic background, and other factors. Parents

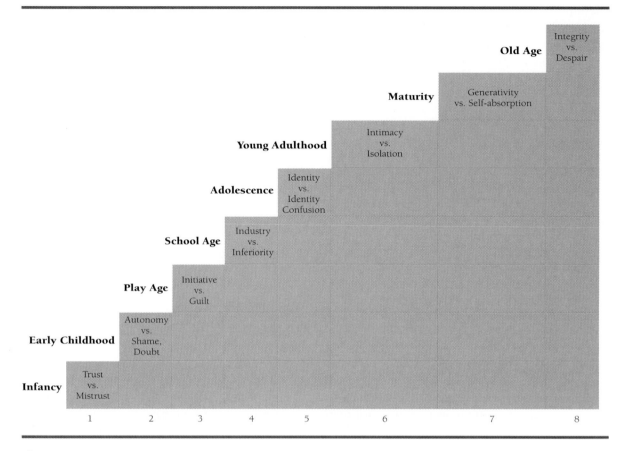

Figure 4-2   *Erikson's "Eight Stages of Man"*

According to Erikson, new issues come to dominate each stage of the life course, but old ones never entirely go away. The way we've dealt with them remains the foundation for later development.

Source: Reprinted with permission of *Daedalus, "*Adulthood," *Journal of the American Academy of Arts and Sciences* [105 (2) Spring 1976], Cambridge, MA.

are not the only source of differences. For example, a child who is raised in a dangerous housing project in the inner city may not have the same opportunities for exercising autonomy and initiative as a child who is raised on a farm or in a suburb. A youngster whose English is poor may not be given the same chance to develop industry in school.

Adolescence

Adolescence—the stage in the life course that extends roughly from puberty to age 20—is a modern invention. In most preindustrial societies, young people progress directly from childhood to adulthood, with no in-between stage. Often the transition is clearly marked by *rites of passage:* rituals or

ceremonies to mark the transition from one stage of life to another. In many traditional societies, a boy or girl undergoes initiation and thereafter is considered an adult. In these societies, young people are expected to work as soon as they are physically able, and the majority marry in their teens. This was the common pattern in the United States into the early decades of the twentieth century. The institutionalization of adolescence was in large part the result of industrialization and the declining need for young laborers, especially after the passage of child labor regulations and the extension of compulsory, full-time schooling to age 14, 15, or 16 in the early twentieth century.

Adolescence is an ambiguous stage in the life course. Adolescents are not quite adults: they are

According to Erikson, the task of the toddler stage is to seek autonomy. Toddlers are eager to explore on their own but have no sense of the possible dangers of their environment.

not expected to support themselves; they cannot vote or drive an automobile until age 16 or 18; they are discouraged from getting married and starting a family. But neither are they children: older adolescents have the bodies and intellectual abilities of adults, if not the experience.

Forming an Identity

Erikson saw the central task during adolescence as achieving an identity in the face of role confusion. In traditional societies, identity is given or ascribed. The individual's place in society is determined by the family, community, and social class into which he or she is born.

In modern western societies, young people are expected to form an identity of their own, distinct from that of their family. This process begins in adolescence. A young girl is so-and-so's daughter and so-and-so's sister. By adolescence, she wants to be her own person. This means moving away from the family and home, psychologically and socially, and orienting herself toward her peers and the adult world. It also means working to fit her hopes for the future to her actual talents and skills.

In the face of changes from within and without, adolescents seek continuity and sameness. They compare the person they feel others see in themselves with the person they feel themselves to be; they search out connections between the skills and talents they have cultivated and the occupational and role opportunities of the adult world. Lacking a

firm identity, adolescents may overidentify with athletes, movie stars, rock musicians, and other celebrities, or they may fall desperately in love, hoping to find an identity in their connection to another person. Some adolescents experience an **identity crisis:** they are unable to reconcile the image they have of themselves with their actual skills, potential, and activities or with the image of themselves they see reflected in other people's eyes.

Erikson saw the achievement of identity as a prerequisite for intimacy in young adulthood. Until young people are sure of who they are, they do not feel secure enough to make a commitment to another person. Others suggested that males and females follow somewhat different paths toward adulthood (Gilligan, 1982, 1986; Marcia, 1980). Traditionally, a woman's identity depended on getting married and having children. Establishing and maintaining relationships (being popular and having good friends) came first in young women's lives; identity (academic success, planning a career) came second. As a result, the order of psychosocial events in young men's and women's lives was reversed. In general, young men attempted to establish an identity before they risked committing themselves to an intimate relationship with the opposite sex. Young women more often attempted to establish an intimate relationship first, postponing identity issues until their early thirties or later. But the later ages at which women are marrying and bearing children today suggest that this is changing; at least for many middle- and upper-class girls, college and careers come first, and family, later.

Changing Views of Adolescence

Conventional wisdom holds that adolescence is a period of storm and stress for both males and females. The typical adolescent is moody, rebellious, self-centered, and (not infrequently) reckless. Adolescents will try anything to impress their peers—and upset their parents. Acting up and acting out are normal parts of adolescent development, or so conventional wisdom holds. This storm-and-stress model of adolescence was based largely on case studies of troubled adolescents who sought psychological counseling and on the memories of adults who were in therapy. In the last two decades, researchers have begun to collect data from large samples of adolescents about their feelings about themselves, their families, and their friends, and a different picture has emerged (Csikszentmihalyi and Larson, 1984; Flaste, 1988; Offer et al., 1988; Steinberg, 1990).

Adolescents are prone to emotional highs and lows, but these moods are usually short-lived. The vast majority of adolescents report that they are happy most of the time and that they get along well with their parents as well as their peers. They say that they are able to cope with their problems and feel positive about their futures. Adolescents (and young adults) do tend to take risks, testing the limits of their own abilities (and other people's tolerance) (Figure 4-3). They may develop a myth of invulnerability (Elkind, 1982; Lapsley et al., 1986)—a belief that they are somehow magically protected from the consequences of their actions. For example, they may believe that they can experiment with drugs without experiencing negative side effects or becoming addicted or that they can engage in unprotected sex without becoming pregnant or contracting AIDS. But only about 10 percent of adolescents could be described as psychologically disturbed or alienated. In most cases, troubled adolescents were troubled children; their problems did not begin at puberty.

Although young people become more peer-oriented in adolescence, this does not mean that they are alienated from their families. Young adolescents, especially, often quarrel with their parents about little things—dress, neatness, chores, curfews, and schoolwork. But they generally agree with

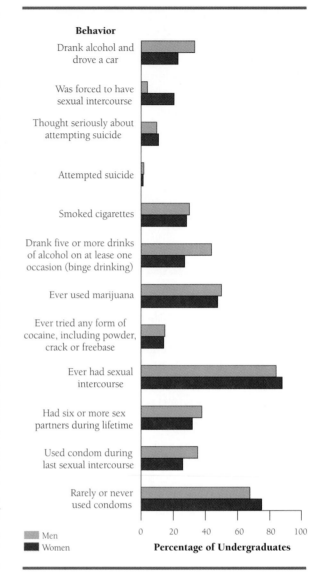

Figure 4-3   *Risky Behavior on College Campuses*

One might think that college students know what's good for them, but many take chances with their health and even their lives. Indeed, undergraduates tend to engage in more risky behavior (especially binge drinking) than young people who do not attend college.

Source: Centers for Disease Control and Prevention; in *The Chronicle of Higher Education;* September 5, 1997, p. A66.

their parents on bigger issues, such as the importance of education, religion, or political activism. The great majority of adolescents like and respect their parents, believe that their parents are proud of them, and feel that their parents are fair with them most of the time (Offer et al., 1988; Chase, 1989). Contrary to stereotypes, about three in four adolescents say they feel close to and identify with their parents (Steinberg, 1990).

Furthermore, adolescent peer groups can sometimes be an influence for the good, prodding friends to do well in school, to be active in the church or community, to stay away from drugs, and to care about other people's feelings. When adolescents are asked what makes them feel proud, one common response is "Helping out a friend" (Offer et al., 1988).

To be sure, adolescence is a time of rapid physical, emotional, and intellectual change. Finding out who you are isn't easy, but neither is it inevitably and always an ordeal.

Transitions to Young Adulthood

In some ways, today's adolescents are behaving more like adults (dating at an earlier age, working during high school, and the like). At the same time, young adults are postponing assumption of full-scale adult roles (Buchmann, 1989; Woodward, 1989). Many young people today are still in school at age 25 or 30. The proportion of young Americans who go to college has grown, but fewer go straight through, largely because of the high cost of tuition. Many work part-time while in college, move back and forth between full-time jobs and full-time schooling, or graduate from college, work for a few years, and then return to school for an advanced degree.

The number of adult children who live with their parents has also increased, especially in middle-class families (Schnaiberg and Goldenberg, 1989) (see Figure 4-4). The growing demand for higher education, the high cost of housing, and a tighter job market have made it harder to establish total independence. Delayed departure is not always happy for either generation. Young adults complain that their parents still treat them as children, while parents complain about the hours their adult children keep and their unwillingness to help with household chores.

Most young adults are postponing marriage. In part as a result of extended education, in part because of women's greater participation in the workforce, family patterns are changing. Since the 1960s, the median age of first marriage has risen

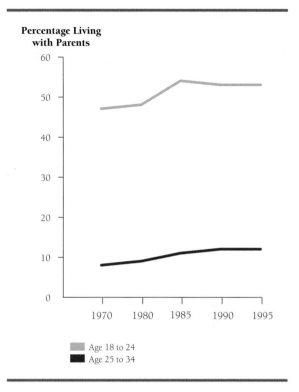

Percentage Living with Parents

Figure 4-4 *The (Not So) Empty Nest: Young Adults Who Live with Parents*

When young adults live at home (with their parents), both go through a period of resocialization. Young adults cannot expect their parents to pay their bills, do their laundry, and generally behave like "parents"; parents must "unlearn" such previous behavior as setting curfews, checking on their child's whereabouts, reading his or her "report card" (or job review), and otherwise taking charge of their now-adult child's life.

Source: U.S. Bureau of the Census, *1970 and 1980 Census of Population,* PC (2)-4B and *Current Population Reports,* p. 20–410 and p. 20–450; and unpublished data.

from 19 or 20 to 23 or 24 for women and from 22 or 23 to 26 for men. The median age at which women have their first child is now about 27 (U.S. Bureau of the Census, 1996). But these averages conceal a wide range of variations. Some men and women marry soon after graduation from high school or college, but an increasing number remain single through their twenties and into their thirties. Some women become mothers in their teens, while others postpone motherhood until their thirties.

Young adulthood is usually a time of assuming complete responsibility for one's life. Although increasing numbers of young adults continue to live with their parents, many strike out on their own.

In short, transitions to adulthood have become increasingly unpredictable, varied, and individualized. Age (and sex) no longer allow you to assume that someone is a student or a worker, financially dependent on parents or a parent with dependents, living with parents or independent. In these respects, the boundary between youth and adulthood has blurred.

Patterns of Middle Adulthood

Two or three decades ago most Americans might have agreed that middle age begins around age 40. But as members of the huge baby boom generation began turning 40, they began moving the boundary of middle age back to age 50 and beyond. In the early 1990s, the American Board of Family Planning asked a random sample of 1,200 Americans when middle age begins. Of the respondents, 41 percent said it begins when you start worrying whether you have enough money to pay health care bills; 42 percent said it begins when your last child moves out; and 46 percent pointed to the stage when you do not recognize the names of music groups on the radio anymore.

Like young adulthood, middle age has become more variable. Men in their fifties who married for a second time are pushing strollers and paying college tuition at the same time. Some have been pushed into early retirement and are wondering what to do with the next twenty or thirty years of their lives. Women "over 40" no longer see them-

selves as "over the hill" in terms of fashion and sexual attractiveness. Some, who saw making a home and raising children as the center of their lives, go back to school or launch careers; successful career women may change fields (a professor becomes a businesswoman, a businesswoman enters politics) or devote more time to an interest they set aside earlier (painting, wilderness expeditions, community or church activities). Many Americans in their middle years today are part of the so-called "sandwich generation," caught between the needs and demands of their not-yet-adult children and those of their aging parents.

Wherever the boundary to middle age lies, this stage of the life cycle seems to be characterized by change more than stability. Whether individuals follow a traditional or an unconventional lifestyle, remain in the marriage and career they chose as young adults or change partners and pursuits, middle age involves **resocialization:** "unlearning" norms and values that were adaptive and considered culturally appropriate in the past in order to take on new social positions and roles.

"Seasons of a Man's or Woman's Life"

Psychologist David Levinson, like Erikson, believed that much as there are seasons to the year, so there are seasons to adults' lives. Seasons are predictable periods of growth (summer), retreat (fall), inactivity or quiescence (winter), and rejuvenation (spring), a cycle that is repeated—with variations—each year. In a similar way, Levinson argued, adults go through periods when their lives seem stable and set, only to find that this stability is temporary, that their social position, their bodies, their relationships, their sense of themselves have changed and they must reorient themselves toward the future. At the beginning of each adult season or era, people make certain key choices regarding identity, family, occupation, religion, leisure, and so on; these choices create the structure within which they pursue their values and goals. During periods of transition, they reappraise this structure—this life plan—and explore possibilities for change in themselves and in their relations with the world. Gradually or suddenly, peacefully or painfully, they create a new structure for the next season of their lives. (See Figure 4-5.)

Levinson's first study (Levinson et al., 1978) was based on in-depth interviews with forty men from

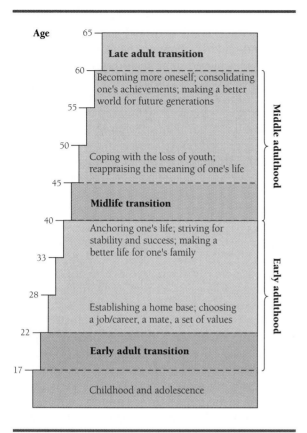

Age

Late adult transition — 65

60 — Becoming more oneself; consolidating one's achievements; making a better world for future generations

55 —

50 —

Coping with the loss of youth; reappraising the meaning of one's life

45 —

Midlife transition

40 —

Anchoring one's life; striving for stability and success; making a better life for one's family

33 —

28 —

Establishing a home base; choosing a job/career, a mate, a set of values

22 —

Early adult transition

17 —

Childhood and adolescence

Middle adulthood

Early adulthood

Figure 4-5 *Levinson's Stages and Transitions of Adulthood*

Like Erikson, Levinson holds that adults go through more or less predictable stages, characterized by alternating periods of stability and uncertainty about their life choices.

Source: Adapted from Daniel J. Levinson et al., *The Seasons of a Man's Life* (Knopf: New York, 1978), p. 57.

different walks of life (business executives, scientists, novelists, and laborers). Levinson found that in young adulthood, men focus on getting established: launching a career, starting a family, formulating a dream. As this era draws to a close (about age 36 to 40), a man seeks to be taken seriously on his own terms, to speak in his own voice, to be recognized as his own man. This quest often leads to a "culmination event"—a promotion, an award, the publication of a major novel or scientific study. The man is poised to move from being a junior adult to being a senior one. But what comes next is uncertain.

During the midlife transition (roughly age 40 to 45), Levinson found, men become less concerned with being viewed as successful in the eyes of the world and more concerned about whether they find their work rewarding. A man is more willing to pursue his own goals even if others ignore or oppose what is important to him. He wants to make a significant contribution, to create a legacy for his family, his clients or students, his colleagues, or his field. His relationship with his spouse (who is becoming more her own woman), his children (who are approaching young adulthood), his parents (who are aging), and his co-workers (more of whom may be subordinates now) are all in a state of flux. Career changes and divorce are not uncommon during this transitional period.

Some men may go through a "midlife crisis," attempting to recapture their vanishing youth by having affairs, seeking adventure, and generally acting out of character (what psychologists call "acting out"). Others become more reflective, while still others muddle through. By age 50, some men have achieved a new sense of self in relation to society; some have accepted a more limited version of themselves and their dreams; and some, unwilling or unable to change, are bitter that "life passed them by." Other researchers have found that adaptation and change in middle age are the exception and that stagnation is the rule (Weiss, 1990).

In a second study (1996) Levinson and his collaborator Judith D. Levinson collected life stories from forty-five women approaching middle age. They were interested, first, in learning whether there is an overall, human pattern of adult development that applies to both sexes or whether men and women develop along different paths. They were also interested in the impact of social change on women's lives. The subjects of this study included some of the first women to pursue careers, as well as traditional housewives. To their surprise, the Levinsons found that *"women go through the same sequence of eras as men and at the same ages"* (p. 5). However, the issues women face during transitional periods are different from those men confront, and there is greater variation among women, not just as individuals but also in the social roles they choose in early adulthood.

The mothers of the women in this sample (the grandmothers of today's young adults) were traditional homemakers who sought fulfillment in the domestic sphere and defined femininity in terms of being good wives and mothers. They may have pursued interests in the outside world through volunteer work, community groups, amateur creative pursuits, and, less often, paid jobs, but their families came first. One-third of those in Levinson's sample followed in their mothers' footsteps: in young adulthood they married, had children, and dedicated themselves to caring for others. At midlife, however, most found that being a "good girl" hadn't paid off as they had expected. Their marriages were stale or over (50 percent were divorced or in a second marriage); their "job" as mother was drawing to a close; they wanted more from life but hadn't developed the personal or social resources required for interesting opportunities in the outside world. Determined to make something of them*selves*, they realized that they were starting almost from scratch.

The career women in the sample had decided in their teens that their mothers represented everything they did *not* want to be (that is, their mothers were a negative reference group). From the outside, their mothers appeared to have it all: husbands who were good providers, children with bright prospects for the future, and material comfort and security. Yet the daughters sensed that their mothers were trapped in rounds of trivial activities, superficially busy but underneath angry and/or depressed. To some degree their mothers supported their wish to be independent, but they had no advice to offer their nontraditional daughters.

The career women in the study created different life structures, some with and some without marriage and children. Forging their own paths, at 40 many had achieved more than they might have anticipated: the top level of middle management in a corporation or a full professorship. Having climbed one ladder to success, they found themselves at the bottom of another ladder, whose steps were less clear. As the first women to reach the senior levels of their fields, they found themselves more isolated—and less welcome among male colleagues—than before. Those who had combined marriage, motherhood, and career felt less like "superwomen" than like jugglers who had often "dropped the ball" in one area of their lives or another. Tired of proving themselves, they wanted more time to love and to play and more opportunity to experience creativity, satisfaction, and social contribution in their work.

At 50, some homemakers were enjoying freedom from the responsibility of caring for others, while others were consumed with caring for aging parents as well as not-quite-independent children. Some career women were enjoying a sense of freedom from the pressure to "make it" in a male world and were involved in helping their daughters, and young women generally, chart a path in a society where gender equality is still an ideal, while others were struggling anew with definitions of gender and success. As with men, some had scaled down their dreams, while others were struggling to survive on their own and/or were chronically discontent.

The "empty nest" syndrome seems to have given way to the "sandwich" generation, as many middle-aged American women are taking care of aging parents while they still have teenage children living at home.

A major question regarding Levinson's work (and other life-cycle theories) is whether he identified a *universal* pattern of adult development or captured the biographies of *one* generation—or what sociologists call a *cohort*—during a *particular* period of social history. If Levinson had studied men and women who were born in the 1920s and became teenagers during the Great Depression, for example, a different pattern might have emerged (Elder, Modell, and Park, 1993). Subjected to hardship and uncertainty at a young age, men of that generation usually picked a line of work early in life and stayed in that field, often working for the same company, until they retired. Women of that generation tended to marry young, perhaps to make up for the "psychic disruptions" of their youth. Because it was a relatively small generation and the U.S. economy grew rapidly after World War II, workers were in short supply and men could pressure for higher wages. Men's incomes were usually sufficient to support a family comfortably, allowing the wives to stay home and give birth to the baby boomers. "Stability" was the watchword for that generation. By and large, they made lifelong commitments in their early twenties and followed a straight and narrow path through adulthood.

In contrast, the baby boom generation grew up in relative affluence. Its members were the first generation of Americans to grow up in suburbs, hang out in shopping malls, go to college in large numbers, and also fight in or protest against an unpopular war in Vietnam. Many did not have to go directly from high school to work; the economy was booming, so they could afford to try on different identities, sure that jobs would be waiting when they were ready to settle down. Raised in the child-centered families of the 1950s, creators of the youth-centered culture of the 1970s and 1980s, the baby boomers have divorced more often, changed jobs more often, and moved more often than their parents or grandparents did. This pattern reflects, in part, a mind-set for seeking the newest and the best and, in part, slower economic growth. To "get ahead," members of this generation have depended on having two-salary families and on changing companies and locations in pursuit of opportunity. Levinson's description of adult development captures the many changes this generation has been through.

Finally, Erikson's and Levinson's life-cycle theories were based primarily on well-off, well-educated, middle-class samples. Whether they apply to working-class and poor Americans, to minorities, or to first- or second-generation immigrants with different cultural backgrounds is questionable.

Menopause: Fact and Fiction

Menopause, long mired in myth and controversy and shrouded by a cloak of embarrassed silence, is fast becoming the leading women's health issue of the decade. (J. Brody, 1992)

The term **menopause** refers to the cessation of ovulation and menstruation in human females, as a result of changes in the levels of sex hormones (especially estrogen) produced in the woman's body. The timing of menopause is highly variable. Some women go through menopause at age 40; others, not until age 58; for some, the transition takes two years; for others, twelve years (Treloar, 1982).

Both popular and scientific descriptions of menopause are as variable as the individual experience. Some women, such as feminist Germaine Greer (1992), see menopause as liberating. Anthropologist Margaret Mead talked of "post-menopausal zest" (A. S. Rossi, 1992, p. 2). Others describe the transition to menopause as a chaotic time, during which women's moods as well as their bodies go through sudden, unpredictable changes, punctuated by "hot flashes" (internally generated heat, flushing, and sweating) (Sheehy, 1992). Wulf Utian, a gynecologist who established the first U.S. menopause clinic a decade ago, warns of an "impending epidemic" as members of the huge baby boom generation move toward middle age. To cope with the symptoms and aftereffects of menopause, many physicians recommend hormone replacement therapy (HRT). Although controversial, estrogen already is the second-most-prescribed drug in the American pharmaceutical market, with profits of some $750 million a year (A. S. Rossi, 1992).

What are the facts? Is menopause a medical crisis or simply a change? An ongoing five-year study by Katherine Matthews and her colleagues found that "natural menopause is a benign event for the majority of middle-aged healthy women" (Matthews et al., 1990). The study found no significant difference in women's scores on tests of anger, anxiety, depression, self-consciousness, or body worries before and after menopause. In other studies only about one in ten women experienced severe hot flashes (Voda, 1982) and only 5 percent were troubled by vaginal dryness (McKinlay et al., 1987). Most studies find that depression is more likely to be a predictor of menopausal problems than a consequence (for example, Avis et al., 1992).

Sociologist Alice Rossi (1992) looks beyond this research to cultural influences. The biological significance of menopause is the end of fertility. But in western societies, most women have their last child long before menopause. In other cultures, where women spend most of their lives either pregnant or nursing small children, women often welcome menopause, particularly if their culture holds older women in high regard. In our culture, however, older women are regarded as "has-beens." That's why after age 28 or so, most women wish they were younger than they are, and many spend extravagantly on antiaging creams, if not cosmetic surgery.

Rossi concludes that the crisis, if there is one, is not biological or medical. It results from normal aging and from women's fear of losing their sex appeal, not from menopause itself. But she adds that social expectations can function as a self-fulfilling prophecy. Thus most studies find that premenopausal women who expect to become irritable, angry, and depressed and to experience hot flashes, night sweats, aches, and pains are far more likely to do so than are women who have no such negative expectations. As long as there are profits to be made from the "medicalization" of menopause, the warnings are likely to continue. Indeed they are spreading.

In recent years, a number of researchers have begun to talk of "male menopause" (in Liebmann-Smith, 1992). They hold that a drop in levels of the hormone androgen in men, like the drop in estrogen in women, can bring on numerous physiological and psychological changes, including lessened interest in sexual activity, changes in body shape, weight gain, bone loss, skin changes, hot flashes, memory loss, mood swings, and lowered self-esteem. There is much debate about whether a male menopause actually exists and, if it does, how many men are affected and whether these men should be treated with hormone replacement therapy. Most researchers hold that changes in men's attitudes and appearance reflect the interaction of natural aging, health (and medications), and lifestyle (McKinlay and Feldman, 1994). But given the huge numbers of Americans entering middle age and the potential market for books, workshops, and therapies, the subject of menopause—both male and female—is likely to remain in the public eye.

Late Adulthood

> When asked when old age begins, people over 50 typically say "80." (in Rosenthal, 1997, p. 42)

At the turn of the century, life expectancy in the United States was 49.[2] Today it is 79, and many Americans who reach age 65 can expect to live into their eighties. In 1990, 3 million Americans were age 65 or older; today there are 33.5 million senior citizens (a number equal to the entire population of Canada) (*Statistical Abstract,* 1996). Increased longevity is due in part to medical advances, in part to changes in lifestyle (such as better diets, regular exercise, and not smoking). Not only has the number of older persons grown, but the proportion of older people in our society has grown—a phenomenon known as "the graying of America." In 1990, one in thirty Americans was 65 or older; today the figure is nearly one in eight. Once a small minority, older people make up 12.5 percent of the U.S. population today—a figure expected to rise to more than 20 percent by the year 2030 (U.S. Bureau of the Census, 1996). The change in our society's age structure is due in part to people's living longer, in part to a declining birthrate (see Chapter 1).

Demographers used to consider people over 65 a single category. However, people in their sixties and seventies are becoming "younger," in terms of both their health and their lifestyles. For example, in the 1950s, the average age of admission to nursing homes in the United States was about 70; today it is 81 (Norman, 1997). At the same time, more people are surviving into their eighties and nineties. Indeed, people age 80 and older are the fastest-growing population segment, not only in the United States and other advanced countries but around the world (Crossette, 1996). In response to increased vitality and increased longevity, demographers now distinguish between the "young old" (about ages 65 to 80), who often are active and in-

---

[2] This average included a higher number of deaths in infancy and early childhood. Life expectancy for those who survived early childhood was probably closer to 60.

dependent, and the "oldest old" (age 80 and beyond), whose activities are limited and who often require a significant amount of care.

Growing old involves not just physical change but also social change in the roles people play and their relationships to others. As in middle age, these changes or transitions entail resocialization.

Retirement

One transition almost all older people will face is retirement. In the years following World War II, retirement usually meant an abrupt, irreversible, and often mandatory switch from full-time work to full-time leisure at age 65 (Treas, 1995). After thirty or forty years of working, often for the same company, the typical rite of passage was a farewell dinner and presentation of a gold watch. For men whose status and self-esteem were based on the role of breadwinner, the experience could be traumatic. Women of that generation were less likely to work throughout their adult years, if at all, and more likely to think of themselves as homemakers first, workers second.

Today retirement is better described as a process than as an event. More than 3.8 million people age 65 and older remain in the workforce, including almost one in four men age 65 to 69 but only one in eighteen men age 75 or older. Consistent with their generation's pattern, older men are twice as likely as older women to work. Some elderly people—especially professionals and people in creative fields—continue to work in the same career but cut back their hours. Some leave active practice but teach or become consultants or board members. The majority of Americans do not have these options, however; most employers do not offer workers a gradual retirement plan. A substantial minority of older Americans move in and out of the workforce, depending on their health, opportunities, or interests, for a number of years. Others are "discouraged workers," who give up looking for work after a long period of unemployment. Thus there are many routes to retirement today.

Mandatory retirement policies were phased out for most jobs in the late 1970s and 1980s, leaving older people the option of continuing to working or retiring (Treas, 1995). Most Americans retire, increasingly before age 65. If they can afford to retire in comfort, most Americans want to do so while they are still fit enough to enjoy their free time. Furthermore, spouses usually retire at about the

Henri Matisse, a master of twentieth-century art. He is shown here in 1950, at age 81. Many elderly people continue to do productive work long after the traditional retirement age.

same time, suggesting that they plan to enjoy more leisure activities together. Early retirement in good health has created a new stage in the life cycle and a new "leisure class." In addition, a significant number of retirees continue to work, but as volunteers. Schools, hospitals, and local government agencies in Florida and other places with large numbers of retirees depend on elderly volunteers (Rosenthal, 1997).

Health

Even for the young old, health is a major issue. A majority of Americans age 65 and older report at least one chronic ailment (Treas, 1995). In some cases the condition is potentially life-threatening and requires constant medication and frequent visits to a physician or the hospital. An example is heart disease, reported by almost one-third of older people. In other cases, the condition is not life-threatening but may cause pain, inconvenience, and a lower quality of life. Almost half of Americans 65 and older suffer from arthritis, for example, and many have visual or hearing impairments that interfere with everyday activities. But national surveys indicate that only 5 to 8 percent of older people living in the community (as opposed to a nursing home or other institution) need help with physical self-care (such as bathing, dressing, or getting out of bed into a chair) or everyday tasks (such as preparing meals or handling money) (Weiner et al., 1990).

Older people may also be affected by mental conditions (Treas, 1995). About one in ten older Americans experiences some memory loss, but it is rarely severe enough to interfere with daily functioning (Norman, 1997). Alzheimer's disease, the leading cause of senile dementia,[3] is rare. However, the risk increases sharply with advanced age—from less than 4 percent for 65- to 74-year-olds to 48 percent (almost half) for people age 85 and older. Severe dementia is a main reason why older people are institutionalized. A major, but less well known, mental health problem among the elderly is depression, sometimes brought on by poor health or prescription medications. Depression has been linked to the high suicide rate among the elderly: white males age 85 and older are six times more likely to kill themselves than are members of the general population (see Chapter 1).

Aging does take a toll. But many adults age 80 or older (the oldest old) and the great majority of adults age 65 to 75 (the young old) are active and alert. Nearly a half-million Americans over 50 have gone back to school—to learn new skills, to complete educations cut short in their younger years, or simply for the joy of learning—raising the average age of junior college students to 40. Senior citizens are among the nation's most frequent travelers, accounting for 70 percent of recreational-vehicle trips and cruise passengers. And although sexual desire does decline with age, in one survey 40 percent of Americans over 65 reported that they were sexually active and had sex two or three times a month (compared with seven times a month for people under 65); half of those in committed relationships were very satisfied with the quality of their sex lives (Manton et al., 1997).

Living Arrangements

The majority of older Americans maintain independent households, often into their eighties (see Figure 4-6). Most older men and young-old women live with their spouses. However, because women usually marry men who are older than they are and because women often live longer than men, they are more likely to outlive their spouses. A majority of women age 75 and older continue to maintain their own homes after they are widowed. Widowers are also more likely to live on their own than with relatives.

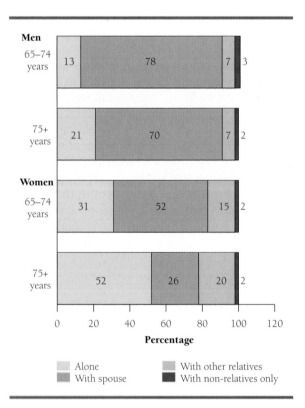

Figure 4-6   *Living Arrangements of Older Americans*

Contrary to stereotypes, most older Americans live with their spouse or alone, not with their adult children or in nursing homes.

Source: J. Treas, "Older Americans in the 1990s and Beyond," *Population Bulletin* 56, May 1995.

---

[3] *Senile dementia* refers to severely impaired memory, concentration, and judgment, often combined with emotional disturbance and personality change.

Relationships between adult children and their older or aging parents are characterized by mutual support, not dependence (Cooney and Uhlenberg, 1992). These relationships include having frequent face-to-face contact, keeping in touch by phone or letter, exchanging care during illness, running errands, giving financial assistance and gifts, and providing one another with emotional support and affection. This does not mean that all adult children and their parents have close relationships; national surveys indicate that half of all adults are not in frequent contact with their parents (Hogan, Eggebeen, and Clogg, 1993). But most aging Americans have a close relationship with at least one of their children. The pattern of relationships varies according to the needs and resources of the generations. For example, on average, African-American and Latino adults receive less assistance from their parents than white adults do, in large part because their families include more brothers, sisters, and grandchildren; but having more adult children and grandchildren can also mean greater support for older minority members.

By age 80, many older people need help with such activities as personal care, meal preparation, and money management (Treas, 1995). Fewer families take in a disabled parent today, whether because both spouses work, because they still have children to raise and support, or for other reasons. But neither do families turn away from elderly parents. Although there are a number of other alternatives, from nursing homes and assisted-living complexes to paid home caregivers and adult day care, most families care for aging parents themselves. Two-thirds of disabled older people living in the community rely on informal help from family and friends—most often the spouse (if he or she is alive), a daughter, or, if they have no daughter, a daughter-in-law. Many of the elderly will enter a nursing home at least once, either for short-term convalescence or because of a terminal illness. But only 5 percent of all older Americans live in nursing homes. The majority of long-term nursing-home residents are white widows in their eighties, admitted after a stay in the hospital; two-thirds suffer from mental as well as physical health problems that require high levels of care and constant supervision. But family care does not stop when an older person is institutionalized; family members visit, monitor the person's care, participate in treatment decisions, manage finances, and otherwise continue to assist and support an aging parent.

Dying

In many cultures and times, people have accepted and even welcomed death (Stolberg, 1997b). In Renaissance Europe, painters, poets, and musicians celebrated a good death as the *ars moriendi* (the art of dying). Death, like birth, was viewed as part of the cycle of life, even a cause for celebrating the salvation of the soul. Buddhism has many stories of Zen masters who wrote poems in the final moments of life to express their first experience of total freedom. In the words of a contemporary Buddhist priest, "Death [is] a mystery to be embraced, entered into and respected" (in Stolberg, 1997b, p. E1).

America has often been described as a "death-denying" society. Our hospital-based medical system is designed to conquer or at least postpone death. For much of the twentieth century, death has been a taboo subject. A book by Elisabeth Kübler-Ross, *On Death and Dying* (1969), broke through this silence. Interviews with the terminally ill had convinced Kübler-Ross that dying, like living, involved a series of predictable stages: *denial* ("It can't be me"), *anger* ("Why me?"), *bargaining* (usually with God, for extra time), *depression* (an overwhelming sense of loss), and finally *acceptance* (accompanied by a sense of tiredness and need to "rest before the final journey," in one patient's words). Kübler-Ross found that family and friends go through similar stages, often complicated by guilt for things they did or did not do. She argued that denying death deprives people who are terminally ill and their loved ones of the opportunity to work through these stages. (See also Becker, 1973.)

More recently, in his book *Dying Well* (1997), physician Ira Byok emphasizes that death is as natural a part of life as birth and that both can promote growth and understanding. Americans often say the best death is a quick one: a fatal accident or falling asleep and never waking up. But few get this wish. The main causes of death in advanced societies are heart disease, cancer, and stroke; a terminally ill patient may live for months or even years. To enable people to die well, Byok argues, we must not only minimize pain but also reduce fear and loneliness. Dying well, he argues, depends on reaching certain landmarks: asking forgiveness, accepting forgiveness, finding dignity, and saying good-bye.

Seventy percent of the Americans who die each year are age 65 or older. A majority want to be told they are dying. They are frightened not of death itself but, rather, of dying alone, in pain and distress. A report by the *Institute of Medicine* (1997) indicates that such fears are not unfounded. Whether they are living on their own, in a nursing home, or with family, when death seems imminent most people still are taken to the hospital. Hospitals—and American medicine generally—emphasize high-tech cures, surgery, and aggressive treatment to save patients; death is viewed as failure. Physicians and other health providers have little training in managing pain or in helping patients to prepare for death. In addition, federal and state laws limit the use of narcotics and other powerful pain-reducing drugs. As a result, terminally ill patients may suffer unnecessarily. A study of 9,000 terminally ill patients, found that half spent their last days in moderate to severe pain (Lynn, 1996). Instead of resting, they may be subjected to hospital routine (such as being woken every four hours to have their temperature taken) and stressful procedures that would be appropriate for a patient with a chance to live, not for one about to die.

Another fear among the terminally ill is being imprisoned between life and death, as a "vegetable" on life-sustaining equipment. New technology has

SOCIOLOGY ON THE WEB

Bookends

Use the web to learn more about the stages of the life cycle—you will find information, statistics, and chat groups. For example, a large number of sites and groups are devoted just to menopause. Do a search of that topic, focusing either on social issues or on biology. What kinds of sites do you find when you narrow your search to either of those areas? Who maintains the sites you find? What kinds of information do different kinds of sites provide? A large part of using the Internet as a source of information is learning how to evaluate the information you find there.

Below is a collection of sites that will start you on a search for information about socialization at the beginning and end of the life cycle: infancy and old age. Use the links provided at these sites to explore one of these topics. Again, evaluate the types of information you come across in your search, and think about what sources of information would and would not be useful in your sociology coursework.

http://idealist.com
At the Child Development web site, you will find a tutorial on the theories of Freud, Mahler, and Erikson. There is also a message forum, where readers can post specific child-development questions and answers. Finally, there's a list of multimedia resources on child development.

http://ericps.ed.uiuc.edu/nccic/nccichome.html
From the National Child Care Information Center, this site offers the text of articles on the effects of child care, the economics of child care in the United States, and socialization and child care.

http://library.utoronto.ca/www/aging/depthome.html
The web site of the Institute for Human Development, Life Course, and Aging at the University of Toronto provides links to Internet resources on aging from Canada, the United States, and the entire world. This is the place to start a search for information on old age as a life stage.

http://www.aoa.dhhs.gov/
A good source for up-to-date statistics on the elderly population, the U.S. Administration on Aging's web site provides a 1997 statistical profile of older Americans, including information on ethnic and racial composition, poverty rates, and income distributions.

enabled physicians to sustain life in patients who only a decade ago would have died. Some of this technology (such as improved cardiac surgery and the use of kidney dialysis machines) provides people with "a new lease on life." But sometimes the technology maintains life without restoring health—hence the attention given to "living wills" (which proclaim a person's desire to die naturally) and even the notion of physician-assisted suicide. The right to choose the time of one's death might not be as big an issue if treatment of the terminally ill were more logical and more humane.

The field of palliative medicine—dedicated to soothing or relieving the symptoms of a disease or disorder for which there is no cure—is gaining support. So are hospices—home care programs or homelike facilities designed to make dying less physically painful and less emotionally trying for patients and their families. Implementing palliative care will depend in part on resocialization of doctors. One resident explained:

"In medical school, we learn how to keep people alive. . . .This [palliative medicine] is almost unlearning all that and learning how to be in tune with what the patient wants. It's a new set of rules." (Jones, in Stolberg, 1997a, p. B7)

Many physicians would agree that addiction to painkilling drugs is not an issue for someone who is dying, but most do not know how much medication an acutely ill person needs to feel comfortable (Byok, 1997). Most physicians do not know that death from (voluntary) starvation usually is not painful. Many patients would prefer to die at home, but believe—incorrectly—that this is illegal. They want to make their own decisions about whether or not to undergo treatments or continue medications, but they may passively follow doctors' orders, if only out of consideration for their families. Palliative medicine and hospices are based on the belief that death is not the enemy and medicine is not the only cure—for most Americans, perhaps especially physicians, a reversal of current beliefs and practices.

Summary

1. **Why is socialization so important?** Our identities, understandings, and behavior are shaped by the lifelong process of *socialization*.

   For many years social scientists were divided into two camps: those who believed that our behavior is the product of nature (or genes) and those who saw our behavior as determined by nurture (or socialization). Today nearly all agree that nature and nurture interact. Studies of "feral" (unsocialized) children, observation of other cultures, and new discoveries in neurobiology underscore the fact that we must learn to be human and that what we learn depends on our cultural environment.

2. **How does socialization occur?** Freud saw socialization as a struggle between a willful, pleasure-seeking child and parents intent on proper behavior. *Personality* develops in stages and consists of three parts: the *id,* the *ego,* and the *superego.* To some degree individuals are always at war with society—and with themselves.

   Charles Cooley and George H. Mead stressed the role of symbolic interaction in the development of the self. Cooley introduced the concept of the *looking-glass self.* Mead held that children learn to take the role of the other in the *play stage* and that they develop a *generalized other* in the *game stage.* The socialized *"me"* continues to provide direction for the spontaneous, impulsive *"I."*

3. **Who is responsible for socialization?** Major *agents of socialization* include the family (which lays the foundation), peers (who introduce children to a new subculture and egalitarian relationships), school (which teaches children how to function in an impersonal organization), and television (which exposes children to a variety of mixed messages regarding violence, gender roles, and sex).

4. **How does socialization change over the life cycle?** Socialization begins at birth and continues throughout the life cycle. Erikson held that the major challenge for adolescents is the development of an identity. Current research indicates that this does not necessarily involve storm and stress or alienation from parents.

The timing of transitions to young adulthood—a full-time job, independent residence, marriage, and parenthood—has become increasingly variable.

Middle age is a time of challenge rather than stability, as people complete (or fail to complete) the tasks they had set for themselves and develop new ideas about what they have accomplished so far and what they want to do in coming years. Levinson's studies of men and women at midlife found they were more alike than different. But the pattern of adult development he described may reflect the experience of middle-class members of one generation, not a universal sequence.

The social meaning of "old age" has also changed, as more people are healthy and active beyond retirement. Most senior citizens live independent, contented lives, and some enjoy lives of leisure.

The taboos banning discussion of the final stage of the life span, death, have been relaxed somewhat, but medical practice still emphasizes maintaining life rather than easing death.

Key Terms

agent of socialization   131

anticipatory socialization   134

ego   129

game stage   130

generalized other   131

the "I"   131

id   129

identity crisis   143

looking-glass self   129

the "me"   131

menopause   149

personality   128

play stage   130

primary group   130

reference group   131

resocialization   146

rites of passage   142

self   129

significant others   131

socialization   122

superego   129

symbolic interaction   130

Recommended Readings

Erikson, E. (1962). *Childhood and Society,* 2d ed. New York: Norton.

Gilligan, C. (1982). *In a Different Voice: Women's Conception of the Self and Morality.* Cambridge, MA: Harvard University Press.

Huston, Althea, Donnerstein, Edward, Fairchild, H., Feshbach, Norma D., Katz, P. A., Murray, J. P., Rubenstein, Earl A., Wilcox, Brian I., & Zuckerman, D. (1992). *Big World, Small Screen: The Role of Television in American Society.* Lincoln: University of Nebraska Press.

Levinson, Daniel J., et al. (1978). *The Seasons of a Man's Life.* New York: Knopf.

Levinson, Daniel J., & Levinson, Judy D. (1996). *The Seasons of a Woman's Life.* New York: Knopf.

Mead, G. H. (1934). *Mind, Self, and Society.* Chicago: University of Chicago Press.

Mead, M. (1935). *Sex and Temperament in Three Primitive Societies.* New York: Morrow.

Rymer, R. (1993). *Genie: An Abused Child's Flight from Silence.* New York: Harper Collins.

Tobin, Joseph J., Wu, David Y. H., & Davidson, Dana H. (1989). *Preschool in Three Cultures: Japan, China, and the United States.* New Haven, CT: Yale University Press.

Chapter

Five

Social Structure

When Lisa Leslie, a 6-foot-tall seventh-grader, played basketball, people would come up to her mother, shaking their heads. "Lisa is so good, it's a shame she isn't a boy." Looking back, Lisa's mother asks, "Can you believe that? . . . I always told them I love Lisa the way she is, and that her day would come" (Sports Illustrated, June 30, 1997, p. 45). Lisa's mother was right. On Saturday, June 21, 1997, at the Great Western Forum in Inglewood, California, 14,284 fans stood cheering as Lisa and her teammates on the Los Angeles Sparks were introduced. Less than a minute later, Sparks guard Penny Toler cut around New York Liberty guard Vickie Johnson to hit an 11-foot jump shot. Those points will go down in sports history as the first scored in the Women's National Basketball Association (the WNBA). Covered live by NBC, the first WNBA game won out over every other national sports event in the Nielsen ratings for that time slot.

After the game, sportswriters and broadcasters interviewed individual players, seeking out tomorrow's celebrities. In the Liberty's locker room, Teresa Weatherspoon was asked about rumors that she had a rose tattoo on her stomach. "Flowers? Are you kidding?" she growled. "Hey, baby, it's a tiger, not flowers. I ain't that sweet." After a Liberty home game in New York City, Tina Trice told reporters, "My daughter's four years old, and she's so excited to see her mommy play in Madison Square Garden" (Orleans, 1997, p. 25).

A sociologist looking at the WNBA would not be as interested in individual players as in the social patterns or structure of the sport itself. How did the game invented in 1891 by James Naismith, a physical education instructor at the YMCA college in Springfield Massachusetts—a game originally played with two peach baskets nailed to the gymnasium walls and a soccer ball—become the preeminent American sport, rivaling (some would say outranking) baseball and football? How did basketball become a multimillion-dollar enterprise, with franchises selling for $125 million and players earning more than the highest paid bankers, doctors, and real estate developers? How has the way basketball is played changed over its first hundred years? How have basketball players changed? Why was the WNBA launched now? How does women's professional basketball compare to men's? Sociologists do not discount the importance of individuals. A sociologist might analyze how an individual player, such as Michael Jordan or Rebecca Lobo

5

(a star center/forward in the WNBA), influences the way the game is played or why certain players receive more attention from the media and from fans than others do. But their primary focus would be on the social structure of the game.

Social structure refers to the relatively stable and enduring patterns that organize social relationships and provide the basic framework for what we call "society." Social structure is essential to ordinary, everyday social interaction; to the functioning of small groups like the family and huge government bureaucracies; and to the social institutions (politics, the economy, the family, education, and religion) that hold a society together. Social structure limits individual freedom to act in some ways, but it also frees us to act by enabling us to coordinate our actions with those of other people, to achieve both individual and collective goals. It allows us to anticipate how other people will act in a given situation, reduces some of the guesswork in social encounters, and makes social interaction more orderly and predictable.

Social structure is not fixed, once and for all. For example, through most of the twentieth century, sports was a male domain. The idea that males were meant to be players and women were meant to be cheerleaders, confined to the sidelines, was taken for granted, as being only natural. The WNBA is one sign that this element of social structure is changing. Similarly, until the 1950s, basketball was an almost all-white game. Racial segregation was part of this country's social structure. To be sure, there were black players and black teams, but hardly anyone considered that blacks might play in the

same leagues, much less on the same teams, as whites. Obviously, this, too, has changed—but not as much as the million-dollar salaries of leading African-American players would suggest. Most "hoop dreams" do not come true. Just as social structure creates limits and opportunities for individual action, so it creates both boundaries and frontiers for social change.

There are two basic approaches to studying social structure: the microperspective and the macroperspective. The **macroperspective** uses a wide-angle lens to analyze the overall patterns and long-term trends of populations, societies, and the world as a whole. Looking at social behavior from the macroperspective is similar to looking at the diagrams basketball coaches and broadcasters use to describe the patterns of play. The diagram is an abstraction; one doesn't have to know who was playing to see the moves and countermoves, and the technique can be used on any team, playing at any level. But a chart of social structure—if such were possible—would be three-dimensional, with many overlapping layers to show the patterns of interaction among individuals and groups, related formal organizations (such as the NBA), how all these are linked to other activities and enterprises via social institutions, and global relationships among this society and others.

The **microperspective** is a zoom lens that yields close-up, detailed analysis of "what people do, say, and think in the actual flow of momentary experience" (Collins, 1981, p. 984). Sportswriters use a version of the microperspective when they analyze a specific game and seek quotes from players. But sociologists go one

Coaches use diagrams to help players understand the overall picture as well as grasp patterns that are difficult to see when the players are in action on the court. Similarly, sociologists use the macroperspective to explain social structure and illuminate the roles, relationships, groups, organizations, and institutions we take for granted in daily life.

step further; they ask, "Why?" For example, in the interviews at the beginning of this chapter, why did one player distance herself from traditional femininity (in effect saying, "I'm a tiger, not a rose") whereas another emphasized her role as a mother? Why did the reporter choose their two quotes?

In this chapter we will look at social life from the macroperspective. We begin with an overview of social structure, using basketball as an illustration. Then we look at the different elements of social structure, beginning with social relationships and building up to society as a whole. In the final section we look at the structure of relationships among societies, or the world order. In Chapter 6 we will use the microperspective to look at everyday behavior, alone and in groups, in public and private. Just as photographs of the same scene taken with a zoom lens and a wide-angle lens will look quite different, so sociological studies conducted from a microperspective and a macroperspective may appear unrelated. It is important to remember that whichever lens sociologists are using, they are trying to understand and explain the same world.

Key Questions

1. *What is social structure?*
2. *How does social structure affect individual behavior?*
3. *What are the basic elements of social structure?*
4. *How do social structures provide the framework for societies?*
5. *How have societies and relations among societies changed over time?*

Social Structure and Individual Behavior

The central question, at the heart of sociology, is: *How does social structure affect individual and group behavior?* Basketball provides concrete illustrations of social structure at work. Whether in college or professional basketball, men's or women's games, all basketball teams have a common structure. Teams today generally have twelve players, only five of whom are on the floor at any given time. Each

player occupies a specific position: one plays center, two are guards, and two are forwards. Each position is associated with a specialized role. Guards—usually the fastest, most agile players, good ball handlers, and high scorers—specialize in offense. The "point guard" moves the ball upcourt and sets up plays, much like a quarterback in football, while the "shooting guard" plays around the perimeter. The forwards are equally active on offense and defense. The "small forward" moves around, shooting from the baseline or from outside, beyond the 3-point arc, while the "power forward" generally stays close to the basket and goes for rebounds. The "center," usually the tallest player, is the cornerstone of most plays, setting up near the basket and waiting for passes and opportunities to score, rebound, or block shots.

The structure of positions and roles enables players to function as a team, coordinating their activities. In different ways, each player contributes to the team's common objective: scoring (or blocking) points. They are able to play together because each player has a general idea of what other players will do and what they expect of him or her. In the words of one coach, "It's a game that parallels life's challenges in that you are able to achieve certain things on your own, but the bulk of what happens is with the team. The bottom line is to mesh your skills with the . . . other people" (Decourcy, 1996, p. 10). Structure also provides continuity. Each season, and sometimes midseason, some new players join the team and other players leave; one player may be substituted for another during the game; but the structure of the team, and thus the game, remains essentially the same.

So it is in everyday life. The roles of husband and wife, parent and child, and grandparent and grandchild structure American families. Of course, no two families are alike. Moreover, families change over time. We may still consider the nuclear family of the 1950s (a married couple and their children living in a home of their own) ideal; but the majority of Americans today live in single-parent families, stepfamilies (which may include children from either partner's or both partners' previous relationships), childless families, unmarried partnerships, or three-generation households or live alone (see Chapter 11). Moreover, individuals vary in how they define their roles, how committed they are to a particular role, and how well or poorly they perform their roles. The sociological perspective shows that the roles of husband or wife, player or coach, marketing manager or consumer have as much impact on people's attitudes and behavior as do their individual characters and temperaments. To a significant degree, roles transcend individual wants, needs, and personality. (See *Close Up:* Are We Prisoners of Society?)

In order to play games, teams must agree on rules and regulations; otherwise, the game would deteriorate into a free-for-all. In fact, one reason why Naismith (1941/1996) invented basketball was to prevent gymnasium brawls during winter months. The football season had ended, the baseball season wouldn't start for months, and the young men were bored. The college president challenged Naismith to restore order by inventing a new game. Naismith reasoned that to appeal to young men, the new game had to have a ball, since most popular team sports did. To minimize injuries to players, running and tackling had to be banned. The solution was a game in which players passed the ball toward a goal placed overhead, so that offensive players could not fire at point-blank range and defensive players could not block shots with their bodies. With the help of the school custodian, Naismith nailed peach baskets to the gymnasium wall, acquired an old soccer ball, and posted a list of thirteen rules. And so basketball was born. Professional basketball, as played today, bears little resemblance to the original game, played on December 21, 1891. But rules still play a critical role in the game.

Likewise, to function as a family, members have to establish certain rules and routines. Someone has to buy groceries, make dinner, and clean up. The wife/mother or husband/father may do this every night, or they may alternate or divide tasks ("You cook; I clean up") with participation of older children; the family members may eat together every night or separately, depending on their schedules and ages. Individuals may argue about whose turn it is to wash the dishes or walk the dog and about who monopolizes the TV zapper or leaves dirty clothes and wet towels on the bathroom floor. But even these familiar quarrels are patterned and structured. If family members have no mutual expectations, they cease to be a family in any meaningful sense. But family structure is difficult to perceive, precisely because it is "close to home."

The history of women's basketball illustrates how social structure affects behavior, as well as the impact of structural change (Bjarkman, 1996). Women played basketball from the beginning, but because it was considered too rough-and-tumble a sport for "young ladies," athletic directors instituted different rules. Teams consisted of six players. The court was divided lengthwise into three zones, and players were required to stay in their assigned zone. Offensive players were limited to one-half the court and defensive players to the other; none were allowed to cross the center court line, and dribbling was prohibited. The result was a largely stationary, "stand-and-pass" game that was almost as dull to play as it was to watch. So it remained for decades. Conflict theorists (see Chapter 2) and feminist sociologists see the tighter rules imposed on women's basketball as designed to restrict, not protect, female players, and they see the fact that women's sports generally were neglected as one of many ways our patriarchal or male-dominated society denied women power and prestige.

In the 1970s, as part of the rising tide of feminism, high school and college teams all over the country rebelled and switched to a five-player, full-court game with "men's rules." The biggest boost to women's basketball was Congress's passing the law known as Title IX, which prohibited dispersal of federal funds to colleges and universities that practiced any form of sex discrimination. The National College Athletic Association (NCAA), which had recently taken over the administration of women's athletics—in some cases, against the protests of female coaches and players—soon mandated equal spending for men's and women's sports. Suddenly women basketball players had uniforms, full-time coaches, scheduled practices, conferences and tournaments, and even athletic scholarships. Still, women's basketball was more than fifty years behind men's. At the 1976 Olympics, the Russian women's team, which had always played with men's rules, easily defeated the first U.S. women's team in the Gold Medal game (Bjarkman, 1996). Twenty years would pass before women's basketball would generate enough star power and public appeal to support a major professional league.

Even though today's NBA and WNBA follow the same rules, men and women play different games (Bjarkman, 1996; Decourcy, 1996). Women tend to play close to the floor, running complex multipass patterns; men race up and down the court with the point guard controlling the ball. Women specialize in layups; men, in airborne jump shots and dunks. Women score a high percentage of foul shots; some of the best male players have mediocre records from the foul line. Of course, some of these differences are physiological: women do not have the height or strength to slam-dunk like 7-foot-1-inch, 300-pound Shaquille O'Neal. But differences in style also reflect gender roles and gender history. Much as women (especially traditional housekeepers) tend to be family-oriented, coordinating family activities and keeping the peace at home, on the basketball court women are team players. Said one young WNBA fan, "There are no big heads and no big salaries, and I love it" (*Sports Illustrated,* June 30, 1997, p. 46). Male basketball is a game of stars, in which players compete with each other to lead their teams to victory. Michael Jordan is without question the best-known athlete in America (and, indeed, much of the world) today; like baseball stars Babe Ruth and Joe DiMaggio in their day, he is an all-American hero. Most basketball fans have never heard of former college all-Americans and women's basketball Hall of Famers Ann Meyers (now an NBC analyst) and Carol Blazejowski (now vice-president and general manager of the New York Liberty's). Because women basketball players didn't have a well-financed league to play in until recently, they usually graduated from college and started careers and families (Orlean, 1997). For example, Cleveland Rockers forward Lynette Woodard is a registered stockbroker and Liberty guard Rhonda Blakes, a nurse practitioner. Increasingly, male players often turn pro before they graduate from college; most have never held an ordinary job, and some have never even had their own apartment. Male pros are basketball players first and foremost, an identity that overshadows any other social roles they play even after they retire. Liberty forward Trena Trice (quoted earlier) is a mother first and a basketball player second.

As this comparison of men's and women's basketball demonstrates, social structure casts individuals into different roles but does not determine how they play their parts or prevent them from changing the rules and breaking through boundaries. People use the social structure they inherit to organize and carry on their lives. But individuals can—and do—improvise. At the same time, changes in social structure may force individuals to adapt. For example, functionalist sociologists might see the creation of the WNBA as an adaptation to women's gaining greater equality in other spheres. Conflict theorists would more likely see the creation of the WNBA as another example of exploitation—a commercial decision designed to extend the basketball season and thus increase profits for organizations. In this view, the WNBA games are only a sideshow, and WNBA players a novelty act, not serious contenders. Many NBA players earn as much as an entire WNBA team earns (see Figure 5-1). Functionalists might see women working outside the home as one reason for the decline in traditional marriage. Conflict theorists might see the decline in traditional marriage as one reason why women need independent incomes. Neither position is necessarily right or wrong. Both

Player Averages	WNBA	NBA
Years of pro experience	4.3*	4.6
Age	27 yrs.	27.7 yrs.
Height	6 ft.	6 ft. 7 in.
Weight	164 lb.	223.7 lb.
Salary	$30,000	$2.3 million
Shooting Percentages		
Field goals	41%	45.5%
Free throws	71%	78.8%
Three-pointers**	31%	36%
Points per game (avg.)	69	96.9
League Data		
Number of teams	8	29
Games per season	28	82
Reg. season attendance (avg.)	9,391†	17,077
Ticket price (avg.)	$14–$15	$34

*Includes overseas experience.

†September, 1997.

**Men's 3-point line is 22 ft.; Women's is 19 ft. 9 in.

Sources: WNBA, ABL, NBA, Nielsen Sports Marketing

Figure 5-1   *One on One: Comparing the NBA and WNBA*

Professional women's basketball is earning a place in sports. In the WNBA's first year, an average of 1.4 million households tuned in to its games. However, WNBA players earn only a small fraction of the salaries their male counterparts in the NBA command.

Are We Prisoners of Society?

On a quiet evening, a police squad car moved into a university neighborhood in California with a list of addresses. Before the evening was out, a dozen male college students had been arrested. The students were searched, handcuffed, and taken to the Palo Alto station house for fingerprinting and booking. They were then transferred to a local prison, where guards on the night shift introduced them to "life on the inside." Each prisoner was stripped, deloused, given a uniform and an identification number, and marched to a cell. A few of the students were released after four days; the rest, after six days. What crime had they committed? Why were they released?

The answer to the first question is none. The young men had not been accused or convicted of any crime. None of them had a criminal record. Rather, they had answered an ad in the newspaper calling for volunteers to participate in a social-psychological experiment. The prison was not an actual prison, but a laboratory at Stanford University built to resemble a jail. The prison guards were also student volunteers.

Social psychologist Philip Zimbardo and his colleagues had designed an experiment to test popular assumptions about prison life. "Everybody knows" that prisons are violent. Reports

> **It was no longer apparent to most of the subjects (or to us) where reality ended and their roles began. The majority had indeed become prisoners and guards.**
> —Philip Zimbardo

of assaults and riots and allegations of guard brutality appear regularly in the mass media. Without really thinking about it, most people attribute the brutal atmosphere in prisons to the personal characteristics of the inmates. After all, they are convicted criminals. Some people would add that the kinds of people who choose to become prison guards have an authoritarian streak and enjoy pushing people around.

To test these popular assumptions, Zimbardo built a number of controls into the experiment. Volunteers were carefully screened. More than seventy people had responded to the ad. Of these, the researchers selected two dozen middle-class white students with similar personality characteristics. Interviews and tests indicated that they were mature, intelligent, and emotionally stable—in Zimbardo's words, "the cream of the crop." There was no indication that any of the young men had either "antisocial" or "authoritarian" tendencies. Their motivation for participation was straightforward: the opportunity to make $15 a day for two weeks. A flip of a coin determined whether a student was assigned the role of prisoner or guard.

Although designed to run two weeks, the experiment was stopped after only six days.

point to the degree to which individual behavior and social structure are intertwined.

The Basic Elements of Social Structure

The concept of social structure may seem abstract. When you examine the basic elements of social structure, however, they are immediately recognizable. The basic elements of social structure are:

1. statuses and roles
2. social relationships
3. groups
4. formal organizations

Statuses and Roles

You and virtually all students act in one way toward your professors, another toward your classmates, and yet another toward your parents. The professor-student relationship is a formal, hierarchi-

Why? Zimbardo and colleagues were frightened by what they saw. The student guards had been told that they were responsible for maintaining law, order, and respect in the mock prison. They were asked to establish their own rules and regulations. And they were alerted to the potential dangers of running a prison and to their own vulnerability. Within a matter of days, some of the guards were treating the prisoners like vermin, inventing ways to make them feel worthless and taking obvious pleasure in cruelty. Not all the guards behaved this way. Some were tough but fair with prisoners, and others were kind. But not once did a "good" guard interfere with a command by a "bad" guard, or suggest that another guard ease up because it was only an experiment, or complain to Zimbardo about what was happening.

Changes in the student-prisoners' behavior were equally frightening. One might expect students to rebel against harsh treatment, banding together to oppose the guards. (After all, they had not committed any crime.) They did not. The guards had little trouble destroying prisoner solidarity. When one prisoner was put in "solitary confinement" (a small closet) for refusing to eat, the guards gave the other prisoners a choice: give up their blankets for a night and the prisoner would be released, or keep their blankets and the prisoner would remain in the lockup. Abandoning their brother, the prisoners voted to keep their blankets. By the end of six days the student-prisoners had become "servile, dehumanized robots." At a mock parole-board meeting some begged to be released and offered to forfeit the money they had earned so far. But not one demanded to be released. When requests for parole were denied, they meekly accepted their sentence. Three were released after four days because they were becoming visibly depressed. The entire experiment was canceled after six days.

Zimbardo's experiment provides a dramatic illustration of how the roles people play shape their thoughts, feelings, and behavior. All the students knew that they were participating in an experiment and that, in effect, they were playing a game of prisoner and guard. Yet by the end of the week, the experiment had become reality. In Zimbardo's words, "It was no longer apparent to most of the subjects (or to us) where reality ended and their roles began. The majority had indeed become prisoners and guards" (Zimbardo, 1972).

To what extent is each of us a "prisoner" of the roles we play, the relationships in which we are involved, the society in which we live? To what extent do we build and maintain the walls of our "jail" through our own actions? One experiment cannot answer all the questions raised.

cal relationship in which one person has more power and authority than the other (much like employer-employee or sergeant-private relationships). Friendship is an informal, egalitarian relationship; the parent-child relationship is informal but hierarchical (though it tends to become more egalitarian as children become adults). As a result, different rules apply.

Ordinarily you wouldn't ask your professor where she is going for lunch, although you regularly invite yourself to lunch with classmates. If you meet with your professor, it will almost certainly be in her office, not in your dorm room or apartment. You would not beg your professor for money to carry you through to your next paycheck, though you might regularly appeal to your parents for help or ask a friend for a loan. Your parents or friend may say no, but they won't see the request as inappropriate. When you want to have a talk with a classmate, you make a "date," not an "appointment" as you would with a professor. But you don't make "dates" with your parents; you phone to say you're coming home, or you just arrive on their doorstep. However, you might not be pleased if your parents suddenly arrived at your dorm room, announced that they were staying for the weekend, and asked, "What's for dinner?" Student-professor, student-classmate, and child-parent relationships differ in these and countless other ways. The social scripts for these relationships are based on statuses and roles.

Sociologists use the term *status* to describe a position an individual occupies in society.[1] A status functions as a social address. It tells people where the individual "fits" in society, as a father, fashion designer, senior citizen, or prison inmate. Knowing a person's status tells you something about how that person will behave toward you and how you are expected to behave toward him or her. Misjudging status is a frequent cause for embarrassment, as when a graduate student mistakes a young-looking professor for a fellow teaching assistant and asks her out.

Some social statuses are *achieved,* or attained through personal effort. Individuals achieve the status of senator or sales representative, concert pi-

anist or soccer coach, through their own choices and behavior. The statuses of convict, junkie, and high school dropout are also "achieved," in that they are the consequence of the person's own behavior. Of course, not everyone has the resources to run for elected office or, for that matter, easy access to drugs. Even achieved statuses are shaped by social forces.

Other social statuses are *ascribed,* or assigned to the individual at birth or at different stages in the life cycle. Men and women, whites and people of color, occupy different statuses in American society because our culture attaches significance to sex and skin color, not because of anything they do. Age is another ascribed status. Children occupy one position in society, adults another, and elderly people still another. Individuals at each stage are expected to "act their age."

Individuals occupy a number of different statuses at the same time. For example, the same person may be a female Mexican-American (ascribed statuses), a city planner (achieved status), and a wife (achieved status). In some cases, however, one status in large part determines a person's social identity. A *master status* is a social position that tends to override everything else the person is or does in life (Hughes, 1945). The fact that a child is a girl, for example, may have more influence on how people see her than the fact that she has athletic ability (as Lisa

---

[1]The word "status" may also refer to the degree of prestige an individual is accorded in his or her community, profession, or business; in this context the term is neutral.

These two individuals share ascribed statuses: both are African American women. But Lilly Swinney, a Mississippi sharecropper, and poet Maya Angelou, shown here at President Clinton's inauguration, differ greatly in achieved status.

Leslie's mother pointed out in the quotation at the beginning of this chapter). Her parents might be more likely to give her a musical instrument than a basketball hoop or a chemistry set and more likely to reason with her than to use physical punishment—just because she is female. Clearly, Lisa Leslie's parents did not let traditional gender roles blind them to her talent for sports. The concept of master status is most closely associated with criminal or deviant behavior, which tends to overshadow other social characteristics. For example, hardly anyone remembers the name of the Unibomber, Son of Sam, or Boston Strangler, much less what they did for a living, what kind of family life they had, or other social identifications; rather, they are known for their crimes. Asked what they remember about President Richard M. Nixon, people are more likely to say the Watergate scandal than Nixon's opening relations with communist China.

A **role** is the collection of culturally defined rights, obligations, and expectations that accompany a status in a social system. For example, children are expected to need guidance, obey their parents, like toys and games, attend school regularly, tire more easily than adults, and so on. Parents have a cultural and legal obligation to provide and care for their children; they also have the right to make decisions for them (such as what religion they will practice) and to issue orders (such as the hour when they go to bed). Parents do not have the right to treat children any way they like, however. Laws against child abuse and neglect are designed to protect children from mistreatment by their parents or other adults.

The "sick role" provides another illustration of patterned expectations (Parsons, 1951). Individuals who occupy the status of "patient" are exempted from many everyday obligations. They are allowed to take time off from work or school, to stay in bed all day, and to ask others to help them. At the same time, they are expected to want to get well, to see a doctor if the illness is deemed serious, and to cooperate with attempts to bring about a cure. Someone who plays the role too long may lose the status of sick person and be labeled a malingerer. Someone who plays the role too often may be considered a hypochondriac. Thus by declaring themselves to be "sick," people are freed in some ways but restricted in others.

Status and role are opposite sides of the same coin. One could not exist without the other. Thus the word "father" designates a position in society: a male with children. The word also refers to a set of behavioral expectations: a father is expected to support his children financially and to give them nurturance and guidance, at least until they reach adulthood. A man can earn the position of father by playing the role with children who are not his biological offspring (as stepfathers and adoptive fathers do). A man can also lose the status of father, in the eyes of the law as well as his family, if he abandons his children or abuses them.

Roles not only invoke norms and expectations but also provide opportunities. A role can be thought of as a *resource:* a means of claiming, bargaining for, and attaining membership and acceptance in a social community as well as gaining access to social, cultural, and material assets or capital (Baker and Faulkner, 1991). In other words, individuals do not merely fill roles, they also use roles to pursue their interests and to create positions for themselves.

To illustrate this more dynamic aspect of roles, the sociologists Wayne Baker and Robert Faulkner (1991) turned to Hollywood. In the 1940s, 1950s, and 1960s, a few major motion-picture studios dominated film-making in the United States. Studio executives decided what films would be made, who would direct them, who would play leading roles. Although careful with big-name stars, studios hired and fired other talent at will. The finished movie was the product of collaboration between three different people enacting specialized roles: a producer (who arranged financing and assembled and supervised the production team), a screenwriter (who might be asked to develop a new idea or to adapt a novel, play, or musical for the screen), and a director (who visualized the script and guided the crew and actors toward that vision). Hollywood movies were popular worldwide, but audiences in the United States were declining as more people acquired TVs and went to "art cinemas" to see foreign films.

The film *The Godfather* (1972) took the movie industry by surprise; no other movie had ever earned so much so quickly. At the time, many observers saw *The Godfather* as a unique moment in the history of film. Then *Jaws* opened in June 1975, grossing $8 million in its first three days. *Jaws* was followed by *Star Wars, Saturday Night Fever, Animal House, The Empire Strikes Back, Raiders of the Lost*

Ark, and *Close Encounters of the Third Kind*—to name a few that earned hundreds of millions of dollars. *The Godfather* had not been one-of-a-kind, but rather it marked the beginning of a new era of Hollywood blockbusters. The winning blockbuster formula was an epic fantasy that featured dazzling special effects and extraordinary stunts.

The possibility of spectacular profits attracted outside investors. Many studios were bought by large conglomerates whose main business lay elsewhere but saw the movie industry as a good investment. As a result, the new studio executives were not interested in producing a series of good films with moderate profits. In the words of one producer, Hollywood moviemaking became a "home-run business" in which minor hits no longer counted. Moreover, the new "mega-studios" had the financial resources to meet the skyrocketing costs of blockbuster production. But they were not filmmakers. Producers who knew their way around Hollywood stepped into the gap. Using their financial role as a launching pad, they became dealmakers by buying rights to stories; negotiating with writers, producer, actors; and presenting studios with a complete package. At the same time, a new generation of filmmakers, influenced by the independence of European filmmakers, expanded and consolidated their roles to director-screenwriter. Some, such as Stanley Kubrick (*2001: A Space Odyssey,* 1968) and Francis Ford Coppola (*Apocalypse Now,* 1979), worked with studios, but as independents. Others, such as Robert Altman (whose film *M*A*S*H** of 1970 became a long-running TV series) and actor-director John Cassavetes (*A Woman under the Influence,* 1974), bypassed the Hollywood system. A few produced, wrote, directed, and often starred in their own films—notably Woody Allen (from *Take the Money and Run,* 1969; to *Bullets over Broadway,* 1994) and Spike Lee (*Do the Right Thing,* 1989; *Four Little Girls,* 1997).

Thus the structure of the Hollywood film industry changed as individuals used their roles as resources to create new positions. In the pre-blockbuster era, producers, directors, screenwriters, actors, and actresses worked *for* Hollywood studios. Today, most studios do not make films but rather buy and distribute films packaged by producers and made by director/writers or actors. The key point is that social structure depends in large part on how people enact their roles, which is an active process that can produce change.

Of course, many would-be blockbusters fail at the box office. Likewise, many attempts to claim a role and establish a new status flounder. A graduate student cannot become a professor unless his or her dissertation is accepted by established professors. Many artists, such as Vincent Van Gogh, were not accepted by the artistic community until after they died. A husband or wife may find that marriage does not automatically confer the position and role they anticipated; rather, in-laws dominate their family life. In some cases, roles provide opportunities; in others, they create problems.

Role strain occurs when a single status makes contradictory or conflicting demands on a person. For example, the status of U.S. senator requires that a person represent the people of his or her state and defend their interests; it also requires that the senator consider the best interests of the nation, which may or may not be the same. It is in the best interests of the nation to reduce the budget deficit, but it may be in the best interests of a senator's state to keep building submarines if the state's shipyards employ thousands of workers. The status of newspaper reporter requires that a person collect the facts and verify information; it also requires that he or she present this information in a clear and interesting style, to promote sales of the paper. Journalistic standards may run counter to commercial considerations, creating role strain.

Role conflict occurs when the different positions an individual occupies make incompatible demands. An employed mother is the classic example. In meeting the requirements of a full-time job, she automatically violates the expectation that a mother will put her children's needs before everything else. In meeting the cultural demands of motherhood (staying home if the child is sick, attending school plays) she automatically violates the expectation that she will be in her office, and give her full attention to her job, during business hours.

A single social status gives rise not to one but to an array of different roles. A professor, for example, plays the role of lecturer with students, supervisor with research and teaching assistants, colleague with other faculty members, employee with university administrators, boss with departmental secretaries, and other roles in addition. The term ***role set***

Figure 5-2   *A College Student's Role Set*

This diagram shows, in simplified form, the role set of a college student, "Joe College," who works at the campus bookstore and is captain of the basketball team. Joe's role in relation to these other social actors is in brackets.

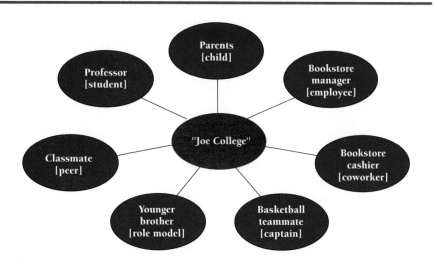

refers to the cluster of different social relationships in which a person becomes involved because she or he occupies a particular social status (Merton, 1968).

A hypothetical student's role set is shown in Figure 5-2. But social reality is far more complex than the diagram shows. "Joe College" probably has four or five professors in a given semester, ten to twelve teammates, as many coworkers, dozens of classmates, old high school friends, dorm mates, aunts, uncles, cousins, and more.

Social Relationships

Statuses and roles lay the foundations for social relationships. Before entering into a relationship, however brief, we assess the other person's status in relation to ours; this, in turn, provides us with information about role expectations and what kind of relationship might develop.

Relationships take many different forms. Some are multifaceted (for example, two people who live in the same neighborhood, work for the same company, and have many of the same friends). Others are single-purpose (coworkers who never get together outside work; dog owners who meet almost every day, share anecdotes and advice about their pets, but don't even know one another's names).

In our society, we distinguish among friends, lovers, and acquaintances. Friendships are warm, enduring relationships that link us to groups (male buddies, "girlfriends," or couples who make up a "crowd"), stages in our life (high school friends we keep in touch with over the years), or interests (someone who shares our passion for jazz or the opera). Friendship is voluntary: friends talk about intimate matters, call on each other in times of need or celebration, but remain independent. Romance is more intense, private, and exclusive; for as long as the relationship continues, lovers are "bound" to one another as to no one else. Acquaintances are people we know, greet, and recognize as being like us in certain ways. Acquaintances maintain a certain distance: ordinarily they do not discuss intimate topics. The relationship is largely coincidental: people who work for the same company, live in the same neighborhood, have a friend or interest in common. These relationships are not fixed: an acquaintance may become a friend or a lover; friendships wax and wane; romance may lead to marriage or to a breakup.

In every social interaction, every situation in which one participant's behavior influences another's behavior, individuals define, negotiate, and redefine their relationship. (We examine social interaction in detail in Chapter 6.) Some relationships involve direct face-to-face interaction; others are indirect. Students and the dean of their university are involved in a relationship, even though they may never meet. The dean sets policies that affect students' everyday lives and college careers; if students refuse to abide by these policies or protest violently against them, the dean's job will be in jeopardy. Their relationship is mediated by third parties, such as resident advisers in dormitories who are responsible for enforcing the dean's policies among students and communicating student grievances to the dean.

Groups

Groups are the next level of social structure. We will discuss this topic in more detail in Chapter 6, where we talk about leadership and behavior in groups. Here we want to introduce the basics. Seven people sitting in a doctor's office are *not* a group; they just happen to be in the same place at the same time. Each has a relationship with the doctor, but they have no connection with one another. They may also share certain social characteristics. If the doctor is a gynecologist, for example, almost all will be women (though some may be accompanied by their male partners). Women are members of a social category, but this does not make them a group. When a new patient arrives, the others may look up and smile, but then they return to the magazine they're thumbing through to pass the time. To stare at another patient or to initiate more than casual conversation would be a violation of privacy. Two women who are in the same stage of pregnancy and have met in the office before may greet each other and exchange experiences and information; but unless they discover some other connection, their acquaintanceship will be limited to the doctor's office.

The people who work in the doctor's office *are* a social group. They see each other frequently; working together gives them a common purpose, common goals, and a shared sense of identity; and their interactions are structured by their different positions and roles, as physician, radiology technician, nurse, office manager, receptionist, and so on. In public, they put on a united front of polite efficiency, though in private they may joke about patients or disagree about office procedures. The physician is the final authority on medical questions. But he or she may exercise tight control over the office and staff, or leave the role of "boss," and decisions about hiring and firing, schedules and responsibilities, to a manager. The receptionist may be the office "cheerleader," chatting with patients, listening to the nurse's, radiologist's, and physician's complaints about one another, and smoothing things out. These unofficial roles are as important to

the group's functioning as a team as their formal positions in the medical office hierarchy.

Groups come in many shapes and sizes, as described in Chapter 6. Each of us belongs to a number of groups over the course of our lives. Group membership adds another dimension to our social identities or addresses. Being a member of a family, college team, choir, country club, or neighborhood association strengthens our connections to society as a whole.

Formal Organizations

When a group grows beyond a certain size, or when a goal requires the coordinated skills and efforts of a number of people, a formal organization is likely to emerge. A *formal organization* is a group designed and created to pursue specific goals, and held together by explicit rules and regulations. Formal organizations differ from small groups in their scale, structure, and emphasis on getting things done, or goal orientation. They tend to be larger, more complex, and more enduring than informal social groups (Aldrich and Marsden, 1988; Scott, 1987). Once firmly established, organizations seem to assume a life of their own. The personnel may change, but the organization remains intact.

How Organizations Develop

The emergence of basketball as one of America's top professional sports illustrates both the importance and the impact of formal organization. Basketball might have remained a form of exercise and recreation (like hiking) and not become a competitive sport, were it not for the YMCA (an organization), which published Naismith's original rules in its newsletter. Graduates of Springfield College (another organization) also helped popularize basketball, introducing the new game to the colleges where they taught physical education and to the armed forces (Bjarkman, 1996).

Local Leagues   In 1901, seven schools in New England formed an Intercollegiate Basketball League; gradually other schools followed their lead. The formation of college leagues and regional conferences brought standard rules and equipment and scheduled tournaments to basketball, raised the level of competition by setting the stage for team rivalries, and, equally important, created a training ground for officials (Patterson and Deutsch, 1996).

Going National   Another level of organization was required to make college basketball a national sport. In the 1920s and early 1930s, basketball was played in small gymnasiums with limited seating capacity, although games attracted overflow crowds. Recognizing the game's spectator potential, in the mid-1930s the Metropolitan Basketball Writer's Association staged a series of double-headers between local college teams at New York City's new showcase, Madison Square Garden. These events attracted such large crowds that the sponsors decided to organize a National Invitational Tournament (the NIT) for college teams from around the country (selected by sportswriters). Not to be outdone, the National Association of Basketball Coaches convinced the NCAA to stage a championship tournament at the end of the 1938–1939 college season. Thus coalitions of reporters and coaches, college administrators and auditorium owners created a superstructure to link the nation's more than 300 college and university basketball teams. National tournaments, with seasonal championship teams, elevated basketball from a winter diversion to a major sport. "March Madness"—the month the annual NCAA men's and women's tournaments are played—has become one of the most popular sports events, not only in the United States but also abroad. The Final Four games attract as many TV viewers as the Superbowl or the World Series (Decourcy, 1996).

Professionalization   In basketball's first fifty years, a number of professional leagues were created, but none was successful enough to do more than pay its way. Although games drew fair-sized audiences, pro basketball remained in the shadow of college ball. Then, in the mid-1950s, a series of scandals (players taking bribes from gamblers to lose games or reduce the point spread) hit college basketball, weakening its appeal. The NBA, a relatively low-profile, low-profit league formed in the late 1940s, saw an opportunity. NBA management calculated that to compete with other professional sports, it would have to make the game more exciting. In 1954, the NBA instituted a new rule to speed up play: the twenty-four-second shot clock put an end to end stalling or "the freeze"[2] and pro-

moted the fast break. Attendance at NBA games grew steadily.

The short-lived, rival American Basketball Association (ABA, 1967–1976), with its signature red, white, and blue ball, added style to speed. The ABA recruited players who had not been drafted into the NBA, including some who decided to turn pro before graduating from college or, in a few cases, right out of high school (so called "hardship cases"). The ABA also encouraged the razzle-dazzle style of "street basketball," with its emphasis on one-on-one shoot-outs and three-on-three contests, urban cool, and "in-your-face" play, a style the NCAA and NBA had spurned. Although ABA games were not widely televised, players like Julius "Dr. J" Erving and Earl "The Pearl" Monroe earned word-of-mouth reputations as the most exciting players in basketball. Not a commercial success, the ABA was forced to agree to a merger; its stars took their slam dunks and "shake-and-bake" moves with them into the NBA. College basketball had also undergone a revival, producing a series of sensational players like forward Larry Bird and guard Earvin "Magic" Johnson. The result was the fast-paced, airborne, improvisational game played in the NBA today.

Commercialization   Finally, perhaps most significantly, the NBA courted TV coverage (Decourcy, 1996). In many ways, basketball is "made for TV." Unlike baseball and football fields, a basketball court fits neatly into a 25-inch diagonal screen; none of the action is hidden. Basketball superstars are easier to identify—and idolize. Football players, hidden by helmets and shoulder pads, disappear into piles of colliding players. Baseball players appear in the batter's box only four or five times a game. Basketball players are in full view, hurtling from one end of the court to the other, for most of the game. Their skills, as well as their height, make them "larger-than-life" heroes. In baseball and football, the action is stop and start, with long periods of waiting. In basketball, the action is nonstop, with teams regularly scoring more than a point a minute. Positions in baseball and football are highly specialized: pitchers are not expected to be good batters and never play in the outfield; in football different squads play offense and defense. Basketball players must do it all, whatever position they play. The fast pace, continuous action, "swirling controlled violence," and breath-taking airborne athleticism of basketball could be a formula

---

[2]The tactic of passing the ball around a wide circle to maintain possession, and hold onto a lead, without scoring.

The development of pro basketball. (a) In 1942, the Oshkosh Wisconsin Stars won the national pro basketball championship. (b) In the 1970s, ABA players like Julius Erving were the most exciting players in basketball. (c) In the late 1990s, fans flock to WNBA games.

for MTV (Bjarkman, 1996, p. ix). When CBS-TV began broadcasting NBA finals live (rather than as late-night, tape-delayed broadcasts), pro basketball came into its prime.

The WNBA, with its official slogan, "We Got Next," is part of the NBA/CBS complex (*Sports Illustrated,* June 30, 1997). Although women athletes had gained prominence in other sports (especially tennis and track and field) in the 1980s and early 1990s, women's basketball attracted only local interest. The 1996 Olympics (a global organization) brought the best women players together for the first time. The NBA and Nike sponsored a year of training and practice plus a pre-Olympic tour for a women's "dream team," which went on to win the Gold Medal in Atlanta. By chance, the same year the Lady Huskies of the University of Connecticut won their second NCAA women's finals, after two unbeaten seasons, picking up regular coverage on the ESPN all-sports channel and local newspapers. Building on this momentum, the NBA lined up TV contracts and commitments from corporate sponsors. Together they spent almost $15 million on promotion, transforming a minor-league women's game into a media attraction. Without the NBA—a sports/entertainment/ product-promotion conglomerate—the WNBA's future would be more uncertain. One question is whether the "adoption" of women's basketball by huge organizations (the NBA and CBS) will change the nature of the game, eliminating some of the "spirit of sisterhood" its original fans so admire.

In short, the growth of basketball was both a cause and an effect of increasingly formal organization. If basketball had remained a pastime between the baseball and football seasons or had not attracted spectators, formal organization would not have been necessary. At the same time, formal organization changed the way the game is played. This is a common social phenomenon. Medicine provides another familiar example. In the early twentieth century, the family doctor was one of the most prominent people in his (or less often her) community. A one-person operation, he treated patients in his office or made home visits, had to know something about every aspect of medicine, and charged modest fees. Advances in medical technology required increasing specialization, which in turn required more formal organization. Today, to perform specialized tests and treatments, physicians have to

be affiliated with hospitals, laboratories, and hi-tech clinics. To pay for costly treatment, patients must rely on private insurance companies or government assistance. The American Medical Association (AMA) grew in tandem with modern medicine, protecting the physician's central role in health care. However, with the emergence of health maintenance organizations (HMOs)—organizations that provide total medical care to subscribers for a fixed annual fee—this may be changing. The "private physician" is being replaced by both nonprofit and for-profit corporations. The trend toward increasingly formal organizations affects all areas of social life. The result is what George Ritzer (1998) called the "McDonaldization of society," in which standardization and efficiency override other considerations, and opportunities for human decisions and creativity are reduced to a minimum.

The Structure of Organizations

Whatever the purpose of an organization— providing services, producing goods, or promoting a cause—all large-scale organizations share certain characteristics. These include formal structure, participants, goals, and technology (see Figure 5-3).

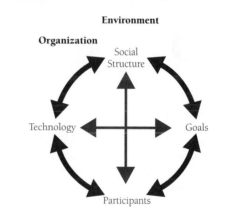

Figure 5-3   *The Elements of Organizations*

Whatever the purpose of an organization, all formal organizations have certain elements in common.

Source: Adapted from Harold J. Leavitt, "Applied Organizational Change in Industry: Structural, Technological, and Humanistic Approaches," in J. G. March (Ed), *Handbook of Organizations,* Chicago: Rand McNally, 1965; as it appeared in W. R. Scott, *Organizations: Rational, Natural, and Open Systems,* 2nd ed., Englewood Cliffs, NJ: Prentice-Hall, 1987. Reprinted by permission of James G. March.

Formal Structure   Relationships among the members of a large-scale organization ideally follow regular, predictable patterns. There are norms governing the means by which short- and long-term goals ought to be pursued and expectations concerning the way people who occupy different positions in the organization ought to act. Often, regulations and responsibilities are printed, as in the *NBA Rule Book.*

Participants   Most formal organizations can count on only partial involvement of their members. This is because most of us are members of an array of groups and organizations. A single person may be a dean at a university, a member of a church or synagogue, a volunteer at a shelter for the homeless, a member of an amateur tennis team, as well as a client of an HMO, a customer at numerous stores, a member of a political party, a citizen of a state, and so on. The individual's level of commitment to these different organizations will vary. To some degree, all formal organizations must compete for participants' time and loyalty.

Goals   Formal organizations are established to meet more or less clearly defined objectives. Goal orientation is part of the standard definition of formal organizations. To pursue their goals, organizations compete with one another for supplies and markets, participation and loyalty. Employees may go on strike, demanding more flexible hours; consumers may look for a different type of product; the government may impose new restrictions. To survive, organizations have to adjust their goals to changing conditions.

Technology   Whatever their goals, and however these may change, formal organizations exist to "get something done." Technology, conceived of broadly here, describes whatever means an organization uses to pursue its goals. Some organizations transform raw materials into hardware and equipment; they may do this by hand or by machine, with people or with robots. Other organizations "process" people—for example, transforming uninformed children into knowledgeable citizens (schools) or helping sick or injured people become healthy (hospitals or clinics). This processing may be highly impersonal or personal. Whether products are handmade or machine-produced and whether servicing is standardized or personalized, the technol-

ogy an organization employs affects its members, goals, and structure. For example, a retail company that decides to computerize its inventory records and billing system must either retrain its clerical staff or hire new staff and rearrange its office. Once it has taken these steps, it may decide to enter the mail-order business—a new goal.

Environment   No organization is totally self-sufficient; all are part of a larger community, whether local, national, or global. Organizations depend on their environment for resources. For instance, a McDonald's franchise recruits employees (participants); appoints managers and assistants (structure); installs soda dispensers, fry machines, and calculators (technology); and locates itself in a busy area that will attract customers (goal). At the same time, organizations affect the environment of which they are a part. For example, when Wal-Mart, the huge discount warehouse chain, opens a store in a community, local stores and small businesses often suffer. That is why several New England towns have fought the location of Wal-Marts in their area. As a result of competition from Wal-Mart, Kmart, and other mass-market discount chains, Woolworth's—the country's original "5 & 10"—went out of business in 1997.

Bureaucracy

The word "bureaucracy" comes from the French *bureau,* which means "office," and the Greek suffix *-ocracy,* which means "rule by." Sociologists define **bureaucracy** as a hierarchical organization that is governed by formal rules and regulations.

The word "bureaucrat" is often used as an insult. Most of us associate bureaucracies with inefficiency, red tape, frustration, and waste. When we are billed by computer for something we didn't buy, spend hours waiting in line for a driver's license, or waste a weekend trying to figure out how to fill out an income tax form, we blame bureaucracy. But consider the alternatives.

You take on the job of collecting dues for a club to which you belong (Blau and Meyer, 1987). If your club is small (fifty members) and you know everyone, including those least likely to pay, you won't have a problem. But suppose your club has 500 members. It would be too time-consuming for one person to contact all the other members, and so five people are assigned the job. Unless these five dues collectors get organized (hold a meeting, divide up the membership list, keep records, and so on), they may separately and repeatedly ask some people for dues and never ask others. Multiply the numbers by several hundred or thousand, and the need for organization becomes even clearer.

Weber's Model   Sociologist Max Weber was among the first to recognize the importance of bureaucracy to the large organizations of modern society. He asserted that "for the needs of mass administration today, [bureaucracy] is completely indispensable" (1922/1968). Weber intended his model of bureaucracy as an ***ideal type.*** That is, it was meant to capture the essential characteristics of bureaucratic organization, not to describe how any particular bureaucracy was organized or how one ought to be organized. According to Weber, there are six key features of a bureaucracy (based on Weber, 1922/1968; Blau and Scott, 1962; Blau and Meyer, 1987):

1. Bureaucracy is based on a clear-cut *division of labor.* Each position in the organization is tied to a particular task. The division of labor permits a high degree of specialization and encourages the development of expertise.

2. Positions in a bureaucracy are ranked one above the other, in a *hierarchy.* Officials are responsible to their superiors for the activities of their subordinates. This ensures that decisions made at the top are passed down the chain of command and that someone can be held responsible for mistakes. While each official has authority over the people who work under him or her, this authority is clearly defined and limited to the business at hand.

3. Formal *written rules and regulations* govern all activities in a bureaucracy, specifying the procedures to be followed and thus giving bureaucracies stability: the organization can continue to function despite changes in personnel.

4. Bureaucrats tend to be *impersonal* in their official dealings with others. They treat clients as cases and subordinates as more or less replaceable parts of the bureaucratic machine. Rational judgments take precedence over personal considerations. Ideally, each individual receives fair and impartial treatment.

5. The individual's position in a bureaucracy is based on *technical qualifications,* not on personal or family "connections." Both *performance* and *seniority* determine advancement within a bureaucracy. Ideally, this system ensures that the organization

hires a competent staff and that staff members have job security.

6. Finally, bureaucracies draw a *clear line between the public and official sphere and the private sphere.* Authority is vested in the position or office, not in a particular person, and the officeholder's authority is clearly defined and limited. Official statements are distinguished from personal opinions; the organization's funds and equipment are separate from the individual's money and possessions; the office is separate from the home.

Weber saw bureaucracy as a powerful organizational tool for achieving efficiency. Figure 5-4 shows the organization of the U.S. Department of Defense, one of the largest bureaucracies in the world. Under the direction of the president as commander in chief, the secretary of defense is in charge of separate military departments of the Army, Navy, and Air Force; the joint chiefs of staff; separate security, defense, and intelligence agencies; and a variety of defense agencies created for special purposes. Each of these agencies and departments is a bureaucracy within a bureaucracy. Altogether, the Department of Defense is staffed by 3.6 million people, including 1.1 million troops on active duty, 1.7 million reserve troops, and 800,000 civilians. Its main headquarters, the Pentagon, is the largest office building in the world.

One of the tasks of the Department of Defense is to coordinate the movement of troops into combat. This is a complex operation, one that requires planning down to the last detail. Consider, for example, the logistics involved in the war in the Persian Gulf. Thousands of combat-ready soldiers had to be moved into the area as quickly as possible. These soldiers had to be supplied simultaneously with food, water, tents, weapons, appropriate camouflage uniforms, vehicles and aircraft repainted to blend with the desert, and even seemingly trivial items like sunscreen. The department had to purchase, transport, and distribute all these items expeditiously. At the same time, on the strategic level, the joint chiefs and the secretary of defense had to negotiate and coordinate all military plans with the other nations participating in this United Nations–sponsored action.

It is impossible to conceive how the Department of Defense could function in such instances without a hierarchy of authority, a complex division of labor, technical training, clear procedures for work,

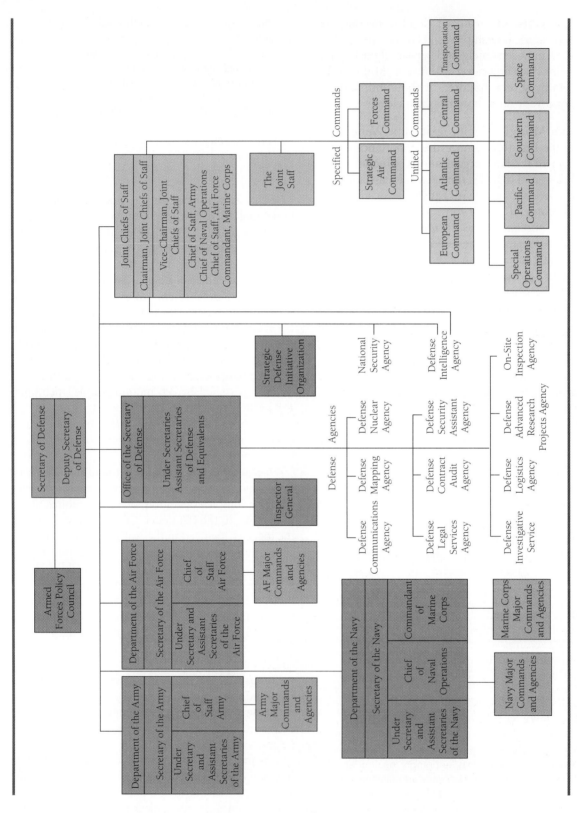

Figure 5-4 *U.S. Department of Defense*

The U.S. Department of Defense (diagrammed above), one of the largest bureaucracies in the world, is staffed by 3.6 million people, organized into a rigid chain of command. Its headquarters, the Pentagon, is the world's largest office building.

Source: The United States Government Manual 1988/89, Office of the Federal Register National Archives and Records Administration.

accepted rules of behavior, and a hierarchy of rewards—in other words, a bureaucratic structure.

Formal versus Informal Structure   Weber held that the key to bureaucracy is a set of formal rules and regulations defining each position in the chain of authority, spelling out the correct procedures for getting things done, and identifying rewards and punishments for conformity and nonconformity. Ideally, bureaucratic organization promotes efficiency through impartiality.

Do actual organizations conform to Weber's model? Yes and no. Bureaucratic organizations have both a formal and an informal structure (roughly equivalent to "ideal" and "real" culture; see Chapter 3). The *formal structure* consists of official rules and regulations, explicit job descriptions, an organizational chart that describes the job hierarchy (who reports to whom), and promotion and pay scales. The *informal structure,* in contrast, lies outside it and consists of unofficial norms that both workers and management devise to cope with situations not anticipated in the official rules, to protect their own positions, and to avoid unpleasant work. The informal structure involves personal relationships, deals and agreements made "off the record," and so on. The informal structure often is an "open secret," a system most people use without acknowledging so in public.

In some cases, the informal structure may undermine organizational goals. For example, a group of factory workers may establish their own limits on productivity and enforce these limits by isolating or harassing individuals who work too slow or too fast, while rewarding those who play by the group's rules by teaching them strategies for avoiding work (how to look busy when they aren't, when it is safe to leave a machine untended, and so on). In this way, workers establish some control over their own work (Roy, 1952). Likewise, the informal structure of a high school student "counterculture" may undermine formal educational goals.

In other cases, however, the informal structure of an organization improves and enhances performance. Middle managers view knowing how to get things done informally as one of their chief assets. To achieve their assigned goals and meet quotas, managers often bend the rules or work around the official chain of command, exchanging favors with other managers (Dalton, 1959). Employees who play along and put getting a job done ahead of following the rules may be rewarded with raises. Managers who meet or exceed their quotas may be rewarded with promotions and bonuses. If something goes wrong, however, someone will be held responsible for breaking the rules. The manager's dilemma is whether to follow the letter or the spirit of company policy.

According to our cultural ideals, corporations and other bureaucracies are meritocracies, in which promotions are based on performance. In reality, above a certain level, a manager's fate depends as

A manager's success often depends on the image she or he projects, on how well she—or, more likely, he—fits in with the group.

much on relationships with superiors and on the image he or she projects as on personal accomplishments (Jackall, 1988). Most large corporations give employees regular, formal evaluations; many assign them a numerical grade or rank on the basis of their achievement and skills. But when decisions about promotions are actually made, they are based on the gut feeling that a manager is "our kind of person" or "one of the gang" (which is one reason why female or minority managers may be passed over).

Corporate executives are often held responsible for events over which they have no control (such as shifts in the economy that cause their departments or units to flounder). When things go badly, the most common response is to replace someone in top management. Typically, the new CEO's first act is to replace the heads of the divisions with his or her own people. Division heads bring in their people, and so on down the line. Major upheavals have become a regular feature of corporate life and may occur even when things are going well. To get ahead, managers must hitch themselves to a star, but stars can fall.

The informal structure of an organization is not necessarily inefficient or corrupt; it supplements the formal and provides a laboratory for change. "Temporary" functions and "makeshift" procedures may later be formally recognized. To some degree, the informal structure allows power struggles to be settled behind the scene, so that no one suffers public humiliation. Contemporary business analysts speak of corporations and other organizations as having their own "culture," which embodies the informal structure, the corporation's characteristic work style, and key moments in its history (Deal and Kennedy, 1982; Ott, 1989).

The Dysfunctions of Bureaucracy Everyone has a favorite example of bureaucracy gone haywire—for example, the Pentagon purchasing $600 toilet seats and $400 hammers. Sociologists are interested not in individual cases of fraud or abuse but in the types of problems that seem to be built into bureaucracy (Merton, 1968).

First, bureaucracies depend on *routinization*. They are efficient because they establish rules and regulations that apply to a wide range of cases. But rules that make sense in one context may be complete nonsense in another. Bureaucracies are ill-equipped to deal with unusual situations or individual problems.

Second, bureaucracies tend to promote what Thorstein Veblen (1922) called *trained incapacity*—

the inability to perceive or respond to change. Bureaucrats are trained to abide by the regulations. In a sense, they are trained to wear blinders. But in blindly following the rules, a bureaucrat may undermine the goals of the organization. As a result, bureaucrats tend to become "ritualistic" (Merton, 1968): they go through the motions of filling out forms, obtaining the required documents and signatures, and the like without concerning themselves about whether this will solve—or exacerbate—the problem. Abiding by the regulations becomes an end in itself.

A third problem is *depersonalization*. Bureaucrats are supposed to be impartial, dealing with everyone's problems in a uniform way. Yet in many cases the decisions they make (for example, whether to grant welfare or disability benefits) have a direct, personal impact on individuals. Workers may be treated like robots—the "McDonaldization" effect (Ritzer, 1998). At McDonald's and other mass producers, an operations manual provides exact instructions for every activity and workers are strictly controlled via technology: the soft drink machine shuts off automatically, a bell rings when the french fries are done, and the cash register is preprogrammed. The chances for human error—or human originality—are reduced to a minimum.

A fourth problem is *vested interests*. Weber's friend and colleague Robert Michels (1915/1962) argued that large organizations tend to concentrate power in the hands of a few. According to his **iron law of oligarchy,** even the most democratic, idealistic organizations inevitably become oligarchies, dominated by a small, self-serving elite. (The term "oligarchy" comes from the Greek for "rule by a few.") Drawing on his study of the labor movement in Germany, Michels reasoned that in large organizations it may be physically impossible to get the rank and file together every time a decision needs to be made. Moreover, most members lack the knowledge or the interest to deal with complex issues. This is why responsibility is delegated to elected leaders. Once in office, leaders have both the means and the incentive to take control. They have access to data, can manipulate communications, and have political skills that others lack (which is why they were elected). They may also manage organizational funds. As they come to appreciate the power and prestige that go with the office, they begin to concentrate on maintaining their elite position rather than furthering the organization's cause. They may suppress internal opposition in the name of presenting a united front, and come to see themselves as indispensable. Michels blamed this sequence of events not on individual character flaws but on the nature of formal organizations.

A fifth problem is a built-in tendency toward *excessive growth* in bureaucracies. Some years ago C. Northcote Parkinson (1957) noted that in the years following World War I, the numbers of ships and sailors in the British navy declined but the administrative staff continued to grow. Why? Parkinson reasoned that lower-level bureaucrats, who typically depend on the organization for their livelihood, have a vested interest in promoting the organization and the units they supervise or manage. One way in which bureaucrats protect their positions is by looking busy. If they succeed in creating new work for themselves, they may be rewarded with assistants. Supervising assistants adds work to their original tasks, and filing reports to the supervisor increases the assistants' load. In time, they too may need assistants. And so bureaucracies grow, without any increase in productivity. According to *Parkinson's law,* "work expands to fill the time and staff available." Parkinson was only half-jesting when he proposed this law.

Formal organizations are both a distinctive type of social structure and a part of larger social structures. Hence they reflect the society and culture in which they are rooted (see *A Global View: The Japanese Corporation*).

The Structure of Society

In everyday life, most of our experiences involve statuses and roles, social relationships, small groups, and formal organizations. These familiar elements of social life depend on social institutions and the system of social stratification that transforms a population into a society.

Social Institutions

By far the most important structural element of human societies is social institutions. **Social institutions** are stable and enduring sets of norms and values, statuses and roles, and groups and organizations that provide a structure for behavior in a particular area of social life. They are time-honored, widely accepted social arrangements that people regard as vital to their well-being. All large-

scale societies have five major social institutions: the family, education, religion, politics, and economics. Although these institutions serve the same basic needs in every society, there is much cross-cultural variation in how families are structured, what values and behavior education promotes, how religion is linked to other institutions, and so on.

Sociologists (especially those who use the functionalist perspective) view institutions as crucial in meeting society's needs. The *family* is responsible for raising and caring for children, and thus replacing members of society who have died or moved away (see Chapter 11). *Education* ensures that cultural norms and values are passed from one generation to the next and that young people acquire the knowledge and skills to perform adult roles (Chapter 12). *Religion* reinforces shared values, thus giving meaning and purpose to life (Chapter 13). *Political institutions* maintain social order, protecting members of society from invasions from without, controlling crime and disorder within, and providing channels for resolving conflicts of interest (Chapter 14). *Economic institutions* organize the production and distribution of goods and services (Chapter 15). Science, the arts, health care, the legal system, the military, and leisure-time pursuits have also been institutionalized in modern societies.

Although each of the major institutions deals with a different aspect of life, they are interrelated; all are parts of an integrated whole. For example, to get married and start a family in the United States, a couple must obtain a license from the state (one link between the family and politics). Americans have the option of getting married in a religious ceremony at a church or synagogue or in a civil ceremony performed by a judge or justice of the peace at City Hall or anywhere else. In countries that have an official religion (unlike our separation of church and state), such as Germany, marriages are considered legal only if they take place in a church. In traditional societies, the family is a single economic unit: family members (including children) work together as a team; whatever individuals produce or earn belongs to the "family pot." In western societies, the family's role in the economy is greatly reduced. Children are not expected to be productive members of their households; as adults, they are not expected to work with or for their families. Our economic institutions favor individual enterprise. But the family still plays a role

The Japanese Corporation

One key difference between American and Japanese corporations is the practice of lifetime employment. When Japanese workers are hired by a large company or government agency, they are generally hired for life. New positions are filled from within; dismissals are a matter of last resort, only after cuts in managers' pay and in dividends have been made. The advantages of this system for the company are employee loyalty, highly trained workers, and the benefit of the accumulation of experience (Dore, 1992). Lifetime employment and lifetime commitment to a company also allow decision makers the luxury of long-term planning. They know they can't be fired for bad short-term results. American companies often suffer from decisions made to earn short-term gains at the expense of long-term goals and strategies. ("Lifetime employment" may be something of a misnomer, however. "Midlife employment" might be a more accurate term:

all except the very top executives are forced to retire at age 55. They receive a generous severance pay but no pension or social security. Moreover, some Japanese corporations are taking a second look at lifetime employment as they experience economic downturns.)

A second key difference in the Japanese corporation is an emphasis on collective performance, not individual achieve-

> **The common denominator is a weakened worldwide economy.**

ment. This approach reflects Japanese culture, which values group loyalty, conformity, cooperativeness, and belongingness as highly as American culture values individualism and independence (Takayanagi, 1985; Zandu, 1983). Members of an age group tend to move up the corporate ladder together, with minimal salary differences. In many firms, all employees from

the managing director down wear a company uniform. A president's salary is rarely more than ten times that of the average employee (compared with hundreds of times in most American firms) (Dore, 1992). Workers tend to be organized into teams of eight to ten for various tasks and evaluated on the basis of team, not individual, performance. Workers at every level are also given a role in designing their own jobs.

In American companies, responsibilities are clearly defined; a division manager knows that the "buck stops here." In Japanese companies, decision making is collective. Typically, two or three younger employees will consult with those to be affected by a decision, draft a proposal, submit it for consideration, and redraft it until a consensus is reached. A decision that might require one phone call to a division manager in an American company may take two or three weeks in a Japanese company. Once a decision is reached,

in the distribution of wealth through inheritance laws that ensure that some property (houses, investments) stays within the family.

The different institutions in a society also tend to uphold similar norms and values. Americans place a premium on individual freedom and achievement, values that are reflected in our political institutions (democracy and the Bill of Rights), our economic institutions (capitalism and the accumulation of personal wealth), our religious institutions (religious freedom and the separation of church and

state), our educational institutions (equal opportunity and personal performance), and our family institutions (the independent nuclear family and family privacy).

Because social institutions are interconnected, change in one usually leads to change in others. For example, the growth of higher education has contributed to the trend toward smaller families in two ways. First, it has encouraged men and women who want to complete college and perhaps attend graduate school to postpone getting married and however, everyone is committed to the plan.

The third major difference between Japanese and American companies is the former's holistic concern for employees (Pascale and Athos, 1982). The firm is defined as a community of people rather than just the property of shareholders (Dore, 1992). Japanese firms take responsibility for their employees' general welfare. They provide recreational facilities, vacations, parties, and family services. American firms operate on the principle that the connection between the company and employees is limited to activities directly connected to business.

Many doubt that Japanese strategies would work well in western societies, which emphasize individualism and mobility, even though the Japanese system was based in part on theories of "humanistic management" developed by Rensis Likert, Douglas McGregor, and other American social scientists. However, there are signs today that Japanese firms are learning from the American system at the same time that American firms are adopting some conventions of the Japanese organization. The common denominator is that both must cope with a weakened worldwide economy. Mass layoffs are still taboo in Japan, and so less drastic solutions are being tried, such as voluntary early retirement (offered to some as young as 35), pay based on merit rather than on seniority, fewer meetings, fewer levels of management, transfer of employees to other plants, "loaning" workers to other firms, cutting back on recruitment, and retraining surplus workers.

Meanwhile, American firms are looking at ways to "empower" their employees to enhance efficiency and competitiveness in the world market. In July 1993, the Clinton administration sponsored a Conference on the Future of the American Workplace. Some of the possibilities considered at the conference were getting workers to participate in skills training, to work closely with management in setting pay levels and production goals, to take a part in hiring coworkers, to carry out quality control, to reorganize assembly lines, to share in company profits, to earn bonuses based on production, and so on. It was hoped that the "cooperative workplace" would help slow the need for layoffs or at least make the process more just.

As Ronald Dore puts it,

> There are grounds . . . for arguing that, incrementally, the U.S. system is edging toward the Japanese more than vice versa. I would put my money on the probability that those trends will continue. (1992, p. 25)

having children until their mid- or late twenties. Second, it has raised the cost of rearing children (college students may be financially dependent on their families until age 21 or 22); the more children a couple have, the less they are able to invest in each child. Studies of developing countries show that women's education is inversely linked to family size: that is, the more education a women has, the fewer children she is likely to have.

Institutions are so firmly rooted in custom and tradition that people rarely consider alternative social arrangements. No American politician who hoped to remain in office would dare to propose that religion be outlawed, that all babies be raised in communal nurseries by professional caretakers, or that banks and major industries be taken over by the government. (All these arrangements have been tried in other societies.) Politicians nearly always support traditional institutional forms (as in the debates over "family values" in the 1992 and 1996 presidential elections). We regard freedom of religion, the family, education, free enterprise, and

Social institutions such as religion create deep convictions about what is vitally important to our well-being. These Saudi women would never consider appearing in public without wearing their abbayas *(or coverings). At a private family gathering such as a wedding, however, their religion permits them to dress more fashionably.*

democracy as sacred; challenges to these institutions meet with passionate resistance. Institutions can also function to maintain continuity through periods of social change, establishing links between the past, present, and future. For example, Americans no longer take lifelong marriage for granted. The United States presently has one of the highest divorce rates in the world: about one in two marriages ends in divorce. Furthermore, many people are choosing to remain single, to live with someone without getting married, to get married but not have children, or to raise children by themselves as single parents. One might conclude that the family is a dying institution in the United States. But despite high divorce rates, nine out of ten Americans get married at least once in their lives, and most of those whose first marriage fails try again. One can no longer assume that a child's mother's husband is also the child's father. Yet families struggle to apply old kinship terms to new social arrangements. Children may refer to "my other Dad"; new spouses ask youngsters to think of them as a second father or mother. Behavior has changed, but the ideal of establishing a traditional family—the social institution—remains strong.

Social Stratification

An equally pervasive feature of human societies is structured inequality. No society, past or present, has allowed all members to benefit equally from so-cial arrangements. **Social stratification** refers to the division of a society into layers or social classes whose members have unequal access to wealth, power, and prestige. The degree of inequality, the manner in which rewards are distributed, and the extent to which individuals are able to influence their own fortunes all vary. In the smallest, simplest societies, people draw distinctions between males and females, young and old, and one kin group and another. Many societies have kept slaves, including the ancient Greeks, the inventors of democracy. As societies became larger and more complex, social stratification became more entrenched. The feudal societies of medieval Europe, for example, recognized three classes or "estates": the aristocracy, who held title to land and maintained private armies of knights to protect their position; the church and clergy, whose support gave legitimacy and authority to the monarch and his or her lords; and commoners, who had no significant property or rights but lived in semiservitude as vassals or serfs. In modern democracies, almost all citizens have the right to own land and other property; to exercise power through political parties and the vote; to enjoy equal treatment under the law; and to receive at least minimal life chances, via various state welfare programs. Nevertheless, huge inequalities in wealth, power, and prestige still exist.

Americans, in particular, pride themselves on being a free society in which people earn their positions in life, whether high or low. Yet only in the

All societies practice age stratification, but cultural ideas about different stages in the life cycle vary from one society to another. In China, old age confers prestige and respect. In the United States, by contrast, we view the elderly as past their prime.

last twenty-five years have African Americans, as well as other ethnic and racial minorities, and women won the right to equal opportunity in education, employment, political representation, and housing—and these rights are still being contested. Some Americans enjoy the best educations, the best medical care, the best legal representation, the most access to high-level politicians that money can buy—advantages that other Americans only dream about. Wealthy, white, male, Protestant professionals enjoy privileges that are not available to poor, nonwhite, female, Catholic, Jewish, or Muslim high school graduates or dropouts.

We will examine socioeconomic, racial and ethnic, and gender discrimination in detail in Chapters 8, 9, and 10. Here we want to look at a form of social stratification that is so ingrained in our social institutions that we rarely notice it: age stratification.

Age Stratification

All societies use age as a basis for assigning rights and privileges. An individual's position in the life cycle in part determines the roles that are available to him or her, and the rewards and punishments for conformity or nonconformity. For example, in our society murderers are not confined to prison or sentenced to death *if* they are small children; college students may be exempt from full tuition payments *if* they are age 65 or older; nude sunbathers may be arrested *if* they are over age 10. Age determines whether a person is allowed to drive a car, to vote

or serve on a jury, to run for president (one must be 35), or to get married. Children under age 16 are not allowed to work without a special permit; certain federal employees and airline pilots are required to retire at a specified age. Age stratification creates inequalities in wealth, power, and prestige. It also tends to promote segregation by age, conflict between generations, and role strain for people who are not ready to take on a new role, or relinquish an old one, at the age society deems appropriate.

In some respects, age stratification resembles stratification by sex, race, and ethnicity. Age grades are ascribed statuses over which the individual has no control. They are also master statuses that tend to override most other traits, such as individual talent and skill. But age-linked status is unique in one respect: it keeps changing. People are expected, and in some cases required, to change statuses at certain points in their lives. Still, individuals have no more control over their age than they do over their sex or skin color.

Aging in Historical Perspective   In most societies and times, the elderly have been revered. Young and middle-aged adults, as well as children, were expected to defer to their elders and to seek their advice and guidance. In traditional societies, counsels of elders made final decisions on matters affecting their village or clan. As a result, the oldest members of a society wielded considerable power. So it was through much of this country's history.

In colonial America, indeed through most of the nineteenth century, the United States was primarily an agrarian society. Older men maintained possession and control of the most important economic resource, land, usually until their deaths. As a result, children often were financially dependent on their parents through much of their adulthood. In the early days of the nation, people made most of the goods (tools, clothes, etc.) they needed for themselves, in their homes. Older people continued to produce goods and perform farmwork long after they reached age 65. Formal retirement was unknown. Moreover, the elderly were admired for their crafts expertise and respected as teachers of their trade. Of course, not all elderly people had land or large families to provide for them when their health began to fade. Some were forced to depend on charity or to enter the local almshouse. Even so, the image of the elderly was one of power and authority.

As the nation began to industrialize, the position of older people in society started to change. Many young people left farms for factory jobs and independent lives in the growing cities of the northeast. At the same time, manufactured, store-bought goods began to replace handmade products. Older workers' skills lost value in two ways: older people were no longer valued as teachers, for younger generations were entering occupations that hadn't existed before; and the demand for their crafts declined. In the small number of families that amassed fortunes, patriarchs and matriarchs exercised power over inheritance. But in most families, and hence society at large, the power and prestige of older people declined. Much the same pattern has been observed in other industrializing societies, from England to Japan.

Age Discrimination   The lowered status of elderly people is reflected in *ageism:* subtle (and not very subtle) forms of prejudice and discrimination against older people. We like to think of America as innovative, energetic, and forward-looking—qualities we associate with youth. We associate aging with physical, mental, and social decline. Children may look forward to growing up, but Americans in their thirties and forties generally do not look forward to growing older.

Consider age discrimination in employment. A majority of Americans retire, increasingly before age 65 (as noted in Chapter 4). But how many choose to retire and how many are pushed out of the labor force is not known. Of men age 55 and older who either quit their jobs, were laid off, or were fired, one-third go back to work, usually within a year. Two out of three of those who are reemployed work full-time (though not necessarily at the same-level job for the same level of pay), and one in three, part-time. But what about the other two-thirds?

Some of the obstacles facing middle-aged and older workers are structural. Changes in the global economy have created jobs at the top and bottom of the occupation and pay scale, but eliminated many jobs in the middle—jobs acquired through years of work for the same company and through seniority. To cut costs, it makes financial sense for a corporation to offer attractive early retirement bonuses to older employees who have accumulated pensions and other privileges and then to hire younger workers, who are not entitled to as many benefits. But perhaps the major obstacle facing middle-aged and older job applicants is prejudice or ageism. The federal Age Discrimination in Employment Act prohibits decisions to hire or fire, promote or demote, workers age 40 and over solely on the basis of age. But age discrimination is difficult to document—and to fight. Employers may assume that if a man hasn't established his worth in a company or career by age 55 there must be a reason and that employees age 60 to 65 and older are slower, more set in their ways, and less motivated than are new, young employees. In fact, studies show that older workers may be slower but more than compensate for this through greater accuracy, lower rates of absenteeism, and loyalty (Treas, 1995). Older workers are less likely to be offered, or to accept, another job with another company.

Age Inequality   Without question, older Americans in the U.S. today enjoy a higher standard of living than did any previous generation of elderly Americans (Treas, 1995). In 1959, more than one-third (35 percent) of Americans age 65 and older lived below the poverty line; today, less than 12 percent do. In contrast to their grandparents, today's elderly benefit from Social Security (since the 1960s, tied to the cost of living) and Medicare (virtually free government-backed health insurance for all Americans age 65 and older). In addition, many older Americans receive income from private pension plans; thanks to government programs, many were able to buy their own homes (which often could be sold for a substantial profit) and save for retirement. But not all older Americans are part of the new "leisure class" of happy, healthy, financially comfortable retirees (see Table 5-1).

When they stop working, most older Americans see their incomes drop by one-third to one-half (Treas, 1995). Freedom from work-related expenses compensates for some of this loss, but not all. Social Security benefits are pegged to previous earnings, which means that whites, who on average had higher incomes, receive more than Hispanics, who in turn receive more than African Americans. Likewise, women, who were less likely than men to work full-time throughout their adult lives (especially in the generations now age 65 and over), receive less than men. Married couples fare best under current programs, and individuals living alone (usually widows), worst. Although fewer older Americans qualify officially as poor, one in ten households headed by an elderly person and one in four older persons living apart from kin are "near poor" (with incomes slightly above the official poverty line). Moreover, once poor, older Americans are more likely to remain so.

Table 5-1 *Median Household Income by Age, Race, and Household Type*

Household Characteristics	Median Household Income, 1993
Age of householder	
Less than 64 years	$35,956
65–69 years	23,753
70–74 years	18,970
75+ years	14,328
Householders age 65 and older	
Race/ethnicity:	
White	18.471
African American	11,926
Latino/Latina	13,284
Household type:	
Married-couple family	26,197
Male-householder family	27,855
Female-householder family	22,522
Male householder living alone	13,896
Female householder living alone	9,980

Note: Latino/Latina may be of any race.

Source: U.S. Bureau of the Census, *Current Population Survey,* March 1994; J. Treas., "Older Americans in the 1990s and Beyond," *Population Bulletin* 56, May 1995, table 7.

Future Prospects Early in the twenty-first century, members of the huge baby boom generation—nearly one-third of the population—will begin entering their sixties. This simple demographic fact will lead to dramatic changes in social structure. Inevitably, the dependency ratio—the number of people too old or too young to work in relation to the number of working-age Americans—will increase. Social Security and Medicare are funded through the FICA tax on working people. Whether a smaller number of workers will be willing to pay higher taxes to maintain these programs at current levels is unknown. The higher cost of taxes, housing, and college tuition for children, combined with layoffs and cutbacks in private pension plans, has made saving for retirement increasingly difficult. Many baby boomers will enter their sixties in better health but with fewer personal resources than their parents had. Yet because of their numbers, this generation will exercise considerable political influence. Already, the American Association of Retired Persons (AARP) is one of the most powerful political organizations in the country.

Three other demographic factors will influence the futures of older Americans (Treas, 1995). The first is increasing racial and ethnic diversity, which will create a new mix of needs and perhaps a greater variety of services for the elderly. The second is changing family patterns: smaller family size, increased childlessness, and high divorce rates will leave today's middle-aged adults with fewer family resources to draw on as they age. The demand for formal as opposed to informal and paid as opposed to familial elder care will likely grow. The third is increasing longevity and the possibility that the average American will live longer, increasing not only the number and proportion of elderly Americans in the twenty-first century but also the costs of programs like Social Security and Medicare, as well as the kinds of programs and services older Americans will need in their final years. Adapting to an aging population is one of the major challenges facing our society (and others) in the twenty-first century.

Society

A **society** is an autonomous population whose members are subject to a common political authority, occupy a common territory, have a common culture, and have a sense of shared identity. A society is the largest group with which most people can identify, and it has more influence on individuals than any smaller group. Members of a society are mutually interdependent: they are held together by sustained patterns of direct and indirect interaction, they depend on society to maintain their culture and way of life, and they often act collectively to defend the territory they occupy from other societies. A society may or may not have formal organizations, including government bureaucracies. But society is more than a formal organization writ large.

No society is fixed or static. Indeed, maintaining traditions over long periods of time requires frequent adjustment to accommodate changes in the population and its social and natural environment. However, rapid social change is one of the defining characteristics of contemporary societies in an age of global communications. Throughout most of human history change was gradual, as the pace of life was slower and the contacts between societies were less frequent.

Relations among Societies

No society exists in total isolation. The earliest archaeological sites show evidence of wide-ranging intergroup contacts. But the nature of relations among societies has changed over time. Most societies today are nation-states or countries, like Mexico or France. But in some parts of the world there are still small, isolated societies that are more or less independent of the nation-states in which they are located.

We begin this section by tracing the evolution of human societies, pointing out how changes in technology and social structure have influenced both relationships among members of a society and relations between societies. With this background, we look at the pattern of relations among societies in the world today.

Evolutionary Trends

Along with other sociologists, Gerhard and Jean Lenski (Lenski, Lenski, and Nolan, 1991) view the history of society as a process of sociocultural evolution, from simpler to more complex forms. The Lenskis see technology as the driving force in sociocultural evolution. To simplify a bit, new technologies enable a society to support a larger population, and a larger population requires more complex so-

cial organization. This is not to say that the history of human societies followed a neat, linear, evolutionary path or that the smaller, more traditional societies in the world today are "living relics" of earlier stages in the evolution of societies. The emergence of new, more complex forms of social organization did not automatically mean that older, simpler forms were abandoned or destroyed. Moreover, the fact that a society is "bigger" does not necessarily mean that it is "better." Nor does more advanced technology always improve the quality of life. Evolution should not be equated with progress.

Four basic types of societies have emerged over the course of human history: hunter-gatherer bands, horticultural villages, agrarian states, and, most recently, industrial nations (see Figure 5-5). These societies differ in their level of technological development, their population size, and their institutional arrangements (Chagnon, 1968; M. Harris, 1977; Lee and DeVore, 1976; Lenski, Lenski, and Nolan, 1991).

Hunter-Gatherer Bands

For 99 percent of human history, our ancestors were hunters and gatherers who neither produced nor preserved food. They lived in nomadic bands of

Until recently the !Kung San of the Kalahari Desert (Number 1 on Map 5-1) were nomadic hunter-gatherers, living as all humans lived for millions of years. However, encroachment by outsiders, dwindling populations of wild animals to hunt, and other factors have led many to settle down.

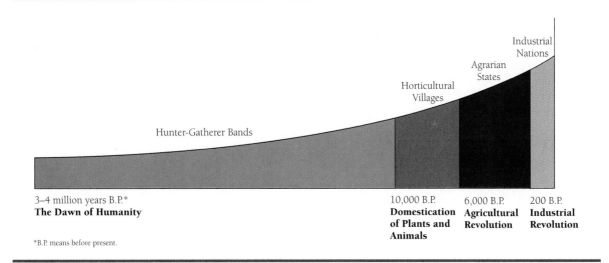

Figure 5-5 *The History of Human Societies*

Viewed from the macroperspective, horticultural villages and agrarian states are modern developments and industrial nations are a modern invention. For 99 percent of human history, our ancestors lived in hunter-gatherer bands.

ten to fifty, whose members were free to come and go. The basic unit of social structure was the nuclear family. There were no formal economic institutions: the exchange of goods and services was governed by informal norms of reciprocity. Although each family was able to provide for itself, food was shared with other members of the band. Hunter-gatherers had no formal political leaders. Individuals might earn special respect for their skills or knowledge and wisdom. People looked to them for advice but had no obligation to follow it. Religion was woven into everyday life; what we might call rituals or prayers were considered an integral part of such practical activities as carving arrows or cooking food. Children learned the skills they would need as adults by observing adults, listening to their stories and gossip, imitating adult activities in play, and working alongside them. Every adult male was a hunter, and every adult female, a gatherer. Within the confines of these roles, hunter-gatherers enjoyed a high degree of individual freedom. No one worked for anyone else, and no one had the right to issue commands.

Warfare was unknown in this stage of the evolution of societies. The human population of the world was small, and natural resources were abundant. When families or bands could not get along, they simply moved apart. Only a few such societies have survived into modern times (see Map 5-1).

Horticultural Villages

About 10,000 years ago, some groups of hunter-gatherers discovered how to plant and harvest crops and to tame and herd animals. For the first time, human beings became food *producers.* Slash-and-burn agriculture (burning down a patch of forest and planting in the cleared area) enabled people to establish larger, semipermanent villages. The domestication of plants and animals did not create a "Garden of Eden." To the contrary, attacks and raids on neighboring villages were frequent. But village or tribal warfare was largely a ritual activity, staged to settle disputes and restore balance, in which few people were killed.

Horticultural villages ranged in size from 40 to 250 members. There were no formal political, economic, or religious institutions in these villages, but the beginnings were there. Kinship was more clearly defined, and membership in a clan (or extended-kinship group) determined the individual's rights to land and to marriage partners. There was little formal trade (direct, calculated exchange of one item for another), but feasts and gifts were used to cement alliances between villages. Each

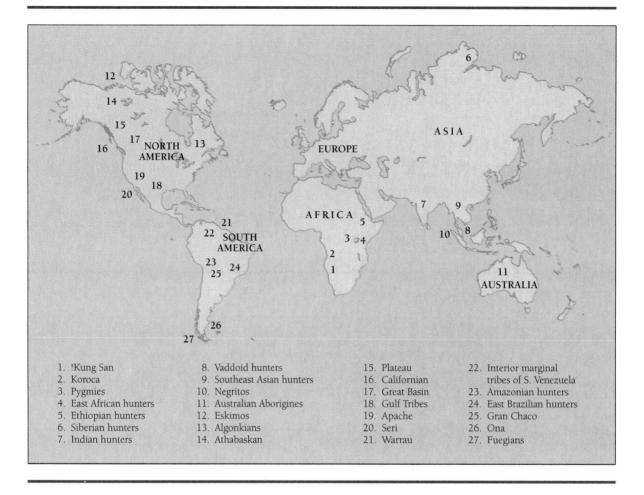

1. !Kung San
2. Koroca
3. Pygmies
4. East African hunters
5. Ethiopian hunters
6. Siberian hunters
7. Indian hunters
8. Vaddoid hunters
9. Southeast Asian hunters
10. Negritos
11. Australian Aborigines
12. Eskimos
13. Algonkians
14. Athabaskan
15. Plateau
16. Californian
17. Great Basin
18. Gulf Tribes
19. Apache
20. Seri
21. Warrau
22. Interior marginal tribes of S. Venezuela
23. Amazonian hunters
24. East Brazilian hunters
25. Gran Chaco
26. Ona
27. Fuegians

Map 5-1 *Distribution of Recent Hunters and Gatherers*

Hunter-gatherer societies are among the endangered species of humankind. Their numbers are declining rapidly, due to civil wars, encroachment on traditional lands, disease, outright slaughter, and forced assimilation. When a culture dies, irreplaceable knowledge about traditional medicines and adaptation to particular ecosystems disappears as well.

Source: Richard B. Lee and Irven DeVore (Eds.), *Man the Hunter,* Chicago: Aldine, 1968, p. 14.

village had a head man or chief—a temporary position that depended on the man's ability to earn respect and/or inspire fear. A man or woman could earn the status of shaman (or spiritual healer). But because men had the additional status of warrior, women were often regarded as inferior, stolen in raids, or traded.

Agrarian States

The period between 6,000 and 3,000 B.P. (before present) was one of the most productive in all human history. The invention of the wheel, pottery, bronze, writing, calendars, and money, the first cities, the first formal governments and religions, the first kingdoms and empires—all can be traced to this period.

The emergence of large-scale, complex societies followed the Agricultural Revolution (intensive agriculture using plows, irrigation, and other innovations), which began around 6,000 years ago in Mesopotamia and Egypt, and occurred at different times in China, India, and other places. For the first time, the land yielded more than was needed to feed those who worked it, and some people could devote themselves full-time to nonfarming activi-

The Aztecs dominated central Mexico for almost two centuries. In this advanced agrarian state, the nobility, priesthood, and military maintained their positions of power by conquering neighboring peoples and sacrificing war captives to Aztec gods. In 1519, when Cortés and his soldiers landed, many subject people joined the Spanish to overthrow Aztec ruler Montezuma. This modern mural by Diego Rivera shows the Aztec capital, Tenochtitlán, which is the site of present-day Mexico City.

ties. The combination of new technology, increased productivity, and greater population density encouraged—and perhaps required—the development of more efficient forms of social organization. Small-scale irrigation works might be organized informally, but large-scale irrigation works require a centralized authority.

Between 3000 B.C. and A.D. 300, agrarian states appeared throughout the world: the ancient kingdoms of Mesopotamia and Egypt, the empires of China and Rome, the Olmec and Mayan states of Central America. (The feudal societies of Europe, which appeared much later, were also agrarian states.) These states differed from the other types of society we have described in four main ways: (1) Political organization was based on territory (rather than kinship), (2) a small elite, and often a single ruler, controlled key resources, (3) political and economic affairs were administered by bureaucratic officials, and (4) society was divided into sharply unequal social classes. Chiefs became absolute monarchs (even, in the case of pharaohs, gods), with divine rights of life and death over their subjects. Their power depended on a combination of religious authority, military might, and control of information (through control of writing and record keeping). Societies were stratified in a hierarchy of ruler, priest, warrior, scribe, peasant, and slave castes. The individual's status in the hierarchy was determined largely by birth. The vast majority of those living in agrarian states remained farmers. But unlike horticulturalists, they did not work for themselves. Rather, they were peasants, with little or no control over the resources needed to grow food (land, water, capital) or the distribution of produce.

The emergence of wealthy agrarian states with fortified cities also marked the beginning of modern warfare—large-scale, long-term, armed aggression to acquire territory, laborers, and/or power. For the first time, societies had a centralized government, territorial boundaries, and wealth, a combination that both enabled them to launch wars and made them desirable acquisitions for other states (Dyer, 1985; Giddens, 1985). Smaller societies were no match for a giant agrarian state. Some were taken over, their populations enslaved or conscripted as peasants; some were pushed off their traditional lands into less hospitable territories; and others were allowed to remain intact, as long as they paid tribute.

On the eve of the Industrial Revolution, the average size of human societies had grown, the number and size of towns and cities had increased, and humans had expanded into new environments, with profound consequences for the biosphere. They had developed new symbol systems and storage systems, produced monuments that survive to this day, and developed complex forms of social organization. Inequality both within and between societies had increased tremendously. The rate of social and cultural change had been gathering momentum and was about to explode (Lenski, Lenski, and Nolan, 1991).

Industrial Nations

The Industrial Revolution, which began in England about 200 years ago, ushered in a new era. Tasks once performed by humans were soon performed by machines, on assembly lines, at a much faster speed and lower cost.

Changes in the structure of work had a profound impact on the structure of society (see Table 5-2). Among the most significant were changes in institutions. For example, in preindustrial societies education, occupation, marriage, care of the sick and elderly, and many religious observances were "family affairs," organized by and for family members. In industrial societies, the family's functions have been greatly reduced. The job of educating young people has been taken over by formal schools; most people work for somebody else; health care has been professionalized; the government is the main supplier of social security; individuals choose their own marriage partners (and, indeed, whether to marry or not); married couples usually live apart from their extended families and kin; and many people look to political ideologies, secular philosophies, science, and psychology rather than religion to answer questions about the meaning of life. The main role of the family today is ordering its members' private lives.

Industrialization has also influenced the institutions of politics and economics (Lenski, Lenski, and Nolan, 1991). In agrarian states, most people had no say in political decisions. Industrialization seems to encourage mass participation in government, in the form of either voting (in democracies) or party organizations (in socialist nations). Whether democratic, totalitarian, or some combination of the two, virtually all modern governments at least claim to be acting in the name of the people. Likewise, the epic wars of the past were fought by professional soldiers and combat usually was limited to battlefields and/or to sieges of forts or capital cities. Modern warfare recognizes few boundaries between bat-

Table 5-2   *All This in Only 200 Years!*

1. World population has multiplied nearly sevenfold (from 725 million to 5 billion) just since 1750, a rate of growth more than fifteen times higher than the rate between the time of Christ and 1750.
2. The rural-urban balance in advanced industrial societies has been nearly reversed: agrarian societies were approximately 90 percent rural; several advanced industrial societies are more than 80 percent urban.
3. The largest urban communities of the industrial era are more than fifteen times the size of the largest of the agrarian era.
4. Women in industrial societies give birth to only about one-third as many children as women in preindustrial societies.
5. Life expectancy at birth is almost three times greater in advanced industrial societies than it was in agrarian.
6. The family, for the first time in history, is no longer a significant productive unit in the economy.
7. The role of women in the economy and in society at large has changed substantially.
8. The role of youth has also changed, and youth cultures have become a significant factor in the life of industrial societies.
9. The *per capita* production and consumption of goods and services in advanced industrial societies is at least ten times greater than in traditional agrarian societies.
10. The division of labor is vastly more complex.
11. Hereditary monarchial government has disappeared in industrial societies, except as a ceremonial and symbolic survival.
12. The functions of government have been vastly enlarged.
13. Free public educational systems have been established and illiteracy has been largely eliminated in all industrial societies.
14. New ideologies have spread widely (notably socialism, capitalism, and nationalism), while older ones inherited from the agrarian era either have been substantially altered or have declined.
15. Worldwide communication and transportation networks have been created that have, for practical purposes, rendered our entire planet smaller than England in the agrarian era.
16. A global culture has begun to emerge, as evidenced in styles of dress, music, language, technology, and organizational patterns (e.g., factories, public schools, small families).
17. Global political institutions (e.g., the United Nations, the World Court) have been established for the first time.
18. A number of societies have acquired the capacity to obliterate the entire human population.

Source: G. Lenski, J. Lenski, and P. Nolan, *Human Societies: An Introduction to Macrosociology,* 6th ed., New York: McGraw-Hill, 1991, pp. 211–213.

tlefields and civilian territories, citizens and soldiers. Waging a world war or a guerrilla war depends on the ability of the government (or a rival faction) to mobilize and support citizen armies. Thus in industrialized societies ordinary people play active roles in war and peace. At the same time, however, the power and size of government have increased dramatically. At the turn of the century, most Americans had contact with only one government agency: the post office. Today the federal government has a hand in almost everything we do, from birth to death.

Over time, industrialization seems to reduce the extreme inequalities found in agrarian states. Political and economic institutions require mass education to produce committed citizens and skilled workers. The overall standard of living rises and the distribution of wealth becomes somewhat more even—on average—because of the development of a large middle class. (Of course, there are still wide gaps between rich and poor, all the wider because today's wealthy may be richer than were the kings of agrarian states.) But while industrialization has reduced inequalities within developed nations, it has had the opposite effect on the global community. The gap between rich (industrialized) and poor (nonindustrialized) nations has widened.

In a mere 200 years, industrialization has made its impact felt all over the globe. Independent hunter-gatherer and horticultural societies have all but disappeared, their traditional homelands taken over by governments and/or commercial enterprises. The peasant communities characteristic of agrarian societies are also dwindling. The mechanization and commercialization of agriculture has driven many peasants off the land and into cities. Likewise the independent farmers of rural America have given way to agribusiness and factory farms. Whereas the rise of agrarian states led to the elaboration of distinctive cultures, the spread of industrialization has reduced cultural diversity. Modern transportation and communication systems have brought once-remote groups into contact with other societies and ways of life. People everywhere are beginning to look and act like members of a single, worldwide industrial society—a "global village" (McLuhan and Fiore, 1967).

The historical developments described in this section are summarized in Table 5-3. Some sociologists (for example, Bell, 1973) maintain that in the second half of the twentieth century, a new type of "postindustrial" society has emerged. In technologically advanced societies such as the United States, automation has reduced the number of people involved directly in the production of goods. At the same time, the number of people working in science and technology and in services (health care, education, and the like) has increased. Other sociologists (for example, Mann, 1987) maintain that the notion of society as an autonomous social unit has become obsolete. Globalization—the distribution not only of money and products but also of information (via satellite communications), political disputes (via terrorism), pollution, and population (whether immigrants or refugees) across national borders—has reduced the power and influence of national governments. The peoples and nations of the world today are linked in a single world system, such that what happens in one nation or one region affects others.

The World System

Sociologist Immanuel Wallerstein (1980) pioneered the world system approach to the study of social structure. Wallerstein argued that economic relationships extend beyond the borders of nation-states and operate independently of the political systems of those nation-states. The result is a *world system:* an economic network that links the nations of the world into a single socioeconomic unit.

Writing before the rise of global corporations, the Internet, or the revolutions in eastern Europe and breakup of the Soviet Union, Wallerstein identified three positions in the world system.[3] *Core* nations (the United States, western European nations, and Japan) dominated this world system, not because of their political or military power (though these were important), but because of unequal terms of exchange. They provided most of the management and machinery for the world system. The manufactured goods they produced (automobiles, computers, spacecraft, weapons) commanded much higher prices than the agricultural products, handicrafts, and raw materials poorer nations traded.

---

[3]Wallerstein did not include former Communist nations in his model because, at the time, these nations had either chosen or been forced to operate outside the world system.

Table 5-3   *The Changing Structure of Human Societies*

Type of Society	Size	Technological Innovations	Social Roles	Social Institutions
Hunter-gatherer bands	Nomadic bands of 10–50	Simple technology	All adults involved in food collection; roles based on sex and age—males hunt; females gather	No formal social institutions other than the family
Horticultural villages	Autonomous, semipermanent villages of 40–300	Food production: substitution of farming and stock raising for gathering and hunting	All adults involved in food production; division of labor based on sex and age; roles of head man, shaman, and warrior added	The extended-kin group or clan becomes basic unit of social organization
Agrarian states	City and surrounding villages link tens of thousands in a territorial unit	Agricultural Revolution (irrigation, crop rotation, etc.); wheeled vehicles and sailing ships; ceramics and bronze; writing and calendars; money; etc.	Occupation specialization and inequality lead to emergence of hereditary social castes; majority of the population belongs to peasantry	Religion and politics become separate institutions, less dependent on the family or clan
Industrial nations	Nation-state links millions; urbanization spreads	Industrial Revolution (harnessing of new sources of energy; mechanization of work; adoption of factory system); advanced systems of communication, transportation	High level of differentiation and specialization in occupations; social ranks based on achieved as well as ascribed status; higher level of individual choice in social roles	Distinct religious, political, economic, and family institutions; emergence of new institutions, such as education and science; shifts in the balance of other institutions

Peripheral nations (often former colonies) operated on the outskirts of the world system. They sold some raw materials to and purchased some manufactured goods from the richer nations, but for the most part, their populations were engaged in subsistence agriculture and their governments depended on foreign aid and investment. Because core nations determined the terms of trade in the world system, peripheral countries were essentially locked into their dependent, outsider status.

Semiperipheral nations were those that were moving up or down in the world system. Upward movement was difficult. For example, a poor nation in Latin America or Africa could not follow the British or American pattern of industrial development, precisely because it would forever lag behind. But some countries (such as South Korea) were able to improve their position by offering very cheap labor to the richer nations and undergoing rapid technological change. Low-cost labor plus

technological advances in semiperipheral countries attracted international investment and trade, taking business away from some of the older core nations, such as Great Britain (Mandel, 1975). Politically, today's Britain is still an important member of the western community of nations, but economically it is semiperipheral.

A nation's position in the world system determined not only its economic well-being but also many features of its internal social structure. For example, in peripheral nations, members of the upper class were likely to be oriented toward core nations: they purchase goods and emulate the lifestyle of these nations, work for foreign companies (and perhaps hope to emigrate one day), and depend on foreign aid or investment for domestic ventures. In semiperipheral nations such as Brazil or South Korea, rapid economic gains led to demands for higher wages, shorter workweeks, the protection of unions, and a greater voice in political

A Chrysler factory in Toluca, Mexico. In Immanuel Wallerstein's model, Mexico is a semiperipheral nation, whose low-cost labor and technological advances make it attractive to American corporations.

SOCIOLOGY ON THE WEB

The Nets on the Net

To explore the way in which bureaucracies present themselves to those outside the organization, log on to the web sites of a number of corporations, non-profit organizations, and government agencies. The possibilities are limitless: below are a few suggested sites to begin with, but you will easily find more. With a few mouse clicks in any search engine, you'll find hundreds of corporate and government sites.

As you explore different types of sites, think about these questions: What kind of information is provided in corporate sites? in government sites? in nonprofit sites? How do the different kinds of organizations present themselves through their web sites? What can you find out about each organization? What can you *not* find out? Compare the sites, for example, of the NBA and the WNBA, of a public and a private university, of IBM and a research consortium. As you think about these questions, consider what the text has to say about the purposes and functions of large bureaucracies.

Here are a few web sites to get you started:

Companies

http://www.wnba.com   (WNBA)

http://www.ibm.com   (IBM)

http://www.elektra.com
(Elektra Records)

http://www.nike.com   (Nike)

Governments

http://www.presidencia.gob.mx/
welcome/gov_hp.tm
This site, maintained by the government of Mexico, has links to many government agencies and departments, some in English and Spanish and some in Spanish only.

http://www.state.nj.us/
This is the state of New Jersey's site. Other states' web sites can be reached by changing the "nj" in this address to the postal abbreviation of the state you are interested in.

Nonprofit Organizations

http://www.audubon.org   (National Audubon Society)

http://www.npr.org   (National Public Radio)

affairs (again, characteristics of core nations). But core nations were not exempt from the impact of the world system. The decline of manufacturing jobs, the increase in the trade deficit, and restructuring of the economy and the job market in the United States in recent decades are the result of globalization.

The world system is not a recent phenomenon. Wallerstein traces it back to the beginnings of capitalism, in the fourteenth century. By 1600, the East India Company, chartered in Britain, was one of the most powerful "global corporations" the world has ever known. Twentieth-century advances in communication and transportation technology have made this global network even stronger. The cre-

ation of the European Union, the North Atlantic Free Trade Agreement (NAFTA), linking Canada, the United States, and Mexico, and the Association of Southeast Asian Nations (ASEAN), linking Brunei, Indonesia, Malaysia, Philippines, Singapore, Thailand, and Vietnam; economic development in China (with the largest population, and hence the largest pool of workers and potential consumers of any nation on earth); and the participation of the former Communist nations of eastern Europe and countries that were part of the Soviet Union in the world economy—all have the potential to restructure the current world system. What shape relations among nations and regions will take in the future is an open question.

Summary

1. **What is social structure?** *Social structure* refers to the regular, predictable, enduring patterns that organize everyday interaction, social relationships, societies, and relations among societies. Social structure can be studied on two levels: the *microperspective,* which focuses on everyday life, and the *macroperspective,* which looks at larger, long-term patterns.

2. **How does social structure affect individual behavior?** Social structure provides patterns for interaction that enable people to coordinate their actions in pursuit of individual or collective goals.

3. **What are the basic elements of social structure?** The primary links between the individual and social structure are *statuses* (positions in society) and *roles* (cultural scripts for different positions). Statuses and roles establish a template for social relationships, which may be multifaceted or single-purpose; involve friendship, love, or mere acquaintance; be direct and face-to-face or indirect and mediated by other people. Groups (discussed in detail in Chapter 6) link individuals to one another and to the wider society.

    Formal organizations are likely to emerge when a goal requires the coordinated skills and efforts of a number of people. The basic elements of formal organizations are explicit social structure, limited participation of members, emphasis on goals, and dependence on technology. Many formal organizations are bureaucratic in structure. Weber's *ideal type* of bureaucracy emphasized a clear-cut division of labor, a clearly defined hierarchy and authority, formal rules and regulations, impersonality, positions based on technical qualifications and performance, and a clear line between the public and private spheres. In reality, bureaucratic organizations have both a formal and an informal structure, which may improve or impede efficiency.

4. **What social structures provide the framework for societies?** The structure of society derives in large part from *social institutions.* Each of the major institutions—the family, politics, economics, education, and religion—fills a specific need, but all are interrelated. Social institutions help preserve continuity but also act to channel social change. No society treats all its members equally. *Social stratification* refers to the division of society into layers or classes whose members have unequal access to wealth, power, and prestige. Our society is stratified not only in terms of wealth, race and ethnicity, and gender but also by age.

5. **How have societies and relations among societies changed over time?** The evolutionary perspective traces the emergence

of different types of societies (hunter-gatherers, horticultural villages, agrarian states, and industrial nations) to the impact of new technologies on social structure. The *world system* approach focuses on the economic links among nations, and their social consequences.

Key Terms

achieved status 166	macroperspective 160	social institutions 179
ageism 184	master status 166	social stratification 182
ascribed status 166	microperspective 160	social structure 160
bureaucracy 174	role 167	society 185
formal organization 170	role conflict 168	status 166
ideal type 175	role set 168	world system 191
iron law of oligarchy 178	role strain 168	

Recommended Readings

Blau, Peter M., & Meyer, M. W. (1987). *Bureaucracy in Modern Society,* 3d ed. New York: Random House.

Dalton, M. (1959). *Men Who Manage.* New York: Wiley.

Diamond, Jared. (1997). *Guns, Germs, and Steel: The Fates of Human Societies.* New York: Norton.

Lenski, G., Lenski, J., & Nolan, P. (1991). *Human Societies: An Introduction,* 6th ed. New York: McGraw-Hill.

Lipset, Seymor Martin, Trow, Martin A., & Coleman, James S. (1962). *Union Democracy.* New York: Anchor.

Mulkey, Lynn M. (1995). *Seeing and Unseeing Social Structure: Sociology's Essential Insights.* Boston: Allyn and Bacon.

Scott, W. Richard. (1987). *Organizations: Rational, Natural, and Open Systems,* 2d ed. Englewood Cliffs, NJ: Prentice-Hall.

Wallerstein, I. (1974). *The Modern World System,* Vol. I. New York: Academic.

Wallerstein, I. (1980). *The Modern World System,* Vol. II. New York: Academic.

Wallerstein, I. (1989). *The Modern World System III: The Second Era of Great Expansion of the Capitalist World Economy, 1730–1840s.* New York: Academic.

Six

Social Interaction and Social Groups

Watching television is the number-one recreational activity in the United States (Robinson, 1990). An average couple watches TV at least two or three hours a day and considerably more during events such as the Olympics or fast-breaking news stories such as the Oklahoma City bombing. Much has been written about the impact of TV on children, but adult TV-viewing habits have largely been ignored. "Couch potatoes" hardly seem worthy of research. The microsociological perspective shows that even the most commonplace activities are socially structured.

Use of the TV remote control is an example. Sociologist Alexis J. Walker (1996) became interested in this subject when her parents bought a second TV set. The reason, her mother explained, was "I can't stand the way he flips through the channels" (p. 183). Anecdotal evidence suggests men are far more likely than women to use the remote to switch from channel to channel looking for something of interest ("grazing" or "surfing") and to "zap" between channels, watching two programs simultaneously and avoiding commercials—much to their female partners' irritation. Walker wanted to know whether there is, in fact, a gender difference, and if so, why.

Thirty-six married or cohabiting couples were selected as subjects. Working in teams of four, students from Walker's undergraduate course on gender and family relationships conducted a survey (see Chapter 2). The student-interviewers asked semistructured questions about how many televisions the couple owned and where they were located, how often they watched TV together, what other activities they engaged in while watching TV, and patterns of remote-control use. They also asked open-ended questions about how the couple decided what to watch, how each partner got the other to watch a show he or she wanted to watch, and whether they enjoyed watching TV together.

The survey found that in most households men controlled the remote, which enabled them to watch what they wanted, when they wanted, however they wanted, and without regard to their partner's preferences:

"I'm the guilty party. My [family members] would leave it there and watch the commercial. I just change it because I'd rather not be insulted by commercials." (husband, p. 818)

"I don't hold [the remote] but I pretty much have control of it, and if I don't care what's on, then I let her have it." (husband, p. 817)

6

The casual, everyday activity of watching TV demonstrates who wields the power in a marriage. By studying such seemingly mundane behavior, sociologists can reveal a great deal about social structure.

"I usually have the remote because I know how to use it." (husband, p. 817)

One husband routinely kept the "zapper" in the pocket of his shirt or bathrobe.

Most women said that they found their partners' use of the remote control irritating:

> "[What's] frustrating for me is when we first turn on the TV and he just flips through the channels. It drives me crazy because you can't tell what's on, because he just goes through and goes through and goes through." (female cohabitor, p. 817)

> "I get hooked into one show and then he flips it to another one. As soon as I get hooked into something else, he switches to another one." (wife, p. 817)

Women were far more likely than men to say that the last show they had watched (indeed most shows they watched) was their partners' choice:

> "He just watches what he wants. He doesn't ask." (wife, p. 819)

> "I tell him that would be a good one to watch, and he says, 'No,' and keeps changing [channels]. I whine, and then usually I don't get [my way]." (cohabiting female, p. 818)

The men did not deny this; to the contrary, most saw choosing what the couple watched as their prerogative:

> "I mean, if there's sports on, that's usually what we watch. . . . Oh, I guess, *if there's not anything that I'm real big on watching* then I'll let her choose, or she, you

know, she's interested in something. . . . A bunch of times, we watch TV, and it's like, well, we'll go back, and, well, that's kind [of] interesting, we go back and forth." (husband, p. 818; emphasis added)

His wife agreed. Asked how she got him to watch something she wanted to see, she laughed:

> "I tie him down and say, 'You're watching this.' I don't know. He usually just comes over, and if it's not what he wants, then he'll take the remote and try to find sports." (wife, p. 818)

In other words, this couple watched sports most of the time. If and only if there was no sports show or other program the husband really wanted to watch, he let his wife choose—but even then he used the remote control to "graze" for sports during her show.

Thus watching TV—an apparently casual, routine, everyday activity—is in reality, a battle of the sexes. When men or women watch television alone, there is no discernible difference in the way they use the remote control; rather, being together brings out sex-typed behavior and power plays. The idea that a man is the "head of his household" is so embedded in culture and social structure that it is rarely questioned. The men in this study took their control of the TV for granted. The women had to struggle to get their partners to watch their choice of programs, and they often lost. Even when their partners "let" or "allowed" them to choose a program, the men "reminded" the women who was in charge by keeping the remote within easy reach and flipping channels during commercials.

Men exercise power not only in direct, observable actions (manifest power) but also in subtle, indirect ways (latent power) that are reflected in their female partners' behavior (Komter, 1989). As a rule in relationships of unequal power, the dominant partner usually does as he or she pleases; the job of adjusting and keeping the relationship intact falls to the subordinate partner (Farrington and Chertock, 1993). So it is in marriage. Typically, husbands are able to prevent issues from being raised, often by changing the subject (or the channel). Consciously or unconsciously, wives attempt to anticipate their desires. The wife cooks her husband's favorite dishes, serves dinner when he wants it served, watches his favorite TV shows, devotes much of her "leisure time" to housework and child care, and caters to him in countless other small ways (Hochschild, 1989). Going along with a husband or male partner is easier—and safer—than standing up to him. To avoid conflict, women often resign themselves to undesirable situations, worry that change might harm their relationship, and hide their deferral of their own wishes and desires even from themselves.

Despite the discontent evident in the comments cited here, most of the women in this study described themselves as happy with the status quo. Less than half said they resented the partner's control of the remote, even fewer said they would like him to stop surfing and flipping channels, and only four thought there was a possibility he might change. The few who asserted their preferences did so indirectly, watching on a second TV or taping shows to watch later, a strategy that did not "interfere" with their partners' choices.

A couple's behavior, in the privacy of their home and during leisure time, both reflects social structure and helps create and maintain that social structure. Through couple interaction, women and men behave in ways that affirm that they are separate and unequal. The roles they play and the norms they follow in watching TV recreate and reinforce gender inequality in the most intimate of primary groups. And their behavior serves as a model for their children. Following Dad, sons use the remote control more often than their sisters or their mothers.

Each of us likes to think he or she is a unique individual whose behavior, especially at home and among friends, is spontaneous. Yet as this analysis of watching TV illustrates, much of our behavior falls into regular, predictable patterns. The goal of microsociology is to expose the hidden structure of everyday social behavior.

Key Questions

1. How do people establish and maintain rules for social interactions?
2. How do individuals establish and maintain a social identity?
3. How do networks take shape?
4. What is a social group?
5. What are the main types of social groups?
6. How does the size of a group affect the way the group functions?
7. What effect does the structure of a group have on individual and group behavior?

Social Interaction

A conversation, a game of cards, a dinner party, making love—what do these activities have in common? They cannot be accomplished by only one person (McCall and Simmons, 1972). All are examples of **social interaction,** in which one person's actions depend on the actions of the other, *and vice versa.* Social interaction is the result of mutual influence, not simply parallel or simultaneous activity.

Social interactions range from the most superficial contacts—strangers passing in the street or attending the same concert—to deep, long-lasting, complex relationships, such as those between husband and wife or parent and child. Some are formal—for example, a job interview. Others are much more free-form—two children meet in a park and start to play. But even apparently spontaneous interactions fall into patterns.

When you are seated on an airplane, you glance at the person next to you; take note of that person's sex, age, and clothing; and adjust your behavior accordingly. If she is an older woman, you might offer to help her stow carry-on luggage in the overhead compartment; if he is an athletic-looking young man, you would not. You might initiate a conversation with a comment on the weather, a remark about something the other person is reading or carrying ("I see you play tennis"), or a statement of what's wrong with airlines today. The person in the next seat may respond to an overture with a nod and then open her book, signaling that she isn't interested in talking. If, however, she continues the conversation, the two of you would probably talk about your jobs or why you are both flying to Seattle; you would not discuss your sex lives, and you would probably avoid getting into deep political or religious debate. Your interaction is further limited by the physical layout of the plane and by the other people on the plane. At a party you can easily end a conversation by saying you see an old friend across the room and moving away; in a plane there is no place to go, except to the bathroom and then you have to return to your assigned seat. Because you are surrounded by other passengers, even if you and the other person are strongly attracted to one another, you probably would not become physically intimate; nor, if you find the other person supports everything you oppose, would you engage in a shouting match. Without half thinking about it, you are following a ready-made cultural script.

Cultural Scripts and Ethnomethodology

The most important and revealing studies of everyday social behavior come from symbolic interactionists (see Adler and Adler, 1987). Symbolic interactionists emphasize the role of language and other symbols (such as fashion) in the social construction of identity and in the structure of relationships. Some sociologists in this school (for example, Goffman, 1959, 1967) draw an analogy between real life and the stage—*the dramaturgical approach* (see Chapter 2). In a drama, the playwright sets the scene and introduces the characters in the first act. When the curtain falls, the audience is left in suspense about what will happen in Act Two. Even if some audience members know the play, they do not know how these particular actors will interpret their roles. So it is in everyday life. Social expectations set the stage for interaction but do not dictate behavior. Individuals do not perform their roles automatically like puppets on a string. As on the stage, each person interprets a role in his or her own way. Some learn their parts well, while others continually bungle their lines. The unexpected—a heckler in the audience or a falling prop—intervenes. In some situations, there are strict rules governing interaction, and participants are expected to follow the script closely. Other situations are more improvisational, with participants making up the "story" as they go along.

In many cases, we are so accustomed to our culture's scripts that we take expected role behavior for granted. In a restaurant, for example, we greet our waitperson, perhaps exchange a pleasantry or two, and listen politely to the recitation of that day's specials, but for the most part we act as if he or she were not there. For diners to invite their waitperson to sit down and join them for coffee and dessert, or the waitperson to enter into the discussion the diners are having (instead of acting as if he or she hears nothing) would be considered distinctly odd. Children frequently break the rules of restaurant etiquette, but gradually, with corrections by their parents, come to take them for granted. Sociologist Harold Garfinkel (1967) coined the term ***ethnomethodology*** (or "people rules") for the countless unspoken, often unconscious rules people use to maintain order and predictability in everyday social interaction.

To demonstrate the power of such seemingly trivial social understandings, he invented a technique called the "breaching experiment," in which he and his students deliberately violated unspoken assumptions and recorded how other people responded. In a classic experiment, he asked students to behave as guests the next time they visited their families. The students maintained a polite distance, avoiding personal topics, asked permission to get a glass of water or use the bathroom, and thanked their "host" and "hostess" for their gracious hospitality.

> Family members demanded explanations: What's the matter? What's gotten into you? Did you get fired? Are you sick? What are you being superior about? Why are you mad? Are you out of your mind or just being stupid? (Garfinkel, 1967, pp. 47–48)

Even though few students were able to keep up the experiment for very long, their parents quickly became annoyed and angry. In breaking unstated rules, students uncovered the rules about family interaction most of us take for granted. In other breaching experiments, students tried to bargain for the price of items in stores (which Americans generally do not do), erased their opponents' moves in games of tic-tac-toe, and closed in until they were almost nose to nose during an ordinary conversation. In each case, the response was much the same as in the family experiment. Perhaps most interesting, the student-experimenters became as confused as their unsuspecting victims, and reported feeling anxious and even angry during the experiment. A question for ethnomethodologists is the degree to which unconscious rules vary from culture to culture (see *A Global View:* Smiling Across Cultures: The United States and Japan).

Defining the Situation

As breaching experiments demonstrate, in many situations we know exactly how we are expected to behave. For example, our culture, family traditions, and experience provide clear guidelines for behavior at a Thanksgiving dinner. You get together with your extended family at grandmother's house, rather than meeting friends at an ethnic restaurant. Your grandmother cooks a turkey, not hamburgers; everyone eats too much, and everyone raves about one another's special pies. After dinner, the men watch football and the women wash dishes, even though you spurn gender-typed roles on other occasions. In other cases, however, the required behavior isn't clear at all. For example, an attractive man or woman from your history class asks if you're free that evening. Is this a date? When a situation is ambiguous, you hesitate, look for clues about how to behave, explore the various possibilities, and test the limits. If the classmate then suggests dinner at a nearby Thai restaurant, it sounds more like a date. If he or she says, "A group of us want to get together to talk about holding ethnic dinners; Sukanya, a Thai student in my dorm, suggested it," it's probably not a date, or not yet. Gradually you arrive at a **definition of the situation**—an overall idea of what is expected. And this definition establishes a framework for social interaction.

Defining the situation is a collective process: the important clues about what is appropriate and the main limits on behavior come from other people. A friend calls to tell you she is pregnant. You bubble over with congratulations. Your friend is silent for a moment; then you hear a muffled sob. "But we can't afford a third child! I haven't even told Michael yet." Immediately you change your tone of voice and ask how you can help. Would she like to meet for lunch? Your friend has defined the situation as a crisis.

Arriving at a collective definition isn't always quick or easy. Two people may disagree completely on what the scene calls for. For example, one roommate may see college as liberation from parental surveillance and the beginning of an extended party and may thus want his room to become a social gathering place; the other roommate may see college as serious preparation for a career and may thus want his room to be a study hall. Reconciling opposing definitions may entail hours of discussion, bitter conflict, or the manipulation of one social actor by the other (Garfinkel, 1967; Heritage, 1987).

Backstage and Frontstage

According to sociologist Erving Goffman, there are two main areas of behavior: the public, or "frontstage," and the private, or "backstage." Every marriage, for example, has frontstage (public) and backstage (private) areas. In public, the couple works to create the impression of a happy marriage. The partners avoid open conflict, try not to criticize or contradict one another directly, and work to prevent each other from doing something that creates a bad impression. For example, if the husband makes an insensitive or rude remark, the wife may protect his act by saying something like "He was only joking" or "What he really means is . . ." When they give a dinner party, their husband-wife act may be so successful that their guests never know that a terrible fight was transpiring when they arrived and that the argument continued backstage in the kitchen all through dinner. When the guests have left, the frontstage masks of a happy couple can be let down and the argument resumed at full pitch. One of the reasons why a couple may have trouble when in-laws come for an extended visit is that both partners are forced to be "on stage" so much of the time.

As ethnomethodology reveals, often our patterns of interaction become so ingrained that they are unconscious, especially in a long-term, multifaceted relationship such as that of husband and wife. In other cases, however, our behavior is more calculated.

The Presentation of the Self

Goffman (1959, 1967) emphasized the social ploys all of us use but seldom admit. Goffman held that each of us has an image of how he or she wants to be seen by others. Far from passively accepting the roles "society" writes for us, we actively work to

A GLOBAL VIEW

Smiling across Cultures: The United States and Japan

Smiling is an integral part of everyday social interaction. In some cases, smiles are conscious and intentional signals of happiness, friendliness, or amusement; in other cases, smiles are unintentional communications that betray emotions the person would rather conceal, especially nervousness or ridicule. In some social situations, smiling is required, as when a salesperson greets a customer, a host or hostess introduces a new arrival at a party, or a performer accepts the audience's applause. In other situations, smiling is considered inappropriate—for example, when you are told that someone you know (indeed, anyone) is dying or when you witness another person in physical or emotional pain.

Do norms for smiling vary across cultures? To investigate this question, sociologists Kenji Nagashima and James Schellenberg (1997) presented forty-two college students in the United States and forty-eight in Japan with three situations involving student-professor or student-student interaction:

1. A student goes to the professor or another student to ask about classwork (a friendly smile)

2. A student hears a professor or another student tell a joke that he or she does not consider funny (a forced smile)

3. A student receives the information he or she wanted from a professor or another student (a genuine smile)

The researchers asked students in both countries to rank the likelihood that the student would smile in each of these situations on a 7-point scale from 1 (not smile at all) to 7 (smiles very much).

> **Cross-cultural research that uncovers or confirms similarities is as important as research that identifies cross-cultural differences.**

Cultural stereotypes hold that the Japanese are more formal and polite, and show more respect for rank, than do Americans. Nagashima and Schellenberg hypothesized that out of respect for status differences, Japanese students would be less likely than American students to smile when asking a professor a question (situation 1) and more likely to smile at a professor's joke (situation 2). They made no prediction for situation 3. The results?

Japanese students indicated they would be somewhat less likely to smile when asking a professor, rather than another student, for information. So did the American students. Japanese students indicated they would be more likely to force a smile in response to a professor's bad joke than to another student's. Again, so did American students. Students from both countries indicated that the other person's status would not affect a genuine smile. In short, the study found no significant cultural differences.

Does this mean the study was a failure? Not at all. Cross-cultural research that uncovers or confirms similarities is as important as research that identifies cross-cultural differences. The samples and the scope of this particular study were too small to permit generalization. But combined with other research, this bit of information suggests that expressions of emotion may be universal, a nonverbal form of communication all human beings use and understand.

Source: K. Nagashima, and J. A. Schellenberg, "Situational Differences in Intentional Smiling: A Cross-Cultural Exploration," *Journal of Social Psychology* 137(3), 1997, pp. 297–301.

present ourselves in a certain light. To some extent, Goffman argued, we are all putting on an act. In numerous books and articles, Goffman detailed the **presentation of the self,** that is, the ways in which people attempt to direct and control the impression they make on others and on how others see them. Goffman called this *impression management.*

Social Identities

A **social identity** is "our sense of who and what we are" (F. Davis, 1992, p. 24). Whereas our personal identity is based on our individual biography and idiosyncrasies, our social identity derives from the positions we occupy in society, as student, daughter, friend, poet, vegetarian, and the like. It includes roles to which we aspire as well as the positions we currently occupy. Our social identity depends in large degree on our perception of how others see us, what Charles Horton Cooley (1902) called "the looking-glass self" (see Chapter 4). Our private identity may include thoughts and experiences we never divulge to anyone; our social identity requires public validation. This is particularly true when we are taking on a new role or leaving an old one: entering college, starting a new job, becoming a parent, or becoming single again after a divorce. In addition, each of us has various *situational identities* that become dominant in certain settings. A woman may be a professor in class, at faculty meetings, and at professional conferences; when she gets home, however, her identity as "Mommy" comes first.

The social self tends to be an idealized version of how we would like to see ourselves perform a given role (McCall and Simmons, 1972). Each of us spends a good deal of time imagining and often play-acting (in private) future performances—asking a grandparent for a loan, explaining our grades to parents and friends, telling the boss we are going to quit, making an entrance at a party, hitting a grand-slam home run, or getting a role in a Broadway play. In the rehearsal hall of our minds we play these scenes over and over, working out the smallest details. Imagining how the audience will react is an integral part of this process. We may hope that the action or announcement we are contemplating will not change other people's perception of us (in asking for a loan or admitting a poor performance); that we will change other people's perception of us by doing something extraordinary (hitting a grand slam or landing a Broadway role); or simply that we will

get through an occasion without damaging our identity (a party). In each case, our feelings about ourselves depend on whether other people support or reject the social identity we seek. But often we are our own harshest critics. Just before giving a speech, you discover a stain on your shirt or a blemish on your face; you imagine everyone is staring at this imperfection, not listening to what you say. After a job interview, you think of everything you should have said but didn't, and you suspect the interviewer immediately rejected your application.

Social identities are not simply daydreams (or nightmares). They are a major source of plans for action (helping us decide whether to do this or that); they provide the criteria for evaluating our actual performances (making us feel good or bad about ourselves); and they give meaning to our daily lives (helping us interpret the situations, events, and people we encounter). Identities arise from a need to find stable social footing in a chaotic social world (H. C. White, 1992). But social identities are fragile. Because they tend to be idealized, they often get bumped and jarred by reality. There is no guarantee that others will accept the image we wish to project. One of the main goals of social interaction, therefore, is to create and maintain our social identities.

Looking the Part: Fashion and Fitness

To affirm a social identity, people strive to "look the part." Dress serves as a "visual metaphor" for identity (F. Davis, 1992, p. 25). A police officer's uniform, a rock star's hairstyle, or a convict's prison gray is intended to reveal at a glance what kind of person this is. So are the "looks" individuals create with everyday clothes. For example, a woman who dresses in a tailored suit and carries an expensive handbag is attempting to project an image of respectability and prosperity; a man who wears wire-rimmed glasses and an old tweed jacket is signaling that he sees himself (and wants to be seen) as an intellectual; an adult who dresses in jeans almost all the time wants to be seen as youthful, carefree, and a little rebellious.

All societies use clothing and ornamentation to distinguish among categories of people (male and female, young and old, powerful and lowly). But *fashion* is a relatively recent phenomenon, one that has almost reached a fever pitch in contemporary societies (and their imitators) (F. Davis, 1992).

Fashion differs from style and other related phenomena in that it is constantly changing: what is in this year may be out next year, and trendsetters pay attention to the subtlest nuances. Only in contemporary western society (and its imitators) has this continual, uninterrupted succession of stylistic changes become institutionalized.

Sociologist Fred Davis (1992) holds that fashion is a reflection of cultural ambivalences, of unresolved conflicts over the meaning and significance of youth versus age, masculine versus feminine, work versus play, conformity versus individuality, success versus failure, snobbery versus egalitarianism. These cultural ambivalences create personal insecurities, which may be resolved (at least temporarily) through fashion.

Consider, for example, the recent history of the female executive's office clothes. In the 1970s, when more and more women began seeking jobs in management and the professions, the "dress for success" style came into vogue. A woman who wanted to be taken seriously in the world of work dressed in conservatively tailored suits, not unlike the male executive uniform, but softened by a silk blouse with a flowing scarf or ruffled collars and cuffs. By the mid-1980s this ensemble had lost its impact: no longer did it reassure career men, or career women themselves, that there was "still a woman" behind the business veneer. Dresses, knit ensembles, and pants suits became acceptable office attire. But gender ambivalence resurfaced in the 1990s, most notably in a series of ads that combined the traditional banker's pinstriped suit with skirts slit thigh-high and exposed black-lace underwear. "Dress for success" had merged with "dress for sex."

Like clothing, bodies have become the objects of impression management. Looking slim, fit, youthful, and sexy, at every age, from the preteens to the sixties, almost has become a moral imperative. Sociologist Barry Glassner (1992) points out that our culture's ideal body type is based in large part on what we see in ads. This image has little basis in reality; even the models who pose for these pictures seldom look as perfect in person: photos are usually touched up, and models have enhanced their looks via plastic surgery. Nevertheless, the fitness ideal is powerful. On the one hand, it reflects such time-honored cultural values as self-control, hard work, achievement, and prosperity. On the other hand, fitness has become an integral part of our economy. Americans spend an estimated $50 billion a year on diets, cosmetics, plastic surgery, health clubs, and workout equipment. And with good reason: Studies show that overweight, nonathletic, not-very-beautiful applicants are discriminated against in both college admissions and

We are so accustomed to our culture's scripts that we take expected role behavior for granted. Both these Japanese businessmen and American vacationers would be disconcerted if their companions suddenly began to breach their expected social rules.

employment. How we see ourselves also depends on our bodies; few Americans today escape "the tyranny of perfection."

To be sure, exercising and eating lean are good for our health. But is that why we pursue the perfect shape? Glassner thinks not. Fitness, he argues, has become a status symbol, a way of announcing one's social class. As the saying goes, "You can never be too rich or too thin." Glassner cites a survey in which the respondents, a cross section of Chicagoans, were asked to define health. Two distinct views were expressed. Middle-class professionals saw health as something you achieve through discipline and self-control, much as you achieve wealth through hard work and wise investments. To them flabbiness was a sign of laziness (not heredity, age, or ill health) and therefore a pitfall to be avoided at all costs. Working-class and poor people, in contrast, saw health as something you enjoy, a winning ticket that allows you to let go and kick up your heels. In practical terms they do not have the time and money to prepare a lean cuisine or to join health clubs. More subtly, their experiences in the workplace have undermined the myth that hard work pays off, in health or wealth. Meanwhile countless middle- and upper-class girls and women literally make themselves sick (becoming anorexic or bulimic), striving to achieve the perfect body, regardless of whatever limitations their heredity and everyday lives might impose. Glassner writes, "The ideal body isn't so ideal after all[;] it stands not only for beauty and health but also for false hopes and prejudices" (1992, p. 258). Our bodies and body images remain crucial components of our identities.

Negotiations and "Face-Work"

In all social encounters, participants' identities are on the line. In order to define the situation, participants must negotiate who will play which roles and to what degree they will support one another's acts (see Figure 6-1). At first, social actors hint at the image they want to present, without fully committing themselves. (Goffman called these hints *deniable communications*.) Tentatively, they edge into the positions they would like to claim. At the same time, they observe other people's reactions, note what roles they want to play, and perhaps adjust their own lines. At an informal brunch before a convention, you don't see anyone you know. You

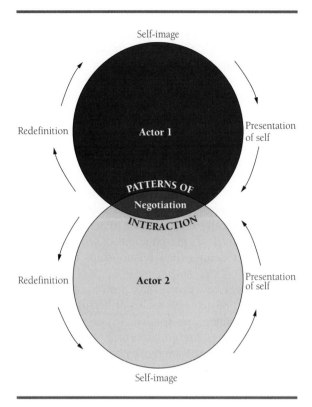

Figure 6-1   *Social Interactions: Identity Defined and Redefined*

Individuals bring memories of their previous social encounters to every new meeting. Their behavior is in part a response to an immediate situation and a reflection of previous encounters. A person's self-image is modified according to the degree of success or failure experienced in each interaction.

spot an animated group, ask if a seat in their circle is taken, and they invite you to sit down. You decide to try playing the role of sophisticate, and casually mention "The last time I was in Budapest . . ." A group member responds, "Ah, Budapest. The treasures I've found at Escery! I think it's the best flea market east of Paris, don't you? I'm sure you know Kecskenet: the artists, the apricot brandy. . . ." Realizing that you are in over your head, you switch to your athlete role: "Actually, I was on my way to Zermatt and the plane was diverted. Do you ski?" Another person joins in: "I started skiing this year, in Colorado, but I'm not very good" (acknowledging your hinted expertise). "You need to spend a week, maybe two, taking lessons; then you'll be on your feet," you counsel, adding, "That's what I did" (to show you're not a skiing snob). "Zermatt? in Switzerland? That's near where they found the 4,000-year-old ice man. Fascinating!" a third person pipes in, seizing an opportunity to play the role of amateur archaeologist. And so you and the other parties experiment with different lines, testing each other's reactions, until you find a comfortable niche.

For participants to arrive at a workable definition of the situation, there must be a certain amount of give-and-take. Each participant knows that to some degree he or she and everyone else are posturing. Ideally, they all agree to act *as if* they believed one another's presentations of self. This negotiated order defines their relationships toward one another.

Moreover, everyone has a stake in the encounter. If one actor blows his or her part, the others' performances are spoiled. If one person loses face, the others are embarrassed. Hence people tend to support one another's efforts at impression management. Goffman calls this *face-work* (as in "saving face"). "Much of the activity during an encounter can be understood as an effort on everyone's part to get through the occasion and all the unanticipated and unintentional events that can cast participants in an undesirable light, without disrupting the relationships of participants" (Goffman, 1967, p. 41).

When someone does something out of character, others protectively turn away to give the person time to pull himself or herself together. For example, if you realize that someone is on the verge of tears in a public place, you are likely to look the other way. When a professor who is trying to act dignified in front of a guest lecturer belches or yawns, everyone pretends not to notice. (Goffman called this reaction *civil inattention*.) When one member of a group unintentionally insults another, others quickly change the subject to cover up the mistake. These courtesies are an expected part of social interaction. Ideally, individuals are "expected to go to certain lengths to save the feelings and face of others present, and . . . to do this willingly and spontaneously because of emotional identification with the others and with their feelings" (Goffman, 1967, p. 10). Embarrassment must be avoided (see *Close Up:* Embarrassment: The Last Taboo). Public figures do not enjoy this immunity, however.

Exchange and Reciprocity

Why do we go to such lengths to protect and support one another's acts? A number of sociologists see social exchange as the key ingredient in interpersonal relations (Blau, 1964; K. Cook, 1990; Gouldner, 1973; Homans, 1990). The glue that binds individuals to one another is the **norm of reciprocity,** which demands that we respond in kind to certain behavior ("You scratch my back, I'll scratch yours"). When one person gives another person a gift, assistance, advice, compliments, intimate revelations, or even love, the giver expects to get something of equivalent value in return. By the same token, when a person accepts a gift, invitation, admiration, etc., he or she is obliged to reciprocate.

The norm of reciprocity is far more pervasive, and powerful, than most of us realize: "Neighbors exchange favors; children, toys; colleagues, assistance; acquaintances, courtesies; politicians, concessions; discussants, ideas; [cooks], recipes" (Blau, 1964, p. 88). Because of the norm of reciprocity, you are not free to ignore a greeting from a friend you meet walking across campus, for example. If you do not return the hello or do not offer an explanation or excuse the next time you meet, you may lose the friend. We feel uncomfortable in the presence of someone who is far more (or less) physically attractive, intelligent, sophisticated, wealthy, or talented than we are in large part because the exchange is unequal. We (or the other person) cannot repay in kind, and so we are less likely to form a lasting bond.

Social exchange differs from purely economic exchange in that the terms are subtle and diffuse rather than specific and concrete. As in economic exchange, participants seek to maximize their profits and minimize their losses. But three types of "currency" are involved in social exchanges: material rewards (money, labor, goods, information, prestige); intrinsic rewards (the satisfaction of doing a good job, bodily pleasure, simple joy); and identity support (confirmation of one's self-image) (McCall and Simmons, 1972). Some exchanges are primarily material. People cannot live on imagined role performances alone; to pursue their goals and plans they require material resources. Some interactions or performances are rewarding in and of themselves: pure pleasure overrides other considerations. And some exchanges are sought primarily be-

Some social exchanges, such as close, warm interactions between friends, are intrinsically rewarding because of the pleasure they provide.

cause they enable the participants to live up to their imagined performances, to see themselves and to be seen by others as they wish to be seen. Which of their various identities actors put forward in a given situation depends on many factors, including the amount of time and effort they have invested in that identity, the self- and social support they have received in the past, the intrinsic and extrinsic rewards associated with it, and the degree to which they believe others will support their current performance. People tend to gravitate toward the situations and relationships that offer material rewards, intrinsic satisfaction, and identity support.

Networks: The Social Fabric

A **network** is the web of relationships that connects an individual to many other people, both directly and indirectly. The diagram of Joe College's role set (Figure 5-1, p. 169) included seven relationships. For simplicity's sake, let's say this comprises Joe's entire social circle. Each of these people has a social circle of his or her own. A more complete picture of Joe's social world would connect their orbits to his. In some cases these connections would overlap. Joe's professor teaches one of his teammates in another class; the bookstore manager is dating a woman who is Joe's brother's teacher. In other cases, these connections lead to new relationships. One of Joe's classmates invites him home for the weekend

and takes him to a party given by a high school friend; someone he meets there tells him about a summer job opening at a dude ranch in Wyoming; at the ranch he meets a young woman whose mother works for the same company as Joe's mother, but in a different city; and so on and on. Joe's actual social network would include hundreds of connections, some close and multifaceted (a classmate who lives in the same dorm, whose father went to college with Joe's father, whose mother is Joe's sister's boss) and many more loose and distant (the friend of a friend's second cousin).

Networks are a familiar part of our everyday lives. For example, when businesspeople meet someone in their line of work at a cocktail party or a sports club, they exchange cards, expanding their networks. When we apply for admission to college, attempt to change jobs, or purchase a big-ticket item, we try to think of who we know (or who among our acquaintances knows someone) who can give us inside information and perhaps open doors. People are more likely to get a job through their networks than through newspaper ads, employment agencies, or other formal, conventional means (Granovetter, 1974). One reason why it is difficult for minority members, women, and other "outsiders" to get top jobs is that they are not part of the "old-boy" network and often do not learn about opportunities to advance their careers.

There are several approaches to studying networks. One, a microapproach, is to examine actual

CLOSE UP

Embarrassment: The Last Taboo

Embarrassment is an inevitable part of social interaction. People routinely monitor their own performances and so cannot help but notice slips and blunders. But while we consider it socially acceptable to express pride, acknowledging feelings of embarrassment is taboo. As Erving Goffman noted, to admit embarrassment is "considered evidence of weakness, inferiority, low status, moral guilt, defeat, and other unenviable attributes" (1967, pp. 101–102).

As part of a larger study of heterosexual dating patterns, C. Lee Harrington (1992) analyzed videotaped interviews of five men and five women between the ages of 20 and 23. Harrington focused on the emotions involved in asking for a date. He found that subjects used a variety of verbal and nonverbal techniques to cover up or minimize the expression of embarrassment.

One technique was *verbal mitigation,* or downplaying the intensity of the experience or the importance of the event.

Verbal qualifiers (in italics) were common:

> "Uhm: even if it's a friend *sometimes* you get embarrassed."

> "You *kinda* fear rejection a *little bit.*"

> "I *guess* I don't like rejection." (p. 208)

> **Open expression of feelings, especially negative feelings, is considered a form of "public littering."**

A second technique was *projection.* Instead of admitting the emotion as his or her own, the speaker projects it onto other people, using "you," "they," or "people" rather than the personal pronoun "I":

> "Uhmm: even if it's a friend sometimes *you* get embarrassed because *you* don't know really what they think or if they really want to go."

> "Well, *no one* likes to be rejected."

> "[When rejection occurs] it's not like *you* feel sorry for *yourself* but . . . *you* lower *your* own esteem." (p. 211)

Projection gives the speaker a built-in ally: "*I'm* not alone, *anyone* would feel embarrassed," defending himself or herself from social isolation and stigmatization.

Another common strategy is to add the verbal tag "*Ya know.*" In this way the speaker invites the listener to share in, and agree with, the emotion:

> "I've tended not to let it bother me anymore *ya know* if a girl rejects me she rejects me."

> "'Cause you're like *ya know* is she gonna say yes or is she gonna say no or what is she gonna say?" (p. 212)

"Ya know" transforms an isolating experience into a common or collective one.

Some speakers deny embarrassment altogether, by inserting

networks within a particular social unit. A sociologist might ask the fifty members of a sorority to list their five closest friends. This simple exercise would reveal whether cliques are sharply defined (each member of the clique names all the others, but no outsiders) or diffuse (the people who Sue named as friends did not necessarily name one another). We would probably also learn that some people were named more often than others and by several women whom they did not include on their own list. Another sociologist, looking at these findings, could rank the most popular women (who was selected most often, second most often, etc.) and predict something about the dynamics in the sorority, without ever meeting the young women involved. For example, if there are several cliques in the sorority rather than diffuse friendships, the sociologist would predict conflict.

Another approach is to analyze different types of networks (see Figure 6-2). For example, a network of five people might take the form of a clique (in which everyone is connected to everyone else), an

"*I dunno.*" This verbal tag not only signals uncertainty but also distances the speaker from the emotion:

> [How come you've never asked anybody out?] "I *dunno* I guess I'm shy about things like that."

> "Oh I like it if guys're taller 'n me too."
> [How come?]
> "Jus' I *dunno* I jus' it I it jus' bothers me when they're shorter." (p. 214)

Even after they have denied having the requested information ("I dunno"), most speakers still attempt to answer the question.

Finally, the speaker may use *laughter* to buffer an admission of embarrassment:

> "I called a girl on the phone and (*laugh*) asked her out and I sounded like a fool 'cause I had planned everything I was gonna say."
> [Did you go out with her?]

"No: cuz I sounded so stupid (*laugh*) she didn't want to go out (*laugh*)." (p. 217)

"I mean I won't be really rude but I'll kinda let them know that I'm not interested. I'll just pretty much just get up and walk away I think."
[And they get the hint?]
"Pretty much and then they call me names (*laugh*) or something."
[Do they really?] (p. 216)

Emotion researchers have long recognized the relationship between laughter and embarrassment. Some hold that laughter is a bid for intimacy, an attempt to reduce the social distance between the speaker and the listener; others see laughter as a form of catharsis, as a way of reducing tension. What is significant here is that the laughter is one-sided. In most talk, laughter is mutual; the conversational partners share their amusement. In "troubles-talk," however, the confessor or complainant may laugh, but it would be rude for the listener to do so. (Note that in all the examples here, the speaker uses more than one device to deny embarrassment.)

Harrington concludes that people avoid direct, frank expressions of embarrassment for two reasons. One is the general social rule that people are supposed to control their emotions. Open expression of feelings, especially negative feelings, is considered a form of "public littering" (Gaylin, 1979; Scheff, 1988). Another is the rule that participants in social interaction must be poised from the outset: to admit embarrassment is to lose poise, spoiling the encounter. Analyzing speech patterns, as Harrington did, shows how far we go to live up to these implicit rules even when we all have shared in the emotion and felt humiliated.

---

orbit (in which one person serves as the connection to all the others), a chain (in which connections become increasingly distant), or a ring (in which each person has more than one connection). If one member of a clique moves, the network is likely to remain intact; if the central member of an orbit moves, this is less likely. Information may travel faster around a ring than along a chain.

A macroapproach requires the use of computers and advanced statistical methods to analyze the actual networks that develop among different cate-

gories of people or even whole populations. Sociologists who work at this level ask such questions as these: Which is more likely to lead to friendship, living near someone or working with someone? What proportion of the people who are linked through their jobs are also linked as members of the same church or voluntary organization? To what extent do the friendship networks of African Americans, Latinos, Asians, and whites overlap? Networks are created through social interaction, but do not depend on frequent contact. The popularity of

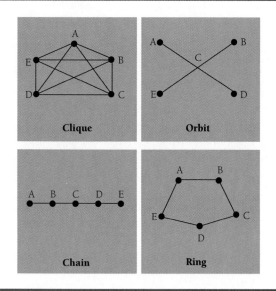

Figure 6-2 *Four Different Network Patterns*

The interactions among members of a five-person network may be overlapping (as in a clique), focused on a key person (as in an orbit), or diffuse and indirect (as in a chain or ring).

high school, college, and family reunions reflects the ease with which old connections can be renewed after years, even decades, of separation.

Social Groups

Groups are the crucible of social structure, the setting in which positions and roles, as well as norms for social interaction, are enacted, tested, and negotiated. Groups are more structured than networks or everyday interaction in the sense that they require leadership, agreement on values and established patterns of interaction, regular contact, and clear boundaries. But groups are also dynamic: leadership may change, members may switch roles, and the group's size may expand or contract.

What Is a Group?

In ordinary conversation, "group" is a multipurpose word. Sometimes people use it to refer to an **aggregate,** or a collection of people who just happen to be in the same place at the same time. People sitting in a doctor's reception room or waiting on a corner for the traffic light to change or an audience in a theater would constitute an aggregate. These individuals are close to one another physically and have an activity in common. But they do not interact with one another unless something happens, say, an accident on the street or a fire in the theater. Even then, their connections to one another would be limited and brief.

Sometimes people use the word "group" to describe a **social category**—individuals classified together because they share a certain characteristic, such as playing for the NBA or WNBA, being overweight, being very rich, or being homeless. We lump these people together in our minds. But they do not congregate in one place, they do not interact with one another, and they may or may not attach any significance to the characteristic they share.

A **social group** differs from these haphazard collections of individuals in four ways. First, members of a group have *shared identity*. They believe they have something in common and that this "something" makes a difference. Female representatives in a legislature are aware that some of the other legislators are members of their sex; if they attach no special significance to this, they are not a group. However, they may become a group—by forming a women's "caucus," for instance—if they come to see their sex as a basis for common interests and develop a sense of "we" (women) as opposed to "them" (men).

Second, members of a social group *interact regularly*. If three alumni of Notre Dame University meet for lunch and then go their separate ways, they are not a group in the sociological sense. If they make a point of getting together every so often, and see their lunches as special, they tend to become a group.

Third, social groups have a *social structure*. Members do not interact on a random basis. Formally or informally, they establish a structure of roles and statuses to coordinate their activities. However subtly, some become leaders, some lieutenants, and some followers. The degree of structure in a group may change. A group of office friends who regularly lunch together will likely be loosely structured. If rumors of a layoff or a case of sexual harassment prompts them to take action, they are likely to organize, establish a division of labor, select a spokesperson, and so on. This more structured group may dissolve after the issue is resolved, or it may persist over time and despite changes in membership.

Fourth, social groups depend on *consensus*. Members must agree to some extent on values, norms, and goals. Suppose a group of neighbors get together to discuss the problem of stray cats and dogs in their neighborhood. If some see the purpose of forming the group as getting rid of the strays by rounding them up and sending them to the pound where they will likely be euthanized, while others want to take the animals in, get them veterinary care, and find homes for them, the group is likely to fall apart at the start. Indeed, they might stop talking to one another. The greater the consensus on values, norms, and goals and the more likely that group members can engage in friendly debate, the less likely that friction will break a group apart.

To sum up, then, a social group is a number of people who feel a common identity and interact in a regular and structured way, on the basis of shared norms and goals.

Types of Groups

Groups vary along a number of dimensions, including degree of intimacy and involvement, size, structure, and impact on behavior.

Primary and Secondary Groups

Clearly, different kinds of groups carry different meanings. It is one thing for a man to learn that his retirement planning committee is disbanding; another, that his wife wants a divorce after their youngest child leaves for college. The family is an example of what sociologists call a primary group; the committee, an example of a secondary group.

Charles Horton Cooley (1909) coined the term ***primary group*** to describe a small, warm association based on ongoing, personal, intimate relationships. Members of primary groups care about one another as people; they share experiences, opinions, and fantasies and feel "at home" together. They may occasionally argue with one another, especially if they think one member is being disloyal or if they feel they are not receiving the attention and support they expect, but they nevertheless remain united. Members of primary groups identify with one another's triumphs and disasters. To a significant extent, they derive their individual identi-

ties from membership in the group. In Cooley's words:

> [Primary groups] are fundamental in forming the social nature and ideas of the individual. The result of intimate association, psychologically, is a certain fusion of individualities in a common whole, so that one's very self, for many purposes at least, is the common life and purpose of the group. Perhaps the simplest way of describing this wholeness is by saying that it is a "we." (1909, p. 23)

A ***secondary group*** is a "cool," impersonal association whose members' relationships are limited and instrumental. Secondary groups are created to achieve a specific goal. They are a means to an end, not an end in themselves (as primary groups are). Individuals are valued for what they can do for the group, not for who they are as individuals. Members need not know much about one another. They don't even have to like one another. Conversation in secondary groups is usually limited to polite small talk and to discussion of the business at hand. A committee is a typical secondary group (Olmsted and Hare, 1978, p. 8).

The concepts of primary group and secondary group are summarized in Table 6-1. In reality, few groups are purely primary or purely secondary. For example, a theater company may begin its existence as a secondary group, but as the members of the company rehearse and perform together, they are likely to turn more and more into a primary group and perhaps even feel like a family. Members become involved in one another's personal lives and are sensitive to one another's moods. When the play closes, however, this "family" typically breaks up.

Table 6-1   *Primary and Secondary Groups*

Primary Groups	Secondary Groups
1. Frequent face-to-face association	1. Occasional face-to-face interaction
2. Diffuse relationships (involving numerous activities and interests)	2. Limited relationships (interaction limited to the task at hand)
3. Relationships valued in themselves	3. Relationships are instrumental (seen as a means to an end)
4. High level of intimacy	4. Low level of intimacy
5. Small number of persons; members irreplaceable	5. Group size flexible; members replaceable

Reference Groups

We all use certain groups as a touchstone for evaluating ourselves and monitoring our behavior. As we saw in Chapter 4, such groups are known as **reference groups.** For an inner-city teenager the reference group might be a street gang or a rap group; for a politician running for office it might be a local political club; for a woman making a career or marriage decision, her reference group might be her family, her friends, or female public figures she admires. Reference groups may be primary or secondary; it is not even necessary to belong to a group to use it for reference. Thus, a reference group is not always a social group. Some groups serve as negative reference groups; they are groups that we do not want to belong to or to be identified with. For instance, a "metal head" dressed in grunge would probably not want to be associated with preppies in khakis and crew necks.

Reference groups serve two main functions. One is *normative*: we look to the group to set and enforce standards of behavior and belief. In recent years, the impact of normative reference groups on young people, in particular, has raised concern. For example, superthin models, as a normative reference group for adolescent girls and young women, may contribute to unrealistic ideas of what is normal and to eating disorders. In urban ghettos, where few adult men are steadily employed, drug dealers and their young employees, who flaunt large amounts of cash, and wear expensive clothes and jewelry (or gang colors), may serve as a normative reference group for young children. On college campuses, fraternities may set standards for self-destructive drinking patterns and abusive attitudes and behavior toward women (Sandy, 1990).

The other function of reference groups is *comparative*: the group provides standards by which we can measure ourselves. An individual's self-esteem—and aspirations—depend in part on whom he or she uses as a comparative reference group. Suppose a student finishes her freshman year of college with a 3.8 grade point average (out of a possible 4.0). Compared with other students at her college, she is doing extremely well. This student attends a state university. It has a good reputation—but it isn't Harvard or Stanford. If she uses other freshmen at her university as a reference group, she will have a high evaluation of her abilities and career potential. If, however, she compares herself with all college freshmen, her feelings about herself and her aspirations will be more moderate. Thus, depending on whom she uses as a reference group, she may see herself as a big frog in a small pond or as a small frog in the large pond of all American college students (see Figure 6-3).

Research over many years suggests that most students use the entire college community as a reference group (e.g., Bassis, 1977). In high school, if not before, they learn that some colleges and uni-

Figure 6-3   *First Choose the Frog Pond: The Comparative Function of the Reference Group*

Depending on the choice of reference group, a student may have a high, moderate, or low view of his or her abilities and achievements.

versities are far more selective, and therefore more prestigious, than others. In the ranks of colleges and universities, students know approximately where their school stands. Moreover, they know that when they apply for a job or graduate school, they will be competing against students from the entire array of universities. Most students want an accurate assessment of their career prospects.

A classic study conducted during World War II demonstrates the power of reference groups from a somewhat different angle (Stouffer et al., 1949). One part of the study asked soldiers to evaluate their chances for promotion within their branch of the service. The results might be considered surprising: Soldiers in branches with low promotion rates evaluated their chances for promotion more optimistically than did soldiers in branches with high promotion rates. But consider the reference groups that these soldiers used for purposes of evaluation. A soldier in a branch with a low promotion rate compared himself with a group that had not been promoted much; therefore his own chances seemed better than average. The soldier who compared his lot with others who had experienced high rates of promotion rated his own chances less optimistically. It seems, then, that our individual impressions are not governed so much by the absolute state we are in as by our relative state, as compared with some reference group.

In-Groups and Out-Groups

In-groups and out-groups express the idea of "us" versus "them." Opposing sports teams, rival gangs, political parties, and competing schools are examples. The **in-group** is a group to which people feel that they belong; it commands their loyalty and respect. The **out-group** is, by contrast, a group one feels opposed to or in competition with. These terms, introduced by William Graham Sumner (1906/1959), apply not only to specific social groups but also to entire nations, regions, religions, and ethnic groups. Members of in-groups often consider themselves not just different from but superior to members of out-groups. The ongoing conflict among Croats, Bosnians, and Serbs in the former Yugoslavia is an extreme example of the consequences of in-group and out-group beliefs and behaviors (see Chapter 9).

American colleges and universities are becoming increasingly multicultural, as the numbers and pro-

A Muslim man begs Serbian commandos for his life in Bosnia. The conflict in the former Yugoslavia is an extreme example of the consequences of in-group/out-group beliefs and behaviors.

portions of immigrants and foreign students grow. Given racial tensions on many campuses, ethnic conflicts are a distinct possibility. To what extent do American students accept classmates of other nationalities? Janet Ruscher and her colleagues conducted an experiment on in-group–out-group perceptions at a private southern university (Ruscher, O'Neal, and Hammer, 1997). The subjects, 135 male undergraduates, were divided into control and experimental groups. The control groups were shown a taped interview with a student identified as "Latvian," who described his impressions of the United States in neutral or benign terms. The experimental groups watched an interview in which the supposed Latvian described the students at the participants' university as materialistic, shallow, uninterested in world events, and conceited. The subjects were also shown slides depicting eight positive and four negative actions performed by other Latvians or by Senegalese. Their actions were identical; the only difference was their national identity. (The experimenters chose Latvians and Senegalese because prior testing showed that the American students were not familiar with, and therefore had no preconceptions about, either nationality.)

The subjects were asked to rate the "Latvian" interviewee in terms of likability, friendliness, and similarity to American college students (the in-group). Not surprisingly, the subjects who watched the provocative interview gave him low ratings. Next, subjects were asked to rate the students in the slides in terms of their similarity to American students. The control groups, who had not been provoked, saw few differences between either the Latvian or the Senegalese students and themselves. The experimental groups rated the Senegalese as "similar," but the Latvians as "different," as an out-group. Thus one negative impression of a student from another country led the subjects to generalize this impression to others from the same back-ground and view "them" as different from "us." This finding does not bode well for intergroup re-lations on campus. By extension, a cultural misun-derstanding may lead to stereotypes and avoid-ance. For example, Middle Easterners consider it only polite to praise and do favors for an older per-son in a position of authority, such as a professor; American students consider this "apple polishing," even a violation of the code that students should be graded on the basis of their work, not personal-ity or liking. Likewise, Americans may violate other students' cultural norms, such as *not* taking off their shoes before entering an Indonesian's home or refusing a cup of tea, acts Indonesians see as ex-tremely rude. One or two bad experiences may lead students to seek out members of their in-group and avoid members of out-groups, increas-ing the possibility of misunderstandings and mu-tual distrust. (See Chapter 10 for more on ethnic relations.)

Peer Groups

A **peer group** consists of people who share similar characteristics. In some cases, the term "peer group" is used to describe a category of people (who often serve as a reference group) or people who are about the same age and social status: fourth-graders, medical residents, or senior citizens. The American legal system, for example, grants ac-cused criminals the right to be tried by a "jury of their peers" (meaning fellow citizens, as opposed to judges only). Today, the term is used to apply to a social group whose members not only are the same age and status but interact frequently. In this sec-tion we look at social peer groups.

Most discussions of peer groups focus on ado-lescence, when young people may use peers as a wedge between themselves and their families (in-deed, adults in general), as a first step toward es-tablishing independent identities. But peer groups are important at all ages. New parents tend to so-cialize with other new parents and to measure their success as parents in terms of their friends' chil-dren, not in terms of their parents' and in-laws' standards. Classical musicians may or may not so-cialize with other musicians, but their self-image and self-esteem depend more on their colleagues' evaluations than on their friends' and families' opinions.

Peer groups are particularly important to the elderly, who tend to be highly social and spend a great deal of time with their peers.

Peer groups seem to be particularly important to older people. Many of us assume that the elderly tend to be lonely. In fact research shows that older Americans (who are not physically or mentally disabled) often are highly social and spend a lot of their time visiting with and talking to peers. Much as they enjoy seeing their children and grandchildren, senior citizens often consider people their own age as more reliable sources of support and assistance (FitzGerald, 1986). With peers they can relax and admit frailties, without feeling they are burdening their busy middle-aged children with their problems or interrupting their children's schedules. In one study, half of the older Americans questioned said they had between eleven and forty friends with whom they were in frequent contact and whom they felt comfortable asking for help in their daily lives. Friends form car pools, cook for one another, read to a friend whose eyesight is failing, and the like. Some studies have found that older people who live among peers in retirement communities enjoy better health and even live longer than do older people in other settings (Quadagno, 1986).

The Importance of Group Size: Dyads and Triads

Numbers have an independent effect on groups (Simmel, 1905/1964). Regardless of a group's other characteristics, the addition or subtraction of members will alter relationships.

The smallest possible social group is a *dyad,* or two-person group. Compared with other groups, a dyad is extremely fragile. If one member leaves, the group ends. Dyads depend on a high degree of commitment; the members must feel that this relationship is unique and irreplaceable. Often dyads are highly personal, intimate associations. For example, married couples reveal things to each other that they do not show to other people. The same is true of close friends or business partners. Dyads frequently confront all-or-nothing situations. There is no third party to mediate in disputes. Members must reconcile their differences, endure hostilities, or part.

A *triad,* or three-person group, differs from a dyad in two important respects. First, a triad can suffer the loss of one member and still be a group. Second, the addition of a third person creates the possibility of coalitions and exclusions. Consider what happens when the first child arrives in a family. Suddenly, the marriage partners do not have exclusive time for each other. If the mother is the primary caretaker, the father may feel neglected and left out of the bonding process. The abrupt change from dyad to triad often requires a period of adjustment—the root of the saying "Two's company; three is a crowd."Another characteristic of triads is that they have a tendency to divide into two against one (Caplow, 1969). This tendency can be seen among business partners as well as cliques of teenage girls. Still, members often shift alliances from one dispute to the next, and this helps maintain group solidarity.

With the addition of a fourth member, the number of possible relationships and the complexity of the group increase significantly. For example, two members may line up on one side of an issue and two on the other, creating a stalemate, or one member may oppose the other three. Communication also becomes more problematic. With five the group becomes even more complex, and so on. The larger a group, the more vulnerable it is to subdivisions. (See Figure 6-4.)

Behavior in Groups

Group structure has a significant impact on the way individuals act and even think. Without knowing the particular individuals who compose a group, it is possible to predict regular patterns in the emergence of leaders, responses to group pressure, and group decision making.

Leadership

Common sense holds that "some people are born leaders," that leadership depends on special personality traits. In fact, sociologists have found that leadership is as much a function of the requirements of the group as of the personalities of individuals (Neville, 1983). Whether elected, appointed, or chosen informally during the course of interaction, leaders tend to be self-confident and talkative, offering numerous suggestions and opinions. Others see them as deeply committed to the group's values and determined to achieve its goals (Trice and Beyer, 1991). The individual's prestige outside the group and competence in areas that might facilitate group goals are also important. But

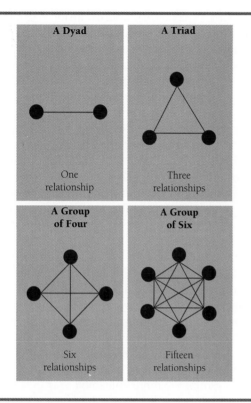

A Dyad

One relationship

A Triad

Three relationships

A Group of Four

Six relationships

A Group of Six

Fifteen relationships

Figure 6-4   *The Incremental Effects of Group Size on Relationships*

traits that have no obvious connection to ability to lead also count. People who are tall and considered good looking are more likely to become leaders than are short, average-looking people (Stodgill, 1974; Crosbie, 1975). (But see *Close Up:* Status, Emotions, and Getting Ahead.)

Sociologists distinguish between two basic types of leadership: *instrumental leadership* (organizing work, setting standards, and keeping the group's attention and energy focused on achieving its goal) and *expressive leadership* (building team spirit, maintaining group morale, mediating disputes, and being supportive). Groups, even small ones, seem to need both types. In the early stages of group formation, one individual may fill both roles (Slater, 1955; Olmstead and Hare, 1978). Because an instrumental leader is task-oriented and pushes group members to "stick to business," he or she often becomes unpopular and may create friction in the group. Because an expressive leader wants to make everyone happy and give everyone a chance to be

heard, he or she may have difficulty getting anything done. With a division of leadership, one complements the other.

Furthermore, different situations call for different styles of leadership. If a group is not under any pressure to get something done, a *laissez-faire,* or laid-back, leadership style is appropriate. When a group of friends get together on a Saturday afternoon, for one person to take charge would interfere with the group's goal, which is simply to have fun. Such groups may appear leaderless but in fact usually depend on one person to say, "Okay, let's go." Looking back, most people can clearly identify the "ringleader" in the group of kids they hung out with in high school.

When a group needs to take care of business, a *democratic* style—soliciting ideas and opinions from group members, delegating authority, and helping a group achieve consensus—seems to work best. Many studies show that workers have higher morale, are more motivated to achieve, and perform better when they are given some control over their tasks (Burger, 1987). When a group is faced with a difficult assignment that must be accomplished under pressure, a *directive* style—making unilateral decisions, issuing orders, and insisting on compliance—may be called for. If warning lights begin to flash at a nuclear power plant, there isn't time for discussion; someone has to take command and see that emergency procedures are followed. Likewise, if a group of friends are deep-sea fishing and a storm suddenly appears on the horizon, someone must take command, acting as captain.

Emergencies are not the only situations in which directive leadership is effective. If a complex task requires the contributions of a number of highly trained specialists, a combination of democratic meetings and directive leadership may work best. If the task is demanding and participants receive periodic progress reports, directive leadership promotes motivation to achieve (Locke and Latham, 1990). If the work is dull and repetitive and workers have no control over their activities and receive no acknowledgment or information from managers, however, motivation and productivity decline.

The same basic principles of leadership apply not only to small groups but also to large formal organizations. The heads of corporations, for example, set the leadership style for middle management, establishing a "corporate culture." IBM, once

Like Apple Computer in the 1970s, many small, highly successful software companies exhibit a freewheeling, informal corporate style and a willingness to take risks. These young video and computer game programmers clearly enjoy their work.

the undisputed king of the computer industry and considered one of the most powerful corporations in the world, followed a strict policy of directive leadership. During its heydays in the 1950s and 1960s, its management policy was to encourage loyalty by maintaining stability, rarely firing or reassigning employees, and rarely bringing in "new blood." Executives and salespeople were expected to follow orders, down to wearing nearly identical blue suits and adopting similar lifestyles. Apple Computer was the opposite, an advocate of laissez-faire leadership. Created in a garage in the early 1970s by two computer hacks and college dropouts, Steve Jobs and Steve Wozniak, Apple bypassed larger companies (especially IBM) in a remarkably short time by selling personal, "user-friendly" computers to the general public. By 1980 it was a multimillion-dollar corporation. Apple's phenomenal success was based on a freewheeling corporate style and willingness to take risks. Apple prided itself on being "a corporation made up of a

new generation, unencumbered by the traditions of corporate America" (Sculley, 1987, p. 134). Weekend retreats replaced traditional boardroom-style meetings. The company hero was the "lone cowboy," the creative person who could do it all alone, exemplified by the company's maverick founders. Insofar as Apple had a structure, it was designed to protect individuals from any kind of managerial interference. Which leadership style was most effective? As it turned out, neither. Structured to avoid risk, IBM failed to anticipate the growing market for personal computers and user-friendly software; the corporation lost billions. In the early 1990s IBM's board of directors brought in a new CEO who promoted democratic leadership (as well as closing plants and laying off more than 60,000 employees). Structured to invite innovation, Apple's huge success with the first-generation MacIntosh was followed by new products (such as the hand-held "communicator" called Newton) that no one wanted. The CEO and other managers left, leaving

Status, Emotions, and Getting Ahead

In President Bush's White House, two senior staff members, Dick Darman and John Sununu, "each scored the maximum 1600 on the Scholastic Aptitude Tests [and] neither was at all reluctant to remind others of the fact" (Bromley, 1994, p. 43). Such status displays go on in all task-oriented or work groups. The degree of influence individuals exercise within a group depends in part on their status outside the group. Knowing this, people commonly find ways to display their credentials and thus enhance their standing. Dangling a Phi Beta Kappa key, beginning a sentence with "When I was at Harvard," and casually dropping a phrase in Latin (as if everyone knew Latin) are examples. In general, high-status group members have more opportunities to perform, receive higher evaluations, and have more influence on group decisions than do low-status members.

The hierarchical structure of a group, in turn, influences how people feel about a group. High-status group members are more likely to feel happy and satisfied with their experience in a group than are low-status members. Low-status group members have fewer opportunities to participate, have little influence on group decisions, and receive lower evaluations for their performance and thus are more likely to feel anger and resentment to-

This advice is not for women only.

ward the group. The result is a self-fulfilling prophecy (Merton, 1968). Positive emotions tend to enhance the motivation, commitment, and performance of top-ranking group members, "proving" that higher expectations for them were warranted. Conversely, negative emotions tend to dampen low-ranking group

members' motivation, commitment, and performance, "proving" that lower expectations for them were justified.

Reviewing the evidence of the impact of group structure and status on emotions, Michael Lovaglia and Jeffrey Houser (1996) wondered if the opposite might be true. Do emotions have an impact on status? In a series of experiments, they found that subjects who were designated high status were more positive than the others and that subjects who were in a good mood were more open to suggestions and more cooperative than those in a bad mood. In one experiment, 245 student subjects were given a test of leadership. The results were announced the following week, and much attention was given to the high scorers. In fact, the test had nothing to do with leadership; the "high scorers" were chosen at random, and the

---

Apple in disarray. In 1997, a new giant in the computer industry, Microsoft, stepped in to save Apple from self-destructing.

As these cases suggest, effective leadership—in formal organizations as in small groups—depends on a balance of expressive and instrumental, democratic or laissez-faire and directive styles. Studies conducted in India, Taiwan, and Iran found that the most effective supervisors in coal mines, banks, and government offices scored high on tests of both instrumental and expressive leadership (Smith and Tayeb, 1989). They were concerned about sched-

ules and productivity *and* sensitive to their subordinates' needs; they invited participation in decision making *and* inspired confidence and loyalty by consistently sticking to their goals.

Group Influence

The movie *Twelve Angry Men* (1957) opens with twelve hot, tired jurors filing into the deliberation room after a murder trial, eager to deliver a quick verdict of guilty and go home. One dissenter, played by Henry Fonda, refuses to vote guilty. Through heated debate, others jurors join him, one other participants were told they had scored below average. The subjects were divided into groups of six, each including one "high scorer" as the designated leader. As predicted, high-status subjects, who received more attention and deference than other group members, reported more positive emotions than did the other members. But the data revealed a twist: regardless of status, women reported more positive emotions than did men.

The researchers suggest that gender is a "diffuse" status, which ranks females lower than males in almost any situation. Yet gender roles inhibit women from expressing negative emotions.* In the workplace, this creates a double-bind. Women who consciously or unconsciously accept their lower status vis-à-vis men assume that males are more competent and have more to contribute than they do, leave decision making to them, and do not seek responsibility. They are the stereotypical secretaries, always cheerful and ready to follow the boss's orders. Because upbeat, cooperative people evoke positive emotions in others, these women are considered competent enough but thought to lack the drive that might lead to promotions. Women who believe themselves to be as competent as their male coworkers, resent being treated as inferior, and let their anger show evoke negative emotions in others. They may be labeled pushy and aggressive and viewed as unfeminine ("the bossy woman"). They aren't likely to be promoted, on the grounds that they are not "team players."

Lovaglia and Houser suggest a way out of this trap: impression management. To get ahead, a woman has to recognize the obstacles in front of her, but not let her frustration show. If a woman suppresses her resentment and expresses positive emotions, she is likely to be seen as motivated by group success. This evokes positive emotions in others, which in turn makes them more likely to listen to her suggestions and recognize her contributions. As a result, her chances of a positive job evaluation and promotion increase. The key is to recognize and resist negative preconceptions, while managing to appear content and cheerful.

This advice is not for women only. Anyone who is automatically perceived as low in status—because of race, ethnicity, disabilities, lesser educational credentials, or another reason—can benefit from this strategy.

*As in the television study at the beginning of this chapter, which found a majority of women claim to be "happy" even though their husbands bully them with the remote control.

---

by one, until they reach a unanimous verdict, "Not guilty." Fonda plays the all-American hero, the individual who defends what he believes regardless of what others think. All of us like to believe that we would stand up to group pressure in a situation like this. But the character Fonda plays is the exception. The reality is that the groups to which we belong exert a powerful influence on what we do and even what we think (Myers, 1993). (Recall Asch's experiment, described in Chapter 1.)

For example, you're not thirsty, but when your companion suggests stopping for something to drink, you suddenly feel parched. You begin each day with a 2-mile jog; when a friend or acquaintance joins you, you finish your laps much quicker. Sociologists call this *social facilitation*: the mere presence of another person or other people influences our desires and performance, even in noncompetitive situations—with an important qualification. If you feel you are good at an activity (say, singing), you'll do your best when other people are present; if you don't feel confident, you'll perform better alone (singing in the shower).

Social loafing occurs when people are working toward a common goal and individuals are not accountable for their own efforts. The game tug-of-war is an example. Do people working in teams of eight exert as much effort as they do in individual contests? Apparently not. Almost a century ago, a French engineer found that collective force in a game of tug-of-war was only half the sum of individuals' best efforts (Kravitz and Martin, 1986). When individuals are being evaluated for group performance—whether in a game, on a work crew, or on a classroom project—they tend to "coast," relying on the group to make up for their diminished effort. When students are assigned "joint" or collaborative term papers, almost invariably one student will complain that he or she did all the work while the partner or other group members slacked off.

The combination of excitement (social facilitation) and diffusion of responsibility (social loafing) in groups tends to *reduce inhibitions.* Under some circumstances, groups may encourage deviant or antisocial behavior. A famous example was captured in a videotape of four police officers beating unarmed motorist Rodney King, fracturing his skull in nine places, while twenty-three other officers passively stood by. In an equally disturbing incident in 1967, 200 University of Oklahoma students gathered to watch a disturbed student who was threatening to jump from a tower. The crowd began chanting "Jump. Jump!" and the student did (Zim-

bardo, 1969). In seems unlikely that a single officer, acting alone, would have committed such a savage beating or that one observer would have encouraged a potential suicide to jump. (We discuss behavior in crowds in more detail in Chapter 17.) In a more benign example, a team of researchers (Diener, 1976) observed 1,352 children on Halloween. Dressed in costumes, the children were (or believed they were) unidentifiable. In the homes with observers, the experimenter welcomed the children warmly, invited them to "take *one* of the candies," and left the room. Children in groups were twice as likely to take extra candy as children who were by themselves; but children who were asked their names and where they lived, whether alone or in a group, were half as likely to take more than one. Being part of a group does not necessarily unleash antisocial impulses; it may also encourage generosity and altruism. At a charity auction, for example, one high bid tends to promote even higher bids as people get caught up in the spirit of giving (Spivey and Prentice-Dunn, 1990).

Decision Making in Groups   Membership in a group may also promote what Irving Janis (1968) called *groupthink.* Once a tentative group decision has been made, discussions tend to center around rationalizing that decision, rather than considering alternatives. Leaders may use jokes and sarcasm (rather than information and reasoning) to pres-

Being part of a group may allow people to be less inhibited.

sure dissenters to agree. Under pressure, members may exercise self-censorship, withholding or discounting their personal misgivings. Some group members act as mind guards, "protecting" the group from information that might raise questions about the effectiveness or morality of the decision. If outside experts or skeptics raise questions about the wisdom of their decision, the group unites in opposing and discrediting the source of contrary views. Social pressure to support the group's decision, combined with self-censorship, creates an illusion of unanimity.

Groupthink is most likely to develop in highly cohesive groups with directive leadership that are operating under stress and insulated from outsiders (McCauley, 1989). The president and his hand-picked advisers, who often make decisions in closed meetings on the basis of information not available to the public, are a prime example.

Groupthink played a role in the decision to ignore intelligence reports that the Japanese were preparing to attack the United States, a decision that resulted in the bombing of Pearl Harbor in 1941; it was also a factor in the 1961 Bay of Pigs invasion of Cuba and in the escalation of the war in Vietnam (1964–1967), against advice that aerial bombardment and search-and-destroy missions would not succeed in bringing North Vietnam to the peace table.

NASA's decision to launch the space shuttle *Challenger* in 1986 is an often cited example of groupthink (McCauley, 1989; Myers, 1993). Public enthusiasm for the space program was on the decline, and NASA officials were determined to launch a successful mission. Engineers at Morton-Thiokol and Rockwell International, who manufactured critical parts of the shuttle, had expressed misgivings long before the launch. At issue were O-

(a) The Challenger *disaster illustrates what sociologists call the "risky shift," the tendency for groups to take more risks than people working alone. (b) At hearings held to investigate the failed launch, physicist Richard Feynman explained the O-ring problem that caused the disaster, a problem that NASA officials knew about before the launch but considered an acceptable risk.*

rings, which were installed to protect the rocket motor from propellant gases generated during the launch. The engineers were not convinced that the O-rings could withstand freezing temperatures on the launch pad. Reluctant to let NASA down, company managers dismissed the engineers' misgivings. As a result, NASA was operating under the illusion of unanimity.

The night before the launch the engineers again argued their case with managers and NASA officials in telephone conversations. The dissenters were asked to document their recommendation that the launch should be postponed. But tests of the O-ring had produced inconsistent findings; all the engineers could say was that they were uncertain. Exercising pressure to conform, one NASA official complained, "My God, Thiokol, when do we launch, next April?" Acting as a mind guard, the Morton-Thiokol executive polled his company's managers, not its engineers. The NASA executives who made the final decision to proceed with the fatal launch acted on the information they had, unaware that their enthusiastic and insistent leadership might have promoted groupthink.

When the sociologist Diane Vaughan (1996) began her investigation of the *Challenger* launch, she, like most others, believed the tragedy was the result of group pressure, violations of safety precautions, and miscommunication. But a careful, systematic examination of NASA's extremely detailed records convinced her otherwise. Engineers rarely can say with 100 percent certainty that a particular part or plan will work, especially with equipment as complex and sophisticated as a space shuttle. Rather, they define a level of "acceptable risk." The O-rings and many other parts fell into this category. NASA officials did know about the O-ring problems, but procedures required so many reports on various aspects of the project that these warnings were buried. Vaughan concluded that, ironically, the *Challenger* tragedy was a result of the strict scientific standards and organizational procedures specifically designed to prevent such accidents by eliminating guesswork and hunches. Given the use of technology that pushes the limits of physical and biological phenomena, accidents are inevitable (Tenner, 1996). Certainly, the last thing NASA wanted was for the shuttle to explode within minutes of the launch, incinerating a guest school teacher as well as trained astronauts.

The *Challenger* tragedy illustrates another dimension of group influence, what J. A. Stoner (1961) called the *risky shift*. When making decisions in groups, people tend to take more chances than they do when making decisions alone. In a series of experiments, Stoner presented subjects with various dilemmas—for example: "A man with a severe heart ailment must seriously curtail his customary way of life if he does not undergo a delicate medical operation which might cure him completely or might prove fatal" (Stoner, 1961, p. 58). Stoner asked subjects what they would advise the man to do. He found that when subjects made this decision alone, they usually recommended the conservative choice (in this case, that the man curtail his activities). When subjects made the decision as a group, however, they tended to recommend the more daring course (risk the operation). Stoner hypothesizes that groups made the risky shift for a number of reasons: because the group members diffuse responsibility (one person will not be blamed for making a poor choice), because American cultural values favor risk (in a group, individuals want to seem "with it"), and because groups tend to reduce individual inhibitions and release a desire for adventure.

The Case of Juries   Some of the most interesting research on group influence concerns juries. In the United States alone, 300,000 times a year, groups of citizens must reach a unanimous decision about whether a defendant is guilty or innocent, and of what crime (Kagehiro, 1990). Do the group pressures we have described affect their decisions? Neither sociologists nor reporters are permitted to observe jury deliberations directly; however, simulated trials with "mock juries" provide insight into the delivery of justice.

In two out of three cases, when a trial is completed and jurors retire to consider a verdict, they do *not* agree. Yet, after deliberation, more than 90 percent of juries deliver a unanimous verdict. Clearly the group influences individual decisions. What goes on behind those closed doors? Common sense suggests that group discussion provides individuals with new information, exposes them to different interpretations of the facts, and so may persuade them to change their minds. In fact, the reverse is true.

Dozens of studies have found that the group discussion often strengthens participants' original opinions, a phenomenon known as *group polarization* (Myers, 1993). Several factors contribute to polarization. When people know they will be expected to discuss an issue, they get their thoughts together and often adopt a more emphatic or extreme position. The very act of stating their opinions in their own words, taking a public stand, tends to increase commitment to a position. Hearing others express their points of view magnifies this effect. Individuals tend to assume (usually incorrectly) that other members of a group hold more conservative opinions than they do. As they learn that others share their view, they may take an even stronger stand. On questions of fact (is he guilty?), persuasive arguments are most likely to cause dissenting jurors to join the majority; however, on questions of value judgment (how long a sentence should he serve?) group pressure comes into play (Kaplan, 1989). The higher the status of a juror arguing a position, the more influential he (or less often she) will be.

In nine out of ten cases, juries reach the verdict favored by the majority on the first ballot (Davis et al., 1989). If jurors are split 50/50, a hung jury is likely. In contrast to the movie *Twelve Angry Men,* lone dissenters rarely prevail in jury deliberations. But a persistent, consistent, and self-confident minority can influence the majority. A steadfast minority prevents others from developing an illusion of unanimity and may influence jurors who otherwise would self-censor their doubts. A convert from the majority to the minority position has more influence on original minority members, with the result that when one person defects, others often follow, in a snowball effect. Interestingly, a minority that favors acquittal is more likely to make converts than one that favors conviction (Tindale et al., 1990). Indeed, one exception to the risky shift is that deliberation often makes jurors more lenient, erring on the side of caution.

Social pressure is a powerful force (as shown in Asch's experiment, described in Chapter 1). But conformity is not necessarily "blind, unreasoning slavish adherence to the patterns of behavior established by others or to the demands of authority" (Shaw, 1981, p. 280). Some degree of conformity is a necessary part of social life. If members of a soci-ety did not agree on minimal standards of behavior, such as norms of reciprocity, everyday interaction would dissolve into chaos. Consciously or unconsciously, we often follow well-known cultural scripts. But which script is appropriate, what role we will play in a given situation, and even our social identities are subject to negotiation.

Most of our activities take place in groups. For better or worse, group discussion more often leads individuals to strengthen their personal views and convictions (polarization) than the reverse. Groupthink, the risky shift, and giving in to group pressure are not inevitable. The presence of just one "confederate" makes it easier to stand up to group pressure; the risky shift is not as common as was once thought; and groupthink is preventable (see Figure 6-5). Membership in groups shapes the way people behave in more or less predictable ways. At the same time, however, groups and networks provide opportunities for spontaneity, creativity, and change.

Figure 6-5   *How to Avoid Groupthink*

1. Tell group members about groupthink, its causes, and its consequences.
2. Be impartial; do not endorse any position.
3. Ask everyone to evaluate critically; encourage objections and doubts.
4. Assign one or more members the role of "devil's advocate."
5. From time to time subdivide the group. Have the subgroups meet separately and then come together to air differences.
6. When the issue concerns relations with a rival group, take time to survey all warning signals and identify various possible actions by the rival.
7. After reaching a preliminary decision, call a "second-chance" meeting, asking each member to express remaining doubts.
8. Invite outside experts to attend meetings on a staggered basis; ask them to challenge the group's views.
9. Encourage group members to air the group's deliberations with trusted associates and report their reactions.
10. Have independent groups work simultaneously on the same question.

Source: Adapted from I. L. Janis, "Counteracting the Adverse Effects of Concurrence-Seeking in Policy-Planning Groups: Theory and Research Perspectives," in H. Brandstätter & others (Eds), *Group Decision Making,* New York: Academic Press, 1982, pp. 477–501. As appeared in D. G. Myers, *Social Psychology,* 4th ed., New York, McGraw-Hill, 1993.

SOCIOLOGY ON THE WEB

The On-Line Community

As the web grows and evolves, it fosters many new kinds of groups, as well as research about them. Begin this exercise by logging on to a few chat rooms or newsgroups and observing the interactions among members. These groups are easy to find. If your server does not maintain any groups, a quick search of the net, on almost any topic, will locate some for you.

Think about these questions: Is a chat room a social group? If so, what type of group? Are there leaders? What kind of leadership style is apparent? What kinds of group pressures and influences exist? Continue your exploration of these questions by logging on to the following sites, all maintained by researchers who study group processes:

http://www.sscnet.ucla.edu/soc/csoc/
The Center for the Study of the On-Line Community, at UCLA, posts research articles on its web site. Access them by clicking on "Usescan."

http://www.uiowa.edu/grpproc/
http://www.workteams.unt.edu/
These two sites, maintained by the Center for the Study of Group Processes (University of Iowa) and the Center for the Study of Work Teams (University of North Texas), provide links to other sites on work groups and group process, as well as research papers on group process.

Summary

1. **How do people establish and maintain rules for social interactions?** Everyday interaction depends on countless unspoken and often unconscious assumptions about how people ought to behave (ethnomethodology). In many cases, however, the situation is ambiguous. How people interact depends, first, on their definition of the situation and on whether the action takes place backstage or before an audience.

2. **How do individuals establish and maintain a social identity?** Our social identity—our image of ourselves and how we feel about ourselves—reflects how other people see us. Goffman emphasized the degree to which people attempt to manage the impression they make on others, or the "presentation of the self." To claim a desired role, social actors first must look and dress for the part. Even in private imaginings, other people affect our social identity. In public, which of many possible roles we play is the result of subtle negotiations with other participants in the interaction. Once identities are established, people generally cooperate to protect one another's performances. The collective effort to save face is based on norms of reciprocity.

3. **How do networks take shape?** The different roles people play and the groups and organizations to which they belong link individuals to one another, even though they may never have met.

4. **What is a social group?** A social group is distinguished from aggregates and social categories by four characteristics: shared identity, regular interaction, social structure, and consensus.

5. **What are the main types of social groups?** Social groups can be primary (based on intimate personal relationships) or secondary (based on impersonal instrumental relationships). Groups that we look to for models of behavior or attitude are known as reference groups. In-groups and out-groups are those we feel we belong to or we feel opposed to. Peer groups (in the social sense) are primary groups consisting of people in the same social status and usually of the same age.

6. **How does the size of a group affect the way the group functions?** Group size has an effect on group relationships. Dyads, or two-person groups, depend on a high degree of commit-

ment and are extremely fragile. Triads, or three-person groups, make coalitions and shifting alliances possible. The addition of more members increases the number of relationships and complexity of the group.

7. **What effect does the structure of a group have on individual and group behavior?**
Group structure creates predictable patterns of behavior, which can be seen in the emergence of leaders, responses to group pressure, and group decision making. Instrumental leaders coordinate activities to meet group goals, while expressive leaders specialize in interpersonal relationships; even small groups seem to need both. Different situations call for different styles of leadership (laissez-faire, democratic, or directive). Studies of large corporations suggest that too much emphasis on one style can be counterproductive.

Social facilitation, social loafing, and reducing inhibitions are some of the ways groups influence individuals. Small, cohesive, insulated groups are susceptible to groupthink, in which group members withhold opinions that might cast doubt on an agreed-upon course of action. Group decision making may encourage people to make more daring decisions than they would as individuals (the risky shift). Studies of simulated juries find that discussion leads to polarization (strengthening original beliefs). In most cases, the original majority decision prevails; lone individuals seldom convince the majority to change its opinion, but forceful minorities can.

Key Terms

aggregate   210

definition of the situation   201

ethnomethodology   200

in-group   213

network   207

norm of reciprocity   206

out-group   213

peer group   214

presentation of the self   203

primary group   211

reference groups   212

secondary group   211

social category   210

social group   210

social identity   203

social interaction   199

Recommended Readings

Berger, Peter and T. Luckmann. (1967). *The Social Construction of Reality.* New York: Doubleday.

Crosbie, Paul V. (Ed.) (1975). *Interaction in Small Groups.* New York: Macmillan.

Davis, Fred. (1992). *Fashion, Culture, and Identity.* Chicago: University of Chicago Press.

Garfinkle, Harold. (1967). *Studies in Ethnomethodology.* Englewood Cliffs, NJ: Prentice-Hall.

Goffman, Erving. (1959). *The Presentation of Self in Everyday Life.* New York: Anchor Books.

Hare, A. Paul, Edgar F. Borgatta, and Robert F. Bales. (1965). *Small Groups: Studies in Social Interaction,* rev. ed. New York: Knopf.

Homans, George C. (1950). *The Human Group.* New York: Harcourt Brace.

Janis, Irving L. (1989). *Crucial Decisions: Leadership in Policymaking and Crisis Management.* New York: The Free Press.

McCall, George J. and J. L. Simmons. (1972). *Identities and Interactions: An Examination of Human Associations in Everyday Life.* New York: The Free Press.

Vaughn, Dianne. 1996. *The Challenger Launch Decision: Risky Technology, Culture, and Deviance at NASA.* University of Chicago Press.

Chapter

Seven

Deviance and Social Control

The "beer crisis" of February 1621 was a major turning point in early American history (Lender and Martin, 1987). The Mayflower had set anchor in Cape Cod Bay two months earlier. The pilgrims had chosen a site and were laying the foundations of Plymouth colony. Until now the colonists had been living onboard ship, sending out work parties to erect permanent shelters on land. But the ship's beer supplies were running low, and the captain ordered the settlers ashore, where they would be forced to drink water. William Bradford, a future governor of the colony, begged for mercy. Finally, the captain relented and promised to provide "beer for them that need it" during the cold, hungry months that lay ahead.

Alcohol wasn't a luxury in the colonists' minds; it was a necessity. The pilgrims believed that drinking water was a serious health hazard—with reason. In seventeenth-century Europe, sanitation was primitive and the water supply in most towns and cities was contaminated. The colonists felt as vulnerable as modern tourists would feel if they were deep in the Amazon rain forest and lost their water purification kit. The pilgrims would learn that the water in the New World was pure and drinkable; even so, the wisdom of the day held that alcohol was essential to good health. A drink before breakfast lifted the spirit; several glasses with meals

aided digestion and strengthened the constitution; a nightcap warded off chills and fevers. At sea, it was critical. On long voyages, liquor kept well in wooden barrels, whereas water soon became foul. In leaving the pilgrims a supply of beer, the Mayflower's captain risked his own and his sailors' health on the voyage home.

On their own in the New World, the colonists began to experiment with local ingredients. Brewing ale, like baking bread, was part of a colonial housewife's regular routine. At mealtimes the usual beverages were beer and hard cider, served to children as well as adults. Farmers took a flask to the fields to dull the pain of backbreaking labor. A cask of spirits was considered essential to community activities, such as holding town meetings, clearing common fields, or raising the town church. Taverns were among the first structures to be put up in colonial towns, not only to accommodate travelers but also to serve as meeting places for local people. Tavern keepers were among the most respected town citizens. Libations were also enjoyed at weddings, baptisms, funerals, ordinations, and militia drills.

Drinking at meals and at work, at the tavern and on special

occasions, added up. Estimates are that by the 1790s, the average Anglo-American age 16 and older consumed 34 gallons of beer and cider, a little more than 5 gallons of distilled liquor, and a gallon of wine a year. This is twice the current average. History books rarely mention the great beer crisis of 1621, much less the fact that the pilgrims we learned to revere in grade school were, by today's standards, problem drinkers, if not outright alcoholics! Some readers will be surprised by this revelation; some will be amused; and a few will suspect that we made this up. We won't say yet which of you is right or wrong. But we will say that one goal of the sociology of deviance is to debunk common assumptions about what is normal, rational, acceptable behavior—and what is not.

We begin this chapter by introducing sociological perspectives on deviance; then we focus on crime and the criminal justice system in the United States.

Key Questions

1. *How do societies decide what behavior is deviant and attempt to control deviance?*
2. *What are the consequences of being labeled "deviant"?*
3. *What is the main difference between biological and psychological theories and sociological theories of deviance?*
4. *What are the main sociological theories of deviance?*
5. *What are the most common types of crime in our society, and how does our criminal justice system operate?*

What Is Deviance?

Deviance is a violation of social rules (Rubington and Weinberg, 1995). It occurs when someone breaches a society's or group's widely held values and norms. Behavior that is unconventional or atypical is not necessarily deviant. For example, vegetarians are a minority in North America. While many people may consider not eating any meat a bit odd, vegetarians are not considered deviant. But North Americans who love hamburgers and steak

would find the sight of puppies for sale in markets in Southeast Asia, where dog meat is considered a delicacy, repugnant. To us, dogs are pets, not dinner.

Some acts of deviance (such as sexual abuse of children) are widely condemned. In prisons, child molesters may be isolated from other inmates for their own safety. Other violations of social codes are so common that hardly anyone notices. For example, most people occasionally tell a "white lie" when they want to get out of a social engagement (saying "I've got a cold" or "I forgot I had other plans"). Everyone commits minor acts of deviance from time to time, usually without attracting public attention. But some behavior is considered beyond the limits.

From an **absolutist perspective,** deviance lies in the act itself, which may be viewed as a violation of natural law or a transgression against God's commandments (Clinard and Meier, 1992). The right-to-life movement, for example, considers abortion "absolutely" wrong, no matter where, when, or why a pregnancy is terminated. In their view, abortion is murder regardless of the circumstances surrounding the pregnancy (including rape or incest), risks to the mother's health, or knowledge that a baby will be born with a serious genetic defect or other disorder. Similarly, animal rights activists consider trapping animals for fur, confining them in factory farms, using exotic animals in circuses and films, and conducting scientific experiments with animals absolutely wrong. They believe that nonhuman animals are sentient (thinking, feeling) beings with the same rights to protection from torture and exploitation as human beings have. People who take an absolutist perspective may view violations of the laws of society as acceptable or even necessary to enforce the laws of God or nature. Thus some antiabortion groups rationalize bombing abortion clinics on the grounds that they are saving the lives of unborn babies; some animal activists rationalize breaking into laboratories and liberating animals from experiments as a humane act.

The absolutist perspective is not confined to groups that others might regard as extremist. For example, most Americans consider democracy the only legitimate form of government and view dictatorships and totalitarian governments as absolutely wrong, regardless of the time or place (see Chapter 14). And almost all of us believe that some acts (for example, cannibalism, slavery, or torture) are inherently deviant and must be stopped. As individuals, sociologists would agree; however, as scientists they are not "in the business" of deciding what is right or wrong, normal or abnormal. Rather, they seek to describe and explain patterns of deviant (as well as routine, everyday) behavior.

The Social Definition of Deviance

People everywhere distinguish between two broad categories of behavior: the good and desirable and the bad and undesirable (Goode, 1990). Every society establishes rules and regulations, experiences violations of those rules, and in one way or another punishes offenders. Deviance is universal. Behavior is seen as deviant when people are alarmed, angered, outraged, or threatened by violations of what they consider right and proper. But the social definition of deviance—what people view as right or wrong, praiseworthy or blameworthy—is highly variable. Acts that are considered sacred in some cultures may be viewed as sin, sacrilege, or sickness in another.

Cultural Variations

Social rules vary from one culture to another. Islam prohibits drinking even mildly alcoholic beverages. In Saudi Arabia, importing, manufacturing, or consuming alcohol are punishable by jail terms, fines, flogging, and/or deportation (*The Economist,* September 13, 1997). In contrast, Judaism and Christianity incorporate wine into their religious rituals (the Sabbath and other Jewish holy days; the Christian Eucharist). Beginning in the Middle Ages, Christian monasteries produced some of the finest wines and ales in Europe, a practice that continues today. A recent survey found variations from country to country in the amount of alcohol people consume as well as patterns of consumption. (See *A Global View:* International Trends in Alcohol Consumption.)

Historical Change: A Brief History of Drinking in America

Definitions of deviance also change over time. In this country, both patterns of drinking and attitudes toward drinking have varied from period to period (Figure 7-1).

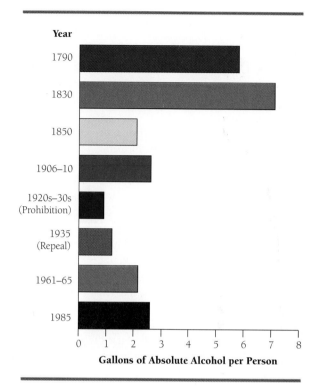

Figure 7-1   *Changing Patterns of Drinking in America, 1790–1985*

In our own society patterns of alcohol consumption have fluctuated widely over the past 200 years.

Source: M. E. Lender and J. K. Martin, *Drinking in America: A History,* 2d ed., New York: Free Press, 1987, pp. 205–206.

The early colonists did drink ale and cider often and abundantly, but they strongly condemned drunkenness, as witnessed by sermons on the evils of intemperance and laws against inebriation, backed by the threat of imprisonment, fines, the stocks, and public flogging (Conroy, 1991). These penalties were seldom applied, however—not because judges were lenient but because violations were rare. Informal social pressure kept most individuals from chronically abusing alcohol. In small, close-knit colonial communities, people felt they had a right, even a duty, to get involved in other people's business. If self-control failed, family members, friends, community leaders, and clergy were there to shepherd a problem drinker back into the fold. The colonists did not view drinking as a social problem; nor did they consider liquor dangerous, at least for themselves. They did not trust Native

A GLOBAL VIEW

International Trends in Alcohol Consumption

As awareness of the social costs and health risks of alcohol has grown, levels of alcohol consumption and changes in drinking patterns have become matters of worldwide concern (Edwards et al., 1994). There are three main ways that per capita consumption in a given country can change. The first is change in the number of people who drink alcohol: people who had previously abstained (including children) may begin drinking, and/or drinkers may give up alcohol, often because of increasing health consciousness. Second, the frequency and amount people drink may change. For example, drinking may become an everyday activity, rather than being confined to weekends and special occasions. Third, the context in which people drink may change. In Europe's wine-drinking countries, drinking with meals has increasingly been replaced by leisure-time drinking. Such social drinking is more likely to lead to intoxica-

tion—both because alcohol has less impact when consumed with food, and because people usually drink less at home with their families than they do with friends and acquaintances at restaurants, bars, and private parties.

Drinking levels in economically developed countries are shown in Table 1. In some countries (such as Australia and the United States) drinking increased in the 1970s, peaked in

Drinking levels in almost all countries fluctuate.

the early 1980s, and then declined. In other places (notably Italy, France, and Sweden) consumption of alcohol has decreased more or less steadily. Yet in countries as different as Luxembourg and Japan, alcohol consumption increased. The one common pattern in economically developed countries is that drinking different beverage types (beer, wine, and liquor)

has replaced a strong preference for one or the other. On average, national levels of alcohol consumption represent a mix of 50 percent beer, 35 percent wine, and 15 percent distilled beverages.

Because of social and economic instability, data on central and eastern European countries are less reliable. The available evidence suggests that in the former Soviet republics drinking rates dropped during an anti-alcohol campaign launched in 1985 but began to climb when this policy was abandoned in 1987 and are still climbing. In Russia, the Ukraine, and Estonia, drinking problems, measured in terms of alcohol-related hospitalizations and arrests, are increasing. Likewise, in Poland, the Czech Republic, Slovakia, and Bulgaria, both drinking levels and drinking problems are on the rise.

Data on alcohol consumption in developing countries are virtually nonexistent, in part because collecting statistics is diffi-

Americans to "hold their liquor," however, and banned the sale of beer or whiskey to Indians (Lender and Martin, 1987). Colonists were not above exploiting this alleged weakness: when they wanted to expand their territory, they brought along barrels of liquor and encouraged Native American leaders to drink heartily during negotiations.

Around the time of the American Revolution, distilled (or hard) liquor began to replace beer and cider. Hard liquor keeps longer than beer and is easier to transport. It is also more potent: beer is

about 12 percent alcohol; rum or whiskey, 70 to 90 percent. In addition, the colonial population had grown and dispersed, and informal social controls were weaker, especially in frontier settlements. Public drunkenness became more common—and more disruptive. Drinking abundantly, once considered normal, came to be seen as deviant.

The temperance movement, which began in the early 1800s, took an absolutist position toward alcohol, similar to public attitudes toward illicit drugs today. Alcohol was considered dangerous and ad-

Table 1   *Per Capita Alcohol Consumption (Liters of Ethanol) in OECD Countries, 1970–1990*

	1970	1980	1990
Australia	8.1	9.6	8.4
Austria	10.5	11.0	10.4
Belgium	8.9	10.8	9.9
Canada	6.1	8.6	7.5
Denmark	6.8	9.1	9.9
Finland	4.4	6.4	7.7
France	16.2	14.9	12.7
Germany	10.3	11.4	10.6
Great Britain	5.3	7.3	7.6
Iceland	3.2	3.9	3.9
Ireland	5.9	7.3	7.2
Italy	13.7	13.0	8.7
Japan	4.6	5.4	6.5
Luxembourg	10.0	10.9	12.2
Netherlands	5.6	8.8	8.2
New Zealand	7.6	9.6	7.8
Norway	3.6	4.6	4.1
Portugal	9.9	11.0	9.8
Spain	11.6	13.6	10.8
Sweden	5.8	5.7	5.5
Switzerland	10.7	10.8	10.8
Turkey	0.5	0.7	0.6
United States of America	6.7	8.2	7.5

Source: G. Edwards et al., *Alcohol Policy and Public Good,* Oxford, New York, Tokyo: Oxford University Press, 1994, p. 35, table 2-1.

cult, in part because people traditionally have made their own alcoholic (and nonalcoholic) beverages. Sale of commercially produced beer has increased in many countries in Central and South America, Africa, and Asia, but whether this represents an increase in alcohol consumption is not known.

What conclusions can be drawn from these statistics? Attempts to explain changes in levels of drinking and problem drinking in terms of increased buying power, more leisure time, social misery, industrialization and urbanization, or other single causes have failed, suggesting that rates of alcohol consumption reflect the interplay of numerous factors. The one certainty is change: regardless of the level of economic development and cultural attitudes toward alcohol, drinking levels in almost all countries fluctuate. This in itself is significant. The fact that patterns and levels of drinking in a society are not "set for all time" has important implications for health and social policies.

dictive; drinking was linked to poverty, crime, and a decline in family values; people who sold (or "pushed") alcoholic beverages in saloons were villains; and drinking any alcohol at all was deviant. The movement faded into the background during the Civil War, then reemerged as a "women's war" against saloons in the early 1890s, gradually gaining public and political support. The temperance movement finally achieved its goal: the eighteenth amendment to the Constitution, which prohibited "the manufacture, sale, or transportation of intoxicating liquors," went into effect at midnight on January 16, 1920.

Prohibition was relatively short-lived (1920–1934). Popular descriptions tend to glamorize Prohibition as an era of giddy lawlessness that opened the door to organized crime, undermined respect for law enforcement, and ultimately backfired. In this view, "forbidden fruit" is always enticing, and drinking increased, rather than decreased, during Prohibition. In fact, crime syndicates emerged in only a few cities, and drinking rates

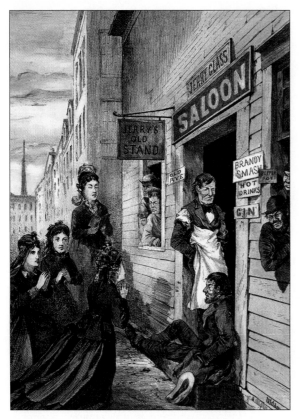

The nineteenth-century temperance movement took an absolutist position toward alcohol, similar to public attitudes toward illegal drugs today. As shown here, by late in the century the movement had evolved into a women's war against saloons.

dropped, as did alcohol-related hospitalizations and deaths, arrests and crimes. Americans did not suddenly, en masse, give up alcohol. In rural areas people continued to brew beer, wine, and spirits for home use and local sale, while in cities well-off, otherwise law-abiding citizens frequented "speakeasies" (illegal saloons). But most Americans apparently supported Prohibition, at least for a while.

By the end of the 1920s, public concern about alcohol had waned. A number of groups began to call for repeal on the grounds that Prohibition was a violation of individual liberty (much as the National Rifle Association views gun control as a violation of personal freedom). The final blow was the Great Depression. Anti-Prohibition leaders argued persuasively that repeal would create thousands of jobs in a revived liquor industry, while liquor taxes would provide federal, state, and local governments with badly needed revenues. And so, in December 1933, Prohibition was repealed.

During the political struggle for repeal, hard liquor lost its cultural association with working-class, immigrant, backward lifestyles and acquired a new upper-class, cosmopolitan, progressive chic (Barrows and Room, 1991). In the 1930s and 1940s, the mixed drink or cocktail, an American innovation, came into its own. Drinking, and getting drunk, became a regular and expected feature of many social activities, from the cocktail hour in upper-class social circles to beer on "boys' night out" in working-class culture. On college campuses, drinking became a ritual part of fraternity parties, football weekends, and other occasions.

In the 1950s, the medical community drew a new line between "normal" and "abnormal" drinking. New research suggested that *alcoholism* was not just a matter of drinking to excess but a chronic, usually progressive, often fatal disease that affects people in all social classes and walks of life. The redefinition of alcohol abuse as a medical problem, not a moral weakness or vice, removed some of the social stigma so that family members (if not alcoholics themselves) were less likely to conceal the problem and alcohol abusers were more likely to seek treatment. One of the most effective programs has been Alcoholics Anonymous (AA), a support group started in 1935 by a surgeon and a stockbroker who vowed to help one another stay sober, which has grown into a network of more than 85,000 groups and 2 million members. AA teaches that some people cannot tolerate alcohol, just as diabetics cannot tolerate sweets; hence alcoholics cannot simply cut back but must abstain from liquor one drink, and one day, at a time.

In the 1970s and 1980s, concern about alcohol began to grow again. Medical researchers had learned more about the impact of alcohol on health (especially during pregnancy). Public health agencies reported that 10 percent of Americans are alcoholics (who are psychologically or physically addicted to alcohol) and perhaps another 25 percent are problem drinkers (whose consumption of alcohol interferes with their personal relationships, their work, or their health) (Lender and Martin, 1987, pp. 181–182). They also called attention to the social costs of drinking—in health care expenses, lost production, traffic accidents, violent

By the 1930s, with Prohibition in force, alcohol had acquired an upper-class, progressive chic. Many Hollywood movies of the period portrayed rich, glamorous characters whose sophisticated lifestyle included alcohol.

crime, and fires. The "new temperance movement" defined drinking as a social problem that required social solutions. Grassroots organizations such as Mothers Against Drunk Driving (MADD), founded by a mother whose child was killed in an automobile accident caused by a drunk driver, rallied popular support for stronger controls on drinking, including raising the minimum age for buying alcohol, imposing stiffer penalties on drunk drivers, and holding bars, restaurants, and, in some cases, private hosts and hostesses liable if they served drinks to someone who was already intoxicated and that person injured others or damaged property. Neither public health agencies nor groups like MADD advocate a return to Prohibition. Rather, they are using the law and the media in much the way the pilgrims used sermons and gossip: to mobilize social pressure and hold the community responsible for preventing and controlling drunkenness.

Contemporary attitudes toward alcohol and drinking are ambivalent (Lender and Martin, 1987). Most Americans see drinking as part of our culture (even if they themselves don't drink), but they also want stricter controls on how drinkers behave in public. Knowledge of fine wines is a status symbol; heavy drinking on some occasions may be tolerated but is not encouraged. Thus, during different periods of American history alcohol has been viewed as a healthful tonic, a social evil (and, during Prohibition, a crime), a "happy-time" release for some and a disease for others, and a gourmet beverage (wine) or an adult soft drink (beer).

Where, When, and with Whom: Drinking on College Campuses

Social definitions of deviance also depend on the setting, the situation, and the participants. One of the last places where public drunkenness is tolerated, and often expected, today is the American college campus (Mathews, 1997). A recent survey of representative campuses found that almost half of American college students engage in "binge drinking," usually defined as having five or more drinks at one sitting (Wechsler, 1996) (Figure 7-2). Campuses tend to be divided into two subcultures: one emphasizes personal and social responsibility, while the other glamorizes being out of control; one defines drunkenness as deviant, while the other views *abstinence* as deviant. The division varies from one school to another: on some campuses 1 percent of students binge; on others, 70 percent. First-year students, recently liberated from parental supervision, are most likely to describe their evening schedule as "drink, dance, scream, puke, pass out" (Mathews, 1997, p. 84). Binge drinkers are much more likely than other students to have unprotected sex, to drive after drinking, and to miss classes. They are also more likely to damage property, get into fights, experience injuries, and have trouble with the police or campus security. Drinking too much, too fast can be lethal: every year perhaps a

Public health agencies and groups like MADD use advertising to mobilize social pressure against the dangers of alcohol and to hold the community responsible for controlling drunkenness.

Figure 7-2 *Binge Drinking on College Campuses*

A study of drinking on college campuses found clear patterns in binge drinking: men, students under 24, fraternity and sorority residents, whites, students involved in athletics, and students who socialize more are most likely to binge while drinking.

Source: Wechsler, 1996 as cited in: "Drinking and Dying," *Newsweek,* Oct. 31, 1997, p. 69.

	Percent		Percent
Gender		**Age**	
Male	50	Under 21	45
Female	39	21–23	48
		24+	28
Race			
White	48	**College Residence**	
Hispanic	38	Fraternity/sorority	84
'Other'	34	Co-ed dorm	52
Nat. Amer./Nat. Alask.	34	Off-campus housing	40
Asian/Pacific Islander	21	Single-sex dorm	38
African American	16		

Causes of Death from Binge Drinking

- Drinking a lot of alcohol quickly, without eating, raises the blood-alcohol level fast.
- When the level reaches between 400 and 500 milligrams per deciliter, breathing may stop.
- Thickening blood cuts off oxygen supply to brain.
- Choking on own vomit may occur.

*Among 17,592 college students surveyed at 140 campuses, binge drinking (five drinks in a row for men, four for women) is common.

dozen students die because they pass out and choke on their own vomit, or their blood becomes so thick that oxygen can't reach the brain; others have died because they were too drunk to escape fire, fell off a roof, or suffered some other alcohol-related accident (Rosenberg and Bai, 1997).

The effects of binge drinking are not limited to students who participate. At schools with high binge rates, a majority of students report that they have been unable to study or sleep because of bingers. Many sober students have had to care for drunken friends, endured drunken insults, and fended off drunken sexual advances. Administration attempts to control drinking have not met with much success, in part because of a "conspiracy of silence" among responsible students, who are reluctant to report their peers to authorities. Even if they view drunkenness as deviant, out of generational loyalty students attempt to handle such problems themselves.

Finally, whether binge drinking or other behavior is viewed as deviant or not also depends on the actor, the audience, and the situation. A student whose friend binged regularly would probably be more concerned if that friend were a female than a male (*the actor*). College norms define deliberately getting drunk as a "guy thing"; getting women drunk so that they are less "inhibited" and more "cooperative" is also a guy thing. With a female binger, a good friend would intervene to prevent her from becoming a victim or developing a reputation as "easy." If the binger were male, a friend would more likely express annoyance, not concern, and say, "It's your problem." However, a student who took his friend home for a holiday would be less tolerant if the friend got drunk in front of his parents (*the audience*). Likewise, a professor who has "a few too many" with his or her colleagues would not be considered deviant (unless this were a regular occurrence). For that professor to "tie one on" with a group of students, to the point where he or she begins flirting, gets hostile, or reveals personal problems, or to come into class obviously drunk or even slightly inebriated is another matter. Faculty are expected to act dignified and serve as role models for students. For students to get "wrecked" on weekends (even if the "weekend" begins Thursday night) and at parties may be considered fine in some college circles. But for a football player to show up drunk before a big game, or for a student to drink privately and secretively, rather than socially, is not "cool" (*the situation*). Even bingers set limits.

Meanwhile, the tug-of-war between college administrations and student groups (especially fraternities), colleges and the surrounding community, drinking and nondrinking students, continues. Attempts to reduce drinking by banning alcohol on campus or in fraternity houses have generally resulted in parties moving off campus and out of fraternity houses into the street, where college administrations have no authority.

The key point here is that deviance is the result of *social interaction* between people who do not accept or abide by the norms of their group or society,

but have their own definitions of what is normal and acceptable, and people who see such behavior as immoral, dangerous, disgusting, or just "no good."

Deviance and Social Control

Social control refers to any and all efforts to prevent and/or correct deviant behavior. The most powerful instrument of social control is socialization. Ideally, socialization leads people to want to do what they are supposed to do. But socialization is never perfect; human beings are not social robots. To achieve control, all societies depend on **sanctions,** that is, on rewards for conforming behavior and punishments for deviant behavior (see Chapter 3).

A broad distinction can be made between formal and informal social controls. **Informal social controls** are unofficial pressures to conform to society's norms and values. They are so tightly woven into the fabric of everyday life that we often overlook their impact—a smile or nod that indicates one person approves of what another has said (positive sanction); the averted eyes or stiff handshake that indicates the other person wants to maintain distance (negative sanction). Gossip is one of the most familiar and pervasive forms of informal social control. When people chat about who was invited to a party and what everyone wore, why a friend behaved in some unusual way, why a couple has sued for divorce, or how the man down the street treats his dog, they are testing and reaffirming shared norms and values. Symbolic interactionists point out that a breach of social rules embarrasses the people who witness the mistake as well as the individual who commits it (Goffman, 1967). In offering an apology, making an excuse, pretending it was just a joke, or changing the subject, people attempt to erase the social error and thus restore order. Through gossip, people may reinterpret a breach of propriety as a mistake or establish their own distance from the offender and the offense. Such informal social controls deploy a great deal of power.

In small primary groups and traditional societies, informal social controls may be sufficient. Thus the New England colonists were able to control drunkenness through social pressure and only rarely invoked the law. But in large secondary groups and complex societies, more formal mechanisms of control are needed. **Formal social controls** are institutionalized, codified, public mechanisms for preventing or correcting deviant behavior. Prohibition was an example. In modern societies, certain institutions and organizations specialize in formal social control. The police, courts, and prisons are responsible for enforcing the law by apprehending and punishing criminals. Psychiatrists and other mental health workers have the authority to diagnose psychological disorders. If a person is deemed mentally incompetent or considered dangerous to himself or herself or to other people, that individual may be involuntarily confined to a psychiatric hospital or unit. Other formal social controls are built into the structure of organizations. Businesses reward employees who meet or exceed expectations with promotions and raises and punish those who do not by demoting or firing them. Universities use admissions, scholarships, grades, probation, and expulsion to reward or penalize students for their performance. Individuals may be subject to social controls in many different domains at the same time—at home, at school and at work, in church, or even on the street, where police exert formal social control and the stare of the crowd exerts informal social control.

One of the more powerful forms of social control is branding behavior and people who engage in such behavior "deviant." A key question for sociologists is why some behavior, and some individuals, are labeled as "nuts," "sluts," "crooks," and "perverts" and shunned by people who consider themselves respectable (Liazos, 1972).

The Labeling Perspective: Creating Outsiders

To understand and explain the social dynamics of deviance, many sociologists employ a labeling perspective. Avoiding absolutist definitions of deviance, the **labeling perspective** focuses on the process of interaction between those who make and enforce the rules and those who are identified as breaking the rules. According to this view, deviance and social control are opposite sides of the same coin: One could not exist without the other. Whereas common sense suggests that deviance creates a need for social controls, the labeling perspective shows how social controls can create deviance and even a need for deviance. The classic statement of this position comes from the introduction to Howard Becker's *The Outsiders* (1963):

> Social groups create deviance by making the rules whose infraction constitutes deviance, and by applying those rules to particular people and labeling them as outsiders. From this point of view, deviance is not a quality of the act the person commits, but rather a consequence of the application by others of rules and sanctions to an "offender." The deviant is one to whom that label has been successfully applied; deviant behavior is behavior that people so label. (p. 9)

According to this view, no act is deviant in and of itself. Rather, deviance is an interactive process whereby a society, or a group within society, defines

Criminal laws, which give the police and courts the authority to put people whose behavior is deemed deviant behind bars, are an example of formal social controls. The United States has a higher proportion of its population in prison than any other developed nation. Yet the deterrent effect of heavy prison sentences remains hotly debated.

certain behavior as deviant, labels people who engage in that behavior as deviants, and then treats them as outcasts. Labeling theorists do not deny that some actions (such as torture or mass murder) are wrong. But they would point out that such acts have been considered normal and even "good" in certain societies over the centuries (during the Spanish Inquisition or in Nazi Germany). In looking at our own society, labeling theorists tend to focus on controversial behavior, such as prostitution or drug use.

Who Creates the Rules?

Before an act can be labeled as deviant and the people who do it can be labeled outsiders, there must be a rule against it. Such rules do not spring into being by themselves. Someone must call public attention to a perceived problem and make people feel that something must be done about it immediately. In other words, the creation of rules requires social action. So does enforcement. Rules are not likely to be enforced unless somebody insists on it.

Becker (1963) used the term **moral entrepreneurs** to describe people (or groups) who make it their business to see that offenses are recognized and offenders treated as such. Leaders of the temperance movement were moral entrepreneurs. Some recent examples are Mothers Against Drunk Driving (MADD), described earlier; Greenpeace, the environmental organization that has campaigned for bans on activities ranging from the slaughter of baby seals to nuclear testing; Operation Rescue and other groups that oppose abortion; and the many groups that have fought for laws banning cigarette smoking in public places. The mass media also play a role in raising public consciousness about an issue, as well as identifying and labeling individuals or groups as deviant.

The Consequences of Labeling

Sociologists distinguish between **primary deviance,** or the initial violation of a social rule, and **secondary deviance,** or deviance that results from other people's reactions to the initial violations (Lemert, 1951). Most people break social rules from time to time but do not think of themselves as deviants. Suppose, for example, a schoolteacher who enjoys pornographic movies occasionally rents videos involving sadism or child pornography

when his wife is not home. Although he keeps his taste for pornography secret, he sees nothing wrong with his behavior and assumes that many other men do the same. If no one ever discovers or publicizes his interest in pornography, his life will go on as usual and his identity as a good teacher and a family man will remain intact. If his wife discovers his secret, however, she may insist that he seek psychiatric treatment and threaten divorce if he refuses. If the store where he rents videos is raided and his name made public, he may lose his job as a teacher. Suddenly people see him in a different light.

The classic example of secondary deviance is the drug user (primary deviance) who turns to crime (secondary deviance) to support his or her habit. Labeling theory holds that the addict's crimes are not the result of drug use per se but a consequence of society's labeling certain substances as illicit drugs, pushing those substances onto the black market, and thereby raising the cost of those drugs. As a result, the drug user may become a drug dealer or commit other crimes (such as robbery or prostitution) to feed his or her habit.

A "deviant" label can create a *master status*—one that overrides all others (see Chapter 5). When people discover that an individual is a drug addict, for example, they often reinterpret the person's past behavior in light of this new identity. Suppose, for example, that a teenager fails a drug test before an athletic meet. Before, her parents saw the hours she spent listening to music through headphones, her insistence on privacy and tantrums when she suspected someone had gone into her room, her laughter at jokes her parents didn't understand, and the way she dressed as typical adolescent behavior; now they see the same behavior as symptoms of a drug problem.

Erich Goode (1984) identified six elements of deviant stereotyping—assumptions people tend to make about deviance and individuals they consider deviant. The first is *exaggeration:* conventional people tend to focus on an extreme form of deviant behavior and to assume that this is typical of all individuals who fit into that category. The label "drug addict" calls to mind a gaunt, incoherent street person, seen in an urban neighborhood or on TV, who has thrown his or her life away. The second element in deviant stereotyping is *centrality:* people tend to assume that deviance plays a central part in the labeled individual's life, consuming most of the person's waking hours and dominating his or her thoughts. Thus a teenager who uses drugs is presumed to have no interest in school, sports, current events, and so on. The third element is *persistence*: conventional people tend to assume "once a deviant, always a deviant." Even if the teenager successfully completes a drug treatment program, her parents remain watchful and suspicious. The fourth element is *dichotomizing*: people tend to think of deviance in either-or terms. A person is a drug addict or not. Popular stereotypes of deviance do not admit the possibility that a person may shift back and forth between conventional and deviant behavior or occupy some middle ground in between. The fifth element is *homogeneity*: many people assume that all drug abusers are basically alike. The last element is *clustering*: people tend to assume that deviance is a "package deal"; it is rarely seen as an isolated trait or activity but is linked with a number of related characteristics. Teenage drug users are presumed to be delinquent in every way, from stealing to sexual promiscuity.

Such assumptions have the effect of isolating or segregating the person who has been labeled deviant from "respectable society." They contribute to the process by which the individual himself or herself may develop a "deviant identity." Thus Marsh Ray (1964) found that drug users develop an "addict identity" in part as a result of their experiences among nonaddicts, who tend to regard them as being degenerate, lacking in willpower, and willing to lie, cheat, or steal from anyone to "feed their habit." Even when people have given up drugs, they must deal with the skepticism of nonaddicts who doubt the possibility of permanent cure or rehabilitation. A key point is that we do not make such assumptions about the much larger categories of people who consume legal mood-altering substances, such as caffeine, nicotine, or medications obtained with a doctor's prescription, even though these drugs may be as potent, addictive, and dangerous as illicit drugs. Antidepressive drugs (such as Prozac) and antianxiety drugs (such as Valium) are two of the most widely prescribed medications in the United States, but we don't label people who take them as "drug users." And this, according to the labeling perspective, makes all the difference.

As Erving Goffman pointed out, "One response to this fate [of being labeled deviant] is to embrace it" (1961, p. 30). An individual who has been labeled may be pushed into a ***deviant career,*** a lifestyle that includes habitual or permanent deviance. And this may draw him or her into a ***deviant subculture,*** a group that is distinguished from other members of society by deviant norms, values, and lifestyle. This completes the break with conventional, "straight" society. One heroin user told Ray she did not think of herself as a junkie until one day she realized that all her friends were junkies.

Self-segregation in a deviant subculture is a logical, protective reaction to humiliation and ostracism. The irony is that by shunning people who are alleged to have committed deviant acts, conventional society encourages secondary deviance, the development of deviant subcultures, and commitment to deviant careers. The application of a deviant label can become a self-fulfilling prophecy (Merton, 1968).

This sequence of events, from primary deviance to labeling and secondary deviance, is not inevitable. In some cases violations of the rules are not detected or not labeled as deviant. Even if they are, many people successfully reject the label "deviant" through a process that Gresham Sykes and David Matza (1957) called ***neutralization:*** they rationalize (make excuses for) their deviant behavior in ways that both relieve their feelings of guilt and turn aside other people's expressions of disapproval.

Sykes and Matza describe five major techniques of neutralization: (1) denial of responsibility ("I couldn't help it"); (2) denial of injury ("I didn't really hurt anybody"); (3) denial of the victim, if there is one ("They had it coming"); (4) condemnation of the condemners ("The cops are all corrupt"); and (5) appeal to higher loyalties ("I did it for my friend, not myself").

Diana Scully and Joseph Marolla (1984) studied how convicted rapists used neutralization. They found that some of the men denied that they had committed a rape, justifying their behavior on the grounds that the woman seduced them, that her clothing was provocative, that her "no" really meant "yes," that she enjoyed herself, or that she wasn't a "nice" girl and so deserved what she got. Those who admitted they had raped the victim excused themselves, usually on the grounds that they were using alcohol and/or drugs and were out of control or that they are emotionally disturbed. Virtually all the men condemned rape and rejected the label "rapist" for themselves.

An Evaluation

Labeling theory shifts attention away from the individuals who violate social rules and focuses on the social dynamics of deviance and the processes of defining deviance and of identifying and excluding those labeled as deviant. But the strengths of labeling theory are also its weaknesses.

First, labeling theory implies that the social definition of deviance is arbitrary. For the most part, labeling theorists have focused on "crimes without victims" (Schur, 1965; Meier and Geis, 1997), that is, on crimes that injure no one except (perhaps) the person who commits them. Illegal use of drugs, prostitution, pornography, and unconventional sexual behavior between consenting adults all fall within this category. In such cases, the label "deviant" may be arbitrary in the sense that some people are imposing their definition of normal behavior on others. But other acts are clearly seen as deviant by almost all individuals and societies. We can all usually agree that such actions as robbery, rape, drive-by shooting, or terrorist attacks on public places are wrong.

Second, labeling theory fails to explain why people break social rules, often with full knowledge of the possible consequences, in the first place (primary deviance).

Theories of Deviance

Why do people engage in deviant behavior? How one explains deviance depends in part on what questions one asks. In general, biologists and psychologists attempt to answer the question of why certain individuals engage in particular forms of deviance. No matter what society's view of drinking alcohol, some people drink, some do not, and the amount of alcohol drinkers consume, as well as their drinking pattern, varies from individual to individual. Likewise, in a given society at a given time, some people steal, some commit violent crimes, some join gangs or cults, some are preoccupied with suicide, some seem disconnected from everyday reality. What explains these individual differences?

Sociologists ask: Why is deviance more common in some societies and times, and in some subcultures within a society, than in others? Why are some social categories (males, young people) more prone to deviance than are others (women and older people)? Why does the social definition of deviance change from one period to another? Is deviance an inevitable part of social life? Or is it a sign of breakdowns or malfunctions in the social order?

Psychological and Biological Theories

As recently as the nineteenth century, deviants were viewed as sinners who had succumbed to temptation or, in extreme cases, been taken over by evil spirits or the Devil himself. The publication of Charles Darwin's *The Origin of Species* (1859), and his revolutionary theory of evolution, suggested a different explanation: like other traits, deviant or criminal tendencies were inherited as part of the individual's biological makeup. In the late nineteenth century a number of *biogenic* theories of deviance were put forward. According to one theory, criminals were subhuman, a throwback to an earlier stage of evolution. According to another, a perverted or depraved personality was caused by a hereditary defect or "bad seed." The term "psychopath" (from the Greek words for abnormal or "sick mind"), or more popularly, "psycho," dates from this period.

In the early twentieth century, influenced by sociology as well as the work of Sigmund Freud, psychologists began to reject the simple biological theories of the day and focus on the individual's environment and early experience (Bootzin, Acocella, and Alloy, 1993). Individuals who casually and callously mistreat other people came to be known as "sociopaths." Psychodynamic theorists trace this syndrome to infancy and a mother (or other caretaker) who treats the baby mechanically and impersonally, neglecting the baby's inborn need for attachment. Behaviorists theorize that children learn sociopathic behavior from parents who are both arbitrary and punitive, with the result that their children do not see any connection between their own behavior and the treatment they receive. The main criticism of both theories is that they are based on hindsight and cannot be proved or disproved scientifically.

Recent advances in genetics and neuroscience have led to renewed interest in the role of biology

At the end of the nineteenth century, biological criminologists tried to identify the physical features that would enable them to classify a person as a criminal type on the basis of appearance alone.

in criminal behavior (Fishbein, 1990). Studies of identical twins and of adopted children and their biological or birth parents have found evidence that criminal tendencies may be inherited in a small number of cases (Brennan, Mednick, and Volavka, 1995). But the most interesting studies lie at the intersection of psychology, sociology, and biology. Researchers have long known that a high proportion of serial killers and other extremely violent criminals, including child abusers, were themselves abused as children. However, the "why" eluded them. One might expect that someone who was abused as a child would be exceptionally sensitive to pain and helplessness, not cruel and heartless. Neurobiologists are finding answers in brain studies (summarized in Gladwell, 1997). At birth, the sections of the brain that control basic functions—breathing, blood pressure, body temperature, and so on—are fully developed. But the cerebral cortex—the gray matter that enables humans to control impulses, make judgments, learn from experience, and use memory to organize responses—is only beginning to mature. Experiences in early childhood shape the anatomy or structure of the brain and hence thought, emotions, and behavior. Brain injuries at an early age (from being shaken or thrown on a hard surface) can interrupt normal cortex development. Traumatic experiences send waves of hormones through the brain—including cortisol, which in large or repeated "doses" can dis-

rupt memory. In computer lingo, someone who can't access memory cannot learn from past experience. Excess cortisol may also weaken the fibers that connect the right and left hemispheres, resulting in what we call a "split personality." Furthermore, researchers have found that birth complications, mild retardation, or slowed development, when combined with maternal rejection (perhaps because the baby is not "easy" or "perfect"), increase the potential for antisocial and violent behavior. In short, new research is beginning to not only document but also explain "organic rage." This, in turn, may lead to medical treatments for antisocial behavior. But however promising, this research applies only to a small percentage of deviants.

Sociologists look at the bigger picture. Neither psychological nor new neurological theories explain why rates of deviance vary from group to group, community to community, region to region, or time to time.

Deviance and Anomie

Emile Durkheim, a pioneer in the sociology of deviance, linked deviance to a breakdown in the social order. Specifically, Durkheim saw high rates of deviance as the result of ***anomie,*** a condition of "normlessness," or loss of accepted social rules within a society. When anomie sets in, human desires run wild:

From top to bottom of the [social] ladder greed is aroused without knowing where to find [the] ultimate foothold. . . . A thirst arises for novelties, unfamiliar pleasures, nameless sensations, all of which lose their savor once known. . . . [People] cannot form a solid foundation of happiness. (Durkheim, 1895/1951, p. 256)

Durkheim traced anomie to the breakdown of small, close-knit, traditional communities and the rise of modern, urban, ever-changing social structures. He believed that there were too many inconsistencies and ambiguities in modern societies. In traditional societies people "know their place" in the social order and can expect to live much as their parents did. Their lives are predictable; they know what to expect from others and what others expect of them. In periods of social change, the old rules no longer apply. People have to find their own way. The future is unpredictable. Without clear, time-honored social rules and regulations, Durkheim argued, people lose control, acting on every whim.

For example, after the Communist government that had ruled the Soviet Union for seventy years collapsed, organized-crime syndicates took over many activities and even local government in some places, individual crime rates soared, drinking rates remained high, and drug use, prostitution, pornography, and other activities banned by the former Communist government spread. In former Yugoslavia, the demise of formal dictator Marshal Tito's central government led to civil war and "ethnic cleansing," with atrocities committed by all groups (see Chapter 9).

Control Theory

Travis Hirschi's control theory (1969) both refines and expands Durkheim's theory of anomie. Hirschi reasons that most people are tempted to engage in forbidden behavior from time to time. The puzzle is not why people engage in deviant behavior but why most people *conform* most of the time. Hirschi concluded that the more attached people are to family, friends, and neighbors, the more involved they are in socially approved activities (such as school and work), and the stronger their belief in legitimate opportunities, the more likely they are to conform. Conversely, few or weak attachments, low levels of commitment and involvement, and lack of opportunity or the *belief* that conformity will not be rewarding promote deviance.

One of Hirschi's primary interests was juvenile delinquency. He identified four controls on youthful deviance:

1. The most important control on delinquent behavior is adolescents' attachment to their parents. Obviously, parents cannot follow teenagers around; what counts is that they are "psychologically present." Delinquents are less likely than nondelinquents to say that their parents know where they are most of the time and to value their parents' approval.

2. A second source of control is the school. Delinquents are far more likely than law-abiding teenagers to say that they dislike school, do not do homework, and do not care what their teachers think about them. In contrast, when students want to succeed, school acts as a moral force.

3. A third control is the peer group. Hirschi holds that delinquent youth have fewer close ties with friends than do their nondelinquent peers. Other researchers have found that the difference lies in the characteristics of the peers with whom an adolescent associates, not time spent with age-mates. Some peer groups encourage conformity to mainstream cultural goals and values, while others approve or tolerate antisocial behavior.

4. The fourth control on delinquency, according to Hirschi, is aspiration to conventional goals, especially in education and work. When young people want to lead the "good life" and believe society will give them the chance to do so, they are more likely to complete high school and stay out of trouble. They do not want to risk their futures for a few kicks now. Delinquent youth, in contrast, have few hopes or plans for the future; they live for the present. Hirschi found that one predictor of delinquent behavior was the age at which young people began engaging in three adult activities: smoking, drinking, and dating. The earlier these started, the weaker the youngsters' attachments and aspirations and the greater the chance that they would become involved in delinquency.

See Figure 7-3 for an overview of Hirschi's model.

More recently, Hirschi has focused on *self-control* (Gottfredson and Hirschi, 1990)—on willingness to defer gratification, perseverance, caution, patience, planning, and sensitivity to others. Hirschi traces low self-control to faulty socialization. Whether because of their personal traits, their social circumstances, or both, parents are not very

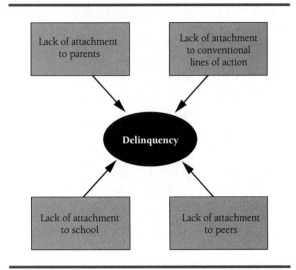

Figure 7-3   *Hirschi's Model of Control Theory and Juvenile Delinquency*

Hirschi emphasized the power of attachments as agents of social control. Delinquency, he argued, was likely when four kinds of controls were weak or absent.

Source: Based on Travis Hirschi, *Causes of Delinquency,* Berkeley: University of California Press, 1969, in John Conklin, *Criminology,* New York: Macmillan, 1992, p. 249.

attached to the child, fail to supervise his or her behavior, do not recognize deviance, and are inconsistent in punishing deviant acts. Inadequate parental control, Hirschi argues, leads to inadequate self-control. Other control theorists (Sampson and Laub, 1990) emphasize that social ties must be maintained over the life span. Steady employment and commitment to marriage can reverse a developmental path toward deviance and inhibit criminal or antisocial behavior in adulthood. Conversely, unemployment and marital instability may weaken bonds established in childhood. These ties may also be weakened by historical change, as when a society enters a period of high unemployment and high divorce rates. We would add that social controls may be weaker in some environments than in others. For example, freshmen who go away to college are beyond parental surveillance, often for the first time. In most cases they are also leaving old friends behind for a social setting in which hardly anyone knows them personally. Weak social controls may partially explain high rates of binge drinking on campus, while weak self-control may explain why some students participate in the drinking culture but others do not.

The main critique of control theory is that it is incomplete. Attachment and aspirations may explain why neglected children or adults whose personal lives or plans for the future have been disrupted engage in deviance. But what causes a person who is close to his or her family, spouse, and children, who is steadily employed and earns a comfortable income, to begin cheating customers or embezzle from the company, spend time with prostitutes or commit adultery, knowing there may be serious personal and/or legal consequences? A second critique is that control theory assumes that the relationship between social bonds and deviance is a one-way street. It does not consider the possibility that deviance is a cause, not a consequence, of weak social ties. For example, if a man begins to get drunk more and more often, his wife may leave him, his friends may stop seeing him, his employer may fire him, and so on. In other cases, deviance may be the result of reciprocal influences. For example, a student whose first college friends or fraternity brothers approve of binge drinking may participate to gain acceptance, they do the same, and so the culture of drunkenness is reinforced.

Deviance and Social Structure

One of the major challenges to Durkheim's theory of anomie (and, by extension, control theory) was put forward some years ago by American sociologist Robert Merton (1938, 1968). Durkheim described human passions as a powerful, independent force that must be socially controlled. By implication, control theory also endorsed that view. In contrast, Merton argued that our desires are created by the sociocultural system.

Every culture has its own notions as to which goals are worth pursuing in life. Every culture also prescribes legitimate means of working toward those goals. Americans, for example, place a high value on material success, or wealth. The "American dream" holds that hard work is the legitimate route to wealth. Our culture teaches that anyone and everyone can win at this game; in reality, however, there are only a few prize positions. The possibility of becoming wealthy is virtually nonexistent for most Americans because of their position in the social structure. A high rate of failure is inevitable;

it is built into the social system. Failure is doubly painful in a system such as ours. First, the individual fails to get all that money can buy (not only goods and services, but also respect and social esteem). Second, the individual, not the system, is blamed for the failure. Just as we admire the "self-made man or woman," so we condemn the loser, the person who doesn't "make it."

Merton described five possible responses to a gap between culturally prescribed goals and socially structured opportunities (see Table 7-1). *Conformists* accept both the goals their culture holds as desirable and the socially approved means of pursuing those goals, whether or not such behavior "pays off." Most people are conformists in this sense. *Innovators* are determined to achieve conventional goals but are willing to use unconventional means of doing so—to cut corners, "play dirty," cheat, bribe, steal, or do whatever else is necessary to succeed. *Ritualists* are the opposite of innovators. Compulsive about following the rules, they often lose sight of the goals; complying with the means becomes an end in itself. Although many people consider ritualists annoying or eccentric, they are not usually regarded as deviant. *Retreatists,* Merton's fourth type, have given up on both the goals and the accepted means of achieving them. They are society's dropouts—psychotics, homeless people, chronic drunkards, and drug addicts. *Rebels* reject both the values and the norms of their society, substituting new goals and new means of achieving them. Members of survivalist or militia groups and other countercultures are examples. Innovators, retreatists, and rebels are the most likely to be regarded as deviant.

Merton's key point was that deviance is a *product of the social system,* not of abnormality within the individual. People turn to deviance when a culture stimulates appetites that cannot be satisfied by culturally approved means.

Reviewing Merton's ideas some years later, Richard Cloward and Lloyd Ohlin (1960) came up with an interesting addition. Merton focused on the availability of legitimate opportunities as a factor in deviance. Cloward and Ohlin raised questions about the availability of *illegitimate opportunities.* To violate the laws against insider trading on the stock market, for example, one must first be an insider and know how the stock market works. If the drug traffic in a community is controlled by a particular ethnic group, members of that ethnic group have more opportunities to meet dealers and to observe drug deals—and are more likely therefore to be invited to participate—than outsiders. Cloward and Ohlin's point is that illegitimate opportunities for success may be distributed throughout society as unevenly as are legitimate opportunities. At least one reason few middle-aged, middle-class men and women become loan sharks or hired guns is that most never have the opportunity. (Control theorists would add that an equally important reason is that middle-class men and women have a vested interest in conformity.)

Cultural Transmission

Another challenge to the theory of deviance and anomie is the theory of cultural transmission. This view is based on the observation that some of the people society at large considers deviant are in fact conformists in their own social world. Cultural transmission theory views deviance as the result of socialization to a subculture that applauds attitudes and behavior that the mainstream culture rejects.

Criminologist Edwin Sutherland (1949/1983) belonged to this school. Sutherland reasoned that in a heterogeneous society such as ours there are many different groups, each with its own set of norms. Some place a high value on being able to get along with other people; others demand a violent response to the mildest challenge. Some reward effort and hard work; others advocate "easy living."

Table 7-1   *Merton's Five Modes of Social Adaptation*

Modes of Adapting	Accepts Culturally Approved Goals	Accepts Culturally Approved Means
Conformist	Yes	Yes
Innovator	Yes	No
Ritualist	No	Yes
Retreatist	No	No
Rebel	Creates new goals	Creates new means

Source: Adapted with permission of The Free Press, a Division of Macmillan, Inc., from *Social Theory and Social Structure* by Robert K. Merton. Copyright 1967, 1968 by Robert K. Merton.

According to Sutherland, individuals become delinquent or criminal through **differential association,** that is, when they are exposed to more pro-criminal than anticriminal norms and values for long periods or when they generally find themselves in situations that reward criminal behavior. Sutherland believed that in the delinquent's "education," acquiring attitudes that support criminal activities is just as important as learning the techniques for committing a crime. And we acquire our attitudes from those with whom we associate. Sutherland thus disagreed sharply with the idea that criminal behavior is an expression of "something inside" that sets deviants apart from other people. For Sutherland it was all a matter of exposure and associations, the balance of "good" and "bad" influences.

Differential association also helps explain noncriminal but "problem" behavior. For example, even before they enter college, students may expect that binge drinking will be accepted and approved on campus. In the United States, age 18 to 21 is the period of heaviest drinking. The culture of drinking on campuses might explain why binge drinking is far more common among college students than nonstudents (National Institute on Alcohol Abuse and Alcoholism, 1995).

The major flaw in Sutherland's theory of differential association is that it does not explain why deviant subcultures emerge in the first place. Conflict theory suggests an explanation.

Conflict Theory

The conflict perspective on deviance is rooted in the work of Karl Marx (see Chapter 2). Although Marx did not write extensively on this subject, he saw crime as derived from the division of capitalist societies into two separate and unequal classes: the owners of the means of production and the workers. To simplify a bit, the poor commit crimes to obtain material goods they have been denied and to express their anger and frustration. Members of the ruling class also violate norms in order to maintain their position and privileges. But, unlike the "masses," they have the power to prevent their actions from being labeled as deviant or criminal. Thus conflict theory focuses not on the groups that break the rules but on the groups that *make* the rules. In this view, social definitions of deviance are "first and foremost a reflection of the interests and

ideologies of the ruling class" (Quinney, 1976, p. 192).

According to conflict theory, the temperance movement was not only an attempt to ban drinking but also an attempt to retain power and privilege. It was, according to Joseph Gusfield (1986, 1991), a **symbolic crusade:** an effort by members of a social class or ethnic group to preserve, defend, or enhance their position in relation to other groups in their society. Whereas political movements seek to replace one form of government, a particular group of leaders, or the prevailing political ideology with another, symbolic crusades focus on lifestyles and public morals. They are most likely to develop when a group is *losing* power but seeks to maintain its status and prestige. Prohibition was also an example of a symbolic crusade.

The Politics of Prohibition

The founding fathers of the United States, or Federalists, were aristocrats who expected, after independence, to act as "stewards" or protectors who would govern in the name of the common good; they had no intention of sharing power with the "common man." In the early years of the republic, only white male *property owners* were permitted to vote. Alarmed by electoral defeats in the early nineteenth century, the Federalists allied themselves with the temperance movement, which was expanding. The Federalists needed organized political support as well as votes. In private, most Federalists enjoyed moderate drinking, but they were not convinced the "common man" would exercise self-restraint. In public, the Federalists supported the temperance movement's goal of abstinence.

During the mid- to late nineteenth and early twentieth centuries, the numbers and influence of new non-Protestant, often non-English-speaking immigrants grew, and modern, industrial cities began to overshadow this country's traditional, agrarian heartland. Patterns of drinking vary from one subculture or social class to another and thus serve as "cultural markers." Among rural, native-born, American Protestants, abstinence had become a marker of middle-class status, a symbolic line that divided industrious, respectable citizens from ne'er-do-wells and drifters. The new immigrants brought their drinking customs with them from Europe: the Irish were known for their use of hard liquor and bachelor drinking bouts; the Germans, for their love of beer;

the Italians and to a lesser extent Jews, for their fondness for wine. The temperance movement was one way that native-born Protestants could demonstrate that "it was not yet somebody else's America" (Gusfield, 1986, p. 6). As the temperance movement grew, it came to symbolize the struggle between native and immigrant, Protestant and Catholic, rural and urban, traditional and modern lifestyles. It also became increasingly democratic, condemning the lavish lifestyles of the upper class as well as the squalor of the urban poor, and increasingly radical as its goal shifted from reforming drinkers to outlawing alcohol. Prohibition was concrete evidence of the victory of "middle America" over its enemies, though the victory was only temporary.

Symbolic crusades, from the Salem witch-hunts to today's women's movement, have been a regular feature of American politics. For the most part, however, the law reflects—and protects—the interests of the predominantly white, male, older, wealthy ruling class. Often the behavior of nonwhites, juveniles, the poor, and some women is criminalized. Thus street crime (committed by the poor) tends to be penalized more strictly than white-collar and corporate crime (committed by the rich); marijuana (smoked primarily by the young) is criminal but alcohol (enjoyed by the wealthy as well as the working class) is not; the penalties for possession of small amounts of crack (usually by inner-city blacks) are higher than those for possession of larger amounts of cocaine (usually by well-

off whites); prostitutes (females) are arrested while their clients or "johns" (males) usually go free.

Changing Definitions of Rape

The changing legal definitions of rape also illustrate the role of power in defining what is and is not criminal (Bourque, 1989; Schur, 1980). Until quite recently, the burden of proof rested on the victim in rape cases, preserving male dominance and rights over women. Certain kinds of women (prostitutes, heavy drinkers, hitchhikers, divorcées) were not thought credible rape victims; they "brought it on themselves." A woman could not charge her husband with rape: a husband had the legal right to his wife's sexual services, and she had no right to refuse him.

By the mid-1970s, the women's movement had acquired the power to redefine rape as a crime of violence (not passion) and to provide victims with support in bringing charges. Since then, rape trials have become easier to prosecute, the victim is less often blamed, and public attitudes have changed (Caringella-MacDonald, 1988; Hamlin, 1988). The definition of rape also expanded, for example, to include date rape and similar violations between acquaintances rather than only between strangers (Coller and Resick, 1987; Koss et al., 1988). In the past, a woman who went to a man's apartment or dorm room, or had too much to drink, effectively gave up her right to say "no" to the man's sexual advances. Today men have lost some of their rights over women's sexual behavior, and the courts are

Alex Kelly, a handsome, wealthy high school wrestling star, was accused in 1986 of raping a 16-year-old girl and a 17-year-old girl in separate incidents. With his parents' financial help, Kelly fled to Europe, where he traveled through fifteen countries and evaded authorities for eight years. Ten years after these crimes were committed he turned himself in. Found guilty of the first rape, he is now in prison and faces another rape trial next year. Attitudes toward date or acquaintance rape are changing, and juries today are less willing to believe that a woman who said "no" really meant "yes."

less willing to believe that a woman who said "no" meant "yes." But most experts agree that only a small number of the women who are raped by a date or acquaintance report the assault, either because they fear being stigmatized, feel guilty, or want to avoid being sullied in the press. (See the discussion of sexual harassment in Chapter 10.)

In short, sociologists focus on patterns of deviance rather than on individual cases. While not minimizing the impact of individual psychological and biological factors, they attempt to identify the "social facts" of deviance: where and when deviance is most likely to occur and why members of some social groups and categories are more likely to engage in deviance than others. Sociologists also seek to determine the circumstances under which certain acts—and social actors—are likely to be labeled and treated as deviant.

Crime and the Justice System

A *crime* is the violation of a norm that has been codified in a law and is backed by the power and authority of the state. Although deviance and crime often overlap, they are not the same. Not all crimes are regarded as deviant. Littering, driving above the speed limit, and cheating a little on income taxes are all illegal, but many Americans do not consider these acts deviant. By the same token, not all acts that are considered deviant are crimes. Many people would consider going to a funeral in biking shorts or owning a hundred house cats deviant, but these are not crimes. Deviance, then, may be criminal or noncriminal. The most significant difference between the two is that criminal deviance may result in formal, official sanctions, such as arrest and imprisonment.

In addition, the law distinguishes between two broad categories of illegal activities. Violations of the *criminal law* are acts that the state has declared injurious to public safety and morals—from physical violence, theft, and vandalism to treason and prostitution. Violations of the *civil law* (or torts, from the Latin for "crooked") are acts of injustice for which the injured party may be entitled to compensation, such as slander, negligence, trespassing, and the like. The legal procedures for dealing with these two categories of wrongdoing are quite different. In criminal cases, the state initiates police investigation and court action. The burden of proof is on the state, and the accused is presumed innocent until proven guilty. In civil cases, private citizens must initiate court action by filing suit. The burden of proof is on the plaintiff (or person who initiated the case), not the state. For example, in a criminal trial O. J. Simpson was found not guilty of murdering Nicole Brown Simpson and Ron Goldman. Simpson's legal team persuaded the jury that the prosecution had not proved, as they must, that he was guilty beyond a reasonable doubt. This was the trial that received so much publicity. In a civil case brought by the victims' families, however, Simpson was found liable for wrongful death and ordered to pay monetary damages.

Types of Crime

Crime itself can be divided into five basic types: (1) violent and property crimes (or "common" crime), (2) white-collar crime, (3) corporate crime, (4) organized crime, and (5) crimes without victims.

"Common" Crime

Violent crimes—murder, rape, robbery, and assault—involve a direct confrontation between the criminal and the victim. Muggings—physical assaults with intent to rob, usually on the street or in a hallway—are the crimes Americans seem to fear most (Flanagan and Maguire, 1992, table 224). Unlike the perpetrator of a "crime of passion," the mugger is usually a stranger to the victim. The attack is sudden, unpredictable, and impersonal. *Property crimes* include burglary (theft without confrontation), larceny, auto theft, and such "minor" crimes as shoplifting and pickpocketing. Because the thief does not confront the victim face to face, the thief may feel that no "real" harm is involved (though certainly the victim feels differently).

Who commits these crimes? According to the most recent analysis of the FBI's *Uniform Crime Report (UCR)*, most violent and property crimes were committed by young males (Table 7-2). The crime rate for African American and Latino offenders is higher than that for white offenders; that is, the percentage of crimes known to be committed by these groups exceeds their proportion in the population. In terms of absolute numbers, however, most known criminals are white. Consistent with popular beliefs, most criminals are male; most are

Table 7-2 *Violent and Property Crimes in the United States, 1995 (UCR)*

Crimes	
Total crimes reported	23,876,143
Violent crimes reported	1,789,785
Violent crime rate per 100,000 population	984.6
Property crime rate per 100,000 population	4,593
Arrests	
By age:	
Under age 15	6.2%
Under age 18	18.3
Under age 25	44.5
By sex:	
Male	79.6
Female	20.4
By race:	
White (including Latino)	69.2
African American	27.9
Other	3.0

Note: Many crimes go unreported. These statistics represent only those crimes that were formally reported to the police.

Source: U.S. Department of Justice, Federal Bureau of Investigation, *Crimes in the United States, 1995,*. Washington, DC: GPO, 1996, pp. 5, 10, 35, 218–227.

also young—and getting younger (Fox, 1996). The homicide rate for adults age 25 and older has declined 25 percent since 1985. But the homicide for young adults (age 18 to 24) increased 61 percent; most disturbing, the rate of homicides committed by *juveniles* (age 14 to 17) increased by 172 percent. Although only 8 percent of the population, males age 14 to 24 commit 48 percent of murders; they are also 27 percent of murder victims. All the increase in juvenile murder involved guns; homicide rates with other weapons have not increased. In most cases, the victim and offender are friends or acquaintances.

The stereotype of muggings holds that the victims of common crime are most likely to be white and middle-class. Not so: young, African American males and Latino males are most likely to be the victims of violent or property crime, followed by women (see Table 7-3). Most criminals do not travel very far from their homes to commit burglaries or robberies. With most violent crimes, the attacker and victim know one another, sometimes intimately. One in four aggravated assaults reported to the police is committed in the home, and a large percentage of murders are committed by family members (U.S. Department of Justice, 1996).

In some cases, the victim of common crime is not a person but a company. What we might call "lifestyle crime" is more widespread, and more costly, than most people realize. For example, illicit taping of movies and videocassettes, fraudulent use of credit cards, and fraudulent use of automatic teller machines cost banks billions of dollars each year. Individuals who commit such crimes may rationalize (or neutralize) their behavior on the grounds that they are not really harming anyone, but they are in fact robbing the public. The costs are not simply absorbed by the bank or company; rather, they are passed on to consumers. Almost everything you buy has a built-in crime "tax."

White-Collar Crime

If the FBI measured crime in terms of financial costs, the demographic portrait of property criminals would change to white, middle-aged, middle-class males. Sociologist Edwin Sutherland introduced the term "white-collar crime" in his presidential address to the American Sociological Association in 1939 (Braithwaite, 1985; Sutherland, 1949/1983, p. 7). **White-collar crime** refers to violations of the law committed by middle- and upper-middle-class people in the course of their business and social lives. Crimes in this category range from stealing paper clips and using the office copying machine for personal reasons to multimillion-dollar stock swindles (Reichman, 1993).

In contrast to street criminals, white-collar offenders usually are employed at the time they commit their crimes. Some hold managerial, technical, or professional positions, and a few are business owners or corporate officers, but most are lower-level employees. They are more likely than street criminals to be white. They are also older than most common criminals (mean age 40 at time of conviction) (Weisburd, Chayet, and Waring, 1990).

Whereas street criminals use violence or the threat of violence, white-collar criminals use lies, misrepresentations, and deception to convince victims to part with their money or property (Shapiro, 1990). Whereas common criminals break and enter, white-collar criminals use "social technology" (skills, charm, networks) to become insiders in organizations that provide opportunities for fraud. Common offenses include misappropriation of

Table 7-3   *Victims of Crime, 1994 (NCVS)* (Victimizations per 1,000 Persons Age 12 or Older)

Characteristics	All Crime	All Crimes of Violence	Rape/Sexual Assault	Robbery	Crimes of Violence — Total	Assault — Aggravated	Assault — Simple	Personal Theft
Sex:								
Male	61.7	59.6	.2	8.1	51.3	15.3	35.9	2.0
Female	45.1	42.5	3.7	4.1	34.7	8.1	26.6	2.5
Age:								
12–15	117.4	114.8	3.1	12.0	99.7	22.2	77.6	2.6
16–19	125.9	121.7	5.1	11.8	104.8	33.7	71.1	4.2
20–24	102.5	99.2	5.0	11.3	82.9	26.6	56.4	3.3
25–34	63.2	60.9	2.9	7.5	50.6	13.7	36.9	2.3
35–49	41.4	39.5	1.6	5.2	32.8	7.6	25.2	1.9
50–64	16.8	15.1	.2*	2.3	12.6	3.3	9.3	1.7
65 or older	7.2	5.1	.1*	1.4	3.6	1.2	2.4	2.1
Race:								
White	51.5	49.4	1.9	4.8	42.7	10.9	31.8	2.1
African American	65.4	61.8	2.7	14.0	45.0	16.6	28.4	3.6
Other	49.1	47.6	2.5*	9.0	36.1	11.9	24.2	1.6*
Ethnicity:								
Latino	63.3	59.8	2.6	9.8	47.4	16.2	31.2	3.5
Non-Latino	51.9	49.8	2.0	5.6	42.1	11.1	31.0	2.1
Household income:								
Less than $7,500	88.3	83.6	6.7	11.1	65.8	20.5	45.3	4.7
$7,500–$14,999	60.8	58.6	3.3	7.1	48.1	13.8	34.3	2.2
$15,000–$24,999	51.7	49.9	2.3	5.9	41.7	13.2	28.5	1.8
$25,000–$34,999	51.3	49.3	1.2	4.6	43.5	11.3	32.3	2.0
$35,000–$49,999	49.3	46.8	.9	4.8	41.1	10.1	31.0	2.6
$50,000–$74,999	47.6	46.1	.8	4.2	41.1	9.5	31.6	1.5
$75,000 or more	42.7	40.0	.9*	4.5	34.6	8.0	26.5	2.7
Residence:								
Urban	67.6	63.6	2.7	10.9	50.1	14.8	35.2	4.0
Suburban	51.8	49.6	1.8	5.1	42.7	11.0	31.7	2.2
Rural	39.8	39.2	1.7	2.6	34.9	9.2	25.8	.6

Note: The victimization survey cannot measure murder because of the inability to question the victim.

*Estimate is based on about 10 or fewer sample cases.

Source: U.S. Department of Justice, *Criminal Victimization in 1994,* Washington, DC: Federal Bureau of Investigation, 1996.

funds (embezzling, padding expense accounts, taking unauthorized commissions and fees, inflating their own salaries and bonuses), conflict of interest (using their positions for personal benefit, for example, by investing pension funds in ventures in which they have a financial interest), and corruption (in effect, selling or renting their positions to the highest bidder, who then receives special consideration in the form of corporate contracts, votes in Congress, etc.).

The cumulative cost of white-collar crime is enormous. According to one estimate, embezzlement and pilferage by employees cost American businesses an estimated $10 billion a year (*The Wall Street Journal,* August 17, 1993, p. A4). The cost of white-collar crime cannot be reckoned in dollars alone, however (E. Moore and Mills, 1990; Shapiro, 1990). Whether as salaried employees or public officials, white-collar criminals occupy positions of *trust:* they have the authority to make decisions and to manage and spend other people's money. Their misuse of assets or power is a violation of that trust and may weaken public faith in a free economy and its business leaders, democracy and our political leaders, and public morality generally.

James McDougal was convicted of 18 counts of fraud and conspiracy—white-collar crimes—in connection with the Whitewater land deal, in which President Clinton and Hillary Rodham Clinton were also involved. Shown here displaying a copy of the Whitewater deed, McDougal began cooperating with special prosecutor Kenneth Starr while serving his prison term. McDougal's failing health and memory lapses raised questions about his credibility, and in March 1998, he died in jail of a heart attack.

Though both expensive and widespread, white-collar crime usually does not generate the public concern of street crime. The main reason is that "abuses of trust are hard to detect, . . . victimization subtle, offenses ongoing, culpability difficult to assign, conclusive evidence hard to amass, [and] harsh sanctions spill over onto innocent parties" (Shapiro, 1990, p. 359). Often the crime is not discovered, the criminal cannot be located, and the victims may not even know they have been robbed. The victim may be an organization rather than an individual or even a class of individuals. When detected, white-collar offenses are more likely to be handled privately (by the person's boss or by a pro-

fessional association) than through the police and courts. Even when brought to trial and convicted, white-collar criminals are more likely than common criminals to receive fines and/or suspended sentences rather than time in prison. Although they often are repeat offenders, white-collar criminals apparently seem less threatening to police, judges, and juries (Weisburd, Chayet, and Waring, 1990). As a result, the white-collar criminal may avoid being publicly labeled as a thief, a criminal, or a crook.

Corporate Crime

Corporations can also be guilty of crimes—false advertising, price fixing, violation of safety regulations for employees or consumers, stock manipulation, copyright infringement, and mislabeling food and drugs, to name a few common violations (Eitzen and Baca Zinn, 1992). Whereas white-collar crime consists of crimes against the corporation, **corporate crime** consists of crimes committed by the corporation, on behalf of the corporation. Whereas white-collar crime usually consists of individual acts, corporate crime is the result of collective action.

In recent years major corporations have been found guilty in court or exposed by the press for:

- *The sale of products they knew to be defective and dangerous:* Examples are products such as the Ford Pinto, which exploded on impact; the Dalkon shield, an intrauterine birth control device linked to infections and infertility; faulty airplane brakes (Vandiver, 1996)—and cigarettes.
- *Industrial pollution:* An Environmental Protection Agency report estimated that American industry released or disposed of 22.5 billion pounds of toxic substances into surface waters, underground wells, landfills, and the air in a single year (in Yeager, 1993).
- *Discrimination in hiring and promotion:* In this category are AT&T, General Motors, and Libby-Owens-Ford, among others.
- *Negligence:* There have been more than 800 health and safety violations, including willful exposure to lead and arsenic, by General Motors.
- *Bribery, especially of foreign governments:* Exxon, Gulf Oil, Mobil Oil, Ashland Oil, Northrop, Lockheed, United Brands, and others, have engaged in bribery.

The human and financial costs of such actions far exceed those from other types of crime. But as with

The environmental costs of industrial crime and negligence are enormous. Here cleanup workers deal with the after-effects of the Exxon Valdez oil spill in Prince William Sound, Alaska, in 1989. Exxon and the pipeline company deemed responsible for the spill eventually paid over $1 billion in fines and restitution for the largest oil spill in U.S. history.

white-collar crime, our society has been lenient toward business (Ermann and Lundman, 1996; Tonry and Reiss, 1993).

Many corporate offenses are handled by regulatory agencies, not the courts. Studies of these agencies (for example, A. J. Reiss, 1983, 1984) found that officials saw their goal as achieving compliance with regulations, not identifying criminals; moreover, these officials believed that they were most successful when they dealt with businesses through negotiation, threats of negative publicity, bluff, and other informal sanctions. The corporation might be let off with a "consent decree," in which it consents to end violations but neither admits nor denies the allegations. In this way it avoids public exposure in an open courtroom, as well as liabilities toward victims. The Environmental Protection Agency (EPA), for example, does not have the staff or the funds to conduct regular inspections and so relies on companies to file reports voluntarily and monitor themselves. A study of 220 "nonminor" effluent or sewage violations (all in New Jersey) found that in most cases the EPA took no action or merely issued a warning letter; administrative orders, requiring that the company take action, were rare (eight cases), and only two cases were referred to the criminal or civil courts (Yeager, 1993).

Weak enforcement of laws and regulations is not necessarily the result of bureaucratic inefficiency or the "fault" of overburdened and uncommitted inspectors (Tonry and Reiss, 1993). Regulatory agencies are responsible for finding a balance between public health and safety and economic growth—no easy task. Just as people do not want nuclear waste dumped in *their* backyards, so they do not want to lose *their* jobs to save the spotted owl. Rapidly changing technology (whether pollution control devices or investment strategies) requires ever more complex regulations, a spiral that leads to inaction. Finally, corporations are not the only culprits: government agencies and not-for-profit groups also commit organizational crimes.

Many corporate violations are legally defined as torts, not crimes. Moreover, usually the corporation is held responsible, not the people who made decisions or carried out illegal activities. If individuals become ill because of exposure to toxic substances, for example, they must bring their own cases to court, suing the manufacturer and/or dumper for damages. The civil courts do not send guilty parties to prison but award compensation. In a civil action, the victims cannot call on the police or other public agencies to help in the investigation. They (and, in many cases, their attorneys) must bear the costs of investigation and court proceedings, in the hope that the court will order them repaid. Large corporations can afford to drag out legal battles for years; often the victims cannot. When found guilty, the fines are so small that they are more than offset by the profits from the offense and are simply written off as part of the "cost of doing business." (Indeed, in some cases court costs and fines may be tax-deductible!)

The case of the tobacco industry illustrates the complexity of regulating corporations. For three decades, public health officials have warned that smoking can cause cancer, heart disease, emphysema, and other fatal diseases. With their vast resources, cigarette manufacturers were able to fend off lawsuits by smokers suffering from these ailments (or their survivors) on the grounds that the companies did not force people to smoke. In the 1980s and 1990s, public attitudes toward smoking changed, leading to widespread bans on smoking in public places. Then, in a 1997 civil suit, the attorneys general of twenty (eventually forty) states accused the Liggett Group, the smallest of the five leading tobacco companies, of hiding knowledge of the adverse health effects of cigarettes and sought compensation for the billions of dollars the states spend annually in Medicaid for people with smoking-related ailments. In an attempt to plea-bargain, Liggett admitted that it knew that smoking causes cancer and nicotine is addictive, and even that it had aimed ads at teenagers, who are least likely to pay attention to health warnings and more likely to develop a lifelong smoking habit than are adults who start smoking. Liggett also agreed to turn over company records thought to reveal that it and other manufacturers not only knew smoking was lethal and addictive but also conspired to manipulate levels of nicotine and target teenagers. Soon after, the other leading tobacco companies reluctantly came to the bargaining table. The agreement worked out with the federal and state government requires that they pay close to $350 billion in damages, health care, and antismoking campaigns; put strict limits on the advertising and sale of cigarettes; and agree that nicotine is a drug and so subject to Federal Drug Administration (FDA) controls. Before the agreement goes into effect, however, Congress, the president, and possibly the U.S. Supreme Court will have to agree on numerous details. The tobacco industry may be gambling that the approval process will take so long that current sales will offset much of the cost. Meanwhile, the companies have stepped up advertising and sales abroad, especially in developing countries.

Organized Crime

The study of white-collar and corporate crime concerns the illegal activities of individuals and organizations engaged primarily in legitimate businesses.

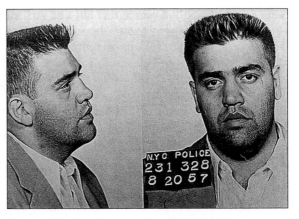

Vincent "The Chin" Gigante, alleged boss of the Genovese crime family, in a New York City mug shot from 1957. Gigante evaded the law for decades, in part by claiming (through his lawyers) mental incompetence. He was notorious for wandering the streets in his pajamas, which was all part of an act according to prosecutors. Finally, at age 67, Gigante was brought to trial and found guilty of racketeering and conspiracy to commit murder in 1997.

The study of **organized crime** deals with organizations that exist primarily to provide, and profit from, illegal goods and services.

Organized-crime groups typically specialize in three types of activities. The first and most obvious is the sale of forbidden goods and services. Drugs and prostitution are familiar examples. Prostitution violates the official norms of "respectable" society yet provides a service many people (including "respectable" citizens) want. In this case, organized crime profits from society's moral ambivalence.

Second, organized crime provides goods and services in forms and in places where legitimate businesses will not work. Loan-sharking, or providing loans at exorbitant rates to individuals or businesses that cannot obtain credit through conventional channels, is an example. Smuggling cigarettes from low-tax southern states to high-tax northern states or automatic weapons from states where their sale is legal to states where it is not are other examples.

The third area in which organized crime does business—perhaps the majority of its business—is providing legal goods and services by illegal means. Crime groups control garbage collection or taxi and limousine service in many cities by using intimidation to eliminate competitors. Some also use legitimate businesses to "launder" (that is, disguise the origins of) profits from illegal activities.

The term "organized crime" conjures up images of Italian mobsters who came to public attention during Prohibition. But there is nothing intrinsically Italian about organized crime. It exists in some form throughout the world. In the United States, some members of almost every new wave of immigrants have been involved in organized crime for a period of time. Black Americans became involved in organized crime when they found themselves concentrated in urban ghettos and blocked from legitimate careers. Of course, the great majority of immigrants from Europe, Asia, and Latin America and of African Americans attempt to work their way out of poverty through legal activities, often accepting the most menial jobs so that their children may have better lives. But the pattern of "ethnic succession" suggests that organized crime is, in part, a product of social arrangements that create a high-risk, but high-profit, market for illegal goods, on the one hand, and of social arrangements that limit opportunities for some groups to engage in legitimate businesses, on the other.

The successful investigation and prosecution of organized crime is a long-term, information-intensive process. While it may be relatively easy to capture and convict "small fry," major figures often evade the law. The scale of the enterprise and tight control over information shield the bosses, while intermediaries do much of the "dirty work" on the front lines. When bosses do go to prison, it is usually for a less serious offense, such as income tax evasion (Edelhertz, Cole, and Berk, 1984). In this, organized crime is similar to white-collar and corporate crime.

Crimes without Victims/Victims without Crime

Edwin Schur (1965) coined the term **crimes without victims** to describe activities that have been declared illegal because they offend public morals, not because they cause anyone direct harm. Prostitution, most pornography, illegal sex acts between consenting adults, the sale and use of illegal drugs, public drunkenness, and illegal gambling all fall into this category. These activities may be *self-destructive,* but the criminal and the victim often are one and the same. They are crimes because some segments of the population view such behavior as immoral, indecent, and harmful to public order and had the power to see that it was banned by law.

People who favor criminalization of personal behavior believe that all societies must define and enforce a common morality. They hold that society has an obligation to protect people who cannot or do not protect themselves, just as society has an obligation to protect children. Furthermore, these crimes do have victims. Prostitutes spread sexually transmitted diseases (including AIDS). Babies born to women who use drugs or drink suffer from multiple problems, including addiction at birth. Drunkenness not only leads to traffic accidents and fatalities but is also associated with (but not necessarily the cause of) violence, spouse abuse, and date rape.

Those who support decriminalization of personal behavior hold that for the government to legislate morality is an abuse of power and, in many cases, a violation of the right to privacy (especially in sexual acts) and the right to free speech (in the case of pornography). They point out that many of these laws are arbitrary. There is no intrinsic reason why cigarettes and alcohol should be legal and marijuana and heroin illegal, for example. All are harmful to health, and all are potentially addictive. Other laws are so vague (for example, laws against loitering, disorderly conduct, and vagrancy) that they are enforced arbitrarily (for instance, against African American inner-city youth and the homeless). Finally, they hold that outlawing personal behavior is seldom effective; pushes goods and services onto the black market, which leads to secondary deviance or other, more serious crimes (from addicts stealing to support their habit to the murder of innocent bystanders by rival gangs and drug cartels); and adds to the cost of law enforcement.

In recent years, the trend has been toward decriminalization (with the notable exceptions of drugs and drunk driving). Gambling, once illegal, is now permitted in most states, and buying lottery tickets at local grocery stores or from news venders has become an everyday activity. Laws against sodomy are no longer used to prosecute—or blackmail—homosexual men. In the landmark *Roe v. Wade* decision, the U.S. Supreme Court declared laws against abortion in the first trimester of pregnancy unconstitutional. Decriminalization has not eliminated controversy, however. The debate over abortion and the organized effort to reverse the Supreme Court's decision are as strong as ever. In some states the law protects homosexuals from discrimination, but there is much debate over whether homosexual couples should be permitted to get married and enjoy the legal advantages of marriage (especially tax breaks and inheritance laws). When the Disney Corporation extended health care benefits to same-sex partners of its employees, the Southern Baptist Conference urged its 16 million members to "boycott Disney Company stores and theme parks if they continue this anti-Christian and anti-family trend" (Niebuhr, 1996, p. A10).

Sociologists Robert Meier and Gilbert Geis (1997) point out that sociologists who study crimes without victims have ignored a second and related category of offense, *victims without crimes*. A person who contracts AIDS from someone he or she is dating, people maimed or killed by land mines left behind by soldiers, and employees laid off when a company decides to close a plant and move production to another state or country are examples. All suffer because of actions society has not defined as criminal. In the United States the "good samaritan" might become a victim without crime. Almost all European countries have laws that *require* bystanders to intervene if they witness a crime or accident and are able to assist the victim or call for help. In France, it is a crime for a doctor to drive by the scene of an accident and not offer assistance, and prosecutions are not uncommon. In the United States, the opposite is true: in most states, bystanders have no legal obligation to intervene and, indeed, can be held liable for the consequences, say, if their efforts to help cause unintentional harm.[1] Most Americans would agree that good samaritans are essential to a decent society and that someone who does not stop a blind person from walking into traffic or help an elderly person who falls on the sidewalk is inhumane. Yet our laws, in effect, encourage us to be "bad samaritans."

---

[1] The exceptions are Vermont and Minnesota, whose laws require that bystanders intervene in accidents or face criminal penalties, and Massachusetts, where bystanders are required to report violent crimes.

The scene of Princess Diana's fatal crash in a Paris highway tunnel in August 1997. In France, it is illegal for a doctor to drive by an accident scene without stopping to help. In the United States, laws are very different.

Pornography and prostitution are readily available in many U.S. cities, despite laws that attempt to eradicate them. However, if a law is not backed by social consensus about the problem it is designed to solve, it is likely to be ineffective.

The central questions in both crimes without victims and victims without crimes are whether it is possible to legislate morality and, if so, where to draw the line. Meier and Geis (1997) suggest two criteria: What kinds of problem can the law solve? and, What kinds of problem can the law create? They conclude that if a law is not backed by social consensus regarding the problem it is designed to solve, that law is likely to be ineffective at best and, at worst, create more problems than it solves, as happened to some degree under Prohibition.

Crime in the United States

By almost any measure, the United States is one of the most violent nations in the world. According to FBI statistics, for 1995, a murder was committed every twenty-four minutes; a rape, every five minutes; an assault, every twenty-nine seconds. About 7 out of every 1,000 Americans were victims of violent crimes; 4.5 in every 100, victims of property crimes (see Figure 7-4).

Why are crime rates, especially violent crime rates, in the United States so high? To answer this question, sociologist Rosemary Gartner (1990) conducted a cross-cultural survey. Gartner analyzed data from eighteen nations over a thirty-year period. She found that four social structural variables were associated with higher rates of homicide. These included:

1. *Economic stress*—measured in terms of inadequate or unequal distribution of income
2. *Social disintegration*—measured in terms of divorce rates and cultural diversity, which may both weaken group ties and lead to intergroup friction
3. *Demography*—the percentage of teens and youth in a population (the age groups with the highest crime rates), and the percentage of households with working women
4. *The cultural context*—specifically, the existence of officially approved violence, such as recent war or state executions

All these variables are found in the United States: a wide gap between the rich and the poor, cultural diversity, large numbers of unsupervised and unemployed young people, and a culture that is permissive toward violence.

To understand whether crime in the United States is increasing or decreasing, we first must interpret crime statistics. The FBI's *Uniform Crime Report* includes two sets of data. For "Type I" crimes (homicide, aggravated assault, forcible rape, robbery, burglary, larceny-theft, and motor vehicle theft), the FBI records all crimes reported to, or discovered by, the police, as well as data on the number of arrests made, the number of cases sent to trial, and the characteristics of those arrested and convicted. Note that only those crimes *known* to the police are included. If a crime is not reported (because the victim knows the offender, fears retaliation, fears the police, or simply does not want to be bothered), it does not appear in the FBI's reports. For "Type II" crimes (white-collar crimes and crimes without victims), the FBI records only the number of *arrests*. Moreover, white-collar crimes handled as civil, not criminal, cases are not included.

In addition to recording the number of crimes, the FBI calculates crime rates in terms of the num-

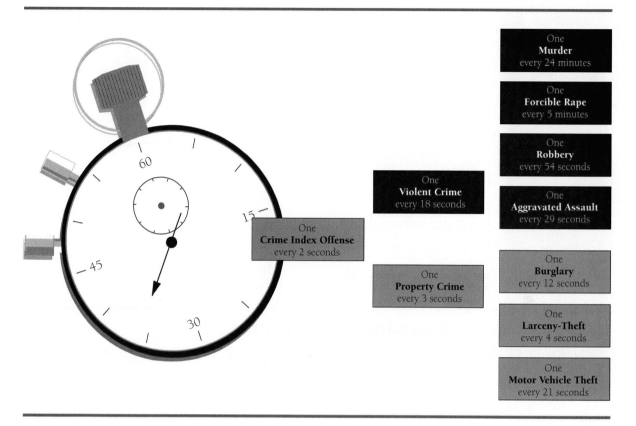

Figure 7-4   *The Crime Clock*

The crime clock should be read with care. It does not describe an actual interval in the commission of the "Type I" crimes; rather, it represents the annual ratio of crime to fixed time intervals.

Source: Uniform Crime Reports for the United States, 1995, Washington, DC: GPO, U.S. Department of Justice, Federal Bureau of Investigation, 1996, chart 2.1.

ber of crimes per 100,000 inhabitants. The distinction between the **absolute number of crimes** and the **crime rate** is an important one. Suppose the violent crime rate for Middletown in 1990 was 5.95. If Middletown has a population of 100,000, that means about 6 violent crimes were committed that year. However, if Middletown's population is 2 million, a rate of 5.95 means that 120 violent crimes were committed. The FBI's *Uniform Crime Report* shows that both the total number of offenses known to the FBI and the rate of offenses declined between 1991 and 1995. The rate declined by 10.5 percent, and the total number of offenses by 6.8 percent (see Figure 7-5).

Another source of data is the *National Crime Victimization Survey (NCVS),* launched by the Department of Justice in 1973 because research had shown that most crimes are not reported. This annual report includes data on victimization from a representative sample of about 60,000 American households. Respondents are asked about six crimes: assault, forcible rape, robbery, burglary, larceny, and motor vehicle theft. (Homicide and thefts from businesses are not included.) According to this survey, 27 million crimes were not reported to the police in 1994.

The gap between the *UCR* and *NCVS* data does not necessarily mean that one is better or more accurate than the other. Rather, they measure different things (Steffensmeier and Harer, 1991). For example, in the *UCR* each "criminal incident" is recorded once, in terms of the most serious offense committed; in the *NCVS,* when several crimes are committed together, all are reported. Respondents in the

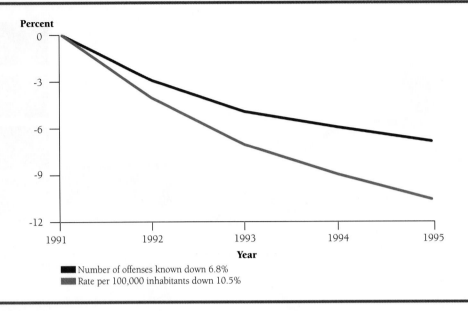

Figure 7-5   *Changes in Number and Rate of Offenses, 1991–1995*

According to the FBI's *Uniform Crime Report* (a count of crimes reported to police), crime in the United States has declined significantly in recent years.

Source: Uniform Crime Reports for the United States, 1995, Washington, DC: GPO, U.S. Department of Justice, Federal Bureau of Investigation, 1996, chart 2.1.

NCVS cite numerous offenses they did not bother to report to the police. The *UCR* is best seen as a measure of serious crimes; the *NCVS,* a measure of all crimes, large and small.

The available data from both the *Uniform Crime Reports* and the *National Crime Victimization Survey* agree that the rate of violent crime peaked in the early 1980s, fluctuated during the 1980s and early 1990s, and has decreased since 1994 (see Figure 7-6). According to the *NCVS,* 27 million crimes were *not* reported to the police in 1994. The rate of crime victimization fluctuated between 1973 and 1995. Between 1993 and 1995, the rate declined.

The current rate of serious violent crimes is about equal to the previous low in 1986. The latest data on violent crime, recently released by the FBI, show that the murder rate continued to drop between 1995 and 1996 (Butterfield, 1997).

Even though the crime rate is declining, most Americans agree that the levels of violence and theft in our society are unacceptably high. What can be done to control crime?

Equal Justice for All?

The criminal justice system can be seen as a funnel or filter. For a variety of reasons—some practical, some political, some social—only a tiny fraction of the crimes actually committed are punished. In general, the poor, minority-group members, and young males are more likely to be subject to formal sanctions than are well-off, white, middle-aged, and older men. Women are far less likely than men to commit crimes, and also less likely to be arrested, convicted, imprisoned, or executed when they do.

The selection process begins with ordinary citizens. As noted above, only about one-third of all crimes committed are ever reported to the authorities. The selection process continues with the police.

The Police

The police become involved in social control when they witness a crime, when they uncover one crime in the course of investigating another, or when a private citizen registers a complaint. In theory, the police are responsible for investigating all crimes that

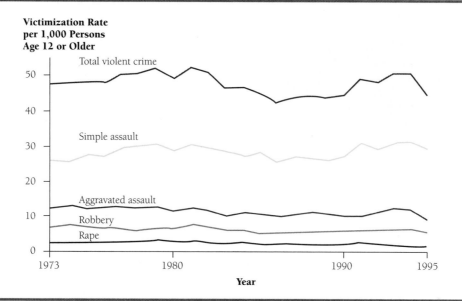

Figure 7-6   *Violent Crime Rates, 1973–1995*

According to the Department of Justice's *Victimization Surveys* (which includes crimes *not* reported to police) the rate of criminal victimization fluctuated in recent years.

Source: M. Rand, J. P. Lynch, and D. Cantor, *Crime Victimization, 1973–1995,* Washington, DC: U.S. Department of Justice, Office of Justice Programs, 1997.

come to their attention and for arresting and interrogating suspects. In practice, they are selective about which crimes they investigate, whom they arrest, and what testimony they give in court. In some cases the police do not pursue an investigation because they do not consider the charges serious. In other cases an investigation is undertaken but leads nowhere. Most crimes are not solved through detective work but because the victim is able to identify the offender or because witnesses come forward. All told, only a fraction of the crimes reported to the police, usually violent crimes rather than property crimes (see Figure 7-7), result in arrests.

In recent years, charges of racial discrimination and police brutality toward minorities have mounted. The 1992 riots in Los Angeles and other cities were touched off by the acquittal of four white police officers accused of brutally beating a black motorist, Rodney King. Are these charges justified?

The evidence is mixed. In a classic study of police discretion, observers rode in patrol cars in Boston, Chicago, and Washington, D.C. (Black and Reiss, 1970; Black, 1980). They found that police

were far more likely to arrest black than white juveniles and that black juveniles were more likely to be stopped and questioned about serious crimes. Most complaints about black juveniles came from black adults in the community, who were more likely than white adults to demand that the police make an arrest. Other research has found evidence that blacks and Latinos are disadvantaged at various points in the judicial process (Humphrey and Fogarty, 1987; Mieth and Moore, 1986; Zatz, 1984), but this pattern is not always present or uniform. Rather, it seems to depend on such factors as the location of the crime (the ghetto or suburbia) and the social makeup of the community (ethnically and racially mixed or homogeneous) (Frazier, Bishop, and Henretta, 1992). African Americans and other minorities tend to be treated more harshly when the victims of a crime are white and the crime occurs in a predominantly white suburb.

The Courts

The courts become involved in social control when the police make an arrest. The courts are responsible

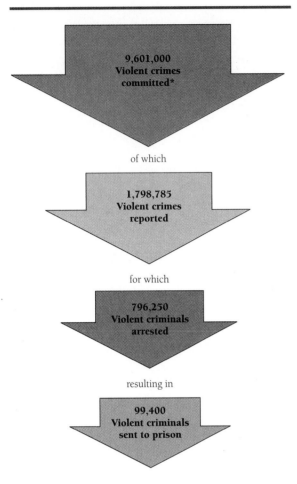

*Figures are for major categories of violent crime: murder, rape, robbery, and aggravated assault.

Figure 7-7   *A Violent Criminal's Chances of Going to Prison in 1995*

Only a fraction of crimes reported to the police result in arrests, and of those, a much smaller fraction will ultimately result in a prison sentence.

Source: U.S. Department of Justice, *Bureau of Justice Statistics Bulletin*, and Federal Bureau of Investigation.

for charging suspects, bringing them to trial, and determining penalties for those who are convicted. Only a fraction of the suspects who are arrested are ever brought to trial, however.

As a representative of the state, the prosecutor is the one who decides whether to bring a case to trial and what charges to press. In some cases, charges are dropped because the prosecutor feels there is

insufficient evidence. In many cases, the defendant waives the right to a trial and agrees to plead guilty in exchange for a lesser charge or the promise of leniency; this is known as *plea bargaining*. An estimated 90 percent of convictions in our courts are the result of plea bargaining (Senna and Siegel, 1996). Given the case overload in our judicial system, plea bargaining is a practical necessity, but it undermines the presumption of innocence guaranteed by the Constitution. The cases most likely to go to trial are those that have attracted public attention and those the prosecutor expects to win. Many prosecutors are elected officials who may see their court position as a way to further their political careers. As a result, many prefer not to risk losing a case in public.

The selection process continues in the courtroom. Our courts operate as an adversary system, in which the state and the accused engage in a public debate before an impartial judge or jury (Eitzen and Baca Zinn, 1992). For this system to be fair, the two adversaries would have to be equal in abilities and resources. But the state obviously has more resources than the individual defendant, particularly if the defendant is poor and must accept a court-appointed lawyer and remain in jail while awaiting trial. Not surprisingly, about nine out of ten defendants in criminal trials are found guilty (Eitzen and Baca Zinn, 1992, p. 506).

The Prisons

Although the number of serious crimes declined in the 1990s, the number of convicted criminals sentenced to prison, which had remained more or less steady for almost fifty years, climbed steadily (see Figure 7-8). The United States has one of the highest incarceration rates in the world (see Figure 7-9). In 1996, almost 1.7 million Americans were confined to prisons and jails, up 19 percent from 1990 (Mumola and Beck, 1997). If crime rates are falling, why is incarceration increasing?

One reason is statistical: The FBI does not include drug offenses in its annual report, in part because they are "crimes without victims." Crimes from murder to burglary may be declining, but apparently drug offenses are not. Between 1985–1986 and 1995, drug arrests increased by 64 percent; prison sentences for drug offenders rose 478 percent and account for almost half of the growth in prison populations over the past fifteen years

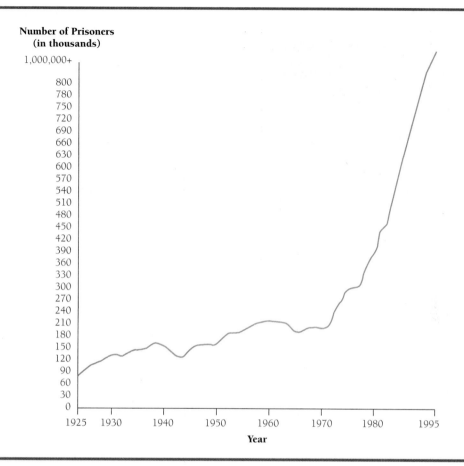

Number of Prisoners
(in thousands)

Figure 7-8   *The Growth of the U.S. Prison Population, 1925–1995*

Although the number of crimes reported to police declined in the early 1990s, the number of offenders sent to prison climbed, in large part because of an increase in drug arrests and longer sentences for both drug abuse and violent crimes.

Source: Bureau of Justice Statistics, 1982, *Prisoners 1925–1981,* Washington, DC: GPO, 1982, and ibid., *Correctional Populations in the United States,* 1995.

(Maguire and Pastore, 1997; Mumola and Beck, 1997). The rationale for imprisoning drug offenders is that they are likely to have committed other, often violent crimes. But a study in New York State estimated that a quarter of new inmates were "drug-only offenders," who had never been charged with any other crime (DiIoulio in Butterfield, 1997). A second reason for the growing prison population is that judges are imposing longer sentences and sending more people back to prison (often because of parole or probation violations, such as failing a urine test for drugs) and that parole boards are releasing fewer inmates who are eligible for parole. As

a result, inmates are spending more time behind bars than was true ten or fifteen years ago.

An alternative explanation is that crime rates have fallen because so many offenders have been locked up. There is no precise way to prove or disprove this line of reasoning. Estimates are that rising rates of imprisonment account for about 15 percent of the recent decrease in crime.

Alfred Blumstein and other criminologists think this prison boom may backfire (in Whitmire, 1995). When such large numbers of people (many from the same neighborhoods) are arrested, going to prison may lose some of its stigma (much as

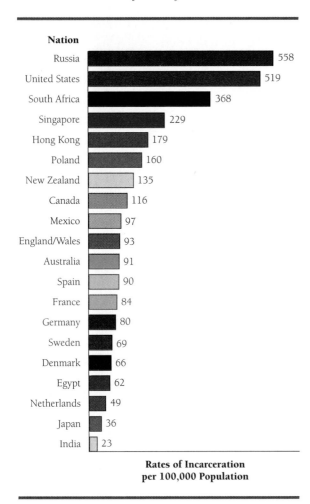

Figure 7-9   *Incarceration Rates for Select Countries*

The United States is a "world leader" in rates of imprisonment, exceeded only by Russia. Although Russia has a higher incarceration rate, there are more people in U.S. jails and prisons.

Source: Marc Mauer, *Americans Behind Bars: The International Use of Incarceration, 1992–1993,* Washington, DC: The Sentencing Project, 1994.

rising divorce rates have removed the stigma of a failed marriage). In Washington, D.C., half of black men age 18 to 35 are either in jail or prison or on probation or parole on any given day (Butterfield, 1997). Serving time in prison is almost as common as serving time in the military was when the United States had a universal draft policy. Imprisoning such large numbers of young men disrupts families and communities, on the one hand, and strength-

ens connections between criminal groups in prison and those on the street, on the other. Moreover, almost all these inmates will eventually be released and, whether because of their own criminal inclinations, their experiences in prison, or lack of legitimate opportunities and networks, may return to crime.

The growth of prison populations also diverts resources from other social institutions (Butterfield, 1997). For example, in California the number of inmates in state prisons grew from 19,000 to 150,000 in the last two decades. California's highly respected public university system is suffering as a result. During this time, California built twenty-one new prisons but added only one new university. State universities have laid off 10,000 employees, including many professors; state prisons have hired 10,000 new guards. The share of state revenues going to universities has fallen from 12.5 to 8 percent, while the share going to corrections has risen from 4.5 to 9.4 percent. The state now spends about $6,000 per student, compared with $34,000 a year for prison inmates.

The Goals of the Criminal Justice System

Does our criminal justice system work? The answer depends in part on what we want the system to do. There are four main reasons for imposing criminal sanctions: retribution, incapacitation, deterrence, and rehabilitation.

Retribution

The goal of **retribution** is to restore social balance by forcing criminals to pay back society for the crimes they committed. This approach to social control is an ancient one, dating back to the biblical principle of "an eye for an eye, a tooth for a tooth." In modern times, retribution has been refined by the concept of "just deserts," which holds that the punishment should fit the crime. Thus the penalty for murder should be more severe than that for assault, the punishment for grand larceny more severe than that for petty theft, and so on. Advocates of retribution hold that the sanction should be based on the crime, not the criminal, and that like crimes deserve like penalties. The circumstances in which a crime was committed and the character and history of the defendant are irrelevant. Ideally, this approach would make the delivery of justice more even-handed.

Determining the seriousness of a crime and the appropriate response is often subjective, however. With heinous criminals, such as a serial killer who tortured and raped his victims, most people would agree that the person should be "put away." But there is little consensus on other crimes. Suppose a woman who has been frequently battered by her husband gets a gun and kills him. Some people might feel that her husband got his "just deserts"; others, that murder is murder, regardless of the circumstances.

Mandatory-minimum sentences (in which a person found guilty of a particular crime must serve a specified period in jail) are designed to reduce bias and subjectivity on the part of judges and jurors. Where such laws have been in place for some time, research shows that prosecutors sometimes circumvent mandatory sentences by exercising discretion in deciding how a defendant will be charged and that juries and judges may reduce the charge when they feel the defendant is not a threat to other people or the circumstances to some extent justified the crime. For example, in one highly publicized case, a young British woman, hired as an "au pair" or "nanny" by a couple in Massachusetts, was accused of killing the infant under her care. She was found guilty of second-degree murder, which in Massachusetts carries a mandatory-minimum sentence of fifteen years. The judge changed the verdict to manslaughter, which freed him from mandatory sentencing, and released her on the basis of time served in jail awaiting trial. The Federal Judicial Center (1994) found that mandatory-minimum sentences were applied in only half of all potentially eligible cases. Furthermore, 68 percent of African American defendants received minimum sentences or more, compared with 57 percent of Latinos and 54 percent of whites found guilty of the same or similar crimes.

Incapacitation

Often prosecutors decide whether to bring charges or plea-bargain, and juries decide whether or not to convict, not on the basis of what crime the person allegedly committed but on the basis of whether they perceive the defendant to be a threat. **Incapacitation** is designed to protect society by confining criminals to prison or otherwise preventing them

from committing additional crimes. Judging by rising rates of imprisonment, the "lock 'em up and throw away the key" approach is gaining popular support.

Imprisoning all the 4 million or so people convicted of crimes in the United States each year would be unfair as well as impossible. Most Americans agree that first-time offenders who are unlikely to commit a serious crime again should not be treated as harshly as "career criminals." For these reasons, advocates of incapacitation support so-called *three-strike laws,* which target repeat offenders. In California, for example, the courts are required to give a person with a prior conviction for a serious or violent felony twice the usual sentence for a second felony, and a sentence twenty-five years to life if convicted of a third felony. Whether such laws can be applied is questionable. A study by the RAND Corporation estimated that full compliance might reduce serious felonies by 22 to 34 percent but at a cost (in new prisons and longer internment) of $4.5 to $6.5 billion a year (Greenwood et al., 1994). Critics point out that three-strike laws might have unintended consequences. Given the higher stakes, second- and third-time offenders might demand jury trials, increasing the caseload of already overburdened courts; and facing the possibility of life in prison, a third-time offender might attempt to shoot down police rather than surrender (Kaminer, 1994). Furthermore, third-time offenders tend to be older than first-time offenders and thus are "locked away" at an age when they are less likely to commit crimes.

Deterrence

Deterrence refers to using sentences to set an example, convince individuals and society as a whole that the state is determined to control crime, and thus inhibit or prevent potential criminals and future crimes. *Specific deterrence* means using penalties to convince specific individuals not to commit the same crime or crimes again; *general deterrence* means reducing the desire to commit crimes in the general public by penalizing certain offenders. In either case, the rationale for arrest and imprisonment is to prevent future crimes, not to exact vengeance or "payment" for past crimes.

The deterrence model of criminal justice rests on the assumption that human beings are rational creatures who stop to calculate the relative costs and benefits of a certain course before acting. This may be true for "instrumental" crimes like burglary or embezzlement. Indeed, there is some evidence that criminal sanctions are most effective against white-collar crimes, such as income tax evasion and insider trading (Klepper and Nagin, 1989). Potential white-collar criminals have more to lose than "common criminals," not only financially but also in terms of their respectability and standing in the community.

It seems doubtful that rational calculation plays a major role in "emotional" crimes, such as assault or murder committed in an outburst of rage. Many, if not most, violent crimes are impulsive. Moreover, many conventional offenders (or street criminals) may calculate that, given their limited educational and work opportunities, they have little to lose. As control theory suggests, they have a low stake in conformity. Indeed, the risk and excitement may outweigh the possible costs. One offender described his first mugging:

> I was scared, but it was exciting. You see, the whole thing, I was scared and excited. I knew, you know, I had a fifty-fifty chance of either getting away or getting caught. But I figured that was the chance I was going to take. I wanted to get the money. (From Lejeune, 1977, p. 129; cited in Conklin, 1992, p. 439)

In fact, this man's chances of getting caught were much lower than he calculated—about one in eight, not one in two. But he took the risk anyway.

Does strict law enforcement deter crime? In general, research suggests that the *certainty* of punishment has more impact on crime rates than does the severity of punishment (Conklin, 1992). For example, since the fall of Communist governments in eastern Europe and the Soviet Union, crime rates have risen as much as 25 percent (Greenhouse, 1990). Apparently the former police states in those countries were effective in suppressing crime as well as civil liberties (if one does not count government corruption and persecution as crimes). Likewise, most studies have found that the number of police on the streets or in patrol cars, the frequency with which they make arrests, or the appropriateness of their tactics have little effect (Conklin, 1992). However the recent decline in violent juvenile crime, especially in New York City, which adopted a strong policy of deterrence, has raised new questions. See *Sociology and the Media:* Crime Rates Drop in a Sociological "Whodunit."

Rehabilitation

In the 1960s, many prisons were renamed "correctional facilities," and prison guards were given the new job title "correction officer." These labels reflected the view that the goal of imprisonment was not just to punish criminals but also to reform them and provide them with the social and practical skills that would enable them to become self-sufficient, law-abiding citizens upon release from prison. Underlying this **rehabilitation** approach was the belief that in some sense, society promoted criminal activities by allowing high rates of unemployment, deepening poverty, and the deterioration of school systems and neighborhoods, especially in black inner-city ghettos. When crime rates began to rise in the 1970s, however, rehabilitation was declared a failure. Critics asked, Why provide services and benefits to convicted criminals that are not available to law-abiding residents of poor neighborhoods? (Senna and Siegel, 1996). High rates of recidivism (rearrest and perhaps return to prison) indicated that few prisoners were rehabilitated.

A number of sociologists have argued that imprisonment does more to *promote* than to prevent crime. In prison, the individual is exposed to a criminal subculture that provides rationales for illegal activities; the prisoner is also educated into "new" techniques for committing crimes. (Recall Sutherland's theory of differential association.) Furthermore, because of the label "ex-con," a person may have difficulty finding legitimate work after he or she is released (leading to secondary deviance). The evidence for this view is weak, however. Surely, prison can be a brutalizing experience, especially for young, first-time offenders who are likely to be victimized by other prisoners. But high rates of recidivism may be the result not of judges' sending individuals with previous records to prison but, rather, of giving first-time offenders probation—in part because prisons are so overcrowded.

Interestingly, the general public may not be as tough on criminals as are public officials and law enforcement agencies. Surveys find that a majority of respondents still believe that at least some offenders can be rehabilitated. When asked where the government should make a greater effort, however, most choose punishment over rehabilitation (Maguire and Pastore, 1997).

Capital Punishment

The ultimate and perhaps most controversial form of social control is the death penalty. In 1972, the U.S. Supreme Court ruled the death sentence unconstitutional on the grounds that it had been applied selectively and therefore constituted "cruel and unusual punishment" (*Furman v. Georgia*). This decision was based in part on sociological research showing that blacks were far more likely to be given death sentences than whites, especially when the crime was rape and the victim white. In 1976, however, the Supreme Court ruled that laws with clear standards for the death penalty are constitutional (*Gregg v. Georgia*); since then, thirty-eight states have passed laws allowing the death sentence in specific cases, such as murder of a police officer or premeditated murder.

Although increasing, executions still are relatively rare (see Figure 7-10). Most convicted murderers are not sentenced to death, and most who are given death sentences are never executed. Between 1977 and 1995, the FBI recorded about 450,000 cases of homicide and nonnegligent manslaughter. From these, 4,857 persons were sentenced to death. More than one-third were removed from death row by new trials, new sentences, commutations, or natural death; almost two-thirds remain on death row. Since 1977, when a firing squad in Utah ushered in a new era of capital punishment, 313 prisoners have been executed (Snell, 1996).

Whether a criminal receives a death penalty depends in part on where the crime took place. States vary widely in what crimes they consider eligible for capital punishment, who decides to impose a death sentence (the judge or jury), how often district attorneys ask for this decision, procedures for appeal, and even the method of execution (see Figure 7-11). In 1995, a total of fifty-six people were executed in the United States, including nineteen in Texas, six in Missouri, five each in Illinois and Virginia, and one to three in other states. Race also influences decisions to impose the death penalty. Although African Americans make up only about 12 percent of the population, as of December 1995, almost as many African American prisoners (1,275) as white (1,730) were on death row (Snell, 1996). The race of the *victim* also appears to influence sentencing. Roughly half of the murder victims in the United States each year are African American. Yet the great majority (85 percent) of recent executions were for crimes in which the victim was white. Regardless of the race of the defendant, if the victim was white, the odds of a death penalty double (Eckholm, 1995).

One argument for the death penalty is that it acts as a deterrent for potential or future murders (see Stack, 1990). The more publicity an execution receives, the greater its deterrent effect. Critics argue the opposite, that capital punishment has a

Karla Faye Tucker was executed in 1998 for a double murder committed almost a dozen years earlier. Despite Tucker's conversion to born-again Christianity, and pleas on her behalf by many religious and secular leaders, including the Pope, she became the first woman to be executed in Texas since the Civil War.

Crime Rates Drop in a Sociological "Whodunit"

When crime dipped in the early 1990s, crime experts thought it was a statistical anomaly. By 1996, however, the evidence was incontrovertible. Led by murder rates, crime rates were falling. The biggest surprise was that the greatest decrease in serious and violent crime was in the nation's largest cities, especially New York City (see Figure 1). And the most surprised witnesses of this trend were sociologists and other scientists who study crime: "This is getting to be like the sun setting in the west," said Jeffery A. Fagan, director of the Center for Violence Research and Prevention at Columbia University, in a *New York Times* interview (December 20, 1996): "Something has changed on the street, and we don't know exactly what it is" (p. B4). "This is a humbling time for all crime analysts," echoed John J. DiIulio, Jr., a professor of politics and public affairs at Princeton University (*New York Times,* January 19, 1997, p. E1).

Most sociologists had long held that the roots of inner-city crime lay in poverty, joblessness, and demographics, social forces that law enforcement cannot control. Yet crime rates declined most in areas where rates of unemployment, teenage births, welfare dependency, and other measures of socioeconomic decline were increasing—precisely the areas where sociologists

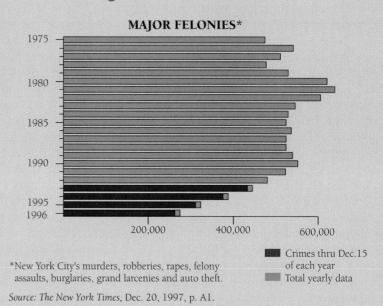

MAJOR FELONIES*

*New York City's murders, robberies, rapes, felony assaults, burglaries, grand larcenies and auto theft.

■ Crimes thru Dec.15 of each year
■ Total yearly data

Source: The New York Times, Dec. 20, 1997, p. A1.

> **Something has changed on the street, and we don't know exactly what it is.**

would have predicted crime would increase. In particular, many sociologists were convinced that tougher law enforcement would not have much effect. As Michael Gottfredson and Travis Hirschi (cited in this text's discussion of control theory) wrote in their 1990 book, *A General Theory of Crime:*

> No evidence exists that augmentation of police forces or equipment, differential patrol strategies or differential surveillance have any effect on crime rates.

Politicians were quick to credit tougher law enforcement for dropping crime rates, however: "I don't think there has ever, in history, been a city with three consecutive years of double-digit drops in crime statistics," claimed New York City Mayor Rudolph Giuliani (*New York Times,* December 20, 1996, p. B4).

In 1994, following the advice of the criminologist George Kelling, New York instituted a new policy of attempting to prevent more serious crimes by cracking down on minor ones like jumping turnstiles in the subway, graffiti vandalism, and panhandling. In many cases, people arrested for misdemeanors were wanted for more serious crimes and, in plea bargains, gave police information on local crime networks. The city closed small grocery stores where drugs were being sold, as well as secondhand jewelry shops and car repair shops that were dealing with stolen goods. Using computer analysis of current statistics, the city identified "hot spots" where crime was on the rise and flooded these neighborhoods with undercover and uniformed police. Said Mayor Giuliani:

All the strategies that have been put in place are working better than anyone, including me, thought they would when we devised them. (*New York Times,* December 20, 1996, p. B4)

Some sociologists were not convinced. Criminologist James Q. Wilson of UCLA pointed out that murder rates had also dropped in Los Angeles, where the police department was plagued by poor leadership and low morale, and arrest rates had fallen (*New York Times,* January 19, 1997, p. E6). Possible explanations included the creation of hospital trauma units that saved the lives of gunshot victims; the ban on assault weapons and the Brady Law, which requires a five-day waiting period to purchase a handgun; longer sentences for "career criminals" (repeat offenders); and a high death rate among urban youth.

Wilson, criminologist John Laub of Northeastern University, and others suggested that fighting crime is like fighting an epidemic, which doesn't follow neat mathematical formulas (*New York Times,* January 19, 1997, pp. E1, E6). With a disease, such as AIDS, apparently isolated, unrelated cases quietly spread contagion; suddenly a "tipping point" is reached and the number of cases explodes. With AIDS in the United States, the tipping point may have been gay baths, where men engaged in sex with strangers. With crime in U.S. cities, the tipping point may have been the appearance of crack. A relatively cheap and highly addictive form of cocaine, crack drew young people into the drug trade with the promise of quick, easy cash. This, in turn, increased the demand for automatic handguns, not only among drug dealers and users but also among teenagers who, in this atmosphere, wanted guns for protection or prestige. Teenagers are less likely than adults to consider the consequences of their actions. Random and drive-by shootings and firing at someone who "dissed" them was almost a fad, as sudden as a fashion or music craze. Most of the increase in murder rates in the 1980s was due to an increase in juvenile violence. By the early 1990s, members of the teenage

crack subculture were becoming young adults. A significant proportion were in prison, and many had been killed. This, combined with other factors (including tougher law enforcement), led to a sudden decrease in murder and other violent crimes. Said William J. Bratton, the former New York Police Commissioner: "I think we are at another one of those tipping points, only on the way down" (*New York Times*, January 19, 1997, p. E1).

Sociologists are also at a "tipping point," in terms of reevaluating existing theories and explaining a trend they not only failed to anticipate but also thought couldn't happen. New Orleans was one of a few cities where violent crime and murder rates increased in the early 1990s. When New Orleans adopted a preventive crime control strategy similar to New York's, it became a "natural experiment" on the impact of law enforcement on crime. "If it works," Princeton crime expert DiIulio told *Newsweek,* "a lot of criminologists would have to jump out the window" (December 23, 1996, p. 29).

The latest report from New Orleans is that crime rates dropped in 1996 and 1997, suggesting that New York's approach might work in other communities.

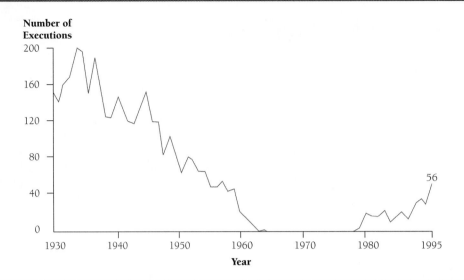

Figure 7-10   *Executions in the United States, 1930–1995*

The United States is the only western democracy that applies capital punishment. Since the U.S. Supreme Court reinstated the death penalty in 1976, 313 prisoners have been executed.

Source: T. L. Snell, *Capital Punishment 1995,* Washington, DC: U.S. Department of Justice, Office of Justice Programs, 1996, p. 2.

"brutalization effect" (King, 1978; Lempert, 1983). In this view, executions by the state may encourage unstable people who feel they have been wronged to take matters into their own hands. In their minds, an execution by the state legitimizes personal retribution. Studies of the murder rate around the time of a publicized execution (for example, Bailey, 1990) find no consistent pattern to support either the deterrence or the brutalization argument. Looking at capital punishment from a different perspective, Amnesty International (1995) points out that there is no evidence of an *increase* in homicide rates when the death penalty is abolished. For example, in Canada the homicide rate fell from a high of 3.09 per 100,000 population in 1975, the year before the death penalty was revoked, to 2.41 in 1980, and has continued to fall. But this is similar to the pattern in the United States, which abolished but then restored the death penalty (in most states).

A main argument against the death penalty is that innocent people may be executed. Between 1900 and 1985, 350 people convicted of capital crimes in the United States were later found innocent. Most escaped the death penalty through appeals or grants of clemency, sometimes just minutes before execution, but twenty-three were killed. Since 1972, when the death penalty in the United States was temporarily suspended, forty-eight men on death row have been found innocent (Amnesty International, 1995).

About half the countries in the world (ninety-seven nations) have either abolished the death penalty for all crimes, limited execution to exceptional circumstances (such as wartime crimes), or not carried out an execution in the past ten years. The other half retain and sometimes apply the death penalty. Amnesty International documented 2,331 executions in 37 countries in 1994, although the actual number was certainly higher. Three countries—China (1,791 executions), Iran (139), and Nigeria (100)—accounted for 87 percent of all known executions. The United States is the only western democracy that still applies the death penalty. It is also one of only five countries known to have executed a prisoner who was under age 18 at the time of the crime, the others being Iran, Pakistan, Saudi Arabia, and Yemen.

Capital punishment apparently enjoys widespread support in the United States. Gallup polls

New Jersey Pop. 7,904,000*	Texas Pop. 18,378,000*
Enacted: Aug. 6, 1982	**Enacted:** June 14, 1973
On death row: 9	**On death row:** 400
Executed since 1976: 0	**Executed since 1976:** 92
Capital offenses: First-degree murder, felony murder	**Capital offenses:** First-degree murder, felony murder
Public defenders office: Established in 1967, the statewide system has offices in all 21 New Jersey counties. Represents all indigent defendants from trial to state appeals to the United States Supreme Court.	**Public defenders office:** Texas does not have a public defender's office. Indigent defendants are represented by counsel appointed by county judges. Guilty convictions in capital cases are automatically appealed to the Court of Criminal Appeals.
Costs: Defense costs in capital cases are paid by the state. There is no cap on money spent in defending capital cases.	**Costs:** For the trial and direct appeal, the county provides the defense and sets a fee schedule. Fees are determined by the judge and defense attorney. There is no set standard for the state as a whole, and many counties have no such schedule. Counties are not required to provide compensated counsel for Federal appeals.
New evidence: There is no time limit for filing a new trial motion based on undiscovered evidence.	**New evidence:** The law provides 30 days after conviction for filing a new trial motion based on undiscovered evidence.

*Population figures are Census Bureau estimates for July 1, 1994.

Figure 7-11   *Two States, Two Death Penalties*

Use of the death penalty varies from one state to another. Even the method of execution (lethal injection, electrocution, hanging, the gas chamber, or a firing squad) depends on where the crime was committed.

Source: The New York Times, Feb. 23, 1995, p. B6.

(Gallup, 1995) find that three-quarters of Americans (77 percent) favor the death penalty—but only in some cases. Most Americans also say that the brutality of the crime, as well as the circumstances and characteristics of the defendant, should be taken into account. The number-one reason given by those who favor the death penalty is not deterrence but retribution—"an eye for an eye," a life for a life.

The execution of Karla Faye Tucker in 1998—the first execution of a woman in Texas since the Civil War and second execution of a woman in the nation since 1976, when the U.S. Supreme Court allowed capital punishment to resume—focused world attention on this issue. Tucker was sentenced to death for the ax murder of two people. At the time of the crime, she was a self-admitted drug addict and sometime prostitute; at the time of her execution (by lethal injection), she was a soft-spoken, gentle-looking, 38-year-old born-again Christian,

married to her prison minister. Her pleas for mercy were denied, in part to uphold retribution and in part to demonstrate that neither remorse nor rehabilitation, sex nor race, counts in the eyes of the law (deterrence). In the United States, Tucker's execution generated controversy, especially among evangelical Christians who have supported the death penalty on biblical grounds but identified with Tucker's religious conversion. In Europe, the verdict was unanimous: the U.S. death penalty is not only barbaric but also hypocritical, given the nation's stand on global human rights (*The New York Times,* February 4, 1998, p. A20).

Why do a majority of Americans deviate from international norms on this issue? One possibility is that support for the death penalty is a reaction to the still high levels of violent crime in our society; another possibility, that *both* murder and execution reflect a violent streak in our culture.

SOCIOLOGY ON THE WEB

Alcohol Use Today

This chapter traces the history of alcohol use in the United States as well as changing attitudes toward alcohol use and abuse to illustrate the social definition of deviance. The web sites listed below will allow you to explore alcohol use today. How much drinking is too much drinking? Where should we draw the line? Use the information you gather on the web to test your own ideas about the impact of alcohol on health, behavior, and public safety. The first two sites contain general information, statistics, and links to many related sites; the last one is a research database that allows you to access sociological research on alcohol use and abuse.

http://www.niaaa.nih.gov/
The web site of the National Institute on Alcohol Abuse and Alcoholism, part of the National Institutes of Health, is a good beginning for on-line research into the topic of alcohol abuse in the United States today. It contains answers to common questions on alcohol use and abuse, information about treatment programs, and many links.

http://alcoweb.com/
This web site has a European focus but contains links to both U.S. and international organizations concerned with alcohol abuse and prevention of alcoholism. Particularly interesting are sections on sites relating to young adults and the elderly.

http://sunspot.health.org/
This site includes IDA, "Information on Drugs and Alcohol," a searchable database of research. For example, by typing in the terms "sociology" and "alcohol," you can access hundreds of abstracts of recent sociological studies on alcohol use, abuse, and prevention. Search for information about current definition of alcohol abuse. By searching articles published over the past five or ten years, can you find evidence that the definition has changed?

Summary

1. **How do societies decide what behavior is deviant and attempt to control deviance?** *Deviance* is a matter of social definition. What is considered deviant varies not only from culture to culture and time to time but also according to the actor, the situation, and the audience. The prevention and correction of deviance depend on both *formal* and *informal* social controls.

2. **What are the consequences of being labeled "deviant"?** The *labeling perspective* emphasizes the social creation of deviance and how labeling may lead from *primary* to *secondary deviance,* including a deviant identity, lifestyle, and subculture. But this progression is not inevitable.

3. **What is the main difference between biological and psychological theories and sociological theories of deviance?** Whereas psychological and biological theories of

deviance focus on the reasons particular individuals might be predisposed to commit particular deviant acts, sociological theories emphasize the social conditions that allow or even encourage deviant behavior.

4. **What are the main sociological theories of deviance?** We discussed five theories of deviance. The first emphasizes a breakdown in social understandings (*anomie*); the second, a weakening of *social controls;* the third, the ways in which social structure produces deviance; the fourth, the cultural transmission of deviant behavior and attitudes; and the fifth, the conflict inherent in a society that provides different groups with unequal rewards.

5. **What are the most common types of crime in our society, and how does our criminal justice system operate?** A *crime* is a violation of the law (and may or may not be considered

deviant by most members of a society). There are five basic types of crime: "common" (violent and property) crime, *white-collar crime, corporate crime, organized crime,* and *crimes without victims.* Although the public tends to focus on "common" crime, white-collar and corporate crime cost the nation much more, in terms of lives as well as dollars. So does the victimless crime, especially when linked to organized crime.

Analysis of the criminal justice system in the United States reveals that formal social controls operate in a selective way that tends to favor the wealthy. Only about 50 percent of the crimes committed are reported to the police, and at each stage of the criminal justice process (arrest, trial, punishment) significantly fewer cases remain. Only a fraction of the people who commit crimes are ever imprisoned. The goals of our criminal justice system (*retribution, incapacitation, deterrence,* and *rehabilitation*) and whether prison sentences—and capital punishment—achieve these goals are the subjects of much debate.

Key Terms

absolute number of crimes   255

absolutist perspective   228

anomie   240

conformists   243

corporate crime   249

crime   246

crime rate   255

crimes without victims   252

deterrence   261

deviance (deviant behavior)   228

deviant career   238

deviant subculture   238

differential association   244

formal social controls   235

incapacitation   261

informal social controls   235

innovators   243

labeling perspective   236

moral entrepreneurs   237

neutralization   238

organized crime   251

primary deviance   237

rebels   243

rehabilitation   262

retreatists   243

retribution   260

ritualists   243

sanctions   235

secondary deviance   237

social control   235

symbolic crusade   244

white-collar crime   247

Recommended Readings

Becker, Howard S. (1963). *The Outsiders.* New York: Free Press.

Clinard, M. B., & Meier, R. F. (1992). *Sociology of Deviant Behavior.* Fort Worth, TX: Harcourt Brace Jovanovich.

Erikson, Kai. T. (1966). *Wayward Puritans: A Study in the Sociology of Deviance.* New York: Wiley.

Ermann, M.D., & Lundman, Richard J. (Eds.). (1996). *Corporate and Governmental Deviance,* 5th ed. New York: Oxford University Press.

Gottfredson, Michael, & Hirschi, Travis. (1990). *A General Theory of Crime.* Stanford, CA: Stanford University Press.

Gusfield, Joseph R. (1986). *Symbolic Crusade: Status Politics and the American Temperance Movement,* 2d ed. Urbana: University of Illinois Press.

Hirschi, Travis. (1969). *Causes of Delinquency.* Berkeley, CA: University of California Press.

Meier, R. F., & Geis, Gilbert. (1997). *Victimless Crimes?* LA: Roxbury Publishing.

Sampson, Robert J., & Laub, John H. (1993). *Crime in the Making: Pathways and Turning Points Through Life.* Cambridge, MA: Harvard University Press.

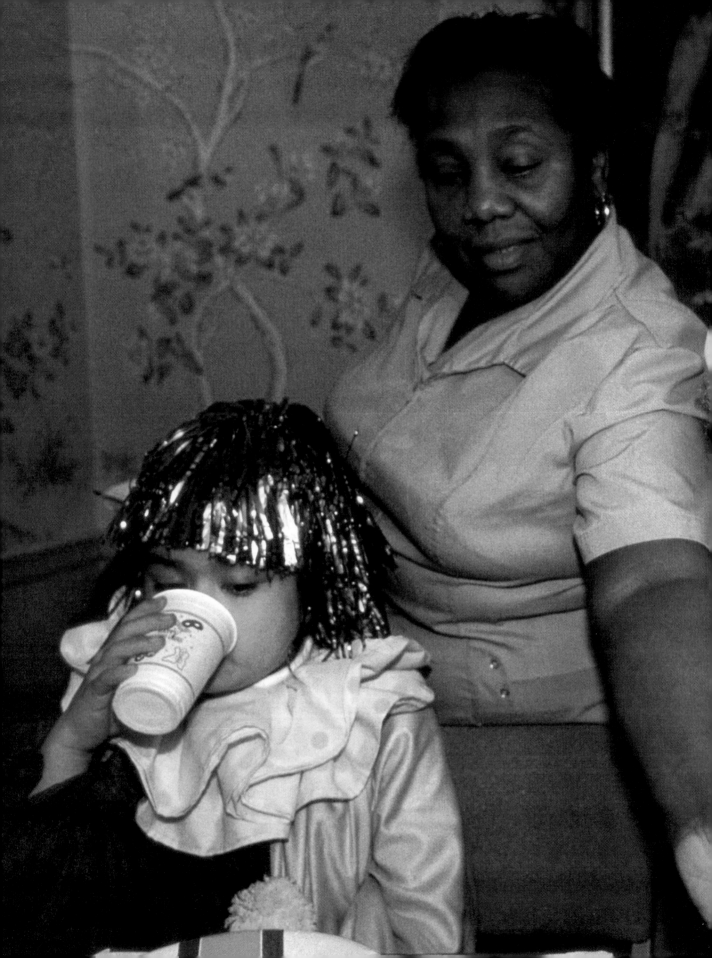

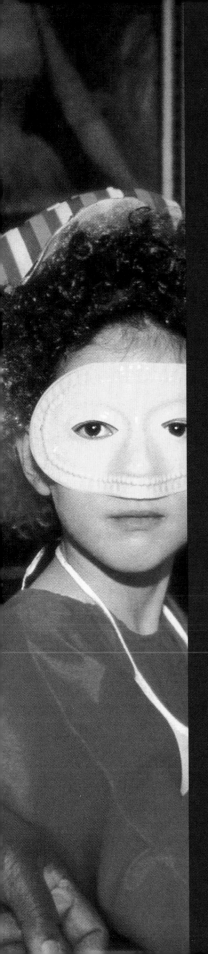

Part

Social Inequality

3

A sociologist can reasonably predict many aspects of a child's future, based on a few simple facts: the child's parents' income and education, their ethnic origin, and the child's sex. To be sure, some youngsters will escape the sociologist's crystal ball, but most will not. The "crystal ball" in this case is an understanding of social inequalities.

Chapter 8 explores the origins and consequences of social stratification: the growing gap between the very rich and the chronically poor, the declining fortunes of middle- and working-class Americans, and the impact of global stratification.

Chapter 9 examines changing patterns of racial and ethnic stratification. The history of intergroup relations in this country (including the civil rights movement) helps explain the current standing of racial and ethnic minorities.

Chapter 10 focuses on gender stratification: actual and alleged differences between the sexes, gender inequality, the century-old women's movement, and the dilemmas caused by society's expectations for men.

Chapter

Eight

Social Stratification

We Americans like to believe that our nation is the land of opportunity, where anyone who works hard can get ahead. But the notion of equal opportunity in the United States is greatly exaggerated. In reality, the deck is often stacked. Consider two children:

Jimmy is a second grader. He pays attention in school, and he enjoys it. School records show that he is reading slightly above grade level and has a slightly better than average IQ. Bobby is a second grader in a school across town. He also pays attention in class and enjoys school, and his test scores are quite similar to Jimmy's. Bobby is a safe bet to enter college (more than four times as likely as Jimmy) and a good bet to complete it—at least twelve times as likely as Jimmy. Bobby will probably have at least four years more schooling than Jimmy. He is twenty-seven times as likely as Jimmy to land a job which by his late forties will pay him an income in the top tenth of all incomes. Jimmy has about one chance in eight of earning a median income.

These odds are the arithmetic of inequality in America. They can be calculated with the help of a few more facts about Bobby and Jimmy. Bobby is the son of a successful lawyer whose annual salary. . . puts him well within the top ten percent of the United States income distribution. . . . Jimmy's father, who did not complete high school, works from time to time as a messenger or a custodial assistant. His earnings . . . put him in the bottom ten percent. Bobby lives with his mother and father and sister. Jimmy lives with his father, mother, three brothers, and two sisters. (de Lone, 1979, pp. 3–4)

This capsule description of inequality was written by Richard deLone in 1979, for a classic study of children entitled Small Futures. *But it still applies today. In fact, the gap between the rich and the poor has widened, and the number of children affected by this gap has increased since 1979. The distribution of social rewards— not only high-income jobs and "all the things money can buy," but also political influence, social esteem, and simple respect—is far from equal. Opportunities are determined as much or even more by race, ethnic origin, gender, and social class as by individual talent and effort.*

This is the first of three chapters on social stratification. In this chapter we look at socio-economic stratification. In Chapter 9 we analyze stratification based on race and ethnicity, and in Chapter 10 stratification based on gender. (We looked at stratification based on age in Chapter 5.)

Key Questions

1. *What is social stratification?*
2. *How do sociologists explain social stratification?*
3. *How have patterns of social stratification in the United States changed over the past 30 years?*
4. *How widespread is poverty in the United States?*
5. *What are the causes and consequences of global stratification?*

What Is Social Stratification?

The term **social stratification** refers to the division of a society into layers (or strata) whose occupants have unequal access to social opportunities and rewards. People in or near the top strata (such as Bobby and his family) enjoy privileges that are not available to other members of society; people in the bottom strata (like Jimmy and his family) face obstacles that other members of society escape. In a stratified society, social inequality is institutionalized; that is, it is part of the social structure and is passed from one generation to the next (see Chapter 5). Certain individuals and groups exercise more influence, command greater respect, and have greater access to goods and services than others do. To some degree, people accept inequality as "the way things are" (Kerbo, 1996).

In this context, **status** refers to a person's position in the system of stratification. A **social class** is a grouping of individuals who occupy similar statuses or positions in the social hierarchy and therefore share similar political and economic interests (Kerbo, 1996). Social class is grounded in economics. But economics have consequences for life chances—for how people live their lives, how healthy they are, and even how long they live (Gerth and Mills, 1946). Most sociologists today agree that social class is multidimensional and that it includes such attributes as educational attainment, occupation, political influence, prestige, and celebrity, as well as economic position.

These various measures of social status usually overlap. People who are wealthy usually went to college and work in prestigious occupations; people who are poor are likely to be high school dropouts who work at menial jobs, if they work at all. But this is not always the case. A poet or a minister may enjoy great prestige but have little personal wealth. Conversely, a drug dealer may be wealthy but has little social prestige. **Status inconsistency** occurs when one marker of social standing is out of sync with the others—for example, a Ph.D. who drives a cab for a living, or a high school dropout who earns millions as a boxer. Further, some markers of social standing operate more or less independently of other factors. Children occupy a lower status than their elders, regardless of whether they are rich or poor. In some situations the fact that a person is a

In the United States, doctors enjoy high status based on a combination of education, occupation, and income.

member of a minority group or a female overrides other indicators of social standing.

Social stratification dates back to the emergence of agrarian states, as described in Chapter 5. Hunter-gatherers and horticulturalists had no concept of private property and few possessions; rather, they "lived off the land," which belonged to everyone. Institutionalized inequality was a consequence of the agrarian revolution, which led to surplus food and other goods, a division of labor, the emergence of cities, centralized government, and the rise of elites who did not have work but had the power to control the distribution of goods (Kerbo, 1996). Thus "in the simplest societies, or those which are technologically most primitive, the goods and services available [are] distributed wholly, or largely on the basis of need, [whereas] with technological advance, an increasing proportion of the goods and services available to a society [are] distributed on the basis of power" (Lenski, 1966, p. 46).

All modern societies are stratified, but the structure of stratification varies.

Open and Closed Social Systems

There are two basic forms of social stratification: closed and open systems. In a *closed system*, a person's position in the social hierarchy is ascribed; people are assigned a more or less permanent social status on the basis of traits over which they have no control (such as blood relationships, skin color, sex, or age). Social position usually is hereditary; individual ability and effort do not count.

The traditional caste system in India is the classic example of a closed system of social stratification. According to ancient Hindu traditions, society is divided into four main castes: the Brahmins (the priests and scholars); the Kshatriya (nobles and warriors); the Vaisya (merchants and traders); and the Sudra (peasants, laborers, and artisans). The Harijans, or "untouchables" (street sweepers, scavengers, leather workers, and swineherders), have no status under this system. They are, literally, out-castes. Considered unclean, they are thought to pollute everything they touch. Even today, despite laws against caste discrimination, in many rural villages they are not permitted to enter Hindu temples, draw water from wells used by higher castes, or walk on certain paths. In the Hindu caste system, individuals are born and die in one caste or another. The only

way to improve one's status is through reincarnation. Birth into a higher caste is believed to be a reward for correct behavior in one's previous life.

Nearly a quarter of a billion people in Hindu-dominated societies, chiefly India and Nepal, call themselves *Dalits,* a Hindi word meaning "the oppressed" (Burns, 1997; Crosette, 1996). Modern India has taken steps to change this system. *Dalits*, or untouchables, as well as tribal people and members of the lowest Hindu castes are protected under India's constitution, which grants them full political rights. Some have benefited from a broad affirmative action program that sets aside "reservations" or quotas in government jobs, schools, and universities. At the local level, untouchables are gaining political power. Weeks before India celebrated fifty years of independence, an untouchable, K. R. Narayanan, was sworn in as India's president, a ceremonial position. But the caste system is deeply entrenched, in part because it is supported by religious institutions. In cities, reinforcement of caste lines may be subtle. For example, advertisements for arranged marriage nearly always specify caste. In rural villages, punishment for alleged violations

India officially abolished the ancient Hindu caste system in 1950, but caste discrimination is still widespread. The untouchables, like this street sweeper in New Delhi, are at the bottom of the social hierarchy. The kinds of work they do are considered so dirty that they are literally "untouchable" by members of upper castes.

of caste taboos can be brutal and humiliating. Indian newspapers often print reports of upper-caste village men raping untouchable women, marching them naked through the village, or shaving their heads to "put them in their place." Most untouchables still sweep floors, wash clothes, and clean latrines for members of higher castes and lead lives of extreme poverty and social degradation. As many as 115 million untouchable and lower-caste children work instead of attending school; more than 15 million are bonded laborers, bought or kidnapped from their parents and virtually enslaved by their employers. The Hindu caste system may be an extreme example of rigid stratification based solely on birth; unfortunately, it is not unique.

In an *open system* of social stratification, status is achieved: a person's position in the social hierarchy is awarded on the basis of individual ability and effort, or merit. Such factors as family of origin, skin color, sex, and age are not supposed to count. In its ideals, the American class system is an open system. Americans believe that all individuals are equal "under God." Our traditions emphasize individualism, hard work, competition, and freedom of choice. Theoretically, people are free to be whatever they want to be. We like to think that our institutions are designed to provide everyone with the same political and legal rights and the same educational and occupational opportunities. Ideally, this system is like a giant marathon race with a few first prizes, more second prizes, and many third prizes. In theory, all individuals start at the same point but where they finish depends on their ability and the effort they put into the race.

Social inequality is attributed to differential ability and/or achievement, particularly in economic pursuits. Thus an open stratification system attempts to reduce the obstacles to advancement by providing equal opportunity to all.

No society is entirely open or entirely closed. In India, members of a low caste may improve their position by taking over a valued new occupation, adopting upper-caste or western customs, or converting to Christianity or another religion that does not recognize castes. Indian civil rights leaders view caste discrimination as a violation of human rights, on a par with the old system of apartheid in South Africa and "ethnic cleansing" in Bosnia (Burns, 1997; Crosette, 1996). In the United States, we say that any child can grow up to be president—but it certainly helps to be white, male, and Protestant. Furthermore, because of the family into which they were born, the wealth they inherit, the schools they attend, the connections they make, and other class-related factors, some white males have far greater opportunities than others do. But social mobility is possible.

Social Mobility

The term ***social mobility*** refers to movement up or down the socioeconomic ladder. Social mobility can be measured by comparing an individual's position with that of his or her parents or by assessing the degree of success or failure experienced in a lifetime. Individuals whose incomes, lifestyles, and working conditions are better than their parents' were or improve over the course of their own lives are said to display *upward mobility*. Examples include a physician whose father was an automobile worker or a high school dropout who heads a multimillion-dollar company. People whose jobs are less well paid or prestigious and who do not live as well or stylishly as they or their parents once did are said to display *downward mobility*. A salesclerk whose mother was a judge or an engineer who works as a building superintendent are examples.

Oprah Winfrey exemplifies the American dream of upward mobility. Born in rural Mississippi, the child of what she later described as a "one day fling under an oak tree" (in Mair, 1996, p. 3) with a soldier on leave, Oprah spent her early childhood on her grandmother Hattie Mae's pig farm, tending chickens and cows barefoot, saving her shoes for school and church. At age 6, she was sent to Milwaukee to join her mother, who was working as a maid and living with her current boyfriend, another "love child," and various drop-in relatives in the heart of Milwaukee's black ghetto. Victimized by classmates who considered her a show-off, often ignored at home, she began "running the streets." At age 14, when she was sent to Nashville to live with her father and his wife, Oprah's life began turning around. An almost model daughter and straight-A student, she was invited to speak at churches as far away as Los Angeles and enrolled in local beauty pageants, which she invariably won on the strength of her outgoing personality. At age 17, Oprah asked

Oprah Winfrey, born to a "dirt poor" single mother in rural Mississippi but now one of the wealthiest women in the world, embodies the American dream of upward mobility.

a local radio station to sponsor her in a walkathon. They not only sponsored her but hired her on the spot as an announcer at $100 a week, at that time a spectacular sum for a high school senior. In her sophomore year at Tennessee State University, Oprah was offered "the job of a lifetime," as a TV anchor on the local CBS affiliate—and never looked back.

Today, Oprah Winfrey is one of the wealthiest women in the world, earning more than $250 million a year as the star and producer of her own talk show, for which she holds syndication rights. She is one of only five African Americans, and also one of only five women, who through their own enterprise (not marriage or inheritance) made the *Forbes* 400 list. Oprah is an all-American success story. Such leaps from rags to riches are rare, however (see Blau and Duncan, 1967). Rather, upward mobility usually involves a small step up: the child of a factory

worker becomes a supervisor; the child of a high school teacher becomes a professor.

Much of the mobility in the United States (and other countries) is the result of structural change, not individual success stories. **Structural mobility** occurs when technological change, urbanization, economic booms or busts, wars, and other events alter the number and kinds of occupations available in a society. As a result, people are "pulled" onto a higher social level or "pushed" onto a lower one. Thus when the United States began to industrialize in the late nineteenth century, the children of farmers (and European peasants) became factory workers; many of their children became office workers; some of their children and grandchildren went to college and became managers; and some of theirs became professionals (doctors, lawyers, and so on). Not everyone prospered, but, except during the Great Depression, the standard of living rose for almost everyone. In some developing countries today, agricultural exports, manufacturing, and education have made small segments of the population upwardly mobile, but many more people have become the poorest of the poor—displaced from their traditional villages and farms by commercial ventures and forced to work as migrant laborers in the countryside or to move to squatter settlements outside cities and survive on the outer edges of a wage economy that has not grown quickly enough to absorb them—a case of downward structural mobility.

Theories of Social Stratification

Social stratification is a persistent social fact in the United States and other modern societies. Why should this be so? Why are social rewards, and even life chances, distributed unevenly? Theories of stratification attempt to answer these questions. The functionalist approach was introduced by Emile Durkheim and other European sociologists but found its chief support among American sociologists. Whereas functionalists see social stratification as a stabilizing force, Karl Marx viewed economic inequality—the division of society into "haves" and "have-nots"— as the major source of conflict and social change. Max Weber was more interested in the subjective and cultural dimensions of social stratification, or prestige.

Functionalists and Meritocracy

Functionalists hold that social stratification is an inevitable and necessary element of modern societies. The classic statement of this view was made by sociologists Kingsley Davis and Wilbert Moore (1945). Davis and Moore reasoned this way: Complex societies depend on individuals occupying a variety of interdependent social positions and performing the roles associated with those positions. If everyone had the ability and skills to fit any role, and if all roles were equally desirable and important, it would not matter who occupied which position.

In fact, however, some roles are far more important and demanding than others. Moreover, everyone is not qualified to fill every role. Some roles require special talents, skills, and extensive training. To ensure that the right people take on important positions and that they are motivated to do their best, societies develop systems of unequal rewards. For example, in our society, physicians are rewarded with high income and prestige for the many years they spend in training and for the important, risky, and sometimes unpleasant work they do. Digging ditches may also be socially necessary and unpleasant, but the job of ditchdigger does not require a high degree of intelligence or a long period of training. For these reasons it is not highly rewarded. Functionalists maintain that this system of distributing unequal rewards ultimately benefits everyone.

Underlying this theory of stratification is the American ideal of a *meritocracy*—a system in which social rewards are distributed on the basis of achievement. What matters is what you yourself do. A meritocracy is based on equality of opportunity, not equality of outcome. Functionalists argue that some degree of inequality is necessary to motivate people to fill socially important roles. Indeed, one of the most common explanations of the economic collapse of Communist Europe and the Soviet Union was lack of motivation. The reasoning: If basic necessities are guaranteed, and individual enterprise is not rewarded, why should people try to be productive? (Of course, these revolutions were also sparked by food shortages, the lack of consumer goods, and the general feeling that communism had produced a lower standard of living.) Much the same arguments are used by critics of the U.S. welfare system (discussed in more detail below).

A more recent functionalist theory holds that stratification promotes social stability and solidarity by answering the question of who gets what and why in a society, at least temporarily (Kerbo, 1996). In this view, without a system of stratification, a society would experience perpetual conflict over scarce resources. To the degree that people accept and agree on the existing distribution of wealth, "little contest need take place concerning the sharing of resources. The contest has already taken place and has been settled—at least for a time" (van der Berghe, 1978, p. 54). Thus in large part Americans accept inequality on the grounds that people who inherit or make their own fortunes deserve to live better than the rest of us. By extension, the poor have only themselves to blame for their hardships.

Taking the functionalist position to its extreme, Herbert Gans (1995) analyzes the ways society benefits from poverty. Because Americans focus on the personal deficiencies of the poor, elected and appointed officials can blame the poor for social problems the government has not been able to solve, such as the drug culture, violent crime, and the deterioration of inner cities. The so-called culture of poverty supposedly undermines "family values"—values that better-off Americans preach but may have difficulty practicing. For example, a social worker will not lose her job because she lives with her boyfriend, but a welfare recipient can be denied benefits if she is living with a man to whom she is not married. Poverty creates jobs—for the administrators, investigators, and clerks who run the welfare system; the police, judges, lawyers, prison guards, and parole officers assigned to "control" the poor; the social scientists and journalists who study and write about the poor; as well as the "salvation industries"—religious and secular charities who hire professional fund-raisers and hold charity balls for the downtrodden, which provide work for caterers, musicians, fashion designers, and others. By working as migrant laborers, the poor reduce the costs of fruits and vegetables for other Americans. By working as domestics, they free middle- and upper-class people to pursue their careers and other interests full-time. Perhaps most significantly, by *not* working they free up jobs for other, "deserving" Americans.

As Gans suggests, social stratification is "functional," but more functional for some segments of the population than for others.

Conflict and Class

Conflict theorists, in contrast, view social stratification as "dysfunctional" in that it benefits a small elite at the expense of the masses. Karl Marx, the founder of this approach, saw institutionalized inequality as the engine driving history.

"The history of all hitherto existing society," wrote Marx and his collaborator, Friedrich Engels, in *The Communist Manifesto* (1848/1960), "is the history of class struggles." Marx believed that the emergence of a division of labor laid the foundation for the division of society into antagonistic classes. For Marx, a social class is a category of people who have a common relationship to the means of production (to the raw materials, technology, and so on). Those who control the means of production (the landed aristocracy in a feudal society, the factory owners and bankers in a capitalist society) exploit those who do not (the serfs or workers). Although the subordinate class provides all or most of the labor, the dominant class reaps all or most of the benefits. In feudal societies, barons exploited serfs by imposing high taxes and tithes (a proportion of the serf's produce); in capitalist societies, business owners pay workers less than the value of what they produce.

Marx argued that the class that controls the economic life of a society is in a position to control other aspects of social life as well. He taught that the law is designed to protect the interests of the dominant class and that religion supports the status quo (for example, by teaching that those who accept hardship in this life will be rewarded in the next), and so on. "The ruling ideas of each age have ever been the ideas of its ruling class" (1884/1975). Marx argued, further, that the class into which a person is born largely determines that individual's modes of thinking and behaving. "It is not the consciousness of men that determines their existence, but on the contrary their social existence determines their consciousness" (1859/1980). He called the failure to recognize exploitation, and the belief that inequality was inevitable, "false consciousness." For Marx, economic relationships and material conditions were all-important.

Marx's theory of social stratification was grounded in his reading of history. He held that each stage in history is defined by a particular *mode of production,* which in turn gives rise to a distinctive form of social stratification. Capitalism, for example, depends not only on industrial technology (a mode of production) but also on private ownership of the means of production; this draws owners and nonowners into specific social class relationships. Although Marx acknowledged periods of stagnation and historical "dead ends," he believed the overall trend was toward higher levels of production and higher standards of living. Feudalism represented an advance over tribalism, and capitalism, an advance over feudalism. In advanced capitalist societies there is greater choice of occupation, more room for personal development, more leisure time.

As a society progresses, according to Marx, its own achievements make it obsolete, provoking revolution. For example, feudal societies laid the foundation for capitalism by producing surplus goods that could be traded or sold and the raw materials for industrialization. But capitalism could not develop under the existing social system. Feudal society was based on inherited social position and land; capitalism required opportunities for personal advancement based on technological innovations and investment of profits. According to Marx, the revolutions in England, France, and America in the sixteenth and seventeenth centuries, which replaced monarchy with democracy, were revolutions on behalf of the rising capitalist class—what he called the "bourgeoisie"—against the constraints imposed by the old aristocracy.

Similarly, Marx predicted that capitalism would eventually reach a point where its own advances could no longer be contained in a system where a relatively small number of people owned and controlled the means of production. Like the bourgeoisie before them, the workers—"the proletariat"—would unite to overthrow the system that held them back. For the first time in history, a class representing the majority of the population would control the means of production. Marx believed that ultimately the workers' socialist state would give rise to a communist society without class distinctions. Communism would mark the end of history based on class struggle, and the beginning of a new history determined by human potential.

Contemporary conflict theorists have compared Marx's predictions with recent history. Most revolutions inspired by Marx occurred in less advanced countries during the transition from feudal, agricultural to industrial, capitalist production—the former Soviet Union, eastern Europe, Cuba, and, on the other side of the world, China. Nor was the outcome as Marx predicted. The ouster of feudal elites and state seizure of the means of production in these countries led to the emergence of new government and party elites, totalitarian political systems, and stratification based on position in the political structure, which in command economies translates into "control over the means of production." Government bureaucrats used their power to acquire goods and services not available to ordinary citizens, from better food at special stores, to chauffeur-driven cars and summer houses, to better educations and job opportunities for their children. The resentment of this new class and its growing wealth and privilege contributed to a second round of revolutions in the late 1980s and early 1990s, beginning with the Solidarity movement in Poland and culminating in the overthrow of the Communist party in the former Soviet Union.

Why have capitalist societies "avoided" revolution? In Marx's theory, revolution depends on increasing polarization—on a clear separation of class interests that provides the basis for organization, mobilization, and eventually revolutionary collective action (see Chapter 17). Marx believed that the common experience of economic exploitation would override other sources of group identity (religion, ethnicity, occupation, even nationality) and that workers would unite in a revolution against capitalism and its ruling elite. However, structural mobility and the growth of the middle- and upper-middle classes have worked against class consciousness by creating divisions among the ranks of nonowners below the level of capitalist elite. Top managers and highly paid professionals who enjoy high status and high incomes tend to identify more with capitalist interests than with the working class. The working class in capitalist societies has also enjoyed a rising standard of living and, where unions and labor parties are strong, both protection from economic downturns and, through politics, some control over working conditions. In the United States, Japan, and other capitalist countries, some "workers" participate in "ownership of the means of production" through the stock market, mutual funds, and pension plans, as well as companies that pay workers bonuses in the form of stock or stock options. Moreover, new technology is changing the composition of the capitalist class: control of the means of *communication,* and hence access to information, is becoming as significant as control of production.

What Marx failed to anticipate was the *globalization* of capitalism. If one looks at the world as a whole, his prediction of a division between owners and workers, haves and have-nots, remains valid. In effect, developed nations have become a global capitalist elite and poor countries, a global working class. Rich nations prosper from their resources and labor, while living and working conditions in poor nations grow worse as traditionally self-sufficient local economies are bulldozed to make way for "development." (See the discusssion of global stratification at the end of this chapter.)

Wealth, Power, and Prestige

Although Max Weber agreed with many of these points, he found Marx's analysis of social stratification oversimplified. Weber did not believe societies inevitably divide into two opposing camps of haves and have-nots, as Marx had argued. Where Marx saw sharply divided classes, Weber saw subtle, continuous gradations, with many intermediate groups. Moreover, he did not believe that politics, religion, and ideas are simply reflections of economic relationships. Although in some cases, economics may determine the shape of religion, in others, religious beliefs shape economic pursuits (Weber, 1904/1958). Whereas Marx was a strict materialist, Weber was more of an idealist, concerned with the meanings people attach to their actions in different social and historical contexts (see Coser, 1977).

Weber held that social stratification depends on the distribution of three resources: wealth (economic resources), power (political resources), and prestige (social resources). Whereas Marx saw wealth as the decisive factor in social stratification, Weber believed that power and prestige were also significant. Each element in Weber's model requires elaboration.

Ordinarily we think of wealth in terms of possessions: money, a house, a car. Both Marx and Weber used the term "wealth" to refer to rights over socially desirable objects as well as to ownership of the objects themselves. For example, oil companies can purchase the right to drill in the ocean (although they cannot buy the ocean itself). Writers can copyright their ideas. A slave in Greece or the American south was "property" in the sense that the slave owner exercised rights over that person. But Marx and Weber differed on a central point. Marx emphasized control of the means of production. He analyzed class position by asking, "What does a person do?" (Is he an owner capitalist or a worker?) Weber emphasized the marketplace. For him the question was "How much does a person get?" (Is she rich or poor?)

Weber defined *power* as the ability of individuals or groups "to realize their own will in a communal action even against the resistance of others who are participating in that action" (1946, p. 180). Marx believed that power is always rooted in economic relations. Weber agreed that this is often the case but argued that power may come from other sources, too. For example, in some cases power automatically accompanies a social role. Thus in our society the president, police officers, professors, and parents exercise power over certain other people by virtue of their social positions. In other cases power depends on the threat or use of physical force. Generals have power; so do street gangs. In still other cases, power derives from personal qualities such as intelligence, charm, and the ability to inspire and organize others—what Weber called "charisma" (see Chapter 14).

Prestige refers to social standing, to the degree of respect or esteem a person receives from others. Marx believed that the way a person earns a living determines his or her status, or position, in the social hierarchy. Weber held that the way a person *spends* his or her earnings is also significant. Cultural notions of proper consumption patterns and proper lifestyle influence social standing. According to Weber, status also depends on how highly a culture values such characteristics as a person's ethnic and family background, religion, occupation, and education. It depends on what people in a society define as beautiful or as courageous, intelligent, or holy. For example, in industrial societies, occupation is a major source of prestige.

Weber held that because stratification is multidimensional, the formation of groups depends on which interests or identities people choose to emphasize. In capitalist societies, for example, ethnic and national identifications have proved more important than economic or class identification. Nationalism and ethnic identity played a major role in the anti-Communist revolutions of 1989–1990 in eastern Europe, which were in large part rebellions against Soviet domination (and within the Soviet Union, Russian domination). Ethnicity continues to fuel rebellion and civil war in that and many other parts of the world (see Chapter 9).

The respect accorded General Colin Powell results from a combination of the power he wielded and the prestige he earned in his tenure as Chairman of the Joint Chiefs of Staff (during which he coordinated and supervised all military activities relating to the national security) and from what Weber called charisma, which is personal ability to inspire and lead.

In Weber's view, Marx's division of society into two opposing classes ignored the complexities of social conflict in modern societies. The relationship between economics and power and prestige is variable. Modern societies are divided into different political parties and status groups as well as different economic classes. Sometimes the wealth, power, and prestige coincide, but other times they do not. Nowhere is this clearer than in the United States, which has never had an official aristocracy.

Social Stratification in the United States

America, as every schoolchild knows, was founded on the principle that "all men [*sic*] are created equal." Yet some Americans have always been "more equal" than others. Americans recognize and in large degree accept distinctions based on social class. (Stratification based on race or ethnicity and on gender is more controversial, as we'll discuss in Chapters 9 and 10.)

The American Class System

Americans rank one another into social classes according to a multitude of different criteria (C. Jencks, 1992). Income is important, but we also take into account the way people make their money (say, from a family trust, a salary, or public assistance), their cultural skills (how they talk, how they dress, how they deal with other people, how much they know), their lifestyle (how they spend their leisure time and their tastes in consumer goods and services), their address or neighborhood, and their moral norms or "values" (especially attitudes toward work, family, and violence).

In studying the American class structure, sociologists look at both objective criteria (such as level of education, amount and source of income, occupation or type of work, and type and place of residence) and subjective criteria (how individuals rank themselves and/or other members of their community). Dennis Gilbert (1998) divides American society into six social classes (see Figure 8-1). Not everyone fits into these molds, of course, yet most Americans recognize these groupings.

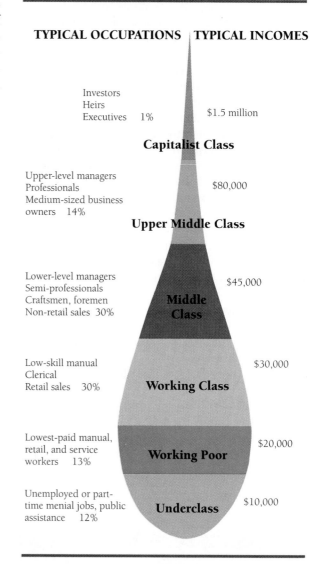

TYPICAL OCCUPATIONS	TYPICAL INCOMES
Investors Heirs Executives 1%	$1.5 million
Capitalist Class	
Upper-level managers Professionals Medium-sized business owners 14%	$80,000
Upper Middle Class	
Lower-level managers Semi-professionals Craftsmen, foremen Non-retail sales 30%	$45,000 **Middle Class**
Low-skill manual Clerical Retail sales 30%	$30,000 **Working Class**
Lowest-paid manual, retail, and service workers 13%	$20,000 **Working Poor**
Unemployed or part-time menial jobs, public assistance 12%	$10,000 **Underclass**

Figure 8-1   *The American Class Structure*

Gilbert's model of the American structure emphasizes *sources* of income. The incomes of the upper (or capitalist) class are derived largely from returns on assets, while the incomes of the bottom or underclass depend in part on government payments. The classes in between rely on earnings from jobs at different occupational levels.

Source: D. Gilbert, *The American Class Structure,* 5th ed., Belmont, CA: Wadsworth, 1998, p. 18, fig. 1-1.

The *upper (capitalist) class* is a small, exclusive "club" of families who have accumulated wealth and privilege over a number of generations. Their wealth is based on inherited assets, which they, in turn, pass on to their children. Although they do not need to work, they often serve on the boards of major corporations (and so make decisions that affect millions of workers and stockholders, not to mention consumers) and are the main source of "soft-money" contributions to political parties (and so have easy access to the politicians whose campaigns they helped to finance; see Chapter 14). They fund private foundations and public policy "think tanks," own newspapers and television stations, and may be appointed to cabinet or other powerful government positions or run for public office (as well as making substantial campaign contributions), and so wield considerable power and influence. Although wealth is a prerequisite for membership in the upper class, it does not guarantee admission (Kerbo, 1996). Membership in this elite also depends on going to the "right" prep schools and colleges and belonging to exclusive, invitation-only clubs, as well as knowing and socializing with the "right" people.

The *upper-middle class* is composed of top-level executives, highly paid professionals, and owners of medium-size businesses who have "made it" by most people's standards. The key to success for this class is education, which has become increasingly valued in today's "information economy." Virtually all have college degrees, and most have postgraduate education as well. High incomes enable them to afford comfortable suburban homes, country clubs, travel, expensive cars, and other symbols of success. They tend to live in exclusive, class-segregated neighborhoods and to send their children to exclusive, class-segregated schools. Career-oriented, they expect their children to do as well as they have. They are often active in local political and cultural affairs.

At the top of this class is a small but growing number of extremely wealthy entrepreneurs who head large corporations or founded corporations of their own; they are what some sociologists call "the corporate class" (Kerbo, 1996). They may exercise as much or more political influence as the upper class (Ross Perot, for example). Their business decisions can affect thousands of working Americans—

indeed millions, if one includes stockholders, mutual funds, and pension plans. (We'll say more about America's very rich in the next section.)

The *middle class* is composed of small-business owners, semiprofessionals (police, clergy, social workers), low-level managers, crafts people, foremen, and nonretail salespeople (such as insurance salespeople, real estate agents, and manufacturers' representatives). Many have a college education. They hold respectable jobs that require social and other skills, but their authority and opportunities for advancement at work are limited. Whereas members of the upper-middle class often *make* decisions, the middle class more often *implement* decisions. Their incomes allow them to lead comfortable, if not extravagant, lives.

The *working class* is made up of traditional blue-collar workers (factory workers, construction workers, and so on) and low-level white-collar workers. This class also includes "pink-collar workers" in traditionally female occupations: clerical workers and retail salespeople. Their jobs tend to be routine, mechanized, and closely supervised. They may or may not have some college education or technical training, and they work hard to maintain a simple but decent lifestyle. Many blue-collar workers, in particular, have been laid off in the transition from an industrial to postindustrial economy and work at lower-paying, lower-benefit jobs. Union membership, and hence the political influence of the working class, has been greatly reduced.

The *working poor* are people who work full-time but do not earn enough to raise their total household income over the poverty level and are barely able to make ends meet. Typically, they work at minimum-wage jobs with few, if any, benefits as unskilled laborers, as service workers, and in bottom-level sales positions (cashiers, stockroom workers, and the like).

The *lower class* (sometimes referred to as the "underclass") is composed of individuals who live in a chronic state of poverty, often magnified by discrimination, physical or mental illness, and other problems. Some have graduated from high school, but many have not. Many are single mothers. Some work at low-wage seasonal or part-time jobs in the mainstream economy or at various legal and illegal jobs in the informal or underground economy (as handymen, unlicensed mechanics, street vendors, and household helpers or as shoplifters, numbers runners, and drug dealers). All experience frequent spells of unemployment. With low, often erratic household incomes, they are rarely able to save or plan ahead and thus live in a state of constant financial insecurity. Given this precarious position, having an extended family and friendship network to rely on during hard times takes on added importance.

The distinction between the middle and working class is somewhat blurred because a number of occupational categories, such as factory operative and clerk, include some people with relatively high educations, solid incomes, and considerable job independence but also other people with far less income, education, and autonomy. The boundary between the working poor and the lower class is also permeable, with a number of people moving back and forth, temporarily or permanently.

The American class system has remained relatively stable over the past fifty years. To be sure, chief executive officers (CEOs) of large corporations have largely replaced small-business owners as the VIPs (very important people) in their communities; some entertainers and professional athletes, once considered marginally respectable, earn top salaries

and enjoy considerable prestige, in part because of the mass media. But today, as in 1950, the majority of Americans consider themselves "middle class"— whether they are would-be actors earning minimal wages as wait staff or entrepreneurs with six-figure incomes. However, the gap between the richest Americans and the rest of the population has widened.

The Changing Distribution of Wealth and Income

In the last two decades, the distribution of wealth and income in the United States changed dramatically. In brief, the rich got richer, the poor got poorer, and the dream of a better life dimmed for the working and middle classes. The gap between the richest Americans and the rest of the population was at a low point from 1965 to the 1970s, and then rose dramatically in the 1980s, reaching the highest point since the Great Depression in the early 1990s (Danziger and Gottschalk, 1995). (See Figure 8-2.)

In measuring economic inequality, social scientists distinguish between wealth and income. **Wealth** refers to the things people own, to such

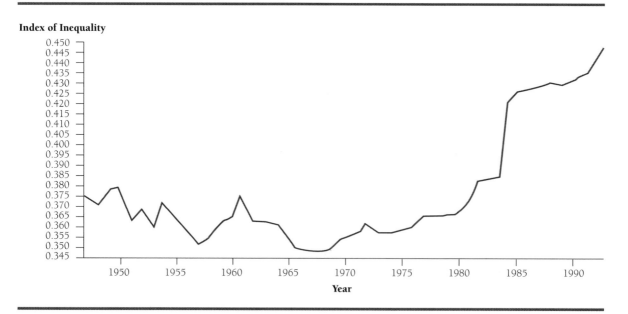

Index of Inequality

Figure 8-2   *Family Income Inequality in the United States, 1947–1992*

Income inequality is calculated by computing how far the richest and the poorest households in a country diverge from the national median. Note the large rise in inequality since 1980.

Source: H. R. Kerbo, *Social Stratification and Inequality,* 3d ed. New York: McGraw-Hill, 1996, p. 24, fig. 2–1.

assets as stocks, bonds, real estate, savings accounts, and life insurance policies, as well as such consumer durables as houses, cars, personal computers (PCs), and stereos. *Income* refers to the money people earn in the form of wages or salaries, interest or dividends from investments, rent on property, and the like. A person may draw a high salary but spend everything he or she earns and so have little wealth. Conversely, an individual may own valuable property (prime real estate or a collection of Picasso's paintings) but earn little or no income from his or her assets.

One way to analyze the distribution of wealth and income is to divide the population into fifths and compare each segment's "share of the pie." As shown in Figure 8-3, the wealthiest fifth of the population earns more than ten times as much as the poorest fifth. Moreover, the income gap between the rich and the poor has widened. Between 1973 and 1994, the average income of the wealthiest fifth of Americans jumped from $83,300 to $105,900 (in constant dollars), while that of the poorest fifth slipped from $8,100 to $7,800 (Weinberg, 1996). But the most significant change in recent decades

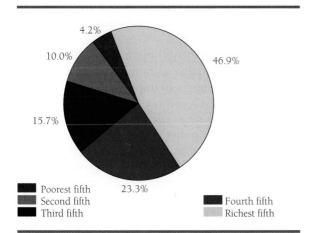

Figure 8-3 *The Distribution of Income in the United States, 1994*

This figure shows how income is distributed among each fifth of the earning population. The richest fifth of the population earns about ten times the income of the poorest fifth.

Source: U.S. Bureau of the Census. *Statistical Abstract of the United States, 1996,* Washington, D.C.: GPO, p. 467, table 719.

has been the declining fortunes of the working and middle classes (Kerbo, 1996). Between 1970 and 1992, the proportion of poor families with annual incomes of $15,000 or less remained about the same (16 to 17 percent). During the same period, the proportion of middle-income families, earning between $15,000 and $49,999, decreased substantially (from 61 to 50 percent). Meanwhile, the proportion of affluent families, with annual incomes of $50,000 or more, rose from 23 to 33 percent, and those with incomes of $100,000 or more rose 4 percent (*Statistical Abstract*, 1993).

Inequality in wealth is even more pronounced than inequality in income in the United States today. Looking at net worth (assets minus debts), Gilbert (1998) identifies three groups:

1. *The nearly propertyless class* (about 45 percent of the population) is worth $30,000 or less. Many have few or no assets, and a number owe more than they own. Ninety percent of these families own cars; most have bank accounts with modest balances; only 36 percent own homes.

2. *The "nest-egg" class* (about 45 percent of the population) is worth $30,000 to $300,000. Gilbert describes these families as "savers not investors" (p. 103). For example, virtually all households in the $50,000 to $100,000 range have safe, interest-earning investments such as savings accounts, certificates of deposit (CDs), and government bonds, worth about $10,000; less than one-quarter have money in corporate or mutual funds, and only 11 percent own small businesses or professional practices. Their primary assets are their homes and their cars.

3. *The investor class* (about 10 percent of the population) is worth $300,000 or more and controls almost two-thirds of the nation's wealth. Most have diversified investment portfolios worth an average of $385,000; many also own small businesses, professional practices, and rental properties. Their homes and cars account for only about 15 percent of their wealth.

As a measure of the concentration of wealth, the net worth of the top 1 percent of wealthy Americans is roughly equivalent to that of the bottom 90 percent.

America's Rich

Who are the wealthiest Americans? How wealthy are they? How did they acquire their wealth? Each year, *Forbes* magazine publishes a list of the 400 wealthiest Americans, based on income, property, and investments. In 1996, *Forbes* identified 400 Americans with assets of $400 million or more, including 137 with personal fortunes in excess of $1 billion. Each of the six men at the top of the list was worth over $5 billion (more than the tax revenues of Oregon or Colorado) (Hacker, 1997). At least half of the wealthiest Americans are self-made multimillionaires or billionaires At the top of this group are Bill Gates, who founded Microsoft; Warren Buffet, investor; John Kluge, who started Metromedia; and Philip Knight, founder and chief executive officer of Nike. A second group run businesses started by earlier generations, including Johnson's wax, Wrigley's chewing gum, and Mars candy bars. Some members of this group translated a modest inheritance into a fortune, such as Rupert Murdoch, who built his father's Australian newspaper chain into a worldwide media empire. A third group consists of individuals and families who inherited substantial fortunes but do little or no work, such as the widow and children of Sam Walton, who founded Wal-Mart, and Beverly Kroc, widow of Ray Kroc, who still earns a penny or two from every hamburger sold by McDonald's. A fourth group, heirs to old family fortunes (the Astors, Vanderbilts, Morgans, Rockefellers, Mellons, and Fords), are notable for their absence, largely because family fortunes have been dispersed among descendants. Only one member of these legendary dynasties—a du Pont—made the list of the twenty wealthiest Americans in 1996. Thus much of the wealth in America today is "new wealth." The *Forbes* 400 list tends to support the functionalist view that our economy is in large part a meritocracy in which fortunes are earned.

This new wealth differs from "old money" in several ways (Hacker, 1997). When *Forbes* published its first list in 1918, eight of the ten wealthiest Americans had made their fortunes through mining and manufacturing (oil, steel, automobiles, and railroads); today's superrich made their fortunes in computers, the media, investments, and consumer goods (sneakers and fast food). Henry Ford's fortune consisted of the cash profits made from selling automobiles; Bill Gates's fortune consists largely of "paper wealth" made by selling stock in a rising stock market. Today's superrich are wealthier than their predecessors were: in 1996, the cutoff figure for the *Forbes* 400 list was $400 million, up from $150 million (in constant dollars) in 1982. In addition, many of today's wealthiest Americans "got rich quick." It took Andrew Carnegie three decades to accumulate $100 million from steel; it took Jeff Bezos only three years to make this much from his idea for an Internet bookstore (amazon.com). Eight of the *Forbes* top twenty in 1996 were just getting started in 1982.

Not only have the rich gotten richer, but more Americans are wealthy. The number of households reporting annual incomes of $1 million or more has climbed from 13,505 in 1980 to 68,064 in 1995 (Hacker, 1997). Nine out of ten millionaires reported some earnings from wages and salaries, but most of their incomes (67 percent) came from investments. However, the great majority of Americans live from one paycheck to the next, and the average American family earns no more today than it did twenty-five years ago (in constant dollars).

The Shrinking Middle

Lauren Caulder enjoyed a stable, happy childhood in a middle-class suburban community (Newman, 1993). Her father, a quiet man of working-class origins, worked all his life as an advertising copywriter. Despite a modest salary, he and his wife, a full-time housewife and mother, were able to provide their children with a comfortable New England–style home, a solid education at a good public high school, music lessons, lazy summers around the club pool, and occasional travel to vacation spots.

Lauren Caulder played by the rules. She studied hard in school, graduated from a good college, and worked her way up to an important job in the public sector. At age 40, she is better educated than her father was, earns more than he ever did, and has a professional identity her mother never dreamed of. Yet she feels that even her parents' lifestyle is beyond her grasp. Caulder and her husband are able to pay their bills, but only because both work full-time. They could never afford the house her father bought in the 1950s for $15,000 and sold for $400,000 in 1990. Instead, they rent. They see children as a luxury they may never be able to afford. And they cannot anticipate the leisurely retirement Caulder's father (now a widower) will enjoy. Lauren Caulder feels cheated:

> Even if you are a hard worker, did everything they told you you were supposed to do . . . you don't get where you were supposed to wind up. . . . *They lied to me.* (Newman, 1993, p. 3)

If Oprah Winfrey and Bill Gates of Microsoft represent the American dream, Lauren Caulder is closer to the reality for many Americans today. Raised to expect upward social mobility, they are struggling just to maintain the lifestyle they enjoyed as children. (See Figure 8-4.)

Modest homes like this one built for the working and middle class are now out of the reach of many two-earner middle-class families.

Nearly all Americans are descended from immigrants who saw this nation as the land of opportunity. In large part they were right. Despite occasional setbacks (most notably, the Great Depression of the 1930s), for generations the majority of Americans have been upwardly mobile. The two decades following World War II were a period of exceptional growth and prosperity for this country (Hacker, 1997; Kerbo, 1996). Americans at all socioeconomic levels saw their incomes and standard of living rise—an example of structural mobility, as noted earlier. Because the United States entered the war relatively late and the war was fought overseas, this country did not suffer the destruction of its factories, transportation systems, cities, and farms, as European nations and Japan did. Whereas it took our allies (and enemies) nearly two decades to rebuild, the United States was in high industrial gear when the war ended. Military service and wartime civilian employment had given Americans new skills and high self-confidence. Growing industries could afford generous settlements with unions, which raised blue-collar wages and benefits to new highs. Advances in technology increased the demand for professionals, managers, and office workers. In the 1950s, median family income (in 1995 dollars) rose 37 percent, the largest increase ever recorded in this country or any other. In the 1960s, family income rose another 16 percent (Hacker, 1997).

Figure 8-4 *Upward Mobility at the Top; Stagnation in the Middle*

For most of the twentieth century, Americans could expect that they would be better off than their parents were (due to structural upward mobility). In recent decades, however, only a small proportion of Americans have been upwardly mobile, as middle- and working-class incomes stagnated.

Note: Income data are shown in constant 1994 dollars.

Source: U.S. Bureau of the Census, *Statistical Abstract of the United States,* 1996, Washington D.C.: GPO, p. 461, table 710 (median income); p. 467, table 719 (top 5 percent).

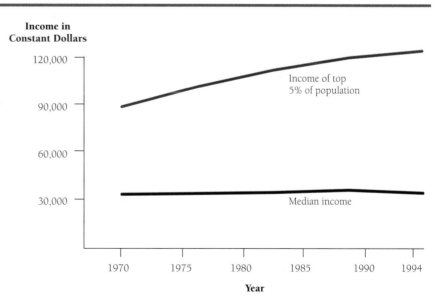

Income in Constant Dollars

Income of top 5% of population

Median income

Year

The middle class expanded steadily. Many families were able to exchange renting for home ownership; move from the city to the expanding suburbs; buy a first or second car, a washing machine, a dishwasher, and a color television; and send their children to college. Lauren Caulder's parents were beneficiaries of this boom. Because of rising income tax revenues, government support for poor families also increased. Americans enjoyed the highest standard of living the world had ever seen. And they came to expect that their standard of living would continue to improve over their working lives and that they would be better off at retirement than their parents had been. As a measure of this optimism, parents at all social levels were having three or four children, confident that the economy would provide the same upward mobility for their children as it had for them.

During the past twenty-five or thirty years, however, opportunities to "get ahead" have dwindled. The 1970s, 1980s, and 1990s brought economic stagnation. The country did not fall into a deep, prolonged depression, but the rate of economic growth slowed. Between 1973 and 1994 median family income (in constant dollars) rose a mere 2 percent (O'Hare, 1996). Men's median earnings fell 16 percent during this period (Danziger and Gottschalk, 1995). This means that the main reason family income even remained stable was that women entered the workforce in unprecedented numbers. Most households depend on two (or more) earners today, and many people work longer hours or at two jobs to maintain their standard of living (Newman, 1993). More blue- and white-collar workers face periods of unemployment. And many young adults find they cannot afford to live as well as they did as children. Between 1970 and 1994, the median family income (in constant dollars) of a family in which the wife was not in the labor force dropped from $33,386 to $31,176 (*Statistical Abstract,* 1996). Clearly, in order to get ahead, families need two workers, but this increases family expenses because of day care and work-related expenses (clothes, transportation, and the like). The average family has been treading water for two decades.

A number of other signs show that the American dream of upward mobility is withering (Newman, 1993). The proportions of young working adults who still live with their parents, delay getting married, and postpone having children have all increased. Fewer and fewer young people are able to buy a home. The average age of first-time home buyers rose from 28 in 1976 to 32 in 1995 (*Statistical Abstract,* 1996). Owning the roof over one's head is one of the entrance requirements for full membership in the middle class. For most people, buying a home is the largest purchase they will ever make; in time, that investment will become the nest egg on which they retire. But like Lauren Caulder, more and more Americans who started in the middle class and "played by the rules" are unable to make that first step.

For most people, the American dream of upward mobility has not come true. Recent Gallup polls found that 52 percent of Americans believe they are worse off than their parents were; 52 percent believe the future will be worse than the present; and 57 percent agree that no matter how much the economy improves, good economic times will not last as long as they used to (Golay and Rollyson, 1996). Even so, a majority (52 percent) say they are satisfied with their financial status. (Marx would see acceptance of growing inequality as "false consciousness.")

America in a Changing Global Economy

From the end of World War II in 1945 to about 1975, the United States enjoyed "shared prosperity" (Gilbert, 1998). The economy was booming, the gap between the rich and the poor narrowed, and the middle and working classes saw their incomes and lifestyles improve steadily. Beginning in 1975, however, Americans' fortunes took a "great U-turn" (Harrison and Bluestone, 1988). The gap between the rich and poor increased, and the working and middle classes found themselves working harder to stay in the same place and, not infrequently, losing ground. What happened? No one knows exactly, but the short answer is that the economy changed (Danziger and Gottschalk, 1995; Gilbert, 1998).

The shift from shared prosperity to growing inequality coincided with changes in the structure of the economy. By 1970, deindustrialization—the shift from an economy based on manufacturing to one based on information and service—was well under way. Two forces fostered deindustrialization. The first was *globalization.* In the 1950s and 1960s, American corporations hired American workers, paid dividends to American stockholders, and sold their products both at home and abroad. In the 1970s and 1980s, corporations began to close factories in the United States and transfer manufacturing to Third World countries, where wages were much lower and they did not have to negotiate with unions or to comply with U.S. safety and environmental regulations. Not only were millions of blue-collar workers laid off (especially in the steel and auto industries), but young, less-educated workers were deprived of the job ladders that enabled previous generations to work their way out of poverty into steady, relatively high-paying, union-protected jobs and a comfortable working-class lifestyle.

The second force behind deindustrialization was *technology* (especially computers and robotics). With new technologies, one skilled worker at a control panel can produce as much as, say, twenty semiskilled workers on an assembly line. Complex technology increases the demand for engineers, scientists, technicians, and people who manage technology, while reducing the demand for crafts people, operatives, and laborers. The combination of globalization and technology increased the flow of capital and goods around the world. This favored investors, accountants, aeronautical engineers, and systems analysts, but it undercut factory workers in western nations.

In short, the new "postindustrial" economy created a small number of well-paid, skilled jobs for highly educated workers (in communications, research and development, finance, law, advertising,

In the developed world, well-paying factory jobs like this one in France are threatened by deindustrialization and the globalization of the workforce.

and the like) and a much larger number of low-paying jobs with no health or pension benefits and few, if any, opportunities for advancement for young less-educated and older laid-off workers (as salespeople and cashiers, waiters and waitresses, fast-food workers, janitors and porters, nurse's aides and hospital orderlies, messengers and deliverers).

Faced with an increasingly competitive global market, corporations sought additional ways to cut costs. Moving production abroad was the first step; "downsizing" and "outsourcing" were the second. Corporations save money by laying off full-time middle- and low-level managers, designers and editors, and clerical and other office workers and hiring consultants, independent contractors, freelancers, and part-time workers, who do not receive benefits (including Social Security), require office space, or use office equipment and supplies. The "temp" industry (agencies that supply companies with part-time workers) employs almost as many workers today as the auto and steel industries combined. Corporations are earning more with fewer workers (see Figure 8-5). Between 1993 and 1995 alone, 10.1 million American workers were laid off.

Finally, the programs and policies that helped reduce inequality before 1975 have been weakened. Today, far fewer workers are protected by labor unions and collective bargaining. The minimum wage was created after the Great Depression to ensure that workers received what President Franklin Roosevelt called "a fair day's pay for a fair day's work." Although the minimum wage was increased in the 1980s and 1990s, inflation reduced its value or purchasing power. Programs to provide a social safety net for the poor have been cut. At the same time, government policy provided tax breaks for the wealthy (for example, lowering the tax rate on capital gains, the profits from buying and selling real estate or stocks). Supporters of this policy argued that "a rising tide lifts all boats": tax breaks for the wealthy would free up capital, increase spending, stimulate the economy, and thus benefit everyone. Barriers to international trade were lowered, again to stimulate the economy.

As a result of these changes, the U.S. economy is in better shape, but most American workers are not. Globalization, new technology, and market forces have improved the fortunes of some individuals who are well educated, well financed, or simply lucky but created structural *immobility* (stagnant or declining wages, reduced job security, and lower benefits) for

Corporate Fields

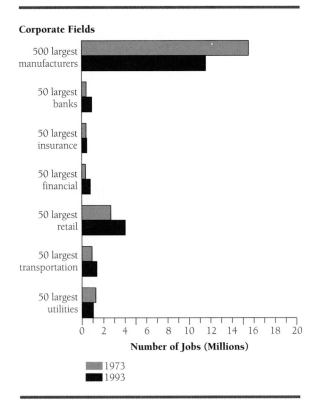

Figure 8-5   *Corporate Wealth / Corporate Workers*

In the 1990s corporations became "leaner and meaner," in part by exporting and automating jobs and also by laying off well-paid, full-time employees and relying more on part-time workers.

Source: A. Hacker, *Money: Who Has How Much and Why,* New York: Scribner, 1997, p.47.

the average worker. The United States today ranks highest among the advanced nations on the "index of inequality"—in part because the rich are richer than their counterparts in other countries, in part because the poor are poorer. (See Table 8-1.) Many observers worry that the widening gap between the rich and poor will create a two-tier system of stratification and a divided society, with a small number of well-off people at the top and much a larger number of people who struggle to make ends meet at the bottom.

Poverty in America

As a result of the changes we have described, the poor are poorer than they were twenty years ago. Between 1974 and 1994 the "poverty gap"—the amount of money the average poor family would need to rise above the poverty level—increased by 16 percent for families, to $6,097, and by 25 percent for unrelated individuals, to $3,574. Not only has the number of Americans living in poverty swelled in recent decades, but poverty has become more common. Nearly one-quarter of the U.S. population experiences poverty or near-poverty at some point in their lives (O'Hare, 1996). And for some, poverty has become a chronic condition, more and more difficult to escape.

During the prosperous 1960s, the percentage of Americans living in poverty dropped by half, hitting an all-time low of 11 percent in 1973. The number of poor Americans increased sharply during the recession of the early 1980s, remained high during the rest of that decade, and rose again in the early 1990s (Figure 8-6). In 1995, 36.4 million Americans—13.8 percent of the population—were officially counted as poor. About 40 percent of the poor—more than 15 million people—were extremely poor, getting by on incomes of less than half the poverty threshold. Another 25 million Americans lived close to the poverty line, just one or two paychecks away from being poor (O'Hare, 1996).

Table 8-1   *Inequality in Fourteen Countries: Rich/Poor Ratio*

Country	Best-Off Tenth	Poorest Tenth	Inequality Index
Finland	153%	59%	2.6
Sweden	152	56	2.7
Belgium	163	59	2.8
Netherlands	175	62	2.9
Norway	162	55	2.9
Switzerland	185	54	3.4
New Zealand	187	54	3.5
France	193	55	3.5
United Kingdom	194	51	3.8
Australia	187	47	4.0
Canada	184	46	4.0
Italy	198	49	4.1
Ireland	209	50	4.2
United States	206	35	5.9

Percentages show the proportion of each nation's median income received by the midpoint household within its poorest 10% and also for its best-off 10%. The *index of inequality* is the ratio of the two percentages for each country.

Source: A. Hacker, *Money: Who Has How Much and Why,* New York: Scribner, 1997.

The official ***poverty line*** is based on the federal government's estimate of a minimal budget for families of different sizes (in 1995, $15,569 for a family of four) (U.S. Bureau of the Census, 1996a). The poverty line is used to count the number of people who are poor and also to determine who is eligible for various government programs.

The poverty line has been the subject of much debate (O'Hare, 1996). Some critics argue that it is too high because it fails to take into account such "in-kind" (noncash) aid as food stamps and Medicare. If this aid were treated as income, they maintain, the poverty count might drop by 4 million or more. In addition, the poverty line is based on income only and does not take into account such assets as a home or farm. Others argue that the poverty line is too low. The formula for measuring poverty is based on the cost of basic necessities and does not allow for taxes, alimony, child support, work-related expenses, or out-of-pocket health care, which cut into the money available for food, clothing, and shelter. Neither does the poverty line consider variations in the cost of living from state to state, city to small town. Commissioned by Congress, the National Research Council (NCR) (1995) recommended that the poverty line be calculated on the basis of food, clothing, shelter, and "a little bit more"; that government subsidies and benefits be counted as income, and money spent on taxes, child care or child support, work-related expenses, and health expenses be deducted; and that the poverty line be adjusted for geographic differences in the cost of living. If these standards were adopted, the poverty rate would rise by 3 to 4 percent.

Who Are the Poor?

Many Americans think of the poor as a stable, uniform segment of the population, distinct from the "not poor." Stereotypes feature the so-called welfare queen, an unmarried mother who relies on welfare, odd jobs, or crime, and the male wastrel, a homeless alcoholic or predatory criminal who could work but doesn't. In fact the poor population is quite diverse, including inner-city ghetto residents, Native Americans living on reservations, rural families in Appalachia and the Deep South, displaced workers in the midwest, teenage mothers, and elderly widows (O'Hare, 1996). The poor population is also in flux. The groups at greatest risk of becom-

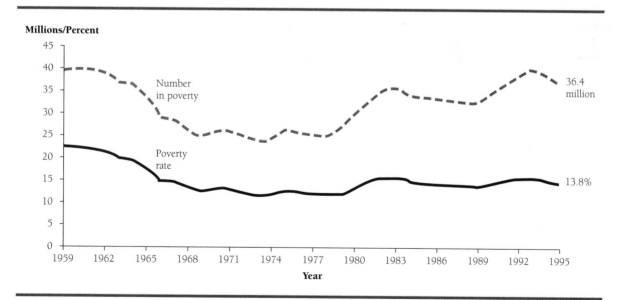

Figure 8-6   *Changes in the Number and Percentage of Americans in Poverty, 1959–1994*

The 1980s and 1990s produced a new, more desperate, and longer-lasting poverty, symbolized for many people by the presence of the homeless. But the greatest change has been in the number of working poor, whose jobs do not pay a living wage.

Source: U.S. Bureau of the Census, *Current Population Reports*, Series P60–189, Washington, DC: GPO, 1996, table B–5.

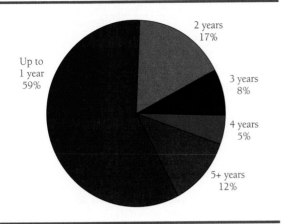

Figure 8-7   *Time Spent in Poverty, 1968–1987*

For most of America's needy, poverty is not "a way of life" but a temporary setback.

Figures do not add to 100 because of rounding.

Source: Gottschalk, McLanahan, and Sandefur, in *Confronting Poverty: Prescriptions for Change,* eds. Danziger, Sandefur, and Weinburg: 89, figure 4.1.

ing poor haven't changed much (except for the elderly and children, discussed below), but the specific *individuals* living in poverty constantly change. Longitudinal studies, which track the same families and individuals over a number of years, indicate that for most Americans, poverty is only a temporary condition (see Danziger and Gottschalk, 1995). (See Figure 8-7.) The same people are not poor year in, year out; rather, they fall into or out of poverty because of personal fortune, economic cycles (and structural unemployment), and/or their stage in the life cycle. Two out of three people who experience spells of poverty recover within a year; about 12 percent remain poor for five or more years.

Other misconceptions or, at best, "half-truths" about the poor include the following (O'Hare, 1996):

1. *The great majority of America's poor are African American or Latino.* The most numerous racial and ethnic group living in poverty is non-Latino whites, who make up 48 percent of the poor (Figure 8-8). However, the *risk of poverty* is much higher for minorities. African Americans and Latinos are nearly three times as likely as white Americans to be poor.
2. *Most people are poor because they do not want to work.* Half of the poor are either too old (age 65 and older) or too young (under age 18) to work; about 25 percent are disabled and cannot work. Almost

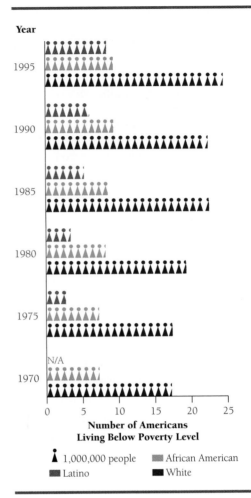

Figure 8-8   *Poverty and Race*

Although the risk of poverty is higher for minorities, almost twice as many whites as African Americans, and three times as many whites as Latinos, are poor.

Source: U.S. Bureau of the Census, *Current Population Reports,* Series P60–194, *Poverty in the United States: 1995,* Washington DC: GPO, 1996.

half of poor adults age 22 to 64 work at least some months out of the year or part-time.

3. *The majority of the poor live in inner-city neighborhoods.* Less than half (42 percent) of the poor live in urban areas, and less than one-quarter in high-poverty inner-city ghettos. The majority (58 percent) live in suburbs, small towns, or rural areas.
4. *Most of the poor are single mothers and their children.* The majority of the poor (63 percent) are either married or living alone or with nonrelatives. But female heads of households stand a much greater risk of being poor. Never-married, deserted, or

divorced mothers (and their children) are three times more likely to be poor than are two-parent families. Since 1960, the proportion of the poor living in female-headed households doubled, reaching 37 percent in 1995. Many single mothers do not receive child support from their children's father; many work only part-time at low-paying jobs; many who work full-time spend a large proportion of their incomes on child care (see Chapters 10 and 11). The risk of poverty is greatly increased for single mothers who are African American or Latina.

5. *Poor mothers live off government welfare.* Only 40 percent of the poor collect cash welfare benefits; roughly half of the income of poor adults comes from wages, and 22 percent from Social Security. Only about one-third of the poor population received benefits from Aid to Families with Dependent Children (AFDC), the main public assistance program

in 1995 (O'Hare, 1996). Half of the women who received AFDC support were off the welfare rolls within two years; only about 2 percent became chronically dependent (Bane and Ellwood, 1994).

6. *Welfare programs for the poor strain the federal budget.* In 1996, federal programs for the poor cost $217 billion, about 14 percent of federal expenditures. A much larger share (43 percent) went to Social Security and Medicare, which primarily benefit middle-class Americans, than to welfare

7. *Antipoverty programs are designed to reduce poverty.* Most welfare programs are designed to sustain the poor, not to lift them out of poverty. Only about 10 percent of the welfare budget goes to education and job training, which lowered the poverty rate by only one-half of 1 percent in 1994.

For an overview, see Figure 8-9.

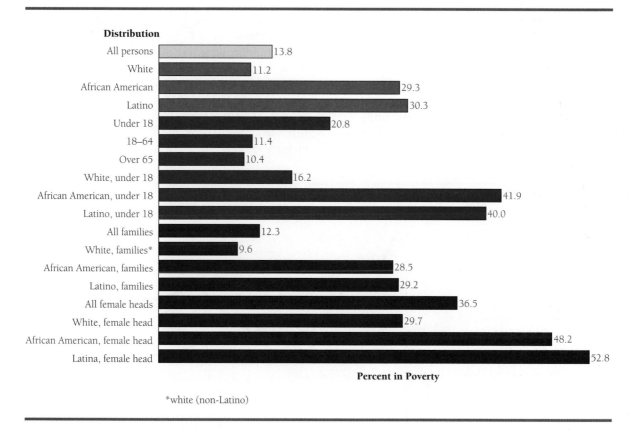

*white (non-Latino)

Figure 8-9   *Poverty in the United States: An Overview*

Poverty is not "distributed equally" in our society. Perhaps the saddest aspect of today's poverty is the high proportion of needy children and adolescents. Nearly half of America's children cannot count on having a home, enough to eat, and adequate clothing.

Source: U.S. Bureau of the Census, *Current Population Reports*, Series P60–185, *Poverty in the United States: 1995*, Washington DC: GPO, 1996.

Poverty and Age

One of the major changes in the poor population in recent decades is age. While the proportion of elderly Americans living in poverty has dropped, the proportion of poor children has climbed (Figure 8-10). In 1960, 35 percent of Americans age 65 and older lived below the poverty line, the highest poverty rate of any age group in the population. Although the number of older Americans has increased, their poverty rate has dropped to 12 percent, about the same as that for working-age Americans. Most of this decline is due to higher Social Security benefits (adjusted to the cost of living), Medicare, and Supplemental Security Income (SSI). Today's elderly also were beneficiaries of post-World War II economic growth and are more likely to have accumulated wealth (especially through home ownership and private pension plans) than their parents were.

In contrast, the poverty rate for children has nearly doubled since 1960. In 1995, 21 percent of Americans age 18 and younger—more than 15 million young people, including nearly 6 million under age 6—were poor. Young people are more likely to be poor than are members of any other age group. One in five American children under age 18—and two out of five African American and Latino children—are growing up in families whose incomes fall below the poverty level (U.S. Bureau of the Census, 1996a). Children account for about 50 percent of the increased poverty rate since the 1970s. Compared with other developed countries, the United States does far less to help poor children (Table 8-2).

The Working Poor

A second trend is growth in the ranks of the working poor: people who work but do not earn enough to keep themselves and their families out of poverty (O'Hare, 1996). In 1995, 13 percent of the adult poor (2.3 million people) worked full-time, year-round and still did not earn enough to rise above the poverty line. The decline in wages hit young men—the traditional breadwinners for families with dependent children—hardest. The proportion of men in poverty-wage jobs rose from 13 to 23 percent during this period, while the share of women in such jobs, always much higher, declined slightly (from 39 to 37 percent). One reason is that the minimum wage (as of September 1997, $5.15 an hour, or $10,300 a year) has not kept pace with inflation. In the 1960s, someone who worked full-time, year-round at a minimum-wage job earned enough to keep a family of three above the poverty line. In 1996, the same worker earned barely enough to keep himself or herself above the poverty

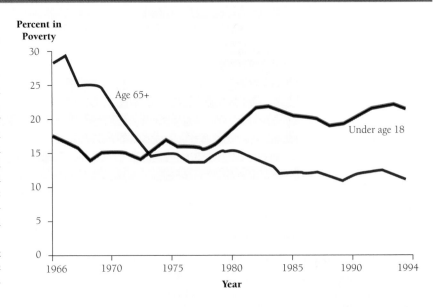

Figure 8-10   *Divergent Rates of Poverty for Children and the Elderly, 1966–1994*

Thanks to higher Social Security benefits, Medicare, pension plans, and home ownership, the poverty rate among older Americans has dropped, but the poverty rate for American children has risen. The United States is the only western democracy that does not have a national program to help parents to support their children during hard times.

Source: W. P. O'Hare, "A New Look at Poverty in America," *Population Bulletin* 51(2), September 1996, p. 16, fig. 4.

One of the major changes in the composition of the poor population in the United States in recent decades is in age structure. The poverty rate for children has increased, while that for the elderly has decreased.

Table 8-2   *Government Assistance to Poor Children in Seventeen Developed Countries*

Country*	Year	Percent of Children in Poverty		Percent of Children Lifted Out of Poverty by Gov't Programs
		Before Assistance	After Assistance	
United States	1991	25.9	21.5	17
Australia	1989	19.6	14.0	29
Canada	1991	22.5	13.5	40
Ireland	1987	30.2	12.0	60
Israel	1986	23.9	11.1	54
United Kingdom	1986	29.6	9.9	67
Italy	1991	11.5	9.6	17
Germany	1989	9.0	6.8	24
France	1984	25.4	6.5	74
Netherlands	1991	13.7	6.2	55
Norway	1991	12.9	4.6	64
Luxembourg	1985	11.7	4.1	65
Belgium	1992	16.2	3.8	77
Denmark	1992	16.0	3.3	79
Switzerland	1982	5.1	3.3	35
Sweden	1992	19.1	2.7	86
Finland	1991	11.5	2.5	78

*Ranked by postassistance poverty rate.

Sources: Lee Rainwater and Timothy M. Smeeding, "Doing Poorly: The Real Income of American Children in a Comparative Perspective," Working Paper No. 127, Luxembourg Income Study, Maxwell School of Citizenship and Public Affairs (Syracuse, NY: Syracuse University, 1995); W. P. O'Hare, "A New Look at Poverty in America," *Population Bulletin* 51(2), September 1996.

line,[1] but $2,064 below the poverty line for a family of two, and $7,563 below for a family of four (U.S. Bureau of the Census, 1996a). In short, a job no longer guarantees that a worker and his or her family will not be poor (Bane and Ellwood, 1994).

Because the number of well-paying, blue-collar jobs has decreased, more young adults work for minimum wages in service sector jobs. In addition, to cut costs, many employers have eliminated full-time jobs and fill in with part-time, temporary, or seasonal workers. Furthermore, an unknown number of poor adults work for less than the minimum wage, whether in illegal "sweatshops," at odd jobs (such as housecleaning or gardening), or doing piecework in their homes. Poverty for this large group cannot be explained by their failure to work or to seek jobs when they are out of work. Rather, their subemployment is built into the economic system.

Public Policy

In the booming 1960s economy, most Americans supported government efforts to help the poor. President Lyndon B. Johnson's "war on poverty" enjoyed widespread support. The public is less sympathetic today and more likely to see the poor—especially "welfare mothers"—as undeserving (Gans, 1995). Indeed, some analysts (e.g., Murray, 1984; Rector and Lauber, 1995) blame government programs for the persistence of poverty. They reason this way: Aid to Families with Dependent Children, until 1996 the major cash assistance program for the poor, was designed to help single, low-income women with dependent children. The more children a woman had, the higher the benefits she received. In most cases, poor married couples were not eligible for welfare, and women found to be living with a man could be denied benefits. These critics argued that AFDC discouraged couples from getting married (because they would lose benefits), led young women to bear children out of wedlock to become eligible for welfare (and independent of their parents), and perhaps caused women already on welfare to have another child to increase their welfare checks.

There is some evidence to support this view. For example, single mothers who switch from welfare to work often find that, when they deduct the cost of child care and work-related expenses such as transportation, their incomes decline, and so they go back to welfare (Edin and Lein, 1997). However, the bulk of the evidence indicates that welfare and other social programs have little impact on family structure (O'Hare, 1996). States with generous AFDC benefits did not have a higher percentage of female-headed families than did those with low benefits. For example, in 1994 the proportion of families with single parents was 26 percent in California (which offered the highest welfare benefits) compared with 34 percent in Louisiana (which offered far lower benefits). If welfare promoted single parenthood, one would expect both indicators to rise or fall together. In fact, the opposite was true. In real value, the average monthly welfare check declined from $657 in the 1970s to $378 in 1994 (in 1994 dollars); during this same period, female-headed households expanded from 13 to 24 percent of all families. Nevertheless, welfare was cast as the "villain" in public perceptions of poverty.

In the summer of 1996, Congress enacted broad changes in federal assistance to the poor. Under the Temporary Assistance to Needy Families (TANF) program, the federal AFDC or welfare program was replaced with block grants to states, with a number of new regulations. Among other features, the new program:

- Imposes a five-year lifetime limit on federal cash assistance for at least 80 percent of the state's recipients.
- Ends cash assistance to able-bodied adults after two years unless they get a job
- Limits receipt of food stamps by unemployed individuals to three months in any three-year period
- Allows states to deny welfare to unwed teenage mothers unless they attend school and live with an adult
- Rewards states that reduce births to unwed mothers by giving the states additional cash grants
- Increases funds for child care
- Allows individuals no longer eligible for welfare to continue receiving Medicaid (for one year if they are employed)

The goal of welfare reform is to reduce welfare rolls in both the short and the long terms. In the

---

[1]This also meant he or she did not qualify for Medicaid or other government benefits.

short term, the aim is to move people away from welfare and toward work. In the long term, the aim is to reduce incentives to have children out of wedlock. Each state can establish its own rules and limits for benefits. In the robust economy of 1997 and 1998, many states reported reductions in their welfare rolls. What will happen if the economy turns down or when time limits for benefits run out, no one really knows.

The Ghetto Poor

Although they are only a small proportion of America's poor, low-income, minority residents of inner-city poverty tracts are the focus of public perceptions and social policies toward the poor. As William J. Wilson (1987, 1996) has emphasized, to understand the ghetto poor one has to understand the changing structure of the ghetto itself.

In the 1950s, Woodlawn, on Chicago's South Side, was a thriving African American community of 80,000 with its own doctors and lawyers, schools and churches, theaters and clubs, markets and retail stores (A. Duncan, 1987; Wacquant and Wilson, 1989; Wilson, 1996). Because of segregation, which prevented better-off blacks from moving into better ("white only") neighborhoods, the black ghettos of this period enjoyed a high degree of social class integration. Some blocks and apartment buildings were considered "middle class" and others viewed as "lower class," but everyone shopped at the same stores, went to the same churches, and sent their children to the same schools. In 1950, Woodlawn boasted more than 800 commercial and industrial establishments. Residents remember a time when the streets were so packed at rush hour that you had to elbow your way to the train station.

Today Woodlawn looks like a bombed-out war zone (Wacquant, 1991). The main commercial strip has become an unlit tunnel of abandoned buildings and vacant lots littered with broken glass and garbage. A barber shop, thrift store, and small caterer huddle behind iron gates. There is only one supermarket, but dozens of lottery agents, currency exchanges,[2] and liquor stores. Since 1960,

---

[2]Establishments that, for a fee, cash checks, issue money orders, and the like—the "bank of the poor."

half the housing units have disappeared; what remains is deteriorating. The middle- and working-class exodus of the 1960s and 1970s reduced the population by almost two-thirds, leaving many streets deserted.

In the 1950s, a majority of adults (69 percent) in Woodlawn and other black Chicago neighborhoods had jobs; in 1990, when Wilson and his colleagues collected data, two out of three were unemployed. Half had not completed high school. Six in ten were on welfare. Median income had dropped to one-third the city average; half of South Side families made do with household incomes of less than $7,500. During the mid-1980s, a period of economic recovery for most of the nation, residents of South Side reported that their situation had stayed the same or had deteriorated. Three-quarters did not have even one of the following assets: a personal checking or savings account, a retirement account or pension plan, or a prepaid burial plan. Owning a home and a car—staples of the American dream—were well beyond reach. A stable family life was also elusive. In Chicago's inner-city neighborhoods, almost 60 percent of African American adults age 18 to 44—including 56 percent of parents—had never been married (Wilson, 1996). Only 15.6 percent of parents in these neighborhoods were currently married. As many as six out of ten babies were born to unmarried women, and two-thirds of households were headed by single mothers (W. J. Wilson, 1987).

Ghetto youth were especially disadvantaged. The unemployment rate for young African Americans, age 16 to 19, reached a staggering 48.3 percent. Of the original class of 1984 enrolled in inner-city Chicago schools, only two-thirds were still in school in ninth grade. Of these 25,500 ninth-graders, only 16,000 graduated from high school and only 2,000 read at or above the national average. In the late 1980s, there were more young African American males in prison than on college campuses (Duster, 1988). Perhaps two-fifths of these ghetto African American youths will never find a decent job or stable marriage partner, and their children may share the same fate (Adams, Duncan, and Rodgers, 1988).

The South Side story is not unique. In city after city, the numbers of impoverished African Americans (and other minorities) concentrated in deteriorating neighborhoods have increased.

Explaining Ghetto Poverty

As sociologist Herbert Gans (1995) points out, the term "underclass" has become a code word for the "undeserving" poor. This underclass was defined not just by acute or chronic poverty but also by deviant behavior and values; not by lack of money, but by lack of morals. The underclass was portrayed as the antithesis of the middle class. Lacking a work ethic, stable family values, respect for law and order, and even self-respect, the underclass stood for everything the middle class opposed (e.g., Auletta, 1982).

One of the first to oppose this negative characterization was University of Chicago sociologist William Julius Wilson (Wilson, 1987, 1991b, 1996; see also Gans, 1995). Wilson argued that ghetto poverty is due to a combination of structural and social changes, not to a "culture of poverty" with its own values and norms (see Chapter 1).

According to Wilson, a major reason for the increase in ghetto poverty is the **deindustrialization** of the nation's big cities (especially in the northeast and midwest). In recent decades, these cities have been transformed from industrial to information-processing centers (Kasarda, 1989). Factories were moved from the inner city to the suburbs, the sun belt, and foreign countries where labor is cheap, and warehouses were relocated in rural areas and the suburbs. For example, in the 1950s and 1960s, the economy of North Lawndale on Chicago's South Side was grounded in the Hawthorne plant of Western Electric (which employed more than 43,000 workers), an International Harvester factory (14,000 workers), and the headquarters of Sears, Roebuck and Company (10,000 jobs) (Wilson, 1996). In the 1970s, all three closed. In a domino effect, the departure of large companies triggers the closure or relocation of other, smaller businesses that relied on their employees' wages. The employees of these businesses lost their jobs. When a neighborhood appears in decline, banks are reluctant to grant loans to start new businesses or to renovate or rebuild housing, and so deterioration continues. Bypassing the city, new office buildings and stores—and hence most new jobs—are opened in the suburbs.

Even when the national economy was growing, ghetto residents were stranded. One study found that, in the 1980s, the United States lost 16 blue-collar jobs per 1,000 of the working-age population, and gained 27 clerical, sales, and service jobs (McKinsey & Company, 1994). But most good jobs in the urban information sector—accounting, advertising, brokerage, and law—require advanced education. Low-level service jobs—such as messenger, hamburger flipper, gas station attendant, dry cleaner assistant—do not pay enough to keep one person out of poverty. Between 1970 and 1989, the real value of wages for the bottom fifth of workers dropped 30 percent (Wilson, 1996). Other new jobs—in warehouses, construction, offices, and stores—are geographically out of reach. In the past two decades, 60 percent of new jobs created in the Chicago metropolitan area were in the suburbs. Most ghetto residents do not own (and cannot afford) cars. The wages for low-skilled workers do not offset the cost of commuting from the inner city to the suburbs on public transportation (say, $7 to $9 a day for a two-hour trip each way). In the 1990s, the sons of factory assemblers and operators worked as janitors and waiters, if and when they found work.

A second reason for the increase in ghetto poverty and joblessness is *social isolation*. Poor whites, who are less likely to live in areas of concentrated poverty, often find jobs through their better-off relatives, friends, and neighbors; their children have opportunities to observe and learn from these working adults. When *most* people in the neighborhood are unemployed, informal job networks disintegrate. Ghetto children are deprived of role models of successful working adults and stable families and lack opportunities to learn how to apply for a job, what to wear and what to say, how to deal with an annoying boss or coworkers, and the like. Children in single-parent homes are doubly isolated. As a result, the gap between ghetto residents and the mainstream widens.

Social isolation also occurs *within* urban ghettos (Wilson, 1996). When stable, working families leave the area, formal institutions (such as churches and political organizations), voluntary associations (such as block clubs, parent-teacher associations, men's lodges, and women's groups), and informal networks (neighborhood friends and acquaintances, coworkers, marital and family ties) that make a geographic area a "community" may weaken or disappear. Stores close, people move away, and the number of vacant lots and abandoned buildings increases, so it's more difficult for people to develop a sense of community or feel they can find safety in numbers. The informal social organization of a neighborhood depends on networks of adults who, first, interact on the basis of personal relationships and mutual obligations and expectations and, second, take some responsibility for the quality of neighborhood life—most importantly supervising young people.

High levels of joblessness undermine informal social organization. Neighbors come and go, adults are unable to provide for themselves and their families on a regular basis, children are subject to fewer rules, and distrust is more widespread. The appearance of crack, in the mid-1980s, accelerated this trend. Heroin was readily available in urban ghettos, but heroin is expensive. Crack, a form of cocaine that produces an instant though short-lived "high," cost as little as $3 to $5 for a single hit. The heroin market was structured, in the sense that established dealers, who tended to be middle-aged, recognized one another's territories and operated according to shared standards of how to conduct their (illegal) business. Crack suppliers bypassed this "establishment," recruiting young suppliers with few, if any, reciprocal obligations. As opportunities for legitimate, stable employment declined, the incentive to earn quick money by selling drugs increased. Given weak informal social controls, young crack dealers became more powerful, and the "crack culture" exercised more influence on behavior and norms, even of people not directly involved. Crack suppliers provided their dealers with guns and encouraged them to fight for turf among one another. On the one hand, this frightened adults with no connection to drugs into remaining silent; on the other, it encouraged young people to see owning a weapon "as necessary or desirable for self-protection, settling disputes, and gaining respect from peers and other[s]" (Wilson, 1996, p. 21). During the crack epidemic, the homicide rate among black inner-city males tripled. Crack and drug-related violence began to subside in the mid-1990s, but ghetto poverty persists.

In Wilson's view, what sets the ghetto poor apart is the *combination* of joblessness and social isolation (W. J. Wilson, 1991, 1996). Wilson does not dismiss the role that racial discrimination and cultural differences play in ghetto poverty. Numerous studies have found that employers are reluctant to hire inner-city African Americans, especially black males, whom they perceive as uneducated, unstable, uncooperative, and dishonest (T. Bailey, 1989; Neckerman and Kirschenman, 1990). To survive in the ghetto, young people may learn attitudes and behavior patterns that are alien or frightening to employers. But well-educated African Americans have made significant progress in recent years. This suggests that the social disorganization of the ghetto is the result of structural changes in the urban economy, not of African American cultural patterns or individual deviance.

Sociologist Christopher Jencks (1992) questions Wilson's explanation of ghetto poverty. Indeed, Jencks questions the very existence of a special category of ghetto poor (or "underclass"). Analyzing data on the problems associated with membership in this class one by one, rather than lumping them all together, Jencks found that some had gotten worse over the past twenty-five years (especially joblessness and the proportion of babies born out of wedlock), that some seem to have leveled off (welfare dependency and violent crime), and that some have lessened (school dropout rates and functional illiteracy).

Jencks argues that in assuming these problems are interlinked, we perpetuate class (and racial) stereotypes. Just as few individuals meet all the criteria for membership in the middle class, so few meet all the negative criteria for the ghetto poor. Further, in lumping problems together, we imply that reducing ghetto poverty will require fundamental social change. Because few policy makers are willing to recommend, much less fund, massive change, little or nothing is done. The belief that the problems of the inner-city poor are pervasive and self-perpetuating becomes an excuse for inaction.

The Homeless

They lie in doorways and sleep on park benches. They beg for money outside banking machines. They talk to themselves or to the sky. They line up at soup kitchens. The homeless seem to have become a permanent part of the American landscape, especially in big cities. No one knows exactly how

Residents of most American cities have become accustomed to the sight of people living on the street in numbers not seen since the Great Depression of the 1930s.

many Americans are homeless. Estimates range from 250,000 to 3 million or more. The truth may lie between these extremes: on any given night, about half a million Americans have no place to stay, while a million more may be at risk for homelessness (Jencks, 1994; Rossi, 1994).

Who are the homeless? Twenty years ago the typical street person was a white, alcoholic male, age 50 or older, who lived on Skid Row and survived off charity and odd jobs (Barak, 1992). Today's homeless are more varied and more visible (see Table 8-3). The largest group of the homeless are single males age 21 to 64; almost 40 percent never married, and virtually none of the rest are currently living with their spouses. The proportion of homeless women is smaller but growing (see *Close Up*: "Tell Them Who I Am": An Intimate Portrait of Homeless Women). Since the 1980s, the number of homeless families, especially young unmarried mothers and their children, has also grown (Rossi, 1994). The average length of homelessness is almost four years for single males, less than three years for single women, and sixteen months for women with children. The ethnic composition of the homeless population varies from place to place. In general African Americans are overrepresented compared with their presence in the local area, while Latinos tend to be underrepresented. Taken together, minority representation in local populations ranges from 20 to 88 percent (Baker, 1994).

A number of factors contributed to the increase in homelessness in recent decades (Jencks, 1994; P. H. Rossi and Wright, 1989). First, changes in the structure of the economy (as described above) reduced the demand for low-skilled workers. The proportion of working-age men who reported no paid job for a full calendar year grew from 5 to 10 percent in the 1980s; the proportion who go through periods of unemployment in a given year is even higher (Jencks, 1994). Second, virtually all assistance programs for the poor have been cut back. These cutbacks had both direct and indirect effects. It is all but impossible for a single person with a poverty-level income to afford even the cheapest housing today, and the declining value of welfare benefits made it more difficult for families to shelter an adult relative who had fallen on hard times.

Third, subsidies for the disabled were cut back, reducing both the number of people eligible for disability support and the amount of support. Changes in policy regarding the mentally ill also played a major role in homelessness. In the 1960s, the government set out to reduce the number of patients confined to mental hospitals. This policy, known as *deinstitutionalization*, was based on good intentions. State mental institutions had offered little more than custodial care for the mentally ill. New drugs promised that many of these patients could function satisfactorily outside the hospital, and community centers were to be set up to ease the transition, helping them cope with the problems of everyday life on their own. Between 1960 and 1980, the rate of hospitalization for mental illness dropped by about 75 percent. But plans and funding for a network of community clinics and halfway houses did

Table 8-3   *A Profile of Homeless Adults*

Characteristic	Large Cities, 1987*	All Local Surveys, 1981–1988[†]
Demographic:		
Male	84%	74%
African American	45	44
Latino	10	12
Over 65	3	na
Mental Health:		
Spent time in mental hospital	22	24
Attempted suicide	24	na
Diagnosed as currently mentally ill	na	33
Substance abuse:		
Currently addicted to alcohol	na	27
Spent time in residential treatment program	na	29
Social ties:		
Never married	53	na
Not currently with a spouse	97[‡]	na
No friends	na	36
No contact with relatives	na	31
Spent time in jail or prison	41	41
Current health "fair" or "poor" (self-report)	44	38

*Weighted mean of estimates for service users and nonusers in cities of 100,000 or more; from Martha Burt and Barbara Cohen, *America's Homeless: Numbers, Characteristics, and the Programs That Service Them,* Washington, DC: Urban Institute Press, 1989, pp. 69–71.

[†]Unweighted mean of fourteen to forty local surveys, depending on the measure; from Anne Shlay and Peter Rossi, "Social Science Research and Contemporary Studies of Homelessness," *Annual Review of Sociology* 18, 1992, pp. 129–160. Many of Shlay and Rossi's samples are restricted to shelter residents, who are more likely to be women and tend to be in better mental and physical health than those not in shelters.

[‡]Adults using shelters or soup kitchens.

Source: C Jencks, *The Homeless,* Cambridge, MA: Harvard University Press. 1994, p. 22, table 4.

not materialize. After release, many patients were on their own.

Fourth, the supply of low-income housing decreased. Cutbacks in federal spending for low-income housing, reductions in tax incentives for private investment in housing, the deterioration of housing projects built in the 1950s and 1960s, and "gentrification" of urban neighborhoods (destroying and replacing or renovating old, low-cost housing for higher-income residents) all combined to decrease the amount of housing available to the poor during a period when the number of poor was growing. The greatest decline has been in low-cost housing for single people (Jencks, 1994).

A fifth factor was the arrival of crack in the mid-1980s (Jencks, 1994). Alcoholism has been a significant cause of homelessness for generations, but drug addiction was rare, if only because hard drugs were expensive. On the basis of drug tests of shelter users, as well as arrestees, Christopher Jencks estimates that perhaps half of single homeless adults in

big cities, and one-third of the homeless nationwide, used crack at least occasionally (1994, pp. 42–43). Whether crack use was a cause or a consequence of homelessness is impossible to say. Undoubtedly heavy drug use makes marginally employed adults even less employable, makes relatives and friends less willing to take a person in, and uses up money that might be put toward rent. At the same time, however, crack is readily available in big-city shelters and other places where the homeless congregate, and it may have become part of social routines, much as sharing a bottle has always been.

Among the factors that push the homeless over the edge and distinguish them from other chronically poor Americans are long-term unemployment (more than four years); a combination of poor physical health, drug or alcohol abuse, psychological problems, and/or a criminal record; and social isolation (P. H. Rossi, 1988; P. H. Rossi and Wright, 1989). But here we have a chicken-and-egg dilemma: Which came first? Are these

"Tell Them Who I Am": An Intimate Portrait of Homeless Women

People used to call them "bag ladies": unkempt, ill-dressed women who carried their possessions in a motley assortment of shopping bags, rarely confronted strangers, and often muttered to themselves as they went about their rounds. Although not as threatening as homeless men, homeless women were somehow more disturbing. Their apparent wish to keep to themselves made their situation all the more tragic.

Elliot Liebow (1993) broke through this silence in several years of participant observation at a shelter for homeless women in Washington, D.C. The women he got to know were a varied group: Betty, a 50-year-old white woman who used to be a heavy drinker but has been sober for more than four years and is sometimes mistaken for the director, not a client, of the

shelter; Ginger, a pretty, white 24-year-old, who has been designated as "retarded" but is seen as competent and kind by other women in the shelter; Lisa, a 300-pound African American who exudes confidence and cheer and is seen as somewhat intimidating by the other women and the staff. Although not a representative sample of

> **I'm not homeless, I'm familyless.**

homeless females, these women gave Liebow insights into what life is like for the poorest of the poor.

Among the biggest problems these women faced in their daily lives were getting a good night's sleep (almost impossible in the barracks-like conditions, where snoring, shouting, and the like, were common); killing time

during the day (when they were neither permitted to remain in the shelter nor admitted to many public places); finding safe places to store their possessions (however few); maintaining their health (when even simple cures, like a day's rest in bed, were difficult or impossible to carry out); and dealing with harassment (such as a restaurant insisting they pay before they ate or a security guard barring them from a public bathroom).

Most of the women wanted to work and actively sought work. But with no home phone or address, problems keeping themselves clean and their clothes neat, and stereotypes about the homeless being lazy and violent, finding a job was difficult. Even those who did work could not earn enough to support themselves, by themselves.

problems a cause of homelessness or a result of homelessness?

The Impact of Poverty

Social stratification can be a matter of life and death (Table 8-4). The impact of poverty on life chances begins even before birth. Poor women are more likely than other women to suffer from protein, vitamin, and mineral deficiencies, untreated infections, and emotional stress during pregnancy. They are less likely to seek prenatal care. They are often younger when they have their first baby, and older when they have their last child, than are other mothers. As a result, their babies are more likely to

be born prematurely, to have low birth weights, and even to die during infancy.

Thanks to Medicaid, poor children today visit a doctor nearly as often as middle-class children do. Even so, they have many more health problems growing up, ranging from dental cavities and poor eyesight to tuberculosis and dysentery (diseases often associated with Third World populations) (Physician Task Force on Hunger, 1985).

As adults, America's poor are more likely than other Americans to suffer from chronic and infectious diseases, to feel sick, and to worry about their health. They lose more days of work because of illness and injury. They are also more likely to suffer from occupational diseases, such as black-lung dis-

"I'm not homeless," one woman told Liebow, "I'm fami-lyless" (p. 81). Liebow described the women he met as the left-over bits and pieces of broken families. Some had been abandoned or beaten by their husbands; some could not get along with their parents or stepparents; some had lost touch with both their parents and their grown children. Usually, the last place they had lived was with a family member, but the situation had not worked out well. Typically, these women came from lower-class or working-class families who did not have the resources to help them through hard times.

Liebow described their lives on the streets and in the shelters as "brutish." Although violence was not a frequent problem (as it sometimes is for homeless men), they lived in an atmosphere of mistrust. The homeless women both feared, and were feared by, the social workers and shelter staff who were supposed to help them. The women resented the loss of privacy, the imposition of shelter rules, and the "hurry-up-and-wait" atmosphere of social service agencies. To keep going, they turned to one another (old friends invariably spurned them), to God (nearly all were deeply religious), and into themselves (sometimes withdrawing).

Some of the women Liebow came to know had abused alcohol or drugs, had been in prison, or had been institutionalized for mental illness. But Liebow found that these problems were episodic, rather than chronic. Thus a woman might seem incoherent at some times but rational and intelligent at others. As one said to him,

> You talk to us as if we were normal people who can hold a normal conversation. That's naive. No one can live this way and be normal, no matter how they were when they first came. (p. 210)

Liebow did not believe that personal problems caused their homelessness. Homelessness, he argued, is a social, not an individual, problem. What happened to these women is the result of the declining standard of living for the working and lower classes; their tragedy is the tragedy of a society that does not provide jobs with living wages for all its members. Quite simply, and sadly, they are too poor to afford a place to live.

ease among coal miners. Yet they are much less likely to see physicians, dentists, or other medical professionals. It is not simply that they cannot afford medical care, although this is a problem, especially for the "working poor" who do not qualify for Medicaid. Mild illnesses have a low priority in poor households. A slight fever is tolerated in the face of more pressing problems, such as putting food on the table. Moreover, to receive medical treatment, poor people may have to travel long distances to a clinic and wait there for hours. Treatment is impersonal, and rarely is the same doctor seen twice. Many seek medical attention only as a last resort. When they do receive treatment, it may not be the same quality treatment as wealthier Americans receive.

Broad social and economic trends also affect different classes in different ways. In times of inflation or recession, the poor suffer more from rising prices and are more likely to lose their jobs (Caplovitz, 1979). Because they have no "disposable income" (money left over when necessities are paid for), the poor are hit hardest by rises in the cost of living. Suppose, for example, that the cost of food for a family of four is $5,800 a year. This represents 33 percent of the budget of a family with an income of $17,500 a year (about half the median income and $5,000 above the poverty line). Food would amount to only 19 percent of the budget of a family with an income of $30,000 a year. If food prices rise by 25 percent, the additional cost ($1,450)

Table 8-4   *Life Chances by Social Class*[a]

	Lower Class	Middle Class	Upper-Middle and Upper Class
In excellent health[b]	28%	37%	53%
Victims of violent crime per 1,000 population	50	29	21
Psychological impairment index[c]	217	62	21
Feel lonely frequently or sometimes	46%	35%	27%
Obesity in native-born women	52%	43%	27%
Children, 18–24, in college	15%	38%	54%
Dissatisfied with personal life	22%	15%	5%
Favor liberal economic policies[d]	48%	38%	28%

[a]Classes defined by income.

[b]Self-assessment, U.S. Public Health Service.

[c]Moderate to serious symptoms.

[d]In a 1984 survey, favored increased federal spending on at least three of five social programs (food stamps, Social Security, Medicare, public schools, job creation).

Source: D. Gilbert, *The American Class Structure,* 5th ed., Belmont, CA: Wadsworth, 1998.

represents a much larger share of the poorer family's income (8 percent) than of the moderate family's income (5 percent). The same principle applies to housing, utilities, and other necessities. Efforts to cut the federal budget also have a greater impact on the poor than on those who are well-to-do (Waxman, 1983, chap. 7). This was particularly true of the budget cuts made in the early 1980s, which hit social welfare programs particularly hard (W. J. Wilson and Aponte, 1985).

The poor are more likely to be arrested and sent to prison for committing crimes and also more likely to be the victims of crime (Chapter 7). They are more likely to be divorced or separated than are affluent Americans (Chapter 11). Schools in low-income neighborhoods are more likely to emphasize discipline and vocational training, whereas schools in affluent neighborhoods encourage academic performance and college preparatory programs (Chapter 12). The poor are less likely to vote or to participate in political and other organized social activities (Chapter 14). In short, few areas of a person's life are not affected by poverty.

Global Stratification

So far in this chapter, we have focused mainly on social stratification within the United States. The same concepts and theories apply to the international scene. Immanuel Wallerstein (1974, 1980, 1989) was one of the first social scientists to point out that economic relations are no longer confined within national boundaries but form an international capitalist "world system." Wallerstein did not include the former Communist countries of eastern Europe and China in his analysis because they had essentially opted out of the world system and traded only among themselves at the time he was writing. Even today these countries are a special case whose economies reflect the legacy of communism and command economies. (See *A Global View:* Poverty in Russia before and after the Anti-Communist Revolution.)

Following Wallerstein, Daniel Chirot (1986) shows how the industrial prosperity that Europe and North America achieved over the last century was due in large part to the development of a global system of social stratification. In 1900, Europeans and Americans controlled much of the world, directly (as colonies) or indirectly (through influence and power). This led to a global division of labor.

The wealthy, economically diversified, industrial powers of the northern hemisphere operated as an international upper class. These nations owned or controlled the means of production on a global scale. The undeveloped nations of the southern hemisphere—what we call the Third World—functioned as an international lower class, supplying raw materials and cheap manual labor. Europeans ran their colonies like plantations. The government of, or companies from, the colonial power controlled mineral rights, transportation sys-

Table 8-5   *Gross National Product per Capita and Life Expectancy for Selected Countries, 1995*

	GNP per Capita[†]	Life Expectancy at Birth (Years)*
Ethiopia	$ 100	47
Bangladesh	240	58
China	620	69
Egypt	790	63
Bolivia	800	60
Thailand	2,740	69
Turkey	2,780	67
Mexico	3,320	72
Brazil	3,640	67
Greece	8,210	78
Korea, Republic of	9,700	72
Saudi Arabia	7,040	70
Spain	13,580	77
Israel	15,920	77
Australia	18,720	77
Canada	19,380	78
France	24,990	78
Singapore	26,730	76
United States	26,980	77
Japan	39,640	80
Switzerland	40,630	78

*Note that while life expectancy in general is correlated with gross national product per capita, there are striking exceptions. China, for example, has a very high life expectancy for its income group, due largely to its advanced health care policies and the fairly even distribution of income. Saudi Arabia has a relatively low life expectancy for its income level because that income is very recent and based overwhelmingly on one product (oil) not yet matched by the overall level of economic development.

[†]In 1994 dollars.

Source: Adapted from *World Development Report 1997* by the World Bank. Copyright © 1997 by the International Bank for Reconstruction and Development/The World Bank. Reprinted by permission of Oxford University Press, Inc.

Exporting raw materials can bleed a Third World country of its natural wealth without creating jobs and profits at home. These diamond miners in the Congo have few if any alternatives to working in the mines, but neither they nor their country reaps the profits of their labor.

tems, the import-export business, and sometimes land. Their representatives acted as top executives, making decisions about what would be produced in the colony and sometimes employing forced labor. A few nations like Japan, which were neither colonized nor industrialized in 1900, took on the characteristics of an international middle class.

Although virtually all former colonies have won political independence, the global system of stratification remains intact. Indeed, the rich nations have grown richer and the poor nations poorer (see Table 8-5). While western nations became increasingly diversified economically in recent decades, former colonies were encouraged to specialize in

Poverty in Russia before and after the Anti-Communist Revolution

Officially, poverty did not exist in Russia during the Soviet period (Braithwaite, 1997). In broad terms, the Communist system guaranteed universal employment, controlled prices, and provided retirement and social insurance to everyone. The cornerstone of the Soviet philosophy was the right to work: the state provided every able-bodied adult with a job; in return, all adults were obligated to work. Indeed, people who did not work could be charged as "social parasites" and sentenced to time in a labor camp. (Studying full-time and caring for small children or for invalids were considered work.) Employees of high-priority enterprises were rewarded with such noncash benefits as desirable housing (in short supply throughout the Soviet period); on-the-job child care centers, cafeterias, clinics, and recreational facilities; and preferential access to waiting lists for cars and other scarce consumer goods. The elderly, disabled adults, and orphans received pensions. In the 1970s the government recognized that some families were "underprovisioned" (a euphemism for poverty) and provided a small monthly stipend for the children of these families.

Estimates are that 13 percent of the Soviet population, about 36 million people, was "underprovisioned" in 1990, the year before the Communist government was overthrown. More

The first to suffer are children.

than half of the people in this category were families with children; a second large group consisted of pensioners who lived alone; another was workers in low-paying occupations (often women); and there were a smaller number of homeless, many of whom had spent time in prisons or mental hospitals. Rural Russians, who often lacked such modern facilities as indoor plumbing or access to telephones, earned about half the average income and received only half the pension provided to other workers.

Since the Communists were overthrown in 1991, the poverty rate in Russia has tripled. One reason is inflation. Under communism the government set prices according to what most people could afford, regardless of the costs of production. Goods were scarce but affordable. When controls were removed, the cost of consumer goods skyrocketed. The real value of the average wage fell from 70 rubles per month in 1990 to 35 in January 1995. But average wages conceal an increase in "hidden unemployment." In the new market economy, the government and private enterprises have not been able to meet payrolls. Rather than lay off workers, they delay paying wages and/or put workers on forced part-time schedules or forced "vacations." In 1993, about 37 percent of industrial, construction, and agricultural enterprises were more

exporting agricultural crops and raw materials—coffee, peanuts, rubber, tin, and the like. This specialization has two main negative consequences. Growing crops for export disrupts traditional patterns of food production, undermining agricultural self-sufficiency. Land that used to feed the local population is used for cash crops for the world market. A few large landowners may benefit, but peasants are left without fields and pastures or other means of support. Many are forced to migrate to cities, swelling the ranks of the urban poor and straining already-overburdened city structures.

Exporting raw materials, such as copper or oil, can bleed a Third World nation of its natural wealth (Kerbo, 1996). In developed, industrialized nations, natural resources generate a chain of economic activity. Suppose the resource is copper. The first step, mining copper, creates jobs and profits.

than twenty days late in paying workers; in 1994, between 40 and 60 percent of Russians employed in the textile, farm equipment manufacture, and electro-technical fields experienced reduced work time. Thus even though unemployment remains low, underemployment—and poverty—has increased.

Russia's new market economy has pushed increasing numbers of rural residents, pensioners, and low-wage workers into poverty. But the group hardest hit by economic change is families with children, especially young couples and single mothers. When a paycheck is late or a parent's hours are cut back, the first to suffer are children.

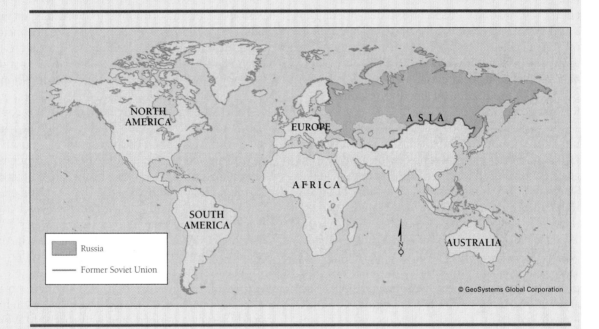

Map 8-1   *Russia and the Former Soviet Union*

The copper must then be refined, creating more jobs and profits. The metal is used by other companies to produce consumer goods, creating still more jobs and profits. These goods are sold by retail firms, yet again generating jobs and profits. The net result is economic growth. When a Third World nation exports natural resources, native workers may mine the ore, but all the other jobs and profits go to other nations. Furthermore, the price of raw materials on the world market fluctuates widely, leaving these countries exceptionally vulnerable to external forces.

Equally problematic, the populations of Third World nations have expanded rapidly (see Chapter 16). In many, a substantial majority of the people are dependents, too young or too old to work. Even though these nations are predominantly agricultural, they do not produce enough food to feed their populations; they depend on imports and aid from rich nations. Though necessary, such aid can be disruptive. For example, free or low-cost food undercuts domestic food prices.

Furthermore, although Third World nations control their own natural resources, industrial nations control most of the technology of mining, transportation, and trade (Goldthorpe, 1985). Third World nations must buy equipment, and sometimes hire technicians, from industrial nations. Wealthy nations also control the world currency system, shipping, and communications. Capital for investments is scarce. When foreign investors build factories and plants, opportunities for internal development decline. For example, Coca-Cola may replace local beverages produced by small entrepreneurs. Multinational corporations that operate in Third World nations create low-level jobs but often fill top managerial positions with personnel from industrial nations. Even when they do hire local managers, they tend to create a class of well-to-do people who are dependent on, and responsible to, foreign interests.

The global stratification system is not fixed and unchanging. Clearly Japan has moved into the ranks of "upper-class" nations, with a per capita gross national product exceeding that in the United States in 1995. Southeast Asian nations (Taiwan, Korea, Singapore, and Hong Kong) industrialized rapidly, joining the ranks of "middle-class" nations; Thailand, Malaysia, Indonesia, India, and, perhaps, Brazil and Mexico were not far behind. In the fall of 1997, however, the "little tigers" of Southeast Asia plunged into financial crisis. Thailand, Malaysia, and Indonesia had experienced rapid economic growth, driven by exports. These countries began to consume more than they produced and to invest in assets such as commercial real estate and golf courses. At the same time, China began to emerge as an economic powerhouse, competing with the "little tigers" in the export market. To match China, Thailand had to lower its prices, which it did by devaluing its currency. Overseas investors began to withdraw their money from Thailand and other little tigers to invest elsewhere. As a result, Thailand could not pay its foreign debts. Seemingly overnight, Thailand's stock market plunged, a pattern repeated in Malaysia, Indonesia, and the Philippines. For the time being, the little tigers have become (literally and figuratively) "paper tigers," and their movement into the international middle class has been halted. So far, the only impact of the Asian crisis on western nations was that their stock markets also fell, but they soon recovered.

By almost any measure, the United States today is an upper-class nation. Nevertheless, its position has slipped and may continue to do so. Sociologist Linda Brewster Stearns (1993) argues that a major reason for our precarious position is our failure to recognize the global economy. "The global market has changed the nature of economic competition," writes Stearns (p. 632). "Where once the competitive unit was the company, today it is the company/nation-state." In most highly developed industrial nations (Germany, France, Japan), government and business work together in pursuit of a national industrial policy. In the United States, both government and business have endorsed a laissez-faire, or "hands-off," policy, in which the government intervenes only in emergencies. We have no clear national policy for competing in the global economy; rather, it is each company for itself. The result, says Stearns, is equivalent to a pickup team of eleven individuals trying to play football against a coordinated team that is highly trained, heavily equipped, and well coached. In her view, the United States must shift its attention from intramural (within country) competition to the big league (the global market), or the lifestyles and life chances of U.S. citizens may suffer.

SOCIOLOGY ON THE WEB

A Wealth of Information about Poverty

The web contains numerous sources about poverty in America. Before you begin researching this huge and complex subject, decide what questions you want to answer.

One question might be, has the distribution of poverty in the United States changed since the text was written (1997–1998)? To find out, you need to break down this general query into more specific questions. For example, how many children under age 18 are poor? How many old people? What proportion of Americans living in poverty are white, African American, Latino, or Asian? You can obtain this information and much more at the sites listed below. Then, use your data to generate graphic displays that present the information clearly. Experiment with different ways of presenting the same data.

When this text was written, the Temporary Assistance to Needy Families (TANF) program, which replaced the federal AFDC or welfare program, had only been in effect for a short time. What impact has this program had on poverty rates?

A third possibility is to search for information about ways to fight poverty and its concurrent problems, such as homelessness. What tactics have been tried? What new programs and initiatives are being developed by government and private organizations? What has worked? What hasn't? The sites listed here will get you started.

http://www.fedstats.gov/
http://www.census.gov/
Either of these addresses will allow you to access the federal government's wealth of data on poverty and related problems, such as homelessness. Within Fedstats, begin by searching "Poverty" or "Income" in the A to Z index. The Census Bureau's site provides direct access to household income data, as well as historical tables and breakdowns by region.

http://www.ssc.wisc.edu/irp/
The best place to start any research on poverty in the United States is the web site of the Institute for Research on Poverty at the University of Wisconsin–Madison. It contains answers to frequently asked questions about poverty, as well as many, many links, organized by subject.

http://www.nlchp.org/
The National Law Center on Homelessness and Poverty provides information on causes of poverty and possible solutions, as well as links to regional antipoverty programs, both private and governmental.

http://cpmcnet.columbia.edu/dept/nccp/
The National Center for Children in Poverty at Columbia University posts articles from its newsletter that identify strategies intended to reduce the number of children living in poverty.

http://www.ris.org.uk/
Begin a search for information on poverty in countries outside the United States by checking out this British site. It discusses causes of poverty in the United Kingdom and provides links to many international sites.

Summary

1. **What is social stratification?** A system of *social stratification* exists when social inequalities are institutionalized so that society is divided into layers, or social classes, whose occupants do not have equal access to social opportunities and rewards. In a *closed system* of stratification, a person's position on the social ladder is ascribed on the basis of characteristics over which he or she has little control; in an *open system,* a person's position depends largely on achievement and there are opportunities to move up or down the social ladder. *Social mobility* usually takes the form of small steps up or down the social ladder, not giant leaps from rags to riches or the reverse, and often is the result of structural change rather than individual success or failure.

2. **How do sociologists explain social stratification?** Functionalists maintain that society needs a system of unequal rewards to ensure that qualified people will fill important but demanding positions—and accept existing inequalities. Marx emphasized the relations of production and saw society as divided into opposing camps of haves and have-nots. Weber argued that there are many gradations in a society and that *power* and *prestige* (or social esteem) can be as important as *wealth* in determining social positions.

3. **How have patterns of social stratification in the United States changed over the past thirty years?** Most sociologists divide American society into six social classes. At one extreme is the upper class, which controls a major share of the nation's wealth. At the opposite extreme are the ghetto poor and the homeless. Social class depends in part on wealth but also on social connections, occupational prestige, and lifestyle.

   In recent decades the distribution of wealth in the United States has changed. The gap between the rich and the poor has grown; the very rich are wealthier, and the number of affluent families more numerous, than their counterparts in the past; and the middle and working classes are working harder for lower incomes and reduced lifestyles. Especially since World War II, most Americans have enjoyed (and expected) upward mobility, but this pattern—and the American dream—may be changing.

   Growing inequality reflects globalization, new technology, and public policies related to these changes.

4. **How widespread is poverty in the United States?** The percentage of Americans who live below the federal *poverty line* in a given year rose in the 1980s and remains high. For most Americans, poverty is a temporary setback. The majority of the poor are white single or married adults who work at least part of the year, live outside cities, and do not depend on government assistance. However, the risk of poverty is greatest for minorities, children, and female heads of households. The chronic, severe poverty in the nation's inner-city African American ghettos is the subject of much debate. Whereas popular explanations invoke a "culture of poverty," Wilson holds that the ghetto poor are victims of the combined effects of deindustrialization and social isolation. Jencks holds that ghetto poverty is a variable phenomenon with multiple causes. Most researchers trace homelessness to a decline in low-skill jobs, a shortage of low-cost housing, cutbacks in social welfare programs, and social isolation. Whatever the explanation, the consequences of poverty include shorter life spans and generally poor health, as well as greater vulnerability to economic swings.

5. **What are the causes and consequences of global stratification?** The colonization and/or domination of much of the world by the wealthy industrial nations of Europe and North America produced a global system of stratification. Although former colonies have gained political independence, economic inequality continues. Today the United States is unquestionably an "upper-class" nation, but competition from "middle-class" nations is increasing.

Key Terms

Recommended Readings

Bane, Mary Jo, & Ellwood, David. (1994). *Welfare Realities: From Rhetoric to Reform.* Cambridge, MA: Harvard University Press.

Danziger, Sheldon, & Gottschalk, Peter. (1995). *America Unequal.* Cambridge, MA: Harvard University Press.

Gans, Herbert J. (1995). *The War Against the Poor: The Underclass and Antipoverty Policy.* New York: Basic Books.

Gilbert, D. (1998). *The American Class Structure: A New Synthesis.* 5th ed. Belmont, CA: Wadsworth.

Hacker, Andrew. (1997). *Money: Who Has How Much and Why.* New York: Scribner

Jencks, Christopher. (1994). *The Homeless.* Cambridge, MA: Harvard University Press.

Liebow, Elliott. (1993). *Tell Them Who I Am: The Lives of Homeless Women.* New York: Free Press.

Polakow, Valerie. (1993). *Living on the Edge: Single Mothers and Their Children in the Other America.* Chicago: University of Chicago Press.

Chapter

Nine

Racial and Ethnic Stratification

The former nation of Yugoslavia sits at the crossroads of Europe and Asia. Along with the other Balkan nations, the republics of Yugoslavia have been traded among superpowers for centuries. At various times they have been ruled by the Ottoman Turks, the Austro-Hungarian Empire, the Nazis, and, most recently, the Communists. Although the peoples of former Yugoslavia share common Slavic roots (the name "Yugoslavia" means "pan-Slavic"), their turbulent history has divided them into distinct ethnic groups: Serbs, most of whom belong to the Eastern Orthodox church; Croats, most of whom are Roman Catholic; Bosnian Muslims; Macedonians; Albanians; and other smaller groups.

From World War II until the early 1990s, Yugoslavia was a federation of six republics, each with its own Communist party, held together by the totalitarian government of Marshal Joseph Tito. Each republic was named for its dominant ethnic group, but all included members of other groups. (See Map 9-1.) Tito's hope was that equal treatment under the law and modernization—industrialization, urbanization, education, and a rising standard of living—would lead people to think of themselves as "Yugoslavs," rather than as members of rival groups. When Tito died in 1980, a Serbian nationalist came to power and Serbs dominated the federal government, the state-run economy, and the Yugoslav army.

In the wake of the anti-Communist revolutions that swept eastern Europe during 1989 and 1990, Yugoslavia began to come apart. Economic conditions in the country had deteriorated. One republic after another declared its independence. Serbs living outside Serbia, primarily in Croatia and Bosnia-Herzegovina, feared they would be expelled from their homes, jobs, and government positions. With the help of the Yugoslav army and the federal government in Belgrade, they began fighting to expand their ethnic territory and create a "Greater Serbia." Tens of thousands were killed, and millions uprooted from their homes. Only when the United States and other NATO countries sent in ground troops to enforce peace, in 1995, did the fighting stop. The troops were supposed to be there for only eighteen months, but their stay has been extended (as of this writing, indefinitely). In 1997, hostilities flared again, this time in the province of Kosovo, where an independence movement by ethnic Albanians was met with violent reprisal by Serbian troops. Apparently only a totalitarian

9

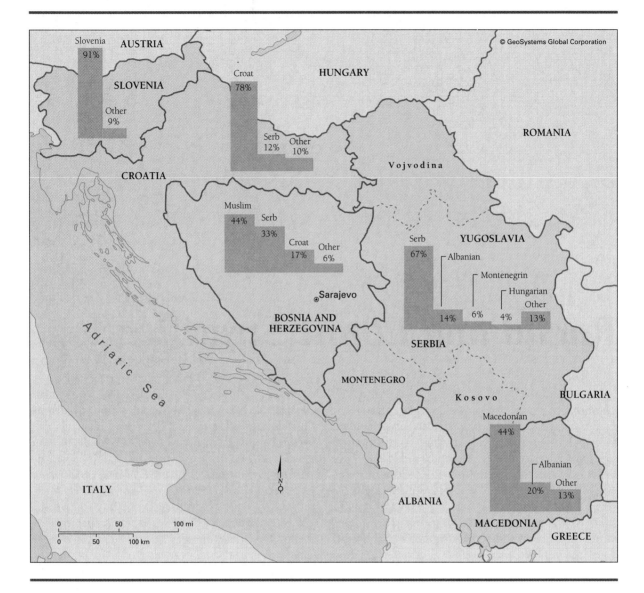

Map 9-1 *An Ethnic Map of Former Yugoslavia*

The former nation of Yugoslavia was a patchwork of different ethnic groups, who speak different languages and practice different religions. The collapse of communism in Yugoslavia and other European countries set off one of the bloodiest civil wars of recent times.

Sources: Center for Strategic and International Studies, International Institute for Strategic Studies; Misha Glenny, *The Fall of Yugoslavia: The Third Balkan War*, New York: Penguin, 1992; Ralph D. Kaplan, *Balkan Ghosts: A Journey through History*, New York: St. Martin's 1993; Geoffrey Barraclough (Ed.), 1989, *The Times Atlas of World History*, Maplewood, NJ: Hammond, Inc.

dictatorship or military force can control ethnic conflict in this region.

Some observers see the Slavic war of the mid-1990s as a revival of old antagonisms. Bosnian Muslims were a living reminder of 400 years of Turkish domination.

During World War II, Croats sided with the Nazis, helping send thousands of Serbs, Jews, and Gypsies to their deaths in concentration camps. The Serbs fought back, setting off a civil war (1941–1945) that killed an estimated 1 million Yugoslavs. According to this view,

Tito's iron rule held ethnic rivalries in check, but group hatred continued to smolder under the surface. After Tito died, old antagonisms flared up. Other observers see the recent war as a battle for political and economic control (Hodson, Sekulic, and Massey, 1994). Under communism, rival political parties were banned. The collapse of communism left a void. In the absence of other forms of political organization, opportunistic leaders fanned the fires of old ethnic conflicts to mobilize support for their own political goals. According to this view, ethnic conflict was an "excuse" for armed conflict over scarce economic resources. One explanation doesn't necessarily cancel out the other, however. If "Yugoslavs" had not maintained their separate identities, appeals for ethnic solidarity would have failed. Likewise, if economic development had been more even across regions and among groups, civil war on any grounds would have been less likely.

Racial and ethnic conflict is a global phenomenon. In the 1990s, as many as fifty ethnic wars raged worldwide. In eastern Europe, as in former Yugoslavia, the collapse of communism and the resulting economic and political chaos have rekindled old ethnic rivalries. In western Europe, new political groups based on ethnicity are forming, partly in response to increasing numbers of immigrants. In African nations, struggles between rival ethnic groups or tribes began soon after independence from colonial rule and, in many places, continue today.

In some ways, the United States is unique. It is one of very few "settler societies," in which a majority of the population consists of immigrants or descendants of immigrants. (Other settler societies are Canada, Australia, and New Zealand.) Americans have roots in every continent on earth (Figure 9-1). Compared with the situation in former Yugoslavia and elsewhere, racial and ethnic relations in the United States seem relatively tranquil. Yet national origins continue to play a major role in determining a person's social identity and opportunities in our society.

Key Questions

1. *What are the social definitions of race, ethnicity, and minority group?*
2. *How do patterns of intergroup relations vary across cultures and over time?*
3. *What patterns have racial and ethnic relations taken in the United States?*
4. *What explains racial inequality?*
5. *How did the struggle for civil rights begin, and where did it lead?*
6. *What is the extent of racial and ethnic inequality in the United States today?*

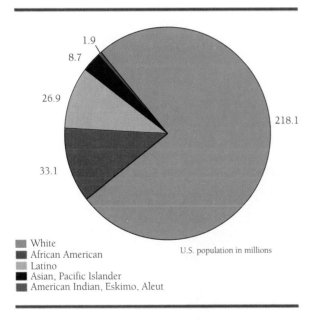

■ White
■ African American
■ Latino
■ Asian, Pacific Islander
■ American Indian, Eskimo, Aleut

U.S. population in millions

Figure 9-1   *The Ethnic Composition of the United States, 1995*

The 1860 U.S. Census used three categories: "white," "black," and "mulatto" (mixed). The 1990 Census had seventeen (distinguishing among different Hispanic or Latino, Native American, and Asian/Pacific Island groups).

The Social Definitions of Race, Ethnicity, and Minority Group

In everyday conversation the terms "race," "ethnic group," and "minority group" are rarely defined. The result is a good deal of vagueness, confusion, and disagreement. For example, some people think that Jews are a race; others would argue that Jews form an ethnic group. Some Jews consider themselves as members of a minority group, while others see themselves simply as members of a religion. The purpose of this section is to clarify these terms.

Races and Ethnic Groups

Many people take for granted the idea that the human species can be divided into a number of biologically distinct races. In fact, racial categories are products of *social* definition. For example, in central Africa, the Tutsi and Hutu consider one another as separate races. The two have similar coloring and features, but the Tutsi are tall, the Hutu short. In the United States we assign individuals to races primarily on the basis of skin color and facial features; height doesn't count. Neither system of classification has any more biological significance than the other. However, both have social consequences.

From a sociological perspective, a **race** is a category of people who see themselves and are seen by others as different because of characteristics that are assumed to be innate and biologically inherited. What matters is that people believe that there are innate, genetic differences among categories of human beings and that these differences are meaningful. The concept of race is usually found in association with **racism:** the belief that another group is innately inferior to one's own group.

Whereas racial categories are based on physical differences, ethnic categories are based on cultural differences. The former focuses on "looks"; the latter, on "outlooks" (P. I. Rose, 1974, p. 9). An **ethnic group** is a category of people who see themselves and are seen by others as set apart because of their cultural heritage. Italian and Irish Americans are examples. Ethnic groups are maintained by "consciousness of kind" and the assumption that people who share your ethnic background are likely to have similar values. Language and culture establish ethnic boundaries. Not only do "one's own kind" speak one's own language but they speak it "correctly." Food preferences, traditional (or "folk") art, music and dance, religion, occupational specialties, family names, and a shared myth of the group's origin and history can all be important in establishing ethnic identity.

One might think that racial and ethnic identities are fixed and immutable; for example, you are black or white or Asian or your ancestors come from Poland, El Salvador, or Vietnam. In fact, race and ethnicity are dynamic and changing. For example, Americans of European descent tend to think of Hispanics or Latinos as a single, undifferentiated bloc. But people of Latin American heritage, especially recent immigrants from Central and South America, refer to themselves by their *country* of origin. New immigrants from Africa and the West Indies have made the category "African American" more variable. During the 1970s, the number of people identifying themselves as "American Indian" on U.S. census forms increased by 1.4 million. But birth and death records for that decade show that the number of American Indians increased by only 760,000. Obviously, immigration could not account

A wedding of Ethiopian Jews in Tel Aviv. To some people, Jews comprise a race, while others think of them as an ethnic group, a minority group, or, simply, a religion.

for this increase. The most likely explanation is that people of mixed parentage or grandparentage were reclaiming their Indian ancestry (Nagel, 1996). (See *Close Up:* Racial Classification and the U.S. Census.)

People may change their ethnic identities, as individuals or as groups, for political or for personal reasons. For example, the Census Bureau used to classify people from the Indian subcontinent as "Caucasian/white." However, the Association of Indians in America successfully lobbied to have themselves reclassified as "Asian," distinguishing themselves from people of European ancestry. On an individual level, the same person may feel 100 percent American while traveling abroad, self-consciously "white" when looking for housing, but unquestionably Irish on St. Patrick's Day (Waters, 1990). In general, Americans of European background are free to pick and choose among their ancestors, selecting the ethnic identity they like best and sometimes changing identities to fit the situation. However, persons of color usually do not have that option. A persistent question for sociologists is why the color line tends to be more rigid and to have more social meaning than ethnicity.

Minority Groups

In a classic essay written during the last days of World War II, when the world was learning about Nazi concentration camps and the massive death toll of the Holocaust, Louis Wirth (1945) defined a *minority group* as a category

> of people who, because of their physical or cultural characteristics, are singled out from others in the society in which they live for differential and unequal treatment, and who therefore regard themselves as objects of collective discrimination. (p. 347)

"Minority group" is a sociological, not a statistical, concept. It does not depend primarily on numbers. The fact that a group is small and physically or culturally distinct does not automatically mean that it will be treated as inferior. (For example, neither redheads nor Bostonians are treated as minority groups in the United States.) In some cases, the "minority" outnumbers the "majority." Black South Africans are clearly a majority of the South African population, but until recently they were systematically denied the rights and privileges of citizenship in their own land.

A group's status as minority or mainstream can change. For centuries, Jews were a persecuted minority throughout Europe, where they were prohibited from owning land or living among Christians, restricted to small rural communities (or *shetls*) and walled urban districts (ghettos), and subjected to frequent pogroms (organized massacres). In the early twentieth century, German Jews became increasingly assimilated, or part of the cultural and socioeconomic mainstream. Many identified themselves as Germans and not as Jews. When Hitler came to power in 1933, the German economy was in shambles. In a classic example of scapegoating, Hitler blamed an "international conspiracy" of Jews for Germany's problems. The Nazi government imposed laws and restrictions that deprived Jews of their rights and possessions. Jews were prohibited from attending universities, their property and businesses were seized, they were required to carry identity cards and wear yellow Stars of David, and they were victimized by street gangs as well as police. After Germany overran Poland in 1939, Jews in conquered countries were forced to live in ghettos and to work as slave laborers. But only after Germany invaded the Soviet Union in 1941 did Hitler implement the so-called final solution: a systematic campaign to exterminate Jews throughout Europe. Jews were rounded up, packed into cattle cars, and shipped to death camps, along with Poles, Gypsies, and other groups. Some were gassed immediately, their corpses cremated in huge ovens; others were kept barely alive to assist in the murder and disposal of new arrivals. At least 6 million died.

In the United States today, most Jews have joined the mainstream and are seen by many as a successful, even privileged group. Yet Jews are conspicuously absent on the boards of major corporations, and anti-Semitic epithets and jokes, vandalism of synagogues, and hate attacks on individuals are not uncommon. A group's status also can vary from society to society. Jews were an oppressed minority in the former Soviet Union, but at the same time they were the dominant group in the state of Israel.

There are four key points in Wirth's definition of a minority group:

1. Minority groups are *disadvantaged* groups. Their members are excluded from full participation in society. In some cases they are not allowed to vote or hold public office. They may be denied certain

Racial Classification and the U.S. Census

For the past twenty years, the U.S. government has listed five races on census questionnaires and other forms: (1) white, (2) black, (3) American Indian or Alaskan Native, (4) Asian and Pacific Islanders, and (5) Hispanic. People filling out the form are asked to choose one of these categories or to identify themselves as "other." They are also asked if they are Hispanic. A main reason for asking people to identify their race or ethnicity is to enforce the Voting Rights Act, which requires that the federal government ensure that minority-group voters are not "silenced" by being assigned to predominantly white voting districts. Government officials use census data to identify patterns and allocate funds related to health, education, employment, housing, and the like. So do sociologists and other scientists (as you can see if you look at the source notes for many tables and charts in this book).

As the census for the year 2000 approaches, the idea of asking Americans to identify

themselves by race and/or ethnicity was questioned (Cose, 1997; Fuchs, 1997). The main opponents were "Hispanics" (Diaz-Calderón, 1997). This term is widely used to refer to people with ties to Mexico and Central and South America, as well as the islands of Cuba and Puerto Rico. Clearly, Hispanics are not a "race." The peoples of Latin America are extremely di-

> The new census form will make possible a more complex and accurate picture of the U.S. population.

verse, including Cubans of Spanish, African, or mixed descent; Peruvians of Inca or Japanese ancestry; Mexicans of French, Mayan, Spanish, Yaqui, or Basque descent; Venezuelans of Portuguese, Italian, or Middle Eastern ancestry; and many others. Nor are Hispanics an "ethnic group," in the sense that Italian Americans are. People of Italian descent share a common

cultural background. Cubans—whether black or white, of predominantly Spanish or African ancestry—are an ethnic group in this sense. But Cubans and Costa Ricans, Mexicans and Argentineans, though all considered "Hispanic," are culturally distinct. The differences between, and often within, people from these countries are as great as their similarities. All speak Spanish, but they have no more in common than do English-speaking North Americans, South Africans, Australians, and Jamaicans. Where do Brazilians, a racially diverse population who speak Portuguese, fit? Suppose Peruvian President Alberto K. Fujimoro's children emigrated to the United States. How would they choose to identify themselves: as "Asian," because of their Japanese ancestors, or as "Hispanic," because of their South American homeland?

The category "Hispanic" is misleading in several ways. First, it creates the false impression among *non*-Spanish-speaking Americans of a single,

---

property rights. Often they do not receive equal treatment under the law (indeed, they may be subject to special laws). Their access to education, and through education to high-prestige, high-income occupations, may be limited.

2. Minority groups are held in *low esteem* and often become objects of suspicion, contempt, hatred, and violence. The physical or cultural characteristics associated with minority groups are devalued. The

way their members look, act, and dress is ridiculed. As a result, minority groups are socially isolated.

3. Membership in a minority group is *involuntary;* it is an ascribed status, not an achieved one. Individuals are born into the group. They do not choose to join and are not free to leave. Individuals are treated as members of the category, regardless of their individual behavior. This has been called

monolithic group. Mexicans and Bolivians, or a third-generation Mexican college graduate and a recent immigrant from rural Mexico who has no formal education, have little in common. Yet other Americans tend to attribute common characteristics to this artificial category. Employers may treat a schoolteacher from Ecuador, a Dominican with a degree in horticulture, and a U.S.-born Puerto Rican high school dropout as alike, as part of a "mass" of replaceable workers.

Second, data on "Hispanics" can create false generalizations. For example, census data indicate that "Hispanics" have higher-than-average fertility rates. While rural immigrants from Mexico may have large families, established residents and urban immigrants do not. Averages conceal wide variations in family size, education, income, and other socioeconomic characteristics. Moreover, the actual number of American citizens or residents is probably much larger than the data indicate—

not just because of illegal immigrants. Because racial and ethnic identity are mixed together on the census and other questionnaires, Spanish-speaking people may check off "white," "black," or "Hispanic." Well-off people of Latin American background often identify themselves (and are seen by others) as "white," thus skewing information on Hispanics toward the poorest and most recent immigrants.

Finally, the old forms virtually required that people with Spanish surnames choose between their racial or ethnic/linguistic identity, while denying them the opportunity to express their own sense of identity. Other, perhaps more cohesive categories—such as Arabic speakers—had to choose between the race of people who colonized their countries (white) and "other." Furthermore, non-Hispanic whites had only one choice, whether their family dates back to the *Mayflower* or they are recent emigrants from Russia or Greece. And a growing number of people of mixed an-

cestry—the child of a black and a white parent, of a fourth-generation Japanese father and Irish mother, or of any other combination—were required to choose one part of their heritage over another.

After much debate, the U.S. Office of Management and Budget (OMB) decided that for the first time, the 2000 census will ask about ethnicity first and race second; provide more choices under the question about race; and allow people to check more than one race.* (See Figure 9-2.) Responses will be analyzed in terms of the older racial categories (except that Asian and Native Hawaiian or Other Pacific Islander have been separated), but data on more specific groups will be available. The new form will make possible a more complex and accurate picture of the U.S. population, but it might also make comparisons with previous census data problematic (*Population Today*, January 1998).

*The more-than-one-race provision creates 57 possible categories, and when combined with Hispanic or non-Hispanic, 114 possibilities.

the "ultimate attribution error" (Pettigrew, 1976). Negative acts are attributed to group dispositions ("That's the way they are"); positive behavior that does not fit the stereotype is attributed to luck, special advantages, or unusual circumstances and is written off as "the exception that proves the rule."

4. Minorities are *self-conscious*. Their history, their values and beliefs, and the unequal treatment they

experience make them see themselves as "a people apart."

The existence of minority groups implies the existence of a **majority group** that has gained the upper hand in society and guards its power and privilege, excluding outsiders from its ranks. A majority group is able to impose its norms and values on others.

(A) RACE AND ETHNICITY QUESTIONS FOR 1990 CENSUS

Standard Form 181 (Rev. 5–82)
U.S. Office of Personnel Management
FPM Supplement 296–1

RACE AND NATIONAL ORIGIN IDENTIFICATION
(Please read the instructions and Privacy Act Statement before completing form)

Agency Use Only	Name *(Last, First, Middle Initial)*	Social Security Number	Birthdate *(Month & Year)*
		⎹ ⎹ – ⎹ ⎹ – ⎹ ⎹ ⎹	

NAME OF CATEGORY (Mark **ONE** only)	DEFINITION OF CATEGORY
	Categories for Use in All Jurisdictions Except Hawaii* and Puerto Rico
A ☐ American Indian or Alaskan Native	A person having origins in any of the original peoples of North America, and who maintains cultural identification through community recognition or tribal affiliation.
B ☐ Asian or Pacific Islander	A person having origins in any of the original peoples of the Far East, Southeast Asia, the Indian subcontinent, or the Pacific Islands. This area includes, for example, China, India, Japan, Korea, the Philippine Islands, and Samoa.
C ☐ Black, not of Hispanic origin	A person having origins in any of the black racial groups of Africa. Does not include persons of Mexican, Puerto Rican, Cuban, Central or South American, or other Spanish cultures or origins (see Hispanic).
D ☐ Hispanic	A person of Mexican, Puerto Rican, Cuban, Central or South American, or other Spanish cultures or origins. Does not include persons of Portuguese culture or origin.
E ☐ White, not of Hispanic origin	A person having origins in any of the original peoples of Europe, North Africa, or the Middle East. Does not include persons of Mexican, Puerto Rican, Cuban, Central or South American, or other Spanish cultures or origins (see Hispanic). Also includes persons not included in other categories.
	Categories for Use in Puerto Rico
D ☐ Hispanic	A person of Mexican, Puerto Rican, Cuban, Central or South American, or other Spanish cultures or origins whose official duty station is in Puerto Rico. Does not include persons of Portuguese culture or origin.
Y ☐ Not Hispanic in Puerto Rico	A person not of Mexican, Puerto Rican, Cuban, Central or South American, or other Spanish cultures or origins whose official duty station is in Puerto Rico.

*Reproduce OPM Form 1468 from FPM Supp. 298-1 for data collection in Hawaii.

(B) RACE AND ETHNICITY QUESTIONS FOR 2000

❺ Is this person Spanish/Hispanic/Latino? Mark ☒ the *"No"* box if *not* Spanish/Hispanic/Latino.
☐ **No**,not Spanish/Hispanic/Latino ☐ Yes, Puerto Rican
☐ Yes, Mexican, Mexican Am, Chicano ☐ Yes, Cuban
☐ Yes, other Spanish/Hispanic/Latino — *Print group.* ⟍
⎹ ⎹

❻ What is this person's race? Mark ☒ one or more races *to indicate what this person considers himself/herself to be.*
☐ White
☐ Black, African Am, or Negro
☐ American Indian or Alaska Native — *Print name of enrolled or principal tribe.* ⟍
⎹ ⎹

☐ Asian Indian ☐ Japanese ☐ Native Hawaiian
☐ Chinese ☐ Korean ☐ Guamanian or Chamorro
☐ Filipino ☐ Vietnamese ☐ Samoan
☐ Other Asian—*Print race.* ⟍ ☐ Other Pacific Islander—*Print race.*
⎹ ⎹

☐ Some other race—*Print race.* ⟍
⎹ ⎹

Figure 9-2   *Census Forms, 1990 and 2000*

Due largely to lobbying by Hispanics who are neither a race nor a unified ethnic group, the U.S. Census form for the year 2000 will permit a wider variety of choices, reflecting the increasing diversity of the U.S. population.

Source: 1990, Office of Management and Budget Form 181; *2000,* Census Race and Ethnic Categories Retooled, 1998. *Population Today,* 26 (4) (January).

Patterns of Intergroup Relations: A Global View

Relations between racial and ethnic groups that are part of a single society can be seen as a continuum, ranging from mutual tolerance and accommodation to mutual hatred and violent conflict.

Amalgamation

One pattern of intergroup relations is **amalgamation,** or the formation of a "melting pot." The different ethnic and racial groups that make up the society intermingle, producing a new and distinctive genetic and cultural blend. For example, in colonial Brazil, descendants of Native Americans, Portuguese conquerors and settlers, and African slaves mixed far more freely than they did in North America. Although colonial Brazil was by no means an egalitarian society, color was not an absolute social barrier. Slaves could and did obtain their freedom, and mulattoes (individuals of mixed racial ancestry) were socially accepted. The population and culture of Brazil today reflects over four centuries of "cross-pollination."

African American culture can also be seen as a product of amalgamation. Prevented from maintaining their different tribal traditions under slavery and denied access to white institutions, African Americans created new and unique cultural forms. Jazz, for example, began as an amalgam of African rhythms and harmonies and Christian hymns and folk music.

Assimilation

A second pattern is **assimilation,** which occurs when ethnic and racial minorities are absorbed by the dominant culture and differences are forgotten or destroyed. Assimilation may be voluntary or involuntary, partial or total. The rate and degree to which different racial and ethnic groups, or different members of the same group, become assimilated into a society may vary.

Studies of European immigrants to the United States suggest that assimilation occurs in stages (Gordon, 1964). *Cultural assimilation*—adoption of the dominant group's food, dress, customs, and language—is often only partial among first-generation immigrants, who tend to form ethnic communities of their own. Full cultural assimilation more often takes place in the second generation, which has been exposed to the dominant culture through education and the mass media. As a rule, cultural assimilation is a prerequisite for *structural assimilation*: admission to major businesses and professions. But interaction on the job does not necessarily bring about *primary assimilation*: acceptance into private clubs, friendships, cliques, and ultimately the family, through intermarriage. Primary assimilation does not mean that ethnicity disappears, however. *Symbolic ethnicity,* or voluntary identification with an ethnic group, may increase as the third and fourth generations seek to establish their identities (Gans, 1979; Jiobu, 1988).

Pluralism

A third pattern is **pluralism,** in which ethnic and racial groups maintain their own language, religion, and customs and socialize mainly among themselves. In this way, each group maintains its distinct identity. Yet all participate jointly in the same political and economic systems. This does not necessarily mean that all groups are equal and that they treat one another with mutual respect. It's important to distinguish between *functional* integration (mutual interdependence) and *social* integration (mutual respect). Intergroup relations in a pluralist society may be harmonious and egalitarian or hostile and nonegalitarian.

The classic example of egalitarian pluralism is Switzerland, in which four ethnic groups—Schwyzerdütsch, French, Italians, and Romansh—coexist as equals. Each has maintained its distinctive cultural heritage and group identity, but no one group dominates the others. Other examples are Belgium, Brazil, and the state of Hawaii; Yugoslavia under Marshal Tito also would have qualified. Some of the troops who slaughtered one another were formerly friends and neighbors—one reason why the war there was so tragic.

Unfortunately, egalitarian pluralism is the exception. More often relations between the different groups in a pluralist society are characterized by tension and conflict. In a nonegalitarian pluralist state the dominant group usually controls the government and the economy. Members of other groups are "subjects, not citizens" (M. G. Smith,

1969, p. 33). The former Soviet Union was a pluralist society, composed of more than ninety distinct ethnic groups. But ethnic Russians controlled the Communist party as well as the central government, and hence the economy. Education and government business were conducted in the Russian language, supervised by Russian officials. Ethnic activities and nationalist movements were suppressed. South Africa under apartheid also was a pluralist society in that its economy depended on blacks, whites, Indians, and "Coloureds." But these groups were strictly separated, with the white minority retaining wealth, power, and privilege for themselves. Similarly, in the United States, African Americans

Proponents of multiculturalism argue that our society should encourage cultural diversity, rather than cultural sameness. Here, an elementary-school class studies Indonesian culture.

were segregated by law (*de jure* segregation) for 100 years, from the end of slavery to the passage of civil rights legislation in the 1960s, and to some degree are still segregated in practice (*de facto* segregation). (We discuss segregation in more detail below.)

In the United States today there is much debate about whether our institutions should promote assimilation or harmonious pluralism. Advocates of **multiculturalism** argue that there is strength in diversity and that our society should respect cultural differences, rather than require cultural sameness. Critics argue that a society depends on shared cultural values—especially a common language (English)—and that emphasizing differences promotes intergroup distance, not tolerance. In the past, families, churches, and local social and civic groups assumed responsibility for teaching children about their heritage. At issue in the multicultural debate is whether *schools* should teach African, Latino, American Indian, and Asian history, literature, and art—not just western (white, European, male) civilization—and what these groups have contributed to American society and culture. Sociologist Nathan Glazer (1997) traces the rise of multiculturalism to the failure of our schools—and our society—to assimilate minorities, especially African Americans. Given continuing prejudice and discrimination, he sees multiculturalism as the next best choice.

Exploitation

A fourth pattern is the use of race and ethnicity to rationalize exploitation of minority groups. Exploitation takes different forms: *colonization,* in which outsiders claim a territory, impose their own government and economic institutions, and usually appropriate native people's land and require local people to work in fields and mines or as servants; isolation, or *segregation,* of groups within a society; or the importation of laborers and servants from other countries. Typically, the exploited group is viewed as innately inferior and is systematically denied political rights, education, and economic opportunities.

Slavery, in which members of a group are kidnapped, held captive, forced to work for their captors, and treated as property, is the most extreme form of exploitation. Slavery has been practiced throughout history and on every continent, from ancient Babylon to the present. Indeed, the word "slave" refers to the eastern Europeans (or Slavs) the Vikings captured and forced into bondage in the ninth and tenth centuries. The Roman Empire used slaves to row its Mediterranean war boats; Arab and Berber caravans captured West African tribal people to labor for their rulers; the ancient Inca and Aztec Empires held slaves for use in rituals involving human sacrifice. But no group suffered more from slavery than the Africans who were brought to the Americas, where they and their descendants were treated as chattel, bought and sold, used and abused for more than 300 years.

Slavery is still practiced in some places (Crossette, 1997). Debt bondage is common throughout South Asia (working without wages, or giving away a child, to repay a loan); Islamic tribes in southern Sudan capture non-Muslim animists to use as forced laborers unless their clans buy them back; well-organized smuggling rings capture and mutilate poor children in India and transport them to Saudi Arabia to beg outside mosques; although formally outlawed, hereditary slavery is still practiced in Mauritania (Burkett, 1997).

In some cases, people may voluntarily relocate without understanding the consequences. In the United States today, unskilled and/or illegal immigrants from Mexico, China, and elsewhere work long hours for less than the minimum wage in private households, on farms, or in factories that resemble the "sweatshops" of the turn of the century. In several recent cases, including one involving deaf-mutes from Mexico, police found workers who were confined to barracks or apartments, kept under surveillance, and not allowed to communicate with their families in their home countries or with outsiders. Immigrants (legal or illegal) who do not know anyone in the country where they work, do not speak the language, and do not know the law are most vulnerable to such exploitation. Migrants within their own countries, such as poor Brazilians lured to the Amazon to work on isolated plantations, are equally vulnerable. In some cases, however, what we might see as virtual "slave labor"—for example, poor rural women in Bangladesh or Indonesia who work long hours in garment factories for pennies—looks more like opportunity to the workers themselves, who have no other employment options.

Segregation refers to laws or customs that impose physical and social separation on racial or ethnic minorities, denying members of these groups equal rights as citizens, equal justice, and equal opportunity in education, housing, and employment. Under segregation, the privileges of the dominant ethnic or racial group, and prejudice against minority groups, are institutionalized. The two primary examples of segregated societies in the twentieth century were the United States, as described below, and South Africa. (See *A Global View:* South Africa and the Legacy of Apartheid.)

Ethnic Conflict

A fifth pattern, *ethnic conflict,* is most likely when ethnocentrism (or a sense of "cultural superiority," see Chapter 3) is combined with the struggle for land and other scarce resources. Ethnic conflict may take the form of hate crimes (such as the attacks by neo-Nazi groups on immigrants and refugees in Germany); riots (as in the clashes between Muslims and mostly Hindu government troops in the Indian state of Kashmir); terrorist attacks (such as the Irish Republican Army's bombings of public buildings in London); uprisings (the Shining Path guerrillas in Peru and the Tamil rebels in Sri Lanka); or civil war.

The civil war in central Africa, which began in Burundi in 1993, is an ethnic war, grounded in the long-standing rivalry between the Hutu and the Tutsi: two nationalities (or "tribes") who see themselves as racially and culturally distinct and have long sought independence, but whose traditional homelands overlap. The former Belgian colony of Rwanda-Burundi had split into two nations soon after achieving independence, with the idea of creating one country for the Tutsis (Rwanda) and another for the Hutu (Burundi) (see Map 9-3 on page 326). But a Tutsi rebel army in Burundi blocked Hutu independence and effectively controlled its government. A short-lived coalition between an elected civilian government headed by a Hutu president and the Tutsi army in 1993 collapsed when the president was assassinated in an attempted military coup. Hutu extremists launched a campaign of terrorism against Tutsi civilians in which more than 500,000 people were killed. Tutsi soldiers retaliated, killing thousands and sending an estimated 1 million Hutu

South Africa and the Legacy of Apartheid

Apartheid means "separate development" in the language of Afrikaners, the descendants of Dutch settlers who emigrated to southern Africa in the seventeenth century. On one level apartheid was a philosophy of white supremacy grounded in Afrikaner history and religion (Fredrickson, 1981; Lelyveld, 1985). On another level, it was a system of overlapping laws, regulations, and agencies designed to maintain separation of the races and white *baaskap,* or "bossdom."

The country called South Africa today began as a supply station and "company town" for the Dutch East India Company. Most of the early settlers came as indentured servants and laborers and then moved into the countryside to become free farmers, or "Boers." The company made little attempt to govern the Boers. Visitors described them as renegades and adventurers who held civilized society in contempt (see Map 9-2).

Great Britain seized control of the Cape colony in the early 1800s. When the new British colonial government outlawed slavery and drew up plans to reserve lands for native tribes, the Boers rebelled. In the Great Trek of 1836 to 1845, more than 6,000 left the colony for the highlands beyond, where they declared independent Boer republics. Identifying with the ancient Israelites, the Boers likened British rule to the

Pharaoh's yoke; they also compared their Great Trek to the exodus from Egypt and the South African veld to the Promised Land. They believed themselves

> **South Africa belongs to all of us who live in it, united in our diversity.**
> —preamble to South Africa's 1996 constitution

to be God's chosen people. And they interpreted the biblical story of the Tower of Babel as a sign that racial mixing was a sin against God and nature.

After a long and bloody struggle, the British won the war against Boer independence: the Union of South Africa became a self-governing British dominion in 1910. But military defeat merely reinforced Afrikaner defiance. For the first half of this

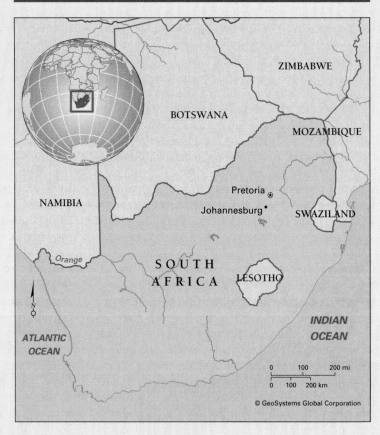

Map 9-2   *South Africa*

century the pro-British United party governed South Africa. But in 1948, Afrikaner nationalists came to power and began to put together the legal apparatus of apartheid.

Under apartheid, every South African was assigned to one of four racial categories at birth: "white" (European ancestry), "black" (African ancestry), "Indian" or "Coloured" (mixed ancestry), or "other." A person's racial classification determined his or her opportunities from birth to death. White people, who made up only 15 percent of the population, enjoyed the political freedoms and economic opportunities of citizens of western democracies. Nonwhite people lived under what was, effectively, police state rule. Under the law, black South Africans were considered citizens of ten "homelands" created and operated by the government, not citizens of South Africa itself. Black people were not permitted to vote. They were not allowed to own land or live in areas reserved for white citizens only, and whole black townships could be "relocated" to make room for white development. Black people were not allowed to enter white neighborhoods without official permits, and they were banned from virtually all public facilities: hospitals, hotels, buses and trains, parks, public toilets, and even elevators. Interracial marriage was illegal. Under "emergency power" decrees, anti-apartheid protestors could be arrested and detained without trial. Hundreds of demonstrators were killed by government troops—most notably in Sharpesville in 1960, in Soweto in 1976, and on the anniversaries of these massacres. Indians and Coloureds were only slightly better off.

All told, 17 million black South Africans were arrested for entering areas reserved for white citizens only; 3.5 million were dispossessed from their homes; 80,000 were detained without trial; and perhaps 40,000 were forced into exile. The impact of inadequate education, families torn by violence and arrest, and grinding poverty is more difficult to measure (Wren, 1991).

When F. W. de Klerk was elected president in 1989, South Africa was under increasing pressure from the world community to end apartheid. Economic sanctions had taken a toll. In early 1990, de Klerk stunned the world by lifting the thirty-year-old ban on the African National Congress (ANC) and other black political groups and releasing Nelson Mandela, long the symbolic leader of the fight against apartheid. Over the next two years, most of the legal structure of apartheid was dismantled. Mandatory racial classification was abandoned; public facilities were desegregated; restrictions on travel, residence, and home ownership lifted; and emergency powers canceled.

In a national referendum in 1992, nearly 70 percent of voters (all white) ratified de Klerk's plan to negotiate an end to apartheid. The first multiracial elections in South Africa's 350-year history took place in April 1994. And a new constitution was ratified in 1996.

The new South Africa has not produced the miracles some hoped for, but neither has it fallen into the chaos others feared (*The Economist*, December 13, 1997). Under the leadership of Nelson Mandela and the ruling ANC party, the government has kept the commitment stated in the preamble to the new constitution: "South Africa belongs to all of us who live in it, united in our diversity." The ANC did not follow its previous policy of nationalizing industries but, rather, has taken steps to increase free-market competition. Nor has the government confiscated property, sought legal retribution, or otherwise penalized former apartheid supporters. However, it does give preferential treatment to blacks in government appointments, in an effort to have the staff of institutions reflect the racial makeup of the population. Homes in some of the poorest townships now have electricity and freshwater taps. A small middle class of

continued

South Africa and the Legacy of Apartheid *(concluded)*

black businesspeople is growing. But progress has been slow.

In most respects, black and white South Africans still live in different worlds. With 85 percent of the land, rich farms and vineyards, abundant minerals, a high level of industrial development, advanced communication and transportation systems, "white" South Africa ranks as an upper-middle-income country. "Black" South Africa, in contrast, remains one of the poorest nations on earth. After four decades of apartheid, the majority of blacks are too poor to afford decent housing in the better neighborhoods now open to them. A majority do not have the education and job skills to make use of equal opportunity. Integrated schools, neighborhoods, and workforces are still the exception. With South Africa's old police state dismantled, law and order have proved elusive. Crime rates have climbed, especially in Johannesburg. South Africa has the highest murder rate in the world— nearly seven times that in the United States. Organized-crime syndicates from as far away as Russia and Colombia, Nigeria and China provide a risky source of income for some of the estimated 20 to 30 percent of adults who do not have regular jobs, as well as supplying guns to rival taxicab cartels and other local business rivals (*The Economist,* December 13, 1997). Such is the legacy of four decades of apartheid.

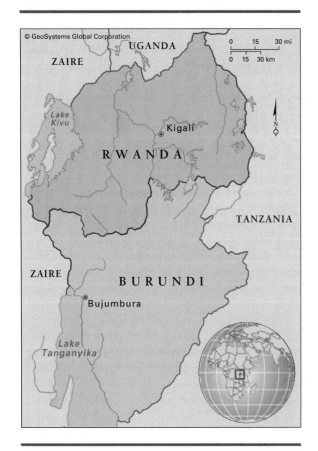

Map 9-3   *Rwanda and Burundi*

refugees across the border into the Congo. Apparently Hutu militia used refugee camps as bases for continued guerrilla warfare against Tutsis (McKinley, 1997). To stop the killing, the government of Rwanda sent troops into the Congo, joining forces with Congolese rebel leader Laurent Kibali. Most of the fighting took place in remote jungle, out of sight of the rest of the world. But reports suggest that hundreds of thousands of Tutsi villagers and Hutu refugees were massacred. With the backing of Rwanda, Uganda, and Angola, Mr. Kibali occupied the Congolese capital of Kinsasha in May 1997, ousting Mobuto Sese Seko, who had ruled Zaire (now the Democratic Republic of Congo) for three decades. At least a million people have been murdered or have starved to death since 1994, and sporadic guerrilla warfare continues along the Congo-Burundi-Rwanda borders.

The classic explanation of continued ethnic and political conflict in Africa is that the boundaries drawn by European colonial powers, meeting in Berlin in 1885, created artificial nations without regard to the continent's ethnic, historical, or economic realities (French, 1997). (See Map 9-4.) Kwame Nkrumah, the founding father of modern Ghana, preached pan-Africanism: To prosper, he argued, Africa would have to unite (following the model of the colonies that became the United States). But for most of the postcolo-

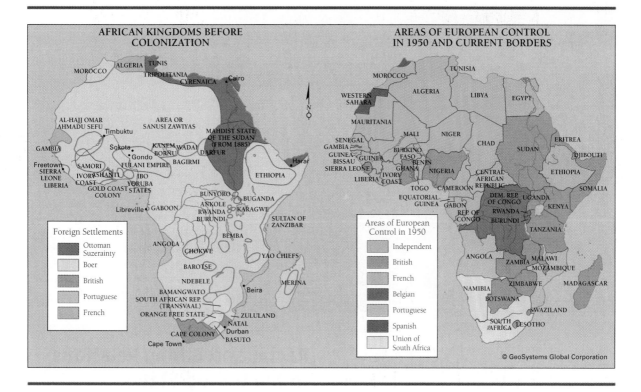

Map 9-4   *Drawing the Map of Africa*

Source: The New York Times, Nov. 23, 1997.

nial era (the 1960s to the present), African leaders have maintained colonial borders and followed a policy of noninterference in one another's internal affairs, a strategy supported by alliances with the United States or the Soviet Union during the long cold war. African nations can no longer count on outside support—or, as shown in Burundi-Rwanda-Congo, neighborly nonintervention. Thus the instability in Africa today reflects these recent changes in the structure of global politics, as well as its colonial past. Some observers foresee a new map of Africa emerging, composed of regional powers and surrounding, tributary states, led by Nigeria in west Africa, Angola in central Africa, South Africa in its region, and perhaps Uganda and Rwanda in east Africa. Ideally this arrangement would combine economic and military cooperation with local self-rule for Hutus, Tutsis, and Africa's many other nationalities.

The "ultimate solution" to intergroup conflict is *genocide:* the intentional mass murder of an ethnic,

religious, racial, or political group. The best-known example in modern history was the Holocaust in Nazi Germany. Less than fifty years later, Bosnian Serbs launched a campaign of "ethnic cleansing" to rid the country of Muslims through displacement or death. Thousands of Muslim men were taken to detention camps, where some were shot and others beaten, tortured, or starved to death. The Serbs also practiced a policy of mass rape. Muslim girls and women were assaulted in their homes, in front of their families; others were taken to hotels or camps where they were locked up and raped repeatedly by soldiers. Adding to this humiliation, many of the survivors had been impregnated by their captors. In a sense, genocide was applied to the next generation, as yet unborn.

One of the most horrific chapters of modern history took place in Cambodia. After seizing power from Prince Norodom Sihanouk in 1976, the week after the United States pulled out of Vietnam, Khmer Rouge leader Pol Pot set out to

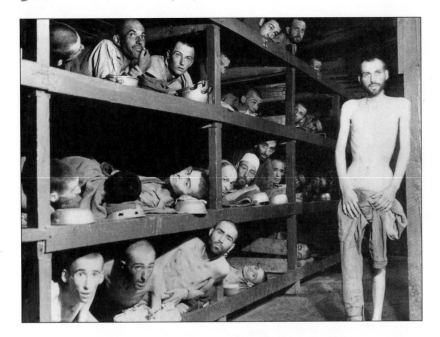

The worst though not the only episode of genocide in history was the Nazis' extermination of millions of Jews. This photograph was taken when American troops liberated the concentration camp at Buchenwald, Germany, in April 1945. The Noble Prize–winning writer Elie Wiesel is the prisoner at the far right of the center bunk.

rebuild Cambodian society by destroying it from the top down (Chandler, 1992). Private property, money, and family life were outlawed; Cambodia's central bank was dynamited; schools, Christian churches and Buddhist temples, and other institutions were closed and later destroyed. Virtually all citizens of the capital city Phnom Penh, plus other "intellectuals" (anyone else who had education, wealth, or even eyeglasses), were sent to the countryside and forced to labor in rice paddies. In a case of political genocide, tens of thousands were executed outright for alleged offenses against the revolutionary regime; thousands more were worked to death or succumbed to disease and starvation. The killing continued until 1979, when neighboring Vietnam took over the Cambodian government. By then, Pol Pot's troops had "eliminated" at least one-sixth of his country's population, as many as 2 million people. In 1998 Pol Pot died of natural causes.

The pattern of intergroup relations in a particular society at a particular time depends on a number of social factors, including economics, the size of different groups, and their histories and cultures, as illustrated by the racial and ethnic history of the United States.

Racial and Ethnic Relations in the United States: Changing Patterns

"The peopling of America is one of the greatest dramas in all of human history" (Sowell, 1981, p. 3). More than 45 million people—speaking virtually every language and representing almost every race, nationality, and religion in the world—have crossed oceans and continents to reach the United States. There are more people of Irish descent in the United States today than in Ireland, more Jews than in Israel, more African Americans than in many African nations. The setting in which this drama has unfolded is itself impressive. The United States today is larger than the Roman Empire at its greatest. The distance from San Francisco to Boston is about the same as that from Madrid to Moscow. Whereas Europe is divided into many nations whose citizens speak different languages, the United States is a single political and linguistic unit. The unity of the American people is as extraordinary as its diversity.

Each chapter of U.S. history has added new racial and ethnic stocks to the population and has defined new relationships between society as a whole and minority groups (Steinberg, 1981). The United States has seen the full continuum, from assimilation and pluralism to slavery and genocide.

Settlement: The English Protestant Foundation

On the eve of the Declaration of Independence, three-quarters of the colonial inhabitants traced their origins to the British Isles. Although population shortages forced them to admit "foreigners," the early colonists were determined to maintain their white Anglo-Saxon, Protestant heritage. *Nativism*—protecting majority institutions and privileges from immigrant influences (or "America for Americans")—is a recurring theme in our ethnic history. The irony, of course, is that those who established this doctrine for the United States were not natives of this continent.

Expansion, Conquest, and Genocide

When the first Europeans arrived in North America, the native population was about 2 million. Scattered across 3 million square miles, American Indians had developed diverse cultures and lifestyles. European settlers may have considered American Indians "uncivilized," but few Europeans would have survived their first winters without them. British and French soldiers competed for their services in colonial wars. For a time, the colonies were pluralist in the sense that European settlers and Native Americans lived in separate communities and neither group attempted to impose its culture or way of life on the other. This period of relatively peaceful coexistence did not last, however.

The expansion phase of U.S. ethnic history began after the Revolution. As the flow of European homesteaders picked up, the nation was infected with "land fever." American Indians in the areas being settled were soon outnumbered and, more significantly, outgunned. Typically, settlers would negotiate for territory but soon push beyond its borders, provoking an attack. The attack would be used as an excuse for "punishing" the defending American Indians, who would then cede another piece of territory and sign another treaty. But the Europeans kept coming. Under the Indian Removal Act of 1830, all tribes in the eastern United States were forced to move west—a "Trail of Tears" for Cherokees and others.

This cycle of trespassing, warfare, broken treaties, and dispossession was repeated time and again, to the point of genocide. When American Indians made their last military stand at Wounded Knee, South Dakota, in 1890, their total population had been reduced to about 250,000 (Figure 9-3). Some had been killed in battle, but many more had died because they had been exposed to diseases for which they had no immunity or had been forced into regions that could not support their way of life. Between the 1880s and 1930s, the Bureau of Indian Affairs, created to protect

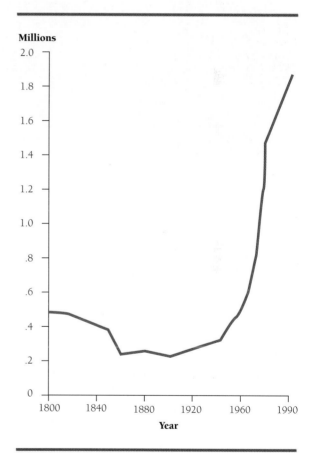

Figure 9-3   *The Decline and Recovery of the American Indian Population*

Driven to the brink of extinction during the Indian Wars of the nineteenth century, the American Indian population began growing in the 1960s, in part because more people were reclaiming their Indian ancestry.

White soldiers bury the Sioux massacred at Wounded Knee, South Dakota, in 1890. Popular opinion and government policy toward Native Americans can be summed up in the reprehensible remark often heard at the time, "The only good Indian is a dead Indian."

Native Americans, sold off 90 million acres, almost two-thirds of their remaining land. In the 1950s, the Eisenhower administration "terminated" 100 Indian governments for small cash payments (Egan, 1998).

The second chapter of U.S. expansion also involved conquest. In 1846, U.S. troops seized Mexico City, forcing the Mexican government to cede half its territory—what is now Arizona, California, Nevada, New Mexico, Utah, and parts of Colorado and Texas. And so the west was won by force. Most of the 80,000 or more Mexicans who lived in the ceded territory decided to remain. Under the Treaty of Guadalupe Hidalgo (1848), Mexicans were guaranteed rights as citizens. In practice, however, these rights were rarely granted. As Anglo-Americans poured west, Mexican Americans became "foreigners in their own land" (Takaki, 1993, p. 178). Through force and fraud, millions of acres of private and communal land were seized. Ejected from their own farms and ranches, many Mexicans became agricultural workers or miners.

No attempt was made to assimilate these ethnic groups (although American Indians later were forced to give up traditional practices and send their children to Anglo schools); once conquered, they were treated like colonial subjects.

To aid expansion, Chinese laborers were recruited to work on the railroads beginning in the 1840s, followed by Japanese agricultural workers in the 1890s.

Agriculture, Slavery, and Segregation

Meanwhile, another story was unfolding in the south. With its warm climate and vast stretches of flat land, the south was ideal for agriculture. But there was no class of serfs or peasants to provide agricultural labor; European workers were scarce and expensive; and conscription of Native Americans was impractical (escape would have been too easy). African slaves were the "obvious" solution to this labor shortage.

The first Africans arrived at Jamestown, Virginia, in 1619, a year before the *Mayflower* (Pettigrew, 1976). Like many white immigrants, they came as indentured servants, not as slaves. In 1661, Virginia enacted the first slave code, singling out black people for "perpetual servitude." By the early 1700s most other states had followed suit. Racial and cultural differences made it easier to rationalize and enforce slavery. Africans were viewed as "heathen children." By introducing them to civilization and Christianity, the white master was "saving their souls."

In the nineteenth century, the south became one of the most economically specialized regions in the world; cotton was king, and cotton depended on year-round, backbreaking labor. The number of slaves in the south grew from less than 1 million in 1800 to almost 4 million in 1860 (Pettigrew, 1976).

The Emancipation Proclamation was signed in 1865, a year before the Civil War ended, in part to free slaves to fight against the Confederacy. After the war, during the period known as the Reconstruction, northern troops occupied the south and the federal government set up Freedmen's Bureaus to protect black rights. African-American men were given the vote, and some were elected to public office.

Economic freedom proved elusive, however (Steinberg, 1981, chap. 7). Further deterioration of the southern economy would have hurt the northern businesses that supplied them. Freedmen's Bureaus helped re-create black servitude with the system called *sharecropping*. White landowners advanced supplies to freed slaves against future earnings, setting up a cycle of borrowing and indebtedness that tied African Americans to the land as surely as slavery had. Materially, many were worse off than they had been under slavery (Fogel and Engerman, 1974).

Around the turn of the century, southern states passed a series of Jim Crow laws that institutionalized racial separation and inequality. In *Plessy v. Ferguson* (1896) the U.S. Supreme Court gave segregation its blessing, declaring "separate-but-equal" facilities constitutional. But "separate" never meant "equal." Throughout the south, "coloreds" or "Negroes" were forced to live in segregated neighborhoods, attend segregated schools, and work at menial jobs, as janitors, porters, machine operators, manual laborers, and domestics. (The few black professionals—teachers, doctors, lawyers—could serve only black clients.) African Americans were denied the vote through such measures as poll taxes, literacy tests, and the "grandfather clause."[1] They were also denied equal protection under the law. White police imposed fear and humiliation on black communities, while white judges and juries treated African Americans as guilty almost by definition, especially if the alleged crime was interracial (A. D. Morris, 1984). Segregation under the law was reinforced by burnings, lynchings, and other acts of terrorism, especially by the Ku Klux Klan. This period has been described as the low point of African American fortunes (Pettigrew, 1976).

Industrialization and Immigration, Assimilation and Discrimination

The cotton boom in the south spurred industrial development in the north, which began with textile mills. Although many northerners had opposed slavery, few believed in racial equality. Fear of an influx of freed slaves after the Civil War made the new industrialists look elsewhere for workers. As the south had come to depend on slave labor, so the north came to depend on labor imported from Europe.

Between 1820 and 1880, more than 10 million Europeans crossed the Atlantic, leaving Germany, Britain, Ireland, and Scandinavia behind. Between 1882 and 1920, they were joined by 23 million Italians, Poles, Russian Jews, and other eastern and southern Europeans. (See Figure 9-4.) By 1910, one-quarter of the nation's workforce was foreign-born and a majority of workers in major port cities were immigrants.

Did the United States provide a haven for Europe's "huddled masses"? Or were foreign workers the victims of false promises and exploitation?

---

[1]A "grandfather clause" was a clause in the constitution of several southern states before the year 1915 that was intended to deny blacks the right to vote. Grandfather clauses exempted individuals from stringent voting laws, such as poll taxes and literacy tests, if they were descendants of persons who were registered to vote before 1867. Thus, white southerners who could not pass literacy tests or pay poll taxes could vote if their grandfathers had registered to vote. (Women did not yet have the right to vote; see Chapter 10.) African Americans were not able to vote if they failed the literacy test and could not pay the poll tax, because few of their grandfathers were registered to vote before 1867.

Lewis Hine took many photographs of immigrants to the United States. This one shows Italian men newly arrived at Ellis Island. Like their counterparts from other European countries, they probably encountered a combination of opportunity and exploitation in the United States.

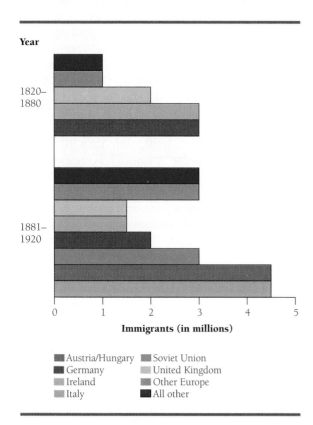

Figure 9-4   *Immigration from Europe, 1820 and 1920*

Source: INS, *Statistical Yearbook of the Immigration and Naturalization Service,* various years.

Probably both. Pushed out of Europe by a population explosion—and by food and job shortages—and pulled to the expanding American economy, these immigrants came to the United States of their own free will (unlike Native, African, and the first Mexican Americans). But mass immigration created a labor surplus, enabling industrialists to pressure immigrant workers into accepting long hours, unhealthy working conditions, and low pay. Nativist antagonism against non-English-speaking, Catholic, and Jewish immigrants ran high, and intergroup ethnic conflict was common. Even so, these immigrants had a foot in the urban industrial economy. Whether by using ethnic networks to go into business for themselves or by moving into semiskilled and skilled occupations, most eventually improved their standard of living. By the second or third generation, most European immigrants were becoming assimilated.

World War I cut off immigration from Europe in the midst of an economic boom, forcing employers to recruit African Americans. Over the next decade, several hundred thousand southern blacks moved north in search of jobs. The passage of restrictive immigration laws in the 1920s, and the heightened demand for labor during World War II, accelerated the exodus of African Americans from the south. Their experience in northern cities was quite different from that of Europeans.

The Making of the Ghetto

African American ghettos seem so much a part of the urban social landscape that one might assume that the ghettos have always been there. In fact, they are a comparatively recent social creation (Massey and Denton, 1993). Before 1900, both black and white people in northern cities lived, studied, and worked side by side. Blacks were more likely to live in poor areas, but most cities also had a black elite, made up of professionals, business owners, and skilled craftspeople who mingled freely with their white colleagues and customers. African Americans certainly did not enjoy equal opportunities, but the two racial groups lived in the same social worlds and interacted regularly.

By 1940, most urban African Americans lived in all or mostly black neighborhoods. The creation of the black urban ghetto was not a matter of chance or choice but the result of both personal and institutional decisions. The white working class saw the growing number of black workers as unwelcome competition for jobs. Between 1900 and 1920, a wave of racial violence swept through northern cities: individuals were attacked and many black homes firebombed. In white middle-class communities "neighborhood improvement associations" were formed, whose primary goal was to exclude black residents; so African Americans fled or were forced into segregated neighborhoods.

During the second half of the century, government policies had the (mostly) unintended consequence of reinforcing residential segregation. During the economic boom that followed World War II, a number of government programs (from highway construction to low-cost mortgages) enabled white middle-class families to leave the city for the suburbs. Such assistance was not available to urban minorities, who were considered a "poor risk." But not all whites left the city. Urbanites associated with elite institutions such as universities, hospitals, and museums stayed on. In the late 1950s and early 1960s they took advantage of government urban renewal programs to reclaim and refurbish old housing and rebuild downtown shopping and theater districts. "Urban renewal" often translated into "black removal," as slums were razed to make room for development. Displaced African American families were pushed into high-rise public housing. By the end of the decade these projects had begun to resemble African American "reservations."

Today one-third of African Americans live in large, run-down, crime-ridden, densely populated urban neighborhoods that show no signs of recovery. "People growing up in such an environment have little direct experience with the culture, norms, and behaviors of the rest of American society and few social contacts with members of other racial groups," wrote sociologists Douglas Massey and Nancy Denton in a book entitled *American Apartheid*. Citizens of a large, culturally diverse, highly mobile society, "blacks living in the heart of the ghetto are among the most isolated people on earth" (Massey and Denton, 1993, p. 77).

To a large degree the United States seems to have given up the goal of assimilation or full integration and embraced multiculturalism (Glazer, 1997).

Explaining Racial Inequality in the United States

By and large, European ethnic groups have followed the assimilationist path into the mainstream of American social and economic life. Why have certain minorities—African Americans, Latinos, and Native Americans—been left behind?

Innate Differences: Real or Imagined?

The idea that racial differences in aptitude and achievement are grounded in biology has intuitive appeal. If observable differences in appearance are inherited, why not differences in talent, intelligence, and ambition?

The IQ Controversy

For some decades, debates over innate racial differences have focused on intelligence quotient (IQ) and other aptitude and achievement test scores. During World War I, the U.S. Army administered intelligence tests to some 2 million recruits. It found that, on average, immigrants scored lower than did native-born Americans; immigrants from southern and eastern Europe, lower than immigrants from northern and western Europe; and

African American recruits, lowest of all groups. Discounting differences in language or education, nativists and segregationists viewed these data as "scientific proof" that the northern Europeans were superior. Although the Army study was discredited, new evidence and new arguments for or against racial and ethnic differences in intelligence continue to appear (e.g., Jensen, 1969).

The most recent controversy over race and IQ was sparked by the publication of *The Bell Curve* (1994), by Richard Herrnstein and Charles Murray (see Figure 9-5). The authors begin, in their preface, with the idea that our society is becoming increasingly divided between a highly educated, well-paid elite at one extreme and an undereducated, impoverished, and troubled underclass at the other—an observation few social scientists dispute. What provoked debate was Herrnstein and Murray's explanation: that social inequality is the natural result of differences in intelligence.

In the first half of their book Herrnstein and Murray cite evidence that they interpret as demonstrating that IQ (and related) tests are accurate measures of intelligence; that intelligence is in large part inherited, and therefore fixed and immutable; and that intelligence has a significant impact on where people end up in life. The authors analyze data

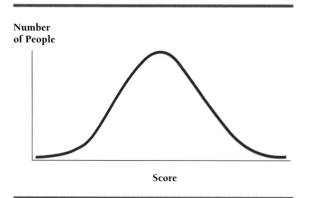

Figure 9-5   *The Bell Curve*

The bell curve is a statistical device for illustrating the normal distribution of any measurable traits of a group, such as differences in IQ scores. Most people score about average on a bell curve, producing the center or top of the bell. The numbers decline as one moves toward the highest and lowest scores, producing the bell's sloping sides.

from the National Longitudinal Survey of Youth (NLSY), which began in 1979 with a sample of 12,500 whites age 14 to 22 who have been followed ever since. As a rule, participants with higher-than-average IQ scores graduated from college, entered high-status, high-paying occupations, maintained stable marriages, and enjoyed an affluent lifestyle. In contrast, participants with lower-than-average IQ scores tended to drop out of school, have problems holding a job, engage in crime, bear children out of wedlock, and end up in poverty. The authors hold that IQ overrides such socioeconomic factors as parents' income and education in determining opportunities for success.

In the second half of their book, Herrnstein and Murray apply the same reasoning to group differences. The average IQ score of Asian Americans is a few points higher than that of non-Hispanic white Americans, and the average IQ of African Americans and Latinos, 10 to 15 points lower. This, they argue, explains not only higher rates of school failure, unemployment, and poverty for these groups but also poor job performance, illegitimate children, broken families, welfare dependency, neglectful parenting, and a host of other ills. They acknowledge that the IQ gap closed somewhat during the 1970s and early 1980s, thanks to programs like Head Start, but feel such efforts have reached their limit. They worry about "dysgenesis" (or the "dumbing" of America)—in part because the low-IQ underclass has higher fertility rates than the high-IQ elite; in part because our society spends too much on children who have (innate) problems in learning and too little on (innately) gifted children.

The Bell Curve was a magnet for opposing views (see Fischer et al., 1996; Fraser, 1995). Critics pointed out, first, that intelligence is far more complex, variable, and changeable than a single test score suggests (Gardner, 1995; Gould, 1995). Many cognitive psychologists hold that just as ranking people by height does not tell you anything about their build, strength, or coordination, so ranking people by IQ does not tell you anything about their creativity, practical sense, social skills, or other qualities we associate with intelligence (Sternberg, 1997). Others point out that IQ tests are as much a measure of cultural knowledge as of innate ability. White, middle-class children are more likely to understand questions with terms like "regattas" and "esthetics" than are poor, minority children who have never seen a yacht race or visited an art museum. Support for the view that such tests are culturally biased comes from a study at Washington University (Meyerson et al., 1998). The researchers compared IQ test scores of black and white students at the end of high school and again at the end of college. Given the same education in the same cultural setting, blacks' scores improved four times as much as whites' did, reducing the average difference by half.

Second, a large body of evidence refutes the idea that group differences in intelligence are hereditary. If group differences are innate, how do we explain that average scores for racial and ethnic groups change significantly over time, even when their rates of intermarriage (which would introduce genetic change) are very low (Sowell, 1995)? For example, tests given to Jewish, Polish, Chinese, Italian, and Greek immigrants on their arrival showed these groups to be below-average in intelligence; as they became more integrated into American culture, however, their IQ test scores rose to average and above-average. If intelligence is fixed and stable, how do we explain the finding that—worldwide—average IQ scores have risen 15 points in the past 65 years (Flynn, 1987)? Is the human race becoming "smarter"? A more likely explanation is that urbanization, access to the mass media, and other, unknown factors have widened people's intellectual horizons.

Third, there is little evidence that IQ or other test scores predict future success. To the contrary, a number of studies—of medical school, law, and psychology graduate students, and three different classes admitted to the Harvard Graduate School of Education during the 1950s, 1960s, and 1970s—found little or no correlation between scores on standardized admissions tests and success in school (measured in terms of grades and completion) or success in careers (measured in terms of level of achievement, income, and professional satisfaction) (Bronner, 1997). To cite one example, Martin Luther King, Jr.—widely recognized as one of our nation's great orators—scored "below average" in verbal aptitude on the Graduate Record Exam. (Nevertheless, he was admitted to Boston University, where he received his doctoral degree.)

What, then, explains why African Americans and Latinos score lower than non-Hispanic whites on standardized tests? This turns out to be a sociological, not a biological, question. Around the world,

members of minority groups score lower than the majority group, regardless of their racial identity (Sowell, 1995; Fischer et al., 1996). In Japan, Koreans (many of whom were brought to Japan as slave laborers when Korea was a colony of Japan; still do menial jobs or "dirty work," if they work; and are widely regarded as violent and stupid) score below average on intelligence tests. In the United States, Koreans do as well academically as Japanese Americans—that is, above average. The Irish and Scottish in Great Britain, Maoris in New Zealand, Flemish in Belgium, Eastern European Jews in Israel, and Gypsies in Czechoslovakia score lower on intelligence tests than other groups in their country (Fischer et al., 1996). Obviously these groups are not genetically related; what they do have in common is that they are minority groups and, as such, are outside the cultural mainstream.

In short, research supports the view that an ethnic or racial group's position in society has a significant impact on measurements of intelligence, rather than the reverse Herrnstein-Murray hypothesis (that intelligence has a significant impact on a group's or an individual's social position). (See Figure 9-6.)

Prejudice and Discrimination

A second explanation of racial inequality focuses on the attitudes and actions of the white majority.

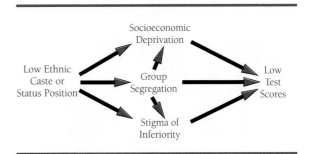

Figure 9-6 *A Model of the Impact of Minority Status on Test Scores*

Cross-cultural comparisons find that group differences in test scores are a reflection of a group's status in society, not biological or cultural differences. This figure shows why.

Source: C. S. Fischer et al., *Inequality by Designs: Cracking the Bell Curve Myth*, Princeton, NJ: Princeton University Press, 1996, p. 174, fig. 8.1.

Prejudice is an unfavorable and rigid opinion of members of a social group or category. The word "prejudice" comes from the Latin for "prejudgment." People make social prejudgments all the time: we think that knowing a person's age, sex, or occupation tells us something about that person. Opinions become prejudice when they cannot be altered by new information. The statement "Juan is bright—for a Puerto Rican" is an example. The fact that Juan is an A student has not altered the speaker's opinion that Puerto Ricans are not very intelligent.

Prejudice rests on *stereotypes*: overgeneralizations about a group and its members that go beyond existing evidence (Feagin and Feagin, 1996). The beliefs that all Asians are smart, that all Jews are cheap, that all African Americans are lazy, and that all Italians belong to the Mob are examples. Stereotypes may be concealed in polite, "politically correct" conversation but often leak out in the form of racial and ethnic jokes. The mass media enforce stereotypes, often in subtle ways. For example, although two out of three poor Americans are white, 65 percent of the people chosen to represent the poor on major television networks and 62 percent of the poor photographed in major news magazines are black (Boston Globe, July 23, 1997, p. A-17).

Prejudice and discrimination against Chinese immigrants were rife on the American west coast in the second half of the nineteenth century.

(See *Sociology and the Media:* Hispanics, TV's Missing Persons.)

The term "prejudice" refers to attitudes; the term "discrimination" refers to behavior. *Discrimination* is the denial of opportunities and social esteem to individuals because they are members of a devalued social group or category. It is the "unequal treatment of equals" (Yinger, 1986).

Years ago, Swedish social scientist Gunnar Myrdal (1944) showed how prejudice and discrimination created a *self-fulfilling prophecy* (Merton, 1968). Because whites believed African Americans to be racially inferior, they denied blacks equal education, job opportunities, quality housing, and ordinary everyday respect. Because African Americans were discriminated against, many African Americans were illiterate, employed at menial jobs, ill-housed, and impoverished. This lower standard of living "confirmed" the belief that the black race was inferior. Thus an originally false belief (racial inferiority) affected behavior in such a way (lack of opportunity) as to make the false belief seem true.

How much have attitudes and behavior changed? Surveys suggest that white prejudice toward African Americans has decreased but not as much as many whites believe. The great majority of white Americans support racial equality in principle; in practice, however, many want to maintain social distance. For example, though most whites do not oppose intermarriage, the majority say they would feel "uneasy" if a close relative planned to marry an African American. Similarly, most white parents think classrooms should be integrated, but if the proportion of black students in their child's class or school approaches 50 percent, they are not so sure. Thus, whites generally endorse racial equality but only up to a point. When certain boundaries are crossed—when too many black people are involved or interracial contact is too frequent or too close—white people tend to back off or back away (National Research Council, 1989).

When asked about discrimination, blacks and whites have different views about how blacks are treated in the United States today (Gallup, 1997). In a 1995 poll, more than two out of three whites agreed with the statement, "Blacks have as good a chance as white people in your community to get any type of job for which they are qualified"; about the same proportion of blacks disagreed. More than seven in ten black respondents said that job

SOCIOLOGY & THE MEDIA

Hispanics, TV's Missing Persons

Hispanic Americans, who currently number more than 28 million people, will be the country's largest ethnic group by the year 2005. Yet they are virtually invisible on commercial television. A study conducted by the Center for Media and Public Affairs for the National Council for the Raza, aptly titled "Don't Blink," found that representation of Hispanics on television has decreased over the past thirty years. Although they now make up 10 percent of the population, only 2 percent of characters on 139 prime-time series were Hispanic. When they do appear, Hispanics are usually portrayed as drug pushers, maids or gardeners, gang members, and Latin American drug lords. Should we care? Does it matter?

Independent film producer Paul Espinosa believes "it matters deeply—both for the larger society and for the Hispanic community itself" (1997, p. B7). Espinosa suggests that when Americans think of race and ethnicity, they tend to think in bipolar terms of black and white. Our national consciousness has not yet grasped the diversity of our population; neither has television, "a medium that follows rather than leads" (p. B7). What little the average Anglo-American learns about the Hispanic world from TV is bleak and frightening, fostering stereotypes that link economic problems and crime with a growing Hispanic presence. To be sure, African Americans have been portrayed in terms of demeaning stereotypes. So have women. But blacks and women clearly have made progress in recent years, in terms of telling their stories on their terms, hosting talk and news shows, and appearing as multidimen-

> **What happens when a significant group in our society consistently perceives that no one in the larger world hears its stories, no one knows its heroes, no one paints its pictures, no one sings its songs?**

sional characters. With the notable exception of Jimmy Smits's role in *NYPD Blue,* Hispanics are almost invisible.

There is no precise way to measure the impact of misrepresentation and nonrepresentation on the Hispanic community. But Espinosa believes it is profound:

We don't really know what happens when a significant group in our society consistently perceives that no one in the larger world hears its stories, no one knows its heroes, no one paints its pictures, no one sings its songs. But surely the damage to the human soul wounds us all. (p. B8)

Although proving cause and effect is impossible, Espinosa asks whether it is a coincidence that high school dropout rates for Hispanics are higher than those for other minorities? As our culture's dominant symbol system, TV is as "real" to most Americans as their personal, everyday experiences. Why should Hispanic teenagers pursue learning and careers when the symbolic world of television tells them that they do not exist, except at the bottom of society? Espinosa argues that educators have a responsibility to teach all students, of all races and ethnic groups, to think critically about the images that are constructed and presented on television, to understand the politics and economics of the TV industry, and to learn how to bring about change.

discrimination was a "major" problem for black men; fewer that four in ten whites agreed (Gallup, 1995, in Golay and Rollyson, 1996). In a 1997 Gallup poll, a majority of blacks said they thought race relations were generally getting worse. Blacks were still more likely than whites to say that African Americans are treated unfairly at work and in stores, but a majority of blacks said they themselves were treated fairly, except by police (see Figure 9-7). Three out of four blacks said that their relations with whites were generally good and that they had a close white friend. Moreover, very few had experienced discrimination personally in the previous month.

What explains the gap between general impressions and personal experiences? Sociologist Orlando Patterson (1997) holds that the answer is the media. In reporting the 1997 Gallup poll, for example, the press emphasized the one negative finding (race relations are getting worse), ignoring the positive findings. Television news and tabloids focus on urban crime and racial incidents. Hence the general impression that race relations are getting worse comes from the media itself. Patterson suggests that "pessimism results from a strange collision of interests" (p. WK15). White liberals tend to accept the stereotype that African Americans are a victimized group and that any problem blacks encounter stems from racism. (In fact, in the 1997 Gallup poll poor blacks said that money, not racism, was their biggest problem.) Likewise, black political leaders have a vested interest in racial pessimism. Like white liberals, their legitimacy depends on defending entitlement programs. Leaders and scholars on

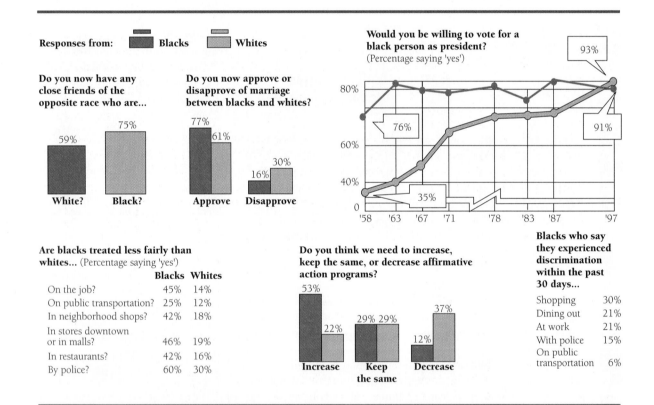

Figure 9-7 *Race Relations in the United States Today*

Media headlines tend to emphasize negative racial relation incidents. However, there are many positive strides in racial relations to be found when data are closely examined. This poll, for example, found that three-quarters of blacks and two-thirds of whites have a close friend of the opposite race; about the same percentage approve of interracial marriage; and the great majority of black respondents had not experienced discrimination themselves in the previous month.

Source: USA Today, June 11, 1997, p. 9a.

the political right use the crisis in race relations to illustrate the failure of liberal programs. Patterson does not argue that racism has disappeared. To the contrary, his own research indicates that about one in five white Americans opposes full racial assimilation. Rather, he argues that ignoring progress (for example, in the proportion of whites who would vote for a black presidential candidate) diverts attention from the bigger problems (chronic poverty and growing inequality) and plays into the hands of racial separatists on the right and the left.

Institutionalized Racism

A third explanation of racial inequality involves social institutions. *Institutionalized racism* refers to established social patterns that have the unintended consequence of limiting the opportunities of certain racial groups. Inequality is built into customs and practices that, on the surface, have nothing to do with racial discrimination. Inequality persists not because white Americans deliberately discriminate against minorities but because they go about business as usual. Thus a person who commits a racist act may not be prejudiced personally and may not even know that the consequences of the act will be discriminatory.

For example, banks are in business to make a profit, and they have a legal obligation to protect investors' money. In deciding whether to grant a home mortgage or a small-business loan, banks rely on statistical predictors. Many banks use zip codes to "redline" (mark off) neighborhoods that their statistics indicate are high risks. The statistics are "color-blind," but the consequences are not. Because minorities are more likely than white residents to have low incomes, the redlined districts are often predominantly nonwhite. This, in turn, makes it more difficult for members of minorities to own their own homes or start their own businesses or for others to provide goods and services to minority communities.

Cuts in the federal budget provide another example. One way to reduce government spending is to reduce the number of government employees. Because African Americans were discriminated against in the private sector in the past and the government made a point of hiring minority members, they are now overrepresented in federal bureaucracies. As a result, more African Americans than

white Americans are hurt by federal cutbacks. Seniority and the principle of "last hired, first fired" were not designed to exclude blacks. But because of past discrimination, black workers often have less seniority than their white counterparts. In all these examples, behavior that has widespread social approval and no intent to discriminate has the unintended consequence of perpetuating racial inequality. Once established, then, patterns of racial inequality tend to take on a life of their own.

Race or Class?

Another explanation of racial inequality emphasizes discrimination based on social class and the cumulative effects of poverty, not race itself. Almost two decades ago, in a controversial book entitled *The Declining Significance of Race* (1980), sociologist William J. Wilson argued:

> Race relations in America have undergone fundamental changes in recent years, so much so that now the life chances of individual blacks have more to do with their economic class position than with their day-to-day encounters with whites. (p. 1)

Wilson reasoned that laws banning racial discrimination and affirmative action programs had lowered the barriers to social mobility for African Americans. In the 1970s, blacks with higher education had made significant progress in income and occupation vis à vis whites. This suggested that race was not the only or primary cause of continuing inequality. Rather, the income gap between blacks and whites was primarily the result of prior discrimination, which had limited opportunities for older blacks.

In a second book, *The Truly Disadvantaged* (1987), Wilson focused on the extreme poverty in black ghettos, which he attributed primarily to structural changes in urban economies or institutionalized racism. To review: The transformation of cities from industrial to information-processing centers, the movement of entry-level factory, clerical, and sales jobs to the suburbs, and cutbacks in government jobs stranded African Americans who lacked the educational credentials for jobs in the information sector and could not afford to move or commute to the suburbs. The result, according to Wilson (1991b, 1993), was a new kind of poverty—and new prejudices. For many

Americans, "minorities [had come to] symbolize the ugly urban city left behind" (Wilson, 1993, p. 1). While acknowledging that prejudice played a role in racial inequality, Wilson maintained that poverty (or class) is as much a *cause* as a consequence of prejudice.

In a more recent work, Wilson (1996) addressed the growing reluctance of employers to hire inner-city blacks. In today's economy, employers are looking for both "hard skills" (literacy, numeracy, mechanical skills, and other testable attributes) and "soft skills" (good attitudes, good grooming, skill dealing with the public and getting along with coworkers). When there is high unemployment, they can afford to raise requirements for education and previous experience, both of which are in short supply among poor inner-city youth. Hired only for menial jobs, workers often become resentful and sometimes "just walk off the job." This confirms employers' suspicions that inner-city workers in general are unreliable, and it makes them less likely to consider other ghetto residents who apply for jobs. Wilson agrees that racism created and to some degree maintains today's ghettos, but he believes that the solution lies in employing unskilled workers of all races, for example, to repair the aging infrastructure of major cities (transportation and communication systems, water and power lines, and public institutions such as schools and post offices). If minorities were given jobs, he argues, racism would become a minor issue.

Many sociologists disagree—some, strongly. Citing Wilson's own description of employer prejudices, Donald Massey (1996) argues that the proposal of "color-blind" poverty programs is naive at best. Once a program is perceived to benefit high proportions of African Americans, it is likely to be attacked. Massey points out that opponents of welfare succeeded in mobilizing support by constantly invoking the stereotype of the "welfare queen"—an unwed *black* mother who had children in order to increase her welfare check. In his view, racism, not opposition to poverty programs, swayed public opinion. At the opposite end of the socioeconomic spectrum, studies of middle-class blacks who entered previously segregated occupations and corporations in the 1970s suggest that their "success story" may have been exaggerated (Benjamin, 1991). Black executives hired by major corporations tend to be viewed as "tokens" by colleagues, must outperform their white counterparts to receive

recognition (though their mistakes are immediately recognized), and often are assigned positions with few opportunities for advancement. Indeed, many were hired for new positions dealing with "minority issues" (community, personnel, and public relations)—jobs that are important to a corporation but are not related to profits or expansion and do not prepare an executive to become a CEO. A study of black and white wages that controlled for education, previous experience, years with current employer, and other factors found that racial differences in wages and promotions increased significantly in the 1980s, a decade during which the government cut back on enforcement of antidiscrimination laws (Cancio, Evans, and Maume, 1996). This suggests that hiring African Americans may have been based more on corporate self-protection than on commitment to equal opportunity.

In short, prejudice, discrimination, and institutionalized racism—including recent changes in the economy and social class distinctions—all play a role in racial inequality.

Fighting Racial Inequality

Of all minority groups in this country, only African Americans were enslaved by law. African Americans never "accepted" discrimination and exploitation. Whether resistance was expressed subtly, in a sermon with double meaning or in feigned ignorance, or outright in slave revolts or urban riots, it was never far beneath the surface. Yet equal rights remained a distant goal for African Americans until the 1950s.

The Civil Rights Movement

The turning point came in 1954. In *Brown v. Board of Education,* the Supreme Court rejected the separate-but-equal doctrine that had provided the legal foundation for racial segregation, declaring that segregated schools were "inherently unequal." By implication, all forms of segregation were unconstitutional. The *Brown* decision raised hopes in the black community and provoked defiance among southern whites (A. D. Morris, 1984). Southern governors declared that they, personally, would prevent black children from attending white public schools. Southern prosecutors moved to outlaw the National Association for the Advancement of Colored People

(NAACP), which had taken the case to the Supreme Court. "White Citizen Councils" and other racist groups stepped up violence against black people. But neither Republican President Eisenhower nor the Democratic Congress wanted to intervene. This combination of rising expectations among black citizens, white lawlessness, and government inaction set the stage for a mass movement.

On December 1, 1955, Rosa Parks, an African American seamstress and former state secretary of the Alabama NAACP, was arrested in Montgomery, Alabama, for refusing to give her seat on a public bus to a white man. Under Jim Crow laws, seats in the front of the bus were reserved for white riders, and seats in the back, for black people. If the seats in the white section were filled, black riders were expected to give theirs to white passengers. Segregated buses were visible, daily reminders of racial inequality.

News of Rosa Parks's arrest spread rapidly (A. D. Morris, 1984). Within a week, local African American leaders founded the Montgomery Improvement Association; elected a young minister, the Reverend Martin Luther King, Jr., as its president; and mobilized virtually the entire black community for a one-day boycott of city buses. The boycott lasted a year, attracted national attention and support, and became the model for the movement as a whole.

As the head of the Southern Christian Leadership Conference (SCLC), King led the movement on to Selma and then to Birmingham, Alabama.

The SCLC advocated nonviolent resistance. Demonstrators would deliberately violate a Jim Crow law (for example, by lining up to drink from a "whites-only" water fountain) and then go limp when the police attacked them. The goals of nonviolent resistance are to create civil disorder, to demoralize the police, and to create sympathy by making the police look brutal in the public eye. In 1959, SCLC was joined by black college students, who began holding sit-ins at segregated lunch counters, led by the Student Nonviolent Coordinating Committee (SNCC). The Congress of Racial Equality (CORE) sent busloads of "freedom riders" from the north to organize demonstrations in Alabama and other southern states.

From the beginning, the civil rights movement encountered organized, official, often violent resistance. Four black churches in Montgomery were firebombed. The governor of Arkansas used the national guard to prevent nine black students from entering Little Rock's Central High School. President Eisenhower sent the 101st Airborne to Little Rock to guarantee the enrollment of the nine children at that school. In Birmingham, Sheriff "Bull" Connor ordered police to use clubs, high-pressure fire hoses, electric cattle prods, and police dogs on nonviolent protesters.

Newsreels and still photographs of police attacking unresisting men, women, and children awakened the conscience of America. In 1963, 250,000 black and white Americans marched on Washington, D.C.,

An indelible image of official resistance to desegregation and the civil rights movement was the sight of police dogs being used to disperse peaceful demonstrators.

where they heard Dr. King deliver his famous "I have a dream" speech. A year later Congress passed the Civil Rights Act, outlawing discrimination.

The civil rights movement was a true grassroots movement. To explain this, sociologist Aldon Morris (1984) contrasts the structure of the movement to that of the NAACP. The NAACP was (and is) a formal, national organization with headquarters in New York City. The civil rights movement was not a single, homogeneous organization but was composed of dozens of local protest groups with their own structures, leaders, and strategies. In order to present a united front, the NAACP adopted bureaucratic procedures: all decisions had to be cleared at the top. In contrast, decision making among the grassroots protest groups was more ad hoc, the result of face-to-face discussions among local ministers, community leaders, and laypeople. As a result, the protest groups were more flexible and innovative and could respond quickly to the situation at hand. While most African Americans supported the NAACP, its active members were predominantly educated and middle-class. Protest groups used familiar spirituals, prayers, and sermonlike speeches to attract the entire spectrum of black southerners. Meetings were emotionally charged, and everyone was involved. The NAACP was committed to working within the system, slowly chipping away at the legal foundations of segregation. Protest groups actively confronted the system, employing such peaceful, yet disruptive, tactics as economic boycotts, marches, sit-ins, and mass submission to arrest. Their goal was broadly (rather than narrowly) defined and immediate (rather than slow and incremental): "Freedom Now."

This does not mean that the civil rights movement was completely spontaneous and unstructured. Rather, in Morris's words, the movement succeeded in "organizing the organized" (1984, p. 42). Black churches played a key role (Findlay, 1993). As the one black institution that the southern white community permitted, the church provided the black community with leaders who were independent of white society, a meeting place, and experience in forming committees, raising funds, and other collective activities. "The church was a place to observe, participate in, and experience the reality of owning and directing an institution free from the control of whites" (A. D. Morris, 1984, p. 5). Contacts among black clergy allowed news to travel

quickly, giving the movement a rapid and independent communications network. Finally, through its traditions of music, oratory, and charismatic leadership, the church maintained a shared symbolic world, a means of expressing black hopes and containing black fears.

In Morris's view, the church was pivotal. Indeed, the civil rights movement might be described as the transformation of an already existing cultural institution (the church) into a political instrument.

The impact of the civil rights movement was not confined to the black community. Never before in U.S. history had large masses used nonviolent confrontation to upset the political status quo (A. D. Morris, 1984). The movement demonstrated to other minority groups that nontraditional political strategies could bring about rapid and dramatic social change. It provided the inspiration, tactical models, and training ground for the student movement of the next decade, the modern women's movement, the migrant farmworkers' movement led by Cesar Chavez, the pan-Indian movement, the gay rights movement, and mobilization of the disabled. American politics would never be quite the same again.

Minority Rights and Affirmative Action

The civil rights legislation of the early 1960s brought an end to legally sanctioned segregation and discrimination but not to racial inequality and separation. While many whites thought of race as a "southern problem," anger and frustration were building in inner-city ghettos in the northeast, midwest, and far west. In 1965, a riot erupted in the Watts section of Los Angeles, leaving thirty-four dead. Riots broke out across the nation in the summers of 1966 and 1967, and again in 1968, following the assassination of Dr. Martin Luther King, Jr. (National Advisory Commission on Civil Disorders, 1968) (see Chapter 17). Partly in response to these riots and partly in response to peaceful pressure, the federal government decided that ending segregation was not enough; the government would have to play an active role in promoting integration.

Affirmative action refers to programs designed to open educational and job opportunities to minorities (Golay and Rollyson, 1996). Affirmative action programs have ranged from voluntary outreach programs and special on-the-job training or in-school tutorial programs to mandatory preferential treatment and numerical quotas for women and minorities and "set-aside" programs in which a certain percentage of government contracts are awarded to firms owned by minorities. For example, most colleges and universities use a combination of grade point average and test scores to establish a threshold for admissions; applications by students who do not meet this standard are automatically rejected. Under affirmative action, this standard was adjusted for minority applicants to reduce the impact of the test gap (described above).

From the beginning, the concept of affirmative action was controversial (A. Hacker, 1992). Supporters maintained that African Americans and other minorities deserved compensation for policies that excluded them from educational and employment opportunities in the past; that unless organizations were rewarded for admitting minority members or penalized for excluding them, they were unlikely to change; and that affirmative action would benefit society as a whole, by reducing alienation among minorities and by creating situations in which members of different ethnic and racial groups get to know one another. "Affirmative action" toward members of one's own group, they argued, is an established tradition: employers have always given preferential treatment to job applicants who come with personal recommendations; likewise, colleges and universities have always made special allowances for children of alumni. Because of past discrimination, members of minority groups are less likely to know people who can help them.

Critics of affirmative action held that opportunities for higher education and jobs should be awarded solely on the basis of individual merit. In their view, affirmative action amounts to "reverse discrimination" against the white (male) majority. Critics maintained that far from improving race relations, affirmative action tends to stigmatize minority individuals who acquired a position through their own talents and efforts; harm individuals who are not fully prepared for competitive colleges and jobs; and reinforce negative stereotypes regarding minorities (Jencks, 1992).

When Californians voted to ban preferential admissions for minorities to state colleges and universities, followed by a similar decision in Texas, many observers believed a backlash against affirmative action was beginning. (See Chapter 12 for a discussion of the impact of those decisions.) However, a recent poll conducted by *The New York Times* and CBS (1997) suggests mixed feelings rather than rejection. The poll found widespread support for the goals of affirmative action but disagreement about the means. The majority of whites and blacks agreed that diversity in the nation's universities and workforce is important; supported special educational and job training programs to help minorities compete; and said that laws to protect minorities from discrimination were still necessary. A majority also favored preferential treatment in college admissions and hiring for people from *poor* families as opposed to middle-class and rich families. But a majority of whites did not think that blacks should be given preference in hiring and promotions to make up for past discrimination or that affirmative action was necessary to achieve diversity; a majority of blacks disagreed. When asked if affirmative action should be continued or abolished, 52 percent of whites said "abolished." When given a choice between ending affirmative action now, phasing it out over the next several years, or continuing it for the foreseeable future, only 13 percent of whites (and 1 percent of blacks) chose ending it now. (See Figure 9-8.)

Racial and Ethnic Inequality in the United States Today

Given the changing attitudes and opportunities, where do minority groups stand in the United States today? To what extent is our society stratified by race and ethnicity? (See Figure 9-9 for an overview.)

African Americans

In the 1980s, the National Research Council (1989) conducted the first comprehensive survey of the position of blacks in American society since Swedish social scientist Gunnar Myrdal's classic work, *An American Dilemma* (1944). The survey followed black Americans from the eve of World War II to the mid-1980s. The researchers concluded that by almost every measure—education, income, health, political participation—African Americans are far better off than they were fifty years ago. Yet,

Figure 9-8 *Attitudes toward Affirmative Action, 1997*

Although a majority of blacks favored keeping all current affirmative action programs while a majority of whites opposed it, neither favored an immediate ban on all programs.

Source: The New York Times/CBS Poll, 1997, in *The New York Times*, Nov. 14, 1997, p. A1.

QUESTION: What is the best thing to do with affirmative action programs giving preference to some minorities?*

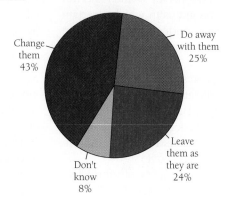

Change them 43%

Do away with them 25%

Leave them as they are 24%

Don't know 8%

*Based on nationwide telephone interviews with 1,258 adults, including 173 black respondents, conducted Dec. 6-9, 1996. The margin of sampling error is plus or minus 3 percentage points.

by the same measures, blacks are still far behind their white counterparts:

> The status of black Americans today can be characterized as a glass that is half full—if measured by progress since 1939—or as a glass that is half empty—if measured by the persisting disparities between black and white Americans. (National Research Council, 1989, p. 4)

African Americans have made significant gains in politics. Black voters have become the swing vote in many elections and a political force in their own right locally. The number of blacks elected to political office nationwide grew from 1,500 in 1970 to 7,500 in the early 1990s (Joint Center for Political and Economic Studies, 1992). In 1996, thirty-eight African Americans were elected to Congress, including the first black woman senator, Carol Mosley Braun (Democrat-Illinois), for a second term. Even so, the proportion of black elected officials (2 percent) is well below the proportion of black people in the population (12 percent) (Joint Center for Political and Economic Studies, 1992).

The economic picture for African Americans continues to be mixed (Marger, 1994). During the 1950s and 1960s, a period of growth and prosperity for America as a whole, the economic status of African Americans as a group improved substan-

tially. Largely as a result of moving from the rural south to northern industrial cities, many African Americans were able to climb out of poverty. Male farmhands became construction and factory workers, while female domestics went to work in factories, shops, and offices. During the 1960s, a significant number were able to translate civil rights into higher education and economic gain; the percentage of middle-class African Americans doubled, from about one in eight to one in four workers (Landry, 1987). But the 1970s was a decade of retrenchment; upward mobility stalled. In the 1980s, the economic gap between whites and blacks widened. In addition, economic divisions within the black population increased. Some African Americans have found a place in the working and middle classes, but others, primarily the ghetto poor, have fallen further behind.

In some ways, the educational gap between the black and the white communities has narrowed. In terms of the median years of school completed, both groups are almost equal. But equal quantity of education does not necessarily mean equal quality of education. In largely segregated, inner-city schools more than half the students score below the national average on achievement tests. Moreover the percentage of African Americans who graduate from college or obtain advanced degrees—prerequisites for most

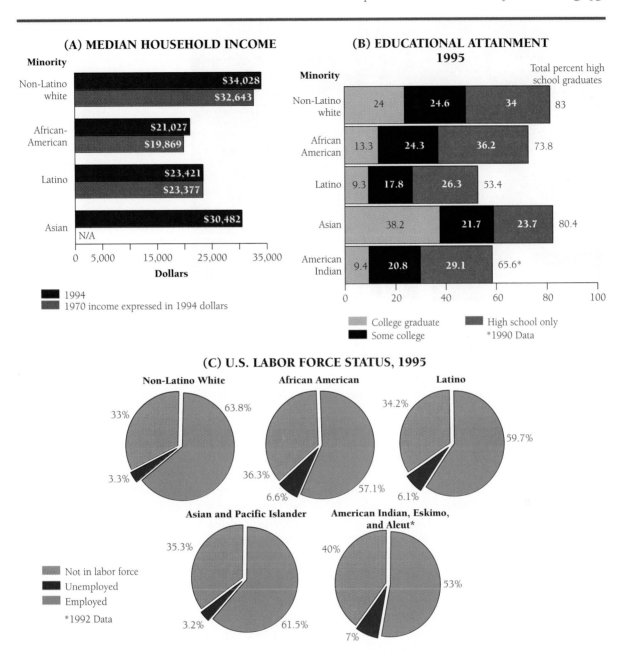

(A) MEDIAN HOUSEHOLD INCOME

Minority

Non-Latino white: $34,028 (1994); $32,643 (1970)

African-American: $21,027 (1994); $19,869 (1970)

Latino: $23,421 (1994); $23,377 (1970)

Asian: $30,482 (1994); N/A (1970)

Dollars: 0, 5,000, 15,000, 25,000, 35,000

■ 1994
■ 1970 income expressed in 1994 dollars

(B) EDUCATIONAL ATTAINMENT 1995

Minority — Total percent high school graduates

Non-Latino white: 24 | 24.6 | 34 — 83

African American: 13.3 | 24.3 | 36.2 — 73.8

Latino: 9.3 | 17.8 | 26.3 — 53.4

Asian: 38.2 | 21.7 | 23.7 — 80.4

American Indian: 9.4 | 20.8 | 29.1 — 65.6*

0, 20, 40, 60, 80, 100

■ College graduate   ■ High school only
■ Some college   *1990 Data

(C) U.S. LABOR FORCE STATUS, 1995

Non-Latino White: 63.8%, 3.3%, 33%

African American: 57.1%, 6.6%, 36.3%

Latino: 59.7%, 6.1%, 34.2%

Asian and Pacific Islander: 61.5%, 3.2%, 35.3%

American Indian, Eskimo, and Aleut*: 53%, 7%, 40%

■ Not in labor force
■ Unemployed
■ Employed
*1992 Data

Note: The labor force includes individuals age 16 and over who were working in the week preceding the survey plus those who were actively seeking a job (the unemployed).

Figure 9-9   *Racial and Ethnic Inequality in the United States Today*

In recent decades, African Americans have made significant gains in politics. In 1992, thirty-eight African Americans were elected to Congress, including Senator Carol Mosley Braun.

high-income, high-prestige jobs—leveled off and even declined somewhat in the 1980s and early 1990s (Marger, 1994).

African Americans are still the most residentially segregated group in our society, but there are signs of small steps toward change (Farley, 1997; Farley and Frey, 1994). Social scientists measure degrees of segregation with an *index of dissimilarity*: if all whites live on exclusively white blocks and all blacks on exclusively black blocks, the index would be 100; if race made no difference in where people lived, the index would be zero. Studies of 232 metropolitan areas with substantial black populations found that between 1980 and 1990, the average black-white index fell from 68 to 64. In 1980, thirteen metropolitan areas had indexes above 85; in 1990, only four were that extremely segregated. The number of locations that could be considered moderately integrated (a score less that 55) more than doubled. (See Table 9-1.) Eight of the ten most segregated places were older midwestern industrial centers; the least segregated places were those with military bases and university towns. Decreases in residential segregation were most common and most extensive in the south and west, where new construction rates are much higher than in the north and midwest.

Several trends explain the decline in segregation in the 1980s, and suggest that the 2000 census may find more blacks and whites living in the same neighborhoods (Farley, 1997; Farley and Frey,

1994). First, white attitudes have changed. In the 1940s, four out of five whites favored racial segregation; in the 1990s, fewer than one in five did. Second, the Fair Housing Act has been reinforced by a number of Supreme Court rulings, which strengthened enforcement, especially for developers who use government-backed loans. Third, whereas old neighborhoods and suburbs often have histories of segregation and reputations for discrimination, new developments usually start out as "open housing" with no or few established biases. Fourth, the proportion of black families who can afford better housing and have the upper- and middle-class social characteristics (in terms of education, occupation, and lifestyle) doubled between 1970 and 1990. Finally, the 1990 census suggested that more African Americans are leaving highly segregated areas in the northeast and midwest for more integrated locations in the south and west.

Despite progress, neighborhood segregation is still the rule in most older cities with long-established ethnic and African American communities, including Chicago, Detroit, Cleveland, Philadelphia, St. Louis, and New York. Rates of segregation remain substantially higher for blacks than for Latinos (average index score 42.7 in 1990) or for Asians (43 in 1990) (Farley and Frey, 1994). Apparently some whites are still uncomfortable—and leave—when large numbers of blacks move into "their" neighborhoods (and rarely move into predominantly black neighborhoods) but are less

Table 9-1   *The 10 Most Segregated and Least Segregated Metropolitan Areas: Blacks and Whites, 1980 and 1990*

1980		1990	
Metropolitan Area	Index of Dissimilarity	Metropolitan Area	Index of Dissimilarity
Most Segregated			
Bradenton, FL	91	Gary, IN	91
Chicago, IL	91	Detroit, MI	89
Gary, IN	90	Chicago, IL	87
Sarasota, FL	90	Cleveland, OH	86
Cleveland, OH	89	Buffalo, NY	84
Detroit, MI	89	Flint, MI	84
Ft. Myers, FL	89	Milwaukee, WI	84
Flint, MI	87	Saginaw, MI	84
Ft. Pierce, FL	87	Newark, NJ	83
West Palm Beach, FL	87	Philadelphia, PA	82
Least Segregated			
Jacksonville, NC	36	Jacksonville, NC	31
Lawrence, KS	38	Lawton, OK	37
Danville, VA	41	Anchorage, AL	38
Anchorage, AL	42	Fayetteville, NC	41
Lawton, OK	43	Lawrence, KS	41
Fayetteville, NC	43	Clarksville, TN	42
Honolulu, HI	46	Ft. Walton Beach, FL	43
Anaheim, CA	47	Cheyenne, WY	43
San José, CA	48	Anaheim, CA	43
Colorado Springs, CO	48	Honolulu, HI	44

Note: These indexes were calculated from block-group (contiguous blocks averaging 564 residents) data for persons reporting white or black as their race on the 1980 and 1990 census forms.

Source: R. Farley, "Modest Declines in U.S. Residential Segregation Observed," *Population Today* 25, 1997, p. 2.

uncomfortable with Latino or Asian neighbors. As we have emphasized, poor blacks who cannot afford to buy or rent new, more open housing or to move to a different state are the most likely to live in highly segregated neighborhoods.

Latinos

Latinos are the second-largest minority group in the United States and will outnumber African Americans early in the twenty-first century, in part because of immigration, and in part because many Latinos are in their childbearing years and tend to have larger families than non-Hispanics. People of Spanish heritage have lived in what is now the United States since the sixteenth century, but nearly two-thirds of those who identify themselves as Latino or Hispanic today are immigrants or the children of immigrants (del Pinal and Singer,

1997). A diverse population, they come from varied national backgrounds and social classes and have followed different immigration and settlement patterns. Latinos may have European, Amerindian, or African ancestors or—perhaps most often—some combination thereof. Latinos have been described as the "in-between" minority, whose ethnic status lies between European Americans and African Americans (Marger, 1994).

In socioeconomic terms, Latinos are among the most disadvantaged groups in our society (del Pinal and Singer, 1997). Many Latino families are solidly middle-class: one in five has a household income of $50,000 or more, about the same percentage as for African Americans. But more than one-quarter (28 percent) have incomes below the poverty level. Latinos have the lowest rates of high school and college graduation of any major population group. On average, Mexican Americans have the lowest education levels and incomes, and Cuban Americans the highest (though below levels for non-Hispanic whites). Why do Latinos have such low incomes and high poverty levels? Many are recent immigrants who have few marketable skills, speak little English, and work for entry-level salaries at low-level jobs. Many face discrimination in the workplace, particularly if they are dark-skinned and have strong accents. In school, Latino youth face numerous barriers, including limited proficiency in English, low expectations on the part of teachers, and overcrowded and poorly funded schools. Although Latinos make up 11 percent of the population, in 1997 only 1 percent of all elected officials and 17 members of Congress were Latino.

The Latino population includes three main ethnic groups (as well as many smaller ones, including many recent immigrants from Central and South America) (see Figure 9-10 and Map 9-5). The largest group, Mexican Americans, are concentrated in the southwest. Some trace their ancestry to colonial days, while others are recent immigrants. Up through the 1960s, a majority worked as agricultural laborers. Viewed as "peasants" and "foreigners" by the Anglo majority, little effort was made to assimilate Mexican Americans. In the 1970s and 1980s,

Mexican Americans began moving into cities, where eight out of ten reside today. But the pattern of low levels of education and low-wage employment, especially among recent immigrants, has continued.

The second-largest group is Puerto Ricans, most of whom live in New York City. Puerto Ricans were declared American citizens in 1917, but the first large wave of immigrants did not arrive until the 1950s, when airlines introduced relatively inexpensive flights between the island and the mainland. By 1970 there were half as many Puerto Ricans on the mainland as in Puerto Rico, but migration back and forth is common (Fitzpatrick, 1987). Due to low levels of education, poor English, recent entry into the labor force, and discrimination, especially against those who are

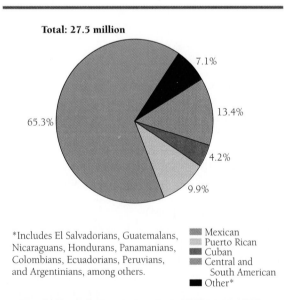

Total: 27.5 million

65.3%

7.1%

13.4%

4.2%

9.9%

*Includes El Salvadorians, Guatemalans, Nicaraguans, Hondurans, Panamanians, Colombians, Ecuadorians, Peruvians, and Argentinians, among others.

■ Mexican
▦ Puerto Rican
■ Cuban
▦ Central and South American
■ Other*

Figure 9-10 *Latino Americans*

Although a majority of Latino immigrants are from Mexico, immigration from countries in Central and South America is increasing.

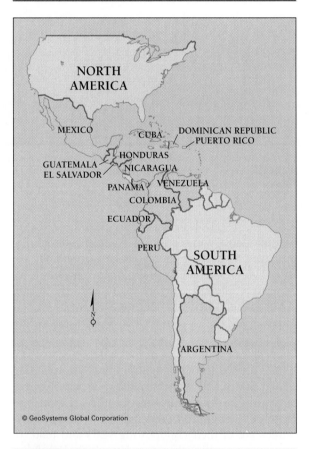

Map 9-5 *Countries of Origin of Hispanic Immigrants, 1980s and 1990s*

Source: J. del Pinal and A. Singer, "Generations of Diversity: Latinos in the United States," *Population Bulletin* 52 (3), October 1997, p. 10, fig. 8.

Eight out of ten Mexican Americans live in cities, particularly in the southwest. El Paso, Texas, is shown here.

dark-skinned, Puerto Ricans are among the poorest Latinos (del Pinal and Singer, 1997).

Another prominent group of Latinos in the United States is Cuban Americans, who began arriving in 1959, the year Fidel Castro seized control of the Cuban government. The first large group of refugees to move to the United States en masse, Cuban Americans have also been one of the most successful non-English-speaking immigrant groups.

Cuban Americans differ from Mexican Americans and Puerto Ricans in a number of ways. Many of the early Cuban refugees were educated urban business owners and professionals. They arrived not as poor individuals but as a relatively well-off group with established social networks. As political refugees, they had access to government programs not available to other immigrants. A majority settled in Miami, where they established an economic enclave with businesses run by and catering to Cubans (Portes and Bach, 1985; Feagin and Feagin, 1996). As a result they did not have to learn a new language and new ways of doing business or to accept entry-level jobs in the mainstream economy. Subsequent waves of Cuban (and other Latino) immigrants supplied both the labor and the consumers to maintain and expand this enclave.

Second- and third-generation Latinos tend to be "bicultural" as well as bilingual: although Americanized in some ways, they have maintained their language, religion (Roman Catholicism), family traditions, and contacts with their homelands over the generations.

Native Americans: American Indians, Aleuts, and Eskimos

The category "Native American," like that of "Latino," includes people with different histories and cultures (see Figure 9-11 and Map 9-6). The

Total: 2 million

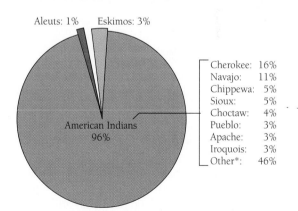

*Includes 100 major tribes, and 500 with populations of 1,000 or less.

Figure 9-11   *Native Americans*

The concept of a Native American or American Indian ethnic group was a white construct. But although tribal identities remain strong, many Native Americans see advantages in "Pan-Indianism."

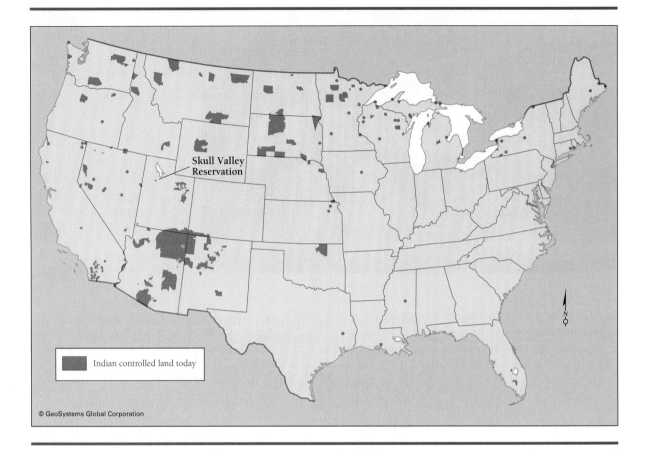

Skull Valley
Reservation

Indian controlled land today

© GeoSystems Global Corporation

Map 9-6   *Indian Country Today*

Two centuries ago, Indians controlled three-quarters of the United States' eventual landmass. That has shrunk to just 2 percent, on 314 scattered reservations.

Source: The New York Times, Mar. 8, 1998, p. A24.

1990 census counted nearly 2 million Native Americans. Eskimos and Aleuts are concentrated in Alaska and the Pacific Coast states. American Indians—comprising 554 nations that control more than 300 reservations, a total of 56 million acres—live primarily in the west, a legacy of the relocation policies of the nineteenth century. About 1.4 million live on or near tribal land, while an additional 500,000 live primarily in urban areas (Egan, 1998).

American Indians have long been the poorest of America's poor. In 1995, unemployment was more than 30 percent, and nearly one-third of those who had jobs earned less than $10,000 a year (Egan, 1998). Many rural American Indians live in severe poverty, with no indoor plumbing, running water, or access to modern transportation. American Indi-

ans have unusually high rates of accidents, alcoholism and liver disease, homicide, suicide, diabetes, influenza, and tuberculosis (U.S. Department of Health and Human Services, 1991). Life expectancy for American Indians is ten years shorter than the average, the shortest of any group in our society (Yetman, 1992).

Conditions are changing, however. Indian nations occupy a unique status, as "domestic, dependent nations," which means in part that they are subject to federal but not to state law. This was the basis for Congress's passing the 1988 Indian Gaming Act, which allows tribes to offer games of chance for a profit—sometimes referred to as the "new buffalo" (replacing the great herds on which Plains Indians depended for their living). One-third

American Indians remain among the poorest groups in the United States. However some tribes have benefited from the 1988 Indian Gaming Act, which allowed casinos on reservation lands. In January 1998, the Foxwood Casino's net revenues from slot machines alone were $52 million.

of tribes now operate some gambling enterprise. Although spread unevenly, combined profits are estimated at more than $6 billion a year. Some tribes have generated full employment, built housing and schools, created a scholarship fund for all Indians, and invested in businesses outside reservations. They have also begun to exercise political muscle, with $2 million in campaign contributions, mostly to Democrats, in the 1996 elections. But development on reservations may be producing a backlash: in several cases, neighboring, non-Indian communities feel that the "new buffalo" is trampling on states rights (Egan, 1998).

Asian Americans and Pacific Islanders

Although a small proportion of the total U.S. population, Asians and Pacific Islanders are the fastest-growing racial and ethnic group in the United States. Their numbers increased by 123 percent between 1980 and 1990, reaching 9.9 million in 1996 (U. S. Bureau of the Census, 1997). Almost all this increase has been due to immigrants and refugees (see Chapter 3).

This category is extremely diverse, including peoples whose origins lie in the Far East, Southeast Asia, the Indian subcontinent, or the Pacific Islands. This vast territory embraces people from dozens of different cultures with religious affiliations ranging from Buddhist to Zoroastrian. (See Figure 9-12 and Map 9-7.)

The Asian experience in the United States can be divided into two distinct chapters (Marger, 1994). The early Asian immigrants (first Chinese, then Japanese) came between the mid-nineteenth century and the early twentieth century. Nearly all were unskilled laborers, recruited to work in construction or agriculture. From the beginning, these immigrants were subjected to intense discrimination, culminating in the Oriental Exclusion Act of 1924. Chinese workers retreated to ethnic enclaves, or "Chinatowns," where many lived until recently. Working as small farmers, Japanese Americans carved a niche for themselves in the California economy. After the outbreak of World War II, however, nearly 12,000 were forced to abandon their homes and businesses and were sent to internment camps for the duration of the war. The incarceration of people of Japanese ancestry was clearly racially motivated. Most of the detainees were American citizens, born in the United States. But unlike German and Italian Americans, Japanese Americans were declared an "enemy race." Not until 1987 did the U.S. government issue an official apology and offer compensation to the survivors.

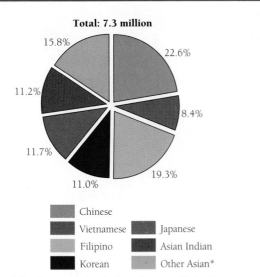

Total: 7.3 million

15.8%
22.6%
11.2%
8.4%
11.7%
19.3%
11.0%

Chinese
Vietnamese   Japanese
Filipino   Asian Indian
Korean   Other Asian*

* Includes Hawaiians, Cambodians, Laotians, Thais, Hmongs, Pakistanis, Samoans, Guamanians, and Indonesians, among others.

Figure 9-12   *Asian Americans*

Asian Americans (and Pacific Islanders) are the fastest-growing minority group in the United States, largely because of immigration. Except for Japanese Americans, the majority of Asian Americans are foreign-born.

The second chapter in Asian immigration began after the 1965 Immigration Act, which ended national quotas. The new act gave preferential treatment to family members and people with valuable vocational skills. Since immigration from Asia had been banned for several decades, most new Asian immigrants came as skilled workers who helped fill shortages in such fields as engineering and medicine. Some (notably Koreans) used their skills to open small family businesses. Other Asian immigrants, including many Vietnamese and recent Chinese, came as political refugees. Nearly two-thirds of today's Asian Americans and Pacific Islanders are foreign-born (Hsia and Hirano-Nakanishi, 1989; Bennett, 1992).

Asian Americans and Pacific Islanders rank higher than other minority groups on every measure of socioeconomic status. Asian American adults are as likely as native-born whites to have graduated from high school and far more likely to have graduated from college. They are more likely than any other group to work in professional and white-collar occupations, although they are under-represented in the ranks of corporate management (unless they start their own companies). A high proportion of recent Asian immigrants earned educational credentials and professional status before migrating. This, plus cultural values that emphasize education, hard work, and sacrifice to get ahead and the pooling of family labor and resources, helps explain their success. Median Asian American family income is significantly higher than average. In addition, Asian Americans are more likely than other non-Europeans to move to the suburbs and live in integrated neighborhoods.

In recent years, Asian Americans have been hailed as a "model minority." Former pariahs have become paragons (P. I. Rose, 1985). But this apparent praise is problematic. The stereotype of a model minority conceals the fact that many Asian Americans, especially recent refugees from Southeast Asia, are poor, uneducated, and struggling to survive. It puts extreme pressure on Asian American students, who are expected to outperform their non-Asian peers. It can be used as an excuse to blame other minorities for problems not of their own making. By extension, if Asian Americans are successful despite their racial visibility, why aren't the ____? (Fill in the blank with "African Americans," "Latinos," or "Native Americans.") The notion of a model minority may provoke a backlash of envy and hostility in other groups. Thus, much of the anger during the L.A. riots of 1992 was directed specifically at Korean-American shopkeepers, who were seen as taking business, jobs, and dollars away from the black community (see Chapter 17). Finally, the notion conceals subtle but continuing prejudice against people of Asian ancestry. No matter how successful they are or how assimilated, because of their racial visibility Asian Americans continue to be seen as not quite American, not one of "us" (P. I. Rose, 1985).

"The United States is going through a historic transition from a predominantly white society rooted in western culture to a global society composed of diverse ethnic and racial minorities," says demographer William P. O'Hare (1993b, p. 1). Today's 64 million African Americans, Latinos, Asians, and Native Americans make up one-fourth of the total U.S. population (more than the entire population of Great Britain, France, Italy, or Spain) (O'Hare, 1993a). By the mid-twenty-first century, minorities will constitute almost one-half of the U.S. population (Figure 9-13). Moreover, in recent

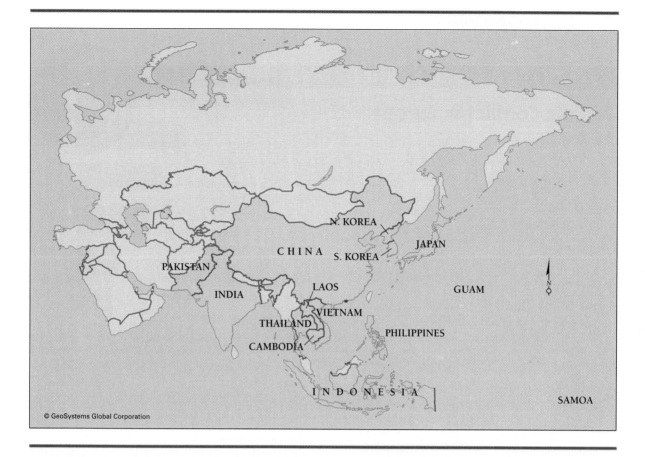

Map 9-7   *Countries of Origin of Asian Immigrants, 1980s and 1990s*

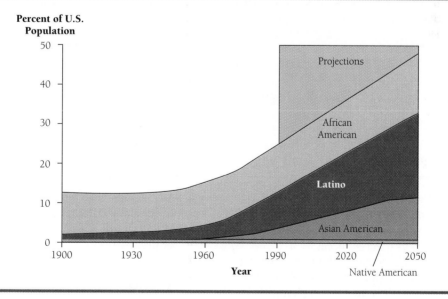

Figure 9-13   *Share of Minorities in the U.S. Population, 1900–2050*

Sources: Jeffrey S. Passel and Barry Edmonston, "Immigration and Race: Recent Trends in Immigration to the United States" (Washington, DC: The Urban Institute, 1992), table 3; and U.S. Bureau of the Census, *Current Population Reports,* P-25, no. 1092 (Washington, DC: GPO, 1992), table 1.

SOCIOLOGY ON THE WEB

Ethnic Conflict in Europe

Ethnic conflict is not just something that happens in heterogeneous societies like the United States or in former colonial areas like Africa. The sites listed below will help you begin to see it as a near-universal occurrence. As you explore them, take note of the number and kinds of ethnic conflicts that exist in Europe and in other parts of the world today. What is the basis for the different conflicts described at these sites? Which are potential, and which actual, conflicts? What kinds of solutions have been proposed for the conflicts? You may be amazed at the sheer number of potential ethnic conflicts in Europe, especially since the collapse of communism has given rise to the reassertion of ethnic rights in many eastern European countries.

The first two sites listed here discuss local and international initiatives aimed at easing specific ethnic conflicts. The last sites provide background information in the form of data, maps, and news reports.

http://www.ecmi.de/
The European Center for Minority Studies (ECMI) is located in Flemsburg, a German city with a large Danish population. The web site offers a unique European perspective on the causes and cures of ethnic conflicts.

http://www.pw1.netcom.com/~ethnic/
The Project on Ethnic Relations at Princeton offers reports on attempts to ease conflict in several European trouble spots. Highlighted are efforts to obtain rights for the Romani (Gypsy) people, an ethnic group that has been subject to discrimination throughout Europe for hundreds of years and that suffers severe social and economic problems.

http://www.incore.ulst.ac.uk/
INCORE, a joint initiative of the United Nations University and the University of Ulster, provides lists of Internet resources on ethnic conflict in many specific countries. You can obtain maps, local news reports, data, and background information on ehtnic conflicts around the world.

http://www.unhcr.ch/
The web site of the United National High Commission on Refugees provides background information, maps, and photos pertaining to specific countries, such as Burundi, that are experiencing ethnic conflict.

decades the number and diversity of immigrants have increased. As a result, the United States has more and more minorities, who look and act less and less alike. Patterns in racial and ethnic relations will play a major role in America's future.

Summary

1. **What are the social definitions of race, ethnicity, and minority group?** A *race* is a category of people who see themselves and are seen by others as different because of characteristics that are assumed to be inherited. An *ethnic group* is a category of people who are distinguished by their ancestry and cultural heritage. Either one becomes a *minority group* when its members are disadvantaged, held in low esteem, involuntarily excluded from valued social positions, and conscious of being a "people apart."

2. **How do patterns of intergroup relations vary across cultures and over time?** Patterns of intergroup relations can be seen as a

continuum, ranging from *amalgamation* (blending) to *assimilation* (absorption of minority groups into the majority's culture and social institutions), *pluralism* (the coexistence of different racial and ethnic groups, whether egalitarian or not), *exploitation* (the majority using minorities for its own benefit), and *ethnic conflict* (from hate crimes to civil war and genocide). The particular pattern of racial and ethnic relations in a society reflects its unique history.

3. **What patterns have racial and ethnic relations taken in the United States?** Each chapter of U.S. history has produced its own patterns of intergroup relations: settlement (which established white Anglo-Saxon or WASP dominance); expansion (in which American Indians and Mexicans were subjugated by force); agricultural development (which rested on the enslavement of African Americans); industrial development (which brought millions more Europeans to this country and attracted many African Americans to the north); and the making of the ghetto (which continues to isolate African Americans).

4. **What explains racial inequality?** There are four main theories as to why racial minorities are disadvantaged. The IQ debate highlights the persistence of, and flaws in, theories of innate differences. The theory of prejudice and discrimination traces inequality to the attitudes and behavior of the white majority. *Prejudice*

(an unfavorable opinion of members of a group) and *discrimination* (unequal treatment of members of a group) do not necessarily go together, however. The theory of *institutionalized racism* holds that inequality is the unintended consequence of established social patterns that on the surface seem to have nothing to do with race. The debate over race versus class centers around the question of whether racism causes inequality or whether inequality promotes racism.

5. **How did the struggle for civil rights begin, and where did it lead?** African Americans led the modern struggle for equal rights for minorities in the United States. The civil rights movement built on existing organizations and networks (especially the black church) and added a new dimension to American politics.

6. **What is the extent of racial and ethnic inequality in the United States today?** African Americans have seen much improvement since the days before the civil rights movement, but they are far from achieving equality with white Americans. Latinos are a diverse group whose present circumstances reflect the conditions under which they arrived in this country. Native Americans (American Indians, Aleuts, and Eskimos) are among the poorest of the poor. Although some Asian Americans and Pacific Islanders have achieved the American dream, their reputation as a "model minority" is a mixed blessing.

Key Terms

affirmative action   342

amalgamation   321

assimilation   321

discrimination   336

ethnic group   316

genocide   327

institutionalized racism   339

majority group   319

minority group   317

multiculturalism   322

nativism   329

pluralism   321

prejudice   336

race   316

racism   316

segregation   323

slavery   322

stereotype   336

Recommended Readings

Anderson, Elijah. (1990). *Streetwise: Race, Class, and Change in an Urban Community.* Chicago: University of Chicago Press.

Fischer, Claude S., Hout, Michael, Sanchez, Martin, Lucas, Samual R., Swidler, Ann, & Voss, Kim. (1996). *Inequality by Design: Cracking the Bell Curve Myth.* Princeton, NJ.: Princeton University Press.

Gann, Lewis H., & Duignan, Peter J. (1986). *The Hispanic in the United States: A History.* Boulder CO: Westview.

Glazer, Nathan. (1997). *We Are All Multiculturalists Now.* Cambridge, MA: Harvard University Press.

Hacker, Andrew. (1992). *Two Nations: Black and White, Separate, Hostile, and Unequal.* New York: Scribner.

Herrnstein, Richard J., & Murray, Charles. (1994). *The Bell Curve.* New York: Free Press.

Massey, Douglas S., & Denton, Nancy A. (1993). *American Apartheid: Segregation and the Making of the Underclass.* Cambridge, MA: Harvard University Press.

Morris, A. D. (1984). *The Origins of the Civil Rights Movement: Black Communities and Organizing for Change.* New York: Free Press.

Nagel, Joane. (1996). *American Indian Ethnic Renewal: Red Power and the Resurgence of Identity and Culture.* New York: Oxford University Press.

Rose, Peter I. (1994). *They and We: Racial and Ethnic Relations in the United States,* 5th ed. New York: McGraw-Hill.

Takaki, Ronald. (1993). *A Different Mirror: A History of Multicultural America.* Boston: Little, Brown.

Chapter

Ten

Gender Stratification

In the rural Chinese village of Xiamen, only one girl was born in 1992. All the other babies were boys. What accounts for this "miracle"? Chinese culture assigns a higher value to sons than to daughters. Tradition holds that Chinese sons will carry on the family line and provide for their parents in old age, whereas girls merely become part of their husbands' families. A strong desire for sons collides with China's "one-child-per-family" policy, which is designed to slow population growth. Doctors can identify the sex of an unborn child with ultrasound, which creates a video image of a fetus. For a bribe of $35 to $50, many doctors will tell a woman whether she is pregnant with a boy or a girl. Then, if it is a girl, the woman can get an abortion. While technology makes sex selection possible, social forces in China make it almost inevitable (see Chapter 16).

Since the introduction of ultrasound technology, the proportion of baby boys to baby girls in China has climbed steadily (Figure 10-1). Worldwide, the sex ratio at birth is about 105 or 106 males to 100 females. In China in 1992, the ratio was 118.5 males to 100 girls. Given China's huge population, this means that more than 1.7 million girls are "missing." Some girl babies are not registered with authorities, some are given to other families for adoption, and still others are aban-

doned, drowned immediately following birth, or aborted (Kristof, 1993). In China, sex discrimination begins even before birth.

China may be an extreme case, but it is not unique. Of 8,000 abortions performed in Bombay after the parents had learned the sex of the fetus, only 1 child would have been born a male (United Nations, 1991). Around the world, females are subject to violence at the hands of family members throughout the life cycle. The practice of female genital mutilation is widespread (see Chapter 3). In many places girls and women are systematically denied equal education, shut out of the paid labor force, and excluded from politics.

Compared with women in these other countries, women in the United States seem well off. The number of American women in government is increasing. As of this writing, there are 2 women on the U.S. Supreme Court; 4 women in the cabinet, including the first female attorney general, Janet Reno, and the first female secretary of state, Madeleine Albright; 51 women in the House of Representatives and 9 women in the Senate. At

**Male Births for Each
100 Female Births**

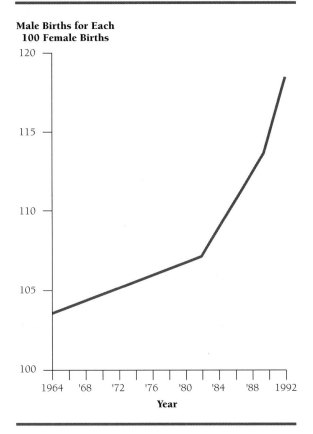

Figure 10-1   *The Chosen Sex*

China's one-child policy was designed to slow runaway population growth. One of the unintended consequences of this policy is that parents are choosing boy babies over girl babies. A generation from now, the uneven sex ratio will produce a marriage squeeze: Who will the boys marry?

Source: Chinese census and unpublished data, cited in *The New York Times,* July 21, 1993, p. A1.

present 2 governors and 22 percent of state legislators are women (Neft and Levine, 1997).

Women earn more than half of the B.A.s and more than one-third of the Ph.D.s and professional degrees awarded by American colleges and universities. Three-quarters of women work in the paid labor force today. They are moving into formerly all-male occupations, from management and medicine to law enforcement and construction work. In 1997, American women earned, on average, 75 cents for every dollar men earned—up from 59 cents in 1970 (Bianchi and Spain, 1997).

Equally important, women have succeeded in making wife battering, acquaintance rape, and sexual harassment—abuses that used to be discussed behind closed doors and not even whispered to friends—into major social issues.

That's the good news. The bad news is that even with these gains, American women are a long way from achieving equality. Despite talk of the new "sorority" in Washington, men outnumber women by ten to one in state legislatures. The 25-cent gap between men's and women's median wages means that a woman has to work ten days to earn as much as a man earns in seven days. The median annual income for female college graduates exceeded that for male high school graduates for the first time in 1989, but the difference was a mere $100. The majority of working women still hold low-paying, gender-segregated, traditionally female or "pink-collar" jobs, such as secretary or waitress. When women do work for major corporations or in prestigious professions (such as law or medicine), they usually do so at the lower levels; very few advance to the top. Women are far more likely than men to live in poverty, at every age (Bianchi and Spain, 1997). The income gap between mother-only and married-couple families is widening. New welfare reforms will have more impact on women than on men, especially unmarried minority mothers whose children's fathers are more likely to be unemployed or to earn lower wages than do white men. Moreover, women at all socioeconomic levels work a "second shift" at home (Hochschild, 1989), taking primary responsibility for housework and child care.

Finally, the advances women have made have not protected them from harassment or abuse. Courts still place much of the blame for rape on the victim rather than on the rapist—as if the victim's dress, the amount of alcohol she had consumed, her sexual history, her relationship to the rapist (if any), or her failure to fight back "caused" the rape, rather than the man who committed the act (Tavris, 1992).

Full equality for women remains a distant goal.

Key Questions

1. What is gender?
2. How different are the sexes?
3. What are the social and economic consequences of being a woman in our society today?
4. How do sociologists explain gender stratification?

5. *How did the women's movement begin, and where is it headed?*
6. *How are men and masculinity changing?*
7. *Have attitudes toward sexual orientation changed?*

Defining Gender

Talking about gender for most people is the equivalent of a fish talking about water. Gender is so much the routine ground of everyday activities that questioning its taken-for-granted assumptions and presuppositions is like thinking about whether the sun will come up. (United Nations Development Programme, 1995, p. 9)

"Masculine" and "feminine" can mean different things. When we describe a person by using either of these terms, we may be referring to that person's biological identity as male or female, to the fact that the person exhibits traits traditionally considered ideal for his or her sex, or to the fact that the person is attractive to the opposite sex (Maccoby, 1987). Thus these terms have many uses.

To clarify discussion, sociologists distinguish among three concepts: **Sex** refers to the biological differences between males and females; **sex role** refers to the behavior, attitudes, and motivations that a particular culture considers appropriate for males or females; **sexual orientation** refers to an individual's attraction to members of the opposite sex, the same sex, or both sexes. **Gender** refers to the "complex of social meanings that is attached to biological sex" (Kimmel and Messner, 1995). Gender is part of social structure: a set of social and cultural practices that both reflect and reinforce assumptions about differences between men and women.

Sociologists who study gender emphasize three points (Riley, 1997). First, gender is a *social institution*. Like the family, religion, and other institutions, it affects the roles men and women play in society. Gender also interacts with other institutions, such as the economy. The labor force in the United States is based on the assumption that most workers are men with families to support. Salaries, the 9-to-5 workday, employers' expectations, and the structure of business reflect this assumption and, in turn, influence the way women are hired, fired, and paid.

Second, gender involves differences in *power.* Like race and social class, gender assigns roles in ways that afford women fewer opportunities and privileges than men enjoy. Nancy Riley (1997) distinguishes between two kinds of power. "Power to" refers to the ability to act, which often requires such resources as education, money, land, and time. Typically, women have less "power to" pursue education, inherit land, get high-paying jobs, or choose to get married or divorced. "Power over" refers to the ability to assert one's will even against opposition from others (Weber's definition of power). Women usually have less say in family decisions, lower positions in the workplace, and little representation in government or influence on public policies.

Third, gender is a *cultural construct.* Gender shapes the lives of people in every society, but assumptions about and expectations for men and women vary widely (as described below).

How Different Are the Sexes?

The list of actual and alleged male-female differences is potentially long. Obviously, males and females differ anatomically. As a rule, boys are more physically active than girls. Girls tend to be more verbal than boys and may begin speaking earlier. Men tend to be aggressive; women tend to be compliant. Men value independence and achievement; women value intimacy and attachment. Men are action-oriented; they "take care of business." Women are people-oriented; they take care of others.

Opinions on the origins and extent of male-female differences tend to polarize (Tavris, 1992). On the one hand are the "maximalists," who believe there are major, fundamental, deep-rooted differences between males and females. Maximalists may believe that males are superior or, conversely, that females are superior. What unites them are their beliefs that the sexes are *different,* that these differences are significant, and that they are "built in." On the other hand are the "minimalists," who believe that the differences between males and females are minor and superficial, a product of the different roles assigned by society. Whereas maximalists assume that gender differences derive from the way men and women are, minimalists assume that gender differences reflect what men and women *do* at a particular time in history, in a particular culture, and in a given situation.

Biological Differences

Are gender differences natural expressions of biological dissimilarity, or are they social creations that have little or no biological foundation?

Let's start with something "everybody knows": males excel in athletics. The reason seems so obvious as to require no explanation: After puberty, men are taller, bigger-boned, and more muscular, on average, than are women, and so "naturally" they are better athletes. This is true, but only up to a point (Fausto-Sterling, 1985). Strength and endurance depend on sufficient levels of physical activity and training, as well as on good genes and hormones. Until recently, only boys were allowed to roam and were expected (even required) to be athletes; girls were "tied to their mother's apron strings," almost literally. But as girls have been encouraged to take sports seriously, the gap between males' and females' athletic performances has narrowed.

For example, between 1964 and 1984, women marathon runners cut their running times by an hour and a half, while men's times decreased by only a few minutes. Similar trends are notable in other track events and in swimming. If the gap continues to close at the current rate, in a mere thirty to forty years males and females could compete in these sports as equals. It seems unlikely that women athletes will compete as near-equals in sports requiring height, bulk, or upper-body strength (basketball, football, tennis, golf), but they might catch up in other sports, such as gymnastics.

Turning from brawn to brains, recent studies reporting sex differences in neuroanatomy have attracted widespread attention (Fausto-Sterling, 1985). The brain is divided into two hemispheres of equal size, connected by a bundle of fibers. Scientists used to think that one hemisphere dominated the other. In the 1950s, however, Dr. Roger Sperry and others found that the two hemispheres are not so much dominant and dominated as they are different. The left hemisphere was associated with verbal ability and reasoning, and the right hemisphere with spatial skills and artistic talent. Soon other scientists began using the discovery of hemisphere specialization to explain alleged differences in the way men and women think and feel.

Scientific opinion on sex differences and brain specialization has fluctuated widely in the intervening years (Tavris, 1992). At first, studies found that the left hemisphere, the presumed seat of intellect, was more developed in males. Then, when the right hemisphere was pinpointed as the source of brilliance and creativity, studies uncovered greater right-hemisphere specialization in males. To confuse the issue, more recent research suggests that males have greater left-and-right hemisphere specialization, whereas abilities in the female brain are

In recent years women have greatly decreased their performance times in marathons. If the gap between women and men continues to close at the current rate, they may eventually compete against one another as equals.

more diffused. Thus whichever way opinion flowed, females ended up on the wrong (inferior) side. Meanwhile, the numerous studies that found no differences between male and female brains were generally disregarded. And the many scientists who maintained that the brain functions as an integrated whole, in which each hemisphere complements the other, were largely ignored.

At issue, of course, is the question, Which sex is smarter? Conventional wisdom holds that girls excel in verbal skills (supporting the cliché that women talk too much), whereas males have superior spatial and mathematical abilities (supporting the stereotype that males are too calculating). An early review of the existing research (Maccoby and Jacklin, 1974) supported this picture. However, more recent research tells a different story. A study of 100 tests of mathematical ability, representing tests of 3.9 million students, found a very small sex difference *in favor of females* in the general population. Only in studies of exceptional individuals (or "math geniuses") did males come out ahead (Hyde, Fennema, and Lamon, 1990). A recent analysis of past and present scores on more than 400 different tests, taken by millions of students, found only minor gender differences among high school seniors, with boys scoring slightly higher (on average) on tests of mechanical/electronic skills and girls somewhat higher (on average) on tests of verbal skills, especially writing and language use (Willingham and Cole, 1997). Contrary to the belief that these differences are inborn, boys and girls in fourth grade are roughly equal; by eighth grade, girls begin pulling ahead in verbal skills; and between eighth and twelfth grade, boys pull ahead in math, science, and geopolitics. This suggests that social and cultural forces come into play. In one study, researchers hypothesized that playing sports, building model airplanes, and doing other traditionally masculine activities give boys an edge in math and science, while the cultural belief that girls aren't very good with numbers and machines and that these skills are "unfeminine" may reduce self-confidence in girls (Casey, Nuttall, and Pezaris, 1997). This study, like many others, found that the variations *within* each sex are greater than the variations *between* the sexes—and this is the crux of the matter.

The problem with biological theories of gender differences is that they draw attention away from gender similarities (Tavris, 1992). Studies reporting that the sexes are more alike than different rarely make the news (see Chapter 1). Moreover, when researchers and the public hear that a study found differences between males and females, they tend to ignore the size of the difference. In their mind's eye they imagine two nonoverlapping curves, with females all below average and males all above average (as in Figure 10-2A). In fact the difference usually is a matter of a few percentage points, and the great majority of males and females overlap (Figure 10-2B).

As a final note, studies of everyday conversation find that men outtalk women in the workplace and that they are far more likely to dominate the conversation, change the subject, and interrupt than are women (Tannen, 1990). And despite women's alleged inferiority in math, about half of all accountants today are female.

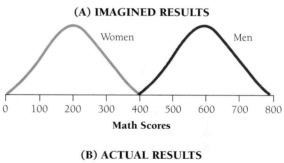

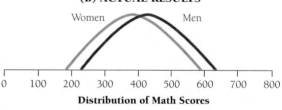

Figure 10-2   *Evaluating Studies of Sex Differences*

When people learn through the media that researchers have found evidence of sex differences, they tend to assume that all males are superior to all females, or vice versa (A). In fact, the differences within the sexes almost always are greater than the differences between them (B).

Sources: Carol Tavris, *The Mismeasure of Woman: Why Women Are Not the Better Sex, the Inferior Sex, or the Opposite Sex,* New York: Touchstone, 1992, pp. 41 and 42; based on Robert Sapolsky, "The Case of the Missing Night-Watchmen," *Discover,* July 1992, pp. 42–45.

Cultural Influences

If sex roles and gender identities were firmly rooted in biology, one would expect ideas about gender to be universal. They are not. All known societies attach social significance to the differences between the sexes. In most societies, boys and girls are taught different games and given different rewards for good behavior. Men and women distinguish themselves with different clothing and body ornaments and follow different rules of etiquette in dealing with members of the same or opposite sex. All preindustrial societies have a division of labor based on sex. But what people consider masculine or feminine behavior is quite variable (Mead, 1935; Sanday, 1981; Ashmore et al., 1986).

In western societies people tend to think men are better-suited to strenuous labor. However, in most societies in sub-Saharan Africa, women are expected to haul firewood, carry crops to market, and do the construction work on houses. There is no concept of women as weak or delicate. In traditional Balinese villages, men are as slender and graceful as women; big shoulders and bulging biceps are considered abnormal and ugly. The Toda of India thought women incompetent at housework and left the job to men. Iranians are convinced that women are cool and logical and men emotionally volatile. In Russia, nearly all physicians are female. This list could go on and on. The many cultural variations seem to make a case for the social determination of gender differences.

The puzzle is that although gender roles differ cross-culturally, gender stratification is universal (Marini, 1990). Virtually all societies place a higher cultural value on men's roles than on women's roles. For example, in some New Guinea societies women are responsible for growing sweet potatoes and men for growing yams. Invariably, the sweet potatoes are considered ordinary, everyday food, while yams are a delicacy to be saved for feasts. "Everywhere, in every known culture, women are considered in some degree inferior to men," wrote anthropologist Sherry Ortner (1974).

But the degree of inequality between the sexes varies. In general, the more economic power women have, the more egalitarian the society (Blumberg, 1984; Chafetz, 1984). Thus in societies where women make a vital contribution to the production and distribution of essential goods, women are likely to be treated as almost equal. Hunter-gatherer bands and some horticultural villages fit this pattern. But in societies where men control the means of production and the marketplace, women are more likely to be subordinate. Pastoral groups, agrarian states, and industrial societies tend to be more gender-stratified.

Gender Socialization

Gender socialization begins soon after birth. The first question people ask of new parents is not "Is the baby healthy?" but "Is it a boy or a girl?" We feel uncomfortable commenting on a baby's appearance

Some societies view women as weak and delicate; in others, women are expected to do much of the heavy labor. These Rwandan women haul wood while caring for infants at the same time.

or activity, or selecting a baby present, until we know the child's sex. The answer to the question "Boy or girl?" has immediate social consequences.

Without realizing it, parents subtly prepare their infants and small children for traditional sex roles. When questioned a few days after birth, parents of girls describe their infants as soft, delicate, and somewhat passive; parents of boys describe their infants as strong, hardy, and alert. For the first year of life, it is often difficult for a stranger to tell whether a baby is male or female—one reason parents dress boys in blue and girls in pink. Most parents are upset if a stranger perceives their infant or toddler as a member of the opposite sex. Parents engage in more physical play with male babies and more talk with girl babies. Boys are roughed up and tossed into the air; girls are held far more gently (Walum, 1977).

Parents today are more likely than past generations to encourage girls to be athletic and boys to be considerate of others' feelings. But other forms of gender stereotyping persist. For example, parents rarely give a boy a doll or a girl a truck. In assigning household chores, parents tend to ask boys to do yardwork and repairs and girls to help cook or baby-sit. These messages are reinforced if children see their mothers playing the role of "helper" and their fathers the role of "handyman."

Even when parents try to "socialize children of both sexes toward the same major goals, . . . they believe they are starting from different points, with each sex having a different set of 'natural' assets and liabilities" (Maccoby and Jacklin, 1974, p. 344). Parents tend to describe growing boys as messy and noisy, girls as neater and better mannered. This gender stereotyping extends to intellectual achievements. Thus parents are more likely to attribute a girl's success in math to effort and a boy's success to talent. By implication, the girl has to work hard at something that comes naturally to the boy.

Gender socialization is continued and reinforced in school, as part of a "hidden curriculum" (see Chapter 12). Even when teachers try to treat both sexes alike, biases slip through. Boys are more likely to be asked to wash the blackboard and girls to pass the cookies (Richmond-Abbott, 1992). In nursery school, girls tend to get attention for being obedient, boys for misbehaving. In grade school, girls tend to be praised for being neat, boys for doing a good job. Attempts to get boys to enroll in

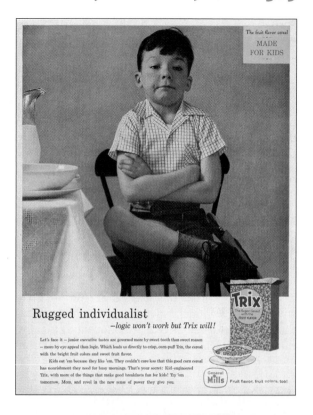

Gender socialization for future roles extends even to "correct" body postures for males and females. This advertisement showing a male "rugged individualist" (top) and the photograph of teenage girls at "charm school" (bottom) both date from the 1950s. If the sitting positions were reversed, would they look appropriate to us today?

home economics or girls in shop have not been very successful; efforts to organize coeducational sports programs have met with similar failure.

Peer groups also reinforce gender distinctions. In fact, other children make stronger judgments of what toys or clothes are appropriate for boys or girls than their parents do and tend to shun children who engage in "gender-inappropriate" play. Gender stereotyping can be especially strong among adolescents (Richmond-Abbott, 1992).

Given this bombardment of subtle and not-so-subtle messages, the surprise is that boys and girls are more alike than different! Gender differences in children at play are in the expected direction—for example, girls spend more time playing house, and boys spend more time roughhousing—but the differences are generally small. "There is no consistent evidence . . . that the sexes differ in cognitive style, creativity, independence, susceptibility to influence, general self-esteem, emotionality, empathy, nurturance, sociability, or loquaciousness" (Marini, 1990, p. 98).

"The Mismeasure of Women"

If men and women are more alike than different, why do adolescent girls often suffer crises in self-esteem (Gilligan, 1982)? Why do adult women buy so many self-help books that promise to improve their sex lives, their relationships with their lovers and their mothers, their moods, their bodies, their confidence? Part of the answer, according to Carol Tavris in her book, *The Mismeasure of Women* (1992), has to do with the "universal man." In virtually every realm, men are considered the norm, and women are seen as "abnormal," deficient, the sex that needs to be explained. "Male behavior, male heroes, male psychology, and even male physiology continue to be the standards of normalcy against which women are measured and found wanting" (Tavris, 1992, p. 17). In politics, we distinguish between the "big issues" (war economics, crime, drugs) and "women's issues" (day care, birth control, peace). In economic theories, "women's work" (caring for the home and family) is simply not counted. In our schools the study of western civilization focuses almost exclusively on what "great (white) men" did and said; the study of western literature concentrates on (white) male writers. "Women's studies" and "women's literature" are con-sidered specialties (as are courses on nonwhite societies and arts).

Even in medicine, males are the norm. Medical students first learn anatomy and physiology by studying a male model. "The 70-kilogram (154-pound) male" is the standard for all patients. Only later do medical students study female anatomy, physiology, and health problems. Likewise, most medical research is based on a male standard of normalcy. Studies of drug effects, diseases, and treatments regularly exclude women; studies of men are frequently generalized as applying to all patients; studies that include both sexes often fail to look for gender differences; and far more research is devoted to men's primary health problems (such as heart disease) than to women's (such as breast cancer).

Tavris shows how the "universal male" is so ingrained in our thinking that we often fail to notice him. She cites a researcher who gave men and women a test of creativity (C. B. Olson, 1988). The researcher was not interested in which sex was more creative (they were equal) but in how men and women explained their success or failure during a mock job interview. She found that women were more likely to attribute their success to luck and that they were less confident of their own ability than were men. Why do women give "less self-serving" explanations? she asked. She concluded, "The feminine goal of appearing modest inhibits women from making self-promoting attributions in achievement situations." Hidden in this conclusion is the assumption that men are the norm, and the problem is to explain why women don't behave like men. To see this assumption more clearly, turn the question around so that women are the norm. Now the question would be "Why do men make more self-serving explanations than women do?" And the conclusion: "The masculine goal of appearing self-confident inhibits them from making modest explanations of their abilities or acknowledging the help of others and the role of chance" (Tavris, 1992, p. 28).

Tavris holds that one reason for the mismeasure of women is that we tend to assume that "equal" means "the same." Whether we view women as the better sex, the inferior sex, or the opposite sex, we fall into the same trap of using males as the standard. Until we develop *human* standards, and recognize that women can be different and equal, gender bias and discrimination are likely to persist.

Women: The 52 Percent Minority

Women are a numerical majority in the United States, comprising more than 52 percent of the population. Nevertheless, they fit Louis Wirth's classic definition of a minority group (see Chapter 9). To review, a minority group is "a group of people who, because of their physical or cultural characteristics, are singled out from others in the society in which they live for differential and unequal treatment, and who therefore regard themselves as objects of collective discrimination" (Wirth, 1945, p. 347). Women are no longer "segregated" in the sense that they are expected to stay at home, care for the children, and keep house while men take care of business and run the country. Most women work today. Most are also housewives, who take responsibility for keeping the house clean, putting food on the table, dressing and chauffeuring their children, and the like. In effect, many women lead two lives. But neither in the workplace nor in the home are they equal partners with men.

Inequality at Work

That women work outside their homes is no longer news. But it is worth recalling how much women's participation in the labor force has grown. Back in 1960, only 35 percent of American women held jobs outside their homes; today 59 percent of all women are employed. But this figure, which includes teenagers and women over 65, gives a somewhat distorted picture. More than three-quarters (76 percent) of women age 24 to 54 work, including 77 percent of women age 35 to 44. In the 1950s and 1960s, most women quit their jobs when they got married or had their first child. No longer. Today a majority (59 percent) of married women work, almost twice as many as in 1960 (Neft and Levine, 1997). The greatest increase has been working mothers. In 1960, only 16 percent of mothers with children under age 16 were in the job force; today more than 79 percent are, including 68 percent of those with children under age 6 (Bianchi and Spain, 1996). And more women work full-time, year-round, than before, whether out of economic necessity or because their jobs require this commitment.

Women flocked to well-paying factory jobs during World War II, and "Rosie the Riveter" became a popular symbol of the war effort. When the soldiers returned home, women were expected to give up their jobs to men.

Unequal Pay

For almost two decades, the wage gap between men and women closed steadily (Figure 10-3). In 1993, the median earnings of women who worked full-time were 72 percent of men's median earnings—up from 60 percent in 1979. In the mid-1990s, however, the pay gap began widening again. In 1995, women earned an average of 71 cents for every dollar men earned. Why women's earnings appear to be slipping is uncertain, but three hypotheses have been suggested. One is that the wage difference has reached an equilibrium because of family arrangements. Mothers (not fathers) are still the ones who change diapers and push strollers. As a result, their wages tend to fluctuate over the life cycle. When women first enter the job market, between ages 16 and 24, they earn almost as much (more than 90 percent) as men do. When they become mothers, the gender gap begins to widen. Women age 25 to 54 earn about 75 percent as much as men do—whether because they lose ground if they take time off when a new baby is born, because they spend more time and energy on child rearing than fathers do and so cannot devote as much to their jobs, or because employers tend to see mothers as a "bad risk" and are less likely to promote them. Women 55 and over earn about

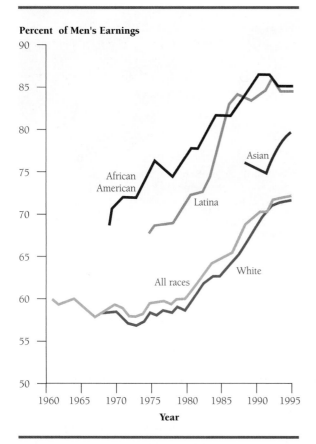

Percent of Men's Earnings

Figure 10-3   *Women's Earnings as a Percentage of Men's Earnings, by Race and Ethnicity, 1960–1995*

Despite significant progress, women still do not earn as much as men.

Note: Percentages are based on three-year moving averages of median annual earnings of full-time, year-round workers.

*Latinas may be of any race.

Source: U.S. Bureau of the Census, unpublished tabulations, in S. Bianchi and D. Spain, "U.S. Women Make Workplace Progress," *Population Today* 25, 1997, p. 24, fig. 5.

65 percent as much as men do, probably because they were the first modern generation of women to become breadwinners, experienced more discrimination, and have not worked as steadily as younger women.

The second explanation is that men's wages are rising. A main reason that the pay gap narrowed in the 1980s was that men's wages declined, not that women's wages increased (Bianchi and Spain, 1997; Ries and Stone, 1992). For women to keep up,

their wages would have to rise even faster. A third hypothesis is that more women are taking low-skill, low-paying jobs—in part because the job market is becoming more divided between high-level and low-level jobs (and has few in the middle), in part because of welfare reform. Unmarried mothers with little education or work experience entering the job force might exert a downward pull on women's median wage.

The Equal Pay Act of 1963 and the Civil Rights Act of 1964 made it illegal to pay a member of a particular group or category less than another person for the same job. But even when the laws requiring equal pay for equal work are enforced, women, on average, earn less than men with the same levels of education and years of experience. For example, nurses who worked for the city of Denver found that they were paid considerably less than tree trimmers and sign painters, most of whom were male, even though the nurses' jobs required more education and life-and-death decisions. In California, school librarians, who often held master's degrees, were paid less than school custodians and groundskeepers, whose jobs did not require even a high school diploma (England, 1993). Fifty-five percent of the 3 million or more women who work for state and local governments are in the lowest-paying categories (primarily clerks and health aides), compared with one-quarter of men and just one-fifth of white men in particular (Berheide, 1992). As a rule, occupations dominated by women pay less than those dominated by men.

Gender Segregation

In the last two decades, women have broken into many formerly all-male occupations. Increasing numbers of women are becoming lawyers, doctors, dentists, bankers, stockbrokers, professors, and journalists. More and more are working as bartenders, police officers, typesetters, and telephone installers. But the woman surgeon and the woman soldier are the exception (see Table 10-1).

To a high degree, the job market is still segregated by gender. The worlds of "men's work" and "women's work" are as different as Norway and Brazil; they are vastly unequal in power, pay, and prestige. In some cases, whole industries and occupations are dominated by one sex or the other, such as coal mining and logging (virtually all male occupations) or nursing and textile manufacturing (al-

Table 10-1   *Gender Segregation in the Workplace*

	1983	1991	1995
Female-Dominated Occupations	**Percent Female**		
Registered nurses	95.8	94.8	93.1
Elementary school teachers	83.3	85.9	84.1
Retail salesclerks	69.7	66.7	65.6
Secretaries	99.0	99.0	98.5
Receptionists	96.8	97.1	96.5
Bank tellers	91.0	96.0	90.1
Private household workers	96.1	96.0	95.5
Male-Dominated Occupations	**Percent Male**		
Physicians	84.2	79.9	77.1
Lawyers and judges	84.2	81.1	75.8
Engineers	94.2	91.8	91.6
Teachers—college and university	63.7	59.2	54.8
Executives, administrators	67.6	59.4	62.0
Managers	78.2	69.4	64.3
Protective service personnel*	87.2	84.8	84.1
Precision artisans, repair persons	91.9	91.4	91.1
Motor vehicle operators	90.8	89.4	89.0

*Firefighters, police, detectives, guards.

Sources: Adapted from U.S. Bureau of Labor Statistics, *Employment and Earnings,* January 1984, U.S. Bureau of the Census, *Statistical Abstract,* 1992, Washington, DC: GPO, 1992, table 692, pp. 392–394; ibid., *Statistical Abstract, 1996,* table 637, pp. 405–407.

most all female). In other cases, men and women work in the same setting but hold different positions; men manage the office, while women do the clerical work. Half of all working women are employed in occupations that are at least 80 percent female, such as secretary, waitress, and health aide (V. Taylor, Whittier, and Huber, 1993). "Female" occupations not only pay less than "male" occupations but usually offer fewer benefits (such as health insurance and pension plans), fewer opportunities for promotions, and less job security.

When women do go into prestigious and high-paying fields, it is usually into positions that are lower in pay, authority, and status than men's jobs in the same field. Most of the women the government classifies as "professional/technical workers" are nurses, social workers, elementary school teachers, and hospital technicians—not physicians, lawyers, or college professors. Moreover, women who have entered professions often specialize within those professions. For example, female MDs tend to be pediatricians, gynecologists, and psychi-

atrists (performing the "feminine" functions of caring for children, women, and emotional problems), rather than surgeons (who perform the "masculine" function of repairing broken bodies). A study of lawyers found that ten years after graduating from law school, female attorneys earned $40,000 less, on average, than their male peers (Hagan, 1990). They were more likely than male lawyers to work for small firms that represented individuals than for large firms that represented major organizations. Even when they worked in large firms, they tended to work in less prestigious areas (family versus corporate law) and to receive fewer promotions. Moreover, when women enter an occupation in large numbers, the pay and prestige of that occupation usually decline.

Comparable worth is the effort to correct gender bias in wages. The idea is that male and female jobs that require comparable skill, training, effort, responsibility, and ability to cope with unpleasant conditions should pay the same. Comparable worth extends equal pay for equal work to different jobs that are equally demanding. To apply the concept of comparable worth, an employer would conduct a job evaluation of male- and female-dominated occupations, assigning each a numerical score for degrees of difficulty. Ideally, the pay for female jobs would then be raised to the level of male jobs with the same or similar scores. To date, the courts have not endorsed comparable worth, but a number of state and local governments have passed laws mandating job evaluation and salary adjustments, usually called "pay-equity" programs (England, 1993; R. J. Simon and Danziger, 1991).

Job Mobility

Women executives are a particularly interesting case. In the mid-1990s, 43 percent of female workers were managers and administrators, though the proportion was much higher in some fields than in others (Bianchi and Spain, 1997). The typical woman executive is 44 years old, white, married, and has zero to two children. She works fifty-six hours a week and earns $187,000—twice what she earned ten years ago but only two-thirds what male executives earn (Korn/Ferry International, 1993). She is also the exception to the rule.

Very few women make it to the top of corporate ladders and government bureaucracies. Nearly one-fifth of the *Fortune* 500 corporations, the nation's largest companies, have all-male boards of directors; in most cases their corporate officers are all men as well (Catalyst, 1995). In 1995, only 10 percent of corporate officers were women. Female executives often find that they are trapped under a *glass ceiling:* they run into barriers so subtle as to be invisible. For example, the types of corporate jobs held by women tend to be on a sidetrack that doesn't lead to promotion. Of 978 women corporate vice-presidents in 1995, only 28 percent were responsible for revenues or profits and losses—the positions that lead to the very top. The glass ceiling translates into lost dollars and cents. At *Fortune* 500 corporations, only 50 of the 2,500 top earners (or 2 percent) were women. On average, female administrators earn 68 percent of male managers' incomes (U.S. Department of Labor, Bureau of Labor Statistics, unpublished data). A U.S. Chamber of Commerce survey found that corporate women at the vice-presidential level or higher earn 42 percent less than men at the same level (in Simon and Danziger, 1991). According to separate surveys conducted by Harvard, the Rand Corporation, Stanford, and the Columbia University Graduate School of Business, female M.B.A.s are paid the same starting salaries as male M.B.A.s. But regardless of the company they work for or the job they hold, within ten years they are earning about 20 percent less than their male colleagues (Gerhart and Milkovich, 1989).

A main reason for the glass ceiling is that stereotypes are still entrenched at many companies.

When looking for a personnel manager, male corporate officers are likely to consider women; when looking for a plant manager, however, female candidates are not even mentioned. Women are still excluded from the "old-boy network." Male executives may feel women interfere with the "clubby atmosphere" of the boardroom. Accustomed to exchanging information and reaffirming friendships on the golf course or the squash court and indulging in humor based on athletic, sexual, and military allusions, they feel uncomfortable with a woman in the next office or boardroom. Women who do reach the top levels of management usually had a mentor. But senior executives may be reluctant to take on a woman as a protégé. Similarly, junior executives may be less willing to offer a woman assistance or to admit her to informal networks and after-work activities, in part because they see her as a "poor investment." At some point, they assume, she will interrupt her career to raise a family. And so the female manager is passed over for promotions or new jobs with another company.

Women executives (and would-be-executives) are responding to these barriers by forming networks of their own, looking for jobs at corporations with females in high positions, participating in social activities like golf, and starting businesses of their own (Blum, Fields, and Goodman, 1994; Fagenson, 1993). According to the latest available Census Bureau data, women owned more than 6.4 million businesses, employing 13 million peo-

Women executives are still excluded from the "good old boy network" and the clubby atmosphere of the golf course or boardroom.

ple and generating $1.6 trillion in revenues in 1992 (U.S. Department of Labor, Women's Bureau, 1994).

Of course, most women do not have to worry about the glass ceiling for the simple reason that they never get even close to the top. Rather, they are confined to low-paying, dead-end jobs. What holds them down, says sociologist Catherine Berheide (1992), is the "sticky floor." Looking at government jobs, Berheide notes that women are hired primarily to deal with frustrated, angry people (as clerks) or to work with children and the elderly (as child care workers and health aides). Their job descriptions do not acknowledge their "people skills," nor do pay scales. Once in a "woman's job," employees stay there. Men entering "female" professions, such as nursing, librarianship, kindergarten and elementary school teaching, and social work, often have the opposite experience. Far from being discriminated against, men often are given preferential treatment in hiring, welcomed by supervisors and colleagues, and invited into informal networks and the workplace subculture. Far from being held back, they may be promoted faster and further than they wish to move—a phenomenon Christine Williams (1992) calls the "glass escalator." Thus a man who wants to be a first-grade teacher may be pushed out of the classroom into administration. Men in "female" occupations do encounter prejudice outside their profession, however. Clients are suspicious of their motives (why would a man want to work with small children?); friends wonder why they couldn't get a "real job"; parents may brag about "my son, the doctor," but not about "my son, the nurse."

Work and Family

A UCLA survey conducted twenty years ago found that only half of female executives were married, and 60 percent of married women executives did not have children. Women paid for success with their personal lives. Today seven out of ten women executives are married, and most have children (Korn/Ferry International, 1993). Yet, no matter what their level of employment, working women experience role conflicts that working men do not encounter in trying to combine work and family.

The problem begins even before conception: How many women of childbearing age are not hired or not promoted because they *might* become

pregnant is unknown. A 1978 law prohibits discrimination against women in the workplace simply because they are pregnant. But women often find that the workplace becomes hostile when they become pregnant; their clients may be assigned to other employees, promotion offers may be withdrawn, and the like (Swiss and Walker, 1993).

Among industrialized nations, only the United States and New Zeland do not have a national policy guaranteeing parental leave—time off *with pay* for the mother and/or father—when a baby is born or adopted. (Seventy other nations do, including India, Egypt, Poland, and Argentina.) The 1993 Family and Medical Leave Act requires that companies with fifty or more employees grant up to twelve weeks of unpaid leave (with health benefits) a year for family medical emergencies, childbirth, or adoption. But part-time workers and recent hires are not entitled to family leave, and many workers cannot afford to give up their salaries. The United States is the only industrialized nation that does not have a national program for child care, such as income support for a parent who stays home to care for an infant, free or subsidized day care for most children, or universal preschool programs. In the United States licensed day care centers (most of which are privately run) can accommodate only about one out of five preschoolers, and the government provides day care only for children of poor women.

Given the high cost of day care or baby-sitters, new mothers may be forced to accept part-time, low-paying jobs near home. This is true not only for women in low-level occupations but also for highly trained, well-paid female professionals. A survey of more than 900 female graduates of Harvard's law, medical, and business schools found that 53 percent changed jobs or specialties as a result of family responsibilities. The survey also revealed that 25 percent of Harvard female M.B.A.s left the workforce entirely when they became mothers—not so much because they wanted to as because they were unable to juggle their professional and private lives (Swiss and Walker, 1993). Proposals to give parents (not just mothers) such options as flexible schedules, job sharing, or telecommuting from home have not caught on with corporations or, apparently, with employees.

Arlie Hochschild (1997) spent three summers observing and interviewing managers and employees at a *Fortune* 500 company with a reputation for "family-friendly" policies. To her surprise, she found that parents did not take advantage of offers of flexible jobs and schedules. Indeed, many saw work as a refuge from the stresses and strains of family life (rather than the reverse). Consciously or unconsciously, parents (especially women) feared being shunted onto a "mommy track" of lower-level jobs, interrupted careers, and part-time work. Hochschild argues that our job-oriented culture creates a vicious circle: to get ahead, people work longer hours; the more they work, the more stressful their home lives become; the greater the tensions at home, the more they see work as an escape. Advising coworkers becomes a substitute for guiding children; discussing problems with coworkers, a substitute for the companionship side of marriage: "work becomes home and home becomes work." Children, whose natural desires and needs make them "time thieves," are the first to suffer. Hochschild warns that this time bind also threatens democracy: if "workaholics" have no time for their families, how much care and concern can they devote to their communities?

Work and Sex

Finally, women encounter another problem that men rarely face: sexual harassment. **Sexual harassment** is a form of discrimination in which sexual advances, requests for sexual favors, or demeaning sexual references are (1) a condition for employment or promotion, and/or (2) create a work environment that is hostile, intimidating, or offensive (Neft and Levine, 1997). The 1964 Civil Rights Act prohibited sex discrimination in employment, housing, and education. Women could—and did—file charges when they believed they were denied an opportunity just because they were women. But sexual harassment did not receive much attention until recently. In our culture (and many others) the line between sexual harassment and flirtation, on the one hand, and between harassment and sexual abuse, on the other, is blurred. If a man made advances to a female subordinate, commented on her appearance, decorated his work space with erotic pictures, or told sexually derogatory jokes in her presence—but did not physically force her to engage in sexual acts—where was the harm? If a woman consented to sexual relations with a man in a position to promote or demote her, again, where was the harm? The idea that such actions might be an abuse of power and thus a form of discrimination was slow to catch on. The key difference between sexual harassment and romantic overtures or friendly joking is that the social relationship between the initiator and the victim is one of unequal power and authority—for example an employer and employee, a teacher and student, a physician and a patient, or a police officer and a civilian.

The case of Clarence Thomas versus Anita Hill marked a turning point in public awareness of sexual harassment. In 1991, during Senate hearings on Judge Thomas's appointment to the Supreme Court, law professor Anita Hill told a reporter that when she worked for Thomas at the Equal Employment Opportunity Commission during the early 1980s he had harassed and embarrassed her with repeated requests for dates and graphic descriptions of pornographic films. Reluctantly, Hill agreed to testify. Under pressure from women's groups, the Senate Judiciary Committee reversed its decision to close the hearings: Hill's testimony and Thomas's rebuttal were televised live for three days. The fact that both the accuser and the accused were highly successful African Americans added racial overtones to the hearings. Judge Thomas denied the charges outright, accusing the all-white Senate Judiciary Committee of a "high-tech lynching." Professor Hill was charged with being a "vindictive woman" and a "traitor to her race." In the end, Judge Thomas's appointment to the Supreme Court was confirmed, and Professor Hill became a feminist heroine.

"They [men] just don't get it" became a rallying cry among women across the country. The image of Anita Hill trying to explain her actions or lack of action to a panel of all-male, all-white senators who appeared to be putting her on trial came to symbolize the position of all women in a male-dominated society. The senators couldn't understand why she didn't file a complaint or quit her job at the time of the incidents she described, but women did understand. The hearings struck a chord that continues to reverberate. Books questioning Hill's credibility (Brock, 1994), Thomas's competence and political agenda (Roberts, 1995), and behind-the-scenes political machinations (Mayer and Abramson, 1994) continue to appear—most recently Hill's own statement, *Speaking Truth to Power* (1997).

There are no reliable statistics on how many women have been sexually harassed, but estimates range from about 50 to 80 percent. Harassment may take the form of irritating catcalls on the street, frightening encounters in dark corridors and locked offices, or the humiliation of giving in. In the past, most women kept silent because they feared losing their jobs; being labeled as "poor sports," lesbians, or liars; being ostracized by coworkers; and becoming the target of additional insults and jokes. Sexual harassment was "accepted" as one of the prices women paid for entering the workforce—and simply for being women. After the Thomas hearings, charges of sexual harassment increased, not because offensive behavior increased but because women (and men) were emboldened to speak out.

In a sense, the military has provided a natural experiment in sexual politics. Women have served in the military since World War I, but until recently they were restricted to auxiliary units, such as the Women's Army Corps (WAC) and Women Accepted for Voluntary Emergency Services (WAVES), a branch of the Navy. Not until 1973 did the Department of Defense begin to admit women into regular Army, Navy, Air Force, and Marine units (in noncombat positions). Women were first admitted to service academies in 1976. After much debate, sex-integrated training was initiated in the Air Force in 1976, the Army in 1993 (after failed attempts at some bases in the 1970s), and the Navy in 1994, but not in the Marines. Since 1993, women have been allowed to fly combat aircraft and to serve aboard warships, but not in ground combat units. Even so, 80 percent of jobs and 92 percent of all career fields in the military are open to women, who today make up 12.6 percent of the armed forces (see Figure 10-4).

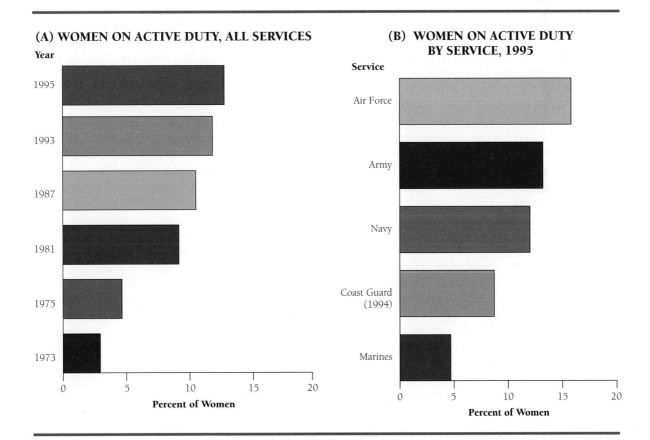

(A) WOMEN ON ACTIVE DUTY, ALL SERVICES

(B) WOMEN ON ACTIVE DUTY BY SERVICE, 1995

Figure 10-4   *Women in the Armed Forces*

Since women were admitted to regular army units in 1973, female enlistment has increased steadily.

Source: U.S. Department of Defense.

Intended to promote equality and camaraderie, sex integration also led to scandal. The Tailhook debauch (group sexual harassment by Navy and Marine Corps pilots at a 1991 convention in Las Vegas) was followed by charges of harassment and abuse of female recruits by male drill sergeants at the Aberdeen Proving Ground in Maryland. At first the Pentagon treated such cases as exceptions to the rule. But mounting negative publicity prompted investigations, trials, and controversial decisions and proposals.

An inspection of fifty-nine Army installations around the world revealed that Aberdeen was not unique. According to an Army report issued in 1995, 47 percent of female troops in a general survey had experienced "unwanted sexual attention," 15 percent had endured "sexual coercion," and 7 percent had been victims of "sexual assault." Although the numbers were smaller, 30 percent of male troops reported "unwanted sexual attention," and 7 percent, "sexual coercion." The survey found that only 12 percent of recent victims had filed reports, while 55 percent ignored the harassment or dealt with it personally. Apparently, victimized soldiers believed (with reason) that their complaints would either be ignored or lead to ostracism by soldiers in their unit, lowered reviews by superiors, and often transfers. "Victims are re-victimized by the system," the report said. "We are firmly convinced that leadership is the fundamental issue. Passive leadership has allowed sexual harassment to persist" (in Shenon, 1997). By implication, the top ranks at Aberdeen and other locations tolerated harassment, partly on the grounds that "men will be men" and partly out of resentment of female soldiers.

Among those charged during this period was Sergeant Major Gene McKinney, the Army's highest-ranking enlisted soldier and a member of the panel investigating misconduct at Aberdeen. In 1993, six female soldiers accused McKinney of propositioning, groping, and otherwise sexually harassing them. In 1998, after a lengthy court-martial, a military jury exonerated McKinney on eighteen of nineteen charges, finding him guilty on one count, obstruction of justice. Faced with "he said/she said" testimony, six female accusers whose credibility was questioned, and a soldier with an otherwise sterling reputation, the jurors decided they could not conclude beyond a reasonable doubt that the alleged crimes took place. Feminists were stunned by the verdict, accusing the Army of a "mock trial" in which a high-ranking male was judged more credible than six female soldiers and the verdict was based on sex and rank, not justice.

In 1997, an advisory committee appointed by the Secretary of Defense to investigate sexual behavior on military bases issued its report. To the Pentagon's surprise, the panel was more disturbed by the impact of consensual sex among trainees than about harassment or abuse (Meyers, 1997). The panel concluded that sex integration was a distraction that lowered morale and led to "softer" training. It recommended that men and women be organized into all-male or all-female basic training units, housed in separate barracks, and assigned more same-sex drill instructors. In other words, the other services should follow the model of the Marine Corps, in which men and women recruits both undergo twelve weeks of physically and emotionally difficult training on the same fields and obstacle courses but rarely have contact with one another. After basic training, the Marine Corps is coed, on the assumption that once "raw recruits" are transformed into disciplined soldiers, sexual misconduct will not be a problem. Critics see sex segregation in the other forces as a step backward for women in the military, in part because one of the goals of basic training is to promote bonding, which is essential on the battlefield.

All coed institutions face similar issues, especially when there are clear differences in power and status, as at colleges and universities. Schools no longer act as surrogate parents; the days are gone when male and female students were required to live in separate dormitories and sign in at a specified time each night and coed visits were limited and closely supervised. But the potential for harassment remains. In the past, "affairs" between a faculty member and an undergraduate were seen as scandalous, particularly if the professor was married, but propositioning a student or fondling her (or him) was not a crime. But under sexual harassment statutes, even consensual sex may be seen as a crime, because faculty have the power to improve or lower a student's academic record and to provide or withhold recommendations. To reduce opportunities for harassment, Yale, the University of Pennsylvania, and other private universities have banned *social* relations between faculty and undergraduate students. At state universities, outright bans on interaction between consenting adults would violate state laws, but intimate relationships between faculty and undergraduates are strongly discouraged. Liaisons between professors and undergraduates are grounds for dismissal at most schools. Colleges and universities also face the problems of date rape and other forms of sexual harassment or abuse by students. Many now discuss these issues during freshman orientation, provide counseling and support to victims who come forward, and impose sanctions (suspension or dismissal) on offenders. Often, however, victims of sexual abuse blame themselves and fear being ostracized by other students, particularly if the abuser is a star athlete or president of a fraternity or is prominent and popular for other reasons.

Since the Thomas hearings, laws against sexual harassment have been strengthened. In 1991, Congress passed an amendment to the Civil Rights Act that enables women to seek compensatory and, in some cases, punitive damages for sexual harassment, as well as back pay for discrimination. One consequence is that lawyers, who may work for a percentage of the damage settlement, are more willing to take on sexual harassment suits. A recent U.S. Supreme Court ruling (*Harris v. Forklift Systems, Inc.*) held that a woman does not have to prove that she suffered discrimination in job assignments or psychological damage to bring charges of sexual harassment. The Supreme Court also ruled that the Civil Rights Act applies to same-sex harassment. Pending cases involve whether school districts can be held liable under federal law for a teacher's having sexual relations with a student or for sexual harassment of one student by another and whether a company can be held liable for a supervisor's sexual harassment of a lower-level employee. At the same time, judges and juries seem to be setting limits on what constitutes a "hostile environment." When Miller Brewing Company fired an executive for describing a racy episode of the TV sit-com *Seinfeld* to a female colleague, he sued and won millions in damages.

Moreover, not all cases of sexual harassment are treated equally. Paula Jones's charge that President Clinton, while he was governor of Arkansas, summoned her to a motel room and humiliated her with a crude request for sex is an example. Feminists and organizations such as the National Organization for Women (NOW) and the Feminine Majority did not rally behind Jones, for several reasons. Feminists supported President Clinton, who has been a strong advocate of women's issues and appointed more women to high government positions than any president before him. Paula Jones was defended by people who defended Oliver North (in the Iran-Contra affair), Justice Clarence Thomas, and Operation Rescue (a radical branch of the right-to-life movement that has taken "credit" for bombing abortion clinics) and funded by conservative, right-wing organizations such as the Rutherford Institute and the Landmark Legal Foundation. Feminists saw the Jones case as a "front" for a right-wing attack on women's rights and a pro-feminist president. Status was also a factor: Professor Hill is a well-educated, conservatively dressed, articulate professional; Paula Jones is a high-school-educated, low-level clerk whose speech and appearance reflected her lower-class background. Interestingly, as allegations of sexual harassment against President Clinton grew, support for Clinton in public opinion polls increased. Part of the reason might have been "scandal fatigue." But on some level Americans may believe that women are attracted to men in high places (i.e., "willing victims") and that, given the history of past chief executives, "presidents will be presidents." In April 1998 (seven years after the alleged incident), Jones's civil suit against Clinton was dismissed by a federal judge on the grounds that, even if true, Jones had not shown that the encounter caused her injury, either personally or in her career.

The current ambivalence and confusion about sexual harassment reflects a clash between a culture and social institutions grounded in clear distinctions between men's and women's gender roles (men as heads of the families and wives as "helpmates"; men as bosses, women as secretaries; men as soldiers, women as nurses) and contemporary social conditions, in which men's and women's roles increasingly overlap.

Inequality in the Family

For much of the twentieth century, American husbands were expected to be the sole breadwinners for their families, and wives were expected to be full-time homemakers. The family's lifestyle and status depended on the income and occupation of the husband. He made the major decisions for the family (such as buying a house), and his wife was

Is he "helping" his wife with "her" chores, or is he doing his fair share of the housework and cooking?

responsible for implementing them (decorating the home) (Safilios-Rothschild, 1970). She did the shopping; he paid the bills. Sexual intimacy was considered a husband's prerogative and a wife's obligation. Because most women had little work experience and even less earning power than they have today, a wife who was unhappily married or even physically abused had few options.

The division of labor and balance of power in the family have changed, but not as much as one might think. As unpaid laborers, housewives are not even listed on scales of occupational prestige; their prestige is assumed to be zero (see Oakley, 1985). Even when both spouses work, the husband's job usually is considered more important than the wife's. If a husband is offered a better job in another city, a majority of men and women (72 and 62 percent, respectively) believe the wife should quit her job and relocate. But if the wife received such an offer, only 20 percent of men and

women think that the husband should quit and relocate (Roper Organization, 1980–1985, in Simon and Danziger, 1991). Marital rape is now considered a crime in all fifty states, but thirty states allow some exemptions, for example, if the husband did not use physical force.

How do contemporary husbands and wives view their respective roles in the family? With so many women in the labor force, how do couples divide up housework and child care?

"The Second Shift"

In a classic study, Arlie Hochschild and her colleagues (1989) conducted intensive interviews with fifty dual-earner families over a six-year period and observed a dozen families in their homes. She found three basic orientations toward sex roles. Even though she works, the *traditional* wife bases her identity on her activities around the home (as wife and mother), sees her husband's identity as grounded in his work, and wants him to be the head of their household. The traditional husband holds the same views.

The *egalitarian* man or woman believes that a husband and wife should identify with the same spheres and share power within the family equally. Some want the couple to put the home first; some, to put careers first; and some, to achieve a balance between the two. But the egalitarian spouse does not see work or the family as the exclusive right or responsibility of either sex.

In between these two types are the *transitional* spouses. The transitional wife wants to be seen as a worker and a wife/mother but expects her husband to focus on earning a living; the transitional husband applauds his wife for working but also expects her to assume primary responsibility for the home and children. Most of the couples Hochschild studied were transitional, even though many professed egalitarian ideals.

A major question for families in which both the husband and the wife work is, Who should do the housework? The great majority of husbands and wives say that when the wife works, the husband should do more around the house (Ferree, 1991). But the reality falls far short of this ideal (see Figure 10-5). Hochschild calculated the amount of time men and women devote to their paid jobs, housework, and child care. She found that on aver-

Household Task

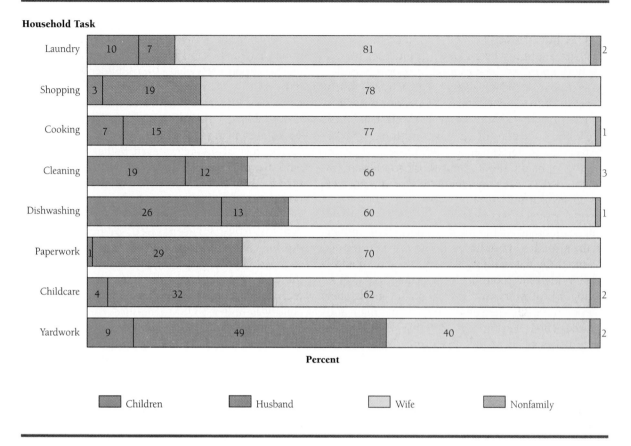

Figure 10-5 *Distribution of Household Tasks by Family Members*

Entering the labor force has not liberated women from their role as housewife. Husbands and children may "help out," but housekeeping is still viewed as women's work.

Source: Frances K. Goldscheider and Linda J. Waite, *New Families or No Families? Demographic Change and the Transformation of the Home,* Berkeley: University of California Press, 1991, p. 176.

age, women work about fifteen hours more (or two extra workdays) than men do each week: "Just as there is a wage gap between men and women in the workplace, so there is a 'leisure gap' between them at home. Most women work one shift at the office or factory and a 'second shift' at home" (Hochschild, 1989, p. 4).

Hochschild found that many couples develop a "family myth" that rationalizes or covers up the unequal division of labor in the home. One middle-class couple who claimed to be egalitarian explained that the wife was responsible for upstairs and the husband for downstairs. "Upstairs" turned out to mean the first-floor living areas and second-

floor bedrooms; "downstairs" was the basement, where the husband kept his tools and extra TV set. The wife took care of the children; the husband cared for the dog. They rationalized this arrangement in terms of personalities: she was "compulsive," they claimed, while he was "lazy."

A traditional, working-class couple Hochschild studied also had a myth. Both the husband and the wife believed that the man should be the "head of the house" and the family breadwinner. But because they could not make ends meet on his $12,000-a-year salary, the wife cared for neighbors' children in her home. Both described this situation as "temporary." To explain away the fact that he did nearly half the work around the house, they invoked the myth of female helplessness. He paid the bills because she was helpless with a calculator; he took her shopping because she could not drive a car; and so on. As these examples suggest, middle-class couples are more likely to preach egalitarian ideals than to practice them, while working-class couples are somewhat more likely to practice equal role division while preaching traditional gender ideals (see also Berardo et al., 1987).

Why is the division of housework so uneven? so stereotyped? Most researchers believe the answer lies in gender socialization. Following their own parents' model, the wife cleans while the husband watches football. If the husband does cook dinner or do a load of laundry, it usually is defined as "helping" the wife with what is still her job. In addition, women are more likely than men to say that having a neat home and eating quality meals (not takeout pizza) are personally important (Blair and Lichter, 1991; Ferree, 1991). Wives tend to see dirty dishes piled in the sink, unmade beds, and "dust bunnies" under the furniture as a reflection on them as women. As a result, they put more time into housework and pick up the wet towels if their husbands or children "forget."

Likewise, women tend to see unruly, unhappy, or unkempt children as a reflection on them as mothers. Final responsibility for child care nearly always falls to the woman. Whether a mother has a full-time job or career or not, the chances are she is the one who takes the day off if the child is sick or the baby-sitter does not show up. Many fathers change diapers and give babies their late-night bottle, put older children to bed, take them on Saturday outings, teach them to ride bicycles, and the like. But it is usually the mother who takes responsibility for the routine, mundane, never-ending aspects of child rearing: seeing that the children have enough socks, wear their mittens, eat their vegetables, do their homework every night, and so on.

Divorce

Contemporary no-fault divorce laws, which allow a marriage to be ended without accusations or blame, were written with the intention of treating both parties fairly. But no-fault divorce has caused many women more harm than good (Weitzman, 1985). In no-fault divorces, judges generally treat both partners as equals. This means that each receives half of their family assets; it also means that the ex-wife is expected to be able to support herself. Less than 15 percent of divorced women are awarded alimony payments, and less than 10 percent actually receive support (Hewlett, 1986). Older women who have been homemakers for all their adult lives or worked at low-level jobs for supplemental income nearly always experience a sharp decline in their standard of living.

The cost of divorce is even higher for ex-wives who are mothers. When a family breaks up, the man is likely to become *single* and, more often than not, the woman becomes a *single parent*. The latest available data indicate that more than half (56 percent) of divorced, separated, or never-married mothers with children under age 21 had been awarded child support payments. But only half of these women received full payments; one-quarter received nothing. The average amount received per child was under $3,000 (*Statistical Abstract,* 1996). Support payments are rarely enough to cover the costs of raising a child (England, 1993). Divorce means an economic setback for most women and economic disaster for those already living close to the poverty line.

Female poverty and divorce are opposite sides of the same coin. If women earned as much as men, many fewer female-headed households would live in poverty; conversely, if fewer people lived in poverty, divorce rates might decline.

Explaining Gender Stratification

The universality of gender stratification and the persistence of gender inequality in societies such as our own, where a majority of men and women say they endorse gender equality, demand explanation: (See *A Global View:* Women as "Missing Persons.") Why are women still the "second sex"?

Sociological Perspectives on Gender Stratification

The two main sociological perspectives—functionalism and conflict theory—differ both on why the gender gap exists and on what should be done about it.

In November 1997, President Clinton and seventeen other Pacific Rim leaders posed for photographers at a Vancouver conference. The universality of gender stratification, even in societies where a majority of people endorse gender equality, demands explanation.

The Functionalist View

Functionalists maintain that gender stratification is rooted in the biological differences between the sexes. Throughout history, most women spent their prime years bearing and rearing children. Pregnancy and nursing required that women stay near their homes. Because of their superior strength and speed, as well as their mobility, men became hunters (providing the main meal for their families) and warriors (defending the community). They also had more time to devote to learning and perfecting specialized skills. The division of labor by sex made sense; male and female roles were complementary.

The Industrial Revolution threw these social arrangements out of balance. Such technological innovations as relatively effective birth control, safe alternatives to breast feeding, and labor-saving devices for the home freed women from their biological and domestic constraints. At the same time, automation reduced the importance of male strength for most work. Women began entering the labor force in increasing numbers. But attitudes and expectations about the proper roles for men and women have changed more slowly than technology—a case of cultural lag (see Chapter 3).

Functionalists argue that expectations have to be brought back in line with actual conditions. Some advocate a return to traditional roles and the stable families those roles produced. Others urge a redefinition of gender roles, to allow both sexes to participate equally in public (work-oriented) and private (family-oriented) life.

Conflict Theory

Conflict theorists see gender inequality as part of the universal problem of exploitation of the weak by the strong. According to this view, throughout history men used their superior strength and women's vulnerability to create institutions that supported and maintained male power and authority. Men controlled the means of production, and women were seen as men's domestic servants.

With the coming of the Industrial Revolution, women were freed (to some extent) from domesticity. Because they had fewer skills and little experience working outside the home, women were willing to work for low wages. Threatened by a new source of competition, the emerging labor movement excluded women from union ranks. At the same time, the early women's movement, led primarily by educated, upper-class women, sought to protect working women—especially working mothers—by limiting the hours they worked and the kind of jobs they filled (Lenski, Lenski, and Nolan, 1991). In hindsight, this legislation "protected" women from equal employment opportunities as well as unsafe working conditions (Simon and Danziger, 1991). As a result, women were confined to a marginal role in the workforce and were dependent on their husbands. The main beneficiaries of this arrangement were not so much working men but capitalists: the existence of a female "underclass" allowed the captains of industry to keep wages for male workers low and, at the same time, gave working men the illusion of power in the workplace.

Women as "Missing Persons"

In many ways, the world's girls and women are "missing persons." They are missing from schools. Worldwide, about 100 million children enter primary school each year. Of the estimated 130 million children who do not attend school, a substantial majority (60 percent) are girls (Neft and Levine, 1997). The degree of educational inequality varies widely by region. In Latin America and western Asia, girls are beginning to catch up with boys; in North America and Europe, female enrollment generally is equal to, and even exceeds, male enrollment in colleges and universities as well as secondary schools. In sub-Saharan Africa and southern Asia, however, girls still lag far behind boys. The education gap is far wider in rural than in urban areas, and it increases with age. In these regions, three-quarters of women age 25 and over are still illiterate. (See Map 10-1.)

Enrollment in school does not tell the whole story (Riley, 1997). In less developed countries girls are much more likely than boys to be chronically absent from school or to drop out altogether. When they do attend school, they may study different subjects (home economics and the like) and tend not to receive as much attention from teachers or as much encouragement from parents. One reason girls skip school is that they are expected to care for younger siblings, perform household chores, or earn wages. In China, the number of girls kept out of school is reportedly increasing. New economic reforms allow families to supplement their meager wages from state-run employment with private enterprise, and parents are putting girls to work. A second reason for devaluing female education is that in China and other countries, when daughters marry, they leave their parents' households and become members of their in-laws' families, whereas sons stay

> No country treats its women as well as its men.

home. Hence educating sons is viewed as a better investment.

Education is one of the most important sources of opportunity in all societies (Riley, 1997). Learning to read and write gives individuals access to knowledge; school exposes people to social life outside the family, opening doors to better jobs and a higher standard of living. Schooling is important for both sexes, of course, but educating girls may produce greater benefits (Neft and Levine, 1997). Education not only improves the individual woman's opportunities and her family's income but also makes it more likely she will have fewer children, spaced farther apart.* As a result, she and her children are likely to enjoy better health, and population growth is slowed. Furthermore, women in developing countries share what they learn with friends and family members, especially daughters, multiplying the benefits of their own education. Sadly, in regions where population growth erodes development, women are least likely to obtain any education, much less equal education.

Women are missing from the paid labor force, especially the well-paid labor force. Women work as hard as or harder than men (on average, thirteen more hours a week worldwide). But the work women do—caring for children, providing food and health care to their families, and, in less-developed countries, tending gardens and livestock, processing crops, gathering firewood and hauling water, weaving cloth, carpets, and baskets, and selling home-grown food and homemade crafts at local markets—is not considered "real" work. It is not counted in calculations of gross national product (GNP), the standard measure of a country's economic health; nor is it entered into the formulas used to design aid and development programs. Worldwide, 70 percent of women age 15 to 64 work outside the home today. Labor-force participation

---

*In Brazil, for example, women with no formal education have an average of six or seven children, while those with secondary or higher education average only about three children (Riley, 1997).

is highest (50 percent or more) in developed countries and sub-Saharan Africa and lowest (25 percent or less) in Arab Muslim countries.

Women everywhere encounter discrimination in the workplace. In industrialized as well as less industrialized countries, they earn less than men; are segregated in low-paying clerical, sales, and service occupations, and excluded from higher-paying jobs in manufacturing, transportation, and management; and are less likely to be promoted to jobs with higher pay, authority, and prestige. Worldwide, women hold only about 14 percent of managerial and administrative *continued*

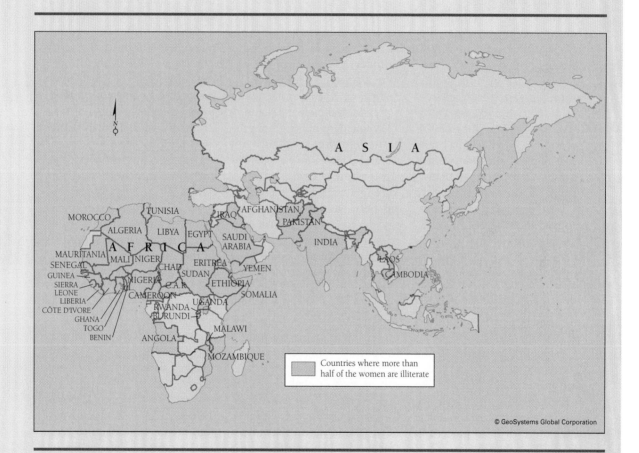

Map 10-1   *Countries Where More Than Half of Women Are Illiterate*

Source: N. Neft and A. D. Levine, *Where Women Stand: An International Report on the Status of Women in 140 Countries, 1997–1998,* New York: Random House, 1997, pp. 33, 34.

Women as "Missing Persons" (continued)

positions in corporations, national or local government, and traditional villages (Neft and Levine, 1997). Only in Brazil and the Philippines do women hold more professional jobs than do men (Riley, 1997). Even when women have similar qualifications and do the same work as men, they earn—on average and worldwide—30 to 40 percent less. In four countries—Tanzania, Vietnam, Australia, and Sri Lanka—women earn 90 percent or more of men's wages; in five—Syria, China, South Korea, Japan, and Bangladesh—the proportion is 60 percent or less (Neft and Levine, 1997). Before the Soviet Union broke apart in 1991, Russian women earned 75 percent of men's wages; in the transition to a market economy, this ratio dropped to 40 percent in 1994. The perception that women's family responsibilities might interfere with performance at work or that women simply are not as good as men at leadership and management is almost universal (Riley, 1997).

Women are missing in the halls of power, policy, and decision making. Although women make up more than half the world's population and in some cases more than 50 percent of voters, less than 5 percent of heads of state, cabinet members, and directors of international organizations are female. (See Table 10-2.) On average, 10 percent of the world's parliamentary representatives are

women. Only five countries, all in Europe (Sweden, Norway, Finland, Denmark, and the Netherlands), have reached the 30 percent threshold recommended by the United Nations Commission on the Status of Women in 1990 (Neft and Levine, 1997). Although the United Nations Charter, adopted in 1945, prohibits sex discrimination, fifty years later, the UN had never had a female secretary-general, only five ambassadors to the United Nations were women, and 40 percent of delegations had no women with professional diplomatic status.

Women are missing from the battlefield, but tragically not from the ranks of war victims (Neft and Levine, 1997). Throughout history, mass rape has been employed as a "strategy" to conquer, terrorize, and punish civilian populations, especially in cultures where violence toward women is regarded as an attack on family honor. (In some cultures, the victims are seen as "defiled" and are disowned by their parents and/or husbands.) In recent times, widespread sexual abuse as a result of wars or civil unrest has been reported from Bangladesh, Burundi, Cambodia, Liberia, Peru, Somalia, and Rwanda. During the first months of the war in the former Yugoslavia, an estimated 20,000 or more women and girls were raped as part of a policy of "ethnic cleansing" (see Chapter 9). The UN estimates that almost half of the 14

million refugees in the world (more than half in Africa) today are women (United Nations High Commissioner for Refugees, 1995). Physical and sexual violence against female refugees—during the events that forced them to leave their home countries, during their flight to a new area, and in resettlement camps and refugee communities—is common.

Often, violence against women is committed not by "the enemy" but by their "loved ones": women the world over are regularly abused sexually, physically injured, and even killed by their families. The most dramatic form of domestic violence occurs in Bangladesh, India, and other countries where a bride is expected to provide her groom's family with large amounts of money, gifts, and other valuables, sometimes in the form of "installment payments" (Neft and Levine, 1997). Despite a law holding the husband and in-laws responsible for a wife's unnatural death during the first seven years of marriage, India reported 7,000 "dowry deaths" in 1995 (up from 5,400 in 1994). In some countries (Nigeria, Mexico, Turkey), the law and local custom permit a husband to "correct" his wife as long as the injury is not incapacitating or does not require extended hospital treatment. Not until 1991 did the Brazilian Supreme Court outlaw the "honor" defense, which excused a man who

Table 10-2   *Women in Government as of October 1997*

Name	Country	Position
Heads of State		
Chandrika Kumaratunge	Sri Lanka	President
Sirimavo Bandaranaike	Sri Lanka	Prime minister
Sheikh Hasina Wajed	Bangladesh	Prime minister
Janet Jagan	Guyana	Prime minister
Heads of Parliament		
Millicent Percival	Antigua and Barbuda	President, Senate
Bridget Harris	Antigua and Barbuda	President, House of Representatives
Sylvia Walker	Antigua and Barbuda	Secretary-General, Parliament
Katica Ivanisevic	Croatia	President, House of Zupanije
Margaret A. Jno. Baptiste	Dominica	Secretary-General, House of Assembly
Riitta Uosukainen	Finland	President, Eduskunta-Riksdagen
Rita Sussmuth	Germany	President, Deutscher Bundestag
Alice Roberts	Grenada	Secretary-General, Senate
Kirsti Kolle Gröndahl	Norway	President, Stortinget
Frene Noshir Ginwala	South Africa	President, Volksraad
Birgitta Dahl	Sweden	President, Riksdagen
Jacqueline Sampson	Trinidad and Tobago	Secretary-General, House of Representatives
Norma Cox	Trinidad and Tobago	Secretary-General, Senate
Betty Boothroyd	United Kingdom	President, House of Commons
Foreign Ministers		
Nazdezhda Mihailova	Bulgaria	
Maria Emma Mejia Velez	Colombia	
Tarja Halonen	Finland	
Andrea Willi	Lichtenstein	
Shirley Gbujama	Sierra Leone	
Zdenka Kramplova	Slovakia	
Lena Hjelm-Wallen	Sweden	
Madeleine Albright	U.S.A.	
Janet Bostwick	Bahamas	
Billie Miller	Barbados	
U.N. Ambassadors		
Penny Wensley	Australia	
Cristina Aguiar	Dominican Republic	
Aksoltan Ataeve	Turkmenistan	
Mahawa Bangoura Camara	Guinea	
Patricia Durrant	Jamaica	
Akmaral Arystanbekova	Kazakhstan	
Claudia Sritsche	Lichtenstein	
Annette Des Iles	Trinidad and Tobago	

Source: Providence Sunday Journal, Oct. 19, 1997, p. B1.

continued

Women as "Missing Persons" (concluded)

murdered an adulterous wife (a defense still allowed in Morocco, Somalia, and other countries). In much of the world, wife battery is ignored, accepted, or even expected.

Involuntary prostitution is another form of violence against women. In the "sex capitals" of Asia, remote lumber camps in Brazil, and the Middle East tens of thousands of women and girls from poor countries and rural villages, lured by promises of employment, are enslaved as prostitutes. In some cases, families turn over their daughters to recruiters in exchange for a "cash advance." The AIDS epidemic has increased the demand for younger and younger prostitutes, in the belief they are less likely to be infected with HIV. (In fact, immature girls are more

vulnerable to infection because their skin and tissues are more fragile.)

Sexual violence against women and girls is not confined to developing countries (Neft and Levine, 1997). Surveys in Canada, the Netherlands, Norway, New Zealand, and the United States find that one-quarter to one-third of the women interviewed said they had been sexually abused during childhood, usually by a family acquaintance or a relative.

Finally, violence is not the only reason that females "disappear." Biologically, women are the stronger sex: given equal nutrition and medical attention, women, on average, outlive men. Yet in a number of countries female life expectancy is the same as or shorter than that for

males. Because of sociocultural preference for sons, an unknown number of unborn or newborn females are aborted, abandoned, or allowed to die of neglect. In rural Bangladesh and elsewhere, tradition dictates that men and boys be served first; often there is little food left for women and their daughters. Given limited resources, parents may be more likely to seek medical attention for sons than daughters. Female genital mutilation and early and frequent pregnancies and births, often with no medical attention and under unsanitary conditions, further compromise women's health.

"No country treats its women as well as its men," declared a report by the United Nations Development Programme (1993).

In most societies and times, men have controlled the means not only of production but also of *reproduction* (Riley, 1997). Women were viewed as property, whose main function was to bear children (especially sons). When women have frequent and numerous births, their autonomy and opportunities to participate in the public sphere, such as paid employment or political office, are restricted. Such is the case in many developing countries today, especially in rural areas. Frequently wives want birth control, but their husbands refuse, especially in cultures where masculinity is measured in part by the number of children a man fathers. When women have access to safe and effective means of controlling their reproductive lives, maternal and child health generally improve, the differences between men's and women's roles may be reduced, and women tend to gain status and power in their families and their societies.

Conflict theorists hold that social change depends on social action, which in turn depends on the development of "class consciousness." The contemporary women's movement (discussed below) has helped women find common ground and articulate their grievances. Conflict theorists urge women to band together—joining forces with other oppressed groups—and challenge white male capitalist dominance.

Middle-Range Theories of Gender Stratification

In analyzing trends and conducting research, sociologists employ a number of middle-range theories that focus on specific areas of gender stratification, such as inequality in the workplace. The *human capital* theory holds that women earn less than men because they have fewer assets to "sell" on the labor market. Older women tend to have less education and less work experience than do men their age. Younger women may have the same educational credentials as their male peers, but they are expected to take time off to have children. As a result, they are worth less to employers. While this may explain some inequality in pay, it does not explain why highly educated women who pursue careers full-time earn less than men do.

The *overcrowding* theory holds that gender inequality in the workplace is caused by women crowding into a relatively small number of occupations. According to the laws of supply and demand, the more workers there are competing for a job, the less an employer has to pay. This, too, may explain some gender inequality. But it does not explain why men in traditionally female occupations (such as social work) earn more than women do. Nor does it explain shortages in such "female" occupations as nursing.

A third explanation is the *dual labor market* hypothesis. This view holds that the job market is divided in two. The *primary* job market is characterized by high wages, good working conditions, fringe benefits, job security, opportunities for advancement, a high degree of unionization, and due process with regard to job rights. There are relatively few entry-level jobs in the primary market but long promotion ladders. In contrast, the *secondary* job market is characterized by low wages, poor working conditions, low job security, part-time and seasonal employment, few fringe benefits, low levels of unionization, and little protection from arbitrary action on the part of employers. There are many entry-level jobs in the secondary market but few opportunities for advancement. The primary and secondary job markets are separate worlds; individuals rarely move from one to the other. And the majority of women workers are trapped in the secondary job market (for example, as secretaries, waitresses, beauticians, garment workers).

Underlying all these middle-range theories is the belief that prejudice and discrimination, based on stereotypes of sex differences in abilities, keep women "in their place." But if this were the main reason for job inequality, laws against sex discrimination and changing attitudes toward women working should have reduced the earnings gap. While women have made some progress in relation to men, the gap is far from closed.

The explanation of persistent gender inequality lies in **institutionalized sexism**: established social patterns that have the unintended consequence of limiting women's opportunities. Gender inequality is a by-product of practices and policies that, on the surface, seem to have nothing to do with sex. For example, the 9-to-5 business day was not designed to keep women "in their place," but it has the unintended consequence of making it difficult for women with small children to hold full-time jobs or to pursue careers without interruptions. Pension plans requiring that an employee work for the company for a number of consecutive years were not designed to discriminate against women, but a woman who takes time off to rear children loses benefits. Health insurance policies that cover only full-time employees are not part of a plot against women, but they have the consequence of excluding part-time workers, many of whom are female.

It is between the ages of 25 and 35 that men "get ahead." This is the decade in which lawyers become partners in their firms, academics get tenure in universities, and blue-collar workers move into skilled, highly paid trades. Workers who do not advance during this period often stay where they are, in terms of job and income level, for the rest of their working lives. And this is the decade during which women who are going to have children are most likely to leave the labor force. For this reason alone, gender inequality will persist even without discrimination.

The elimination of gender inequality would require structural changes in both child care and work. As long as combining work and family and rearing children are seen as "women's problems" rather than as society's problems, significant change is unlikely.

Equality for Women: A Century of Struggle

Women's liberation is not a modern phenomenon. *Feminism*—the belief that women are equal to men and should have equal rights and opportunities—has a long history in the United States (see Figure 10-6). The first Women's Rights Convention was held more than a century ago. In its Declaration of Sentiments, its delegates decried the "history of repeated injuries and usurpations [meant to] destroy woman's confidence in her own powers, to lessen her self-respect, and to make her lead a dependent and abject life" (in Chafe, 1972, p. 5). Support for

Figure 10-6 *The Course of Feminism in the United States*

1750–1850	1850–1900	1890–1920	1920–1945
Colonial America Women are a vital part of the family workforce but are prohibited by law from voting, owning property, making contracts, or bringing suit in court.	**Birth of Modern Feminism: Women and Social Reform Movements** A period of social upheaval beginning with the Civil War. Women are active in the abolition (antislavery), temperance (antialcohol), and progressive movements (the drive to protect children's rights and provide social services for immigrants) but often find that their efforts are ridiculed or ignored. Feminists begin working for women's rights. Elizabeth Cady Stanton and Susan B. Anthony found the National Woman Suffrage Association (NWSA).	**Industrialization** Work moves from the home to the factory. Immigrants and farm girls join the urban workforce, but most married, middle-class women stay at home. Female suffragettes encounter strong, violent opposition, but in 1920, the Nineteenth Amendment is ratified. Women can vote.	**The Static Years** Period of retrenchment on women's rights, as the country celebrates prosperity in the "roaring twenties," and then struggles with the Great Depression, followed by World War II. "Rosie the Riveter" becomes the symbol for millions, as women fill jobs vacated by soldiers. When soldiers return, women are sent home.

women's rights peaked around the turn of the century, as women organized to demand the right to vote, and then faded for several decades after the right to vote had been obtained. The contemporary women's movement began to take shape in the 1960s. Why the 1960s?

The Modern Women's Movement

A number of factors contributed to the resurgence of feminism in the 1960s and 1970s (Chafe, 1991; J. Freeman, 1973; Simon and Danzinger, 1991). The first was a *climate of social change* launched by the civil rights movement and culminating in the antiwar movement. These movements raised the expectations of social equality for all. Young women who were active in these movements gained experience in the politics of protest, but they found that movement leaders often viewed women's issues as trivial and relegated women to gender-stereotyped jobs (typing, answering phones, serving coffee).

A second factor was the emergence of a sense of *collective injustice*. As long as people see their problems as private troubles (Mills, 1959), they are unlikely to take action. Only when they realize that others share their grievances and develop a common explanation of their plight are they likely to participate in collective action. Betty Friedan's book *The Feminine Mystique* (1963) served as a catalyst for the women's movement. Analyzing the loneliness and frustration of full-time housewives, as well as women trapped in dead-end jobs, Friedan identified "the problem that has no name." But discontent alone does not produce a social movement.

A third factor was *organization*. The protest movements had created communications networks

1950s	1960s	1970s	1980s	1990s
The Ozzie and Harriet Decade	**The Protest Years**	**Progress and Promise**	**Backlash**	**Regrouping**
As couples flock to the suburbs, the myth of the happy homemaker rationalizes discrimination against women in higher education and in the workplace. Cultural ideals hold that "a woman's place is in the home." Married women begin returning to the workplace, but usually in such low-paying "pink-collar" jobs as secretary and waitress.	A period of social upheaval. The civil rights movement focuses national attention on social injustice and provides a model for the Chicano, Native American, and antiwar movements, in which many young women are active. In 1964, the Civil Rights Act bans discrimination because of race, nationality, religion, or sex. The birth control pill contributes to the "sexual revolution."	Through the efforts of NOW and other formal organizations, as well as small, informal, local "consciousness-raising" groups, women's rights attract national attention. In *Roe v. Wade,* the U.S. Supreme Court rules that a woman has a right to terminate a pregnancy during the first six months. Age at first marriage and the divorce rate climb; family size declines. The percentage of women seeking higher education and jobs in traditionally "male" occupations increases.	The election of President Reagan in 1980 confirms a rising tide of opposition to the reforms of the 1960s and 1970s. Segments of the New Right accuse the women's movement of being "antifamily." Congress and the Supreme Court place restrictions on abortion. The media begin to portray the women's movement as women's own worst enemy.	Paradoxically, the setbacks of the 1980s reinvigorate the women's movement, awakening women to the need for continued action. In "The Year of the Woman," 1992, six new women are elected to the U.S. Senate and nineteen to the House. For the first time, a woman becomes attorney general. In 1994, Congress passes the Violence Against Women Act, inspired in part by widespread coverage of the murder of Nichole Brown Simpson and the trial of her ex-husband, O. J. Simpson. In 1996, serious allegations surface of sexual harassment in the U.S. Army; similar allegations are made against the president of the United States in 1997–1998. In 1997, Madeline Albright becomes the first woman secretary of state.

among politically conscious young women. At the same time, the appointment of women's commissions at the federal and state levels brought together women who were active in mainstream politics, ultimately leading to the creation of the National Organization for Women (NOW). Organization is critical in mobilizing people and resources for collective action.

A fourth factor was *structural change.* By the 1960s the average family was having fewer children. Motherhood was no longer a lifelong job. In their late thirties, many women found themselves with time on their hands and began entering the workforce. And many younger women were delaying marriage and motherhood to pursue higher education and careers.

In short, the women's movement did not create the desire to be "more than a housewife" or propel women into the labor force. Rather, the movement was a reflection of a general climate of social change, of rising expectations among female activists, and of the fact that many women were already working and pursuing higher education.

From the beginning, the women's movement included two main branches (Boles, 1991; Stoper, 1991). *Liberal feminists* used such tactics as lawsuits, boycotts, and demonstrations to press for equal rights under the law. *Radical feminists* held that true equality was not possible in a patriarchal, misogynist (woman-hating) society and that fundamental social change was required. Radical feminists concentrated on developing women's health clinics, day care centers, shelters for victims of rape and intimate violence, feminist bookstores and theaters, and college courses in women's studies.

Victories, Setbacks, and Institutionalization

In the early 1970s, it looked as though the women's movement had a major impact on national public policy (Chafe, 1991). The movement had scored many victories, particularly in female educational and career opportunities and in abortion rights. But, as often happens, the women's movement provoked a countermovement (Chafe, 1991; Taylor, Whittier, and Huber, 1993). (See also Chapter 17.) The New Right saw feminists as the embodiment of everything that was wrong with the 1960s. Feminists, they argued, wanted to undermine the traditional religious and family values that had made America great. As the 1970s passed, the New Right gained numbers and influence, culminating with the election of conservative Ronald Reagan as presi-

In the 1960s and 1970s, liberal feminists used boycotts, lawsuits, and demonstrations to press for equal rights under the law and to lobby for ERA, the Equal Rights Amendment to the U.S. Constitution. After a ten-year struggle for ratification, the ERA was defeated at the state level in 1982.

dent in 1980. The New Right's main targets were the Equal Rights Amendment to the Constitution (ERA), which was defeated at the state level, and abortion, in a battle that continues today. In the early 1980s, both Congress and the Supreme Court placed restrictions on abortions. "Pro-life" groups such as Operation Rescue became more organized—and more violent.

At the same time, the women's movement became institutionalized. NOW and other women's organizations began to employ paid leaders and professional staff, who used such mainstream tactics as lobbying and forming electoral alliances to guard women's rights. Many of their members are "conscience constituents," who contribute money and occasionally participate in protest marches but are not true activists (Zald and McCarthy, 1987). They have added new issues to the women's agenda, including affordable day care and flexible work schedules for parents, women's health, violence against women, and sexual harassment and assault. Radical feminists are still active in academia, the arts, and health and social services.

Social movements thrive when a defining issue galvanizes grassroots support. The groundswell of support for Anita Hill, which many believe helped sweep a number of women into elected offices in the fall of 1992, showed that American women have a sense of collective interests (or "class consciousness"), as well as the organizations, resources, and networks to mobilize when the need or the opportunity arises. In the absence of a clear cause, however, social movements tend to fade into the background. Such seems to be the case with the women's movement today. In a CBS News poll (1997), three-quarters of women said that the status of women in our society had improved over the past twenty-five years. A large majority (69 percent) applaud the women's movement, although they do not consider themselves "feminists," a term that may be linked to radical fringe activities. Yet a minority of women (43 percent) said the movement had had a positive impact on their lives. What explains this apparent contradiction? One reason may be that many women feel the gains they have made in their careers have come at the expense of their children. Interestingly, women under age 30 are more likely to say the movement has made their lives better but also more likely to perceive discrimination in the workplace than are women over age 30 (see Figure 10-7).

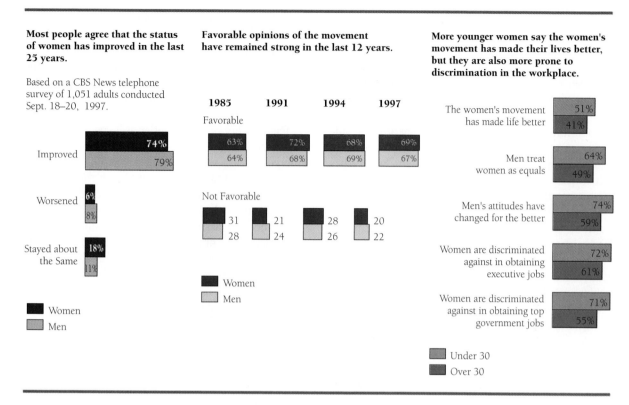

Most people agree that the status of women has improved in the last 25 years.

Based on a CBS News telephone survey of 1,051 adults conducted Sept. 18–20, 1997.

Favorable opinions of the movement have remained strong in the last 12 years.

More younger women say the women's movement has made their lives better, but they are also more prone to discrimination in the workplace.

Figure 10-7   *Current Views of Women's Status and the Women's Movement*

A recent poll found that women believe they enjoy more respect today than they did twenty-five years ago yet are ambivalent about whether the women's movement improved their own lives.

Source: The New York Times, Dec. 14, 1997, p. wk3.

Based on national polls conducted by *The New York Times,* CBS News, the Roper Organization, Gallup, Princeton Survey Research Associates, the National Opinion Research Center, Yankelovich Clancy Shulman, and *The Los Angeles Times.* Compiled by Marjorie Connelly.

Men and Masculinity

A review of the status of women in the United States creates the impression that men—particularly white middle-class men—are a very privileged class indeed. In many ways this is true. However, closer examination shows that gender stratification is a double-edged sword, creating conflicts and constraints for both sexes.

Men have long been considered the normative gender, the standard against which women have been measured and found wanting (Kimmel and Messner, 1995; Tavris, 1992). Yet their very prominence has made men invisible. To be sure, library shelves are crammed with books by and about men in their public roles as political leaders, scientists, authors, and such. But very little has been written about men *as men.* Just as whites rarely think of themselves as being defined by their race and middle-class people rarely think about the impact of social class on their lives because they take these social attributes for granted, so "men often think of themselves as genderless" (Kimmel and Messner, 1995, p. 3). But gender and social definitions of masculinity shape men's identities and experiences as well as women's.

The Hazards of Being Male

Men, we are reminded over and over, are the stronger sex. Yet in terms of health, males are more vulnerable than females at every age. More males than females are miscarried, are stillborn, or die in their first year of life. In all societies, men die earlier than women do (an average of seven years earlier in the United States). American men are more likely than women to die from heart disease, lung disease, and cirrhosis of the liver (a disease strongly associated with alcoholism). They are more likely to suffer from stress-related diseases, such as hypertension, ulcers, and asthma. They are hospitalized for mental illness more frequently. Women attempt suicide more often than men, but men succeed in killing themselves three times as often (largely because they use violent means—guns rather than sleeping pills). Men are twice as likely as women to die in motor vehicle (and other) accidents. They are almost four times as likely to be victims of homicide.

Some of these health differences are undoubtedly due to genetic factors (especially prenatal and infant mortality), but others are linked to the male role (Kimmel and Messner, 1995). For example, in our culture "being able to hold your liquor" is viewed as a sign of masculinity; alcohol may also serve as an escape from pressures to achieve. Four times as many men as women drink to excess. Alcohol is a factor in many auto fatalities and in other deaths from external causes (accidents, suicide, and homicide). The cultural notion that high-risk activities (such as fast driving) and physical aggression (from fistfights to "packing a gun") are validations of masculinity is also a factor in male deaths. Clearly, being "macho" is hazardous to your health.

"The Good Provider"

In our society, a man's status depends on what he does for a living and how successful he is in his occupation—on being a "good provider." Women also seek recognition on the job, but their femininity does not depend on it. A steady job or successful career (depending on social class) is a cultural option for a woman but an obligation for a man. Men have a cultural ultimatum to achieve in the workplace, whether or not they consider their jobs personally rewarding or socially valuable. Many women can choose to emphasize their work or their family; men have no such choice.

The association of masculinity with the provider role is relatively recent (Bernard, 1992). Throughout much of human history, women played a vital role in providing for their families. In this country, as recently as colonial days, husbands and wives ran farms, shops, or businesses together, as part-

ners. Under the law, men were the heads of their households and owned and controlled their wives' property. In practice, however, women often were in charge. Thus John Adams was able to spend time in Philadelphia, working on the Constitution, because his wife Abigail Adams managed the family estate.

The concept of the provider as a specialized male role dates to the Industrial Revolution and the emergence of a wage economy. The new industrial order was a competitive one, in which the male role of provider soon escalated to good provider. A man was judged by the level of luxury he provided; the family became a showcase for his financial virility. In exchange for financial support, the husband was exempted from domestic chores. But there was a negative side to masculine privilege: If a husband/father failed in business, he could not make up for poor performance by displaying excellence in other roles. "The good provider played an all-or-nothing game" (Bernard, 1992, p. 208).

Beginning in the 1970s, more and more families found that they could not maintain their standard of living, or even pay the bills, on a single income. Married women began joining the workforce in increasing numbers. The recessions of the mid-1980s and early 1990s, which left many men unemployed or underemployed, further eroded the role of good provider. Still saddled with the drive to succeed in the workplace, men also faced new demands at home, for intimacy and nurturance and for help with housekeeping and child care.

"The New Father"

Our culture's definition of what it means to be a "good father" is changing (Pleck, 1988; LaRossa, 1997). In the eighteenth and early nineteenth centuries, fathers were expected to be the "moral overseers" for their families. Women were considered "too weak" to guide their children's education and development. Because work was still a family enterprise, fathers were in regular contact with children. In cases of marital separation, both the right and the obligation of child custody were automatically assigned to the father.

In the early nineteenth century, with the rise of industrialization, these roles were almost reversed. With men at the office or factory all day, parenting was redefined as women's work. As distant breadwinners, fathers often lost touch with their families.

The father-child relationship is probably the one that has benefited the most from the emerging redefinition of masculinity.

"The suburban husband and father is almost entirely a Sunday institution," noted *Harper's Bazaar* in 1900 (Pleck, 1988, p. 88). In cases of marital separation, child custody was routinely awarded to the mother.

During World War II, psychologists and journalists began to worry about what happened when the father was absent. Left home alone during the war (and after the war, when their husbands returned to work), the argument went, mothers became too involved in their children. "Momism" was especially bad for boys, who were likely to become "sissies" (a code word for "homosexuals") or delinquents as a result. (The contradiction implied by these two outcomes was blindly overlooked.) Fathers were assigned a new responsibility as sex-role models.

In the late 1960s and early 1970s, as the women's movement gathered momentum and more mothers went to work, a new image of the good father began to take shape. The "new father"

is present at the birth [of his child]; he is involved with his children as infants, not just when they are older; he participates in the actual day-to-day work of child care, and not just play; and he is as involved with his daughters as much as his sons. (Pleck, 1988, p. 93)

How common is the new father? The culture of fatherhood (ideals of what makes a good father) probably has changed more rapidly than the conduct of fatherhood (what fathers actually do)—another case of cultural lag (LaRossa, 1997). Today's fathers may spend more time at home, but relatively little time in direct interaction with their children, and they see their wives as responsible for basic care and daily routines. The lag between performance and ideals creates several problems. Marital conflict may increase when the mother finds she is doing more than she planned because her husband is doing less than he promised; she feels cheated and he gets defensive. In addition, many fathers feel ambivalent or guilty about their performance. Guilt more often leads to tension than to change. Ironically, the men most likely to fit the model of the "new father" are those (relatively few) divorced men who remain involved with their children, and so spend time alone with them, as single parents.

Redefining Masculinity

Old definitions of masculinity required that men control their emotions, prove their virility through heterosexual conquests, see other men as competitors more than as brothers, and accept long hours of drudgery in the workplace as the price for fulfilling the role of good provider and being the head of their households.

New definitions of masculinity are emerging. (See *Close Up*: The Men's Movement: Promise Keepers or Patriarchs?) These new ideals have not replaced the old ones but, rather, have developed alongside them. The result is "a dynamic tension between ambitious breadwinner and compassionate father, between macho seducer and loving companion" (Kimmel, 1988, p. 9). Men today appear to be at a crossroad. They do more housework and spend more time with children than their fathers did, but women still carry a far heavier domestic load. Men are breaking out of old career molds and paying more attention to their physical and emotional

CLOSE UP

The Men's Movement: Promise Keepers or Patriarchs?

Masculine revivals, like women's liberation, are not new to the United States. In the early 1900s, men across America flocked to male-only prayer meetings to hear Billy Sunday's sermons on "Muscular Christianity." Sunday preached that changes in the nature of work, the closing of the frontier, and changes in the family were undermining American values in general and the male role in particular. Numerous fraternal lodges, wilderness retreats, rodeos, and dude ranches were organized to provide settings where "men could be men," without female interference or approval. The Boy Scouts and all-male classrooms were designed to protect the next generation of boys from feminization (Kimmel, 1996).

Likewise today, a men's movement seems to be taking shape. Organizations such as the Coalition for Free Men, the National Congress for Men, and Men's Rights, Inc. (MR, Inc.), have formed to seek equal rights for males (see Baber, 1992). They argue that men are discriminated against in the military (because women are ex-

> **. . . a Christ-centered ministry dedicated to uniting men through vital relationships to become godly influences in their world.**
> —Promise Keepers

> **The hottest religious-right marketing tool since televangelism . . .**
> —Patricia Ireland, president of the National Organization for Women (NOW)

empted from combat), in divorce and child custody proceedings, and in abortion laws (which do not require that a woman obtain the father's consent). Inspired by poet Robert Bly's *Iron John* (1990) and Sam Keen's *Fire in the Belly* (1992), both best-sellers, men from all walks of life—including *Fortune* 500 CEO's, senators, and two presidents (Reagan and Nixon)—attended weekend retreats designed to encourage male bonding and to help men rediscover the "inner warrior" through adapted Native American rituals. In 1995, the Million Man March organized by Louis Farrakan, head of the Nation of Islam, drew an estimated 900,000 African American men to Washington for a day of brotherhood, black solidarity, and prayer.

The group that has attracted the most participants, and the most public attention, is Promise Keepers, which describes itself as a "Christ-centered ministry dedicated to uniting men through vital relationships to become godly influences in their world." Founded in 1990 by former University of Colorado football coach Bill McCartney, Promise Keepers (PK) has grown from a prayer group of 72 men who met in a local gymnasium to a network of 20,000 local "fellowship groups," huge stadium rallies (called "conferences") attended by a total of more than 2.4 mil-

Men pray together at a Promise Keepers rally in Dallas, Texas, in 1995.

lion men, and, in October 1997, one of the largest assemblies ever held in the nation's capital. The crowd of well over a half-million people packed the Mall stretching from the Capitol to the Washington Monument for six hours of hymns, prayer, and repentance. Although the gathering included large numbers of blacks and other minorities, as well as wives and other female supporters, the great majority of participants were white men. With national headquarters in Denver, Colorado, PK boasts an annual budget of $87 million and 360 paid staff members.

Promise Keepers has been described as "a men's movement that blames men for every modern malaise" (Goodstein, 1995). Leaders emphasize that men are more likely than women to break their marriage vows (through infidelity, abuse, or desertion); to impregnate young women and leave them alone to deal with the consequences; to abuse drugs and alcohol and then engage in criminal, often violent, behavior (McCartney, 1997). The basic message is twofold. First, most of societies ills are the result of broken promises in every sphere of life, from friendship to global treaties. Second, it is not just "those guys" (politicians, liberals, criminals, etc.) who have broken promises; "us guys"— that is, men claiming to be Christians—have broken promises to the family, to the com-

munity, to one another, and to God. Promise Keeper's popular rallies combine familiar rituals from sports events—cheering, stomping, doing "the wave" for Jesus—with elements of old-fashioned religious revivals—hymns, prayer, and repentance. By the thousands men fall to their knees weeping and beg forgiveness for sins ranging from reading pornography to abusing their wives, from literally abandoning their children to spending every weekend working, from drinking and gambling to having feelings of racial hatred. Then, with gusto, men sing out traditional hymns such as "Amazing Grace" to rock rhythms.

The male-only nature of PK is based in part on the idea that just as the male role holds that "real men don't cry," so real men do not pray, sing, admit their feelings to others, or form close friendships. The movement aims to release men from these cultural inhibitions by creating a setting in which men are more likely to examine themselves and their lives honestly. At the same time, PK urges men to reclaim the role assigned to them in the Bible, as the religious head of their households. In the words of founder Bill McCartney, "From a Christian Perspective, men have a unique, God-given responsibility for the spiritual health of their families" (1997, p. 18).

Like other social movements, Promise Keepers is not a formal organization: "We are not, never have been, and never will be a church or denomination," declared one executive (in Abraham, 1994, p. 67). Individuals cannot join or become members of PK. They are simply asked to make six promises: Trust in Christ; form close friendships with a few men; practice moral and sexual purity; love your wife and children; support your church; and encourage others to do the same.

Promise Keepers has achieved considerable support, in terms of both the numbers of men who participate in its activities and the endorsements it has received. Hillary Clinton praised the group in her book, *It Takes a Village* (1996). Pat Funderburk Ware, an African American expert on teenage pregnancy, is a supporter: "So many white women . . . don't know what it is not to have their men there. . . . We've suffered enough." Spokeswomen for mainline Protestant, Orthodox, and Roman Catholic churches have praised PK as an important correction of the "radical feminist fixation on power." Even journalists who have gone undercover to investigate the group—including Donna Minkowitz, on assignment for *Ms. Magazine,* who attended a rally

continued

The Men's Movement: Promise Keepers or Patriarchs? *(concluded)*

disguised as a teenage boy—have been impressed. Participants are not simply "angry white men," they report, but men who want to help one another change in important ways (in Stodghill, 1997).

The movement has also attracted strong criticism. Many observers view PK as the third wave of the Christian right, as a political organization masquerading as a religious movement. Groups ranging from the Center for Democratic Studies to the ecumenical Equal Partners in Faith hear the admonition that participants must "take back the nation for Christ" as a political agenda for imposing a strict, fundamentalist moral code on all Americans and a serious threat to both religious freedom and civil rights, especially women's rights. Some of the strongest opposition to PK comes from women's groups. Patricia Ireland, president of the National Organization for Women (NOW), characterizes the group as "the hottest-religious-right marketing tool since televangelism . . . portrayed women's equality as the source of society's ills" (Ireland 1997, p. C03). Ireland makes three main points. First, PK claims it has no political agenda. Yet it has accepted funds from such conservative political activists as Jerry Falwell, Pat Robertson,

and James Dobson, who have also supported Operation Rescue, the group that claimed "credit" for firebombing abortion clinics. "When I look out on the [Washington] Mall and see hundreds and thousands of people," said Ireland, "I see hundreds and thousands of names on direct mail lists" (in Goodstein, 1997). Second, PK asks men to "honor" their wives. Certainly, most women want men to contribute their fair share of child care and housework. But PK is not preaching equality; rather, it preaches patriarchy, or male dominance. In the words of PK spokesman Tony Evans, "I'm not suggesting that you ask for your role [as head of household] back, I am urging you to take it back. There can be no compromise here." Third, PK preaches love and tolerance. Yet founder Bill McCartney was instrumental in passing Colorado's antihomosexual Amendment 2 (later ruled unconstitutional by the Supreme Court) and has been a strong supporter of the Right to Life Movement, once describing abortion as "a violation of the heart of God" (in Stodghill, 1997). All of this suggests that PK's concept of "love and tolerance" is limited.

It is tempting to view Promise Keepers and today's men's movement as a whole as a

"backlash" against feminism, a revolt against the loss of male privilege that accompanies greater female equality. To some extent this may be true. But other social forces are at work. As at the turn of the century, the nature of work is changing. Jobs requiring muscle-power are dwindling; working- and middle-class men have been hit hardest by changes in the global economy. Unemployment undermines the role of "good provider"—even, perhaps especially, if the wife earns enough to support the family. The so-called American Century, during which the United States was an unquestioned world leader, may be drawing to a close. And American families are clearly in a state of flux. As husbands and wives, mothers and fathers, both sexes are struggling to reconcile traditional gender roles with current economic and social realities. In times of rapid, unpredictable social change, groups that offer a simple explanation of what is wrong (broken promises) and clear guidelines (turn to God and each other) have widespread appeal.

Whether the men's movement will become institutionalized and be a significant political force or whether it will fade from the scene, as the "inner warrior" has, remains to be seen.

health, but they still suffer from stress-related diseases and early death. They seek to get in touch with their feelings and to develop deeper, more intimate relationships both with the women in their lives and with their male buddies, yet violence against women and against homosexuals seems to be increasing. What directions men will choose, who they will see when they look in the mirror, is still undecided.

Sexual Orientation

Much as our social institutions are based on the assumption that men and women are inherently different, so they assume that the only "normal" or "natural" form of sexual interaction is between adults of the opposite sex. We do not see homosexuality (sexual interest in members of one's own sex) simply as a personal choice, equivalent, say, to a preference for classical rather than popular music. Gay (male homosexual) and lesbian (female homosexual) are a *social identity* that shapes the way other members of society view a person and how they interact with him or her. People who have sexual relations with a member of the same sex during a brief period in their lives, occasionally, or even exclusively may or may not see themselves as "homosexuals" (their personal identity). But our culture defines homosexuality as an either-or characteristic. Like gender, this distinction is not a "biological given" but is socially constructed.

Attitudes toward homosexual behavior have varied with the time and place (Greenberg, 1988). In some small, traditional societies, homosexual relationships are seen as a normal part of adolescence. Often boys are isolated in special houses or villages during their training for manhood; the homosexual relationships they develop during this period may or may not be continued after the boys grow up and marry. In other societies, homosexual acts with older partners are part of the initiation ceremonies that transform boys into men. Some peoples believe that a shaman's healing powers can be transmitted to an apprentice only through his semen. Others recognize a special role (called *berdache* by French researchers) for men who dress as women and perform "female" tasks (such as gardening and weaving). Still others do not regard affection and physical intimacy between men or between women as "sex."

Not all traditional societies approve of or tolerate homosexuality. While some groups revere berdaches, others ridicule them. Some peoples have never heard of homosexual behavior; some are indifferent on the subject; a few require that individuals caught in homosexual behavior choose between ritual purification and expulsion. (See Table 10-3 for examples of current attitudes toward homosexuality.)

The historical record is equally varied. Conventional wisdom holds that the ancient Greeks approved of homosexual relationships, especially between young boys and their teachers. This is only partly true. The classical Greeks had no word for a homosexual (or heterosexual) person, for they did not recognize these as mutually exclusive categories. They believed that most people could be sexually attracted to beauty in either sex and that choice of a same-sex or opposite-sex partner at one time did not preclude choice of the other at another time. The Greek gods Zeus, Apollo, and Poseidon wooed both sexes, as did the Hindu god Samba, son of Krishna, and many Roman gods. These cultures did not draw a distinction between homosexual and heterosexual relations or between people who favored one over the other.

In general, Judeo-Christian teachings have condemned homosexuality, along with any other sexual activities not associated with procreation. Homosexuality was viewed as immoral and sinful, but like other "vices" (such as masturbation), it was considered an expression of human weakness, not a sickness that marked the individual as different from other people.

The idea that homosexual behavior is pathological dates to the late nineteenth century and the work of Sigmund Freud. Freud himself did not develop a specific explanation of, or "treatment" for, homosexuality. Indeed, in his "Letter to an American Mother" he stated that whatever its origin, homosexuality was not a sickness, and in 1930 he signed a statement declaring the punishment of homosexuals an "extreme violation of human rights" (in Greenberg, 1988, pp. 425–426). But his other writings strongly implied that erotic attraction to the same sex resulted from an arrested state of development. Expanding on Freud, other psychologists declared that homosexuality was a sign of maladjustment, even mental illness.

The medicalization of homosexuality did not lead to greater tolerance; it led to the reverse. **Homophobia** (prejudice and discrimination against gays and lesbians), the equivalent of sexism and racism, became entrenched. For the first half of the twentieth century, homosexuals were subject to systematic persecution. In Nazi Germany, they were sent to death camps; in the United States, they were treated as criminals. One state after another passed sodomy laws banning "unnatural" sexual acts, even between consenting adults. (These laws applied to heterosexuals as well as homosexuals, but they were rarely enforced against heterosexuals.) Stereotypes depicted male homosexuals as effeminate, lesbians as mannish, and both as oversexed and potential child molesters. As a result, homosexual activities were hidden, the subject was not discussed in the open, and homosexuals were vulnerable to blackmail. Alfred Kinsey, the first modern scientist to study sexual behavior in the United States, found that homosexual behavior was more common than anyone suspected, occurring in all walks of life and at every socioeconomic level (Kinsey, Pomeroy, and Martin, 1948). Kinsey maintained that homosexual activity was not an either-or "condition"; rather, sexual activities spanned a continuum from exclusive heterosexuality to exclusive homosexuality, with many degrees in between. His research played a role in the American Psychiatric Association's decision to eliminate homosexuality from its list of mental disorders in 1973, but it had little impact on popular opinion.

The first public protest against harassment of homosexuals, generally seen as the beginning of the gay rights movement, was the 1969 Stonewall riot in New York City, prompted by a police raid on a gay bar (see Chapter 17). Emboldened by the so-called sexual revolution among students in the 1960s and 1970s, which changed cultural attitudes toward premarital sex and cohabitation, homosexuals began to "come out of the closet," protest discrimination, and create gay communities in San Francisco, New York, and other urban centers. The Gay and Lesbian Task Force, the Lambda Fund, and numerous other groups challenged discrimination against homosexuals in housing, employment, and other areas on the grounds that existing laws and policies were a violation of their civil rights. As a result of activism, twenty-six states repealed their antisodomy laws and nine passed laws banning discrimination against homosexuals.

The AIDS epidemic, which began among homosexuals in the United States, made some people more sympathetic to homosexuals and convinced others that homosexuals deserve punishment and isolation. Both gay rights organizations, which did not want homosexuals to be stigmatized, and federal agencies were slow to respond (Shilts, 1987). Eventually, however, the gay community, with help from Elizabeth Taylor and other celebrities, mobilized public support. (See the discussion of protest movements in Chapter 14.) A safe-sex campaign lowered the rates of new infection with the HIV virus among gays.

In the 1990s, the gay community itself became divided (Stolberg, 1997). Mainstream gay groups focused on family rights, such as marriage (which affects health care plans, taxation, and inheritance), parental rights, and adoption. More radical groups, such as Sex Panic, called for a return to sexual liberation and opportunities for anonymous sex with multiple partners, which they view as central to the gay identity. They see members of

Table 10-3   *Attitudes toward Homosexuality:* How Do You Feel about Each of the Following Homosexual Rights?

	Approve	Disapprove
Health insurance for gay spouses	67%	27%
Inheritance rights for gay spouses	70	25
Social Security for gay spouses	58	35
Legally sanctioned gay marriages	35	58
Adoption rights for gay spouses	32	61
Should homosexuals have equal rights in job opportunities?	78	17
Is homosexuality an acceptable alternative lifestyle?	41	53
Are gay rights a threat to the American family and its values?	45	51

Note: For this *Newsweek* poll, the Gallup Organization interviewed 547 registered voters by phone Aug. 27, 1992. Margin or error +/-5 percentage points. "Don't know" and other responses not shown.

Source: Newsweek, Sept. 14, 1992, p. 36. The *Newsweek* Poll © 1992 by *Newsweek,* Inc.

the traditional organizations as "assimilationists," who seek mainstream acceptance by living according to prevailing, middle-class family values. More conservative gays see liberationists as suicidal, both literally, in exposing themselves to AIDS, and socially, in alienating mainstream supporters.

Social attitudes toward homosexuality have changed, but prejudice and hate crimes against gays and lesbians have not disappeared. President Clinton's first act as president was to ban discrimination against homosexuals in the military. He was forced to retreat to a "don't ask, don't tell" policy designed to allow homosexuals to serve in the military while protecting individual privacy and troop morale, which the Pentagon believes would be lowered by the knowledge of homosexuals in the ranks. Under this policy, recruiters are not allowed to ask prospective enlistees about their sexual orientation, commanders are not permitted to investigate suspected homosexual conduct in the absence of compelling evidence, and gay and lesbian soldiers are forbidden from disclosing their sexual orientation.

Whether this policy has helped or hurt homosexuals is a matter of debate. Between 1994 (when the policy was put into effect) and 1997, the proportion of gay and lesbian troops dismissed from the military increased by 67 percent—a pattern gay rights activists see as evidence of continuing harassment (Weiner, 1998). There still is no federal law protecting homosexuals against discrimination. And in many places gays can lose their jobs, their homes, and their children because of their sexual preference. Homosexuals remain a minority group: they do not enjoy equal rights; they may be treated with "suspicion, contempt, hatred, and violence"; and many see themselves as "a people apart" (Wirth, 1945).

Clearly, cultural definitions of what it means to be male or female, gay or straight, have social and economic consequences. Even when attitudes and behavior change, old norms and values, embedded in social institutions, continue to influence social structure, social identities, and social interaction.

Summary

1. **What is gender?** In comparing males and females, it is important to distinguish between *sex* (biological differences), *sex roles* (expected behavior), *sexual orientation* (choice of sex partners), and *gender* (the social meanings attached to sex). Gender is a culturally constructed social institution that maintains inequality between the sexes.

2. **How different are the sexes?** Males and females play different roles in reproduction, but other biological differences (in males' and females' brains, thinking, and even sports performance) have been exaggerated. Gender stratification is universal, but the roles men and women play in different cultures and the degree of inequality vary. Given the many conscious and unconscious attempts to fit boys and girls into gender molds, the wonder is that they are so alike. Too often men's behavior is seen as normal and women's behavior as the "problem" that needs to be explained.

3. **What are the social and economic consequences of being a woman in our** society today? Despite gains, women still fit Wirth's definition of a minority group. In the workplace, women earn less than men with comparable education and experience; tend to be segregated in low-income, low-prestige service occupations; and encounter hidden cultural and structural obstacles to getting ahead, including prejudice against working mothers and sexual harassment. In the family, women still bear the primary responsibility for housework and child care, whether they work or not, and they "pay" more for divorce than men do.

4. **How do sociologists explain gender stratification?** Sociologists differ in their views of the causes of gender stratification. Functionalists see gender stratification as the product of a biologically based division of labor that, until recently, benefited both sexes. In contrast, conflict theorists see gender stratification as a design to maintain male privilege and appease working men. In explaining specific areas of gender

SOCIOLOGY ON THE WEB

It All Depends on Your Point of View

Feminism

The following sites will allow you to research the topic of feminism from both a U.S. and a global perspective. As you explore these sites and others they lead you to, note the kinds of problems feminists in different countries address and the different means they employ. Pick two countries to study, such as the United States and India or another developing country. What issues are feminists concerned about in the two countries? How does a country's relative economic condition reflect the status of women?

The first site listed below, maintained by an MIT professor, is an enormous set of links to other sites about women and feminism. Then there are two sites from U.S. feminist groups, followed by two with a global focus.

http://www.mit.edu:8001/people/sorokin/women/index.html
Start researching the topic of feminism here by exploring some of the many links provided to women's, feminist, and lesbian organizations, individuals, and political action groups.

http://www.feminist.org/
The Feminist Majority is a U.S. organization whose web site provides news about women, current events of interest to feminists, reports on the organization's activities, and lots of links.

http://www.now.org/
At the web site of the National Organization for Women, you will find information on such topics as economic equity and woman-friendly workplaces, as well as position papers and links to related sites.

http://un.org/womenwatch/
At this United Nations site, you can obtain data about family structure, household makeup, and women's health, education, and work, by region of the world. The information here can be the basis for a cross-cultural examination of the status of women.

http://www.igc.org/
The Global Fund for Women supports international women's rights groups. The site contains many links to international organizations that work on behalf of women's social and economic rights.

Men's Issues

The following sites provide three different "takes" on men's issues and the men's movement. Compare the point of view each provides on such issues as domestic violence, feminism, and fathers' rights. As you review the information at each site, think about how the sponsoring organization would view the topics presented in this chapter. How would Promise Keepers explain and defend gender stratification? How would the editors of *XY* magazine consider the same topic?

http://www.vix.com.men/
http://www.vix.com.menmag/menmag.html
These are the addresses of the Men's Issues Home Page and *MenMag, The Men's Voices Magazine*. Especially interesting is the viewpoint on child abuse and domestic violence that you will find here. Compare it with the text discussion, and list the differences and similarities you find.

http://coombs.anu.edu.au/~gorkin/XY/welcome.html
XY magazine, published from the University of Coombs in Australia, is a feminist men's magazine.

http://www.promisekeepers.org/
At Promise Keepers' web site, you can find out about the organization's activities and take its current survey. To what degree are the results of such surveys statistically reliable? Compare the information at this site with NOW's information about Promise Keepers.

stratification, sociologists often employ middle-range theories, including overcrowding, the dual labor market, and *institutionalized sexism*.

5. **How did the women's movement begin, and where is it headed?** Feminism is not a modern phenomenon. The early women's movement emerged during a period of rapid social change in the late nineteenth century. Feminism seemed to disappear in the early twentieth century, after women won the vote, but resurfaced in the 1960s—another period of social upheaval. After a period of more or less steady victories in the 1970s the movement encountered organized, government-backed opposition in the 1980s. To a large degree, the women's movement has become institutionalized: women's issues have gained a respected place on the national agenda.

Without a unifying, urgent issue, the movement is quiet.

6. **How are men and masculinity changing?** Often overlooked is the fact that gender stratification affects males as well as females—most obviously in terms of their health. Old cultural definitions of what it means to be a man (especially "the good provider") remain powerful, but new ideals (especially "the new father") are emerging alongside the old.

7. **Have attitudes toward sexual orientation changed?** During the first half of the twentieth century, *homophobia* was widespread in the United States. The gay rights movement succeeded in decriminalizing homosexuality, but gays and lesbians remain a minority group in the sociological sense and are still subjected to prejudice and discrimination.

Key Terms

comparable worth 369	homophobia 395	sex role 361
feminism 385	institutionalized sexism 385	sexual harassment 372
gender 361	sex 361	sexual orientation 361
glass ceiling 370		

Recommended Readings

Farrell, W. (1993). *The Myth of Male Power.* New York: Berkley Books.

Fausto-Sterling, A. (1985). *Myths of Gender: Biological Theories About Men and Women.* New York: Basic Books.

Friedan, B. (1963). *The Feminine Mystique.* New York: Norton.

Hochschild, A., & Machung, A. (1989). *The Second Shift: Working Parents and the Revolution at Home.* New York: Viking.

Kimmel, M. (1996). *Manhood in America: A Cultural History.* New York: Free Press.

Kimmel, M., & Messner, M. A. (1995). *Men's Lives,* 3d ed. New York: Macmillan.

LaRossa, Ralph. (1997). *The Modernization of Fatherhood.* Chicago: University of Chicago Press.

Neft, Naomi, & Levine, Ann D. (1997). *Where Women Stand: An International Report on the Status of Women in 140 Countries, 1997–1998.* New York: Random House.

Simon, R. J., & Danziger, G. (1991). *Women's Movements in America: Their Successes and Disappointments.* New York: Praeger.

Tannen, J. (1990). *You Just Don't Understand: Women and Men in Conversation.* New York: Morrow.

Tavris, C. (1992). *The Mismeasurement of Women.* New York: Simon & Schuster.

Part

Social Institutions

This part looks at social institutions: time-honored, widely accepted sets of norms and values, statuses and roles, and groups and organizations that provide a structure for behavior in a vital area of social life.

Chapter 11 puts in sociological perspective the controversy over changes and variations in American families.

Chapter 12 examines the goals of education in the United States, whether our schools provide all students with equal educational opportunity, who has access to the best school systems, and how schooling in the United States compares with schooling in other cultures.

Chapter 13 analyzes the relationship between religion and society across several cultures and historical periods. Particular attention is given to the current status of religion in America.

Chapter 14 looks at the origins of modern political institutions; compares our democratic political ideals with the realities of big government, campaign financing, interest-group politics, and voter apathy; and then surveys different types of political systems around the world.

Chapter 15 analyzes the impact of changes in the economy on both the kinds of work available in the United States (and other countries) and workers themselves.

4

Chapter

Eleven

The Family

Marriage is certainly a *transformed* institution, and it plays a smaller role than ever before in organizing social and personal life. . . . Although fewer women stay single all their lives than in 1900, a higher proportion of women than ever before experience a period of independent living and employment before marriage. Women's expectations of both marriage and work are unlikely to ever be the same as in the past.
    —*The Way We Really Are* (Coontz, 1997, p. 31)

Shouldn't we do more to protect and strengthen the American family? The American family is at the heart of our society. It is through the family that we learn values like responsibility, morality, commitment, and faith. Today it seems the family is under attack from all sides—from the media, from the educational establishment, from big government.

   Our Family Responsibility Act is pro-family because it recognizes the value of families. We will strengthen the rights of parents to protect their children against education programs that undermine the values taught in the home. We will crack down on deadbeat parents who avoid child support payments. Pay up, or be forced to work by the state.
    —*Contract with America* (Republican National Committee, 1994, p. 79)

Merle, 14, lives north of Boston with her mother Molly, and her mother's partner, Laura. Over the years she has learned to ignore the name-calling . . . from kids who know her mother is a lesbian and assume she must be one, too (as far as she knows she isn't). And there are other painful memories. . . . One day in sixth-grade health class, the teacher asked for examples of different kinds of families. When Merle raised her hand and said "lesbian," the teacher responded: "This is such a nice town. There wouldn't be any lesbians living here." (*Newsweek,* November 4, 1996, p. 52)

By what they say and sometimes even more importantly, by the information they omit, [college textbooks on marriage and family] repeatedly suggest that marriage is more of a problem than a solution. . . . The potential costs of marriage to adults, particularly women, often receive exaggerated treatment, while the benefits of marriage, both to individuals and to society, are frequently downplayed or ignored.
    —*Institute on American Values' Council on Families* (in Lewin, 1997)

Everyone pays allegiance to "family values," but there is little agreement as to what kinds of families they mean. Lesbian and gay families, single-parent families, and blended families are just three of the many contemporary family forms.

As we approach the year 2000, the family is yet again at the center of a storm of controversy. On the one hand are those who applaud the diversity of "postmodern" families as healthy, ingenious, even courageous adaptations to the economic and social/cultural uncertainties of our times (Stacey, 1996). On the other hand are those who see the "breakdown" of conventional, stable families as a serious threat to the welfare of our nation's children and even to the future of our society (Blankenhorn, 1995). Families are held responsible for all manner of social problems, from declining educational standards to violent crime. At the same time, families are being called upon to solve those problems. For example, supporters of welfare reform argued that the only way to reduce poverty in the United States was "to end welfare politics that discourage marriage and reward irresponsible behavior" (California Governor Pete Wilson, State of the State Address, January 1996). Gay and lesbian parents, who have children from previous heterosexual partnerships or who start new families by adopting or through artificial insemination or surrogate mothers, are cautiously coming out of the closet. Leaders as far apart as Pat Robertson, founder of the Christian Coalition, and Louis Farrakhan, head of the Nation of Islam (or Black Muslims), call on their male followers to take back their rights and responsibilities as "head of their households." Feminists suggest that with men becoming part-time, sometimes absentee fathers, "The Family of Man"—a phrase that once stood for all humankind—is becoming "The Family of Woman." Politicians of every stripe proclaim their allegiance to "family values." But

for some this phrase means communities and kin playing an active role in bringing up related (and unrelated) children, as in Hillary Rodham Clinton's book, It Takes a Village (1996); for others it connotes rejection of recent advances in racial and ethnic, women's, and gay rights. Even college textbooks are drawn into the fray. No one disputes that American families are struggling or that they are changing; but there is little consensus over whether this is good, bad, or neutral—simply "the way we really are" (Coontz, 1997).

Concern about the family dates back at least as far as the Greek philosopher Plato, who thought the family was too weak to be entrusted with the socialization of children. Bright young people, Plato argued, should be made wards of the state and trained and educated in schools. In the early 1800s, Auguste Comte, one of the founders of sociology, worried that the social disorganization created by the French Revolution would break the patriarchal backbone of the family, undermining commitment to lifelong monogamy. In twentieth-century America, the argument has shifted from whether traditional three-generation households were enriching or stifling, to whether the independent nuclear family promoted togetherness or neurosis, and, most recently, to whether the family as a social institution is coming apart at the seams.

The intensity of the debate over the family illustrates how social institutions shape our values; affect and are affected by other major institutions (politics, economics, education, and religion); and influence the most ordinary and intimate details of our lives.

Key Questions

1. *How do families vary across cultures?*
2. *How have American families changed?*
3. *How do contemporary Americans choose a partner, decide to get married, and balance work and family?*
4. *How do sociologists explain family violence?*
5. *What are the causes and consequences of today's high divorce rate?*
6. *What will the family look like in the future?*

Cross-Cultural Similarities and Differences

The *family* is a social group, and social institution, with an identifiable structure based on positions (breadwinners, child rearer, decision maker, nurturer) and interaction among people who occupy those positions. Typically, the family carries out specialized functions (such as child rearing), involves both biological and social kinship, and shares a residence (Gelles, 1995, p. 10). The family, as a social institution, is universal; every known society has families. But what form the family takes and what functions it performs vary widely over time and among societies.

In traditional Navajo society, for example, a wife and husband never live under the same roof. Rather, she lives with her mother, sisters, and their children; he lives in a communal men's house. Their "conjugal relations" are limited to discreet visits. The Maasai of east Africa consider it normal and proper for a man to ask permission to sleep with a good friend's wife. For either the husband or his wife to refuse "sexual hospitality" is considered rude. There are even societies where parents do not have final authority over their children. In Samoa, children are considered members of an extended family and wander from one relative's house to another, deciding for themselves where to live. In the United States and other western societies, we expect individuals to choose their own marriage partners and to marry for love. In India, China, and other societies, marriages are arranged by the bride's and groom's parents on the basis of what they consider best for their respective lineages. In many ways, the marriage of Britain's Prince Charles and the late Diana Spencer was arranged.

Family Structure

To most Americans, the word "marriage" is synonymous with **monogamy**—marriage involving only one woman and one man. Although we recognize that such unions may not last, we assume that monogamy is the ideal in most societies and cultures. Not so. According to the *World Ethnographic Survey* (Murdock, 1957)—a survey of all societies known to social scientists through history, exploration, and anthropology—monogamy is the preferred form of marriage in only 25 percent of societies.

In 75 percent, the *preferred* arrangement is *polygamy*—marriage involving more than one wife or husband at the same time. Most often this takes the form of *polygyny,* marriage of one man to two or more women. Polygyny was practiced in ancient China, hardly a small, primitive society. It is part of Judeo-Christian cultural history: the ancient Hebrews (including Kings David and Solomon) were polygynists. Up until 1890, so were the Mormons of Utah. Islam, the second-largest religion in the world today, allows a man four wives (providing he treats each wife equally). Only four known societies have practiced *polyandry*—marriage of one woman to two or more men.

Group marriage—marriage of two or more men to two or more women at the same time—is the rarest family type. Indeed, there has been some debate about whether this arrangement exists at all (Linton, 1936). Group marriage is most likely in a society where polyandry is the cultural ideal, but if the first wife proves infertile, a second wife joins the marriage to provide children.

Most of the men in the societies that permit polygyny do not actually practice it, for the simple reason that there aren't enough women to go around. Even if there were an excess of women, most men could not afford the cost of marrying and maintaining several wives. In practice, polygyny is a privilege that accompanies wealth, power, status, and, in most societies, old age. As a result, monogamy is the most commonly *practiced* form of marriage in the world.

Ironically, it may be more common for a person to have more than one spouse in the United States and other "monogamous" societies than in societies that permit polygamy. The only difference—and one we consider crucial—is that a person must divorce (or outlive) one spouse before acquiring another. More than half of first marriages in America end in divorce today (Bumpass, Sweet, and Martin, 1990). Most divorced people remarry, however, and even when second marriages end in divorce, most of these people try a third time. Thus, some Americans practice **serial monogamy:** one exclusive, legally sanctioned, but relatively short-lived marriage after another (M. Mead, 1970).

Family Functions

Family functions, like family structures, vary widely. In most traditional, preindustrial societies, the family performs four central functions (Murdock, 1949). The first is the *regulation of sexual activity*. No society leaves people free to engage in sexual behavior whenever they want, with whomever they want. Some societies place a strict ban on sexual intimacy before marriage; others require that a woman demonstrate that she is fertile by becoming pregnant before she marries. All societies place a taboo on incest, though which family members are included in this taboo varies.

The second function of the family (which follows from the first) is *reproduction*. The family perpetuates itself by having children to carry on their lineage, replace members of society who have died or emigrated, and thus keep society "alive" from generation to generation.

The third function is the *socialization of children*. It is not enough simply to produce children; they must be given physical care and trained for adult roles. The family bears primary responsibility for teaching children the language, values, norms, beliefs, technology, and skills of their culture.

The fourth function of the family is *economic maintenance*. The family bears primary responsibility for providing food, shelter, protection, health care, and other necessities for its members, including those who are too young, too old, or otherwise unable to provide for themselves.

In modern, industrial societies, some of these traditional functions have either changed or been taken over in part by other institutions. For example, with effective birth control and safe, legal abortions, the regulation of sexual activity became less urgent. During the so-called sexual revolution of the 1960s and early 1970s, "sex lost not only its biological connection to reproduction but also its normative connection to marriage" (Skolnick, 1991, p. 89). It became an accepted—and even expected—part of dating and premarital relationships. But although most Americans consider sex before marriage permissible, the great majority disapprove of sex outside marriage (extramarital sex) (Smith, 1996).

The family's role in socialization has changed significantly. In traditional societies, family members teach young people all they need to know for a life that will resemble their parents' lives. The emphasis is on well-defined traditional social roles and skills. Education is continuous and largely informal, woven into the fabric of everyday life. In modern societies like our own, a child's future occupation is unpredictable. Furthermore, technical skills and even knowledge quickly become obsolete. Schools (including colleges and universities) have taken over responsibility for preparing young people for occupational roles. Day care centers now expose children to "professional socialization" at a younger age than ever before (see Chapter 4). The mass media also have a powerful impact on young people. Much of the debate over "family values" concerns whether the schools and the media have usurped the family's authority over children. For example, should the family or the school be responsible for sex education? Should the family, the media, or the government be responsible for deciding what kinds of shows young people watch on television? what information they have access to on the Internet?

Government also has taken over some of the family's former economic functions—for example, the care and financial support of the elderly through Medicare and Social Security. When one of their members is injured or sick, families turn to the medical establishment (physicians, hospitals, insurance companies, and most recently health maintenance organizations, or HMOs).

The overall trend is for functions that were previously matters of personal care within the family to be taken over by (1) professional experts, (2) large-scale markets, and/or (3) bureaucratic formal organizations.

In traditional societies, such as the Uygur of western China, families teach children all they need to know. In modern societies, schools and day care centers have taken over much of the educational function.

While many of the family's functions have diminished, one that has become increasingly important is emotional gratification. Although schools teach children skills, the family still provides "nurturant socialization" or emotional support and caring. Children are not the only ones to receive emotional gratification from the family. For most of us, the family is the group we count on to satisfy emotional needs on a continuing basis. In one poll, three out of four participants defined the family as "a group of people who love and care for one another" (*Newsweek,* 1990, in Stacey, 1996). We expect—or feel we have a right to expect—to find understanding, companionship, and affection at home. In the words of poet Robert Frost,

> Home is the place where, when you have to go there,
> They have to take you in.

The more depersonalized our work and school lives become, the more we come to depend on the family. The modern family is an "intimate environment" (Skolnick, 1996), distinguished from other social groups by the erotic attachment between husband and wife and the affectionate attachment of parents and children. Ideally, the family is a safe, secure, nurturant "haven in a heartless world"—the world of capitalism, careers, and competition (Lasch, 1977).

The American Family in Historical Perspective

When considering other social institutions—education, politics, the economy—we often equate change with progress. We look for new and better ways of teaching science, delivering health care, or boosting the economy. Change in the family, however, is more often viewed as a sign of decay and decline. Rather than look forward, we look back to the "good old days," when families were stable, self-sufficient, and caring—or so we like to imagine. But our image of the past is based more on fiction than on fact (Coontz, 1992, 1997). Moreover, cultural notions of the ideal family change. In the 1950s and 1960s, Americans saw the extended family as ideal; today the emphasis is on the nuclear family.

The Extended Family

In the 1950s and early 1960s, when those couples who could afford to were flocking to the suburbs and single-family homes, many Americans mourned the death of the big, multigenerational families of the past, where grandparents were the heads of the household, everyone worked together, and children grew up respecting their elders. This is what sociologists call an **extended family:** members of three or more generations, related by blood or marriage, who live together or in close proximity.

There were always plenty of children down on Grandpa's farm and plenty of adults to look after them. No one was lonely or idle. The family produced and preserved its own food, repaired its own equipment, educated its young in vocational skills (namely, being a farmer or a farmer's wife), settled its own disputes, and cared for its own sick, disturbed, and elderly members. Births out of wedlock and divorce were unheard of. Family pride rested on self-sufficiency. The head of the household was stern but fair, and everyone in the family knew his or her place. Furthermore, the extended family was part of a close-knit community in which doors were left unlocked, neighbors came and went, and everyone minded everyone else's business. Life may sometimes have been hard, but it was secure.

The problem with this image of the extended family is that it seldom existed. As William Goode wrote, this was the "classical family of Western nostalgia" (1963, p. 6). Multigenerational families have never been the norm in the United States; at most they accounted for 20 percent of households (Coontz, 1992). A century ago most people lived in one-room cottages, not in big houses. Few farms were large or diversified enough to be self-sufficient. In order to scrape by, families depended on child labor. Many children did not have shoes, and most did not attend school regularly—if at all.

Death was a constant presence in the extended families of old (Skolnick, 1991; Whitehead, 1993). Women frequently died during childbirth; perhaps half of all children died before reaching adulthood; and few of the survivors lived beyond age 50. Because of early death, only one-third of marriages lasted more than ten years, and a quarter of the children born in 1900 lost at least one parent before reaching age 15. Some children lived with a widowed parent and other relatives; others were sent to orphanages or foster homes.

Family Networks

Ironically, the generations that mourned the death of the large, multigenerational family in the 1950s and 1960s may have had longer and closer relationships with their extended families than did Americans at the turn of the century. In a classic study of middle-class urban families in the 1950s, Marvin Sussman (1959) found that over 90 percent received some kind of aid from extended-family members. Direct financial aid (say, the down payment for a house), indirect financial aid (a gift of a major appliance or a savings account for grandchildren), help during illness, and baby-sitting were all cited. In most cases aid flowed from parents to children, but adult children also helped their parents and one another. It did not seem to matter how far apart members of the family lived; they came to one another's aid when the need arose.

Family ties remain strong. Indeed, the special relationship between grandparents and grandchildren, which leaps a generation, may be growing stronger (Cherlin and Furstenberg, 1986). More people live long enough to become grandparents (and even great-grandparents) today than in the past. Moreover, many of today's grandparents have more time and money to devote to their grandchildren, and advances in transportation and communication make it easier for them to keep in touch, even though they probably do not live together.

The result is the **modified extended family:** a network of relatives who live in separate residences, often miles apart, but maintain ties (Litwak, 1960). These interlocking families often provide significant aid to one another. But their feeling of being connected does not depend on living near one another, working together, or falling under the authority of a strong parent, as in classical extended families. Participation in the modified extended family is voluntary, not obligatory; some individuals do "drop out." Kinship has become more like friendship (Skolnick, 1996).

The Nuclear Family

Today when people talk of the golden age of families, they usually are referring to the 1950s, known affectionately as the "Ozzie and Harriet" decade. The ideal family type in this era was the **nuclear family,** consisting of a husband, his wife, and their dependent children living in a home of their own. In the ideal nuclear family, the husband/father was the sole breadwinner (an element of the "good-provider" role; see Chapter 10). Each morning he went off to work for a corporation or branch of government (not, as in generations past, for a family-owned enterprise). Although still the head of his household, he worked for somebody else. The wife/mother was a full-time homemaker. Although she had a variety of labor-saving devices (the more the better), it was assumed that she delighted in baking brownies and sewing Halloween costumes for the children herself.

"A new standard of family security and stability was established in postwar America," writes Barbara Whitehead of the Institute for American Values (1993, p. 50). At first glance, the statistics support this view (Coontz, 1992). In the 1950s rates of divorce and out-of-wedlock births were half what they are today; the family was seen as the core social institution, the heart and soul of society; nine out of ten Americans told pollsters that getting married and raising a family were the most important goals in life; many couples married in their late teens or early twenties; and the average couple had at least two and sometimes three, four, or more children. The "only child" was an object of pity and concern. During this era, America often was described as a "child-centered" society.

In discussions of family values, we tend to use the nuclear family of the 1950s as the baseline, and find contemporary families wanting. But the Ozzie

The cast of Leave It to Beaver, *which, like other TV series of the time, reflected the ideal type of American nuclear family in the 1950s: breadwinner husband and father, full-time homemaker wife and mother, and two or three children.*

and Harriet standard is misleading, for a number of reasons. The 1950s was a unique period in American family history. The early marriages and large families of the postwar period were exceptions to a trend of later marriage and smaller-size families that had begun at the turn of the century. For more than fifty years, the ages at which women married and bore their first child had been increasing, the gender gap in education narrowing, and the divorce rate rising. In the 1950s—and only the 1950s—these trends reversed. Far from exemplifying traditional family values, the nuclear family of the 1950s was a break with a long-term pattern of social change. Moreover, our image of the families of this period is based more on media portrayals than on real life (see *Sociology and the Media:* Prime-Time Families).

The 1950s also was a decade of unparalleled prosperity for Americans. Never before had so many people had money to spare after meeting basic needs. By 1960, 62 percent of American families owned their homes, 75 percent had a car in the garage, and 87 percent had purchased a television set (Coontz, 1992). Middle- and working-class wives could be full-time homemakers because their husbands earned enough to support the family in comfort.

Not all families participated in the postwar economic boom, however. In the mid-1950s, 25 percent of the population—40 to 50 million people—lived in poverty. Two out of three Americans age 65 or older subsisted on incomes of less than $1,000 a year. But poverty was "socially invisible": most people did not know, or want to know, about the poor (Harrington, 1963). African Americans were systematically excluded from the American family dream through legally sanctioned segregation and socially accepted terrorism in the south as well as discrimination and harassment in the north. During this "golden age of the family," 50 percent of two-parent black families lived in poverty, and 40 percent of mothers in these families with small children worked outside their homes (Coontz, 1992).

A distant dream for some women, the full-time homemaker role was a nightmare for others. The ideal nuclear family depended on the wife's subordinating her needs and aspirations to those of her husband and children. "Rosie the Riveter" was forced out of the challenging, relatively high-paying job she had filled during World War II and either sent home or, if she had to work, demoted to a lower-paid, less interesting "female job." Even

SOCIOLOGY & THE MEDIA

Prime-Time Families

The changing image of the family on television provides insights into changing attitudes toward the family in society. This is not to say that portrayals of the family on TV sit-coms mirror reality; they do not. But television speaks to our collective desires, our shared worries and concerns, our wish to improve or repair our own lives (E. Taylor, 1989)—and to our stereotypes (Butsch, 1992).

The 1950s and 1960s were the decades of the happy TV family. The family that viewers saw on prime-time television, for the most part, was an intact, white, comfortable (though not conspicuously wealthy), middle-class, suburban, nuclear family—as presented on *Father Knows Best, Ozzie and Harriet,* and *Leave It to Beaver.* Parents on these shows had an endless supply of time, energy, and wisdom, which they devoted to guiding their children toward adult lives that presumably would resemble their own. Blessed with all the modern conveniences, these families also were firmly grounded in traditional values. The outside world of public issues rarely, if ever, intruded on this contented domestic circle.

Other prime-time shows from this period appealed to the dream of professional success, a beautifully decorated suburban home, and an affluent middle- to upper-middle-class lifestyle, often with servants (Butsch, 1992). Writers, with no other apparent source of income, appeared well-off (*The Dick Van Dyke Show, My World and Welcome to It,* and *The Debbie Reynolds Show,* featuring Ms. Reynolds as a magazine reporter); the father in *Life with Father* was not just a banker but a Wall Street banker; on an architect's income, *The Brady Bunch* had a housekeeper. On these shows, Mom and Dad were intelligent, mature, successful "superparents." On the rare sit-coms featuring working-

. . . the way we never were.

class characters, family life was chaotic and gender roles were reversed, with the husband playing a lovable but incompetent buffoon whose wife always knows best. Thus on *The Honeymooners* (still popular in reruns), bus driver Ralph Cramden engages in endless, hair-brained get-rich-quick schemes, while his wife Alice waits to tell him, once again, "I told you so."

Many family sit-coms of the 1970s focused on change. One of the most popular shows of this decade was *All in the Family,* the story of a white, middle-aged, working-class couple, living in a soon-to-be-integrated neighborhood in Queens, New York. The show was a battle of the generations, which pitted unrepentant bigot Archie Bunker, with his constant stream of racial and ethnic slurs, against his muddleheaded but kindly wife Edith, his feminist daughter Gloria, and her Polish American husband Michael, who was studying to become a sociologist. Social problems that had been taboo for the situation comedies of the 1960s were "lined up like ducks in a shooting range and argued back and forth in a contest between tradition and modernity," between the political conservatism of the 1950s and the liberalism of the post-Vietnam years (E. Taylor, 1989, p. 69). The gender-role reversal of *The Honeymooners* was replaced by a generation-role reversal, in which "children know best." The husband's moral authority was also questioned on *The Bob Newhart Show,* which featured an indecisive, self-doubting psychologist; *The Jeffersons,* in which George provides a middle-class standard of living but fails miserably to acquire middle-class manners; and *Maude,* where an outspoken feminist (and one of the first "older" women to star in prime time) exasperates her husband, their daughter, and their friends.

Prime-time soap operas in which superrich families were divided against themselves (*Dallas* and *Dynasty*) made their first appearance in the 1970s. Two of the only popular shows with happy, "intact" families—*The Waltons* and *Little House on the Prairie*—were set in the past.

The 1980s was a decade of reorganization for TV families. Alternative family forms—single parents, all-female and all-male households, mixed-race families—were treated as (almost) normal. But by far the most popular program about families was *The Cosby Show.* In many ways the Huxtables resembled the happy prime-time families of the 1950s and 1960s. Despite high-powered careers (Claire was a lawyer and Cliff, a physician), the Huxtables always had plenty of "quality time" to devote to their children. "There is no dissent, no real difference of opinion or belief, only vaguely malicious banter that quickly dissolves into sweet agreement—all part of the busy daily manufacture of consensus" (E. Taylor,

1989, p. 161). Almost all the action took place within the Huxtables' elegant brownstone; the outside world did not intrude on this charmed family circle.

Why was *The Cosby Show* so popular? With his impish grin and affluent lifestyle, Bill Cosby implicitly reassured the audience that the American system is fair to everyone, black or white. "Look!" he seemed to be saying, "even I can have it all!" (M. C. Miller, 1988, p. 71). The difficulty of combining two careers and family life, as well as the ongoing racial tensions in our society, were swept aside. *The Cosby Show* appealed to our nostalgia for "the way we never were" (Coontz, 1992).

In the early 1990s, the portrayal of a variety of family types continued, but with a new touch of cynicism. All but one of the lead characters on *Murphy Brown* were single: the news team functioned as a substitute family, and Murphy Brown, a famous, affluent single parent, struggled to disavow maternal feelings. *Cybil,* a mother of almost-adult children and a would-be actress who can't quite get her career together, was Murphy Brown's mirror image.

Roseanne was the story of an intact working-class family, in

which the heavy-set, brash, tough-talking wife leads a one-woman crusade against middle-class hypocrisy. Dan, her husband, is loving, sensible, and respected by his children. The fact that they were working-class helped make the idea that they were not superparents with all the answers, but a couple whose life did not revolve around their children, more acceptable. At the same time, however, *The Simpsons* brought back the incompetent working-class father in cartoon form. Homer, who can't even afford a TV, demonstrates fatherly love by waving to his son and thereby causing an accident at a nuclear power plant. Though his wife, Marge, is somewhat more level-headed, son Bart and even baby Lisa are clearly smarter. *Married with Children*—featuring a domineering, do-nothing wife, a blustery, incompetent husband, a stereotypical "blonde bimbo" daughter, and a nerdy son—was designed to insult everyone. The overall message seemed to be that conventional families don't work very well but neither do the alternatives.

continued

Prime-Time Families *(concluded)*

As the 1990s draw to a close, families—even dysfunctional families—are disappearing from prime-time television. *Roseanne* and her blue-collar family live on only in reruns; the last episode of *Married with Children* ran in 1997. To be sure, families appear here and there: On *Mad about You*, Jamie and Paul have a new baby; Raymond Romano copes with his wife, daughter, and twin sons, as well as his parents and divorced brother, who live across the street, in *Everybody Loves Raymond*. But, for the most part, prime-time television focuses on relationships, as in *Seinfeld* (now discontinued) and *Friends*. If TV sit-coms reflect our dreams and fears, the family is something we want to tune out when we tune in.

The cast of Everybody Loves Raymond.

(perhaps especially) women college graduates were expected to seek fulfillment in the family and to base their identity on it. For many wives, the suburban nuclear family spelled isolation and boredom. By the end of the decade, the women's magazines that once glorified the happy housewife were printing stories about runaway wives. Physicians were among the first to notice the mounting discontent among middle-class housewives. Their solution? Tranquilizers (Coontz, 1992).

Finally, the happy, smiling Ozzie and Harriet families on television concealed a host of problems, from alcoholism and mental illness to wife battering and sexual abuse of children. In the 1950s, such problems were largely unrecognized, unreported, and untreated. The family of the fifties kept up appearances at all costs. Problems were swept under the rug. Only in the plays of Tennessee Williams, Eugene O'Neill, Arthur Miller, and Edward Albee did we glimpse loveless marriages and families torn by drug addiction, madness, incest, and unrealistic expectations.

The 1950s were not all bad, of course; many people cherish happy family memories from this time. But in some ways the nuclear family contained the seeds of its own destruction (Coontz, 1992). Women who "played dumb" to catch a husband ended up resenting him for not living up to the fantasy of male superiority. Early marriage and family planning left women with time on their hands after their children left home. And the ethic of family closeness fostered a search for authenticity and a sensitivity to hypocrisy that fueled the student ("hippie") rebellion of the 1960s and 1970s—a rebellion that turned family values inside out. Most student rebels had grown up in Ozzie and Harriet families.

Contemporary Families

Americans continue to see family ties as their main source of happiness and meaning in life (Skolnick, 1996). But social and economic conditions have

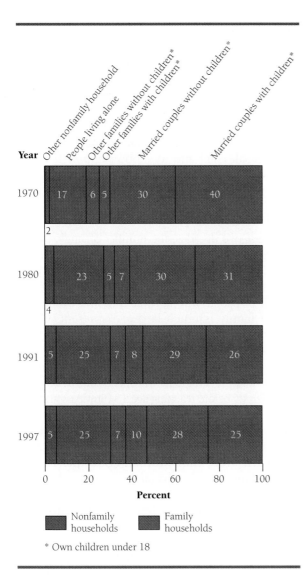

Figure 11-1   *Today's Changing Family*

There is no one, typical family type in the United States today. Furthermore, most people will live within several different types of family over the course of their lifetimes.

Sources: Current Population Reports, series P-20, no. 468, December 1992, p. 3, fig. 1; U.S. Census Bureau, *Current Population Survey,* March 1997.

changed dramatically since the 1950s. So have families.

Today's families are characterized not by one dominant family type but, rather, by variation (see Figure 11-1). Less than one in four households in the United States today consists of a husband, a wife, and their children at home. The numbers of single people living alone, single parents, married

couples with no children (or no children living at home), and unmarried couples living together have grown steadily. Furthermore, nuclear families have changed. Most two-parent families today have two or fewer children; very likely, the mother is employed outside the home; and the odds are about 50/50 that the parents will divorce before the children grow up (Ahlburg and De Vita, 1992). Single-mother families outnumber families with a married, stay-at-home mom by more than two to one (Stacey, 1996).

Singlehood

One reason for the changing composition of American households is that more people remain single for longer periods of time. In 1960, only 28 percent of American women age 20 to 24 had not yet married; today more than 66 percent of women in this age group are single (*Statistical Abstract,* 1996). The main reason for this increase is that more young adults are postponing marriage, not that a significant number are deciding never to marry. A larger proportion are going to college and to graduate or professional school, which tends to delay marriage. Marriage is no longer a prerequisite for a satisfying sex life, for women or men; nor is marriage a prerequisite for parenthood.

The category "single" is a diverse group, however. Some single people are students or young adults who have not yet found "Mr. or Ms. Right." Others are cohabiting couples, individuals "between marriages," people who have chosen not to marry, or elderly widows or widowers. Some live alone, some with roommates, and others with their parents, grown children, or other family members. The rising cost of housing, slow wage growth, and the increased cost of higher education (and repayment of student loans) have made it increasingly difficult for young people to establish an independent household. More than half (53 percent) of 18- to 24-year-olds still live at home with their parents (up from 47 percent in 1970). So do 12 percent of 25- to 34-year-olds (up from just 8 percent in 1970) (*Statistical Abstract,* 1996).

Singlehood changes over the life cycle. Often young adults in their twenties try out different lifestyles and make provisional choices but delay full commitments. They can have a good deal of company in this stage. The early thirties tend to be a period of reevaluation, when individuals weigh the possibilities of changing careers and/or living arrangements. People who are married may consider the alternatives; those who are single may feel increased internal and external pressure to marry. The number of single people declines in this stage. Among persons 30 to 34 years old, 28 percent of men and 19 percent of women have never married (*Statistical Abstract,* 1996). But the never-married single people are joined by those who are newly divorced. The middle years reveal a different pattern. Only 8 percent of men and 6 percent of women age 45 to 54 have never married. The ratio of unmarried men to unmarried women also changes over the life cycle. In their twenties and thirties, more men than women are single; from age 40 on, more women than men are likely to be divorced or widowed.

Given current patterns of marriage, divorce, and widowhood, the United States' single population seems likely to continue growing in the future.

Families without Children

Thirty-five percent of today's families consist of married couples without children at home (*Statistical Abstract,* 1996). This category, too, includes several distinct groups. Some of these couples are "pre-parents": they plan to have children, but not in the immediate future. Others are "empty-nesters," couples whose children have grown up and moved out of the family home. Still others are "nonparents," couples who either decided not to have children or were unable to have children because of infertility.

Voluntary childlessness is the exception to the rule. Although many young couples see parenthood as an option, not an obligation, most want to, and plan to, have children. A survey by the U.S. Census Bureau found that more than half of married women under age 35 still plan to have a child someday (O'Connell, 1991). Among married women in their twenties, the proportion rises to 80 percent.

Most studies of childless couples suggest that few decide never to have children before they get married or in the early years of their marriage (L. S. Gilbert, 1988; Houseknecht, 1987; Neal, Groat, and Wicks, 1989; Jacobson and Heaton, 1991). Rather, they decide to postpone parenthood until one or both complete school, until they are established in their careers and can afford to buy a home, or until they feel financially secure. This decision may escalate into a series of "temporary" postponements. In a small percentage of marriages, the couple make a conscious decision never to have

children. The main reasons such couples give are freedom from responsibility, greater opportunity for self-fulfillment and career development, and a happier marital relationship. More often, couples drift into childlessness. Adoption and new technologies to combat infertility make it possible for older women (40 and over) to have children. But post-poners may decide that they are too old to keep up with a small child and to support him or her into adulthood, when they themselves would be entering or past retirement age.

Single-Parent Families

In the last two decades, the number of single-parent families nearly doubled, reaching 15 million in 1995 (*Statistical Abstract,* 1996). This figure represents only the number of *current* single-parent families; the number of people who at some time will live in this type of family is much larger. At present, about 27 percent of children live in one-parent families (*Statistical Abstract,* 1996). But estimates are that 50 percent of all American children (and 80 percent of African American children) will spend time in a single-parent family before reaching age 18 (Bumpass, 1990).

The great majority of single parents (about 88 percent) are mothers. Single mothers usually have lower incomes than single fathers, mainly because men earn more than women (Cherlin, 1996). Whether unmarried, separated, or divorced, single mothers bear most of the cost of raising their children alone. More than half of single mothers (56 percent) are awarded child-support, but only 37 percent receive full or partial payment (an average of slightly more than $3,000 a year) (U.S. Department of Health and Human Services, 1997). A majority of single mothers (51 percent) do not receive any help from the father, either because they do not seek child support, the noncustodial father is unable to pay, or he simply does not pay.

Since 1960, births to unmarried mothers have climbed steadily. Almost one-third of all births in the United States today are to single women (*Statistical Abstract,* 1996) Unwed mothers have come to symbolize the supposed decline in family values in America today. People who supported the federal welfare reform legislation of 1996, which allows states to deny aid to children born to unmarried teenagers and to unmarried women already receiving aid for other "illegitimate" children, viewed aid to single mothers as a cause, not a consequence, of out-of-wedlock births, poverty, and

The great majority of single parents are mothers, and single mothers usually have lower incomes than single fathers.

related social problems. The popular stereotype of unwed mothers is a poor, minority, teenage high school dropout.

A profile of actual unwed mothers suggests the reality is more complex (Figure 11-2). The majority of never-married women who bear children outside marriage are poor or working class: 60 percent had annual family incomes of less than $25,000, of whom 43 percent lived on less than $10,000 a year. Many are poorly educated: 47 percent are high school dropouts; 30 percent are high school graduates; only 6 percent are college graduates. Although the number of out-of-wedlock births is higher for white mothers, the rates are higher for minorities. More than two out of three African American babies were born to unmarried mothers in 1992, compared with slightly more than one in five (23 percent) of white babies. Finally, teenagers account for less than one-third of all births outside marriage, and black teenagers for less than 12 percent. The rate of out-of-wedlock births has been growing fastest among women in their twenties (the age that our culture considers appropriate for women to become mothers), who now account for seven out of ten such births.

There is little evidence that increasing numbers of women *want* to become single parents or that more men want to become absentee fathers (Usdansky, 1996). Almost nine in ten unwed mothers report that their pregnancies were accidental (either unwanted or mistimed). Moreover, unwed motherhood is often a temporary state. One-quarter of single women who give birth have been married in the past, but were divorced, separated, or widowed when they conceived. Four out of ten women whose first birth occurs outside wedlock marry within five years. One in four is currently living with a man (often, but not always, the child's father).

Polls consistently show that the overwhelming majority (90 to 95 percent) of young adults want and expect to marry, consider a good marriage and family life quite important, and think children are better off when raised within marriage (National Opinion Research Center, in Usdansky, 1996). Why, then, are births to single mothers increasing?

Part of the reason is cultural. Much of the stigma attached to "illegitimate births" has disappeared: bearing a child out of wedlock is no longer a cause for lifelong shame. Given high divorce rates, as many as half of married mothers become single parents before their children grow up, so unmarried mothers "have company"; they are not as conspicuous or isolated as their counterparts were in the past. So-called shotgun weddings (hastily arranged after the woman becomes pregnant but before she gives birth), unwed mothers' giving babies up for adoption, and abortion have all declined (Usdansky, 1996).

Part of the reason for births outside marriage is economic. Our culture holds that a man who wants to marry should be able to support a family, but this standard is becoming more difficult to meet, especially for young men without a college degree. For non-college-educated youth, a "family wage" has become a goal that fewer and fewer expect to achieve. As sociologist Andrew Cherlin told *The New*

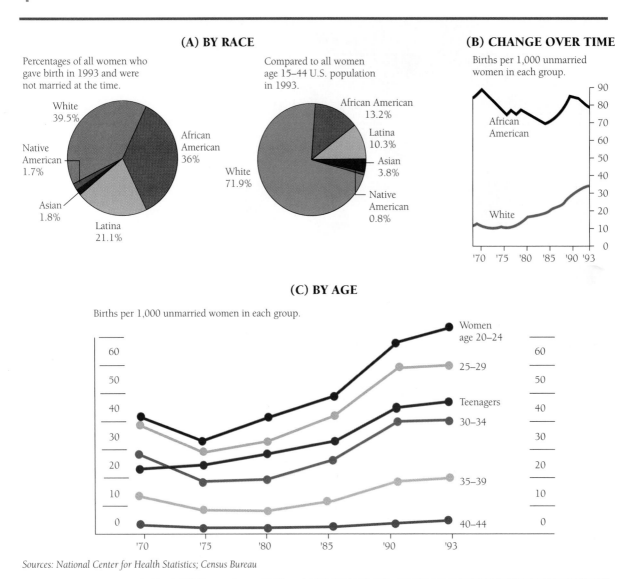

Figure 11-2   *A Demographic Portrait of Single Mothers*

"Single mothers" is not a homogeneous category but includes women of different ages, races, and ethnic groups.

Source: M. L. Usdansky, "Single Motherhood: Stereotypes vs. Statistics," *The New York Times*, Feb. 11, 1996, p. E4.

York Times, "Marriage is still highly valued, but people don't think it's a realistic possibility" (Usdansky, 1996, p. E4). But babies "happen": the rate of unwanted or mistimed pregnancies in the United States (40 percent for married women, 88 percent for unmarried women) is much higher than in Europe.

The United States also has the highest rate of *teenage* pregnancy of any western nation, even though teenagers in Canada and Europe have as high or higher rates of sexual activity (Pittman, 1993). Each year more than a million American teenagers become pregnant. In 1993, 501,000 teenagers gave birth. (See Figure 11-3.) The teenagers most at risk for unmarried pregnancy become sexually active at a young age, are African American or Latina, live in poor neighborhoods, attend segregated schools, and perform poorly in school (Pittman, 1993). Although the rate of pregnancy is higher for inner-city, minority teenagers, two

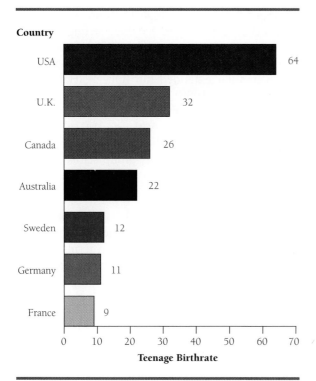

Country

Figure 11-3   *Births to Teenage Mothers in International Perspective*

American teenagers are no more likely to be sexually active than are Canadian or European teenagers. Why, then, are teenage birthrates much lower in other countries? Many believe the reason is that Canadian and European nations have mandatory sex education programs and their schools provide teens with free birth control.

Source: U. Bronfenbrenner, P. McClelland, E. Wethington, P. Moen, and Stephen J. Ceci, *The State of Americas,* New York: Simon and Schuster, 1996, p. 117.

out of three teen births are to white teenagers who live in rural areas and small cities. Moreover, the birthrate for white teenagers is growing, while that for minority teenagers has leveled off. When one adjusts for income and academic skills, the difference between whites and minorities disappears. Regardless of race or ethnicity, one in five young women who come from poor families and are doing badly in school becomes an unwed mother—compared with only one in twenty young women who are better off, financially and academically (Pittman, 1993). This, in turn, suggests that teenagers who grow up surrounded by poverty and have limited opportunities, either to break out of poverty themselves or to find a

husband who is a "good provider" (since most young men they know are unemployed), may feel they have little to lose by becoming teenage mothers. Indeed, they may feel they have something to gain. Realistically or unrealistically, low-income teenage girls may believe that having a baby will affirm their adult status, make the father stay in their lives, and provide love and affection.

In addition to financial problems, single mothers report less satisfaction with their lives and higher levels of stress than do single women with no children. Single mothers also report poorer relations with their children than do married mothers (McLanahan and Booth, 1989). Children in single families are worse off, on average, than children who live with both of their parents regardless of the parents' race or educational background, whether the parents were married when the child was born, and whether the parent with whom the child lives remarried (McLanahan and Sandefur, 1994). Children of single mothers are more likely to have low educational goals, to drop out of high school, to get into trouble with the law, to abuse alcohol and drugs, to marry and bear children at an early age, to get divorced, and to remain poor into adulthood.

The New Extended Family

In recent years, extended or multigeneration households are making a comeback. The high cost of housing, particularly in urban areas, combined with flat or declining wages has made it increasingly difficult for young people to establish independent households. More single adults return to their parents' households after completing school or after a divorce than in past generations. Some single parents (16.2 percent) live with their parents; some, with other relatives (U.S. Bureau of the Census, 1996). Even two-parent families are "doubling up." In the early 1990s, less than half of adults under age 35 were the head (or married to the head) of an independent family household (Ahlburg and De Vita, 1992). These households constitute the *new extended family.*

Ethnic and Racial Variations

Ethnic and racial variations add to the diversity of family life in America. A group's history, cultural ideals, and economic circumstances all affect family structure and experience.

African American Families

African American families tend to be young; they most often live in cities or in southern states; and they are more likely than other families to be headed by a woman (*Statistical Abstract,* 1996). The so-called matrifocal (mother-centered) African American family has been the subject of ongoing debate. Some observers view female-headed families as the cause of poverty and other problems African Americans endure, while others see female-headed families as a consequence of the legacy of slavery, racism, and economic inequality. This debate tends to obscure both the diversity and strengths of African American families.

African American families may be affluent professionals, working-class, or poor (Willie, 1988). Contrary to stereotypes, almost half (47 percent) of these families include two parents, and seven out of ten of the adult men work to support their households (*Statistical Abstract,* 1996). At the same time, two-thirds of African American children are born to single mothers, and four out of five will live in a female-headed household at some time in their childhood. One reason is that African Americans have a higher risk of divorce than white Americans, partly as a function of economic disadvantage. A second reason is a shortage of black men; among African Americans, because of the high rate of homicide among teenagers and premature death due to illness, women outnumber men at every age past childhood.

The outstanding feature of African American families is strong extended-family ties. They are far more likely than whites to live in three-generation or "classical" extended families (Beck and Beck, 1989). Even if they do not live together, members of extended families frequently "pool" or share economic resources and provide one another with other various kinds of assistance and support (such as child care). Strong kin and friendship networks act as a buffer against discrimination as well as economic insecurity.

Latino Families

The category "Latino" includes a range of Spanish-speaking ethnic groups (see Chapter 9), but some generalizations are possible. Latino families, like African American families, tend to be young and to experience high levels of poverty. Latino families are distinguished by their high birthrates, compared with other groups, and by their strong sense of familism. Many Latinos see *la familia* as the center of their lives; they maintain close kinship ties and live near their extended kin (Queen, Haberstein, and Quadango, 1988). The family plays a key role in assisting kin to immigrate to the United States and find employment (Wilson, 1991a). Latino familism may be part of the Latino cultural heritage or an adaptation to minority-group status and economic disadvantage, or both.

Asian American Families

Asian Americans and Pacific Islanders are an even more diverse group than Latinos in terms of place of origin, time of arrival in the United States, circumstances of their arrival, and family structure (see Chapter 9). Some migrants are single individuals, forced by war or economic hardship to leave their families behind; some are intact nuclear families; and some are incomplete extended families, composed of a couple, their children, grandparents, and other relatives (Tran, 1988).

Despite their varied origins, traditional Asian American families have some common features. They tend to be strictly patriarchal: men are the wage earners, decision makers, and disciplinarians. Even when Asian American women work, as many do, they assume near-total responsibility for housework and child rearing. Children are raised to be cooperative, obedient, and loyal and to defer to their parents' wishes (Kitano and Daniels, 1988). Marriage rates for Asian Americans are very high, and divorce rates lower than average (*Statistical Abstract,* 1996).

Minority families and new immigrants add to the variety of family experiences people encounter over the life cycle. One team of demographers has compared the American family to "a patchwork quilt—composed of many patterns yet durable and enduring even when it becomes frayed around the edges" (Ahlburg and De Vita, 1992, p. 38).

Courtship, Marriage, and Children

Despite changes in the family, the great majority of Americans get married and become parents. Women, in particular, wait somewhat longer to get

Table 11-1   *Median Age of First Marriage, 1900–1994*

Year	Men	Women
1900	25.9	21.9
1910	25.1	21.6
1920	24.6	21.2
1930	24.3	21.3
1940	24.3	21.5
1950	22.8	20.3
1960	22.8	20.3
1970	23.2	20.8
1980	24.7	22.0
1990	26.1	23.9
1995	26.9	24.5

Source: Adapted from U.S. Bureau of the Census, "Marital Status and Living Arrangements: March 1994," *Current Population Reports,* series P-20, no. 484, Washington , DC: GPO, 1994, p. vii, table B; Statistical Abstract, 1996, Table 149, p. 105.

In some developing countries, such as India, marriages are arranged when the bride and groom are still children. The two families participate in the wedding ceremony, but the husband and wife do not live together until they are older.

married than they did in the past (Table 11-1). But every year millions get married (2.3 million marriages in 1994). Over 95 percent marry at least once in their lives. Indeed, the United States has one of the highest marriage rates in the world (Ahlburg and De Vita, 1992). Why do people get married? Who marries whom? How do contemporary couples combine work and family?

Choosing a Mate

Why do people get married? Most Americans think the overarching reason is—or should be—"for love." This is not a universal view. Nearly all societies recognize that, on occasion, a man and a woman may develop a "violent emotional attachment" to each other—what we call love (Linton, 1936). But few societies consider this attachment desirable, much less a basis for marriage. In most societies marriages are arranged by older relatives, with an eye to expanding their network of kin. The most important criteria in mate selection are economic security and family background, not mutual attraction.

The notion of arranged marriages strikes most westerners as barbaric. Yet research suggests that in arranged marriages, the couples' romantic attachment to one another grows over the years, whereas couples who married for love report that their attraction to one another dropped precipitously after the first two to five years of marriage (Gupta and Singh, 1982). (See Figure 11-4.)

Analysis of marriage patterns shows that even in our own society, Cupid's dart is highly selective. In principle, we are free to marry anyone we like. In practice, however, our choices are limited by social forces—the same social forces that influence the neighborhood in which we live, the school we attend, and the people we meet. In sociological terms, we practice **homogamy:** the tendency to marry someone who is like ourselves in the social attributes our society considers important. Thus most Americans (95 percent) marry someone of the same race, social class, age, and educational level. Each of these criteria reduces an individual's "pool of eligibles" (see Figure 11-5).

In the past, religion played a major role in defining a person's pool of eligibles: most Americans did not marry outside their religion (whether Protestant, Catholic, or Jewish). However, to some degree educational criteria are beginning to replace religion

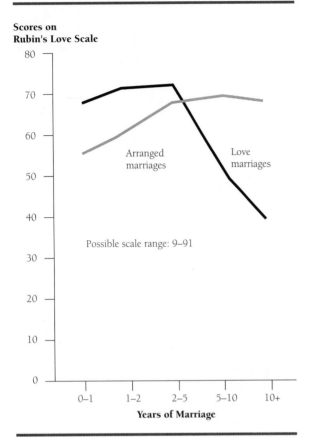

Scores on Rubin's Love Scale

Possible scale range: 9–91

Years of Marriage

Figure 11-4   *Love and Marriage*

A study of romantic and arranged marriages in India found that love and marriage do go together but not necessarily in that order. Couples who marry for love may become disillusioned when the romance fades.

Source: V. Gupta and P. Singh, 1982, in D. G. Meyers, *Social Psychology*, 4th ed., New York: McGraw-Hill, 1993, p. 495, fig. 13-7.

in the choice of mates (Kalmijn, 1991). Intermarriage between people of different religions has increased, while intermarriage between people with different levels of education has decreased. Why? First, education plays a major role in determining people's future earning potential and hence their social class and lifestyle. Second, level of education has a strong impact on the values people hold with regard to marriage and family. Whatever their class background, Americans with college educations tend to be more liberal in their attitudes toward sex roles, to have more permissive attitudes toward sex, to want fewer children, and to place less impor-

tance on obedience in child rearing. They are likely to hold similar moral and political views and to enjoy similar leisure-time pursuits. Finally, young people spend more time in school today than in the past, and so they have more opportunities to meet and date other students. College graduates often meet their future spouses in school (Mare, 1991). As more and more people postpone marriage, however, new ways of meeting potential mates are emerging, including newspaper personal columns, singles clubs and outings (often designed around special interests), and even e-mail computer networks (Hanson, 1993, personal communication).

By one means or another, a person may meet dozens of people who fit his or her basic criteria for a future mate; how does the person choose among them? Exchange theory is a middle-range theory that holds that mate selection is the result of a series of conscious or unconscious calculations (Murstein, 1986). Each of us has an image of our value on the dating market, based on cultural standards and previous experience. In deciding whether to approach a member of the opposite sex, we compare the other person's assets to our own. If the other person has a much higher value, the potential risk of being rejected outweighs the possibility that he or she may be interested. We do not ask for a date. (To simplify, a man who considers himself successful but not good-looking might approach a woman who is good-looking but not high on the career ladder or a woman who is successful but not strikingly attractive. He would be less likely to approach someone who is both beautiful and successful.) Thus self-esteem plays as important a role in courtship as does physical attraction.

After the initial attraction and beginning of the relationship, couples spend much of their time comparing values. He asks what she thought of the party where they met; she asks what he usually does on weekends; the conversation may turn to elections, sports, religion, or food. The couple are most likely to develop a strong liking for one another if their values are similar. Values are the goals people hold in life; roles can be seen as the means to those goals.

Progress beyond attraction and liking depends on role fit. If both like to play a nurturant role (the one to whom others turn for comfort), they are less likely to get together than if one sees himself or herself as supportive and the other sees himself or her-

POOL OF ELIGIBLES FOR SUZIE:
A Single, White, Catholic College Student of Average Height

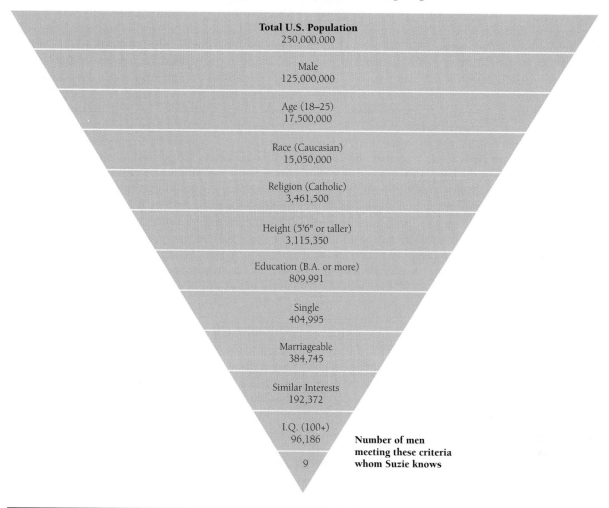

Total U.S. Population
250,000,000

Male
125,000,000

Age (18–25)
17,500,000

Race (Caucasian)
15,050,000

Religion (Catholic)
3,461,500

Height (5'6" or taller)
3,115,350

Education (B.A. or more)
809,991

Single
404,995

Marriageable
384,745

Similar Interests
192,372

I.Q. (100+)
96,186

Number of men meeting these criteria whom Suzie knows

9

Figure 11-5   *The Dating Game*

Who marries whom?

self as needy and dependent. Thus similarity may "heat up" a relationship in the dating stage but "cool it down" in the decision stage. Moreover, each measures the other against the image of an ideal mate. If the fit is close enough, they may become engaged or—almost as likely—try living together.

Living Together

The number of unmarried couples who live together has increased sixfold since 1970, reaching 3.6 million in 1995 (*Statistical Abstract,* 1996). (Note that this figure represents opposite-sex couples only, or, to use the Census Bureau's term, "POSSLQ's": "persons of the opposite sex sharing living quarters"). Most cohabitors (60 percent) are under age 35; a majority (58 percent) have never been married; one-third are divorced; 4 percent are widowed; and the remainder are married but living with someone other than their spouses. About one-third have children under age 15 living in their households.

Only a small percentage of couples see cohabitation as a substitute for, or alternative to, marriage. For most it has become a stage en route to marriage, somewhat like engagement, a time that allows a couple to find out whether they are compatible before getting married. At least one partner expects to get married in 90 percent of cohabitations (Bumpass, 1990). Within a year and a half of moving in together, most couples either get married (about 60 percent) or break up (about 40 percent) (Bumpass, Sweet, and Cherlin, 1991).

One might expect that couples who "look before they leap" are more likely to stay together after marriage. In fact, a national survey of married people found the reverse (Booth and Johnson, 1988). Those who had lived with their spouses before they were married reported that they argued more and spent less time together than did couples who married before living together. They also were more likely to separate or divorce. Does this mean that cohabitation has a negative effect on marriage? Not necessarily. Cohabitors may be "poor marriage risks" before they marry, either because one or both had personal problems (such as unemployment or drug use) or because they had different ideas about marriage (such as how much time and energy to invest in their careers or whether and when to have children).

Work and Families

One of the major issues confronting married couples in the 1990s is how to combine work and family life. A majority (61 percent) of married women are employed today, including 63 percent of mothers with children under age 6 and 76 percent of mothers with children age 6 to 17 (*Statistical Abstract,* 1996). Women's earnings play an important role in family income. In 1993, the median income of married-couple families in which the wife worked was $50,798 compared with $28,799 when the wife did not work and $16,000 for female-headed households (*Statistical Abstract,* 1996). Even though women still earn less than men, on average, the wife's income can lift a family out of poverty or enable a family to remain in the middle class. In polls, most women say they work to support themselves or their family (Yorburg, 1993). But 85 percent say they would continue working even if they did not need the money because they enjoy the

sense of accomplishment and the social contacts (Eggebeen and Hawkins, 1990).

Working women are not a modern phenomenon. On the contrary, in most societies and times women have played a critical role in providing for their families. American families of the 1950s and 1960s, in which most husbands were the sole providers and most wives were full-time homemakers and mothers, were not a "natural" arrangement but an unusual one (Skolnick, 1996). Nevertheless, there are two distinctive features about women's reentry into the labor market in recent times. The first is that work nearly always requires that a woman be away from her home and children; the second is that the sharp distinction between men's and women's jobs found in most earlier societies has faded.

When asked to name the major problems in a two-job marriage, men chose "time for each other" first, followed by child care and housework; women chose housework first, followed by time for each other and child care (Vannoy-Hiller and Philliber, 1989).

Housework

Regardless of whether they have a full-time job or not and no matter how much they earn, wives devote significantly more time to housework than husbands do (Ferree, 1991). Almost 80 percent of all household chores are performed by women (Berardo, Shehan, and Leslie, 1987).

Not only do women do more work around the house but they do different work (Blair and Lichter, 1991) (Figure 11-6). Women are more likely to perform the dull, routine tasks that lock them into rigid daily schedules, such as vacuuming, bed making, diapering babies, and cooking and cleaning up after meals. Women also do more of the undesirable jobs (scrubbing the bathroom or ironing). Men typically take responsibility for such nonroutine tasks as household repairs, auto maintenance, lawn mowing, snow shoveling, and disciplining children. These jobs do not require tight daily schedules; moreover, for some men, home and auto repair may be enjoyable hobbies, and yardwork allows a husband to be out of doors.

Child Care

In 1995, 21 million American children under age 6 had mothers who were employed outside their homes. Who is minding the kids? About 40 per-

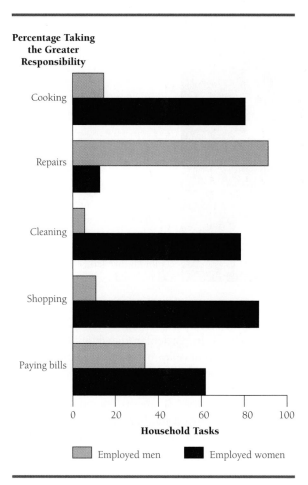

Percentage Taking the Greater Responsibility

Cooking

Repairs

Cleaning

Shopping

Paying bills

0   20   40   60   80   100

Household Tasks

☐ Employed men   ■ Employed women

Figure 11-6   *A Woman's Work*

A comparison of women and men in dual-earner families shows that, except for repairs, women assume far more responsibility for household tasks.

Source: Families and Work Institute, *The New York Times,* Sept. 19, 1993, p. F21.

cent of preschoolers are cared for in their homes by a parent (often with the mother and father alternating "shifts"); 31 percent go to day care centers; 18 percent are in family day care (a nonrelative who may care for several children in her own home); 21 percent are cared for by a relative in the relative's or the child's home (*Statistical Abstract,* 1996). Employed mothers are increasingly choosing day care centers for their youngest preschool child (31 percent in 1995, compared with only 6 percent in 1960). Of children age 6 to 13 whose mothers are employed, about 18 percent go to a family or day

care center after school, about 10 percent take lessons, roughly 5 percent go home to a parent, and most of the others go to a relative's or neighbor's home. Only about 2 percent are "latchkey" children, who are at home alone after school (Hoffreth et al., 1991).

More than nine out of ten parents in this survey said they were either "satisfied" or "very satisfied" with their child care arrangements. But one-quarter said they would prefer another arrangement or a combination of settings. At the same time, many found their arrangements less than totally reliable. Overall, employed mothers miss about one and a half days of work each month because of breakdowns in their child care arrangements. Low-income mothers are particularly hard hit because their child care arrangements tend to be less reliable; thus they miss more time at work, and may not be paid for time off.

In terms of sharing, today's fathers get better reports for child care than for housework. A national survey found that fathers and mothers generally agree that they share child care equally (Chapman, 1987). Fathers also share some of the worry and guilt about leaving their children in someone else's care.

How much time fathers devote to child care depends on several factors. One is the wife's schedule: the more hours the mother works, the more the father pitches in. Another factor is the *mother's* gender-role attitudes: if the mother believes the husband is competent at child care, the father is likely to be more involved (though which is cause and which is effect is difficult to say). The father's relationship with his own father is also a factor: fathers who were dissatisfied with their own fathers are likely to devote more time to their children than are fathers with happier memories. Finally, fathers are more likely to take part in child care if the child is a boy.

The Impact of Work on Families

In the not-too-distant past, the impact on the family of women working was almost universally viewed as negative. But attitudes have changed. What does research show?

Do young children suffer when their mothers work? Most contemporary researchers agree that the real issue is not so much who cares for a child but whether the child gets *good-quality care* (APA

How much time fathers spend caring for their children depends on the mother's work schedule, the mother's gender-role attitudes, the father's relationship with his own father, and the sex of the child.

Task Force, 1993). The most appropriate care for infants and toddlers is either a single caregiver or a small group (no more than four children per caregiver), where the small child can receive individual attention. In general, when the mother works, parents prefer care by a relative, especially the father or grandmother, for children up to age 3. Older preschoolers, age 3 to 5, can benefit from group care, especially if the caregivers are trained in early childhood education and if they interact verbally with each child, provide a safe environment but are not overly restrictive or punitive, and offer both continuity and new experiences. Parents often choose day care centers or nursery schools for their 4- to 5-year-olds. In addition to the caretakers' training and experience, parents also consider convenience and reliability, the attractions of the physical environment, agreement on cultural and religious values, discipline, and cost.

Care by others does not mean that children forgo maternal love and attention. Working women (especially college graduates) spend almost as much time in direct interaction with children (talking, reading stories, baking cookies) as do full-time homemakers. These career women sacrifice sleep and leisure time rather than time with their children (Hoffman, 1987).

In general, studies of school-age children show that maternal employment, by itself, has little effect (Hoffman, 1989). Children whose mothers work do as well in school as children whose mothers stay at home, and perhaps slightly better (Moore and Sawhill, 1984). In particular, daughters of working mothers tend to develop more flexible sex-role attitudes and to have higher career aspirations than do other girls (Hoffman, 1984; Lamb, 1984; Moore and Sawhill, 1984). Some studies also find that children of employed mothers are somewhat more responsible and independent than children with mothers at home (Hoffman, 1984; Moore and Sawhill, 1984). Maternal employment is most likely to have positive effects if the father is involved in family tasks (housework and child care) and the husband and wife agree about the wife's work (Lerner, 1993).

Does working improve or undermine a couple's relationship? The answer depends on a number of factors. One is the nature of the wife's job. Long hours, frequent travel, or a demanding boss can spill over into family stress (Spitze, 1988). A second factor is attitudes toward gender roles, whether traditional, egalitarian, or transitional (Hochschild, 1989). Employed wives tend to be happier and healthier than full-time homemakers, particularly when they and their husbands approve of women working; married women are most likely to be depressed when they are at home full-time but would like to be working (Ulrich, 1988). Not surprisingly, marital satisfaction tends to be highest among working wives with high levels of education who work out of choice, enjoy their jobs, and receive help from their husbands; marital satisfaction tends to be lower among women who have low incomes from undesirable jobs (Voydanoff, 1989). Time together is a problem for most working couples (Kingston and Nock, 1987). The less time they spend together, the less likely they are to be satisfied with their marriage.

The risk of divorce is higher when the wife works, particularly if she works in an unconventional (traditionally male) occupation, such as medicine, law, architecture, or engineering (Bumpass, Martin, and Sweet, 1991). This does not mean that female employment, by itself, causes divorce. Rather, women who work have greater opportunity and choice in both marriage and divorce (Spitze, 1988). Women in high-paying occupations, in particular, do not have to consider potential earning power when choosing a spouse; nor do they have to choose between an unhappy marriage and downward mobility or poverty.

Behind Closed Doors: Violence in the Family

"And they lived happily ever after." Hundreds of stories about marriages and families end with this line. Loved ones are reunited, obstacles to marriage overcome, problems with children resolved. Indeed, the very idea of living happily ever after is linked, in our minds, with the special warmth of the family. Yet if we look behind the closed doors of many American households, we discover that all is not peace and harmony.

Myths and Realities

With the exception of the police and the military, the family is the most violent social group in American society (and most other contemporary societies). The home is a more dangerous place than a dark alley. A person is more likely to be assaulted or murdered in his or her home, by a member of the family, than by anyone else, anywhere else, in society.

Thirty years ago, few Americans would have believed these statements. But things have changed. The sad case of Lisa Steinberg, a young girl killed in New York City in 1987, galvanized public attention around the issue of child abuse and neglect. Hedda

Nussbaum, who acted as Lisa's "mother,"[1] clearly was a battered wife and evoked mixed reactions: yes, she was a victim, but even so, why didn't she protect the child under her care? At that time, violence against women had not captured the interest of the public or policy makers.

The brutal murders of Nicole Brown Simpson and her friend Ron Goldman in June 1994 broke the wall of selective inattention to battered wives. Nicole Brown's ex-husband, former football star O. J. Simpson, was accused of the crime. His arrest and criminal trial galvanized public attention for nearly three years; five years later this case is still the focus of numerous books, talk shows, and articles. O. J. Simpson was an authentic American hero: a child of the ghetto who became a multimillionaire on the strength of his athletic talents; an African American, best known to the public through his ads for Hertz Rent-a-Car, who has seemingly escaped racial classifications. His marriage to Nicole Brown, a glamorous blonde, their luxurious home in Brentwood, an elite neighborhood in Los Angeles, and two beautiful children added to their allure. They were a couple who "had it all." Yet even before the trials began, the media released tapes of Brown's frantic calls to 911, suggesting a pattern of spousal threats and abuse. O. J. Simpson was found "not guilty" of the murders, in part because his defense team revealed a pattern of racism among the police who investigated the crime. But the image of the dark underside of a "perfect marriage" lingers.

Two months after the murders, Congress passed the Violence Against Women Act as part of the crime bill. The act defined "violence inspired by gender" as a violation of civil rights, created an office for domestic violence within the U.S. Justice Department, and provided funds for a national hotline and for innovative state programs to reduce domestic violence and protect victims (Gelles, 1997). Up for reauthorization in 1998, there is little doubt that it will be renewed. Innumerable state laws were enacted. If domestic violence suffered from selective inattention in the 1980s, the reverse is true at the end of the 1990s. Yet myths about family violence abound.[2]

---

[1]Lisa Steinberg had not been legally adopted: Hedda Nussbaum was neither her biological nor adoptive mother.
[2]Unless otherwise noted, the data and conclusions in this section are from Gelles and Straus, 1988, and Straus and Gelles, 1990.

Myth 1: Family violence is rare or epidemic. Public attention to family violence has led some people to believe we are in the midst of an epidemic. Others have concluded that all this attention is "hype." Both are wrong. Family violence is not a modern phenomenon; it has existed in virtually all societies and times. Experts may disagree about whether family violence is increasing or decreasing, but all agree that it is a serious problem that will not go away by itself.

Myth 2: Abusers are mentally ill. When we read a description of family violence, we would like to believe that only someone who is "sick" could beat up a pregnant woman or torture a child. Health workers often find that abusers are disturbed. But whether they committed a violent act because they were disturbed or whether they became disturbed after the act is impossible to say. Only about 10 per-

cent of abusers are clinically diagnosed as mentally ill.

Myth 3: Abuse occurs only in poor, minority families. Rates of abuse are higher in poor and minority households, but violence occurs in families at all socioeconomic levels. One reason that the poor and nonwhites are greatly overrepresented in official statistics is that they are more likely to be labeled as "abusers" or "victims." Sociologists Patrick Turbett and Richard O'Toole (1980) gave groups of physicians and nurses a file describing an injured child and the child's parents. These professionals were more likely to conclude the child was a victim of abuse when they were told the father was a janitor than when they were told he was a teacher and when they were told the child was black as opposed to white. Except for these social markers, which were varied at random, the files were identical.

Myth 4: The real causes of family violence are alcohol and drugs. A news report might highlight the fact that a man who murdered his family was a "crack addict." Victims of family violence often say, "He only did it when he was drunk." Does this mean drugs cause abuse? No. Cross-cultural studies show that the effects of alcohol vary from society to society. In some, people become quiet and withdrawn when they drink; in others, they become loud and aggressive. Our society is one of the latter. We define being drunk as a "time-out" from normal rules of behavior, when a person can claim "I didn't know what I was doing." As a result, both abusers and victims often cite alcohol as the excuse for violence. In one study half the men arrested for beating their wives claimed that they had been drunk, but only 20 percent had enough alcohol in their blood to be considered legally intoxicated (Bard and Zacker, 1974). Frequent drunks (and nondrinkers) are less likely than occasional drinkers to become violent. Much less is known about the effects of illegal drugs on behavior. The only drug that has been conclusively linked with increased aggression (in studies with monkeys) is amphetamine.

Myth 5: Children who are abused grow up to be abusers. Children who are victims of family violence are more likely to be abusive as adults than are children who did not experience family violence. But this does not mean that all abused children become abusive parents. Studies of the intergenerational transmission of family violence are difficult to eval-

Public-service announcements like this one have helped to redefine family violence as a social problem, not a private matter. Until recently, few people considered verbal abuse a form of violence—one that could be as harmful as physical abuse.

uate because they usually rely on self-reports of events that occurred years earlier. The best estimate is that about 30 percent of adults who were abused as children treat their own children the same way (Gelles and Conte, 1990). A follow-up study of children who were abused or neglected twenty years ago found that they did have higher rates of juvenile delinquency, adult criminality, and violence than a matched group of controls (Widom, 1989). But this does not mean that all violent adults were abused as children, or that all abused children grow up to be violent. Abuse makes children more vulnerable to a host of social and emotional problems, but it does not determine how they will behave as adults.

Myth 6: Battered women provoke their offenders, and/or the solution is for them to leave their partners. Most people are angered and saddened by reports of battered children but puzzled by reports of battered wives. After all, the woman is an adult; if her husband beats her, why doesn't she leave him? Abused wives are often assumed to be masochists or, worse, to have provoked their husbands to violence ("She asked for it!"). Anyone who has been through a divorce knows that there is more to ending a marriage than simply walking out the door. In most cases, violence is not an everyday event. It may be easier to talk oneself into believing it will not happen again than to face the world on one's own, with little money, credit, or experience—and perhaps with children to care for as well. Where can the battered wife go? Because our society has mixed feelings about battered wives, we have been slow to build shelters.

If you reread this list of myths, you will see a common theme: Only people *other than* us assault their loved ones. Assigning family abusers to deviant categories (mentally disturbed, poor, drunk) allows us to avoid thinking that it could happen to us. These myths also blind us to the structural characteristics of the family that promote or at least allow violence.

Sociological Explanations

The potential for violence is built into the family. Many of the characteristics we cherish most about families also make us most vulnerable within the family. One is *intimacy.* Family members are intensely involved with one another. They know the private details of one another's lives and what makes the others feel proud or ashamed. When quarrels break out or problems arise, the stakes are higher than in other social groups. For example, a man who is amused by the behavior of a female colleague who is drunk may become enraged if his wife were to have a little too much to drink. A politician who has been an active supporter of gay rights, at some risk to her career, may be appalled to discover that her own child is homosexual. Why? Because we perceive the behavior of a member of our family as a direct reflection on ourselves. The intensity of family relationships tends to magnify the most trivial things, such as a burned dinner or a whining child. When did you last hear of someone beating up the cook in a restaurant for preparing an unacceptable meal? But minor offenses and small oversights often spark violent family fights.

A second factor contributing to violence in the home is *privacy.* Because family affairs are regarded as private, there are few outside restraints on violence. When a family quarrel threatens to become a fight, there are no bystanders to break it up, as there might be on the street or in some other public place. The shift from extended to nuclear families, the move to detached single-family houses in the suburbs, and the trend toward having fewer children have all increased the potential for family violence, simply because there are fewer people around to observe (and try to stop) abuse. Children in isolated single-parent families are at high risk (Gelles, 1989).

A third factor is *inequality.* Few social groups routinely include members of both sexes and different ages. In school, for example, we are segregated by age; at work we are often segregated by sex—for example, men doing heavy labor, women doing clerical work. Because men are usually bigger and stronger than women, and women bigger and stronger than children, they can get away with violent behavior that would provoke retaliation from someone their own size and strength. Moreover, the costs of leaving an abusive family—of becoming a runaway child or a single mother—may seem higher to some family members than to others.

From a feminist perspective, violence toward women in the home is an extension of male dominance in society as a whole. Acts of violence are one of many ways men control their wives, including intimidation, isolation, emotional abuse, economic abuse, using children as pawns, and invoking male privilege. "Domestic violence is not just an individual problem," writes Kerstie Yllo, "but a social and political one. Violence is a means of social control that is at once personal and institutional, symbolic and material. The restrictions on women's psychic and physical freedom created by the fear and reality of male violence are inescapable" (1993, p. 59).

Fourth, and perhaps most disturbing, there is a good deal of *social and cultural support* for the use of physical force in the family. Parents are allowed—indeed, sometimes expected—to spank their children. "Spare the rod and spoil the child," the saying goes. Most people do not think of spanking a child as violence. Indeed, in a recent survey almost three out of four Americans said they saw slapping a 12-year-old as often necessary, normal, and good. But suppose a teacher slapped the child, or a stranger slapped you for something you did or said in the supermarket? Either would constitute assault and battery in a court of law—but not in the family. In effect, a marriage license in our society is a license to hit. This applies not only to children but also to spouses and partners. In the same national survey one in four wives and one in three husbands said that slapping a spouse was sometimes necessary, normal, and good.

Finally, in the process of *socialization* we learn to associate violence with the family. Our first experience of force nearly always takes place at home. Most of our parents use physical punishment on occasion—"for our own good," of course, and "because they love us" go the excuses. (The child is told, "This hurts me more than it hurts you.") From here it is only a small step to the conclusion that the use of violence is legitimate whenever something is really important. And the things that are most important to us are often family matters.

Intimate Violence: The Victims

Three decades of research have shown that virtually any family or intimate relationship has the potential to become violent (Gelles, 1997). Clinical studies, official crime statistics [the *Uniform Crime Reports* (*UCR*) and the Justice Department's annual *National Crime Victimization Survey* (*NCVS*); see Chapter 7], and social surveys (see Chapter 2) lead to the same conclusion. Who are the victims of domestic violence? How big is the problem?

Children

Infants and very young children are at greatest risk of abuse and most likely to be severely injured or even die as a result. Child maltreatment may take the form of physical assault, sexual molestation, emotional abuse (deliberately confining or withholding sleep, food, or shelter from a child or threatening to do so), physical neglect (including abandonment or expulsion from home; failure to provide adequate food, clothing, or health care; and lack of protection or supervision), educational neglect (inattention to schooling), or emotional neglect (including inattention to developmental needs for nurturance and frequent exposure to adult violence, substance abuse, and the like).

A survey of cases reported to (or recognized by) social service agencies found that 2.9 million American children were recognized by professionals as maltreated in 1993 (National Center on Child Abuse and Neglect, 1996). Of these children, an estimated 630,000 (9.2 per 1,000 children) were physically abused; 302,000 (4.4 per 1,000) were sexually abused; and 536,400 (7.9 per 1,000) were emotionally abused. Almost 2.5 million children suffered physical, emotional, or educational neglect.

Surveys in which adults are asked to report (anonymously) their own behavior toward their children during the previous year suggest physical abuse is more widespread than recognized or reported cases indicate (Gelles, 1997). While mild forms of violence toward children, acts that many people consider appropriate physical punishment, were most common, the rates of abusive violence—kicking, punching, hitting with an object, burning, and other acts likely to cause serious injury—were surprisingly high. Slightly more than one in twenty parents (2.3 percent) reported at least one act of abusive violence toward a child, and 7 in 1,000 children were injured as a result. Projecting this rate to all children living with one or both parents means that at least 1.5 million American children experience physical abuse each year—more than twice the number known to authorities.

Child abuse and neglect can be deadly: an estimated 1,215 children under age 18 were killed by their parents or caretakers in 1995, or 1.8 children per 100,000 (Daro, 1996). The rate for children under age 4 is even higher: 11.6 children per 100,000 according to one estimate (U.S. Advisory Board on Child Abuse and Neglect, 1995). Because killing one's child is viewed as reprehensible (so that confessions are less likely) and because children are fragile and inexperienced and suffer more injuries than do adults, child deaths may sometimes be misclassified as accidental. The actual number of parental homicides is probably higher. (See Figure 11-7.)

Intimate Adults

Violence between adults who are attached to one another begins before couples become committed and continues or sometimes escalates if they separate. No one knows how much violence occurs in dating and courtship relationships; estimates of physical coercion range from 10 to 67 percent and of abusive violence, from 1 to 27 percent (Sugarman and Hotaling, 1989; Arias, Samios, and O'Leary, 1987).

In surveys of couples, more than one in four (28 percent) report violence at some point during their relationship and 16 percent, in the last year (Gelles and Straus, 1988; Straus and Gelles, 1986). More than 30 of 1,000 women said they had suffered abusive violence at the hands of their spouses or partners in the preceding year. In 1992–1993 when the *NCVS* began asking women not just *whether* they had been victimized but also *who* had victimized them, it found that 78 percent of women victims knew their attackers, often intimately: 9 percent reported the offender was a relative; 29 percent, an intimate (a spouse or ex-spouse, boyfriend or girlfriend, or ex-boyfriend or ex-girlfriend); and 40 percent, an acquaintance. Thus the idea that women are most vulnerable when they are alone in a strange place is false. Women are three times more likely to be assaulted or raped by someone they know than by a stranger. In contrast, men are about as likely to be victimized by a stranger (49 percent) as by someone they know. In most cases, intimate violence against women is not an isolated event but part of a pattern of abuse. On average, female victims of intimate violence are battered three times a year. Women are also more likely to be murdered by an intimate than are men (see Figure 11-8).

Male victimization has been the subject of much controversy (Dobash, Dobash, Wilson, and Daly,

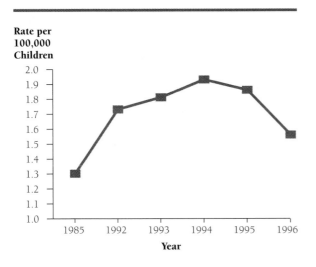

Rate per 100,000 Children

Figure 11-7   *Child-Abuse- and Neglect-Related Deaths, 1985–1996*

This figure shows a decline in *known* homicides related to abuse and neglect. The actual number may be higher.

Source: C. Wang and D. Daro, *Current Trends in Child Abuse Reporting and Fatalities: The Results of the 1996 Annual Fifty State Survey,* Chicago: National Committee to Prevent Child Abuse, 1997.

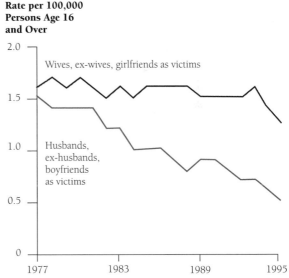

Rate per 100,000 Persons Age 16 and Over

Figure 11-8   *Intimate Homicide, 1977–1995*

Rates of murder by a "loved one" are falling for both sexes, but women are still twice as likely to be killed by an intimate as men are.

Source: D. Craven, *Female Victims of Violent Crimes,* Washington, DC: U.S. Department of Justice, 1996.

1992). Early studies found that female violence toward men they love (or had loved) was almost as common as the reverse. Closer analysis found that female violence often occurs as self-defense; that women inflict less injury than men do, whether because of size and strength or of cultural constraints; and that women rarely engage in a pattern of violent abuse. Anecdotal evidence and case studies suggest that men are more likely to stalk and kill their victims (often spouses who left them); more likely to kill their wives after a long period of physical and emotional abuse; and far more likely to kill their wives and children, in acts of familicide.

Other "Loved Ones"

Family violence is not limited to spouses and lovers or to parents who abuse their children. Children also abuse their parents. Although elder abuse is difficult to measure, estimates are that 5 percent of people age 65 or older are victims of physical abuse, verbal aggression, financial exploitation, and/or neglect at the hands of their grown sons and daughters or grandchildren (Wolf, 1995). Data on parents who are victimized by children are even more elusive, in large part because parents are reluctant to seek help for fear of being blamed for the violence. Estimates suggest that between 750,000 and 1 million American parents are assaulted by their teenage children each year (Cornell and Gelles, 1982).

"Everybody knows" that brothers and sisters fight; physical fights between siblings are by far the most common form of family violence (Straus, Gelles, and Steinmetz, 1980). For the most part, parents, physicians, and social workers consider "sibling rivalry" normal. But violence between siblings often goes far beyond so-called normal violence: each year, almost 110,000 use guns or knives to "settle their differences."

In short, no one is immune to violence by the people he or she loves (or are supposed to love). As a nation, we tend to pay more attention to violence on the street and violence on TV than to what is happening in our own homes. In part because we expect so much from our family, guard our privacy (and respect other people's), view family problems as personal failures, and learn from our parents and siblings to use force to settle disputes, we take out frustrations on those to whom we are closest.

Physical fights between siblings are by far the most common form of family violence. Although most experts consider sibling rivalry to be normal, it often escalates into abusive violence.

Divorce

Marriages end every day, for all sorts of reasons—of which violence is one, cited in 20 to 40 percent of divorce suits. Indeed, divorce is becoming an accepted part of our way of life, or so it appears. What can sociology reveal about divorce?

Understanding Divorce Statistics

Raw data can be deceptive, as statistics on divorce make quite clear. In 1994 there were about 2.3 million marriages in America. The same year, 1.19 million marriages ended in divorce (*Statistical Abstract*, 1996). This means that half of today's marriages end in divorce—right? Not necessarily. Direct comparisons of marriage and divorce rates for a given year are based on a fallacy. The pool of men and women eligible for marriage in a year is relatively small. It consists primarily of single people about 18 to 30 years old, plus some younger and older single people, widows, and divorced people. The pool of men and women "eligible" for divorce, in contrast, includes everyone who is currently married, whether the wedding took place yesterday or fifty years ago. That is, the "divorce pool" includes most of the adult population. Thus, measuring the marriage rate against the divorce rate for a given year is highly misleading. Comparing the number of divorces issued this year with the number issued five or ten years ago is also misleading, for the population is growing and changing.

The **divorce rate** is the number of divorces per 1,000 married women (or men) age 15 or older in a given year. For example, in 1960 there were 42.6 million married women in the United States; 393,000 got divorced that year. Thus the divorce rate for 1960 was 9.2 divorces per 1,000 married women. The divorce rate climbed steadily during the 1970s, reaching a peak of almost 23 divorces per 1,000 married women in 1979–1980; it then leveled off and dropped somewhat in the 1980s. The rate for 1994 was 20.5 (*Statistical Abstract,* 1996). Today—as in much of the past—the United States has the highest divorce rate in the industrial world (see Table 11-2).

Who Gets Divorced and Why

At current rates, scholars estimate that at least half of marriages formed today are likely to end in divorce (Cherlin, 1992). But all marriages do not have an equal chance of success or failure; some segments of our population are more prone to divorce than others.

The likelihood of divorce depends, first, on *age at first marriage.* Couples who get married in their teens are twice as likely to get divorced as are couples who marry in their twenties (L. K. White,

Table 11-2 *Divorce Rates for Selected Countries, 1960–1994*

| Divorces per 1,000 Married Women | | | | | |
Country	1960	1970	1980	1990	1994
United States	9.2	14.9	22.6	21	21
Canada	1.8	6.3	10.8	12.6	11
France	2.9	3.3	6.3	8	N/A
Germany	3.6	5.1	6.1	8	7*
Japan	3.6	3.9	4.8	5	6*
Sweden	5.0	6.8	11.4	11.4	12*
United Kingdom	2.0	4.7	12.0	13	13*

*1993 data.

Sources: Statistical Abstract, 1991, in Dennis A. Ahlburg and Carol J. De Vita, "New Realities of the American Family," *Population Bulletin* 46(2), 1992, p. 15, table 3; U.S. Bureau of the Census, *Statistical Abstract, 1996,* Washington, DC: GPO, p. 833, table 1329.

1990). Not only are young marrieds more emotionally immature; they are more likely to be poor, and they are more likely to have rushed into marriage because of an unhappy family life or because of a premarital pregnancy.

Socioeconomic status is also correlated with divorce. Divorce rates are highest in lower socioeconomic groups, and they decline as one moves up the socioeconomic ladder (L. K. White, 1990). Presumably this is because poor families experience more stress than do families who are better off. Also, higher-income couples have more to lose (the house, the cars, and so on). But divorce may be a cause of low income, rather than a consequence. Women with children nearly always experience a decline in standard of living after a divorce, and many slip into poverty.

Race is another factor in divorce. Most studies report that African American couples are more likely to separate or divorce than are white couples (L. K. White, 1990). The main reason is that black men and women are more likely to be young and poor when they marry. African Americans who own their own homes and have the same incomes and the same-size families as white Americans have a divorce rate 6 percent lower than whites in similar circumstances.

A fourth factor in divorce is *religion.* In general, divorce rates for Protestants are higher than those for Catholics, although separation rates are higher for Catholics. The more often a person attends religious services, the less likely he or she is to be divorced, no matter which religion. And interfaith marriages tend to be less stable than same-faith marriages—whether because such couples are more unconventional to begin with or their families oppose the marriage, or for other reasons.

A fifth factor is *children.* The birth of a first child reduces the chances of divorce to almost zero for the year following birth, but subsequent births have little effect (L. K. White, 1990). Older children may slow the pace of divorce but do not stop it altogether. At the same time, childlessness is associated both with higher rates of divorce and with speedier divorces.

Other factors that influence divorce include premarital births (which increase the chances of divorce), cohabitation (which reduces the chances that a marriage will last), the length of time the couple knew each other before marriage (two years appears to be optimal), the divorce of their own parents, and the influence of their friends and family. When a couple's "nearest and dearest" approve of the marriage and view their own marriages as stable, the new marriage has a greater chance of survival (Gelles, 1995).

Why did divorce rates rise steadily in the late 1960s and the 1970s and then stabilize at relatively high levels in the 1980s? There is no simple explanation for high divorce rates, but several contributing factors stand out (Cherlin, 1992; L. K. White, 1990). One was changes in the divorce laws: no-fault divorce made it easier and faster to end a marriage. The movement of women into the labor force was another factor—in part because jobs made women feel freer to divorce and in part because two-worker families may experience more role conflicts than breadwinner-housewife families. At the same time, men's position in the labor force was weakened: middle-class men struggled to maintain the relatively high standard of living their parents enjoyed; increasing numbers of working-class men experienced layoffs and long spells of unemployment; and poor men found it harder and harder to break into the working class.

A third factor in changes in the divorce rate is cultural: a general shift from faith in institutions to concern with individual fulfillment. One study compared interviews with men and women who divorced in the late 1940s (Goode, 1956) with similar interviews of men and women who divorced in the 1980s (Bloom, Niles, and Tatcher, 1985). In the earlier interviews, the main reasons given for divorce were failure to live up to instrumental family roles (nonsupport, lack of interest in the home, excessive drinking and gambling). In the more recent interviews, the main reasons given for divorce were related to personal fulfillment and growth (problems in communication, conflicts over values, boredom, sexual incompatibility). Thus our definitions of a successful marriage have changed from living up to social responsibilities to finding individual happiness (Price and McKenry, 1988). Many couples want both togetherness and individual freedom—a difficult balance to achieve.

In addition, formal marriage may have lost some of its cultural significance (L. K. White, 1990). The distinctions between cohabitation and marriage and between premarital and marital childbirth are becoming increasingly blurred. One seldom hears the terms "living in sin" or "illegitimate child" anymore. But changes in attitude often follow changes in behavior (rather than precede them), as people try to explain their new and unexpected life situations.

Sociologist Andrew Cherlin (1992) put recent changes in historical perspective. When you compare divorce rates in the 1960s and 1970s with rates in the 1950s, it looks as if the family is falling apart. When you look further back in history, however, a somewhat different picture emerges (see Figure 11-9). Divorce rates have been climbing more or less steadily since the late nineteenth century. The 1950s were an exception to this trend. Perhaps in reaction to the instability of the Great Depression and World War II, Americans placed an unusually high value on family life in this decade. In the 1970s the pendulum swung the other way. Comparing these two exceptional decades creates the false impression of a divorce "boom." How divorce rates might change in the future is impossible to predict. But most indicators suggest that divorce rates have peaked and may decline somewhat.

Children and Divorce

Each year about 1 million children—almost 2 percent of all children in the United States—are involved in a divorce (Ahlburg and De Vita, 1992). But this is only a fraction of the number of children who have been or will be directly affected by divorce. Estimates are that as many as two-thirds of all children, including one-third of white children and two-thirds of African American children, will see their parents divorce before they reach age 18 (Bumpass, 1990). The number of children involved in a divorce soared in the 1960s and 1970s, then dropped slightly. Even so, a child's odds of seeing his or her parents divorce are twice as high today as they were a generation ago.

In the 1950s and 1960s, parents were admonished to stay together "for the sake of the children." In the 1970s, opinion shifted and parents were told that an unhappy family was worse for children than divorce. Current research suggests that the impact of divorce on children is more complicated than either of these recommendations suggests.

Andrew Cherlin and his colleagues followed national samples of American and British children for four to five years (Cherlin et al., 1991). At the end of the study, the children were divided into two groups: those whose parents had divorced and

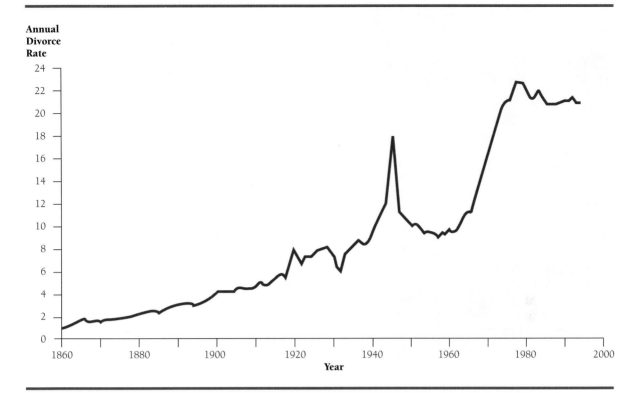

Annual Divorce Rate

Figure 11-9 *Annual Divorce Rate, United States, 1860–1994*

U.S. divorce rates have been rising more or less steadily since the mid-nineteenth century, with two exceptions: the Great Depression of the 1930s and the "family boom" of the 1950s and early 1960.

Sources: 1860–1920: Paul H. Jacobson, *American Marriage and Divorce,* New York: Rinehart, 1959, table 42; 1920–1967: U.S. National Center for Health Statistics, *100 Years of Marriage and Divorce Statistics,* series 21, no. 24, 1973, table 4; 1968–1987: U.S. National Center for Health Statistics, *Monthly Vital Statistics Report* 38(12), suppl. 2, "Advance Report of Final Divorce Statistics," 1987, table 1; 1988: ibid., (13), "Annual Summary of Births, Marriages, Divorces, and Deaths: United States, 1989," 1989; from Andrew J. Cherlin, *Marriage, Divorce, and Remarriage,* rev. ed., Cambridge, MA: Harvard University Press, 1992, p. 21, figs. 1–5.

those whose parents had stayed together. As expected, the children whose parents had divorced showed more behavior problems and scored lower on reading and mathematics tests than did the children whose parents were still married. But when the researchers looked back at records from the beginning of the study, they found that the children whose parents would later divorce *already* showed more problems. This suggests that conflict between parents and the process of divorce affects children before parents actually split up.

Psychologists Judith Wallerstein and Joan Kelly conducted an in-depth study of 131 children from 60 families in which the parents had recently divorced (J. B. Kelly and Wallerstein, 1976; J. S. Wallerstein and Kelly, 1976). All the subjects were

middle-class, suburban families, and the children, by and large, were happy, healthy youngsters. Wallerstein and Kelly made this selection deliberately to eliminate the effects of poverty, urban living, and preexisting emotional disturbance on families, thus highlighting the impact of divorce.

The researchers found that divorce hit almost all children like a bolt of lightning. None of the children were prepared for divorce, no matter how much their parents had fought; many reacted to the news with stunned silence. The children's short-term reactions varied by age. The youngest children were frightened and bewildered. Some pretended that their families were not really breaking up; many worried that the parent who moved out (usually the father) would forget them. Older children

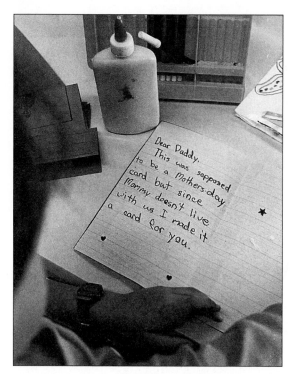

Divorce means adjustment in every area of life, for the children as well as the couple involved.

reacted with shame and anger. They took the divorce personally, as a rejection of themselves, and were embarrassed that their families were breaking up and ashamed of their parents' behavior. Adolescents were more likely than younger children to understand why their parents divorced and also more likely to worry about the impact on their own futures.

Follow-up interviews, conducted five years after the divorce, produced a mixed picture. Some of the children (29 percent) were doing reasonably well. Others (39 percent) were either moderately or severely depressed. Their most frequent complaint was loneliness. Still others (34 percent) appeared to be thriving. Surviving the divorce seemed to have strengthened them.

Interviews conducted ten years after the divorce (J. S. Wallerstein and Blakeslee, 1989) painted a more pessimistic picture. The older males (age 19 to 29 at the time of these interviews) were generally found to be lonely and unhappy; few had been able to establish lasting relationships with the opposite sex. Many of the young women who had appeared

well adjusted at the five-year mark seemed to be suffering delayed reactions to their parents' earlier divorce—in what Wallerstein and her coauthor Sandra Blakeslee called "sleeper effects." At age 19 to 23, they reported intense fear and anxiety about making an emotional commitment to a man.

Although Wallerstein's studies contain illuminating case histories, they cannot be generalized to all children of divorce. First, the sample was small and select. Second, she did not compare the subjects with a control group of children whose parents did not break up, and so it is impossible to know how common or uncommon their problems are in the population at large. Third, the subjects were referred to her clinic for short-term therapy by lawyers, clergy, and the courts. Many of the parents had suffered mental health problems in the past, including "disabling neuroses and addictions" and "chronic depression." Wallerstein did not consider how the parents' personal problems affected their children (Cherlin and Furstenburg, 1989). Given these histories, the surprise is that 60 percent of the younger children and 40 percent of the older subjects were doing so well (Cherlin, 1992).

Looking at nationally representative samples of children whose parents divorced, Andrew Cherlin (1992) concluded that most children suffer intense emotional upset at the time their parents separate, that most recover within a year or two, but that a minority suffer long-term, sometimes severe psychological problems as a result of their parents' breakup. Cherlin suggests two conditions that foster healthy recovery. First, children do better when the custodial parent (usually the mother) is able to maintain orderly household routines in the aftermath of a divorce. Second, children do better when their divorced parents are able to communicate and cooperate on child rearing and when they do not use the children as pawns or urge them to take sides. But Cherlin added, "I think it is clear that most children do not benefit from divorce" (1992, p. 88).

Remarriage and Blended Families

For most Americans, divorce and single parenthood are temporary. Divorce seems to be a rejection of a specific, unsuccessful relationship, not a rejection of the idea of marriage and family (Spanier, 1989). Put another way, people may give up on a particular marriage, but they have not given up on the institution of marriage. About two out of three divorced women and three out of four divorced men remarry, usually after cohabiting with their new partners (Cherlin, 1992). But Americans are not returning to the altar as quickly as they did in the past. In 1970 the average interval between divorce and remarriages was two and a half years; today it is three and a half to four years (B. F. Wilson and Clarke, 1992). The sharp decline in the rate of remarriage over the past two decades means that more children spend more years in single-parent homes (Bronfenbrenner et al., 1996).

The likelihood of remarriage varies among social categories. Although African Americans are more likely to separate or divorce than white Americans, the latter are more likely to remarry. Despite their tendency to say they are not interested in marriage, men are more likely to remarry than women. Social class has different effects on divorced men and women. The more education a man has and the higher his income, the more likely he is to remarry. The reverse is true for women—either because women who are better off feel less need to remarry than do women with little education and low-paying jobs or because they have more trouble finding a mate who is their educational and occupational equal.

About 24 percent of remarriages are between a divorced woman and a single man; 24 percent, between a divorced man and a single woman; and about 42 percent, between two divorced persons (B. F. Wilson and Clarke, 1992). In general, remarried couples report levels of marital satisfaction that are as high as those for couples who are in their first marriage. Yet the divorce rate for remarried couples is as high as or higher than the rate for first-time marriages (Cherlin, 1992; Furstenberg, 1990). The reason is not necessarily that certain individuals are divorce-prone but that second marriages face special problems, particularly when one or both partners have children from a previous marriage.

About eight in ten remarriages involve children. As a result, more than 7 million children live with a stepparent today. Estimates are that one-third of all children will participate in a blended family before they reach age 18. **Blended families** take different forms: a mother, her children from a previous marriage, and a stepfather; a father, his children from a previous marriage, and a stepmother; a mother, father, and children from both of their previous marriages; any of the above combinations and a new child from the current marriage. The children of previous marriages may live with the couple full-time or part-time, or one spouse's children may live with the couple and the other spouse's children may visit.

Blended families are not simply new families. They differ from other families in a number of ways. First, some members of the family have recently experienced a disruption in a close relationship (with a parent, a child, and/or a spouse), an experience that shapes their attitudes toward the new family. Second, the relationship between the parent and child predates that between the new husband and wife. The parent and child have a longer history together and may know one another better than the new spouse does. Third, the children usually belong to more than one household, for they have another parent living elsewhere. The couple may not have exclusive control over the child; comparisons between the two homes are perhaps inevitable. Fourth, there is no legal tie between the stepparent and stepchild. Neither has legal rights and responsibilities toward the other.

These special characteristics create special problems. The couple may have unrealistic expectations of righting past wrongs and solving everyone's problems with the new marriage. A spouse who has never had children may have fantasies of instant parenthood and see herself or himself as "coming to the rescue." These fantasies soon collide with unanticipated realities. The new spouse may have underestimated the amount of time and attention the parent is accustomed to giving his or her children. The couple may find that they have established very different styles of being a parent with their respective children. For small children, the new marriage may mean giving up a secret dream that their parents will get back together. For older children, the new marriage may mean giving up the position as second in command and special friend to their custodial parent. Within a year or two of the remarriage, about half of the children living in blended families are faced with a new baby. Although parents may hope that a new baby will bring the family closer together, it may have the opposite effect of making older children feel like outsiders. All blended families go through a period of adjustment. Many settle

A GLOBAL VIEW

Beyond the Nuclear Family: The Case of Sweden

In his book *Disturbing the Nest* (1988), David Popenoe warned that the family was in danger of disappearing in Europe's social democracies, especially Sweden. Marriage rates have declined more rapidly, and more dramatically, in Sweden than in any other nation. To a large degree, Sweden has moved beyond the traditional nuclear family. The only lasting family tie is between a mother and her child(ren). The family as an institution, he argued, is "losing social power and functions, losing influence over behavior and opinion, and generally becoming less important in [Swedish] life" (p. xii).

Popenoe cited three main indicators of family change in Sweden. The first is the declining marriage rate. Sweden today has the lowest marriage rate in the industrial world. Swedes also postpone marriage longer. (The mean age of first marriage for men is 30 and for women, 27.) According to one estimate, more than one-third of Swedish women born in 1955 will never have married by the time they reach age 50. Only 75 percent of Swedish men ever marry (compared with 95 percent of men in the United States). The first generation of Sweden's unmarried mothers are now becoming grandmothers.

The second measure of change is the rise in nonmarital cohabitation. Most single mothers in Sweden are living with the father, at least when the child is born; they just don't see

> **The family as an institution . . . is losing influence over behavior and opinion.**

the point of marrying him. Swedes view living together as a couple not just as a prelude to marriage but as an *alternative* to marriage. When asked, they tend to say marriage is "just a piece of paper." Marriage—the formal, public commitment to live together in an exclusive sexual union and to rear one's offspring together—has not disappeared in Sweden. Rather, it has become a matter of personal choice. Half of all births in Sweden are to unmarried parents.

The third indicator is family breakup, or dissolution. Even though the marriage rate has dropped and nonmarital cohabitation has increased, the divorce rate in Sweden is as high as ever. If one assumes that as many unmarried as married couples break up, this means that a large majority of Swedes do not spend their adult lives with the same partner and that a majority of Swedish children do not live with both of their biological parents throughout their childhood.

In large part, the Swedish government had taken over the role of breadwinner and extended family. The government provides all parents and children with extensive support, including parental leave at 90 percent of salary, free day care, child support payments and housing subsidies (at a higher level for single than married parents), free medical and dental care, and free education to

down into comfortable patterns after a year or two, but a relatively high proportion fall apart.

The Future of the Family

No one disputes the fact that American families are changing. The question is what do these changes mean? Do the variety of household arrangements in the United States today mean that the family, as a social institution, is doomed? Or are these changes a sign that the family, as a social institution, is adapting and developing (and perhaps experiencing "growth pains")?

Some sociologists, such as David Popenoe (1993), are pessimistic. Popenoe makes three the university level. Materially, Swedish children undoubtedly are better off today than in the past. Parents do not have to worry about the cost of quality day care or whether they will be able to send their children to college. Never-married or divorced mothers are not plunged into poverty, and no child grows up hungry, unsupervised, or undereducated.

Nevertheless, in Popenoe's view the nonmaterial costs outweigh the benefits. Popenoe laments the decline of *familism:* "the belief in a strong sense of family identification and loyalty, mutual assistance among family members, and a concern for the perpetuation of the family unit" (1988, p. 212). In mother-only families, children have fewer (if any) sibling companions and adult role models. Even if fathers live with or maintain contact with their children, the parents and children do fewer things together as a family; they have less time to develop family-centered routines and

traditions. Also, children lack the security of knowing their parents will try to stay together and provide the continuing love, understanding, guidance, and protection that every child needs. Couples may not need marriage certificates, says Popenoe, but children need parents.

In the decade since Popenoe issued his warning, the trend toward mother-only families has spread from Scandinavia to France, England, Austria, and Germany and is increasing in other countries (Bogert, 1997). (See Map 11-1.) Increasingly marriage is viewed as unnecessary and single motherhood as normal. Almost one in three babies in France and England is born to unmarried parents, and women in the first large generation of single mothers in Scandinavia are becoming grandmothers. Even Ireland, long a bastion of Roman Catholicism, is changing. Divorce was legally recognized in 1997 (though abortion is still illegal), and the number of unmarried mothers is grow-

ing. "The feeling is, why bother to live with [men] and wash their socks?" says Noreen Byrne of Ireland's National Women's Council.

Although some European countries are facing severe cuts in government spending, reducing family subsidies is last on the list. Given years of falling birthrates (and fears that pension plans similar to Social Security in the United States—indeed, national economies—would crash for lack of young workers), European governments have actively promoted childbirth. Billboards proclaim, "Every baby is welcome in France." Motherhood (whether within marriage or not) is politically untouchable. Yet some European social scientists are beginning to worry that high rates of unemployment among single mothers promote other social problems. Whether the revolution against marriage and family will provoke a counterrevolution remains to be seen.

points. First, the American family is not simply "changing"; it is becoming weaker. Second, the disintegration of the family is behind many of our most urgent personal and social problems, including delinquency and crime, drug and alcohol abuse, suicide, depression, and long-term poverty. Third, "the heart of the problem lies in the steady breakup of the two-parent home" (1993, p. A48). The main

victims of the weakening of the family, according to Popenoe, are children: "Across society, children's needs are often placed behind those of adults" (1993, p. A48). Popenoe adds that the United States is not alone (see *A Global View:* Beyond the Nuclear Family: The Case of Sweden).

Other social scientists are cautiously optimistic, including Stephanie Coontz (1997), Arlene

Beyond the Nuclear Family: The Case of Sweden *(concluded)*

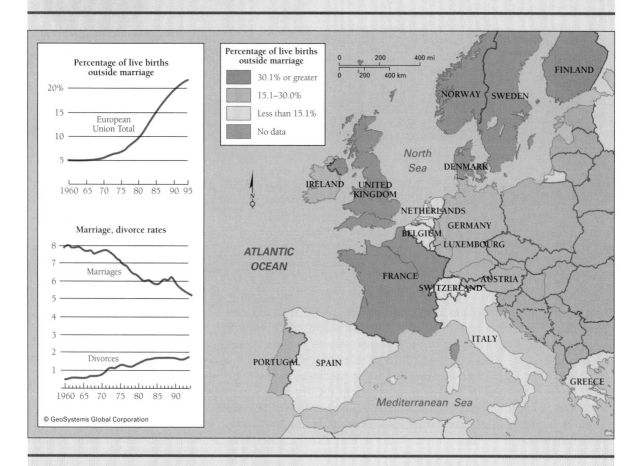

Map 11-1   *Where Wedding Bells Aren't Ringing*

Source: Newsweek (International Edition), Jan. 11, 1997, p. 43.

Skolnick (1996), and Judith Stacey (1996). They maintain, first, that the idea that contemporary American families are in crisis is based on a misreading of history. In "days gone by," as many families were disrupted by death as are disrupted by divorce today, and the children often were sent to orphanages. The Ozzie and Harriet decade of two-parent families with a home of their own and a white picket fence was a unique period in American family history. Moreover, many families could not

live up to the Ozzie and Harriet ideal, and many who did found the arrangement less than ideal.

Second, to blame society's ills on families is to "blame the victim." Laments over the family divert attention from the social sources of many "private troubles" (declining wages, unequal pay for women, cutbacks in public spending for housing and social services, and so on). Many parents cannot afford a "lifestyle" choice regarding the neighborhood in which they live, the type of job at which they work, and the number of times they have to take off to attend to family matters. Cherlin (1992) recommends that instead of bemoaning the changes that have taken place in American families, we should seek to change other institutions (such as the workplace) to reduce the social, psychological, and financial costs of family change.

Third, whether one is optimistic or pessimistic depends in part on how one defines the family (Gelles, 1995). If one sees the family as "primarily a social instrument for child rearing," as Popenoe does (1988, p. viii), one is likely to be pessimistic. However, if one sees the family as primarily an institution for providing intimacy and companionship, one might be more optimistic (Skolnick, 1996). In one survey three out of four respondents defined the family as "a group of people who love and care for one another." Although a majority of those surveyed said they thought that the quality of American family life in general was declining, 71 percent said they were "at least very satisfied" with their own family lives (*Newsweek,* 1990, in Stacey, 1996, p. 9).

But even the optimists are concerned. They are concerned, first and foremost, about children. In every racial group, more children live in poverty than was true a decade ago. And these children are at significant risk for disease, violence, and other threats. The optimists are also concerned that the gains women made in the workplace in the 1970s and 1980s have produced a "backlash" (Faludi, 1991) and that the increase in the number of "good (involved) dads" has been counterbalanced by an increase in "bad dads" (who walk out on their children, emotionally and financially) (Furstenberg, 1988). They are concerned about the "stalled revolution" in the family division of labor, which allows women to pursue careers but still allows men to avoid housework (Hochschild, 1989). And they are concerned about the unknowns (Gelles, 1995).

- Will the proportion of single-parent families increase, and children continue to suffer adverse consequences?
- Will our society, the last industrial society on earth without a government-funded child care program, develop a national day care policy and program? If not, what will be the consequences for families and children? Given the work requirements of the new welfare law, who will care for children of poor mothers?
- When the time limits for welfare run out, what will happen to families and children?
- What new forms might families take, and what will this mean for adults and especially for children?

Arlene Skolnick calls the family an "embattled paradise," a seeming contradiction in terms. But this phrase captures the ambivalence most people feel toward family. "For better or worse," writes Skolnick, "family life, and an idealized image of what the family should be, remain at the source of our greatest joys, our deepest worries, and our most painful hurts" (1991, p. 220).

Summary

1. **How do families vary across cultures?** Every known society has families. But the structure of the family (the number of spouses a man or woman may have and household composition) varies from culture to culture, and the functions the family performs have changed over time. In postindustrial societies, the family's main function has become providing intimacy and emotional gratification.

2. **How have American families changed?** Images of the "traditional" family tend to be based more on ideals than on realities. Today nostalgia for the *extended family* (several generations in one household) has been largely replaced by nostalgia for the *nuclear family* of the 1950s (a husband, wife, and their children, living in a home of their own). In fact neither family type was universal, and both had weaknesses as well as strengths. The biggest change in the family has been the increase in the variety of family arrangements, including singles, single parents, and childless couples.

3. **How do contemporary Americans choose a partner, decide to get married, and balance work and family?** Most Americans say they marry for love, but sociological research shows that love is highly selective. Most people marry someone with similar social characteristics (the

SOCIOLOGY ON THE WEB

Children at Risk?

The chapter notes that family structure is undergoing rapid change, as couples find new ways to form families, balance work and home, and care for children. How are children affected by rapid social change? Socially and economically, are children better or worse off than they were in more traditional families? What proportion of children live in poverty in your state, and how does that compare with the national average? How many mothers work outside the home, and who is taking care of their children? What government programs support parents' need for quality child care? Are rates of child abuse and neglect rising or falling?

Pick one of these questions, or one of your own, and begin to look for answers by exploring the following sites and the many others you will find that provide information and data about children's issues:

http://ericps.ed.uiuc.edu/nccic/nccichome.html
The web site of the National Child Care Information Center provides state child care profiles and demographic information on children, families, and child care in each state.

http://www.aecf.org/aeckids.htm
The Annie E. Casey Foundation maintains the Kids Count project, which tracks child welfare throughout the United States. The foundation's web site provides a wealth of demographic data on children and families. For example, you can compare a number of criteria of child well-being between 1985 and 1994 on a state-by-state basis. You can also obtain data on such factors as teen birthrates, immunization rates, health insurance, poverty rates, and school attendance by year and by state.

http://www.childrensdefense.org/
The Children's Defense Fund's web site gives information on lobbying and current political initiatives on behalf of children, as well as discussions of current issues, such as day care and immunizations.

http://www.acf.dhhs.gov/programs/cb/stats/ncands/
At this site, you can find state-by-state data on rates of child abuse and neglect, as well as information about victims and perpetrators. For example, did you think that most child abuse was perpetrated by strangers lurking near the playground? Think again.

---

principle of *homogamy*). Exchange theory portrays courtship as an exchange of assets and liabilities in which people weigh the costs and benefits of a potential partner. With wives working, the daily routine may become more hectic, but there is little evidence that two careers either harm or improve the quality of family life.

4. **How do sociologists explain family violence?** All families do not live happily ever after: violence in American families at all socioeconomic levels is surprisingly common. Intimacy, privacy, cultural support for the use of force, and socialization all contribute to this social problem.

5. **What are the causes and consequences of today's high divorce rate?** The *divorce rate* reached an all-time high in the United States in 1979, and the number of divorces involving children has grown. Studies find that virtually all children are upset by a divorce; most recover in a few years, but some suffer lasting and/or serious problems. The high rate of remarriage after divorce and the number of *blended families* indicate that people believe as strongly in the institution of marriage as they ever did.

6. **What will the family look like in the future?** Some social scientists see the breakup of the two-parent family as a major social problem and as the cause of other problems. Others see

changes in American families as adaptations to changing social circumstances, and they view many of the problems these families face as the result of uneven changes in other institutions.

Key Terms

blended family   435

divorce rate   431

extended family   407

family   405

group marriage   405

homogamy   419

modified extended family   408

monogamy   405

new extended family   417

nuclear family   408

polyandry   405

polygamy   405

polygyny   405

serial monogamy   406

Recommended Readings

Blankenhorn, David, Bayme, Steven, & Elshtain, Jean Bethke (Eds.). (1990). *Rebuilding the Nest: A New Commitment to the American Family.* Milwaukee, WI: Family Service America.

Cherlin, Andrew J. (1992). *Marriage, Divorce, Remarriage.* Cambridge, MA: Harvard University Press.

Coontz, Stephanie. (1992). *The Way We Never Were: American Families and the Nostalgia Trap.* New York: Basic Books.

Furstenberg, Frank F., Jr., & Cherlin, Andrew J. (1991). *Divided Families: What Happens to Children When Parents Part.* Cambridge, MA: Harvard University Press.

Gelles, Richard J. (1997). *Intimate Violence in Families,* 3d ed. Thousand Oaks, CA: Sage Publications.

Gutman, Herbert G. (1976). *The Black Family in Slavery and Freedom: 1750–1925.* New York: Pantheon.

Hochschild, Arlie, with Machung, Anne. (1989). *The Second Shift.* New York: Viking Penguin.

McAdoo, Harriette Pipes (Eds.). (1993). *Family Ethnicity: Strength in Diversity.* Thousand Oaks, CA: Sage Publications.

Popenoe, David. (1988). *Disturbing the Nest: Family Change and Decline in Modern Societies.* New York: Aldine DeGruyter.

Rubin, Lillian. (1994). *Families on the Fault Line: America's Working Class Speaks about the Family, Economy, Race, and Ethnicity.* New York: HarperCollins.

Skolnick, Arlene. (1991). *Embattled Paradise: The American Family in the Age of Uncertainty.* New York: Basic Books.

Wallerstein, Judith S., & Blakeslee, Sandra. (1990). *Second Chances: Men, Women, and Children a Decade after Divorce.* New York: Ticknor & Fields.

Chapter

Twelve

Education

Our nation is at risk. . . . While we can take justifiable pride in what our schools and colleges have accomplished and contributed to the United States and the well-being of its people, the educational foundations of our society are presently being eroded by a rising tide of mediocrity that threatens our very future as a nation and a people.

—*A Nation at Risk* (1983)

Written sixteen years ago, this dire prediction could have been written yesterday. It was part of a report released by the National Commission on Excellence in Education (1983), which had the ominous title A Nation at Risk. *The report prompted a great deal of concern and attention and placed education prominently on the national political agenda.*

Americans claim to value education. Believing it is the key to success in life, most parents want their children to graduate from college. Traditionally, our educational system was a source of national pride: the United States pioneered in providing universal elementary and secondary public education; its academic curriculum was considered comprehensive and rigorous; its teachers were well respected and well qualified; America had one of the highest literacy rates in the world.

Nearly two decades after the warnings in A Nation at Risk, however, the risk remains. Standard Aptitude

Test (SAT) scores have risen only slightly in the last few years and are still well behind scores of the late 1960s (Chronicle of Higher Education, *September 5, 1997). In 1997, math scores reached 511, their highest level since 1971, while verbal or reading scores remained stagnant at 505. Though fourth-graders in the United States were well above average in math and science when compared with their peers in twenty-six countries, eighth-graders were below average, finishing twenty-eighth in math and thirteenth in science in a forty-one-country study* (The Economist, *March 29, 1997). So while there are signs of progress, there is still plenty of cause for concern, particularly since it appears students may be losing ground during their middle school years. Remaining in school is also a problem. As Figure 12-1 shows, dropout rates in the United States are as high as 13 percent in some states. Nearly one-third of young Latino adults are high school dropouts, a rate that has held steady for twenty years, though dropout rates for African Americans age 16 to 24 have fallen* (U.S. Bureau of the Census, *1996).*

Education is a process, but it is also a major social institution, carrying an established set of

12

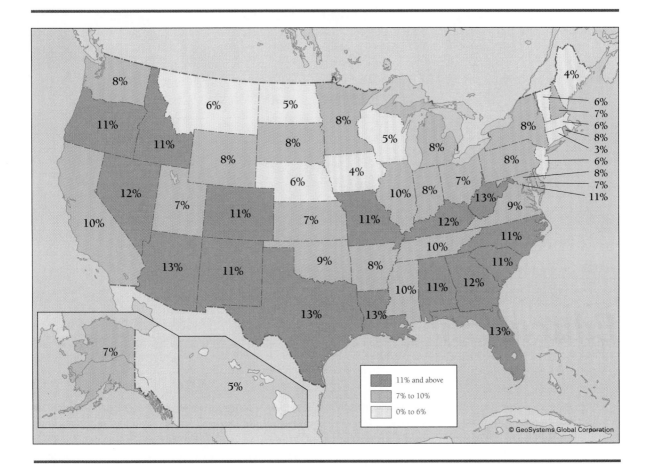

Figure 12-1   *High School Dropout Rates in the United States*

High school dropout rates vary from a low of 3 percent in Connecticut to a high of 13 percent in Florida, Louisiana, Texas, and Arizona. In sixteen states, more than one in ten students does not complete high school.

Source: Annie E. Casey Foundation.

norms, values, statuses, roles, and organizations. It is the institutional function of education that we examine here.

Key Questions

1. *What caused the schooling revolution—the expansion of education—in the United States?*
2. *Do schools provide a fair and open environment for achievement and social mobility, or is inequality a part of education as a social institution? If inequality is a part of education, why should that be so?*

3. *Why has the overall quality of education in the United States declined?*
4. *How does the American system of education differ from the systems in other countries?*

The Schooling Revolution: Three Interpretations

The term *education* refers to the formal or informal transmission of knowledge and skills. The term *schooling* refers more specifically to formal instruction in a classroom setting. The United States has experienced a "schooling revolution" (Hurn, 1978). A century ago many American children did not receive even an elementary school education. Most of those who did go to school attended only irregularly and dropped out before their teens. But beginning in the late nineteenth century and continuing into the 1970s, the number of young people receiving formal education climbed steadily. So did the number of years of school attendance. By World War I every state had declared primary education compulsory; between the two world wars secondary education became compulsory as well. The biggest changes since World War II are in the levels of education attained by African Americans and women. Today a vast majority of young Americans complete at least high school (Figure 12-2). This schooling revolution has not been confined to the United States. Virtually every nation on earth has embraced the goal of universal education. While still a dream for many poor countries, mass education is an accomplished fact in most industrial nations. (See Figure 12-3.)

What caused the schooling revolution at home and globally? Sociologists have proposed three major answers: One stresses the impact of modernization; one, capitalism; and one, status competition.

Schooling for Industrial Society

Many popular beliefs about the value of education are captured in the *functionalist perspective* (see Chapter 2). Functionalists hold that education expanded to meet the demands of an increasingly complex industrialized society—the demands for skilled workers, for moral and cultural consensus, and for equality of opportunity.

In preindustrial America, responsibility for educating the young was divided among the family, religious institutions, and the school. The family was the most important of the three. Children learned to be farmers, blacksmiths, seamstresses, or traders by observing their parents and other adults and by serving as apprentices. Older brothers and sisters or aunts and uncles were available to teach children how to read. Religious institutions dealt with the larger

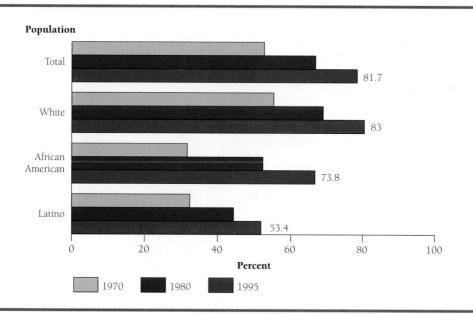

Figure 12-2   *Percentage of Persons Completing High School or More, 1970–1995*

More than 81 percent of adult Americans in 1995 reported completing at least high school. The biggest gains in the last two decades have been made by African Americans.

Source: U.S. Bureau of the Census, *Statistical Abstract of the United States, 1996,* Washington, DC: GPO, 1996, p. 159.

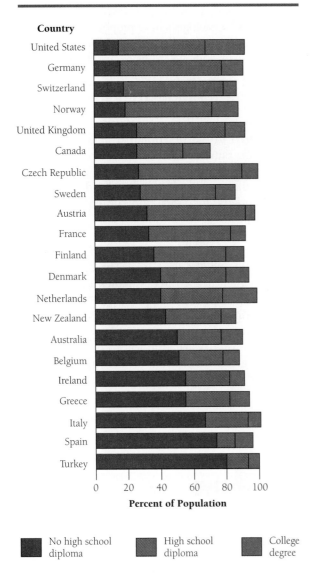

Country

Percent of Population

■ No high school diploma ■ High school diploma ■ College degree

Note: Figures are for 1994 and cover 25- to 64-year-olds.

Figure 12-3 *Educational Attainment in Twenty-One Industrialized Countries*

Of twenty-one industrialized countries, the United States has the lowest percentage of high school dropouts and the highest percentage of college graduates.

Source: Chronicle of Higher Education, Dec. 13, 1996, p. A45.

meaning of life, reinforcing attitudes of piety and respect for authority taught in the home. Schools (where they existed) provided little more than ad-ditional help in reading and another dose of discipline.

With the Industrial Revolution, the function of schools began to change, for many reasons. First, the early colonists had attempted to re-create in the New World the towns and communities they had left behind in the Old World. Now the new nation had to develop a national character of its own. Par-ents were not equipped for this job. Second, the lo-cation of work began to shift from the home to the factory and shop. As industrialization spread, fewer adults were at home to oversee the education of children. Third, factory and white-collar jobs re-quired new skills and work habits. Fourth, indus-trialization led to urbanization. When families moved from farms to cities, the norms and values of rural communities in which parents had been reared no longer applied. Their social environment changed as much as their physical environment. Fi-nally, industrialization attracted waves of new im-migrants from southern and eastern Europe, whose languages and customs differed from those of previ-ous immigrants (see Chapter 9). If they could not be "Americanized," their children could be.

By the late nineteenth century, schools had over-taken families as the primary educator of children. The nation began to look to its schools to transform rural and foreign-born children into "modern Americans." Schools were held responsible not only for teaching academic subjects but also for instilling good work habits and civic pride. Equally impor-tant, they were assigned the custodial function of keeping youngsters off the streets.

These trends accelerated in the twentieth cen-tury. Increasingly parents looked to schools to in-troduce youngsters to skills and knowledge they themselves did not possess. The roles of teacher and administrator were professionalized, accentuat-ing the difference between home- and school-based education. Each generation obtained more school-ing than the last. Just as industrialization spurred the expansion of secondary school education, the technological advances during and after World War II placed a premium on a high school education; and the current postindustrial economy requires skills developed through higher education.

Today, the service economy needs people who not only are equipped with basic skills (reading, writing, and arithmetic) but also possess good writ-ten and oral communication skills and can access

At the turn of the twentieth century, compulsory education was an important means of integrating the children of European immigrants into mainstream American society.

new, often highly specialized, information and use it. The ability to use a computer and the Internet is now essential. As a result, college and graduate education expanded in recent decades to provide these skills (see Figure 12-4).

As the importance of schools grew, so did expectations. Over time, schools were assigned the task of translating democratic, egalitarian ideals into social realities. Functionalists hold that schools can serve these ideals in two ways. First, education helps youngsters become informed citizens, better able to participate in the democratic process. Second, schools give every child an equal opportunity to excel. An English nobleman writing over a century ago about this distinctly American goal of social equality said:

> In a country where there is no distinction of class, a child is not born to the station of its parents, but with an indefinite claim to all the prizes that can be won by thought and labor. It is in conformity with the theory of equality . . . to give as near as possible to every youth an equal state in life. (quoted in Kozol, 1991)

Ideally, rich and poor, native and foreign-born, white and black children compete on an equal foot-

ing in school. They are judged by the same standards and awarded grades and degrees on the basis of individual performance, and they trade these credentials for jobs, income, and status. From the individual's point of view, education opens avenues of social mobility that might otherwise be closed. From society's point of view, the educational system locates, trains, and motivates the most able individuals to enter demanding occupations that are important to society as a whole. Through schooling, a meritocracy in which social positions are awarded on merit, not class privilege, becomes possible and everyone benefits.

Over time, then, schools acquired five basic functions: (1) instruction (equipping future workers with basic knowledge and technological skills), (2) socialization (equipping youngsters with the attitudes, values, and interpersonal skills society endorses), (3) custody and control (taking responsibility for the care of children during specified hours), (4) certification (awarding credits, diplomas, and other signs of competence that other organizations recognize), and (5) selection (sorting individuals for future educational, occupational, and social positions) (Sprady, in Boocock, 1980).

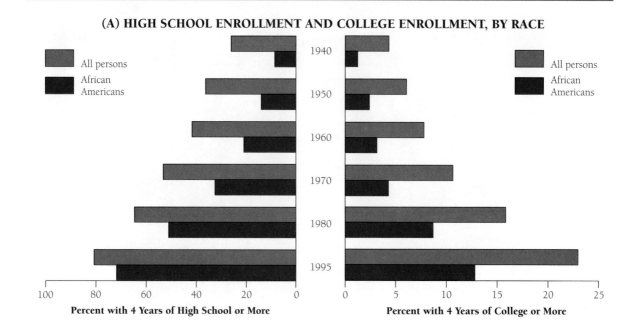

(A) HIGH SCHOOL ENROLLMENT AND COLLEGE ENROLLMENT, BY RACE

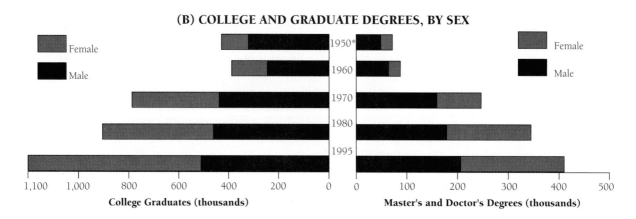

(B) COLLEGE AND GRADUATE DEGREES, BY SEX

*High college enrollment for men in the 1950s was the result of the GI bill, which provided educational subsidies for veterans of World War II.

Figure 12-4   *The Expansion of Higher Education*

The number of African Americans completing high school and college has steadily increased since World War II, as has the number of women earning college and graduate degrees. The need for new and more highly specialized skills in the marketplace has contributed to the spread of higher education.

Sources: Adapted from U.S. Bureau of the Census, *Statistical Abstract of the United States, 1985,* Washington, DC: GPO, 1985, pp. 134, 149; ibid., *Statistical Abstract of the United States, 1992,* 1992, pp. 144, 173; ibid., *Statistical Abstract of the United States, 1996,* 1996, pp. 15, 19.

Schooling for Capitalism

From the functionalist perspective, the expansion of education constitutes definite progress. From the conflict perspective, in contrast, it is "a story of betrayals and false promises" (Hurn, 1978, p. 66). Education expanded not to meet the needs of society as a whole but to serve the interests of the capitalist elite.

Bowles and Gintis's *Schooling in Capitalist America* (1976) was written from the **conflict perspective** (see Chapter 2). In it, the authors argue that for the early industrialists, schools were merely another kind of factory—one that turned raw material (rural and foreign immigrants to cities) into finished products (compliant workers). Public schools were designed primarily to instill respect for authority, obedience, discipline, and punctuality—the qualities industrialists wanted in their workers. Basic skills came second.

Industrialists played a prominent role in the nineteenth-century movement for compulsory education. And many educational progressives of the day were more concerned with reforming the "character" of the poor than with opening avenues of opportunity or spreading literacy. Horace Mann, for example, described the function of education as "the removal of vile and rotten parts from the structure of society as fast as sound ones can be prepared to take their place." Others saw schools as a tool for clearing "moral jungles" and cleaning up "the infected and waste districts of society" (in Hurn, 1978, p. 67). Reading, writing, and arithmetic were rarely mentioned.

Bowles and Gintis trace the expansion of secondary education in the twentieth century to the changing demands of capitalist production. As the economy expanded and changed, the elite needed more and more white-collar workers and managers. Their jobs required not only more education but also initiative, self-direction, and interpersonal skills. Educators obliged by introducing electives into high school programs, encouraging greater flexibility, and urging students to go to college. Large amounts of money were poured into athletic programs designed to teach team loyalty, which could later be translated into company loyalty. Sorting youngsters into "bright," college-preparatory programs and "slow," vocational programs ensured a steady supply of both management material and laborers.

Far from opening routes to social mobility, the educational system protects the status quo, according to Bowles and Gintis. In the early twentieth century, schools began to use standardized tests, grades, and other "objective" criteria to sort young people into different elementary school classes, high school programs, and colleges. Is it coincidence that children from upper- and middle-class backgrounds tend to do better on these tests? Conflict theorists think not. They argue that IQ and other tests were not developed as tools for discovering hidden talent among the poor, as their supporters have sometimes claimed. Rather, the tests provided "scientific" justification for maintaining the existing system of social stratification. Psychologist Lewis Terman (1923), a pioneer in testing, described the results of early tests of Native Americans, Mexican Americans, and African Americans in this way: "Their dullness seems to be racial. Children of these groups should be segregated into special classes. . . . They cannot master abstractions, but they can often be made efficient workers."

By creating the illusion of equality of opportunity, the school system fosters acceptance of the status quo and thus perpetuates social inequality (Bowles and Gintis, 1976). The use of tests to select students and education credentials to select workers suggests that individuals in high places earned their positions through intelligence and hard work and that those who fall behind have only themselves to blame. (Later in this chapter we discuss the use of testing and the role schools play in social stratification.)

In addition, the continuous expansion of education created a surplus of trained personnel. An employer's power over workers derives from the ability to hire and fire more or less at will. This weapon is effective only if there are other, equally qualified people waiting to take a worker's place. In creating a "reserve army" of skilled labor and management, the educational system increased the power of the elite.

From the conflict perspective, the system of education under capitalism uses the illusion of equality to promote the status quo. Are socialist and communist societies any more successful in achieving real equality of opportunity? Not necessarily. For example, despite its intention to provide equal access to education, Russian educational reform under communism fell short of its goals. (See *A Global View:* Education Stratification in Russia.)

A GLOBAL VIEW

Educational Stratification in Russia

Equal access to education was seen as crucial to achieving the communist goal of a classless society. Communists reasoned that if educational stratification ended—if all citizens had the same educational opportunities—the advantages enjoyed by those who were better educated and trained would disappear.

Under the old tsarist regime, education was a privilege reserved for Russia's elite—and for men. After the Russian Revolution of 1917, the new Communist regime launched a campaign to end illiteracy. Education was highly centralized, standardized, and regimented. School enrollments climbed. In the late 1920s the government decided to replace academic courses for the eighth and ninth grades with vocational training and to recruit adult workers to higher-level technical institutes. But by 1934, these early experiments proved unmanageable and more traditional education—with primary, lower-secondary (or middle), and secondary (high school) stages—emerged. A separate vocational track that coincided with and extended some-

what beyond secondary school was also established. Eventually there were two types of vocational schools: general professional-technical schools, known as PTUs, which combined vocational training with a secondary school diploma; and *technikum,* which were more specialized and trained nurses, librarians, technicians, and elementary school teachers.

> **In Russia, increased enrollments actually created an *increase* in educational stratification based on social origins, despite intentions to the contrary.**

In the years leading up to World War II the enrollment of students in primary and secondary schools soared. After the war, these students began to compete for a much smaller number of places in institutions of higher education, as shown in Figure 12-5. From 1927 to 1985 enrollments in all types of educational institutions grew at a rate that was more than twice that of the population.

Ironically, it was this increase in enrollments that undermined the Communist goal of universal access to education. To cope with the large numbers of students trying to gain admittance to nonvocational postsecondary institutions, the government restricted admission to higher-education institutes (VUZs) to applicants who had completed tenth grade at a general secondary school and passed an entrance exam. In most cases, the students who did well enough were those whose parents had a higher education and those who attended urban primary and secondary schools, where the quality of education was superior to that offered in rural areas.

The rapid growth in secondary school enrollments followed by the lack of growth in openings in VUZs meant that by 1956 many young people were underemployed and overeducated, a situation that created a new set of social problems. Khrushchev's regime tried to open up enrollments by lowering standards and requiring resentful faculty to teach evening hours, but these reforms were reversed following his downfall in 1964.

Source: T. P. Gerber and M. Hout, "Educational Stratification in Russia During the Soviet Period," *American Journal of Sociology,* 101, 1995, pp. 611–620.

Status Competition and Credentials

It may be that education is neither the tool of the elite that conflict theorists claim nor the logical and direct extension of societal needs as envisioned by the functionalists. It may be that functionalists tend to overlook the irrational aspects of educational expansion (for example, the fact that the system produces many more people in certain occupations than society needs and not enough in

The children of peasants and workers did benefit from the Communist expansion of secondary education, but this increase in educational opportunity did not extend to higher education because opportunity at that level did not expand as it had at the secondary level. In Russia, increased enrollments actually created an *increase* in educational stratification based on social origins, despite intentions to the contrary. Children of less-educated parents, particularly those living in rural areas, were less likely to go on to achieve a higher education under socialism.

Only gender stratification improved. Under Communism, men no longer enjoyed an advantage over women when it came to access to higher education. In fact, in some cases the reverse was true.

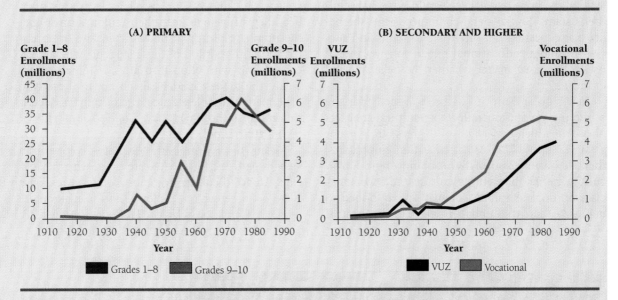

(A) PRIMARY

(B) SECONDARY AND HIGHER

Grades 1–8 Grades 9–10

VUZ Vocational

Figure 12-5 *Educational Enrollments in Communist Russia*

In Communist Russia, enrollment in primary school increased, then leveled off, while enrollment in secondary schools continued to climb, resulting in "educational inflation."

Source: T. P. Gerber and M. Hout, "Educational Stratification in Russia During the Soviet Period," *American Journal of Sociology* 101, 1995, p. 618.

others) and that conflict theorists like Bowles and Gintis tend to overlook the fact that much of what schools teach—such as French grammar or Shakespeare—is irrelevant to capitalist goals (Hurn, 1978). In fact, in the case of the study of Marx in sociology, the goals of education may even be subversive. Both explanations neglect the difficulty that schools have in controlling and motivating their captive populations enough to teach them anything.

According to Christopher Hurn (1978), an alternative explanation for the schooling revolution is **status competition,** or the quest for prestige and social esteem. (This view derives from Max Weber, who held that prestige is as important as wealth and power in maintaining social stratification; see Chapter 8.) Education has long been a status symbol in America. At the turn of the century middle- and lower-class families saw the upper classes sending their children to high school. They wanted their children to get ahead, so they demanded more education for them. Enrollment in high schools grew. As the educational gap between classes began to narrow, the upper class raised the educational "ante." They sent their children to college. In time, middle- and lower-class families followed their lead, in the hope that college would raise their children's status. So the spiral continued. Thus the belief that education is a sure route to status and success promotes educational expansion, in and of itself. (It doesn't matter whether the belief is valid or not.)

In a similar vein, it has been argued that the schooling revolution reflects a "cultural marketplace," in which *credentials* (or degrees) are a major asset (Collins, 1979). What education emphasizes, then, is given prestige. By teaching Anglo-Saxon culture rather than ethnic cultures and working-class norms and values, colonial settlers hoped to maintain their traditional privileges. The contro-versy over bilingual education today shows that the battle for cultural dominance continues. According to this view, academic credentials are not merely a matter of status competition; they can give you "money in the bank" (Collins, 1979). For example, doctors' and lawyers' educational credentials give them a monopoly over certain kinds of knowledge and practical activities. A person who attempts to practice medicine or law without proper certification can be sent to jail.

The current trend in rating colleges and universities is an example of how the ante in status competition is being raised even higher. There have always been college guides, but recently news magazines such as *U.S. News & World Report* have begun publishing rankings of the top schools. Even though colleges and universities publicly decry this practice, they struggle to keep their rankings up so that the numbers of applicants and the rate of acceptance (the proportion of those students who are accepted and who choose to attend) remain high. Today, the highest credentials go not to those who have merely completed a college or university education but to those who have done so at an elite or high-status school.

Recent history supports the status competition view in part. When students are asked why they decided to go to college, the most common response is "to get a better job," followed by "to make more money" (*Chronicle of Higher Education,* August 28,

Some sociologists believe that status competition is what drives the expansion of education in the United States. In the forefront of that quest for prestige and credentials would be these new graduates of Harvard.

1997, p. 20). Does a college education pay off, in terms of better jobs and higher incomes? In general, the answer is still yes (see Figure 12-6). But the details of this picture have changed. It used to be that a college education in the liberal arts served as a guarantee of upper-middle-class prosperity. That is no longer the case.

In the late 1960s and 1970s, when the large baby boom generation was completing its education, there was an oversupply of college graduates. The average male with a college degree earned only about 18 percent more than the average high school graduate. During the 1980s, international competition and technological advances led to massive lay-offs in the manufacturing sector of the economy. At the same time companies providing services (such as credit card companies or investment banking services) grew. As a result, oversupply shifted to high school graduates, who were forced to compete for a smaller number of jobs in manufacturing and were often driven to lower-wage jobs in the service sector. There has been a decline in the number of jobs available to those without college education and in the hourly wages for those jobs.

The earning gap between a high school and a college graduate jumped to over 50 percent for both men and women in 1992 (Harrington and Fogg, 1994). The requirements for many blue-collar jobs have risen. For example, in the past, all a textile worker needed to know was how to operate a machine. Today's more sophisticated machines are run by microprocessors, and many textile workers must be able to decipher complex computer manuals. Telephone operators, clerks, salespeople, and truck drivers today work with computers. The "up-skilling" of jobs has further reduced the number of jobs available to high school graduates. Not going to college has become expensive.

At the same time, even those with liberal arts degrees have found their earning power may no longer qualify them for the upper middle class. Advanced degrees or more specialized majors (in areas like engineering, computer science, health, or business) are needed to guarantee the earning power necessary to maintain or attain that status (Harrington and Fogg, 1994).

Schooling and (In)Equality

Americans consider promoting social equality one of the most important functions of education. We like to believe our schools invite fair and open competition for "credentials" and serve as a channel for upward social mobility. In fact, research shows that our educational system usually preserves the status quo. Not only do schools often fail to promote social equality but they may contribute to social inequality by limiting the opportunities of women and racial, ethnic, and social minorities. Sometimes this limiting is deliberate discrimination, but most often it is simply a reflection of the institutionalized sexism and racism that are built into the structure of education as a social institution.

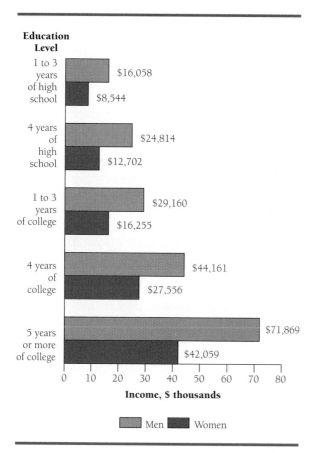

Figure 12-6   *Education and Income, 1996*

The bars indicate the median annual income of full-time male and female workers 25 years old and over according to the level of school completed. As the graph shows, schooling does have financial rewards.

Source: U.S. Bureau of the Census, updated Sept. 29, 1997.

Academic Achievement and Social Class

Countless studies have found that the higher a student's social class, the more likely he or she is to do well in school and to continue his or her education. The classic, as well as one of the most extensive, studies of the relationship between socioeconomic status and academic achievement were conducted by William Sewell and his colleagues (Sewell, 1971; Sewell and Hauser, 1976, 1980). Sewell's team of researchers collected data on the social origins, academic ability, school performance, and educational careers of more than 10,000 Wisconsin students over a period of twenty years. Analysis of these data suggests that social class has strong effects on students' achievements. For example, Sewell found that students from upper-class families are two and a half times as likely as students from lower-class families to go to college, six times as likely to graduate from college, and nine times as likely to obtain a graduate or professional education (Sewell and Hauser, 1980). Whatever measure of socioeconomic status researchers use (family income, parents' education, parents' occupation) and whatever measure of academic achievement they employ (grades, test scores, course failures, dropout rates, college plans, actual years of schooling), the results are the same. Children from lower-class homes do not do as well in school as those from upper-class homes.

Moreover, all academic credentials are not equal. Students who receive degrees from certain elite schools have greater opportunities for financial success than those with equivalent degrees from other colleges and universities. In one study (R. P. Coleman and Rainwater, 1978) researchers divided American colleges and universities into three categories: a small number of very elite private institutions that serve about 15 percent of college students; a large group of good private institutions and better state universities, attended by 45 percent of students; and "all others." The researchers found that getting a B.A. from the first, "elite" group increased lifetime earnings by almost 85 percent; graduating from the second, "good" group increased expected income by over 50 percent. But B.A.s from all other schools provided no advantage; expected lifetime earnings for graduates of this group were no better than those for the population

at large, which includes large numbers of noncollege graduates. More recent studies confirm this pattern: the academically and socioeconomically "rich" get richer (attend the best colleges and universities), while the poor get poorer (Hearn, 1984).

To be sure, some disadvantaged students overcome the odds and reach the highest educational levels, while some advantaged students do not go beyond high school. But they are exceptions to the rule.

Can the link between social status and academic achievement be broken? One of the goals of the Cultural Revolution in China was to fracture the connection between social origins and academic achievement. A study of men's academic achievement using data from the 1982 census of the People's Republic of China found that this effort was largely successful, unlike the similar effort undertaken in Communist Russia (described in this chapter's *Global View* box). The study found that large-scale state intervention, particularly during the Cultural Revolution, greatly reduced the advantage that children of the upper classes had enjoyed and has made educational attainment in China highly egalitarian (Deng and Treiman, 1997). A father's socioeconomic status is no longer closely associated with his son's academic achievement. However, the gains in educational opportunity set in motion in China have been sustained largely by educational expansion, rather than continued government intervention (Deng and Treiman, 1997).

There is no simple explanation for the relationship between socioeconomic status and educational attainment. Socioeconomic background affects the scores students receive on tests of intellectual ability, the way they are perceived by significant others (parents, teachers, classmates), the educational level to which they aspire, the number of years they remain in school, and the level they eventually attain, as well as the kind of job they acquire. These sorts of influences—parents' or teachers' expectations that a daughter will not become a scientist, for example—are another way in which education can promote inequality. The African American child who is not expected to go on to college and so has no such expectations or aspirations for himself or herself is likely to receive quite a different education from the child who is preparing for a college admission.

Race, Gender, and Academic Achievement

Education is not the great equalizer many Americans would like to believe it is. As a group, white men earn about one-third more than both white women and African Americans of both sexes (see Table 12-1).

Racial differences in academic scores can be seen by age 9, are entrenched by age 13, and continue to increase throughout high school (Oakes, 1988). African Americans and Latinos consistently score lower than whites on measures of achievement at the end of high school. African American and Latino students are less likely than their white peers to enter college, less likely to enter four-year colleges, and less likely to enter and complete graduate programs. Considering the disproportionate number of African Americans and Latinos who drop out of high school, this measure of low achievement is perhaps even more serious than the test results imply. It is estimated that 40 to 60 percent of low-income minority students drop out of schools in urban areas (M. Fine, 1991).

By far, the highest percentage of high school dropouts nationwide (more than 30 percent) are Latino (*Statistical Abstract*, 1996). (See Figure 12-7.) One study of the dropout rates for Latinos found that cutting classes, getting suspended from school, dating, being older, and being female greatly increased the odds of dropping out; having a high socioeconomic status and a stable two-parent family decreased the odds (Velez, 1989).

Minority status affects test scores and academic performance in several ways (Fischer et al., 1996). One is socioeconomic deprivation. In the United States, black and Latino children are more likely to grow up in poverty, eat less nutritious foods, live in unhealthy environments, and receive little or poor medical care—all conditions that can impair learning—than are white children. Often they live in overcrowded homes in dangerous neighborhoods. Their families may value education but lack the skills to help with homework, talk with teachers, or use cultural resources (libraries, museums, etc.) in the wider community.

Second, African Americans and to a lesser degree Latinos tend to be physically and socially isolated. Many live in segregated neighborhoods, attend segregated schools (especially in large cities), and so-

Table 12-1 *Education and Income, by Race and Sex*

	White Americans		African Americans	
	Male	Female	Male	Female
Percent completing high school	83%	83%	73.4%	74.1%
Median income*	$32,440	$23,894	$24,405	$20,628

*For full-time workers.

Source: Adapted from U.S. Bureau of the Census, *Statistical Abstract of the United States, 1996,* Washington, DC: GPO, 1996, pp. 159, 469.

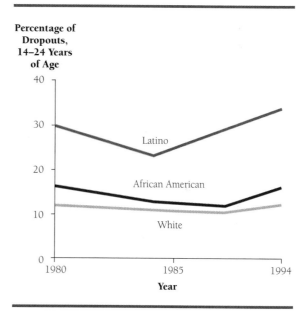

Figure 12-7 *Dropout Rates, 1980–1994*

Latino youngsters are more likely than African American or white students to drop out before graduating from high school.

Source: U.S. Bureau of the Census, *Statistical Abstract of the United States, 1996,* Washington, DC: GPO, 1996, p. 175.

cialize among themselves. Interracial friendships or marriages are rare. As a result, poor black and Latino children have less exposure to the majority culture, and more exposure to failure and problems, than do well-off white children.

Third, and perhaps most significantly, both groups are stigmatized as inferior. The larger society's expectation that they will fail affects their sense of themselves. This negative identity makes some young people anxious, hopeless, and resigned; others rebel, rejecting and defying the wider culture. Either reaction—resignation or rebellion—tends to lower academic performance and test scores (Fischer et al., 1996). Rejecting mainstream values and academic achievement may function as a form of self-protection: if you don't try, you can't fail (Steele, 1993). Several studies have demonstrated a direct effect of minority status on test performance. For example, African Americans score higher on IQ and other tests when the person administering the test is also African American (Graham, 1992). Black students at Stanford University who were told a test measured personal ability and were asked to check off their ethnicity on a questionnaire scored much lower on a selection of questions from the GRE than did black students who were told they were participating in a psychological study and not asked about race (Steele and Aronson, 1995). (The same was true for female students and for white males who were told they were being compared with Asians.) In contrast, youth from advantaged ethnic groups are able to interact with adult friends and neighbors who do well and can help them get started and who instill confidence in their futures.

Gender, too, plays a role in academic achievement and academic inequality, though as we saw in Chapter 10, sex differences in academic achievement are diminishing. Boys tend to get more encouragement from parents and teachers to take math and science courses as well as to enroll in higher-level courses. They are similarly encouraged by sex segregation in the marketplace, which has tended to shut women out of professions using higher math and science skills. One cross-cultural study has found that in countries where women have something approaching equal access to higher education and the job market, there are smaller sex differences in mathematical performance in school (Baker and Jones, 1993).

Encouragement and rising expectations can undermine the inequality in education women and African Americans have experienced, but what about more blatant inequities such as underfunded schools where textbooks are decades old, walls and ceilings are crumbling, and classes are twice the size

of those in affluent suburbs? One of the major controversies in education concerns the role that schools and communities play in students' achievement. To what extent does the socioeconomic status of a community affect the quality of its schools? How do tracking programs within schools affect students' achievement? Many observers argue that low achievement among African Americans and Latinos has more to do with these students' schools than with their abilities. We focus now on the interactions between communities, schools, and educational achievement. Later on we will take a look at the role peers play in devaluing educational achievement.

Unequal Schools

Funding schools through local taxes naturally makes some districts better equipped than others. Moreover, neighborhood schools bring together students from similar socioeconomic backgrounds, with similarly high or low educational aspirations. Common sense suggests that the better the school and the better the education that children receive, the further they will go. The 1954 Supreme Court decision outlawing school segregation was based, in part, on this reasoning.

School Funding

The social structure of education in the United States is unique in that rather than being organized nationally, as it is in most other countries, the primary source of funding for local school districts is the local property tax. Since wealthy communities tend to have higher property tax rates than poorer towns, schools in well-off districts have more money. One town in Vermont had a tax base of $140,000 per pupil and spent $3,743 per student, while another (in a prime ski area) had a tax base of $2.2 million per student and spent $6,476 on each (Goldberg, 1997). Schools in well-to-do districts tend to be newer, better-equipped, better-staffed, and less crowded than schools in low-income districts. Average expenditures per pupil in New York City's public schools in 1987 amounted to about $5,500, yet in neighboring suburbs per-pupil expenditures were twice that figure (Kozol, 1991). Jonathan Kozol provides a graphic description of what that means for inner-city schoolchildren:

The primary source of school funding in the United States is the property tax. Since wealthy suburban communities raise more money in property taxes than do poor urban ones, there tends to be a great disparity between school facilities.

If the New York City schools were funded . . . at the level of the highest-spending suburbs of Long Island, a fourth grade class of 36 children such as those I visited in District 10 would have had $200,000 more invested in their education during 1987. Although a portion of this extra money would have gone into administrative costs, the remainder would have been enough to hire two extraordinary teachers at enticing salaries of $50,000 each, divide the classes into two classes of some 18 children each, provide them with computers, carpets, air conditioning, new texts and reference books, and learning games—indeed, with everything available today in the most affluent school districts—and also pay the costs of extra counseling to help those children cope with the dilemmas that they face at home. (1991, pp. 123–124)

In recent years many poor school districts across the country have sued to challenge school funding inequities. A number of state courts have ruled that property tax funding of schools is unconstitutional and have ordered the states to equalize the funds that go to the local school districts. Only two, Kansas and Vermont, have enacted statewide property taxes that say, in effect, that the high tax base of one community does not belong to that community but is part of the educational budget for the state. This solution is not without its critics. Residents of the wealthier districts worry that the quality of their schools will decline in the process of improving other schools. In several states wealthy districts are

countersuing, arguing that they are being unfairly deprived of their own money.

Private versus Public Schools

The first large-scale, nationwide study of American high school sophomores and seniors was sponsored by the National Center for Educational Statistics in 1980. It included students attending public and private schools (primarily Catholic schools). The survey found that by almost any measure, students who attended private schools performed better than students from similar socioeconomic backgrounds who went to public schools. On tests of vocabulary, reading, and mathematics, private school students averaged about one grade level above their public school peers. Catholic schools were particularly effective with poor and minority students.

A follow-up study found that during the last two years of high school, Catholic school students made greater advances than public school students in verbal and mathematical skills but not in science or civics (Coleman and Hoffer, 1987). Students at non-Catholic private schools also made greater gains in verbal skills (but not in mathematics, science, or civics). High school dropout rates were much lower in Catholic schools than in public schools or other private schools, even for students who had been considered high risks in their sophomore year. Graduates of both Catholic and

Studies have found that students who attend private schools do better than students in public schools. This finding has helped fuel debate over voucher programs, which would enable children from poor families to attend parochial and other private schools. Here first-graders work on math problems at Union Baptist Excel Academy in Denver.

non-Catholic private schools were much more likely to enroll in college than were graduates of public schools. After parents' education and income, the main reason for higher college enrollment was that private school students were more likely to take traditional, college-preparatory courses (English composition, European history, science, foreign languages, and the like). Public school students were more likely to take nontraditional electives. Finally, private school graduates were slightly more likely to remain in college or, if they dropped out of college, to return. Again, Catholic schools had the greatest impact on poor and minority students.

The success of Catholic schools may be because they are part of a community (Coleman and Hoffer, 1987). Private schools attract families with similar values and aspirations, but these families do not necessarily live near one another or interact regularly. Religion is one of the few institutions that

brings together people of different generations and (particularly in the case of the Catholic Church) different socioeconomic backgrounds who have an interest in preserving continuity. More concretely, Catholic schools are demanding, in terms of both academic work and discipline. Their students do more homework, cut fewer classes, and fight with each other less often. And these differences in student behavior and school climate translate into better academic performance. Of course, there is a possibility that private school students do better because they were better students in the first place or because their parents are more concerned about education than are public school parents. Critics were quick to point to this possibility (for example, McPartland and McDill, 1982).

Unfortunately, there have not been many studies of the differences in academic achievement between public and private schools. Private and parochial schools seldom release test scores, nor do they often use the same tests as public schools. Thus, it has been difficult to make comparisons. But in 1990 the National Assessment of Educational Progress reported on the results of a math test administered to both private school and public school students. The differences were far from dramatic: on a 500-point scale, seniors in private school scored on average just 6 points higher than public school seniors (National Center for Educational Statistics, 1992). A recent review of studies comparing public and private schools found that when variables such as the selectivity of the schools are adjusted for, the superior performance of the private school students nearly evaporates (White, 1997).

School Resegregation?

The Supreme Court decision in *Brown v. Board of Education* (1954) mandated one of the most ambitious (and controversial) programs for reducing educational inequality in this nation's history: school desegregation. The decision was aimed at southern states, in which schools were segregated by law (*de jure*). However, it soon became clear that segregation was just as pronounced in northern states, where the combination of residential segregation and the neighborhood school tradition concentrated minority students in some schools and white students in others (*de facto* segregation). Ending de jure segregation in the south proved to be an easier task than combating de facto segregation in the north. Today, an African American student in the south is more likely to attend an integrated school than is an African American student in the north. Although neighborhood segregation has decreased in recent decades, the proportions of minority families living in the inner city and of white families moving to the suburbs have increased steadily. The result: Schools are experiencing resegregation at the fastest pace since the *Brown v. Board of Education* ruling was handed down (*Providence Journal,* April 8, 1997, p. A5).

In every major city, the school system has lost white enrollment. The overwhelming majority of public school students in Los Angeles, New York, Chicago, Cleveland, Miami, Houston, and Washington today are nonwhite. In a series of studies, Gary Orfield and his colleagues found that African American and particularly Latino students are increasingly being isolated in schools that are poor (Orfield, Bachmeier, and Eitle, 1997). Not all the resegregation is the result of shifting demographics, however. In the south, court challenges to school desegregation have resulted in previously integrated schools' becoming resegregated as schools find ways to avoid desegregation orders.

Does integration reduce racial inequality in education? Does attending integrated schools result in improved academic performance among minority students? The findings are mixed (Rist, 1978; St. John, 1975). There is no evidence that desegregation has a negative impact on white students. However, neither is there evidence that desegregation, by itself, has a strong, positive effect on minority students. Economic integration does seem to have an impact, however. Minority students placed in classrooms with a majority of middle- to upper-class students show substantial gains in academic achievement (Weinberg, 1975). One obvious reason is that desegregated schools are more likely to be under community pressure for college-track education and to have the resources to meet this demand than are segregated minority schools. As a result, there may be more college-track slots for minority students (Longshore and Prager, 1985). There may be subtler gains as well. Some researchers have found that minority students who attend integrated, middle-class schools aspire to higher levels of education, show more awareness of career opportunities, and feel more hopeful about their own futures than those who attend predominantly minority schools (Daniels, 1983).

Placing disadvantaged minority students in white, middle-class classrooms does not guarantee that the minority students will benefit from the experience or that race relations will improve, however. Students may simply work side by side, and relations between races may be tentative and superficial. When students are required to work together in small mixed-race groups on tasks that require cooperation, both white and nonwhite students score higher on subsequent achievement tests (Longshore and Prager, 1985).

Tracking

Another explanation of differences in academic achievement is unequal treatment within schools. Three out of four American schools use some form of ***tracking:*** assigning students to different classes and programs on the basis of perceived ability and interests. In some schools all students take the same subjects but are assigned to different-level classes. In other schools students are assigned to different programs (vocational, general, or college-preparatory) and study different subjects.

Advocates hold that tracking allows each student to work at his or her own pace. Bright students can move ahead. Slower students are relieved of the burden of constantly being compared with students who have more ability and/or experience than they have, and they can get extra help when they need it. All students benefit. Critics maintain that tracking creates a system of social stratification within the school, undermining the goal of equal education for all. Students in college-preparatory and advanced groups are treated as the school's elite, while students in lower tracks and groups are stigmatized as the school's "dummies." In the view of these critics, tracking provides an example of how the "Pygmalion effect" can influence a child's academic achievement (see *Close Up:* Pygmalion in the Classroom).

Another criticism of tracking is that grouping by ability also stratifies classes by race, ethnicity, and socioeconomic status. A national study of 14,000 eighth-graders in public schools in 1988 discovered that among students from the top quarter of the socioeconomic spectrum, 39 percent were assigned to high-ability groups, whereas only 13 percent of those in the bottom quarter were in high-ability tracks (*The New York Times,* April 4, 1993, pp. 14–16). Overall, 47 percent of Asian students and 35 percent of white students were in high-ability math groups, compared with 18 percent of Latinos, 15 percent of African Americans, and 10 percent of Native Americans; the low-ability math and English groups were disproportionately black, Latino, and Native American.

One study found that 80 percent of high school sophomores from the highest socioeconomic level with high test scores were assigned to a college track, compared with only 52 percent of high scorers from the lowest socioeconomic level (Vanfossen et al., 1987). Not counting past performance, students from the highest socioeconomic level had a 53 percent chance of being assigned to the college track, compared with only a 19 percent chance for students from the lowest level (see Figure 12-8). Even schools with a policy of inclusion—in which students from many different cultures and socioeconomic backgrounds are encouraged to explore their

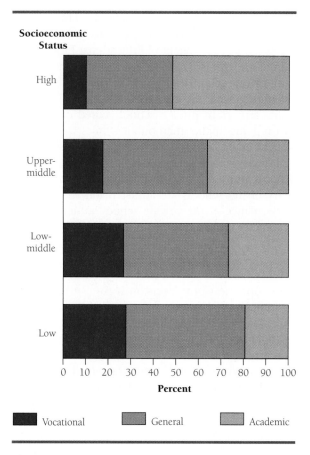

Figure 12-8   *Track Location by Socioeconomic Level*

Students with high socioeconomic status are far more likely to be placed in academic tracks and are less likely to be in vocational tracks than students from the lower socioeconomic levels.

Source: From B. E. Vanfossen, J. D. Jones, and J. Z. Spade, "Curriculum Tracking and Status Maintenance," *Sociology of Education* 60, April 1987, p. 109, fig. 2. Reprinted by permission of the American Sociological Association.

differences—may find that white, non-Latino students are vastly in the majority in advanced placement classes (Holmes, 1997).

Another study found that there is some evidence of affirmative action in the nation's high schools; females and blacks were slightly more likely to be assigned to a college track than male whites who had similar test scores (Gamoran and Mare, 1989). But in general the academic hierarchy in high schools reflects the social hierarchy in society at large.

Tracking influences student achievement in direct ways, but this influence depends on the kind of

CLOSE UP

Pygmalion in the Classroom

Teachers tend to expect different levels of performance from different students—from male and female, poor and middle-class, white and nonwhite, and high- and average-intelligence students. Do these expectations have any effect on student performance? Robert Rosenthal and Lenore Jacobson (1968) became interested in whether teacher expectations could become *self-fulfilling prophecies*—false predictions that influence behavior in such a way that the predictions come true (Merton, 1968). Rosenthal and Jacobson suspected they did.

To test their hunch, Rosenthal and Jacobson conducted an experiment at a grade school in California in which they manipulated variables so that they could study the effect teachers' expectations had on their students (see the discussion of experimental methods in Chapter 2). At the beginning of the school year, all the children in grades one through six were given a test. Then Rosenthal and Jacobson gave teachers a list of children whom they said the test had identified as "bloomers"—children who could be expected to show significant intellectual growth over the year. In reality, they were planting false expectations. The test was an ordinary intelligence test that did not predict intellectual growth. And the children on the list of bloomers were chosen at random, without regard to scores. Thus, the difference between these and the other children (the control group) existed only in the minds of the teachers.

If the teachers' expectations functioned as self-fulfilling prophecies, Rosenthal and Jacobson reasoned, the children identified as bloomers would make greater strides than the other children would. At the end of the year they administered the test again to measure progress. Looking at all the students, the researchers found that the bloomers made the greatest gains in test scores—an average of 12 points, compared with an average of 8 points for the other youngsters.

They found no real differences in the higher grades but did find differences in the lower grades. The most improvement

> **Self-fulfilling prophecies may help explain the unequal school performance of white and nonwhite, middle-class and lower-class, and male and female students.**

occurred among first-graders (suggesting that young children are most susceptible to teacher influence) and among Mexican American students (suggesting that racial prejudice had had a negative effect on their performance in the past). In the lower grades, then, the self-fulfilling prophecy seemed to occur: children of whom more was expected tended to do better than children in the control group. Rosenthal and Jacobson named this the "Pygmalion effect," after the king in Greek mythology who loved the statue of a maiden so much that she sprang to life.

Subsequent studies have not been able to replicate Rosenthal and Jacobson's results, casting some doubt on the validity of the Pygmalion effect. If the effect is real, however, as many sociologists have come to believe, then self-fulfilling prophecies may help explain the unequal school performance of white and nonwhite, middle-class and lower-class, and male and female students (in math). Published studies and past performances lead teachers to believe that certain categories of students are capable of performing better than other categories. Acting on these expectations, however subconscious they may be, the teachers unwittingly encourage the "better" students and discourage the "inferior" ones. More attention, praise, and challenging work are given to those considered to be achievers; those labeled as underachievers are not required to give as much effort to their less challenging academic work. Since these attitudes and expectations form early in a child's schooling experience, the cumulative effect over time can be devastating. Students are in a sense "trained" to perform the way their teachers expect them to; as a result, the teachers' expectations are confirmed. Some educators believe that this vicious circle must be broken before educational inequities can be remedied (Oakes, 1988).

tracking system a school uses (Gamoran, 1992). Tracking that is rigidly organized results in greater gaps in achievement between the academic and nonacademic tracks as well as a lower overall achievement rate for the school than tracking that is more flexible and includes more students in the academic track. Presumably, more is demanded of a student body with a large number of students in the academic track (or with the possibility of moving into that track).

Tracking has indirect effects as well, especially in the way it influences social behavior. Young people tend to make friends with the kids they see every day in class. College-track students usually report that their closest friends like school, get good grades, go to class regularly, and plan to go to college (Vanfossen, Jones, and Spade, 1987). Doing well in school is socially acceptable, even mandatory. In contrast, students in general and vocational tracks may find that good grades and academic aspirations are a social liability.

The classroom environment also differs from one track to another (Vanfossen, Jones, and Spade, 1987). College-track seniors recall few incidents of other students' cutting class, talking back to teachers, or refusing to follow instructions. For students in general and vocational tracks, these are common experiences. Classroom observers (see Oakes, 1985) find that teachers in the lower tracks spend more time on discipline and less on teaching. They tend to emphasize learning basic skills and memo-rizing facts and to make frequent use of drills. College-track teachers are more likely to emphasize conceptual learning, to encourage independent projects, and to enjoy teaching. Their students generally report that the teachers are warm and fair, that they treat everyone with respect, that they are clear in their assignments and lectures, and that they seem to enjoy being teachers. General- and vocational-track students are more likely to describe their teachers as unclear, unenthusiastic, and punitive.

Taking other factors into account, assignment to a noncollege track increases the likelihood that a student will drop out of high school before graduation (Gamoran and Mare, 1989). Whereas there is a direct connection between a college-preparatory program and the next stage of a student's life (college), general and even vocational education may seem to have little application to life after high school.

In addition, tracking has led to resegregation, especially in inner-city schools (Slavin, 1987). Schools that serve predominantly poor and minority students usually offer fewer advanced courses and more remedial courses in academic subjects, they have smaller advanced tracks and larger vocational tracks, and they demand less of students who are in the college track (Hanson, 1986). Even courses for the vocational track are different. For example, a vocational track at a predominantly white, middle-class school might offer courses in

In college-track classes, doing well in school is socially acceptable. College-track students usually report that their closest friends like school, get good grades, and go to school regularly.

business and science or technology; a vocational track at a predominantly minority school tends to offer classes in low-level trades and such unskilled work as building maintenance (Oakes, 1985). Enrollment in the latter school, on a lower track, begins a cycle of restricted opportunities and poor performance (Oakes, 1987).

In summary, the evidence suggests that tracking may be good for students with high ability, but it reinforces and perpetuates social inequality among other students.

The Quality of Education

Today educators are wrestling not only with problems of social, racial, and sexual inequality but also with educational standards. As we saw in the chapter introduction, there are many signs that the quality of education continues to lag behind the needs of society, despite the calls of alarm that were sounded in the 1983 report *A Nation at Risk.*

Student Achievement

Standardized tests show that student performance in the United States has, for the most part, been declining. As we saw in the introduction to this chapter, scores on the SAT have been languishing or declining for over two decades, though the average mathematics SAT score rose in 1997 (*Chronicle of Higher Education,* September 5, 1997, p. A68). The fact that more Americans, from a wider range of socioeconomic and educational backgrounds, were applying to college and therefore taking the test has been used to account for some of this decline, but only for some of it.

What explains the overall drop in scores? Some educators blame the schools: In a push to raise the grades of average students, schools lowered their academic standards and the top students suffered. The number of students with an A average taking the SAT increased by 9 percent while their average combined scores have fallen by 14 points (*Chronicle of Higher Education,* September 5, 1997), suggesting grade inflation is indeed widespread. Other educators note that the decline in verbal scores began with the students who were the first to be raised with television. Watching television takes time away from other activities that stimulate academic

achievement. Today's eighth-graders, for example, spend an average of twenty-one hours per week watching television, compared with less than two hours devoted to outside reading and less than six hours to homework (*American Educator,* 1992, p. 4). Critics of television argue, "If you want higher scores, turn the TV off or throw it out."

SAT results refer only to those high school students who plan to go to college. Studies of the more general population of elementary and secondary students reveal significant deficits in standard and basic skills. In 1992, the Department of Education tested 140,000 students across the nation for their ability to read for literary experience (novels, short stories, essays), for information (newspaper and magazine articles, encyclopedia entries, textbook chapters), and for performing a task (such as reading directions). One quarter of high school seniors, nearly one-third of eighth-graders, and two out of every five fourth-graders read so badly that they could not understand material considered basic for their levels (National Center for Educational Statistics, 1993b). Again, the more television the students watched, the lower their scores.

American students are only average when compared with their counterparts in other industrialized nations. In the Third International Math and Science Study, which tested students from forty-one countries, American 13- and 14-year-olds outperformed students in thirteen other nations in math, and came in seventeenth in science (see Figure 12-9). The countries whose students scored the highest—Singapore, South Korea, and Japan—have all raised educational standards in an effort to improve their economies by improving education (*The Economist,* March 29, 1997, pp. 21–23).

The international picture may be distorted, however, by the fact that the pool of students being compared is sometimes quite different (P. B. Walters, 1993). In many European countries academic schooling is the province of elite students; low-ability students have already been steered away from the academic track and onto vocational tracks before the tests are given. American students, by contrast, are encouraged to stay in school and complete their secondary education. But even when only twelfth-grade students on an academic track are compared, Americans still do not perform as

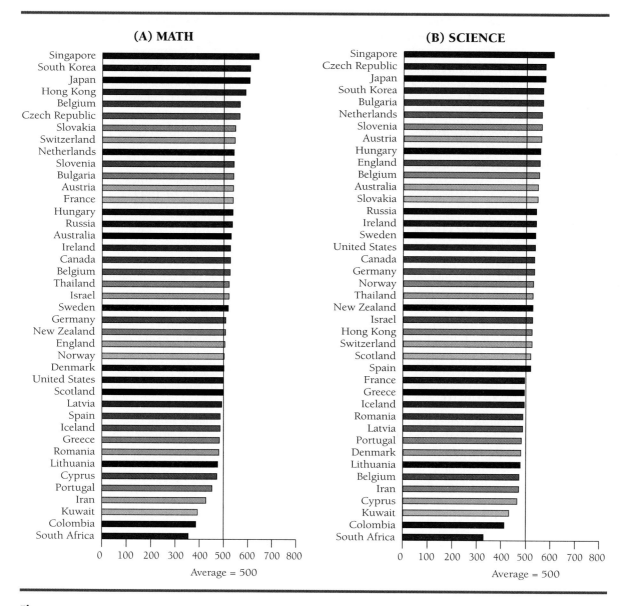

Figure 12-9   *International Comparison of Academic Achievement, Select Countries, 1996*

The figure shows the scores of 13-year-olds on the Third International Math and Science Study (TIMSS). The international average was found and then set at 500.

Source: The Economist, Mar. 29, 1997.

well on comparative tests as students from other countries. One reason may be the difference in curriculum: European schools tend to require more demanding subjects, while American high schools offer many more nonacademic subjects and put more emphasis on extracurricular activities, as we will now see.

Academic Standards

A number of critics blame reduced standards for the decline in achievement by American students. In the 1960s and 1970s, junior and senior high schools moved away from the basics and began offering students a wide range of nontraditional programs and courses. A study of fifteen schools over a five-year period compared high schools with shopping malls, where students browse, decide what they want to "buy" (what courses to take) and how much they want to spend (how much effort they want to invest), see their friends, and pass the time (Powell et al., 1985). A typical high school attempts to please every consumer of education by offering a wide range of subjects at different levels of difficulty.

Instead of setting standards, some high schools see their job as devising a curriculum that everybody can do. Instead of requiring that students adapt to the curriculum, they adapt the curriculum to students. This approach is based on the widespread American belief that almost everyone should go to high school, almost everyone should graduate, and almost everyone should get something out of the experience. While these might be noble sentiments, the approach in effect dilutes the quality of education. Too many decisions are left in the hands of students. Special students (the very bright and the disabled) can thrive in this environment, but "only-average" students are often lost in the shuffle.

Learning Environments

As the children of the baby boom generation enter and proceed through elementary school, enrollments are skyrocketing and, as a consequence, overcrowding is widespread in many areas of the country. It will take years to build the schools needed to accommodate the students. In many school systems portable classrooms are being set up and classes are held in lunchrooms and former closets. As these children reach high school age, the problem will only become worse: to excel, students need more expensive facilities such as language and science labs. The average elementary school costs $6.3 million to construct; the average high school, $15.3 million (*Providence Journal Bulletin,* August 24, 1997, p. A21).

Added to this is the fact that many existing facilities have been so poorly funded (as described earlier) that they are desperately in need of repair. This is particularly true in urban areas where students whose lives reflect many of the social problems of our times are asked to study in aging schools that are crowded and crumbling. These factors have many ramifications—from the physical well-being of both student and teacher to the level of academic achievement that is possible.

> The deteriorating physical condition of inner-city schools has been well documented. The Carnegie Foundation reported in 1988 that one high school in Cleveland is near a once bustling intersection of commerce, but so many surrounding buildings have been razed that now the vacant land makes the school look like a forgotten outpost in an underdeveloped country. A sprawling playground is rendered useless by a carpet of glass. Inside, lavatories for students have no light bulbs, the stalls have no doors, and there is no toilet paper in the dispensers. There is an atmosphere of hopelessness among the students, mirroring the outside world. (in Louv, 1990, p. 334)

New York City public schools opened two weeks late in the fall of 1993 because of concern about exposed asbestos in the peeling walls and ceilings of the classrooms. The news cameras that documented this problem also revealed broken windows, dilapidated furniture and dysfunctional toilets, filthy halls and classrooms, and severe overcrowding. In some schools classes are held in gyms or converted restrooms, and guidance counselors work out of closets. Custodians, many of whom earn more than teachers, are often creative in finding ways to cut corners on maintenance, which contributes to the

The deteriorated conditions of many inner-city schools have widespread ramifications, ranging from the physical well-being of students and teachers to the level of academic achievement it is possible for students to attain.

dilapidated condition of the buildings. In September 1997, a new New York City school opened to help alleviate this crowding and was immediately closed because toxic fumes from the dry-cleaning plant that it used to be remained at dangerous levels.

Illiterate? Who, US?

Undoubtedly the most alarming educational information to come to light in the 1980s was the number of adult Americans who cannot read or write. Most Americans associate illiteracy with Third World nations and previous generations. Unfortunately, they are wrong. Illiteracy rates in the United States are quite high. The nation ranks an embarrassing forty-ninth among the 158 members of the United Nations in literacy. A four-year government study of a representative sample of 26,000 adults found that nearly half were not sufficiently well versed in English to write a letter about a billing error. Nor were they proficient enough in math to calculate the length of a bus trip from a schedule, fill out a bank deposit slip, compute the cost of carpeting a room, or extract information from a table or a graph (National Center for Educational Statistics, 1993a). That translates to approximately 90 million adult Americans with very limited literacy skills.

Illiteracy is expensive, for individuals and for societies. The Senate Select Committee on Equal Educational Opportunity estimates the unrealized earning potential forfeited by men age 25 to 34 who have less than high school–level skills at $237 billion. Half of the heads of households classified below the federal poverty line cannot read an eighth-grade book; more than one-third of mothers on welfare are functionally illiterate, as are 60 percent of the adult prison population and 84 percent of juveniles who come before the courts. Businesses have difficulty filling such entry-level jobs as clerk, bank teller, and paralegal assistant. A major insurance firm reports that 70 percent of dictated letters must be retyped "at least once," because secretaries cannot spell and punctuate correctly. The military also pays a price for illiteracy. The Navy has stated that 30 percent of new recruits are "a danger to themselves and costly to naval equipment" because they cannot read or understand simple instructions.

The human costs of illiteracy are difficult to grasp for those of us who take reading for granted.

Illiterate people cannot read notices from the IRS, a welfare office, or a housing bureau, and so they do not know what rights they have or what deadlines and requirements they must meet to obtain them. For the most part, they do not vote. As a result they are "half-citizens," whose rights exist on paper they cannot read. Illiterate people lack freedom of choice in our print society. They cannot read the TV listings in the newspaper or the menu in a restaurant. In a grocery store, they depend on familiar packages. They cannot travel where they like because they cannot read street or bus signs or train destinations. Their health is uninsured, in several ways. They cannot read a medicine bottle's instructions and warnings, a health insurance form, or the waiver they sign before undergoing surgery. They cannot help their children with homework and often do not visit the school for fear of embarrassing their children or themselves.

Critics of our educational system see illiteracy as only "the tip of the iceberg." In the "information age," most people will earn their living by working with their heads, not their hands. An average job will require a twelfth-grade reading level (Wagner, 1987). Yet two out of three American students who graduate from high school read at only a ninth-grade level. The notion of educational excellence has become synonymous with our ability to survive in the global marketplace (Timar and Kirp, 1988). International comparisons suggest that today's American students—tomorrow's American workers—are not prepared for the economic olympics. (See Map 12-1.)

School Reform: The Policy Debates

Dozens of reports on the problems in our schools and recommendations for reform were published during the 1980s, in part in response to the warnings of *A Nation at Risk* (P. B. Walters, 1993). The reports gave rise to reforms such as creative ways of funding schools, school choice, charter and magnet schools, and efforts to raise the quality of teaching. In his 1997 Call for Action for American Education in the Twenty-First Century, President Clinton emphasized reform efforts aimed at rigorous national standards, teacher recruitment and training, and school choice. Yet there are those who believe that just setting standards and increasing school budgets produce few beneficial effects on student achievement in and of

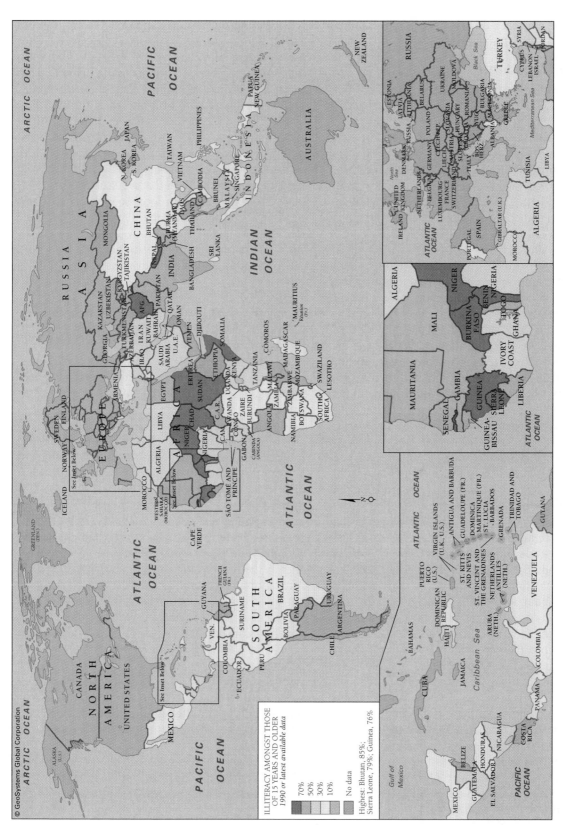

Map 12-1   Illiteracy Rates around the World

The highest rate of illiteracy is in Bhutan, where 85 percent of the population cannot read or write.

Source: Michael Kidron and Ronald Segal, *The State of the World Atlas,* 5th ed. 1995. New York: Penguin, p. 42.

ILLITERACY AMONGST THOSE
OF 15 YEARS AND OLDER
1990 or latest available data

70%
50%
30%
10%
No data

Highest: Bhutan, 85%;
Sierra Leone, 79%; Guinea, 76%

themselves. They see the problems of education as extending beyond the classroom.

National Standards

Nearly all other industrial nations have a national education system that sets goals, establishes curricula, and evaluates performance for the country as a whole. Traditionally Americans have opposed national standards as interfering with local control of schools, but by 1989 a large majority of those polled favored national regulation. In November 1997 President Clinton signed into law a bill to fund a pilot program of voluntary national tests as part of his call for all children to be reading independently and well by the end of third grade. When fully instituted, his plan for national standards will require that children take national tests of reading skills in the fourth grade and math skills in the eighth grade.

Americans take standardized tests every year. What would be different about national examinations? Most current tests give scores based on how children compare with other children their age—a grading curve. The new tests would rate children according to an absolute standard of what they should know about a given subject at a given age. Supporters claim that this would produce an annual "report card" that would allow politicians, educators, and parents to evaluate their local schools and prod schools and teachers whose students performed poorly into doing better.

Most of the criticism of national standards has come from educators. Who, critics ask, would decide what students should know? The idea of national standards is based on the assumption that scholars in a given field agree about what is important and about what skills children should have mastered at a given age. They do not. It is also based on the assumption that all children can or should learn at the same pace. Few educators agree. Critics argue that standardized tests (usually in the form of multiple-choice questions) call for standardized answers. They tend to reward memorization and rote learning and to penalize critical thinking and creativity. Teachers who want their students to do well would be pressured to cram students full of facts and formulas.

Then there are those who fear that such standardization will result in mediocrity. Rather than "raising the bar" for students, national standards will become minimum standards. As mentioned earlier, some schools have shown a tendency to lower their requirements when they are faced with increasing numbers of students who cannot meet them. Critics also argue that national tests would emphasize knowledge of white, western, middle-class culture and values, at the expense of other ethnic traditions, and thus encourage teachers to ignore cultural diversity. Finally, some educators are concerned that national standards would spawn a rigid national curriculum that would have the effect of wresting control from local school districts, removing any local or regional flavor from the curriculum, stifling teacher innovation in the classroom, and increasing the disparities between schools in poor and affluent districts (Celis, 1993).

Magnet Schools and Vouchers

During the 1980s **school choice,** a plan that allows parents to choose their children's schools, emerged as a popular reform proposed to solve the problem of unequal schools. During the 1990s school choice has come to refer to a number of arrangements. Where national standards rely on a centralized educational system, school choice reforms take a market approach to education and encourage a diversity of schools, in some cases allowing groups of individuals to start their own *charter schools*, which are public schools permitted to operate on their own without public oversight (Cohn, 1997).

In some cases, school choice means the ability to choose among the public schools in one's district; in others, it means that a portion of funds usually allocated directly to schools would be given to parents in the form of vouchers or tuition tax credits. After shopping around for the best school, the parent gives the school that is chosen the voucher, which can then be "cashed in." In some areas, vouchers can be used at public or private schools (Cookson, 1994). Some school districts have attempted to provide parents with a degree of choice through the creation of **magnet schools.** These are schools with a specialized focus or teaching style— for example, computer applications, performing arts, math and science, foreign language centers, honors classes, or the "new basics." In a magnet school program, the parents can choose whichever school fits their child's needs and interests. Spots in these schools may be awarded on the basis of test scores (for math and science schools), auditions (for performing arts), lottery, or simply a first-come, first-served basis. Some schools may be placed in predominantly minority neighborhoods and others in predominantly white neighborhoods, so that students are encouraged to move around.

Polls show that a majority of the public, but especially nonwhite people and young Americans, support choice in public education (Sandy, 1997). Moreover, the freedom to choose seems to raise student motivation and performance, heighten parental involvement, and even attract some parents back into the public school system (Armor, 1989). In fact, one of the greatest benefits of the school-choice movement may be its ability to engage parent and community participation (Cookson, 1994). The danger, critics warn, is that neighborhood schools will be worse off after the more motivated and able students—and a disproportionate share of resources—are drawn to magnet schools.

Proponents of school choice believe it improves the incentive for education among school administrators and teachers as well as parents and students (J. S. Coleman, 1992). Schools would try to attract and keep the best students, while parents and students would try to get into the best schools and stay there. Without school choice, the only way parents can find a better school is to move into another school district. Since the parents who do so tend to be white and middle-class, the result is a school system increasingly stratified by income and race.

Critics of school choice fear that it will only increase the social stratification that already exists in schools (Ambler, 1997; Astin, 1992). In the "free-market" atmosphere of school choice, the most attractive schools would indeed become the most successful at enrolling the best students. But instead of responding to success by growing (as a private company would), they would simply become more and more selective. The most talented, highly motivated, and highest-achieving students would end up being concentrated in the best schools. Since these students tend to come from the most affluent and advantaged families, students from lower socioeconomic levels would be relegated to less attractive schools and concentrated there. A study of school-choice experiments in Britain, France, and the Netherlands found that it tended to intensify class segregation (Ambler, 1997).

Teacher Credentials

In the 1970s and 1980s the number of college freshmen who planned to become teachers dropped dramatically as women and African Americans, who had traditionally made up a majority of the ranks of teachers, found employment opportunities elsewhere. By 1985, less than 10 percent of college women planned to become teachers, the number of minority education majors had declined, and many teachers were leaving teaching for other jobs. At the same time, the qualifications of education majors declined. Between 1973 and 1982, the gap between the average SAT score for all high school seniors and the average for those who planned to major in education grew from 59 to 80 points (Carnegie Foundation for the Advancement of Teaching, 1986).

The training and evaluation of teachers remain controversial reform issues, however. Two reports attracted both positive and negative attention in the 1980s: *Tomorrow's Teachers* (1986), prepared by the Holmes Group (a committee of chief academic officers of schools and colleges of education), and *A Nation Prepared: Teachers for the 21st Century* (1986), issued by the Carnegie Forum on Education and the Economy (a task force of businesspeople, elected officials, and the heads of state departments of education and teacher unions and associations).

Both the Holmes and the Carnegie reports argued that the most important reform would be to professionalize teaching through (1) requiring national certification, (2) shifting teacher education to graduate programs, (3) upgrading the status and income of teachers, and (4) giving teachers more autonomy in the classroom. Although some teachers applauded these recommendations, many others did not. Critics argued that national examinations would promote a technical and scientific view of teaching, as if mastering certain information would automatically make a person a good teacher (Cornbleth, 1987). Motivating students and promoting intellectual curiosity require subtle skills.

Both reports advocated giving teachers a greater say in the way their schools are run—a greater voice in designing curricula, scheduling classes, preparing budgets and allocating funds, hiring and evaluating other teachers, and the like (point 4). This suggests that schools should become more flexible organizations, where problem solving and creativity are valued more than one's position in a bureaucratic hierarchy or strict adherence to rules and regulations created by the top of the bureaucratic pyramid (see Chapter 6). Both reports implied that schools have become too bureaucratic. At the same time, however, both recommended creating a new hierarchy of teachers, a new national regulatory board, and a new set of national standards and procedures—all of which would add to the educational bureaucracy (Popkewitz, 1987; Tom, 1987). At best, the reports sent a mixed message; at worst, they betrayed a basic distrust of teachers. Virtually everyone agrees that finding ways of improving the professionalization, pay, and status of teachers is crucial to improving the quality of education. The question is how to do this. Years after the reports were issued, few of the recommendations have been implemented or even tried.

In the 1990s, as the children of the baby boom generation entered the educational system, many schools saw their enrollments rise as much as 20 percent. With fewer new teachers, retirement and career changes, and growing school enrollments, schools experienced a shortage of teachers, and many school districts have had to offer higher salaries and better working conditions. As a result, the number and qualifications of college students planning to enter teaching are inching upward. In the 1997 State of the Union Address, ensuring that "a talented and dedicated teacher is in every classroom" was part of President Clinton's ten-point call to action on education. Clinton's education budget includes money to certify 100,000 master teachers over the next ten years.

Minority Students and Teachers

Many see equal education for disadvantaged children as the major challenge of the 1990s and the twenty-first century. Because of high birthrates in poor and minority communities, high immigration rates, and increasing poverty, as many as 40 percent of American students will fall into this category by the year 2000.

Study after study has shown that poor and minority children are at risk. They receive lower test scores, even before they begin school. They fall further and further behind as they move through school. And they are almost twice as likely as middle-class white students to drop out of school before the end of high school. If current trends continue, we will become a two-tiered society with a large number of poorly educated, unemployable youth (most of whom will be African American or Latino) on the bottom and a smaller number of highly educated, affluent adults (most of whom will be white) on the top (Levin, 1986). As job requirements increase and the pool of qualified workers declines, more and more jobs will be shipped to other countries or computerized. Unemployment will rise, and with it the costs of public assistance and law enforcement. This grim scenario can be avoided.

Preschool programs, such as Head Start, enable poor and minority children to enter school on a more equal footing with their advantaged peers.

Educating the disadvantaged must begin with preschool programs that enable poor and minority youngsters to enter school on an equal footing. Graduates of Head Start, a federal preschool enrichment program, have shown immediate gains in basic skills and school readiness and have outperformed other low-income children on standardized tests of IQ and achievement in elementary school (R. C. Collins, 1983). But only a small percentage of the children eligible for Head Start participate in the program, and these gains may not last beyond the first years of formal schooling.

One of the most effective classroom techniques with disadvantaged children is cooperative learning (Committee on Education and Labor, 1988). Students are divided into small mixed-ability (and ideally mixed-race and mixed-gender) groups, and the group is held responsible for learning, and helping individual members learn, the material being studied. When properly implemented (and that is essential), all children can benefit from this approach. High-ability students learn more when they play the role of tutor, helping low-ability students master the material. And low-ability students benefit from the extra help and attention. Cooperative learning can also enhance all students' self-esteem, improve race relations among students, and promote acceptance of disabled students.

In-classroom techniques need to be supported by out-of-classroom opportunities, such as providing after-school study space (in schools, libraries, or local organizations) for students whose parents both work and for those with no quiet place to study at home, access to computers programmed to tutor students whose parents do not have the time or skills to help them with homework, and summer programs that combine learning with field trips, movies, sports, and other enjoyable activities. For older students, both work-study programs, which enable potential dropouts to see direct connections between school and earnings, and mentor programs, which provide disadvantaged students with successful role models from the business community, would be helpful.

Minority teachers, at all levels, are essential to educating the disadvantaged (Grant and Gillette, 1987; Spellman, 1988). This is not to say that African American children need African American teachers, Latino children need Latino teachers, and female students need female teachers, but the presence of minority teachers on the faculty is important. Minority teachers serve as role models, for white as well as minority students. Their very presence promotes multicultural education, something that will become increasingly important as the ethnic composition of the United States becomes more diverse and as the United States becomes even more involved in the global market. They are in a unique position to help minority children reconcile what they are being taught in school with the realities of their everyday lives.

For many disadvantaged children, school represents a shelter from the outside world. Some social scientists have come to believe that the key to making education work for these students is to turn the school into the hub of the community, a "home away from home," where children can find the warmth and adult contact they do not get at home. Psychiatrist James Comer, director of Yale's Child Study Center, is a leading proponent of this idea. His recommendations call for parents and teachers to get together and design their own school plans to create a sense of belongingness. In approximately fifty Comer-influenced schools across the country parent-teacher teams have devised such techniques as keeping students with the same teacher for two years, painting walls to look more like home, and paying parents to work as class aides. The tactics seem to be working: In New Haven, Connecticut, where Comer's ideas were first tried, the dropout rate fell 26 percentage points and the number of

Cooperative learning programs, such as this one for third-graders in Hoagland, Indiana, have been found to enhance students' self-esteem, improve race relations among students, and promote acceptance of disabled students.

students going on to higher education increased from 45 to 73 percent during the 1980s (Louv, 1990).

In short, educators do know a number of ways to help disadvantaged children take advantage of education. Whether schools will be given the resources to implement these programs is another matter.

Affirmative Action

Affirmative action is one of the methods educators have used to help disadvantaged children. As discussed in Chapter 9, affirmative action programs in education began in response to the civil rights movement of the 1960s. Just how much help disadvantaged students deserve is the issue now threatening this reform. Initially affirmative action took the form of establishing quotas for minority students' admission to colleges and universities. In its 1978 *Bakke* decision the Supreme Court rejected quotas but said universities could still treat race as a positive factor in admissions.

Since then, affirmative action has suffered a number of setbacks. In 1996, Californians (by a margin of 54 percent) approved Proposition 209, which prohibits the use of racial or gender preferences in hiring, contracting, and education. Implementation of Proposition 209 was delayed, temporarily, by court appeals. In 1997, the Supreme Court decided not to hear the case, in effect giving the law its approval. In Texas, a 1996 court ruling (*Hopwood v. Texas*) held that race would not be used as a factor in granting admission to schools. The University of Texas Law School once led the nation in education of minority lawyers. For decades, the school had admitted about 40 African American and 60 Latino students a year under an affirmative action policy, graduating a total of 650 black and 1,300 Latino lawyers. After a court order to abandon this policy, the first-year law class of 1997 included only 4 African Americans and 26 Latinos. In both California and Texas, minority enrollment in colleges and universities appears to be declining. About two dozen other states are considering similar repeals of affirmative action.

Given the possibility that affirmative action will be cut back across the country, many educators are questioning the use of standardized tests in college and graduate school admission (Bronner, 1997). Although a simple and inexpensive way of comparing

students who attended different schools having varying programs and standards, tests do not predict how well students will perform in school in the future or whether they will graduate. Nevertheless, lower scores do disqualify a proportion of minority (and other) applicants.

University officials who seek a diversified student body and believe that one of the goals of education is to provide opportunities to people who have been denied them in the past are looking for alternatives to affirmative action. Several hundred colleges have stopped requiring that applicants submit test scores. Bates College in Maine is one. In a retrospective study, Bates found that students who chose not to submit SAT scores with their applications for admission scored, on average, 160 points lower (out of a possible 1,600) on their SATs than did students who submitted their test scores. Yet there was no difference in the two groups' grades or graduation rates. The low scorers included not only minorities but also white students from blue-collar backgrounds, students who grew up speaking another language at home, more women than men, and students with special talents, for example, for music or athletics. Under the no-test admissions policy, minority enrollment at Bates doubled (Bronner, 1997).

Beyond School

Is school reform the solution to the problem of lower academic achievement? There are those who believe improved teachers, affirmative action programs, school choice, and other reforms ignore the main source of the problem: disengaged students. In his book, *Beyond the Classroom* (1997), Laurence Steinberg describes students' disengagement from school as both a cause and a symptom of other difficulties they are having in their lives. In addition to being a source of poor academic performance, a student's disengagement may also indicate depression, drug use, delinquency, and sexual precocity (see *Close Up*: Violence in the Schools). It is not that students of today are less intelligent than those in the past; they simply are less interested in education.

According to Steinberg, while it is important for schools to be made more engaging, it is equally necessary to try to find ways to make students more willing to be engaged. School reform has focused on only the former, but Steinberg believes it is time to focus on what it takes to make students see education as interesting and valuable.

Why have students become disengaged? One answer seems to be related to the idea, discussed earlier, of education as conferring status. In his research Steinberg found that students tend to see education as *only* a credential: while students believed in general that a degree would help them in life, they were less sure that *learning* itself was necessary to success. This may also reflect a difference between **ideal culture** and **real culture** (discussed in Chapter 3):

> Within a belief system in which all that counts is graduation—in which earning good grades is seen as equivalent to earning mediocre ones, or worse yet, in which learning something from schools is seen as unimportant—students choose the path of least resistance. And because schools hesitate to give students bad grades, hold them back, or fail to graduate them, students believe, with some accuracy, that there are no real consequences of doing poorly in school, as long as their performance is not poor enough to threaten graduation. Under these conditions, getting by, rather than striving to succeed, becomes the operating principle behind most students' behavior. (Steinberg, 1997, p. 75)

Parents, too, play a role in the undervaluing of education. They also can play a big part in raising their children's motivation to succeed in school rather than just get by, according to Steinberg. As discussed in Chapter 4, parents who are *authoritative*—who are accepting, firm, and supportive of their children—raise children who have more self-esteem and negotiate life more successfully than children of *permissive* parents (who set few limits on their children's behavior) or of *authoritarian* parents (who use force to discipline their children and are rarely nurturing and affectionate) (Baumrind, 1971, 1980). Steinberg found that the compassionate engagement with a child's life that is key to an authoritative parenting style also helped produce engaged students. Such parents not only paid attention to their children's learning (as opposed to the authoritarian approach of simply demanding certain grades) but were engaged with their children's schools as well.

Peers, too, play a role in helping one another remain engaged in learning. Steinberg found that the peer environment in which students operate may provide incentives or disincentives to succeed in school. This peer environment is one reason why minority students may do poorly in school even when their parents value education and try to create a home environment in which learning is important. But "it is important to understand that the pressure against academic excellence that is pervasive within African American and Latino peer groups is not unique" (Steinberg, 1997). Peers who tend to shun those who strive for academic success come in every race, ethnicity, and sex.

Reforming schools does not begin to address these issues, issues that are central to the values each student brings with him or her when coming to school. In this sense, how the child is socialized to think about education and learning is as important as the educational system itself.

Education in Global Perspective

Through education, a society socializes children in its own image. Schools reflect the ideals of a society. American schools emphasize individual achievement, academic studies, and equal education for all, but these goals are by no means universal (Boocock, 1980). Cross-cultural studies of education can illuminate the distinctive structure of schooling in the United States and, by implication, certain distinctive features of American society. In this section we will look at educational systems in western Europe, as well as in Japan and China, whose day care programs were considered in Chapter 4.

Education in China

The American educational system emphasizes individual ability and achievement. From the day children enter school, they are evaluated on the basis of personal performance. Grades, promotions, and degrees are awarded to the individual. The goal is to provide each individual with an equal education. In Communist societies, the emphasis is more on the group than on the individual, and the "better" students are given more educational opportunities than others are.

The curriculum in the People's Republic of China is a unified one imposed by a central governmental structure (Yao, 1992). Its primary focus is

CLOSE UP

Violence in the Schools

A security guard is jumped by students engaged in a food fight in the school cafeteria. A girl sprays a corrosive acid in a crowded hallway. A boy knifes a classmate he has been feuding with. These recent incidents, all in one urban school district, illustrate why teachers, administrators, students, parents, and policy makers are increasingly concerned about violence in the schools. One survey found that, after drugs, parents' main concerns about their children's education centered on violence (see Table 12-2). Parents are troubled by the perceived increased rate of violence in schools—both between students and by students toward teachers and administrators—as well as by the perception that, increasingly, students are bringing

deadly weapons, especially guns, to school.

Their concerns are justified. According to a report by the U.S. Department of Health and Human Services, 26 percent of high school students admitted carrying a weapon to school in 1991 (up from 20 percent in 1990) (Maguire, Pastore, and Flanagan, 1993). Of that group,

> **Violence in the schools is the result of deeply held values. . . .**

almost half carried handguns. More boys than girls carry weapons: 41 percent as compared with 11 percent. The weapons are not confined to high school students; younger and younger children are coming to school armed, including a

5-year-old boy who entered his kindergarten class with a fully loaded pistol (Prothrow-Stith, 1991). Gone are the days of the fistfight: "It's just guns now," says a young man in Detroit (Prothrow-Stith, 1991, p. 18). Complicating the problem of proliferating guns is that "good" kids are getting armed to protect themselves from the "bad" ones. It is becoming "normal" behavior to carry a weapon.

The presence of weapons, especially guns, in a school naturally arouses fear. A 1989 survey found that 22 percent of boys and 21 percent of girls feared an attack in school; 6 percent reported that they avoid certain places in school out of fear of being attacked (Maguire, Pastore, and Flanagan, 1993). The presence of metal detectors to screen for knives and guns and of uniformed guards patrolling the hallways contributes to the atmosphere of fear. Some schools even practice "duck-and-cover drills" to train children to protect themselves from neighborhood shootings (Henslin, 1994).

The ingredients for violence in schools are admittedly there, but just how extensive are actual

Table 12-2   *Top Parental Concerns about Education*

Issue	Percent Rating as Top Concern*
Drugs	78
Violence	68
Low academic standards	62
Quality of teachers	59
Poor curriculum	50

*Survey of 400 parents.

Source: The Gallup Organization, Princeton, N.J., 1993.

on moral education. In particular, the students are taught love for the Communist party and patriotism, but they also learn respect for elders, good manners, self-control, and discipline. Children are encouraged to place the needs of the state and the group ahead of individual preferences. This does not mean that such academic subjects as math, sci-

ence, and foreign languages are neglected: students spend long days at school, six days a week, 250 days a year, with several hours of homework each evening.

Chinese students spend six years in elementary school, three years in lower secondary school, and three years in upper secondary school, which is incidents? Sensationalized media reports lead one to believe that school violence has become commonplace, but in fact, the reality is less extreme. Crime in school tends to reflect conditions in the community: areas where there is poverty, unemployment, high crime and delinquency, drug dealing, and a tradition of violence tend to have schools that are most susceptible to violence (Scarpitti and Andersen, 1992). But most schools do not fall into that category, and most students and teachers do not need to live in fear for their lives. A *National Crime Victimization Survey* conducted in 1989 found that only 2 percent of all students reported being victims of violence in school. From 1980 to 1992 there were only slight fluctuations in the reports of violent victimization among high school seniors (Maguire, Pastore, and Flanagan, 1993).

One statistic is disturbing, however. The rate of violent victimization of 12- to 15-year-olds is greater at school than at any other location (Whitaker and Bastian, 1991). This means that even though the actual rate of violence is low, schools are still the place where young adoles-cents are most likely to encounter violence. For teenagers over 16, the risk of violence is greater outside school, and schools are actually the least likely place where they will be victimized by weapons.

While metal detectors and guards can help reduce the number of weapons brought into school buildings and the number of violent incidents, the problem will never be fully resolved until solutions are found to the more fundamental social problems embedded in homes and communities. A recent analysis of violent incidents among middle school– and high school–age students by Daniel Lockwood (1997) found that violence is usually unintended and is the result of a sequence of events that become more and more aggressive until they culminate in a violent act.

Retribution is usually the reason behind such incidents. The "opening move" is typically quite minor: a student feels he or she has been laughed at or otherwise disrespected, often for something as trivial as a mishap like dropping books or tripping. In the next move, that student seeks to retaliate to save face, and the cycle of escalating interactions begins.

In this sense violence in the schools and among school-age children is actually the result of deeply held values (including the notion that violence is an acceptable solution to problems) rather than an example of amorality as some have claimed (Lockwood, 1997).

Seen this way, one way to prevent violence is to work to change the values that lead the slights and careless comments, common among school-age children, to be interpreted as disrespect and to teach students that there are more acceptable ways to deal with the feelings they have about such interactions. Role playing can give students a repertoire of nonviolent ways to resolve conflicts and thus prevent opening moves from escalating into violent incidents. School-based violence prevention programs also need to set the standard that all types of offensive touching—from throwing something to grabbing, shoving, slapping, or hitting—are serious and wrongful behavior (Lockwood, 1997).

equivalent to senior high school in the United States. The educational system is highly centralized, particularly at the highest levels (Deng and Treiman, 1997). The vast majority of China's people were illiterate at the time of the Chinese Revolution (1949). Within forty years the majority of young people had basic reading and writing skills (though for many, education did not go far beyond this minimum). With the opening of China to the west in the late 1970s and its attempt to modernize industry and technology, the emphasis shifted at least in part toward providing better higher education, but only for the most educable students. A crucial examination at the end of the high school years determines whether a student can proceed to higher education and be guaranteed a good job on graduation. In 1989, of the high school seniors who took the exam, 28.1 percent entered colleges and universities, 8.3 percent got into junior colleges, and 2.5 percent went into technical schools. The majority—60.1 percent—failed the exam altogether (Yao, 1992, p. 233). Intellectual competence is the only criterion in this examination (Deng and Treiman, 1997). Because of the entrance examination, Chinese students work very hard, with little time for social or leisure activity.

Education in Western Europe

Americans believe in equal education for all. We see free elementary and high school education as a basic right of citizenship and believe that as many young people as possible should go on to college. Put another way, Americans believe in mass education.

In western Europe, higher education traditionally has been viewed as a privilege for the upper classes or for those of unusual intellectual ability (as in China). For example, until quite recently all British schoolchildren were required to take a rigorous examination at age 11. The small percentage of youngsters who earned high scores on these exams were admitted to *grammar schools,* which prepared students for university careers. The majority of students were sent to *secondary modern schools* that offered a combination of basic academic classes and vocational training, with the emphasis on the latter. The educational system in France was similar.

The educational system in Germany is even more selective. On the basis of performance in grades one through four, many German children are assigned to, or choose to attend, a *hauptschule,* which offers vocational training through ninth grade. After grade six, more children will go on to a *realschule,* which offers a higher level of technical training through tenth grade. Only one in four German children is permitted to attend a gymnasium, a rigorous program to prepare students for university work. A final exam, taken at the end of the thirteenth year of school, determines which students will go on to universities.

In Europe vocational training is highly respected, unlike in the United States. It provides a workable alternative for the students who will probably not

do well in college, and it supplies a pool of skilled, well-trained workers for business and industry. Most of the schools combine classroom academic instruction with paid apprenticeships. The problem with the vocational schooling system is that it can be inflexible. It sometimes forces children and their parents to make a choice too soon between academic and vocational schooling. Some children, too, are "late bloomers," who may find themselves shut out of the avenue to higher education just at the time they feel ready for it.

The American and European educational systems reflect two different systems of social mobility: *contest mobility* and *sponsored mobility* (R. H. Turner, 1968). Under contest mobility, illustrated by the system in the United States, everyone is eligible to compete for society's prizes and there is more than one strategy for winning. Status is seen as the result of individual talent and effort. Under sponsored mobility, illustrated by the British system, "elite recruits are chosen by the established elite or their agents, and elite status is given on the basis of some criteria of supposed merit and cannot be taken by any amount of effort or strategy. Upward mobility is like entry into a private club where each candidate must be 'sponsored' by one or more members" (R. H. Turner, 1968, p. 220).

Neither of these educational systems is a "pure type." Through ability grouping in elementary school and the assignment of high school students to different tracks (discussed above), schools in the United States practice a form of selection (the sponsorship model). Graduates of vocational schools in Britain and Germany sometimes end up in high-paying, prestigious jobs, especially in technical fields (the contest model). On the whole, however, occupational status in the United States usually reflects the number of years a person has remained in school, whereas occupational status in Britain and Germany usually reflects the type of school a person attended (Kerckhoff and Everett, 1986).

The system of sponsored mobility in Britain was reformed in the late 1960s. Today secondary education in Britain resembles that in America. But differences remain at the university level. About 40 percent of high school graduates in the United States enroll in college. In Britain, only about 12 percent of 18-year-olds are enrolled in universities. The proportions of students who attend universities in other European nations are equally small (see Figure 12-3). In general, European universities have higher standards of instruction but offer this opportunity to a smaller segment of the population.

Education in Japan

In some ways the educational system in Japan resembles that in Europe, and in other ways, that in China. The result is uniquely Japanese.

As in western Europe, Japanese education is structured like a pyramid, with broad-based elementary education, a narrower selection of academic high schools, and a very small number of elite universities at the top (Shields, 1989). Early achievement is critical. Japanese students take their first national examination at age 14. Scores on this test determine which young people will go to academic high schools and which will go to vocational schools. Students who do not make it past this first cutoff can give up any hope of advanced education or occupational success. A second make-or-break examination at the end of twelfth grade determines who will be admitted to elite universities or to any college at all. Education and business are closely allied in Japan (Rosenbaum and Kariya, 1989). Graduation from an elite university virtually guarantees employment by a top company, at least for males, and failure means low-level employment with little hope of advancement.

Education in Japan is a family undertaking, and the child's success a matter of family honor. Japanese mothers, most of whom are not employed, prepare their toddlers for school by teaching them how to draw, make paper toys, and recognize letters and numbers. As discussed in Chapter 4, by 4 years of age, 90 percent of Japanese children are enrolled in preschools in which their teachers issue few commands to individuals; rather, they rely on peer pressure.

Three features distinguish Japanese from American schooling (Stevenson, 1989). The first has to do with how the two societies view achievement. Americans think of each child as a unique individual and attribute success in school to a combination of innate or inherited ability and opportunity. They see scores on IQ and other ability tests as a measure of innate ability, a sign of "academic predestination" (Shields, 1989, p. 7). Children who perform better than the tests predict are considered "overachievers," and those who perform below their tested potential, "underachievers." In contrast, the Japanese believe that all children are born equal: "We are all one white silk sheet." If some children achieve more than others, it is because of effort and *garanbu,* or persistence. The Japanese do not recognize a ceiling on achievement. Students who perform poorly are urged to work harder; children at the top of their class receive the same message. When asked how far their kindergartners would go in school, half of Japanese mothers said it depended on how hard the child worked. Only 5 percent of American mothers gave this answer; rather, they stressed "natural

In Japan, childhood and adolescence are devoted to education. After a full day of regular school, students prepare for national exams at a juku, or "cram school."

ability" and such external factors as whether the family would have enough money for college (Stevenson, 1989).

Second, the Japanese tend to have higher standards for performance than Americans do (Stevenson, 1989). In general, Americans have very good opinions of themselves. American fifth-graders give themselves high ratings on mathematical ability, brightness, and school performance. They believe that their parents and teachers are happy with their schoolwork. When asked how well they will do in high school math, nearly two out of three say they expect to be above average or near the top of their class. Only one out of four Japanese students is so optimistic. American mothers are "very satisfied" when their children score in the seventieth percentile on tests of mathematics and reading; Japanese mothers are not satisfied until their children reach the eighty-fourth percentile. Stevenson thinks that our self-satisfaction works against achievement: If children are already doing well, why try harder?

Finally, Japanese students work much harder than American students do (Stevenson, 1989). The average American student attends school six or seven hours a day, five days a week, for 180 days, with three months off in the summer. The average Japanese student attends school eight hours a day five days a week plus a half day on Saturday, 240 days a year. For all their classes except physical education and laboratory work, students stay in their homerooms and their teachers come to them (Johnson and Johnson, 1996).

During the forty-day summer break, Japanese students have assignments to complete each day. During the school year, two out of three junior high school students spend one and a half hours each afternoon at a *juku*, or privately run "cram school," to prepare for the national examination. As the final examination approaches, the average high school student spends four to five hours a night studying (compared with an average of one-half to one hour in the United States). Life is not all work and no play for the Japanese, however. Some of the school day is given over to nonacademic activities, and there is a play break before each class. High school students take part in club activities such as swimming, calligraphy, softball, kendo, broadcasting, and volleyball after school every day. However, students may join only one club and remain in the same club throughout high school (Johnson and Johnson, 1996). Japanese

children even manage to watch as much television as American children.

Japanese schools teach many of the same subjects as American schools, but they introduce new concepts and skills about a year earlier. By fifth grade there is a substantial achievement gap between the two countries. By the time they finish high school, Japanese teenagers have completed the equivalent of three or four more years of school than American high school graduates have; about half know as much as the average American college graduate. By comparison, college in Japan is relatively easy. There are few tests, no term papers, and no one flunks out. Japanese freshmen call college "leisure land."

In short, childhood and adolescence in Japan are dedicated to education—or, more accurately, preparation for examinations. Japanese teenagers do not date, drive cars, work at part-time jobs, or even perform household chores. They study full-time. This hard work pays off in terms of higher achievement scores. But there are costs. The school system depends on standardization, uniformity, and conformity in every aspect of the child's life, at every age. Youngsters who are different in some way (such as *kikokushijo*, who have spent time abroad) are treated as "outsiders" by teachers and peers alike (Kobayashi, 1989).

Finally, Japan does not provide equal opportunity for all its citizens. Girls have the same curriculum and the same examinations as boys do in elementary and secondary school, but many fewer women attend universities. Their subordination to males begins early in their school experience: for example, before each class it is customary in Japanese schools to call a roll of the boys before that of the girls. One Japanese educator notes that "the practice of placing girls in a secondary position to boys within the roll call is repeated on a larger scale by the relative dearth of female role models within the secondary school system" (Kanamura, 1993, pp. 77–78). In high school less than 20 percent of the teachers are female, and only 2.4 percent of the principals are. The *Burakumin*, who have long been treated as outcasts in Japanese society, have had to fight for equal access to education (Hawkins, 1989). (Although racially and linguistically Japanese, the Burakumin are associated with "unclean" occupations, such as butchering and cremation, and are treated as a minority group.) Moreover, Japan has lagged behind other nations in efforts to integrate disabled children into mainstream education (Goldberg, 1989).

In summary, Japan has an impressive record in terms of academic achievement. But this record depends on sacrifices few Americans are prepared to make. The total dedication to education among Japanese youth runs counter to our concept of being "well rounded." The emphasis on uniformity stands in opposition to our reverence for individuality. The restricted access to higher education is contrary to our belief in giving everyone a chance. And the unequal treatment of whole categories of people violates our belief that education is (or should be) an avenue for social mobility.

Challenge for the Future

Sociological analysis of the history of education in the United States, the complex relationship between education, social class, race, and gender, and the structure of American education in comparison with other nations' educational systems suggests that achieving educational excellence will not be easy.

One problem with recent proposals is that they focus narrowly on school reform or incentives for teachers, neglecting the pervasive and powerful effects of family, community, social class, race, and sex on students. To say that certain groups of students are "deprived" oversimplifies the issue. Different aspirations and different skills must also be taken into account. Sociological research shows that schooling is not "neutral." Schools not only train young people for success but also select and socialize them for different, unequally rewarded social roles. Though occasionally a poor youngster does superbly in school and wins a scholarship to an elite college, education does not erase the effects of class background for most Americans. Studies show that students who recognize that the odds are stacked against them (despite the ideology of

SOCIOLOGY ON THE WEB

How Are We Doing?

The text gives the big picture of how schooling in America has been revolutionized over time in response to society's needs for an educated workforce. But what about shorter time periods? How have educational outcomes changed in the last twenty or thirty years? What changes have occurred in educational attainment, graduation and dropout rates, and educational levels of people of different ethnic groups? How are our schools doing? The following sites provide data that allow you to track the answers to these and other questions over time, both within the United States and internationally:

http://www.census.gov/
The Census Bureau provides data on educational trends, among many other topics. You can access historical tables, for instance, that track educational attainment, fields of training, and school enrollment over time. For example, using data from the past fifty years, you can chart dropout rates among people of both sexes and all racial groups or trace the percentage of adults who have completed high school or college, by sex and race. How can you use the text discussion to help explain the trends in the data? What additional information do you need to make sense of what you find?

http://www.nces.ed.gov/timss/
The Third International Math and Science Study (TIMSS), run by the National Center for Educational Statistics, compares the achievement of half a million students in forty-one nations at five different grade levels. The findings are fascinating and puzzling—and in the newspaper all the time. For example, why do U.S. fourth-graders underperform Japanese fourth-graders in math but not in science, while middle school students score higher in science than in math? Why do our twelfth-graders underperform students from all other countries included in the study? Findings such as these, presented at this site in great detail, have important implications for national education policy and funding.

equality) may resist the system and contribute to their own failure (Willis, 1977; Ogbu, 1974).

At the same time, sociological research shows how urgently America needs better-educated citizens and workers. Reforming education may not be the whole solution, but it is a crucial step. When there is widespread educational failure, not only individuals but the whole society suffers—especially in this age of high technology and international competition. Thus, the question for the next century is not whether equality or quality in education is more important but whether we can merge the goal of equality with the quest for quality.

Summary

1. **What caused the schooling revolution—the expansion of education—in the United States?** There are three main explanations of the "schooling revolution" in this country. The first is that mass education fills the need of complex industrial societies for skilled workers, moral and social consensus, and equal opportunities. The second is that our educational system was designed, and has been maintained, by capitalists to further their own goals. The third explains the schooling revolution in terms of *status competition*.

2. **Do schools provide a fair and open environment for achievement and social mobility or is inequality a part of education as a social institution? If inequality is a part of education, why should that be so?** Despite our ideal of equal opportunity in education, young people from upper-income families do better in school, on average, than poor children do. There are also inequalities between whites and nonwhites and between boys and girls. Why? Early studies suggested that the school environment has little impact on a student's achievement. However, more recent studies suggest that teaching strategies, commitment to learning, respect for students, and consistent discipline have a positive effect. Continuing racial and economic segregation and *tracking* may have a negative impact. Funding inequities also can contribute to inequalities between schools, shortchanging the students in the less affluent school districts.

3. **Why has the overall quality of education in the United States declined?** Our educational system seems to have reached a crisis point. Deteriorating learning environments, declining test scores, changes in curricula, teacher shortages, and rising illiteracy rates have all raised questions about how to achieve excellence in education. Would national standards interfere with local control? What are the costs and benefits of professionalizing teaching? How can we strive for educational excellence for all students, including the increasing number of disadvantaged pupils?

4. **How does the American system of education differ from the systems in other countries?** Cross-cultural comparisons help identify the unique features of our own system of education. Americans value individual rather than group achievement (as in Communist societies), they favor contest over sponsored mobility (as in western Europe), and they do not believe that children should be full-time scholars (as in Japan).

Key Terms

conflict perspective   449
education   444
functionalist perspective   445
ideal culture   473

magnet schools   468
real culture   473
school choice   468
schooling   444

self-fulfilling prophecies   461
status competition   452
tracking   459

Recommended Readings

Arnove, Robert, Altbach, Philip G., & Kelly, Gail P. (Eds.). (1992). *Emergent Issues in Education: Comparative Perspectives.* Albany: State University of New York Press.

Bowles, S., & Gintis, H. (1976). *Schooling in Capitalistic America.* New York: Basic Books.

Coleman, James S., & Hoffer, T. (1987). *Public and Private High Schools: The Impact of Communities.* New York: Basic Books.

Cookson, Peter W., Jr. (1994). *School Choice: The Struggle for the Soul of American Education.* New Haven, CT: Yale University Press.

Hurn, Christopher. (1978). *The Limits and Possibilities of Schooling.* Boston: Allyn and Bacon.

Jencks, Christopher, et al. (1972). *Inequality: A Reassessment of the Effect of Family and Schooling in America.* New York: Basic Books.

Kozol, Jonathan. (1991). *Savage Inequalities: Children in America's Schools.* New York: HarperCollins.

Louv, R. (1990). *Children's Future.* New York: Anchor Books.

Persell, Caroline Hodges. (1977). *Education and Inequality: The Roots and Results of Stratification in America's Schools.* New York: Free Press.

Chapter

Thirteen

Religion

In the 1960s many observers of American society were convinced that religion was defunct. In The Secular City (1966), for example, theologian Harvey Cox argued that religion had become irrelevant. Modern men and women had moved on to other things. At the rate things seemed to be going, churches would be little more than museums by the late twentieth century. The pundits of the day proclaimed "God is dead." Today, however, we have come full circle: a recent poll found that 71 percent of respondents "never doubt the existence of God," up from 60 percent ten years ago (Providence Journal-Bulletin, December 22, 1997, p. A11). The number of Americans attending religious services regularly is pretty much the same as it was fifty years ago (The New York Times, December 15, 1997, p. 55).

The obituaries written for religion three decades ago have been replaced by cover stories such as "The Meaning of Mary" (Newsweek, August 25, 1997) and "The Mystery of Prayer: Does God Play Favorites?" (Newsweek, March 31, 1997). Religious groups have become more active in politics and are credited with the Republican congressional victory in 1994. They are also influential closer to home—supporting candidates for local offices and school committees in addition to taking stands and influencing public opinion on a wide range of social issues including the legality of abortion, aid to parochial schools, the death penalty, and the nuclear arms race.

The baby boomers who came of age in the "God is dead" decade are finding religion on somewhat different terms than did Americans fifty or even thirty years ago. Skepticism is as active an element in modern religion as belief. Religion is more often seen as a social institution operating at the individual rather than the societal level (Miles, 1997). A sociologist who studied the spiritual beliefs of the baby boomers found that about one-third of them never stopped going to church or synagogue; around one-quarter of them have returned to religion; 28 percent can be classified as "believers," who are interested in religious questions but remain unaffiliated; and 9 percent are "seekers," trying out various faiths. Only 5 percent claim to be atheists or agnostics (Roof, 1993). The openness, experimentation, and concern with social issues that typified the baby boomers in the 1960s can be seen in their fluid religious styles today:

Religious and spiritual themes are surfacing in a rich variety of ways in Eastern religions, in

13

evangelical and fundamentalist teachings, in mysticism and New Age movements, in Goddess worship and other ancient religious rituals, in the mainline churches and synagogues, in Twelve-Step recovery groups, in concern about the environment, in holistic health, and in personal and social transformation. (Roof, 1993, pp. 4, 5)

Religion is still very much alive in the rest of the world as well. Locate the "hot spots" on the globe, where nations or groups are taking up arms against one another, and you will find that the source of conflict is frequently religion-based: Muslims against Jews in the Middle East, Muslims against Christians in Bosnia and Croatia, Hindus versus Muslims in India, and Catholics versus Protestants in Northern Ireland. Where so many are dying for their religious beliefs, religion can hardly be dead.

The aim of this chapter is to explain the persistence of religion as a social institution. This point is an important one. As individuals, sociologists may or may not be committed to a particular religious faith. As scientists, however, they are not qualified to comment on such things as the validity of different religions or the existence of God. Rather, they study the organization of religion, the way it affects members of a society, the relationship between systems of belief and social structure, and the manner in which that relationship changes over time.

Key Questions

1. *Why is some form of religion found in all human societies? What are the basic elements of religion as a social institution?*
2. *How have sociologists explained the link between religion and society?*
3. *What are the different types of religious organizations? What distinguishes them? What central dilemma do all religious organizations face?*
4. *How has the role of religion changed in modern society? How has religious life changed in America in the 1990s?*

Religion: An Overview

Religion is any set of institutionalized beliefs and practices that deal with the ultimate meaning of life.

Religions provide blueprints for social behavior based on a divine, supernatural, or transcendental order.

The question of why people hold religious beliefs has long intrigued social scientists. Anthropologist Bronislaw Malinowski (1931) saw religion as filling a gap between human aspirations and abilities. The power of humans to control events is limited. Accidents happen; unforeseen factors disrupt the best-laid plans; the most advanced technology cannot control the weather, predict or prevent earthquakes, or eliminate premature death. Religion provides an institutionalized means of adjusting oneself to life's uncertainties and risks. Sociologist Talcott Parsons (1952) saw religion as filling the gaps between social expectations and experiences. In all societies, some expectations are doomed to failure. Pain and deprivation are distributed haphazardly, violations of moral standards sometimes are rewarded, and upstanding behavior may end in personal loss and defeat. Religion explains suffering and evil as part of a divine or supernatural plan. Anthropologist Clifford Geertz (1965) sees religion as relieving the intense anxiety people feel when they are at the limits of their analytical capacities and moral insights. Humans need to feel that the world is comprehensible, that there is a reason for the events of their lives. Religion accounts for, and indeed celebrates, the puzzles, ambiguities, and paradoxes of life. In Max Weber's words, religion deals with "problems of meaning" and serves as a motivator, with different religions functioning much like switchmen, directing human behavior onto various tracks (Wuthnow, 1993).

The earliest evidence of religious behavior dates back over 50,000 years. In Europe and southwest Asia, Neanderthals buried their dead with tools and other supplies, suggesting that they had some notion of a "world beyond." We cannot know exactly what Neanderthal groups believed or how they enacted their beliefs in ritual. But we do know from historical records and ethnographic studies that all societies tend to have some form of religion. Specific beliefs and practices vary widely. Some groups attribute powers to ancestors; others, to supernatural forces. Some believe in one supreme deity; others, in many gods; still others, in the essential harmony of the universe. Some see their gods as benevolent; others see them as mischievous, hostile, or indifferent. Some seek affirmation of their faith

The earliest human societies had burial customs that showed respect for the dead. This, in turn, suggests a belief in an afterlife. This ancient jade burial suit was found in China.

Some religious rituals are aimed at inducing encounters with the supernatural. Leaders like this shaman in eastern Borneo are trained in the performance of such rituals.

in solitude and wilderness; others erect pyramids, cathedrals, or other monuments and maintain hierarchical priesthoods to intercede with the divine. But some form of religion has been found in all societies (D. Brown, 1991).

To devout Christians, who believe in God the creator, ruler of heaven and earth, the belief that ancestors are all-powerful or that nature is alive with spirits may bear little resemblance to what they call "religion." But even though their "truth," meanings, and practices may be very different, all religions draw on certain common features of human social life and have similar elements and implications.

The Elements of Religion

The religious framework is composed of four basic elements: beliefs, rituals, subjective experiences, and community (Glock, 1962; M. B. McGuire, 1981).

Beliefs

Religious beliefs affirm the existence of a divine or supernatural order, define its character and purposes, and explain the role humans play in that order. (A **belief** is a conviction that cannot be proved or disproved by ordinary means; see Chapter 3.) Religious beliefs organize an individual's perceptions of the world and serve as a guide for behavior. For example, animist religions hold that the world is inhabited by spirits with motives and emotions like our own. Although believers do not worship these spirits as gods, they do attempt to influence their behavior through magic. This animist belief in spirits explains the occurrence of illness or accidents and prescribes a course of action. Similarly, the Christian belief in original sin, Christ and his miracles, and eternal salvation or damnation shapes perceptions and establishes a code of conduct. Religious beliefs differ from other types of beliefs in that they are based on faith in powers and processes whose existence cannot be proved by simple observation (Wuthnow, 1993; Yinger, 1970).

Rituals

Religious **rituals** are formal, stylized enactments of religious beliefs—processions, chants, prayers, sacraments, and the like. Religious rituals differ from other activities in that believers attach a symbolic meaning to them. For example, lighting candles on a menorah to commemorate Hanukkah, the Festival of Lights, means something quite different to Jews from decorating the table with candles on an ordinary night. Religious symbols are concrete embodiments of values, ideals, judgments, longings, and beliefs.

Western religions tend to emphasize symbols and rituals in part because these religions emphasize abstract beliefs. Religion is a separate institution, and religious activities are clearly distinguished from other activities. In other societies, however, religion is woven into the fabric of everyday life. Like the weather, the desires of spirits or ancestors must always be taken into account. In these societies, the distinctions between religious and secular events, rituals and practical activities, belief and action, are blurred (Bourdieu, 1977; Leenhardt, 1981).

Subjective Experience

The subjective experiences of religion grow out of beliefs and rituals. Beliefs direct people to interpret certain inner states and group experiences as "religious." Rituals may be used to invoke or recall communion with the supernatural. Religious experiences range from the quiet sense of peace that comes from the belief that one's life is in the hands of a divine power to the intense mystical experiences that inspire terror and awe. Individuals may

feel transported from everyday reality or experience being outside their own bodies or in the presence of supernatural beings (what psychologists call "altered states of consciousness"). Some religious groups actively seek visions and mystical experiences; these groups feature specialists (shamans or "medicine men") who undergo intensive training for encounters with supernatural forces (see Harner, 1980). Other groups do not define such experiences as "religious"; some define them as sacrilege. Even though religious experiences may be intensely private and personal, they tend to fall into patterns. Like other experiences, they are shaped by norms.

Community

Belonging to a community of believers is a central part of religious experience (Wuthnow, 1993). Shared beliefs, rituals, and subjective experiences heighten group identification. In a tribe or other small-scale society, religion may be accepted as part of the natural order. There is only one religion, and traditional beliefs and practices are rarely if ever questioned. In more complex societies, religion tends to be compartmentalized and to have institutions of its own, such as churches. These institutions may help knit together specific communities of believers, both as local parishes within a national or international church and as followers of one religion rather than another. Despite the diversity of religions in most complex societies, community remains a vitally important element of religion. There may be private beliefs, but there are no private religions (Durkheim, 1912/1947).

Religion and Society: Three Views

Three nineteenth- and twentieth-century thinkers have provided contrasting views of the relationship between society and religion. Emile Durkheim emphasized the function of religion as a celebration of the social order. Karl Marx, on the other hand, saw religion as an instrument of oppression used by a ruling class to cover up economic exploitation of the masses. For Max Weber, in addition to being a motivator, religion was an agent of social change.

The Sacred, the Profane, and the Collective: Durkheim

Emile Durkheim was, among other things, a pioneer in the sociology of religion. Other nineteenth-century thinkers addressed the topic of religion from different perspectives. Some of Durkheim's contemporaries such as Sir James Frazer and Edward B. Tylor were interested in the historical origins of religion and speculated on its evolution from "primitive" beliefs. By implication, they viewed religion as a relic of earlier stages of human social evolution. Others such as Sigmund Freud and William James were concerned with the psychological origins and functions of religion and probed individual motives, purposes, and religious experiences. They saw religion as springing from a deep psychological need. In contrast, Durkheim

In many societies, such as the traditional aboriginal culture of Australia, totems of animals and plants serve as links to the supernatural. To Durkheim, worship of a totem amounts to worship of the society, because the totem represents the society.

was interested in the social sources of religion and in what the study of religion could reveal about the nature of social life. His analysis relied on the functionalist theoretical model (see Chapter 2).

Durkheim's reading of historical and ethnographic literature convinced him that all societies distinguish between the **sacred**—that which is holy, inspires awe, and must be treated with respect—and the **profane**—ordinary, everyday things that may be treated casually. If religion is universal, he reasoned, it must perform some vital function in human society. Rejecting the search for "first beginnings" and psychological motives as unscientific, Durkheim (1912/1947) sought the "ever-present causes" of religion, the social forces that maintain religion in all societies.

Durkheim began his search in descriptions of totemism among Australian aboriginal groups, which he believed represented the simplest form of human society and would therefore reveal the "elementary forms" of religious life. A **totem** is a sacred emblem that members of a group or clan treat with reverence and awe. The things chosen as totems (a lizard, a caterpillar, a fish, a tree) are not, in themselves, awe-inspiring. But members of a clan see the object as their link to the supernatural. They call themselves by its name, observe taboos in approaching it, and consider its appearance or behavior as specially significant. A totem is both a symbol of god and a symbol of the clan. Durkheim saw this association between the sacred and the clan as a clue to the function of religion. In worshiping the totem, members of the clan were worshiping society: "The god of the clan, the totemic principle, can be nothing less than the clan itself, personified and represented to the imagination under the visible form of the animal or vegetable which serves as totem" (Durkheim, 1912/1947, p. 206).

Durkheim reasoned this way: Many of the sentiments and experiences that people categorize as "religious" are responses to unseen but powerful social forces. For example, the religious belief that human beings are the product of divine creation reflects the social fact that we are creatures of our culture and time. The religious sensation of eternity reflects the social fact that society existed before we were born and will continue after we die. "We speak a language that we did not make; we use instruments that we did not invent; we invoke rights that we did not found; a treasury of knowledge is transmitted to each generation that it did not gather itself, etc." (Durkheim, 1912/1947, p. 212). Is it any wonder, Durkheim asked, that we feel as if our lives are designed and controlled by outside forces? that we treat these forces with awe, as if our lives depended on them? They do.

Durkheim extended this line of reasoning to other aspects of intellectual life as well. We do not learn about time and space, good and evil, through personal experience. Time and space are not empirical facts but social concepts. (Recall the different conceptions of time in Vietnamese and American cultures, discussed in Chapter 3.) In prescientific societies (and, to some extent, in all societies), religious rituals and beliefs teach these basic concepts, creating and re-creating both the faith and the intellectual categories necessary for individual and collective action. Thus religion arises from our experience of social forces and gives this experience concrete form and expression.

Durkheim held that religions create and maintain "moral communities," or collectives. Religious beliefs reinforce group norms and values by adding a sacred dimension to everyday social pressure. Religious rituals bolster social solidarity by bringing people together to reaffirm their common bonds and recall their social heritage. Participation in rituals heightens the feeling of being part of something larger than oneself. This, in turn, helps individuals adjust to loss and pain. Durkheim believed that if science were to undermine belief in the sacred, some functional equivalent would arise to replace traditional religion. In offering new explanations of nature and causality, science inevitably weakens religion's hold on us. But, in Durkheim's view, science can never replace religion altogether: "Faith is before all else an impetus to action, while science, no matter how far it may be pushed, always remains at a distance from this. Science is fragmentary and incomplete; it advances but slowly and is never finished; but life cannot wait" (1912/1947, p. 479). Science can provide us with facts, but it cannot establish morality; science can tell us what is possible and likely, but it cannot tell us what we should do. Durkheim believed that modern societies would require either a renewal of religion in revised forms that accommodated modern science or a new type of sociopolitical faith (what students of religion today call "secular humanism"). It is this kind of sociopolitical faith that led to the belief that "God is dead" in the 1960s. However, as we have seen, as the 1990s come to a close with a renewed interest in religions of all kinds, it appears Durkheim was quite accurate in his description of the role of religion versus science in society.

Religion as Opium: Marx

Writing a half-century before Durkheim, Karl Marx also portrayed religion as a reflection of society (not as an expression of "primitive" or psychological needs). Whereas Durkheim emphasized the positive functions of religion, Marx used a conflict perspective (see Chapter 2). Durkheim saw religion as benefiting all segments of society by promoting social commitment; Marx held that in stratified or class societies, religion serves the interests of the ruling elite at the expense of the masses. "Religion," he wrote, "is the sigh of the oppressed creature, the sentiment of a heartless world, and the soul of soulless conditions. It is the opium of the people" (K. Marx, 1844/1963, p. 27). Just as a painkiller masks the symptoms of disease, lulling the sick person into the illusory belief that he or she is well, so religion masks the exploitation of workers, lulling them into the false belief that existing social arrangements are just or, if not just, inescapable. Thus a religion may teach that the individual's position on earth is preordained or that suffering on earth will be rewarded in heaven, obscuring the class structure and the elite's vested interest in the status quo.

Marx saw religion in capitalist societies as the epitome of alienation: the self-estrangement people experience when they feel they have lost control over social institutions. Marx used the term "alienation" to describe the modern worker's experience of being nothing more than a "cog in a machine." He also used it to describe what he saw as the dehumanizing effect of religion. "The more the worker expends himself in work the more powerful becomes the world of objects which he creates in the face of himself, the poorer he becomes in his inner life, the less he belongs to himself. It is just the same as in religion. The more of himself man attributes to God the less he has left in himself" (K. Marx, 1844/1963, p. 122).

Marx's view of religion was based on his belief that man created God in his own image. In the earliest, primitive societies, people attributed human-like powers and feelings to trees, rivers, and other natural objects. They assumed the existence of many individual spirits, some good, some bad. As societies progressed from small, scattered tribes to large nation-states with centralized governments, religion progressed toward monotheism and the idea of one "supergod." This god embodied the power of the state and the potential power of human collective action. The next step, according to Marx, was to recognize that there was no god, only nature and humanity. This, in turn, would inspire human beings to focus on developing their own capacities.

Although Marx held that religion had been associated with progress in the distant past, his indictment of religion in modern, capitalist society was total. He argued that only when people give up the illusory happiness of religion will they begin to demand real happiness. "The criticism of religion," Marx continued, "disillusions man so that he will think, act and fashion his reality as a man who has . . . regained his reason" (1844/1963, p. 44). In a classless society religion would become irrelevant and unnecessary.

Marx might well have predicted the "God is dead" movement of the 1960s. In fact, this philosophy was related to the rise in popularity of Marxist theory on college campuses at that time. It was a time of questioning social values and struggling against the injustices of poverty, racism, and sexism. Activists rejected most social institutions, including religion, as embodiments of the status quo as well as the source of alienation, inequality, injustice, and unhappiness. Marxism may not have been openly avowed by the "God is dead" generation, but it exerted a strong influence. Perhaps it is no coincidence that as the influence of Marxist communism has waned in the last decade, the influence of religion has been on the rise.

Religion as an Agent of Social Change: Weber

Max Weber's interest in religion was inspired to some degree by Marx. Like Marx, Weber devoted much of his intellectual life to investigating the history of capitalism. He credited Marx with highlighting the role of economic arrangements in history. But whereas Marx believed that all history can be explained as class struggle, Weber viewed economics as only one of many influences on the course of history. Whereas Marx held that religion is an obstacle to social change, Weber argued that religion may also be an agent of social change. Weber's *The Protestant Ethic and the Spirit of Capitalism* (1904/1958) has been described as a "dialogue with the ghost of Karl Marx" (Coser, 1977, p. 228).

Weber began this work by observing that in countries with both Protestant and Catholic populations, the business leaders, the bankers, even the highly skilled workers were "overwhelmingly Protestant." Why should this be? Weber asked.

As the influence of Marxism has waned in the former Soviet Union, the influence of religion has been on the rise. This woman lights candles in an Orthodox church in the Republic of Georgia.

What is there about Protestant beliefs and practices that fosters economic enterprise? Weber found an answer in the Calvinist phase of the Protestant Reformation. His explanation focused on two elements of Protestant belief: the redemptive value of work and worldly asceticism.

The doctrine of predestination was central to Calvinist thinking. The Catholic Church taught that the route to salvation led through the church, that one earned a place in heaven through participation in the sacraments (mass, confession, penance, and so on). The Calvinist belief that God decided before a person was born whether that individual would be "elected to the saints" or damned to hell and that nothing, not even the good works a person might do on earth, could alter that determination freed individuals from the bonds of the church. But this belief also created intense anxiety. How could a person know whether he or she was one of God's elect? Some Calvinists resolved this psychological dilemma by regarding worldly achievement as a sign of God's favor. Good works might not earn one salvation (as Catholics believed), but they did ease the fear of damnation. As the Bible states, "Seest thou a man diligent in his business? He shall stand before kings" (Proverbs 22:29).

The Calvinist belief in the redemptive value of work was combined with what Weber called "worldly asceticism." Calvinists condemned self-indulgence, the pursuit of luxury, and the pleasures of the flesh. But they also rejected the belief that one could earn salvation by giving away one's possessions and living in poverty (something they associated with Catholic monks). What, then, were successful entrepreneurs to do with their wealth? Calvinism's answer: Put those profits to work. Calvin "did not wish to impose mortification on the man of wealth, but the use of his means for necessary and practical things" (Weber, 1904/1958, p. 171). And so the Protestant ethic, with its peculiar combination of hard work and self-denial, was born. For centuries, the Catholic Church had condemned the pursuit of profits, especially through money lending and trade. Calvinism elevated saving, investing, rational calculation, and profit making to a moral duty. Indirectly, then, Calvinism gave capitalism moral sanction and created a pool of dedicated entrepreneurs.

Weber did not maintain that these beliefs alone could explain why capitalism emerged in Protestant Europe rather than, say, in China or India. He saw Protestant beliefs as one of many factors that contributed to the rise of capitalism. Although he disagreed with Marx's economic determinism, Weber did not set out to disprove the role of economics in history: "It is not . . . my aim to substitute for one-sided materialistic an equally one-sided spiritualistic causal interpretation of culture and history" (1904/1958, p. 183). Rather, his aim was to show that history could not be reduced to one-factor explanations and that religion could be an agent of social change.

In the conclusion to his book, Weber described the spirit of capitalism and the near-worship of rational instrumentalism in modern times as an "iron cage" in which "the technical and economic conditions of machine production . . . determine the lives of all individuals." He continued, "In the field of [capitalism's] highest development, in the United States, the pursuit of wealth, stripped of its religious and ethical meaning, tends to become associated with purely mundane passions, which often actually give it the character of sport." The religious spirit that had inspired the growth of capitalism has fled the cage, leaving behind "specialists without spirit, sensualists without heart." For Weber, a society in which human activities and relationships are governed by rational calculation and "economic compulsions" was devoid of meaning (1904/1958, pp. 181–183).

The Nature of Religious Organizations

Religions are not only sets of beliefs and practices but also social organizations (Troeltsch, 1931; Niebuhr, 1929; B. Johnson, 1963; Swatos, 1975). Sociologists recognize four distinct types of religious organization: the established church, the sect, the denomination, and the cult. (In this context, "church" does not refer specifically to a Christian organization but refers to any established religion.) The differences among them lie in their relationship to the social environment (McGuire, 1992). This relationship is determined, first, by whether a religion accepts or rejects the dominant social order and, second, by whether it considers itself uniquely legitimate ("the one true faith") or accepts religious pluralism.

Types of Religious Organizations

Established Church

The term "church" may be used in a generic sense, to refer to all varieties of religious organization. We use the term **established church** to refer to a religious organization that claims unique legitimacy and has a positive relationship to society. Declaring itself "the one true faith," it does not recognize other religions or tolerate dissent within its ranks. Nonbelievers are subject to conversion and/or persecution. An established church is the official religion of its society. It endorses existing political and economic institutions and is, in turn, endorsed by the state. In its pure form, such a church is a "life-encompassing" organization (Swatos, 1975). All members of a society belong to the church, and all facets of life are subject to direct or indirect religious control.

The Catholic Church in medieval Europe and the Anglican Church in Elizabethan England are familiar examples. Explaining the mutually reinforcing relationship between church and state in the latter period, one Anglican declared:

> We hold, that seeing there is not any man of the Church of England but the same man is also a member of the commonwealth; nor any man a member of the commonwealth which is not also of the Church of England. (Hooker in Swatos, 1975, p. 180)

In Japan, the Shinto religion dates from before the fifth century. Its emphasis on the worship of natural phenomena and its belief in *kami,* kindly supernatural beings who looked out for people, led to its being made the national religion, reaching its peak in the years just before World War II. State Shintoism emphasized nationalism, obedience, and loyalty to the emperor. Though it is no longer the official religion of Japan, Shinto shrines can still be found at the headquarters of such corporations as Hitachi and Toyota. The United States is one of the few countries that has never had an established church embracing the entire nation.

Sect

A **sect** is a religious organization that asserts its unique legitimacy but stands apart from society. Like an established church, a sect claims to have a monopoly over the route to salvation. But whereas an established church enters into society in order to influence it, a sect views society as "too sinful to influence except from without" (Bellah et al., 1985, p. 243). A sect dissociates itself from existing political and economic institutions. Its members may withdraw from "worldly" affairs, creating a separate community, or they may engage in open attacks on the system. Put another way, a sect is a protest movement. Often sects are groups that have broken away from an established church, which they view as corrupted, to re-create the "pure" religious community they believe existed in the past. Examples include the Puritans in sixteenth-century England; the Quakers and Mormons in some communities in eighteenth- and nineteenth-century America; the Amish, Jehovah's Witnesses, and Jewish Hasidim in the United States today.

Denomination

A **denomination** is a religious organization that has a positive relationship to society and accepts the legitimacy of other religions (Niebuhr, 1929). Like an established church, it is at ease with the norms, values, and practices of society. But unlike either an established church or a sect, it does not claim to have "the answer." Not claiming unique legitimacy, denominations view religious participation as a voluntary activity. They are most often found in societies where religion is compartmentalized, that is, where all aspects of life are not thought to have religious significance and where other institutions (such as politics and education) are seen as independent and legitimate in their own right. Most of the major religious groups in the United States today—Methodists, Lutherans, Episcopalians, Baptists, and Reform and Conservative Jews—can be seen as denominations.

The term "the public church" has been used to describe the major Christian denominations in the United States today (Marty, 1981). Although each retains the integrity of its distinctive beliefs and practices, many often join together on issues and programs of common interest. They also seek contacts with Jewish and other non-Christian religious groups and with secular organizations. Some see this as evidence that separate denominations are a thing of the past, but for the most part, Americans are members of a particular religious denomination (Wuthnow, 1993).

Cult

In March 1997, thirty-nine members of Heaven's Gate, a religious cult, inspired by the proximity of the Hale-Bopp comet, killed themselves, shedding their "containers" in a bid to ride the comet to their true home in the heavens (Miller, 1997). A *cult* is a religious organization that accepts the legitimacy of other religions but has a negative relationship to society. Like a sect, a cult holds that there is "something wrong" with the way most people in society live. But whereas sects are often "at war" with society, cults tend to focus on the individual. They are often more concerned with getting the individual in tune with the supernatural, and with individual peace of mind, than with social change. Because the emphasis is on the individual, they tend to be more tolerant of other religions. Cults frequently form around charismatic leaders (people who are believed to have unique insights or powers) and dissolve when the leader dies. They are more transient than other religious organizations. They are also more loosely organized. Most cults are not as extreme as Heaven's Gate, but because of the attention the actions of such groups receive in the media, the public tends to think of cults as extremist groups.

Cults tend to remain small and informal. Members may even be allowed to retain other religious affiliations. In some cases followers are better described as clients or as an audience than as members of a congregation (Stark and Bainbridge, 1980). Their participation may consist only of reading books or magazines. Contemporary examples include American Zen, transcendental meditation, scientology, and snake-handling groups. Twelve-step programs are another example (Wuthnow, 1993).

Some cults, however, like Heaven's Gate, are far from casual. Their members take the ties that bind them to the extreme, even to the extent of dying for their leader. The Branch Davidians, followers of a charismatic leader named David Koresh, who saw himself as a warrior angel destined to cleanse the earth (see Chapter 17), were another such cult. Koresh attracted devotees from all over the world to his compound outside of Waco, Texas, mesmerizing his followers with his superhuman command of the scriptures and his apocalyptic visions of the imminent end of the world (Thomas et al., 1997). To prepare for "Armageddon," Koresh stocked the compound with firearms and ammunition. This strategy attracted the attention of federal agents, who staged an unsuccessful raid on the compound in March 1993. Following a standoff of several weeks, the federal agents moved in with tanks to break open the compound. Before they could enter, a raging fire consumed the building. Eighty-five Branch Davidians, including seventeen children under 14 years of age, perished in the flames. It is not known whether they were held against their will or elected to die. But in a similar cult in South America in 1978, it is known that more than 900 members drank poisoned Kool-Aid at the behest of their leader, Jim Jones.

Not all cults are self-destructive. In fact, many religious experts agree that the negative connotations of the word "cult" stigmatize the many minority religious communities that are quite benign (Richardson, 1990). According to James Richardson (1990), 99 percent of minority religious groups are benign and peaceful and just want to be left alone. These experts recommend replacing the word "cult" with such terms as "new" or "minority" or "exotic" religion.

Where a religion fits in this typology depends on its relationship to the social environment. The same religion may be an established church in one society, a sect or cult in another. For example, Roman Catholicism can be seen as an established church in modern Italy (though the Italian state has become increasingly secular). In the United States, Catholicism is more like a denomination. In many Latin American nations, Catholicism plays a double role: it is an established church that claims a majority of the population as members and plays a dominant role in social life; but where elites have seemed to betray religious values, and priests and nuns have played an active part in revolutionary movements, Catholicism is more like a sect.

Religions are not static; neither is the larger social environment. The relationship between a religion and the social environment can, and often does, change. In sixteenth-century England, for example, the Puritans were a sect. They saw "the Bible [as] a complete guide to Christian living, a digest of all the statutes and regulations necessary for human government" (K. T. Erikson, 1966, p. 47). But they regarded the Church of England, with its hierarchy of bishops and elaborate rituals, as an obstacle that

Catholicism serves as a sect in parts of Latin America, where priests and nuns often play an active part in liberation movements. Here, priests and worshipers honor the memory of six murdered Jesuits in Chalatenango, El Salvador.

society had erected between people and God—as a corruption of "the Word." They therefore set out to found a holy commonwealth, in which political, economic, and all other institutions were to be based on the Bible. In Massachusetts Bay, the Puritans were no longer a sect but an established church. Church elders were given authority over all aspects of social life; dissenters were banished.

A similar transformation occurred in the recent history of Iran (see Chapter 17). Prior to the 1979 revolution, the Shiite Muslims were a sect—a group of dissenters who on religious grounds opposed the rule of the Shah and his efforts to modernize Iran. Today the Shiite branch of Islam in Iran is an established church in the sociological sense; it is a religion that is aligned with political and economic institutions and claims to be the one true faith. Such changes in structure may change the content and practice of religion. (See *A Global View:* Islam: East and West.)

The Dilemmas of Institutionalization

To a greater or lesser degree, all religious groups face a central problem. If a religion is to have any impact on society, it must create a structure for realizing its goals and values. A "mood" is not enough. The religion must be institutionalized. Yet the process of institutionalization may subtly change the goals and values of a religion and separate members of the group from the original shared experience of belief and faith. As a result, religious organizations are often confronted with one or more of five dilemmas (O'Dea, 1966):

1. The first is mixed motivations. Most religions are founded by a charismatic leader (Jesus, Muhammad, Buddha) and a group of followers who are single-minded in their devotion to the leader and/or his or her cause. In the process of institutionalization, however, a religion must appeal to a wide range of motivations (the desire for

Islam: East and West

The Muslim religion, also known as Islam, originated some fourteen centuries ago in the Middle East when the prophet Muhammad claimed to have received a series of visions that revealed the will of God. Islam means "submission," and a Muslim is "one who submits" to God's will. The revelations that came to Muhammad are recorded in the Koran, the sacred Muslim text, which Muslims believe is a correct version of the divine message that God had attempted to convey to a long line of prophets from Abraham to Jesus. As a result of an ancient split, there are two major subgroups of Islam today: the Sunnis and the Shiites (found mainly in Iran and Iraq). Muslims now constitute the second-largest religious group in the world, with close to 1 billion adherents.

For a Muslim, to submit to God's will means to follow the Islamic law specified by the Koran and by traditions that have grown up around Muhammad's life and words. The Five Pillars of Islam require that an adherent (1) profess faith in one God and his messenger, (2) pray five times a day, (3) give alms to those in need and support the Muslim community, (4) fast one month a year, and (5) make a pilgrimage to Mecca. Muslims are expected to dress modestly, to maintain separate roles for males and females, and to observe certain dietary restrictions (alcohol and pork are prohib-

> **By persisting in the view that all Muslims are fanatics, Americans may . . . push moderate Muslims into alliances with terrorists.**

ited). In keeping with Muhammad's role as both political and spiritual leader, Muslims have traditionally made no distinction between their religious and secular way of life. The Islamic ideal is to create a Muslim community with no boundaries and no national divisions.

The earliest Muslims to come to the United States were probably slaves in the seventeenth and eighteenth centuries. In the nineteenth century a few

Map 13-1   *Iran, Iraq, and Surrounding Middle Eastern Countries*

Sources: Barry A. Kosmin and Seymour P. Lachman, *One Nation under God,* New York: Harmony Books, 1993; Bruce B. Lawrence, *Defenders of God: The Fundamentalist Revolt against the Modern Age,* San Francisco: Harper & Row, 1989; ibid., "Muslims between Nationalism and Religion: Rethinking Islam as an Ideology of Violence," in Bruce Kapferer (ed.), *Anthropology of Nationalism,* New Brunswick, NJ: Rutgers University Press. In press.

Malcolm X was one of many thousands of young African Americans who turned to Islam in the 1960s in order to establish contact with their preslavery culture and to impose meaning and order on their lives by adhering to Islamic law.

Lebanese immigrants found their way to the midwest where they established a small Muslim community. Then, in the 1960s, two events caused an explosion in the number of Muslims in the United States: thousands of African Americans converted to Islam as a means of finding their preslavery roots, and new immigration laws relaxed restrictions on a number of countries with large Muslim populations. Today American Muslims number in the range of 3 to 4 million; it is thought that about two-thirds of them are immigrants and one-third are con-verts (Kosmin and Lachman, 1993). American Muslims have established their own schools, social clubs, magazines, book-stores, and marriage services, as well as more than 1,000 mosques across the country.

The majority of Muslims in the United States are like any other immigrant group: they want to assimilate into Ameri-can life and yet maintain their religious identity. Many of their values coincide with those of other conservative religious groups: antiabortion, an-tipornography, close family ties, no sex outside of marriage. Like funda-mentalist Christians, fundamentalist Muslims believe in the literal interpretation of their sacred text.

Unfortunately, many Ameri-cans equate fundamentalism in Islam with fanaticism. They have little understanding of ei-ther the background or the be-liefs of the Islamic religion. Their exposure via the media to violent events in Iran, Iraq, Lebanon, India, Egypt, and other Muslim countries has led them to link Islam in general with violence, terrorism, sexism, and intolerance. It is true that a small minority of devout Mus-lims seem bent on establishing the dominance of Islam by whatever means possible, but the vast majority of Muslims, es-pecially in this country, do not advocate violence or terrorist tactics. They do, however, share many traditions and rituals—indeed, an entire way of life—with their more extreme coreli-gionists. Some observers fear that by persisting in the view that all Muslims are fanatics, Americans may eventually push the moderate Muslims into al-liances with the terrorists. Pow-erful splits now occurring within the Muslim movement in the Middle East could well be put aside in order to present a united front to the "decadent" west.

prestige, respectability, power, economic advantage, and so on). To survive, it must "mobilize the self-interested as well as the disinterested" (McGuire, 1992). But this appeal to mixed motivations may corrupt or compromise its original values.

2. The second dilemma relates to the religion's symbol system (its prayers, ceremonies, and insignia). Symbols are a necessary part of institutionalization. They transform subjective religious experiences into concrete images, enabling believers to express and reaffirm their common faith. Yet continual, routine use of religious ceremonies and symbols tends to rob them of their emotional impact.

3. The third dilemma involves organization. Charismatic leadership is precarious. To secure permanence, a religion must develop an administrative structure (a division of labor, standardized procedures, and so on). But in creating a permanent (usually bureaucratic) structure, a religious group may create a class of individuals who have more interest in maintaining their own positions in the organization than in preserving religious ideals. Moreover, impersonal, bureaucratic structure may alienate the rank and file.

4. The fourth dilemma relates to the letter versus the spirit of religious law. If a religion is to affect people's lives, its message must be translated into concrete rules that apply to everyday activities and concerns. But ethical insights may lose something in the translation. In following the letter of religious law, members may forget the spirit of the law.

5. The fifth dilemma involves conversion versus coercion. Ideally, membership in a religious group is based on voluntary commitment and internal conviction, what we call "an act of faith." In the early stages, a religion may depend entirely on conversion to attract members. But in the process of institutionalization, it must develop strategies for combating doubt. These strategies may range from subtle social pressure to the threat or use of torture (as in the Spanish Inquisition). In combating doubt, a religion may lose its spontaneous and voluntary character. Members who conform because of external pressures, not out of personal conviction, are not "believers" in the true sense.

Institutionalization is necessary if a religion is to pursue its original goals (influencing society and affecting individuals' lives), yet it may transform those goals, alienate believers, and sow the first seeds of disbelief. All religions face this dilemma of institutionalization (O'Dea, 1966).

Religion in Contemporary Societies

Nearly all social scientists would agree that the role religion plays in society has changed. In traditional societies, religion was seen as an authority in all areas of social life; few activities remained unaffected. Farmers prayed or made offerings to their gods or ancestors before planting crops. Priests or shamans were responsible for curing. Conflicts within and between families or villages were acted out in religious rituals; disputes were settled through religious trials. Formal education was in the hands of the clergy. The chief or king ruled by divine right.

In modern industrial societies, religion is one of many specialized institutions. Farmers go to agricultural experts and the weather bureau for advice on crops; the sick put their lives in the hands of physicians; conflicts are settled in courts run by legal experts; and so on. As a result, religion has been stripped of many of its former functions and must compete with other institutions for authority. To the extent that individuals accept religious teachings and incorporate them into their business, politics, education, or family life, religion has an indirect influence on these spheres. But religious institutions in most industrialized nations have no direct authority or control. Today a religious organization may declare that one should give generously to the poor or that using birth control is a sin, but individuals or society as a whole may choose not to take these declarations seriously. In medieval Europe or Puritan New England, however, religion was considered a complete guide for living.

The Trend toward Secularization

The term *secularization* refers to the removal of religious control over social life. Secularization occurs on two levels. On the institutional level, the church loses control over such things as marriage, schooling, and law enforcement. (Religious trials are replaced by trials by the state, civil marriages are considered acceptable, and so on.) This loss of control greatly reduces the power of the church and of church officials. On the individual level, religion loses its control over personal decisions as religious interpretations of reality are replaced by more scientific, rational expectations of human behavior and other events.

Marriage decisions over the last century reveal the increasing secularization of society. Religious homogamy, marrying within one's religion, used to be considered very important. But as we saw in Chapter 11, fewer individuals today are marrying someone from the same religious group; instead, more and more individuals are marrying a person with the same level of educational attainment (Kalmijn, 1991). In other words, the social boundaries between educational levels have strengthened at the same time that the boundaries between religious groups have been breached in marriages.

Most social scientists agree that there is a clear trend toward secularization in modern societies. But they do not agree on what this trend means. Some see it as evidence that the importance of religion is declining. Others see it as evidence of a transformation but not necessarily a decline. Indeed, some observers cite the revival of fundamentalist beliefs and attempts to turn religious values into law as evidence that the trend toward secularization has been halted or even reversed.

Change as Decline

Weber was one of many social scientists who view changes in the relationship between religion and society as evidence of decline. Weber (1904/1958) saw secularization as part of an overall trend toward rationalization in modern societies. By "rationalization," Weber meant the adoption of norms and values that emphasize effectiveness, efficiency, and cost-benefit equations. In a rational economy, business decisions are based on a rational calculation of profit and loss. Traditions and social obligations have no place in a rational economy. Such nonutilitarian values as generosity and compassion are considered irrelevant. In a rational society, the emphasis on effectiveness, efficiency, and cost-benefit analysis extends also to politics, education, and other spheres, including personal relationships. Working, learning, and even the institution of marriage are seen as means to an end, not as intrinsically valuable in themselves. The result of rationalization is, in Weber's words, "disenchantment." Things people once regarded with reverence and awe are stripped of their religious meaning and rendered mundane.

Other social scientists have pointed to a decline in belief in supernatural or divine forces, a preoccupation with "this world," the replacement of religious explanations of life with philosophies that emphasize human responsibility for social arrangements, and the confinement of religion to the private sphere (summarized in Shiner, 1967). In *Religion and Society in Tension* (1965), Charles Glock and Rodney Stark argued that religions themselves had become secularized and offer members "demythologized, ethical rather than theological religion." Harvey Cox summarizes the view that religion is fading: "For some, religion provides a hobby, for others a mark of national or ethnic identification, for still others an esthetic delight. For fewer and fewer does it provide an inclusive and commanding system of personal and cosmic values and explanations" (1966, p. 3).

Change as Transformation

What some sociologists see as decline others see as transformation and evidence of the durability of religion (Parsons, 1963; Bellah, 1964; Luckmann, 1967; Wuthnow, 1988, 1993). Robert Bellah has been one of the most forceful proponents of the transformation view.

Bellah (1964) sees current changes in belief and practice as the result of a process of religious evolution. He maintains that religions evolve from simple to more complex forms and that in the process they become more independent of their social environments and more adaptable.

Primitive religion, according to Bellah, consists of a fluid mythology that unites humans and animals, past, present, and future in a meaningful whole. In this stage religion does not have a separate social structure, and the religious role is fused with other roles.

In *archaic religion,* mythical figures become gods with distinct characterizations and power over human and natural events. Ritualistic systems for communicating with the gods (worship and sacrifice) are created. But religious structures are still merged with other social structures, and the individual and society are seen as merged with a natural-cosmic order.

The defining characteristic of *historic religion* (the "major" religions: Judaism, Christianity, Buddhism, Hinduism, Islam) is the emergence of dualism. All

C L O S E   U P

Women and the Church

What happens when long-cherished religious beliefs and practices clash with a sweeping social movement? Bitter controversy, agitation, dissatisfaction, protest, confusion, and disaffection, to name just a few reactions. This has been the state of affairs in major Christian denominations for at least half of this century as women press for ordination as priests and ministers. Some feminist activists feel caught up in a reformation second only to the great Protestant Reformation of the sixteenth century.

The basis for the controversy is the patriarchal theology, which holds that only men can represent Christ Jesus at the altar and that Jesus set a precedent for a male priesthood by selecting only men to be his apostles. Those who hold this view believe that God intended different roles for men and women in his service.

> The beginning of a new age in the church for all Catholics who care about justice—a Catholic nun

They cite verses from Paul's writings to lend biblical authority to their position: "I permit no woman to teach or have authority over men" (I Timothy 2:12); "The women should

The presence of women ministers and rabbis is one indication of the increased liberalization of several major religions and denominations.

such religions draw a sharp distinction between this world and another, more perfect realm (or this life and the life hereafter). In varying degrees, they are oriented toward the other world and preoccupied with salvation. Historic religions are also characterized by the emergence of a religious elite that is separate from the political elite and by the establishment of a specialized religious organization. The separation of church and state heightens the possibility of conflict between political and religious elites and within the religious ranks.

Bellah cites early Protestant denominations as the prime example of *early modern religion*. Protestants rejected the need for saints and clergy to me-

diate between the individual and God. They rejected the emphasis on sacraments, ceremonies, and the other world. Most significantly, they began to press for "social change in the direction of greater realization of religious values" in this world (Bellah, 1964, p. 370). This change set the stage for modern religion.

In *modern religion* the dualism of historic religion breaks down. The idea that each individual must personally reinterpret religious teaching gains widespread acceptance. Organized religions lose their monopoly on the creation of sacred symbols. The search for meaning is no longer confined to the church. The church is seen as providing a favorable keep silence in the churches" (I Corinthians 14:34). This patriarchal point of view went unchallenged for close to 2,000 years, building credibility through its longevity. On the other side of the issue are those who argue that sex should have nothing to do with the ability to serve God and minister to others. They regard Paul's dictums as applying to situations in the first century A.D.—not for all eternity.

The first barriers against women fell in the Protestant churches. In 1853, Antoinette Brown was ordained in the Congregational Church. But other mainline Protestant churches did not follow suit until the 1950s, when Methodists and Presbyterians began ordaining women. Sweden's Lutheran Church led the way in Europe. In 1972 the first woman rabbi in the United States was ordained. The Epis-copal Church permitted ordination in 1976. The biggest stir was caused by the change of heart of the Anglican communion in Great Britain in November 1992. The Anglicans have been very close to Roman Catholics in their theology; their decision (by two votes) to allow women in the priesthood broke off long-term discussions concerning the merger of the two denominations.

The battle for ordination of women continues in the Catholic Church. The Vatican remains opposed to the idea, but various groups are agitating for and against letting women become priests. About 67 percent of American Catholics are in favor of ordaining women (Gallup Organization, 1992). They have seen laywomen and nuns performing every priestly function except the consecration of the eucharist. Of the nearly 300 parishes in the United States without a priest, three-fourths are currently being led by women—either nuns or lay leaders (Wallace, 1992). At a time when the numbers of male priests are declining, many religious females stand ready to take up the slack. A glimmer of hope for activists came in late 1992 when American Catholic bishops voted not to adopt a document that took a stand against ordination of women and other aspects of the feminist movement. One activist nun regarded the vote as the beginning of "a new age in the Church for all Catholics who care about justice. For the first time, we saw bishops willing to make their dissent from official teaching public" (*Providence Journal-Bulletin,* (November 19, 1992, p. A13).

environment for this quest, not as providing prefabricated answers. In Bellah's words, "modern religion is beginning to understand the laws of the self's own existence and so to help man take responsibility for his own fate" (1964, p. 372). In other words, modern religion stresses personal autonomy and the ability of individuals to change themselves and their social world.

For Bellah, then, neither a decline in belief in the supernatural nor movement away from organized religion and orthodox creeds signals indifference to religion. Rather, he sees these developments as evidence of new ways of practicing and interpreting religion (see, for example, *Close Up:* Women and the Church).

Civil Religion

The emergence of civil religion is evidence of the transformation of religion in modern societies. A *civil religion* is a set of beliefs, rituals, and symbols that define a nation's special relationship with God. Civil religions are composed of sacred symbols conceived outside the church and are independent of both the church (or denominations) and the state. Bellah (1967, 1975; Bellah and Hammond, 1980) discusses the emergence of civil religion in the United States.

Civil religion in the United States is based on the belief that America has a mission to carry out God's

Civil religion is based on the belief that the nation has a mission to carry out God's will on earth. All U.S. presidents have invoked the name of God in their oaths of office and their inauguration speeches.

will on earth. Every president has invoked God in his inaugural address. John Kennedy, for example, ended his address this way: "With a good conscience our only sure reward, with history the final judge of our deeds, let us go forth to lead the land we love, asking His blessing and His help, but knowing here on earth God's work must truly be our own." Our pledge of allegiance to the flag declares us "one nation under God"; our national motto, "In God we trust," is printed on every dollar bill. During the Revolutionary War, political leaders described themselves as leading the American people out of Egypt (away from European tyranny) into the promised land. The Civil War introduced the themes of death, sacrifice, and rebirth into our civil religion—themes personified in our martyred president, Abraham Lincoln, July 4, Memorial Day, Lincoln's birthday, and other national occasions celebrate and sanctify the American way of life.

Bellah's description of civil religion is reminiscent of Durkheim's theory that all religion is the worship of society. He maintains that civil religion played a crucial role in the development of American institutions by supplying religious legitimization of political authority. Our civil religion draws on Judeo-Christian tradition, but it does not compete with personal beliefs and practices, which it regards as private and sacred. "Civil religion at its best is a genuine apprehension of universal and transcendent religious reality as seen in, or one

could almost say, as revealed through the experience of the American people" (Bellah, 1967).

Critics argue that this nation's civil religion is a watered-down version of religion at best. Americans are devoted not to God but to the "American way of life," a materialistic creed that supports our addiction to consumerism. In brief, religious rhetoric is used to disguise highly secular attitudes and beliefs.

World Religions

Even though there are thousands of different religions being practiced around the world, religion's standing as a social institution becomes clear when one considers that over three-quarters of the world population belong to one of six major religions. Each of these world religions—Buddhism, Christianity, Confucianism, Hinduism, Islam, and Judaism—has millions of members (see Table 13-1). They are also quite different—not only in their beliefs but also in terms of their development and relation to other social institutions.

Buddhism

Siddhartha Gautama "founded" Buddhism in India, 2,500 years ago and five centuries before the birth of Christ. It is a religion based on the enlightenment he achieved after many years of travel and

The six major world religions—Buddhism, Christianity, Confucianism, Hinduism, Judaism, and Islam—each have millions of adherents. They differ greatly in their beliefs, in their historical development, and in their relationships to other social institutions. (A) Buddhism: a pilgrim at Thimpu, Bhutan. (B) Christianity: a Lutheran altar boy in Philadelphia. (C) Confucianism: Lungshau Temple in Taipei, Taiwan. (D) Hinduism: worshipers pray and make offerings at Varanesi, India. (E) Islam: men at prayer in a Haydar mosque in Kuliab, Tadjikistan. (F) Judaism: a bar mitzvah in Harrisburg, Pennsylvania.

meditation. Having come to understand the essence of life, Gautama became a Buddha. According to Buddhism, this essence is contained in the Four Noble Truths: (1) that all people experience suffering, some more than others, according to their *karma* or spiritual level; (2) that attachment and desire are the root of suffering; (3) that suffering can be overcome if one achieves a state of emptiness and lets go of attachment and desire; and (4) that nirvana can eventually be achieved by following the Eightfold Path, which involves behaving ethically, having a simple life, renouncing material pleasures, and meditating.

Because Buddhism is more concerned with righteous living than formal doctrine and is frequently followed in combination with other religions such as Taoism and Confucianism, its membership worldwide is difficult to estimate but it is probably around 300 million people, or 6 percent of the world's population. There are several branches of Buddhism. The oldest group, sometimes called *Hinayana,* is part of local cultures and traditional politics in Myanmar, Laos, Cambodia, Sri Lanka, and Thailand. *Mahayana* Buddhism is practiced in China, Korea, and Japan and is part of the cultural fabric of those countries. *Vajrayana* or "Vehicle of the Thunderbolt," the Buddhism of Tibet and Mongolia, is interwoven with politics. Tibet's Dalai Lama is considered both a political leader, committed to achieving that country's independence from China, and the incarnation of Buddha. In Japan there are also Zen and Nichiren Buddhism.

Table 13-1 *Religious Population of the World, 1995*

Religion	Total Population (Thousands)
Christians	1,927,753
Roman Catholics	968,025
Protestants	393,867
Orthodox	217,948
Anglicans	70,530
Other Christians	275,593
Muslims	1,099,634
Nonreligious	841,549
Hindus	780,547
Buddhists	323,594
Atheists	219,925
Chinese folk-religionists	225,137
New religionists	121,294
Ethnic religionists	111,777
Sikhs	19,161
Jews	14,117
Spiritualists	10,170
Bahia'is	6,104
Confucians	5,257
Jains	4,886
Shintoists	2,844
Other religionists	2,156
Total population	**5,716,425**

Source: U.S. Bureau of the Census, *Statistical Abstract of the United States, 1996,* Washington, DC: GPO, 1996, p. 826.

Christianity

Like Buddhism, Christianity is a religion inspired by the life of one man. The belief that Jesus of Nazareth, a Jew, was the Christ or Messiah foretold in the Bible is one of the core beliefs binding the huge variety of Christian denominations, sects, and cults. Christians believe that Jesus's teachings of personal salvation provide the key to an ethical life and humans' redemption from their fallen state. Most Christians also believe that Christ was the Son of God and rose from the dead after being crucified in Jerusalem for being a threat to the established political leaders of the Roman Empire of the time.

A total of 1.9 billion people, about one-third of the world's population, are Christians, most of them living in Europe and the Americas. Originally a persecuted sect, Christianity divided between the Roman Catholic Church in Rome and the Eastern Orthodox Church of Turkey in the eleventh century. It divided again in the sixteenth century during the Protestant Reformation, which eventually led to the Protestant denominations, such as Methodists, Baptists, and Presbyterians. Unlike the Roman Catholics, who believe that the church hierarchy is the authority on salvation, Protestants place their faith in an individual's direct relationship with God.

Christianity grew as a result of European conquest and colonization. Missionaries spread Christian teachings, particularly to the poor, who came to view it as a means of upward social mobility. Such efforts continue today. Because of the diversity of Christian groups, it is difficult to characterize the relationship between Christians and other social institutions. Even within Catholicism there is a tradition of support for both revolutionary causes (as in Central America) and the status quo (as in much of Europe). The current peace in northern Ireland comes after centuries of often violent conflict between Catholics allied with the Republic of Ireland and Protestants who supported English sovereignty.

Confucianism

Named for its founder, K'ung-Fu-tzu (551–479 B.C.), Confucianism is more a set of philosophic teachings on living ethically than a religion concerned with redemption or transcendence. The official religion of China until the revolution in 1949, Confucianism served as the basis for ethics and politics in China for over 2,000 years. The teachings of Confucius (as he is known in the west) had an enormous influence on that country as well as Korea, Japan, and Vietnam.

Confucianism sees opposites as part of a harmonious whole rather than at odds with one another. This whole is constantly changing, thanks to the dynamic interaction of *yin* (the female) and *yang* (the male). The *I Ching* or *Book of Changes* presents teachings regarding this dynamic. It also offers a technique for understanding one's present circumstances and taking actions that are philosophically sound.

Even though Confucianism is no longer an "official" religion and is estimated to have just over 5 million adherents worldwide, the rapid economic growth that countries such as Singapore, China, and Taiwan have enjoyed until recently was powered in part by Confucianism's emphasis on discipline and respect for authority. These beliefs and their overall effect on Chinese thinking have also made Confucianism useful to rulers and administrators.

Hinduism

The oldest of the world's religions, Hinduism is the source of both Buddhism and Sikhism. It began in the Indus River Valley in India about 4,500 years ago. It, too, is concerned with an ethical force (*dharma*) and a universal ideal way of life; but it is not based on the teachings of any one person, nor do its followers believe in a single God. It has no sacred writings like the Bible or Koran (see below) and teaches that life is *maya* or illusion and that what is important is the spiritual progress of the soul, one's *karma*. Karma works through reincarnation—death and rebirth at a new spiritual level. The practice of Hinduism is extremely diverse. In fact, Hindu religious services can occur anywhere, for though there are temples and sacred sites, holiness can be found in any location.

Nearly 800 million people, about 13 percent of the world's population are Hindus. Most Hindus continue to live in India and Pakistan, though they are also found in significant numbers in parts of southern Africa, Indonesia, and the United States. Over the centuries Hinduism and Indian culture have blended together, and it is now difficult to consider them separate from one another.

For example, Hinduism is the basis for the social structure in India. As we saw in Chapter 8, the caste system, though abolished in 1949, remains an integral part of Indian society. Hindu beliefs serve as the basis for this system, and an important example of *dharma* is living in concert with its responsibilities. Hindu teachings describe a series of four stages of life for upper-caste males. These stages include a student stage; a householder stage; a period of spiritual seeking, in which men leave their families after their children have grown and live in the forest; and a period of renunciation, in which men give up all attachments to worldly things in order to attain enlightenment (recall the journey of Siddhartha Gautama).

Islam

Islam is the main religion of the Middle East. Its growing numbers of adherents call themselves Muslims and are presently about 1 billion strong—roughly 18 percent of the world's population. As its numbers suggest, Islam is widespread: it is practiced in the former Soviet Union, Europe, China, India, Pakistan, and Indonesia. It is estimated that there are about 5 million Muslims in North America (*Statistical Abstract* 1996). Though Islam is the official faith of Arabs, the number of non-Arab Muslims greatly exceeds that of Arab Muslims.

As described in this chapter's *Global View* box (see page 494), the Five Pillars of Islam, as revealed to the prophet Elijah Muhammad (570–632), govern all aspects of Muslim practices of worship, ethics, and daily life. In addition, Muslims believe that devotion to Allah, the only God, must be absolute and unquestioning. The Sunni sect of Islam, to which most of the leaders in the Middle East belong, is committed to the separation of church and state, while the Shiite Muslims (who overthrew the shah of Iran) strongly believe there should be no separation between church and state. These beliefs have greatly influenced governments in Arab countries.

The social position of women under Islam is quite restrictive—many would say, oppressive. It has been improving somewhat, and women figure prominently as leaders in some Islamic countries. It is important to keep in mind that the patriarchal structure of Middle Eastern society was already established by the time of Elijah Muhammad.

Judaism

Small by comparison to other world religions and made considerably smaller by the extermination of about 7 million Jews during the Holocaust, Judaism still occupies a central place among world religions. It has served as the basis for two of those religions—Christianity and Islam. As we have seen, Jesus was himself Hebrew; and Muhammad claimed that the teachings of the Hebrew prophet Abraham served as the basis for Islam. About 14 million people around the world identify themselves as Jewish, and half of this number live in the United States.

Judaism began about 4,000 years before Jesus's birth, among the cultures of Mesopotamia. It was one of the first monotheistic religions. Like the adherents of many other religions, Jews believe they are God's chosen people, but unlike other religions, they do not seek to convert others to their faith.

Religious law for the Jews is based on the Torah, a scroll inscribed with the first five books of the

Bible, as well as the practice of publicly studying and writing expositions on the Torah (collected in the Mishna and Talmud). The three principle divisions of Judaism today offer differing views of this biblical law. Orthodox Judaism sees the Bible as coming directly from God and holds, therefore, that its teachings are to be taken literally and accepted as totally binding. Reform Judaism takes the perspective that while the Bible is a historic document containing important ethical guidelines, it is subject to interpretation. The stance of Conservative Judaism is somewhere between these extremes. Though it retains many traditional religious practices, it also adapts others to the demands of modern society.

Because Jews resisted conversion to other religions and assimilation to surrounding cultures, because they viewed themselves as "the chosen people" and made no effort to convert others to their faith, and because they had no homeland, Jews were subject to frequent persecution. Starting in the twelfth century, Jews in Europe and Russia were forced to live in isolated rural communities (or *shetls*) and walled urban districts (*ghettoes*), were denied full rights as citizens, and were subjected to periodic massacres (*pogroms*). The growing tide of nationalism in nineteenth-century Europe led to divisions between Jews who sought to adapt their religious life to European culture and Zionists ("Zion" is the ancient name for Jerusalem) who sought to reclaim their ancient homeland in Palestine. In the aftermath of the Holocaust in Nazi Germany, Jewish settlers fought the British colonialists who controlled Palestine and established the modern nation of Israel, while others fled to other counties, especially the United States. Two leading issues for Jews today are whether the state of Israel represents all Jews and whether this ancient religion will survive in the United States and elsewhere, where Jews are increasingly assimilated and rates of intermarriage between Jews and members of other faiths are high.

Religion in the United States

The United States is one of the most "religious" nations in the western industrial world (see Table 13-2). Americans donate more time and money to religious organizations than to all other voluntary associations combined (Bellah et al.,

Table 13-2 *Religious Beliefs and Practices: A Cross-Cultural Look*

Consider selves religious persons	
Italy	83%
United States	81
Ireland	64
Spain	63
Great Britain	58
West Germany	58
Hungary	56
France	51
Nonethnic Lithuanians	50
Czechoslovakia	49
Ethnic Lithuanians	45
Scandinavia	46
Attend church at least weekly	
Ireland	82%
United States	43
Spain	41
Italy	36
West Germany	21
Czechoslovakia	17
Ethnic Lithuanians	15
Nonethnic Lithuanians	12
Great Britain	14
Hungary	13
France	12
Scandinavia	5
Average ratings of importance of God in one's life (10 = highest importance)	
United States	8.2
Ireland	8.0
Northern Ireland	7.5
Italy	6.9
Spain	6.4
Finland	6.2
Belgium	5.9
Great Britain	5.7
West Germany	5.7
Norway	5.4
Netherlands	5.3
Hungary	4.8
France	4.7
Denmark	4.4

Source: "Religion in America 1992–1993," *The Gallup Report,* Princeton, NJ: The Princeton Religion Research Center, The Gallup Organization, 1993, p. 70.

1985; Gallup and Castelli, 1989; Gallup Organization, 1993). Two out of three Americans are now or were "churched"; that is, they either are members of a church (or synagogue) or attended services in the last six months, not counting holidays. Only 11 in

100 say that they have no religious preference, do not go to services, and do not consider religion very important in their lives (Gallup Organization, 1993; Gallup and Castelli, 1989). But interest in religion is not distributed evenly throughout the population. Women, African Americans, and Americans age 50 or older attend church (or other religious) services more often than do other members of the population; married and widowed Americans are more active than those who are single or divorced; and Catholics attend services more regularly than do Protestants, and Christians as a whole more often than do Jews (Jacquet, 1989). As a general rule, young adults (age 18 to 24) have been the least involved in religion.

What do Americans believe? Polls indicate that the vast majority hold traditional beliefs (Gallup Organization, 1993; Golay and Rollyson, 1996). More than nine out of ten believe in God, and most (84 percent) see God as a "Heavenly Father, who can be reached by prayer" (Gallup Organization, 1993, p. 20). Only 5 percent say that they do not believe in God or a universal spirit, while 4 percent "do not know." Nearly nine out of ten Americans pray. Almost two-thirds believe in life after death. Interestingly, more believe in heaven (78 percent) than in hell (60 percent) (Gallup Organization, 1993, p. 27). In spiritual matters, Americans appear to be optimists.

How important is religion to Americans? Interest and confidence in religion dropped sharply during the 1960s and 1970s but then began to recover. A majority of Americans today say that religion is "very important" in their lives and that "religion can answer all or most of today's problems" (Gallup Organization, 1993; Golay and Rollyson, 1996). A large proportion also believe that the influence of religion in our society is increasing, not decreasing.

Religious participation in the United States is characterized by two apparently contradictory trends. Most Americans hold traditional religious beliefs, and many are members of a church or synagogue. Yet actual participation in organized religion has declined (see Figure 13-1). In 1995, less than 42 percent of those polled said they had attended services in the last week (Golay and Rollyson, 1996). Even that figure may be inflated. Several sociologists, intrigued by the discrepancy between the numbers of Americans who claimed to attend

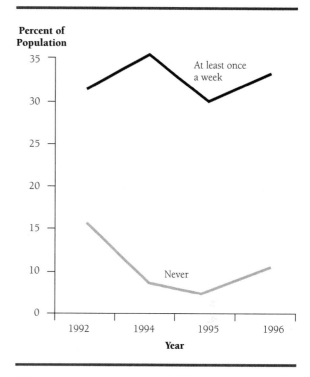

Figure 13-1   *Americans' Attendance at Religious Services*

Those answering the question, "How often do you attend church or synagogue?"
Source: The Gallup Poll, 1996.

church weekly and the numbers of churches that have reported losing millions of members, conducted an exhaustive study of an area in Ohio. They found that a head count of congregants was considerably lower than the number of people who in a telephone poll reported going to church that week. They attribute the discrepancy to a tendency for people to want to report socially desirable behavior (Hadaway, Marler, and Chaves, 1993).

What might explain the decline in church participation? A number of sociologists (for example, Bellah et al., 1985) believe that religion in America has been privatized. Most Americans say that a person does not have to attend church or synagogue to be a good Christian or Jew (Shriver, 1979). In other words, they are religious individualists and draw a distinction between their personal relationship to God and participation in a religious organization. "It's not the religion or church you go to that saves you," said one devout Christian; it is your "personal relationship" with God (quoted in Bellah et al., 1985, p. 234).

Individual freedom has always been a dominant theme in American culture, and religious individualism has a long tradition in our society. Over the centuries many Americans who considered themselves religious or "spiritual" have rejected organized religion, preferring to find their own way. Thomas Jefferson, for example, declared, "I am a sect unto myself." Some religious individualists have been attracted to nontraditional religions. But in most cases religious individualism is based not on alternative beliefs but on disillusionment with church institutions. Some individualists charge churchgoers with hypocrisy, with failing to practice what they preach. Others feel that religious leaders are too busy with administrative affairs to provide guidance on personal problems or to help members of their congregations gain insight into the meaning of life and death (Gallup and Castelli, 1989). But this does not necessarily mean that they are nonreligious. Most "unchurched" Americans are believers.

Summarizing more than fifty years of polling Americans on their religious beliefs and practices, George Gallup concludes:

> Religion in America has been remarkably stable, both in terms of religious beliefs and practices. Essentially, America's religious beliefs have been orthodox, relative to other nations. I would say that the Americans of 1989 are very much like Americans of 1939 in many of their beliefs and values. . . . There's much more stability than people realize. (interview by T. K. Jones, 1989, p. 23)

Others disagree, however.

The Restructuring of Religion in America

Sociologist Robert Wuthnow (1988, 1993) surveyed the past four decades of religious life in America. Looking beyond polls to patterns of religious activity, the structure of religion, and the relationship between religion and other institutions, Wuthnow concluded that the nature of religion in America—indeed, what it means to be "religious"—has changed dramatically.

In the 1940s, religious life in America centered around neighborhood churches and synagogues. People's social identities were based in large part on membership in one or another religious denomination (Presbyterian or Baptist, Catholic or Jew). Church and state enjoyed an easygoing alliance: although legally separate, they usually reinforced one another. By the 1980s, television ministers had become as influential as neighborhood churches (see Table 13-3). People's identities and affiliations were based more on where they stood on social issues than on membership in one or another denomination. Religion had become an active voice in politics, often speaking out against government policies, court rulings, and elected officials. Wuthnow traces this transformation.

Mainstream Denominations after World War II

The years following World War II were a period of reaffirmation for mainstream religious denominations in America. The forces for good had triumphed in Europe, and the nation could settle back and enjoy the pleasures of everyday life. As Wuthnow writes, it was "a time of peace and prosperity when people moved to the suburbs, bought Chevrolets, went to bed early, and repopulated the churches" (1988, p. 35). Religion was viewed as the conscience of America (an inner voice, not an active political force). Polls showed that a majority of Americans endorsed traditional values, were members of a religious congregation, and went to church on Sundays.

The major divisions in American religion were between Protestantism, Catholicism, and Judaism. Americans saw membership in one of these three religious categories as a central part of their identity. But a spirit of mutual tolerance and cooperation prevailed, and interfaith councils of various sorts were common. Gradually, the traditional religious boundaries began to blur. Increasing numbers of people switched from one denomination to another, attended services in other denominations, and/or married across denominational boundaries. Americans were becoming more religiously mobile (see Table 13-4). Wuthnow sees the decline of denominationalism as "sweeping the decks" for change (1988, p. 11).

Table 13-3   *Church Membership Status for Selected U.S. Denominations*

Denomination	Year			
	1960	1970	1980	1996
Mainline Protestant:				
Evangelical Lutheran	(5,295,502)*	(5,650,137)	(5,384,271)	(5,190,489)
Disciples of Christ	1,801,821	1,424,479	1,177,984	1,655,000
Episcopal	3,269,325	3,285,826	2,786,004	2,536,550
United Methodist	10,641,310	10,509,198	9,519,407	8,538,662
United Presbyterian USA	(4,161,860)	(4,045,408)	(3,362,086)	(3,669,489)
Evangelical Protestant:				
Assembly of God	508,602	625,027	1,064,490	2,387,982
Jehovah's Witness	250,000	388,920	565,309	966,243
Mormon	1,486,887	2,073,146	2,811,000	4,711,500
Seventh Day Adventist	317,852	420,419	571,141	790,731
Southern Baptist	9,731,591	11,628,032	13,600,126	15,663,296
Roman Catholic	42,104,900	48,214,729	50,449,842	60,280,454

*Data in parentheses include denominations that later merged.

Sources: Adapted from Constant H. Jacquet, *Yearbook of American and Canadian Churches,* Nashville, TN: Abingdon, 1991, pp. 272–273, copyright © 1991 by The National Council of the Churches of Christ (USA). Kenneth B. Bedell (Ed.), *Yearbook of American and Canadian Churches, 1997,* Nashville, TN: Abingdon Press, 1998, p. 2, used by permission of the publisher, Abingdon Press.

Table 13-4   *Changes in Religious Preference*

Denominational Category	Affiliates	Dropouts	Converts	Net Change
Pentecostal/Sects	64.4	35.6	52.4	+35.3
Conservative Protestant	73.7	26.3	17.3	−10.9
Mainline Protestant	68.0	32.0	23.5	−11
Liberal Protestant	63.4	36.6	36.1	—
Catholic	83.1	16.9	10.3	−7.3
Other Christian	55.4	44.6	61.0	+41.9
Non-Christian	79.8	20.2	22.8	+3.4
None	39.9	60.1	83.0	+134.8

Note: Percentage of religious category who practice the religion in which they were raised ("affiliates"), left their childhood religion ("dropouts"), and converted to that religion. Pentecostal/Sects include Assemblies of God, Church of God in Christ Holiness, Church of Holiness, Churches of God, Holiness, Holiness Church of God, Pentecostal, Pentecostal Assembly of God, Pentecostal Church of God, Pentecostal Holiness or Holiness Pentecostal, United Holiness, Christian Science, Church of Jesus Christ of Latter Day Saints (Mormons), Seventh Day Adventists, and Jehovah's Witnesses. Conservative Protestant churches include Baptist, Churches of Christ, Evangelical Congregational, Evangelical Evangelist, Christian and Missionary Alliance, and Brethren. Mainline Protestant churches include Presbyterian, Lutheran, Methodist, and Christian Church. Liberal Protestant churches include Unitarian, Episcopal, and United Church of Christ. Other Christian includes a diverse set of churches (e.g., Quaker, Mennonite, Dutch Reform). Non-Christian falls outside Christian tradition (e.g., Buddhist, Moslem, Shinto).

Source: L. D. Nelson and D. G. Bromley, "Another Look at Conversion and Defection in Conservative Churches," in D. G. Bromley (Ed.), *Falling from the Faith: Causes and Consequences of Religious Apostasy,* Newbury Park, CA: Sage, 1988, table 3.2, p. 54. Copyright © 1988 by Sage Publications, Inc. Reprinted by permission.

The Liberalization of Mainstream Denominations

During the 1960s and 1970s, the spell of calm consensus in American society was broken first by the civil rights movement and then by the war in Vietnam. Could religions maintain a position of neutrality on these issues and still retain credibility as "the conscience of America"? Many denominations, and many congregations, were deeply divided on this question. On one side were liberal religious leaders and lay members, who thought religion must not only take a stand but also become actively involved. On the other side were conservatives, who believed that the church should confine its activities to spiritual matters. As the sixties progressed, it became clear that protest movements were only the tip of the iceberg of social unrest. American society was experiencing dramatic shifts in attitudes and values. A large segment of the population was becoming more egalitarian in attitudes toward women, African Americans, and other minorities; supporting civil liberties and freedom of speech for communists, atheists, homosexuals, and others outside the American mainstream; and becoming more tolerant on such lifestyle issues as premarital sex, cohabitation, and divorce.

The government both influenced and was influenced by these trends. For example, in 1964 Congress passed the Civil Rights Act, which empowered the Justice Department to take action against individuals and organizations who discriminate against racial or religious minorities or against women. The Supreme Court ruled that prayer in school is a violation of the separation of church and state. Later it held that laws against abortion are unconstitutional. A presidential commission reported that pornography is harmless.

Religion played an active role in social change. Led by the National and World Councils of Churches, a number of mainstream denominations and congregations began moving toward the liberal end of the spectrum. Many Jewish groups also played an important role in American liberalism. Numerous special-religious-interest groups were formed in this period, dedicated to causes ranging from nuclear arms control to updating religious rituals. Some of these groups were formed within congregations or denominations, while others were interdenominational or nondenominational. Wuthnow credits special-interest groups with helping maintain interest in religion in an increasingly secular society.

Fundamentalism after World War II

Fundamentalism has a long history in the United States (Alhstrom, 1975; Kosmin and Lachman, 1993). Religious revivals have come in waves, sweeping the country and then subsiding, only to rise again. Despite many variations, fundamentalist Christianity generally emphasizes a literal interpretation of the Bible, the living presence of Christ, the importance of a personal experience of conversion (being "born again"), and the need to "spread the Word" (or missionary activity). Fundamentalists believe that the Bible provides unambiguous answers to all moral questions, and they contrast the purity within the church to the wickedness without. There are prominent fundamentalist strains in other religions, for example, Judaism and Islam, as well.

At the close of World War II, pockets of fundamentalism could be found in the southern Bible belt, but, in general, fundamentalism seemed to be in retreat. Its basic tenets ran counter to popular sentiments. At a time of national confidence, fundamentalists talked of the second coming and divine judgment. In an era of prosperity, they rejected worldly aspirations. In a period of interfaith tolerance, fundamentalists preached separatism. While most of America was enamored with science and technology, fundamentalists saw the Bible as the ultimate source of truth. Many Americans viewed fundamentalism as an anti-intellectual reaction to modernism and as a religious backwater.

In the 1950s, a new generation of "evangelical" ministers emerged. Eager to distance themselves from the extreme, sectlike fundamentalism of the past, they emphasized basic Christian values, Bible study, and one's own personal experience of Christ. During the 1950s and 1960s, they worked on building regional and interdenominational coalitions. The number of evangelical congregations and special-interest groups within mainstream congregations, colleges, and seminaries grew steadily. Evangelist Billy Graham became the unofficial chaplain of the White House. In Gallup polls taken in the mid-1970s, fully one-third of Americans described themselves as "born-again" Christians. When Jimmy Carter, himself a born-again Christian, was elected president in 1976, it seemed that evangelicalism had "arrived" (Wuthnow, 1993). From 1986 to 1990 the percentage of those who described themselves as born-again or evangelical Christian went from 32 to 37 percent (T. Smith, 1992). Over the last thirty years, the fastest-growing church in America was a Pentecostal denomination, the Church of God in Christ, which grew by 863 percent (Bedell, 1997).

Just as mainstream denominations had moved left, evangelists had moved toward the political center. For a time it looked as if mainstream denominations and evangelical forces might reach a common ground. But a new set of issues and a new set of leaders, using a new medium, entered the picture.

Televangelism and Mobilization of the Religious Right

The Federal Communications Commission (FCC) has always required that broadcasters allot time for public-interest messages. Traditionally, TV stations satisfied part of this requirement by granting free time to mainstream religious denominations. In 1960, however, the FCC ruled that stations could sell airtime to religious organizations and still receive "credit" for public-interest broadcasting (Hadden, 1987). A new generation of fundamentalist ministers seized the opportunity.

The new televangelists differed from evangelist and mainstream ministers in significant ways. Nearly all were headquartered in the south. They were willing, even eager, to be associated with fundamentalism and "that old-time religion." They preached a literal interpretation of the Bible and often the literal existence of the devil, hell, and the second coming. Other ministers felt uncomfortable about going on television and asking people to give themselves to Jesus, much less asking for donations. In their zeal for saving souls and raising money, the televangelists had few such qualms (Hadden, 1987).

From the beginning, fundamentalists dominated religious broadcasting. Between 1959 and 1979, the proportion of paid religious broadcasts grew from 53 to 92 percent (Hadden, 1987). According to the National Religious Broadcasters, there are now 1,588 religious radio stations and 191 religious television stations (National Religious Broadcasters, 1997). How many people actually watch these broadcasts is debatable. But a conservative estimate

suggested that in 1984, 13 million Americans were tuning in—more than the combined memberships of the United Methodist, Presbyterian, and Episcopalian churches (Ostling, 1986, p. 63). In 1987, about 7 million Americans contributed money to TV ministries. Half said they had given less than $100 in the preceding year, and half, more. By 1987, the electronic church had become a $2 billion enterprise (*Gallup Report,* 1987).

Televangelists appealed to segments of the population (especially older Americans, southerners, and Americans with lower-than-average educations) that had been largely ignored in the political debates of the 1960s and 1970s (Wald, Owen, and Hill, 1989). Many of these people felt outraged at the "unpatriotic" demonstrations against the war in Vietnam and felt humiliated when the United States ultimately withdrew. Many were alienated by a government that allowed, and a culture that applauded, behavior that they believed to be sinful. And many felt betrayed by the evangelical ministers who had attempted to accommodate cultural change, and by President Jimmy Carter, whose liberal positions (they thought) violated religious teachings. "I will pray for him daily," declared one televangelist (Jerry Falwell, in Wuthnow, 1988, p. 204).

Earlier generations of fundamentalists had remained aloof from politics, indeed from secular society in general. But the new televangelists saw morality as a public issue and their mission as saving America's soul. Reverend Jerry Falwell took the lead in forging an alliance between Christian fundamentalists and the political right. After a series of "I Love America" rallies on the steps of state capitols, Falwell founded the Moral Majority in 1979 (renamed "Liberty Federation" in 1985). Falwell's basic message could be summarized as follows: America is God's chosen instrument for bringing good into the world. But America is in a state of moral decay. Unless this decline in public morals is reversed, the government will be replaced by an atheistic dictatorship. Christians have a moral duty to back candidates who endorse traditional religious and patriotic values.

In terms of membership and political power, the Moral Majority was never as strong as its supporters or critics claimed (Hadden and Shupe, 1988; Wuthnow, 1988). Some observers (including Wuthnow) feel that the Moral Majority was largely the creation of the mass media and of pollsters, who were eager to spot and report a new trend. Others argue that televangelists tapped into a growing disillusionment with liberalism and a general cultural shift toward conservatism (Hadden and Shupe, 1988). Whichever view is correct, Falwell and other televangelists succeeded in gradually transforming their religious audiences into a political constituency: the "New Christian Right."

Several television ministries lost followers in the late 1980s after a series of sexual and financial scandals. Jim Bakker was dismissed as a minister by the Assemblies of God after admitting adultery; he was subsequently convicted of financial fraud in his TV ministry. Also defrocked by the Assemblies of God was Jimmy Swaggart, who confessed to hiring prostitutes for pornographic purposes. Such scandals caused the ratings of television evangelists to fall from 41 percent of those surveyed in 1980 to 23 percent in 1989 (T. Smith, 1992). But fundamentalist beliefs in general appeared not to have been shaken. In 1994, the Christian Coalition, a fundamentalist group led by Ralph Reed, aligned itself with Newt Gingrich's "Contract with America" and helped the Republicans gain the majority in the House and Senate. Though it appeared from these victories that the fundamentalist agenda was becoming a major player in U.S. politics, its influence appears to be waning. Many of the legislative items on this agenda, such as prohibition of late-term abortions and the Parental Rights and Responsibilities Act, have failed to be enacted. Ralph Reed's departure from the Christian Coalition and Bill Clinton's defeat of Republican Bob Dole in 1996 are further evidence of this decline, though Republicans have retained their majorities in the House and Senate. As mentioned earlier, however, fundamentalist Christian groups are having some success in school board and other local elections.

Religion in America Today

Religion in the United States has become polarized, with religious conservatives on one side of the great divide and religious liberals on the other. The old boundaries between Protestantism, Catholicism, and Judaism have lost much of their relevance. For example, Christian fundamentalists, Mormons, Catholics, and politically conservative Jews have joined forces to oppose abortion (Kosmin and Lachman, 1993). The new boundaries are issue-oriented.

Religious liberals and religious conservatives are equally concerned about the relationship between government and morality. But religious liberals define morality in terms of individual choice and worry about government invasion of privacy. Religious conservatives define morality in terms of traditional values and the health of society as a whole; they argue that the government has betrayed these values. Each sees the other in a negative light. Asked to pick phrases that describe religious conservatives (from a list of nineteen phrases, some positive, some negative), liberals chose "intolerant of other religious beliefs," "too concerned with their own salvation," "close-minded," "too rigid and simplistic," and "too harsh an emphasis on guilt, sin, and judgment." Conservatives were equally unflattering, describing religious liberals as follows: "morally loose," "do not truly know Christ," "knowledge of the Bible is shallow," "not interested in sharing their faith," "tend to be unloving in their attitude," and "don't believe in the Bible" (Wuthnow, 1988, p. 216).

As a result of this polarization, religion is often in the forefront of political debates. Whether the issue is school prayer or abortion or gun control or military readiness, religion is there, in the thick of it. Far from being an institution in retreat, religion has become more active in recent decades.

SOCIOLOGY ON THE WEB

Cyber Religion

This exercise will help you explore the capabilities of the web as a research tool. Use the web to investigate the religion topic of your choice, but do the search in two different ways and compare your findings. First, pick a topic. Some suggestions are Judaism and feminism, Buddhism in the United States, Islam in the United States, evangelicalism, or New Age religion. Then look for information on your topic, starting with two different sites, an academic search engine and a commercial one. A good place to start is the first site listed below. (If your university has a department of religious studies or a divinity school, its web site would be another good place to start.) Then search the same topic again, this time using a commercial search engine such as Yahoo.

http://www.academicinfo.net/religindex.html
This is the address of the religion page at Academic Info, a search engine that brings together links to academic sources of information on many different topics. You will find links to libraries and research institutions as well as university departments of religious

studies and academic databases. Search for information about your chosen topic, noting the links you pursue and the types of information you find.

http://www.yahoo.com/Society_and_Culture/ Religion/
This is the address of the religion listings at Yahoo. Compare what you find here with what you found at Academic Info. What links do you find here? What kinds of information can you obtain? How do the results of this search differ from what you found by searching Academic Info? Write a brief evaluation of the capabilities of the two search engines.

Compare the web sites for one of each of the types of religious organizations described in the text: established church, sect, denomination, and cult. Look up groups mentioned in the text or others of your choice. Is there a difference in the way each type of organization presents itself at its web site? How would you explain the differences you find, based on the text's discussion of religious organizations?

Summary

1. **Why is some form of religion found in all human societies? What are the basic elements of religion as a social institution?** *Religion* is a set of institutionalized beliefs and practices that deal with the ultimate meaning of life. It is found in all societies because it fills a gap between human aspirations and abilities and between social expectations and experiences; it helps account for life's paradoxes. The basic elements of religion are *beliefs* (which affirm the existence of a supernatural order), *rituals* (formal, stylized enactments of beliefs), subjective experiences, and community.

2. **How have sociologists explained the link between religion and society?** Sociologists

have offered three different views of the relationship between society and religion.

Durkheim saw religion as defining a realm of the *sacred,* as distinct from the *profane.* Using *totemic* religions as an example, he argued that all religions reflect social forces and thus that they are a celebration of the social order.

Marx saw religion as an instrument of oppression. Just as opium and other painkillers mask the symptoms of disease, he argued, so religions mask the symptoms of exploitation, lulling the masses into the false belief that the existing social order is just.

Weber saw religion as an agent of social change. Using the Protestant Reformation as an example, he showed how religion might support a cultural revolution, in this case, the rise of capitalism.

3. **What are the different types of religious organizations? What distinguishes them? What central dilemma do all religious organizations face?** Sociologists distinguish among four types of religious organizations: the established church, the sect, the denomination, and the cult. An *established church* claims unique legitimacy as the official religion of its society and has a positive relationship with society. A *sect* also claims unique legitimacy but stands apart from society; sects are often protest movements that have split off from established churches. A *denomination* is at ease with the norms of society but does not claim to have the only answer to spiritual questions. *Cults* vary widely in their manifestations, but generally they do not have a positive relationship with society and do not claim unique legitimacy. Cults tend to be small, informal, and transient, often forming around a particular charismatic leader.

All organized religions face a central dilemma: The process of institutionalization may alter or dilute the original doctrine and so alienate true believers.

4. **How has the role of religion changed in modern society? How has religious life changed in America in the 1990s?** The trend toward *secularization* (the removal of religious control over social life) in modern society is undeniable. But sociologists disagree as to what this trend means. Some are convinced that religion is in decline. Others see signs of transformation, or evolution, rather than decline. Bellah cites the *civil religion* in America as evidence of the continuing importance of sacred symbols.

The existence of many, mutually tolerant denominations in the United States is unique in the western world. Polls show that faith in religious institutions remains high in the United States and that a majority of Americans hold traditional religious beliefs. Nevertheless, participation in organized religion has declined. One reason may be an increase in religious individualism.

Surveying the recent history of religion, Wuthnow concludes that the structure of religion in America has changed and that the most important boundaries in American religion today are not between major denominations but between conservatives and liberals.

Key Terms

belief 485	established church 491	sacred 487
civil religion 498	profane 487	sect 491
cult 492	religion 484	secularization 496
denomination 491	ritual 486	totem 487

Recommended Readings

Bellah, R. N., & Hammond, P. E. (1980). *Varieties of Civil Religion.* New York: Harper & Row.

Durkheim, E. (1912/1947). *The Elementary Forms of Religious Life.* J. W. Swan, trans. New York: Free Press.

Finke, R., & Stark, R. (1992). *The Churching of America: 1776–1990: Winners and Losers in Our Religious Economy.* New Brunswick, NJ: Rutgers University Press.

Glock, C. Y., & Stark, R. (1965). *Religion and Society in Tension.* Chicago: Rand McNally.

Kosmin, Barry A., & Lachman, Seymore P. (1993). *One Nation under God: Religion in Contemporary America.* New York: Crown.

Marty, M. (1981). *The Public Church: Mainline Evangelical-Catholic.* New York: Crossroad.

Roof, W. C. (1993). *A Generation of Seekers: The Spiritual Journals of the Baby Boom Generation.* New York: Harper & Row.

Schoenherr, R. A., & Young, L. A. (1993). *Full Pews and Empty Altars: Demographics of the Priest Shortage in United States Catholic Dioceses.* Madison: University of Wisconsin Press.

Weber, M. (1925/1964). *The Protestant Ethic and the Spirit of Capitalism.* T. Parson, trans. New York: Scribner.

Wuthnow, R. (1989). *The Struggle for America's Soul: Evangelicals, Liberals, and Secularism.* Grand Rapids, MI: Eerdmans.

Wuthnow, R. (1993). *Christianity in the 21st Century: Reflection on the Challenges Ahead.* New York: Oxford.

Chapter

Fourteen

Politics

The 1996 presidential election was, in the eyes of many observers, unusually dull. From the end of primaries, through the national party conventions, to election night, the incumbent Democratic President Bill Clinton, held the lead in public opinion polls. The Republican challenger, Senator Bob Dole, offered voters clear choices in terms of policy and programs but failed to capture public support. The outcome of the election was not "a sure thing," but neither was it a surprise.

After the votes were counted and Bill Clinton returned to office, attention turned to the election process, especially campaign financing. In large part because of the high price of television advertisements, the cost of elections has soared (Figure 14-1). An estimated $2 billion was spent on the 1996 presidential and congressional campaigns, almost twice the amount spent four years earlier (Rosenbaum, 1996). Most of the cost was paid with so-called soft money—donations by corporations, unions, trade associations, and interest groups to the Democratic and Republican National Committees, rather than donations to specific candidates, which are more strictly limited by law. The only restrictions on the parties is that they not accept donations from foreign nationals or from foreign companies that do not have at least subsidiaries in the United States. Both candidates took advantage of soft money during the 1996 campaign. But because Bill Clinton was the incumbent president and did not face serious opposition in the primaries, the Democrats could spend more on the election itself.

Questions about Democratic fund-raising had surfaced during the campaign but attracted little attention. After the election, in March 1997, the Republican chairs of the Senate and House Government Affairs Committees launched formal investigations and scheduled hearings on Democratic campaign finances. As the majority party, Republicans now had the power to probe deeper. Aided by the press, these committees uncovered a number of irregularities. The first series of allegations focused on fund-raising in the White House. The law does not permit campaign activities in government offices, where soliciting or accepting a donation would appear to be a bribe. Apparently Vice President Al Gore, and possibly the president, phoned major donors from their offices. But laws governing access to the White House and high-level federal officials are less clear. Most presidents have rewarded major donors with invitations to receptions, state dinners,

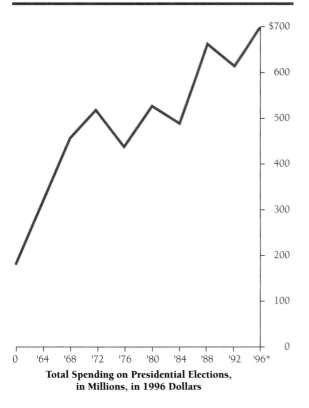

$700

600

500

400

300

200

100

0

0   '64   '68   '72   '76   '80   '84   '88   '92   '96*

**Total Spending on Presidential Elections,
in Millions, in 1996 Dollars**

*Estimate

Figure 14-1   *The Rising Cost of Becoming
President*

Much of the soaring cost of presidential election campaigns is due to the rising cost of television advertisements.

Source: D. E. Rosenbaum, "Cash Overflow: Fixing Politics, More or Less," *The New York Times.* Dec. 22, 1996, p. E1.

and the like. Investigation found that some Democratic National Committee (DNC) fund-raisers were unusually blunt: dinner and a photograph with the president cost $12,500; coffee with the president and other high-level officials at the White House, $50,000; an overnight stay in the Lincoln bedroom or another White House suite, at least $250,000 (Newsweek, March 10, 1997). The latter attracted the most attention. Technically, the second floor of the White House is the presidential family's private residence. The Clintons often invited old friends and celebrities to stay there; late-night talk sessions with the president and first lady were legendary. But the idea that the president was "renting" rooms to the highest donors caused outrage.

In the late spring another set of allegations surfaced regarding an "Asian connection," perhaps leading directly to the Chinese government. The vice chairman of the DNC finance committee was an old friend of the Clintons, a Chinese American named John Huang. They met in the 1980s when Clinton was governor of Arkansas and Huang was an executive for the Lippo Group, an investment conglomerate based in Indonesia. The Lippo Group is owned by the powerful Riady family, ethnic Chinese who have maintained contacts with their homeland and launched several major development projects in mainland China. Huang raised $1.6 million for the DNC. Where did this money come from? Was he still acting as an agent for the Riadys? Yuan Lin "Charlie" Trie ran a popular restaurant in Little Rock that Clinton had frequented as governor. How were Trie and his family, whose restaurant reported modest earnings, able to donate almost a million dollars to the DNC and Clinton's legal defense fund? Underlying these specific queries was the more general question, Were Asian businesses—perhaps acting as "fronts" for the government of China—contributing to the Clinton campaign through "straw donors" (people who wrote checks for which they were reimbursed)? Each year the president and Congress debate whether to grant China most-favored-nation trade status or to deny this because of well-documented human rights violations in China. Had Asian money influenced President Clinton's position?

When these allegations made front-page news, the reaction in Asia was primarily surprise (WuDunn, 1997). In Asia, guanxi (the Chinese word for "connections") are essential in establishing credibility. Whether in politics or business, relationships are considered more important than written contracts. And relationships depend in part on the exchange of favors, gifts, and money. Prestigious connections are also important. A photograph or personal letter from the president of the United States is a valuable asset in international commerce. Asian political and business leaders were surprised at the outrage in the U.S. press—and amazed that distributing a few thousand dollars here and there raised eyebrows in America. In Asia, influence costs millions!

In the end, the DNC quietly returned several million dollars in questionable contributions, and the investigation was unable to produce concrete proof of criminal wrongdoing. Nevertheless, one might expect that these allegations would lead to a strong campaign-finance reform bill. They did not. The McCain-Fiengold bill, a bipartisan proposal that the national parties and presidential candidates voluntarily agree to restrictions on campaign contributions and expenditures, was defeated in 1997 and again in 1998. The reason is simple: Republicans as well as Democrats benefit from legal loopholes and weak enforcement of campaign-finance laws. Indeed, the Republicans raised and spent more soft money during the 1996 campaign than the Democrats did. Both parties and presidential candidates seemed to treat campaign-finance laws like parking rules—a nuisance, but not a crime. Paying fines and returning contributions are costly but, after the election is over, inconsequential (Rosenbaum, 1997).

The cost of elections is higher in the United States than in any other democracy. Most European countries control spending by funding election campaigns through tax dollars, strictly limiting party donations and expenditures, providing candidates and parties with free airtime to promote their positions, and the like. The U.S. Supreme Court has ruled that limiting contributions to political parties would be a violation of free speech and, therefore, unconstitutional. The unintended consequences of this decision include an entire industry devoted to "packaging" candidates for political office, politicians devoting considerable time to fund-raising rather than governing, and opportunities to "buy" access to (if not influence over) government officials. Certainly, allegations and cases of bribery and corruption are not unique to the United States. But our elections, like our Oscar Awards, are uniquely American: in both cases, the most appealing people and the most lavish productions often win.

And so politics goes on as usual—mixing high finance, foreign intrigue, media savvy, public opinion polls, hearings and investigations, presidential celebrity, and the symbolism embodied in the White House with formal, official democratic institutions.

Politics refers to the social processes by which people gain, use, and lose power. Power plays a role in virtually all human relationships. When we speak of "sexual politics," we're talking about the ways men and women try to gain the upper hand in their intimate relationships, as well as in society at large. "Office politics" refers to the strategies and ploys people use to enhance or maintain their positions in the workplace. Sociologists who adopt the conflict approach investigate the role of power in all areas of social life. In this chapter, however, we look at politics as a social institution: as an enduring, widely accepted set of norms and values, statuses and roles, and groups and organizations that are directly concerned with the distribution of power.

Key Questions

1. What is the difference between power and authority?
2. How has the development of modern political institutions affected the distribution of authority?
3. What are the basic elements of the American political system?
4. Who actually rules America today?
5. How do political systems vary around the world?

Power versus Authority

Power is the ability to control what other people do, even when they resist (Weber, 1925/1964, p. 152). In its raw form, power is the use of intimidation or physical coercion to force someone else to do one's bidding. All societies distinguish between the legitimate and the illegitimate use of power. For example, in our society most people consider it legitimate for the government to require that citizens pay income taxes but illegitimate for a politician to demand or accept a bribe. Most Americans consider it legitimate for the government to require that parents send their children to school but illegitimate for public schools to teach a particular set of religious beliefs. Following Max Weber, sociologists use the term **authority** to refer to the legitimate use of power. Authority depends on agreement that certain uses of power are valid and justified—not only by those who make decisions and issue commands but also by those who are subject to those orders. Whereas power depends only on *might*, authority depends on cultural ideas of what is *right*.

Virtually all political systems depend on a combination of authority and coercion. For example, the U.S. government uses force when police arrest and detain a suspected criminal or when they issue a speeding ticket or tow away an illegally parked car; when it sends armed agents of the Bureau of Alcohol, Tobacco and Firearms onto private property to confiscate weapons or illegal drugs; when the IRS confiscates the property or garnishes the paychecks of individuals accused of income tax evasion; or when it sends troops to another country. Most Americans approve the use of force against people (and countries) who resist authority. Yet on

Adolf Hitler was an absolute dictator who used power to create the first modern totalitarian state, to invade and conquer most countries in continental Europe, and to carry out a policy of genocide on a scale never seen before. President Franklin D. Roosevelt, in contrast, exercised rational-legal authority. Roosevelt went before Congress to ask for a declaration of war, which was granted with only one dissenting vote, and he was the only American president to be elected for four terms.

many occasions the FBI, CIA, and IRS have been accused of overstepping their authority; at the local level, allegations of police brutality surface regularly. Debate over where to draw the line between the legitimate and illegitimate uses of power underlies the most controversial political issues on the public agenda today—for example, abortion, gun control, affirmative action, even child protection laws. The militia movement (introduced in Chapter 3) regards the government's collecting income taxes, requiring children to attend school, controlling guns, mandating racial integration and women's equality, and indeed the government itself as illegitimate. But many less extreme groups view certain government actions as illegitimate uses of power. One example is Victims of Child Abuse Laws (VOCAL), whose members argue that mandatory reporting laws have led to excess government intrusion in the way parents raise their children.

No government can rule through force alone, however. Political regimes created by military coups and maintained through martial law tend to be unstable and short-lived. To stay in power and govern effectively, political systems depend on at least some degree of legitimacy and consent from the people. Fear without allegiance is not enough. For example, the government of China could not have implemented its one-child-per-family policy if most of the Chinese population did not agree that the government has a legitimate right to issue orders regulating family life; that the needs of the state override many individual rights; and that the government as a whole has the people's best interests at heart (even though individual leaders may take advantage of their position). In contrast, the governments of the former U.S.S.R., Romania, East Germany, and other eastern European countries collapsed when they lost legitimacy in the eyes of the people, who came to see the Communist party as corrupt and the Communist system as failing to meet their basic needs for food, medicine, and the like.

One of the central functions of political institutions is to legitimize the ways in which power is exercised in a society. Americans usually assume that democracy—rule by the people—is the only legitimate form of government. But in different times and places, other political systems have enjoyed widespread popular support and voluntary allegiance.

Max Weber (1946) identified three main sources of political legitimacy: traditional, charismatic, and rational-legal authority. **Traditional authority** is based on customs handed down through the generations. It is the sacred right of a king or queen, an emperor or tribal chief, to command his or her subjects. In many cases, traditional authority is inherited. Although custom may impose some limits, traditional leaders are free to make unilateral decisions. A modern example of traditional leadership, although outside politics, is the pope, whom many Roman Catholics recognize as the supreme authority on issues of morality.

Charismatic authority is based on special personal qualities. Charismatic leaders have no traditional or legal claim to power; indeed, they often oppose prevailing custom and existing laws. Their authority derives from their followers' belief that they have exceptional insight and ability or, perhaps, supernatural powers. Mahatma Gandhi, who used nonviolent resistance to oppose British rule and lead India to independence, is an example of a charismatic leader. Another example is the Reverend Martin Luther King, Jr., who viewed Gandhi as a model. Although King never held public office, he was considered the spokesperson for African Americans and he inspired collective action, against violent opposition, in the civil rights movement. By its very nature, charismatic leadership is short-lived; followers are unlikely to accept a successor. Thus no single person has replaced Dr. King, though a number of leaders have carried on his tradition (including his widow Coretta Scott King and his close associate the Reverend Jesse Jackson). In some cases, charismatic leadership becomes "routinized" in the sense that past heroism serves as the foundation continuing legitimacy. For example, Fidel Castro began his political career as a charismatic leader who led the fight to overthrow the pre-

Fidel Castro came to power as a charismatic freedom fighter but retained his position as Cuba's leader by exercising such dictatorial power as banning religion. On this historic visit to Cuba in January 1998, Pope John Paul II used the traditional authority of the papacy as well as his personal charisma to urge Castro to grant Cuban citizens greater civil rights and religious freedom. The pope also urged the United States to end the long embargo against Cuba that has contributed to that country's poverty.

vious, U.S.-backed Cuban dictator, Fulgencio Batista; to remain in power, however, Castro developed a political system that suppressed opposition.

Rational-legal authority derives from a formal system of rules or laws that specify who has the right to make which decisions and under what conditions. Authority is vested in the position or office, not in the person who temporarily occupies that position, and the officeholder's authority is clearly defined and limited. For example, the president of the United States does not have the authority to tell American couples to limit their families to two children; our Constitution protects individual liberty and our culture holds family matters as private.

While in office, the U.S. president is commander in chief of the armed forces. Once retired, the president has no more power over the armed forces than any other citizen, though he (and perhaps someday she) may exercise considerable influence on current leaders and public opinion.

Traditional, charismatic, and rational-legal authority are "ideal types," or abstractions of key characteristics. In practice, political systems depend on varying combinations of all three. Charisma plays a role in who gets elected president of the United States; once elected, the president has both rational-legal authority and the traditional authority that accompanies this position. Each year the president delivers a State of the Union address. This is the only occasion on which the three branches of government—members of the House and Senate, the justices of the Supreme Court, and cabinet ministers—gather on Capitol Hill. When President Clinton spoke in January 1998, a scandal regarding his personal behavior dominated the news. Yet for this hour, personal criticism and, to some degree, partisan politics were suspended:

> The strength of our country really does lie in the fact that when the President of the United States gives the State of the Union address we all rise and we all salute that office. [Representative John B. Kasich (Republican, Ohio), quoted in *The New York Times,* January 28, 1998, p. A1]

The United States and other modern political systems are the product of a long process of social and cultural evolution. Although the historical details vary from one country to another, certain basic patterns stand out.

The Development of Political Institutions

One of the defining characteristics of modern societies is the development of specialized political institutions. Modern societies have courts, legislatures, political parties, government agencies, a military, and an executive branch of government (the office of president, prime minister, or chair). Together these entities make up what sociologists call "the state."

Through most of human history, politics was woven into the fabric of everyday life. People did not distinguish between politics and kinship, civilians and police, social obligations and the law. An individual's personal responsibilities as the head of the household and public duties as an elder or warrior were one and the same. Kinship (extended to lineages, clans, and tribes) was the basis of social order, and power was concentrated in the hands of elders or heads of kin groups, not organizations.

The development of separate and distinct political institutions can be traced to the emergence of large-scale agrarian states about 3,000 years ago

President Bill Clinton delivered the State of the Union address on January 28, 1998, under a cloud of personal and political scandal. For this state occasion, politics were temporarily set aside; even Clinton's adversaries attended. The office of the President of the United States embodies rational-legal authority, regardless of the person who occupies that office at a given time.

(see Chapter 5). The most successful states were those in which a single ruler—supported by a hereditary elite, a priesthood, and an army—controlled key resources, including land and labor. Over time, the kingship, or office of king, came to be seen as sacred and eternal—above any particular king. In the great African kingdoms of Swazi and Zulu, for example, special care was taken to keep the kingship pure and its authority intact. Defeat in battle and other setbacks were blamed on lower officials; the absolute wisdom of the king was never questioned. The expression "The king is dead, long live the king" captures this idea. In other words, the kingship continues to operate, even though specific rulers come and go (Gluckman, 1965). The separation of the office of the king (or emperor or pharaoh) from the person who was king at any given time, the distinction between the public office and the private person, was a first step toward the development of states.

The kings and emperors in Europe during the Middle Ages were absolute monarchs who ruled by divine right, but their control over their dominions was more symbolic than actual. France, for example, was a patchwork of small, semiautonomous feudal territories. People were loyal to the church or to the local baron, not to the French monarch; they identified themselves as Burgundians or Normans, not as French. The same was true elsewhere. Monarchs of this period depended on the church to legitimize their rule and on the landed aristocracy to pay tribute and raise armies and thus enable them to remain in power.

The birth of nations in Europe was the result of two converging forces: (1) territorial expansion and (2) the growth of international trade (Mann, 1993). Between the sixteenth and nineteenth centuries, monarchs expanded and consolidated their territories through dynastic marriages, wars of conquest, and colonization of the Americas, Africa, and Asia.

The Aztec emperor Montezuma and Carlos V, the Spanish king whose soldiers deposed him, were both absolute monarchs who ruled by divine right. Both empires—Aztec and Spanish—had traditional kingships. The Spaniards were able to conquer the Aztecs by virtue of superior technology, including ships, horses, and guns.

By the mid-seventeenth century, Europeans saw the world as carved up into separate nations and their colonial territories, represented not only by lines on a map but also by a single monarch and a centralized government. At the same time, international trade—in grain, textiles, precious metals, spices, tea, and other "goods," including slaves—was expanding. The members of a newly rich merchant class called on kings to protect them from banditry within national boundaries and piracy on international routes. In turn, members of the merchant class or bourgeoisie were useful allies of the monarchs in their continuing struggles to limit the power of the landed aristocracy.

These new demands and responsibilities eventually led to the creation of large-scale public bureaucracies (Weber, 1922/1968). The consolidation of national territories and protection of trade required that rulers collect taxes, build roads, mobilize armies, and engage in innumerable other activities. The most effective states were those in which monarchs (1) established clear hierarchies of control, (2) created formal rules and regulations for state activities and rational criteria for the appointment of officials, and (3) emphasized separation of the public and private spheres.

The transition to rational-legal authority occurred in fits and starts. Many of the practices we consider "corruption" today—bribing officials, using public office for personal gain, and nepotism (family favoritism)—were accepted practice for some time to come. In structure, Europe's emerging states combined new political institutions with archaic methods of administration (J. Anderson, 1983). For instance, most European monarchs still raised revenues through "tax farming." Individuals were sold the right to collect taxes, with the understanding that they would pay a portion of what they collected to the king and keep the remainder for themselves. Tax collection was a private business, much like a McDonald's franchise or Ford dealership today. The military also reflected this combination of new and old methods of governing. As recently as World War I, the rank of officer in most European armies was restricted to "gentlemen," and men born into wealthy families could buy commissions as senior officers. This arrangement helped the government raise funds for war and allowed members of the elite to avoid the hazards of the front line. But it did not win wars. Establishing more efficient, ratio-

nal control of taxation and the military played a central role in the expansion and strengthening of modern states (Weber, 1922/1968; Tilly, Tilly, and Tilly, 1975; Levi, 1988).

The Modern State

In the twentieth century, the size and scope of the state increased dramatically. Prior to this time, the role of the state had been confined largely to providing defense against external threats and maintaining internal law and order. Except during times of war, most citizens had little contact with the government. Then, in the late nineteenth and early twentieth centuries, western (and other) nations began to take on responsibility for a wide range of collective goods (M. Olson, 1965). *Collective goods* are products and services that cannot easily be bought and sold by individuals but require major investments and coordinated efforts. An example is the U.S. National Park System, which was created in 1872 when Congress established Yellowstone National Park and today encompasses forty national parks and other areas totaling over 80 million acres. Beginning with the expansion of transportation and communication systems, the state became more involved in public education, housing, social security,

In the late nineteenth century, governments began to take on responsibility for collective goods. One result in the United States was the National Park Service, which administers parks such as Yellowstone, created in 1872.

public safety, and working conditions. The state also became more involved in managing the economy, using government spending and hiring, as well as government control over the printing and circulation of money and over interest rates, to buffer the public from sudden economic reversals.

This expansion of government activities and authority led to the evolution of the **welfare state,** in which the government assumes varying degrees of responsibility for the well-being of citizens. The Scandinavian countries, especially Sweden, and most western European countries are *social democracies,* in which most businesses are privately owned but the government protects workers (with a relatively high minimum wage, stringent safety standards, and extensive unemployment benefits) and provides a number of social services, including child care, national health programs, university tuition, and pensions, and its tax policies are designed to reduce economic inequality.

In the United States, the welfare state increased dramatically with President Franklin D. Roosevelt's New Deal, which established a wide range of programs [including Social Security, unemployment insurance, and the Federal Deposit Insurance Corporation (F.D.I.C.), which guarantees bank deposits] to help the country and individuals recover from the Great Depression of the 1930s. The welfare state grew again under the administration of President Lyndon B. Johnson with the passage of civil rights legislation and the creation of the Equal Opportunities Commission; the "War on Poverty" and the creation of Medicare and Medicaid, the expansion of Aid to Families with Dependent Children (or "welfare"), and cost-of-living increases in Social Security benefits; and the creation or expansion of federal regulatory agencies such as the Environmental Protection Agency.

One consequence of the adoption of welfare-state principles was enormous growth of the federal bureaucracy. In 1900, the federal government employed 26,000 workers; today some 3 million people (not counting armed forces) are on the federal payroll. In their campaigns and policies, Presidents Reagan and Bush targeted "big government" both as a drain on the federal budget and taxpayers and as an intrusion on individual liberty and private enterprise, and hence as an abuse of government authority. Under Prime Minister Margaret Thatcher, Britain also cut spending on social programs.

Citizens' Rights

Another major theme in modern history is the expansion in people's ideas of their rights (Barber, 1983). Whereas traditional political systems assign people different rights on the basis of kinship, gender, and age, modern rational-legal political systems usually ascribe the same basic rights to all (or most) citizens. In western nations, the spread of written constitutions in the eighteenth century played a key role in this development. Prior to this time, states did not have written rules and regulations that officials were obliged to follow if they wished to maintain legitimacy. Constitutions, as the name implies, constitute or create a rule-governed sociopolitical order. They may be based, as ours is, on philosophical traditions. But they always come into being through an act of political creation. As often as not, constitutions are the product of revolution. Moreover, where constitutions exist and are recognized, they are important vehicles for citizens to use in demanding their rights and enforcing ideas of legitimacy. For example, the U.S. Supreme Court does not decide on who is right and who is wrong in a case; rather, it decides whether the law being applied is constitutional.

In the second half of the twentieth century, the concept of *human rights,* rights that override any political or social system, gained at least verbal acceptance. Most modern political systems have adopted constitutions, hold elections, and claim to be acting in the people's name. But many are democracies in name only. Iraq, for example, holds elections, but all candidates are selected by the ruling Baathist party. The National People's Congress in China, also elected, is composed exclusively of members of the Communist party and serves as a rubber stamp for policies decided by the party's leadership. Opposition to nonrepresentative government may take the form of nationalist or religious movements (by the Kurds and Shiite Muslims in Iraq, for example), as well as calls for democracy. Even in democracies, women are still regarded as "outsiders" in politics. (See *A Global View*: Women and Politics.)

Politics in the United States

The political system of the United States is based on the ideal of democracy. Our political system emphasizes four main points:

A GLOBAL VIEW

Women and Politics

Opportunities for women have greatly increased in the past quarter-century, but women still do not enjoy full participation in society. Nowhere is this more evident than in the world of politics. Women have the right to vote almost everywhere; in fact, they make up over half of most electorates. But, with few exceptions, they still play only a very minor role in high-level political and economic decision making.

In top leadership positions, women are vastly underrepresented. Of the 159 member states of the United Nations, only six had women ambassadors in 1997 (Guinea, Jamaica, Kazakhstan, Liechtenstein, Trinidad and Tobago, and Turkmenistan). Women account for 30 percent of all UN employees, but less than 15 percent of senior management.

The story is much the same in national legislatures (see Table 14-1). Overall, only 10 percent of national parliamentarians are women. There is, however, considerable variation among countries. Only five countries in northern Europe have achieved the 30 percent threshold recommended by the United Nations Commission on the Status of Women in 1990.

> **Women in politics face most of the same barriers that limit them in other areas.**

The proportion of female legislators is highest in Scandinavia (on average, 37 percent) and Oceania (24 percent in New Zealand/Australia); moderate in Europe and North America (13 to 14 percent); and lowest in Asia, Africa, and South America (7 to 8 percent). Worldwide, very few women are cabinet ministers, and most are in such "soft" areas as education, culture, and women's affairs.

Women in politics face most of the same barriers that limit them in other areas (see Chapter 10). In addition, they may be held back by special circumstances that characterize politics. Traditionally, people have achieved decision-making government positions either through election or through a career in the civil service. Candidates for election are usually recruited from political parties, labor unions, and special-interest organizations, and women's access to leadership in these institutions has been limited. Likewise, though many women hold public sector jobs, the vast majority of these are at the lowest echelons.

Source: Naomi Neft and Ann D. Levine, *Where Women Stand: An International Report on the Status of Women in 140 Countries, 1997–1998,* New York: Random House, 1997.

- *Importance of the individual:* Our political institutions are designed to help the individual live a fuller life. The individual has "inalienable rights," which are specified in the Declaration of Independence as the right to life, liberty, and the pursuit of happiness. These rights existed before the state, and it is the state's duty to uphold them on behalf of the individual. At the same time, the Constitution is designed to protect individuals from unnecessary interference, or tyranny, by the state.
- *Consent of the governed:* Government derives its authority from the people. Every citizen has both the right and duty to participate in the democratic process—by voting, joining local party groups or interest groups, voicing political opinion in letters to elected representatives, and the like.

- *Majority rule and minority rights:* Elections are won and laws passed in accordance with the will of the majority, but this does not mean that minorities can be neglected or oppressed. Their rights—to vote, to be heard, to dissent—must be protected and upheld no less vigorously than those of the majority.
- *Equality of opportunity:* The Declaration of Independence proclaims that "all men are created equal." Obviously, some people are more intelligent, more creative, or more ambitious than others. In this sense, all people are not created equal. But in a democracy all individuals have the same freedom and rights and should have the same opportunities. The question of how to achieve equality of opportunity has been the subject of much

Table 14-1   *Women in National Legislatures Worldwide* (Percentage of Total Legislature and Cabinet)

Country	Legislature	Cabinet	Country	Legislature	Cabinet
Sweden	41%	52%	United States	11%	29%
Norway	39	39	Czech Republic	10	0
New Zealand	29	4	Dominican Republic	10	38
Germany	26	12	United Kingdom	10	8
South Africa	25	11	Israel	8	6
Cuba	23	12	Cambodia	6	0
Argentina	22	0	Bosnia-Herzegovina	5	0
China	21	8	France	5	13
Canada	19	23	Kenya	4	5
Vietnam	19	6	Korea, South	3	5
Costa Rica	16	8	Egypt2	9	
Nicaragua	16	6	Morocco	1	0
Mexico	14	12	Togo	1	5
Philippines	13	14	Kuwait	0	0
Bangladesh	11	10	Somalia	0	0

Source: Naomi Neft and Ann D. Levine, *Where Woman Stand: An International Report on the Status of Women in 140 Countries, 1997–1998,* (New York: Random House, 1997.

controversy in recent decades, as black citizens, women, and others have challenged the privileges traditionally granted only to white males. Programs designed to assist minorities (such as affirmative action, described in Chapter 9) have provoked mixed reactions.

One of the distinguishing features of American democracy is the *separation of powers.* The executive and legislative branches of government are elected separately and to some degree operate independently. The same is true at the state and local levels: the election of a governor or mayor is not tied to the election of state legislators or city council representatives. In addition, the judicial branch of government is separate from the other two. Federal judges are appointed by the president, subject to approval by Congress. Once appointed, however, judges are not responsible to either but are authorized to interpret the law according to their reading of the Constitution, which can be challenged only by a higher court. Justices to the Supreme Court (and other federal courts) are appointed for life, based on the ideal that they will not be influenced by political considerations or shifts in public opinion (as they might be if subject to periodic elections). In addition, American democracy is based on the concept of a federation, in which political authority is shared among national, state, and local jurisdictions. In Great Britain, parliament has to approve local laws; in the United States, state and local laws may be challenged through the courts but are not subject to review by the president or Congress. This complex system of overlapping jurisdictions was designed to create "checks and balances" that would make it difficult for any individual, party, or citizen group to seize control of the government.

How do the people exercise their democratic rights in the United States? What means are available for ordinary citizens to influence decisions about social programs, military expenditures, and other issues? Here we will look not only at the two traditional forms of political participation, voting and political parties, but also at interest groups, political action committees (PACs), and protest movements.

Electoral Politics: The American Voter

In the United States today, we consider the principle of "one person, one vote" a cornerstone of democracy. This was not always so. When this nation was founded, voting was a privilege, not a universal right. Only white male property owners were eligible. In the nineteenth century, the vote was extended to all adult men (including, in theory, black men). Only in the twentieth century were women (1920), Native Americans (1924), and 18-year-olds (1972) included. And not until 1965 did the Voting Rights Act make the right to vote a political reality for African Americans.

In practice, however, few Americans take advantage of their basic right of suffrage. About one-third of eligible voters (70 million people) are not registered to vote, and many of those who are registered do not vote, even in presidential elections. Only 63 percent of registered voters went to the polls in 1960 (Kennedy versus Nixon), and slightly more than 50 percent did so in 1988 (Bush versus Dukakis), the lowest turnout in sixty-four years (*Congressional Quarterly,* 1989). In 1992, the presidential race was a three-way contest among Bush, Clinton, and maverick Texas billionaire, Ross Perot. This election did draw the highest number of voters ever (104 million) and 55 percent of eligible voters cast their ballots. (See Figure 14-2.) In 1996 (Clinton versus Dole), less than half of eligible voters

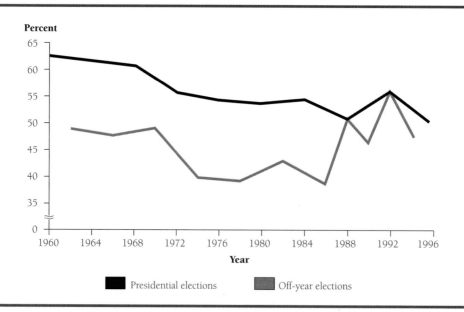

Figure 14-2   *Voter Turnout in National Elections, 1960–1996*

Low voter turnout suggests that many Americans view politics as something "other people do."

Sources: Committee for the Study of the American Electorate; U.S. Bureau of the Census, *Statistical Abstract of the United States, 1992,* Washington, DC: GPO, 1992, p. 269, table 435; *Current Population Survey,* November 1994, table 14.

(48.8 percent) went to the polls. (The voter turnout in nonpresidential elections is even smaller—about one-third of eligible voters.) This pattern contrasts sharply with that of other western nations, where 70 to 85 percent of citizens vote regularly. In Australia, there is a penalty for not voting!

One reason voter turnout in the United States is low may be obstacles to voter registration. In the nineteenth century, elections typically drew between 70 and 80 percent of eligible voters. Around the turn of the century, however, state governments imposed numerous legal restrictions, such as literacy requirements and grandfather clauses, designed to prevent, or make it difficult (and dangerous) for, African Americans in the south and immigrants in the north to register and vote. Even after the Voting Rights Act was passed, complicated procedures discouraged some citizens (especially poor minority-group members and non-English speakers) from exercising their rights. In recent years, both federal and state governments have liberalized electoral procedures. In 1993, Congress passed the National Voter Registration Act, known as the "motor voter" bill, which requires states to provide voter registration forms at motor vehicle offices, military recruiting stations, and welfare offices. In just the first three months after the bill went into effect, on January 1, 1995, 2 million Americans registered to vote for the first time, the largest increase in U.S. history; 20 million more were expected to register before the 1996 elections (National League of Women Voters, 1997). But this does not explain the low turnout of registered voters.

Low voter turnout may be an expression of apathy and alienation from the political system. Some people may ignore politics because they find the issues confusing; others may feel that regardless of who gets elected, nothing much changes; and still others may see politics as something "other people take care of" (Lapham, 1991). Or, apathy may indicate that most people are satisfied with the current state of affairs (Kaplan, 1997).

One observer summarized political participation in the United States this way:

> About one-third of the American adult population can be characterized as politically apathetic or passive; in most cases they are unaware, literally, of the political part of the world around them. Another 60 percent play largely spectator roles; they watch, they cheer, they vote, but they do not battle. . . . The percentage

of gladiators does not exceed five to seven percent. (Milbraith, quoted in Verba and Nie, 1972, p. 28)

As a general rule, white, affluent, college-educated Americans are most likely to exercise their political rights, not only by voting but also by working for a political party or candidate, contributing to campaigns, participating in community groups, and the like. Poor, young members of minority groups with little education have historically been the least likely to do so. This situation may be changing, however. Increasing numbers of African Americans and, to a lesser degree, Latinos are both registering and voting. As a result, members of previously unrepresented minorities have been elected mayor in a number of major cities. On the other hand, more well-educated, well-off, and/or white citizens are choosing not to vote (Teixeira, 1988).

Party Politics

A ***political party*** is a collectivity organized to gain and hold legitimate control of government. (The difference between a party and a social movement, described in Chapter 17, is that a party has a formal, bureaucratic structure.) Ideally, political parties function to link individual citizens to the government by translating public opinion into legislation and mobilizing popular support for government policies. They also serve to recruit candidates for public office and to link the various branches of government (state, federal, and local; the executive, legislative, and judicial). In many ways, the two-party, presidential system in the United States is unique.

Party politics in this country are shaped by the fact that our political system is a *presidential democracy,* in which the executive and legislative branches of government are separate. The president is elected directly by the people,[1] as are members of the House and Senate. Thus a Democratic president may preside over a predominantly Republican

---

[1] Actually, the president and vice president are not elected directly by voters but by the electoral college. Each state is represented by a number of electors based on the number of senators and representatives that state sends to Congress. Because some states have more electors than others do, a candidate who wins a majority of votes in the electoral college but not a majority of the popular vote may be elected. We have had ten "minority" presidents, including Bill Clinton, Richard Nixon, John Kennedy, Harry Truman, and Abraham Lincoln.

Congress (as Clinton has since 1994), or a Republican president may preside over a predominantly Democratic Congress (as in the Reagan and Bush administrations). The president has the authority to veto laws passed by Congress; likewise, Congress can override presidential vetoes with a two-thirds majority vote.

In the *parliamentary democracies* of Europe and Asia, people do not vote directly for the head of state. Rather, they vote for local representatives or for a party; the party that wins a majority of seats in parliament then selects a prime minister from within its ranks. There are no primary elections; rather, candidates for the different seats are selected by party officials. As a result, political parties tend to be highly organized and exercise strict discipline over their active members. A prime minister can count on votes from members of his or her party. A representative who does not vote the party line will not be nominated in future elections. If a prime minister cannot deliver a majority vote, however, he or she is required by law to call for new elections.

In contrast, political parties in the United States are loosely organized coalitions of national, state, and local groups. There are as many divisions within parties as between them. Because members of Congress are elected independently, the president has no control over how members of his party vote, and he may spend as much time courting them as he does battling the opposition. An example was the 1993 North American Free Trade Agreement (NAFTA) between the United States, Canada, and Mexico, which eliminated tariffs, licensing requirements, and other barriers to free trade among these countries. Both the Democratic leaders in Congress and labor leaders (who traditionally support Democrats) opposed NAFTA, while many Republicans and some Democrats supported the agreement. To get NAFTA through Congress, Democratic President Clinton had to persuade Democrats as well as Republicans. Clinton also faced opposition within his own party in the 1996 and 1997 debates over welfare reform and a balanced budget.

In parliamentary democracies, minority parties can have a significant impact. For many years, Italians voted for political parties, not specific candidates, and party leaders selected individual representatives proportionately. Thus a party that received 10 percent of the vote was allocated 10

In parliamentary democracies such as Israel, small, minority parties can wield considerable power. Here right-wing demonstrators protest then–Prime Minister Yitzak Rabin's 1993 agreement with the Palestinians. Israel's religious right led not only to Rabin's assassination in 1995 but also to a change in government and the eventual stalemate of the peace process.

percent of seats in the legislature.[2] If no one party wins a majority in an election, the leading party has to form a coalition with one or more smaller parties. In proposing legislation, the majority party has

---

[2] Since 1994, three-quarters of national representatives in Italy are elected directly.

to take the wishes of this minority party into account. In Israel, for example, orthodox religious parties, representing a small minority of voters, exercise considerable power because neither of the two major parties has been able to capture a majority in the legislature. The orthodox parties want to retain the West Bank and build settlements there. Although a majority of Israelis are willing to return the land, the orthodox minority has blocked such an agreement in parliament.

Unlike most other democracies, the United States has only two major political parties. In Germany, by contrast, voters choose among five parties: the Christian Democratic Union (CCU), the Socialist Democratic Party (SPD), the Free Democratic Party (FDP), the Party of Democratic Socialism (PDS), and the Green Party. European political parties offer quite specific policies and programs to voters. Our Democratic and Republican parties are less ideological. Democrats tend to be liberal; Republicans, conservative. But the differences between them are not always clear. With some exceptions, both have avoided taking strong political positions in order to appeal to a wide range of voters. As sociologist Robert Michels observed long ago (1915/1949), in a two-party system both parties tend to voice "centrist" opinions. Since Democrats can count on nearly all "left-wing votes," and Republicans on nearly all "right-wing votes," both must compete for the center. In his first term—and before the 1996 election—President Clinton moved toward the center by signing a welfare reform billing and submitting a deficit-reducing balanced budget—two acts Republicans had long supported and Democrats had opposed. When there are three or more parties, each is likely to adopt a specific ideology that appeals to a specific sector of the electorate.

Third parties (such as New York's Liberal party) have had some impact at the state and local level, but rarely at the national level, in the United States. The 1992 presidential election was an exception. In the most successful third-party bid for national office in recent decades, Texas billionaire Ross Perot received 19 million of 104 million votes.[3] Perot

campaigned for more financially responsible, businesslike government, beginning with reduction of the national deficit and a balanced budget. Clearly, Perot struck a responsive chord. But exactly what chord is unknown. Perhaps people voted for Perot because of his outspoken manner; perhaps they felt that a successful businessman could do a better job of running the country than a politician; perhaps they were casting a protest ("none of the above") vote. Although Perot did not receive nearly enough votes to be elected president, if all the votes cast for Perot had been cast for President George Bush, Bush might have been elected to a second term. Perot ran again in 1996, but attracted little attention and received less than 9 percent of votes. In general, third-party candidates are seen as "spoilers" who may affect the outcome of an election even though they have no chance of winning, and votes for third-party candidates are considered a waste.

Most European political parties are closely associated with a particular social class (for example, labor parties represent the working class; social democrats, the middle class; and conservatives, the upper class). In this country, the Democratic party traditionally has been identified with the working class, minorities, and "the underdog"; the Republican party, with business and "fat cats." For much of this century, Americans did vote along social class lines. Unionized workers and members of minority groups (especially African Americans) still tend to be pro-Democrat; college graduates, professionals, and people with high incomes, to be pro-Republican. But party loyalty in the United States is on the decline.

In the 1940s and 1950s, study after study found that Americans sided with either one party or the other—usually the one their parents supported—and voted for that party's candidates in almost all elections. In the 1960s and 1970s, however, this began to change: more voters identified themselves as "independents" or were "crossovers," who voted for a different party from that in which they registered (see Figure 14-3).

Increasingly, politics in the United States has become less party-oriented and more issue-oriented. For example, the Republican party has aligned itself with right-to-life or antiabortion forces, an issue that cuts across party lines. Indeed, in 1997–1998 the Republican National Committee (RNC) refused to support Republican candidates who were

---

[3] In 1968, the American Independent Party candidate, George Wallace, received 9.9 million of 73.2 million votes cast in the presidential election. In 1980, John Anderson got 7 million of 85.5 million votes—just a million short of the margin by which Republican Ronald Reagan beat Democratic incumbent President Jimmy Carter.

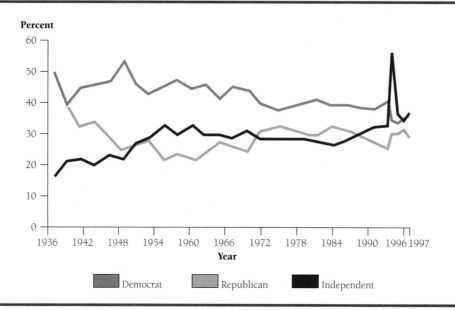

Figure 14-3   *Declining Party Loyalty?*

For more than fifty years, the Gallup poll has asked voters, "In politics, as of today, do you consider yourself a Republican, a Democrat, or an Independent?" (Respondents who gave replies other than Democrat, Republican, or Independent were excluded.)

Source: The Gallup Organization, data compiled November 21 to 23, 1997.

pro-choice. The Democratic party supports abortion rights. Democrats have taken a strong stand on gun control; Republicans have taken a strong stand on crime control and are more likely to support imprisonment of "drug-only offenders" so-called three-strike laws, and the death penalty (see Chapter 7). Democrats are more likely to support environmental protection, while Republicans oppose any government regulation. In general, Democrats support increases in welfare and social spending, while Republicans seek to cut social spending and increase the budget for defense.

Likewise, American voters have become more issue-oriented—more inclined to see such issues as economic policy, environmental pollution, and abortion as having a direct impact on their lives. They vote for a candidate because that person supports their own views on particular issues, not simply because he or she is a Democrat or Republican. This has been more of a blow to Democrats than to Republicans. Although registered Democrats outnumber registered Republicans by a wide margin, Republicans won a majority of seats in Congress in

1994 and again in 1996. Yet the same voters reelected a Democratic president. One consequence of the decline in party loyalty is that candidates have turned increasingly to special-interest groups, the media, and media consultants for assistance.

Interest Groups and Political Action Committees

An *interest group* is an organization created to pressure public officials to make decisions that will benefit its members or promote a particular cause. Many Americans think of lobbyists as operating outside the conventional or legitimate political system. When asked why our government is not working better than it is, a large majority cite "too much influence on government by special interest groups and lobbies" (Etzioni, 1982). In fact, interest groups have been part of the American political system from the beginning. The term "lobbies" comes from the old practice of cornering officials in the lobbies of government buildings to plead a case. The First Amendment to the Constitution recognizes the right of citizens to petition the government. But it is doubtful that the authors of that amendment envisioned lobbying as we know it today.

Under a lobby reform act that took effect on January 1, 1996, lobbyists and lobbying firms are required to register with the Senate, provide a list of their staff and their clients, and submit a general description of the issues they are lobbying for. According to the first report, 9,219 lobbyists (almost 20 for every member of Congress) were working for 2,929 firms or organizations, including such diverse groups as the National Association of Manufacturers and the AFL-CIO, the National Milk Producers Association and the Distilled Spirits Council, the John Birch Society and the American Civil Liberties Union, the National Organization for Women (NOW) and the right-to-life movement. The giant delivery firm Federal Express—alone—employs twenty-eight lobbyists to represent its interests in aviation, highways, and labor and pension laws among other issues. Lobbying firms often hire former government officials and government employees who are familiar with how things are done in Washington. For example, the staff of Preston Gates & Rouvelas Meeds—which represents clients ranging from Microsoft and Court TV to the Muckleshoot Indian tribe in Washington state—includes previous aides to the Senate Foreign Relations

"Gucci Gulch," where well-heeled lobbyists congregate in the corridors of the U.S. Capitol. Lobbyists' power is derived from two main sources: money and information.

Committee, former House Speaker Thomas Foley, former Senator Bob Packwood, and two members of the House of Representatives.

One of the most powerful and successful pressure groups is the National Rifle Association (NRA). For years the NRA blocked gun control legislation, even though polls showed that the majority of Americans, along with most law enforcement agencies, favored strong controls. The NRA both lobbied Congress and made large contributions to legislators who support its position. The Brady bill, named for James S. Brady, the White House press secretary who was severely wounded in a 1981 assassination attempt on President Reagan, was first proposed in 1987. The bill requires that the purchaser of a handgun wait five business days before taking possession, so that local law enforcement can check the person's background for evidence of criminal activity or mental instability. The bill makes no mention of assault or hunting rifles. Even supporters of the bill acknowledged that it was only a first step. Still the NRA fought it, on the grounds that once the door was open, stricter gun controls would be imposed. The Brady bill was passed in 1993 after a seven-year battle and perhaps 70,000 handgun homicides. The NRA continues to lobby to repeal or at least revise this law and spent more than $1 million to support friendly candidates (mostly Republican) in the 1996 federal election campaigns.

Interest groups derive power from two main sources: information and money. In a single session of Congress, a legislator may be asked to vote on hundreds of bills dealing with issues ranging from sex education in high schools to nuclear energy plants. Lobbyists are walking encyclopedias in their particular areas. They may answer legislators' questions about a particular bill, draft speeches for them, or even draft legislation. This is not necessarily as sinister as it sounds. A lobbyist's effectiveness depends in part on trust. Supplying misinformation would be a violation of that trust and would limit the lobbyist's influence in the future. Nevertheless, expertise does give lobbyists a hold over public officials.

But the most direct and effective way of influencing elected officials is through campaign contributions, as suggested at the beginning of this chapter. Between January 1995 and June 1996, the fifty largest campaign donors—corporations, unions, and trade associations, all prohibited by law from making direct contributions to candidates—

donated more than $800,000 each to the candidates they supported (see Figure 14-4 for the top fifteen donors). How was this possible? Did these donors violate the law? The answer (in almost all cases) is, no; rather, they took advantage of loopholes.

In 1974, after the Watergate scandal that drove President Richard Nixon from office, Congress passed the Federal Campaign Finance Law, which sets limits on the amount of money that can be collected and spent by candidates for the presidency and Congress during election campaigns. At the same time Congress created the Federal Election Commission (FEC) as an independent regulatory agency charged with administering and enforcing campaign statutes. Under the 1974 law, corporations and unions are prohibited from making direct contributions to candidates for federal office. Individual contributions to federal elections are limited to $2,000 per candidate ($1,000 each for a primary and general election) and a total of $25,000 per

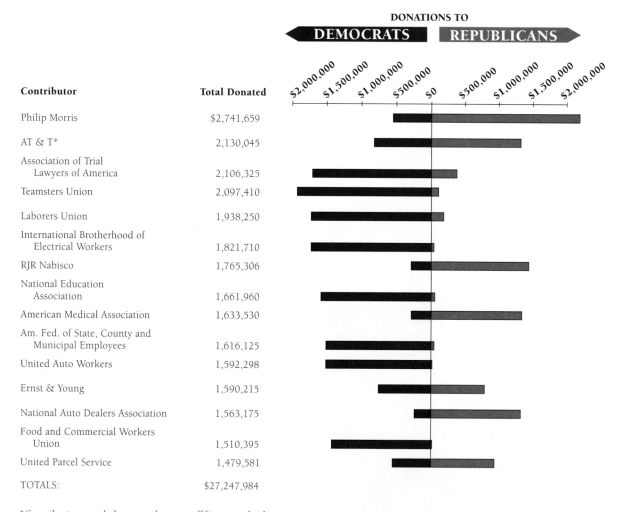

Contributor	Total Donated
Philip Morris	$2,741,659
AT & T*	2,130,045
Association of Trial Lawyers of America	2,106,325
Teamsters Union	2,097,410
Laborers Union	1,938,250
International Brotherhood of Electrical Workers	1,821,710
RJR Nabisco	1,765,306
National Education Association	1,661,960
American Medical Association	1,633,530
Am. Fed. of State, County and Municipal Employees	1,616,125
United Auto Workers	1,592,298
Ernst & Young	1,590,215
National Auto Dealers Association	1,563,175
Food and Commercial Workers Union	1,510,395
United Parcel Service	1,479,581
TOTALS:	$27,247,984

*Contributions made by more than one affiliate or subsidiary.

Figure 14-4   *The Fifteen Largest Contributors to the 1996 Federal Campaigns*

This figure shows only the tip of the iceberg: the fifty largest donors together contributed $63.7 million to the 1996 federal campaigns.

Source: Center for Responsible Politics: *The Providence Sunday Journal,* Jan. 5, 1997, p. D4.

year. Individual donations to a political party are limited to $20,000 a year. The 1974 law also provides grants to presidential candidates in the form of matching funds: candidates who accept the federal grant must agree not to exceed the spending limit determined by the FEC (in 1996, $62 million). As is often the case, however, a law limiting certain activities opens a door for other activities that law does not cover.

For example, the 1974 campaign law did not cover combined contributions and so led to the growth of political action committees. **Political action committees (PACs)** are organizations formed by interest groups to collect small contributions from large numbers of people to be donated to candidates who support their particular cause or position. Because PACs make contributions to more than one candidate, individuals are allowed to make donations of up to $5,000 for a given primary or election. And because PACs pool donations from many individuals, they wield considerable political influence. Although most of the first PACs were organized by the so-called New Right, they now cover the political spectrum.

Another loophole was party contributions or "soft money"—now the most rapidly growing source of political financing (as discussed at the beginning of this chapter). The 1974 campaign-finance law applies only to contributions to and expenditures by *candidates*. It does not place limits on the amounts corporations, unions, or other organizations may donate to *parties* or the amounts parties may spend for administrative and other general or "party-building" activities. Indeed, in the summer of 1996, the U.S. Supreme Court ruled that legal restrictions on the amount political parties collect from organizations or spend on "issue advertising" are a violation of the right to free speech under the First Amendment (*Colorado Republican Federal Campaign Committee et al. v. Federal Election Committee*). Since 1992, when the FEC ruled that party donations must be reported, soft money contributions have climbed from $89 billion to $107 billion in 1994 (a nonpresidential election) to an estimated $250 billion in 1996, about evenly divided between the Democratic and Republican parties. The ways in which parties use soft money have also expanded. At first used for such activities as distributing "Vote Democratic" or "Vote Republican" bumper stickers and voter registration and get-out-

the-vote drives, a large proportion of party funds is now spent on television advertisements. Especially in the 1996 elections, the line between advertisements for issues and those for candidates became increasingly blurred. As long as the ad did not specifically say, "Vote for Candidate X," it qualified as an issue ad and thus as legal use of soft money. One example was a short biography of Senator Bob Dole, produced and aired by the Republican National Party (RNC), which failed to state directly that Dole was running for president (Rosenbaum, 1997).

Television advertising plays a key, if not deciding, role in U.S. elections at all levels (and is a major reason for the high cost of running for office). For example, in 1994 the Republicans captured a majority of the seats in Congress for the first time in forty years. Many observers attributed this victory to a powerful, issue-oriented TV campaign, financed by the Republican party, to discredit Clinton's health care initiative (and, by extension, Democratic support of "big government"), on the one hand, and to promote Newt Gingrich's "Contract with America" (and, by extension, Republican advocacy of cutting big government), on the other. As a result, Clinton lost not only a Democratic majority in Congress but also support among Democratic party members, many of whom blamed him for the Republican landslide. Reportedly, Clinton and his campaign advisers decided to "fight fire with fire." Beginning in August 1995, and continuing through the election, the Democratic National Committee (DNC) saturated the media with ads attacking Republican positions. Although none of the ads specifically said "Support President Clinton," the implication was clear. Clinton's ratings in public opinion polls, and therefore his credibility in his own party, rose steadily. The ad campaign cost an estimated $1 to $1.5 million a week.

What impact have campaign-finance regulations and loopholes had on the political scene? When PACs first appeared, they seemed to dilute the power of the major political parties (Stanley and Niemi, 1988). For example, in the past, business groups usually supported Republican candidates. But PACs, in particular, are interested in specific issues, not party policy. They support candidates who are likely to further their interests, regardless of their party affiliations. For example, a PAC representing mining interests might support a Republican candidate for the Senate who opposes strict environmental regulations or a Democratic candidate for the state senate who is looking for ways to create new jobs in his or her district. A second effect of PACs has been the promotion of single-issue politics and elections in which the candidate's stand on a particular issue (such as regulation of car insurance or the establishment of the death penalty) counts more than general political philosophy or experience.

Critics argue that PACs have undermined the goals of campaign reform, that they have too much influence on politics and politicians, and that their contributions should be strictly limited. However, others feel PACs perform useful functions: they provide a new avenue through which citizens can influence the government, introduce new issues into political debates, and serve as checks and balances on each other.

The Supreme Court ruling on contributions to parties and increasing importance of soft money has had the opposite effect, at least to some degree. Now corporations, unions, and other organizations that seek "access" to high-level government officials and no doubt hope to influence decisions must make donations through national parties. But this does not necessarily mean that parties have more power. To the contrary, large donations may cause parties to support candidates and espouse policies that favor their donors.

To deny the influence of campaign donations on party politics would be wishful thinking. To cite just one example, over the past quarter-century Archer-Daniels-Midland Co. and its chairman, Dwayne Andreas, have contributed millions of dollars to both parties and to numerous candidates. Is it coincidence that the government has allowed multibillion-dollar tax breaks for ethanol, one of the company's chief products (Rosenbaum, 1997)?

Clearly, big money counts, which may be a reason why many Americans do not bother to vote. But just as clearly, citizens can and do have an impact on government policies and decisions.

Protest Movements

A *protest movement* is a grassroots effort to change established policies and practices (see Chapter 17). The 1960s and 1970s were decades of protest in the United States, beginning with the civil rights movement and continuing with the antiwar movement, the women's movement, and others. The overall level of political activism may have declined in the 1980s and 1990s, but protest remains an important form of political expression. Laws prohibiting smoking in public places and stricter enforcement of laws against drunk driving are just two examples of grassroots movements.

Protest movements mobilize people who either had not been aware of an issue or had not had the power or organization to make themselves heard. Like other interest groups, they may hire lobbyists and seek to influence legislators through contributions and letter-writing campaigns. But they are also willing to use social disruption as a tactic for capturing public attention, attracting the media, and persuading legislators of their strength. The movement to alert the public to the AIDS epidemic illustrates the strengths and weaknesses of protest movements. The fight against AIDS began not in the gay community but among the group of doctors who identified the HIV virus and described how it was transmitted. They then had to convince homosexuals that the dangers of the epidemic vastly outweighed the potential backlash against gay people (Shilts, 1987). By the mid-1980s the gay community had mobilized with the help of celebrities, notably Elizabeth Taylor after the death from AIDS of her fellow actor and friend, Rock Hudson. But this was—and still is—an uphill battle.

Some AIDS groups used conventional tactics, such as lobbying the government and holding fund-raisers, while others, notably Act Up, employed shock—disrupting church services, "outing" (publishing the names of) high-status homosexuals who had remained in the closet, and attempting to deliver a casket bearing an AIDS victim to the White House. Perhaps due to continuing pressure, the Clinton administration has stood by its promise to increase funding for AIDS research and appoint an AIDS "czar" to coordinate government activities. A red AIDS ribbon in coat lapels is a common sight. The approximately 3,500 AIDS organizations in the United States today seek to educate the public and lobby the government, as well as offer information about treatment, support groups, and care to AIDS victims. But mobilization has become more difficult as new groups (especially intravenous drug users, their partners, and their babies, most of whom are poor members of minority groups) become infected. Moreover, public recognition may prove as

Protest movements, such as the fight against AIDS, use both conventional means of influencing opinion and legislation and unconventional means, such as protests and social disruption.

much of an obstacle as initial public revulsion. AIDS is in danger of becoming "old news." Shortly before he died, journalist and AIDS victim Jeffrey Schmalz (1993) wrote:

> Now, 12 years after it was first recognized as a new disease, AIDS has become normalized, part of the landscape. It is at once everywhere and nowhere, the leading cause of death among young men nationwide, but little threat to the core of American political power, the white heterosexual suburbanite. . . . The world is moving on, uncaring, frustrated and bored, leaving by the roadside those of us who are infected and who can't help but wonder: Whatever happened to AIDS?

"Normalization" is a problem for all protest movements, particularly for groups who, as Schmalz notes, lack conventional political power.

Protest movements may be narrowly self-interested, concerned with only a minor reform, such as a community group that organizes to fight plans to run a highway through its neighborhood. Or they may be radical in their aims, seeking fundamental changes in existing institutions. The animal rights movement is an example. For thousands of years, people have used animals for food and clothing, as beasts of burden, as pets, as entertainment, and most recently in scientific experiments. The idea that nonhuman animals are sentient creatures (conscious beings with feelings and emotions) and have rights, just as human animals do, challenges basic beliefs and practices. Activists have used a wide range of tactics, from lobbying for stronger legislation and enforcement of existing laws to organizing demonstrations and boycotts, undercover investigations, and laboratory break-ins by the Animal Liberation Front.

Although the AIDS and animal rights movements may seem to have little in common, both developed outside conventional political channels. Both seek to change public attitudes and influence government policy. And both have had an impact. Increasingly, AIDS victims are viewed less often as "immoral lepers" (Schmalz, 1993), and fur coats are no longer universally accepted as status symbols.

Power in America: Who Rules?

The preceding discussion of participation in the American political system addressed the question of whether it is indeed "we the people" who govern—whether through voting, political parties, and collective action—or whether our government is itself governed by well financed, organized private interests. What light can sociology shed on who actually rules America?

Since President Clinton was elected to his first term in 1992, Congress and the executive branch (the president and his cabinet) have addressed such important issues as health care reform, which Congress rejected in 1993–1994; welfare reform, which stalled in 1995 but passed in 1996; and a balanced budget, which was enacted in 1997. Trade agreements, tax cuts, a ban on late-term abortions, and other social issues are the subjects of ongoing, heated debate. The federal government also confronted such issues as whether to maintain peacekeeping forces in the former Yugoslavia, whether to use bombs to force Iraq's president, Saddam Hussein, to comply to UN sponsored inspection of arms production, and whether to maintain trade ties with China despite the Chinese government's well-documented violations of human rights. Why did the drive for welfare reform succeed whereas calls for health care reform failed? What determines which proposals become the law of the land and which do not? The answer depends on how one views the structure of power in the United States. Different sociologists have suggested different answers.

The Pluralist View

Pluralists hold that power in the United States is shared among a multitude of competing interest groups, some represented by elected officials, lobbyists, and PACs, and others more diffuse. The advantage of pluralism, according to sociologist David Riesman (1950), is that competition among these interest groups prevents power from being concentrated in the hands of a ruling elite. Although groups may develop alliances around a given issue, these alliances are constantly dissolving and reforming. The disadvantage of pluralism is that interest groups may become "veto groups": even though a group lacks the resources to push through a program, it may be able to block other programs. The result may be "gridlock": with many groups pushing in different directions, nothing gets done.

In his campaign for president, Clinton pledged to "end welfare as we know it," but what exactly that would entail was uncertain. The issue moved to center stage in the 1994 federal and state elections. Cutbacks in welfare benefits, time limits for welfare recipients, work requirements, and other limits were supported by Republicans, some conservative Democrats, and state legislatures and governors but opposed by liberal Democrats, child and family advocates, and others. Various proposals were negotiated and renegotiated for more than two years before the Personal Responsibility and Work Opportunity Act of 1996 was passed by both houses of Congress and signed into law by the pres-

ident in the summer of 1996 (see Chapter 8). In the next session of Congress, however, some of the more controversial provisions (such as denying benefits to legal immigrants) were repealed. This is a common pattern: bills are debated and negotiated, enacted into law, and later revised.

As pluralists would predict, in some cases (such as health care reform) opposing and crosscutting interests lead to inaction. Indeed, in the winter of 1995–1996, the federal government was shut down for nearly a month because opposing groups in Congress and the president could not agree on the issue of a balanced budget.

The Power Elite

C. Wright Mills (1956) advanced a very different view of American society, the power-elite perspective. According to Mills, the pluralist view is a romanticized distortion of the truth. Yes, interest groups and lobbies exist, he wrote, but they—and Congress as well—make up a secondary level of power in American society. Most decisions of real national and international importance are made on a primary level, by the power elite. (Ordinary citizens, powerless and unorganized, make up the third level.)

The power elite is not a conspiracy but a dominant set of groups—almost entirely male—who occupy the highest positions in the executive branch of the government, in the military, and in giant corporations and financial institutions. Frequently members move from one of these three power centers to another, as when a business leader is named to the president's cabinet or a retired general joins the board of a large corporation. No one of the three components dominates; rather, each cooperates with the others, manipulating the public through the mass media. The power elite is motivated by the desire to maintain power and behind-the-scenes control, as well as by opportunities for financial gain. Although inherently conservative, the power elite may support or oppose social change to protect its position and advance its interests.

According to this view, the power elite supported welfare reform because it transferred power from the federal to state governments and hence reduced the power of both the president and Congress. The power elite opposed health care reform because a federal program would weaken the power of business leaders [who are now free to select or reject health insurance programs and health maintenance organizations (HMOs) from the private sector] and top military officials (who oversee plans for veterans and military retirees).

The influence of this ruling clique is most obvious in military appropriations. The military not only provides for national defense but also awards multimillion-dollar contracts to defense manufacturers, which in turn make large contributions to political parties and candidates and provide high-level jobs for former government officials, as well as employing large numbers of civilians. Mills referred to this coalition of economic, political, and military interests as "military capitalism." With the collapse of the Soviet Union and the end of the cold war, the military had to justify its requests for peacetime appropriations. The official explanation for the war in the Persian Gulf was that Iraq violated international law when it invaded neighboring Kuwait. From the power-elite perspective, the underlying motive was to demonstrate the ongoing need for a well-equipped military. In September 1997, 100 nations endorsed a land-mine treaty that would ban the use, production, and development of antipersonnel land mines and require that countries destroy their stockpiles and remove any mines they have laid (Bonner, 1997). The U.S. rejected the treaty on grounds of national security. From the power-elite perspective, the underlying motive was to protect military capitalism: profits from the sale of land mines and other military equipment to other countries average $12 billion a year. In October 1997, the president and members of Congress blocked passage of a "Code of Conduct" bill that would ban military aid to countries with undemocratic governments and records of human rights abuse (Gedda, 1997). Opponents claim the code might be used to block arms sales to Israel and other U.S. allies. An equally plausible explanation is that the power elite depends on military ties to other countries and does not want "civilian interference."

The Instrumental View

A third way of looking at power in America, the instrumentalist perspective, was advanced by G. William Domhoff (1967, 1983). Domhoff argues that power resides not in the hands of a small clique who occupy positions of authority but in a national upper class. Members of this class may use their wealth to run for public office, sit on corporate boards, or serve in the military. What distinguishes them is not their personal achievements but their inherited wealth. Members of the upper class are recognizable by such criteria as listing in the Social Register, education at certain schools, membership in certain clubs, and family connections through intermarriage. Power is wielded by "members of the upper class who have the interest and ability to involve themselves in protecting and enhancing the privileged social position of their class" (1983, p. 2).

This view explains why proposals for health care reform failed. The current system, in which the quality of care a person receives depends in large part on ability to pay, serves upper-class interests. Doctors—whose six-figure incomes place them in this category—were among those mobilizing to protect their incomes and prevent their costs from rising. Even before specific proposals were put forward, the American Medical Association began a massive ad campaign and wrote to over 700,000 physicians and medical students, warning that the administration's plan threatened to limit patients' choices and undermine the quality of treatment.

In contrast, NAFTA and other trade agreements serve the interests of big business, against the opposition of labor unions, who fear loss of jobs, as well as environmentalists, who fear current regulation of fishing and other activities will be diluted or ignored. Likewise, welfare reform—often referred to as "workfare"—expands the pool of workers who will be forced to accept minimum-wage jobs with few or no benefits, as well as part-time, seasonal employment.

The Structuralist View

Sociologists who adopt the structuralist perspective agree that power is concentrated in the hands of a few but argue that social class is less important than influence over corporate profits and the stock and bond markets. Above all, the government must maintain a healthy economy (Neubeck, 1991). To do so, politicians must satisfy the demands of corporate boards of directors, the heads of financial institutions, and stock and bond traders. In setting the political agenda, proposing legislation, and voting for or against bills, government leaders first consider the potential impact on large-scale investors (Woodward, 1994).

From the structuralist perspective, public policy reflects capitalist interests. Policies are most likely to be translated into programs, and proposals enacted into law, if they benefit all sectors of this economic structure. Structuralists would argue, for example, that U.S. foreign policy is based more on what is best for the U.S. economy than on such stated principles as promoting democracy, civilian government, and human rights.

These different views of the structure of power in the United States are not mutually exclusive: opposing interest groups, members of both the power elite and the upper class, and economic considerations all influence the outcome of political debate. In some cases, the power elite or a strong, well-funded interest group may prevail; in most cases, the translation of policies and proposals into laws is the result of trade-offs and compromise.

Politics around the Globe

How does the American political system compare with the systems in other countries? Only by comparing our system with others can we recognize and evaluate our own political institutions and our own cultural assumptions about power and authority.

Types of Political Systems

Political systems can be divided into two broad categories, authoritarian rule, in which the state claims a monopoly on the legitimate uses of power, and democratic government, in which authority rests in the hands of the people. Within these categories, there are a number of variations. Here we will analyze different types of political systems and describe contemporary examples.

Authoritarian Political Systems

In **authoritarian political systems**, the state claims an exclusive right to exercise political power, and ordinary people are denied the right to participate in government. The three main types of authoritarian rule are monarchy, dictatorship, and totalitarianism.

In a *monarchy,* one person inherits the right to be head of state, as king or queen, emperor or empress, czar, or kaiser. Up to the eighteenth century, monarchy was the main form of government in Europe, Asia, and parts of the Americas. Drawing on traditional authority, monarchs of this era claimed the divine right to exercise absolute power (that is, without legal restraints). Today, the once all-powerful royal families of Europe have either been dethroned (in Russia, Germany, and Austria) or been restricted to ceremonial roles. Great Britain, the Netherlands, Norway, Sweden, Denmark, Belgium, and Luxembourg are *constitutional monarchies,* in which members of royalty have no formal authority to rule and little political power. As symbols of national unity, however, they may perform an important service, especially during wars and other national emergencies. The same pattern can be seen in Asia. The royal family of Thailand (which has reigned as long as the Windsors) and the once-sacred emperor and empress of Japan are, today, constitutional monarchs.

Hereditary rule has not disappeared, however. Contemporary monarchs include King Fahd of Saudi Arabia, King Hussein of Jordan, the emirs of Kuwait, Qatar, and other Arab nations, and the sultan of Brunei, a tiny but oil-rich nation in northern Borneo. Today, as in the past, these monarchs rule not so much through coercion as through the exercise of traditional authority with the consent of powerful religions and financial groups, as well as much of the population.

The founder of modern Saudi Arabia was Ibn Saud, a leader of the Wahhabi Muslim sect, who expelled Turkish colonial governors and went on to conquer neighboring tribes and territories, declaring himself king of a United Saudi Arabia in 1932. (See Map 14-1.) Since then, the country has been ruled by his family. Succession to the Saudi throne is not hereditary; rather, a crown prince is selected from the royal house by the family, in consultation with religious leaders and members of other prominent families. Saudi Arabia has no legislature, political parties, or other means for citizens to participate in the government. Laws are decreed by the king and his ministers, based on the traditional authority of Islamic codes. In 1992, King Fahd created the Shura council, composed of sixty advisers selected by the king. The council has the right to review, but not to overrule, government acts. The Saud royal family remains all-powerful.

Dictatorship is another, and today more common, form of one-person authoritarian rule. The word "dictator" comes from ancient Rome, where in times of civil disturbance the Senate awarded a single magistrate emergency powers for a limited period. Over time, various politicians usurped this position, culminating with Julius Caesar's declaring himself dictator for life in 45 B.C. Caesar was assassinated the following year, and the position of dictator abolished. Familiar recent dictators include Mao Zedong in China, Francisco Franco in Spain, Fidel Castro in Cuba, Ferdinand Marcos in the Philippines, Juan Perón (and his wife Evita) in Argentina, Col. Muammar al-Qaddafi of Libya, Mobuto Sese Seko in Zaire (now the Republic of Congo), and Saddam Hussein in Iraq.

In contrast to monarchs, dictators usually do not enjoy traditional authority. To the contrary, dictators often come to power by overthrowing the existing government and dissolving traditional political institutions. Some were leaders of popular uprisings and enjoy charismatic authority and widespread popular support, at least at the beginning of their rule. Others are political rivals, perhaps unknown to much of the public but supported by their own country's military and/or business leaders or by outside forces. During the long cold war, when the U.S. and U.S.S.R. dominated global politics, dictators could maintain their power, buy arms, and acquire funds for aid and development by threatening to abandon the camp of one superpower for the other. In still other cases, such as Iran and Afghanistan, revolutions have given dictatorial powers to Islamic *mullahs* (or teachers), who also

Contemporary hereditary rulers, such as King Fahd of Saudi Arabia, remain in power by exercising traditional authority and enlisting the consent of powerful religious and financial groups. Here the king meets with former CIA director William Casey.

Map 14-1   *Saudi Arabia*

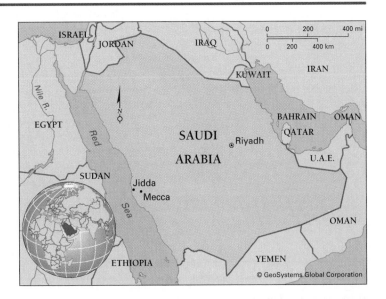

exercise traditional authority. Dictatorships have developed on the far right of the political spectrum (Chile under August Pinto's rule) as well as the far left (North Korea under Kim II Sung).

Regardless of how they came to power and what ideology they profess, all dictatorships have two common characteristics: there is no legal procedure for replacing the ruler or regime; and opposition, whether in the press or the formation of rival parties, is suppressed. To remain in power, dictators typically employ a combination of coercion, intimidation, and financial favoritism (such as granting concessions or monopolies). Nevertheless, dictatorships may be considered legitimate and may even enjoy popular support.

The Republic of Indonesia, the fourth most populous nation in the world, is an example (see Map 14-2). Indonesia's President Suharto[4] came to power in 1965 after an uprising (allegedly led by Communists but more likely due to a split in the military) in which as many as half a million people, including many ethnic Chinese, were killed. Suharto's power derived from strong backing by the military and strict economic controls, as well as substantial popular support. As president, Suharto presided over both the executive and the legislative branches of government and also appointed the judiciary. Indonesia's House of People's Representatives—composed of 360 elected members (most of whom are nominated by the government party, Golkar) and 100 presidential appointees (most from the military)—was essentially a rubber-stamp legislature. The Suharto regime did not tolerate political dissent. Although it recognized two other political parties (one pro-democratic, the other composed of Muslim moderates), outspoken critics and peaceful demonstrators were arrested and detained without trial. Seemingly arbitrary arrests of other citizens ensured compliance. When Indonesia forcibly annexed East Timor in 1975, as many as 100,000 pro-independence citizens were killed, and clashes there continue. With this exception, however, the government generally allowed both cultural and religious pluralism. The Javanese, Sudanese, Mandurians, Malays, and many other ethnic groups were free to maintain their languages and customs. And although almost 90 percent of the population is Muslim, the government protected the religious

---

[4] Suharto resigned as President while this book was in press.

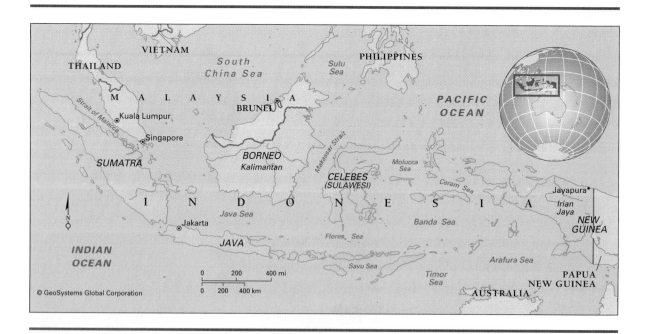

Map 14-2   *Indonesia*

freedom of Protestants, Roman Catholics, Hindus, Buddhists, and traditional animists.

On coming to power, Suharto denounced his predecessor's alliance with the then-powerful Soviet Union and opened Indonesia to western investment and aid. Beginning in 1970s, a combination of central economic planning and private investment led to impressive growth, due in part to the export of oil, timber, and minerals and in part to mostly low-tech manufacturing. Most Indonesians benefited from development. Between 1970 and 1996, the proportion of the population living below the official poverty line dropped from 60 percent to about 11 percent; life expectancy grew from 46 to 63 years; all children receive at least a primary school education; and adult illiteracy was reduced by almost two-thirds (The World Bank Group, 1997). Although the overall standard of living improved, most Indonesians remained poor. At the same time, however, President Suharto and his inner circle amassed fortunes. The Suharto family controls a multibillion-dollar financial empire through ownership of major enterprises (television and radio networks, banks, chemical factories, shopping malls, pulp and paper mills, shipping lines, etc.) and stocks (accepted in exchange for permits) in ventures funded by other Indonesian and foreign companies. One way President Suharto remained in power was by rewarding military leaders and other supporters with licenses and lucrative concessions for oil, mining, timber, and the like.

The financial crisis that spread through Southeast Asia in 1997–1998 hit Indonesia hard, forcing banks to close, factories to lay off millions of low-paid workers, the price of food and other necessities to rise, and the value of the *rupiah* (Indonesia's currency) to fall sharply. The International Monetary Fund (IMF) demanded widespread economic reform in exchange for loans to help Indonesia recover, but Suharto resisted. Re-elected to a seventh term, he again appointed cronies to cabinet posts. Meanwhile, demonstrations at major universities became more frequent and more critical, with students openly demanding that Suharto be replaced. While President Suharto was in Cairo on a state visit, riots erupted in the capital city of Jakarta. Looters moved into shopping malls throughout the city, taking goods they could not afford and burning stores behind them. Their primary targets were stores owned by, and neighborhoods occupied by,

Former President Suharto of Indonesia long relied on strong backing by the military and suppression of political opposition, as well as impressive economic growth, to remain in power.

ethnic Chinese, whom many Indonesians view as the prime beneficiaries of "crony capitalism." In contrast to previous episodes of unrest, the police and military did not intervene. Nevertheless, hundreds died, many in fires set by other looters. By the time Suharto returned, thousands of university students had taken over the Parliament building. The soldiers sent to maintain order attempted to befriend the demonstrators, not to evict them, even after they began hanging banners that read "Hang Suharto." To the surprise of many, Suharto quietly resigned on May 21, 1998, turning over the government to his chosen Vice President Habibie, according to Indonesia's constitution. Although this vast country's future remains uncertain, as of this writing the country is calm.

Why did Indonesians suddenly stand up against the one-man rule they had tolerated for decades? Why did Suharto resign? There are no simple answers. But the pattern suggests that opposition to Suharto was based on an unwritten social contract (Kristof, 1998): Indonesians were willing for Suharto to rule unchecked and enrich his family and friends in exchange for a rising standard of living. During the financial crisis in Southeast Asia, however, that social contract was broken: the government could no longer "deliver the goods." Faced with increasing disorder, unable to stabilize the economy or to maintain the military establishment he had built, Suharto bowed out. In a sense, he was a victim of his own success. In encouraging education and economic development, Suharto raised expectations; when the economy took a sudden downturn, the gap between elite government-connected multimillionaires and average people became intolerable. The mostly peaceful revolution in Indonesia raises questions about the long-accepted belief that, in Asia, authoritarian rule creates stability and promotes economic growth.

Another form of authoritarian government is ***totalitarianism.*** In totalitarian states, the ruling party not only controls the government but also regulates social, economic, intellectual, cultural, and spiritual activities. Under monarchy or dictatorship, ordinary people are mostly free to live and work as they choose, as long as they do not get involved in politics. Under totalitarianism, every aspect of daily life is subject to government intervention.

Totalitarianism is a relatively new type of political system and depends on modern technology to control the entire population. A single political party, often identified with the people or the nation, exercises a monopoly over the use of force. The ruling party ensures compliance, and suppresses opposition, in four main ways. First, it attempts to control communication: The mass media are owned and operated by the government; news and private communications are censored; education and the arts are used to support party ideology; unofficial public gatherings are banned; and travel requires a permit, rarely given. Thus access to information is limited, although modern technology has made such limitation increasingly difficult. Second, the government uses its powers in arbitrary and unpredictable ways. Citizens may be arrested at any time, denied contact with their families or a lawyer, tortured, exiled, or killed. A secret-police force is trained to exact confessions, reward spying against neighbors or even family members, and thus intimidate and terrorize citizens. In effect, people are deprived of what symbolic interactions call a "backstage" area, in which they can express their genuine (as opposed to politically approved) opinions. Anyone might be an informer; any place, from private homes to public restaurants, may be "bugged." Third, the government manages socialization. Not only are children indoctrinated to accept the state's legitimacy, but adults are exposed to constant propaganda. Dissidents may be subject to harsh forms of "resocialization," such as exile to hard-labor camps or confinement to mental institutions. Fourth, the government controls the economy. A totalitarian government may guarantee employment to all adults, but where they work, what kind of work they do, where they live, and even where they shop and what they are able to buy is subject to government regulation. Loyalty is rewarded, and doubt punished.

Nazi Germany, the former U.S.S.R., and China are familiar examples of totalitarian states. Another is the Republic of Singapore (see Map 14-3). Once a crown colony of Britain, this tiny country (popu-

A totalitarian government, such as that of the former Soviet Union, may guarantee employment to all adults. But it cannot guarantee that there will be anything for workers to buy with their salaries.

Map 14-3 *Singapore*

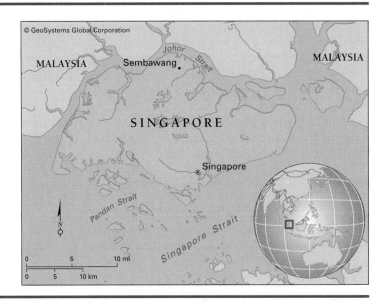

lation, 3 million) became an independent nation in 1959. Under Singapore's constitution, a president, elected to a four-year term, is the head of state, and a prime minister, selected by the dominant party, is head of the government. The country's first prime minister, Lee Kuan Yew, held this position from 1959 to 1990,[5] when he stepped down from office, but he remained chairman of the People's Action Party, which has never faced opposition. Singapore has the highest per capita income and the lowest crime rate in Asia. It is also one of the cleanest countries in the world, reminding North American visitors of a theme park (Braneganm, 1993). But public order and prosperity in Singapore have been achieved through what some have called "soft totalitarianism." Civil liberties are strictly limited. The government holds elections, but candidates are pre-selected by the ruling party. Under Singapore's laws, the police have the right to jail a person suspected of a crime without a charge or trial. Pornography is banned, as is the sale of chewing gum. Smoking in public, eating on a subway, and littering are subject to stiff fines. The penalty for possession or sale of illegal drugs is death by hanging. The government owns and manages almost all housing and has a controlling interest in many businesses, including airlines, television stations, telephone service, and even taxis. Thus, for most people the government is both landlord and employer. Singapore differs from most totalitarian systems in that it encourages private enterprise and does not directly intervene in citizens' private lives, although it provides tax incentives for advanced education, family planning, and caring for elderly parents. Both poverty and political discussion are virtually nonexistent. In short, the government of Singapore demands total loyalty and obedience in exchange for providing security and prosperity. Apparently most citizens of Singapore accept this trade-off.

Democratic Political Systems

In a **democracy,** citizens have the right to run or at least to choose their own government. The word "democracy" means government by the people (from the Greek words *demos,* meaning "the people," and *kratos,* meaning "rule"). Democratic political systems are grounded in rational-legal authority. The legitimate and illegitimate uses of power are usually spelled out in a constitution; the power of government officials is strictly limited by law; and, ideally, all citizens have equal rights under the law. In democracies, the law is designed to protect civil liberties, including freedom of speech and the press, freedom to associate with whomever one chooses, and freedom from unreasonable search and seizure. Individuals and groups accused of

---

[5] Except for a brief period (1963–1965) when Singapore joined but then withdrew from the Federation of Malaysia.

violating the law have the right to legal counsel and usually are seen as innocent until proven guilty; they also have the right to challenge the law through judicial appeals. Citizens owe allegiance to the system itself, not to the party or individuals who are in positions of power. Elections ensure that when citizens do not agree with officials' positions on issues, or when they believe officials have misused their authority, the officials can be voted out of office or, in extreme cases, impeached.

Direct versus Representational Democracy The concept of democracy is an old one, dating back to the Greek city-state of Athens during the fifth century B.C. The Athenian system was a *direct democracy,* in which citizens ran their own government. All citizens gathered to debate and vote on the issues at hand. Direct democracy was possible both because Athens was a small town by today's standards and because not all Athenians were considered citizens: women and slaves, on whose labor the city-state depended, had no say in government.

The one modern nation in which direct democracy is still widely practiced is Switzerland, a federation of twenty full and six half cantons, or states. In the smaller cantons, a *Landsgemeinde,* or assembly of all voting citizens, decides issues by voice vote. At the federal level, major issues, constitutional amendments, and in some cases federal laws are presented to the entire Swiss electorate in the form of referendums, which voters may approve or reject. But, like Athens, Switzerland is comparatively small—about half the size of Maine, with a population of slightly over 7 million, about the same as New York City.

In the United States and other modern democracies, the sheer size of the population and the number and complexity of issues make it impossible for all citizens to assemble in one place or for all voters to decide on every matter. Our government takes the form of *representative democracy,* in which citizens elect representatives who set policies and enact laws in the people's name. The legitimacy of government officials rests on the support they receive in elections. A free press and freedom of speech and assembly, as well as voting, political parties, and the formation of interest groups and protest movements (discussed earlier), are cornerstones of representative democracy.

The United States and other mainly representative democracies also provide opportunities and mechanisms for direct participation in government. At the local level, budget and plans often are decided at town meetings; any resident who attends the meeting may vote. In most states, citizens who collect a requisite number of signatures can place a referendum on the ballot, enabling the public to decide specific issues. In recent years, referendums have been used to ban smoking in public areas, oppose the construction of nuclear power plants, end affirmative action, limit taxation and spending, and deny official recognition of homosexual marriage, among other issues. Citizens also can participate in political decisions by going to public hearings, writing to elected officials, supporting interest groups, and joining social movements.

New technology—fax machines, voice mail, e-mail, computerized mailing lists, and programs for identifying possible sympathizers—has made it easier and less expensive for individuals and interest groups to influence public opinion and mobilize support. Most federal and many state and local government agencies now have web sites, which enable citizens to gain immediate access to information. Countless interest groups use their own web sites to offer supporters e-mail alerts, the names and e-mail addresses or fax numbers of their local representatives or officials in charge of a bill they endorse or oppose, and form letters that can be downloaded, signed, and faxed with minimal time and effort. But technology is politically neutral. New means of communication can be used to invade privacy, spread rumors, manipulate opinion, and control citizens. The best known example was the 1989 student pro-democracy movement in China. Faxes played a key role in enabling students to circumvent censors and exchange information with supporters outside the country. Later, the government reportedly used phone records to trace, arrest, and imprison student protestors. Finally, participation in "electronic democracy" requires access to computers and fax machines, which poor citizens cannot afford.

Presidential versus Parliamentary Democracy
Another distinction can be drawn between presidential and parliamentary democracy. As discussed earlier, the structure of presidential democracies tends to promote two-party dominance and centrist politics. Parliamentary politics tends to promote class-oriented parties with clearly defined policies and programs and to create opportunities for minority parties. Presidential democracies most often devel-

Jomo Kenyatta, first president of Kenya, ruled from the time the country gained independence in 1963 until his death in 1978. Nationalist leaders such as Kenyatta often became their country's first president, but they ruled in large part through charismatic authority, which left a vacuum when they died. Dictatorship often followed.

oped in nations that fought colonial domination—such as the United States, Brazil, and Egypt. In most cases, parliamentary democracies are former monarchies, such as France, Great Britain, and Japan. With the exception of the United States, parliamentary democracies generally have proved more stable than presidential democracies. Most countries in Latin America and sub-Saharan Africa have presidential constitutions but have vacillated between brief periods of democratic government, longer periods of military dictatorship, and in some cases civil war. Clearly, other social factors—from economic hardship to ethnic rivalries—are at work. But the structure of a presidential democracy, in which the head of state is independent of the legislature, might facilitate the emergence of dictators. (See *Close Up:* Is Democracy for Everyone?)

In practice, no political system is purely authoritarian or democratic. Political ideals (whether or not they are embodied in a constitution) establish a vision of how people would like their society to work; they set institutionalized goals. But no society totally succeeds in meeting its goals. Something is always lost in the translation of ideals into a working political system. The former Soviet Union long proclaimed itself a workers' state. In practice, however, only a small percentage of Soviet citizens were admitted to party membership. And those who rose to the top levels of the party enjoyed numerous social and economic privileges that were not available to ordinary workers. The United States has long considered itself a champion of democracy, but until this century it denied full political and legal rights to Native Americans, African Americans, and women. Even today, some citizens (the directors of major corporations, union presidents, spokespersons for large interest groups, and major campaign donors) have more impact on politics than others do. U.S. citizens do have the right to express their opinions and to create organizations that oppose government policy, but they rarely participate directly in party activities or even vote. Individuals in China probably are more active in local politics and community affairs than Americans are—as long as they follow the Communist party line.

Equally important, politics is now a global affair. The exercise of power, whether internally or internationally, is shaped by structural forces that are beyond the control of any one government or nation. Global corporations, world financial markets, and the mass media, aided by new communications technology, play an ever-increasing role in world events. Of the 100 largest economies in the world today, 51 are corporations, not countries (Kaplan, 1997). In some ways global corporations resemble the feudal societies that evolved into modern nation states (see Chapter 15). But they are not tied to a particular territory, population, or local culture. Similarly, the world's financial capitals are beginning to resemble international city-states that are not dependent on the countries in which they are located. How the increasing importance of financial markets that know no borders will influence the political institutions that evolved in the twentieth century is one of the great unknowns.

CLOSE UP

Is Democracy for Everyone?

In a controversial article published in the *Atlantic Monthly* (1997), Robert D. Kaplan argues, "To think that democracy as we know it will triumph—or even that it is here to stay—is itself a form of . . . ethnocentricity." As Americans, we tend to believe that democracy is the best form of government for everyone, everywhere. A main goal of U.S. foreign policy has been to export democracy around the globe (although we have tolerated and even supported dictatorships when they served our interests). Likewise, Americans tend to see the collapse of Communist governments in the former U.S.S.R. and eastern Europe as a victory for democracy. Kaplan contrasts the violence, instability, and poverty of today's democratic Russia to the rising standard of living in Communist China. Which country, which people, are better off? Identifying the social structural conditions under which democracy works best— and worst—Kaplan concludes that it may not be for everyone.

Kaplan holds that democracy emerges more or less naturally in societies that have achieved a certain level of national integration and economic development. Democracy is most likely to succeed in nations that already have established borders, efficient government bureaucracies, a solid middle class, and relative economic stability. Democracy also depends on established *civic institutions*— groups and organizations that are neither run by the state nor run for a profit but structure everyday activities, such as inde-

> **First create an economy, then worry about elections.**
> —unemployed Tunisian student

pendent political groups, professional associations, scientific and literary societies, clubs, lodges, churches, and neighborhood groups. These necessary preconditions developed under the monarchies of western Europe (and European colonies in North America), but from a global and historical perspective, they are relatively rare.

Under different conditions, democracy is more likely to lead to dictatorship or anarchy and civil war. Thus the economic chaos in pre–World War II Germany and Italy led to the democratic election of Adolf Hitler, the "father" of the modern totalitarian state and "ethnic cleansing," and his ally in fascist Italy, Benito Mussolini.

Democracy itself is value-neutral; depending on social conditions, it can work for the people or against them. Latin America provides examples of both failed democracies and successful dictatorships. Most nations of Latin America have alternated between elected governments and (usually military) dictatorships. In Venezuela, which has had an elected civilian government since 1959, coup attempts are frequent, crime is rampant, and the economy is weak. Rated a credit risk by world banks, Venezuela does not attract business; indeed, the country's own elite invests its savings elsewhere. In contrast, Chile was governed by a military dictatorship for most of the

Source: Robert D. Kaplan, "Was Democracy Just a Moment?" *The Atlantic Monthly,* Dec. 6, 1997, pp. 55–72.

1970s and 1980s. Yet it has become one of the region's most stable middle-class societies, with economic growth rates that rival the "little tigers" of the Pacific Rim. In 1990, Peruvian voters elected Alberto Fujimori president. As promised in his campaign, Fujimori disbanded Peru's Congress and used his power to weaken the Shining Path guerrilla movement and to take control of the economy. Governing by decree, much as a chief executive runs a corporation, Fujimori cut inflation and restored order, bringing Peru investment and jobs. An elected dictator, he received three times as many votes as his closest rival in Peru's 1995 elections. In contrast, Colombia has a democratically elected government, but political power has been usurped by rival drug lords. Elected officials are leaders in name only, and many middle-class Colombians have fled.

In a society that has not reached a certain level of social and economic development—one in which most people are poor, many are illiterate rural or transplanted urban peasants, many are young unemployed males, few have experience in government, and civic institutions are weak to nonexistent—free elections are likely to aggravate and harden ethnic and regional divisions. Kaplan quotes Uganda's President Yoweri Museveni, a military dictator: "I happen to be one of those people who do not believe in multi-party democracy. In fact, I am totally opposed to it as far as Africa today is concerned. . . . If one forms a multi-party system in Uganda, a party cannot win elections unless it finds a way of dividing . . . the electorate, and this is where the main problem comes up: tribalism, religion, or regionalism becomes the basis for intense partisanship." Kaplan also quotes an unemployed Tunisian student, who made much the same point: "In Tunisia we have a twenty-five percent unemployment rate. If you hold elections in such circumstances, the result will be [an Islamic] fundamentalist government and violence like in Algeria. First create an economy, then worry about elections."

Kaplan concludes that in underdeveloped, unstable countries the choice is not between democracy and dictatorship. Under these conditions democracy is likely to be short-lived (unpaid soldiers stage a coup) or inefficient (leading to high rates of crime and corruption). Rather the choice is between "bad dictators and slightly better ones." Like the monarchs who set the stage for democracy in Europe, an efficient dictator may create the social stability and economic development necessary for democracy to take root. Kaplan also suggests that democracy may be fading in developed countries such as the United States, where voting rates, participation in civic institutions, and the role of government (as opposed to corporations) may be declining. But that is another story.

SOCIOLOGY ON THE WEB

Liberty and Justice for All

Search for information on political parties on the web. The text describes the characteristics that define true political parties. Use the web to determine whether groups that call themselves political parties meet that definition. Begin by searching the sites listed below.

http://www.politicalindex.com/sect8.htm
http://www.voxpop.org:80/

These are general sites with hundreds of links to sources of information about the U.S. political system. For example, the Political Index lists 123 groups that call themselves political parties. Pick any three of them and read about their goals, aims, and methods of operation. Use the information you obtain from the web and print sources. Using the definition given in the text, are these groups political parties? Write a brief essay that explains why or why not.

Do a web search about a major political controversy that's current at the time you are reading this chapter. Using any search engine you choose, define your topic carefully, do a search, and evaluate the information you find. What types of rhetoric does your topic elicit? What are writers saying about it in political magazines? In chat rooms? Reflect on what the text says about power and politics. What implications does the issue have for the power base of the U.S. political system or for specific politicians? How do those implications affect the kind of commentary you find? As an example, in March 1998, typing the words "Monica Lewinsky" into the Excite search engine yielded 4,700 hits. The equally current topic of a possible U.S. war against Iraq yielded only around 1,200—of a very different type. Why the difference?

Summary

1. **What is the difference between power and authority?** Whereas power rests on coercion, authority rests on cooperation. All political systems depend on some combination of the two. Weber identified three types of authority (or legitimate use of power): *traditional, charismatic,* and *rational-legal authority.* Although rational-legal political systems gradually replaced traditional rulers in western (and other) societies, all three types of authority play a role in contemporary politics.

2. **How has the development of modern political institutions affected the distribution of authority?** The emergence of large agrarian states about 3,000 years ago both promoted and required the development of distinct political institutions. Supported by a priesthood, army, and noble class, the heads of these states claimed a divine right to rule. A major development was the separation of the position of the ruler from the person who occupied that

position. The emergence of nation-states in Europe was the result of territorial consolidation, expanding trade, and a growing merchant class. In the twentieth century the size and scope of government expanded as states took on responsibility for collective goods and, often, social welfare. Most modern states at least claim to represent the will of the people, though not all are democracies.

3. **What are the basic elements of the American political system?** The American political system differs from that of most other stable democracies in the separation of powers. Traditionally, political participation in the United States centered on voting and political parties. Through most of the twentieth century, however, voting rates have declined and party loyalty has declined. The impact of *interest groups, PACs,* and *protest movements* as avenues of political influence and participation has grown, partly in response to the ever-rising

costs of elections and to laws (and loopholes) regarding campaign finance.

4. **Who actually rules America today?** Sociologists have proposed four different models of the structure of power in the United States. Pluralists describe a complex pattern of crisscrossing interest groups, which prevents the concentration of power in the hands of a single group but may also lead to paralysis. Mills and others believe that real authority lies in a power elite, composed of decision makers in the executive branch of government, the military, and large corporations. Domhoff and the instrumentalists argue that a national upper class is in control, while structuralists hold that policies and plans are based on the needs of the capitalist system.

5. **How do political systems vary around the world?** Political systems can be divided into two main categories, authoritarian and democratic. *Authoritarian systems* may take the form of a monarchy (led by a hereditary ruler), dictatorship (in which popular participation in government is limited and opposition banned), or *totalitarian states* (which attempt to control virtually all aspects of citizens' lives). *Democracies* also vary. Ancient Athens (and other city-states and local governments) was a *direct democracy*: citizens ran their own government (though not all members of the population were granted citizenship). In *representative democracy* (most modern democracies) decisions are made by elected officials who are responsible to the people. In presidential democracies such as ours, the president and members of Congress are elected directly by the people in winner-take-all contests, a form of democracy that promotes two-party dominance and centrist policies. In parliamentary democracies, the prime minister is chosen by the party that wins a majority of seats in the legislature; political parties tend to be more organized, ideological, and class-oriented; and minority parties have more impact.

Key Terms

authoritarian political systems   538

authority   517

charismatic authority   519

democracy   543

direct democracy   544

interest group   530

political action committee (PAC)   533

political party   527

politics   517

power   517

protest movement   534

rational-legal authority   519

representative democracy   544

totalitarianism   542

traditional authority   519

welfare state   523

Recommended Readings

Domhoff, William G. (1978). *Who Really Rules? New Haven and Community Power.* New Brunswick, NJ: Transaction Books.

Domhoff, William G. (1983). *Who Rules America Now?* New York: Random House.

Domhoff, William G. (1996). *State Autonomy or Class Dominance? Case Studies on Policy Making in America.* New York: Aldine de Gruyter.

Mills, C. Wright. (1956). *The Power Elite.* New York: Oxford University Press.

Rosenstiel, Tom. (1993). *Strange Bedfellows: How Television and the Presidential Candidate Changed American Politics, 1992.* New York: Hyperion.

Skocpol, Theda. (1992). *Protecting Soldiers and Mothers: The Political Origins of Social Policy in the United States.* Cambridge, MA: Harvard University Press.

Stroessinger, John G. (1992). *Why Nations Go to War,* 6th ed. New York: St. Martins Press.

Chapter

Fifteen

The Economy and Work

In late 1992 the small town of Warren, Rhode Island, received a crushing blow: American Tourister, the luggage manufacturer and Warren's largest employer, announced that it was moving its manufacturing and distribution operations to Florida. The 350 jobs lost would increase Warren's unemployment rate, already the highest in the state. Many other American Tourister employees had been laid off in 1989, when the company opened a manufacturing plant in the Dominican Republic.

American Tourister, like many other U.S. manufacturers, found it could substantially cut costs by opening a plant in a Third World nation. The company pays its Dominican Republic workers 90 cents an hour; the workers in Warren averaged $8 an hour. Health care costs, overhead, and taxes are also lower outside of the United States. Moreover, by moving its remaining operations to the south, American Tourister could be closer to the major retail chains, such as Wal-Mart and Kmart, that account for a large portion of its sales. The company estimates that it can now cut its distribution time to its primary retail customers by about half. Finally, technology and consumer preference drove American Tourister's actions. The Warren plant produced hard suitcases, but consumers now prefer soft-fabric luggage. The plants in the Dominican Republic and Florida are equipped to manufacture this kind of luggage.

American Tourister's actions made economic sense, but they left real human dilemmas in their wake. Some of the Warren employees had worked at the plant for thirty years. What jobs would now be open to them? American Tourister's corporate decisions reveal a great deal about the economy as a social institution. The decisions may have been made for economic reasons, but they affected the structure of society. They directly affected the lives of the people of Warren—not just those laid off, but their children, those who sold them goods in the community, and those who built homes or performed services there. Most of the American Tourister jobs were blue-collar manufacturing jobs, but corporate downsizing in other parts of the country has left many white-collar workers out of work or underemployed. As companies have become more shareholder-driven over the past decade or so, layoffs and downsizing have become a regular part of the U.S. and global economies. In order to boost their bottom lines, companies lay off or

15

A white-collar worker packs up after learning that she has been "downsized" out of her job at AT&T. Downsizing and layoffs have had a profound effect on the way Americans see their jobs and their prospects for the future.

downsize workers to reduce expenses and make their stock performance more attractive to investors. Whirlpool and International Paper each let 10 percent of their workforces go—over 13,000 jobs. Stanley, the tool manufacturer, let go of 4,500 workers, nearly one-quarter of its workforce (Stein, 1997).

Downsizing and layoffs of workers around the country have had a profound impact on the way Americans see work and their prospects for the future. Workers no longer can count on keeping the same job with the same company for their entire career—whether they are white-collar, blue-collar, or service workers. Many workers have had to retool their skills to find jobs. Changes in the economy and work have also affected the institution of government—state and local governments may grant companies tax concessions to keep jobs in the area.

The United States is not the only place experiencing these problems. The growth of a global economy has meant that economic downturns in one part of the world can cause downsizing elsewhere. As financial crises hit Japan and other Southeast Asian countries in late 1997 and early 1998, investors in the United States and the companies doing business with those countries also felt the pressure. In a market economy, no part of the global economy is immune to the quest for higher profits.

Key Questions

1. What is the global economy? How does it affect the structure of the economy? How does it work worldwide and in the United States?

2. What is capitalism, and how does it structure the U.S. economy?

3. How has the world of work changed? What does work mean to Americans?

4. How are new technologies changing the nature of work? What effect have they had on workers' satisfaction and leisure time?

The Global Economy

A number of sociologists argue that the world is no longer composed of separate, individual national economies. Rather, global corporations shape the business opportunities, employment patterns, and standard of living of everyone on earth, including Americans (I. Wallerstein, 1980; Chirot, 1977, 1981; Stearns, 1992).

The World System

In 1900, western nations directly or indirectly ruled most of the world. Virtually every nation in Europe had colonies abroad. Although its colonial possessions were few, the United States exercised indirect control through its economic investments (and later, after World War II, through its economic aid programs and military support of certain governments). Colonialism created a global division of labor and a global system of stratification. The rich, industrialized nations acted as an international upper class. The poor, undeveloped nations of Africa, Asia, and Latin America became an international lower class. Countries that were neither rich nor poor—Spain, Italy, Japan—formed an international middle class.

The colonial system was essentially a plantation system: The colonies supplied most of the raw materials that the European industrialized nations used to manufacture products; the owners and managers from European nations reaped most of the profits. Although nearly all European colonies have subsequently won political independence, they are not economically independent. (But neither, as we shall see, are the industrialized nations.) The global division of labor and the global system of stratification persist. The main difference today is that the less developed nations are providing global corporations with not only the raw materials but the laborers as well.

Multinational Corporations

The key actors in today's global economic system are **multinational corporations:** companies with holdings and subsidiaries in several different nations. Multinationals organize human, natural, and technological resources from all over the globe into single economic units. For example, International Harvester has factories in Turkey, where it assembles chassis built in the United States with engines made in Germany. From its headquarters in Canada, Massey-Ferguson directs plants in Detroit that assemble components from France, Mexico, and Britain. American car manufacturers use parts made in other nations, and they own assembly plants abroad. Toyota and Honda both have manufacturing plants in the United States and import many of their vehicles into Japan. Almost 70 percent of the color televisions made by Japanese companies are manufactured elsewhere.

The first modern multinationals were based in the United States; they emerged to take advantage of the lower costs of manufacturing and doing business overseas. Other nations soon followed. The Japanese, for example, were initially shocked to see the United States forfeit its industrial power when American manufacturers began to move their operations to Asia and sell products made by companies abroad, but the sharp rise of the Japanese currency in recent years and the high wage scale have forced many Japanese corporations to move their operations overseas as well.

Multinationals do not compete with other corporations on an equal footing. By buying from and selling to their own subsidiaries in different countries, they avoid price competition. Because they have bases in many countries, they can shift operations or assets from country to country to avoid taxes, government regulations (such as antitrust and antipollution laws), and labor unions. Their size and global reach enable them to play the world

A Reebok factory in Ho Chi Minh City, Vietnam. Multinational corporations such as Reebok organize human, natural, financial, and technological resources from all over the globe into single economic units.

money and commodity markets almost at will. Their size also enables them to influence local politics, particularly in Third World countries that depend on outside investments.

Multinationals are essentially "stateless." According to *Fortune* magazine's Global 500 list, the top-ranked multinational corporation in 1996 was General Motors. In that year it had sales of more than $168 billion and assets worth $191 billion; it employed 647,000 workers worldwide. Shell Oil, a British-Dutch entity, had sales close to $128 billion, assets of $124 billion, and 101,000 employees. Toyota's sales were $108 billion, its assets were $102 billion, and it employed 150,736; Daimler-Benz, the German car manufacturer, recorded sales of over $71 billion, assets worth $72 billion, and employees numbering more than 290,029. Of the fifty largest multinational corporations, all are in the northern hemisphere; thirteen are in the United States, and twenty are in Japan (*Fortune*, August 4, 1997, pp. F1–F2). Table 15-1 shows the top-ten multinational companies and their revenues, profits, assets, and number of employees.

The growth of multinationals created what Richard Barnet (1980) called "the global factory":

> Viewed from space, the Global Factory suggests a human organism. The brain is housed in steel-and-glass slabs located in or near a few crowded cities—New York, London, Frankfurt, Zurich, and Tokyo. The blood is capital, and it is pumped through the system by global banks assisted by a few governments. The financial centers in New York, London, Frankfurt, and Tokyo, and their financial extensions in such tax havens as Panama and the Bahamas, func-

> tion as the heart. The hands are steadily moving to the outer rim of civilization. More and more goods are now made in the poor countries of the southern periphery under direction from the headquarters in the North. (p. 239)

Advances in two types of technology contributed to the global factory. The first was new technology for conquering distances (computerized shipping, jet cargo carriers, and satellite communication networks). The second was new technology for fragmenting and routinizing production (especially advanced data processing).

The manufacturing of baseballs—an "all-American" product—provides a concrete illustration of the global factory in action. Leather, yarn, thread, and cement produced in the United States are shipped to Haiti. There, women working for some of the lowest wages in the hemisphere assemble these materials into baseballs. The finished product is sold not only in the United States but also in Cuba, Mexico, and Japan.

The reason for shifting production to developing countries was simple: the abundance of cheap labor (see *A Global View*: Life on the Assembly Line). Even with the added costs of shipping, it is less expensive to assemble products in these countries than at home. Migrants from developing nations have also become the "hands" inside wealthier nations: Mexican workers have picked tomatoes in the United States; Turks, Greeks, and Yugoslavs have built roads and washed dishes in northern Europe; a million or more Yemenese were "guest laborers" in Saudi Arabia.

Table 15-1   *Top Ten of the Global 500*

Rank and Company	Nation	Revenues ($, Millions)	Profits ($, Millions)	Assets ($, Millions)	Employees
1. General Motors	U.S.	168,369.0	4,963.0	222,142.0	647,000
2. Ford Motor	U.S.	146,991.0	4,446.0	262,867.0	371,702
3. Mitsui	Japan	144,942.8	321.9	61,144.5	41,694
4. Mitsubishi	Japan	140,203.7	394.1	77,871.5	35,000
5. Itochu	Japan	135,542.1	110.9	59,179.6	6,999
6. Royal Dutch/Shell	Britain/Netherlands	128,174.5	8,887.1	124,373.4	101,000
7. Marubeni	Japan	124,026.9	178.6	60,865.4	65,000
8. Exxon	U.S.	119,434.0	7,510.0	95,527.0	79,000
9. Sumitomo	Japan	119,281.3	(1,292.8)	45,506.3	26,200
10. Toyota Motor	Japan	108,702.0	3,426.2	102,417.0	150,736

Source: Fortune, Aug. 4, 1997, p. F2.

In the 1980s, the traditional model of a multinational corporation with headquarters in one country and subsidiaries in others was expanded through cross-border mergers, strategic alliances, joint ventures, and international licensing agreements. Former international competitors and one-market corporations became transnational partners. The location of a company's headquarters and the place where a product is made have become less and less relevant. For example, Microsoft is headquartered in Redmond, Washington, but the corporation has several international subsidiaries that have helped to contribute to its growth (see Figure 15-1 on page 558).

A major reason for international collaboration is that no one country offers a market big enough to support the cost of developing and producing high-technology products and services. For example, Otis Elevator Inc., a division of United Technologies Corp., marketed an elevator that was developed by five research centers in six countries. The motor drives were designed in Japan, the electronics in Germany, the doors in France, the systems integration in Farmington, Connecticut, and the small-geared components in Spain. Otis estimates that this collaboration saved the company $10 million in development costs and cut two years from the development schedule (*Business Week*, May 14, 1990, p. 101).

As a result of such collaborations, much of the growth in the global market has taken place among developed nations. Foreign investment in developed nations has increased, while foreign investment in developing nations has leveled off or decreased. Production of high-technology goods (and services) often requires skills that are in short supply in developing countries. And the primary markets for high-technology goods are developed, not developing, nations.

Another change in the global market is the emergence of the European Community (EC). The EC consists of fifteen western European nations that have agreed to lift most barriers to the movement of people, goods, services, and money for the benefit of other member nations. With a combined population of 372 million (as of 1997), the EC is the world's largest internal market. In time the new market will pull in 32 million additional consumers in seven nations that have not yet joined the EC but will participate in a "European economic area." The EC has attracted investments by companies based not only in member nations but also in North America and Japan.

Where the newly liberated eastern European countries and Russia will fit is an open question. Eastern European nations might join the EC, remain independent, or form an association of their own. Multinational corporations see the former eastern bloc as a potential market, a pool of low-cost labor, and a source of brainpower (Holusha, 1990). Although these countries have well-deserved reputations for producing shoddy consumer goods, they also have well-earned reputations for producing top-rate scientists. Under Communist regimes, science was largely theoretical. With the notable exceptions of the Soviet space and weapons programs, there were few attempts to translate theoretical advances into technological applications. Already, multinationals are stepping into this gap. For example, the Monsanto Company signed a three-year contract with the Shemyakin Institute in Moscow, a center for biological research. Monsanto is providing the funds and equipment for research in exchange for the right to market discoveries. Chrysler and Mazda are competing for contracts with Skoda, a Czechoslovakian manufacturer, to produce American- or Japanese-designed cars for market in western Europe. The attractions of the eastern bloc (engineering and manufacturing skills plus low wages) may further reduce investment in Third World nations, adding to their problems.

The Economics of Developing Countries

Developing nations were once called "Third World" countries. In modern times the concept of "Third World" (which originally was derived from the old French notion of three estates—the aristocracy, the church hierarchy, and the common people) became associated with the division of Europe into the western, capitalist nations linked to the United States (the First World); the eastern, Communist nations formerly linked to the U.S.S.R. (the Second World); and the poorer nations of the southern hemisphere, comprising the **Third World.** The end of communism in eastern Europe and the former Soviet Union has made the concept of a Second World out of date. Thus, we have today *developed* nations in the northern hemisphere and *developing* nations located mainly south of the equator. These rich and poor nations are worlds apart in every socioeconomic indicator (see Table 15-2 on page 559), although the

Life on the Assembly Line

We need female workers; older than 17, younger than 30; single and without children: minimum education primary school, maximum education one year of preparatory school [high school]: available for all shifts.

—Ad in a Mexican newspaper

The manual dexterity of the Oriental female is famous the world over. Her hands are small, and she works fast with extreme care. . . . Who, therefore, could be better qualified by nature and inheritance, to contribute to the efficiency of a bench-assembly production line than the Oriental girl?

—Malaysian government investment brochure

These advertisements illustrate a little-known fact about overseas laborers in multinational corporations: They are overwhelmingly female. In fact, between 80 and 90 percent of the low-skilled assembly-line jobs in the developing countries are held by women (Ehrenreich and Fuentes, 1983). The global economy depends on the work of these women, and they are regarded as key resources by the ever-expanding multinationals. Why is it that assembly-line work is considered "women's work"?

First of all, women in poor countries are generally willing to work for less money than are men, and most countries make it

> **In the global factory, assembly-line work is considered "women's work."**

legal to pay them less. The great majority of women workers live at or near subsistence level. "Subsistence" usually consists of a diet of rice, dried fish, and water and accommodations in dormitories that sleep four, eight, even twenty to a room. Salaries increase with seniority, but many companies find it more profitable to dismiss the higher-paid, experienced women and replace

Like these workers in Korea, laborers in multinational corporations are overwhelmingly female.

gap in life expectancy between developed and undeveloped regions of the world appears to be narrowing (see Figure 15-2 on page 560).

Some developing nations have recently experienced very rapid economic growth. The so-called Four Little Dragons of South Korea, Taiwan, Singapore, and Hong Kong are examples. In 1950, life expectancy in South Korea was about 50 years of age, and 80 percent of the population was farmers. A mere forty-five years later, South Korea's life expectancy was 72 years, and only 29 percent of the population worked in agriculture (World Bank, 1997). To be sure, such rapid growth has caused cultural and social dislocations. But South Korea them with a fresh supply of teenagers.

Second, many corporations regard women as better suited than men for taking on tedious, repetitive work under adverse conditions. One personnel manager of a Taiwan assembly plant noted that "young male workers are too restless and impatient to do monotonous work with no career value. If displeased, they sabotage the machines and even threaten the foreman. But girls? At most, they cry a little" (Ehrenreich and Fuentes, 1983, p. 381). The work is not only tedious but often hazardous as well. Electronics, generally considered a "clean" industry, uses a surprising number of toxic substances. Few Third World factories issue health warnings or provide for the safe storage of toxic matter. Impaired eyesight is another consequence of even short periods of work on electronics assembly lines. Conditions in textile and garment factories are even worse. Workers labor in overheated, underventilated, and poorly lit facilities, for long hours and with few breaks.

Finally, the low status of women in developing countries makes it easy to keep them in low-status jobs. In the nations with patriarchal cultures, women who accept assembly-line jobs also endure the stigma of being "factory girls"—the modern equivalent of the "loose woman." As one anthropologist has noted, this stigmatization serves indirectly to keep the women in line: "The fear of having a 'reputation' is enough to make a lot of women bend over backward to be 'respectable' and ladylike, which is just what management wants" (Ehrenreich and Fuentes, 1983, p. 388). Women who organize to protest their low wages or poor working conditions are usually restrained by the male-dominated political systems of the Third World nations.

The millions of female industrial workers employed in developing countries constitute an important strategic bloc of woman power. However, for most of us in the First World, "they are still faceless, genderless 'cheap labor,' signaling their existence only through a label or tiny imprint 'made in Hong Kong,' or Taiwan, Korea, the Dominican Republic, Mexico, the Philippines" (Ehrenreich and Fuentes, 1983, p. 380).

Children are another source of unpaid or underpaid labor—in the developing countries, where they are sometimes sold into slavery, and in the United States, where they help produce products for such companies as J.C. Penney, Pillsbury, Sears, and Wal-Mart. Despite labor laws against the exploitation of children, the Associated Press found 165 children working illegally in sixteen states, a number which, when projected using census surveys and other workplace and population data, becomes about 300,000 children nationally (*Associated Press,* December 19, 1997). This number does not include the children of migrant farmworkers, who spend their days working side by side with their parents in the fields.

has joined the ranks of upper-middle-income nations.

Other formerly Third World nations have developed, but more slowly. In India in 1950, life expectancy was 40 years of age. By 1991, life expectancy has risen to 60 years (World Bank, 1997). India is a poor nation, but not the poorest in the world. Moreover, India has developed more rapidly in the past forty years than did rich nations when they were undergoing the transition from agricultural to industrial societies.

Still other developing nations have not made economic progress and have even fallen further behind. Several countries in Africa fit this

(A) EMPLOYEES WORLDWIDE

7,340

United
States
14,936

(B) GROWTH 1988–1997*

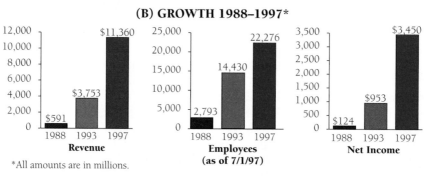

Revenue

$591 (1988)
$3,753 (1993)
$11,360 (1997)

Employees
(as of 7/1/97)

2,793 (1988)
14,430 (1993)
22,276 (1997)

Net Income

$124 (1988)
$953 (1993)
$3,450 (1997)

*All amounts are in millions.

(C) OFFICES WORLDWIDE

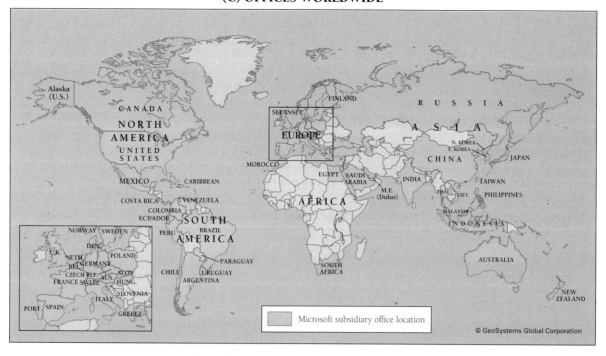

Microsoft subsidiary office location

© GeoSystems Global Corporation

Figure 15-1   *Microsoft: A Global Corporation Without Boundaries*

Microsoft has grown from a start-up based in a garage to a multinational corporation with 22,000 employees worldwide and offices in over fifty-five countries.

Source: www.microsoft.com/corpinfo/fastfact.htm.

Table 15-2   *Socioeconomic Indicators in Selected Countries*

	Population, Mid-1997 (Millions)	GNP per Capita Dollars 1995	GNP per Capita Average Annual Growth Rate, 1985–95 (Percent)	Live Expectancy at Birth, 1995 (Years)	Infant Mortality Rate, 1997 (per 1,000 Live Births)
Low-Income Economies					
Ethiopia	56.4	100	−0.3	49	120
Bangladesh	119.8	240	2.1	58	77
Kenya	26.7	280	0.1	58	120
India	929.4	340	3.2	62	75
Ghana	17.1	390	1.4	59	66
Georgia	5.4	440	−17.0	73	124
China	1,200.2	620	8.3	69	31
Middle-Income Economies					
Sri Lanka	18.1	700	2.6	72	17.2
Bolivia	7.4	800	1.8	60	71
Indonesia	193.3	980	6.0	64	66
Jordan*	4.2	1,510	−4.5	70	36
El Salvador	5.6	1,610	2.8	67	41
Russian Federation†	148.2	2,240	−5.1	65	18
Peru	23.8	2,310	−1.6	66	55
Thailand	58.2	2,740	8.4	69	32
Turkey	61.1	2,780	2.2	67	47
Poland	38.6	2,790	1.2	70	12.4
South Africa	41.5	3,160	−1.1	64	53
Mexico	91.8	3,320	0.1	72	34
Brazil	159.2	3,640	−0.8	67	48
High-Income Economies					
Korea, Republic	44.9	9,700	7.7	70	11
Ireland	3.6	14,710	5.2	72	6
United Kingdom	58.5	18,700	1.4	77	6
Australia	18.1	18,720	1.4	77	6
Hong Kong	6.2	22,990	4.8	79	5
Sweden	8.8	23,750	−0.1	79	4.2
United States	263.1	26,980	1.3	77	7.3
Japan	125.2	39,640	2.9	80	4
Switzerland	7.0	40,630	0.2	78	5

*In all tables, data for Jordan cover the East Bank only.
†Estimates for economy of the former Soviet Union are subject to more than the usual range of uncertainty and should be regarded as very preliminary.
Sources: The World Bank, *World Development Report, 1997,* New York: Oxford University Press, 1997, pp. 214–215; table 28, pp. 292–293. Infant mortality rates from Population Reference Bureau, *1997 World Population Data Sheet,* May 1997.

picture, including Sudan, Ethiopia, Mali, Chad, and Somalia.

There are no simple explanations of the extremes and extent of poverty in the developing countries. Some of their problems are a legacy of colonialism. In Africa and elsewhere, colonial powers practiced a divide-and-conquer strategy. National boundaries were drawn so that in some cases members of hostile religious groups or of tribes that had been at war for centuries were forced together in a single country; in other cases a single tribe was split apart by boundaries; and in still others people were cut off from vital natural resources. Civil wars and tribal rivalries are still a leading problem in Africa

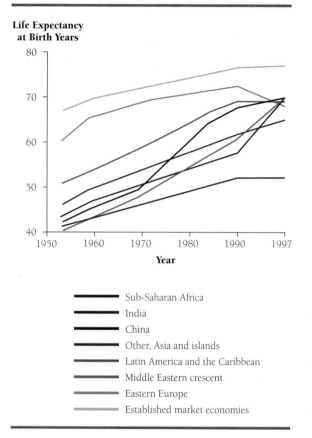

Life Expectancy at Birth Years

Sub-Saharan Africa
India
China
Other, Asia and islands
Latin America and the Caribbean
Middle Eastern crescent
Eastern Europe
Established market economies

Figure 15-2   *Life Expectancy in Global Perspective*

Life expectancy has increased worldwide over the past forty years, but the greatest gap remains between the western nations and sub-Saharan Africa and India.

Source: Development Report, 1993. New York: Oxford University Press, 1993, fig. 1.2, p. 23; Population Reference Bureau, *1997 World Population Data Sheet,* May 1997.

(see Chapter 9). Colonial economic policies disrupted traditional social and economic patterns, sometimes deliberately (as in the British destruction of India's textile industry). Often colonial powers left behind a taste for expensive western goods and lifestyles.

Some of the problems in poor countries are the result of dependency on rich nations. **Dependency theory** (Frank, 1967, 1980) suggests that the developing countries have failed to develop the solid modern industrial base and secure middle class that are characteristic of developed nations because they are economically and politically dependent on foreign corporations. According to this theory, development in these countries began not from within but from without. Foreign companies that bought land for sugar plantations and the like were soon followed by foreign government aid to build schools, roads, and factories. In the short term this may have boosted development. In the long term, however, foreign investment and aid delayed development, causing the dependent countries to remain *underdeveloped.* Raw materials were taken out of these countries, profiting only a few middlemen, rather than being manufactured at home into goods for sale in the capitalist market—thus robbing the developing nations of the profits and jobs they needed to develop a stable middle class. Political leaders acted as intermediaries between their own countries and the rich countries on which they depended. This meant they had to pay as much attention to foreigners' wishes as to the needs of their own people. The best and brightest businesspeople in countries like Brazil and Argentina went to work for foreign companies instead of starting companies of their own. The gift of a shoe factory provided employment for some but put traditional shoemakers out of work. To maintain new factories, local owners had to buy parts and hire technicians from the donor countries with scarce foreign currency.

Over time, foreign aid began to take the form of loans rather than gifts. When development did not occur as rapidly as planned, the countries borrowed more. Today many Latin American nations are essentially bankrupt as a result of accumulated debt. Whatever economic gains they make will go toward paying the interest on past loans. It is estimated that a net total of $20 billion a year is being transferred from developing nations to the developed nations to pay off loans; these repayments and interest charges far exceed any new aid from abroad. Moreover, the international financial community is requiring that the debtor nations impose strict austerity measures in order to qualify for more loans or to renegotiate outstanding debts. As a result, these countries are forced to cut a wide array of health, nutrition, and social service programs, further damaging the already poor prospects of children, women, and other vulnerable populations. This situation prompted Tanzania's president, Julius Nyerere, to ask: "Must we starve our children to pay our debts" (quoted in Bradshaw et al., 1993, p. 630)?

Dependency slowed political as well as economic development in many developing countries. Numerous dictators, armies, and secret police forces, trained and equipped by foreign powers, have used foreign aid and loans to line their own pockets, pay off their supporters, and repress their populations.

Other problems of developing nations derive from their position in the world system. Core nations among the developed countries set the terms of international trade because of their control of currency, shipping, and markets and because they trade relatively high-priced manufactured goods for raw materials, agricultural products, and relatively low-priced goods (baskets, textiles, and the like). One reason that developing countries are behind is that developed countries started out ahead.

A good illustration of the dynamics of the relationship between developed and developing nations is the economic crisis that struck the Asian markets in October 1997. For a number of years foreign investors had poured money into Thailand. As a result, interest rates were so low that it was easy to borrow money to speculate. This easy money built office towers, one after the other, even though none of them were being filled because there were no businesses to fill them (Sloan, 1997a). By the summer of 1997, however, investors began taking their dollars elsewhere, and currency speculators began to bail out of the stagnant economy and to sell the Thai currency, the *baht,* for dollars. This forced the Thai government to devalue its currency (because such a large part of its value had been based on foreign investors' willingness to back it). Other Asian currencies, such as Malaysia's, also lost value. Citizens' savings became worth far less overnight. Finally, in October, Hong Kong, fearing that speculators' sale of its currency would devalue the currency, raised interest rates an enormous 300 percent, thus making its currency more valuable, but also less accessible for development. The Hong Kong stock market plunged immediately, losing about 10 percent of its value in one day (Powell, 1997).

The drop in Hong Kong's market caused U.S. mutual-fund investments in the area to lose value and soured the prospects of companies like IBM,

A collapse in the price of Thailand's currency that began in the summer of 1997 triggered an international financial crisis later that year. Here Hong Kong traders watch as the Hang Seng stock market index plunges in late October, after the government failed in its attempt to support Hong Kong's currency.

which depend on Asian sales to help meet their projected earnings. The U.S. stock market plunged by 554 points. The panicky sell-off was stopped only by a halt in trading on the New York Stock Exchange. Eventually, the fever subsided, and the U.S. markets rebounded in the coming days, but the Asian countries' currencies, as well as their citizens' savings in those currencies, had lost a great deal of their value. As dependency theory predicts, foreign investment had simply served to keep the Thai economy from developing. The crisis arose because developed countries had pumped too much money into the small underdeveloped economy of Thailand and then had pulled it out too fast, thus creating the panic which spread the "Asian Contagion" (Samuelson, 1997).

The problems of developing nations are complicated by rapid population growth (which eats up economic gains), environmental deterioration (including the depletion of resources like forests; see Chapter 16), severe inflation (brought on when governments cannot meet payrolls and other obligations), the "brain drain" (the emigration of skilled workers and professionals to rich nations), and vulnerability to natural disasters (because developing nations do not have reserve food, much less capital, to carry them through difficult times).

One of the consequences of severe economic hardship in the southern hemisphere is that the developing nations became breeding grounds for revolution and civil war. Tamils still fight Sinhalese in Sri Lanka, Eritreans and Tigrayans fought Amhara in Ethiopia, and Maoist followers of the Shining Path in Peru tried to marshal peasants against both the leftist government and the rightist military. Ideologies vary widely, from fundamentalist Islam to nationalism to communism. The common thread is the desperation of people who have little reason to believe the existing world system will ever help them.

With the end of the cold war and the end of conflict between east and west, the conflicts between north and south and between rich and poor countries are moving to the center stage in world affairs. Perhaps the biggest question facing the world today (and facing the United States as part of the world community) is whether we can find a way to close the gap between developed and developing nations. This is an issue not only for citizens of poor countries but also for citizens of rich countries, because both worlds are interdependent. We depend on workers in South Korea to make cars, computers, stereos, and other products that we regard as necessities. We buy copper from Zambia, oil from the Arabian Peninsula, and coffee from South America. We depend on other countries not just for material goods but also for cooperation in the pursuit of peace in an era of nuclear weapons. The problems of the developing world are our problems.

The American Economy as a Social System

The case of American Tourister, described in the opening of the chapter, shows the effect that the workings of the global economy can have on the employment and economy of a small Rhode Island town. Multiply that case by the thousands, and it is easy to see that the flow of jobs and capital out of the country on the part of corporations both large and small has posed enormous challenges for the entire U.S. economy. We turn now to a discussion of the underlying structure of the American economy.

A Market Economy

The economy of the United States is a free-*market* economy; that is, it is not controlled or heavily regulated by a central government. The market is driven by the principles of **capitalism**—the supply of and demand for goods and services. The "bible" of capitalism, the book that set forth a vision of the ideal capitalist society, was Scottish philosopher Adam Smith's *The Wealth of Nations,* published in 1776, the year of the Declaration of Independence. Capitalism, according to Smith, is based on three basic principles: private ownership of property, the profit motive, and free competition.

1. *Private ownership of property:* In a capitalist society, most goods and resources are owned by individuals (rather than the tribe or the state). Of particular significance, the means of production from farms to factories to McDonald's franchises are privately owned. People tend to view private property as a sacred right and to measure a person's worth partly in terms of what he or she owns. Smith believed that private property was a necessary incentive for both productivity and progress. The reason is found in capitalism's second principle, the profit motive.

2. *The profit motive:* Smith reasoned that if people keep the profits of their labor and/or ingenuity, they will be motivated to work harder to produce more. The more they make, the more they get, the more they want. The opportunity to make a profit not only makes people work harder; but encourages them to take calculated risks on new products and new ways of producing goods, thereby stimulating progress. What translates self-interest and acquisitiveness into a functioning economic system?

3. *Free competition:* In the drive for ever-greater profits, capitalists strive to discern what consumers need and want. Suppose an entrepreneur discovers (or creates) a desire for a new product: frozen dinners. If this new business is successful, other producers will be drawn into the market. To attract consumers and earn profits for themselves, they work to produce better frozen dinners at a lower cost. If they

succeed, the first entrepreneur will be forced to improve the product and/or lower prices or go out of business. The same principles of supply and demand apply to workers and wages. Just as businesses that charge too much for their products lose customers to their competitors, so businesses that pay their workers too little lose their best employees. Free competition, then, is the cornerstone of capitalism. It benefits society in two ways. First, it ensures that people's needs are met: where there is a need (or desire), a profit can be made. Second, it promotes efficiency: wasteful businesses and unfair employers are driven out of the market. American Tourister's corporate decisions were determined by the free-market economy: In order to keep the prices of its products low, it had to lower the costs of manufacturing by moving some of its production out of the country to take advantage of low wages and by locating its shipping center closer to major retail outlets. Also, American Tourister had to respond to changes in consumer preference, by switching to the production of soft luggage.

When cellular technology was introduced, cell phones cost hundreds of dollars. Today they are inexpensive and available everywhere. This photo was taken in Moscow.

Smith acknowledged that a capitalist economy would create economic inequalities, but he argued that the distribution of rags and riches would be just. In an ideal capitalist system, the rewards go to the "economically virtuous" (those who produce the best goods for the lowest price). Entrepreneurs reap the first gains. In the long run, however, everyone gains. The possibility of profit encourages the production of better and/or cheaper goods; the laws of supply and demand control prices and wages; the consumer is seen as sovereign. In Smith's often-quoted phrase, a capitalist economy is guided by an "invisible hand." It is this invisible hand that consistently reduces the prices of technological goods. Whether it is computers, cell phones, or VCRs, new technology is always priced high. If there is demand for a product, more and more companies will try to produce it cheaper. When cellular technology first became available, cell phones cost hundreds of dollars; now they are given away to encourage use of the phone and stimulate profits in cellular service companies.

The opposite of a capitalist market economy is the **command economy** found in socialist and communist societies. In a command economy all or most of the means of production are owned by the state. Economic activities are centrally planned: the government decides how much of the nation's resources (including human muscle and brainpower)

will be invested in agriculture, automobiles, arms, and other products. Most people work for the state. In return, the state guarantees employment, housing, health care, and other necessities of life. The major goal of socialist systems is to create an equitable distribution of wealth, a "classless society."

In reality, no economic system is purely capitalistic or communistic. As discussed in Chapter 14, in the *welfare state,* the government assumes some degree of responsibility for the well-being of citizens. The socialist economies of Europe (and, to some degree, the U.S. economy since the New Deal) are examples of modern welfare states, in which the government provides goods and services such as clean air and water, national defense, public transportation, or health care that individual citizens cannot buy because they are either too expensive or too difficult to divide into individual portions.

The command and capitalist economies are blended as well. The government is a major force in the American economy (the world's model for capitalism), and private ownership and a degree of free enterprise were allowed in the former Soviet Union (the archetypal command economy) as well as in today's Communist Chinese economy. In Japan's "state capitalism," the government often works in partnership with business. Nevertheless, ideals shape people's ideas of how their society should work. The ideals of capitalism have not changed very much since Adam Smith's day, even if economic realities have. The result is a distinctively modern, distinctively American form of capitalism.

Big Business: Some Historical Background

The most significant change in the American economy since the birth of this nation is the enormous increase in the scale of manufacturing and distribution. Adam Smith's vision of capitalism was based on society as he knew it. In the eighteenth century, economic activity was primarily local. Local farmers grew nearly all the food their community or region needed; local artisans supplied most other necessary goods, from horseshoes to pots and pans, baskets, and houses. This was even truer in the United States than in Europe. The Atlantic Ocean made international trade prohibitively expensive; within the country, towns and villages were spread out over wide open spaces. Against this background, it was possible to imagine a system of fair competition among individual entrepreneurs.

But even as Smith wrote, the social and economic landscape was changing. Roads and river transportation were improving, the population was growing, and different regions of the country were beginning to specialize in different kinds of products. The pace of change accelerated in the nineteenth century, with the coming of the Industrial Revolution. Industrialization was based on four technological changes. It is referred to as a "revolution" because these innovations were as radical in their social consequences as the French and American political revolutions (Toynbee, 1884/1969). The first technological advance was the harnessing of new sources of power: animals (including humans) and water mills were replaced by steam engines and, somewhat later, the internal combustion engine and electricity. The second advance was a more complex division of labor: production was divided into small tasks, and skilled artisans who created an entire item themselves were replaced by several workers performing simpler tasks under a common manager. The third change was the birth of the factory: the new division of labor required that workers be brought together in the same location. The fourth was the use of machines to perform some or all of the tasks once performed by

people. Equally important were advances in **infrastructure** technology, in techniques for moving raw materials, goods, people, and ideas from one place to another. The spread of railroads was followed closely by the invention of the telegraph (and later automobiles, airplanes, telephones, radio and television, communications satellites, computer modems, fax machines, and cellular phones).

The building of railroads and highways created the potential for a national marketplace. Technological innovations (such as inexpensive methods for producing steel) laid the foundation for mass production. But industrialization involved far more than technological advancement. It required new social structures to manage the technology and the change it brought about, including business transactions on an ever-increasing scale. In terms of its impact on the developing American society, the most important social innovation was the business corporation. Below, we consider the growth of corporations, beginning with the powerful push provided by the railroads.

Corporate Capitalism

According to the business historian Alfred Chandler (1976), railroads played a crucial role in the development of the American corporation. Most obviously, railroads made it possible to unite business activities dispersed over wide geographic areas. Textiles made in Spartanberg, South Carolina, could be shipped to Maine or New Mexico; a corporate headquarters in Pittsburgh could manage a steel mill in Allentown and an iron mine in Michigan. Indeed, a look at a railroad map shows you where the centers of industrial activity were in the late nineteenth and early twentieth centuries.

But, socially, railroads mattered in another way, according to Chandler. They themselves were the first enterprise so vast in scale that they demanded a new form of social organization. First, railroads were extraordinarily expensive; many investors had to pool their money to provide capital for constructing lines and building and maintaining cars and engines. Second, a national system composed of many small, independent railroads was impractical and inefficient. A number of independent lines were started, but it soon became clear that raising capital, coordinating schedules, and establishing a common gauge (size) for the tracks so that trains

Model T Fords roll off an early assembly line. Mechanized production was a major factor in the rise of big business.

could cross the nation were best handled by only a few companies. Third, a national rail network required efficient management. The system would not work if one clerk in Chicago and another in Denver sold different people tickets for the same seat on the same train to Los Angeles or if two dispatchers scheduled two trains to run in opposite directions on the same track at the same hour. A centralized management that delegated authority to, but also coordinated the activities of, many dispersed local managers was imperative. Thus railroads led to the invention of "external capitalization," or raising funds from people who would not be active managers of an enterprise. Too big to be run as family businesses, they also led to management by individuals who were not owners but worked primarily for salaries. In these ways, the railroad became a model for the modern corporation.

The Modern Corporation

A **corporation** is a formal organization (see Chapter 5), created by law, whose existence and liabilities are independent of particular owners and managers. The word "corporation" means, literally, a "created body." Almost any group of people who sign the appropriate papers and register with the state can qualify. A religious institution, a charity, a school, or a medical or dental practice can be a corporation. Most often, however, we use the term in reference to a particular kind of business.

Corporations differ from other business organizations in a number of significant ways. Under the law, a corporation is a kind of artificial person (Dan-Cohen, 1986). Like an ordinary person, a corporation can own property, make contracts, and sue or be sued. Because the corporation itself is a "person" under the law, the actual people who own it or work for it are not legally responsible for its actions. If you have an accident because the brakes on your new Chrysler fail, you sue Chrysler, not the chief executive officer, the engineer who designed the brakes, or the mechanic who failed to insert a critical screw. If Chrysler goes out of business before your accident, you cannot sue anyone. The corporate "person" that was legally responsible for construction of the automobile no longer exists. The principle of limited liability is essential to the workings of modern corporations (Orhnial, 1982). It is the result of nearly a hundred years of controversial court decisions (Friedman, 1973; Horowitz, 1977), and many still oppose it (for example, Nader, Green, and Seligman, 1976).

A second distinction between corporations and other businesses is that they can sell shares of ownership on the stock market. This enables corporations to raise much larger amounts of capital than individual entrepreneurs could on their own. The sale of shares (on the railroad model) not only increases the scale of corporate enterprise but also spreads both the costs and profits among many part owners, diluting the risks of free enterprise.

The trading floor of the New York Stock Exchange, where billions of dollars' worth of stock changes hands each day. Corporations that sell shares on the stock exchange can raise much more capital than individual investors could on their own.

The third distinguishing feature of corporations is the separation of ownership and management (Berle and Means, 1932; Galbraith, 1978). Although an individual or family may hold controlling shares, most large corporations are owned by literally thousands of shareholders. The ownership changes with every trade of stock on the stock exchange. Many of the owners are not individuals but mutual funds, pension funds, and institutional investors (Drucker, 1976). Unlike the owner or manager of a private business, stockholders have little or no direct control over the corporation's activities. In the first place, owner-stockholders are a widely dispersed group with few, if any, social connections; it would be extremely difficult for them to mobilize to push the company in one direction or another. Second, in most cases the owners' shares of the whole are too small to make it worth the time and trouble to play an active role. In principle, if you own ten shares of General Motors stock, you are entitled to a voice in the decisions made at the corporation's annual meeting. In practice, your ten shares are worth only about $650 at current market value. It probably would cost you around that just to go to the meeting! If you do not like the way the company is being run, you are more likely to sell your stock. The same would probably be true if you owned a thousand shares. (Moreover, most investors, large and small, make money buying and selling stock, not from the proportion of profits corporations may distribute as dividends.) Who, then, runs the corporations?

Who Controls Corporations?

The answer to this question is more complicated than one might imagine. The chief executive officer (CEO) manages the daily and yearly activities of a corporation. He or she makes such decisions as whom to hire or promote to top management, whether to enter into a new line of business, how to cut costs, where to apply for major loans, how to handle labor relations, and the like. Often these decisions are made in consultation with subordinate executives; sometimes they are made by the CEO alone. In most cases the CEO is not the owner of the firm (though most own large blocks of stock) but, rather, an employee.

The CEO is responsible to the corporation's board of directors, a group of a dozen or so executive officers of the company, prominent business-people from other companies, and public figures. In addition to protecting stockholders' interests, the board is charged with general oversight of operations and, to some extent, with protecting the public interest (for example, by seeing that the corporation does not engage in illegal activities). The board of directors, in turn, is elected by and responsible to stockholders.

This simple, clear arrangement does not dictate who actually controls corporations, however. Many sociologists argue that corporations are controlled by their CEOs. CEOs usually select members of the board and set their compensation and benefits; the board rarely "interferes" with management unless there is a crisis. Ordinary stockholders do have the right to nominate and approve board members, but this is rarely exercised. As a result, the invisible hand of the market has been replaced by the visible hand of management (Chandler, 1976). Managers are more concerned with improving their personal incomes and advancing their careers than with responding to consumer demand or making a profit for shareholders. Poor corporate performance has recently led to the replacement of many managers by boards, including the CEOs at IBM and Apple Computer, for example (see Chapter 5).

One factor that limits the autonomy of managers is *strategic control*. In this scenario, someone who is not a member of the executive team and is not directly involved in management controls the corporation from the outside, issuing directives to the CEO. If a CEO does not comply, he or she is fired. For example, Howard Hughes, who for many years owned 78 percent of the stock in TWA, reportedly ran the company on a daily basis, even though he was never an executive officer and only briefly sat on its board of directors. All major decisions about personnel, business policy, labor relations, joint ventures, and the like, were cleared with him.

A second limiting factor is *intercorporate control*. A CEO's decision-making options are limited by the willingness of other corporations (especially banks and financial institutions) to permit specific actions. In 1997, Hilton Hotels Corporation, a major investor in and would-be purchaser of ITT, set out to depose the board of ITT so that it could then vote in its own slate of directors, thus paving the way for Hilton's takeover of ITT. Rand Araskog, ITT's CEO, favored the slightly better offer of another company, so Hilton took its offer to the stockholders in a heated and highly visible advertising campaign (Sloan, 1997b).

Some sociologists carry the idea of intercorporate control one step further. They argue that members of corporate boards, top managers, and major stockholders are knit together to form a "capitalist elite" (Mills, 1951) (see also Chapter 14). This hidden class is held together by a web of interlocking directorships (Mizruchi, 1996), exchanges of personnel, and social interaction (they attended the same schools and universities, belong to the same exclusive clubs, and so on). According to Michael Useem's detailed study of financial reports and biographical data (1984), these ties create a feeling of common identity among the owners and managers of different corporations. Useem holds that the level of "class consciousness" among corporate owners and top management is higher than in any other sector of American society.

Other researchers find the notion of a capitalist elite not so much wrong as oversimplified or perhaps outdated (Herman, 1981; Hirsch, 1986). The surge of corporate takeovers in the 1980s and resurgence in the 1990s, in particular, reveal divisions among corporate captains and the heads of financial institutions. Hostile takeovers in which one corporation purchases another by acquiring stock on the open market (often offering stockholders more than the market value for their shares), rather than negotiating with the managers of the company targeted for acquisition, were an invention of the late 1950s and early 1960s.

When takeovers first came to attention, they were a direct challenge to accepted business practice, one that sent shock waves through the corporate community. Executives of major corporations were accustomed to thinking of all but their largest stockholders as insignificant. Occasional proxy fights or lawsuits by disgruntled stockholders were brushed aside. The new mode of acquiring companies through stock transactions, ignoring the wishes and public protests of the target company's managers and board of directors, forced executives to recognize that they were nothing more than hired agents of corporate stockholders. Suddenly, their own positions were not secure. Adding insult to injury, the takeover artists were outsiders, upstarts, or "foxes"; their names, backgrounds, and ambitions were unknown to the "lions" (established corporations), who saw themselves as kings of the corporate jungle. Moreover, the corporation itself was being redefined "as a salable bundle of liquid assets, rather than as a producer of goods and services" (Hirsch, 1986, p. 801).

In the 1970s and 1980s, the volume of takeovers exploded. Acquirers included DuPont, Philip Morris, Pan American, and R. J. Reynolds. Among the targets were 7-Up, Pet Foods, Marshall Field's, National Airlines, Del Monte, and Gulf. Some of the acquirers, like R. J. Reynolds, were then taken over themselves. Established investment banks, brokerage houses, and law firms that had once viewed corporate takeovers as highway robbery jumped on the bandwagon. All this resulted in the issue of billions of dollars in "junk bonds" (poorly secured debt, the equivalent of loans with no collateral) and tempted many speculators to violate laws. In the late 1980s and early 1990s the bubble burst. Leading inside traders (stockbrokers who illegally used inside information, not available to the general public, to make huge profits) were arrested, and once-powerful Wall Street firms that had financed takeovers were forced to file for bankruptcy.

At the peak of the takeover craze, corporate solidarity—the "capitalist elite"—was broken. Corporate raiders and the financial institutions that supported them were in control, and executives were forced to devote much of their time to protecting themselves and their corporations from attack. Although the rate of takeovers slowed, they have not disappeared. In the late 1990s media and investment companies were popular targets. Time Warner purchased Turner Broadcasting; Disney bought ABC; and Westinghouse bought CBS and Infinity Broadcasting (syndicator of radio shows by personalities Don Imus and Howard Stern) (Bagdikian, 1997). The Travelers Group, Inc., bought Salomon Brothers in an effort to create an investment services firm to rival Dean Witter/Morgan Stanley and Merrill Lynch (Meyer, 1997b). In the spring of 1998 Daimler-Benz, makers of Mercedes automobiles and trucks, shocked the economic world by purchasing American automobile manufacturer Chrysler. Experts predict a surge of mergers in the automobile industry in the next few years.

Market Dominance

The issue of control also applies to the role large corporations play in the economy as a whole. *Monopolies*—business firms that control an entire industry—are against the law in the United States. The Sherman Antitrust Act, passed by Congress in 1890, made it a criminal offense "to monopolize or attempt to monopolize" the production and distribution of a product. Nevertheless, large corporations have eliminated much of the competition in a number of industries. For example, in 1904 there were thirty-four automobile manufacturers in the United States, and in 1921, eighty-eight; today General Motors, Ford, and Chrysler dominate the industry, along with Japanese automakers Toyota, Nissan, and Honda. The oil industry is dominated by the "seven sisters"; grain trade, by five companies; and TV broadcasting, by four major networks and two minor networks. Aluminum, tires, soap, cigarettes, and lightbulbs are produced and distributed by a few familiar firms. Microsoft's Windows operating system is a near monopoly, a fact which has not been lost on the federal government. In February 1998 Bill Gates appeared before the Senate Judiciary Committee, which was investigating Microsoft's efforts to dominate the Internet by integrating its net browser into the Windows operating system. The Department of Justice brought suit against Microsoft in May 1998 for engaging in monopolistic practices. Two to four companies also dominate the market for most food products. The term for domination of an industry by a small number of large companies is *oligopoly* (from the Greek word for "few sellers").

But oligopolies are vulnerable. For example, American Telephone and Telegraph, which for decades dominated the telecommunications industry, faces challenges from MCI, Sprint, and regional telecommunications companies like Bell Atlantic. IBM and Apple, which dominated the computer industry in the 1970s and early 1980s, are facing challenges from Dell, Gateway, and other companies. In fact, Apple, which had four different CEOs from 1992 to 1997, is at an all-time low and may not survive (Meyer, 1997a). Microsoft, which dominated the software and Internet industry in the 1990s much as Apple did the computer industry in the 1970s and 1980s, may face similar competition early in the next century. ABC, NBC, and CBS, the three major TV networks, are encountering increasing competition from Fox and cable television (see *Sociology and the Media:* Television as Big Business).

A more recent corporate innovation is the **conglomerate**—a company with holdings and subsidiaries in a number of different industries. In a conglomerate, a core staff of executives manage a "portfolio" of divisions whose products and services have little or no relation to one another. Sheraton Hotels, the Hartford Insurance Company, and Hostess are all owned by ITT, a "telephone" company. [This trend is not confined to the United States. The French conglomerate CGE (Cie Génerale D'Électricité), which acquired ITT's European telecommunications operations in 1988, produces everything from telephones to nuclear power plants.] The acquisition of unrelated companies allows corporations to grow without violating antitrust laws. It also enables them to avoid some of the effects of market pressures: losses in one division may be offset by profits in another.

Finally, large corporations dominate the economy through their sheer size. As shown in Figure 15-3, General Electric is the largest of the large corporations, followed by Coca-Cola, Microsoft, and Exxon. AT&T is actually at the bottom of the list, with IBM and Procter & Gamble just slightly ahead of it. General Motors, not on the list, nonetheless generates the most revenue of the corporate behemoths— $168,369,000,000. It is the third-largest company in terms of employees: 640,000. The biggest employer is the U.S. Postal Service, followed by Wal-Mart.

The result of these developments is what James Coleman (1982) has called an *asymmetric* society. Coleman compares the corporation (a "person" under the law) to ordinary people. Ordinary people have not changed very much over this century: we live a bit longer, and we are slightly taller, heavier, and stronger than our great-grandparents were. In contrast, corporations have grown enormously in size and strength and may live for hundreds of years. If human beings had doubled in size and strength, this would not even approach the enormous expansion of corporations. As a result, individuals and corporations are unequal in both ability and vulnerability. Because of their enormous

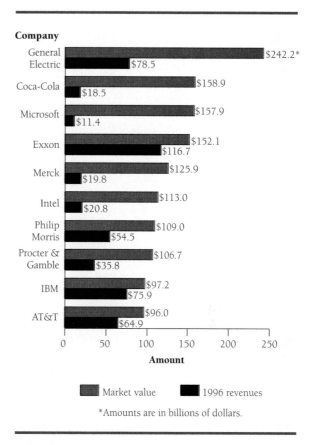

Company

Figure 15-3   *Top-Ten U.S. Companies by Market Value, 1997*

The market value of America's largest corporations exceeds the gross national product (GNP) of many nations. *Source: Newsweek,* Dec. 29, 1997, p. 61.

resources, corporations can accomplish undertakings well beyond the scope of individuals. For the same reason, they are not as vulnerable as individuals are to the law (because of limited liability) or to market pressures. The rise of labor unions, government regulatory agencies, and, most recently, consumer groups all can be seen as responses to this asymmetry.

Government and the Economy: Issues and Policies

Government plays a dual role in the economy. On the one hand, it is an *enabler,* providing goods, such as money, and services, such as the civil courts, that make it possible for individuals and corporations to engage in a wide range of sometimes complex

Television as Big Business

The 1990s witnessed an explosion of new television technologies. Over 62 percent of American households with TVs—approximately 59 million American homes—are now equipped with cable (*Statistical Abstract*, 1996, p. 561). Local cable operators offer their subscribers a selection of the fifty or more broadcast signals. Miniaturized equipment, satellite transmission, and satellite pools enable local news broadcasts to offer on-the-spot coverage of national and international stories, not just local news. Satellite dishes, now frequently installed in homes, allow viewers to capture many of these broadcasts for themselves. VCRs, videocassettes, videodiscs, and video games complete the new television cornucopia. Once dependent on the three major networks for information and entertainment, TV viewers now have a wide range of options.

In theory, the multiplication of channels should lead to greater competition among broadcasters, and competition should lead to diversification. To win audiences via the new technology, broadcasters should be catering to a broader range of tastes in entertainment and a wider range of political points of view. The once-limited "marketplace of ideas" should become a huge bazaar. In practice, however, this is not what has happened. And the primary reason is that television is big business.

Like other businesses, TV networks (of whatever type) are in business to make a profit. In general, advertisers want to avoid programs that deal with complicated themes or controversial topics that might anger potential customers (Herman and Chomsky, 1988). Rather, they want to keep viewers happy and in the "buying mood." To attract the widest-possible audience, television appeals to the "lowest common denominator," supplying programs that will amuse everyone and offend no one. From time to time companies do sponsor serious pro-

> **Economic forces chain commercial broadcasting to the tyranny of the trivial.**
> —Todd Gitlin

grams, often as part of a public relations campaign to upgrade their image. But even then they tend to prefer safe programs (the ballet or a slice of American history) to controversial topics (such as AIDS or the homeless). As a result, much television is apolitical, valuing private consumption above political awareness and emphasizing the pursuit of "private happiness, relief, and self-improvement" (Gitlin, 1985, p. 330).

Increased competition has strengthened, not weakened, this trend, in part because it is not really very competitive.

Major networks and cable franchises operate, in major markets at least, like quasi monopolies—guaranteed to turn a profit simply by virtue of their access to the airwaves reaching a sizable population. Ratings simply determine how much of a profit they make (Bagdikian, 1997). Originally the FCC regulations for radio and television stations limited companies to ownership of seven AM, seven FM, and seven television stations. In 1984 that number was increased to twelve for each type of station. This deregulation has meant that the big business of television is in even fewer hands than it was prior to deregulation. So, even though there are more channels, there is not necessarily more competition. In 1984 there were fifty corporations controlling the media; by 1987, there were only twenty-six. By 1996, the number was down to ten (Bagdikian, 1997).

This "media cartel" is the result of enormous mergers. When ABC/Capital Cities merged with Disney, the deal was worth $19 *billion*. The company that resulted is a conglomerate that is strong in every aspect of media: newspapers, radio, broadcast television, books, magazines, movies, cable systems and programming, videocassettes, and recordings, as well as increasing control of the wires that bring telephone and cable service to homes around the nation.

The political and economic clout of these media giants can be seen in the Telecommunications Act of 1996. Though billed as opening up the media to new competitors such as regional telephone companies, the actual effect of this act has been a further stifling of competition. It is now possible for one media giant to reach 35 percent of all American households in a single market. One company can now own more than one radio station in one market. Companies may also own both cable and TV stations in the same market. There may be 11,800 cable systems, but most are monopolies in their cities. (The same is true for daily newspapers.) Even with four different major networks, programming is still basically of the same type—sit-coms; news magazines; afternoon soap operas and talk shows; and police, medical, and legal dramas. Only the poorly funded public stations offer programming that is considerably different (Bagdikian, 1997). When one considers that the average child spends far more time in front of the television than in front of a teacher, the sameness of programming and the small pool of companies that make up the media cartel suggest that stimulating programming has gone down in direct proportion to the lack of stimulation of competition.

Much of America used to tune in to the evening news on one of the three major networks during the dinner hour. However, during the 1980s the major networks' share of this prime-time audience dropped from about 75 to 63 percent. The public was not switching to other news programs. Less than 1 percent of households that had access to the Turner Network's Cable News Network (CNN) and Cable-Satellite Public Affairs Network (C-SPAN) tuned in during evening hours. The *MacNeil/Lehrer NewsHour* on PBS received similarly low ratings. Rather, people were tuning in to entertainment or turning off their sets (Entman, 1989). Aware of this shift, all three networks announced substantial cuts in their news budgets in the late 1980s. Fewer correspondents and researchers and smaller crews can mean more reliance on statements by government officials, printed handouts, prestaged "photo opportunities," and pooled news services (and therefore more similarity among news programs) and less support for investigative journalism that might or might not turn up usable stories. In other words, economic competition has led to cutbacks and consolidation, not to diversification.

Robert Entman (1989) analyzed the content of the news during this period of intensified competition (1975 to 1986). He found that on national broadcasts, human interest stories (about people involved in situations that are not linked to political or public policy issues) and coverage of foreign policy (based primarily on official statements by government officials) both increased by 50 percent, while coverage of domestic political and policy issues decreased by 37 percent. The content of local newscasts varied from community to community. But, in general, coverage of accidents, sports, weather, and crime increased, while coverage of local political issues decreased. Thus market pressures seem to encourage softer news coverage.

Todd Gitlin (1985) found much the same pattern in entertainment programming. Because of the high cost of installing cables and producing programs, large companies—Warner Amex, Times Mirror, Viacom, Fox, and others—have an edge over smaller companies. They can win local cable franchises by promising more programs at a lower cost and/or by buying out smaller companies. A few suppliers provide most of the programming. Home Box Office (owned by Time Warner) controls more than half the market for recent Hollywood films and made-for-TV movies. The advent of cable TV has led not to a diversity of choices but to more of the same—more sports, more
continued

Television as Big Business *(concluded)*

old movies, more news, more reruns of situation comedies. To be sure, the FCC requires that cable franchises provide public access channels. But programs on these channels usually are poorly advertised, underfunded, and amateurish.

As Entman and Gitlin both point out, the major sources of new political ideas and artistic innovations lie outside the normal marketplace. The media that "articulate, sharpen, ques-

tion world views" (Gitlin, 1985, p. 330)—magazines such as *MS, Mother Jones, The Public Interest, The Economist,* and others—tend to be low-profit or no-profit operations. Economic forces chain "commercial broadcasting to the tyranny of the trivial" (Gitlin, 1985, p. 327):

> To sum up, the brave new cornucopia is likely to create only minor, marginal chances for a diversity of substance and fewer and fewer as time goes

on. The workings of the market give Americans every incentive to remain conventionally entertainment-happy. Conglomeration proceeds apace. Homogeneity at the cultural center is complemented by consumer fragmentation at the margins. Technology opens doors, and oligopoly marches in just behind, slamming them. There can be no technological fix for what is, after all, a social problem (Gitlin, 1985, p. 332).

---

business activities, often involving contracts between strangers. On the other hand, it is a *regulator,* protecting businesses from unfair competition (through antitrust legislation) and workers and consumers from harmful products (for example, through the Occupational Safety and Health Administration and the Food and Drug Administration) and unfair practices (such as the Equal Employment Opportunities Commission's investigation of racial and gender discrimination).

As mentioned earlier, the growth of government that led to today's welfare state began in the 1930s (as described in Chapter 14). President Roosevelt's New Deal was inspired by the theories of the English economist John Maynard Keynes (Schott, 1983). From the point of view of public policy, the central teaching of Keynesian economics was that governments should (1) increase spending during recessions (if necessary, by borrowing) to stimulate the economy and to put people back to work and (2) decrease spending and/or raise taxes during economic booms to prevent inflation. This view guided U.S. government policy for about fifty years, in large part because so many people benefited from it. Businesspeople and other taxpayers might have complained loudly about "big government" and high taxation, but they looked to Washington for better education for their children, national defense, water projects, police protection, national

parks, highways, housing subsidies, and countless other goods and services. The people who benefited most from expanding government programs were not the poor but the middle class.

One leading American Keynesian, John Kenneth Galbraith (1978), maintained that big government had become essential, not only because individuals wanted the goods and services it provided but also because modern business depended on it. If big corporations are to develop new products that require long-range research and expensive capital investment, they need a stable environment. Only the government can provide this. Moreover, the government supports some sectors of the economy directly. The government not only is a very large customer but also is relatively insensitive to price. Many government contracts, especially defense contracts, guarantee manufacturers a profit. Few corporations would undertake such expensive, long-term, risky ventures without guarantees. This is a clear departure from the ideals of capitalism but may result in discoveries and inventions that benefit the public at large. For example, this was a major argument for large investments in the space program. Space technology not only took individuals to the moon but also produced a variety of consumer goods, such as Teflon coatings for nonstick pans. Similarly, the development of the modern computer industry was stimulated by lucrative con-

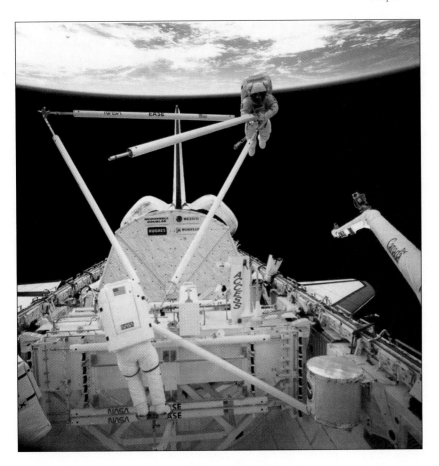

Space exploration has yielded technology that is useful on earth, such as computers and nonstick coatings. Today, space missions, like corporations, are multinational ventures.

tracts from the military and the Internal Revenue Service (Goldstine, 1972).

In the late 1970s, after the league of oil-producing nations (OPEC) hiked the price of oil, the United States (and other western nations) faced an unprecedented set of economic problems. Unemployment rates (associated with recession) and inflation (associated with boom times) were both high. Government policies that had worked in the past now seemed ineffective. As a result of this crisis, many policy makers were drawn to two alternative economic theories, monetarism and "supply-side economics." The leading exponent of monetarism in the United States is Milton Friedman. Friedman argues that the key to a sound economy is control over the supply of money. The government should ensure a stable currency but otherwise adopt a "hands-off" policy toward the economy. This view influenced the Federal Reserve Board's decision to keep interest rates high in the inflationary period of the late 1970s and 1980s.

The Federal Reserve has kept interest rates low in the late 1990s because of the strength of the economy, though there have been a few minor increases in the interest rates in order to prevent inflation. Limiting the growth of the money supply has been seen as the best way to slow inflation.

Supply-side economics is associated with political figures, not with academic theories or research. Its main idea is that Keynesians put too much emphasis on consumer demand, in the belief that increases in the demand for goods and services lead to increases in production. Supply-siders argue that the way to stimulate the economy is to make expansion attractive for businesses by cutting taxes and thus freeing private wealth for investment. Whether people invest the money they save directly in stocks or put their savings in a bank (which pays interest on savings accounts by investing its funds), productivity will increase. And increases in the supply of goods and services will lower costs, reducing both inflation and unemployment. Savings are the cornerstone of supply-side economics. However, during the 1980s, when this theory was put to work, the savings rate in the United States actually fell. The United States lags far behind other industrial nations in overall savings rate. As a result, we have had to borrow heavily from abroad, increasing the national deficit.

In summary, American capitalism has undergone profound changes since the birth of our nation. The growth of corporations changed the financing and organization of business. Oligopolies, conglomerates, and American-based multinationals are pushing many independent entrepreneurs to the outer edges of the economy. The government now plays a major and controversial role in managing the economy. Even so, the American economy is at the mercy of global forces that are beyond our government's control. How does the changing structure of capitalism affect ordinary working people?

The World of Work

The sociology of work focuses on the ways in which technology and organizational structure shape behavior, attitudes, and experiences; it also looks at the social processes that determine who works, what kind of work is performed, and what rewards are given.

The Social Organization of Work

The social organization of work has changed dramatically since the days when this nation was founded. Well into the nineteenth century, most goods were produced by artisans. Even if they worked for someone else, they usually were paid for the product (a piece rate), not by the hour, and so could decide their own hours and set their own paces. Many worked in their own homes or other settings where they were not under direct supervision. Equally important, they were highly skilled and difficult to replace. Employers (and customers) had to treat them with respect.

Industrialization replaced traditional crafts with a combination of machines, low-skilled labor, and managers. How did this affect the worker and the experience of work? Crafts were learned through years of apprenticeship; factory jobs could be learned in a matter of weeks. (Indeed, many tasks were performed by children.) This meant, first, that

workers lost their bargaining power. If they demanded better wages or working conditions or if they refused to work seven days a week or ten hours a day (a typical workweek at the turn of the century), they were easily replaced. Second, factory jobs gave the worker little or no opportunity for creativity. In contrast to crafts, which required judgment and allowed for individual expression, factory jobs were routinized. Finally, control of work was taken over by managers. Managers, not the workers themselves, determined what work was to be done, the speed of the conveyor belt that carried items past workers, and so on. Thus industrialization replaced highly skilled work with low-skill jobs. This trend continues today. The complexity of today's technology often obscures the fact that the human contribution is constantly reduced. For example, most computer programmers have less specialized knowledge and less autonomy than did the coppersmiths, wheelwrights, framework knitters, shipwrights, and other artisans of 200 years ago (Calhoun, 1981).

Today we are a nation of employees. The great majority of Americans work for someone else (or, in the case of corporations, something else). They do not set their own hours or design their own working conditions. Indeed, many consider themselves lucky to have a job at all.

For Better or Worse?

The above sections have emphasized the negative consequences of new technology. But automation has benefits as well as costs. It was technology and the formal business organization—not how hard people worked—that produced the great economic expansion and vast increases in wealth in western nations over the last century. Although this wealth was by no means distributed evenly, the overall standard of living clearly improved. Moreover, there is little dispute about the benefits of automation and increased productivity to consumers. Although some of the distinctiveness of handcrafted goods is lost, many more goods are available, generally at lower prices. What is less clear is how to weigh the gains and losses for workers. Computers and automation make difficult or tedious jobs easier to perform. Few people (including secretaries) who have become familiar with word processors chose to go back to typewriters. As a result, typewriters are completely absent from most workplaces. Some of the jobs that have been automated were dangerous, such as spraying paint on automobiles, which exposed workers to high doses of toxic substances.

What Work Do People Do?

When asked to describe a worker, most Americans picture a laborer with a hard hat, rough hands, and little education. In reality, the average or typical worker in the United States today is a white-collar office worker. The shift from blue-collar to white-collar work is an indirect result of continuing industrialization. Some people call this process deindustrialization. Automation eliminated many jobs in production, but the growth of corporations led to a proliferation of jobs that, though not directly related to production, are designed to maintain profits and/or keep the corporation functioning: selling, billing, advertising, conducting public relations, keeping track of employees (personnel jobs), handling conflicts with the government or private citizens (lawyers), and filing taxes (accountants). Thus the shift from blue-collar to white-collar work represents a shift from a manufacturing to a **service and information economy,** in which most workers are not directly involved in production. Rather they work with people, ideas, and information. Nearly all of the ten fastest-growing occupations in this decade are in the service economy (see Figure 15-4).

White-collar work is not all that it used to be, however. In the past, an office job was "respectable," a guarantee of middle-class status. To some extent this is still true in the public's imagination. But actual white-collar occupations include a mixture of high-paid and low-paid, high-prestige and low-prestige, and high-skill and low-skill jobs. About half of today's white-collar workers are sales and clerical workers, many of whom earn less than assembly-line workers. The other half are professional, technical, and managerial employees. But even the professional category includes a great many jobs that require little training and offer few opportunities for advancement (title searchers, proofreaders, paralegal assistants). (See Table 15-3 for who works in which job categories.)

A number of social scientists (Duster, 1988; Kasarda, 1989; Wilson, 1987) believe that advancing industrialization has created two separate labor markets in the United States and other capitalist nations. The *primary labor market* is composed of workers in large corporations, unionized industries, skilled trades (such as plumbing), government

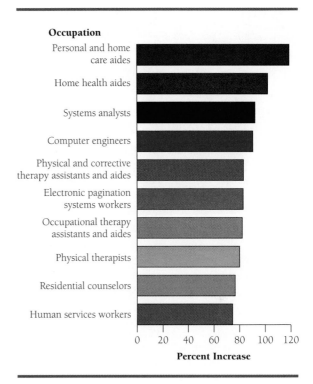

Figure 15-4   *Ten Fastest-Growing Occupations: 1994–2005*

As we enter the twenty-first century, the fastest-growing occupations in the United States are expected to be in service jobs.

Source: U.S. Bureau of the Census, *Statistical Abstract of the United States, 1996,* Washington, DC: GPO, 1996, p. 409, table 639.

agencies, and the professions. Employment in the primary market offers relatively high wages, good working conditions, job security, and opportunities for promotion. The typical worker has specialized skills and/or advanced education.

The *secondary labor market* is composed of workers in local factories, small businesses (such as real estate and travel agencies), personal service enterprises (such as fitness centers and fast-food establishments), and nonfamily farms. Employment in the secondary market is temporary and unstable, wages are low, working conditions are often poor, and there are few, if any, opportunities for promotion. (Waiters and waitresses are rarely promoted to restaurant managers; migrant farmworkers rarely become supervisors.) The typical employee is an unskilled, nonunion, part-time worker. Thus the two labor markets are not only separate but also unequal.

About half of today's white-collar employees are sales and clerical workers, many of whom work for long hours in sterile surroundings for pay that is lower than the earnings of blue-collar workers.

The internal organization of corporations often is a mirror image of the dual labor market (Kanter, 1977, 1989). "Primary jobs" (for example, public relations assistant, sales representative, or executive trainee) offer a high probability of advancement, frequent evaluations and promotions, opportunities to master and use new skills, a high level of challenge, and the possibility of moving to top-level management. "Secondary jobs" (for example, word processor, receptionist, or janitor) are characterized by limited opportunities for advancement, long time lapses between evaluations and job moves, unchallenging tasks, and few opportunities to master new skills. In most corporations it is extremely rare for an individual to move from the slow to the fast track.

In recent years the secondary labor market in the United States has been growing faster than the primary market. Between 1970 and 1994 total employment in the United States increased by just over 44 million workers. Service industries alone accounted for 22 million new jobs, with fast-food establishments, hotels, health services, data processing, personnel, and janitorial services leading the way. At the same time, many industries in the primary sector—steel, mining, and the like—came under attack. More than 600,000 manufacturing jobs were lost (*Statistical Abstract*, 1996, p. 410, table 641). During the 1990s, steep declines oc-

Table 15-3   *Employment and Earnings*

Major Occupation of Longest Job Held	All Workers			
	Women		Men	
	Number (Thousands)	Median Earnings	Number (Thousands)	Median Earnings
Executive, administrators, and managerial	7,570	25,980	9,906	41,410
Professional specialty	10,198	26,449	8,777	41,090
Technical and related support	2,340	22,524	1,977	30,642
Sales	8,626	9,070	8,364	25,790
Administrative support, including clerical	16,085	15,880	4,189	21,023
Precision production, craft, and repair	1,362	15,815	13,333	24,681
Machine operators, assemblers, and inspectors	3,503	12,095	5,303	20,621
Transportation and material moving	589	11,686	5,061	21,546
Handlers, equipment cleaners, helpers, and laborers	1,156	7,893	4,944	10,905
Service workers	12,438	7,059	8,118	11,746
Framing, forestry, and fishing	752	4,223	3,456	10,431
Total*	64,706	14,323	74,264	23,656

Note: Covers civilians 15 years old and over as of March 1995. Based on Current Population Survey.

*Includes persons whose longest job was in the Armed Forces.

Source: U.S. Bureau of the Census, *Statistical Abstract of the United States, 1996*, Washington, DC: GPO, 1996, p. 428.

curred among letterpress operators; typesetting and composing machine operators; directory-assistance operators; data-entry keyers; billing, posting, and calculating machine operators; and central office workers.

In his book, *When Work Disappears, The World of the New Urban Poor* (1996), sociologist William Julius Wilson describes how disadvantaged, under-educated workers have been hardest hit by the changes in labor markets. The technological changes that produce new jobs in the secondary market tend to eliminate jobs in the primary labor market. For example, as the need for educated, skilled workers capable of designing, engineering, and operating computerized machine tools has grown, the need for individuals who used to do such work manually has evaporated. Most of the lost jobs have been in cities, and most of the people affected have been low-educated men, many of them African Americans:

> The manufacturing losses in some northern cities have been staggering. In the twenty-year period from 1967 to 1987, Philadelphia lost 64 percent of its manufacturing jobs; Chicago lost 60 percent; New York City, 58 percent; Detroit, 51 percent. In absolute numbers, these percentages represent the loss of 160,000 jobs in Philadelphia, 326,000 jobs in Chicago, 520,000—over half a million—in New York, and 108,000 in Detroit. (Wilson, 1996, pp. 29–30)

While the rise of the secondary labor market has hurt urban African American men, the secondary labor market has been a boon to female workers. African American women's employment in social service jobs such as in elementary schools, nursing homes and hospitals, and child care rose from 30.5 percent in 1979 to 40.5 percent in 1993. Men, too, are taking these jobs, but in smaller numbers. The earnings for these men and women are 25 to 30 percent less than the earnings from jobs in manufacturing, however (Wilson, 1996).

By the year 2000 the economy is expected to generate 6 million new jobs in skilled executive, professional, and technical occupations, compared with only 1 million new jobs in less skilled and laborer categories. But even low-level clerical, crafts, sales, and service positions will require an ability to use word processors and computers and to read gauges and printouts. Estimates are that 2 to 3 percent of the labor force may need to be retrained each year. As we have seen, nearly one-third

of tomorrow's workforce will come from minority groups, yet almost half of these young people are growing up in poverty. If current trends continue, one-fourth will drop out of high school, and another one-fourth will graduate without the skills needed for employment in a technologically advanced economy. Most observers predict a wide gap between jobs and skills in coming decades. Well-educated young people will face a future of expanding job opportunities and rising wages, while those with little education will face a future of diminishing opportunities and continuing poverty.

The Meaning of Work

Sociologists are interested not only in what work people do but also in their attitudes toward their activities. Work has meant different things to different peoples. In ancient Athens, members of the upper class considered manual work and commerce beneath them. They felt that such work brutalized the mind, corrupted the soul, and robbed a person of independence of spirit. (The Greek word for manual work, *ponos*, means "toil and sorrow.") At the same time, the early Athenians considered it childish to seek entertainment for its own sake. The proper life was one of contemplation (made possible for aristocrats by slave labor).

The Hebrews saw work as a curse brought on by Adam and Eve when they disobeyed God and were cast out of the Garden of Eden. Humankind was sentenced to a life of hard labor. The early Christians introduced the concept of "good works." A person could perform acts of charity for others, and the giver was as blessed as the receiver. But the early Christians did not believe in work for work's sake.

Not until the Protestant Reformation of the sixteenth century did westerners begin to equate hard work with virtue (see Chapter 13). Martin Luther rebelled against the elitism of monks, who considered themselves superior to common people because they devoted themselves full-time to religion. Luther swept away the distinction between religious life and worldly activity. To work was to serve God. For some Protestants, worldly success was a sign of God's grace. The longer and harder a person worked, the better. Idleness was sinfulness. John Calvin urged his followers to accumulate wealth and to use that wealth for charity and for the creation of more work, rather than to spend it on themselves. Thus work was transformed from a regrettable necessity into a moral duty.

The American Work Ethic

The American work ethic is grounded in the Protestant tradition that began with the Reformation. (An *ethic* is a set of moral principles or values.) Many Americans regard earning a living as a moral obligation. Even if they can manage financially, being out of work for any length of time is an extremely demoralizing experience for most Americans. Many do not respect people who live on welfare or private handouts. The American work ethic centers around four themes (Yankelovich, 1974):

1. We tend to equate maturity with being a good provider. Traditionally, men were the breadwinners in our society. As more women moved into the labor force and became heads of households, this ethic began to apply to both sexes.
2. Americans place a high value on "standing on one's own two feet." We see working and getting paid for our work as the way to achieve freedom and independence. Financial dependence on others makes most American adults feel uncomfortable.
3. Americans admire success. Indeed, some observers believe that success has replaced work as the cardinal virtue in American culture. "It does not matter by what means one succeeds as long as one does so. To retrench, to admit defeat—that is the ultimate and unforgivable failure" (Braude, 1975, p. 8). Traditionally, we have defined success in terms of income, occupational prestige, material possessions, and our children's achievements.
4. Most Americans feel that there is built-in dignity in work. It does not matter what the job is, but to do the job well is a source of self-respect. People who work hard at something can feel good about themselves. (And those who do not work or cannot work lose self-esteem.)

People work not only to earn a living but also to maintain or enhance their personal identities and social status. Work provides a rhythm to the days of the week and to the weeks and months of the year. Without work, one day might seem much the same as the next. Work also plays a role in our social lives. Not only does it give us opportunities to meet people, but it can also provide a basis for relationships. (Fellow editors, ski instructors, or auto mechanics have much in common.) Work is a major element of identity. Americans tend to answer the question, "Who are you?" by stating their occupation. Finally, work adds meaning and content to life. A job is an opportunity to demonstrate competence, to develop mastery over oneself and the environment, and to test one's skills in dealing not only with things and ideas but also with people (Slocum, 1966). "A job tells the worker day in and day out that he [or she] has something to offer. Not to have a job is not to have something that is valued by one's fellow human beings" (*Work in America,* 1973, p. 14). The nature of work is changing, however, and so are attitudes toward jobs.

The Coming of Postindustrial Society?

Most of our ideas about what is "modern" are based on a contrast between the industrial societies that emerged in the late nineteenth and early twentieth centuries and the traditional societies that came before. This yardstick is fast becoming obsolete. Computers are the most visible example of new technologies with the potential to change the nature of social organization as well as the structure and experience of work. Along with new communication technologies (such as fiber optics and satellite communications), biotechnology (especially genetic engineering), and new materials (like Mylar plastic, thin insulation materials, and other offshoots of the space program), computers dramatically increase our ability to produce useful goods from the resources available in nature. Computers join a long list of tools that have increased **productivity:** the ratio of goods produced to human effort. Throughout history, people have found artificial means to enhance their human powers: sticks gave early humans a longer reach; pliers give modern humans a better grasp. Some technological changes have been associated with revolutionary social change. The plow, which made it possible to keep fields in continuous cultivation, increasing food productivity, is linked to the rise of state-level societies and cities. The machine, which used interlocking parts and steam, electricity, or other nonanimal sources of power, is associated with the emergence of industrial societies. The question is whether new technologies are leading us toward a new type of society, as yet unimagined.

The Computer Revolution's Evolution

Computers are machines for processing information. Other machines enhance human muscle power; computers augment human brainpower (expanding memory capacity and speeding up data retrieval and calculations).

The Impact of Computers

In one sense, it is possible to say that the original "computer revolution" has ended. Computers are now a basic and integral fact of modern life. They have transformed the way we do business and the way we work. In another sense, as discussed in Chapter 3, the computer revolution has not so much ended as evolved—from a few government mainframes to PCs in many homes and most offices, often with video, sound, and network capabilities. When one considers the latest turn in this evolution—the global use of the Internet, which began during the early 1990s and has enabled PC users to "talk" to each other—one has a revolution that keeps reinventing itself. This rapid rate of technological change shows no signs of slowing. When the revolution began, some felt computers were the saviors of the workforce, freeing people from the drudgery of many tasks. Others saw computers as the beginning of the end, as the tool that was going to usher in a brave new world where human individuality, creativity, and privacy would be crushed and people would become slaves to machines.

The reality seems to lie somewhere between these extremes (Danzinger, 1986). In most settings, the introduction of computers does not lead to dramatic changes in the way people work (or play). As a general rule, people discover ways to make computers conform to their usual behavior patterns, not the reverse. Computers do not "liberate" people from routine work or shorten work periods as some predicted. The increased time necessary to learn and use computer technology tends to take up whatever time might be saved.

Most individuals perceive the impact of computers as benign. Once they overcome their initial fear of the new technology, most appreciate the convenience of automated bank tellers, word-processing systems, automated bookkeeping and record-searching activities, and the like. Wild enthusiasm and extreme frustration are both rare. The main exceptions occur in industries where automation has eliminated jobs, such as automobile production and consumer electronics manufacturing.

Computers have increased the ability of organizations to monitor and control resources, including human resources (personnel). Workloads can be established from a distance, activity levels monitored constantly, a worker's "value" measured in quantitative terms, and all this information entered on his or her record. The networking of computers within a company as well as on the Internet has meant

Rare even twenty years ago, computers are ubiquitous in today's workplace. Their impact is neither wholly benign nor wholly evil. In most settings, people find ways to make computers conform to their usual behavior patterns.

improved opportunities for communication—though along with this has come increased opportunities for miscommunication as well. Information can be shared among a company's entire workforce or among a global audience simply by posting it to the appropriate lists from a personal computer at home or in the office.

Computers increase the opportunities for social control, threatening individual privacy. It is virtually impossible to function in our society without supplying detailed personal information to a variety of public agencies and private companies, from the Internal Revenue Service to local department stores. Some information about you is available on the open market (the sale of magazine subscription lists); other information (the data collected by credit bureaus) is protected by security systems that are, at best, loosely guarded. The number and scale of personal data banks are increasing. Computers tend to reinforce the existing distribution of power and, in fact, have made it more pronounced. Simply put, well-off families and school districts can provide young people with the latest computer hardware and software; schools in low-income districts often have outdated equipment (if even that), and few poor families can afford to buy their children a PC. Those who cannot use computers and who cannot connect to the network are literally left "out of the loop" of the economy, work, and even society. Some social commentators have predicted that the "computer age" would bring to power a new technocratic elite composed of computer specialists; others have predicted that computers would be a force for democracy, distributing "information as power" more widely. But most key decisions about the use of computer technology are made by officials and managers who are already in positions of power and control.

Computers have also made possible the rise of "virtual migrants," workers who are employed by a company in one country, yet live in another (Myerson, 1998). This is increasingly common among software developers and engineers, who as a group are in high demand, and it is the logical extension of the telecommuting many of the "computerati" have been doing within the United States, for example, for some time. Software developers who would make $50,000 in the United States can be hired in India for roughly one-third that amount (Myerson, 1998).

There appears to be no end to the impact and changes the ongoing computer revolution will have. "If history is our guide, even our imaginations cannot grasp what the computer will ultimately become" (Levy, 1997).

The Impact of Automation

One of the more controversial uses of computers is in **automation:** technological control of production that minimizes the need for human workers. Automation reverses the traditional relationship between human beings and tools. In the past, tools were an accessory to human labor and creativity. In the automated factory or office, human beings become accessories to machines. Applying this idea to the modern military, a Vietnam veteran explained, "We used to have armed soldiers. Now we have manned weapons" (Smith, in Garson, 1988, p. 250).

A brief history of the textile industry illustrates the impact of automation on social patterns. With hand looms, a worker could produce, at most, a few yards of cloth per day. In the late eighteenth and early nineteenth centuries, new kinds of looms came into use. These machines not only added external sources of power to the human back, arms, and legs but also made use of "automatic" guidance mechanisms in the form of punch cards, similar to those used much later in computers. They reduced the need for human muscle power and for human brainpower. Productivity increased; a smaller number of weavers could produce far more cloth in a day. There were many social consequences as well. Weaving was moved from the home to the factory; independent, highly skilled, relatively well-paid artisans were replaced by unskilled, poorly paid employees; control of production passed from the weavers to factory managers; and many people were thrown out of work. The mechanization of weaving marked the beginning of the Industrial Revolution. The same basic story has been echoed in almost every line of material production over the last 200 years.

The size of looms and the scale of textile production increased during the first half of this century, but there were no significant changes in the way cloth was made. Then, in the 1950s, a new wave of innovations hit the industry. First, advances in chemistry produced synthetic fibers. Polyesters were manufactured in highly automated plants that required only a few human workers. Second, modern computers began to be used to control weaving (see L. B. Evans, 1981). Again, fewer workers and a lower level of skill were needed to produce the same goods. Finally, the textile industry in the relatively rich nations of Europe and America began to lose business to developing nations, which could supply manufacturers with cheap labor (Rada, 1982). The export of work is an indirect result of automation: jobs can be learned quickly and do not require specialized or technical knowledge.

In the 1980s, automation began to move out of the manufacturing sector of the economy and into the service sector, out of the factory and into the office (Forester 1985, 1987; Garson, 1988). For example, in some welfare agencies social workers, once a profession for people who wanted to work with people, have been replaced by financial assistance workers (FAWs). An FAW simply punches information about the welfare client into a computer, and a program determines what the client will be allowed (so much for a new baby, so much for funeral expenses, and so on). No human judgment is required or allowed. Similarly, stockbrokers with computerized "financial planners" need only type answers to standardized questions into the computer, which then produces a complete plan of investments. One program, called CollegeBuilder, calculates the investments parents will have to make, beginning today, to send three children (fill in the age blank) to three specific colleges (choose which category) fifteen to twenty years from now. These are but a few examples of recent computer innovations. The point is that office automation is changing the nature and experience of work, even for occupations that once required considerable training and skill and allowed a good deal of autonomy and discretion.

The Technology of Management

The standard raison d'être for factories, assembly lines, and other elements of the Industrial Revolution extols the fact that these facilities increased productivity. But industrialization also increased control over workers, turning an independent artisan into a factory hand. And so it is with computers. The general trend has been to maximize managerial power and control at the expense of the autonomy of workers and even at the expense of productivity (Shaiken, 1984; Forester, 1987).

Richard Edwards (1979) identified three types of control. The early days of industrialization were characterized by *simple control*. The "boss" was both owner and manager; supervision was direct, personal, often arbitrary and harsh, and difficult to oppose. The boss's word was law; one wrong word, and you were out. Simple control may still be found in small owner-operated businesses. But as companies grew larger, tasks became more complex, and as workers gained the assistance of trade unions, managers developed two new strategies—two additional types of control. These new forms of control were built into the work itself and into the operation of the organization and were not dependent on close, personal supervision. One of the new controls was *technical control*, in which the physical organization of the work process compelled employees to work in certain ways. For example, Henry Ford invented the assembly line to ensure that all workers produced at a consistently fast speed, not simply because it was a convenient way of coordinating

Robots weld van bodies at a General Motors plant in Baltimore, Maryland. Compare this photo with the earlier one of a Model T assembly line (see p. 565).

production. The conveyor belt was preset to move at a given speed, and workers were penalized if they missed a task and had to slow it down. Edwards calls the third type of supervision *bureaucratic control.* Here compulsion is created through the social relationships of the workplace, in which positions are arranged hierarchically and each layer of the hierarchy has distinct privileges. If the assembly line is a symbol of technical control, the locked executive washroom to which only senior managers get a key is a symbol of bureaucratic control.

Computers enable managers to combine technical and bureaucratic control. Most office computer systems today come with built-in "surveillance" systems that enable managers to obtain detailed information on subordinates at the push of a button (Garson, 1988). Word processors may count the number of keystrokes typists make per minute, allowing their bosses to literally monitor their every move. At telephone companies, sales companies, and airline reservation offices, computers monitor the amount of time operators spend on each call, and print out reports for their bosses. Success on these jobs depends on numbers and speed, not on courtesy and service. Many office computer systems enable managers to look through subordinates' files, letters, and memos. The manager does not have to ask to see a file or actually look over the typist's shoulder, and subordinates do not know whether they are being watched. Access to information is hierarchical: superiors can look at their subordinates' files and monitor their work, but subordinates cannot apply the same scrutiny to their superiors. Supervisors can also monitor employees' personal e-mail messages and use of the Internet. Some companies have banned the playing of computer games after discovering employees were spending much of their workday playing games on-line.

The Impact on Workers

What impact do automation and the reduction in the level of skills required have on workers themselves? The best evidence indicates that **alienation,** the feeling of being separated from one's work and, through one's work, from other people, is widespread (for example, Halle, 1984). The common expressions "I only work here" (implying, "Don't hold me responsible for shabby quality or poor service") and "It's just a job" (implying, "Why should I invest something of myself in this meaningless activity?") capture this feeling.

The idea that industrialization dehumanizes work and alienates workers originated with Karl Marx (1844/1975). Marx believed that the capacity to shape the material world, to produce something of value, sets humans apart from other species—that creative work is a vital part of being and feeling human. He predicted that workers in capitalist, industrial societies would become alienated, first, because they sell their labor to someone else, rather than working for themselves, and, second, because they produce standardized parts of a product rather than individualized, finished goods. The assembly-line worker in an auto plant who turns the same three bolts on car after car, day after day, is a classic example. In assembly-line production, the worker is a replaceable cog in a machine—the ultimate form of dehumanization. Was Marx correct?

Most studies have found that dissatisfaction with work occurs at all occupational levels (Blauner, 1964; *Work in America,* 1973; Quinn and Staines, 1979; R. Howard, 1985). Different kinds of jobs generate different kinds of discontent. "Blue-collar blues" are on the rise (Passell, 1990). The image of blue-collar workers (versus "knowledge workers") in the mass media is far from flattering. On-the-job regimentation resembles that in the military. Bosses have little regard for workers' intelligence. Working conditions may be degrading and dangerous. Blue-collar workers generally do not participate in decisions about what work they do or how they should do it, much less whether a plant will remain open or be closed. In any case, as we have seen, the shift from a manufacturing to a service economy, the globalization of production, and automation and robotics eliminated hundreds of thousands of blue-collar jobs in the 1980s. They also weakened unions, which gave blue-collar workers at least some degree of control over their jobs. As a result, many have been forced into poorly paid service jobs in the secondary labor market. Most of today's blue-collar workers have more education than their parents had, but the educational requirements for many jobs have risen too fast for them to keep up.

Office work has become almost as segmented and subject to authoritarian control as factory work (Garson, 1988). Management often treats white-collar workers as exchangeable and expendable. They have no more job security than blue-collar workers and, in many cases, earn less. The fact that many office workers have attended college and have higher expectations and more skills than their jobs warrant makes their on-the-job experience all the more frustrating. As a young female college graduate put it, "I didn't go to school for four years to type. I'm bored; continuously humiliated" (*Work in America*, 1973, p. 36).

Job dissatisfaction extends into the ranks of middle management. Middle managers feel that they are responsible for implementing policies they had no part in designing and, at the same time, lack the authority and resources to put these plans into effect. They are forced to compete among themselves for the attention and support of top management, which leads to conflict, infighting, backbiting, tension, and anxiety. Given the mergers, takeovers, and corporate downsizing, managerial careers are not as stable as they used to be. Today's managers cannot count on their companies to take care of them or even to remain in business as they reach middle age (Hymowitz, 1987). The "best and brightest" business school graduates are turning down industry jobs—the ones their parents' generation coveted—for jobs on Wall Street or in cutting-edge companies where they have an opportunity to make big money fast. Instead of settling down, managers in their forties and fifties often find themselves looking for new employers or new careers.

The Overworked American

A new concept has gained currency in recent years among those who study work and its impact on workers: that concept is "time squeeze." It refers to the loss of leisure (or nonwork) time at the cost of time spent on the job. According to Harris polls, since the 1970s the amount of leisure time available to the average American worker has declined by close to one-third (L. Harris, 1987). Juliet B. Schor (1992), who has made a study of the "overworked American," estimates that over the two decades of the 1970s and 1980s, the average annual hours of paid employment increased from 1,786 to 1,949 hours, a change that equals an extra month of work a year.

The workday itself has been extended as well. The move to a more global economy, made possible by the computer revolution, has meant that more and more companies are finding that they can do business twenty-four hours a day, seven days a week. As

the population ages, the need for round-the-clock care of the elderly has also grown, so there are more jobs requiring working evenings, nights, and weekends (U.S. Department of Labor, 1997). The "standard" 9-to-5, five-day workweek is becoming more of a rarity. Less than one-third of all employed Americans 18 years old and over work a standard workweek (*Population Today*, December 1997). In some families parents work split shifts, with one parent working while the other stays home. The desire to save on child care costs is not generally the reason for this, however. In most cases, it is simply that these are the only jobs and work schedules available (*Population Today*, December 1997).

The increase in hours affects all income categories, family types, and industries: the corporate executive, the workaholic yuppie, the single parent, dual-career couples, middle managers, small-business owners, assembly-line workers, clerical workers, employees in the service industries. Perhaps the most dramatic increase in working hours has occurred among women; they average about seven and a half added weeks of work a year over the twenty-year period. That is because women are increasingly working full-time and year-round and taking less time off for maternity leave and child care. (This accounting of working hours does not include the number of hours they devote to "housework." Thus the real average workweek of employed mothers reaches a total of about 65 hours; see Chapter 11.)

Many economic factors account for today's time squeeze: economic retrenchments in most American industries, which have resulted in cutbacks in vacation time and increases in overtime for those workers not laid off; moonlighting (holding more than one job) to help meet household expenses and pay debts; competition for well-paid jobs; and the loss of strength of trade unions, which traditionally have fought for shorter workweeks. Those who change jobs frequently lose the longer vacation time they had accrued on their old jobs and have to start over (Ward, 1997).

The capitalist system itself is biased toward long working hours. As productivity increases, employers pay off their employees with extra income, rather than time off (Schor, 1992). Higher income pushes up consumption, which increases the need for productivity (and more working hours). This pattern has led to what Schor calls an insidious cycle of "work and spend": "People buy houses and go into debt; luxuries become necessities; Smiths keep up with Joneses. . . . Work-and-spend has become a powerful dynamic that keeps us from a more relaxed and leisured way of life" (1992, pp. 9–10). Schor notes that western Europe also operates with capitalistic labor markets, yet working hours there are substantially fewer than ours. What accounts for that difference? For one thing, European trade unions are fairly strong, and they have pushed for shorter hours and longer vacations. For another, the European economy is not as driven by consumer wants and preferences as the American economy; it is not yet on the work-and-spend treadmill. Figure 15-5 shows the amount of

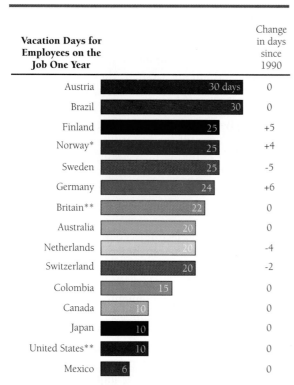

Vacation Days for Employees on the Job One Year		Change in days since 1990
Austria	30 days	0
Brazil	30	0
Finland	25	+5
Norway*	25	+4
Sweden	25	-5
Germany	24	+6
Britain**	22	0
Australia	20	0
Netherlands	20	-4
Switzerland	20	-2
Colombia	15	0
Canada	10	0
Japan	10	0
United States**	10	0
Mexico	6	0

* Based on a six-day workweek.
** No vacation time is required by law, but these are the amounts usually allotted.

Figure 15-5 *Vacation Time*

In most industrialized countries, the amount of paid vacation offered by the private sector is specified by the government.

Source: The New York Times, May 11, 1997, p. F12.

vacation time offered employees on the job for one year in a number of different countries. Only Mexico offers less time off than the United States.

Vacation time may even be decreasing. The pressures of work and the fear of being downsized have meant that many workers are taking shorter and fewer vacations (Ward, 1997). Also, as described above, workers who are forced to change jobs often lose the longer vacation that seniority on a job usually brings. In 1987, U.S. workers spent 22.4 days on the job for each day of vacation; in 1996, they worked 23.9 days for each day of vacation (Ward, 1997). While it is still unclear whether vacations are really dwindling or just growing shorter in relation to the added days of work, the feeling of less vacation is there. Those taking time off may opt to spend it at home catching up on household tasks and spending time with their children, a choice that does not tend to feel like a vacation (Ward, 1997).

Loss of leisure time has its costs. According to Schor (1992), 30 percent of adults report experiencing high stress nearly every day; stress-related diseases, especially among women, have skyrocketed. The highest stress is found among assembly-line workers, who must carry out tedious tasks at a demanding pace. Another problem is sleep deprivation: a majority of Americans are getting an hour to an hour and a half less sleep at night than is optimum for good health. Nutrition has also suffered; fast food and takeouts have replaced the home-cooked meal in many households. Perhaps the most serious consequence of the time squeeze is that working parents have less time for each other and for their children. Marital breakups and the neglect of children have contributed to a whole host of social ailments. Ironically, according to Schor, productivity itself ultimately suffers from long working hours. Studies of companies conducted in the 1970s found that shortening the workweek from forty to thirty-five hours (with no reduction in pay) actually reduced absenteeism, employee turnover, personal business on company time, and overall costs (*The New York Times*, August 29, 1993, p. 9).

While this loss of leisure time and its consequences may be real, the *meaning* of the time squeeze may be different from the picture Schor and others paint. Sociologist Arlie Hochschild studied men and women working for a fairly progressive company in the midwest. She, too, found that men and women put in exceptionally long hours. Yet this company offered flextime, job sharing, paid and un-paid leave—all the sorts of programs thought to be family-friendly. Why weren't employees taking advantage of them? In her book, *The Time Bind: When Home Becomes Work and Work Becomes Home* (1997), Hochschild offers a surprising and controversial interpretation of the loss of family time. Many parents, Hochschild says, spend extra time at the office not because of all the work that needs to be done but because it offers a refuge from the demands of family life. What Hochschild found was that many workers, especially those in higher-level, higher-paying positions, do not use family-friendly policies, preferring instead to devote their time to work, where the problems tend to be more clear-cut and the lines of authority more clearly delineated than at home. In contrast to the volatile family relations and often thorny problems of parenthood, work seemed like an oasis of order. The time squeeze may have set this situation in motion, creating a home life that now seems out of control to many working parents, but the solution they are choosing, working more, is simply adding to the stress:

> Feeling that we are always late and low on time, trying to adapt as best we can to the confines of our time prisons—these are all symptoms of what has become a self-perpetuating national way of life. Even the simple act of trying to imagine other ways of living in time generates a certain amount of anxiety and fear. (Hochschild, 1997, p. 257)

Hochschild believes that what is needed is a movement in which workers seek to regain control of their time. One of the biggest beneficiaries of this movement would be the children in families caught in the time bind. They are rushed to day care early in the morning and spend nine- to ten-hour days away from their parents. Parents who subscribed to the idea that it is not how much time they spend with their children but the quality of that time are finding that that is simply not true. It turns out that raising children works best if one has a fair amount of flexible time to devote to them. An hour of quality time, reading together before bed, or doing homework, is just not enough (Shapiro, 1997).

"The Information Society"

Some social thinkers believe that we are in the midst of a social revolution as profound as the Agricultural and Industrial Revolutions. Sociologist Daniel Bell (1973, 1979) was an early and leading exponent of this view. New information technologies, Bell argued, would change the basis of social organization, producing a new "postindustrial" or "information society." In industrial society, the economy centers on the production of goods. The most important resources are physical capital (such as iron ore) and labor. Most of the workforce is engaged in the production of goods. Ownership of the means of production leads to economic and social power. These characteristics were exemplified by the steel and textile industries. Although declining today (at least in the United States), these industries paved the way for a new kind of society. In the information society, the economy centers on the provision of services. The most important resource is human capital (information, knowledge, expertise). Most of the workforce is engaged in research or the provision of services (for example, health care, education). Power derives from access to knowledge. Microelectronics and other science-based industries are the vanguard, leading the way to a new society. The major differences between an industrial and an information society are summarized in Table 15-4.

Table 15-4   *Industrial versus Information Society*

	Industrial Society	Information Society
1. Economic focus	Producing goods	Service and information
2. Occupational distribution	Workers and managers	Professional and technical workers
3. Critical resource	Harnessing energy	Theoretical knowledge
4. Source of power	Control of capital and labor	Control of technology and assessment
5. Decision making	Ad hoc, based on experience and informal discussion	"Intellectual technology" (computer-assisted decision analysis, etc.)

Source: Adapted from Daniel Bell, *The Coming of Post-Industrial Society,* New York: Basic Books, 1973, p. 14. Copyright © 1973 by Daniel Bell. Foreword © 1976 by Daniel Bell. Reprinted by permission of Basic Books, Inc., Publishers, New York.

In the information society, Bell predicted, technologies that were once used to automate and manage the production of goods will be applied to social planning. In contrast to the hurly-burly of early capitalism, technical efficiency will lead to a more rational and humane society. People's material needs will be met, even beyond the basic level, freeing them to turn their attention to "higher goods":

> If an industrial society is defined by the quantity of goods as marking a standard of living, the postindustrial society is defined by the quality of life as measured by the services and amenities—health, education, recreation, the arts—which are now deemed desirable and possible for everyone. (Bell, 1973, p. 127)

In describing the information society, Bell touched on a basic disagreement among sociologists as to the origins and future of western society. As Anthony Giddens (1982) has pointed out, there are two competing schools of thought, one associated with functionalism, one with conflict theory.

According to functionalists, industrialization was the driving force in creating modern societies. The most significant event (or set of events) in the contemporary world was the transformation of traditional societies, based primarily on agriculture, into industrial societies, based primarily on the mechanized production of goods. Functionalists associate this transformation with progress, material affluence, and the breakdown of rigid social class boundaries. Class conflict did erupt in industrial societies (especially during the early days of labor unions), but this was a transitional phase, soon defused by the rise of the liberal-democratic state and the extension of political rights to all citizens. Although jobs may be less interesting today than in the preindustrial past, workers have been amply compensated with a much higher standard of living. Functionalists argue that all industrial societies are essentially alike, despite differences in political structure and ideology. The United States and even China depend on large bureaucracies, for example. Many (though not all) functionalists agree with Bell that new technology will alter the shape of society.

Conflict theorists, in contrast, hold that the impact of a technology depends on who controls its development and use. According to this view, the most significant event (or set of events) in modern

western history was the rise of capitalism. Conflict theorists see capitalism not simply as one way of organizing economic activity but as a distinctive type of society. Class conflict is built into the structure of capitalistic societies. Capitalists and workers depend on one another: capitalists need workers to produce goods, and workers need the wages that employers pay them. But this dependence is biased in favor of owners of the means of production. The benefits of industrialization for workers have been vastly overrated; no amount of consumer goods compensates for the dehumanizing effects of mass production. Conflict theorists see the state as an extension of elite, upper-class power and the corporation as a means of consolidating power. They argue that the growth of capitalism spurred the technological innovations associated with the Industrial Revolution (not vice versa). Western capitalistic societies may be entering an advanced stage of industrialization, but fundamental power relations remain unchanged.

A growing number of sociologists who do not accept all the tenets of conflict theory have come to reject the functionalist view of both industrial society and the so-called information society. Functionalists tend to assume that technology is a cause and social change an effect. In fact, the creation of technology is a social process. Science entails relationships among scientists and huge educational and research institutions, competition for funding, political disputes, and fashion. If science is not simply the "pure pursuit of knowledge," this is even less true of the development of technology. In the United States today, the development of new technology is usually funded by the federal government or by private industrial corporations. Among other things, this means that technologies that lack government support or a likely market generally will not be developed. For example, most major pharmaceutical companies devote considerable resources to producing new formulas and medicines for headaches and colds—common complaints among citizens of rich countries who can afford medicine. Much less effort and money is devoted to developing treatments for the more serious ailments affecting poor people throughout the world (for example, malaria and dysentery) (Gereffi, 1983; Patel, 1983; Silverman and Lee, 1974). The effects of such priorities are felt throughout the world.

SOCIOLOGY ON THE WEB

Economic Update

The text emphasizes the interconnected nature of the world economic system: stock market rumblings in east Asia cause panic on the U.S. market; layoffs in Europe affect salaries and benefits in many other parts of the world. You can use the resources of the web to update the economic information in the text and to consider what new treads have developed in the global economy since the text was completed in early 1998.

The U.S. Economy

Use the following sites to obtain time-series data that will allow you to plot changes in important economic variables, such as number of people employed, unemployment rate, productivity, or gross domestic product.

http://fedstats.gov/

This extremely useful site contains links to the sites of the U.S. Census Bureau (which can be reached directly at **http://www.census.gov/**), the Bureau of Labor Statistics (**http://www.stats.bls.gov/**), and the Bureau of Economic Analysis (**http://www.bea.doc.gov/**). Obtain economic data for a specific state or county for several recent years and create a graph that shows your findings. For example, you can use the Census Bureau site to obtain 1990 census data for employment in your county; compare these to data found in yearly county business and economic profiles for each of the three most recent years.

The World Economy

Search the following sites to see what kinds of data are available. Then choose a key economic indicator, such as inflation rate or unemployment rate, and obtain time-series data for three different countries. Create a graph that displays your findings.

http://www.census.gov/
http://www.stats.bls.gov/

These two U.S. government sites provide economic data for other countries as well. For example, using BLS data, you could plot the unemployment rates of the United States, Germany, and Japan over the past ten years.

http://globalwarming.mofa.go.jp/

The web site of APEC (Asia-Pacific Economic Cooperation) provides data on member nations' economies. You will find key economic indicators for all Pacific Rim nations.

http://www.unescap.org/

The UN Economic and Social Commission for Asia and the Pacific provides information on social development in the region. Use this site to obtain background reports on poverty, employment, and social change in developing nations in Asia and the Pacific Rim.

Summary

1. **What is the global economy? How does it affect the structure of the economy? How does it work worldwide and in the United States?** The global economy is largely based on the activity of a number of *multinational corporations* that organize resources from all over the world into single economic units. They tend to perpetuate the global division of labor and the system of stratification that began with European colonization. The global economy directly affects American workers because it drains manufacturing jobs into the poor *developing* nations of the southern hemisphere, where manufacturing costs are lower.

2. **What is capitalism, and how does it structure the U.S. economy?** The *capitalist* economy of the United States rests on the ideals of private ownership, the profit motive, and free competition that were set down by Adam Smith in the eighteenth century. As the Industrial Revolution gathered force, the American economy vastly increased in scale. Today the U.S. economy is dominated by *corporations*—business organizations characterized by limited liability, shared ownership (through sale of stocks), and the separation of ownership and management. Who controls corporations internally and to what extent corporations control the economy are matters of intense debate. Clearly, a number of important industries are *oligopolies* and *conglomerates*. The government plays a dual role of enabler and regulator in the economy. Policies based on Keynesian economics, which favor large-scale government intervention to offset depression and inflation, are periodically in and out of favor.

3. **How has the world of work changed? What does work mean to Americans?** The social organization of work has changed dramatically. The shift from a manufacturing to a *service and information* economy in recent decades affects who works and what kind of work is done. The secondary labor market (low-skill, low-paying jobs) is growing faster than the primary labor market (which offers security and promotions). The meaning of work is also changing, though most Americans still endorse the work ethic, which stresses the importance of being a good provider, achieving financial independence, attaining success, and feeling a sense of self-esteem through work.

4. **How are new technologies changing the nature of work? What effect have they had on workers' satisfaction and leisure time?** Computers and other technologies are creating new opportunities and new challenges in what might be called a postindustrial society. Computers permit managers to substitute automated machines for people in the factory and to monitor and control the activity of their employees. The combinations of *automation* and control seem to be increasing the *alienation* of workers. In recent decades, full-time employees have experienced a decline in leisure time as the number of working hours has increased. As a result, workers report an increase in stress, sleep deprivation, and family dysfunction. Longer working hours may also result in a net loss in *productivity*. In addition, the shift to a more global economy and the need for round-the-clock care of the elderly have meant that the workweek is now twenty-four hours a day, seven days a week.

Bell argues that computers and other new technologies are leading toward an information society that will be fundamentally different from the industrial society. Sociologists who agree with Bell tend to believe that technology itself can alter the shape of society (a functionalist view); those who disagree are more likely to believe that the impact of technology depends on which groups control its development and use (a conflict view).

Key Terms

alienation 582	corporation 565	oligopoly 568
automation 580	dependency theory 560	productivity 578
capitalism 562	infrastructure 564	service and information economy 575
command economy 563	monopoly 568	Third World 555
conglomerate 569	multinational corporation 553	

Recommended Readings

Bagdikian, Ben H. (1997). *The Media Monopoly,* 5th ed. Boston: Beacon Press.

Bell, Daniel. (1973). *The Coming of Post-Industrial Society.* New York: Basic Books.

Galbraith, K. (1978). *The New Industrial State,* 3d ed. Boston: Houghton Mifflin.

Hochschild, Arlie. (1997). *The Time Bind: When Work Becomes Home and Home Becomes Work.* New York: Metropolitan Books.

Rifkin, Jeremy. (1995). *The End of Work: The Decline of the Global Labor Force and the Dawn of the Post-Market Era.* New York: Putnam.

Schor, J. B. (1992). *The Overworked American: The Unexpected Decline in Leisure.* New York: Basic Books.

Wallerstein, I. (1980). *The Modern World System,* Vol. 1. New York: Academic Press.

Part

The Changing Shape of Society

5

This section takes an in-depth look at the changing shape of society.

Chapter 16 examines the global problems of population growth, resource depletion, environmental deterioration, and rapid urbanization, with special focus on the problems in developing countries.

Chapter 17 looks at the reasons for seemingly irrational, unpredictable social behavior—from rumors and crazes to riots, to social movements and social revolutions.

Chapter

Sixteen

Population, Global Ecology, and Urbanization

Population growth, environmental strain, and urbanization are the defining characteristics of the late twentieth century. They will continue to be so in the twenty-first century. Our understanding of the ways in which the world population, global ecology, and increasing urbanization interact and affect one another has changed considerably. It used to be that demographers and urban planners assumed that the birthrates of a country would stabilize and fall automatically as the country developed economically. Today, however, the bulk of population growth occurs in the poorest countries, while countries like France and Germany have such low fertility rates that their respective governments offer incentives to women to have more children. This rapid growth in population in developing countries has encouraged intense urbanization. Two-thirds of the world's urban population live in developing countries. Mexico City, Calcutta, and Bombay are each home to more people than New York City (Gugler, 1997).

These population demands are occurring just as environmental resources appear to be dwindling. Famines and chronic hunger are frequent in the developing world, while food surpluses and incentives to farmers not to plant certain crops are not uncommon in developed countries. How can we bring population, ecological issues, and urbanization into balance? Is it even possible? Some argue that widespread famine and environmental catastrophies lie ahead if we do not curb population. Others view these voices of doom as too pessimistic and predict that, as has been the case throughout history, technological advances will make it possible for the earth to support many more people than is presently possible. This chapter looks at these topics, separately and as interacting pieces of a global whole.

Key Questions

1. What stages has population growth undergone in industrialized nations? How does population growth in developing nations differ from this pattern?
2. What two trends have characterized U.S. population development?
3. How is the relationship between population and world resources affected by disparities in distribution and consumption and by environmental hazards?

4. *According to nineteenth-century critics, how did urbanization affect society?*
5. *Through what three stages has U.S. urbanization progressed?*
6. *How does urbanization in developing countries differ from that in rich industrial nations?*

Population: Rates and Trends

Around the world, more than four children are born every second. In the time it takes to read this chapter (about an hour), 15,909 babies will join the human family. Another 15,909 will be born while you watch the late news and fix a snack. About 127,272 more will arrive while you sleep; 15,909 more while you wash, dress, and eat breakfast. By this time tomorrow, the population of the world will have increased by about 381,827 (even though thousands will have died) (*Population Today*, May 1997, p. 2). Every second, world population increases by 2.9 persons (see Table 16-1). The rate of births in less developed countries is three times that in developed countries (Population Reference Bureau, 1997b).

Will the earth be able to support this growing population? The environment is our source of raw materials, our habitat, and our waste disposal site (Population Reference Bureau, 1997c). Will there be enough food, clothing, and shelter, enough fuel, enough drinking water, and enough living space for a world population that may total as much as 10.7 billion by the year 2030? Even at current population levels, there are catastrophic shortages. Twenty percent of the population of developing countries is malnourished (Bender and Smith, 1997). Modern technology may make it possible to increase the production of food and other goods, but many of the techniques used to do this create serious environmental risks. Deforestation may provide land for agriculture, but the loss of rain forest affects the global climate and also means less wood for fuel; according to biologist D. O. Hall, "it often costs more to heat the pot than to fill it" (quoted in Cohen, 1995, p. 196). At current production levels, the air and water of industrial regions are badly polluted. Indestructible toxic chemicals and radioactive wastes compound these problems.

The twin problems of population pressure and pollution meet head-on in the world's major cities. A century ago, most of the people in the world lived in rural villages and small towns. There were only a few cities in the United States whose populations would not have fit comfortably into Yankee Stadium (capacity 54,000). Today three out of four Americans live in cities of 100,000 or more. Nearly half of the world's population lives in cities today (Haub, 1993).

Demography: The Study of Population

The scientific study of population is known as *demography*. The word comes from the Greek for "measuring people." But counting heads is only a small part of what demographers do. They also attempt to calculate the growth rate of a population and to assess the impact of such things as the marriage rate and life expectancy, the sex ratio (the proportion of males to females), and the age structure (the proportions of young, middle-aged, and older people) on human behavior and the structure of society. They are interested in the distribution of population and in movements of people (migration). Put another way, demographers study the effects of social trends on the number of people in a population and the effects of such numbers on social trends.

Demographers use a number of standard measures in translating a locality's raw totals—births, deaths, the number of those moving in and out—into general statistics that allow them to identify trends. The **birthrate** is the number of births per 1,000 people in a given year. Suppose there were 900 births in a city of 50,000 in a specific year. Demographers calculate the birthrate for the city by dividing the number of births (900) by the population (50,000) and multiplying the result (0.018) by 1,000 to get 18. The birthrate in developed countries is 1.6; in less developed countries (excluding China) it is 4.0 (*Population Today*, May 1997). The **death rate** is the number of deaths per 1,000 people in a given year. (The death rate is calculated in the same way as the birthrate.) The **fertility rate** is the number of live births per 1,000 women of

Table 16-1   *World Population Clock, 1997*

Measure	World	Developed Countries	Developing Countries	Developing Countries (Less China)
Population:	5,840,433,000	1,174,792,000	4,665,641,000	3,428,948,000
Births per:				
Year	139,366,897	13,450,155	125,916,742	104,917,695
Month	11,613,908	1,120,846	10,493,062	8,743,141
Week	2,680,133	258,657	2,421,476	2,017,648
Day	381,827	36,850	344,977	287,446
Hour	15,909	1,535	14,374	11,977
Minute	265	26	240	200
Second	4.4	0.4	4.0	3.3
Deaths per:				
Year	53,353,684	12,006,985	41,346,699	33,233,993
Month	4,446,140	1,000,582	3,445,558	2,769,499
Week	1,026,032	230,904	795,129	639,115
Day	146,174	32,896	113,279	91,052
Hour	6,091	1,371	4,720	3,794
Minute	102	23	79	63
Second	1.7	0.4	1.3	1.1
Natural increase per:				
Year	86,013,213	1,443,170	84,570,043	71,683,702
Month	7,167,768	120,264	7,047,504	5,973,642
Week	1,654,100	27,753	1,626,347	1,378,533
Day	235,653	3,954	231,699	196,394
Hour	9,819	165	9,654	8,183
Minute	164	3	161	136
Second	2.7	0.0	2.7	2.3
Infant deaths per:				
Year	8,166,650	116,131	8,050,519	7,391,149
Month	680,554	9,678	670,877	615,929
Week	157,051	2,233	154,818	142,137
Day	22,374	318	22,056	20,250
Hour	932	13	919	844
Minute	16	0.2	15	14
Second	0.3	0.0	0.3	0.2

Source: Population Reference Bureau. *Population Today,* May 1997, p. 2.

childbearing age (15 to 44 years) in a population in a given year; this rate helps demographers calculate average family size. **Life expectancy** is the potential life span of the average member of any given population. The **net growth rate** is the percentage increase in a population, taking into account immigration and emigration as well as birthrates and death rates. Unlike most other demographic measures, population growth rates are calculated as percentages. Suppose a nation has a birthrate of 28 (per 1,000), a death rate of 17, and little immigration or emigration. Its population is increasing at the rate of 11 per 1,000 (28 minus 17); its growth rate is 1.1 percent.

World Patterns

The population of the world reached the 5 billion mark on June 24, 1987, and is growing at the rate of about 90 million per year. By mid-1997 it was 5.84 billion (Population Reference Bureau, 1997b). These fast-growing figures are the result of sudden and dramatic population growth in modern times. It took several hundred thousand years for the population of *Homo sapiens* to reach the 1 billion mark in 1805; only 121 years to reach the 2 billion mark in 1926. Only 60 years later, we exceeded 5 billion (Figure 16-1). But neither population nor population growth rates are distributed evenly throughout

In addition to birthrates and death rates, demographers also study other factors that influence population structure, including marriage rates, life expectancy, age distribution, and migration. In the late 1990s, millions of Hutus fled from Rwanda to the Congo, only to be forced back again.

the world. As mentioned earlier, population and population growth rates are highest in developing nations and lower in western nations. These rates are also complicated by mass movements of refugees to and from certain countries. By 1994 the population of refugees was over 23 million, up from about 10 million refugees worldwide in 1983 (Darnton, 1994). Mass movements of people into and out of Afghanistan, Somalia, Bosnia, and Mozambique have contributed to this sharp increase. Famine and political upheaval are usually behind these mass exoduses.

The Demographic Transition

The term ***demographic transition*** refers to a pattern of major population changes that accompanied the transformation of western nations from agricultural into industrial societies. The demographic transition occurred in three stages.

In *Stage I,* birthrates were high, but death rates were also high. As a result, the population growth rate was low. Thus in eighteenth-century Europe, birthrates were high, but many infants did not survive childhood and many adults did not reach old age. High infant mortality, epidemics, famines, and wars kept the population growth rate low.

In *Stage II,* which began in Europe in the late eighteenth century, birthrates remained high, but

Figure 16-1   *World Population Growth*

Through most of human history, the population was more or less stable. In modern times, however, world population has skyrocketed.

Source: John R. Weeks, *Population,* 5th ed. Belmont, CA: Wadsworth, 1992, p. 30.

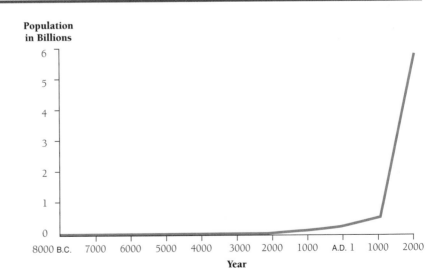

death rates began to fall. Why? Improvements in agricultural technology, the spread of new and hardier crops (such as the potato), and increased food production. Improvements in transportation facilitated food distribution: people were no longer dependent on local supplies or devastated by local crop failures. Better nutrition meant that people were more able to resist and survive disease. During the nineteenth century improvements in public health and sanitation (cleaner water, better sewage disposal, pasteurized milk) and advances in modern medicine contributed further to the decline in death rates. Many more women survived into their childbearing years. The population growth rate soared. (*Note:* The eighteenth-century population explosion was due to lower death rates, not to higher birthrates.)

In *Stage III,* which began in the mid-nineteenth century in western nations, birthrates started to fall. Stage III is associated with industrial development. In agricultural societies, children are an economic asset: the more hands, the better. In urban, industrial societies, however, children become an "economic burden." They are financially dependent on their parents for an extended period. Large families mean crowded living quarters, additional household expenses, and a lower family standard of living. Four additional factors that contributed to falling birthrates in the west in the twentieth century were the decline in infant mortality (which meant that a couple did not have to produce five or six children to ensure that three or four would live), government-sponsored Social Security programs in the 1930s and 1940s (which meant that parents did not have to depend on their children to support them in old age), access to modern birth control devices in the late 1950s and early 1960s, and postponement of the age of marriage. By the 1960s families with only two or three children had become the norm. Today birthrates in most western nations have stabilized at replacement levels, while death rates have continued to decline. [Half of the Americans now alive would have been dead if the death rate had remained at 1900 levels (*Population Today,* February 1997).] Thus the balance between birthrates and death rates has been restored; as in Stage I, the population growth rate is low. (The stages in the demographic transition are summarized in Figure 16-2.)

Population Growth in Developing Nations

In most developing nations today, death rates have fallen, but birthrates remain high. It is tempting to conclude that developing nations are in Stage II of the demographic transition. But their population histories differ from those of western nations in a number of significant ways (van der Tak, Haub, and Murphy, 1979; Yaukey, 1985; Ehrlich, Ehrlich, and Daily, 1995).

First, changes that occurred gradually over a period of 200 years in western nations have been telescoped into a few decades in the developing nations. The drop in death rates and rise in birthrates happened almost overnight. An elderly man living near Calcutta observed: "When I was a boy, they took away forty or fifty bodies after a cholera epidemic. It happened every five or ten years. Now they have come and vaccinated our children. I have lived here almost seventy years. The biggest change in my time is health. We've learned how to keep from dying" (in R. Evans, 1961, pp. 79–80).

Second, changes in the birthrates and death rates in developing nations are largely the result of imported technology, not internal social and economic change. International health agencies and foreign aid programs have initiated public sanitation drives, provided immunizations and antibiotics, helped supply food, and so on. Agricultural and industrial development has not kept pace with population growth.

Third, population growth in developing nations has a built-in **momentum factor:** even if family size declines, populations will continue to grow. Why? Between 40 and 50 percent of the populations of developing nations are in or near their childbearing years—15 to 44 years old—(compared with about 25 percent of the populations of developed nations). If every couple in Mexico, Kenya, or Pakistan decided to limit themselves to two children, it would take a century or more for these countries to achieve **zero population growth** (the point where birthrates and death rates are equal and thus the population is stable). In other words, because of the age structure, a decline in fertility rates would not mean a decline in birthrates for some time to come.

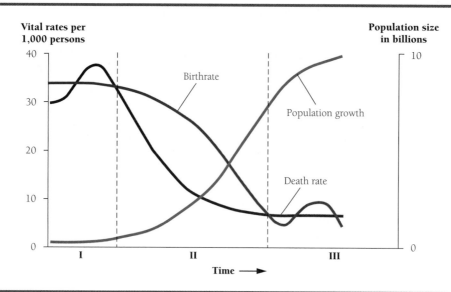

Figure 16-2 *The Demographic Transition in Western Nations*

In Stage I, birthrates and death rates were both high; population growth (the red line) was slow. In Stage II, death rates declined faster than birthrates, so population growth continued to climb. Only when birthrates and death rates are both low, Stage III, does population growth slow down.

Source: John R. Weeks, *Population,* 5th ed. Belmont, CA: Wadsworth, 1992, p. 76.

An immunization program in Ethiopia. Mass immunization can cause the death rate to drop almost overnight in developing nations.

Family Planning: Successes and Failures

The most successful large-scale effort to limit population is taking place in China. There, government-mandated family planning has been in place for nearly three decades. The most populous nation in the world, China is the home of more than 1 billion people. When peace was restored after World War II and the communist revolution, China, like many western nations, experienced a baby boom. The birthrate rose, the death rate fell, and between 1953 and 1970 the growth rate increased from 2.3 to

2.6 percent. At that point China's leaders initiated a policy of strict population control, aiming for one child per family. (Actually, two and sometimes even three children may be allowed, depending on various circumstances.) Enforcement was placed in the hands of local authorities (Kristof, 1993).

The Chinese plan offered both carrots and sticks. The parents of "only children" received preferential treatment in child care, health services, housing, and jobs. Perhaps more to the point, severe penalties were meted out to families that broke the rules. Women were forced to have abortions if they became pregnant with a second or third child. If it was too late for abortion, the parents of such a child might be compelled to undergo sterilization and/or be penalized with stiff fines or confiscations of property. Because males are valued far more highly than females in Chinese society, a pregnant woman may try to undergo ultrasound testing so that she can have the fetus aborted if it is a girl. Authorities claim that the most drastic step of all, infanticide of girls, is extremely rare, but statistics are impossible to obtain (see Chapter 10).

China's severe family planning measures have apparently succeeded. In the 1970s alone, the birthrate was nearly halved, from 34 (per 1,000) to slightly below 18, a level it maintained, though with periodic fluctuations upward, into the 1990s. In two decades, the nation's fertility rate fell to 1.9 lifetime births per woman, about the same rate as that in the United States or Britain (Kristof, 1993). Because China is so

huge, its decline in fertility has actually perceptibly slowed the world growth rate (Haub, 1993).

There are other, less severe and less successful approaches to family planning, however. The experience of western nations implied that "economic development is the best contraceptive." It suggested that a country must reach a threshold of socioeconomic development—a certain level of industrialization, urbanization, child survival, and literacy—before couples see an advantage in having smaller families, and as a result, the birthrate falls. But while China's program successfully cut its average family size in half (to 2.3 children per family) in only ten years, Mexico and Brazil, for example, have showed no such declines in the birthrate despite economic development (Ehrlich, Ehrlich, and Daily, 1995). As early as 1980, demographers began to realize that the relationship between development and the number of children women were having was inconsistent. Only development in certain areas—in health and nutrition, increased security in old age, and the education of women—predicted a lower birthrate.

There are some signs of significant decline in the fertility rates in some developing nations, especially in Asia and Latin America. The growth of world population has slowed down somewhat (Crossette, 1996), but it has not stopped. By 2000 the number of people in their prime reproductive years (age 15 to 49) will have risen 23 percent since 1990 (Ehrlich, Ehrlich, and Daily, 1995).

In addition to its publicity campaigns promoting the one-child policy, China's government has used harsher, more coercive measures to limit population growth.

Raising the Status of Women to Lower the Birthrate

If fertility is rising, development in the form of a higher GNP (gross national product) does not necessarily ensure a drop in the birthrate, and family planning will take too long to show an effect, what is the solution to reducing the birthrate in countries whose populations are growing faster than the nation's ability to provide for them? It turns out that raising the status of women is one of the best ways to lower the birthrate (Bryjak, 1997). Since women often enjoy an increase in status as a country develops, it is possible that this social change and not economic development itself has been behind the population declines in developed nations.

The status of women is both a cause and a consequence of smaller family size (Ehrlich, Ehrlich, and Daily, 1995). In most traditional societies, a woman's status is tied to marriage and motherhood. Most women do not receive formal education or work for wages outside the home. Instead, they marry young and have many children (several of whom usually die in infancy). When women have opportunities for education and employment, they tend to marry later and have fewer children (most of whom live). This, in turn, helps improve their educational level and earnings. For example, in the Kerala region of India, women have always enjoyed high status (Weisman, 1988). In two caste groups, property traditionally was passed down the female line, and women were free to choose and dismiss their husbands (a practice outlawed by the British in the early nineteenth century). But the tradition of respect for women has continued into modern times. In Kerala the literacy rate for women is more than 70 percent—almost three times the average for India. Here the average age of marriage is 22, compared with the national average of just over 18. Women are partners with their husbands in supporting their families, earning money by harvesting tea and coffee, weaving, processing fish, and rolling cigarettes. And Kerala has the lowest birthrate of any region in India (Ehrlich, Ehrlich, and Daily, 1995). Similar patterns may be seen in other regions and countries as women gain more access to education. Reducing the infant death rate also has an effect on the number of births. Parents who expect their children to live are likely to have fewer children (Cohen, 1995).

A woman-owned bank in Bombay. Raising the economic status of women is one of the best ways to lower a country's or region's birthrate, because women who have opportunities to obtain education and employment tend to marry later and bear fewer children.

The Population of the United States

The U.S. Constitution stipulates that for purposes of just representation (as well as taxation) a *census*—a systematic count of the entire population—must be taken every ten years. In addition, the Census Bureau conducts numerous surveys on population trends each year. Census data provide demographers with information for studying fertility patterns and population growth and distribution. Collecting data is only the first step; analyzing it may take years. Actually, figuring out *how* to collect the data for the census in the year 2000 has also taken years (see *Close Up: Census 2000*). We focus now on the social causes and consequences of two major changes in the population of the United States: declining fertility and the changing age structure.

Census 2000

C L O S E   U P

It stands to reason that taking a census of the population of the United States requires lots of advance planning, but even after years of planning, the census to be undertaken in the year 2000 remains controversial. At issue are changes in the four racial categories that have been used for the past twenty years and the new methods to be used to estimate the portion of the population missed by census forms and visits. As discussed in Chapter 9, the old racial categories are being changed. The other issue confronting the 2000 census revolves around the use of sampling to estimate the number of homeless and itinerant people. Demographers have long acknowledged that the census always results in an undercount because the methods traditionally used do not reach this portion of the population.

Those planning the 2000 census intended to use statistical sampling techniques by which the roughly 10 percent of the population not reached by the census mail-in form or personal visit would be *estimated*. The use

of this sampling method, though expected to save money and improve the quality of census data, nonetheless became a political football. Although the National Academy of Science, among other organizations, supported the move to use sampling, believing it to be more accurate and economical, Republicans in Congress opposed it, claiming that the Constitution requires

> **Demographers have long acknowledged that the census always results in an undercount.**

that the census be an actual enumeration or count.

The population as determined by the census is the basis for deciding the number of representatives a state or district will have as well as the amount of government funding and subsidies it will receive. The undercount is generally seen as serving the interests of Republicans, since those who are overlooked by the

census tend to be inner-city minorities. A more accurate count of the population in these traditionally Democratic areas is likely to result in congressional redistricting that will only further erode Republican power in these areas.

In January 1998 the director of the Census Bureau resigned. While the census plan she and the bureau had developed, which relies on statistical sampling, remained in effect, challenges to it continued, and no firm decision on the use of sampling in the census was scheduled to be made until 1999. At the time of this writing, the manner in which Census 2000 will be undertaken remains unclear. A new congressional subcommittee of three Republicans and two Democrats was formed to oversee the census, and the dress rehearsal of the sampling method was proceeding according to plan, though the sampling technique was to be tested in only two, rather than three, sites.

Sources: "Truce on Census Sampling Reached," *Population Today,* January 1998, p. 5; "Census Race and Ethnic Categories Retooled," ibid., p. 4; "Census Bureau Director Martha Riche Resigns," *Footnotes* 26, February 1998, p. 1.

Declining Fertility

The major change in the population of the United States has been a decline in family size. The birthrate began to fall in the early 1900s, hitting a low of 18 (per 1,000) in the 1930s. For a time, it looked as if this trend might reverse itself: in the late 1940s and 1950s the birthrate climbed to 24 or

25. But the "baby boom" was temporary. In the late 1950s the birthrate began to fall, hitting a new low of 16 in 1983 (*Statistical Abstract,* 1992). Fertility has also steadily diminished. In 1800 the American woman had an average of seven children. A century later she could expect to have half that many. By 1976, the average number of children born to each

American woman declined to a low of 1.7. Since then it has increased slightly, to 2.0, about the same as it was at the height of the Great Depression (*Statistical Abstract,* 1992; Population Reference Bureau, 1997b).

One reason for low fertility in the United States is the "contraceptive revolution." Oral contraceptives first became available in this country in the 1960s. "The Pill" was part and parcel of the cultural revolution of the 1960s, which helped make birth control in general more acceptable. A number of state laws banning the sale of contraceptives and the use of public funds to provide birth control to the poor were struck down in this period. Today 68 percent of married couples in the United States practice some form of contraception. Abortions were legalized in 1973. An estimated 25 percent of all pregnancies today end in abortion (mostly among young, unmarried women). In 1995, emergency contraception in the form of a series of pills taken immediately after unprotected intercourse was approved for use in the United States, but a survey of obstetrician-gynecologists ("Kaiser Survey," 1995) shows it is rarely prescribed. As a result of contraception and abortion, the proportion of unplanned babies born in the United States dropped from 20 percent in the early 1960s to 7 percent in the 1980s.

A second reason for low fertility rates in this country is that women are postponing marriage and childbirth (see Chapter 11). The mean age at which women born between 1955 and 1959 had their first child is estimated at 25.3—three years later than that of women born two decades earlier. As discussed above, delayed marriage and motherhood, in turn, reflect the growing numbers of women pursuing higher education or entering the workforce. In this country, as in others, there is a direct relationship between level of education and fertility. Women who drop out of high school have twice as many children as women who complete four years of college.

Economic conditions have also influenced fertility rates, but not as directly as might be thought. The low fertility rates of the 1930s are sometimes attributed to the Great Depression. The idea that couples would be reluctant to have children in times of economic hardship and uncertainty makes sense. But fertility rates began falling in the 1920s, a period of great prosperity. Fertility rates climbed in the 1950s (a period of prosperity) but fell in the 1960s (also a time of prosperity). They are the same today as they were at the height of the Great Depression. One possible explanation is that economic conditions have a delayed effect on family size. People who grew up during the Depression and the war years were used to a lower standard of living. When economic conditions improved, they felt that they could afford more children. In contrast, people who grew up in the prosperous 1950s and 1960s grew accustomed to a higher standard of living. When inflation and recessions forced them to choose between a second or third child and a house or yearly vacations, they chose the latter.

The overall fertility rate in the United States is one of the lowest in the world. Yet the population of the United States continues to grow, for two reasons. One is an "echo boom" (Westoff, 1986, p. 557). Although fertility rates have declined since the 1950s, the number of women still in their childbearing years—women born during the baby boom—remains large. This "inflates" the number of births. The second reason is immigration. Immigration into the United States has dropped considerably since 1991, when it was 1.8 million. Since then it has averaged about 850,000 a year (*Statistical Abstract,* 1997b). The average number of children born to Latina women is high (2.7) compared with the average born to non-Latina white women (1.9).

The Changing Age Structure

The one exception to the pattern of declining fertility in the United States was the postwar baby boom. The average number of children born to a woman began to climb in 1946, reaching a peak of 3.7 children in 1957. One-third of the current population—75 million Americans—was born in the nineteen-year period between 1946 and 1964 known as the "baby boom" (Bouvier and De Vita, 1991).

The baby boom generation provides a clear illustration of the impact of fertility rates on patterns of supply and demand in a society (Merrick and Tordello, 1988). In their early years, baby boomers created a market for delivery rooms and pediatricians, baby food and baby clothes, and child-centered entertainment. As they moved into school, they inflated the demand for classrooms, teachers, and books and created a "youth culture." Today's oversupply of educated workers, slower rates of job advancement, and high unemployment rates are due in part to the fact that this generation has moved out of school and into the job market. As the baby boom generation ages, the demand for retirement facilities and medical services, and the amount paid out in Social Security, will skyrocket. The metaphor of a pig swallowed by a python has been used to describe the movement of this generational bulge through the life cycle.

In part as a result of the baby boom generation, the shape of the U.S. population has also changed (see Figure 16-3). The American population is growing older. More precisely, our population is becoming middle-aged. The median age rose from 20 in 1970 to 33 in 1991 and will probably reach 37 by the year 2000 (*Statistical Abstract,* 1992).

The so-called graying of America (see Figure 16-4) has serious implications. In 1900, only one in ten Americans was 55 or older. By 1987, one in five was 55 or older, and one in eight was 65 or older. In 2011 the baby boom generation will begin turning 65. By 2030, almost one-quarter of the population will be 65 or older, and there will be only two taxpayers for every retiree. European nations are already facing this problem. After a short-lived postwar baby boom, fertility rates began to drop in the 1950s. France and other nations are worried about a potential long-term decline in numbers and about the dependence of a growing elderly population on a shrinking younger population. Many nations have adopted a "pro-natalist" or "pro-birth" policy, offering free child care and tax breaks for families.

The graying of America has social as well as economic implications. Older people in the United States, and in many other industrialized nations, do not have the status accorded them in more traditional societies. This lower status is reflected in *ageism*—subtle (and not so subtle) forms of prejudice and discrimination against older people (see Chapter 5). It is most obvious in the workplace. For a long time, people were forced to retire at the age of 65, no matter how skilled and productive they were. Although mandatory retirement is less common than it used to be, social circumstances still favor retirement at 65, if not earlier. Corporations offer incentives for early retirement, while So-

cial Security benefits are reduced if a recipient earns more than a minimum amount. In living situations, too, the aging face problems. Stereotypes picture them in either fun-filled retirement communities or depressing nursing homes. While neither image fits the reality—the vast majority of elderly people remain in the same communities they lived in earlier—many older Americans suffer loneliness, deteriorating housing, and financial constraints.

What will the future bring? Some demographers think that the baby boom was just one episode in a cycle of recurring population booms and busts. Others, however, believe that although the U.S. fertility rate increased slightly in the early 1990s, there is no evidence that a major increase in the rate will recur.

Population and Global Ecology

In 1798, Thomas Malthus published *An Essay on the Principle of Population,* which became extremely influential in the nineteenth century. Malthus argued that humanity is condemned to cycles of feast and famine. Human population increases faster than the food supply necessary to maintain it. Whereas food supply increases arithmetically, by addition (1, 2, 3, 4, 5, . . .), population increases geometrically, by multiplication (2, 4, 8, 16, 32, . . .) (see Figure 16-5 on page 606). When food supplies are plentiful, the population grows until it outstrips available supplies. Then, because of such checks as "war, pestilence, and famine," population growth slows down or even stops. But as soon as food supplies catch up with population, the cycle begins anew. By implication, efforts to improve the standard of living and augment food supplies are doomed to failure, for they simply encourage people to have large families. The inevitable can be delayed but not avoided. Malthus urged "moral restraint" (sexual abstinence) but doubted that many people would follow his advice.

Malthus failed to predict the technological advances that enabled modern nations to vastly increase the amount of food produced on a given piece of land. He did not foresee technological developments in transportation and communication that made it possible to distribute food all over the

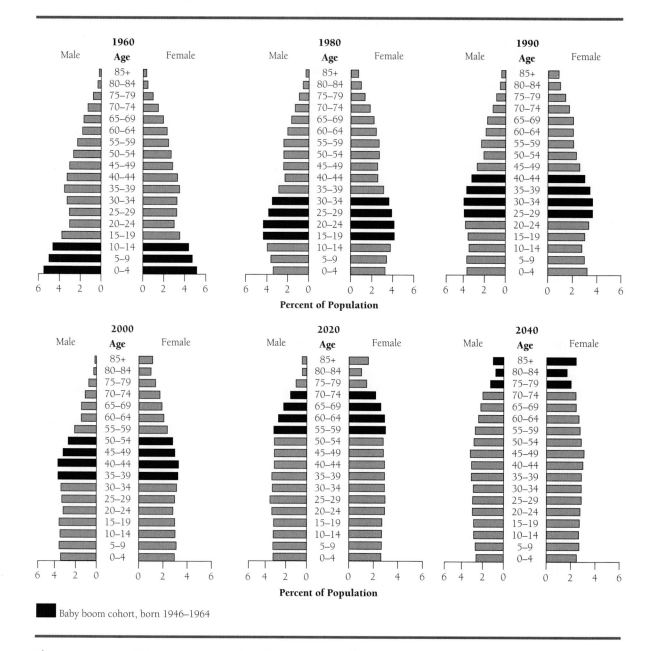

Figure 16-3   *"Pig in a Python": The Baby Boom Generation*

The large baby boom generation created a bulge that alters the shape of the population (like a pig in a python) as it moves through different stages of the life course. In the 1950s and 1960s, the U.S. population was young; today, as baby boomers move through their forties and fifties, our population is becoming middle-aged; in the next century, the proportion of senior citizens and elderly persons in our population will swell.

Source: Leon F. Bouvier and Carol J. DeVita, "The Baby Boom Entering Midlife," *Population Bulletin* 46, November 1991, pp. 1–35.

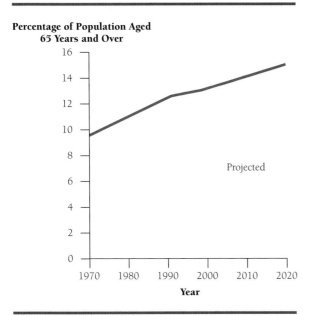

**Percentage of Population Aged
65 Years and Over**

Projected

1970   1980   1990   2000   2010   2020
Year

Figure 16-4   *The Graying of America*

Thanks to improved health and longer life expectancy, the percentage of Americans age 65 and older is growing steadily.

Sources: Adapted from U.S. Bureau of the Census, *Statistical Abstract of the United States, 1980,* Washington, DC: GPO, 1980, p. 338; ibid., *Statistical Abstract of the United States, 1989,* 1989, p. 15.

globe. He did not predict the increased use of birth control devices. He did not consider the possibility that people might respond to a rising standard of living by limiting the size of their families. For a time it looked as if Malthus had been wrong.

But in recent years the population problem and the specter of "war, pestilence, and famine" have reemerged, with new dimensions. If world population does indeed reach 10.7 billion by the year 2030, there is good reason to wonder whether the earth can support its human population.

Food Supplies and Distribution

In the past two and a half decades, worldwide food production increased dramatically. Supplies of cereal crops, for instance, rose about 50 percent; the production of fruits and vegetables also gained significantly. In spite of these increases, however, 43 percent of the population of sub-Saharan Africa is malnourished, along with 22 percent of south

Asia and 15 percent of Latin American and the Caribbean (Bender and Smith, 1997).

The problem of hunger is not so much one of supply as one of distribution. For one thing, the highest-yield crops are concentrated in relatively few "breadbaskets," many of which are found in rich, industrialized nations (notably the United States). Many of the problems of hungry nations, however, derive not from their geographic location but from their involvement in the world capitalist system. Capitalism makes some places richer than others, just as it makes some people richer than others. It concentrates opportunities and crises in specific geographical patterns. Because of uneven development (Gugler, 1997), developing nations do not have the same capacities as richer nations to produce and distribute food. They cannot afford sophisticated irrigation systems; they lack efficient, modern means to transport food; and they must import fertilizers.

In a peasant economy, virtually everyone works in agriculture. The production and distribution of food are governed by traditional social relationships. Communities are self-sufficient; individuals live on what they produce themselves or trade locally. In a commercial system, the production and distribution of food are governed by profits. Land that provided food for local consumption is turned over to the production of cash crops, such as coffee, sugar, or bananas. Food has to be purchased and may have to be imported. How well and how often people eat depends on the fluctuating prices their cash commodities obtain in the world market. People go hungry "not because there is insufficient food grown in the world but because they no longer grow it themselves and do not have the money to buy it" (Barnet, 1980, p. 151).

Most of the increase in food production during the past three decades was the result of the invention of new strains of wheat, rice, and beans that greatly increase the yield per acre. When first introduced in the 1950s, these "miracle plants" were hailed as the solution to the problem of world hunger. In the next ten to fifteen years the grain harvest doubled in Indonesia, tripled in India, and quadrupled in Mexico (L. R. Brown, 1988). But the miracle plants require constant irrigation and large amounts of chemical fertilizers and pesticides, all of which are expensive. The most efficient way to harvest these crops is by machine, which not only is

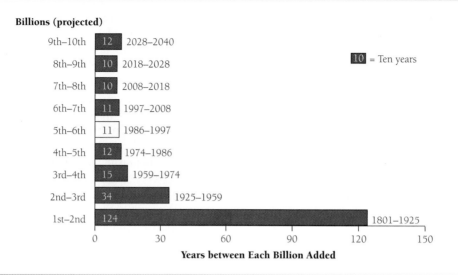

Billions (projected)

9th–10th	12	2028–2040
8th–9th	10	2018–2028
7th–8th	10	2008–2018
6th–7th	11	1997–2008
5th–6th	11	1986–1997
4th–5th	12	1974–1986
3rd–4th	15	1959–1974
2nd–3rd	34	1925–1959
1st–2nd	124	1801–1925

10 = Ten years

Years between Each Billion Added

Figure 16-5   *Billion by Billion*

Human population growth is exponential. Suppose that there are 50 women and 50 men in a population and that over a twenty-five-year period each of those women has 4 children, and each of their daughters also has 4 children. The second generation will consist of 200 children (50 women × 4 children), half of whom are female; the third generation will consist of 400 children (100 × 4). In a mere twenty-five years the population will increase sevenfold: the original 100 people, plus their 200 children, plus their 400 grandchildren, for a total of 700! Looking at world population growth, the numbers are much, much larger, of course. At current growth rates, it takes only about a decade to add a billion people to the world population.

Source: U.S. Bureau of the Census, Center for International Research, *Population Today,* December 1992, p. 4.

expensive but also means that agricultural workers lose jobs. On the national level, governments have had to borrow funds to pay for these changes. On the local level, the changes accelerated the trend away from small, self-supporting farms to large, commercial enterprises. Often only wealthy landowners could afford the new technology, and it was efficient only on large plots. In the Punjab region of India, food production increased dramatically. But as many as half of all agricultural jobs were eliminated, and thousands of peasants were forced off the land. Meanwhile, the increase in food production lowered prices for grains, pushing developing nations and farmers further into debt. There are also environmental costs. Over time, irrigation depletes the soil of vital nutrients. Chemical fertilizers and pesticides pollute the water supply, while insects and diseases develop immunity to chemical pesticides.

The problems of production and displacement in developing nations have been complicated by popu-

lation growth. Overpopulation forces people to move into semiarid grasslands and steep mountainside pastures or to cut down forests in order to create new farmland (Hendry, 1988; Newcombe, 1984). But the soil in these regions is thin and easily eroded. Overpopulation in areas where people depend on wood for fuel and light accelerates deforestation. Farmers begin to use crop residues and animal dung for fuel, instead of using it for fertilizer. As a result, the soil becomes more compacted, and water runs off instead of being absorbed. The water table begins to fall, and wells run dry. Eventually, there is not enough soil or water for even subsistence-level farming. At this point, farmers or herders become "environmental refugees, migrating to the nearest city or relief camp" (L. R. Brown, 1988, p. 20). Thus the amount of arable land is reduced, while the number of landless villagers increases. This pattern is particularly visible, and tragic, in Africa. The growth of cities (discussed below) is both a cause and an effect of deteriorating cropland.

The problem of hunger is largely one of food distribution. U.S. farms produce grain surpluses, unlike farmers in developing nations, who must depend on animal and human power and lack machines and chemical fertilizers.

Since World War II, a huge amount of land—equal in size to India and China combined—has been seriously degraded or taken out of production altogether (*World Resources, 1992*) (see Figure 16-6). In Japan, Taiwan, and South Korea, rapid industrialization has offset declines in local food production, generating the income to import food. In North Korea and Africa this has not been the case (see *A Global View:* The Politics of Famine).

Patterns of Consumption

The problem of overpopulation is not simply a matter of too many people living in poor countries. As Paul and Anne Ehrlich emphasize,

> Numbers *per se* are not the measure of overpopulation; instead it is the impact of people on ecosystems and nonrenewable resources. . . . The birth of a baby in the United States imposes more than a hundred times the stress on the world's resources and environment as a birth in, say, Bangladesh. Babies from Bangladesh do not grow up to own automobiles and air conditioners or to eat grain-fed beef. (1988, p. 915)

Patterns of consumption around the world are extremely lopsided. With only about 22 percent of the world's population, industrial nations consume 75 percent of its resources and generate 75 percent of its waste and pollution (*Population Today,* April 1996). The United States is by far the most extravagant. A child born in the United States will have more than 250 times the impact on the environment than that of a child born in sub-Saharan Africa (*Population Today,* April 1996). American energy consumption is four times the per capita world average (*Statistical Abstract,* 1997, table 1373). Much of the

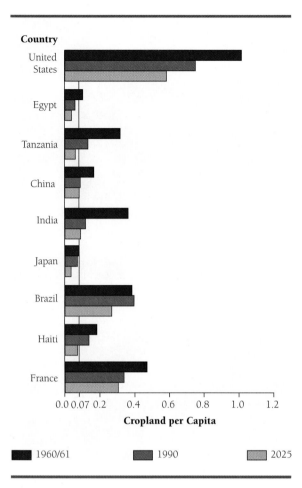

Figure 16-6   *Declines in Available Cropland*

Experts say that the minimum amount of cropland needed to feed an individual is 0.17 acres (0.07 hectares). By 2025 it is projected that an increasing number of countries, some of which are shown above, will be below that minimum level.

Source: Population Reference Bureau, *Population Today,* April 1997, p. 6.

developing world is still living in the "wood age," relying on wood for heat, light, and cooking and on human and animal power for transportation and production. Trees are a renewable resource, unlike oil, gas, coal, and other fossil fuels. But without effective reforestation programs, the world's forests are shrinking rapidly (Postel and Heise, 1988).

Consumption of food is also lopsided. People in industrial nations not only have more to eat than those in developing nations but eat better-quality food. The diet of those in developed countries is about 28 percent meat and dairy products and 31 percent cereals. The diet of people in developing countries is 12 percent meat and dairy and 56 percent cereals (Bender and Smith, 1997). (Sweeteners, oils, and roots and tubers make up the rest of the major sources of food energy in developed and developing nations.) The average American consumes about 120 pounds of meat a year; the average African lives on a diet of grain and root crops that are low in protein and vitamins. North Americans consume about 1,800 pounds of grain a year per capita, most of it indirectly in the form of chicken and cattle feed. In contrast, Indians, Iranians, Thais, and Moroccans consume about 400 pounds of grain a year, most of it in the form of bread, rice, or cereal.

Between 1980 and 1995 the agricultural population dropped 15 percent worldwide and is expected to decline into the next century. While yields have risen, the amount of land devoted to crops has declined (Bender and Smith, 1997). Increased erosion, desertification (the transformation of arable land to desert), and salinization (due to leaching) mean that the land available to grow crops has reached its upward limits (*Population Today,* March 1997). In many places fresh water is also in short supply. Asia has about 36 percent of the global runoff (rainfall that is not absorbed by the soil, but fills streams and rivers) but 60 percent of the world population. The gap between these numbers goes beyond conservation and back to distribution. The Amazon carries 15 percent of the world's runoff, but its waters reach only 0.4 percent of the population (Postel, 1997).

Future supplies of fuel and food depend in part on patterns of consumption. The rates of growth in energy consumption have slowed in recent years (especially in the United States), but continued world population growth means that the absolute amount of energy needed to maintain current standards of living in the future will be greater than it is today. And with living standards rising as countries develop, per capita consumption patterns should *increase* rather than simply remain stable. Increased consumption will drive up prices, making it more likely that the poor will find it even more difficult to feed themselves (Brown, 1997). Reducing consumption is not always the simple answer, however.

Environmental Risks

The world's growing population is menaced not only by shortages of food and fuel but also by major environmental hazards. In many cases, technologies that were developed to make life easier and pleasanter, such as automobiles and air conditioning, have led to harmful consequences undreamed of by their inventors. The wealthiest 20 percent of the population produces two-thirds of the greenhouse gases and 90 percent of the ozone-depleting fluorocarbons (*Population Today,* April 1996). Also at fault is the vast array of modern chemicals—approximately 70,000 different kinds, with 1,000 new ones added every year (Parenti, 1988). Synthetic organic chemicals are found in food, clothing, detergents, pesticides, plastics, and almost everything else.

Air pollution is most noticeable in cities; smog hovers over the palms of Los Angeles, the architectural treasures of Athens, and the office buildings of Seoul. Caused by a mixture of smoke and auto emissions, it is especially dangerous to the health of young children and the elderly. In the form of acid rain—precipitation contaminated with sulfur dioxide—air pollution has destroyed crops, forests, and lakes. Other chemicals pose special dangers to those who manufacture them or who live nearby; the city of Dzerzhinsk, about 250 miles from Moscow, is the site of some of the worst pollution in the world. Its former chemical factories churned out gases like DDT, blister gas, mustard gas, and rocket fuel, as well as Agent Orange. The wastes and unwanted chemical weapons were buried in barrels which have rusted and split open. The earth in Dzerzhinsk now contains the highest concentrations of dioxin in the world. Even a minute amount of this chemical can cause cancer—and the life expectancy in Dzerzhinsk, 42 years for men and 47 for women, reflects this (Specter, 1998). Radiation, another pollutant, is especially dangerous because exposure to it increases the incidence of cancer and birth defects. As a result of the nuclear power accident in 1986 at Chernobyl in the Ukraine, over 300 people died; years later, as many as 150,000 were suffering from serious health problems, and about 4 million were still living on contaminated soil.

Of special concern are the long-term effects of air pollution on the earth's atmosphere. The ozone layer, which protects the earth from the sun's ultraviolet rays, is being depleted by chlorofluorocarbons (CFCs), chemicals emitted by refrigerants and aerosols. A reduction in the use of these chemicals has slowed the damage, however, and scientists hope that the concentration of CFCs will begin to decline around the year 2000. Another long-term danger, the *greenhouse effect,* results from a buildup of carbon dioxide, methane, and other gases that form a shield allowing the sun's heat to enter the atmosphere but not escape (as in a greenhouse). Over time, it is feared, the greenhouse effect will make the earth's climate warmer, melting the polar ice

In Copsa Mica, Romania, a tire-blackening factory blankets the surrounding homes and fields in black soot.

A GLOBAL VIEW

The Politics of Famine

No one who has seen their hollow eyes and wasted bodies in the daily paper or on TV news can easily ignore the suffering of the starving. In the past two decades, famines have devastated Ethiopia, Bangladesh, and Somalia. It is commonly assumed that famine results from a sharp decline in food production when a natural calamity such as flood, drought, or agricultural blight strikes a poor, overpopulated region. But famines are also political. The most recent famine, in North Korea, illustrates how intimately hunger is tied to politics, even if its initial causes have been natural. In 1998 North Koreans were receiving only 750 to 1,000 calories per day. Yet the communist regime of Kim Jong Il resisted the full range of humanitarian aid being offered to its starving people because it feared that the presence of international agencies would weaken its grip on the country. Relief workers, as well as the govern-ments helping to fund their efforts, feared that simply giving the government in Pyongyang the grain and other foodstuffs it needs rather than handling the distribution themselves would

> **There has never been a famine in any country that's been a democracy with a relatively free press.**
> —Amartya Sen

result in the food going to bureaucrats and soldiers and not to the general public. The temptation, for some, is to let this authoritarian regime starve itself out of existence.

Many poor, overpopulated countries manage to avoid starvation in spite of disasters. In sub-Saharan Africa, the same drought that led to famine in Sudan spared Zimbabwe. The key, say experts, is not that food supplies are lacking but that, for political reasons, people are un-able to obtain them, usually because prices are too high (Sen, 1981). In India, the government sponsors make-work jobs to help the poor buy grain. In Zimbabwe, the government provided the relief necessary to stave off mass starvation. In So-malia, on the other hand, warfare between rival clans prevented food from reaching drought-stricken areas. In Bangladesh, the authoritarian government sent out the army to punish hoarders. Rather than convincing people to stop hoarding food, this action sent the message that the government had lost control and could not maintain an adequate food supply. Food prices rose as a result. In North Korea, government officials who allowed the BBC to broadcast pictures of the plight of its citizens lost their jobs. As a result, the famine in North Korea has had little impact on the television-assisted consciences of the governments and citizens of the world.

Sources: Nigel Holloway, "The Politics of Starvation," *World Press Review,* July 1997, pp. 6–7; "The World's Most Obnoxious Beggar," excerpted from "Asiaweek" in *World Press Review,* July 1997, pp. 7–8; Sylvia Nasar, "It's Never Fair to Just Blame the Weather," *The New York Times,* Jan. 17, 1993, pp. E1 ff.

caps and flooding coastal cities, as well as turning farmland into desert.

Widespread water pollution of rivers, lakes, and oceans comes from industries that pour out detergents, solvents, and acids; from farms, with their chemical pesticides, herbicides, and fertilizers; and from cities, which create tons of sewage. And oil spills from tankers and offshore drilling wreak havoc around the globe. The worst oil spill in U.S. history occurred in 1989, when the Exxon *Valdez* ran into a reef in Alaska's Prince William Sound, releasing 35,000 tons of crude oil. Less than 4 percent of the spill was recaptured. In the first weeks after the accident, hundreds of sea birds and animals died. But the real danger lies in the future. Oil deposits on the ocean bottom contaminate microorganisms, then the little fish that feed on them, then the bigger fish, and so on up the food chain.

Another growing problem is soil pollution, especially from hazardous chemical wastes. The amount of such wastes produced in the United States rose

Starving children are treated in an International Red Cross relief tent in Somalia, where widespread famine in the early 1990s resulted not from simple crop failure but from warring clans that prevented food distribution.

What it comes down to, says economist Amartya Sen (1981), is whether or not a nation is democratically ruled. If so, its free press will alert the government to impending catastrophe. If not, the authorities are ignorant and immune to pressure. "There has never been a famine in any country that's been a democracy with a relatively free press," says Sen. "I know of no exception. It applies to very poor countries with democratic systems as well as to rich ones."

While it is true that North Korea's response to the 150,000 tons of grain South Korea shipped to it was a series of commando raids, withholding aid to North Korea would be inexcusable not only on moral grounds but also on political ones. It is unclear what the outcome of a destabilized North Korea would be, but desperation tends to provoke reckless responses, making it unlikely anything good would come from such an action.

from about 9 million metric tons in 1970 to 300 million metric tons less than two decades later. When toxic wastes are disposed of in dumps, dangerous residues leak into the soil and groundwater. The food grown in Dzerzhinsk is contaminated, but the residents eat it anyway, because the industries have all closed down and they lack the money to buy uncontaminated food (Specter, 1998). Solid wastes—garbage—also present a growing problem. Each year Americans throw away 1.6 billion pens, 2 billion razors and blades, 220 million tires, and 16 billion disposable diapers (Langone, 1989). Since much of this waste is not biodegradable, it may be preserved in landfills for hundreds of years. In any case, the United States is running out of landfill space. Recycling is one solution to this problem, but the United States at present recycles only about 18 percent of its waste (*Statistical Abstract*, 1997).

If we know what the environmental risks are, why don't we do more to reverse them? Most of the pollutants result from economic expansion, whether in the form of agricultural production, industrial growth, or energy creation. The poor nations of the world are caught on a population treadmill. With their populations doubling about every forty years, these nations have to run just to stay in the same place; that is, they must attempt to increase food production continuously simply to maintain their current standards of living. Population growth is not the only problem facing these nations, but unless it is slowed, other problems will be magnified.

Western industrial nations have been committed to economic growth—"the treadmill of production" (Schnaiberg, 1980)—for nearly two centuries. Increased production means high profits for business, more jobs and consumer comforts for labor, and higher tax revenues for government. The clearest strategy for increasing production is automation: replacing people with machines. Automation creates short-term gains but long-term problems: unemployment, labor unrest, increased demands on government. Typically, governments solve these problems by helping businesses expand, thus accelerating the treadmill. This strategy creates new jobs and generates new tax revenues. But higher levels of production require higher levels of consumption. Either new consumers have to be brought into the market (through export) or workers have to be paid more so that they can buy more. The solution to this problem is, once again, stepping up production. Once set in motion, industrialized production develops a momentum of its own. Industrial capitalist nations come to depend on economic growth just to maintain their current standards of living. The catch is that each acceleration of the treadmill of production requires higher levels of energy use and produces higher levels of environmental pollution.

In December 1997 a conference in Kyoto, Japan, on reducing global warming by reducing greenhouse gases illustrated this catch. The U.S. government, despite its acknowledgment that global warming is a danger, found itself unable to fully support a group of measures put together by negotiators from around the world that called for the U.S. and other countries to cut emissions 7 percent from 1990 levels in the years 2008 to 2012. Pressures from Republicans and representatives from manufacturing and fossil-fuel industries would have jeopardized other Clinton administration programs. Citizens, too, would need to reduce energy use dras-

tically, making the administration's support of the measures politically dangerous. Another concern involved the degree to which developing countries would be required to reduce emissions, since their emissions are expected to rise considerably in the next two decades as their development progresses (Broder, 1997). The treadmill of production rolls on.

It is difficult to get citizens and their governments to understand the threat of global warming because it is happening so slowly and so incrementally that to many it seems a negligible or even imaginary danger. Others in the northern countries may think, "A little warmer might not be too bad!" However, the health hazards of global warming are real and already beginning to be seen. A heat wave in Chicago in the summer of 1995 left 500 dead. In the tropics, higher temperatures increase the number of insects, and thus increase the incidence of diseases like malaria; warmer waters increase the likelihood of cholera and harmful algae, which can make fish and shellfish toxic (Monastersky, 1996). Warmer conditions will also render some land unfit for agriculture, further depleting food supplies. Since developing countries tend to be in the southern hemisphere, global warming will affect them far more than the developed north.

AIDS and Population

Acquired immune deficiency syndrome (AIDS) is today ravaging every continent, particularly sub-Saharan Africa, where it is expected to reduce life expectancy by nearly twenty years in some countries (Olshansky et al., 1997). This modern plague has the potential to sharply alter world population. AIDS is caused by a virus, HIV, that destroys the body's ability to fight off infections and cancers. It is spread by blood, semen, vaginal secretions, and breast milk. Thus a person may acquire the virus through sexual intercourse, a blood transfusion or shared needle, or being born to or nursed by an infected mother. The virus may remain inactive for years so that a person may not know that he or she is HIV-positive and transmitting the virus to others. New drugs such as AZT and treatment with combinations of drugs may slow the progress of AIDS and even reduce the amount of virus in infected patients, potentially reducing the rate of transmission between adults or from an HIV-positive pregnant woman to her child. However, these drugs are expensive and complicated to administer; only a small percentage of well-off patients can afford treatment. Unfortunately, widespread media coverage of these medical breakthroughs may have had the unintended consequence of leading people to believe that AIDS can be cured. It cannot. The risk of infection may be reduced through abstinence, monogamy, and the use of condoms and sterile hypodermic needles. But when full-blown AIDS develops (the average incubation period is ten years), it is always fatal.

Unknown—or at least, unidentified—before 1981, AIDS has spread rapidly. UNAIDS (1996) estimates that 22 million people worldwide are infected with HIV and that 8,500 new infections occur each day. As shown in Figure 16-7, the disease is most prevalent in sub-Saharan Africa, where at least 8 million people are infected (*Newsweek,* December 29, 1997, p. 8). In some countries, among them Malawi, Tanzania, and Uganda, over one-third of adults are HIV-positive. [In the United States, an estimated 1 million people have been in-

fected, at least 300,000 of whom have died. (National AIDS Clearing House, 1998.)] About 90 percent of AIDS victims live in the developing world, where people have little access to information on preventing infection, much less access to treatment. The World Health Organization estimates that as many as 30 to 40 million people will be HIV-positive by the year 2000.

Sociocultural attitudes have been a major factor in the AIDS epidemic (UNAIDS, 1996). In the United States, AIDS originally was viewed as a "homosexual" disease and therefore something most (heterosexual) people—and serious researchers—need not worry about. In Asia, AIDS is seen as a western disease, best avoided by visiting young prostitutes (who, in fact, are more likely to contract and transmit HIV than are older women). In Latin America, "machismo" attitudes (which encourage promiscuity), lack of basic sex education (partly because of religious taboos), and failure to use condoms have contributed to the epidemic.

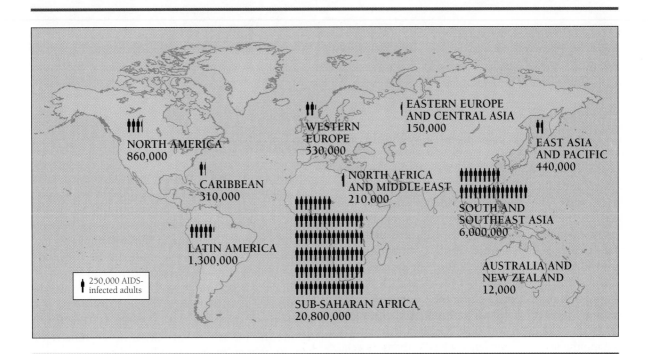

Figure 16-7   *AIDS in Developed and Developing Nations*

HIV is spreading worldwide at a rate of about 16,000 new infections a day. A disproportionate number occur in Africa where the new drugs slowing the disease in developed nations are not yet widely used because of the costs involved.

Source: Adapted from *Newsweek,* Dec. 29, 1997, p. 8.

Kinshasa, in the Congo Republic. One theory holds that the pressures of urbanization in Kinshasa first contributed to the spread of AIDS, now a threat to world health.

Where did AIDS come from? Why did the epidemic break out now? A single plasma sample from the Congo Republic (formerly Zaire) taken in 1959 has repeatedly tested positive for antibodies to the HIV virus. This and other evidence suggests that the disease has been around for some time. But because most people in the area lived in small, isolated villages, had limited contact with outsiders and few sexual partners, it did not spread. One current theory (Garrett, 1994) is that HIV spread because of development along the Congo River, the main "highway" in Central Africa, and the rapid growth of the capital city Kinshasa (formerly Leopoldville). The incidence of HIV today is relatively low in the interior but increases as one moves southwest along the Congo River. Thus urbanization, which brings more people into close contact and erodes traditional sexual taboos, played a key role in starting the AIDS epidemic.

Urbanization

As fast as the world population has grown in the last century, the proportion of people living in cities has increased even more rapidly (World Bank, 1992b). *Urbanization*—an increase in the percentage of a population living in urban settlements and a resulting extension of the influence of urban culture and lifestyles—is a worldwide phenomenon.

Cities of 7,000 to 20,000 people existed on the fertile plains of the Nile, Tigris-Euphrates, and Indus river valleys as early as 5000 B.C. But it was during the Industrial Revolution in the nineteenth century that cities grew rapidly and became a major influence on social life. The many technological changes brought about by the Industrial Revolution affected both rural and urban populations. The mechanization of agriculture increased productivity, creating a surplus of farmworkers. The decline in agricultural jobs pushed workers off the farm; the growing number of factory jobs pulled them to the city. Technological innovations in transportation and communication reduced constraints on the size and density of cities. Railroads, steamboats, streetcars, and elevators in ever-taller buildings helped solve difficulties in moving people and goods.

The first country to industrialize, England, was also the first country to become highly urbanized. Manchester, England—the world's first "factory town"—exemplifies the emergence of the industrial city. In 1790, Manchester was a market town with a population of 25,000. Forty years later, after the construction of seventy-two textile mills, the population had quadrupled; thirty years after that it had quadrupled again (Cousins and Nagpaul, 1970). When other northern European nations, the United States, and Canada were rapidly industrialized in the late nineteenth century, the English pattern was repeated.

Urbanization and Sociology

From the beginning, urbanization fascinated sociologists. Cities played a central role in the transformation of the feudal, agricultural societies of western Europe into modern, industrial-capitalist societies. In the effort to understand what this transformation meant, the founding fathers of sociology looked to cities (Giddens, 1981, 1985a).

Functionalist sociologists saw industrialization and urbanization as destroying traditional communities and primary groups, thus setting the individual adrift. Ferdinand Tönnies (1887/1951) contrasted the social order of small, traditional communities with that of large, industrialized cities (1887/1957). In peasant villages, he argued, shared norms and values, frequent social contact, and warm personal relationships create a sense of belonging and community, or *Gemeinschaft.* People are intimately involved with their neighbors and kin. Little changes from one generation to the next. In modern, industrial cities, by contrast, change is constant. There is little consensus on values and norms. Social contacts are fleeting and impersonal. Individualism replaces group loyalty; anonymity replaces familiarity. People do not feel they belong to a city; they merely use its resources. Tönnies called this cool, impersonal social order *Gesellschaft* (association).

Emile Durkheim painted a similar picture (1893/1966). He held that traditional societies are based on **mechanical solidarity.** In effect, all members of a community are stamped from the same mold. One family's lifestyle is much the same as the next family's. People are united by shared beliefs and shared experiences. In contrast, modern, industrial societies are based on **organic solidarity.** The complex division of labor and the high degree of specialization create differences in both experiences and values. Just as the specialized organs of the body are interdependent, so members of modern societies are interdependent. But although people are more dependent on others for survival, they also have less in common. Whereas mechanical solidarity is based on similarity, organic solidarity is based on interdependence. Alienation, anomie (normlessness), social isolation, and deviance are more likely in organic, urban settings.

Tönnies and Durkheim were concerned with social cohesion; Karl Marx was interested in the sources of social conflict. Marx saw the division between town and country in the nineteenth century as reflecting an underlying conflict between two competing modes of production. The countryside represented a dying feudal order, based primarily on agriculture; cities represented the new capitalist order, based on industrial production. In *The Conditions of the English Working Class in 1844* (1844/1975), Marx's colleague Friedrich Engels used the squalor and misery of Manchester as evidence for the impact of capitalism on working people. Both men thought that the concentration of workers in cities might foster the development of radical class consciousness.

The idea that cities represent modern society in microcosm had a powerful influence on future generations of sociologists. This was particularly true in the United States, where urbanization accelerated rapidly around the turn of the century. Like their European predecessors, American sociologists were drawn to the city. Echoing earlier theorists, they tended to assume that urbanization inevitably meant radical social change. The move from rural communities to urban centers, from family farming to wage labor in factories, stripped people of meaningful social and economic relationships. With Durkheim, they associated urban life with alienation, anomie, social isolation, and high levels of deviance. But American sociologists differed from their European predecessors on a subtle but important point. Whereas European theorists had seen the city as a reflection of changes originating in society as a whole, American sociologists were more inclined to see the city as producing change that then spread through the rest of society (Saunders, 1985).

The Urbanization of the United States

In 1800, nine out of ten Americans lived on farms or in small towns with populations of 2,500 or less. Philadelphia (pop. 70,000) and New York (pop. 60,000) were small towns compared with London (pop. 800,000) and Paris (pop. 500,000). Today, we are an overwhelmingly urban society: three out of four Americans live in or near cities. The urban history of the United States can be divided into three stages.

The first stage was the *emergence of big cities,* beginning in the mid-nineteenth century. As in Manchester, the major stimulus to urban growth was industrialization. The steam engines of the day required coal, and towns on the terminal points of waterways and rail lines leading to northern coalfields boomed. Another factor in the growth of big cities in the United States was immigration. Almost one-third of the entire population of Europe migrated to America between 1850 and 1940, and most immigrants went to work in factories. The industrial cities of the late nineteenth century were highly compact centers of manufacturing and distribution that served as home and workplace to millions of unskilled and semiskilled workers (Kasarda, 1985). Factories, warehouses, shops, and tenement housing were tightly clustered. In 1899, the average New Yorker "commuted" two blocks from home to work (Palen, 1975). Chicago, which had a population of 4,100 when it was incorporated in 1833, had 2 million residents by 1910, the vast majority of whom lived and worked within a 3-mile radius.

The second stage of urbanization, which began around the turn of the century, was the *growth of metropolitan regions.* Cities not only continued to grow in population but also expanded geographically. The electric trolley made it possible for some people to move out of center cities and travel to

Midtown Manhattan, the 1920s. Early in the twentieth century, cities expanded geographically, because of improvements in transportation that allowed people to commute longer distances to work.

work from single-family homes in residential neighborhoods. The mass production of automobiles accelerated this trend. With telephones, keeping in touch with business associates, family, and friends no longer required frequent face-to-face interaction. Radio broadcasts provided news and home entertainment. At the same time, new production technologies drew industry out of center cities. Assembly lines, which require horizontal space, were not suited to the multistory, loft-type buildings of the earlier industrial age. New highways made it more economical to transport freight by truck than by rail or water; inner cities, with their narrow streets designed for horses and carriages, lacked parking space for trucks or workers' cars. After World War II, suburban housing and highway construction accelerated. Retail stores and other consumer services began to follow their middle- and upper-income patrons to the city fringes. Between 1954 and 1975, more than 15,000 shopping centers and malls were built to serve the expanding suburban population (Muller, 1976):

> For the current generation of suburbanites, enclosed regional malls have become their Main Street, Fifth Avenue, and community social and entertainment center all wrapped up into one. The malls not only contain retail establishments of every size, price range and variety, but they also offer professional offices, restaurants, movie theaters, public service outlets, and common space utilized for inexpensive patron attractions. (Kasarda, 1985, p. 41)

By the end of this stage, cities and their suburbs began to run together, producing continuous strips of population. The "Boswash" corridor, which stretches 500 miles from Boston through New York City, Philadelphia, and Baltimore to Washington, is one example; southern California, another.

The third and most recent stage, *suburbanization,* involved major shifts in both population and jobs. In the 1970s, nearly 10 million Americans left the city for suburbs and rural counties. It was the first time in this nation's history that more Americans had moved out of big cities than moved in (President's National Urban Policy Report, 1980, chap. 1). This trend continued through most of the 1980s, but then big cities began to make a comeback. Between 1980 and 1990 San Diego grew by over 26 percent; other big gainers were El Paso, Los Angeles, and Jacksonville, Florida. However, older cities in the midwest and northeast, including Chicago, Cleveland, and New York, lost population. (See Table 16-2.) The thirteen western states have been

Table 16-2   *Big-City Boom: Population of the Twenty-Five Most Populous Cities*

1990 Rank	City	1990 (Thousands)	1980 (Thousands)	Percent Change 1980–1990
1	New York	7,323	7,072	3.5
2	Los Angeles	3,485	2,969	17.4
3	Chicago	2,784	3,005	–7.4
4	Houston	1,631	1,595	2.2
5	Philadelphia	1,586	1,688	–6.1
6	San Diego, CA	1,111	876	26.8
7	Detroit	1,028	1,203	–14.6
8	Dallas	1,007	905	11.3
9	Phoenix, AR	938	790	24.5
10	San Antonio, TX	936	786	19.1
11	San Jose, CA	782	629	24.3
12	Baltimore	736	787	–6.4
13	Indianapolis	731	701	4.3
14	San Francisco	724	679	6.6
15	Jacksonville, FL	635	541	17.9
16	Columbus, OH	633	565	12.0
17	Milwaukee, WI	628	636	–1.3
18	Memphis, TN	610	646	–5.5
19	Washington, DC	607	638	–4.9
20	Boston	574	563	2.0
21	Seattle, WA	516	494	4.5
22	El Paso, TX	515	425	21.2
23	Cleveland	506	574	–11.9
24	New Orleans	497	558	–10.9
25	Nashville, Davidson, TN	488	456	6.9

Source: U.S. Bureau of the Census, *Statistical Abstract of the United States,* 1992, Washington, DC: GPO, 1992, pp. 35–37, table 38.

particularly hard-hit by urbanization because they have experienced several waves of growth during the past four decades and most of this growth has been in cities. Today, Utah has a higher percentage of city dwellers than does New York (Egan, 1996).

These changes point up the significant population shift from the snow belt to the sun belt. For more than two decades, the population of the south and southwest grew at twice the national rate, while the population of north central and northeastern states remained more or less stable. Alaska, Arizona, and Nevada had the fastest growth rates in the 1980s, increasing by 30 percent; California, Texas, and Florida registered the greatest gains in numbers, though New York and New Jersey also gained in population (Waldrop and Exter, 1990). Taken together, these trends add up to a deconcentration of population. Yet the United States is still an urban nation: three out of four Americans live in a city or suburb with a population of 50,000 or more. But the population is more spread out across the nation. More recently, *edge cities*—retail and commercial areas *outside* major cities—have grown up. Edge cities are distinguished from suburbs because they are not bedroom communities—more people leave them at the end of the day than enter them (Garreau, 1991).

Urban Ecology

In the 1920s a group of sociologists at the University of Chicago, led by Robert Park (Park, Burgress, and McKenzie, 1925), began investigating urban changes by treating the city as "a kind of social organism." Borrowing concepts from biology, they compared the city to an ecosystem (biological community). Like an ecosystem, a city was composed of specialized, interdependent parts—a financial district, manufacturing districts, residential districts, and so on. The "urban ecologists," as these University of Chicago sociologists called themselves, argued that the patterns of change in a city could best be understood as the product of competition, natural selection, and social evolution. Some urban ecologists focused on the spatial arrangements of cities at a given point in time, while others focused on patterns of change (see Figure 16-8).

Park, Ernest Burgess, and Roderick McKenzie (1925) compared the pattern of change in the structure and function of city neighborhoods to the

ecological process of **invasion and succession.** Members of one racial, ethnic, or socioeconomic group will begin to "invade" (move into) an area. As their numbers build up, they will eventually "succeed" the group previously living there, replacing it as the dominant group in the neighborhood or in the entire city. The invasion-succession process involves more than just population changes. There are also changes in residential use. A sparsely settled area may become one that is built up; this is the way suburbs are created. Or an area of single-family houses may be "invaded" by high-rise buildings, which attract different kinds of people. In most cases a change in residential land use tends to make an area less desirable; that is, a neighborhood is more likely to deteriorate than to improve as a result of such a change (Gist and Fava, 1974, p. 210).

Another kind of invasion is institutional invasion, as when industry replaces residential use or when commerce moves into a formerly residential area. For example, what happens to the churches, schools, and shops when industry replaces a resident population? They are forced to move, close, or change their functions. However, when industry invades an unoccupied area, it may serve as a beacon for an invasion of residential workers, who bring with them a need for churches, schools, and stores. Sometimes residential land use displaces industry. An area in downtown New York City, known as Soho, was once a center for warehousing and light industry. Today the huge lofts in Soho's buildings have been converted into retail and living spaces, dramatically changing the character of the neighborhood.

But while the invasion-succession process involves more than just population changes, such changes are the most familiar and the most studied. The growth of nearly every American city has been characterized by the general movement outward of immigrant groups. The "old" immigrants—those from western and northern Europe—first settled in the cities. They moved out as they advanced economically and socially and were displaced by the "new" immigrants—those from southern and eastern Europe. African Americans succeeded the new immigrants in the central city. Now both middle-class African American and white residents are "invading" the suburbs, leaving the central cities primarily to lower-class African Americans and Latinos.

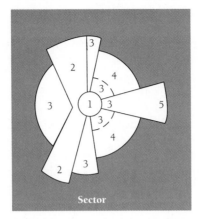
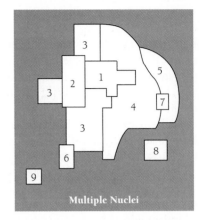

District
1. Central business district
2. Wholesale light manufacturing

3. Low-class residential
4. Medium-class residential
5. High-class residential

6. Heavy manufacturing
7. Outlying business district
8. Residential suburb

9. Industrial suburb
10. Commuters' zone

Figure 16-8   *Changing Models of the City*

Burgess's concentric-circle model of the city, with a central business district, surrounded by rings of light-manufacturing districts, low-income residential districts, and so on, reflected Chicago in the 1920s. Homer Hoyt adapted Burgess's model to reflect the impact of automobiles on cities, using a sector model. In Hoyt's view, cities tend to develop pie-shaped sectors along major transportation routes. Chauncy Harris and Edward L. Ullman's multiple-nuclei model illustrated the shape of highly industrialized cities that had become large and complex enough to support many specialized districts.

Source: Adapted from Chauncy D. Harris and Edward L. Ullman, "The Nature of Cities," *Annals of the American Academy of Political and Social Science* 242, November 1945, pp. 7–17. Reproduced with permission of Chauncy D. Harris and Joan Connelly Ullman (Mrs. Edward L. Ullman).

Generally, groups of the same socioeconomic status invade and succeed one another. For example, "middle-class blacks tend to 'invade' middle-class white neighborhoods and lower-class blacks, lower-class white neighborhoods, so that the character of the neighborhoods remains roughly the same, although the race of the occupants changes" (Gist and Fava, 1974, p. 210). The numbers of people who "invade" an area are not so important sociologically as their character, their relationships with other residents, and the effect of the change on property, social relationships, and institutions (Gist and Fava, 1974, p. 212). An example is the flight of whites to the suburbs in recent years as African American residents and other minorities become more dominant in the central city.

This flight, however, is not always a "natural" occurrence. Sometimes it is the result of the purposeful influence of the power elite, usually based on the profit motive. In only two years Mattapan,

Massachusetts, went from being a predominantly Jewish community to one that was predominantly black, largely as the result of the actions of a group of banks known as the Boston Banks Urban Renewal Group, or B-BURG, and a few opportunistic real estate brokers (Levine and Harmon, 1992). Mattapan is just south of Boston and was originally settled by Jews in the early years of the twentieth century. In the late 1960s, African Americans in Boston were being displaced by urban renewal efforts and needed somewhere to go. The B-BURG bankers targeted the town of Mattapan as a location where they would offer loans to African Americans seeking to buy homes. They did this in part because they figured the liberal Jews there would be less hostile to African Americans and in part because most of the homes in Mattapan were paid off and not providing them with any mortgage interest. Real estate brokers, seeking commission, used scare tactics to get Jewish homeowners to sell their homes for less than they were worth and then sold them to African Americans for two to three times the price. Inspectors for the Federal Housing Administration, which guaranteed the loans to blacks, compounded the problem by conducting slipshod inspections that approved high rates and low down payments without calling attention to needed repairs.

In both the Jewish and the black communities, leaders sent out mixed messages. For instance, although some Jewish groups urged residents to stay and help create a peaceful integrated neighborhood, several synagogues and schools deserted Mattapan for the suburbs. Charges of racism and anti-Semitism added to the tension. The result was that in only three years Mattapan's Jewish population went from 90,000 to 2,500. Its African American population rose from 473 to 20,000 (Levine and Harmon, 1992). Many middle-class black families, finding that their Mattapan houses needed repairs, lacked the money to finance them and at the same time keep up mortgage payments. When the mortgages were foreclosed, houses were frequently abandoned, to be taken over by violent youths and drug gangs. Along the main streets, boarded-up windows and silence replaced the lively scene of earlier years.

In the last twenty years or so, a number of urban neighborhoods have been "invaded" by private homesteaders who buy and renovate old buildings. Former slums have been transformed into chic residential districts that support expensive restaurants, boutiques, and the like—a process known as "gentrification." These urban pioneers tend to be young, two-career, affluent couples, often without children. Because they are visible and attractive, gentrified neighborhoods have received much attention in the media. However, they seem to be exceptions to the rule.

More recently, sociologist Claude Fischer put forth the *subcultural theory of urbanism* (Fischer, 1975, 1995). He argues that subcultural groups do not replace one another, but rather coexist. He suggests that four propositions tend to characterize urbanization: (1) Urbanization gives rise to more specialized subcultures than do less populated places. (2) These subcultures are not only more distinct in urban areas but more intense as well because there are more people in them and because the diversity of urban areas makes identification with a subculture more desirable. (3) Despite the differences among urban subcultures, their proximity leads to more intergroup contact and more mutual influence. Finally, (4) the more urban an area, the higher the rates of unconventional behavior likely to be found there because the diversity of unconventional behaviors of all the various subcultures in an urban area tends to be transmitted from one to another and ends up being shared among the urban population. Urban drug use and the high rates of vice and property crime in urban areas are examples of this aspect of the theory. Fischer's theory applies to ur-

A red-light district in New Orleans. Fischer's theory holds that the more urban an area, the higher the rates of unconventional behavior, such as crime, sexual deviance, and drug use.

banization in general, rather than to the rise of cities at a specific place and time.

Urbanization in Global Perspective

In Japan, children who grow up in beautiful, rural areas such as Hokkaido eagerly head for Tokyo and its suburbs when they are ready to look for work, even though this means they will live in tiny apartments that are enormously expensive and spend an hour or more jammed, standing, on a commuter train to get to work in the city (Kristof, 1996). The snow-capped mountains that surround Mexico City are beautiful, but they also trap the fumes from 3 million cars and 35,000 factories. On windless days, the smog often reaches such high levels that even healthy people are warned to stay indoors. Suffocating air pollution is only one of the many problems of Mexico's capital, a so-called *megacity*—one with a population of 10 million or more. Like many other urban agglomerations, it suffers from inadequate housing, poor sanitation, and high unemployment. And Mexico City is far from alone. In Karachi, Pakistan, water supplies are adequate for only 70 percent of the population; the rest must drink contaminated water that carries the hepatitis virus. In Kinshasa, Congo Republic, the

unemployment rate is 80 percent. Megacities tax the resources of even the richest nations; for instance, Tokyo, the world's largest city, is overwhelmed by the 22,000 tons of garbage it produces each day. But giant urban centers present staggering burdens for developing nations. According to the World Bank, some of Africa's cities are growing by 10 percent a year, the fastest rate of urbanization ever recorded. It is estimated that there will be twenty-one megacities by the year 2000, eighteen of them in developing nations (see Figure 16-9).

Urban growth in developing nations is different from what it is in rich industrial nations. Cities, after all, develop in accordance with the dynamics of the larger economic and political systems of which they are a part (Chase-Dunn, 1984). The rich nations of the world are tending toward deconcentration, with industry, commerce, and population dispersed rather than densely clustered. This is possible because advanced transportation and communication systems transcend space (Gappert and Knight, 1982; Castells, 1985; Calhoun, 1986; Harvey, 1989). Goods can be transported rapidly; deals can be negotiated, instructions communicated, and activities monitored over vast distances via computer. Industrialized nations also have highly developed social organizations (such as the corporation and government bureaucracies) that are capable of exercising long-distance control over employees and citizens. In the early stages of industrialization,

The basin in which Mexico City is built traps the fumes from 3 million cars and 35,000 factories. Like many other megacities, Mexico City suffers from air pollution, inadequate housing, poor sanitation, and high unemployment.

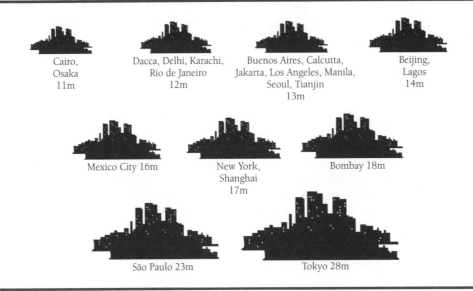

Cairo,
Osaka
11m

Dacca, Delhi, Karachi,
Rio de Janeiro
12m

Buenos Aires, Calcutta,
Jakarta, Los Angeles, Manila,
Seoul, Tianjin
13m

Beijing,
Lagos
14m

Mexico City 16m

New York,
Shanghai
17m

Bombay 18m

São Paulo 23m

Tokyo 28m

Figure 16-9   *Projected Populations of the World's Twenty-One Largest Cities in the Year 2000*

The majority of the world's megacities are found in developing nations.

Source: M. Kidron, R. Segal, and A. Wilson. *The State of the World Atlas,* London: Penguin, 1995, p. 25.

workers lived in housing adjacent to the factory, and the owner in a house on the hill. Today a single company may own and closely control factories and offices all over the country and even throughout the world. Corporate headquarters may be in New York, while research and development are located in Massachusetts, California, and North Carolina; warehousing and shipping, in Chicago or Indianapolis; and actual production facilities, in Georgia, South Korea, and the Philippines. Government agencies are similarly dispersed.

In developing countries, by contrast, *overurbanization* often occurs. Transportation and communications are poorly developed. A few paved roads and railroads link villages to a capital or a port city (but not to one another). Telephone lines are undependable. In Cairo, for example, it is easier to call the United States than it is to call many towns in Egypt (and Egypt is not one of the world's least developed nations). Because of poorly developed infrastructures, economic opportunities are concentrated around ports, primary resource centers (such as mines), and/or the capital. Likewise, the governments of many developing nations are based in the capital city and may have only weak control over the countryside, not only because of poor communication and transportation systems but also because of the na-

tions' relatively short histories. Many do not have highly developed, entrenched government bureaucracies with traditions of coping with crises. (Indeed, one reason military governments come to power in developing nations is that there are few other social institutions with the structure and discipline of the military; military governments are filling an organizational vacuum.) Furthermore, the absence of transportation and communication infrastructures inhibits the development of domestic industries and markets and of national economic self-sufficiency. Populations are growing, but opportunities for employment in the countryside are declining.

Migrants flood into the capital cities of developing nations because there is no place else to go. These cities are growing much faster than the ability of either the government or the private sector to provide jobs, housing, and services. Large percentages of the populations of developing cities live in slums and squatter settlements that lack the most basic facilities (water, sewerage, electricity). Only a few of the migrants find regular employment; others enter the "informal sector" of the economy—a set of marginal economic activities. These activities exist on the fringes of legality, usually uncounted in official statistics and lacking in stability but offering employment to people who do not have the educa-

SOCIOLOGY ON THE WEB

The Numbers Game

Estimates of projected population growth are notoriously unreliable, but they are used all the time by politicians and planners. The text discusses some of the factors that enter into these estimates: changes in birthrates and death rates, improvements in health practices and women's education levels, immigration, and the age profile of the population. As an exercise, use the Internet to obtain estimates of world population growth from two or three different agencies or government sources. Search the sites listed below for estimates of world population in the years 1950, 2000, 2050, 2100, and 2150. (The best place to start is at the first site on the list.) Compare the different estimates you find and plot them on a graph. What factors account for the differences you find? What assumptions are each of the estimates based on?

http:www.prb.org/
The web site of the Population Reference Bureau contains a discussion, "Is the World Population Ex-

plosion Over?" that looks at how population trends are estimated.

http://www.popnet.org/

http://www.undp.org/

http://www.census.gov/ftp/pub/ipc/www/idbnew.html

These three sites are sources of data and information on world population trends. All contain data and background information on world population estimates. POPNET, the first of the three, contains a great deal of information on factors that affect world population growth. The second site, maintained by the United Nations, tracks data on urban, regional, national, and international population trends. The third site, the International Data Base of the U.S. Census Bureau, displays graphs of population trends.

---

tion or connections to enter the formal economy (Hart, 1973). Jobs in the informal sector range from running "gin shops" in private houses to driving unlicensed taxis, trading black-market currency, marketing stolen goods, shining shoes, and engaging in prostitution. In most cities in developing nations, the informal sector is a central source of livelihood for thousands, or even millions, of recent migrants (Castells, 1983).

Rapid urbanization in developing countries reflects all of the topics we have discussed in this chapter: population growth, the commercialization of agriculture and uneven distribution of food, and environmental degradation.

Summary

1. **What stages has population growth undergone in industrialized nations? How does population growth in developing nations differ from this pattern?** Industrialized nations have progressed through the so-called *demographic transition*: Stage I was characterized by high birthrates and death rates; in Stage II, which began in the late eighteenth century, birthrates remained high but death rates fell;

Stage III, beginning in the late nineteenth century with intensive industrialization, was notable for falling birthrates until western population stabilized at replacement levels. At first glance, the developing nations today, with high birthrates and falling death rates, appear to be at Stage II, but there are significant differences from the western experience, namely, the relative suddenness of change, the role of imported technology, and the momentum factor.

2. **What two trends have characterized U.S. population development?** The main change in U.S. population has been a steady decline in family size, due both to a "contraception revolution" and to the postponement of marriage and childbirth, with economic conditions playing an indirect role. The second change has been a "graying" of the population, with the median age constantly rising.

3. **How is the relationship between population and world resources affected by disparities in distribution and consumption and by environmental hazards?** Concern about whether the earth can support its growing population arises from several factors. Unequal distribution of resources results not just from geographic location but also from the increasing commercialization of agriculture, so many developing nations lose self-sufficiency. There are also wide disparities in the use of resources, with industrialized nations consuming a much greater proportion of the world's goods. Environmental degradation, especially from proliferating chemicals, can be seen in increasing air pollution, water pollution, and soil pollution.

4. **According to nineteenth-century critics, how did urbanization affect society?** Tönnies and Durkheim saw *urbanization* as destroying traditional communities and creating instead interdependence and alienation. To Marx, rural-urban conflict pitted a dying feudalism against a triumphant capitalism, a struggle that would produce radical class consciousness.

5. **Through what three stages has U.S. urbanization progressed?** The emergence of big cities, which began in the mid-nineteenth century, was followed after fifty years by the growth of metropolitan regions, a stage that in turn gave way to the most recent era of suburbanization.

6. **How does urbanization in developing countries differ from that in rich, industrialized nations?** In developed countries, the current trend is toward deconcentration. In the developing nations, on the other hand, *megacities* are becoming the rule because only in these giant urban centers are there adequate transportation and communication facilities, and thus the employment opportunities offered by commerce, industry, and government.

Key Terms

ageism 603	fertility rate 594	megacity 621
birthrate 594	*Gemeinschaft* 615	momentum factor 597
census 600	*Gesellschaft* 615	net growth rate 595
death rate 594	invasion and succession 618	organic solidarity 615
demographic transition 596	life expectancy 595	urbanization 614
demography 594	mechanical solidarity 615	zero population growth 597

Recommended Readings

Bryant, Bunyan, & Mohai, Paul. (Eds.). 1992. *Race and the Incidence of Environmental Hazards: A Time for Discourse.* Boulder, CO: Westview.

Gans, Herbert J. 1967. *The Levittowners.* New York: Random House.

Gugler, Josef. 1997. *Cities in the Developing World: Issues, Theory, and Policy.* New York: Oxford University Press.

Lappe, Frances Moore. 1986. *World Hunger: Twelve Myths.* New York: Grove Press.

Menard, Scott W., & Moen, Elizabeth W. (Eds). 1987. *Perspectives on Population: An Introduction to Concepts and Issues.* New York: Oxford University Press.

Nyden, Philip, & Wiewel, Wim. (Eds.). 1991. *An Urban Agenda for the 1990's: Research and Action.* New Brunswick, NJ: Rutgers University Press.

Strauss, William, & Howe, Neil. 1991. *Generations: The History of America's Future, 1584 to 2069.* New York: Morrow.

Weeks, John R. 1994. *Population: An Introduction to Concepts and Issues,* 5th ed. Belmont, CA: Wadsworth.

World Bank, 1997. *World Development Report.* New York: Oxford University Press.

Chapter

Seventeen

Collective Behavior and Social Movements

In the early morning hours of Saturday, June 28, 1969, a confrontation took place in front of the Stonewall Inn in New York City that history now marks as the birth of a new social movement—the gay and lesbian liberation movement. Of course, this movement did not literally begin at that moment. Many other confrontations and individual experiences had led up to it, and many others followed it. These events and experiences, however, became divided into "before Stonewall" and "after Stonewall." Before Stonewall, there was the homophile movement, a loose-knit coalition of homosexual groups in which people tended to hide their identities behind pseudonyms until they knew each other well (Faderman, 1994); after Stonewall, there was the gay liberation movement. As a fairly recent and well-documented movement, gay liberation provides an excellent picture of how social movements occur and the collective behavior that makes them possible.

The Stonewall Inn was a popular bar in Greenwich Village that attracted a diverse crowd of students, businessmen, young people, and old people. It had another bar in back and a jukebox and dance floor (Manford, 1992). For some time, the police had been raiding bars where homosexuals gathered. Generally, the proprietors of these bars paid the police off, and the next day things returned to usual. That night at Stonewall, however, after the people who had been put in the police paddy wagon "escaped" because they had been left unguarded with the door open, they stood in the small park across the street from the bar with the other patrons and talked about why they had to put up with harassment and payoffs (Rivera, 1992). People started throwing money at the police inside the bar. Their anger was also directed at the Mafia, which exacted payoffs from bar owners and cut the chains and police padlocks to reopen the closed bars the next day.

The police inside were frightened and outnumbered. They had expected the raid to be a routine one. Caught unprepared for the reception they were getting, the police barricaded themselves in the bar and called for backup, escalating the level of the confrontation. An upstairs window was broken by a rock; then a downstairs window. Someone threw a burning trash can through the hole in the downstairs window. More police and the fire department arrived. For the next two days the streets around the Stonewall Inn were the scene of a riot in which 400 police battled 2,000 protesters (Cruikshank,

The confrontation that took place in front of the Stonewall Inn in New York City on June 28, 1969, marked the birth of a new social movement. Here, protesters commemorate the twenty-fifth anniversary of Stonewall by marching in front of St. Patrick's Cathedral in 1994.

1992). The immediate message of Stonewall was clear: homosexuals were no longer going to quietly tolerate harassment or ostracism.

The vehicle for this message was **collective behavior,** in which large numbers of people engage in nonroutine activities that violate social expectations. The label "collective behavior" has been applied to everything from sudden shifts in fashion or public opinion to mass panic, riots, and revolutions. Sociologists are, of course, interested in what leads people to engage in collective acts of behavior. The patrons of the Stonewall had long put up with harassment, but what caused them to act?

One view is that collective action is like an infection, spreading as a result of "contagion." "Contagion theory" was first put forward by the French sociologist Gustave LeBon (1895/1960). LeBon held that in mobs, the thin veneer of civilization rubs off and people behave instinctively, losing all reason. In this view, Stonewall's patrons were caught up in the emotions of the crowd, acting without thinking. This theory was accepted by most sociologists during the first half of the twentieth century.

During the protest years of the 1960s, however, sociologists began to look at mass behavior more closely. Many concluded that behavior in crowds is more organized and purposeful than had been previously thought. These sociologists would say that although Stonewall's patrons may not have planned their behavior in advance, they were well aware of what they were doing. They could have just as easily watched from the sidelines or gone home, as they had on other occasions when the police had harassed homosexual patrons of bars and bar owners.

Underlying this debate is the more basic question of whether collective behavior is irrational and a break with everyday behavior or whether it is rational and an extension of everyday norms and values. As you will see, this question has not been settled. The idea that "mob psychology" is an independent force is still part of conventional wisdom.

Key Questions

1. Is collective behavior, ranging from fads to riots, rational or irrational behavior?
2. What explains seemingly sudden and violent riots? What caused the Los Angeles riot of 1992, and how does that riot compare with the urban riots of the 1960s?
3. How does a social movement differ from other forms of collective behavior? What explains the success or failure of a social movement?
4. How is a social revolution a special type of social movement? Are social revolutions rational or irrational behavior?

Rational or Irrational?

Among sociologists, there are two different ways of viewing mass departures from social expectations and normative behavior. The first, especially common among functionalists, interprets collective behavior as a symptom that something has "gone haywire" in the social system: ordinary ways of getting things done and usual methods of social control are not working, and people are behaving irrationally. According to this view, the Stonewall riot was caused by a loss of respect for authority. In 1969 the government was involved in a war in Vietnam that many citizens considered unjust, so the idea that things were not working well was clearly in the air. Add to this the fact that the police allowed bars to reopen so that they could raid them and collect a payoff once again, and one can see why the people in front of the Stonewall might feel that society was not functioning as it should. The mob reacted with frustration to what its members saw as the abuse of their human rights. The criminal acts of assault were irrational responses to what they saw as a miscarriage of justice.

Many symbolic interactionists view collective behavior in a similar way, though they are primarily interested in the social-psychological dynamics, or "group psychology," of collective behavior. For them, the question is, "How do people arrive at a definition of an ambiguous situation?" Sociologists in this school tend to emphasize the spontaneous, unstructured, emotional aspects of collective behavior.

For many years, the functionalist view dominated the study of collective behavior. In recent years, however, a new approach, rooted in conflict theory, has taken shape. **Collective-action theory** sees most (if not all) collective behavior as the result of rational decisions on the part of individuals and of planning and organization on the part of collectivities (Oberschall, 1973; Tilly, 1978). From this perspective, collective action often is the expression of conflicts that have existed for some time but remained hidden and diffuse. It occurs because new social structures have developed or old ones have been revitalized, not because they have broken down. According to this view, the Stonewall riot had deeper social causes, which make the actions of the mob seem much more rational. The participants were reacting to a history of police harassment, to the U.S. involvement in Vietnam, as well as to changing sexual mores. Birth control pills had made the sexual revolution of the 1960s possible, which in turn expanded views of sex to include the recreational as well as the procreational. Against this backdrop of "free love," homosexual sex no longer stood out as being as deviant as it had once been. Finally, the civil rights movement and the women's liberation movement, with their emphasis on the rights of the oppressed, were social movements that served as roots of the gay liberation movement.

Functionalists and collective-action theorists differ not only in their interpretation of social events but also in their definition of the subject. Functionalists see a common thread running from fads and crazes through episodes of mass hysteria to revolutions. In their view, all are examples of collective behavior that can be explained in the same basic terms. Collective-action theorists distinguish between sudden, short-lived outbreaks of unconventional behavior (fads, crazes, hysterias) and more concerted, goal-oriented activities (strikes, certain instances of riots, social movements, and revolutions). They believe that the two types of social phenomena require different types of analysis (see Figure 17-1). A social-psychological approach might be appropriate for studying hysterias and crazes, but it will not explain the Russian revolutions of 1917, 1991, and 1993.

Crowd Violence

Riots hold special interest for sociologists, in part because of the role riots have played in history (for example, the Boston Tea Party was a riot) and in part because they highlight the debate over whether collective behavior is rational or irrational. A riot may seem sensible or senseless, depending on one's point of view. To poor people who are angry about their position in society, a riot may seem a rational way of making their grievances known. For them, a riot is a political act, a rebellion against economic and social oppression. To a shopkeeper trapped in her store as people hurl bricks through the window, the rioters are running amok. To her, the riot is a personal assault, without rhyme or reason. The poor person's rational rebellion is the shopkeeper's irrational mob.

These two different views are echoed in both popular and sociological explanations of riots. Some sociologists (especially functionalists and symbolic interactionists) tend to view riots from the shopkeeper's point of view. They see collective violence as a breakdown in social order and emphasize

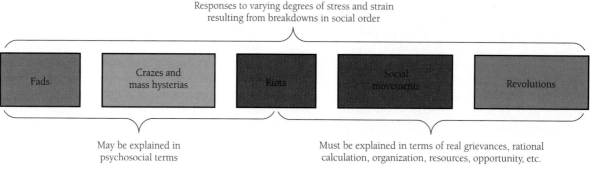

Figure 17-1 *The Functionalist View of Social Events Compared with the Collective-Action Theory*

Functionalists view collective behavior as a continuum, ranging from fads to revolutions. Collective-action theorists distinguish between transient or trivial behavior (fads, crazes and hysterias, and some riots), which can be explained in psychosocial terms, and more purposeful, organized actions (social movements and revolutions, as well as some riots), which can be explained only in terms of social forces.

the irrational, chaotic, and destructive aspects of riots. Other sociologists (especially conflict theorists and collective-action theorists) lean toward the participant's point of view. They see most riots as challenges to the existing social order based on real grievances and emphasize the selective, goal-oriented aspects of crowd violence.

These different points of view are also reflected in our language. **Crowd** is a neutral term that refers to a collection of people who come together on a temporary basis, such as a crowd in a train station or a theater. In most cases, members of a crowd do not behave in a distinctive or unified way. Each goes about his or her business with minimal interaction. On occasion, something provokes a common emotional response and unified action in a crowd. This may be planned (as in a protest march) or unplanned (as when someone yells "Fire!" in a theater). **Mob** is a loaded term that refers to a "*disorderly, riotous, or lawless* crowd of people" (*Random House College Dictionary,* 1984, p. 857, emphasis added). The word "mob" comes from the French for "mobilization" and dates to the French Revolution, when it referred to the moving crowd—the crowd assembled for political purposes. To the ruling class of that period, it conjured up images of

the common people—the "dangerous classes," as they were often called—on the move. When the common people took action together, they were a "mob"; when the nobility assembled for political purposes, they were called a "political party" or a "parliament." The word "mob" retains these pejorative connotations today. When we speak of "mob rule," for example, we mean rule by the (disorderly, lawless, violent) masses; "mob appeal" suggests appealing to the lowest intellectual level. We also use "mob" to refer to criminal gangs. The following sections will use the case of the 1992 riot in Los Angeles to present micro- and macrosociological perspectives on crowd violence.

The 1992 Los Angeles Riot: A Case Study

The riot that broke out in Los Angeles after the not-guilty verdict in the Rodney King trial was the first major upheaval in Los Angeles since the Watts riot of 1965, and the most recent widespread civil disorder in the United States. In the mid-1960s many major cities, including Detroit, New York, Newark, and Baltimore, experienced unrest in what were called the black ghettos, the deteriorating inner-city

(A) *The 1992 Los Angeles riot.*
(B) *This diagram of the first night of the rioting shows how quickly violence erupted—and how slowly police responded.*

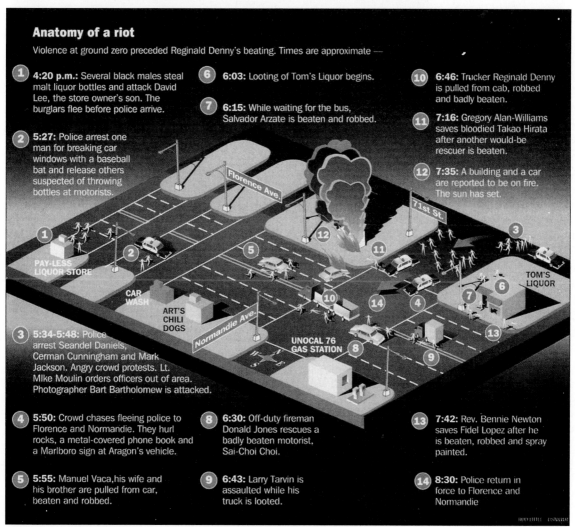

Anatomy of a riot

Violence at ground zero preceded Reginald Denny's beating. Times are approximate —

(1) **4:20 p.m.:** Several black males steal malt liquor bottles and attack David Lee, the store owner's son. The burglars flee before police arrive.

(2) **5:27:** Police arrest one man for breaking car windows with a baseball bat and release others suspected of throwing bottles at motorists.

(3) **5:34-5:48:** Police arrest Seandel Daniels, Cerman Cunningham and Mark Jackson. Angry crowd protests. Lt. Mike Moulin orders officers out of area. Photographer Bart Bartholomew is attacked.

(4) **5:50:** Crowd chases fleeing police to Florence and Normandie. They hurl rocks, a metal-covered phone book and a Marlboro sign at Aragon's vehicle.

(5) **5:55:** Manuel Vaca, his wife and his brother are pulled from car, beaten and robbed.

(6) **6:03:** Looting of Tom's Liquor begins.

(7) **6:15:** While waiting for the bus, Salvador Arzate is beaten and robbed.

(8) **6:30:** Off-duty fireman Donald Jones rescues a badly beaten motorist, Sai-Choi Choi.

(9) **6:43:** Larry Tarvin is assaulted while his truck is looted.

(10) **6:46:** Trucker Reginald Denny is pulled from cab, robbed and badly beaten.

(11) **7:16:** Gregory Alan-Williams saves bloodied Takao Hirata after another would-be rescuer is beaten.

(12) **7:35:** A building and a car are reported to be on fire. The sun has set.

(13) **7:42:** Rev. Bennie Newton saves Fidel Lopez after he is beaten, robbed and spray painted.

(14) **8:30:** Police return in force to Florence and Normandie neighborhoods populated mainly by African Americans. In the summer of 1967 alone, more than 150 cities reported crowd violence (Kerner Commission, 1968). In each case, the riot took place where unemployment, poverty, overcrowded and dilapidated housing, substandard schools, crime, and conflict with police were everyday facts of life. The riot in the Watts section of Los Angeles in 1965 was triggered by the arrest of a speeding black motorist by white police officers. The arrest rapidly got out of hand. Crowds formed, rumors flew, threats received widespread media coverage, and a major riot eventually engulfed almost 50 square miles of the city. In four days of rioting, thirty-four people were killed (including two police officers and one firefighter). More than 1,000 people were injured seriously enough to seek medical attention. Two hundred buildings burned to the ground. Another 700 buildings were damaged by looting or arson. Property loss was conservatively estimated at $40 million. About 4,000 people were arrested, primarily for burglary and theft (McCone, 1966; Task Force Report, 1967).

The Los Angeles riot of 1992 bore an eerie resemblance to the 1965 riot. The precipitating event in both cases was the arrest of a black motorist, and in both cases what started as a neighborhood crowd scene escalated into a citywide, full-scale riot. In 1992 the riot was helped along by the televised absence of police in South Central L.A., where the crowd violence began. Those watching the beatings of motorists on the news at home realized that they could loot without consequence, and thousands of people poured into the streets. According to one eyewitness, "Before long, everybody was outside. Babies, mothers it was like some kind of revolution" (*Newsweek*, May 18, 1992, p. 44).

The speed of the riot was frightening. According to a police commander, "With the Watts riots in 1965 it built and built and on the third day the city went mad. This was completely different—the city went wild in just an hour and a half" (*Newsweek*, May 11, 1992, p. 35). The first targets were liquor stores and gun shops, which fueled the anger and violence of the crowds. Soon fires, looting, and vandalism were spreading from one neighborhood to the next. Within four hours twenty-five blocks of central Los Angeles were burning. Asian-owned stores were especially hard-hit. By the time the Los Angeles police were back on the streets in force,

there were far too many rioters to handle. It took several days, a dusk-to-dawn curfew, and 5,000 federal troops, patrolling the streets in jeeps and armed with M-16 rifles, to bring the riot under control. By then, Los Angeles had suffered $1 *billion* in property damage and had lost more than 50 of its citizens; over 2,000 were injured.

Microperspectives: Crowd Psychology or Collective Action?

Why would "ordinary people" engage in looting and vandalism? Why do crowds become violent? Some sociologists have argued that the answers lie in *crowd psychology*. Gustave LeBon, who has been called the "grandfather of collective behavior theory" (Berk, 1974, p. 20), strongly supported a contagion theory of crowd behavior. LeBon was greatly influenced by the current events of his time. France in his day (the second half of the nineteenth century) was not unlike the United States in recent decades. Everything seemed to be changing. Demonstrations that bordered on riots were almost weekly events. LeBon was also influenced by some of his contemporaries: Charles Darwin, who had traced the origins of humanity back to the animal kingdom, and Sigmund Freud, who was exploring the unconscious levels of the mind.

In crowds, according to LeBon, people cease to act as individuals. People of different ages, sexes, educational levels, and occupations chant the same slogans, do the same things. If one person runs, everybody runs. The crowd develops a mind of its own. Participants become highly suggestible: they'll believe almost anything. Crowds act on unconscious impulses, without thinking. To LeBon, a crowd was an antisocial monster. He attributed the breakdown of individual self-restraint in crowds to behavioral contagion and to the "hypnotic" power of leaders who appeal to participants' unconscious wishes and baser instincts.

Years later, Herbert Blumer (1939) updated LeBon's description of crowds. For LeBon's "contagion" Blumer substituted what he called the "circular reaction." One individual becomes agitated; others pick up the excitement; seeing his or her emotions reflected in others, the individual becomes even more agitated. Instead of evaluating one another's words or actions, crowd members respond reflexively. In this way, tension builds to fever pitch.

According to Blumer, the transformation of a collection of individuals into a mob begins with an exciting event that arouses interest and draws people together (like the acquittal of the Los Angeles police officers in the Rodney King trial, which was televised live). Gradually, attention and emotions focus on a common object (the white truckers, driving through the South Central L.A. intersection, the liquor stores, the Korean-owned markets). At this point, when individuals act (say, by shouting or hurling a brick), others respond. Thus Blumer, like LeBon, believed that rational thought processes break down in crowds and emotions take over. Violence spreads like a contagious disease.

While many contemporary sociologists concede that people in crowds may become excited and emotional, most see contagion theory as overstated. Blumer and LeBon exaggerated the singlemindedness of crowds. Individuals participated in the Los Angeles (and Stonewall) riot for different reasons. Some had observed the videotape of the Rodney King beating and the televised verdict in the trial of the police officers. Others had developed a radical philosophy and saw white authority as the enemy. Some saw the riot as an opportunity to get revenge on a store owner who had insulted them; others, as an opportunity to get free food and appliances. Some were pressured into joining; others joined "for kicks."

Contagion theory also exaggerates the irrationality of crowds. Rioters do not act without thinking. In both Los Angeles riots, the rioters were selective about victims, attacking the symbols of power (police, white people, and Korean-owned stores). One of the first stores to be looted after the Rodney King verdict was a South Central liquor store owned by Koreans. After smashing the padlock and steel gate meant to protect the shop, the looters proceeded to steal or smash every bottle of wine, beer, and liquor in the store.

Not all crowds are violent, however. Some crowds gather to express a common emotion such as joy, excitement, or grief. These types of crowds are **expressive crowds.** A crowd that gathers at a rock concert or at a religious revival is an example of an expressive crowd. Expressive crowds differ from crowds that are violent in that they are more of a means of collectively expressing an emotion and are not intended to lead to violence or political action.

Ralph Turner and Lewis Killian (1972) reject the notion that crowds are normless. To the contrary, they believe that crowd behavior reflects the development of new or **emergent norms.** During the early stages of crowd formation, the meaning of the events that people are witnessing is unclear to them. Then someone offers an explanation. (In Los Angeles, the explanation centered on charges of police brutality and miscarriage of justice.) This view begins to spread, defining the situation. Although all members of the crowd may not agree, group pressure prevents them from expressing different views. When someone starts to chant or hurl bricks and bottles, others follow suit. The riot is under way. Shared definitions and emergent norms rationalize violent action that would not be condoned under other circumstances. But however uncontrolled a crowd may appear, norms set limits on behavior.

Using collective-action theory, Richard Berk (1974) argued that far from being irrational, behavior in crowds is determined by rational calculation. According to Berk, people in crowds weigh the possible benefits of participation against the costs and join a riot only if they believe it will "pay off." The benefits may be tangible (stolen goods) or intangible (the satisfaction of expressing frustration); the costs include the risk of injury or arrest. In Los Angeles, many people apparently felt the benefits outweighed the costs.

These microperspectives explain some of the dynamics of crowd violence and how new norms develop. But they do not explain why riots occur at a particular time and place. Macroperspectives address this question.

Macroperspectives: Rising Expectations and Relative Deprivation

Watts and the other riots of the 1960s caught people off guard. So did the 1992 riot in Los Angeles. After all, nearly thirty years had passed since the last serious urban disorders. Moreover, the crowd violence began in a neighborhood that was relatively successful in comparison with surrounding communities: owner-occupied homes with well-tended lawns and hedges bordered wide, uncluttered streets. In the 1980s the poverty rate had dropped from 33 to 21 percent, and the 1991 homicide rate in Los Angeles was not much above the national average (*U.S. News & World Report*, May 31, 1993, p. 38). Why, then, would the riot begin here and not in one of the worst slums? And why did the riots of the sixties follow a period of improving civil rights for minorities?

Sociologists have identified this pattern in other times and places. Well over a hundred years ago, the French social thinker Alexis de Tocqueville wrote, "Evils which are patiently endured when they seem inevitable become intolerable once the idea of escape from them is suggested" (1856, p. 214). The modern term for this phenomenon is **rising expectations.** James Davies (1969) has argued that rising expectations play a role in many, if not most, outbreaks of civil disorder. Riots and revolutions often take place after a period of political and economic gain. China's student protest movement of 1989 (crushed in the Tiananmen Square massacre) is one example (see Chapter 3). It followed a decade of major economic gains and eighteen months of growing political freedom. The first anti-Communist revolution in the former Czechoslovakia, in 1968, followed a period in which restrictions on the press, education, the arts, and economic activities were slowly lifted. Under the leadership of Alexander Dubcek, during what became known as the "spring thaw," Czechoslovakia moved closer to democracy than had any other Communist state. Then, in August, Soviet troops moved in and installed new leaders who embarked on a program of political purges, mass arrests, and religious persecution. Only during 1989 and 1990 did the Czech Republic and Slovakia finally gain their freedom.

Why should this be? Davies reasons that severe poverty and extreme powerlessness lead to apathy and hopelessness. People who expect little in life and who are preoccupied with the daily struggle for existence are unlikely to take to the streets in protest. If their economic and political situation improves, however, their expectations rise. They begin to believe that a better life is not only possible but lies just around the corner. When these hopes fail to materialize, they become angry. The gap between what they expected and what they have now seems intolerable. Although they may be better off than they were in the past, in relation to what they anticipated, their situation has deteriorated. The result is the *J* curve, shown in Figure 17-2, and uprisings.

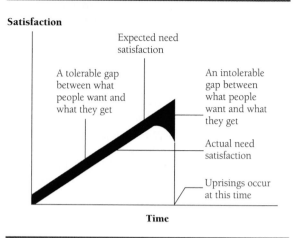

Figure 17-2   *Davies' J Curve*

This curve shows that as the gap between what people anticipate and what they actually get widens over time, the likelihood of uprisings increases. At some point the gap becomes intolerable.

Source: Adapted from James C. Davies, "Toward a Theory of Revolution," *American Sociological Review* 27, February 1962, p. 6, fig. 1.

The concept of rising expectations helps explain why riots in black ghettos took place in the late sixties, not in the forties or fifties. For most of America, the 1950s were a time of economic prosperity. The civil rights legislation of the 1960s and President Johnson's "War on Poverty" led African Americans to believe that they would soon partake of the good life. Expectations rose. By the late 1960s, however, the nation was becoming preoccupied with the war in Vietnam, and the economy was not as strong as it had been. When the better life that African Americans had come to expect failed to materialize—when nothing seemed to change—hopes crashed. Many ghetto residents felt robbed of what they had been promised, and they reacted violently. At this point, violence may have seemed the only way to call attention to problems white America had long ignored.

Another important factor in the Los Angeles riot was **relative deprivation** (Geschwender, 1968). Whether people feel deprived depends in large part on the groups to which they compare themselves—their reference groups (see Chapter 6). In other words, deprivation is relative. The South Central neighborhood where the violence began was the home for a number of upwardly mobile families and the site of successful businesses largely owned by new Asian immigrants. Those residents whose economic situation was stalled or deteriorating could only see themselves as deprived in comparison. The gay men and women at the Stonewall Inn that night had similarly reached a point at which the relative deprivation of their civil rights—to gather, socialize, and pursue their private lives during a period of general sexual liberation—prompted action. To paraphrase de Tocqueville, what had seemed unavoidable became intolerable.

Collective Behavior as a Breakdown in Social Order

Every so often, the media report episodes of "collective madness." For no apparent reason, large numbers of people stop exercising critical judgment and self-control. However, upon closer inspection, such breakdowns may in fact have some rather long-standing reasons, whether one accepts them as justifying outbursts of violent group behavior or not. The terrorist activities of some militia groups are examples of violent collective behavior as an expression of a sense of alienation from national institutions (Tharp and Holstein, 1997). The violent deaths of citizens in Waco, followed by the bombing in Oklahoma City, brought to light a militia movement that is grounded in a deep distrust of the government and an economy that has left many blue-collar workers with greatly diminished prospects for the future. When the contagious element in collective madness is fear or anxiety, rather than anger and frustration, the result is called **mass hysteria.** When the contagion involves wild enthusiasm about some person, object, or activity, the result is called a **craze** (see *A Global View:* Tulipomania: A Historical Perspective). Functionalists see mass hysterias and crazes as collective responses to a breakdown in social order. They occur when large numbers of people are troubled but are not sure why or what to do to alleviate the problem. They become irrational in the sense that they are not aware of the real reason for their distress and their behavior is not aimed at the actual source of the problem (R. H. Turner and Killian, 1972). Their bizarre behavior can be seen as an unconscious attempt to solve undefined and unnamed problems.

The Branch Davidians, Oklahoma City, and the Militia Movement

When the federal agents saw the smoke rise in the large compound near Waco, Texas, their worst fears seemed realized: scores of Branch Davidian cult members apparently were choosing to die with their self-proclaimed leader, David Koresh, rather than surrender. For several hours the agents had pounded holes in the compound and poured in nonlethal gas, but no one came out. Then the flames appeared out of nowhere; whipped by 35-mile-an-hour winds, they rapidly consumed the compound, leaving eighty-six people dead, including seventeen children. The few survivors claimed that the fire was not set deliberately, but authorities subsequently reported finding some evidence of arson. Whether the deaths of the Branch Davidians in April 1993 represented mass suicide or a tragic accident, they still resulted from a collective slavish submission to Koresh's apocalyptic view of the world.

The Branch Davidian cult had started harmlessly enough many years earlier when disaffected members of the Seventh-Day Adventist Church set up a communal farm near Waco. That group also splintered, and one branch, the Branch Davidians, eventually came under the control of a charismatic young high school dropout with an astounding command of the Bible. David Koresh saw himself as an agent of God who would be transformed into a warrior angel at the battle that would end the world, and he predicted that the end would take place in Texas. For a time Koresh traveled widely, attracting devotees from around the world to his Waco compound to await Armageddon and obtain his promised salvation. The cult attracted the attention of federal authorities through rumors of child abuse and stockpiling of arms. In February 1993 a team of more than 100 agents attempted a quick surprise assault on the house but, instead, walked into an ambush. Four agents of the Bureau of Alcohol, Tobacco and Firearms died, along with several Branch Davidians. At this point the federal government laid siege to the compound, providing just the scenario that Koresh had been preaching would happen.

The government was in a dilemma as to how to proceed. Should it just try to wait out the besieged cult members? Or should it act to get them out

Tulipomania: A Historical Perspective

Everyone associates tulips with Holland. But few people realize that our image of Holland today was formed by a "tulipomania" that swept through that country in the seventeenth century. According to legend, a man named Conrad Gesner discovered tulips in Turkey in 1559 and was enchanted by them. He took some bulbs home for his garden in Holland. As the years passed, tulips became a status symbol. No garden was complete without them. Wealthy Dutch citizens competed for rare varieties, paying extravagant prices for bulbs imported directly from Constantinople. By the early 1630s, the rage for tulips had spread to the middle and lower classes. Prices soared, attracting speculators. Merchants paid as much for a single bulb as they would for four oxen, twelve fat sheep, or 1,000 pounds of cheese. Anyone who could do so invested in tulips. Small shopkeepers became rich overnight. Special tulip markets were set up and other industries neglected. A visiting botanist who innocently dissected a priceless tulip bulb was sent to jail.

The craze for tulips peaked between 1634 and 1636. Then,

> **Crazes eliminate ambiguity by providing structure and definition.**

suddenly, the bubble burst. People simply stopped buying. Thousands were caught with huge stockpiles of unwanted bulbs. Rich people became paupers overnight (MacKay, 1932).

Tulipomania takes its place alongside the California gold rush, the Florida land boom of the 1920s, and the stock-buying frenzy that preceded the Great Depression—all "get-rich-quick" schemes that created wild enthusiasm. Like the speculators in these other crazes, Hollanders were troubled by economic uncertainties. Many people had money to spend, but opportunities to invest seemed limited, and the returns on such investments were unpredictable. The Dutch let themselves believe that tulips were the answer—the sure way to protect their economic futures.

Crazes eliminate ambiguity by providing structure and definition. The belief that tulips were worth far more than their weight in gold became the basis for frenzied, overconfident activity. It was, however, a fantasy solution that soon backfired.

---

through forcible means? Those in charge were haunted by the memory of the mass suicide of another cult that had taken place fifteen years earlier. The Reverend Jim Jones was the magnetic leader of a religious group known as the People's Temple, which had established a commune called Jonestown in Guyana. At a time when the commune was coming under investigation by government authorities, Jones called his followers to their central meeting house one day. The time had come to die, he told them; the enemy was at the gates, and life was not worth living. More than 900 men, women, and children then drank from a vat of cyanide-laced grape juice and lay down to die; only a few had to be forced to take the drink (Hall, 1987).

The People's Temple and the Branch Davidians had much in common: messianic leaders, prophetic visions, devoted followers. Both leaders used the women members to serve their sexual needs; both used techniques of humiliation and intimidation to keep their members, including children, in line. And both groups found themselves under "attack" from government authorities. During the several weeks that the Branch Davidians were under siege, the media speculated endlessly about mass suicide. The horrible spectacle of the flame-engulfed compound almost seemed like a self-fulfilling prophecy.

Two years later, in April 1995, 168 people were killed in the bombing of the Oklahoma City Federal Building. A bomb built out of ammonium nitrate

The Branch Davidian Compound in Waco, Texas, goes up in flames on April 19, 1993, leaving 86 followers of messianic leader David Koresh dead. Popular explanations of this tragedy emphasize the charismatic powers of Koresh and such psychological concepts as "brainwashing." Sociologists focus on the social conditions that make apparently irrational behavior possible or even likely.

fertilizer and diesel fuel was placed in a van and the van was parked in the street in front of the building. In the explosion, the child care center on a lower floor of the federal building was destroyed and many children were killed. At first, the media speculated that Middle Eastern terrorists were responsible; but soon after, two members of a militia group, Timothy McVeigh and Terry Nichols, were arrested for the bombing. A letter written by McVeigh revealed that he had planned the bombing to mark the anniversary of the deaths in Waco.

The tragedies of Waco and Oklahoma City brought to light the fact that there is a great deal of antigovernment rage, though not all antigovernment groups subscribe to violence. Militias have grown up as part of a backlash (a response to social movements, discussed below) against civil rights, environmentalism, the pro-choice movement, and gun control (Cooper, 1995). Though the militias differ in some ways, the antigovernment militia movement is united against taxation, corruption, government regulation, gun control, schools as liberalizing influences, the police, nontraditional families, and the jury system. It also believes that citizen militias are needed to police the government (Wills, 1995). It is this distrust of government that enables the Militia of Montana, for example, to boast 12,000 members. There may be only 250 truly active members, but there is an enormous base of support among the discontented people who used to work in the declining mining and timber industries (Cooper, 1995).

The Oklahoma City bombing, in which 168 people were killed, occurred on April 19, 1995, and was timed to coincide with the second anniversary of Waco.

Smelser's Functionalist View

The television news coverage of the fiery end in Waco strained the imagination. Why did it end like this? Most explanations in the press focused on the personality of David Koresh. A paranoid psychotic, Koresh had brainwashed his followers. For sociologists, and many psychologists, this was an insufficient explanation. As psychiatrist Theodore Schwartz pointed out at the time of the Jonestown tragedy, every society has its share of people who claim to be messiahs: "In our mental hospitals you'll find many people who are a cult of one. They don't find a following" (*The New York Times*, November 26, 1978, p. D1). While Koresh may have been psychotic, this does not explain why eighty-six people died with him.

Sociologist Neil Smelser (1963) has argued that for any episode of collective behavior to occur, a number of preconditions must be met. These preconditions lie not in the individual but in the social environment. Smelser takes the functionalist position, that collective behavior represents a breakdown, or "short-circuiting," of the social order.

According to Smelser's theory, the first precondition for collective behavior is **structural conduciveness.** Something about the social environment must invite or drive people to depart from routine behavior. Conditions in the Branch Davidian cult created uncertainty. Koresh kept tight control over communications with the outside world and interpreted outside events to conform to his visions; an armed guard was on duty at all times. The "us-versus-them" mentality that Koresh fostered led the Branch Davidians to rely on one another and mistrust "outsiders."

Structural conduciveness lays the foundation for collective behavior; **structural strain** makes it more likely. Strain develops when people sense an immediate but ambiguous threat, the exact dimensions of which are not known. They know that the situation is getting out of control but feel helpless to do anything about it. The firefight with the Bureau of Alcohol, Tobacco and Firearms and the ensuing siege of the compound for fifty-one days fed the anxiety of the cult members. During that time the FBI cut off electricity, subjected the house to blinding lights at night, and played loud rock music and sounds of rabbits being slaughtered over loudspeakers. The effect of these strategies was only an increase in the Davidians' solidarity.

The third precondition for collective behavior in Smelser's theory is the development of a **generalized belief.** Individuals must develop shared ideas about who or what is threatening them, what the enemy is like, and how they can and should respond. The federal government was the key threat for the Branch Davidians; its representatives were highly visible and audible outside their compound. Moreover, Koresh had prophesied this "battle" with the evil outsiders. It has been speculated that Koresh's followers regarded the FBI's psychological warfare as a manifestation of the Antichrist, whose appearance is a biblical prophecy.

A **precipitating incident** is a dramatic event that confirms people's fears and suspicions. This tips a scale already weighted by structural conduciveness, strain, and a generalized belief. The FBI's April 19 assault on the compound, ramming it with tanks and filling it with gas, was the precipitating incident in the case of the Branch Davidians.

A precipitating incident focuses attention. People are ready to act, but they still require **mobilization** by an official or unofficial leader to suggest a course of action and provide a model for behavior. Koresh supplied both. If the fire was deliberately set, it was certainly on his orders. On many occasions he had made known his willingness to die for his beliefs and his expectation that his followers would do so as well.

At this point, according to Smelser, the ball has been set in motion. How far and how fast it rolls depends on whether or not social control is exercised. If someone is able to correct misinformation, to convince people that the threat is imaginary or that the enemy has been vanquished, to provide leadership and a model for different behavior, or to intervene forcibly, the outbreak may be checked. If there is a **breakdown of social control,** however, collective behavior is all but inevitable. The confusion caused by the gas filling the compound and the sudden fire, which spread rapidly, probably led to a complete breakdown of social control. Some deaths were the accidental result of the fire, but others were undoubtedly suicide. There was time and opportunity for more Davidians to escape the inferno than those who did manage to survive. One woman who found her way outside tried to return to the house when she realized it was taking her "family" up in flames.

Smelser's preconditions for collective behavior are summarized graphically in Figure 17-3.

An Evaluation

Smelser's theory, published in 1963, was one of the first genuinely sociological theories of collective behavior. He did not fall back on individual (or even group) psychology, as others had. Rather, he argued that a number of environmental preconditions must be met before people depart collectively from routine behavior. The existence of strain, a generalized belief, or a leader skilled at mobilization is not enough. All these factors must be operating simultaneously, and at high levels of intensity, for confusion or discontent to be translated into action. Thus Smelser helped explain why collective behavior does not develop in situations that may seem conducive to group panic. For example, if lines of formal and informal communication are not estab-

lished, strain remains a private matter. If people are not mobilized, the excitement created by a precipitating incident fades, and people drift away.

Critics have pointed to a number of flaws in Smelser's theory, however. Some (Oberschall, 1973) argue that he overstated the contrast between collective and everyday behavior. To someone not familiar with American culture, it would be exceedingly difficult to distinguish the phenomena functionalists call collective behavior from behavior at a religious revival meeting, a college football game, a rock concert, or, for that matter, the New York Stock Exchange. All these are regular, traditional features of social life in America (and elsewhere). The Branch Davidian cult and the People's Temple were extreme cases, but other examples of collective behavior might better be described as variations on conventional behavior, not breaks with convention.

Other critics (Currie and Skolnick, 1970; M. Brown and Goldin, 1973) argue that Smelser put too much emphasis on irrational beliefs, implying that real grievances and rational calculations play no role in collective behavior. Collective-action theorists (Oberschall, 1973; Tilly, 1978) concede that rumors and social disorganization may play an important role in the development of mass hysteria and crazes, but they do not explain more "serious" and long-lasting phenomena, such as riots, social movements, and revolutions. Functionalists tend to view collective behavior as having nothing to do with politics; yet recent collective action studies have "restored politics to its central role in the origins, the dynamics, and the outcomes of social movements" (Tarrow, 1988, p. 421).

Finally, functionalist theories of collective (and other) behavior rest on the assumption that stability is the norm in social systems. Conflict theorists, in particular, question this assumption.

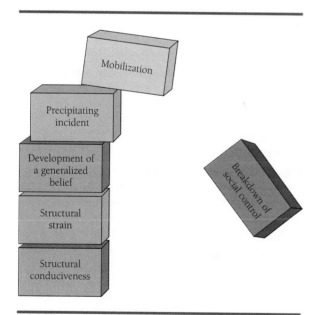

Figure 17-3   *Smelser's Theory of Collective Behavior*

Social collapse does not happen easily. Even when social conditions are unstable, there must be a precipitating incident and mobilization to tip the balance.

Source: Neil J. Smelser, *The Theory of Collective Behavior,* New York: Macmillan, 1963. Adapted with permission of The Free Press, a Division of Macmillan, Inc. Copyright © 1963 by Neil J. Smelser.

Social Movements and Social Change

A **social movement** is the (more or less) organized effort of a large number of people to produce some social change. Examples from recent American history are the civil rights movement, the women's movement, the peace movement, the environmental movement, the movement to ban nuclear weapons, and, as we saw in the opening to this chapter, the gay liberation movement. (See J. Freeman, 1983, and Zald and McCarthy, 1987, for others.) On the surface, social movements resemble collective behavior. Although they are nonviolent, protest demonstrations may seem as spontaneous, unstructured, and emotional as a riot. But social movements differ from collective behavior in four important ways. First, collective behavior is transitory. A riot ignites, spreads, and then burns itself out in a few hours or at most a few days. Social movements are longer-lasting. Second, mass hysteria, crazes, and riots are spontaneous and unplanned. Social movements are purposeful and goal-oriented. Third, collective behavior is more or less free-form. Social movements are more structured. Mobilizing hundreds of thousands of people for demonstrations, as happened in China (and other Communist nations) in 1989, requires organization. Finally, whereas collective behavior may involve a small number of people, social movements involve large numbers.

A social movement depends on the participation of a core of active members. Others may not be active on a regular basis but may contribute critical resources (for example, funds or votes). It can sometimes be difficult for a social movement to attract new members if participation is not necessary in order to benefit from movement efforts. For example, women who are not active in the women's movement still benefit from its successes. People who benefit from a movement but do not participate in it are known as ***free riders.***

In general, all members of a social movement have a sense of group identity because they believe in a common cause. There is an esprit de corps, a camaraderie, when participants meet. All agree, with varying degrees of conviction and urgency, that certain established beliefs and practices are wrong and must be replaced. And all agree, more or less, on how to go about this. Of course, people tolerate injustice more often than they mobilize to end it (B. Moore, 1978). A sense of injustice is basic to social movements. The vision of what ought to be becomes both a license and a duty to violate social expectations and engage in unconventional activities (Blumer, 1939; R. H. Turner and Killian, 1972).

Elements of Collective Action

What does it take to produce collective action? Some sociologists explain social movements in the same terms they use to explain collective behavior, as a breakdown in social order fueled by generalized (often irrational) beliefs and fired by a precipitating (usually ambiguous) incident. However, other sociologists find this functional approach inadequate for explaining goal-oriented activities that involve large numbers of people and persist over long stretches of time.

Those taking a more collective-action approach begin with the assumption that the struggle over power is a universal feature of social life (an assumption they share with more general conflict theories). In every society, there are people who have reasonable, legitimate grievances. Injustices are built into the social system. Riots and revolutions may be unusual, but many other kinds of collective action occur every day. Neighborhoods mobilize to block the construction of a highway. Parents protest inadequate funding for schools. In response to airline layoffs, pilots, mechanics, or flight attendants go on strike. The pattern of collective action changes over time, but not because of breakdowns in social order. When collective action involves large numbers of people organized to pursue common goals and when it persists over time, it becomes a social movement.

Common Interest

Charles Tilly's theory of collective action (1978) illustrates this perspective. Tilly holds that the scale and impact of collective action—whether efforts to alter the status quo are short-lived and localized or whether they develop into large-scale social movements that provoke social change—depend on four factors. These factors provide a useful framework for discussing social movements. According to Tilly's first factor, people are brought together in groups by a common interest. Marx argued that the members of the working class would eventually recognize their common interests and unite in revolution (one form of collective action) against the ruling class of capitalists. Tilly's view of common interests is broader. He holds that there is a wide range of potential interest groups in any society. For example, women have a common interest in equal

Common interest is the first element necessary for collective action. These mothers share an interest in stopping the kind of violence that killed their children.

pay for equal work; small farmers, a common interest in lower interest rates and higher produce prices; hikers, a common interest in preserving national wilderness areas. Moreover, most people have conflicting interests. For example, autoworkers might support quotas on imports of foreign cars, but they are also consumers and import quotas on all manufactured goods would hurt them. But knowing people's interests does not help in predicting which (if any) will move them to collective action. (See Moe, 1982; Taylor, 1988.)

Organization

A key determinant of whether people will pursue a particular interest through collective action is organization, the second of Tilly's four factors. Organization may be formal or informal, designed specifically for a particular cause or developed gradually in the pursuit of multiple and diffuse goals. Social movements require leadership, networks of communication among members, a division of labor, and so forth. As a general rule, initiating collective action is easier if organizations already exist than if new structures have to be built. (See also J. C. Jenkins, 1984; Calhoun, 1982; Przeworski, 1985.)

The type of organization developed or already in place affects the type of collective action pursued. Community-based grassroots organizations have a strong foundation but are usually limited to local issues. Formal organizations are necessary for large-scale collective action and for collective action directed toward precise goals. Residents of South Central Los Angeles were able to organize a riot, calling attention to the problems of black ghettos. But more complex organization is required to organize a nationwide uprising or to pursue specific legislation. One of the dilemmas for social movements is that the development of formal organization may make a movement more conservative and less democratic (Zald and McCarthy, 1987). Sociologists Francis Fox Piven and Richard Cloward (1979) have documented this phenomenon in recent American history, with the civil rights movement, the welfare rights movement, and the unemployed workers' movement. When these movements attempted to capture national attention through disruptive tactics such as civil disobedience or riots, they were able to win some concessions from authorities. When they built lobbying organizations and hired staffs to represent them in Washington, the character of the movements changed. Their goals subtly shifted from radical change to moderate reform; the leaders wanted to fit in with other respectable officials in Washington; the staffs were concerned with protecting their jobs; and the rank and file tended to lose interest. Moreover, when these groups no longer threatened civil disruption, they lost much of their bargaining power.

It is perhaps useful to see organization of social movements as both a blessing and a curse. On the one hand, some social movements may lose energy as their organizations become more concerned with maintaining their own structure than taking action. On the other hand, as research shows, without formal organization a social movement may also lose steam (McNall, 1988). The kind of organization a group adopts is key.

Resource Mobilization

The third important factor in collective action is the mobilization of resources. To succeed in its goals, a social movement must attract money, manpower and womanpower, votes, perhaps weapons, and other resources to its cause. It requires both tangible assets (funds, office space) and intangible ones (endorsement by public figures, an inside knowledge of politics). Preexisting organization is itself an important resource. In order to attract members and donations, a group may form alliances with other groups, seek news coverage, or find other ways of advertising its cause.

Mothers Against Drunk Driving (MADD) is now an established social movement, but it began with the efforts of local volunteers who created more than 400 groups across the country designed to end drunk driving. Effective mobilization of resources enabled MADD to become the strong organization it is today. By affiliating with MADD, local organizers were energized and they benefited in terms of greater legitimacy. By developing an organization structured around task forces that emphasized the idea that individuals could make a difference, MADD chapters succeeded where other groups (such as Remove Intoxicated Drivers, or RID) did not (McCarthy and Wolfson, 1996).

In recent years, direct-mail advertising campaigns based on computerized mailing lists have become an important tool for resource mobilization. By analyzing the magazines people subscribe to, the stores they patronize, the causes to which they have contributed, and demographic factors (age, race, religion), direct-mail specialists are able to tailor a message to fit the background of the recipient. Televangelists (see Chapter 13) and groups like Common Cause have been particularly effective in using direct mail to solicit contributions from people who might never join a march or even write to their representatives in Congress. As this suggests, protests and demonstrations are not the only way in which people participate in social movements.

Some sociologists hold that resource mobilization is the single most important factor in the success or failure of a social movement. Sociologists Mayer Zald and John McCarthy (1987) have developed *resource mobilization theory*. They have argued that many contemporary social movements were planned and directed by outsiders. For example, the drive to obtain Medicare for the elderly was spearheaded by the National Council for Senior Citizens Health Care through Social Security (NCSC)—an organization of young and middle-aged professionals, funded by the AFL-CIO, who lobbied, collected signatures on petitions, and staged rallies around the country. Only after the NCSC began to run into opposition from the American Medical Association and other organized groups did it seek active participants among the elderly. In this case, grassroots support developed after a movement was already under way. In other cases, a movement may depend on a "conscience constituency"—people who have nothing to gain from the movement but sympathize with the cause. In still others, a movement that is well-established and heavily funded may be run by professionals who had no initial interest in the movement but who see an opportunity to advance their careers. Most sociologists, however, view the professionally organized Medicare movement as the exception to the rule (for example, Perrow, 1979). Resource mobilization is one factor in the success of social movements, but only one.

Opportunity

Even if a movement is based on multiple common interests, has strong organization, and marshals substantial resources, it may not have the opportunity to act. Opportunity, Tilly's fourth factor, is as important as the other factors described here. In a democracy, a group can actively campaign for votes; in a dictatorship, this is impossible and armed struggle or passive resistance may be the only options. Even within a democracy, opportunities for collective action are not equally available to all groups. Will the police issue a permit for a peaceful demonstration and protect the demonstrators? (What if group members are neo-Nazis? or members of the Ku Klux Klan?) Will the media cover a demonstration or ignore it? Give it major coverage or bump it to a back page? Are TV and radio stations obliged to accept advertisements from any group that can afford their price? This question reached the courts in 1985, when TV stations in several cities refused to air a documentary made by critics of the U.S. government's operations in Central America. According to Tilly, the degree of government repression or tolerance is among the most important factors in determining what sorts of collective action actually take place (Tilly, Tilly, and Tilly, 1975; Tilly, 1978, 1986).

The Media

Though not included in Tilly's list of factors, the media are also an element of social movements. The media's coverage of student demonstrations against the war in Vietnam—demonstrations that took place around the world—helped define and focus the student organizations that eventually formed the antiwar movement (Gitlin, 1980). Students in Berkeley, Ann Arbor, Paris, and New York City became aware of their common interest in part as a result of the media's coverage of them, and this helped forge the movement to end the war.

The relationship between the media and a social movement works in several directions. Media coverage can help spur a movement, but movements also use the media to gain members and get their message out to more people. Those in social movements often try to get their message publicized by framing or packaging it in a way that makes it more likely the media will cover it. For example, the National Organization for Women (NOW) not only selects issues likely to be covered in the media; the media kits it produces on these issues are "translated" into language likely to appeal to the media. Thus, rather than framing its mission in terms of "feminism" or "women's liberation," NOW's press releases claim to present alternative knowledge—the "truth" behind the news (Barker-Plummer, 1995).

At the same time, the media are tied to the policies and ideologies that are dominant at the time: journalists tend to frame stories on the basis of prevailing government policies (Gitlin, 1980) or social concerns. Consequently, the media are as effective at undermining social movements as they are at popularizing them (see *Sociology and the Media:* Single Women Targeted in the Popular Press).

Psychology or Circumstance? Theories of Social Movements

One of the main questions for sociologists is, "To what extent can social movements be explained in terms of structural causes, such as geographical prox-imity or preexisting organizations, and to what extent must they be explained in terms of participants' aims and motives?" (See J. Coleman, 1973; Giddens, 1985a.) Those emphasizing the structural influences behind social movements assign personal interests and motives a relatively minor role. Early social movement theories focused on individual personalities and the grievances of social movement participants. Relative deprivation (discussed in the section on crowd violence) is one example of these early theories. As you may recall, the relative deprivation theory holds that whether people feel deprived depends in large part on the groups to which they compare themselves. For example, many social movement participants in the 1960s and 1970s belonged to the middle class. According to relative deprivation, their class position—in a society where people expected to be upwardly mobile—allowed them to compare themselves to the upper class, and this comparison contributed to their desire to change society.

Many social protesters of the 1960s and 1970s belonged to the middle class. Relative deprivation theory asserts that these young people compared themselves to the upper classes and that this comparison motivated them to change society.

Single Women Targeted in the Popular Press

In June 1986 *Newsweek* ran an article stating that a single woman had a better chance of being abducted by terrorists than of marrying after 40. The story set off a media frenzy and sent the anxiety levels of a lot of single women up more than a notch. Soon television news shows, radio call-in shows, and women's magazines joined in. The media had supported the feminist movement in the 1970s, but in the 1980s it became the mouthpiece of the threatened status quo.

The *Newsweek* story was based on a Yale-Harvard study showing that women who had remained single into their late thirties and forties were facing tough odds when it came to marriage. It didn't matter that the study was discredited nearly

immediately and, in fact, was not published because of flaws in the research design. Nor did it matter that the U.S. Census Bureau published a far more comprehensive demographic survey of marriage data that

> **The media had supported the feminist movement in the 1970s, but in the 1980s it became the mouthpiece of the threatened status quo.**

painted a different picture. The media had their story and ran it the way they wanted to because, as the lead writer on the story in *Newsweek* said, "we all knew this was happening before that study came out. The study sum-

marized impressions we already had." In other words, the discredited data supported a status quo interpretation of singlehood (that it was against women's nature to remain single rather than marrying and bearing children), and the media were doing their job promoting that position.

In her book, *Backlash: The Undeclared War against American Women* (1991), Susan Faludi details how the media ignored evidence showing that single women are happy and fulfilled and marry if they choose to. Instead, the media preyed upon the fears of baby boom women who had remained single. These women were now facing the fact that their biological clocks were not going to run forever; if they wanted to become mothers, it was now or never. Single

Source: Susan Faludi, *Backlash: The Undeclared War against American Women* (1991). New York: Doubleday, 1991, pp. 98–104.

Two other early theories on social movements also focused on the individual: the **personality theory** of social movements explains participation in social movements as a way to satisfy an individual's personality needs rather than to address actual grievances. Accordingly, this theory sees the social movement participant as deviant or personally troubled. Similarly, **mass-society theory** explains that movement participants feel isolated or alienated in today's society. However, since both of these theories were developed, studies have found that social movement participants do not differ significantly from people who do not participate. Both of these theories viewed participation in a social movement as largely irrational.

Contemporary Theories of Social Movements

Those who attribute social movements to a breakdown in social order also tend to portray social movements as a departure from routine, rational, everyday behavior. Those who attribute social movements to the creation of new social structures (or the revitalization of old ones) tend to analyze the life cycle of social movements, from "birth to death." Contemporary collective-action theorists see social movements as the rational extension, or intensification, of the struggles for power that go on every day, in every society, and have no clear beginning or end. As a result, they draw attention to both the social-psychological factors at work (as in what women were not only facing tough odds when it came to finding a mate, however. According to the media and the pop psychologists they quoted, single women were plagued by loneliness, depression, infertility, and AIDS. The finding that single women were largely satisfied with their accomplishments and their lives was not considered newsworthy. Married women, too, were a target in the media backlash. Married women were encouraged to stay put. The economic and emotional toll of divorce figured prominently in many magazine stories, far more prominently than any benefit that divorce might bring to those in unhappy, abusive marriages.

According to Faludi, the *Newsweek* story was used as a "parable," a cautionary tale of what can happen to women who try to have a life and career:

It presented the "man shortage" as a moral comeuppance for independent-minded women who expected too much. *Newsweek's* preachers found women guilty of at least three sins: Greed—they put their high-paying careers before the quest for a husband. Pride—they acted "as though it were not worth giving up space in their closets for anything less than Mr. Perfect." And Sloth—they weren't really out there beating the bushes; "even though they say they want to marry, they may not want it enough. . . . For years bright young women single-mindedly pursued their careers, assuming that when it was time for a husband they could pencil one in. They were wrong." (p. 100)

In this way the media were acting as the mouthpiece for the backlash against the women's movement, warning younger women that the movement was dangerous and that independence would likely lead to regret. Perhaps the best evidence for this role is what they chose not to report. At one point in the frenzy *USA Today* opened up a hotline for troubled singles. The psychologists answering the phones and those monitoring them were startled to find that male callers outnumbered women two to one.

meaning the movement has for participants) and the structural-organizational aspects of social movements.

The term *collective-action frames* refers to a mechanism through which individuals may understand what happens around them, come to identify the sources of their problems, and devise ways to address their grievances (Snow et al., 1986). Social movements can actually create frames, packaging their positions in a way that makes the issues involved understandable or more appealing to movement participants, potential adherents, and opponents (Snow and Benford, 1992). For example, the civil rights movement, discussed in Chapter 9, framed its activity in terms of deeply entrenched American beliefs such as inalienable rights, "Liberty and justice for all," and being judged by the "content of one's character, not the color of one's skin." The movement understood and framed the problems as a lack of basic constitutional rights, guaranteed by citizenship. These deprivations were then addressed tactically by nonviolent demands for basic rights, such as sitting at a lunch counter. The fact that this collective-action frame struck a chord with dominant cultural beliefs—that anyone who was hungry, behaved with dignity, and could pay was entitled to service—was to a large extent responsible for the movement's success. NOW's strategy described above—focusing on misinformation rather than "feminism"—is another example of how framing collective action can strengthen social movements.

The civil rights movement of the 1960s was successful to a large extent because it was able to frame its actions in the context of basic American beliefs and symbols. Here, Martin Luther King, Jr., delivers his "I Have a Dream" speech on the steps of the Lincoln Monument in Washington, D.C.

Current research on social movements is also concerned with the concept of *new social movements*. Although there is some debate as to what actually constitutes a "new" social movement, the research orientation of many sociologists who study social movements is different from that of the past. In addition to being concerned with the economic structure of society and the role of culture in social movements, they are also concerned with issues of identity and personal behavior within a movement. Unlike previous social movements, new social movements emphasize quality-of-life issues and issues of identity rather than economic grievances.

Are contemporary social movements unique? The theory of new social movements is still being tested, but already it has directed researchers' attention away from choosing between psychological and structural factors. It attempts to encompass both (Pichardo, 1997). The movement to provide better services and access for the disabled is a good example of how issues of identity and structure are addressed in new social movements.

Mobilizing the Disabled

Traditionally, the fight for the disabled was led by organizations like the March of Dimes and the Easter Seals Foundation. By and large the disabled did not speak for themselves; rather, others spoke for them. The emphasis was on raising funds for re-

New social movements today tend to emphasize quality-of-life and identity issues. Here, the Christian Coalition stages a "Faith and Freedom" rally during the Republican National Convention in August 1996.

search, treatment, and care. In the last two decades, however, the disabled have been transformed from passive recipients of private charity and public aid to active demonstrators for full civil rights (Holmes, 1990).

The emergence of the disability rights movement in the 1970s was the result of converging forces. Breakthroughs in medicine and technology (such as motorized wheelchairs and computers that allow the hearing- and speech-impaired to use telephones) were making it possible for severely handicapped people to lead more independent lives. At the same time, returning Vietnam veterans swelled the ranks of the disabled. The Library of Congress estimates that 43 million Americans have some form of physical or mental disability (Holmes, 1990). And the civil rights movement provided a model for those demanding full participation in society.

The early stages of the disability rights movement called attention to the importance of preexisting organization and resource mobilization. The federal government began providing services to people with disabilities (counseling, placement, and the like) in the years following World War I as a result of GI bills for veterans. These services were increased with every war. The Vocational Rehabilitation Act, passed toward the end of the Vietnam war (1973), included a one-sentence section that was hardly noticed at the time. Section 504 stated, "No otherwise qualified handicapped individual in the United States shall, solely by reason of his handicap, be excluded from the participation in, be denied the benefits of, or be subjected to discrimination under any program or activity receiving Federal financial assistance." The wording of Section 504 paralleled that of the Civil Rights Act. The implied commitment to the rights of the disabled, not just to paternalistic care, was revolutionary. It was also ignored. The Department of Health, Education and Welfare (HEW) reacted by stalling. Meetings were held in Washington and around the country; studies were commissioned; regulations were drawn up but not signed.

In 1977, rumors began to circulate about a new set of regulations that would undercut Section 504. The American Coalition of Citizens with Disabilities (ACCD), an organization formed at the 1974 meeting of the President's Committee on Employment for the Handicapped, presented the Secretary of HEW, Joseph Califano, with a deadline of April 4 to address their concerns. Disabled groups across the nation were asked to prepare for mass demonstrations on April 5. When April 4 came and went, sit-ins were held at HEW buildings in ten cities. Most were small and short-lived.

The one exception was San Francisco. Hundreds of disabled people gathered at City Hall on April 5, and when the building was closed at 5 P.M., about 150 refused to leave. At first they planned to stay overnight, and then just for the weekend. But as outside support grew [supplies and assistance from such diverse groups as the Salvation Army, the Black Panthers, a local Safeway, the AFL-CIO, and Werner Erhard of the now-defunct est (Erhard Seminar Training organization)], the demonstrators vowed to stay until Califano endorsed the original Section 504 regulations. California officials and politicians took up their cause. The regional director of HEW called Califano directly; the mayor provided demonstrators with shower facilities, soap, and towels at city expense. On April 19, eighteen of the demonstrators flew to Washington to lobby in person. Although they never met with Califano, they attracted considerable attention from the press. "Two dozen deaf, blind, and mentally retarded demonstrators, many of them in wheelchairs, [were] turned away from HEW by armed guards," reported *The Washington Post*. Finally, on the twenty-fourth day of the sit-in, Califano signed regulations guaranteeing civil rights protection for disabled people.

Why did the San Francisco demonstration succeed where others failed? The first answer is preexisting organization. The Center for Independent Living (CID) in Berkeley (just outside San Francisco) was dedicated to providing disabled persons with the social, psychological, and technical means to lead autonomous lives. A polio victim describes her first encounter with CID:

> I came to Berkeley, was met at the airport by a disabled friend, driving a van with a hydraulic lift. I stayed in a home that was accessible and was given a loaner electric wheelchair to use, and I was assisted with personal care needs by a paid attendant.
>
> My life quickly began to change. I was in charge of my own activities, getting up when I wanted to, going to bed when I wanted, taking a shower when I wanted and the like. All these things may appear small to you, but for me it was the first time that my

handicap did not completely control my life. I decided to stay in California. (R. S. Johnson, 1983, p. 89)

In effect, CID changed what it meant to be disabled—an example of the identity issues addressed by new social movements. The group began in 1972 with one federal grant and a staff of 17 working out of a two-bedroom apartment; By the mid-seventies it had a staff of 117 and an annual budget of $900,000 (R. S. Johnson, 1983). Largely as a result of CID's activities, Berkeley had a much larger proportion of disabled people who were living in the community (not with their parents or in rest homes) and in regular contact with one another. When the demonstration was being planned, CID organized strategy sessions and printed fliers for distribution throughout the community.

The second answer is resources. In part because it was well-organized, the Berkeley group was able to mobilize outside support. Without food, blankets, and assistance from others, the demonstrators could not have remained in the HEW building. Without political support, it seems doubtful that they would have made a strong impression in Washington.

The third answer is rising expectations. Ironically, the government contributed to the movement by creating a new image of people with physical and mental limitations as "second-class citizens." The language of Section 504 legitimized and digni-

fied the movement already under way in Berkeley, redefining the problems of disabled people in terms of civil rights. Section 504 also gave the movement a focal point, a tangible, specific goal. In legitimizing a goal, and then ignoring it, the government set the stage for collective action.

The fight for civil rights for the disabled is by no means over. Disabilities rights groups have formed coalitions with established civil rights organizations, won friends on Capitol Hill, and kept up demonstrations. They won a big victory when the Americans with Disabilities Act became law in 1992. Section 504 protects the disabled from discrimination at the hands of organizations that receive federal funds, but it says nothing about the private sector. The new law provides physically and mentally disabled persons with the same protection against discrimination in employment, transportation, and public accommodations as that now accorded to minorities and women. One section of the law requires that schools, colleges, and universities make provisions for all individuals with handicaps, including learning disabilities. Thus, a student with a documented learning disability must be accommodated in some way, such as by being given longer time to take a test.

The struggle on the part of our nation's disabled population underscores one of the main tenets of collective-action theory: Power struggles are a regular feature of social life and are often necessary to produce basic advances in social conditions.

People with disabilities march for equal access after the Americans with Disabilities Act was passed in 1992. Power struggles like that of the disability rights movement are often necessary to produce basic advances in social conditions.

Social Change

The term "social movement" implies change—change in the way people see themselves and their world and change in the way they behave toward and relate to others. Social movements depend as much on awareness of new possibilities as on discontent. Long-standing grievances or new fears and complaints, rising expectations or relative deprivation—all need to be brought to individual awareness and public discussion. This may result in the development of what Smelser called a generalized belief or in the development of an ideology, a set of convictions about group interests. But, as collective-action theorists remind us, organization, mobilization, and opportunity are also required before a movement can get under way.

The relationship between social movements and social change is complex; outcomes cannot always be predicted from intentions (see *Close Up:* Backyards, NIMBYs, and Incinerator Sitings). In some cases, social movements may delay change by relieving some of the symptoms of a problem without attacking the underlying causes. As a result, public concern may be diverted, and the demand for more fundamental change may decline (for example, anticrime movements focus on rigorous law enforcement and harsh penalties for offenders, diverting attention from the causes of rising crime rates). Such efforts, according to R. H. Turner and L. M. Killian, may simply "channel off much of the protest and potential reform activity into ineffectual work" (1972, p. 409). Thus social movements may inadvertently help maintain the very conditions participants seek to change.

Some movements actively resist change: people are mobilized to defend or restore traditional values that they feel have been undermined. They seek radical change based on old ideals. Such "reactionary radicals" may succeed in toppling the existing government and creating a new one (as in Iran, described later in this chapter). Or (as happened in most socialist revolutions in peasant societies) they may lose control to better organized and more sophisticated groups, such as the Communist party (C. Calhoun, 1983). A social movement that is mounted to resist a movement already under way is known as a **countermovement.** For example, when the women's movement seemed close to getting the Equal Rights Amendment passed in the 1970s, a countermovement sprang into action and ultimately succeeded in blocking passage of the amendment. As a social movement gathers strength, countermovements may form and actively seek to weaken the original movement by organized resistance and efforts to make the most of any weaknesses or blunders (Jasper and Poulsen, 1993).

Social movements may boomerang in other ways, turning formerly neutral or even sympathetic people into opponents. For example, terrorist attacks that injure innocent bystanders may alienate people who would otherwise sympathize with the terrorists' cause. People who oppose abortion have had to contend with a backlash against their cause as a result of the violent tactics some antiabortion groups have used: bombing abortion clinics, attacking and killing abortion doctors, and making public displays of dead fetuses. Because social movements challenge societal norms, people may feel uncomfortable or threatened if they perceive their position of power in the existing structure threatened. Their desire to protect the status quo may produce a backlash: the status quo may become more firmly entrenched with change postponed or avoided.

However, social movements may open people to new ideas. When people participate in a march or a sit-in, they draw the attention of many others to their cause. People who were previously uninvolved may realize that they have accepted existing social conditions out of habit, not conviction. When the possibility of change dawns on large numbers of people, new points of view may attract a wider following.

Social movements also provide an opportunity for individuals to test their convictions. For example, many African Americans who marched for civil rights in the south in the early 1960s were uneasy. They feared that demonstrations would make a bad situation worse. Marching and, in some cases, being harassed, beaten, and jailed served to strengthen their conviction that the time had come to demand change.

The civil rights movement also tested the opposition. On the one hand, some white people who might have accepted a degree of integration changed their minds when they saw thousands of black people marching. Their fear and distrust of African Americans deepened. On the other hand, some who favored strict segregation realized the

CLOSE UP

Backyards, NIMBYs, and Incinerator Sitings

Where should a halfway house for juvenile offenders or for mental patients be established? Where can toxic waste be dumped? Where can trash incineration plants be located? "Not in my backyard!" (NIMBY) is very often the reaction of those who live nearby proposed locations. In recent years some short-term social movements have emerged in response to perceived threats to the environment. When the local opponents organize in protest, they occasionally succeed in blocking the project. What makes such collective behavior successful?

Three sociologists intrigued by this question studied the organized opposition to incinerator sitings in two communities, South Philadelphia and nearby Montgomery County in Pennsylvania (Walsh, Warland, and Smith, 1993). Only one protest

group succeeded: the mayor of Philadelphia announced that the city was dropping the project in July 1988, while the Montgomery County incinerator burned its first load of waste in November 1991. Some differences between the two cases were immediately apparent. Initial survey data gathered by the researchers indicated that the Philadelphia residents were actually more typical of the kind of population that is "least resistant" to incineration projects than were the Montgomery County residents. Moreover, the

> **In recent years some short-term social movements have emerged in response to perceived threats to the environment.**

Montgomery incinerator was slated to accept out-of-town trash, usually a factor that intensifies local opposition. On the other hand, backyard residents at the Montgomery site were offered compensation for allowing the project, whereas no such offer was made to the Philadelphia residents. In many other respects the two cases were quite similar. Both projects were proposed in the early 1980s, neither area had a recycling program in place that would have reduced the need for an incineration plant, both communities organized in opposition within two years, both groups had the help of outside environmental activists, and both had to contend with political leaders who championed the project. What factors, then, can account for the fact that one protest succeeded and one failed? The re-

Source: Edward Walsh, Rex Warland, and D. Clayton Smith, "Backyards, NIMBYs, and Incinerator Sitings: Implications for Social Movement Theory," *Social Problems* 40, February 1993, pp. 25–38.

repercussions of discrimination when they saw black people come under attack. For example, in Birmingham, Alabama, some firefighters who considered themselves staunch segregationists refused to obey an order to turn fire hoses on African Americans gathered outside a church. They may have opposed integration, but they were not willing to brutalize women and children of any color. In this way social movements and the episodes they trigger serve as laboratories for social change. Through their own actions and reactions, people discover where they stand.

Social Revolutions

Revolutions are more than social movements writ large. Sociologist Theda Skocpol (1979) defines a *social revolution* as a rapid, fundamental transformation of a country's political system, social class structure, and dominant ideology. Skocpol takes the unusual view that revolutions are rarely started by intention; they are not planned in secret meetings and orchestrated by central committees dedicated to revolutionary ideals. Rather, they emerge spontaneously when international searchers found the key differences in the ways the protest movements were organized and in the details of the protest activities.

The South Philadelphia opponents organized early, within a year of the first mention of the project. A full-time salaried activist with ties to a member of Congress in the district coordinated the grassroots effort and formed coalitions with other community leaders in the city. The attention of the media was captured by busing thousands of citizens to City Hall and outfitting them with signs and gas masks. The backing of influential outside activists and a key city council member lent legitimacy to the protesters' cause. Finally, by focusing attention on larger environmental issues as well as on alternative technolo-gies, the protesters were able to keep themselves from being portrayed simply as selfish NIMBYs.

By contrast, the organizers in Montgomery did not get started until two years after the incinerator was first proposed, nor were they experienced in organized protest (unlike the Philadelphia activists). The commissioners in the township where the incinerator was to be sited backed the proposal at first, losing crucial time. After they reversed their position, they were not able to win over other municipalities in the county. Too much effort was expended overall on getting the support of experts rather than the support of politicians. Moreover, the incinerator proponents were able to portray the opponents as NIMBYs, involved in their own concerns. Their slow start, lack of experience, isolated position, and poor strategies finally undid the protesters' efforts in Montgomery County.

What the sociologists discovered in their study was that the static variables of traditional social movement theory, such as a community's socioeconomic status, its degree of organization, and its level of discontent, are not the only factors to take into account when evaluating a movement's performance. The outcomes in South Philadelphia and Montgomery County had a great deal to do with less definable, more fluid variables, such as timing and "the complex interactions among individual actors, groups, and larger social structures" (p. 35).

crises heighten internal divisions in a nation. This is essentially a structuralist position. Skocpol holds that social structure (defined broadly in terms of a world system of political and economic interests) is more important than ideology, culture, or other factors.

As with theories on social movements, theories explaining social revolutions have changed from focusing on personal grievances and psychological factors to including structural-organizational aspects. In addition to Skocpol's theory, several other theories also focus on radical forms of social change (Goldstone, 1986). The first, "misery breeds revolts," simply explains that social revolutions are likely to occur when there are actual grievances against the state. Similarly, a second theory holds that citizens revolt when the state faces too many problems and is prevented from governing and providing for people's needs effectively. Another theory views revolutions in terms of changing ideas. Exposed to radical new ideas that shake them out of what they take for granted, people revolt against the status quo in order to put the new ideas into action (Goldstone, 1986).

Victims are treated after a bomb exploded under the World Trade Center complex in New York City in 1993, killing 6 people and injuring 1,000. Such acts of terrorism are intended to frighten people into taking the terrorists' cause seriously, but they are more likely to promote a backlash of anger and rejection.

Marx's theory of rebellion was based on the idea that proletarian revolutions will naturally occur in developed countries as a result of the exploitation of workers. Since, historically, these proletarian revolutions have failed to materialize, Marx's theory has been discredited. Yet there is some evidence that this may be premature. In countries where an economic crisis has hit a working class made large by development, rebellion does occur (Boswell and Dixon, 1993).

Skocpol's Theory of Social Revolution

In her book *States and Social Revolutions* (1979), Skocpol compared the French Revolution against the Bourbons, the Russian Revolution against the tsars, and the Communist Revolution in China to unsuccessful rebellions and to changes in government or social structure that did not involve mass uprisings. She concluded that social revolution depends on four factors:

1. Skocpol holds that *global inequality and international competition* play as great a role in starting revolutions as internal discontent does. Typically, revolutions break out when an undeveloped nation is under military or economic attack by more advanced nations. For example, the Russian Revolution was precipitated by World War I. The German military

machine, not revolutionaries inside Russia, caused the tsar's army and government bureaucracy to collapse.

2. Revolution is more likely if a *clash of interests develops between the state (or government) and powerful groups within the society.* Typically, the state's efforts to resist external threats by raising taxes, increasing social control, or instituting reform alienate the dominant classes. In Bourbon France and Imperial China, the aristocracies resisted modernization, further weakening the state's ability to act and opening the door for revolution from below. (By contrast, in Japan and Turkey, state bureaucrats were able to achieve reform without revolution.)

3. *Popular uprisings* usually play a major role in social revolutions. But, like Tilly, Skocpol argues that discontent alone cannot sustain collective action. Mass uprisings depend on independent, usually preexisting organization among the lower classes that enables them to mobilize the resources for revolution. The weakening of government apparatus for social control and divisions among the elite add opportunity to organization.

4. *Revolutions usually produce a more powerful, centralized, bureaucratic, independent government than existed under the old regime.* But in most cases leaders emerge after the revolution has taken place, not before. Often, their ideology and programs do not reflect the values and goals of groups that produced the revolution. In Russia, for example, the Bolsheviks took much more credit for the revolution than they deserved and few peasants were committed to communism.

Undoubtedly, 1989 will go down in history as the "Year of Revolutions"—the year when the nations of eastern Europe overthrew Soviet domination and Communist dictatorships, the year when the Soviet Union was transformed from a one-party Communist state into a multiparty state, the year when Soviet republics demanded autonomy and in some cases full national independence, the year when the government of South Africa agreed to negotiate with the African National Congress and other previously outlawed antiapartheid groups, the year when Chinese students calling for democracy occupied Tiananmen Square (however briefly). But the revolutions of 1989 are very recent, and scholars have yet to publish detailed analyses of these uprisings. In some cases the revolutions are ongoing, as in Russia and the former provinces of Yugoslavia. Thus, in the following section we will focus on the revolution in Iran.

The Iranian Revolution

At the time it occurred, the Iranian Revolution was described as "the most popular, broad-based, and sustained agitation in modern history" (Ahmad, 1982, p. 292). In 1975, the shah seemed to be in complete control of the country. In a mere twenty years, he had transformed Iran from a minor Third World nation into a regional power. He had one of the most advanced armies in the nonwestern world and one of the most efficient and ruthless secret police forces (called Savak). Thanks to oil revenues, Iran's gross national product had grown from $3 billion in 1953 to $53 billion in 1973; per capita income had risen from $160 to $1,600 per year. Enrollment in universities had increased tenfold; the number of industrial factories had climbed from about 1,000 to 8,000.

The overthrow of the shah therefore took the world by surprise (Skocpol, 1982). What began as a general strike in January 1978 soon turned into mass protests of the shah's rule (Abrahamian, 1985). Approximately 30,000 demonstrators were killed before the shah abdicated in February 1979. Yet the number of workers, students, intellectuals, and business and religious leaders who participated in demonstrations increased steadily. At first, anger was directed at the shah himself, who was seen as a puppet of U.S. imperialism and a traitor to Islam; later, the United States became the main target. The Iranian Revolution differed from other Third World revolutions in two important ways. First, most Third World revolutions (for example, Cuba, Angola, Nicaragua) took the form of prolonged armed struggle between government troops and guerrilla forces based in the countryside. The Iranian Revolution was a nonviolent, urban uprising. Demonstrators were militant in the sense that they demanded the overthrow of the shah and were unwilling to compromise, but they did not take up arms. Violence was directed at the demonstrators, however. Second, other revolutions have replaced old regimes with modern institutions (such as political parties) and modern, secular ideologies (nationalism, socialism, communism). The Iranian Revolution brought to the fore leaders from the Shiite branch of Islam, which is committed to a return to Islamic fundamentalism.

Did the Iranian Revolution fit the broader pattern Skocpol identified in her studies of earlier social revolutions? She believes that it did in some ways but not in others. The following discussion will supplement Skocpol's analysis (1982) with observations by other social scientists (for example, Arjomand, 1986).

Iran was not at war, nor was it even threatened by war (Skocpol's first factor) when the revolution broke out. But it was under subtler forms of international pressure (Ahmad, 1982; Goldfrank, 1982). When the shah's government was threatened in the early 1950s, the CIA had restored him to his throne, creating a "client state." Under President Nixon, the shah was pressured to become the police officer of the Middle East; under President

A crowd of students demonstrate outside the U.S. embassy in Tehran, Iran, in 1980. After the revolution, fundamentalist Shiite Islamic clerics came to power, led by the Ayatollah Khomeini.

Carter, he was pressured to increase civil liberties. In addition, the Iranian government was totally dependent on oil revenues. As a result, it was vulnerable to fluctuations in oil prices on the world market, which were dropping at the time of the revolution. Thus the world system did play an indirect role in the Iranian Revolution.

Skocpol's second factor, conflict between the government and powerful groups within the country, was clearly in place. The shah alienated virtually all segments of Iranian society over the course of his reign. When he was restored to power in 1953, he banned political parties, trade unions, professional associations, and other middle- and working-class organizations. In the 1960s, he replaced large landowners with state overseers, uprooting the landed aristocracy and many peasants as well. And he deliberately prevented the formation of a political elite among members of his own government. No figurehead monarch, the shah made all major decisions himself, playing military and police officers and bureaucrats within his government against one another (Skocpol, 1982). Because the government was supported by oil exports, not by taxes on land or industry, the shah felt no need to develop popular or even elite support. Foreign technicians kept the government and its oil monopoly running. Modernization was accomplished largely by decree. A small group of westernized Iranians profited enormously from this arrangement, but the vast majority were left out or left behind. Thus there were no organic connections between the government of Iran and Iranian society, at any level. There was an exaggeration of the split between the state and the ruling classes that Skocpol had observed in other social revolutions.

The popular uprising in Iran conformed to Skocpol's analysis of earlier social revolutions in most respects. It was a spontaneous uprising; no political party or other group had planned it. And demonstrations succeeded because of organization and resources. Bazaars had long been the center of urban life in Iran. At the time of the revolution, bazaar shopkeepers numbered at least 250,000, controlled about two-thirds of the retail trade in Iran, and employed perhaps 70 percent of Iranian workers (Abrahamian, 1985). When land reform forced thousands of peasants to migrate to the city in the 1960s and 1970s, they turned to the bazaar for jobs and social support. The bazaar, in turn, had long-standing ties with the Shiite religious estab-

lishment. Traditionally, Shiite clergy (not government courts) ruled on commercial disputes within the bazaar; shopkeepers voluntarily paid religious taxes, which enabled the clergy to maintain religious schools and to provide personalized welfare services to the urban poor. Together clergy and shopkeepers organized a never-ending cycle of prayer meetings and celebrations of Islamic holy days.

For most of his reign, the shah did not interfere with these traditions. Although other organizations had been banned, the bazaar's trade and craft guilds were allowed to continue. Although the shah's father had struggled with the Shiite clergy and outlawed traditional Islamic practices (such as the wearing of the *chador,* or long veil), the shah himself did not take old-fashioned, "turban-headed" clerics seriously. In the early 1970s, however, he began to attack both groups. Among other assaults, the government announced plans to bulldoze the huge bazaar in Tehran and undertake a program to "nationalize" religion.

Skocpol suggests that aversion to the shah's militarism and ties to the United States and disgust with the flaunting of wealth and disrespect for Islamic tradition by wealthy, westernized Iranians were widespread. The attacks on the bazaar and the clergy were the last straw. Once protests began, the bazaar contributed critical resources (such as economic aid for striking workers); Shiite prayer meetings and funeral processions provided a framework for political action with which all Iranians were familiar.

Departing from her view that ideologies and leaders emerge after a revolution has succeeded, Skocpol (1982) argues that Shiite Islam provided a tradition of martyrdom that encouraged demonstrators to risk death; it also fostered an image of the Islamic community that would arise when the shah and his foreign supporters were ousted. In Iran, cultural traditions played a major role in the early stages of social revolution, and the postrevolutionary state reflects the wishes of the masses. Others (for example, Keddie, 1982) believe that many Iranians saw the protests as a nationalist uprising, not a religious war. They accepted Shiite rhetoric because it was antishah, anti-imperialism, anti-American, but they assumed the Shiite clergy would step down once the shah was overthrown. Whatever the case, it seems clear that the Shiite clergy control Iran today.

For students of revolutions (as well as political leaders) there are very interesting questions to pose: Was the Iranian Revolution a special case? Or did it mark the beginning of a new era for the Middle East in which revolutionary struggle will take the form of urban protest guided by Islamic ideals?

An Evaluation

Revolutions bring us back to the question raised at the beginning of this chapter: "Is collective behavior rational or irrational?" When revolutions succeed, yesterday's rioters become today's heroes and martyrs. What once seemed irrational now seems ratio-

nal (and vice versa). The shah and most western observers viewed the creation of an Islamic state in Iran as unthinkable. Yet today a movement to westernize that nation, to replace prayer with debate, to value progress over tradition, would be regarded as heresy. Islamic fundamentalists have gained a political foothold in other nations as well—through the ballot box in Algeria, Egypt, and Jordan and via armed opposition to the government in Afghanistan, Lebanon, Tunisia, and Morocco (Ibrahim, 1990).

In 1989, the "unthinkable" happened almost daily. At the beginning of that year no reasonable person would have suggested that the Berlin Wall, long the symbol of the cold war, would be torn

---

SOCIOLOGY ON THE WEB

Gay Rights

The text discusses social movements and explores Tilly's four elements (plus a fifth, media coverage) that define social movements. Use the web, for example, to explore the gay rights movement in the United States and elsewhere, and consider whether gay rights has all the elements of a social movement today. Ask the following questions as you explore the sites listed below and others you will find: To what extent do gays and lesbians have common interests? Are there important areas in which their interests diverge (in other words, is there a single gay rights movement)? What kinds of organizations have evolved to expound gay rights? What resources have been mobilized and by whom? To what degree is the government tolerant of gay causes? How do gay rights organizations use the media?

Any search engine will provide links to gay and lesbian social organizations, Internet groups, and local activist groups. In addition, your server probably maintains chat groups with a gay and lesbian focus. Below are three search engines and three organizations to get your started.

http://qrd.rdrop/com/qrd/
http://www.glweb.com/
http://www.hrcusa.org/
These three databases and search engines contain thousands of links to organizations and social and

political groups. In particular, glweb contains "Rainbow Query," a large, full-text search engine with links to most national activist groups.

http://www.glaad.org/
The website of GLAAD, a media watchdog group, will show you how gay rights advocates are using the media. GLAAD promulgates media alerts, calls to action to the entire gay community. For example, at the time this was written, GLAAD was mobilizing its membership to respond to the cancellation of *Ellen*, the first sit-com with a gay central character.

http://www.gmhc.org/
The Gay Men's Health Crisis is the oldest and largest not-for-profit AIDS organization in the country. What is GMHC's message? What tactic does the organization use to promulgate it?

http://www.actup.org/
Act-Up is an AIDS activist group that uses tactics that are very different from those of the Gay Men's Health Crisis. Compare the aims and agendas of these two groups as you consider the overall question of whether there is one gay rights movement.

down, for example, or that Nelson Mandela would be regarded as an elder statesman by the South African government that had held him in prison for twenty-seven years. All across eastern Europe yesterday's dissidents and political prisoners became today's heroes and even heads of state.

Analysis of revolutionary change highlights the point that explanations of behavior reflect the times in which they are made. Sociological theories of collective behavior are not exempt from this rule. Smelser's functional theory of collective behavior was developed in the 1950s, a period in which conformity was highly valued in the United States. This was the era of the gray flannel suit. Men who wanted to get ahead dressed in uniform (and women did not work outside their homes unless they had to). Everyone knew his or her place, and departures from these norms were scorned. Tilly's collective-action theory was developed in the

1960s, a period of social upheaval and change. The civil rights movement was achieving some of its goals, women were mobilizing, students (both sexes in jeans, beads, and long hair) protested the war in Vietnam. Participation in social movements seemed rational and normal.

Today most sociologists view collective-action theory as an important correction of the more conservative functionalist and psychosocial theories of collective behavior and social movements. But it is important to recognize that taken by itself, each approach has strengths and weaknesses. Functionalism may overstate the irrationality of collective behavior, but collective-action theory tends to underestimate the emotional components. Whereas functionalism risks idealizing the status quo, collective-action theory tends to idealize rebellion. Most researchers try to achieve some balance in their approach.

Summary

1. **Is collective behavior, ranging from fads to riots, rational or irrational behavior?**
Sociological theorists look at *collective behavior* in two ways. *Collective-action theorists* emphasize the real grievances, rational choices, and organization underlying social movements and revolutions, which they distinguish from sudden, short-lived outbreaks of unconventional behavior, such as fads, *crazes,* and hysterias. Functionalists focus on the irrational side: they see mass departures from convention as a short circuit in the social system and emphasize the spontaneous and emotional aspects of all collective behavior. Smelser's functionalist theory identifies six preconditions for collective behavior to occur: *structural conduciveness, structural strain,* a *generalized belief* about a source of threat, a *precipitating incident, mobilization* of participants for action, and a *breakdown of social control.*

2. **What explains seemingly sudden and violent riots? What caused the Los Angeles riot of 1992, and how does that riot compare with the urban riots of the 1960s?** Early sociologists explained sudden and violent riots in terms of group psychology: people cease to act as individuals when the *crowd* takes on a life

of its own; senseless acts get repeated through a form of contagion. Contemporary sociologists think this view exaggerates the irrationality of crowds. They see new *emergent norms* developing in violent crowd situations that serve to define the situation for the participants and rationalize their actions. *Rising expectations* and *relative deprivation* help explain why riots occur at a particular time and place. The 1992 Los Angeles riot was touched off by outrage at police brutality and what was perceived as a miscarriage of justice, but its intensity was fueled by the relative deprivation South Central Los Angeles residents felt when they compared their lot with that of successful immigrants and more upwardly mobile families. The urban riots of the 1960s took place at a time when minorities had come to expect a better life but their expectations were not being met.

3. **How does a social movement differ from other forms of collective behavior? What explains the success or failure of a social movement?** A *social movement* is the organized effort of a large number of people to produce some social change. It differs from other forms of collective behavior in three ways: It is longer-lasting, more purposeful and goal-

oriented, and more structured. According to Tilly, the development of a social movement depends on collective interests, preexisting or new organizations, the mobilization of a variety of resources, and, above all, opportunity. In some cases social movements result in social change, but in others they may delay change by scoring only symbolic victories or by mobilizing opposition. A group that is well-organized, that mobilizes its resources effectively, and that is strengthened by rising expectations is likely to meet with success.

4. **How is a social revolution a special type of social movement? Are social revolutions rational or irrational behavior?** A *social revolution* goes beyond a social movement in that it involves a rapid, fundamental transformation of a country's political system, social class structure, and dominant ideology. Skocpol holds that revolutions emerge spontaneously when international crises heighten internal divisions within a nation. When revolutions succeed, what once seemed irrational now seems rational; yesterday's rioters become today's heroes. Revolutionary change calls attention to historical biases, which exist in all sociological theories.

Key Terms

breakdown of social control   638

collective-action theory   629

collective behavior   628

countermovement   649

craze   635

crowd   630

emergent norm   633

expressive crowd   633

free riders   640

generalized belief   638

mass hysteria   635

mass-society theory   644

mob   630

mobilization   638

personality theory   644

precipitating incident   638

relative deprivation   634

rising expectations   634

social movement   639

social revolution   650

structural conduciveness   638

structural strain   638

Recommended Readings

Burgos-Debary, Elizabeth (Ed.). 1988. *I . . . Riberto Menchu: An Indian Woman in Guatemala,* Ann Wright, trans. London, England: Verso and NLB.

Freeman, Jo (Ed.). 1983. *Social Movements of the Sixties and Seventies.* New York: Longman.

Gitlin, Todd. 1980. *The Whole World Is Watching: Mass Media in the Making/Unmaking of the New Left.* Berkeley: University of California Press.

Goldstone, Jack A. 1986. *Revolutions: Theoretical, Comparative, and Historical Studies.* New York: Harcourt Brace Jovanovich.

Koch, Howard, 1970. *The Panic Broadcast: Portrait of an Event.* Boston: Little, Brown.

McAdam, Doug. 1982. *Political Process and the Development of Black Insurgency.* Chicago: University of Chicago Press.

McAdam, Doug, McCarthy, John D., & Zald, Mayer N. 1996. *Comparative Perspectives on Social Movements.* New York: Cambridge University Press.

Marcus, Eric (Ed.). 1992. *Making History: The Struggle for Gay and Lesbian Equal Rights, 1945–1990.* New York: HarperCollins.

Skocpol, Theda. 1994. *Social Revolutions in the Modern World.* Cambridge, England, and New York: Cambridge University Press.

Glossary

The number in parentheses after each entry refers to the chapter in this book in which each term or concept is discussed in detail.

absolute number of crimes   The number of crimes committed during a given time period, often measured in terms of the number of crimes known to police and/or crimes reported in victimization surveys. (Compare **crime rate**.) (7)

absolutist perspective   The view that deviance lies in the act itself, which is seen as a violation of natural law or a transgression against God's commandments. (7)

achieved status   A social status that is attained through personal effort. (Compare **ascribed status**.) (5)

affirmative action   An approach to compensating minorities for past discriminatory policies by means of programs designed to open educational and job opportunities to members of minority groups. (9)

ageism   Prejudice and discrimination against older people. (5, 16)

agent of socialization   An individual, group, or organization that influences a person's behavior and sense of self. (4)

aggregate   A collection of people who happen to be in the same place at the same time, such as people waiting for a bus. (6)

alienation   The feeling of being separated from one's work and, through one's work, from other people. (15)

altruistic suicide   Suicide that, in Durkheim's view, results from excessive attachment to a group or community. (Compare **anomic suicide; egoistic suicide; fatalistic suicide**.) (1)

amalgamation   A pattern of intergroup relations in which the different ethnic and racial groups that make up the society intermingle, thus producing a new and distinctive genetic and cultural blend. (Compare **assimilation; pluralism**.) (9)

anomic suicide   Suicide that, in Durkheim's view, results from a major disruption of the social order. (Compare **altruistic suicide; egoistic suicide; fatalistic suicide**.) (1)

anomie   A breakdown in social guidelines for behavior and social definitions of right and wrong. (1)

anticipatory socialization   The process of learning about and practicing a new role before one is in the position to play that role. (4)

apartheid   In South Africa, a philosophy of white supremacy grounded in Afrikaner history and religion; a system of overlapping laws, regulations, and agencies designed to maintain separation of the races. (9)

ascribed status   A status that is assigned to the individual at birth or at different stages of the life cycle. (Compare **achieved status**.) (5)

assimilation   A pattern of intergroup relations in which ethnic and racial minorities are absorbed by the dominant culture and differences are forgotten or destroyed. (Compare **amalgamation; pluralism**.) (9)

authoritarian political system   A system in which the state claims an exclusive right to exercise political power and ordinary people are denied the right to participate in government (e.g., monarchy, dictatorship, or totalitarianism). (Compare **democracy**.) (14)

authority   Legitimate power, which depends on agreement among decision makers and those subject to their decisions that certain uses of power are valid and justified. (See **power**.) (14)

automation   Technological control of production that minimizes the need for human workers. (15)

beliefs   Shared ideas about how the world operates that cannot be proved or disproved by ordinary means. (3, 13)

birthrate Number of births per 1,000 people in a given year. (16)

blended family A household that includes at least one spouse with children from a previous marriage. (11)

breakdown of social control Smelser's sixth and final condition for collective behavior; the absence of leadership that is capable of correcting misinformation, convincing people that a threat is imaginary, or intervening to redirect behavior. (17)

bureaucracy A hierarchical organization governed by formal rules and regulations. (5)

capitalism An economic system based on the principles of private ownership of property, the profit motive, and free competition. (Compare **command economy**.) (15)

census A systematic count of an entire population. (16)

charismatic authority Authority based on the belief that a person possesses exceptional personal qualities. (Compare **rational-legal authority; traditional authority**.) (14)

civil religion A set of beliefs, rituals, and symbols that define a nation's special relationship to God. (13)

closed system A society in which a person's social position is ascribed on the basis of traits over which the individual has no control; characterized by little, if any, opportunity to better one's position. (Compare **open system**.) (8)

collective-action theory The view that collective behavior is the result of rational decisions on the part of individuals and planning and organization on the part of collectivities. (17)

collective behavior Nonroutine activities, engaged in by large numbers of people, that violate social expectations. (17)

command economy An economic system in which (ideally) the means of production are owned by the state, economic activities are centrally planned, social welfare is a state responsibility, and the distribution of wealth is more or less even. (Compare **capitalism**.) (15)

comparable worth An effort to correct gender bias in wages by extending the principle of equal pay for equal work to include wages for different jobs that are equally demanding. (10)

conflict perspective An approach to sociological analysis that stresses the differences in people's interests, their clashes over limited goods, and the extent to which society is held together by power. (2, 12)

conformists Merton's term for people who accept both the goals their culture holds out as desirable and the approved means of pursuing them, whatever the consequences. (7)

conglomerate A corporation with holdings and subsidiaries in a number of different industries. (15)

control group The subjects in an experiment who are *not* exposed to the experimental treatment. (Compare **experimental group**.) (2)

corporate crime A violation of the law by a corporation, on behalf of a corporation, such as price fixing and stock manipulation. (7)

corporation A formal organization, created by law, whose existence and liabilities are independent of particular owners and managers. (15)

counterculture A subculture that actively goes against the values and practices of the larger society. (3)

countermovement A social movement mounted to resist another movement already under way. (17)

craze A type of collective behavior that takes the form of wild enthusiasm about some person, object, or event. (17)

crime A violation of a norm that is codified in a law and is backed by the power and authority of the state. (7)

crime rate The number of crimes per 100,000 population in a given time period. (Compare **absolute number of crimes**.) (7)

crimes without victims Activities that have been declared illegal because they offend public morals, not because they harm anyone directly. (7)

cross-cultural study A comparative study of beliefs, customs, and/or behavior among two or more groups of people with different languages and ways of life. (2)

crowd A collection of people who come together on a temporary basis. (17)

cult A religious organization that accepts the legitimacy of other religions but has a negative relationship to society. (13)

cultural integration The degree to which different elements of culture fit well together and support one another. (3)

cultural lag A delay between changes in technology or physical conditions and adjustments in beliefs and values. (3)

cultural relativism The view that a culture must be understood in terms of its own values, attitudes, and meanings. (3)

cultural universal A value, norm, belief, or practice that is found in all cultures. (2)

culture A people's entire design for living, including beliefs, values, norms and sanctions, technology, symbols, and language. (1, 3)

culture shock The feelings of disorientation and stress that people experience when they enter an unfamiliar cultural setting. (3)

death rate Number of deaths per 1,000 people in a given year. (16)

definition of the situation An overall idea of what is expected in a situation; establishes a framework for social interaction. (6)

deindustrialization The transformation of cities from industrial to information-processing centers. (8)

democracy A political system based on popular participation in the decision-making process, or rule by the people. (Compare **authoritarian; political system.**) (14)

demographic transition A three-stage pattern of population change that accompanied the transformation of western nations from agricultural into industrial societies. (16)

demography The scientific study of population. (16)

denomination A religious organization that accepts the legitimacy of other religions and has a positive relationship to society. (13)

dependency theory A theory which suggests that the developing countries have failed to develop a modern industrial base and secure middle class because they are economically and politically dependent on foreign corporations. (15)

dependent variable A change in behavior that is due to the factor whose effects the researcher is studying

(such as the experimental treatment). (Compare **independent variable.**) (2)

deterrence The use of state sanctions to inhibit or prevent criminal activity. (7)

deviance (deviant behavior) Behavior that violates widely held values and norms. (7)

deviant career A lifestyle that includes habitual or permanent deviance. (7)

deviant subculture A group that is distinguished from other members of society by deviant norms, values, and lifestyle. (7)

differential association Sutherland's term for the learning of criminal or violent behavior through exposure to predominantly pro-criminal norms and values or to situations that reward criminal behavior. (7)

direct democracy A political system in which citizens run their own government, deciding issues by voice vote at assemblies or by referendum. (14)

discrimination The denial of opportunities and social esteem to individuals because they are members of a devalued group or category. (9)

divorce rate The number of divorces per 1,000 married women (or men) age 15 or older in a given year. (11)

education The formal or informal transmission of knowledge and skills. (12)

ego According to Freud, the rational part of the personality that deals with the outside world and mediates between the id and the superego. (See **id; superego.**) (4)

egoistic suicide Suicide that, in Durkheim's view, results from lack of attachment to any group or community. (Compare **altruistic suicide; anomic suicide; fatalistic suicide.**) (1)

emergent norm A norm that arises within a crowd when one explanation for the situation spreads and becomes so definitive that group pressure keeps participants from expressing different views. (17)

empty-nest syndrome The dissatisfaction and depression women may feel in middle adulthood when their children leave home and their husbands are still involved in their careers. (4)

enculturation   Immersion in a culture to the point where that particular design for living seems "only natural." (3)

established church   A religious organization that claims unique legitimacy and has a positive relationship to society. (13)

ethnic group   A category of people who see themselves and are seen by others as different because of their cultural heritage. (9)

ethnocentrism   The tendency to evaluate other cultures in terms of one's own and to conclude that the other cultures are inferior. (3)

ethnography   A participant-observer field study in which the researcher lives with the people being studied over an extended period, tries to see the world through their eyes, and attempts to write a description of their culture as a whole. (2)

ethnomethodology   A term coined by Garfinkel in reference to the unspoken, often unconscious rules people use to maintain order and predictability in everyday social interaction. (6)

experiment   A research method involving a systematic, controlled examination of cause and effect. (2)

experimental group   The subjects in an experiment who are exposed to the experimental treatment. (Compare **control group**.) (2)

expressive crowd   A collection of people who gather to express a common emotion, such as joy, excitement, or grief. (17)

extended family   An arrangement consisting of members of three or more generations, related by blood or marriage, who live together or in close proximity. (11)

family   A social group that carries out specialized functions, involves both biological and social kinship, and shares a residence. (11)

fatalistic suicide   Suicide that, in Durkheim's view, results from a hopelessness in not being able to change one's life conditions or situation. (Compare **altruistic suicide; anomic suicide; egoistic suicide**.) (1)

feminism   The belief that women are equal to men and that they should have equal rights and opportunities. (10)

fertility rate   Number of births per 1,000 women in their childbearing years (age 15 to 44) in a population in a given year. (16)

field study   A research method involving direct observation of social behavior in its natural setting. (Also known as **participant observation**.) (2)

folkways   Norms that are not sacred but are so ingrained that people conform to them automatically. (3)

formal organization   A group designed and created to pursue specific goals and held together by explicit rules and regulations. (5)

formal sanctions   Official, public rewards and punishments. (Compare **informal sanctions**.) (3)

formal social controls   Institutionalized, codified, public mechanisms for preventing or correcting deviant behavior. (Compare **informal social controls**.) (7)

free riders   People who benefit from a social movement but do not participate in it. (17)

functionalist perspective   An approach to sociological analysis that stresses the commonality of interests among members of a society and the extent to which the unintended consequences of their actions work together to create a harmonious whole. (2)

game stage   A stage of human development during which children play organized games and, through this participation, come to see themselves as part of an organized structure that has established roles and is governed by rules. (4)

Gemeinschaft   Tönnies's term for the sense of belonging and community that exists in peasant villages because of shared norms and values, frequent social contact, and warm personal relationships. (Compare *Gesellschaft*.) (16)

gender   A set of social and cultural practices that reflect and reinforce assumptions about differences between men and women. (10)

generalized belief   Smelser's third condition for collective behavior; the shared perception among individuals about who or what is threatening them, what the enemy is like, and how they should respond. (17)

generalized other   G. H. Mead's term for an internalized image of the structure, norms, and values of society as a whole. (4)

genocide   The intentional mass murder of an ethnic, religious, racial, or political group. (9)

Gesellschaft   Tönnies's term for the impersonal social order that exists in modern, industrial cities because of little consensus on values and norms, fleeting social contacts, and constant change. (Compare *Gemeinschaft.*) (16)

glass ceiling   A subtle, invisible barrier to promotion for female executives. (10)

group   A number of people who feel a common identity and interact in a regular and structural way, on the basis of shared norms and goals. (5)

group marriage   The marriage of two or more men to two or more women at the same time. (11)

historical study   A research method using sources from an earlier time or from an extended time span. (2)

homogamy   The tendency to marry someone who is similar to oneself in attributes society considers important. (11)

homophobia   Prejudice and discrimination against gays and lesbians. (10)

hospice   A home care or homelike facility designed to make dying less physically and emotionally trying for patients and their families. (4)

hypothesis   A testable statement about a possible relationship. (2)

"I," the   According to G. H. Mead, the impulsive, creative, egocentric part of the self. (4)

id   According to Freud, the part of the personality that serves as a reservoir of innate, primitive, asocial sexual and aggressive urges. (See **ego; superego.**) (4)

ideal culture   Norms and values to which people openly and formally adhere. (Compare **real culture.**) (3, 12)

ideal type   A model that exemplifies the essential characteristics of a general concept or thing. (5)

identity crisis   People's inability to reconcile the image they have of themselves with their actual skills, potential, and activities or with the image of themselves that they perceive others have of them. (4)

idiographic explanation   An explanation based on individualized or unique circumstances rather than global or societal factors. (1)

in-group   A group to which people feel they belong and which commands their loyalty and respect. (Compare **out-group.**) (6)

incapacitation   The process of confining criminals to prison or otherwise preventing them from committing additional crimes. (7)

independent variable   The factor whose effects the researcher studies by control or manipulation in an experiment or by other methodological and/or statistical techniques. (Compare **dependent variable.**) (2)

informal sanctions   Unofficial, sometimes subtle or even unconscious checks on everyday behavior. (Compare **formal sanctions.**) (3)

informal social controls   Unofficial pressures to conform to society's norms and values. (Compare **formal social controls.**) (7)

infrastructure   The means for moving raw materials, goods, people, and ideas from one place to another in a society or region. (15)

innovators   Merton's term for people who are determined to achieve conventional goals but are willing to use unconventional or illegal means to do so. (7)

institutionalized racism   A body of established social patterns built into the social structure that have the unintended consequence of limiting opportunities of certain racial groups. (9)

institutionalized sexism   A body of established social patterns built into the social structure that have the unintended consequence of limiting women's opportunities. (10)

interest group   An organization created to pressure public officials to make decisions that will benefit its members or promote a cause. (14)

invasion and succession   The pattern of change in city neighborhoods in which members of one racial, ethnic, or socioeconomic group begin to move into an area and, as their numbers build up, eventually replace the group previously living there and become the dominant group. (16)

iron law of oligarchy   The belief, according to Michels, that even the most democratic, idealistic organizations inevitably become oligarchies, dominated by a small, self-serving elite. (5)

labeling perspective   The view that deviance is an interactive process whereby a society, or a group within a society, defines certain behavior as deviant, labels people who engage in the behavior as deviants, and then treats them as outcasts. (7)

language A set of shared symbols (spoken and written words) and rules (a syntax) for combining these symbols in meaningful ways. (3)

latent function The unintended and often unrecognized function of a behavior pattern or social arrangement. (Compare **manifest function**.) (2)

law A norm written into a formal code by officials. (3)

life expectancy The potential life span of the average member of a given population. (16)

looking-glass self Cooley's term for the image of ourselves we form by observing how other people react to us. (4)

macroperspective An approach to studying social structure that focuses on the overall analysis of patterns and trends of populations, societies, and the world as a whole. (Compare **microperspective**.) (5)

magnet schools Schools with specialized curricula and/or approaches to teaching; designed to attract a socioeconomically diverse student body. (12)

majority group A category of people who have gained a dominant position in society and guard their power and position, excluding others from their ranks. (9)

manifest function The intended and recognized function of a behavior pattern or social arrangement. (Compare **latent function**.) (2)

mass hysteria Collective behavior that results from the "contagious" spread of fear or anxiety. (17)

mass-society theory The view that participants in social movements feel isolated or alienated in today's society. (Compare **personality theory**.) (17)

master status A social position that tends to override everything else the person is or does. (5)

"me," the According to G. H. Mead, the socialized part of the self that is composed of internalized norms and values and is ever mindful of the impression made on others. (4)

means of production Marx's term for the means by which wealth is created (raw materials, tools, machinery, factories, etc.). (2)

mechanical solidarity The concept that all members of a society are similar; in Durkheim's view, the basis for traditional societies. (Compare **organic solidarity**.) (16)

megacity A city with a population of 10 million or more. (16)

menopause The cessation of ovulation and menstruation in human females, as a result of changes in the levels of sex hormones (especially estrogen) produced in the woman's body. (4)

meritocracy A system in which social rewards are distributed on the basis of achievement. (8)

microperspective An approach to studying social structure that focuses on detailed analysis of human activities and events. (Compare **macroperspective**.) (5)

midlife crisis A condition of middle adulthood, usually in men, characterized by discontent, actions that are out of character, and, sometimes, life changes in an attempt to recapture vanishing youth. (4)

military-industrial complex The web of common interests among high officials in the Pentagon and defense industries. (15)

minimal state A state in which the government does no more than is absolutely necessary to maintain national autonomy and internal order. (Compare **welfare state**.) (14)

minority group A category of people who, because of physical or cultural characteristics, are singled out for differential and unequal treatment and thus regard themselves as objects of collective discrimination. (9)

mob A pejorative term for crowds that are viewed as disorderly, riotous, or lawless. (17)

mobilization Smelser's fifth requirement for collective behavior; the actions of a leader who suggests a course of behavior and provides a model for behavior. (17)

modified extended family A network of relatives who live in separate residences but maintain ties with one another. (11)

momentum factor The continued growth of populations (regardless of family size) owing to the fact that a large percentage of the populations of Third World countries are in or near their childbearing years. (16)

monogamy A marriage involving only one man and one woman at one time. (11)

monopoly A firm that controls an entire industry, eliminating competition. (15)

moral entrepreneurs According to Becker, individuals who make it their business to see that offenses are recognized and that offenders are treated as such. (7)

mores Sacred norms, violations of which are almost unthinkable. (3)

multiculturalism The view that there is strength in cultural diversity and that society should respect cultural differences rather than require cultural sameness. (9)

multinational corporation A corporation with holdings and subsidiaries in several different nations. (15)

nativism The view that majority institutions and privileges must be protected from immigrant influences. (9)

net growth rate The percentage increase in a population, taking into account immigration and emigration as well as birthrates and death rates. (16)

network A web of social relationships that connects an individual to other people, directly and indirectly. (6)

neutralization The rationalization of one's own deviant behavior, in ways that relieve feelings of guilt and turn aside other people's expressions of disapproval. (7)

new extended family An extended family resulting from current economic conditions such as flat or declining wages or the high cost of housing. (11)

nomothetic explanation An explanation based on general or universal factors rather than individual, specific ones. (1)

norm of reciprocity The rule that demands that people respond in kind to certain behavior. (6)

norms Specific rules or sets of rules about what people should or should not do, say, or think in a given situation. (3)

nuclear family A type of family consisting of a mother, father, and their dependent children who form an independent household. (11)

oligopoly The domination of an industry by a small number of large companies. (15)

open system A society in which a person's social position is achieved on the basis of individual ability and effort; characterized by the attempt to provide equal opportunity to all. (Compare **closed system.**) (8)

organic solidarity The concept that all members of a society are interdependent because division of labor and specialization create differences in experiences and values; in Durkheim's view, the basis for modern, industrial societies. (Compare **mechanical solidarity.**) (16)

organized crime A violation of the law committed by an organization that exists primarily to provide, and profit from, illegal goods and services. (7)

out-group A group one feels opposed to or in competition with. (Compare **in-group.**) (6)

participant observation A method of sociological research in which the sociologist joins the people being studied in their daily lives and activities, trying to note their understandings and behaviors in as much detail as possible. (Also known as **field study.**) (2)

peer group An informal, social group whose members have the same social status, are usually about the same age, and interact frequently. (6)

personality The individual's characteristic patterns of behavior and thought. (4)

personality theory The view that participants in social movements are deviant or troubled and that they participate to satisfy their personality needs, rather than to address actual grievances. (Compare **mass-society theory.**) (17)

play stage A stage of human development during which children pretend to be other people, thus vicariously experiencing different perspectives and ultimately acquiring their own sense of themselves. (4)

pluralism A pattern of intergroup relations in which ethnic and racial groups maintain their own language, religion, and customs and tend to socialize mainly among themselves. (9)

political action committee (PAC) An organization formed to collect small contributions from large numbers of people for a candidate who supports its cause. (14)

political party A collectivity organized to gain and hold legitimate control of government. (14)

politics The social process by which people gain, use, and lose power. (14)

polyandry The marriage of one woman to two or more men at the same time. (11)

polygamy The marriage of one man to two or more women or one woman to two or more men at the same time. (11)

polygyny The marriage of one man to two or more women at the same time. (11)

poverty line The U.S. federal government's estimate of a minimal budget for individuals or families. (8)

power According to Weber, the ability to control what other individuals and groups do, regardless of their wishes or resistance. (See **authority**.) (8, 14)

precipitating incident Smelser's fourth condition for collective behavior; the dramatic event that confirms people's fears and suspicions and focuses their attention. (17)

prejudice An unfavorable and rigid opinion of members of a social category. (9)

presentation of the self The ways in which people attempt to direct and control the impression they make on others and the way others see them. (6)

prestige The degree of respect or esteem a person receives from others. (8)

primary deviance The initial violation of a social rule. (Compare **secondary deviance**.) (7)

primary group An association based on ongoing, personal, intimate relationships and strong feelings of mutual identification. (Compare **secondary group**.) (4, 6)

productivity The ratio of goods produced to human effort. (15)

profane That which is ordinary and may be treated casually. (Compare **sacred**.) (13)

protest movement A grassroots effort to change established policies and practices. (14)

race A category of people who see themselves and are seen by others as different because of characteristics that are assumed to be inherited. (9)

racism The belief that a racial group is innately inferior and that this justifies discrimination against and exploitation of members of that race. (9)

random assignment The random division of subjects into experimental and control groups. (2)

rational-legal authority Authority that is based on and limited by a formal system of rules or laws. (Compare **charismatic authority**; **traditional authority**.) (14)

real culture Norms and values that people may not openly or formally admit to but follow nonetheless. (Compare **ideal culture**.) (3, 12)

rebels Merton's term for people who reject both the values and the norms of their society, substituting new goals and new means of achieving them. (7)

reference group A group or social category that an individual uses as a guide in developing his or her values, attitudes, behavior, and self-image. (4, 6)

rehabilitation An approach to social control which holds that imprisonment should not only punish criminals but also reform them and provide them with skills that will enable them to become law-abiding citizens after release from prison. (7)

relative deprivation A condition in which people feel deprived in relation to the group with which they compare themselves. (17)

religion A set of institutionalized beliefs and practices that deal with the ultimate meaning of life. (13)

replication The repeating of a research study with another group of subjects at another place and time; may also include slight modifications in the method. (2)

representative democracy A political system in which citizens elect representatives who set policies and enact laws in the people's name. (14)

representative sampling A sampling technique in which each member of the population being studied has an equal chance of being selected. (2)

resocialization The process of unlearning norms and values that were adaptive and culturally appropriate in the past in order to take on new social positions and roles. (4)

retreatists Merton's term for people who have given up both on socially approved goals and on the means for attaining them. (7)

retribution An approach to social control which holds that criminals must pay back society for the crimes they committed and that the sanction should be based on the crime, not the criminal. (7)

rising expectations Davies's theory that improvements in people's economic and political situation cause them to expect a better life and when their hopes do not materialize, they see their situation as intolerable and civil unrest may occur. (17)

rites of passage Rituals or ceremonies to mark the transition from one stage of life to another. (4)

ritual A formal, stylized enactment of religious beliefs. (13)

ritualists Merton's term for people who are so compulsive about following social rules that they lose sight of the goals. (7)

role The collection of culturally defined rights, obligations, expectations, and emotions that accompany a social status. (5)

role conflict A situation in which the different positions an individual occupies make incompatible demands. (5)

role set The cluster of different social relationships in which a person becomes involved because he or she occupies a particular social status. (5)

role strain A situation in which a single status makes contradictory demands on the individual. (5)

sacred That which is holy, inspires awe, and must be treated with respect. (Compare **profane**.) (13)

sample That portion of the population under investigation that a researcher actually studies. (2)

sanctions Socially imposed rewards and punishments by which people are encouraged to conform to norms. (3, 7)

Sapir-Whorf hypothesis The idea, proposed by Edward Sapir and Benjamin Lee Whorf, that our language causes us to pay attention to certain things and ignore others. (3)

school choice A plan that allows parents to choose which school their children will attend regardless of the district in which they live. (12)

schooling Formal instruction in a classroom setting. (12)

science A set of agreed-upon procedures for establishing and explaining facts. (2)

scientific proposition A statement about the nature of a concept or about the relationship between two or more concepts. (2)

secondary deviance Deviance that results from people's reactions to the initial violation of a social rule. (Compare **primary deviance**.) (7)

secondary group An impersonal association whose members' relationships are limited and instrumental; created to achieve a specific goal. (Compare **primary group**.) (6)

sect A religious organization that asserts its unique legitimacy but stands apart from society. (13)

secularization The removal of religious control over social institutions and individual behavior. (13)

segregation A practice wherein laws or customs impose physical and social separation on racial or ethnic minorities, denying them equal rights and thus institutionalizing the privileges of the dominant group and prejudice against the minority groups. (9)

self The individual's sense of identity or "who I am." (4)

self-fulfilling prophecy A false prediction that influences behavior in such a way that the prediction comes true. (12)

serial monogamy One exclusive, legally sanctioned, but relatively short-lived marriage after another. (11)

service and information economy An economy in which most occupations are not directly involved with production. (15)

sex A person's biological identity as male or female. (10)

sex role The behavior, attitudes, and motivations that a culture defines as appropriate for males or females—that is, as masculine or feminine. (10)

sexual harassment Discrimination in which sexual advances, requests for sexual favors, or demeaning sexual references are a condition for employment or promotion and/or create a work environment that is hostile, intimidating, or offensive. (10)

sexual orientation An individual's attraction to members of the opposite sex, the same sex, or both. (10)

significant others People whose evaluations an individual holds in high esteem. (4)

slavery A practice wherein members of a group are kidnapped, held captive, forced to work for their captors, and treated as property. (9)

social category   People classified together because they share a certain characteristic, such as being left-handed. (6)

social class   A grouping of individuals who have similar statuses or positions in the social hierarchy and thus share similar political and economic interests. (8)

social control   Any effort to prevent and/or correct deviant behavior. (7)

social forces   Forces beyond the control of any individual, which can be explained only in terms of social patterns, not in terms of individual psychology. (1)

social group   A number of people who feel a common identity based on shared norms and goals and who interact regularly in a structured way. (6)

social identity   A person's sense of who and what he or she is derived from the positions the person holds in society. (6)

social institution   A relatively stable set of norms and values, statuses and roles, and groups and organizations that provides a structure for behavior in a particular area of social life. (1, 5)

social interaction   Mutual or reciprocal actions between people in which one person's actions depend on the actions of another and vice versa. (6)

social mobility   Movement up or down the socio-economic ladder that changes a person's status in society. (A move up the ladder is called *upward mobility*; a move down, *downward mobility*.) (8)

social movement   The (more or less) organized effort of a large number of people to produce some social change. (17)

social relationship   A connection between individuals that is shaped by intersecting roles and patterned interaction. (5)

social revolution   A rapid, fundamental transformation of a country's political system, social class structure, and dominant ideology. (17)

social stratification   The division of a society into layers (or social classes) whose occupants have unequal access to social opportunities and rewards. (5, 8)

social structure   The framework of society, consisting of the social positions, networks of relationships, and institutions that hold a society together and shape people's opportunities and experiences. (1, 5)

socialization   The process whereby one acquires a sense of personal identity and learns what people in the surrounding culture believe and how they expect one to behave. (3, 4)

society   An autonomous population whose members are subject to the same political authority, occupy a common territory, and have a common culture and a sense of shared identity. (5)

sociological concept   A general, abstract idea that applies to a number of individual cases and identifies similarities between otherwise diverse social phenomena. (2)

sociological imagination   The ability to see the interplay of biography and history and the connections between public issues and private troubles. (1)

sociology   The systematic study of the groups and societies in which people live, how social structures and cultures are created and maintained or changed, and how they affect our behavior. (1)

status   The position an individual occupies in society. (See **achieved status**; **ascribed status**; **master status**.) (5, 8)

status competition   The quest for prestige and social esteem. (12)

status inconsistency   A situation in which one marker of a person's social standing is out of sync with the others; occurs, for example, when a person with a doctorate drives a cab for a living. (8)

stereotype   An overgeneralization about a group and its members that goes beyond existing evidence. (9)

structural conduciveness   Smelser's first condition for collective behavior; an element within the social structure that invites or drives people to depart from convention. (17)

structural mobility   A change in social position that occurs because technological innovations, urbanization, economic booms or busts, wars, or other events have altered the number and kinds of occupations available in a society. (8)

structural strain   Smelser's second condition for collective behavior; the tension that develops when people sense an immediate but ambiguous threat against which they feel helpless. (17)

subculture   A set of shared understandings, behaviors, objects, and vocabulary that distinguish members of a category or group from other members of the larger society. (3)

superego According to Freud, the part of the personality that contains internalized representations of society's norms and values, especially as taught by parents. (See **ego; id**.) (4)

survey A research method involving the use of standardized questionnaires, interviews, or both to gather data on a large population. (2)

symbol Something (an object, sound, or gesture) that expresses or evokes meaning. (3)

symbolic crusade According to Gusfield, an effort by members of a social class or ethnic group to preserve, defend, or enhance their position in relation to other groups in society. (7)

symbolic interaction The symbolic communication contained in facial expressions, gestures, and, especially, language. (4)

symbolic interactionism An approach to sociological analysis that stresses the basic role of language and other symbols in the social construction of both individual identity and social relationships. (2)

technology A culture's body of practical knowledge and equipment intended to enhance the effectiveness of human labor and alter the environment for human use. (3)

theoretical assumption An untested idea, such as a notion about the nature of human behavior or social systems. (2)

theoretical orientation A general theory that attempts to explain all (or the most important parts of) social life. (2)

theory A summary of existing knowledge that suggests guidelines for interpreting new information. (2)

theory of the middle range A theory limited in scope and generality that relates closely to the empirical data. (2)

Third World The relatively poor nations of the southern hemisphere. (15)

tokenism The practice of making only a token effort, for example, in hiring members of minority groups. (6)

totalitarianism An authoritarian political system in which the ruling party not only controls the government but also regulates social, economic, intellectual, cultural, and spiritual activities. (14)

totem A sacred emblem that members of a group or clan treat with reverence and awe. (13)

tracking Assigning students to different classes or programs on the basis of perceived ability and interests. (12)

traditional authority Authority that is based on and limited by custom. (Compare **charismatic authority; rational-legal authority**.) (14)

urbanization An increase in the percentage of a population living in urban settlements and a resulting extension of the influence of urban culture and lifestyles. (16)

values Broad, abstract, shared standards of what is right, desirable, and worthy of respect. (3)

variable Any condition that can change or have different values, qualities, or characteristics. (See **dependent variable; independent variable**.) (2)

wealth The sum total of a person's assets, such as stocks, real estate, and savings accounts. (8)

welfare state A state in which the government assumes varying degrees of responsibility for the well-being of citizens (e.g., by providing child care, health programs, university tuition, and unemployment compensation). (14)

white-collar crime Any violation of the law committed by middle- and upper-middle-class people in the course of their business and social lives. (7)

world system An economic network that links the nations of the world into a single socioeconomic unit. (5)

zero population growth The point at which birthrates and death rates are roughly equal and thus the population is stable. (16)

References

Abraham, K. *Who Are the Promise Keepers? Understanding the Christian Men's Movement.* New York: Doubleday, 1994.

Abrahamian, V. "Structural Causes of the Iranian Revolution." In J. Goldstone (ed.), *Revolutions,* pp. 119–127. San Diego: Harcourt Brace Jovanovich, 1985.

Adams, T. K., G. J. Duncan, and W. L. Rodgers. "The Persistence of Urban Poverty." In F. R. Harris and R. W. Wilkins (eds.), *Quiet Riots: Race and Poverty in the United States,* pp. 78–99. New York: Pantheon, 1988.

Adler, J., with G. Carroll, V. Smith, and P. Rogers. "Innocents Lost." *Newsweek* (November 14, 1994), pp. 26–30.

Adler, P. A., and P. Adler. "Everyday Life in Sociology." *Annual Review of Sociology* 13 (1987), pp. 217–235.

Ahlburg, D. A., and C. J. De Vita. "New Realities of the American Family." *Population Bulletin* 46, 2 (1992), pp. 1–44.

Ahlstrom, S. E. *A Religious History of the American People,* vols. 1 and 2. Garden City, NY: Doubleday/Image, 1975.

Ahmad, E. "Comments of Skocpol." *Theory and Society* 11 (1982), pp. 293–299.

Aldrich, H. E., and P. V. Marsden. "Environments and Organizations." In N. J. Smelser (ed.), *Handbook of Sociology,* pp. 361–392. Newbury Park, CA: Sage, 1988.

Alexander, J. C. "Watergate and Durkheimian Sociology." In *Durkheimian Sociology: Cultural Studies,* pp. 187–224. New York: Cambridge University Press, 1988.

Ambler, J. S. "Who Benefits from Education Choice? Some Evidence from Europe." In E. Cohn (ed.), *Market Approaches to Education,* pp. 353–379. New York: Pergamon, 1997.

American Psychiatric Association (APA). Task Force for Day-Care for Preschool Children. "Day Care for Early Preschool Children: Implications for the Child and the Family." *American Journal of Psychiatry* 150, 21 (1993), pp. 1281–1287.

Amnesty International. "Death Penalty Facts and Figures." 1995, www.amnesty.org.

Anderson, J. "The Formation of Modern States." In David Held et al. (eds.), *States and Societies.* New York: New York University Press, 1983.

Andreasen, M. S. "Evolution in the Family's Use of Television: Normative Data from Industry and Academe." In J. Bryant (ed.), *Television and the American Family,* pp. 3–55. Hillsdale, NJ: Erlbaum, 1990.

Arias, I., M. Samios, and K. D. O'Leary. "Prevalence and Correlates of Physical Aggression during Courtship." *Journal of Interpersonal Violence* 2 (1987), pp. 82–90.

Arjomand, S. "Iran's Islamic Revolution in Comparative Perspective." *World Politics* 38, 3 (1986), pp. 383–414.

Armor, D. J. "After Busing: Education and Choice." *The Public Interest* 95 (Spring 1989), pp. 24–37.

Asch, S. E. *Social Psychology.* Englewood Cliffs, NJ: Prentice-Hall, 1952.

Ashmore, R. D., F. K. Del Boca, and A. J. Wohlers. "Gender Stereotypes." In R. D. Asmore and F. K. Del Boca (eds.), *The Social Psychology of Female-Male Relationships,* pp. 69–119. Orlando, FL: Academic Press, 1986.

Astin, A. W. "Educational 'Choice': Its Appeal May be Illusory." *Sociology of Education* 65 (1992), pp. 255–259.

Attorney General's Task Force on Family Violence. U.S. Department of Justice. Washington, DC, 1984.

Auletta, K. *The Underclass.* New York: Random House, 1982.

Avis, N. E., D. Brambilla, S. M. McKinlay, and K. Vass. *A Longitudinal Analysis of the Association between Menopause and Depression: Results from the Massachusetts Women's Health Study.* Watertown, MA: New England Research Institute, 1992.

Babbie, E. *The Practice of Social Research,* 7th ed. Belmont, CA: Wadsworth, 1995.

Baber, A. *Naked at the Gender Gap.* New York: Birch Lane Press, 1992.

Bagdikian, B. H. *The Media Monopoly,* 5th ed. Boston: Beacon Press, 1997.

Bailey, J. M., and R. Pillard. "A Genetic Study of Male Sexual Orientation." *Archives of General Psychiatry* 48 (December 1991), pp. 1089–1096.

Bailey, T. "Black Employment Opportunities." In C. Brecher and R. D. Horton (eds.), *Setting Municipal Priorities, 1990,* pp. 80–111. New York: New York University Press, 1989.

Bailey, W. C. "Murder, Capital Punishment, and Television: Execution Publicity and Homicide Rates." *American Sociological Review* 55 (October 1990), pp. 628–633.

Baker, D. P., and D. P. Jones. "Creating Gender Equality: Cross-National Gender Stratification and Mathematical Performance." *Sociology of Education* 66 (1993), pp. 91–103.

Baker, S. G. "Gender, Ethnicity, and Homelessness." *American Behavioral Scientist* 37 (1994), pp. 476–504.

Baker, W. E. *Networking Smart: How to Build Relationships for Personal and Organizational Success.* New York: McGraw-Hill, 1994.

Baker, W. E., and R. R. Faulkner. "Role as Resource in the Hollywood Film Industry." *American Journal of Sociology* 2 (September 1991), pp. 279–309.

Bane, M. J., and D. Ellwood. *Welfare Realities: From Rhetoric to Reform.* Cambridge, MA: Harvard University Press, 1994.

Barak, G. *Gimme Shelter: A Social History of Homelessness in Contemporary America.* New York: Praeger, 1992.

Barber, R. *Strong Democracy.* Berkeley: University of California Press, 1983.

Bard, M., and J. Zacker. "Assaultiveness and Alcohol Use in Family Disputes: Police Perceptions." *Criminology* 12 (1974), pp. 181–192.

Barker-Plummer, B. "News as a Political Resource: Media Strategies and Political Identity in the U.S. Women's Movement." *Critical Studies in Mass Communication* 12 (1995), pp. 306–324.

Barnet, R. J. *The Lean Years: Politics in an Age of Scarcity.* New York: Simon & Schuster, 1980.

Barrows, S., and R. Room. *Drinking: Behavior and Belief in Modern History.* Berkeley: University of California Press, 1991.

Bassis, M. "The Campus as Frog Pond: A Reassessment." *American Journal of Sociology* 82 (May 1977), pp. 1318–1326.

Baumrind, D. "Child Care Practices Anteceding Three Patterns of Preschool Behavior." *Genetic Psychology Monographs* 75 (1967), pp. 43–88.

Baumrind, D. "Current Patterns of Parental Authority." *Developmental Psychology Monographs* 4, 1, Pt. 2 (1971).

Baumrind, D. "New Directions in Socialization Research." *American Psychologist* 35 (1980), pp. 639–652.

Baumrind, D. "Rearing Competent Children." In W. Damon (ed.), *Child Development Today and Tomorrow.* San Francisco: Jossey-Bass, 1989.

Bearman, P. S. "The Social Structure of Suicide." *Sociological Forum* 6, 3 (1991), pp. 501–524.

Beck, R. W., and S. H. Beck. "The Incidence of Extended Households among Middle-Aged Black and White Women: Estimates from a 5-Year Panel Study." *Journal of Family Issues* 10 (June 1989), pp. 147–168.

Becker, E. *The Denial of Death.* New York: Free Press, 1973.

Becker, H. *Art Worlds.* Berkeley: University of California Press, 1984.

Becker, H. *Doing Things Together.* Evanston, IL: Northwestern University Press, 1986.

Becker, H. S. *The Outsiders.* New York: Free Press, 1963.

Bedell, K. B. (ed.). *Yearbook of American and Canadian Churches, 1997.* Nashville, TN: Abingdon Press, 1997, p. 2.

Bell, D. *The Coming of Post-Industrial Society.* New York: Basic Books, 1973.

Bell, D. "The Social Framework of the Information Society." In M. Dertouzos and J. Moses (eds.), *The Computer Age: A Twenty Year View,* pp. 163–211. Cambridge, MA: MIT Press, 1979.

Bellah, R. N. "Religious Evolution." *American Sociological Review* 29 (June 1964), pp. 358–374.

Bellah, R. N. "Civil Religion in America." *Daedalus* 96 (Winter 1967), pp. 1–21.

Bellah, R. N. *The Broken Covenant: American Civil Religion in Time of Trial.* New York: Seabury, 1975.

Bellah, R. N., and P. E. Hammond. *Varieties of Civil Religion.* New York: Harper & Row, 1980.

Bellah, R. N., R. Madsen, W. M. Sullivan, A. Swidler, and S. M. Tipton. *Habits of the Heart: Individualism and Commitment in American Life.* Berkeley: University of California Press, 1985.

Bender, W., and M. Smith. "Population, Food, and Nutrition." *Population Bulletin* 51, 4 (1997).

Benjamin, L. *The Black Elite.* Chicago: Nelson-Hall, 1991.

Bennett, C. *The Asian and Pacific Island Population in the U.S., March 1991 and 1990.* Washington, DC: U.S. Bureau of the Census, 1992.

Berardo, D. H., C. L. Shehan, and G. R. Leslie. "A Residue of Tradition: Jobs, Careers, and Spouses' Time in Housework." *Journal of Marriage and the Family* 49 (May 1987), pp. 381–390.

Berger, P. L. *Invitation to Sociology: A Humanistic Perspective.* New York: Anchor Books, 1963.

Berheide, C. W. "Women Still 'Stuck' in Low-Level Jobs." *Women in Public Service Bulletin* (Fall 1992), pp. 1–4.

Berk, R. A. *Collective Behavior.* New York: Brown, 1974.

Berk, R. A. "Arresting Offenders in Spouse Abuse Incidents: What the Scientific Evidence Shows." In R. J. Gelles and D. Loseke (eds.), *Current Controversies on Family Violence,* pp. 323–336. Newbury Park, CA: Sage, 1993.

Berk, R. A., A. Campbell, R. Klap, and B. Western. "The Deterrent Effect of Arrest in Incidents of Domestic Violence: A Bayesian Analysis of Four Field Experiments." *American Sociological Review,* 57 (1992), pp. 698–708.

Berk, R. A., G. K. Smyth, and L. W. Sherman. "When Random Assignment Fails: Some Lessons from the Minneapolis Spouse Abuse Experiment." *Journal of Quantitative Criminology* 4 (1988), pp. 209–223.

Berkowitz, D. "Television News Source and News Channels: A Study in Agenda Building." *Journalism Quarterly* 64 (1987), pp. 508–513.

Berkowitz, L. *Aggression: Its Causes, Consequences, and Control.* New York: McGraw-Hill, 1993.

Berle, A. A., Jr., and G. C. Means. *The Modern Corporation and Public Policy.* New York: Harcourt Brace & World, 1932.

Bernard, J. "The Good-Provider Role: Its Rise and Fall." In M. S. Kimmel and M. A. Messner (eds.), *Men's Lives,* 2d ed., pp. 203–221. New York: Macmillan, 1992.

Berndt, T., and G. W. Ladd (eds.). *Peer Relationships in Child Development.* New York: Wiley, 1989.

Best, J. *Threatened Children: Rhetoric and Concern about Child-Victims.* Chicago: University of Chicago Press, 1990.

Bianchi, S., and D. Spain. "Women, Work and Family in America." *Population Bulletin* 51, 3 (December 1996), pp. 1–48.

Bianchi, S., and D. Spain. "U.S. Women Make Workplace Progress." *Population Today* 25 (1997), pp. 1–2.

Bishop, D. M., and C. E. Frazier. "The Influence of Race in Juvenile Justice Processing." *Journal of Research in Crime and Delinquency* 25 (August 1988), pp. 242–263.

Bjarkman, P. C. *Hoopla: A Century of College Basketball.* Indianapolis, IN: Masters Press, 1996.

Black, D. J. *The Manners and Customs of Police.* New York: Academic Press, 1980.

Black, D. J., and A. J. Reiss, Jr. "Police Control of Juveniles." *American Sociological Review* 35 (February 1970), pp. 63–78.

Blankenhorn, D. *Fatherless America: Confronting Our Most Urgent Social Problem.* New York: Basic Books, 1995.

Blair, S. L., and D. T. Lichter. "Measuring the Division of Household Labor: Gender Segregation of Housework among American Couples." *Journal of Family Issues* 12, 1 (March 1991), pp. 91–113.

Blau, P. M. *Exchange and Power in Social Life.* New York: Wiley, 1964.

Blau, P. M., and O. D. Duncan. *The American Occupational Structure.* New York: Free Press, 1967.

Blau, P. M., and M. W. Meyer. *Bureaucracy in Modern Society,* 3d ed. New York: Random House, 1987.

Blau, P. M., and W. R. Scott. *Formal Organizations: A Comparative Approach.* San Francisco: Chandler, 1962.

Blauner, R. *Alienation and Freedom.* Chicago: University of Chicago Press, 1964.

Bloom, B. L., R. L. Niles, and A. M. Tatcher. "Sources of Marital Dissatisfaction among Newly Separated Persons." *Journal of Family Issues* 6 (1985), pp. 359–373.

Blum, T. C., D. L. Fields, and J. S. Goodman. "Organization-Level Determinants of Women in Management," *Academy of Management Journal* 37, 2 (1994), pp. 241–268.

Blumberg, R. L. "A General Theory of Gender Stratification." In R. Collins (ed.), *Sociological Theory,* pp. 23–101. San Francisco: Jossey-Bass, 1984.

Blumer, H. *Collective Behavior.* In R. E. Park (ed.), *An Outline of the Principles of Sociology.* New York: Barnes & Noble, 1939.

Blumer, H. *Symbolic Interactionism: Perspective and Methods.* Englewood Cliffs, NJ: Prentice-Hall, 1969.

Blumstein, A. "Youth Violence, Guns, and the Illicit-Drug Industry." *Journal of Criminal Law and Criminology* 86 (1995), pp. 10–36.

Bly, R. *Iron John: A Book about Men.* Reading, MA: Addison-Wesley, 1990.

Bobo, L., and R. A. Smith. "Antipoverty Politics, Affirmative Action, and Racial Attitudes." In S. H. Danzinger, G. D. Sandefur, and D. H. Weinberg (eds.), *Confronting Poverty: Prescriptions for Change,* pp. 365–395. Cambridge, MA: Harvard University Press, 1994.

Bogert, C. "Life with Mother." *Newsweek* (January 20, 1997), pp. 41–46.

Bonner, R. "Land-Mine Treaty Agreement by 100 Countries Ready for Ratification after U.S. Withholds Signature." *The New York Times* (September 18, 1997), p. 42A.

Boocock, S. S. *Sociology of Education: An Introduction,* 2d ed. Boston: Houghton Mifflin, 1980.

Booth, A., and D. Johnson. "Premarital Cohabitation and Marital Success." *Journal of Family Issues* 2 (June 1988), pp. 255–272.

Bootzin, R. R., J. R. Acocella, and L. B. Alloy. *Abnormal Psychology: Current Perspectives,* 6th ed. New York: McGraw-Hill, 1993.

Boswell, T., and W. J. Dixon. "Marx's Theory of Rebellion: A Cross-National Analysis of Class Exploitation, Economic Development and Violent Revolt." *American Sociological Review* 58 (1993), pp. 681–702.

Boudon, R. *The Unintended Consequences of Social Action.* London: Macmillan, 1982.

Bourdieu, P. "Cultural Reproduction and Social Reproduction." In J. Karabel and A. H. Halsey (eds.), *Power and Ideology in Education,* pp. 487–511. New York: Oxford University Press, 1977.

Bourdieu, P. *Distinction: A Social Critique of the Judgment of Taste.* R. Nice (trans.). Cambridge, MA: Harvard University Press, 1984.

Bourdieu, P. "Social Space and Symbolic Power." *Sociological Theory* 7 (1989), pp. 14–25.

Bourque, L. *Defining Rape.* Durham, NC: Duke University Press, 1989.

Bouvier, L., and C. J. De Vita. "The Baby Boom—Entering Midlife." *Population Bulletin* 46 (November 1991).

Bowles, S., and H. Gintis. *Schooling in Capitalist America.* New York: Basic Books, 1976.

Bradshaw, Y. W., R. Noonan, L. Gash, and C. Buchmann Sershen. "Borrowing against the Future: Children and Third

World Indebtedness." *Social Forces* 71 (March 1993), pp. 629–656.

Braithwaite, J. "White Collar Crime." *Annual Review of Sociology* 11 (1985), pp. 1–25.

Braithwaite, J. D. "The Old and New Poor in Russia." In J. Klugman (ed.), *Poverty in Russia: Public Policy and Private Responses,* pp. 29–64. Washington, DC: World Bank, 1997.

Branegan, J. "Is Singapore a Model for the West?" *Time* (January 18, 1993), pp. 36–67.

Braude, L. *Work and Workers.* New York: Praeger, 1975.

Breault, K. D. "A Test of Durkheim's Theory of Religious and Family Integration, 1933–1980." *American Journal of Sociology* 92, 3 (1986), pp. 628–656.

Brennan, P. A., S. A. Mednick, and J. Volavka. "Biomedical Factors in Crime." In J. Q. Wilson and J. Petersilia (eds.), *Crime.* San Francisco: Institute for Contemporary Studies, 1995.

Brock, D. *The Real Anita Hill: The Untold Story.* New York: Free Press, 1994.

Broder, J. M. "The Climate Accord: The Overview; Clinton Adamant on 3d World Role in Climate Accord." *The New York Times* (December 12, 1997), pp. A1, A18.

Brody, J. "Can Drugs 'Treat' Menopause? Amid Doubt Women Must Decide." *The New York Times* (May 19, 1992), p. C1ff.

Bromley, D. A. *The President's Scientists: Reminiscences of a White House Science Advisor.* New Haven, CT: Yale University Press, 1994.

Bronfenbrenner, U., P. McClelland, E. Wethington, P. Moen, and Stephen J. Ceci. *The State of America.* New York: Simon & Schuster, 1996.

Bronner, E. "Colleges Look for Answers to Racial Gaps in Testing." *The New York Times* (November 8, 1997), pp. A1, A12.

Brown, B. B. "Peer Groups and Peer Cultures." In S. S. Feldman and G. R. Elliott (eds.), *At the Threshold: The Developing Adolescent.* Cambridge, MA: Harvard University Press, 1990.

Brown, B. W. "Parent's Discipline of Children in Public Places." *The Family Coordinator* 28, 1 (1979), pp. 67–71.

Brown, D. E. *Human Universals.* New York: McGraw-Hill, 1991.

Brown, L. R. "The Changing World Food Prospect: The Nineties and Beyond." *Worldwatch Paper* 85 (October 1988), Worldwatch Institute.

Brown, L. R. "Tough Choices: Facing the Challenge of Food Scarcity." *USA Today* (July 1997), pp. 30–33.

Brown, M., and A. Goldin. *Collective Behavior: A Review and Reinterpretation of the Literature.* Pacific Palisades, CA: Goodyear, 1973.

Bryjak, G. J. "Is It Possible to Rescue Sub-Saharan Africa?" *USA Today* (July 1997), pp. 34–36.

Buchmann, M. *The Script of Life in Modern Society: Entry into Adulthood on a Changing World.* Chicago: University of Chicago Press, 1989.

Bumpass, L. L. "What's Happening to the Family? Interactions between Demographic and Institutional Change." *Demography* 27, 4 (1990), p. 485.

Bumpass, L. L., T. C. Martin, and J. Sweet. "The Impact of Family Background and Early Marital Factors on Marital Disruption." *Journal of Family Issues* 12 (1991), pp. 22–42.

Bumpass, L. L., J. Sweet, and A. J. Cherlin. "The Role of Cohabitation in Declining Rates of Marriage." *Journal of Marriage and the Family* 53 (November 1991), pp. 913–927.

Bumpass, L. L., J. Sweet, and T. C. Martin. "Changing Patterns of Remarriage." *Journal of Marriage and the Family* 52 (August 1990), pp. 747–756.

Burkette, E. "God Created Me to Be a Slave." *The New York Times Magazine* (October 12, 1997), pp. 56–60.

Burns, J. F. "Lowest-Caste Hindu Takes Office as India's President." *The New York Times* (July 26, 1997).

Butsch, R. "Class and Gender in Four Decades of Television Situation Comedy: *Plus ça* Change. . . ." *Critical Studies in Mass Communication* 9 (1992), pp. 387–399.

Butterfield, F. "Crime Keeps on Falling, but Prisons Keep on Filling." *The New York Times* (September 20, 1997), pp. E1, E4.

Byock, I. *Dying Well: The Prospect for Growth at the End of Life.* New York: Riverhead Books, 1997.

Cairncross, F. *The Death of Distance: How the Communications Revolution Will Change Our Lives.* Boston: Harvard Business School Press, 1997.

Calhoun, C. "The Political Economy of Work." In S. G. McNall (ed.), *Political Economy: Critique of American Society,* pp. 272–299. Glenview, IL: Scott, Foresman, 1981.

Calhoun, C. *The Question of Class Struggle: Social Foundations of Popular Radicalism during the Industrial Revolution.* Chicago: University of Chicago Press, 1982.

Calhoun, C. "Industrialization and Social Radicalism." *Theory and Society* 12 (1983), pp. 485–504.

Calhoun, C. "Computer Technology: Large Scale Social Integration and the Local Community" *Urban Affairs Quarterly* 8 (1986), pp. 204–228.

Calhoun, C. (ed). *Social Theory and the Politics of Identity.* Cambridge, MA: Blackwell, 1994.

Cancio, A. S., T. D. Evans, and D. J. Maume, Jr. "Rediscovering the Declining Significance of Race: Racial Differences in Early Career Wages." *American Sociological Review* 61 (August 1996), pp. 541–556.

Caplovitz, D. *Making Ends Meet: How Families Cope with Inflation and Recession.* Beverly Hills, CA: Sage, 1979.

Caplow, T. *Two against One: Coalitions in Triads.* Englewood Cliffs, NJ: Prentice-Hall, 1969.

Caringella-MacDonald, S. "Parallels and Pitfalls: The Aftermath of Legal Reform for Sexual Assault, Marital Rape, and Domestic Violence Victims." *Journal of Interpersonal Violence* 3, 2 (1988), pp. 147–189.

Carnegie Forum on Education and the Economy. *A Nation Prepared: Teachers for the 21st Century.* Washington, DC: Carnegie Forum on Education and the Economy, 1986.

Carnegie Foundation for the Advancement of Teaching. "Future Teachers: Will There Be Enough Good Ones?" *Change* (September–October 1986), pp. 27–30.

Casey, B., R. L. Nuttall, and E. Pezaris. "Mediators of Gender Differences in Mathematics College Entrance Test Scores: A Comparison of Spatial Skills and Internalized Beliefs and Anxieties." *Developmental Psychology* 33 (1997), p. 669.

Castells, M. *The City and the Grassroots: A Cross-Cultural Theory of Urban Social Movements.* Berkeley: University of California Press, 1983.

Castells, M. (ed.). "High Technology, Space and Society." *Urban Affairs Annual Reviews* 28 (1985).

Catalyst. *Census of Women Directors.* New York: Catalyst, 1995.

CBS News Poll. *The New York Times* (December 14, 1997), p. WK3.

Celis, W., III. "The Fight over National Standards." *Education Life* (August 1, 1993), pp. 14–16.

Chafe, W. H. *The American Woman: Her Changing Social, Economic, and Political Roles, 1920–1970.* New York: Oxford University Press, 1972.

Chafe, W. H. *The Paradox of Change: American Women in the Twentieth Century.* New York: Oxford University Press, 1991.

Chafetz, J. S. *Sex and Advantage: A Comparative, Macro-Structural Theory of Sex Stratification.* Towota, NJ: Rowman and Allanheld, 1984.

Chagnon, N. *Yanomamö: The Fierce People.* New York: Holt, Rinehart and Winston, 1968.

Chalkley, K. "Female Genital Mutilation: New Laws, Programs Try to End the Practice." *Population Today* (October 1997), pp. 4–5.

Chandler, A. *The Visible Hand.* Cambridge, MA: Harvard University Press, 1976.

Chandler, D. O. *Brother Number One: A Political Biography of Pol Pot.* Boulder, CO: Westview Press, 1992.

Chapman, F. S. "Executive Guilt: Who's Taking Care of the Children?" *Fortune* (February 16, 1987), pp. 30–37.

Chase, S. "The Seventeen Survey: My Generation." *Seventeen* (October 1989), pp. 95–106.

Chase-Dunn, C. "Urbanization in the World System." *Urban Affairs Annual Reviews* 26 (1984), pp. 111–122.

Cherlin, A. J. *Marriage, Divorce, and Remarriage,* rev. ed. Cambridge, MA: Harvard University Press, 1992.

Cherlin, A. J. *Public and Private Families: An Introduction.* New York: McGraw-Hill, 1996.

Cherlin, A. J., and F. F. Furstenberg, Jr. *The New American Grandparent: A Place in the Family, a Life Apart.* New York: Basic Books, 1986.

Cherlin, A. J., and F. F. Furstenberg, Jr. "Divorce Doesn't Always Hurt Kids." *The Washington Post* (March 19, 1989), p. C3.

Cherlin, A. J., F. F. Furstenberg, Jr., P. L. Chase-Landsdale, K. E. Kiernan, P. K. Robins, D. R. Morrison, and J. O. Teitler. "Longitudinal Studies of Effects of Divorce on Children in Great Britain and the United States." *Science* 252 (June 7, 1991), pp. 1386–1389.

Chevalier, L. *Laboring Classes and Dangerous Classes in Paris in the First Half of the 19th Century.* Princeton, NJ: Princeton University Press, 1981.

Chirot, D. *Social Change in the Twentieth Century.* New York: Harcourt Brace Jovanovich, 1977.

Chirot, D. "Changing Fashions in the Study of the Social Causes of Economic and Political Change." In J. F. Short (ed.), *The State of Sociology,* pp. 259–282. Beverly Hills, CA: Sage, 1981.

Chirot, D. *Social Change in the Twentieth Century,* 2d ed. San Diego: Harcourt Brace Jovanovich, 1986.

Clinard, M. B., and R. F. Meier. *Sociology of Deviant Behavior.* Fort Worth, TX: Harcourt Brace Jovanovich, 1992.

Clinton, H. R. *It Takes a Village: And Other Lessons Children Teach Us.* New York: Simon & Schuster, 1996.

"Clinton Insists on Third World Emission Role." *The New York Times* (December 12, 1997), pp. A1, A16.

Cloward, R., and L. Ohlin. *Delinquency and Opportunity.* Glencoe, IL: Free Press, 1960.

Cohen, J. E. *How Many People Can Earth Support?* New York: Norton, 1995.

Cohn, E. "Public and Private School Choices: Theoretical Considerations and Empirical Evidence." In E. Cohn (ed.), *Market Approaches to Education,* pp. 3–20. New York: Pergamon 1997.

Cole, J. (ed.). *The UCLA Television Violence Report 1997.* Los Angeles: UCLA Center for Communication Policy, 1997.

Coleman, J. *The Mathematics of Collective Action.* Chicago: Aldine, 1973.

Coleman, J. *The Asymmetric Society.* Syracuse, NY: Syracuse University Press, 1982.

Coleman, J. S. "Some Points on Choice in Education." *Sociology of Education* 65 (1992), pp. 260–262.

Coleman, J. S., and T. Hoffer. *Public and Private High Schools: The Impact of Communities.* New York: Basic Books, 1987.

Coleman, R. P., and L. Rainwater. *Social Standing in America: New Dimensions of Class.* New York: Basic Books, 1978.

Coller, S. A., and P. A. Resick. "Women's Attributions of Responsibility for Date Rape: The Influence of Empathy and Sex-Role Stereotyping." *Violence and Victims* 2, 2 (1987), pp. 115–125.

Collins, R. *The Credential Society.* New York: Academic Press, 1979.

Collins, R. "On the Microfoundations of Macrosociology." *American Journal of Sociology* 86 (1981), pp. 984–1014.

Collins, R. C. "Head Start: An Update of Program Effects." *Society for Research on Child Development Newsletter* (Summer 1983), pp. 1–2.

Committee on Education and Labor, U.S. House of Representatives. *Staff Report on Educational Policies and Practices: Their Impact on Education, on At-Risk Students and on Minority Teachers.* Washington, DC: U.S. Government Printing Office, 1988.

Congressional Quarterly. "Turnout Hits 64-Year-Low in Presidential Race." (January 21, 1989), pp. 135–138.

Conklin, J. E. *Criminology,* 4th ed. New York: Macmillan, 1992.

Conroy, D. W. "Puritans in Taverns: Law and Popular Culture in Colonial

Massachusetts, 1630–1720." In S. Barrows and R. Room (eds.), *Drinking Behavior and Belief in Modern History,* pp. 29–60. Berkeley: University of California Press, 1991.

Cook, K. "Linking Actors and Structures: An Exchange Network Analysis." In C. Calhoun, M. Meyer, and W. R. Scott (eds.), *Structures of Power and Constraint: Essays in Honor of Peter M. Blau.* New York: Cambridge University Press, 1990.

Cookson, P. W., Jr. *The Struggle for the Soul of American Education.* New Haven, CT: Yale University Press, 1994.

Cooley, C. H. *Human Nature and the Social Order.* New York: Scribner's, 1902.

Cooney, T. M., and P. Uhlenberg. "Support from Parents over the Life Course: The Adult Child's Perspective." *Social Forces* 71 (September 1992), pp. 63–84.

Coontz, S. *The Way We Never Were: American Families and the Nostalgia Trap.* New York: Basic Books, 1992.

Coontz, S. *The Way We Really Are: Coming to Terms with America's Changing Families.* New York: Basic Books, 1997.

Cooper, M. "Montana's Mother of All Militias." *The Nation* (May 22, 1995), pp. 714–721.

Cornbleth, C. "Knowledge in Curriculum and Teacher Education." *Social Education* (November–December 1987), pp. 513–516.

Cornell, C. P., and R. J. Gelles. "Adolescent to Parent Violence." *Urban Change Review* 15 (1982), pp. 8–14.

Corsaro, W. A. "Friendship in the Nursery School: Social Organization in a Peer Environment." In S. R. Asher and J. Gottman (eds.), *The Development of Children's Friendships,* pp. 207–241. New York: Cambridge University Press, 1981.

Corsaro, W. A., and D. Eder. "Children's Peer Cultures." *Annual Review of Sociology* 16 (1990), pp. 197–220.

Cose, E. "Census and the Complex Issue of Race." *Society* 34 (1997), pp. 9–13.

Coser, L. *Continuities in the Study of Social Conflict.* New York: Free Press, 1967.

Coser, L. *Masters of Sociological Thought,* 2d ed. New York: Harcourt Brace Jovanovich, 1977.

Couch, C. J. "Toward a Formal Theory of Social Processes." *Symbolic Interactionism* 15 (1992), pp. 117–134.

Counts, D. "Domestic Violence in Oceania: Conclusion." *Pacific Studies* 13, 3 (1990), pp. 225–254.

Cousins, A. N., and H. Nagpaul. *Urban Man and Society: A Reader in Urban Sociology.* New York: Knopf, 1970.

Cox, H. *The Secular City: Secularization and Urbanization in Theological Perspective.* New York: Macmillan, 1966.

Crosbie, P. *Interaction in Small Groups.* New York: Macmillan, 1975.

Crosbie-Burnett, M., A. Slyles, and J. Becker-Haven. "Exploring Stepfamilies from a Feminist Perspective." In S. M. Dornbusch and M. H. Strober (eds.), *Feminism, Children, and the New Families,* pp. 297–326. New York: Guildford Press, 1988.

Crossette, B. "Caste May Be India's Moral Achilles' Heel." *The New York Times* (October 20, 1996a), p. E3.

Crossette, B. "The 'Oldest Old,' 80 and Over, Are on the Increase Globally," *The New York Times* (December 22, 1996b), p. A5.

Crossette, B. "World Is Less Crowded Than Expected, the UN Reports." *The New York Times* (November 17, 1996c), p. A3.

Crossette, B. "Court Backs Eqypt's Ban on Mutilation." *The New York Times* (December 29, 1997a), p. A3.

Crossette, B. "The Unreal Thing: Un-American Ugly Americans." *The New York Times* (May 11, 1997b), pp. E1, E5.

Crossette, B. "What Modern Slavery Is, and Isn't." *The New York Times* (July 27, 1997c), www.nytimes.com/archives.

Cruikshank, M. "The Gay and Lesbian Liberation Movement." New York: Routledge, Chapman & Hall, 1992, pp. 69–70.

Currie, E., and J. H. Skolnick. "A Critical Note on Conceptions of Collective Behavior." *Annals of the American Academy of Political Science* 391 (1970), pp. 34–45.

Curtiss, S. *Genie: Psycholinguistic Study of a Modern Day Wild Child.* New York: Academic Press, 1977.

Czikszentmihalyi, C., and E. Rochberg-Halton. *The Meaning of Things.* Chicago: University of Chicago Press, 1982.

Czikszentmihalyi, M., and R. Larson. *Being Adolescent: Conflict and Growth in the Teenage Years.* New York: Basic Books, 1984.

Dalton, M. *Men Who Manage.* New York: Wiley, 1959.

Dan-Cohen, M. *Rights, Persons and Organizations.* Berkeley: University of California Press, 1986.

Daniels, L. A. "In Defense of Busing." *The New York Times Magazine* (April 17, 1983), pp. 34–37.

Danzinger, S., and P. Gottschalk. *American Unequal.* Cambridge, MA: Harvard University Press, 1995.

Danzinger, J. N. "Social Science and the Social Impacts of Computer Technology." *Social Science Quarterly* 66 (1986), pp. 3–21.

Darnton, J. "U.N. Faces the Refugee Crisis That Never Ends." *The New York Times* (August 8, 1994), pp. A1, A6.

Daro, D. "Current Trends in Child Abuse Reporting and Fatalities: NCPCA's 1995 Annual Fifty State Survey." *APSAC Advisor* 9 (1996), pp. 21–24.

Dash, L. *Rosa Lee: A Mother and Her Family in Urban America.* New York: Basic Books, 1996.

Davies, J. C. "The J-Curve of Rising and Declining Satisfactions as a Cause of Some Great Revolutions and a Contained Rebellion." In H. Graham and T. Gurr (eds.), *Violence in America: Historical and Comparative Perspectives,* pp. 547–576. New York: Bantam, 1969.

Davies, K. "Female Circumcision Triggers Debate on Rites versus Rights." *The Los Angeles Times* (July 14, 1996), p. A1.

Davis, F. *Fashion, Culture, and Identity.* Chicago: University of Chicago Press, 1992.

Davis, J. H., T. Kameda, C. Parks, M. Strasson, and S. Zimmerman. "Some Social Mechanics of Group Decision Making: The Distribution of Opinion, Polling Sequence, and Implications for Consensus." *Journal of Personality and Social Psychology* 57 (1989), pp. 1000–1012.

Davis, K. "Final Note on a Case of Extreme Isolation." *American Journal of Sociology* 50 (1947), pp. 432–437.

Davis, K. *Human Society.* New York: Macmillan, 1948.

Davis, K., and W. Moore. "Some Principles of Stratification." *American Sociological Review* 10 (April 1945), pp. 242–249.

Dawson, G., and A. Levy. "Arousal, Attention, and the Socioemotional Impairments of Individuals with Autism." In G. Dawson (ed.), *Autism: Nature, Diagnosis, and Treatment,* pp. 49–74. New York: Guilford Press, 1989.

Deal, T., and A. Kennedy. *Corporate Culture.* Reading, MA: Addison-Wesley, 1982.

Decourcy, M. *Inside Basketball: From the Playgrounds to the NBA.* New York: MetroBooks, 1996.

de Lone, R. H. *Small Futures: Inequality, Children, and the Failure of Liberal Reform.* New York: Harcourt Brace Jovanovich, 1979.

de Tocqueville, A. *The Old Regime and the French Revolution.* J. Bonner (trans.). New York: Harper and Brothers, 1856.

del Pinal, J., and A. Singer. "Generations of Diversity: Latinos in the United States."

Population Bulletin 52, 3 (October 1997), pp. 1–47.

Deng, Z., and D. J. Treiman. "The Impact of the Cultural Revolution on Trends in Educational Attainment in the People's Republic of China." *American Journal of Sociology* 103 (1997), pp. 391–428.

Diaz-Calderón, J. "The Fallacy of Referring to Hispanics as a Race." Paper presented at the 1997 National Conference of the National Association of African American Studies and the National Association of Hispanic and Latino Studies, San Antonio, TX, 1997.

Diekstra, R. F. W. "An International Perspective on the Epidemiology and Prevention of Suicide." In S. J. Blumer and D. J. Kupfer (eds.), *Suicide of the Life-Cycle.* Washington, DC: American Psychiatric Press, 1990.

Diener, E. "Effects of Prior Destructive Behavior, Anonymity, and Group Pressure on Deindividuation and Aggression." *Journal of Personality and Social Psychology* 33 (1976), pp. 497–507.

Dobash, R. E., and R. Dobash. *Violence against Wives: A Case against the Patriarchy.* New York: Free Press, 1979.

Dobash, R. P., R. E. Dobash, M. I. Wilson, and M. Daly. "The Myth of Sexual Symmetry in Marital Violence." *Social Problems* 39 (1992), pp. 71–91.

Domhoff, G. W. *Who Rules America?* Englewood Cliffs, NJ: Prentice-Hall, 1967.

Domhoff, G. W. *Who Rules America Now?* New York: Random House, 1983.

Dore, R. "Japan's Version of Managerial Capitalism." In T. A. Kochan and M. Useem (eds.), *Transforming Organizations,* pp. 17–27. New York: Oxford University Press, 1992.

Dornbusch, S. M., and K. D. Gray. "Single-Parent Families." In S. M. Dornbusch and M. H. Strober (eds.), *Feminism, Children, and the New Families,* pp. 274–296. New York: Guilford Press, 1988.

Drucker, P. *The Unseen Revolution: How Pension Fund Socialism Came to America.* New York: Harper & Row, 1976.

Duncan, A. *The Values, Aspirations, and Opportunities of the Urban Underclass.* Unpublished B.A. honors thesis. Cambridge, MA: Harvard University, 1987.

Dunford, F. W., D. Huizinga, and D. S. Elliott. "The Role of Arrest in Domestic Assault: The Omaha Police Experiment." *Criminology* 28, 2 (1990), pp. 183–206.

Dunn, J. *The Beginnings of Social Understanding.* Oxford: Blackwell, 1988.

Durkheim, E. *On the Division of Labor in Society.* G. Simpson (trans.). New York: Free Press, 1966. (Original work published 1893.)

Durkheim, E. *Suicide: A Study in Sociology.* New York: Free Press, 1951. (Original work published 1895.)

Durkheim, E. *Suicide.* J. A. Spaulding and G. Simpson (trans.). Glencoe, IL: Free Press, 1951. (Original work published 1897.)

Durkheim, E. *The Elementary Forms of Religious Life.* J. W. Swain (trans.). New York: Free Press, 1947. (Original work published 1912.)

Duster, T. "Social Implications of the 'New' Black Urban Underclass." *The Black Scholar* (May–June 1988), pp. 2–9.

Edelhertz, H., R. J. Cole, and B. Berk. *The Containment of Organized Crime.* Lexington, MA: Lexington Books, 1984.

Edin, K., and L. Lein. *Making Ends Meet: How Single Mothers Survive Welfare and Low-Wage Work.* New York: Russell-Sage Foundation, 1997.

Edwards, G., et. al. *Alcohol Policy and Public Good.* New York, Oxford, Tokyo: Oxford University Press, 1994.

Edwards, R. *Contested Terrain: The Transformation of the Workplace in the Twentieth Century.* New York: Basic Books, 1979.

Egan, T. "Urban Sprawl Strains Western States." *New York Times* (December 29, 1996), pp. A1, A20.

Egan, T. "New Prosperity Brings New Conflict to Indian Country." *New York Times* (March 8, 1998), pp. A1, A24.

Eggebeen, D. J., and A. J. Hawkins. "Economic Need and Wives' Employment." *Journal of Family Issues* 11 (1990), pp. 48–66.

Ehrenreich, B., and A. Fuentes. "Life on the Global Assembly Line." In B. Ehrenreich and A. Fuentes (eds.), *Women in the Global Factory,* pp. 379–393. Boston: South End Press, 1983.

Ehrlich, P. R., and A. H. Ehrlich. "Population, Plenty and Poverty." *National Geographic Magazine* (December 1988), pp. 914–945.

Ehrlich, P. R., A. H. Ehrlich, and G. C. Daily. "What It Will Take." *Mother Jones* (October 1995), pp. 52–55.

Eisenstadt, S. *Revolution and the Transformation of Society.* New York: Free Press, 1978.

Eitzen, D. S., and M. Baca Zinn. *Social Problems,* 5th ed. Boston: Allyn & Bacon, 1992.

Ekman, P., and W. V. Frisen. "A New Pan-Cultural Facial Expression of Emotion." *Motivation and Emotion* 10 (1986), pp. 159–168.

Ekman, P., E. R. Sorenson, and W. V. Frisen. "Pan-Cultural Elements in Facial Displays of Emotion." *Science* 164 (1969), pp. 86–88.

Elder, G. H., Jr., J. Modell, and R. D. Parke. "Studying Children in a Changing World." In G. H. Elder, Jr., J. Modell, and R. D. Parke (eds.), *Children in Time and Place: Developmental and Historical Insights,* pp. 3–21. Cambridge, Eng.: Cambridge University Press, 1993.

Elkind, D. *The Hurried Child.* New York: Addison-Wesley, 1982.

Engels, F. "The Conditions of the English Working Class in 1844." In K. Marx and F. Engels (eds.), *Collected Works,* vol. 4. London: Lawrence and Wishart, 1975.

England, P. "Work for Pay and Work at Home: Women's Double Disadvantage." In C. Calhoun and R. Ritzer (eds.), *Sociology,* pp. 398–415. New York: McGraw-Hill Primus, 1993.

Entman, R. M. *Democracy without Citizens: Media and the Decay of American Politics.* New York: Oxford University Press, 1989.

Erikson, E. *Childhood and Society,* 2d ed. New York: Norton, 1963.

Erikson, K. T. *Wayward Puritans: A Study in the Sociology of Deviance.* New York: Wiley, 1966.

Ermann, M. D., and R. J. Lundman (eds.). *Corporate and Governmental Deviance.* New York: Oxford University Press, 1996.

Ervin, K. "The Shrinking Province of the Primeval." *Sierra* (July–August 1987), pp. 39–45.

Espinosa, P. "The Rich Tapestry of Hispanic America Is Virtually Invisible on Commercial TV." *The Chronicle of Higher Education* (October 3, 1997), pp. B7–B8.

Etzioni, A. "Making Interest Groups Work for the Public." *Public Opinion* 5 (August–September 1982), pp. 52–55.

Evans, L. B. "Industrial Uses of the Microprocessor." In T. Forester (ed.), *The Microelectronics Revolution,* pp. 138–151. Cambridge, MA: MIT Press, 1981.

Evans, P., D. Rueschemeyer, and T. Skocpol (eds.). *Bringing the State Back In.* New York: Cambridge University Press, 1985.

Evans, R., Jr. "India Experiments with Sterilization." *Harper's Magazine* 225, 1338 (1961), pp. 79–80.

Faderman, L. "The Big Bang." In M. Thompson (ed.), *The Long Road to Freedom: The Advocate History of the Gay and Lesbian Movement,* pp. 17–19. New York: St. Martin's, 1994.

Fagenson, E. A. (ed.), *Women and Work: A Research and Policy Series, Vol. 4: Women in Management: Trends, Issues, and Challenges in*

Managerial Diversity. Newbury Park, CA: Sage, 1993.

Faludi, S. *Backlash: The Undeclared War against American Women.* New York: Crown, 1991.

Farley, R. "Modest Declines in U.S. Residential Segregation Observed." *Population Today* 25 (1997), pp. 1–2.

Farley, R., and W. H. Frey. "Changes in the Segregation of Whites from Blacks during the 1980s: Small Steps toward a More Integrated Society." *American Sociological Review* 59 (1994), pp. 23–45.

Farrington, K., and E. Chertok. "Social Conflict Theories of the Family." In P. G. Boss, W. J. Dougherty, R. Larossa, W. R. Schumm, and S. K. Steinmetz (eds.), *Sourcebook of Family Theories and Methods: A Contextual Approach,* pp. 357–382. New York: Plenum, 1993.

Fausto-Sterling, A. *Myths of Gender: Biological Theories about Men and Women.* New York: Basic Books, 1985.

Feagin, J. R., and C. B. Feagin. *Racial and Ethnic Relations,* 4th ed. Englewood Cliffs, NJ: Prentice-Hall, 1993.

Feagin, J. R. and C. B. Feagin. *Racial and Ethnic Relations,* 5th ed. Englewood Cliffs, NJ: Prentice-Hall, 1996.

Federal Judicial Center. *The Consequences of Mandatory Minimum Prison Terms: A Summary of Recent Findings.* Washington, DC: Federal Judicial Center, 1994.

Ferree, M. M. "The Gender Division of Labor in Two-Earner Marriages." *Journal of Family Issues* 12 (June 1991), pp. 158–180.

Findlay, J. F. *Church People in the Struggle: The National Council of Churches and the Black Freedom Movement, 1950–1970.* New York: Oxford University Press, 1993.

Fine, G. A. *With the Boys: Little League Baseball and Preadolescent Culture.* Chicago: University of Chicago Press, 1987.

Fine, G. A. "The Sad Demise, Mysterious Disappearance, and Glorious Triumph of Symbolic Interactionism." *American Review of Sociology* 199 (1993), pp. 61–87.

Fine, M. *Framing Dropouts: Notes on the Politics of an Urban Public High School.* Albany: State University of New York Press, 1991.

Fischer, C. S. "Toward a Subcultural Theory of Urbanism." *American Journal of Sociology* 80 (May 1975), pp. 1319–1341.

Fischer, C. S. "The Subcultural Theory of Urbanism: A Twentieth Year Assessment." *American Journal of Sociology* 101 (November 1995), pp. 543–577.

Fischer, C. S., M. Hout, M. S. Jankowski, S. R. Lucas, A. Swidler, and K. Voss. *Inequality by Design: Cracking the Bell Curve Myth.* Princeton, NJ: Princeton University Press, 1996.

Fishbein, D. H. "Biological Perspectives in Criminology." *Criminology* 28, 1 (1990), pp. 27–72.

FitzGerald, F. *Cities on a Hill: A Journey through Contemporary American Cultures.* New York: Simon & Schuster, 1986.

Fitzpatrick, J. P. *Puerto Rican Americans: The Meaning of Migration to the Mainland,* 2d ed. Englewood Cliffs, NJ: Prentice-Hall, 1987.

Flanagan, T., and K. Maguire (eds.). *Sourcebook of Criminal Justice Statistics— 1991.* Washington, DC: U.S. Department of Justice, 1992.

Flaste, R. "The Myth about Teenagers." *The New York Times Magazine* (October 9, 1988), pp. 19ff.

Flynn, J. R. "Massive IQ Gains in 14 Nations: What IQ Tests Really Measure." *Psychological Bulletin* 101, 2 (1987), pp. 171–191.

Fogel, R. W., and S. L. Engerman. *Time on the Cross.* Boston: Little, Brown, 1974.

Ford, C. S., and F. A. Beach. *Patterns of Sexual Behavior.* New York: Harper & Row, 1951.

Forester, T. (ed.). *The Information Technology Revolution.* Cambridge, MA: MIT Press, 1985.

Forester, T. *High-Tech Society.* Cambridge, MA: MIT Press, 1987.

Fox, J. A. *Trends in Juvenile Violence.* Boston: Northeastern University Press, 1996.

Frank, A. G. *Capitalism and Underdevelopment in Latin America.* New York: Monthly Review Press, 1967.

Frank, A. G. *Crisis in the Third World.* New York: Holmes and Meier, 1980.

Fraser, S. (ed.). *The Bell Curve Wars: Race, Intelligence, and the Future of America.* New York: Basic Books, 1995.

Frazier, C. E., D. M. Bishop, and J. C. Henretta. "The Social Context of Race Differentials in Juvenile Justice Dispositions." *Sociological Quarterly* 33, 3 (1992), pp. 447–458.

Fredrickson, G. M. *White Supremacy: A Comparative Study in American and South African History.* New York: Oxford University Press, 1981.

Freeman, D. *Margaret Mead and Samoa: The Making and Unmaking of an Anthropological Myth.* Cambridge, MA: Harvard University Press, 1983.

Freeman, J. "The Origins of the Women's Liberation Movement." *American Journal of Sociology* 78 (January 1973), pp. 792–811.

Freeman, J. (ed.). *Social Movements of the Sixties and Seventies.* New York: Longman, 1983.

French, H. W. "The World; A Century Later, Letting Africans Draw Their Own Map." *The New York Times* (November 23, 1997), www.nytimes.com/archives.

Freud, S. *The Standard Edition of the Complete Psychological Works of Sigmund Freud,* rev. ed. by J. Strachey. London: Hogarth Press and The Institute of Psychoanalysis, 1964.

Friedan, B. *The Feminine Mystique.* New York: Norton, 1963.

Friedman, L. *A History of American Law.* New York: Simon & Schuster, 1973.

Fuchs, L. H. "Who We Should Count and Why." *Society* 34 (1997), pp. 24–27.

Furstenberg, F. F., Jr. "Good Dads—Bad Dads: Two Faces of Fatherhood." In A. Cherlin (ed.), *The Changing American Family,* pp. 193–218. Washington, DC: Urban Institute Press, 1988.

Furstenberg, F. F., Jr. "Divorce and the American Family." *Annual Review of Sociology* 16 (1990), pp. 379–403.

Galbraith, K. *The New Industrial State,* 3d ed. Boston: Houghton Mifflin, 1978.

Gallup, G., Jr. *The Gallup Monthly,* no. 357 (June 1995).

Gallup, G., Jr., and J. Castelli. *The People's Religion: American Faith in the 90s.* New York: Macmillan, 1989.

Gallup Organization. Princeton, NJ: 1992.

Gallup Organization. *Religion in America 1992–1993.* Princeton, NJ: Princeton Religion Research Center, 1993.

Gallup Organization. "Changes in Race Relations in the USA." *USA Today* (June 11, 1997), p. 9A.

Gamoran, A. "The Variable Effects of High School Tracking." *American Sociological Review* 57 (1992), pp. 812–828.

Gamoran, A., and R. D. Mare. "Secondary Tracking and Educational Inequality: Compensation, Reinforcement, or Neutrality?" *American Journal of Sociology* 94 (March 1989), pp. 1146–1183.

Gans, H. J. "How Well *Does* TV Present the News?" *The New York Times Magazine* (January 11, 1970), pp. 31–45 passim.

Gans, H. J. *Deciding What's News.* New York: Pantheon, 1979.

Gans, H. J. *The War against the Poor: The Underclass and Antipoverty Policy.* New York: Basic Books, 1995.

Gappert, G., and R. V. Knight (eds.). "Cities in the 21st Century." *Urban Affairs Annual Review* 23 (1982).

Gardner, H. "Cracking Open the IQ Box." In S. Fraser (ed.), *The Bell Curve Wars: Race, Intelligence, and the Future of America,* pp. 11–35. New York: Basic Books, 1995.

Garfinkel, H. *Studies in Ethnomethodology.* Englewood Cliffs, NJ: Prentice-Hall, 1967.

Garrett, L. *The Coming Plague: Newly Emerging Diseases in a World Out of Balance.* New York: Farrar, Straus and Giroux, 1994.

Garson, B. *The Electronic Sweatshop: How Computers Are Transforming the Office of the Future into the Factory of the Past.* New York: Penguin, 1988.

Gartner, R. "The Victims of Homicide: A Temporal and Cross-National Comparison." *American Sociological Review* 55 (February 1990), pp. 92–106.

Gaylin, W. *Feelings.* New York: Harper & Row, 1979.

Gedda, G. "Clinton Balking at Arms-Sale Rules." *The Columbian* (October 7, 1997), p. A6.

Geertz, C. *Anthropological Approaches to the Study of Religion.* Association of Social Anthropologists Monographs, no. 3. London: Tavistock, 1965.

Gelles, R. J. "Child Abuse and Violence in Single-Parent Families: Parent Absence and Economic Deprivation." *Journal of Orthopsychiatry* 59 (October 1989), pp. 492–501.

Gelles, R. J. *Contemporary Families: A Sociological View.* Thousand Oaks, CA: Sage, 1995.

Gelles, R. J. *The Book of David: How Preserving Families Can Cost Children's Lives.* New York: Basic Books, 1996.

Gelles, R. J. *Intimate Violence in Families,* 3d ed. Thousand Oaks, CA: Sage, 1997.

Gelles, R. J., and J. R. Conte. "Domestic Violence and Sexual Abuse of Children: A Review of Research in the Eighties." *Journal of Marriage and the Family* 52 (November 1990), pp. 1045–1058.

Gelles, R. J., and C. P. Cornell. "Summing Up." In R. J. Gelles and C. P. Cornell (eds.), *International Perspectives on Family Violence.* Lexington, MA: Lexington Books, 1983.

Gelles, R. J., and M. A. Straus. "Is Violence towards Children Increasing? A Comparison of 1975 and 1985 National Survey Rates." *Journal of Interpersonal Violence* 2 (June 1987), pp. 212–222.

Gelles, R. J., and M. A. Straus. *Intimate Violence.* New York: Simon & Schuster, 1988.

Gelman, D. "The Mystery of Suicide." *Newsweek* (April 18, 1994), pp. 45ff.

Gerber, T. P. and M. Hout. "Educational Stratification in Russia during the Soviet Period." *American Journal of Sociology* 101 (1995), pp. 611–620.

Gereffi, G. *The Pharmaceutical Industry and Dependency in the Third World.* Oxford: Pergamon, 1983.

Gerhart, B. A., and G. T. Milkovich. "Salaries, Salary Growth, and Promotions of Men and Women in a Large, Private Firm." In R. T. Michael, H. I. Hartmann, and B. O'Farrell (eds.), *Pay Equity: Empirical Inquiries,* pp. 23–44. Washington, DC: National Academy Press, 1989.

Gerth, H., and C. W. Mills. *From Max Weber: Essays in Sociology.* New York: Oxford University Press, 1946.

Geschwender, J. "Explorations in the Theory of Social Movements and Revolutions." *Social Forces* 47 (December 1968), pp. 127–135.

Giddens A. *A Contemporary Critique of Historical Materialism.* Berkeley: University of California Press, 1981.

Giddens, A. *Classes, Power and Conflict: Classical and Contemporary Debates.* Berkeley: University of California Press, 1982.

Giddens, A. *The Construction of Society: Outline of the Theory of Structuration.* Berkeley: University of California Press, 1985a.

Giddens, A. *The Nation-State and Violence.* Berkeley: University of California Press, 1985b.

Gilbert, D. *The American Class Structure: In an Age of Growing Inequality,* 5th ed. Belmont, CA: Wadsworth, 1998.

Gilbert, L. S. *Sharing It All: The Rewards and Struggles of Two-Career Families.* New York: Plenum, 1988.

Giles, J. "The Poet of Alienation." *Newsweek* (April 18, 1994), pp. 46–47.

Gilligan, C. *In a Different Voice: Women's Conception of the Self and of Morality.* Cambridge, MA: Harvard University Press, 1982.

Gilligan, C. "Profile." In S. Scarr, R. A. Weinberg, and A. Levine (eds.), *Understanding Development,* pp. 488–491. San Diego: Harcourt Brace Jovanovich, 1986.

Giordano, P. G. "The Wider Circle of Friends in Adolescence." *American Journal of Sociology* 101, 3 (November 1995), pp. 661–697.

Gist, N. P., and S. F. Fava. *Urban Society,* 6th ed. New York: Crowell, 1974.

Gitlin, T. *The Whole World Is Watching: Mass Media in the Making and Unmaking of the New Left.* Berkeley: University of California Press, 1980.

Gitlin, T. *Inside Prime Time.* New York: Pantheon, 1985.

Gitlin, T. (ed.). *Watching Television.* New York: Pantheon, 1986.

Gladwell, M. "Damaged." *The New Yorker* (February 24 & March 3, 1997), pp. 132–147.

Glassner, B. *Bodies: Overcoming the Tyranny of Perfection.* Los Angeles: Lowell House; Chicago: Contemporary Books, 1992.

Glazer, N. *We Are All Multiculturalists Now.* Cambridge, MA: Harvard University Press, 1997.

Glock, C. Y. "On the Study of Religious Commitment." *Religious Education,* Research Supplement (July–August 1962), pp. 98–110.

Glock, C. Y., and R. Stark. *Religion and Society in Tension.* Chicago: Rand McNally, 1965.

Gluckman, M. *Politics, Law and Ritual in Tribal Society.* New York: New American Library, 1965.

Goffman, E. *The Presentation of Self in Everyday Life.* New York: Doubleday, 1959.

Goffman, E. *Asylums: Essays on the Social Situation of Mental Patients and Other Inmates.* Chicago: Aldine, 1961.

Goffman, E. *Interaction Ritual: Essays on Face-to-Face Interaction.* Garden City, NY: Doubleday/Anchor, 1967.

Goffman, E. *Behavior in Public Places: Notes on the Social Order of Gatherings.* New York: Free Press, 1985.

Golay, M., and C. Rollyson. *Where America Stands, 1996.* New York: Wiley, 1996.

Gold, S. J. "Migration and Family Adjustment: Continuity and Change among Vietnamese in the United States." In H. P. McAdoo (ed.), *Family Ethnicity: Strength and Diversity,* pp. 300–314. Newbury Park, CA: Sage, 1993.

Goldberg, M. P. "Recent Trends in Special Education in Tokyo." In J. J. Shields, Jr. (ed.), *Japanese Schooling: Patterns of Socialization, Equality, and Political Control,* pp. 176–184. University Park: Pennsylvania State University Press, 1989.

Goldfrank, W. L. "Comments on Skocpol." *Theory and Society* 11 (1982), pp. 301–304.

Goldstine, H. H. *The Computer from Pascal to Neumann.* Princeton, NJ: Princeton University Press, 1972.

Goldstone, J. A. *Revolutions: Theoretical, Comparative, and Historical Studies.* New York: Harcourt Brace Jovanovich, 1986.

Goode, E. *Deviant Behavior: An Interactionist Approach.* Englewood Cliffs, NJ: Prentice-Hall, 1978.

Goode, E. *Deviant Behavior,* 2d ed. Englewood Cliffs, NJ: Prentice-Hall, 1984.

Goode, E. *Deviant Behavior: An Interactionist Perspective,* 3d ed. Englewood Cliffs, NJ: Prentice-Hall, 1990.

Goode, W. J. *After Divorce.* New York: Free Press, 1956.

Goode, W. J. *World Revolution and Family Patterns.* New York: Free Press, 1963.

Goodstein, L. "Women and the Promise Keepers: Good for the Gander, but the Goose Isn't So Sure." *New York Times* (October 5, 1997), www.nytimes.com/archives.

Gordon, M. M. *Assimilation in American Life: The Role of Race, Religion, and National Origins.* New York: Oxford University Press, 1964.

Gottfredson, M. R., and T. Hirschi. *A General Theory of Crime.* Stanford, CA: Stanford University Press, 1990.

Gould, S. J. *The Mismeasure of Man.* New York: Norton, 1981.

Gould, S. J. "Curveball." In S. Fraser (ed.), *The Bell Curve Wars: Race, Intelligence, and the Future of America,* pp. 1–10. New York: Basic Books, 1995.

Gouldner, A. W. *For Sociology.* London: Allen Lane, 1973.

Graham, S. "Most of the Subjects Were White and Middle Class." *American Psychologist* 47 (1992), pp. 629–639.

Granovetter, M. S. *Getting a Job: A Study of Contacts and Careers.* Cambridge, MA: Harvard University Press, 1974.

Grant, C. A., and M. Gillette. "The Holmes Report and Minorities in Education." *Social Education* (November–December 1987), pp. 506–508.

Greenberg, D. F. *The Construction of Homosexuality.* Chicago: University of Chicago Press, 1988.

Greenhouse, S. "Poles Find Crime Replacing the Police State." *The New York Times* (March 4, 1990), p. 20.

Greenspan, S. I. *The Growth of the Mind: And the Endangered Origins of Intelligence.* New York: Addison-Wesley, 1997.

Greenwood, P. W., et al. *Three Strikes and You're Out: Estimated Benefits and Costs of California's New Mandatory Sentencing Law.* Santa Monica, CA: Rand Corporation, 1997.

Greer, G. *The Change: Women, Aging, and Menopause.* New York: Knopf, 1992.

Gubrium, J. F. *Out of Control.* Newbury Park, CA: Sage, 1992.

Gugler, J. (ed.). *Cities in the Developing World.* New York: Oxford, 1997.

Gupta, U., and P. Singh. "Exploratory Study of Love and Liking and Type of Marriages." *Indian Journal of Applied Psychology* 19 (1982), pp. 92–97.

Gusfield, J. R. *Symbolic Crusade: Status, Policy, and the American Temperance Movement,* 2d ed. Urbana and Chicago: University of Illinois Press, 1986.

Gusfield, J. R. "Benevolent Repression: Popular Culture, Social Structure, and the Control of Drinking." In S. Barrows and R. Room (eds.), *Drinking: Behavior and Belief in Modern History,* pp. 399–424. Berkeley: University of California Press, 1991.

Hacker, A. *Two Nations: Black and White, Separate, Hostile, Unequal.* New York: Scribner's, 1992.

Hacker, A. *Money: Who Has How Much and Why.* New York: Scribner's, 1997.

Hadaway, C. K., P. L. Marler, and M. Chaves. "What the Polls Don't Show: A Closer Look at U.S. Church Attendance." *American Sociological Review* 58 (December 1993), pp. 741–752.

Hadden, J. K. "Religious Broadcasting and the Mobilization of the New Christian Right." *Journal for the Scientific Study of Religion* 26, 1 (1987), pp. 1–24.

Hadden, J. K., and A. Shupe. *Televangelism: Power and Politics on God's Frontier.* New York: Holt, 1988.

Hagan, J. "The Gender Stratification of Income Inequality among Lawyers." *Social Forces* 68 (March 1990), pp. 835–855.

Hall, J. *Gone from the Promised Land: Jonestown as American Cultural History.* New Brunswick, NJ: Transaction Books, 1987.

Halle, D. *America's Working Man.* Chicago: University of Chicago Press, 1984.

Hamlin, J. E. "Who's the Victim? Women, Control, and Consciousness." *Women's Studies International Forum* 11, 3 (1988), pp. 223–233.

Hanson, S. "The College Preparatory Curriculum across Schools: Access to Similar Types of Knowledge?" Paper presented at the annual meeting of the American Educational Research Association, San Francisco, 1986.

Harner, M. *The Way of the Shaman: A Guide to Healing and Power.* San Francisco: Harper & Row, 1980.

Harrington, C. L. "Talk about Embarrassment: Exploring the Taboo-Repression-Denial-Hypothesis." *Symbolic Interaction,* 15 (1992), pp. 203–225.

Harrington, M. *The Other America: Poverty in the United States.* Baltimore: Penguin, 1963.

Harrington, P. E., and W. N. Fogg. "Education and Market Success." Boston, Massachusetts: Northeastern University, mimeographed. (1994).

Harris, L. *Inside America.* New York: Vintage, 1987.

Harris, M. *Cows, Pigs, Wars and Witches: The Riddles of Culture.* New York: Random House, 1975.

Harris, M. *Cannibals and Kings: The Origins of Culture.* New York: Random House, 1977.

Harrison, B., and B. Bluestone. *The Great U-Turn: Corporate Restructuring and the Polarizing of America.* New York: Basic Books, 1988.

Harroff, P. B. "On Language." In J. F. Cuber and P. Harroff (eds.), *Readings in Sociology,* pp. 61–68. New York: Appleton-Century-Crofts, 1962.

Hart, K. "Informal Income Opportunities and Urban Employment in Ghana." *Journal of Modern African Studies* (1973), pp. 70–81.

Hartup, W. W. "Social Relationships and Their Developmental Significance." *American Psychologist* 44 (February 1989), pp. 120–126.

Harvey, D. *The Condition of Postmodernity.* New York: Blackwell, 1989.

Haub, C. "China's Fertility Drop Lowers World Growth Rate." *Population Today* (June 1993), pp. 1–2.

Hawkins, J. N. "Educational Demands and Institutional Response: Dowa Education in Japan." In J. J. Shields, Jr. (ed.), *Japanese Schooling: Patterns of Socialization, Equality, and Political Control,* pp. 194–211. University Park: Pennsylvania State University Press, 1989.

Hearn, J. C. "The Relative Roles of Academic, Ascribed, and Socioeconomic Characteristics in College Destinations." *Sociology of Education* 57 (January 1984), pp. 22–30.

Heider, K. G. "Dani Sexuality: A Low Energy System." *Man* 11 (June 1976), pp. 188–201.

Hendry, P. "Food and Population: Beyond Five Billion." *Population Bulletin* 43 (April 1988).

Henslin, J. M. *Social Problems,* 3d ed. Englewood Cliffs, NJ: Prentice-Hall, 1994.

Heritage, J. *Garfinkel and Ethnomethodology.* Baltimore: Penguin, 1987.

Herman, E. *Corporate Control, Corporate Power.* New York: Cambridge University Press, 1981.

Herman, E. S., and N. Chomsky. *Manufacturing Consent: The Political Economy of the Mass Media.* New York: Pantheon, 1988.

Herrnstein, R. J., and C. Murray. *The Bell Curve: Intelligence and Class Structure in American Life.* New York: Free Press, 1994.

Hewlett, S. A. *A Lesser Life.* New York: Morrow, 1986.

Hill, A. *Speaking Truth to Power*. New York: Doubleday, 1997.

Hirsch, P. "From Ambushes to Golden Parachutes: Corporate Takeovers as an Instance of Cultural Framing and Institutional Integration." *American Journal of Sociology* 91 (January 1986), pp. 800–837.

Hirschell, J. D., I. W. Hutchison, III, and C. W. Dean. "The Failure of Arrest to Deter Spouse Abuse." *Journal of Research in Crime and Delinquency* 29 (February 1992), pp. 7–33.

Hirschi, T. *Causes of Delinquency*. Berkeley: University of California Press, 1969.

Hochschild, A. *The Managed Heart*. Berkeley: University of California Press, 1983.

Hochschild, A. R. *The Time Bind: When Work Becomes Home and Home Becomes Work*. New York: Metropolitan Books, 1997.

Hochschild, A., with A. Machung. *The Second Shift: Working Parents and the Revolution at Home*. New York: Viking, 1989.

Hodson, R., D. Sekulic, and G. Massey. "National Tolerance in the Former Yugoslavia." *American Journal of Sociology* 99, 6 (May 1994), pp. 1534–1558.

Hoffman, L. W. "Work, Family, and the Socialization of the Child." In R. D. Parke, R. N. Emde, H. P. McAdoo, and G. P. Sackett (eds.), *Review of Child Development Research, Vol. 7: The Family*, pp. 223–282. Chicago: University of Chicago Press, 1984.

Hoffman, L. W. "The Effects on Children of Maternal and Paternal Employment." In N. Gerstel and H. Gross (eds.), *Families and Work*. Philadelphia: Temple University Press, 1987.

Hoffman, L. W. "Effects of Maternal Employment in the Two-Parent Family." *American Psychologist* 44, 2 (1989), pp. 283–292.

Hoffreth, S. L., A. Brayfield, S. Deich, and P. Holcomb. *National Child Care Survey, 1990*. Washington, DC: Urban Institute Press, 1991.

Hogan, D. P., D. J. Eggebeen, and C. C. Clogg. "The Structure of Intergenerational Exchanges in American Families." *American Journal of Sociology* 98 (May 1993), pp. 1428–1458.

Holmes, S. A. "The Disabled Find a Voice and Make Sure It Is Heard." *The New York Times* (March 13, 1990), p. E5.

Holmes Group. *Tomorrow's Teachers: A Report of the Holmes Group*. East Lansing, MI: Holmes Group, 1986.

Holusha, J. "Business Taps the East Bloc's Intellectual Reserves." *The New York Times* (February 20, 1990), pp. A1, D5.

Homans, G. "Behaviorism and Rational Choice Theory." In C. Calhoun, M. Meyer, and W. R. Scott (eds.), *Structures of Power and Constraint: Essays in Honor of Peter M. Blau*. New York: Cambridge University Press, 1990.

Horowitz, M. J. *The Transformation of American Law, 1780–1860*. Cambridge, MA: Harvard University Press, 1977.

Houseknecht, S. K. "Voluntary Childlessness." In M. B. Sussman and S. K. Steinmetz (eds.), *Handbook of Marriage and the Family*, pp. 369–395. New York: Plenum, 1987.

Howard, G. S. "Culture Tales: A Narrative Approach to Thinking, Cross-Cultural Psychology, and Psychotherapy." *American Psychologist* 46 (1991), pp. 187–189.

Howard, R. *Brave New Workplace*. New York: Viking, 1985.

Hsia, J., and M. Hirano-Nakanishi. "The Demographics of Diversity: Asian Americans and Higher Education." *Change* (November–December 1989), pp. 20–27.

Hsu, F. L. K. "The Self in Cross-Cultural Perspective." In A. J. Marsella, G. DeVos, and F. C. K. Hsu (eds.), *Culture and Self: Asian and Western Perspectives*, pp. 24–55. New York: Tavistock, 1985.

Huesmann, L. R. "The Effects of Film and Television Violence upon Children." *Children and the Media: First International Conference* (Los Angeles, May 6–8, 1985), pp. 103–128.

Hughes, E. C. "Dilemmas and Contradictions of Status." *American Journal of Sociology* 50 (1945), pp. 553–559.

Humphrey, J. A., and T. J. Fogarty. "Race and Plea-Bargained Outcomes: A Research Note." *Social Forces* 66 (September 1987), pp. 176–182.

Humphreys, L. *Tearoom Trade: Impersonal Sex in Public Places*. Chicago: Aldine, 1970.

Hurn, C. J. *The Limits and Possibilities of Schooling*. Boston: Allyn & Bacon, 1978.

Huston, A. C., E. Donnerstein, H. Fairchild, N. D. Feshbach, P. A. Katz, J. P. Murray, E. A. Rubenstein, B. I. Wilcox, and D. Zuckerman. *Big World, Small Screen: The Role of Television in American Society*. Lincoln: University of Nebraska Press, 1992.

Huston, A. C., B. A. Watkins, and D. Kunkel. "Public Policy and Children's Television." *American Psychologist* 44, 2 (February 1989), pp. 424–433.

Hyde, J. S. *Understanding Human Sexuality*. New York: McGraw-Hill, 1979.

Hyde, J. S., E. Fennema, and S. Lamon. "Gender Differences in Mathematics Performance: A Meta-Analysis." *Psychological Bulletin*, 107 (1990), pp. 139–155.

Hyman, H. "The Psychology of Status." *Archives of Psychology* 37 (1942), p. 15.

Hymowitz, C. "Stable Cycles of Executive Careers Shattered by Upheaval in Business." *The Wall Street Journal* (May 26, 1987), p. 1.

Ibrahim, Y. M. "Islamic Fundamentalism Is Winning Votes." *The New York Times* (July 1, 1990), p. E1.

Institute of Medicine. *Approaching Death: Improving Care at the End of Life*. Washington DC: National Academy Press, 1997.

Ireland, P. "Beware of 'Feel-Good Male Supremacy.'" *The Washington Post* (September 7, 1997), p. C03.

Jackall, R. *Moral Mazes: The World of Corporate Managers*. New York: Oxford University Press, 1988.

Jacobson, C., and T. Heaton "Voluntary Childlessness among American Men and Women in the Late 1980s." *Social Biology* 38 (1991), pp. 79–93.

Jacquet, C. H., Jr. (ed.). *Yearbook of American & Canadian Churches 1989*. Nashville: Abingdon, 1989.

Janis, I. "Group Identification Under Conditions of External Danger." In D. Cartwright and A. Zander (eds.), *Group Dynamics: Research and Theory*. New York: Harper & Row, 1968.

Jasper, J. M., and J. Poulsen. "Fighting Back: Vulnerabilities, Blunders, and Countermobilization by Targets in Three Animal Rights Campaigns." *Sociological Review* 8 (1993), pp. 639–657.

Jencks, C. *Rethinking Social Policy: Race, Poverty, and the Underclass*. Cambridge, MA: Harvard University Press, 1992.

Jencks, C. *The Homeless*. Cambridge, MA: Harvard University Press, 1994.

Jenkins, J. C. *The Politics of Insurgency*. New York: Columbia University Press, 1984.

Jensen, A. R. "How Much Can We Boost IQ and Scholastic Achievement?" *Harvard Educational Review* 39 (1969), pp. 1–123.

Jiobu, R. M. *Ethnicity and Assimilation: Blacks, Chinese, Filipinos, Japanese, Koreans, Mexicans, Vietnamese, and Whites*. Albany: State University of New York, 1988.

Jobes, D. A., A. L. Berman, P. W. O'Carroll, S. Eastgard, and S. Knickmeyer. "The Kurt Cobain Suicide Crisis: Perspectives from Research, Public Health, and the New Media." *Suicide and Life-Threatening Behavior*, 26, 3 (Fall 1996), pp. 260–264.

Johnson, B. "On Church and Sect." *American Sociological Review* 28 (August 1963), pp. 539–549.

Johnson, D. "Uncertain Future, on Their Own, Awaits." *The New York Times* (March 16, 1997), pp. A1, A38.

Johnson, M. L., and J. R. Johnson. (1996). "Daily Life in Japanese High Schools." *Eric Digest,* ED406301. ERIC Clearinghouse for Social Studies/Social Science Education, Bloomington, IN. Posted in U.S. Dept. of Education Database: www.ed.gov/databases/ERIC_Digests.

Johnson, R. S. "Mobilizing the Disabled." In J. Freeman (ed.), *Social Movements of the Sixties and Seventies,* pp. 82–100. New York: Longman, 1983.

Joint Center for Political and Economic Studies. *Black Elected Officials: A National Roster.* Washington, DC: Joint Center for Political and Economic Studies, 1992.

Jones, T. K. "Tracking America's Soul: Our Nation's Most Famous Pollster Talks about American Religion on the Brink of the Nineties." *Christianity Today* (November 17, 1989), pp. 22–25.

Kagehiro, D. K. "Defining the Standard of Proof in Jury Instructions." *Psychological Science* 1 (1990), pp. 194–200.

"Kaiser Survey on Obstetrician/ Gynecologists' Attitudes and Practices Related to Contraception and Family Planning." Fact Finders, Inc. (1995).

Kalmijn, M. "Shifting Boundaries: Trends in Religious and Educational Homogamy." *American Sociological Review* 56 (1991), pp. 780–800.

Kaminer, W. "Federal Offense: Politics of Crime Control." *Atlantic Monthly* 276, 6 (June 1994).

Kanamura, J. "The Second Sex in Practice: A Sexist Practice in Japan's Schools." *Educational Horizons* (Winter 1993), pp. 77–79.

Kanter, R. M. *Men and Women of the Corporation.* New York: Basic Books, 1977.

Kanter, R. M. *When Giants Learn to Dance: Mastering the Challenge of Strategy, Management, and Careers in the 1990s.* New York: Simon & Schuster, 1989.

Kaplan, M. F. "Task, Situational and Personal Determinants of Influence Processes in Group Decision Making." In E. J. Lawler (ed.), *Advances in Group Processes,* vol. 6. Greenwich, CT: JAI Press, 1989.

Kaplan, R. D. "Was Democracy Just a Moment?" *Atlantic Monthly* 820, 6 (December 1997), pp. 55–72.

Kasarda, J. "Urban Change and Minority Opportunities." In P. Peterson (ed.), *The New Urban Reality,* pp. 33–68. Washington, DC: Brookings Institution, 1985.

Kasarda, J. D. "Urban Industrial Transition and the Underclass." *The Annals of the American Academy of Political and Social Science* 501 (January 1989), pp. 26–47.

Keddie, N. R. "Comments on Skocpol." *Theory and Society* 11 (1982), pp. 285–292.

Keen, S. *Fire in the Belly: On Being a Man.* New York: Doubleday Dell, 1992.

Kelly, J. B., and J. S. Wallerstein. "The Effects of Parental Divorce: Experiences of the Child in Early Latency." *American Journal of Orthopsychiatry* 46 (January 1976), pp. 20–32.

Kempton, M. *America Comes of Middle Age.* Boston: Little, Brown, 1963.

Kerbo, H. R. *Social Stratification and Inequality,* 3d ed. New York: McGraw-Hill, 1996.

Kerckhoff, A. C., and D. D. Everett. "Sponsored and Contest Education Pathways to Jobs in Great Britain and the United States." *Research in Sociology of Education and Socialization* 6 (1986), pp. 133–163.

Kerner Commission. *Report of the National Advisory Commission on Civil Disorders.* New York: Bantam, 1968.

Kifner, J., and J. Thomas. "Singular Difficulty in Stopping Terrorism." *The New York Times* (January 23, 1998), p. 23.

Kimmel, M. "Rethinking 'Masculinity': New Directions in Research." In M. S. Kimmel (ed.), *Changing Men: New Directions in Research on Men and Masculinity,* pp. 9–24. Newbury Park, NJ: Sage, 1988.

Kimmel, M. *Manhood in America: A Cultural History.* New York: Free Press, 1996.

Kimmel, M., and M. A. Messner. *Men's Lives,* 3d ed. New York: Macmillan, 1995.

King, D. R. "The Brutalizing Effect: Execution Publicity and the Incidence of Homicide in South Carolina." *Social Forces* 57 (1978), pp. 683–687.

Kingson, P. W., and S. L. Nock. "Time Together among Dual-Earner Couples." *American Sociological Review* 52 (June 1987), pp. 391–400.

Kinsey, A. C., W. B. Pomeroy, and C. E. Martin. *Sexual Behavior in the Human Male.* Philadelphia: Saunders, 1948.

Kitano, H. H. L., and R. Daniels. *Asian Americans: Emerging Minorities.* Englewood Cliffs, NJ: Prentice-Hall, 1988.

Kluckhohn, C. *Mirror for Man.* New York: McGraw-Hill, 1949.

Kluger, J. "Will We Follow Sheep?" *Time* (March 10, 1997), pp. 66ff.

Kobayashi, T. "Educational Problems of 'Returning Children.'" In J. J. Shields, Jr.

(ed.), *Japanese Schooling: Patterns of Socialization, Equality, and Political Control,* pp. 185–193. University Park: Pennsylvania State University Press, 1989.

Kohn, M. L. "Social Class and Parental Values." *American Journal of Sociology* 64 (1959), pp. 337–351.

Kohn, M. L. "Social Class and Parent-Child Relationships: An Interpretation." *American Journal of Sociology* 68 (January 1963), pp. 471–480.

Kohn, M. L. "Social Class and Parent-Child Relationships: An Interpretation." In R. W. Winch and L. W. Goodman (eds.), *Selected Studies in Marriage and the Family,* 4th ed. New York: Holt, Rinehart and Winston, 1974.

Kohn, M. L. *Work and Personality.* Norwood, NJ: Ablex, 1983.

Kohn, M. L., A. Naoi, C. Schoenbach, C. Schooler, and K. M. Sclomczynski. "Position in the Class Structure and Psychological Functioning in the United States, Japan, and Poland." *American Journal of Sociology* 95 (January 1990), pp. 964–1008.

Kohn, M. L., K. M. Sclomczynski, and C. Schoenbach. "Social Stratification and the Transmission of Values in the Family: A Cross-National Assessment." *Sociological Forum* 1, 1 (1986), pp. 73–102.

Komter, A. "Hidden Power in Marriage." *Gender and Society* 3 (1989), pp. 187–216.

Korn/Ferry International. *Decade of the Executive Woman.* New York: Korn/Ferry International, 1993.

Kosmin, B. A., and S. P. Lachman. *One Nation under God: Religion in Contemporary American Society.* New York: Crown, 1993.

Koss, M. P., T. E. Dinero, C. A. Seibel, and S. C. Cox. "Stranger and Acquaintance Rape: Are There Differences in the Victim's Experience?" *Psychology of Women Quarterly* 12, 1 (1988), pp. 1–24.

Kozol, J. *Savage Inequalities: Children in America's Schools.* New York: HarperCollins, 1991.

Kravitz, D. A., and B. Martin. "Ringelmann Rediscovered: The Original Article." *Journal of Personality and Social Psychology* 50 (1986), pp. 936–941.

Kristof, N. D. "4 Years after Tiananmen, the Hard Line Is Cracking" (June 1, 1993, pp. A1, A8); "China Sees 'Market-Leninism' as Way to Future" (September 6, 1993, pp. A1, A5); "Riddle of China: Repression and Prosperity Can Coexist" (September 7, 1993, pp. A1, A10). *The New York Times.*

Kristof, N. D. "Why No One Is Down on the Farm in Japan." *The New York Times* (October 13, 1996), p. E3.

Kristof, N. D. "The Communist Dynasty Had Its Run. Now What?" *The New York Times* (February 23, 1997), pp. E1, E5.

Kübler-Ross, E. *On Death and Dying.* New York: Macmillan, 1969.

Lack, P. B. "The Ways of Americans, through Vietnamese Eyes." *The New York Times* (January 24, 1978), p. 33.

Lake, A. *Somoza Falling.* Boston: Houghton Mifflin, 1989.

Lakoff, R. *Talking Power: The Politics of Language in Our Lives.* New York: Basic Books, 1990.

Lamb, M. E. "Fathers, Mothers, and Child Care in the 1980's." In K. M. Borman, D. Quarm, and S. Gideonse (eds.), *Women in the Workplace: Effects on Families,* pp. 61–88. Norwood, NJ: Ablex, 1984.

Landry, B. *The New Black Middle Class.* Berkeley: University of California Press, 1987.

Langone, J. "A Stinking Mess." *Time* (January 2, 1989), pp. 44–47.

Lapham, S. L. *The Foreign Born Population in the United States.* Washington, DC: U.S. Bureau of the Census, 1992.

Lapsley, D. K., M. Milstead, S. M. Quintana, D. Flannery, and R. R. Buss. "Adolescent Egocentrism and Formal Operations: Tests of a Theoretical Assumption." *Developmental Psychology* 22 (1986), pp. 800–807.

LaRossa, R. *The Modernization of Fatherhood: A Social and Political History.* Chicago: University of Chicago Press, 1997.

Larson, S. G. "Television's Mixed Messages: Sexual Content on *All My Children*." *Communication Quarterly* 39, 2 (Spring, 1991), pp. 156–163.

Lasch, C. *Haven in a Heartless World: The Family Besieged.* New York: Basic Books, 1977.

LeBon, G. *The Crowd: A Study of the Popular Mind.* New York: Viking, 1960. (Original work published 1895.)

Lee, R. B., and I. DeVore (eds.). *Kalihari Hunter-Gatherers: Studies of the !Kung San and Their Neighbors.* Cambridge, MA: Harvard University Press, 1976.

Leenhardt, M. *DoKamo.* Chicago: University of Chicago, 1981.

Lejeune, R. "The Management of a Mugging." *Urban Life* 6 (July 1977), pp. 123–148.

Lelyveld, J. *Move Your Shadow: South Africa, Black and White.* New York: Times Books, 1985.

Lemert, E. M. *Social Pathology.* New York: McGraw-Hill, 1951.

Lempert, R. "The Effects of Executions on Homicides: A New Look in an Old Light."
Crime and Delinquency 29 (January 1983), pp. 88–115.

Lender, M. E., and J. K . Martin. *Drinking in America: A History,* 2d ed. New York: Free Press, 1987.

Lenski, G. *Power and Privilege.* New York: McGraw-Hill, 1966.

Lenski, G., J. Lenski, and P. Nolan. *Human Societies: An Introduction to Macrosociology,* 6th ed. New York: McGraw-Hill, 1991.

Lerner, J. V. *Working Women and Their Families.* Thousand Oaks, CA: Sage, 1993.

LeVay, S. "A Difference in Hypothalmic Structure between Heterosexual and Homosexual Men." *Science* 253 (1991), pp. 1034–1037.

Levi, M. *Of Rule and Revenue.* Berkeley: University of California Press, 1988.

Levin, M. *Educational Reform for Disadvantaged Students: An Emerging National Crisis.* Washington, DC: National Educational Association, Division of Instruction and Professional Development, 1986.

Levine, H., and L. Harmon. *The Death of an American Jewish Community: A Tragedy of Good Intentions.* New York: Free Press, 1992.

Levinson, D. *Family Violence in Cross-Cultural Perspective.* Newbury Park, CA: Sage, 1989.

Levinson, D. J., with J. D. Levinson. *The Seasons of a Woman's Life.* New York: Knopf, 1996.

Levy, S. "The Computer." *Newsweek* (Winter Special Issue, 1997), pp. 28–30.

Lewin, T. "Study Criticizes Textbooks on Marriage as Unscientific." *The New York Times* (September 17, 1997), p. A27.

Liazos, A. "The Poverty of the Sociology of Deviance: Nuts, Sluts, and Perverts." *Social Problems* 20 (1972), pp. 103–120.

Liebmann-Smith, J. "Male Menopause: Fact or Fiction?" *American Druggist* (April 1992), pp. 48–54.

Liebow, E. *Tell Them Who I Am: The Lives of Homeless Women.* New York: Free Press, 1993.

Lindesmith, A. R., A. L. Strauss, and N. K. Denzin. *Social Psychology,* 4th ed. Hinsdale, IL: Dryden, 1975.

Linton, R. *The Study of Man.* New York: Appleton-Century-Crofts, 1936.

Liska, A. E., and W. Baccaglini. "Feeling Safe by Comparison: Crime in the Newspapers." *Social Problems* 37, 3 (1990), pp. 360–374.

Litwak, E. B. "Geographic Mobility and Extended Family Cohesion." *American Sociological Review* 25 (1960), pp. 385–394.

Lockwood, D. "Violence among Middle School and High School Students: Analysis and Implications for Prevention." Washington, DC: U.S. Department of Justice, Office of Justice Programs, (1997).

Longshore, D., and J. Prager. "The Impact of School Desegregation: A Situational Analysis." *Annual Review of Sociology* 11 (1985), pp. 75–91.

Louv, R. *Childhood's Future.* New York: Anchor, 1990.

Lovaglia, M. J., and J. A. Houser. "Emotional Reactions and Status in Groups." *American Sociological Review* 61 (October 1996), pp. 867–883.

Luckmann, T. *The Invisible Religion: The Problem of Religion in Modern Society.* New York: Macmillan, 1967.

Lucy, J. *Grammatical Categories and Cognitive Processes.* New York: Cambridge University Press, 1992.

Maccoby, E. "The Varied Meanings of Masculine and Feminine." In J. M. Reinisch, L. A. Rosenblum, and S. A. Sanders (eds.), *Masculinity/Femininity: Basic Perspectives,* pp. 227–239. New York: Oxford University Press, 1987.

Maccoby, E. E., and C. N. Jacklin. *The Psychology of Sex Differences.* Stanford, CA: Stanford University Press, 1974.

MacKay, C. *Extraordinary Popular Delusions and the Madness of Crowds.* New York: Page, 1932.

Mackie, G. "Ending Footbinding and Infibulation: A Convention Account." *American Sociological Review* 61 (1996), pp. 999–1017.

Maguire, K., and A. L. Pastore (eds.). *Bureau of Justice Statistics Sourcebook of Criminal Justice Statistics 1996.* Washington, DC: U.S. Department of Justice, Bureau of Justice Statistics, 1997.

Maguire, K., A. L. Pastore, and T. J. Flanagan (eds.). *Sourcebook of Criminal Justice Statistics 1992.* Washington, DC: U.S. Department of Justice, Bureau of Justice Statistics, 1993.

Mair, G. *Oprah Winfrey: The Real Story.* Secaucus, NJ: Citadel Stars, 1996.

Malinowski, B. *The Sexual Life of Savages.* New York: Harcourt, Brace & World, 1929.

Malinowski, B. "Culture." In *Encyclopedia of the Social Sciences,* vol. 4, pp. 621–645. New York: Macmillan, 1931.

Mandel, E. *Late Capitalism.* London: New Left Books, 1975.

Manford, M. "Fearless Youth." In E. Marcus (ed.), *Making History: The Struggle for Gay and Lesbian Equal Rights, 1945–1990.* New York: HarperCollins, 1992, pp. 197–212.

Mann, M. *The Sources of Social Power.* New York: Cambridge University Press, 1987.

Mann, M. *The Sources of Social Power, Vol II: The Rise of Classes and Nation-States, 1760–1914.* New York: Cambridge University Press, 1993.

Manton, K. G., et al. Cited in J. Rosenthal, "The Age Boom." *The New York Times Magazine* (March 9, 1997), pp. 39ff.

Marcia, J. E. "Identity in Adolescence." In J. Adelson (ed.), *Handbook of Adolescent Society.* New York: Wiley, 1980.

Mare, R. D. "Five Decades of Educational Assortive Mating." *American Sociological Review* 56 (1991), pp. 15–32.

Marger, M. N. *Race and Ethnic Relations: American and Global Perspectives,* 3d ed. Belmont, CA: Wadsworth, 1994.

Marini, M. M. "Sex and Gender: What Do We Know?" *Sociological Forum* 5, 1 (1990), pp. 95–120.

Martin, P., and E. Midgley. "Immigration to the United States: Journey to an Uncertain Destination." *Population Bulletin* 49 (1994), pp. 2–47.

Marty, M. *The Public Church: Mainline Evangelical-Catholic.* New York: Crossroad, 1981.

Marx, K. "Contribution to the Critique of Hegel's Philosophy of Right" (1844). In T. B. Bottomore (ed.), *Early Writings.* New York: McGraw-Hill, 1963.

Marx, K. "The Economic and Philosophic Manuscripts of 1844." In K. Marx and F. Engels: *Collected Works,* vol. 3, pp. 229–348. London: Lawrence and Wishart, 1975.

Marx, K. "A Contribution to the Critique of Political Economy" (1859). In *Karl Marx/Friedrich Engels, Collected Works,* vol. 16, pp. 465–477. London: Lawrence and Wishart, 1980.

Marx, K., and F. Engels. *The Communist Manifesto* Chicago: Regnery, 1960. (Original work published (1848.)

Massey, D. S. "Featured Essay: Review of 'When Work Disappears: The World of the New Urban Poor,'" *Contemporary Sociology* 26, 4 (1997), pp. 416–418.

Massey, D. S., and N. A. Denton. *American Apartheid: Segregation and the Making of the Underclass.* Cambridge, MA: Harvard University Press, 1993.

Matthews, A. *Bright College Years: Inside the American Campus Today.* New York: Simon & Schuster, 1997.

Matthews, K. A., R. Wing, L. Kuller et al. "Influences of Natural Menopause on Psychological Characteristics and Symptoms of Middle-Aged Healthy Women." *Journal of Consulting and Clinical Psychology* 58, (1990), pp. 345–351.

Mayer, J., and J. Abramson. *Strange Justice: The Selling of Clarence Thomas.* Boston: Houghton Mifflin, 1994.

McCall, G. J., and Simmons, J. L. *Identities and Interactions: An Examination of Human Associations in Everyday Life.* New York: Free Press, 1972.

McCarthy, J. D., and M. Wolfson. "Resource Mobilization by Local Social Movement Organizations: Agency, Strategy, and Organization in the Movement against Drinking and Driving." *American Sociological Review* 61 (1996), pp. 1070–1088.

McCartney, B. "Promise Makers." *Policy Review* (September–October 1997), pp. 14–19.

McCauley, C. "The Nature of Social Influence in Groupthink: Compliance and Internalization." *Journal of Personality and Social Psychology* 57 (1989), pp. 250–260.

McCone, J. A. (ed.). *Violence in the City: An End or a Beginning?* California Governor's Commission on the Los Angeles Riots, 1966.

McGrath, E., G. P. Keita, B. Strickland, and N. F. Russo (eds.). *Women and Depression: Risk Factors and Treatment Issues.* Washington, DC: American Psychological Association, 1990.

McGuire, M. B. *Religion: The Social Context.* Belmont, CA: Wadsworth, 1981.

McGuire, M. B. *Religion: The Social Context,* 3d ed. Belmont, CA: Wadsworth, 1992.

McIntosh, J. "U.S. Suicide." *Newsletter: Michigan Association of Suicidology.* (Winter 1991), pp. 10–11.

McKinlay, J. B., and H. A. Feldman. "Age-Related Variation in Sexual Activity and Interest in Normal Men: Results from the Massachusetts Male Aging Study" A. S. Ross: (ed), in *Sexuality across the Life Course,* pp. 261–285. Chicago: University of Chicago Press.

McKinlay, J. B., S. M. McKinlay, and D. Brambilla. "The Relative Contribution of Endocrine Changes and Social Circumstances to Depression in Middle-Aged Women." *Journal of Health and Social Behavior* 28 (1987), pp. 345–363.

McKinley, J. C., Jr., with H. W. French. "Uncovering the Guilty Path along Zaire's Long Trail of Death." *The New York Times* (November 14, 1997), pp. A1, A14.

McKinsey & Co. *Employment Preferences.* Washington, DC: McKinsey Global Institute, November 1994.

McLanahan, S. L., and K. Booth. "Mother-Only Families: Problems, Prospects, and Politics." *Journal of Marriage and the Family* 52 (1989), pp. 557–579.

McLanahan, S. L., and G. Sandefur. *Growing Up with a Single Parent: What Helps,*

What Hurts. Cambridge, MA: Harvard University Press, 1994.

McLuhan, M., and Q. Fiore. *The Medium Is the Message.* New York: Bantam, 1967.

McNall, S. G. *The Road to Rebellion: Class Formation and Kansas Populism, 1865–1990.* Chicago: University of Chicago Press, 1988.

McPartland, J. M., and E. L. McDill. "Control and Differentiation in the Structure of American Education." *Sociology of Education* 55 (April–July 1982), pp. 77–88.

Mead, G. H. *Mind, Self, and Society.* Chicago: University of Chicago Press, 1934.

Mead, M. *Sex and Temperament in Three Primitive Societies.* New York: Morrow, 1935.

Mead, M. *Culture and Commitment.* New York: Doubleday, 1970.

Meier, R. F., and G. Geis. *Victimless Crimes?* Los Angeles: Roxbury, 1997.

Merrick, T. W., and S. J. Tordello. "Demographics: People and Markets." *Population Bulletin* 4, 1 (February 1988).

Merton, R. K. "Social Structure and Anomie." *American Sociological Review* 3 (1938), pp. 672–682.

Merton, R. K. *On the Shoulders of Giants: a Shandean Postscript.* New York: Free Press, 1965.

Merton, R. K. *Social Theory and Social Structure.* New York: Free Press, 1968.

Meyer, M. "A Death Spiral?" *Newsweek* (July 28, 1997a), pp. 48–49.

Meyer, M. "His Happy Light Is On." *Newsweek* (October 6, 1997b), pp. 46–48.

Meyers, S. L. "To Sex-Segregated Training, Still Semper Fi." *The New York Times* (December 16, 1997), pp. A1, A36.

Meyerson, J., M. R. Rank, F. Q. Raines, and M. A. Schnitzer. "Race and General Cognitive Ability: The Myth of a Diminishing Returns to Education." *Psychological Science* 9 (1998), pp. 61–64.

Michels, R. *First Lectures on Political Science.* Alfred de Grazia (trans.). Minneapolis: University of Minnesota Press, 1949. (Original work published 1915.)

Michels, R. *Political Parties: A Sociological Study of the Oligarchical Tendencies of Modern Democracy.* New York: Collier, 1962. (Original work published 1915.)

Mieth, T. D., and C. A. Moore. "Racial Differences in Criminal Processing: The Consequences of Model Selection on Conclusions about Differential Treatment." *Sociological Quarterly* 27 (1986), pp. 217–237.

Miles, J. "Religion Makes a Comeback. (Belief to Follow.)" *The New York Times Magazine* (December 7, 1997), pp. 56–59.

Milgram, S. "Behavioral Study of Obedience." *Journal of Abnormal and Social Psychology* 67 (1963), pp. 371–378.

Miller, M. "Secrets of the Cult." *Newsweek* (April 17, 1997), pp. 29ff.

Miller, M. C. *Boxed In: The Culture of TV.* Evanston, IL: Northwestern University Press, 1988.

Mills, C. W. *White Collar.* New York: Oxford University Press, 1951.

Mills, C. W. *The Power Elite.* New York: Oxford University Press, 1956.

Mills, C. W. *Sociological Imagination.* New York: Oxford University Press, 1959.

Miner, H. "Body Ritual among the Nacirema." *American Anthropologist* 58 (1956), pp. 503–507.

Mizruchi, M. "What Do Interlocks Do? An Analysis, Critique, and Assessment of Interlocking Directorates." *Annual Review of Sociology* 22 (1996), pp. 271–298.

Moe, T. *The Organization of Interests.* Chicago: University of Chicago Press, 1982.

Monastersky, R. "Health in the Hot Zone: How Would Global Warming Affect Humans?" *Science News* 149 (1996), pp. 218–219.

Moore, B. *Injustice: The Social Bases of Obedience and Revolt.* White Plains, NY: Sharpe, 1978.

Moore, E., and M. Mills. "The Neglected Victims and Unexamined Costs of White-Collar Crimes." *Crime & Delinquency* 36 (July 1990), pp. 408–418.

Moore, K. A., and I. V. Sawhill. "Implication of Women's Employment for Home and Family Life." In P. Voydanoff (ed.), *Work and Family*, pp. 153–171. Palo Alto, CA: Mayfield, 1984.

Moore, S. F., and B. G. Meyeroff. *Symbol and Politics.* Ithaca, NY: Cornell University Press, 1975.

Morley, R. "Wife Beating and Modernization: The Case of Papua New Guinea." *Journal of Comparative Family Studies* 24, 1 (1994), pp. 25–52.

Morris, A. D. *The Origins of the Civil Rights Movement: Black Communities Organizing for Change.* New York: Free Press, 1984.

Muller, P. O. "The Outer City." Resource Paper no. 75-2. Washington, DC: Association of American Geographers, 1976.

Mumola, C. J., and A. J. Beck. *Prisoners in Jail.* Washington, DC: U.S. Department of Justice, Bureau of Justice Statistics, 1997.

Murdock, G. P. *Social Structure.* New York: Macmillan, 1949.

Murdock, G. P. "World Ethnographic Survey." *American Anthropologist* 59 (1957), pp. 664–687.

Murray, C. *Losing Ground: American Social Policy, 1950–1980.* New York: Basic Books, 1984.

Murstein, B. I. *Paths to Marriage.* Beverly Hills, CA: Sage, 1986.

Musgrave, P. W. *Socialising Contexts.* Sydney: Allen and Unwin, 1988.

Mydans, S. "Bad News, Silver Lining for Indonesian Laborers." *The New York Times* (February 6, 1998), p. A6.

Myers, D. G. *Social Psychology*, 4th ed. New York: McGraw-Hill, 1993.

Myerson, A. R. "Need Programmers? Surf Abroad." *The New York Times* (January 18, 1998), p. 4.

Myrdal, G. *An American Dilemma.* New York: Harper & Row, 1944.

Nader, R., M. Green, and J. Seligman. *Taming the Giant Corporation.* New York: Norton, 1976.

Nagel, J. *American Indian Ethnic Renewal: Red Power and the Transformation of Identity and Culture.* New York: Oxford University Press, 1996.

National Advisory Commission on Civil Disorders. *Report.* Washington, DC: U.S. Government Printing Office, 1968.

National AIDS Clearing House. Center for Disease Control and Prevention, fact sheet. (1998), www.cdcnac.org.

National Center of Child Abuse and Neglect (NCCAN). *Third National Incidence Study of Child Abuse and Neglect (WIS-3), Final Report.* Washington, DC: U.S. Department of Health and Human Services, 1996.

National Center for Educational Statistics. *The State of Mathematics Achievement: NAEP's 1990 Assessment of the National and the Trial Assessment of the States.* Washington, DC: U.S. Department of Education, National Center for Educational Statistics, 1992.

National Center for Educational Statistics. *Adult Literacy in America: Executive Summary.* Washington, DC: U.S. Department of Education, 1993a.

National Center for Educational Statistics. *Executive Summary of the NAEP 1992 Reading Report Card for the Nation and the States: Data from the National and the Trial Assessments.* Washington, DC: U.S. Department of Education, National Center for Educational Statistics, 1993b.

National Center for Health Statistics. Press release. (June 24, 1996), www.census.gov.

National Commission on Excellence in Education. *A Nation at Risk: The Imperative for Educational Reform.* Washington, DC: U.S. Department of Education, 1983.

National Institute on Alcohol Abuse and Alcoholism. *Alcohol Alert,* no. 29 PH 357 (July 1995).

National League of Women Voters. (1996). www.lwv.org/nvra.html.

National Religious Broadcasters. *Directory of Religious Broadcasting, 1997.* Parsipanny, NJ: 1997.

National Research Council. *A Common Destiny: Blacks and American Society.* G. D. Jaynes and R. M. Williams (eds.). Washington, DC: National Academy Press, 1989.

National Research Council. *Measuring Poverty: A New Approach.* Washington, DC: National Academy Press, 1995.

Neal, A. G., H. T. Groat, and J. W. Wicks. "Attitudes about Having Children: A Study of 600 Couples in the Early Years of Marriage." *Journal of Marriage and the Family* 51 (May 1989), pp. 313–328.

Neckerman, K. M., and J. Kirschenman. "Statistical Discrimination and Inner-City Workers: An Investigation of Employers' Hiring Decisions. Paper presented at the annual meeting of the American Sociological Association, Washington, DC, August 11–15, 1990.

Neft, N., and A. D. Levine. *Where Women Stand: An International Report on the Status of Women in 140 Countries, 1997–1998.* New York: Random House, 1997.

Neubeck, K. J. *Social Problems: A Critical Approach.* New York: McGraw-Hill, 1991.

Neugarten, B. L., and D. A. Neugarten. "The Changing Meanings of Age." *Psychology Today* 21 (May 1987), pp. 29–30.

Neville, B. "Carkhuff, Maslow, and Interpersonal Perception in Small Groups." *Small Group Behavior* 14 (May 1983), pp. 211–226.

New York Times/CBS News Poll. *The New York Times* (December 14, 1997), pp. A1, A32.

Newcombe, K. *An Economic Justification for Rural Afforestation: The Case of Ethiopia.* Energy Department Paper no. 16. Washington, DC: World Bank, 1984.

Newman, K. S. *Declining Fortunes: The Withering of the American Dream.* New York: Basic Books, 1993.

Niebuhr, G. "Baptists Censure Disney on Gay-Spouse Benefits." *The New York Times* (June 13, 1996), p. A10.

Niebuhr, H. R. *The Social Sources of Denominationalism.* New York: Holt, 1929.

Nielsen Report on Television 1989. Northbrook, IL: Nielsen, 1989.

Nisbet, R. A. *The Sociological Tradition.* London: Heinemann, 1967.

Norman, M. "The Man Who Saw Old Anew." *The New York Times Magazine* (March 9, 1997), p. 54.

Oakes, J. *Keeping Track: How Schools Structure Inequality.* New Haven, CT: Yale University Press, 1985.

Oakes, J. "Curriculum Inequality and School Reform." *Equity and Excellence* 23 (Spring 1987), pp. 8–14.

Oakes, J. "Tracking in Mathematics and Science Education: A Structural Contribution to Unequal Schooling." In L. Weis (ed.), *Class, Race, and Gender in American Education,* pp. 106–125. Albany: State University of New York Press, 1988.

Oakley, A. *Sociology of Housework.* New York: Pantheon, 1985.

Oberschall, A. *Social Conflict and Social Movements.* Englewood Cliffs, NJ: Prentice-Hall, 1973.

O'Carroll, P. W., M. L. Rosenberg, and J. L. Mercy. "Suicide." In M. L. Rosenberg and M. A. Fenley (eds.), *Violence in America: A Public Health Approach,* pp. 184–196. New York: Oxford University Press, 1991.

O'Connell, M. "Late Expectations: Childbearing Patterns of American Women for the 1990s. Studies in American Fertility." *Current Population Reports,* Series P-23, no. 176, 1991.

O'Dea, T. F. *The Sociology of Religion.* Englewood Cliffs, NJ: Prentice-Hall, 1966.

Offer, D., E. Ostrov, K. Howard, and R. Atkinson. *The Teenage World: Adolescent Self-Image in Ten Countries.* New York: Plenum, 1988.

Ogbu, J. U. *The Next Generation: An Ethnography of Education in an Urban Neighborhood.* New York: Academic Press, 1974.

Ogburn, W. *Social Change.* New York: Viking, 1922.

O'Hare, W. P. "America's Minorities—The Demographics of Diversity." *Population Bulletin* 47 (1993a), pp. 1–45.

O'Hare, W. P. "Diversity: More Millions Looking Less Alike." *Population Today* 21 (April 1993b), pp. 1–2.

O'Hare, W. P. "A New Look at Poverty in America." *Population Bulletin* 51, 2 (September 1996) pp. 1–47.

Olmsted, M. S., and A. P. Hare. *The Small Group,* 2d ed. New York: Random House, 1978.

Olshansky, S. J., B. Carnes, R. G. Rogers, and L. Smith. "Infectious Diseases—New and Ancient Threats to World Health." *Population Bulletin* (July 1997), p. 20.

Olson, C. B. "The Influence of Context on Gender Differences in Performance Attributions: Further Evidence of a 'Feminine Modesty' Effect." Paper presented at the annual meeting of the Western Psychological Association, San Francisco, 1988.

Olson, M. *The Theory of Collective Goods.* Cambridge, MA: Harvard University Press, 1965.

Orfield, G., M. D. Bachmeier, and T. Eitle. "Deepening Segregation in American Public Schools.: A Special Report from the Harvard Project on School Desegregation." *Equality and Excellence in Education* 30 (1997), p. 5.

Orhnial, T. (ed.) *Limited Liability and the Corporation.* London: Croom Helm, 1982.

Orlean, S. "The Sporting Scene." *The New Yorker* (July 7, 1997), p. 25.

Ortner, S. B. "Is Female to Male as Nature Is to Culture?" In M. Z. Rosaldo and L. Lamphere (eds.), *Women, Culture, and Society,* pp. 67–68. Stanford, CA: Stanford University Press, 1974.

Ostling, R. N. "Power, Glory—and Politics." *Time* (February 17, 1986).

Palen, J. H. *The Urban World.* New York: McGraw-Hill, 1975.

Parenti, M. *Democracy for the Few,* 5th ed. New York: St. Martin's, 1988.

Parenti, M. *Inventing Reality: The Politics of News Media,* 2d ed. New York: St. Martin's, 1993.

Park, R. E., W. Burgess, and R. D. McKenzie (eds.). *The City.* Chicago: University of Chicago Press, 1925.

Parsons, T. *The Social System.* New York: Free Press, 1951.

Parsons, T. "Sociology and Social Psychology." In H. N. Fairchild et al., *Religious Perspectives in College Teaching,* pp. 286–337. New York: Ronald Press, 1952.

Parsons, T. "Christianity and Modern Industrial Society." In E. Tiryakian (ed.), *Sociological Theory, Values, and Sociocultural Change,* pp. 33–70. Glencoe, IL: Free Press, 1963.

Pascale, R. T., and A. G. Athos. *The Art of Japanese Management.* New York: Penguin Books, 1982.

Passell, P. "Blue-Collar Blues: Who Is to Blame?" *The New York Times* (January 17, 1990), p. D2.

Pate, A. M., and E. E. Hamilton. "Formal and Informal Deterrents to Domestic Violence: The Dade County Spouse Arrest Experiment." *American Sociological Review* 57 (1992), pp. 691–697.

Patel, S. *Pharmaceuticals and Health in the Third World.* Oxford: Pergamon, 1983.

Patterson, O. "Racism Is Not the Issue." *The New York Times* (November 17, 1997), p. WK15.

Pease, J. "Sociology and the Sense of Commoners." *The American Sociologist* 16 (November 1981), pp. 257–271.

Perrow, C. "The Sixties Observed." In M. N. Zald and J. D. McCarthy (eds.), *The Dynamics of Social Movements,* pp. 192–211. Cambridge, MA: Winthrop, 1979.

Peterson, R. A. "Revitalizing the Culture Concept." *Annual Review of Sociology* 5 (1979), pp. 137–166.

Pettigrew, T. F. "Race and Intergroup Relations." In R. K. Merton and R. Nisbet (eds.), *Contemporary Social Problems,* 4th ed., pp. 461–508. New York: Harcourt Brace Jovanovich, 1976.

Phillips, D. P. "The Influence of Suggestion on Suicide: Substantive and Theoretical Implications of the Werther Effect." *American Sociological Review* 39, 3 (1974), pp. 340–354.

Phillips, D. P., and L. L. Cartensen. "Clustering of Teenage Suicides after Television News Stories about Suicide." *New England Journal of Medicine* 315, 11 (September 11, 1986), pp. 685–689.

Phillips, D. P., and L. L. Cartensen. "The Effect of Suicide Stories on Various Demographic Groups, 1968–1985." *Suicide and Life-Threatening Behavior* 18 (Spring 1988), pp. 100–114.

Physician Task Force on Hunger. *Hunger in America: The Growing Epidemic.* Hanover, NH: University Press of New England, 1985.

Pichardo, N. A. "New Social Movements: A Critical Review." *Annual Review of Sociology* 23 (1997), pp. 411–430.

Pittman, K. "Teenage Pregnancy." In C. Calhoun and G. Ritzer (eds.), *Social Problems,* pp. 158–178. New York: McGraw-Hill, 1993.

Piven, F. F., and R. Cloward. *Poor People's Movements.* New York: Vintage, 1979.

Pleck, J. H. "American Fathering in Historical Perspective." In M. S. Kimmel (ed.), *Changing Men: New Directions in Research on Men and Masculinity,* pp. 83–97. Newbury Park, CA: Sage, 1988.

Plog, F., and D. G. Bates. *Cultural Anthropology,* 2d ed. New York: Knopf, 1980.

Popenoe, D. *Disturbing the Nest: Family Change and Decline in Modern Societies.* New York: Aldine De Gruyter, 1988.

Popenoe, D. "Point of View." *The Chronicle of Higher Education* (April 14, 1993), p. A48.

Popkewitz, T. S. "Organization and Power: Teacher Education Reforms." *Social Education* (November–December 1987), pp. 496–500.

Population Reference Bureau. "24-Hour Economy Changing How We Work and

Live." *Population Today* (December 1997a), pp. 1–2.

Population Reference Bureau. "World Population Data Sheet." Washington, DC: Population Reference Bureau, 1997b.

Population Reference Bureau. "World Population and the Environment." Washington, D.C.: Population Reference Bureau, 1997c.

Population Today. "Census Race and Ethnic Categories Retooled." 26, 4 (January 1998), p. 4.

Portes, A., and R. L. Bach. *Latin American Journey.* Berkeley: University of California Press, 1985.

Postel, S. "Dividing." *Technology Review* (April 1997), pp. 54–62.

Postel, S., and C. Heise. *Reforesting the Earth.* Washington, DC: Worldwatch Institute, 1988.

Postman, N., and S. Powers. *How to Watch TV News.* New York: Penguin, 1992.

Powell, A. G., E. Farrar, and D. K. Cohen. *The Shopping Mall High School: Winners and Losers in the Educational Marketplace.* Boston: Houghton Mifflin, 1985.

Powell, B. "The World Economy: Crossed Fingers." *Newsweek* (November 3, 1997), pp. 38–41.

Prasad, B. D. "Dowry-Related Violence: A Content Analysis of News in Selected Newspapers." *Journal of Comparative Family Studies* 24, 1 1994. pp. 71–89.

President's National Urban Policy Report. Washington, DC: U.S. Government Printing Office, 1980.

Price, S. J., and P. C. McKenry. *Divorce.* Beverly Hills, CA: Sage, 1988.

Prothrow-Stith, D. *Deadly Consequences.* New York: HarperCollins, 1991.

Provence, S. "Infants in Institutions Revisited." *Zero to Three* 9 (1989), pp. 1–4.

Przeworski, A. *Capitalism and Social Democracy.* Cambridge, Eng.: Cambridge University Press, 1985.

Quadagno, J. "Aging" In G. Ritzer (ed.), *Social Problems,* 2d ed. New York: Random House, 1986.

Queen, S. A., R. W. Haberstein, and J. S. Quadagno. *The Family in Various Cultures.* New York: Harper & Row, 1988.

Quinney, R. *Criminology.* Boston: Little, Brown, 1976.

Rada, J. "A Third World Perspective." In G. Friedrichs and A. Schaff (eds.), *Microelectronics and Society: For Better or for Worse,* pp. 213–242. Oxford, Eng.: Pergamon, 1982.

Ray, M. "The Cycle of Abstinence and Relapse among Heroin Addicts." In H. S.

Becker (ed.), *The Other Side: Perspectives on Deviance,* pp. 163–177. New York: Free Press, 1964.

Rector, R., and W. F. Lauber. *America's Failed $5.4 Trillion War on Poverty.* Washington, DC: Heritage Foundation, 1995.

Reichman, N. "Insider Training." In M. Tonry and A. J. Reiss, Jr. (eds.), *Beyond the Law: Crime in Complex Organizations,* pp. 55–96. Chicago: University of Chicago Press, 1993.

Reiss, A. J., Jr. *The Police and the Public.* New Haven, CT: Yale University Press, 1971.

Reiss, A. J., Jr. "The Policing of Organizational Life." In M. Punch (ed.), *Control in the Police Organization,* pp. 78–97. Cambridge, MA: MIT Press, 1983.

Reiss, A. J., Jr. "Selecting Strategies of Organizational Control over Organizational Life." In K. Hawkins and J. M. Thomas (eds.), *Enforcing Regulation,* pp. 23–35. Boston: Kluwer-Nijhoff, 1984.

Remick, D. "Dr. Wilson's Neighborhood." *The New Yorker* (April 26 & May 6, 1996), pp. 96–107.

Republican National Committee. *Contract with America. The Bold Plan by Rep. Newt Gingrich, Rep. Dick Armey and the House Republicans to Change the Nation.* E. Gillespie and B. Schellhas (eds.). New York: Times Book/Random House, 1994.

Richmond-Abbott, M. *Masculine and Feminine: Gender Roles over the Life Cycle.* New York: McGraw-Hill, 1992.

Ries, P., and A. J. Stone. *The American Woman, 1992–1993.* New York: Norton, 1992.

Riesman, D. *The Lonely Crowd.* New Haven, CT: Yale University Press, 1950.

Riley, N. E. "Gender, Power, and Population Change." *Population Bulletin* 52, 1 (May 1997), pp. 1–48.

Risen, J. "Promise Keepers Flood D.C." *The Los Angeles Times* (October 5, 1997), www.latimes.com.

Rist, R. C. *The Invisible Children: School Integration in American Society.* Cambridge, MA: Harvard University Press, 1978.

Ritzer, G. *The McDonaldization of Society.* Newbury Park, CA: Pine Forge Press, 1993.

Ritzer, G. *The McDonaldization Thesis: Explorations and Extensions.* Newbury Park, CA: Sage, 1998.

Rivera, R. "Sylvia Lee." "The Drag Queen." In E. Marcus (ed.), *Making History: The Struggle for Gay and Lesbian Equal Rights, 1945–1990.* New York: HarperCollins, (1992) pp. 175–186.

Roberts, R. S. *Clarence Thomas and the Tough Love Crowd: Counterfeit Heroes and Unhappy Truths.* New York: New York University Press, 1995.

Robertson, J. *Children of Choice: Freedom and the New Reproductive Technologies.* Princeton, NJ: Princeton University Press, 1994.

Roof, W. C. *A Generation of Seekers: The Spiritual Journeys of the Baby Boom Generation.* New York: HarperCollins, 1993.

Rose, P. I. *They and We: Racial and Ethnic Relations in the United States,* 2d ed. New York: Random House, 1974.

Rose, P. I. "Asian Americans: From Pariahs to Paragons." In N. Glazer (ed.), *Clamor at the Gates: The New American Immigration,* pp. 181–212. San Francisco: Institute for Contemporary Studies Press, 1985.

Rosenbaum, D. E. "Cash Overflow: Fixing Politics, More or Less." *The New York Times* (December 22, 1996), p. E1.

Rosenbaum, D. E. "In the Political Money Game, the Law Got No Respect in 1996." *The Providence Sunday Journal* (January 5, 1997), p. D4.

Rosenbaum, J. E., and T. Kariya. "From High School to Work: Market and Institutional Mechanisms in Japan." *American Journal of Sociology* 94 (May 1989), pp. 1334–1365.

Rosenberg, D., and M. Bai. "Drinking and Dying." *Newsweek* (October 13, 1997), p. 69.

Rosenthal, J. "The Age Boom." *The New York Times Magazine* (March 9, 1997), pp. 39–43.

Rosenthal, R., and L. Jacobson. *Pygmalion in the Classroom: Teacher Expectations and Pupils' Intellectual Development.* New York: Holt, Rinehart and Winston, 1968.

Rossi, A. S. "Closing the Gap: Bio-medical vs. Social Behavioral Factors in the Experience of Women and Research on the Menopausal Transition." Paper prepared for the symposium, *Development in Midlife: Bio-psycho-social Perspectives.* American Psychological Association, Washington, DC, August 15, 1992.

Rossi, P. H. *Without Shelter: Homelessness in the 1980s.* New York: Unwin Hyman, 1988.

Rossi, P. H. "Troubling Families: Family Homelessness in America." *American Behavioral Scientist* 37, 3 (January 1994), pp. 342–395.

Rossi, P. H., and J. D. Wright. "The Urban Homeless: A Portrait of Urban Dislocation." *Annals of the American Academy of Political and Social Science* 501 (January 1989), pp. 132–142.

Roy, D. "Quota Restriction and Goldbricking in a Machine Shop." *American*

Journal of Sociology 62 (March 1952), pp. 427–442.

Rubington, E., and W. S. Weinberg. *Deviance: An Interactionist Perspective,* 6th ed. New York: Macmillan, 1995.

Ruch, J., and J. Shurley. " 'Genie' as an Adult." Presentation at the Center for Advanced Study in the Behavioral Sciences, Stanford, CA, March 1985.

Ruscher, J. B., E. C. O'Neil, and E. D. Hammer. "The Perception of an Out-Group after Provocation by One of Its Members." *Journal of Social Psychology* 137, 1 (1997), pp. 5–9.

Rutter, M. *The Qualities of Mothering; Maternal Deprivation.* New York: Aronson, 1974.

Rutter, M. "Functions and Consequences of Relationships: Some Psychopathological Considerations." In R. Hinde and J. Stevenson-Hinde (eds.), *Relationships within Families: Mutual Influences,* pp. 332–353. Oxford, Eng.: Clarendon Press, 1988.

Rymer, R. *An Abused Child's Flight from Silence.* New York: HarperCollins, 1993.

Safilios-Rothschild, C. "The Study of Family Power Structure." *Journal of Marriage and the Family* 32 (1970), pp. 539–552.

St. John, N. *School Desegregation.* New York: Wiley, 1975.

Sampson, R. J., and J. H. Laub. "Crime and Deviance over the Life Course: The Salience of Adult Social Bonds." *American Sociological Review* 55 (October 1990), pp. 609–627.

Samuelson, R. J. "Global Boom and Bust?" *Newsweek* (November 10, 1997), p. 35.

Sanday, P. R. *Female Power and Male Dominance: On the Origins of Sexual Equality.* Cambridge, MA: Cambridge University Press, 1981.

Sandy, J. "Evaluating the Public Support for Educational Vouchers: A Case Study." In E. Cohn (ed.), *Market Approaches to Education,* pp. 381–391. New York: Pergamon, 1997.

Sapir, E. *Language: An Introduction to the Study of Speech.* New York: Harcourt, 1921.

Saunders, P. "Space, the City and Urban Sociology." In D. Gregory and J. Urry (eds.), *Spatial Relations and Spatial Structures,* pp. 67–89. New York: St. Martin's, 1985.

Savin-Williams, R. C., and T. J. Berndt. "Peer Relations during Adolescence." In S. S. Feldman and G. R. Elliott (eds.), *At the Threshold: The Developing Adolescent.* Cambridge, MA: Harvard University Press, 1990.

Scarpitti, F. R., and M. L. Andersen. *Social Problems,* 2d ed. New York: HarperCollins, 1992.

Scheff, T. J. "Shame and Conformity: The Deference-Emotion System." *American Sociological Review* 53 (June 1988), pp. 395–406.

Schell, O. *Discos and Democracy: China in the Throes of Reform.* New York: Anchor, 1989.

Schmalz, J. "Whatever Happened to AIDS?" *The New York Times Magazine* (November 28, 1993), pp. 56ff.

Schnaiberg, A. *The Environment: From Surplus to Scarcity.* New York: Oxford University Press, 1980.

Schnaiberg, A., and S. Goldenberg. "From Empty Nest to Crowded Nest: The Dynamics of Incompletely Launched Adults." *Social Problems* 36 (1989), pp. 251–269.

Schor, J. B. *The Overworked American: The Unexpected Decline of Leisure.* New York: Basic Books, 1992.

Schott, K. "The Rise of Keynesian Economics." In D. Held, J. Anderson, B. Gieben, S. Hall, L. Harris, P. Lewis, N. Parker, and B. Turok (eds.), *States and Society,* pp. 338–362. New York: New York University Press, 1983.

Schumann, H., and S. Presser. *Questions and Answers in Attitude Surveys: Experiments in Question Form, Wording and Context.* New York: Academic Press, 1981.

Schur, E. M. *Crimes without Victims.* Englewood Cliffs, NJ: Prentice-Hall, 1965.

Schur, E. M. *The Politics of Deviance: Stigma Contests and the Uses of Power.* Englewood Cliffs, NJ: Prentice-Hall, 1980.

Scott, W. R. *Organizations: Rational, Natural, and Open Systems,* 2d ed. Englewood Cliffs, NJ: Prentice-Hall, 1987.

Sculley, J., with J. Byrne. *Odyssey: Pepsi to Apple . . . A Journey of Adventures, Ideas, and the Future.* New York: Harper & Row, 1987.

Scully, D., and J. Marolla. "Convicted Rapists' Vocabulary of Motive: Excuses and Justifications." *Social Problems* 31 (June 1984), pp. 530–544.

Sen, A. *Poverty and Famines.* New York: Oxford University Press, 1881.

Senna, J. J., and L. J. Siegel. *Introduction to Criminal Justice,* 7th ed. New York: West, 1996.

Sennett, T. *The Fall of Public Man.* New York: Knopf, 1978.

Sennett, T. *The Psychology of Society.* New York: Vintage, 1980.

Sewell, W. "Inequality of Opportunity for Higher Education." *American Sociological Review* 36 (October 1971), pp. 793–809.

Sewell, W. H., and R. M. Hauser. *Recent Developments in the Wisconsin Study of Social and Psychological Factors in Socioeconomic*

Achievements. Working Paper 11. Madison, WI: Center for Demography and Ecology, 1976.

Sewell, W. H., and R. M. Hauser. "The Wisconsin Longitudinal Study of Social and Psychological Factors in Aspirations and Achievements." *Research in Sociology of Education and Socialization* 1 (1980), pp. 59–99.

Shaiken, H. *Work Transformed: Automation and Labor in the Computer Age.* New York: Holt, Rinehart and Winston, 1984.

Shapiro, L. "The Myth of Quality Time." *Newsweek* (May 12, 1997), pp. 62–69.

Shapiro, S. P. "Considering the Crime, Not the Criminal: Reconsidering the Concept of White-Collar Crime." *American Sociological Review* 55 (June 1990), pp. 346–365.

Shaw, M. E. *Group Dynamics,* 3d ed. New York: McGraw-Hill, 1981.

Sheehy, G. *Passages.* New York: Dutton, 1976.

Sheehy, G. *The Silent Passage: Menopause.* New York: Random House, 1992.

Shenon, P. "Army's Leadership Blamed in Report on Sexual Abuses." *The New York Times* (September 12, 1997), www.nytimes.com/archives.

Sherman, L. W., and R. A. Berk. "The Specific Deterrent Effects of Arrest for Domestic Assault." *American Sociological Review* 49 (1984), pp. 261–272.

Sherman, L. W., and E. G. Cohn. "The Impact of Research on Legal Policy: The Minneapolis Domestic Violence Experiment." *Law and Society Review* 23, 1 (1989), pp. 117–144.

Sherman, L. W., and D. A. Smith, with J. D. Schmidt and D. P. Rogan. "Crime, Punishment, and Stake in Conformity: Legal and Informal Control of Domestic Violence." *American Sociological Review* 57 (1992), pp. 680–690.

Shields, J. J., Jr. (ed.). *Japanese Schooling: Patterns of Socialization, Equality, and Political Control.* University Park: Pennsylvania State University Press, 1989.

Shills, E. *Tradition.* Chicago: University of Chicago Press, 1981.

Shilts, R. *And the Band Played On: Politics, People, and the AIDS Epidemic.* New York: Penguin, 1987.

Shiner, L. "Secularization: Its Meaning and Effects." *Journal for the Scientific Study of Religion* 6 (Fall 1967), pp. 207–220.

Shriver, P. A. L. "Do Americans Believe in the Church?" In C. H. Jacquet, Jr., *Yearbook of American and Canadian Churches, 1979,* pp. 255–258. New York: Abingdon, 1979.

Signorielli, N. "Television and Conceptions about Sex Roles: Maintaining

Conventionality and the Status Quo." *Sex Roles* 21 (1989), pp. 341–360.

Signorielli, N., and M. Lears. "Children, Television, and Conceptions of Chores: Attitudes and Behavior." *Sex Roles* 27, 3–4 (1992), pp. 157–170.

Silverman, M., and P. Lee. *Pills, Profits and Politics.* Berkeley: University of California Press, 1974.

Simmel, G. *The Sociology of Georg Simmel.* K. H. Wolff (trans.). New York: Free Press, 1964. (Original work published 1905.)

Simon, R. J., and Danziger, G. *Women's Movements in America: Their Successes, Disappointments, and Aspirations.* New York: Praeger, 1991.

Singer, J. L, and D. G. Singer. "Family Experiences and Television Viewing as Predictors of Children's Imagination, Restlessness, and Aggression." *Journal of Social Issues* 42 (1986), pp. 107–124.

Singer, J. L., D. G. Singer, and W. S. Rapacynski. "Family Patterns and Television Viewing as Predictors of Children's Beliefs and Aggression." *Journal of Communications* 34 (1984), pp. 73–89.

Sisson, M. *Money, Wealth and Class.* London: Oxford University Press, 1970.

Skocpol, T. *States and Social Revolutions.* New York: Cambridge University Press, 1979.

Skocpol, T. *Marxist Inquiries: Studies of Labor, Class, and States.* Chicago: University of Chicago Press, 1982.

Skolnick, A. S. *Embattled Paradise: The American Family in an Age of Uncertainty.* New York: Basic Books, 1991.

Skolnick, A. S. *The Intimate Environment,* 6th ed. New York: HarperCollins, 1995.

Slater, P. E. "Role Differentiation in Small Groups." In A. P. Hare, E. F. Borgatta, and R. F. Bales (eds.), *Small Groups: Studies in Social Interaction,* pp. 498–513. New York: Knopf, 1955.

Slavin, R. E. "Grouping for Instruction Equity and Effectiveness." *Equity and Excellence* 23 (Spring 1987) pp. 31–36.

Sloan, A. "Hong Kong Ain't Sheboygan." *Newsweek* (November 3, 1997), p. 42.

Sloan, A. "They Deserve Each Other." *Newsweek* (November 17, 1997), p. 60.

Slocum, W. *Occupational Careers.* Chicago: Aldine, 1966.

Smelser, N. *Theory of Collective Behavior.* New York: Free Press, 1963.

Smith, L. J. F. *Domestic Violence: An Overview of the Literature.* Home Office Research Study no. 107. London: Her Majesty's Stationery Office, 1989.

Smith, M. G. "Institutional and Political Conditions of Pluralism." In L. Kuper and M. G. Smith (eds.), *Pluralism in Africa,* pp. 27–65. Berkeley: University of California Press, 1969.

Smith, P. B., and M. Tayeb. "Organizational Structure and Processes." In M. Bond (ed.), *The Cross-Cultural Challenge to Social Psychology.* Newbury Park, CA: Sage, 1989.

Smith, T. W. "The Polls: Poll Trends: Religious Beliefs and Behaviors and the Televangelist Scandals of 1987–1988." *Public Opinion Quarterly* 56 (1992), pp. 360–380.

Smith, T. W. *General Social Surveys, 1972–1996: Cumulative Codebook.* Chicago: National Opinion Research Center, 1996.

Snell, T. L. *Capital Punishment 1995.* Washington, DC: U.S. Department of Justice, Office of Justice Programs, 1996.

Snow, D. A., and R. D. Benford. "Master Frames and Cycles of Protest." In A. Morris and C. M. Mueller (eds.), *Frontiers in Social Movement Theory,* pp. 133–155. New Haven, CT: Yale University Press, 1992.

Snow, D. A., F. B. Rochford, Jr., S. K. Worden, and R. D. Benford. "Frame Alignment Processes, Micromobilization, and Movement Participation." *American Sociological Review* 51 (1986), pp. 464–481.

Soldo, B. J., and E. M. Agree. "America's Elderly." *Population Bulletin* 43, 3 (September 1988), pp. 1–53.

Sontag, D. "Making 'Refugee Experience' Less Daunting." *The New York Times* (September 27, 1992), pp. A1, A36.

Sowell, T. *Ethnic America: A History.* New York: Basic Books, 1981.

Sowell, T. "Ethnicity and IQ." In S. Fraser (ed.), *The Bell Curve Wars: Race, Intelligence, and the Future of America,* pp. 170–179. New York: Basic Books, 1995.

Spanier, G. B. "Bequeathing Family Continuity." *Journal of Marriage and the Family* 51 (February 1989), pp. 3–13.

Specter, M. "The Most Tainted Place on Earth." *The New York Times Magazine* (February 6, 1998), pp. 49–52.

Spellman, S. O. "Recruitment of Minority Teachers: Issues, Problems, Facts, Possible Solutions." *Journal of Teacher Education* (July/August 10, 1988), pp. 58–63.

Spitz, R. A. "Hospitalism: An Inquiry into the Genesis of Psychiatric Conditions in Early Childhood." In A. Freud (ed.), *The Psychoanalytic Study of the Child.* New York: International Universities Press, 1945.

Spitze, G. "Women's Employment and Family Relations." *Journal of Marriage and the Family* 50 (1988), pp. 595–618.

Spivey, C. B., and S. Prentice-Dunn. "Assessing the Directionality of Deindividuated Behavior: Effects of Deindividuation, Modeling, and Private Self-Consciousness on Aggressive and Prosocial Responses." *Basic and Applied Social Psychology* 11 (1990), pp. 387–403.

Stacey, J. *In the Name of the Family: Rethinking Family Values in the Postmodern Age.* Boston: Beacon Press, 1996.

Stack, S. "Celebrities and Suicide: A Taxonomy and Analysis, 1948–1983." *American Sociological Review* 57, 3 (1987a), pp. 401–412.

Stack, S. "The Sociological Study of Suicide: Methodological Issues." *Suicide and Life-Threatening Behavior* 17, 2 (Summer 1987b), pp. 133–150.

Stack, S. "Execution Publicity and Homicide in South Carolina: A Research Note." *Sociological Quarterly* 31, 4 (1990), pp. 559–611.

Stanley, H. W., and R. G. Niemi. *Vital Statistics on American Politics.* Washington, DC: CQ Press, 1988.

Stark, R., and W. S. Bainbridge. "Networks of Faith: Interpersonal Bonds and Recruitment to Cults and Sects." *American Journal of Sociology* 85 (1980), pp. 1376–1395.

Statistical Abstract, 1992. U.S. Bureau of the Census. *Statistical Abstract of the United States, 1992.* Washington, DC: U.S. Government Printing Office, 1992.

Statistical Abstract, 1996. U.S. Bureau of the Census. *Statistical Abstract of the United States, 1996.* Washington, DC: U.S. Government Printing Office, 1996.

Statistical Abstract, 1997. U.S. Bureau of the Census. *Statistical Abstract of the United States, 1997.* Washington, DC: U.S. Government Printing Office, 1997.

Stearns, L. B. "How America Can Best Compete in a Global Economy." In C. Calhoun and G. Ritzer (eds.), *Social Problems.* New York: McGraw-Hill/Primus, 1992.

Stearns, L. B. "How the United States Can Compete in a Global Economy." In C. Calhoun and G. Ritzer (eds.), *Social Problems.* New York: McGraw-Hill/Primus, 1993.

Steele, C. "Protective Dis-identification and Academic Performance." Research proposal to NIMH, Stanford University, 1993.

Steele, C., and J. Aronson. "Contending with a Stereotype: American Intellectual Test Performance and Stereotype Vulnerability." Seminar on Meritocracy and Equality, University of Chicago, May, 1995.

Steffensmeier, D., and M. D. Harer. "Did Crime Rise or Fall during the Reagan Presidency? The Effects of an 'Aging' U.S. Population on the Nation's Crime Rate."

Journal of Crime and Delinquency 28 (August 1991), pp. 330–359.

Stein, G. "New Wave of Layoffs Boost Bottom Line." *The Providence Journal* (September 23, 1997), pp. E1–E2.

Steinberg, L. "Interdependency in the Family: Autonomy, Conflict, and Harmony in the Parent-Adolescent Relationship." In S. S. Feldman and G. R. Elliott (eds.), *At the Threshold: The Developing Adolescent.* Cambridge, MA: Harvard University Press, 1990.

Steinberg, L., with B. B. Brown and S. M. Dornbusch. *Beyond the Classroom: Why School Reform Has Failed and What Parents Need to Do.* New York: Simon & Schuster, 1997.

Steinberg, S. *The Ethnic Myth: Race, Ethnicity, and Class in America.* New York: Atheneum, 1981.

Steinmetz, S. K. "Occupational Environment in Relation to Physical Punishment and Dogmatism." In S. K. Steinmetz and M. A. Straus (eds.), *Violence in the Family,* pp. 166–172. New York: Dodd, Mead, 1974.

Sternberg, R. J. *Thinking Styles.* New York: Cambridge University Press, 1997.

Stevenson, H. W. "The Asian Advantage: The Case of Mathematics." In J. J. Shields, Jr. (ed.), *Japanese Schooling: Patterns of Socialization, Equality, and Political Control,* pp. 85–95. University Park: Pennsylvania State University Press, 1989.

Stodghill, R. L., II. "God of Our Fathers." *Time* (October 6, 1997), p. 34.

Stolberg, S. G. "Cries of the Dying Awaken Doctors to a New Approach." *The New York Times* (June 30, 1997a), pp. A1, B7

Stolberg, S. G. "The Good Death: Embracing the Right to Die Well." *The New York Times* (June 29, 1997b), pp. E1, E4.

Stolberg, S. G. "Gay Culture Weighs Sense and Sexuality." *The New York Times* (November 23, 1997c), pp. WK1, WK6.

Stoner, J. A. A Comparison of Individual and Group Decisions Involving Risk. Unpublished master's thesis. Cambridge, MA: MIT, 1961.

Stouffer, S., et al. *The American Soldier: Adjustment during Army Life.* Princeton, NJ: Princeton University Press, 1949.

Straus, M. A., and R. J. Gelles. "Societal Change and Change in Family Violence from 1975 to 1985 as Revealed by Two National Surveys." *Journal of Marriage and the Family* 48 (August 1986), pp. 465–479.

Straus, M. A., and R. J. Gelles (eds.). *Physical Violence in American Families: Risk Factors and Adaptations in 8,145 Families.* New Brunswick, NJ: Transaction Books, 1990.

Straus, M. A., R. J. Gelles, and S. K. Steinmetz. *Behind Closed Doors: Violence in the American Family.* Garden City, NY: Doubleday/Anchor, 1980.

Sugarman, D. B., and G. T. Hotaling. "Dating Violence: Prevalence, Context, and Risk Factors." In M. A. Pirog-Good and J. E. Stets (eds.), *Violence in Dating Relationships,* pp. 3–39. New York: Praeger, 1989.

Sumner, W. G. *Folkways.* New York: New American Library, 1959. (Original work published 1906.)

Sussman, M. B. "The Isolated Nuclear Family: Fact or Fiction?" *Social Problems* 6 (1959), pp. 333–340.

Sutherland, E. *White Collar Crime: The Uncut Version.* New Haven, CT: Yale University Press, 1983. (Original work published 1949.)

Swatos, W. H., Jr. "Monopolism, Pluralism, Acceptance, and Rejection: An Integrated Model." *Review of Religious Research* 16, 3 (1975), pp. 174–185.

Swiss, D. J., and J. P. Walker. *Women and the Work/Family Dilemma: How Today's Professional Women Are Finding Solutions.* New York: Wiley, 1993.

Sykes, G., and D. Matza. "Techniques of Neutralization: A Theory of Delinquency." *American Sociological Review* 22 (1957), pp. 664–670.

Takaki, R. *A Different Mirror: A History of Multicultural America.* Boston: Little, Brown, 1993.

Takayanagai, S. "Japanese Participative Management." In Y. Monden, R. Shibakawa, S. Takanagi, and T. Nagao (eds.), *Innovations in Japanese Management: The Japanese Corporation,* pp. 67–73. Atlanta: Industrial Engineering and Management Press, 1985.

Tannen, D. *You Just Don't Understand: Women and Men in Conversation.* New York: Morrow, 1990.

Tarrow, S. "National Politics and Collective Action: Recent Theory and Research in Western Europe and the United States." *Annual Review of Sociology* 14 (1988), pp. 421–440.

Task Force Report: Crime and Its Impact. President's Commission on Law Enforcement and Administration of Justice. Washington, DC: U.S. Government Printing Office, 1967.

Tavris, C. *The Mismeasure of Woman.* New York: Simon & Schuster, 1992.

Tavris, C., and C. Wade. *The Longest War: Sex Differences in Perspective,* 2d ed. San Diego: Harcourt Brace Jovanovich, 1984.

Taylor, E. *Prime-Time Families: Television Culture in Postwar America.* Berkeley: University of California Press, 1989.

Taylor, M. (ed.). *Rationality and Revolution.* New York: Cambridge University Press, 1988.

Taylor, V., N. Whittier, and J. Huber. "Gender Inequality and Sexism." In C. Calhoun and R. Ritzer (eds.), *Sociology,* pp. 339–371. New York: McGraw-Hill/Primus, 1993.

Teixeira, R. "Will the Real Non-Voters Please Stand Up?" *Public Opinion* (July–August 1988), pp. 41–59.

Tenner, E. *Why Things Bite Back: Technology and the Revenge of Unintended Consequences.* New York: Knopf, 1996.

Terman, L. *Intelligence Tests and School Reorganization.* New York: World Books, 1923.

Tharp, M., and W. Holstein. "Mainstreaming the Militia." *U.S. News & World Report* (April 21, 1997), pp. 25–38.

Thomas, E. "The Next Level." *Newsweek* (April 7, 1997), pp. 28ff.

Thomas, W. I., and D. S. Thomas. *The Child in America.* New York: Knopf, 1928.

Tilly, C. *From Mobilization to Revolution.* Reading, MA: Addison-Wesley, 1978.

Tilly, C. *The Contentious French.* Reading, MA: Addison Wesley, 1986.

Tilly, C., L. Tilly, and R. Tilly. *The Rebellious Century, 1830–1930.* Cambridge, MA: Harvard University Press, 1975.

Timar, T. B., and D. L. Kirp. *Managing Educational Excellence.* New York: Falmer, 1988.

Tindale, R. S., J. H. Davis, D. A. Vollrath, D. H. Nagao, and V. B. Hinsz. "Asymmetrical Social Influence in Freely Interacting Groups: A Test of Three Models." *Journal of Personality and Social Psychology* 58 (1990), pp. 438–449.

Tobin, J. J., D. Y. Y. Wu, and D. H. Davidson. *Preschool in Three Cultures: Japan, China, and the United States.* New Haven and London: Yale University Press, 1989.

Toby, J. "Social Disorganization and Stake in Conformity: Complementary Factors in the Predatory Behavior of Hoodlums." *Journal of Criminal Law, Criminology and Police Science* 48 (1957), pp. 12–17.

Tom, A. R. "A Semiprofessional Concept of Teaching." *Social Education* (November–December 1987), pp. 506–508.

Tönnies, F. *Community and Society—Gemeinschaft and Gesellschaft.* C. P. Loomis (ed. and trans.). East Lansing: Michigan State University Press, 1957. (Original work published 1887.)

Tonry, M., and A. J. Reiss, Jr. (eds.). *Beyond the Law: Crime in Complex Organizations.* Chicago: University of Chicago Press, 1993.

Toynbee, A. *Lectures on the Industrial Revolution in England.* Newton Abbott, Eng.: Davis and Charles, 1969. (Original work published 1884.)

Tran, T. V. "The Vietnamese Family." In C. H. Mindel, R. W. Habenstein, and R. Wright, Jr. (eds.), *Ethnic Families in America: Patterns and Variations,* 3d ed., pp. 276–302. New York: Elsevier, 1988.

Treas, J. "Older Americans in the 1900s and Beyond." *Population Bulletin* 50 (1995), pp. 1–48.

Treloar, A. E. "Predicting the Close of Menstrual Life." In A. M. Voda, M. Dinnerstein, and S. R. O'Donnell (eds.), *Changing Perspectives on Menopause,* pp. 289–307. Austin: University of Texas Press, 1982.

Troeltsch, Ernst. *The Social Teaching of the Christian Churches.* New York: Macmillan, 1931.

Trovato, F., and R. Vos. "Married Female Labor Force Participation and Suicide in Canada, 1971–1981." *Sociological Forum* 7, 4 (1992), pp. 661–677.

Turbett, P., and R. O'Toole. "Physicians' Recognition of Child Abuse." Paper presented at the Annual Meeting of the American Sociological Association, New York, 1980.

Turner, J. H. *The Structure of Sociological Theory,* rev. ed. Homewood, IL: Dorsey, 1978.

Turner, R. H. "Sponsored and Contest Mobility and the School System." In R. R. Bell and H. R. Stub (eds.), *The Sociology of Education,* pp. 219–345. Homewood, IL: Dorsey, 1968.

Turner, R. H., and L. M. Killian. *Collective Behavior,* 2d ed. Englewood Cliffs, NJ: Prentice-Hall, 1972.

U.C.L.A. Center for Communications Policy. *U.C.L.A. Television Violence Report.* 1998. Los Angeles: University of California, Los Angeles.

Ulrich, P. "The Determinants of Depression in Two-Income Marriages." *Journal of Marriage and the Family* 50 (1988), pp. 121–131.

UNAIDS. UN DPI update. (December 1996), www.un.org.

United Nations. *The World's Women 1970–1990, Trends and Statistics.* Social Statistics and Indicators, series K, no. 8. New York: United Nations, 1991.

United Nations Development Programme. *Human Development Report 1993.* New York: Oxford University Press, 1993.

United Nations Development Programme. *Human Development Report 1995.* New York: Oxford University Press, 1995.

United Nations High Commissioner for Refugees (UNHCR). *The State of the World's Refugees.* New York: Oxford University Press, 1995.

U.S. Advisory Board on Child Abuse and Neglect. *A Nation's Shame: Fatal Child Abuse and Neglect in the United States.* Washington, DC: U.S. Department of Health and Human Services, 1995.

U.S. Bureau of the Census. *Poverty in the United States, 1992.* Washington, DC: U.S. Government Printing Office, 1993.

U.S. Bureau of the Census. *Statistical Brief: Who Receives Child Support?* Washington, DC: Economics and Statistical Administration, U.S. Department of Commerce, 1995.

U.S. Bureau of the Census. *Current Population Reports* (August 1996).

U.S. Bureau of the Census. *Educational attainment in the United States: March, 1996.* Document 1237. Washington, DC: U.S. Bureau of the Census, 1996.

U.S. Bureau of the Census. (1997). www.census.gov.

U.S. Department of Health and Human Services. *Health Status of Minorities and Low-Income Groups.* Washington, DC: U.S. Government Printing Office, 1991.

U.S. Department of Health and Human Services. "Suicide among Older Persons— United States, 1980–1992." *Morbidity and Mortality Weekly Reports* 45 (January 12, 1996), pp. 3–6.

U.S. Department of Justice. *A National Crime Victimization Survey Report: Criminal Victimization.* Washington, DC: Department of Justice, 1996.

U.S. Department of Labor, Women's Bureau. "Working Women Count! A Report to the Nation." Washington DC: U.S. Department of Labor, 1994.

U.S. Department of Labor, Women's Bureau. "Care around the Clock." Washington, DC: U.S. Department of Labor, 1997.

Usdansky, M. L. "Single Motherhood: Stereotypes vs. Statistics." *The New York Times* (February 11, 1996), p. E4.

Useem, M. *The Inner Circle.* New York: Oxford University Press, 1984.

van der Berghe, P. *Man in Society: A Biosocial View.* New York: Elsevier, 1978.

van der Tak, J., C. Haub, and E. Murphy. "Our Population Predicament: A New Look." *Population Bulletin* 34 (December 1979).

Vandenberg, L. H., and D. Streckfuss. "Prime Time Television's Portrayal of Women and the World of Work: A Demographic Profile." *Journal of Broadcasting and Electronic Media* 36, 2 (1992), pp. 195–208.

Vandiver, K. "Why Should My Conscience Bother Me? Hiding Aircraft Brake Hazards." In M. D. Ermann and R. J. Lundman (eds.), *Corporate and Governmental Deviance,* pp. 118–138. New York: Oxford University Press, 1996.

Vanfossen, B. E., J. D. Jones, and J. Z. Spade. "Curriculum Tracking and Status Maintenance." *Sociology of Education* 60 (April 1987), pp. 104–122.

Vannoy-Hiller, D., and W. Philliber. *Equal Partners.* Newbury Park, CA: Sage, 1989.

Vaughan, D. *The Challenger Launch Decision: Risky Technology, Culture, and Deviance at NASA.* Chicago: University of Chicago Press, 1996.

Veblen, T. *The Instinct of Workmanship.* New York: Huebsch, 1922.

Velez, W. "High School Attrition among Hispanic and Non-Hispanic White Youths." *Sociology of Education* 62 (1989), pp. 119–133.

Verba, S., and N. Nie. *Participation in America: Political Democracy and Social Equality.* New York: Harper & Row, 1972.

Violas, P. C. *The Training of the Urban Working Class: A History of Twentieth-Century American Education.* Chicago: Rand McNally, 1978.

Voda, A. M. "Menopausal Hot Flash." In A. M. Voda, M. Dinnerstein, and S. R. O'Donnell (eds.), *Changing Perspectives on Menopause,* pp. 126–129. Austin: University of Texas Press, 1982.

Voydanoff, P. "Work and Family: A Review and Expanded Conceptualization." In E. B. Goldsmith (ed.), *Work and Family,* pp. 1–22. Newbury Park, CA: Sage, 1989.

Wacquant, L. J. D. "The Ghetto, the State, and the New Capitalist Economy." *Dissent* (Fall 1989), pp. 508–520.

Wacquant, L. J. D. "The Specificity of Ghetto Poverty: A Comparative Analysis of Race, Class, and Urban Exclusion in Chicago's Black Belt and the Parisian Red Belt." Paper presented at the Chicago Urban Poverty and Family Life Conference, October 10–13, 1991.

Wacquant, L. J. D. "The New Urban Color Line: The State and the Fate of the Ghetto of Post-Fordist America." In C. Calhoun (ed.), *Social Theory and the Politics of Identity,* pp. 231–276. Cambridge, MA: Oxford University Press, 1994.

Wacquant, L. J. D., and W. J. Wilson. "The Cost of Racial and Class Exclusion in the Inner City." *Annals of the American Academy of Political and Social Science* 501 (January 1989), pp. 8–25.

Wagner, D. A. *The Future of Literacy in a Changing World.* New York: Pergamon, 1987.

Wald, K. D., D. E. Owen, and S. S. Hill, Jr. "Evangelical Politics and Status Issues." *Journal for the Scientific Study of Religion* 28, 1 (1989), pp. 1–16.

Waldrop, J., and T. Exter. "What the 1990 Census Will Show." *American Demographics* (January 1990), pp. 20–30.

Walker, A. J. "Couples Watching Television: Gender, Power, and the Remote Control." *Journal of Marriage and the Family* 58 (November 1996), pp. 813–823.

Wallace, R. *They Call Her Pastor: A New Role for Catholic Women.* Albany: State University of New York Press, 1992.

Wallerstein, I. *The Modern World System,* vol. 1. New York: Academic Press, 1974.

Wallerstein, I. *The Modern World System,* vol. 2. New York: Academic Press, 1980.

Wallerstein, I. *The Modern World-System III: The Second Era of Great Expansion of the Capitalist World Economy, 1730–1840s.* New York: Academic Press, 1989.

Wallerstein, J. S., and S. Blakeslee. *Second Chances: Men, Women, and Children a Decade after Divorce.* New York: Ticknor and Fields, 1989.

Wallerstein, J. S., and J. B. Kelly. "The Effects of Parental Divorce: The Experiences of the Child in Later Latency." *American Journal of Orthopsychiatry* 46 (April 1976), pp. 256–269.

Walsh, E., R. Warland, and D. C. Smith. "Backyards, NIMBYs, and Incinerator Sitings: Implications for Social Movement Theory." *Social Problems* 40 (February 1993), pp. 25–38.

Walters, G. D. *The Criminal Lifestyle: Patterns of Serious Criminal Misconduct.* Newbury Park, CA: Sage, 1990.

Walters, P. B. "Education." In C. Calhoun and G. Ritzer (eds.), *Introduction to Social Problems,* pp. 571–596. New York: McGraw-Hill, 1993.

Walum, L. R. *The Dynamics of Sex and Gender: A Sociological Perspective.* Chicago: Rand McNally, 1977.

Ward, L. B. "Working Harder to Earn the Same Old Vacation." *The New York Times* (May 11, 1997), www.nytimes.com/archives.

Waxman, C. J. *The Stigma of Poverty,* 2d ed. New York: Pergamon, 1983.

Weber, M. *From Max Weber: Essays in Sociology.* H. H. Gerth and C. Wright Mills (eds. and trans.). New York: Oxford University Press, 1946.

Weber, M. *The Protestant Ethic and the Spirit of Capitalism.* T. Parsons (trans.). New York:

Scribner's, 1958. (Original work published 1904.)

Weber, M. *The Theory of Social and Economic Organization.* New York: Free Press, 1964. (Original work published 1925.)

Weber, M. *Economy and Society.* E. Fischoff et al. (trans.). New York: Bedminster Press, 1968. (Original work published 1922.)

Wechsler, H. "Alcohol and the American College Campus: A Report from the Harvard School of Public Health." *Change* 28 (July 1996), pp. 20–27.

Weinberg, D. H. "A Brief Look at Postwar U.S. Income Inequality." *Current Population Reports* P60–191. Washington, DC: U.S. Government Printing Office, 1996.

Weinberg, M. "The Relationship between School Desegregation and Academic Achievement: A Review of the Research." *Law and Contemporary Problems* 39 (Spring 1975), pp. 241–271.

Weiner, J. M., R. J. Hanley, R. Clark, and J. F. Van Nostrand. "Measuring the Activities of Daily Living: Comparisons across National Surveys." *Journals of Gerontology* 45, 6 (November 1990), p. S234.

Weiner, T. "Military Discharges of Homosexuals Soar." *The New York Times* (April 7, 1998), pp. A21; A23.

Weinstein, D. *Heavy Metal: A Cultural Sociology.* New York: Lexington Books, 1991.

Weisburd, D., E. F. Chayet, and E. J. Waring. "White-Collar Crime and Criminal Careers: Some Preliminary Findings." *Crime & Delinquency* 36 (July 1990), pp. 342–355.

Weisman, S. R. "Births Are Kept Down but Women Aren't." *The New York Times* (January 29, 1988), p. 4.

Weiss, R. S. *Staying the Course: The Emotional and Social Lives of Men Who Do Well at Work.* New York: Free Press, 1990.

Weitzman, L. *The Divorce Revolution: The Unexpected Consequences for Women and Children in America.* New York: Free Press, 1985.

Westoff, C. F. "Fertility in the United States." *Science* 234 (October 1986), pp. 554–559.

Whitaker, C. J., and L. D. Bastian. *Teenage Victims: A National Crime Survey Report.* Washington, DC: U.S. Department of Justice, Bureau of Justice Statistics, 1991.

White, H. C. *Identity and Control: A Structural Theory of Social Action.* Princeton, NJ: Princeton University Press, 1992.

White, J. F. "Private School versus Public School Achievement." In E. Cohn (ed.), *Market Approaches to Education,* pp. 239–273. New York: Pergamon, 1997.

White, L. K. "Determinants of Divorce." *Journal of Marriage and the Family* 52 (November 1990), pp. 904–912.

Whitehead, B. D. "Dan Quayle was Right." *Atlantic Monthly* 271, 4 (April 1993), pp. 47–87.

Whitmire, R. "Today's Toddler, Tomorrow's Crime Wave." Gannett News Service (January 10, 1995).

Whorf, B. L. *Language, Thought and Reality: Selected Writings of Benjamin Lee Whorf* J. B. Carroll (ed.). Cambridge, MA: MIT Press, 1940.

Widom, C. S. "The Cycle of Violence." *Science* 244 (April 14, 1989), pp. 160–166.

Williams, C. L. "The Glass Escalator: Hidden Advantages for Men in the 'Female' Professions." *Social Problems* 39 (August 1992), pp. 253–267.

Willie, C. V. *A New Look at Black Families,* 3d ed. Dix Hills, NY: General Hall, 1988.

Willingham, W. W., N. S. Cole, and Associates. *Gender and Fair Assessment.* Mahwah, NJ: Erlbaum, 1997.

Willis, P. *Learning to Labor: How Working Class Kids Get Working Class Jobs.* New York: Columbia University Press, 1977.

Wills, G. "The New Revolutionaries." *The New York Review of Books* (August 19, 1995), pp. 50–55.

Wilson, B. F., and S. C. Clarke. "Remarriages: A Demographic Profile." *Journal of Family Issues* 13 (June 1992), pp. 123–141.

Wilson, W. J. *The Declining Significance of Race: Blacks and Changing American Institutions,* 2d ed. Chicago: University of Chicago Press, 1980.

Wilson, W. J. *The Truly Disadvantaged: The Inner City, The Underclass, and Public Policy.* Chicago: University of Chicago Press, 1987.

Wilson, W. J. "Plenary Address." Presented at the Annual Meeting of the National Council on Family Relations, Denver, 1991a.

Wilson, W. J. "Studying Inner City Dislocations: The Challenge of Public Agenda Research." *American Sociological Review* 56 (February 1991b), pp. 1–14.

Wilson, W. J. "President of COSSA Meets with President Clinton." *COSSA Washington Update* 12, 21 (November 22, 1993), pp. 1–2.

Wilson, W. J. *When Work Disappears: The World of the New Urban Poor.* New York: Knopf, 1996.

Wirth, L. "The Problem of Minority Groups." In R. Linton (ed.), *The Science of Man in the World Crisis,* pp. 347–372. New York: Columbia University Press, 1945.

Wolf, R. F. "Abuse of the Elderly." In R. J. Gelles (ed.), *Families and Violence.* Minneapolis, MN: National Council on Family Relations, 1995.

Wolfe, A. *One Nation, After All: What Americans Really Think about God, Country, Family, Racism, Welfare, Immigration, Homosexuality, Work, the Right, the Left and Each Other.* New York: Viking Press, 1998.

Wolff, J. *Aesthetics and the Sociology of Art.* London: Allen and Unwin, 1983.

Woodward, B. *The Agenda.* New York: Simon & Schuster, 1994.

Woodward, K. L. "Young beyond Their Years." *Newsweek Special Issue: The 21st Century Family* (1989), pp. 54–60.

Work in America: Report of a Special Task Force to the Secretary of Health, Education, and Welfare. Cambridge, MA: MIT Press, 1973.

World Bank. *China: Strategies for Reducing Poverty in the 1990s.* Washington, DC: World Bank, 1992a.

World Bank. *World Development Report, 1992.* New York: Oxford University Press, 1992b.

World Bank. *World Development Report, 1993.* New York: Oxford University Press, 1993.

World Bank. *World Development Report, 1997.* New York: Oxford University Press, 1997.

World Bank Group. "Country Brief: Indonesia." (September 1997), www.worldbank.org.

World Resources 1992–93. New York: Oxford University Press, 1992.

Worsley, P. *The Trumpet Shall Sound: A Study of "Cargo" Cults in Melanesia,* 2d ed. New York: Shocken, 1968.

Wren, C. "Apartheid's Laws Are Dismantled, but Not Its Cages" (February 10, 1991, p. E4); "South Africa and Apartheid: No Apologies" (February 24, 1991, p E2); "South Africa Scraps Laws Defining People by Race" (June 18, 1991, pp. A8, 16). *The New York Times.*

WuDunn, S. "Asian Economics, Once a Miracle, Now Muddled." *The New York Times* (August 31, 1997), www.nytimes.archives.

Wuthnow, R. *Meaning and Moral Order: Explorations in Cultural Analysis.* Berkeley: University of California Press, 1987.

Wuthnow, R. *The Restructuring of American Religion.* Princeton, NJ: Princeton University Press, 1988.

Wuthnow, R. *Christianity in the 21st Century.* New York: Oxford University Press, 1993.

Yankelovich, D. "The Meaning of Work." In J. M. Rosow (ed.), *The Worker and the Job,* pp. 19–47. Englewood Cliffs, NJ: Prentice-Hall, 1974.

Yankelovich, D. Quoted in Louis Uchitelle, "The Shift toward Self-Reliance in the Welfare System." *The New York Times* (January 13, 1997), p. A15.

Yao, Y. "American and Chinese Schools: A Comparative Analysis." *Education* 113, 2 (Winter 1992), pp. 232ff.

Yaukey, D. *Demography: The Study of Human Population.* New York: St. Martin's, 1985.

Yeager, P. C. "Industrial Water Pollution." In M. Tonry and A. J. Reiss, Jr. (eds.), *Beyond the Law: Crime in Complex Organizations,* pp. 97–148. Chicago: University of Chicago Press, 1993.

Yetman, N. R. "Race and Ethnic Inequality." In C. Calhoun and G. Ritzer (eds.), *Social Problems,* pp. 416–447. New York: McGraw-Hill/Primus, 1992.

Yinger, J. M. *The Scientific Study of Religion.* New York: Macmillan, 1970.

Yinger, J. M. *Black Americans and Predominantly White Churches.* Paper prepared for the Committee on the Status of Black Americans. Washington, DC: National Research Council, 1986.

Yllo, K. "Through a Feminist Lens: Gender, Power, and Violence." In R. Gelles and D. Loseke (eds.), *Current Controversies on Family Violence,* pp. 47–62. Newbury Park, CA: Sage, 1993.

Yorburg, B. *Family Relationships.* New York: St. Martin's, 1993.

Zald, M. N., and J. D. McCarthy (eds.). *Social Movements in an Organizational Society.* New Brunswick, NJ: Transaction Books, 1987.

Zandu, A. "The Value of Belonging to a Group in Japan." *Small Group Behavior* 14, 1 (1983), pp. 3–14.

Zatz, M. S. "Race, Ethnicity, and Determinate Sentencing: A New Dimension to an Old Controversy." *Criminology* 22 (1984), pp. 147–171.

Zellner, W. W. *Countercultures: A Sociological Analysis.* New York: St. Martin's, 1995.

Zhang, J. "Suicides in Beijing, China, 1992–1993." *Suicide and Life-Threatening Behavior,* 26, 2 (Summer 1996), pp. 175–180.

Zimbardo, P. "The Human Choice: Individuation, Reason, and Order versus Deindividuation, Impulse, and Chaos." In W. J. Arnold and D. Levine (eds.), *Nebraska Symposium on Motivation.* Lincoln: University of Nebraska Press, 1969.

Zimbardo, P. "Pathology of Imprisonment." *Society* 9 (April 1972), pp. 4–8.

Credits

Photo Credits

Part 4: p. 401, Bruno Barbey/Magnum.

Chapter 11: p. 402, Paul Chauncey/The Stock Market; p. 404, James Wilson/Woodfin Camp & Assoc.; p. 407, Ariel Skelley/The Stock Market; p. 407, Paul Conklin/PhotoEdit; p. 409, Archive Photos; p. 412, CBS Photo Archive; p. 415, Gilles Peress/Magnum Photos; p. 419, Raghu Rai/Magnum; p. 424, Bill Horsman/Stock, Boston; p. 426, Courtesy the National Committee for Prevention of Child Abuse; p. 430, Barbara Burnes/Photo Researchers; p. 434, Bob Daemmrich/Image Works.

Chapter 12: p. 442, Bob Daemmrich/Stock, Boston; p. 447, Corbis-Bettmann; p. 452, B. Kraft/Sygma; p. 457, Paul Barton/The Stock Market; p. 457, Stephen Ferry/Gamma Liaison; p. 458, Kerina Maloney/NYT Pictures; p.462, Tom McCarthy/The Stock Market; p. 465, Mark Richards/PhotoEdit; p. 470, Jacques Chenet/Woodfin Camp & Assoc.; p. 471, Marc Pokempner/Impact Visuals; p. 477, Fujifotos/Image Works.

Chapter 13: p. 482, Mark Downey/Gamma Liaison; p. 485, Gamma Liaison; p. 485, Kal Muller/Woodfin Camp & Assoc.; p. 487, Penny Tweedie/Woodfin Camp & Assoc.; p. 489, J. Polleross/The Stock Market; p. 493, Donna DeCesare/Impact Visuals; p. 495, Eve Arnold/Magnum; p. 498, Seth Resnick/Stock, Boston; p. 500, Larry Downing/Sygma; p. 501, Alison Wright, Photo Researchers; p. 501, Joseph Nettis/Photo Researchers; p. 501, James Marshall/Stock Market; p. 501, David Austen/Stock, Boston; p. 501, Abbas/Magnum; p. 501, Blair Seitz/Photo Researchers.

Chapter 14: p. 514, Paula Bronstein/Impact Visuals; p. 518, Topham/Image Works; p. 518, Corbis-Bettmann; p. 519, Gianni Giansanti/Sygma; p. 520, Richard Ellis/Sygma; p. 521, The Granger Collection; p. 521, Corbis-Bettmann; p. 522, John M. Roberts/The Stock Market; p. 528, Ruben Bittermann/Impact Visuals; p. 531, Michael Newman/PhotoEdit; p. 535, Donna Binder/Impact Visuals; p. 539, Chick Harity/Woodfin Camp & Assoc.; p. 541, Michael Nichols/Magnum Photos; p. 542, Swersey/Gamma Liaison; p. 545, Ian Berry/Magnum Photos.

Chapter 15: p. 550, Gabe Palmer/The Stock Market; p. 552, Syracuse Newspapers/Al Campanie/Image Works; p. 553, L. Dematteis/Image Works; p. 556, Nathan Benn/Woodfin Camp & Assoc.; p. 561, Vincent Yu/AP/Wide World Photos; p. 563, R. Poderni/Sygma; p. 565, Owen/Black Star; p. 566, Jose L. Pelaez/The Stock Market; p. 573, NASA/Image Works; p. 576, William Taufic/The Stock Market; p. 579, Mark Richards/PhotoEdit; p. 581, J. Pickerell/Image Words.

Part 5: p. 591, Steve McCurry/Magnum.

Chapter 16: p. 592, Claudio Edinger/Gamma Liaison; p. 596, Scully/Gamma Liaison; p. 598, John Moss/Photo Researchers; p. 599, Alon Reininger/Woodfin Camp & Assoc.; p. 600 Cilene Perlman/Stock, Boston; p. 607, Garry D. McMichael/Photo Researchers; p. 607, Douglas Mason/Woodfin Camp & Assoc.; p. 609, J. Polleross/The Stock Market; p. 611, James Nachtway/Magnum; p. 614, Anthony Suau/Gamma Liaison; p. 616, Topham/Image Works; p. 620, Granitsas/Image Works; p. 621, Alon Reininger/Woodfin Camp & Assoc.

Chapter 17: p. 626, Najlah Feanny/Saba; p. 628, Donna Binder/Impact Visuals; p. 631, Scott Weersing/The Enterprise/Gamma Liaison; p. 631, Rod Little/US News & World Report; p. 637, Greg Smith/Saba; p. 637, Jim Argo/The Daily Oklahoman/Saba; p. 641, Jean-Marc Giboux/Gamma Liaison; p. 643, P. J. Griffiths/Magnum Photos; p. 646, Corbis-Bettmann; p. 646, Mark Peterson/Saba; p. 648, Donna Binder/Impact Visuals; p. 652, Porter Gifford/Gamma Liaison; p. 653, Abbas/Magnum Photos.

Figures, Tables, and Text

Acknowledgments are listed by page number in order of occurrence.

Chapter 1: **12,** *Figure 1–1:* From J. Treas, "Older Americans in the 1990s and Beyond," *Population Bulletin,* 50, 1995, Figure 1, pp. 4–5. Reprinted by permission of the Population Reference Bureau, Washington, D.C.; **20,** *Figure 1–2:* From *Social Psychology* by Solomon E. Asch, Prentice Hall, 1952. Reprinted by permission of Florence M. Asch., **36,** *Figure 1–6:* From Ken Auletta, "The Next Corporate Order AMERICAN KEIRETSU *The New Yorker.* Fall 1997, p. 226. Reprinted by permission; © The New Yorker Magazine, Inc. All rights reserved.

Chapter 2: **46,** *Table 2–1:* Adapted from *The Scientific Approach* by Carlo Lastrucci, Schenkman Books, Inc., Rochester, Vermont, 1967, p. 55. Reprinted by permission. **49,** *Figure 2–1:* Reprinted from *Intimate Violence* by Richard J. Gelles and Murray A. Straus, Simon & Schuster, 1988, p. 227. Reprinted by permission of Lescher & Lescher, Ltd., **56,** *Table 2–3:* From *Policing Domestic Violence: Experiments and Dilemmas* by L. W. Sherman, with J. D. Schmidt, and D. P. Rogan, The Free Press, 1992, p. 129. Copyright 1992 by Lawrence W. Sherman. Reprinted by permission, **67,** *Figure 2–3:* Reprinted with permission from Wallace, Walter, L. (ed.) *Sociological Theory: An Introduction.* (New York: Aldine de Gruyter) Copyright © 1969 by Walter L. Wallace. **67,** *Figure 2–3:* Adapted from *Understanding Sociology* by Ann Greer and Scott Greer, p. 15. Copyright © 1974. Reproduced with permission of The McGraw-Hill Companies.

Chapter 3: **82,** *Figure 3–1:* From Martin and Midgley, "Regions and Countries of Origin for U.S. Immigrants, 1820–1992," *Population Bulletin,* 49, 1994, p. 25. Reprinted by permission of the Population Reference Bureau, Washington, D.C.; **83,** *Figure 3–2:* Population Reference Bureau (1996). From *Population Bulletin,* 51(1), April 1996. Reprinted by permission of the Population Reference Bureau, Washington, D.C.; **94,** *Figure 3–3:* Reprinted by permission of Harvard Business School Press. From *The Death of Distance: How the Communications Revolution Will Change Our Lives* by Frances Cairncross. Boston, MA 1997, p. 88. Copyright © 1997 Frances Cairncross; all rights reserved. **114,** *Figure 3–4:* From "The Rising Standard of Living in China," *The New York Times,* February 23, 1997, p. E–5. Copyright © 1997 by The New York Times Company. Reprinted by permission.

Chapter 4: **135, 136,** *Tables 4–1 and 4–2:* From M. S. Andreasen, "Evolution in the Family's Use of Television: Normative Data from Industry and Academy," tables 1.3, and 1.5, pp. 22 and

24, in *Television and the American Family,* edited by J. Bryant, 1990. Reprinted by permission of Lawrence Erlbaum Associates, Inc. **137,** *Cartoon: Calvin and Hobbes* © 1993 Watterson. Dist. by Universal Press Syndicate. Reprinted with permission. All rights reserved. **142,** *Figure 4–2:* "Erikson's 'Eight Stages of Man' " reprinted by permission of *Daedalus,* Journal of the American Academy of Arts and Sciences, from the issue entitled, "Adulthood," Spring 1976, Vol. 105, No. 2. **147,** *Figure 4–5:* From *The Seasons of a Man's Life* by Daniel J. Levinson. Copyright © 1978 by Daniel J. Levinson. Reprinted by permission of Alfred A. Knopf, Inc. **152,** *Figure 4–6:* From J. Treas, "Older Americans in the 1990s and Beyond," *Population Bulletin,* 50, 1995, Figure 10, p. 30. Reprinted by permission of Population Reference Bureau, Washington, D.C.

Chapter 5: **173,** *Figure 5–3:* From Harold J. Leavitt, "Applied Organizational Change in Industry: Structural, Technological and Humanistic Approaches," in *Handbook of Organizations,* edited by James G. March, Rand McNally, 1965, pp. 114–1170. Reprinted by permission of James G. March. **188,** *Map 5–1:* Reprinted with permission from Lee, Richard B. and deVore, Irven. *Man the Hunter.* (New York: Aldine de Gruyter) Copyright © 1968 by the Wenner–Gren Foundation for Anthropological Research, Inc., **190,** *Table 5–2:* From *Human Societies: An Introduction to Macrosociology,* Sixth Edition, by G. Lenski, J. Lenski, and P. Nolan, pp. 211–213. © 1991. Reproduced with permission of The McGraw-Hill Companies.

Chapter 6: **202,** Box, *Smiling Across Cultures:* From K. Nagashima and J. A. Schellenberg, "Situational Differences in Intentional Smiling: A Cross-Cultural Exploration," *The Journal of Social Psychology,* 137(3), 1997, pp. 297–301. Reprinted with permission of the Helen Dwight Reid Educational Foundation. Published by Heldref Publications, 1319 Eighteenth St., N.W., Washington, D.C. 10036–1802. Copyright © 1997. **223,** *Figure 6–5:* From *Social Psychology,* Fourth Edition, by David Myers. © 1993. Reproduced with permission of The McGraw-Hill Companies.

Chapter 7: **229,** *Figure 7–1:* From Mertin M. Hyman et al., "Drinkers, Drinking, and Alcohol-Related Mortality and Hospitalizations: A Statistical Compendium." Reprinted with permission from *Journal of Studies on Alcohol.* Copyright by Journal of Studies on Alcohol Inc., Rutgers Center of Alcohol Studies, Piscataway, NJ 08855. **231,** *Box, International Trends in Alcohol Consumption, Table 1:* From *Alcohol Policy and Public Good* by G. Edwards et al. Oxford University Press, 1991, p. 35, Table 2–1. Reprinted by permission of Oxford University Press. **234,** *Figure 7–2:* From Debra Rosenberg and Matt Bai, "Drinking and Dying," *Newsweek,* October 13, 1997, p. 69. © 1997, Newsweek, Inc. All rights reserved. Reprinted by permission. **243,** *Table 7–1:* Adapted and reprinted with the permission of The Free Press, A Division of Simon & Schuster from *Social Theory and Social Structure* by Robert K. Merton. **259,** *Figure 7–8:* From *Americans Behind Bars: The International Use of Incarceration 1992–1993,* by Marc Mauer, p. 630. © The Sentencing Project. Copyright © 1967, 1968 by Robert K. Merton. **264,** *Box, Crime Rates Drop in a Sociological "Whodunit":* From Clifford Krauss, "New York Crime Rate Plummets to Levels Not Seen in 30 Years," *The New York Times,* December 20, 1996, p. A1. Copy-right © 1996 by The New York Times Co. Reprinted by permission. **266,** *Figure 7–10:* From "Two States, Two Death Penalties," p. B6. Copyright © 1965 by the New York Times Company. Reprinted by permission.

Chapter 8: **282,** *Figure 8–1:* From D. Gilbert, *The American Class Structure: In an Age of Growing Inequality,* 5th Edition, p. 18. © 1998 Wadsworth Publishing Co. Used by permission. **284,** *Figure 8–2:* From *Social Stratification and Inequality* by H. R. Kerbo, p. 24. Copyright © 1996. Reproduced with permission of The McGraw-Hill Companies. **290,** *Figure 8–5:* Reprinted with the permission of Scribner, a Division of Simon & Schuster, from *Money: Who Has How Much and Why* by Andrew Hacker. Copyright © 1997 by Andrew Hacker. **290,** *Table 8–1:* Reprinted with the permission of Scribner, a Division of Simon & Schuster from *Money: How Has How Much and Why* by Andrew Hacker. Copyright © 1997 by Andrew Hacker. **295,** *Table 8–2:* Reprinted from W. P. O'Hare, "A New Look at Poverty in America," *Population Bulletin,* 51(2 September) 1996, p. 36. Population Reference Bureau, Washington, D.C. **301,** *Table 8–3:* From *America's Homeless: Numbers, Characteristics, and the Programs that Service Them* by Martha Burt and Barbara Cohen, Urban Institute Press, 1989, pp. 69–71, Reprinted by permission. **301,** *Table 8–3:* From Anne Shlay and Peter Rossi, "Social Science Research and Contemporary Studies of Homelessness," with permission, from the *Annual Review of Sociology.* Volume 18 © 1992 by Annual Reviews. **304,** *Table 8–4:* From D. Gilbert, *The American Class Structure: In an Age of Growing Inequality,* 5th Edition, p. 3. © 1988 Wadsworth Publishing Co. Used by permission. **305,** *Table 8–5:* From World Development Report 1997 by World Bank. Copyright © 1997 The International Bank for Reconstruction and Development/The World Bank. Used by permission of Oxford University Press, Inc. **306,** *Quote in box, Poverty in Russia before and after the Anti-Communist Revolution:* From *Small Futures* by Delone, copyright © 1979 by Carnegie Corporation of New York, reprinted by permission of Harcourt Brace & Company.

Chapter 9: **314,** *Map 9–1:* From *Providence Sunday Journal,* May 2, 1993, p. A14. Reprinted with permission of Knight-Ridder/Tribune Information Services. **327,** *Map 9–4:* Howard W. French, "A Century Later, Letting Africans Draw Their Own Map," *The New York Times,* November 23, 1997. Copyright © 1997 by The New York Times Co. Reprinted by permission. **335,** *Figure 9–6:* From C. S. Fischer, M. Hout, M. S. Jankowski, S. R. Lucas, A. Swidler, and K. Voss, *Inequality by Design: Cracking the Bell Curve Myth.* Copyright © 1996 by Princeton University Press. Reprinted by permission of Princeton University Press. **338,** *Figure 9–7:* "Changes in Race Relations in the USA," *USA Today,* June 11, 1997, page 9a. Copyright 1997, USA Today. Reprinted with permission. **344,** *Figure 9–8:* From *The New York Times,* December 14, 1997, p. A1. Copyright © 1997 by The New York Times Co. Reprinted by permission. **347,** *Table 9–1:* From R. Farley and W. H. Frey, "Changes in the Segregation of Whites from Blacks During the 1980s: Small Steps Toward a More Integrated Society," *American Sociological Review.* Vol. 59, 1994, pp. 23–45. Reprinted with permission of the American Sociological Association. **350,** *Map 9–6:* From *The New York Times,* March 8, 1998, p. A24. Copyright © 1998 by The New York Times Co. Reprinted by permission.

Chapter 10: **360,** *Figure 10–1:* From Chinese Census and un-published data, *The New York Times,* July 21, 1993, p. A1. Copyright © 1993 by The New York Times Co. Reprinted by permission. **363,** *Figure 10–2:* Reprinted with the permission of Simon & Schuster from *The Mismeasure of Woman: Why Women Are Not The Better Sex, The Inferior Sex, or The Opposite Sex* by Carol Tavris. Copyright © 1992 by Carol Tavris. **377,** *Figure 10–5:* From *New Families or No Families? Demographic Change and the Transformation of the Home* by Frances K. Goldscheider and Linda J. Waite, University of California Press, 1991, p. 176. Copyright © 1991 The Regents of the University of California. **381,** *Map 10–1:* From *Where Women Stand* by Naomi Neft and Ann D. Levine. Copyright © 1997 by Naomi Neft and Ann D. Levine. Reprinted by permission of Random House, Inc. **383,** *Table 10–2:* From "Women in Government," *Los Angeles Times,* October 19, 1987, p. B1. Copyright © 1977 *Los Angeles Times.* Reprinted by permission. **389,** *Figure 10–7:* From "One Casualty of the Women's Movement: Feminism," *The New York Times,* December 14, 1997, p. wk3. Copyright © 1997 by The New York Times Co. Reprinted by permission. **396,** *Table 10–3:* From *Newsweek,* September 14, 1992 © 1992, Newsweek, Inc. All rights reserved. Reprinted by permission.

Chapter 11: **416,** *Figure 11–2:* From M. L. Usdansky, "Single Motherhood: Stereotypes vs. Statistics," *The New York Times,* February 11, 1996, p. E4. Copyright © 1996 by The New York Times Co. Reprinted by permission. **417,** *Figure 11–3:* Reprinted with the permission of The Free Press, a Division of Simon & Schuster from *The State of Americas: This Generation and The Next* by Uri Bronfenbrenner, Peter D. McClelland, Elaine Wethington, Phyllis Moen, Stephen J. Ceci. Copyright © 1996 by Uri Bronfenbrenner, Peter D. McClelland, Elaine Wethington, Phyllis Moen, Stephen J. Ceci. **420,** *Figure 11–4:* From *Social Psychology,* Fourth Edition by, V. Gupta and P. Singh, p. 495. Copyright © 1995. Reproduced with permission of The McGraw-Hill Companies. **423,** *Figure 11–6:* From "Families and Work Institute," *The New York Times,* September 19, 1993, p. F21. Copyright © 1993 by The New York Times Co. Reprinted by permission. **439,** *Map 11–1:* From "Wedding Bells Aren't Ringing," *Newsweek,* January 20, 1997. © 1997, Newsweek, Inc. All rights reserved. Reprinted by permission.

Chapter 12: **444,** *Figure 12–1:* From "High-School Dropout Rates, 1993–95 Average," The Annie E. Casey Foundation. Reprinted with permission. **451,** *Figure 12–5:* From T. P. Gerber and M. Hout, "Educational Stratification in Russia During the Soviet Period," *American Journal of Sociology,* 101, p. 6. Copyright © 1995. Reprinted by permission of the University of Chicago Press. **460,** *Figure 12–8:* From B. E. Vanfossen, D. Jones and J. Z. Spade, "Curriculum Tracking and Status Maintenance," *Sociology of Education,* Vol. 60, April 1987, p. 109. Reprinted with permission of the American Sociological Association. **464,** *Figure 12–9:* From "World Education League: Who's Top?" *The Economist,* March 29, 1997, p. 21. © 1997 The Economist Newspaper Group, Inc. Reprinted with permission. Further reproduction prohibited. **467,** *Map 12–1:* From *State of the World Atlas,* 5th Edition, by Michael Kidron and Ronald Segal. Copyright © 1995 by Michael Kidron and Ronald Segal, text. Copyright © 1995 by Myriad Editions Limited, maps and graphics. Used by permission of Viking Penguin, a division of Penguin Putnam Inc.

Chapter 13: **505,** Figure 13–1: From *Where America Stands* by Michael Golay and Carol Rollyson. Copyright © 1966. Reprinted by permission of John Wiley & Sons, Inc. **507,** *Table 13–3:* From *Yearbook of American and Canadian Churches, 1991.* Edited by Constent H. Jacquet, Jr. and Alice M. Jones. Copyright © 1991 by the National Council of the Churches of Christ. Used by permission of the publisher, Abingdon Press. **507,** *Table 13–4:* From L. D. Nelson and D. G. Bromley, "Another Look at Conversion and Defection in Conservative Churches," *Falling from the Faith: Causes and Consequences of Religious Apostacy,* edited by D. G. Bromley, p. 54. Copyright © 1988. Reprinted by permission of Sage Publications, Inc.

Chapter 14: **516,** *Figure 14–1:* From D. E. Rosenbaum, "Cash Overflow: Fixing Politics, More or Less," *The New York Times,* December 22, 1996, pp. E1. Copyright © 1996 by the New York Times Company. Reprinted by permission. **526,** *Figure 14–2:* From *USA Today,* November 7, 1991, p. 3A. Copyright 1996 USA Today. Reprinted with permission. **532,** *Figure 14–4:* From "The 50 Largest Political Contributors," *The New York Times,* January 5, 1997, p. D4. Reprinted by permission of NYT Graphics.

Chapter 15: **554,** *Table 15–1:* From "Top Ten of the Global 500," *Fortune,* August 4, 1997, p. F–2. *Fortune Global 500,* © 1997 Time Inc. All rights reserved. **559,** *Table 15–2:* From *World Development Report 1993* by World Bank. Copyright 1993 by The International Bank for Reconstruction and Development. The World Bank. Used by permission of Oxford University Press, Inc. **560,** *Figure 15–2:* From *World Development Report 1993* by World Bank. Copyright © 1993 by The International Bank for Reconstruction and Development/The World Bank. Used by permission of Oxford University Press, Inc. **569,** *Figure 15–3:* From *Newsweek,* December 29, 1997 © 1997, Newsweek, Inc. All rights reserved. Reprinted by permission. **584,** *Figure 15–5:* From "Time Off With Pay," *The New York Times,* May 11, 1997, p. F–12. Copyright © 1997 by the New York Times Company. Reprinted by permission. **585,** *Table 15–4:* Adapted from *The Coming of Post-Industrial Society,* by Daniel Bell. Copyright © 1973 by Daniel Bell. Foreword copyright © 1976 by Daniel Bell. Reprinted by permission of Basic-Books, a subsidiary of Perseus Books Group, LLC.

Chapter 16: **596, 604,** *Figures 16–1 and 16–3:* From John R. Weeks, *Population,* 5th Edition, pp. 30 and 76. © 1992 Wadsworth Publishing Co. Used by permission. **613,** *Figure 16–7:* From *Newsweek,* December 29, 1997. © 1997, Newsweek, Inc. All rights reserved. Reprinted by permission. **619,** *Figure 16–8:* Adapted from Chauncy D. Harris and Edward L. Ullman, "The Nature of Cities," *Annals of the American Academy of Political & Social Science,* Vol. 242, November 1945, p. 717. **622,** *Figure 16–9:* From *State of the World Atlas,* Fifth Edition, by Michael Kidron and Ronald Segal. Copyright © 1995 by Michael Kidron and Ronald Segal, text. Copyright © 1995 by Myriad Editions Limited, maps and graphics. Used by permission of Viking Penguin, a division of Penguin Putnam Inc.

Chapter 17: **639,** *Figure 17–3:* Adapted and reprinted with the permission of The Free Press, a Division of Simon & Schuster from *Theory of Collective Behavior* by Neil J. Smelser. Copyright © 1962 by Neil J. Smelser.

Name Index

Subject Index